JIM MURRAY'S
WHISKEY
BIBLE
2015

This 2015 edition is dedicated with love and pride
to
Eve Beatrice Laurie Rankin
and to the memory of
James Nelstrop
a gentleman and whisky visionary.

This edition first published 2014 by Dram Good Books Ltd.
Distributed in North America exclusively by Whitman Publishing, LLC

10 9 8 7 6 5 4 3 2 1

The "Jim Murray's" logo and the "Whisk(e)y Bible" logo are trade marks of Jim Murray.

Text, tasting notes & rankings, artwork, Jim Murray's logo and the Whisk(e)y Bible logo
copyright © Jim Murray 2014

Design copyright © Dram Good Books Ltd 2014

For information regarding using tasting notes from Jim Murray's Whisky Bible contact:
Dram Good Books Ltd, 9 Edison Close, Wellingborough, Northamptonshire, UK, NN8 6AH
Tel: 44 (0)117 317 9777. Or contact us via www.whiskybible.com

A CIP catalogue record for this book is available from the British Library

ISBN: 978-0-9554729-9-2

Printed in US by Whitman Publishing, LLC. Florence, Alabama, AL 35630

Written by: Jim Murray
Edited by: David Rankin
Design: David Rankin, Dean Ayotte, Jim Murray
Maps: James Murray
Production: Dean Ayotte, Vincent Flint-Hill, Billy Jeffrey
Chief Researcher: Vincent Flint-Hill
Sample Research: Vincent Flint-Hill, Ally Telfer, Julia Nourney, Mick Secor
Other Research: Emma Thomson
Sales: Billy Jeffrey

Author's Note
I have used the spelling "whiskey" or "whisky" depending on how the individual distillers
prefer. All Scotch is "whisky". So is Canadian. All Irish, these days, is "whiskey", though
that was not always the case. In Kentucky, bourbon and rye are spelt "whiskey", with the
exception of the produce of the early Times/Old Forester Distillery and Maker's Mark which
they bottle as "whisky". In Tennessee, it is a 50-50 split: Dickel is "whisky", while Daniel's is
"whiskey".

JIM MURRAY'S
WHISKEY
BIBLE
2015

Contents

Introduction

It is a pretty well known fact that when it comes to whisky I am no great fan of water. But we can safely say this is a watershed edition of Jim Murray's Whisky Bible.

Like usual, I have jam-packed it with over 1,000 new whiskies tasted since last year: 1,145 to be precise. And, after totting up all the figures and an intense taste-off lasting several days, a nation can proudly claim to have made the world's finest whisky for the very first time. Strangely enough, it was not the nation I first thought, or announced to my staff, that would be celebrating that feat. Confused? Believe me, so was I. But all shall be explained...

Events have conspired for me to make a momentous decision on just how the Whisky Bible goes forward. That started last year when flying over the Rockies on my way back to Britain and writing the Introduction to the 2014 edition. Because, unbeknown to me, a pain in my right leg which had given me sleepless nights of agony while tasting the American whiskies turned out to be a blood clot. One which, as is the wont of blood clots, could have killed me at any time I was merrily tapping away on my computer putting the final touches to my latest offering. I had only a day or two in England before I needed to be in Taiwan, not enough time to see my doctor. And while in Taipai a second pain appeared in the leg....a little higher now by the knee. On returning to Britain I was rushed to hospital and ultrasound revealed I had somehow flown 17,000 miles with two blood clots...and lived to tell the tale. Let's just say the fact there is a 2015 Bible is a minor miracle. A big thumbs up to the compression socks I always wear when travelling. And to British Airways' business class beds!

However, the deep vein thrombosis was not a direct result of the flying. It had been caused, ironically, by the thing that year by year created the greatest unhappiness in the production of the Whisky Bible: the receiving of samples from whisky companies. In an ideal world we would have bought them as each brand was released. But as we make profit only by book sales and not advertising, finding at least £50,000 a year would have been a challenge.

We ask bottlers and distillers to send samples no less than 10cl in size and from their latest bottling. When the Bible was first launched in 2003 the internet whisky blogger did not yet exist and I was sent, as often as not, full bottles of product. Those samples became smaller and more haphazard as PR companies rather than the actual blenders I once dealt with became involved in order to cope with the demand from uncle Tom Cobley and all. Sadly agency bods, these passing non-entities of the night, were often incapable of telling the difference between a whisky professional of over 20 years standing and an electrician who writes about whisky on his website when there is nothing decent on television. So pleas for new stock would result in bottling codes showing that the whisky had been around for up to five years and once, memorably, my being sent a dummy bottle made of solid plastic. Or samples so minute they could not be used. Some of the companies we dealt with were model professionals. But the rank amateurism which sometimes resulted in me getting a 5cl sample sloshing around in a 50cl bottle because "it was all they could spare" beggared belief.

This year I tasted a sample which was set to be World Whisky of the Year. The only question was whether it was going to be the first whisky ever to rack up 98 points. I had been working from a 10cl sample so, during Awards showdown time, my research team bought a full bottle for me to taste from. And on pouring I found on the nose light caramel and on the finish the very mildest sulphur, neither trait being in the sample I had originally received. The two samples were only very slightly different. But enough for it to be stripped of World Whisky of the Year . That is why, as you will see on page 13, we are forming a Jim Murray Whisky Bible Tasting Club, allowing members to purchase samples from the very bottle I have worked from. Plans are about three-quarters completed but it will happen. It has to.

Because there is nothing more frustrating than being told by a PR company that your whisky notes don't match the profile of the whisky they sent...only to discover it came from a bottle which had been three quarters open for half a year. Or that the vast majority of the whiskies we receive turn up in the final few weeks of tasting...meaning I'm stuck in the tasting room for over twelve hours a day and getting a blood clot as a result. So there you have it. As in the words of The Stranglers, Something Better Change. Actually, we have already begun the process. More than 400 of the whiskies included in this Bible came from bottles purchased over the counter. As members of the Whisky Bible Tasting Club, you will get a chance to try those very same whiskies out yourself...And, for me, a change will be as good as a rest....

Jim Murray
Willow Cottage
Somewhere in rural Northamptonshire.
Sept 2014

How to Read The Bible

The whole point of this book is for the whisky lover – be he or she an experienced connoisseur or, better fun still, simply starting out on the long and joyous path of discovery – to have ready access to easy-to-understand information about as many whiskies as possible. And I mean a lot. Thousands.

This book does not quite include every whisky on the market... just by far and away the vast majority. And those that have been missed this time round – either through accident, logistics or design – will appear in later editions once we can source a sample.

Whisky Scoring

The marking for this book is tailored to the consumer and scores run out just a little higher than I use for my own personal references. But such is the way it has been devised that it has not affected my order of preference.

Each whisky is given a rating out of 100. Twenty-five marks are given to each of four factors: nose (**n**), taste (**t**), finish (**f**), balance and overall complexity (**b**). That means that 50% of the marks are given for flavour alone and 25% for the nose, often an overlooked part of the whisky equation. The area of balance and complexity covers all three previous factors and a usually hidden one besides:

Nose: this is simply the aroma. Often requires more than one inspection as hidden aromas can sometimes reveal themselves after time in the glass, increased contact with air and changes in temperature. The nose very often tells much about a whisky, but – as we shall see – equally can be quite misleading.

Taste: this is the immediate arrival on the palate and involves the flavour profile up to, and including, the time it reaches maximum intensity and complexity.

Finish: often the least understood part of a tasting. This is the tail and flourish of the whisky's signature, often revealing the effects of ageing. The better whiskies tend to finish well and longer without too much oak excess. It is on the finish, also, that certain notes which are detrimental to the whisky may be observed. For instance, a sulphur-tarnished cask may be fully revealed for what it is by a dry, bitter residue on the palate which is hard to shake off. It is often worth waiting a few minutes to get the full picture of the finish before having a second taste of a whisky.

Balance: This is the part it takes a little experience to appreciate but it can be mastered by anyone. For a whisky to work well on the nose and palate, it should not be too one-sided in its character. If you are looking for an older whisky, it should have evidence of oak, but not so much that all other flavours and aromas are drowned out. Likewise, a whisky matured or finished in a sherry butt must offer a lot more than just wine alone and the greatest Islay malts, for instance, revel in depth and complexity beyond the smoky effects of peat.

Each whisky has been analysed by me without adding water or ice. I have taken each whisky as it was poured from the bottle and used no more than warming in an identical glass to extract and discover the character of the whisky. To have added water would have been pointless: it would have been an inconsistent factor as people, when pouring water, add different amounts at varying temperatures. The only constant with the whisky you and I taste will be when it has been poured directly from the bottle.

Even if you and I taste the same whiskies at the same temperature and from identical glasses – and even share the same values in whisky – our scores may still be different. Because a factor that is built into my evaluation is drawn from expectation and experience. When I sample a whisky from a certain distillery at such-and-such an age or from this type of barrel or that, I would expect it to offer me certain qualities. It has taken me 30 years to acquire this knowledge (which I try to add to day by day!) and an enthusiast cannot be expected to learn it overnight. But, hopefully, Jim Murray's Whisky Bible will help...!

Score chart

Within the parentheses () is the overall score out of 100.

0–50.5 Nothing short of absolutely diabolical.
51–64.5 Nasty and well worth avoiding.
65–69.5 Very unimpressive indeed.
70–74.5 Usually drinkable but don't expect the earth to move.
75–79.5 Average and usually pleasant though sometimes flawed.
80–84.5 Good whisky worth trying.
85–89.5 Very good to excellent whiskies definitely worth buying.
90–93.5 Brilliant.
94–97.5 Superstar whiskies that give us all a reason to live.
98–100 Better than anything I've ever tasted!

Key to Abbreviations & Symbols

% Percentage strength of whisky measured as alcohol by volume. **b** Overall balance and complexity. **bott** Date of bottling. **db** Distillery bottling. In other words, an expression brought out by the owners of the distillery. **dist** Date of distillation or spirit first put into cask. **f** Finish. **n** Nose. **nc** Non-coloured. **ncf** Non-chill-filtered. **sc** Single cask. **t** Taste. ⊹ New entry for 2015. ☉ Retasted – no change. ☉☉ Retasted and re-evaluated. **v** Variant WB15-001 Code for Whisky Club bottling.

Finding Your Whisky

Worldwide Malts: Whiskies are listed alphabetically throughout the book. In the case of single malts, the distilleries run A–Z style with distillery bottlings appearing at the top of the list in order of age, starting with youngest first. After age comes vintage. After all the "official" distillery bottlings are listed, next come other bottlings, again in alphabetical order. Single malts without a distillery named (or perhaps named after a dead one) are given their own section, as are vatted malts.

Worldwide Blends: These are simply listed alphabetically, irrespective of which company produce them. So "Black Bottle" appears ahead of "White Horse" and Japanese blends begin with "Ajiwai Kakubin" and end with "Za". In the case of brands being named after companies or individuals the first letter of the brand will dictate where it is listed. So William Grant, for instance, will be found under "W" for William rather "G" for Grant.

Bourbon/Rye: One of the most confusing types of whiskey to list because often the name of the brand bears no relation to the name of the distillery that made it. Also, brands may be sold from one company to another, or shortfalls in stock may see companies buying bourbons from another. For that reason all the brands have been listed alphabetically with the name of the bottling distiller being added at the end.

Irish Whiskey: There are four types of Irish whiskey: (i) pure pot still; (ii) single malt; (iii) single grain and (iv) blended. Some whiskies may have "pure pot still" on the label, but are actually single malts. So check both sections.

Bottle Information

As no labels are included in this book I have tried to include all the relevant information you will find on the label to make identification of the brand straightforward. Where known I have included date of distillation and bottling. Also the cask number for further recognition. At the end of the tasting notes I have included the strength and, if known, number of bottles (sometimes abbreviated to btls) released and in which markets.

Price of Whisky

You will notice that Jim Murray's Whisky Bible very rarely refers to the cost of a whisky. This is because the book is a guide to quality and character rather than the price tag attached. Also, the same whiskies are sold in different countries at varying prices due to market forces and variations of tax, so there is a relevance factor to be considered. Equally, much depends on the size of an individual's pocket. What may appear a cheap whisky to one could be an expensive outlay to another. With this in mind prices are rarely given in the Whisky Bible.

How to Taste Whisky

It is of little use buying a great whisky, spending a comparative fortune in doing so, if you don't get the most out of it.

So when giving whisky tastings, no matter how knowledgable the audience may be I take them through a brief training schedule in how to nose and taste as I do for each sample included in the Whisky Bible.

I am aware that many aspects are contrary to what is being taught by distilleries' whisky ambassadors. And for that we should be truly thankful. However, at the end of the day we all find our own way of doing things. If your old tried and trusted technique suits you best, that's fine by me. But I do ask you try out the instructions below at least once to see if you find your whisky is talking to you with a far broader vocabulary and clearer voice than it once did. I strongly suspect you will be pleasantly surprised – amazed, even - by the results.

Amusingly, someone tried to teach me my own tasting technique some years back in an hotel bar. He was not aware who I was and I didn't let on. It transpired that a friend of his had been to one of my tastings a few years earlier and had passed on my words of "wisdom". I'd be lying if I said I didn't smile when he informed me it was called "The Murray Method." It was the first time I had heard the phrase... though certainly not the last!

"The Murray Method"

1. Drink a black, unsweetened, coffee or chew on 90% minimum cocoa chocolate to cleanse the palate, especially of sugars.

2. Find a room free from distracting noises as well as the aromas of cooking, polish, flowers and other things which will affect your understanding and appreciation of the whisky.

3. Make sure you have not recently washed your hands using heavily scented soap or are wearing a strong aftershave or perfume.

4. Use a tulip shaped glass with a stem. This helps contain the alcohols at the bottom yet allows the more delicate whisky aromas you are searching for to escape.

5. Never add ice. This tightens the molecules and prevents flavours and aromas from being released. It also makes your whisky taste bitter. There is no better way to get the least from your whisky than by freezing it.

6. Likewise, ignore any advice given to put the bottle in the fridge before drinking.

7. Don't add water! Whatever anyone tells you. It releases aromas but can mean the whisky falls below 40%...so it is no longer whisky. Also, its ability to release flavours and aromas diminish quite quickly. Never add ridiculous "whisky rocks" or other supposed tasting aids.

8. Warm the undiluted whisky in the glass to body temperature before nosing or tasting. Hence the stem, so you can cradle in your hand the curve of the thin base. This excites the molecules and unravels the whisky in your glass, maximising its sweetness and complexity.

9. Keep an un-perfumed hand over the glass to keep the aromas in while you warm. Only a minute or two after condensation appears at the top of your glass should you extend your arms, lift your covering hand and slowly bring the glass to your nose, so the alcoholic vapours have been released before the glass reaches your face.

10. Never stick your nose in the glass. Or breathe in deeply. Allow glass to gently touch your top lip, leaving a small space below the nose. Move from nostril to nostril, breathing normally. This allows the aromas to break up in the air, helping you find the more complex notes.

11. Take no notice of your first mouthful. This is a marker for your palate.

12. On second, bigger mouthful, close your eyes to concentrate on the flavour and chew the whisky - moving it continuously around the palate. Keep your mouth slightly open to let air in and alcohol out. It helps if your head is tilted back very slightly.

13. Occasionally spit – if you have the willpower! This helps your senses to remain sharp for the longest period of time.

14. Look for the balance of the whisky. That is, which flavours counter others so none is too dominant. Also, watch carefully how the flavours and aromas change in the glass over time.

15. Assess the "shape" and mouth feel of the whisky, its weight and how long its finish. And don't forget to concentrate on the first flavours as intensely as you do the last. Look out for the way the sugars, spices and other characteristics form.

16. Never make your final assessment until you have tasted it a third or fourth time.

17. Be honest with your assessment: don't like a whisky because someone (yes, even me!), or the label, has tried to convince you how good it is.

18. When you cannot discriminate between one whisky and another, stop immediately.

Renewing Vows
Staying Committed

It must be 15 years since I sat in the office of one of the world's biggest publishing companies and was told that the Whisky Bible would be a flop.

So I vowed on the central London street their door emptied out onto that I would go home, form my own publishing house and launch a book which I knew would change the whisky appreciating landscape. It was a bright spring morning, the kind of day where green shoots form and buds begin to bloom: where nature cannot be thwarted. The perfect moment, in fact, for the blossoming of a dream.

In fact, it took until 2003 to at last get Jim Murray's Whisky Bible onto the bookshelf. But, since then we are now rapidly heading towards half a million copies sold, an extraordinary number for a book which has only ever appeared in English language. And one now having enough international influence for its World Whisky of the Year to sell more bottles in the 24 hours after the announcement of the award than it had in the entire previous year....

The reason for the delay of the initial launch was because, as it was to be funded by myself, I had to wait until exactly the right time to strike. When I knew that there were a sufficient number of independent bottlers to ensure that each new annual edition would have enough fresh contents to make it a new book in itself, then I made my move. The first year should have been 2002 for a 2003 edition, but it took too long to get the samples assembled and the marketing curtains were drawn closed on that tiny window of opportunity. Instead, I began again in the spring of 2003, this time with an impressive armada of whiskies already gathered and, after spending the hottest-ever summer in Britain indoors tasting, by the autumn of that year the Whisky Bible, comprising of 2,100 whiskies and 256 pages was being read the world over.

Now Jim Murray's Whisky Bible carries 4,700 whiskies over 384 pages. In total, some 13,750 different whiskies have now been tasted and rated by me especially for my Whisky Bible. On average, around 1,200 new whiskies are nosed and tasted by me each year. It is a punishing schedule, one my friends have tried to curtail by suggesting I publish once every two years. But that would lose the rhythm, impact and importance of the Whisky Bible: one of its beauties is that it contains all the newest whiskies from around the world that I and my team of researchers can find. Publish every two years and it would be instantly out of date.

From the very first moment, my concept of the Whisky Bible was for it to serve the general public and support the then small number of shops which were at the vanguard of the whisky movement. And the distillers, too, by rewarding those companies in the business of whisky excellence. The only way it could serve the public was by being fearlessly honest and entirely trustworthy: if a whisky was not of the highest quality, then the Bible would say so. It also had to campaign if need be: to be an independent voice.

It has meant that some distillers and bottlers have not been quite as forthcoming with samples as they might, something we are overcoming by buying in stock. A bottler even told me (in front of witnesses) he would not send samples as I might give a low score. "Why don't you do what some other writers do," he suggested. "If you don't like it, don't include it."

This concept is such anathema to me I refuse to believe anyone could do that. Even so, I can assure you that will never be the way I work. I will, as all my professional and personal instincts and beliefs demand, write as I find...whichever the whisky. And to underscore our independence, we have never and will never carry advertising. The marking of the whiskies will be carried without fear or favour. Not as much as a single half point will be given or subtracted depending on brand or bottler: you don't punish the children because of their parents. And, contrary to what I have read on website forums, we don't take money for awards. Indeed, we don't even charge for whiskies to be included in the Bible. If a whisky gets a high score or an award it is because I, rightly or wrongly, believe it to be of that standard.

And we shall continue to campaign. The first edition carried a withering Bible Thumping on the use of caramel. It was a hard-hitting article which we know led to some independent bottlers discarding colouring altogether and a complete reassessment by many distillers. Ten years on I repeated the dose; while an stance against sulphur received international attention and brought about the bigest-ever debate on the subject, long overdue.

We're proud the way Jim Murray's Whisky Bible has served both the consumer and industry for over ten years. Let's hope my nose and taste buds can carry on for at least ten more...

Bible Thumping
The Spirit Shall
Return Unto Good

Scotch whisky has changed. Dramatically.

Forget the blurb on the back of labels about time-honoured ways and traditions. Ignore the fawning magazine features designed to suck in advertising. Scotch whisky is a significantly different animal to the one it was 25 years ago. Which, in turn, was different to what was produced a generation before.

In some ways we should not be surprised: nothing stands still. Evolution is all around us. Top flight football is unrecognisable to the game played in the 1980s. So is First Class cricket, alas. Novels are now in paper form only as an option. When I drove to Scotland every other week from England in the early 1980s you would spend what seemed a lifetime stuck in traffic queues as far as the eye could see as the modest main route north meandered in single file from bottleneck to bottleneck through little towns barely above village status. Now it is motorway and dual carriageway through rural corridors all the way on less than a tank of diesel allowing the journey to be completed in barely half the time. To see a distillery a generation ago you needed, as I did so many countless times, to undertake a voyage that was as time consuming as it was enlightening. Now you just have to click buttons on your iPhone and you can Google Earth it and find out more still from myriad websites. Little stands still as there is a universal fear that whatever does is likely to wither and die. Meanwhile, people's expectations are higher, their boredom threshold lower.

There is good and bad in all change. But the fact that not a single Scotch whisky was able to make it into my final taste off for World Whisky of the Year — the first time that has ever happened — points to the possibility that not all the changes seen in the Highland glens and Sassenach cities has been to the advantage of the industry. At least in terms of quality. Financially, it may be a different matter entirely. Does Scotland still make outstanding whisky? That is one Yes vote I would unquestionably give to the Scots: of course it does. Just look at some of the massive scores I have given to individual casks. But to paraphrase Aristotle, I think: one single cask does not an industry make. But making good whisky and ending up with an outstanding product are two very different things, though that may be understood less today within the industry than it once was. The fact that the only scotch to get near the Whisky Bible Whisky of the Year taste off, another of The Last Drop's astonishing offerings, had been distilled in 1965 was further evidence that things were not as they should have been. Where were the complex whiskies in the prime of their lives? Where were the blends which offered bewildering layers of depth? Where were the malts which took you on hair-standing journeys through dank and dingy warehouses?

Let us just say that this year they were conspicuous by their absence. There was evidence of some clever work being done in both the wash backs and lab with the anCnoc Rutter. That was achieved by sympathetically using peat to highlight and underline just how sensational that virtually unknown distillery is. However, a lack of years in cask meant it felt like a stunning piece of art still to be completed on the canvas.

For sheer genius, as well as brilliance, I can point you to two whiskies which were launched in time for the 2014 Bible, Glenmorangie Ealanta and Highland Park Loki. The former, which so blew me away I named it World Whisky of the Year for 2014, was 19 years of age and, in effect, an experimental bottling. Loki, bottles of which you might still be able to track down – though only for those with healthy bank accounts – was made 15 years ago and, like the Ealanta, is not something that can be repeated at the drop of a hat.

These one-off bottlings, these unforgettable cameo appearances, are often what add the variety, the spice of whisky life and are national treasures in their own right. But they are seldom cheap and those ordinary whisky lovers with normal pockets who aspire to one day discovering their delights often find the whisky has vanished off the shelves or doubled, trebled even quadrupled in price through scarcity by the time they have saved the money to hunt down a bottle.

There are no shortage of special bottlings - and we all love the cherry on the cake. But what if the cherry is delicious and the cake itself just a stodgy also-ran. Which is why I am a little troubled by the state of Scotland's bread and butter malts and blends. And probably blends in particular. In the last two decades, the number of companies being swallowed by others has been bewildering. We are getting to the stage where independent whisky distillers operating with just a handful of loved and cherished distilleries has reached endangered species proportions. Likewise, we have seen grain distilleries close at an astonishing rate. Thirty years or so ago there was a culling which massively reduced the number of grains available to blenders and therefore the ability to create blends with a unique voice. In more recent times, further closures have narrowed the gene pool down to dangerous proportions. In my time of visiting and writing about distilleries, I have seen the irreplaceable Cambus as well as Carsebridge, Caledonian, North of Scotland and Port Dundas all vanish from the grain producing map. Most shocking, and saddest of all, was the destruction of Dumbarton, for my money the best of all the big guys offering a firmness to a blend, a unique texture, that no other single grain could match.

The reason for its demise was one which the bean counters could justify but no-one with the love of whisky possibly could: finance. In effect, its location sitting on the sea just north-west of Glasgow made it prime real estate. The major upturn in land value in Scotland was its death sentence. So Allied Domecq cashed in and its inferior sister distillery Strathclyde tarted up. It was something akin to closing down Real Madrid so Doncaster Rovers might thrive. Somehow Ballantine's has appeared to have survived the transition so far, digging deep into its vast resources and blending know-how to counter the loss. But other standard brands once dependent on Dumbarton are not doing quite so well – and there is no surprise in that.

If you add these closures to the fact that maturing malt whisky has two potential defects not in existence when all these grain distilleries were in operation, you can see why the blenders' lot is not as happy as it once was. The problem with sulphur-tainted sherry butts has been well covered in previous editions of the Bible, so there is no point in going into detail here. But, as a double whammy, we are now getting problems from ex-bourbon casks, too. Because Kentucky distillers are also shaving costs and the degree of seasoning carried out on the virgin oak before being turned into barrels has been reduced. The result: shorter warehouse life. And that means blenders are finding strange things have been happening to some of their third fill casks which are no longer the safe, trustworthy, semi-neutral receptacles they had been for the previous 50 years.

There is a third factor. With the Chinese and other expanding markets in mind, some larger distillers are hoarding stocks and are less willing to exchange or sell. Which again reduces the number of malts and grains generally available.

And a fourth. In the last decade or so there has been a gradual homogenisation of certain distilleries in Scotland, Speyside in particular. This has a two-fold purpose: one is to make it possible for single operatives to run a distillery more easily, with less to worry about when working from plant to plant. Secondly, if a distillery is shut down for any reason, another malt with a similar, if not identical, profile can take its place. Net result: far less whisky styles to choose from. And, not to put too fine a point on it, it is beginning to show.

The poor old blender has another problem not often talked about: envy and paranoia, with marketing bods wondering why X distillery is doing this and that, and they are not. No greater example of this is there than the folly of the Cask Finishes. When, over 20 years ago, I broke the story in my column in the Sunday Telegraph that Glenmorangie had launched a quite magnificent Port Wood finish, the first-ever pre-designed cask finish whisky, the entire industry appeared to freeze in its tracks and go into meltdown. Soon everyone was doing it, from the smallest independent bottler to the giant Diageo of this world. Some worked. A great many didn't. When I learned the blending craft I was taught that the bread and butter whiskies came first, the experimental side-lines second. And if they were not up to scratch you had to just write it off and tip it discreetly into a blend over several bottlings and out of harm's way. However, marketeers were never trained that way. If they wanted a Tuscany finish, they got a Tuscany finish whether the grape and grain melded together successfully or not. Whether a sulphur stick had been used or not. Often, the decision was taken out of blenders' hands...which had not previously been the case. Money had been spent and a return demanded. And they wanted to be seen as fully paid up members of the Cask Finish Club.

While all this was going on, just how much attention was being paid to the average stocks in the warehouse? Less than usual, sometimes also because of staff cutbacks. The trouble was that everyone thought things were tickety-boo and this feeling of wellbeing thrived as the magazines flourished. Whisky fairs began sprouting up around the world like mushrooms at the end of a long drought. Blenders and brand ambassadors took on minor celebrity status. Flesh was pressed, backs were slapped, bad jokes were laughed at. Revellers, enjoying their tenth unspat sample of the day would tell the kilted ones how wonderful their whisky was, now barely able to distinguish it from the last. The kilted ones wanted to believe it, so did, and everything in the world was not only rosy but golden. Which if you measure things in terms of sales and profits only, it mainly is. But some of us look a little beyond that. So that is why we have reached the point we are at today: some have taken their eye off the ball and not brought into account the changes which have altered the face of whisky. They began to believe their own PR copy and standard brands started standing still or going backwards. Meanwhile around the rest of the world, distillers from Kentucky to Taiwan, from India to Japan paid extraordinary attention to detail in every cask they made or exactly how several casks were vatted together.

Is it the beginning of the end for Scotch? Of course not. You have only to look at the 10-year-olds of Glen Grant and Ardbeg or a Pulteney 17 to see how a great Scotch should be year in, year out. But it is, if anyone is listening, a wake-up call. It is time for a little dose of humility. It is time to focus on the daily brands, to get back to the basics. To realise that, for all the reasons mentioned above, something is missing, especially in the blends. We have had the sleight of hand and the hey-presto moments and, sometimes, they have been wonderful.

But the real magic of Scotch is when you spend less than a single note and end up mesmerised by the complexity and genius of what sits in the glass before you. It still happens, though not as often as before. We need, for once, to suspend evolution: we need go back into the past...and back to basics.

Join our Tasting Club

How would you like to compare your own tasting notes from the very same bottle I have used for each whisky? Set your nose and taste buds against mine.

That is the concept we are now going to make happen – ensuring Jim Murray's Whisky Bible is even more fun, intriguing and informative than ever before. Since the very first edition was launched way back in 2003 readers have asked if we could sell samples of the whiskies I have tasted. I have also had numerous approaches by business types over the years asking me to sell whisky off the back of the Bible...and been offered vast sums to do so.

In order to underline this book's impartiality, the very bedrock of its existence, I declined those offers. I did not want to be incorrectly perceived favouring a whisky; people thinking I was feathering my own nest by making a profit from increased sales of whiskies I had given high scores or even awards to...which would be entirely opposite to absolutely everything I believe in and stand for. So, just like advertising, I turned my back on that potential source of revenue. But within the last year I have had to drastically rethink how to make the Bible happen. Not for commercial reasons But simple health ones. Because, as alluded to in the Introduction, during the writing of the 2014 edition I developed two blood clots which could easily have had fatal consequences. They came about because samples were, as usual, sent to me by some distillers and bottlers so late in the day I had to spend almost six weeks tied to a desk. Tasting twelve to fourteen hours a day, seven days a week in order to somehow hit the publishing deadline. Deep vein thrombosis was, not surprisingly, the result.

So now we will, whenever possible, be buying the whiskies as they are launched and I will be tasting them throughout the year to even the burden, rather than just in the summer months prior to publication. This will also mean we can launch the Whisky Bible in foreign language editions, as we will have time to have my notes translated – something that had been impossible before. For this 2015 edition just over 400 of the 1,145 new whiskies were bought in. Those, like each bottle we will be buying in future, have been split into seven sealed 10cl bottles: one for me to work from, the others to be made available to Whisky Club members on a first come, first served basis. Local whisky clubs can also take advantage.

We are still in the development phase of making this happen and investigating the final mechanics of how. Because of the enormous pressure on time to hit the deadline for this edition we have yet to fully determine just how the samples will be made available. But they will be and we ask you keep a close eye on **Whiskybible.com** to monitor developments and instructions how to join the Whisky Bible Club. The money we raise from this means we then have the funds to buy more whiskies as they become available. Not just the whiskies the distillers and bottlers want us to have. But the ones my researchers find out there.

You will know my score for the samples available for the 2015 Bible. For the 2016 edition onwards you will not. You will have to use your judgement to guess which will be the high flyers because scores will still not be given until the Whisky Bible is launched each October.

This is an exciting new development in the Whisky Bible. It will give you the chance to build your own library and see if you enjoy - or not, as the case may be - the whiskies as I have. Knowing you are tasting exactly the same whisky and not, potentially in non-single cask or batch whiskies, an earlier or later bottling.

I will look forward to welcoming you to the Jim Murray Whisky Bible Tasting Club very soon.

Jim Murray's Whisky Bible Award Winners 2015

In the year when Monty Python reunited and I found myself on a plane randomly sitting next to John Cleese, it just had to happen: Something Completely Different.

Nobody expected the Japanese inquisition – including me. Because, for the first time ever, a Japanese whisky has run off with top billing, scooping Jim Murray's Whisky Bible World Whisky of the Year 2015. And an inquisition it certainly was: The Yamazaki Sherry Cask – though with the number of bottles available, it should probably have been called Casks - was the kind of whisky which asked polite questions of the taster, such as "are you really up to enjoying all I can offer?" And, tauntingly, demanded answers from the world's other finest brands: "can you beat this?" From the glass, with its nose of exquisite boldness, to its very last, fading strain on the finish it teased and mocked: "go on, then. Find something better than me." For a while I thought I had, but that is explained elsewhere in this Bible. In the end I didn't. I know many will be just as surprised. Not so much that I have given the award to a Japanese whisky, but that it is one which owes its personality to sherry casks. As I have always said: I have nothing against good sherry butts. Only bad ones...

Perhaps, though, maybe the most startling thing about this year's crop of award winners was that, when I came down to the shortlist of five for the great taste off of the world's finest, not a single one of them was from Scotland. Another first. And that despite having tasted more new Scotch whiskies this year than I had ever done before. That is not to say that the scotch which gained gongs here weren't superb offerings to live long on the palate and longer in the memory because, obviously, they were. No, it was just that there was a telling and previously unseen gap between the whiskies which radiated near indescribable genius and Scotland's very finest, which were merely magnificent.

In Scotland there were some old faces with new tricks: three gong winners Ballantine's excelled among the blends including a newbie. Glen Grant showed its usual grace at ten years. And what is scary about that brand is that I suspect – no, know - that a tweak here and there could make it even better still. And the chaps from The Last Drop have done it again, scooping two awards, including Scotch Whisky of the Year, with two just-on-the-shelves bottlings. Quite amazing.

Most just, though, and poignant was that the English Whisky Company, which kept missing out on awards last year by mere fractions, deservedly picked up European Whisky of the Year. Though, sadly, just days before I had the chance to tell the distillery's founder, James Nelstrop, who passed away as these very words of congratulation were being written.

2015 World Whisky of the Year
The Yamazaki Single Malt Sherry 2013

Second Finest Whisky in the World
William Larue Weller (68.1 abv)

Third Finest World Whisky in the World
Sazerac Rye 18 Year Old (bottled Fall 2013)

Single Cask of the Year
Four Roses Limited Edition Barrel 3-4P

SCOTCH

Scotch Whisky of the Year
The Last Drop 1965
Single Malt of the Year (Multiple Casks)
Highland Park Loki
Single Malt of the Year (Single Cask)
The Last Drop Glen Garioch 47 Year Old
Scotch Blend of the Year
The Last Drop 1965
Scotch Grain of the Year
The Sovereign Single Cask Port Dundas 1978
Scotch Vatted Malt of the Year
Compass Box The Peat Monster 10th An.

Single Malt Scotch

No Age Statement (Multiple Casks)
AnCnoc Rutter
No Age Statement (Runner Up)
Ardbeg Supernova
10 Years & Under (Multiple Casks)
Glen Grant Aged 10 Years Old
10 Years & Under (Single Cask)
Alexander Weine & Destillate Port Charlotte
10 Year Old
11-15 Years (Multiple Casks)
Highland Park Loki
11-15 Years (Single Cask)
The Balvenie SIngle Barrel Aged 12 Years
16-21 Years (Multiple Casks)
Glenmorangie Ealanta 1993
16-21 Years (Single Cask)
First Editions Clynelish 1996 Aged 17 Years
22-27 Years (Multiple Casks)
Famous Grouse 1986 Glenturret Glasgow
22-27 Years (Single Cask)
Gordon & MacPhail Single Malt Linkwood
28-34 Years (Multiple Casks)
Balblair 1983 Vintage 1st Release
28-34 Years (Single Cask)
Old Malt Cask Caol Ila Aged 29 Years
35-40 Years (Multiple Casks)
Old Pulteney Aged 40 Years
35-40 Years (Single Cask)
BenRiach Batch 11 1977 37 Years Old
41 Years & Over (Multiple Casks)
Gordon and MacPhail Glen Grant 50 Years Old
41 Years & Over (Single Cask)
Last Drop Glen Garioch 47 Year Old

Blended Scotch

No Age Statement (Standard)
Ballantine's Finest
No Age Statement (Premium)
Ballantine's Limited Release no. J13295
5-12 Years
Johnnie Walker Black Label 12 Years Old
13-18 Years
Ballantine's 17 Years Old
19 - 25 Years
Royal Salute 21 Years Old
26 - 50 Years
The Last Drop 1965

IRISH WHISKEY

Irish Whiskey of the Year
Redbreast Aged 21 Years
Irish Pot Still Whiskey of the Year
Redbreast Aged 21 Years
Irish Single Malt of the Year
Bushmills Aged 21 Years
Irish Blend of the Year
Jameson

AMERICAN WHISKEY

Bourbon of the Year
William Larue Weller
Rye of the Year
Sazerac Rye 18 Years Old (Fall 2013)
US Micro Whisky of the Year
Arkansas Single Barrel Reserve Bourbon Whiskey #190
US Micro Whisky of the Year (Runner Up)
Balcones Texas Straight Bourbon VII

Bourbon

No Age Statement (Multiple Barrels)
William Larue Weller
No Age Statement (Single Barrel)
Elmer T. Lee Single Barrel Bourbon 1919-2013
9 Years & Under
Ridgemont Reserve 1792 Aged 8 Years
10-17 Years (Multiple Barrels)
Four Roses 125th Anniversary Small Batch
10-17 Years (Single Barrel)
Four Roses 2013 Limited Edition Single Barrel #3-4P
18 Years & Over (Multiple Barrels)
Elijah Craig 21 Year Old Single Barrel

Rye

No Age Statement
Thomas Handy Sazerac Rye. 132.4
11 Years & Over
Sazerac Rye 18 Years Old (Fall 2013)

CANADIAN WHISKY

Canadian Whisky of the Year
Masterson's 10 Year Old Straight Rye

JAPANESE WHISKY

Japanese Whisky of the Year
Yamazaki Sing. Malt Whisky Sherry Cask 2013

EUROPEAN WHISKY

European Whisky of the Year (Multiple)
English Whisky Co. Chapter 14 Not Peated
European Whisky of the Year (Single)
The Belgian Owl Single Malt '64 Months'

WORLD WHISKIES

Asian Whisky of the Year
Kavalan Single Malt Whisky
Southern Hemisphere Whisky of the Year
NZ Whisky Willowbank 1988 25 Years Old
*Overall age category winners are presented in **bold**.*

The Whisky Bible Liquid Gold Awards (97.5-94)

Jim Murray's Whisky Bible is delighted to again make a point of celebrating the very finest whiskies you can find in the world. So we salute the distillers who have maintained or even furthered the finest traditions of whisky making and taken their craft to the very highest levels. And the bottlers who have brought some of them to us.

After all, there are over 4,500 different brands and expressions listed in this guide and from every corner of the planet. Those which score 94 and upwards represents only a very small fraction of them. These whiskies are, in my view, the elite: the finest you can currently find on the whisky shelves of the world. Rare and precious, they are Liquid Gold.

So it is our pleasure to announce that all those scoring 94 and upwards automatically qualify for the Jim Murray's Whisky Bible Liquid Gold Award. Congratulations!

97.5

Scottish Single Malt
Ardbeg Uigeadail
SMWS Cask 33.120 Aged 8 Years (Ardbeg)
Glenmorangie Ealanta 1993 Vintage
Gordon & MacPhail Linkwood
Old Pulteney Aged 21 Years

Scottish Blends
Ballantine's 17 Years Old

Bourbon
George T Stagg
William Larue Weller
William Larue Weller bott Fall 2011
William Larue Weller bott Spring 2001

American Straight Rye
Thomas H. Handy Sazerac Straight Rye
Thomas H. Handy Sazerac Straight Rye

Japanese Single Malt
Yamazaki Single Malt Whisky Sherry Cask

97

Scottish Single Malt
Aberfeldy Single Cask Aged 21 Years
Ardbeg 10 Years Old
Ardbeg Day Bottling
Ardbeg Supernova
Master of Malt Ardbeg Aged 18 Years
Brora 30 Years Old
The GlenDronach Recherché 1968
Glenfiddich 50 Years Old
Master of Malt Glen Grant 31YO Lost Bott
SMWS Cask 77.28 Aged 25 Years (Glen Ord)

Scottish Grain
Clan Denny Cambus 47 Years Old

Scottish Blends
Johnnie Walker Blue The Casks Edition
Old Parr Superior 18 Years Old

Irish Pure Pot Still
Redbreast Aged 12 Years Cask Strength

Bourbon
Four Roses 2013 Single Barrel #3-4P
Parker's Wheated Mashbill Aged 10 Years

American Straight Rye
Thomas H. Handy Sazerac Straight Rye
Colonel E.H. Taylor Straight Rye
Sazerac 18 Years Old

Japanese Single Malt
Nikka Whisky Single Coffey Malt 12 Years

Indian Single Malt

Amrut Fusion

Taiwanese Single Malt
Kavalan Solist Fino Sherry Cask

96.5

Scottish Single Malt
Ardbeg Corryvreckan
Ardbeg Supernova
AnCnoc Rutter
Balblair 1965
Balblair 1983 Vintage 1st Release
The Balvenie Single Barrel Aged 12 Years
BenRiach Batch 11 1977 37 Years Old
Provenance Benrinnes Over 18 Years
Bruichladdich 1991 Valinch Anaerobic Digestion 19 Years Old
Berry's Own Bunnahabhain Aged 26 Years
Maltman Clynelish Aged 15 Years
Octomore Orpheus 5 Yrs Ed 02.2 PPM 140
Old Malt Cask Caol Ila Aged 29 Years
Port Charlotte PC6
Signatory Glenburgie 1983 Aged 29 Years
The GlenDronach 18 Years Old
GlenDronach Batch 10 1993 21 Years Old
Abbey Whisky GlenDronach Aged 20 Years
The Last Drop Glen Garioch 47 Years Old
First Editions Clynelish 1996 Aged 17 Yrs
Gordon & MacPhail Glen Grant 50 Year Old
Glenglassaugh Aleatico 1939 Aged 39 Years
Cadenhead Glenrothes-Glenlivet 24 Years
Gordon & MacPhail Glentauchers 1994
Glenmorangie Sonnalta PX
Highland Park 50 Years Old
Gordon & MacPhail Highland Park 2003
The Glenlivet Single Cask Inveravon 21 Yrs
Lagavulin 12 Years Old Special Release
Laphroaig Aged 25 Years Cask Strength 2011
Signatory Laphroaig 1998 Aged 15 Years
Berry's Own Linkwood 1987 Aged 26 Years
Chieftain's Port Ellen Aged 30 Years
Master Of Malt Speyside 50 Yrs 3rd Edition
Riegger's Selection Eagle of Spey Glenfarclas 1993
SMWS Cask 4.186 Aged 22 Years

Scottish Grain
Clan Denny Cambus Vintage Aged 25 Years
Clan Denny Dumbarton Aged 48 Years
Sovereign Single Cask Port Dundas 1978

Scottish Vatted Malt

The Last Vatted Malt
The Six Isles St Etienne Rum Cask Finish
Scottish Blends
The Last Drop
The Last Drop 50 Years Old
The Last Drop 1965
Teacher's Aged 25 Years
Irish Pure Pot Still
Midleton Single Pot Still Single Cask 1991
Powers John's Lane Release Aged 12 Years
Redbreast Aged 12 Years Cask Strength
Redbreast Aged 21 Years
Bourbon
Blanton's Gold Original Single Barrel
Blanton's Uncut/Unfiltered
Elmer T. Lee Bourbon 1919 - 2013
Four Roses Single Barrel
Four Roses Single Barrel 12 Years 5 Months
Four Roses 16 Years Old Single Barrel 78-3B
Four Roses 125th Anniversary Bourbon
George T Stagg
George T. Stagg Limited Edition
Virgin Bourbon 7 Years Old
American Straight Rye
Sazerac Kentucky Straight Rye 18 Years Old
American Small Batch
Arkansas Single Barrel Reserve Bourbon
Canadian Blended
Masterson's 10 Year Old Straight Rye
Japanese Single Malt
Chichibu 'The Peated' 2013
Scotch Malt Whisky Society 132.1 28 Years
Swedish Single Malt
Mackmyra Moment "Glöd" (Glow)
Swiss Single Malt
Säntis Swiss Highlander Dreifaltigkeit
Säntis Malt Swiss Highlander
Welsh Single Malt
Penderyn Cask Strength Rich Madeira
Penderyn Portwood Swansea City Special
Australian Single Malt
Sullivans Cove Rare Tasmanian Single Cask
Timboon Single Malt Whisky
Indian Single Malt
Amrut Intermediate
Paul John Edited
New Zealand Single Malt
The New Zealand Whisky Collection
Willowbank 1988 25 Years Oldr
Taiwanese Single Malt
Kavalan Podium Single Malt

96
Scottish Single Malt
Aberfeldy Single Cask Unravel
Aberlour a'Bunadh Batch No. 33
Ardbeg 1977
Ardbeg Kildalton 1980
Ardbeg Provenance 1974
Dun Bheagan Ardberg 15 Year Old
Auchentoshan 1978 Bourbon Cask Ltd Ed.
Master of Malt Balblair 35 YO Lost Bottling
Cadenhead Banff 34 Years Old
The BenRiach Single Cask 1983 Aged 30 Yrs

The BenRiach Single Cask 1996 Aged 17 Yrs
Port Charlotte PC10
Brora 25 Year Old 7th Release
Octomore 5 Years Old
Director's Cut Bruichladdich Aged 21 Years
Duncan Taylor Octave Caperdonich 20 YO
The Dalmore Candela Aged 50 Years
Gordon & MacPhail Glen Albyn 1976
Glencadam 30 Years Old Single Cask 1982
The GlenDronach Single Cask 1992 21 Years
The GlenDronach Single Cask 1994 19 Years
Glenfarclas 1967 Family Casks Release V
Glenfiddich 40 Years Old
Glenglassaugh 40 Year Old
Glenglassaugh Batch 1 1968 45 Years Old
Gordon & Macphail Glen Grant 1948
Gordon & MacPhail Label Glen Grant 1960
Gordon & MacPhail Con. Choice Glenlossie
Glenmorangie Truffle Oak
Glen Scotia 1989 23 Years Old
Master of Malt Glentauchers 15 Year Old
Highland Park Aged 25 Years
Highland Park 1973
Highland Park Loki Aged 15 Years
Highland Park Sigurd
Master of Malt Kilchoman 5 Year Old
The Arran Malt 1996 'The Peacock'
Malts Of Scotland Isle of Arran 1996
Lagavulin 21 Years Old
Laphroaig PX Cask
Laphroaig Quarter Cask
Duncan Taylor Octave Longmorn 15 Years
SMWS 64.42 Aged 22 Years (Mannachmore)
Cadenhead Miltonduff 22 years Old
Gordon and MacPhail Port Ellen 1979
Rosebank 25 Years Old
SMWS Cask 25.66 Aged 23 Years
Single Cask Collection 23 Yr Old Strathmill
Master of Malt Springbank Aged 19 Years
Wemyss Malts 1998 Single Lowland "Tarte
Au Citron"
Scottish Vatted Malt
Big Peat
Big Peat Batch 20 Xmas 2011
Scottish Grain
Cadenhead's Port Dundas Aged 25 Years
Clan Denny Caledonian 45 Years Old
The Pearls of Scotland Invergordon 1972
Scottish Blends
Ballantine's Finest
Dewar House Experimental Aged 17 Years
Irish Pure Pot Still
Redbreast 12 Years Old
Redbreast Aged 12 Years Cask Strength
Redbreast Aged 15 Years bott 12 Nov 12
Irish Blends
Jameson Rarest 2007 Vintage Reserve
Bourbon
Ancient Ancient Age 10 Years Old
Buffalo Trace Master Distiller Emeritus
Elmer T Lee Collector's Edition
Buffalo Trace Single Oak Project Barrel #101
Buffalo Trace Experimental Collection 12
Year Old Bourbon From Floor #9

Four Roses Ltd. Ed. 2012 Small Batch
Old Weller Antique 107
Pappy Van Winkle's Family Reserve 15 YO
Willett Family Estate Bottled 14 Years Old
American Straight Rye
Bulleit 95 Rye
Rittenhouse Very Rare 21 YO Barrel 28
Rittenhouse Rye Aged 25 Years Barrel 19
American Small Batch
Balcones Crooked Texas Bourbon Barrel
Cowboy Bourbon Texas Aged Three Years
Stranahan's Colorado Whiskey Batch #67
Stranahan's Colorado Whiskey Batch #90
Canadian Blended
Alberta Premium bott lott L1317
Crown Royal Special Reserve
Japanese Single Malt
Karuizawa 1967 Vintage
SMWS Cask 116.17 Aged 25 Years (Yoichi)
Japanese Blended
Hibiki Aged 21 Years
Belgian Single Malt
Gouldys 12 Years Old Distillers Range
English Single Malt
Hicks & Healey Cornish Whiskey 2004
The English Whisky Co. Ch. 6 Not Peated
Finnish Single Malt
Old Buck Second Release
German Single Malt
Derrina Einkorn Schwarzwälder Single Grain
Swedish Single Malt
Mackmyra Privus 03 Rökning Tillåten
Mackmyra Moment "Malström"
Swiss Single Malt
Langatun Old Bear Châteauneuf-du-Pape
Welsh Single Malt
Penderyn Bourbon Matured Single Cask
Penderyn Portwood bott 1 Nov 12
SMWS Cask 128.3 Aged 5 Years (Penderyn)
Australian Single Malt
Bakery Hill Classic Malt Cask Strength
Southern Coast Single Malt Batch 002
Indian Single Malt
Amrut Double Cask
Amrut Greedy Angels
Select Cask Peated
Paul John Single Malt Single Cask No 164
Paul John Single Malt Cask No 780
Paul John Single Malt Cask No 1846
Taiwanese Single Malt
Kavalan Single Malt Whisky

95.5
Scottish Single Malt
AnCnoc 1999
Cadenhead's Ardbeg Aged 20 Years
Pearls of Scotland Ardmore 1988 25 YO
Wemyss Ardmore 1992 Single Speyside
"Mellow Mariner"
Cadenhead's Balblair Aged 23 Years
The Whisky Agency Balmenach 1979
The BenRiach Aged 12 Years Sherry Wood
The BenRiach Single Cask 1988 24 Years
Benromach 30 Years Old

Bruichladdich Redder Still 1984
Caol Ila 33 Years
Caol Ila 14 Years Old Unpeated Style
Caol Ila 'Distillery Only'
Caol Ila Special Release 2010 12 Years Old
Old Malt Cask Caol Ila Aged 17 Years
The Warehouse Collection Clynelish 15 Yrs
Cragganmore Special Release 2010 21 YO
The Dalmore Visitor Centre Exclusive
Gordon & MacPhail Cask Highland Park
First Editions Glen Garioch 1993
Berry's Own Selection Glencadam 1991
Glenfarclas 105
Glen Grant Distillery Edition Cask 20 Years
Glenglassaugh Batch 1 1978 35 Years Old
The Glenlivet Archive 21 Years of Age
The Glenlivet Founder's Reserve 21 Yrs Old
The Glenlivet Nadurra Aged 16 Years
Gordon & MacPhail Glenlivet 1974
Glenmorangie 25 Years Old
Glen Moray 1995 Port Wood Finish
The Whisky Castle Glenrothes 21 Years Old
Single Cask Collection Glentauchers 17 YO
Hazelburn Rundlets & Kilderkins 10 Years
Highland Park Aged 18 Years
Highland Park Vintage 1978
Adelphi Selection Highland Park 26 YO
Kilchoman 2007 Vintage
Kilchoman Single Cask Release
Old Particular Highland Leidaig Aged 21 Yrs
Cadenhead's Small Batch Linkwood-
Glenlivet Aged 26 Years
Signatory Vintage Linkwood 1995
Old Malt Cask Arran Aged 15 Years
The Peated Arran "Machrie Moor" 4th Ed.
SWMS Cask 7.75 Aged 27 Years (Longmorn)
SMWS Cask 53.205 Aged 22 Years
SMWS Cask 73.61 Aged 24 Years
The Macallan Fine Oak 12 Years Old
The Macallan Oscuro
Gordon & MacPhail Connoisseurs Choice
Macduff 2000
Gordon & MacPhail Connoisseurs Choice
Mannochmore 1994
Longrow 25 Years
Chieftain's Mortlach Aged 22 Years
Port Charlotte The Peat Project
Alexander Weine & Destillate Port Charlotte
10 Year Old
Cadenhead's Speyside-Glenlivet 18 Years
Cadenhead's Tamdhu-Glenlivet Port Cask
Aged 22 Years
Old Particular Highland Teaninich 30 Years
Tomatin Cù Bòcan Highland 1989 Vintage
Celtique Connexion Origine Islay Affine
Sauternes cask
Wemyss 30 Years Islay "Heathery Smoke"
Scottish Grain
The Coopers Choice Lochside 1964 47 YO
Malts Of Scotland North British 1962
Scottish Vatted Malt
Compass Box Flaming Hart
Compass Box The Spice Tree
Scottish Grain

Clan Denny Invergordon 44 Years Old
SWMS G5.3 Aged 18 Years (Invergordon)
Scottish Blends
Ballantine's Limited Release no. J13295
Johnnie Walker Black Label 12 Years Old
Royal Salute "62 Gun Salute"
William Grant's 25 Years Old
Irish Single Malt
The Tyrconnell Single Cask 11 Year Old
Bushmills Aged 21 Years
Sainsbury's Dún Léire Aged 8 Years
Bourbon
Booker's 7 Years 4 Months
Buffalo Trace Single Oak Project Barrel #27
Buffalo Trace Single Oak Project Barrel #30
Buffalo Trace Single Oak Project Barrel #63
Buffalo Trace Single Oak Project Barrel #183
Buffalo Trace Experiment Hot Box
Buffalo Trace Experimental Collection Entry Proof Rye Bourbon 125
Charter 101
Elijah Craig Barrel Proof Bourbon 12 Years
Elijah Craig 21 Year Old Single Barrel
European Bourbon Rye Association Kentucky Straight Bourbon Whiskey 16 Years
Four Roses Limited Edition Small Batch 2011 Barrel Strength
Smooth Ambler Old Scout Straight Bourbon 10 Years Old
Willett Pot Still Reserve
American Straight Rye
Sazerac Kentucky Straight Rye 18 Years Old
American Small Batch
Bad Guy Bourbon
Balcones Brimstone
Balcones Brimstone Texas Scrub Oak Smoked Corn Whisky
Balcones True Blue Cask Strength
Stranahan's Snowflake Cab Franc
The Notch Aged 8 Years
Canadian Blended
Alberta Premium
Forty Creek Port Wood Reserve
Gibson's Finest Rare Aged 18 Years
Japanese Single Malt
Golden Horse Chichibu Aged 12 Years
Hakushu Single Malt Whisky Agd 12 Yrs
Ichiro's Card "King of Hearts"
Ichiro's Malt Aged 20 Years
Karuizawa 1984
Japanese Single Grain
Kawasaki Single Grain
Austrian Single Malt
Pure Rye Malt J.H. bott code LPR 07
Belgian Single Malt
The Belgian Owl Single Malt '64 Months'
English Single Malt
The English Whisky Co. Ch 14 (Not Peated)
Stephen Notman Whisky Live Taipei 2013
German Single Malt
Austrasier Single Cask Grain
Swiss Single Malt
The Swiss Malt
Swedish Single Malt

Mackmyra Brukswhisky
Mackmyra Moment "Rimfrost"
Welsh Single Malt
Penderyn Portwood
Australian Single Malt
The Nant 3 Years Old Cask Strength
Release The Beast
Sullivan's Cove American Oak Single Cask
Timboon Single Malt Port Expression
Indian Single Malt
Paul John Single Malt Cask No 692
Paul John Single Malt Cask No 784
Paul John Single Malt Cask No 1444
Indian Blends
Rendezvous

95 (New Entries Only)

Scottish Single Malt
Aberlour A'Bunadh Batch No. 45
Darkness! Aberlour Aged 20 Years
The Balvenie Single Barrel Aged 15 Years
BenRiach Batch 11 1976 37 Years Old
Caol Ila Distillers Edition
Montgomerie's Single Cask Caol Ila
Signatory Vintage Un-chillfiltered Collection Caol Ila 1996 Aged 17 Years
Wemyss Malts 1997 Single Highland "Toffee Glaze"
Wemyss Malts 1997 Single Highland "Beach with a Sea View"
Edradour Straight From The Cask Port Wood Finish Aged 13 Years
Berry's Own Selection Glencadam 1991
Cadenhead's Authentic Collection Glenfarclas Aged 25 Years
The Maltman Glen Grant Aged 17 Years
Cadenhead's Glen Moray Aged 21 Years
The Famous Grouse 1986 Glenturret Glasgow 2014 Limited Edition
SMWS Cask 35.110 Aged 17 Years
That Boutique-y Whisky Kilchoman batch 1
Old Malt Cask Laphroaig Aged 15 Years
Old Particular Laphroaig Aged 15 Years
Old Malt Cask Longmorn Aged 18 Years
The Single Malts of Scotland Longmorn Aged 21 Years
Cadenhead's Small Batch Miltonduff-Glenlivet Aged 24 Years
Scotch Malt Whisky Society Cask 72.39
Hazelburn Rundlets & Kilderkins 11 YO
The Whisky Agency Strathmill 1976
Old Malt Cask Tullibardine Aged 23 Years
Blackadder Black Snake Vat No. 2
Master of Malt Speyside 30 Years Old
Scottish Vatted Malt
Compass Box Flaming Heart 4th Edition
Compass Box The Peat Monster 10th An.
Douglas Laing's DB High. Park & Bowmore
Johnnie Walker Green Label 15 Years Old
Norse Cask Selection Vatted Islay 1992
Wild Scotsman Aged 15 Years Vatted Malt
Scottish Grain
Clan Denny Carsebridge Aged 45 Years
The Sovereign Single Cask Strathclyde 1977

Scottish Blends
The Bailie Nicol Jarvie (B.N.J)
Chivas Regal 25 Years Old
Clan Gold 3 Year Old
Compass Box The General
Glen Orin 30 Years old Blend
The Tweeddale Blend Aged 12 Years

Irish Pure Pot Still
Midleton 1973 Pure Pot Still

Irish Single Malt
Tyrconnell Aged 11 Years
Bushmills Select Casks Aged 12 Years
Bushmills Rareg Aged 21 Years

Irish Blends
Jameson
Midleton Very Rare 2009

Bourbon
Big Bottom Straight Bourbon 91
Buffalo Trace Single Oak Project Barrel 14
Buffalo Trace Single Oak Project Barrel 132
Cougar Bourbon Aged 5 Years
Four Roses Single Barrel barrel 4-1F
George T. Stagg (Barrel Proof)
Maker's 46
Orphan Barrel 'Old Blowhard' 26 Years Old
Parker's Heritage Collection "Promise of Hope" Single Barrel 10 Years
Woodford Reserve Master's Four Grain

American Corn Whiskey
Dixie Dew

American Straight Rye
Cougar Rye
High West Rocky Mountain 21 Year Old Rye
Rittenhouse Very Rare 21 YO Barrel 8
Sazerac Kentucky Straight Rye 18 Years Old

American Small Batch
McCarthy's Oregon Single Malt
McCarthy's Aged 3 Years batch W10-01
McCarthy's Aged 3 Years batch W12-01
Stranahan's Colorado Whiskey Batch #83
Westland American Single Malt Whiskey
Woodstone Microspirit 5 Grain Straight Bourbon Single Barrel No. 3

Other American Whiskey
High West Son of Bourye

Canadian Blended
Alberta Premium 25 Years Old
Danfield's Limited Edition Aged 21 Years
Wiser's Legacy
Wiser's Red Letter

Japanese Single Malt
The Hakushu Aged 15 Years Cask Strength
Hakushu 1984
Ichiro's Card "Four of Spades"
Yoichi Key Malt Agd 12 Yrs "Peaty & Salty"
Yoichi 20 Years Old
Pure Malt Black

Japanese Blended
Royal Aged 15 Years

Dutch Single Malt
Millstone Aged 12 Years Sherry Cask

English Single Malt
The English Whisky Co. Ch. 6 (NP) Jan 13
The English Whisky Co. Ch. 6 (NP) Apr 13
The English Whisky Co. Ch. 9 Peated 2012
The English Whisky Co. Ch. 14 Unpeated

Finnish Single Malt
Old Buck

French Single Malt
Kornog Single Malt Tourbé (Peated) Whisky Breton Taourc'h Trived 12BC
P&M Corsican Single Malt Aged 7 Years

German Single Malt
The Alrik Smoked Hercynian 4 Years Old
Derrina Triticale Schwarzwälder Single Grain
Spinnaker 20 Years Old

Swedish Single Malt
Mackmyra Moment "Urberg"
Mackmyra Moment "Skog"
Mackmyra Moment "Mareld" (Sea Fire)

Swiss Single Malt
Interlaken Swiss Highland "Classic"

Welsh Single Malt
Penderyn Madeira bott Jun 11
Penderyn Peated bott 2 Nov 12
Penderyn Madeira bott 4 Feb 13
Penderyn Madeira bott Jul 13
Penderyn Madeira bott Jan 14
Penderyn Sherrywood Limited Edition

Australian Single Malt
Overeem Port Cask Matured Cask Strength
Overeem Sherry Cask Matured Cask
Southern Coast Single Malt Batch 006
Velvet Hammer 13 Years Old

Indian Single Malt
Amrut Two Continents Limited Edition
Amrut Two Continents 2nd Edition
Paul John Single Malt-Classic (Un Peated)
Paul John Single Malt Cask No 777

New Zealand Single Malt
The New Zealand Whisky Collection South Island Single Malt Aged 21 Years

Taiwanese Single Malt
Kavalan Solist Fino Sherry Cask
Kavalan Single Malt Whisky Sherry Oak

94.5 (New Entries Only)
Scottish Single Malt
Aberfeldy Single Cask 1996 Vintage
The Maltman Aberlour Aged 19 Years
BenRiach Batch 11 2005 9 Years Old
Signatory Vintage Single Malt Braeval 1998
Whisky Agency Perfect Dram Caol Ila 1995
Berry's Own Clynelish 1997 Aged 16 Years
SMWS Cask 41.59 Aged 10 Years
GlenDronach Batch 10 2002 12 Years Old
Cadenhead's Glenfarclas Aged 41 Years
Glenglassaugh Batch 1 1975 38 Years Old
Glenglassaugh Massandra Connection 1978 35 Years Old Madeira Finish
Ian Macleod Glengoyne 25 Years Old
Old Malt Cask Glen Grant Aged 18 Years
SMWSsc Cask 9.85 Aged 16 Years
Glenlivet Nadurra Aged 16 Yrs batch 0114A
Cadenhead's Authentic Collection Glenlossie-Glenlivet Aged 20 Years
Signatory Vintage Un-chillfiltered Collection Glenlossie 1992 Aged 16 Years

Cadenhead's Glen Mhor Aged 31 Years
SMWS Cask 93.59 Aged 14 Years
SMWS Cask 121.70 Aged 13 Years
Glen Scotia Legends of Scotia 2nd Release
"Murfield" Heavily Peated
Lagavulin The Distillers Edition
Adelphi Selection Longmorn 28 Years Old
Old Masters Longmorn 17 Years Old
Longrow Aged 18 Years
Pearls of Scotland Macallan 1989 24 Yr Old
Gordon & MacPhail Con. Choice Strathmill
Single Malts of Scotland Tormore 25 YO
Scottish Vatted Malt
Douglas Laing's Double Barrel Ardbeg & Craigellachie
Scottish Grain
Sovereign Single Cask Invergordon 25 YO
Pearls of Scotland North of Scotland 1971
Sovereign Single Cask North British 1962
Sovereign Single Cask Port Dundas 1978
Bourbon
Buffalo Trace Single Oak Project Barrel #11
Smooth Ambler Old Scout Straight Bourbon Aged 7 Years
American Straight Rye
High West Whiskey Rendezvous Rye
Canadian Single Malt
Cadenhead's World Whiskies Canada Potter Distilling Co. Aged 24 Years
Japanese Single Malt
Nikka Coffey Grain Whisky
SMWS Cask 130.1 Aged 4 Years
SMWS Cask 132.3 Aged 20 Years
French Single Malt
Kornog 2013 For The Auld Alliance
German Single Malt
Tronje Von Hagen Single Malt
Liechtenstein Single Malt
Telsington VI Single Cask Malt 5 Years Old
Swedish Single Malt
Mackmyra Midvinter Single Malt
Australian Single Malt
Limeburners Single Malt Barrel M61
Indian Single Malt
Amrut Single Cask
Paul John Single Malt Cask No 1844

94 (New Entries Only)
Scottish Single Malt
Darkness! Aberlour Aged 20 Years
Ardbeg Kildalton
Darkness! Aultmore Aged 16 Years
BenRiach Batch 11 1994 20 Years Old
A.D.Rattray Stronachie 10 Years Old
Blackadder 2001 12 Years Old Bowmore
Riverstown Bowmore Aged 16 Years
Octomore Edition 06.1 Aged 5 Years
The Maltman Port Charlotte Aged 12 Years
Signatory Vintage Collection Bunnahabhain
1997 Heavily Peated Aged 18 Yrs
Old Malt Cask Clynelish Aged 15 Years
SMWS Cask 26.101 Aged 9 Years
Cadenhead's Dalmore Aged 37 Years
Edradour Straight From The Cask 11 Years

GlenDronach Batch 10 1990 24 Years Old
GlenDronach Batch 10 1996 18 Years Old
Cadenhead's Glen Elgin-Glenlivet 22 YO
Old Particular Speyside Glen Elgin 21 Yr Old
Old Particular Speyside Glen Grant 18 Years
The Single Malts of Scotland Glen Grant Aged 22 Years
Signatory Cask Strength Collection Glenlossie 1992 Aged 20 Years
Glenmorangie Dornoch
Old Particular Highland Glen Ord 16 Yrs Old
Pearls of Scotland Glentauchers 1996 17 YO
Old Malt Cask Highland Park Aged 17 Years
Montgomerie's Single Cask Inchgower
The Arran Malt Millenium Casks
Master of Malt Single Cask Arran 17 Yrs Old
Dunc. Taylor Dimensions Linkwood 22 YO
SMWS Cask 39.99 Aged 23 Years
Berry's Own Longmorn 1988 Aged 24 Years
Speyside Longmorn Aged 25 Years
SMWS Cask 72.38 Aged 28 Years
Old Malt Cask Mortlach Aged 13 Years
Directors' Cut Port Ellen Aged 35 Years
Adelphi Selection Royal Brackla 16 Yrs Old
Old Malt Cask Royal Lochnagar Aged 16 Yrs
Single Malts of Scotland Speyside 18 YO
Springbank Aged 9 Years
The Pearls of Scotland Tullibardine 1990
Elements of Islay Cl6
Scottish Vatted Malt
Duthies Islay Region Blended Malt
Scottish Grain
Cadenhead's North British Aged 24 Years
Scottish Blends
Campbeltown Loch
Tweeddale Blended Scotch Aged 14 Years
Irish Pure Pot Still
Master Distiller's Selection Single Pot
Bourbon
Buffalo Trace Single Oak Project #108
Eagle Rare 17 Years Old
American Small Batch
Balcones Fifth Anniversary Single Barrel
Brimstone Resurrection
Umami Under 4 Years
Canadian Blended
Wiser's 18 Year Old
Austrian Single Malt
Single Malt J.H. Rare Selection bott code L
SM 06 TR db (94)
Waldviertler Dinkelwhisky
Waldviertler Limited Edition Hafermalz
Danish Single Malt
Stauning 3rd Edition Peated Single Malt
Danish Single Malt
The English Whisky Co. Chapter 7
French Single Malt
Kornog Single Malt Saint Ivy 2014
German Single Malt
Alt Enderle Neccarus 12 YO Single Malt
The Glen Els Rare & Special Malaga Single
Cask Release Aged 6 Years
Australian Single Malt
Lark Distillery Single Malt Cask Strength

Scottish Malts

For those of you deciding to take the plunge and head off into the labyrinthine world of Scotch malt whisky, a piece of advice. And that is, be careful who you take your advice from. Because, too often, I hear that you should leave the Islays until you have tackled the featherlight Speysiders and the bolder, weightier Highlanders. This is just complete, patronising nonsense. The only time that rings true is if you are tasting a number of whiskies in one day. Then leave the smoky ones to last, so the lighter chaps get a fair hearing.

I know many people who didn't like whisky until they got a Talisker from Skye inside them, or a Lagavulin to swamp their tastebuds with oily iodine. The fact is, you can take your map of malt whisky, start at any point and head in whichever direction you feel. There are no hard and fast rules. Certainly with nearly 3,000 tasting notes for Scottish malts here you should have some help in picking where this journey of a lifetime begins.

It is also worth remembering not always to be seduced by age. It is true that many of the highest scores are given to big-aged whiskies. The truth is that the majority of malts, once they have lived beyond 25 years or so, suffer from oak influence rather than benefit. Part of the fun of discovering whiskies is to see how malts from different distilleries perform to age and type of cask. Happy discovering.

Abhainn Dearg
LEWIS

SKYE
Talisker

Tobermory

MULL
Oban

Isle of Ju

ISLAY

Isle of A

Springbank
Glen Scotia
Glengyle

Islay

Bunnahabhain

Caol Ila

Kilchoman
Bruichladdich

Bowmore

Port Ellen   Ardbeg
Laphroaig   Lagavulin

ORKNEY
ISLANDS

Highland Park
Scapa

Wolfburn

Pultney

Clynelish
Brora

Balblair   Glenmorangie
Dalmore   *Invergordon*
Teaninich

Speyside see page 24

Glenglassaugh   Banff
Macduff

Glen Ord   Royal Brackla   Knockdhu
Glendronach   Glenugie

Inverness   Ardmore
Glen Albyn   Tomatin   Glen Garioch
Glen Mhor
Millburn   The Speyside Distillery
Royal Lochnagar

Aberdeen

Dalwhinnie

Glenury Royal

Fettercairn

Blair Athol   Glencadam   Glenesk
Fort William   North Port
Ben Nevis   Edradour   Lochside
Glenlochy   Aberfeldy

Dundee

Glenturret   Perth   Daftmill

Tullibardine

Deanston   Cameronbridge

Glengoyne
Rosebank   Glenkinchie
St. Magdelene

Loch Lomond   Edinburgh
Dumbarton   North British
Interleven   Glasgow
Littlemill   Strathclyde
Auchentoshan   Port Dundas
Kinclaith

Girvan
Ailsa Bay
Ladyburn

Bladnoch

Key

● **Major Town or City**
▲ Single Malt Distillery
▲ (*Italics*) Grain Distillery
✝ Dead Distillery

Speyside

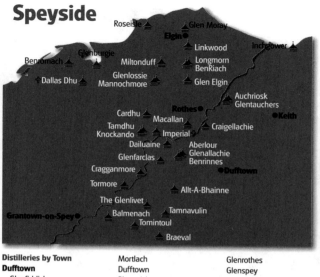

Distilleries by Town

Single Malts
ABERFELDY
Highlands (Perthshire), 1898. John Dewar & Sons. Working.

Aberfeldy Aged 12 Years db (83) n22 t21 f19 b21. The nose is superbly enriched by its usual and uniquely nutty depth. The bitter nougat delivery and finish fails to match the expectation. 40%

Aberfeldy Bits of Strange 16 Year Old db (94.5) n24 that just about unique aroma of a freshly-breeched cask: all dank oak, fruit and barley. Timeless and flawless...; t23.5 magnificent delivery with the sherry ringing loud and clear...and I mean clear...!!! Fabulous spices pepper the palate with oaky splinters; f23 long, forever drying with the oak, but enough voluptuous esters to make a big difference and balance out the finale; b24 one of those lovely casks which combines oaky and sugary bits in just the right proportions. A cracker of a cask – and sublime by present day sherry standards. The perfect way to start or end a day... 55.1%. sc. John Dewar & Sons. Matured in oak for 16 years. 318 bottles.

Aberfeldy 16 Year Old Ramble db (93.5) n23.5 even nuttier than usual, the spices positively pulse. Loads of sharp marmalade and walnut oil combine with stand-your-spoon-in oloroso; t24 heavy molasses notes arrive early and keep their foot in the door. Elsewhere the juiciest of Demerara sugars melt on the palate and begin to form a fabulous Melton Mowbray Hunt Cake richness. Again, walnuts are present and mix perfectly with the syrupy dates; f22 a slight buzz at the death tells its own tale, but before then enjoy the fade to the richest of all fruits cakes with the raisins now at their toastiest; b24 an almost flawless cask good enough for a big, robust, grape-exploding treat. 56%. 643 bottles. Whisky Shop Exclusive.

Aberfeldy Aged 18 Years "Chris Anderson's Cask" db (90) n24 plays the range from bourbon-rich red liquorice right down to diced kumquat; sharp, angular, bold, salty and very enticing; not a single blemish in distillate or wood; t23.5 sharp delivery with a mouth watering malty juiciness, but also weighty, too, with heavy oaks immediately apparent. Any threatening bitterness is seen off by a light dusting of muscovado and dried dates; f21.5 bites deep and caramels out; b22 had the natural caramels just not ticked over a little too exuberantly, this would have headed for a very high score. Aberfeldy in a very unusual light... 54.9%. 248 bottles.

Aberfeldy Aged 21 Years db (92) n24 have I just bitten into a high cocoa Lubec marzipan? The one which has an orange jam topping the almond paste? I must have. Some sublime bourbon hickory and Demerara on show, too. Superb! t23 uniquely nutty delivery screams "Aberfeldy!"; creamy texture without losing complexity. Out of the oils vanilla rises cleanly; f22 reverts to a fruitiness, including, alas, a slightly furry bitter marmalade drawl from, most probably, just one butt...; b23 a distillery I have long held in very high esteem here gives a pretty clear view as to why... 40%

Aberfeldy Aged 25 Years db (85) n24 t21 f19 b21. Just doesn't live up to the nose. When Tommy Dewar wrote, "We have a great regard for old age when it is bottled," as quoted on the label, I'm not sure he had as many as 25 years in mind. 40%.

Aberfeldy Single Cask Aged 21 Years bott 10 Oct 12 db (97) n24 what can you say: the colour of clear honey and with a nose to match...except the salty oakiness adds intriguing depth of fine whisky proportions; t24.5 near enough perfect mouth feel with the kind of punchy bite that every cask strength whisky should have. Actually, make that EVERY whisky. The oak skips around offering a chewy custard tart richness. But that clear honey (perfectly depicted by the bees on the label) is always there or thereabouts; f24 fantastic butterscotch layering, though with delicate marzipan and honey sub layers. The oak is profound but of the highest possible quality, injecting a fabulous drier balance, bordering on cocoa dusting; b24.5 if I find a better single cask this year, it might well be World Whisky of the Year. Just buzzes with magnificence... I have long regarded this not just one of the great distilleries of Scotland, but, even from its Diageo days, one of the true underachievers of world whisky. Not anymore. Someone who knows exactly what they are doing has invaded the Aberfeldy warehouses and made a beeline for the honey casks. This is exactly how malt whisky should bee.... 55.3%. sc. John Dewar & Sons Ltd. 172 bottles.

⁝⁝ **Aberfeldy Single Cask 1996 Vintage** bott 2013 db (94.5) n23 adorable sharp, nutty, honey-tinged malt: like a breakfast cereal with attitude; t24 surprising oaky countenance; definitely on the warm to hostile side but there is something so seductive about the sweet, rambling malt: the bite is from the old school and simply sublime; f23.5 goes into full dry cocoa mode; b24 so rare to fine Feldy this full on and aggressive. But, as usual with this distillery, all the parts feel right and fall into place with majestic ease. Just so my kind of whisky. Brilliant! 61.5%. Exclusive to The Whisky Shop.

Aberfeldy Single Cask Unravel db (96) n24 a beautiful amalgam of dank oak casks (even from the outside) and freshly grated, juicy ginger. The soft distant oak-induced creamed rice and honey, topped with light molasses is superb; some major bourbon traits suggest a pretty virgin type of cask in play here; t24 intense oak but with all the bourbony sugars forming an unforgettable alliance with the black peppers which scorch into the roof of the mouth; like the other two Aberfeldys, the mouth feel is just about perfect...; f24 long, with that formidable coppery flourish sitting happily on the brown sugar and spices; so many layers, you almost give up counting... b24 this completes the best set of single cask malts I have tasted from any Scottish distillery for the last four or five years. Restores one's faith, it does... Oh, and this is supposed to be savoured while listening to some music. Don't bother; it conjures a major symphony of its own...56.5%. sc. John Dewar & Sons.

⁝⁝ **Gordon & Macphail Cask Strength Aberfeldy** refill sherry hogsheads, cask no. 2488, 2489 & 2491, dist 07 Apr 1995, bott 29 Jan 2014 (93) n22 that vague nuttiness...can be from only one distillery. Ultra deft fruit..; t23.5 a perfectly sharp delivery with the alcohohol doing no more than ensuring the intense barley lands with a thump; superb spices and a growing intensity of moist fruitcake; f24 a finish to die for: so busy yet brilliantlystructured with the slow build of Venezualan cocoa finding just the right weight tonaccompany the persistent malt. Really top quality butterscotch, too; b23.5 a fabulous meal of a malt. What a wonderful distillery this is. 55.8%. WB15/113

Gordon & MacPhail Connoisseurs Choice Aberfeldy 1991 (78) n18 t22 f18 b20. Some sensational toffee and raisin moments here, while the sugar-spice combo is in perfect unison. However, also shows what a game of Russian roulette it is now using sherry butts. 46%. ncf.

Old Malt Cask Aberfeldy Aged 18 Years refill hogshead, cask no. 8264, dist Jun 94, bott Jun 12 (92) n23 gorgeous beeswax and vanilla mix; t23.5 not sure if the humming I hear is from the bees or my own happiness: the orange blossom honey and butterscotch is pepped up with just-so black peppers; f22.5 much simpler with more butterscotch and light vanilla; b23 such a charming malt! One for the ladies, too... 50%. nc ncf sc. 306 bottles.

That Boutique-y Whisky Company Aberfeldy batch 1 (83) n21 t22 f19 b21. Didn't know Aberfeldy was in East Anglia. Only explanation for a malt this flat. 47%. 155 bottles.

Wemyss Malts Aberfeldy 1994 Single Highland "Melon Cocktail" hogshead, dist 94, bott 13 (88) n21 t23 f21.5 b22.5. A long way from a perfect dram, but one to seek if character counts for something. 46%. sc. 311 bottles.

⋙ **Wemyss Malts Aberfeldy 1994 Single Highland "Melon Vine"** hogshead, dist 94, bott 14 (**91**) n23.5 milk chocolate Jaffa cake; t23 brilliant delivery: the oak pounds hard, but soft oils, manuka honey and malt keeps it in check; f22 long, with some tangy old tannins but the sugars hold firm; b22.5 sound and lazily complex malt from an effortlessly good distillery. 46%. sc. 242 bottles.

ABERLOUR
Speyside, 1826. Chivas Brothers. Working.

Aberlour 10 Years Old db (87.5) n22.5 t22 f21 b22. Remains a lusty fellow though here nothing like as sherry-cask faultless as before, nor displaying its usual honeyed twinkle. 43%

Aberlour 10 Years Old Sherry Cask Finish db (85) n21 t21 f21 b22. Bipolar and bittersweet with the firmness of the grain in vivid contrast to the gentle grape. 43%

Aberlour 12 Years Old Double Cask Matured db (88.5) n22 t22.5 f22 b22. Voluptuous and mouth-watering in some areas, firmer and less expansive in others. Pretty tasty in all of them. 43%

Aberlour 12 Years Old Non Chill-Filtered db (87) n22.5 t22 f21 b21.5. There are many excellent facets to this malt, not least the balance between barley and grape and the politeness of the gristy sugars. But a sulphured butt has crept into this one, taking the edge off the excellence and bringing down the score like a cold front drags down the thermometer. 48%. ncf.

Aberlour 12 Years Old Sherry Cask Matured db (88) n23 t22 f21 b22. Could do with some delicate extra sweetness to take it to the next level. Sophisticated nonetheless. 40%

Aberlour 13 Years Old sherry cask, hand fill db (84) n21 t22 f20 b21. Skimps on the complexity. 58.8%

Aberlour 15 Year Old Double Cask Matured db (84) n23 t22 f19 b20. Brilliant nose full of vibrant apples and spiced sultana, but then, after a complex, chewy, malt-enriched kick-off, falls surprisingly flat on its face. 40%

Aberlour 15 Years Cuvee Marie d'Ecosse db (91) n22 t24 f22 b23. This always was a deceptive lightweight, and it's got lighter still. It is sold primarily in France, and one can assume only that this is God's way of making amends for that pretentious, over-rated, caramel-ridden rubbish called Cognac they've had to endure. 43%

Aberlour 15 Year Old Sherry Finish db (91) n24 exceptionally clever use of oak to add a drier element to the sharper boiled cooking apple. And a whiff of the fermenting vessel, too; t22 the sharp fruit of the nose is magnified here ten times; f23 wave upon wave of malt concentrate; b22 quite unique: freaky, even. Really a whisky to be discovered and ridden. Once you acclimatize, you'll adore it. 43%

Aberlour Aged 16 Years Double Cask Matured bott 23 Feb 10 db (94.5) n24 a magnificent marriage between sweet, juicy fruit and lively spice; sturdy-framed but giving grape, too; t24 the softest delivery of lightly sugared grape, salivating and sensuous; light spices struggle to free themselves from the gentle oils; f23 pithy with the vanilla determined to ensure a drier finale; b23.5 a joyous malt reminding us of just what clean, fresh sherry butts are capable of. A malt of unbridled magnificence. 43%

Aberlour 18 Years Old db (91) n22 thick milkshake with various fruits and vanilla; t22 immediate fresh juice which curdles beautifully as the vanilla is added; f24 wonderful fruit-chocolate fudge development: long, and guided by a gentle oiliness; b23 another high performance distillery age-stated bottling. 43%

Aberlour 100 Proof db (91) n23 t23 f22 b23. Stunning, sensational whisky, the most extraordinary Speysider of them all ...which it was when I wrote those official notes for the bottling back in '97, I think. Other malts have superseded it now, but on re-tasting I stand by those original notes, though I disassociate myself entirely with the rubbish: "In order to savour Aberlour 100 at its best add 1/3 to 1/2 pure water. 57.1%

Aberlour a'Bunadh Batch No. 31 db (93.5) n24 a resounding Jaffa Cake nose, except someone has extracted much of the sugar from the jam. Some big vanillas amid the cocoa, too; t23.5 a dry delivery with the spices punching hard as the grape unravels; a few maple syrup notes begin to creep in; f23 long, remains dry as the cocoa levels rise enormously; b23 chocolate, anyone...? 60.5%. nc ncf.

Aberlour a'Bunadh Batch No. 32 db (81.5) n20.5 t21 f20 b20. Decidedly acerbic, and this has nothing to do with the strength. Dries far too violently for any balance to be held. 60.4%. nc ncf.

Aberlour a'Bunadh Batch No. 33 db (96) n24 now there's an aroma! A good 20 minute nose, this one, as you try to follow the contours of the Demerara sugar and old sherry Dundee cake on one hand and the far drier, dustier vanillas on the other. The peppers are almost akin to those of a wheated bourbon; t24.5 I think it's the mouth feel that grips the attention first, especially the sheer lusciousness of it. Just as you try to size that up, in pops all kinds of fruit and spice notes, framed by the almost inevitable dark chocolate; those bourbon notes on the nose are backed up by a superb honey-liquorice middle ground; **f23.5** much drier now but the vanillas and other oaky notes show not a degree of bitterness or misalignment; **b24** a masterful dram bubbling over with intense grape....and a whole lot more. Simply gorgeous: the oak involved in this is about as good as it gets. *61.1%. nc ncf.*

Aberlour a'Bunadh Batch No. 34 db (87.5) n21 t23.5 f21.5 b21.5. Overall, impossible not to enjoy. But a bit of a roly-poly kind of malt in which you feel a little short-changed on the complexity front. *59.6%. nc ncf.*

Aberlour a'Bunadh Batch No. 35 db (90) n22 well spiced and heading into red liquorice bourbon territory; **t22.5** silky and toffee-rich delivery. The sugars build cleverly, with the weight firmly on muscovado before the toffee fudge arrives. A light fruitiness mingles with the growing cocoa; **f23** quite complex with the vanillas and cocoa sure footed and well balanced; **b22.5** from the same school as Batch 34, but avoids being bogged down in sticky toffee; *60.4%. nc ncf.*

Aberlour a'Bunadh Batch No. 36 db (94) n22.5 another Kentucky style nose: the liquorice and spiced vanilla take a vice-like grip and refuse to let go; **t24** big and beefy, the sugars arrive with a near treacle thickness, though it is the enormity of the spice which leaves you gasping; **f23.5** calms down but the oils ensure a more gentle version is played out to maximum complexity; the finish displays some flinty fruitiness, not unlike the crisper rye notes in a very good bourbon; **b24** can you find this year another Speyside whisky come with as much muscle as this...? I doubt it. A malt whisky that appears to have spent as much time in the gym as it did the warehouse... *60.3%. nc ncf.*

Aberlour a'Bunadh Batch No. 37 db (94.5) n23 back to a more conventional sherry style here, or seemingly so at first, with what appears to be spiced grape turned up to full volume. However, some powerful bourbon notes are on the prowl and take over proceedings and the fruit effect crumbles...; **t24** spice, as ever, on delivery and as the juiciness grows in intensity, the peppers click up a notch or two; the sugars also arrive early, this time in much lighter mode. Possibly one of the most satisfying deliveries from this brand for some while...which is saying something; **f23.5** vanilla and late molasses interplay superbly; **b24** spice is playing a more central role in a'Bunadh these days and here it is used to excellent effect, putting quite an edge to the fruit. Really beautiful whisky. *59.6%. nc ncf.*

Aberlour a'Bunadh Batch No. 38 db (88.5) n22 t22 f22.5 b22. A heavyweight which maybe overdoes it on the spice. *60.5%. nc ncf.*

Aberlour a'Bunadh Batch No. 39 db (94) n22 wonderful fruit ranging from over-ripe apple to succulent date. The spice is straining at the leash; the grape is encrusted in chocolate; **t24** a graceful dance is being choreographed on my tongue. The spices are at the centre, but swirling around them is a dizzying array of juicy grape and salivating barley. The usual big liquorice sub plot is there and the bourbon theme is underlined with honeycomb. Curiously, there is a small still coppery element to this as well. It does no harm at all; **f23.5** a fabulous denouement of crunchy honeycomb candy and Cadbury's Fruit and Nut...though that is hardly doing justice to the quality of the cocoa...; **b24.5** when they ask for seasoned oak, I am sure the coopers must use pepper. Here, though, as spicy as it may be, everything is under control and weighted superbly. One of the great whiskies of 2012. And confirmation that the best sherry butts on the single malt scene are currently deployed in the a'Bunadh range. *59.8%. nc ncf.*

Aberlour a'Bunadh Batch No. 40 db (93.5) n24 one of the freshest fruit noses you could hope for, with a barrow-full of greengages so ripe they are fit to explode...; **t23.5** silky and succulent, the barley and spice make a big impact after the grape skin introduction; inevitable spices lead to a drier butterscotch tart middle; **f22.5** relatively lightweight for an a'Bunadh with the accent firmly on the barley; **b23.5** a shapely malt with no little barley. *61%. nc ncf.*

Aberlour a'Bunadh Batch No. 41 db (83) n21 t22 f20 b20. By normal standards, not too bad a malt, and another with the emphasis on the barley. But as an a'Bunadh, rather lacking... with one or two unattractive tangs too many. *59.7%. nc ncf.*

⁜ **Aberlour A'Bunadh Batch No. 45** Spanish oloroso sherry butts db (95) n24 Demerara rum meets Java coffee...and dripping grape juice; **t24** fabulous spices give an extra lift to an already full on delivery. Full salivation by about the fifth flavour wave and mocha joins soon after. The fruit is piled high, the sugars higher still; **f23** settles for a more sedate, drier finale, though the dried date and manuka honey tries to have a say about that; late chocolate Swiss roll; **b24** faultless sherry of the old school. *60.2%. sc nc ncf. WB15/332*

⁜ **Aberlour A'Bunadh Batch 47** db (88.5) n22 for oloroso the grape is a little too firm, giving suspicion of perhaps a weakness. And there is nip, too, which bares no relation to the alcohol. But there is a sherry trifle edge to this and black cherry...! **t24** that is one very serious delivery... a warming degree of plum pudding, followed by Melton Hunt Cake doused in brandy; the sugars are gritty and dark, a little treacle and then a return to fruitcake...the burned outside bits; **f20.5** calms as a few caramels appear. But there is grape, too. And now confirmation of only the most distant rumble of sulphur, not easily spotted at first but acting like a slow puncture with the bitterness taking a full five minutes to make its effects felt; **b22** a valued friend of mine, Byron Rodgers, one of Britain's greatest living essayists, asked me over a pint the other night what I thought of the A'Bunadh batch 47 they were selling at our nearest Waitrose. You see, I had recently brought him, wide eyed and innocent, into a world of cask strength whisky; and being a man of infinite curiosity he was determined to learn more very much in the manner of an astronaut having landed on an alien and wondrous landscape. I couldn't tell him, as I had not yet tasted it. Well, I have now. And tomorrow I will advise him to go forth and invest in a bottle, though with a warning. Because as learning curves go, by and large this is a pretty delicious one. Yet perhaps better still for the explorer, it contains a fault from which much can be learned. Like what happens when you pit one bad butt against many good ones. 60.7%.

⁖ **Aberlour A'Bunadh Batch No. 48** Spanish oloroso sherry butts db (**92**) **n24** grape must and nippy mixed spice; **t22** for once, the barley is heard early. But not for long, as lots of natural caramels mix with the grape to make for a thick mouth feel. Elsewhere the spices kick in with a degree of venom; **f23** still nips and tingles, though Demerara sugar tries to heal the wounds; **b23** delicious. But surprisingly aggressive for an a'bunadh. 59.7%. sc nc ncf. WB15/333

⁖ **Cadenhead's Small Batch Aberlour-Glenlivet Aged 23 Years** bourbon hogsheads, dist 1989, bott 2013 (**93.5**) **n23** thin-ish and warming...the spirit safe was taking a bit of a pounding. But the cut was true, leaving the malt to show a rare, warming clarity. The cask is in perfect sync, offering just a light banana and custard accompaniment; **t24.5** astonishingly clean and salivating. The grist appears to have been set in icing sugar; the warm buzz does not appear to be oak-induced spice...; some gorgeous heather-honey adds perfect weight; **f23** more of the same...forever, it seems; and still warms...; **b23** one of the cleanest, sweetest 23 year olds you'll ever encounter. But I suspect the distiller manager of the time, Puss Mitchell, had the stills at full revs when this was made. A hottie! 54.9%. 522 bottles. WB15/069

⁖ **Darkness! Aberlour Aged 20 Years Oloroso Cask Finish** (**95**) **n23.5** rich fruitcake but with demonic amounts of extra spice; **t24** quite brilliant! In true and very old Aberlour style, this not only bristles with spiced sultanas and Demerara sugar but finds the grace to allow in the malt to ensure balance; **f23.5** long, malty but with a lovely fruitcake backing. Delicate for its enormity. And, above all...clean! **b24** "Subtlety, poise and elegance have no place here" claims the back label. Now, I wonder where they get that phrase from...? But, as it happens, this is exactly what the whisky has, helped enormously by the fact that sulphur is wonderfully conspicuous by its absence... 53.4%. 96 bottles. WB15/199

⁖ **Darkness! Aberlour Aged 20 Years Pedro Ximenez Cask Finish** (**94**) **n24** subtle; **t23.5** poised; **f24** elegant; **b23** Thank you for using a PX cask on something that is not a heavily peated monster. Here we can see the sweet sherry at work and play, working alongside the striking intensity of the outstanding barley. In many ways, big, blustery and heavy on the molasses, but beneath the surface a fabulous charm offensive is going on where elegance really is the key. Oh, and for the sheer delight of NOT being assaulted by sulphur...thank you, chaps! 53.7%. 97 bottles. WB15/236

⁖ **The Maltman Aberlour Aged 19 Years** bourbon cask (**94.5**) **n23** wonderful weight to both the barley and the heather honey which also draws in a light mintiness; **t23.5** follows through with an almost identical trick: big malty blast, then heather-honey until the oak makes an impressive incursion without denting the solidity of the bedrock malt; **f24** enriched by copper, almost certainly one of the stills or condensers was repaired/replaced just prior to this malt being made. A real tanginess for the intense malt to grip onto; **b24** absolutely brilliant to see Aberlour naked and not hiding behind sherry: there is rare beauty to behold... 46%

Malts of Scotland Aberlour Christmas 2012 sherry hogshead, cask no. MoS 12053, dist Jun 00, bott Nov 12 (**80**) **n19 t24 f18 b19**. Classic sulphur stain on the nose and finish in particular, though this could be a lot worse. Elsewhere, there's stunning Dundee cake, groaning under the weight of burnt raisins and voluptuous spiced sultana. All the makings of a true superstar dram. What a shame. For the record, the Christmas of 2012 was my worst ever. This didn't improve it. 57.1%. ncf nc sc. 96 bottles.

Old Malt Cask Aberlour Aged 12 Years refill hogshead, cask no. 9340, dist Jan 00, bott Jan 13 (**82**) **n19 t21 f21 b21**. Escapes from the tightened nose of the indifferent cask, displaying a surprising degree of malty versatility, helped by some excellent barley sugar. 50%. sc. Douglas Laing & Co. 312 bottles.

Provenance Aberlour Over 12 Years refill hogshead, cask no. 9074, dist Summer 00, bott Autumn 12 (**88**) **n22 t22 f22 b22**. Well behaved whisky taking a singular malty path. 46%. nc ncf sc.

That Boutique-y Whisky Company Aberlour batch 1 (**92**) **n22** thick with grape, only the spices find a way through; **t23.5** a punchy, blistering delivery with mildly burned sultanas offering a fruitcakey edge to this early on; the mid-ground goes all chocolatey on you...; sugars abound, but are kept honest by the drier, toastier oak notes; **f23** long with those spices continuing their busyness. A silkier element allows the oak to enjoy centre stage late on; **b23.5** the nose warns of a soupy dram. The reality is quite different, with a pleasing complexity unravelling. *53.4%. Master of Malt. 175 Bottles.*

That Boutique-y Whisky Company Aberlour batch 2 (87.5) n22 t23 f21 b21.5. One of those toffee apple fruity guys. With emphasis on the toffee. *52.1%. 298 bottles.*

ABHAINN DEARG
Highlands (Outer Hebrides), 2008. Marko Tayburn. Working.

Abhainn Dearg db (91) n22 the odd feint when pouring, but let the glass warm for a few minutes and the stronger elements soon burn off. What is left is a soft, pulpy gooseberry note as well as barley sugar and vague spice; t22.5 intense and chewy, the delivery confirms the wide cut and for a while the flavours are in suspension. Slowly, a meaningful dialogue with the palate begins and it's those gorgeous barley notes which are first to speak up, soon joined by maple syrup and butterscotch tart; the tongue nearly wipes a hole in the roof of your mouth as it tackles the flavour orgy; f23.5 a wonderful finish, not least because the malt appears to have relaxed into a sugary barleyfest with only a light coppery tang reminding us this is all from a brand new distillery forging its place in island folk lore; b23 so here we go: the 1,000th new whisky of the 2013 Jim Murray Whisky Bible. And this year I give the honour of that landmark to Abhainn Dearg: the first bottling of a brand new Scotch single malt distillery is that very rarest of species. The fact it comes from Lewis really puts the icing on the cake. Some may remember that a couple of years back I made their new make the 1,001st new whisky for the 2011 edition: I have been keeping a close eye on this, now the most western scotch distillery. And it is strange to think that this is the first malt whisky to come from the Outer Hebrides with a licence attached.... My word, it was worth the wait. For after an unsteady start the quality becomes so clearly touched by angels. I can see everyone on the island having no qualms in tucking into this, even on the Sabbath. Well, maybe not... *46%. nc ncf sc.*

Abhainn Dearg New Make db (92.5) n23 t23 f23.5 b23. Exceptionally well made with no feints and no waste, either. Oddly salty – possibly the saltiest new make I have encountered, and can think of no reason why it should be – with excellent weight as some extra copper from the new still takes hold. Given a good cask, no reason this impressive new born son of the Outer Hebrides won't go on to become something significant. *67%*

Abhainn Dearg New Make db (88) n21.5 t23 f21.5 b22. OK. I admit that the 1,001st new whisky for the 2011 Bible wasn't whisky at all, but new make. But, as the Isle of Lewis has made it impossible for me not to visit there by now being an official whisky-making island, I thought it was worth celebrating. The new make in this form is rich, clean and malty but with a much heightened metallic feel to it, both on nose and taste, by comparison to other recently-opened distilleries. This is likely to change markedly over time as the stills settle in. So I had better start looking at the Cal-Mac Ferry timetables to go and find out for myself if it does...

ALLT-Á-BHAINNE
Speyside, 1975. Chivas Brothers. Working.

⊹ **Master of Malt Single Cask Allt-A-Bhainne 20 Year Old** (92) n22 gooseberry jam; t24 salivating barley: grassy, fresh and intense but with a delicate sliver of ulmo honey to thicken things out; f22.5 long, with the oils capturing the vanilla as the sweet spiced barley; b23.5 seeing as this comes in a 3cl bottle, this really is a little gem. *54.9%. sc.*

Old Malt Cask Allt-à-Bhainne Aged 15 Years sherry butt, cask no. 8216, dist Dec 96, bott Mar 12 (89) n22.5 t22 f22.5 b22. Not just is there sherry influence, there isn't the slightest hint of an off note. Delicate and playful. *50%. nc ncf sc. 273 bottles.*

Old Malt Cask Allt-à-Bhainne Aged 21 Years sherry butt, cask no. 8820, dist May 91, bott Jul 12 (71.5) n17 t20 f16.5 b18. The thick, almost concentrated grape does its best to see off the worst excesses of the treated butt. *50%. nc ncf sc. Douglas Laing & Co. 323 bottles.*

⊹ **Old Particular Speyside Allt-A-Bhainne 18 Years Old** refill hogshead, cask no. 10370, dist Jun 96, bott Jul 14 (87.5) n22 heavy oak lightened by malt; t22.5 honeydew melon – with emphasis on the honey; f22 golden syrup with a touch of lime; b22.5 a minor if faultless little gem. *48.4%. nc ncf sc. 275 bottles.*

Provenance Allt-A-Bhainne Over 12 Years sherry butt, cask no. 9219, dist Summer 00, bott Autumn 12 (83) n21 t21.5 f20 b20.5. This may be from a sherry butt, but it has been a long time since a grape has had any kind of influence on this oak. Nothing wrong with the juicy maltiness, however. *46%. nc ncf sc. Douglas Laing & Co.*

Provenance Allt A Bhaine Over 12 Years sherry butt, cask no. 9513, bott Winter 13 (91.5) n22.5 t23.5 f22 b23.5. From the boiled gooseberry school of deliciousness. And about as clean a Speysider as you'll find this year. *46%. nc ncf sc.*

⫶⫶ **Signatory Vintage Cask Strength Collection Allt-A-Bhainne 1991 Aged 22 Years** hogheads, cask no. 90112+90115, dist 09 Jul 91, bott 23 Oct 13 **(90.5) n22.5** the malt is so light and delicate the footprint of the tannins is easily identifiable; soft citrus; a tad earthy; **t23** excellent body: a little more oily than usual but the spices erupt early; massive barley surge; **f22** an impressive biscuit vanilla fade, with a sophisticated dusting of cocoa powder to remind you of its age; **b23** an elegant example of a malt performing beyond the years it was designed for. *54%. nc. 444 bottles. WB15/004*

⫶⫶ **Signatory Vintage Single Malt Allt-A-Bhainne 1995 Aged 18 Years**, hogsheads, cask no. 147071+147072, dist 22 Sep 95, bott 07 Feb 14 **(87.5) n22 t22 f21.5 b22.** A kind of Chivas blending blueprint malt. Cut glass and clean barley: simple with no frills. *43%. nc. WB15/015*

⫶⫶ **That Boutique-y Whisky Allt-A-Bhainne** batch 1 **(77) n19 t20 f19 b19.** Pleasant and sweet...if you like gin! All kinds of botanicals on the nose and follow through on delivery. Maybe the bottling filters had just done a gin run... Disappointing. *49.2%. WB15/193*

⫶⫶ **The Single Malts of Scotland Allt-A-Bhainne 21 Years Old** hogshead, cask no. 2231, dist 20 May 92, bott 12 Sep 13 **(87.5) n22.5 t22.5 f21 b21.5.** Malty and charming, the delicate citrus and kumquat is caught in the surprising oils before vanilla takes a dry grip of the finale. *50.2%. 230 bottles. WB15/307*

ARDBEG
Islay, 1815. Glenmorangie Plc. Working.
Ardbeg 10 Years Old db **(97) n24** more complex, citrus-led and sophisticated than recent bottlings, though the peat is no less but now simply displayed in an even greater elegance; a beautiful sea salt strain to this; **t24** gentle oils carry on them a lemon-lime edge, sweetened by barley and a weak solution of golden syrup; the peat is omnipotent, turning up in every crevice and wave, yet never one once overstepping its boundary; **f24** stunningly clean, the oak offers not a bitter trace but rather a vanilla and butterscotch edge to the barley. Again the smoke wafts around in a manner unique in the world of whisky when it comes to sheer élan and adroitness; **b25** like when you usually come across something that goes down so beautifully and with such a nimble touch and disarming allure, just close your eyes and enjoy... *46%*

Ardbeg 10 bottling mark L10 152 db **(95) n24.5** mesmerising: bigger oak kick than normal suggesting some extra age somewhere. But fits comfortably with the undulating peat and dusting of salt; captivating complexity: hard to find a ten year old offering more than this...; **t23.5** a shade oilier than the norm with orange and honey mingling effortlessly with the smoke: more than a hint of icing sugar; melts in the mouth like a prawn cracker...but without the prawns...; **f23.5** drying oak with cocoa powder. The oils help the sugars linger; **b23.5** a bigger than normal version, but still wonderfully delicate. Fabulous and faultless. *46%. Canadian market bottling in English and French dual language label.*

Ardbeg 17 Years Old earlier bottlings db **(92) n23 t22 f23 b24.** OK, I admit I had a big hand in this, creating it with the help of Glenmorangie Plc's John Smith. It was designed to take the weight off of the better vintages of Ardbeg whilst ensuring a constant supply around the world. Certainly one of the more subtle expressions you are likely to find, though criticised by some for not being peaty enough. As the whisky's creator, all I can say is they are missing the point. *40%*

Ardbeg 17 Years Old later bottlings db **(90) n22 t23 f22 b23.** The peat has all but vanished and cannot really be compared to the original 17-year-old: it's a bit like tasting a Macallan without the sherry: fascinating to see the naked body underneath, and certainly more of a turn on. Peat or no peat, great whisky by any standards. *40%*

Ardbeg Guaranteed 30 Years Old db **(91) n24 t23 f21 b23.** An unsual beast, one of the last ever bottled by Allied. The charm and complexity early on is enormous, but the fade rate is surprising. That said, still a dram of considerable magnificence. *40%*

Ardbeg 1977 db **(96) n25 t24 f23 b24.** When working through the Ardbeg stocks, I earmarked '77 a special vintage, the sweetest of them all. So it has proved. Only the '74 absorbed that extra oak that gave greater all-round complexity. Either way, the quality of the distillate is beyond measure: simply one of the greatest experiences – whisky or otherwise – of your life. *46%*

Ardbeg 1978 db **(91) n23 t24 f22 b22.** An Ardbeg on the edge of losing it because of encroaching oak, hence the decision made by John Smith and I to bottle this vintage early alongside the 17-year-old. Nearly ten years on, still looks a pretty decent bottling, though slightly under strength! *43%*

Ardbeg Alligator 1st Release db **(94) n24** delicate: like a bomb aimer...steady, steady, steady...there she goes...and suddenly spices light up the nose; some coriander and cocoa, too; **t22.5** surprisingly silky, soft and light; milky chocolate hides some lurking clove in the soothing smoke; **f24** hits its stride for a magnificent finale: as long as you could possibly hope for and an-ever gathering intensity of busy, prickly spice. Mocha and a dab of praline see off any potential bitterness to the oaky fight back; **b23.5** an alligator happy to play with you for a bit before sinking its teeth in. The spices, though big, are of the usual Ardbegian understatement. *51.2%. ncf. Exclusive for Ardbeg Committee members.*

Ardbeg Alligator 2nd Release db (**93**) **n24** clove and black pepper; a degree of bourbony polished leather and liquorice, too; **t23** early Demerara sugars and smoke make way for that slow build up of spices again; though perhaps missing the subtlety of the first edition's quietness, it more than has its macho compensations; **f23** curiously, a short finale, as though more energy was expended in the delivery. Much drier with the oak having a good deal to say, though the spices nip satisfyingly; **b23** something of a different species to the Committee bottling having been matured a little longer, apparently. Well long enough for this to evolve into something just a little less subtle. The nose, though, remains something of striking beauty – even if barely recognisable from the first bottling. *51.2%. ncf.*

Ardbeg Almost There 3rd release dist 1998, bott 2007 db (**93**) **n23 t24 f23 b23**. Further proof that a whisky doesn't have to reach double figures in age to enter the realms of brilliance... *54.1%*

⋄ **Ardbeg Aurivedes** American oak casks with specially toasted cask lids. db (**91.5**) **n22** a light Kentucky char nip to this, forming a type of phenol that has nothing to do with peat. Liquorice and butterscotch appear to outdistance the smoke...; **t22.5** astonishingly light delivery: softer than any baby's bottom and maltier, too. Indeed the gristy malt is unusually powerful for an Ardbeg but only because the smoke, which is definitely there, seems preoccupied with a massive surge of vanilla; **f24** way better balanced now as some milky mocha notes take control and a blend of ulmo and manuka honey props up the sugars; the peat remains surprisingly shy and elusive, though the spice tingle on the tongue tells you it is hiding there somewhere; **b23** I have spoken to nobody at Ardbeg about this one but from the slight bourbon character of the nose and the heavy vanilla, this version appears to be about the casks, possibly the char of the barrels. Fascinating, enjoyable...but whatever this is, the usual complexity of the peat feels compromised in the same way a wine cask might. Except here I detect no telling fruit. A real curiosity, whatever it is... *49.9%. Moet Hennessy.*

Ardbeg Blasda db (**90.5**) **n23.5** distant kumquat and lime intertwine with gentle butterscotch tart; it's all about the multi-layered barley and the most vague smokiness imaginable which adds a kind of almost invisible weight; the overall clarity is like that found swimming off a Pacific atoll; **t22.5** sharp barley hits home to almost mouth-watering effect; again there is the most pathetic hint of something smoky (like the SMWS cask, perhaps from the local water and warehouse air), but it does the trick and adds just the right ballast; **f22** soft spices arrive apologetically, but here it could do with being at 46% just to give it some late lift; **b22.5** a beautiful, if slightly underpowered malt, which shows Ardbeg's naked self to glowing effect. Overshadowed by some degree in its class by the SMWS bottling, but still something to genuinely make the heart flutter. *40%*

Ardbeg Corryvreckan db (**96.5**) **n23** excellent, thick, not entirely un-penetrable – but close – nascent smoke and a vignette of salty, coastal references save the day; **t24.5** amazing: here we have Ardbeg nutshelled. Just so many layers of almost uncountable personalities with perhaps the citrus leading the way in both tart and sweet form and then meaningful speeches from those saline-based, malty sea-spray refreshed barley notes with the oak, in vanilla form, in close proximity. The peat, almost too dense to be seen on the nose, opens out with a fanfare of phenols. It is slumping-in-the-chair stuff, the enormity of the peat taking on the majesty of Cathedral-esque proportions, the notes reverberating around the hollows and recesses and reaching dizzying heights; such is its confidence, this is a malt which says: "I know where I'm going...!"; **f24** long, outwardly laconic but on further investigation just brimming with complexity. Some brown sugary notes help the barley to come up trumps late on but it's the uniquely salty shield to the mocha which sets this apart. Simply brilliant and unique in its effortless enormity...even by Ardbeg standards; **b25** as famous writers – including the occasional genius film director (stand up wherever you are my heroes Powell and Pressburger) – appear to be attracted to Corryvreckan, the third most violent whirlpool found in the world and just off Islay, to boot, - I selected this as my 1,500th whisky tasted for the historic Jim Murray Whisky Bible 2009. I'm so glad I did because many have told me they thought Blasda ahead of this. To me, it's not even a contest. Currently I have only a sample. Soon I shall have a bottle. I doubt if even the feared whirlpool is this deep and perplexing. *57.1%. 5000 bottles.*

Ardbeg Day Bottling db (**97**) **n24.5** a dry lead.....seemingly. But it's the busy stuff behind the scenes which intrigues. In typical Ardbegian fashion it's what you have to take a little extra time to find which is the real turn on...apart from the rock pool salt, apart from the squeeze of slightly sugared lime, apart from the thinnest layer of honey, apart from the fracturing hickory, apart from the kelp;...; **t24.5** and while the nose at times seems hard and brittle, the delivery moulds itself into the shape of your palate. Soft oils fill the contours; dissolving sugars counter the well-mannered but advancing oak; the phenols take on an

earthy form, languid spices and omnipresent smoke; **f23.5** dries again in a vanilla direction with the oak determined to have its say. But it is a gentle speech and one inclusive of the delicate phenols encouraging the growing citrus. The oils remain just higher than the norm and thicken the muscovado-sweetened mocha. The finish, one of the longest you will find this year, carries on beyond what you would normally expect of an Ardbeg. And that is saying something; **b24.5** I left this to be one of the last whiskies I tasted this year. I had an inkling that they might come up with something a little special, especially with the comparative disappointment of the fundamentally flawed Galileo. On first sweep I thought it was pretty ordinary. but I know this distillery a little too well. So I left the glass for some 20 minutes to breathe and compose itself and returned. To find a potential world whisky of the year... *56.8%*.
Available at distillery and Ardbeg embassies.

Ardbeg Feis Ile 2011 db **(67) n16 t19 f15 b17.** If anyone asked me what not to do with an Ardbeg, my answer would be: don't put it into a PX cask. And if asked if anything could be worse, I'd day: yeah, a PX Cask reeking of sulphur. To be honest, I am only assuming this is PX, as there is no mention on my sample bottle and I have spoken to them about it. But for something to fail as completely as this my money is on PX. And sulphur. *55.4%*

Ardbeg Galileo 1999 db **(87.5) n23 t23.5 f19 b22.** Today, as I taste this, I am celebrating the first birthday of my grand-daughter Islay-Mae, named after the greatest whisky island in the world. And this was one of half a dozen special whiskies I set aside to mark the event. For it is not often you get the chance to celebrate the first birthday of your first grand-daughter. Nor to taste a malt specially bottled to celebrate some of its fellow Ardbeg whisky that was sent into orbit for experimentation in the Space Station....At least I know a day like this will never be repeated. *49%*

⸭ **Ardbeg Kildalton** db **(94) n23.5** didn't expect that: smoke! Light, dry, ashy but also slightly undercooked in the cask; quite an oily aroma; an unusual, fuzzy aroma of fruit that, for once, isn't citrus-based; **t23** unusually thin first few moments on the palate and takes a while for the smoke, accompanied by the thin layer of plum jam, to make an impact. When it arrives; it stays...; **f23.5** now showing off... the elegance can only be admired as a little ulmo honey and lavender give a deft edge to the already gentle smoke; just a little chocolate raisin on the slightly furry finale; **b24** youthful and lightly smoked, unlike the days when I blended the first-ever Kildalton which was middle aged and, for all intents and purposes, peat free. The most subtle of Ardbegs which whispers its beauty, though quite audibly... *46%*

Ardbeg Kildalton 1980 bott 2004 db **(96) n23 t24 f24 b25.** Proof positive that Ardbeg doesn't need peat to bring complexity, balance and Scotch whisky to their highest peaks... *57.6%*

Ardbeg Lord of the Isles bott Autumn 2006 db **(85) n20 t22 f22 b21.** A version of Ardbeg I have never really come to terms with. This bottling is of very low peating levels and shows a degree of Kildalton-style fruitiness. No probs there. But some of the casks are leaching a soft soapy character noticeable on the nose. Enjoyable enough, but a bit frustrating. *46%*

Ardbeg Mor db **(95) n24** coastal to the point of sea spray showering you, with the smell of salt all the way home until you reach the peat fire. Evocative, sharp with elements of vinegar to the iodine; **t24** one of the biggest deliveries from Ardbeg for yonks; the peat appears way above the normal 50%, thickset and gloriously bitter-sweet, the steadying vanillas carried on the soft oils; **f23** mocha enters the fray with a raspberry jam fruitiness trying to dampen the continuing smoke onslaught; **b24** quite simply Mor the merrier... *57.5%*

Ardbeg Provenance 1974 bott 1999 db **(96) n24 t25 f23 b24.** This is an exercise in subtlety and charisma, the beauty and the beast drawn into one. Until I came across the 25-year-old OMC verson during a thunderstorm in Denmark, this was arguably the finest whisky I had ever tasted: I opened this and drank from it to see in the year 2000. When I went through the Ardbeg warehouse stocks in 1997 I earmarked the '74 and '77 vintages as something special. This bottling has done me proud. *55.6%*

Ardbeg Renaissance db **(92) n22.5 t22.5 f23.5 b23.5.** How fitting that the 1,200th (and almost last) new-to-market whisky I had tasted for the 2009 Bible was Renaissance... because that's what I need after tasting that lot...!! This is an Ardbeg that comes on strong, is not afraid to wield a few hefty blows and yet, paradoxically, the heavier it gets the more delicate, sophisticated and better-balanced it becomes. Enigmatically Ardbegian. *55.9%*

Ardbeg Rollercoaster db **(90.5) n23** youthful malts dominate; a patchwork of smoke on many different levels from ashy to ethereal: almost dizzying; **t23** again, it's the young Ardbeg which dominates; the delivery is almost painful as you shake your head at the shock of the spices and unfettered peat. A genuine greenness to the malts though some natural caramels do make a smoky surge; **f23** long, buttery in part, limited sweetness; almost a touch of smoked bacon about it; **b21.5** to be honest, it was the end of another long day – and book – when I tasted this and I momentarily forgot the story behind the malt. My reaction to one of my researchers who happened to be in the tasting room was: "Bloody hell! They are sending me kids. If this was any younger I'd just be getting a bag of grist!" This malt may be a fabulous concept. And Rollercoaster is a pretty apt description, as this a dram which appears to have the whisky equivalent of Asperger's. So don't expect the kind of balance that sweeps you into a world that only Ardbeg knows. This, frankly, is not for the Ardbeg purist or snob. But for those determined to bisect the malt in all its forms and guises, it is the stuff of the most rampant hard-ons. *57.3%*

Ardbeg Still Young 2nd release dist 1998, bott 2006 db **(93) n24 t24 f22 b23**. A couple of generations back – maybe even less – this would not have been so much "Still Young" as "Getting on a Bit." This is a very good natural age for an Ardbeg as the oak is making a speech, but refuses to let it go on too long. Stylish – as one might expect. And, in my books, should be a regular feature. Go on. Be bold. Be proud say it: Ardbeg Aged 8 Years. Get away from the marketing straightjacket of old age... *56.2%. ncf.*

⠿ **Ardbeg Supernova** db **(96.5) n24.5** rare to find an Ardbeg which positively bristles with peat. Usually it is all smoke and mirrors: here you are steamrollered by the overwhelming peatiness – acrid at its most bruising and direct, smothering once the smoke gets to work... but never less than compelling and not least because of the freshness of the grist which sparkles like the brightest star once the cosmic peat dust has settled...; **t24** for a moment, a gentle silkiness, aided by molten, citrus-molested muscovado, fools you into thinking this is going to be easy. Soon you are jolted into the reality of this dram: it is huge! There is no burn, just a massive piling up of phenols of nuclear fission strength, which erupt around the palate offering a youthful insight into the creation of this malt and a far older tannin-stained echo of passing summers; **f23.5** the finish of a reverberating echo of the explosion before: treacle of subtle finesse, peat which still appears to consist of several different layers of intensity, cocoa still powdery and dry....it just stretches and stretches and stretches...; **b24.5** a spot on bottling which upholds the brand's unique style and never compromises: shows Ardbeg at its biggest and meanest, yet still somehow charms with wondrous intensity and ease. *55%*

Ardbeg Supernova db **(97) n24.5** moody, atmospheric; hints and threats; Lynchian in its stark black and white forms, its meandering plot, its dark and at times indecipherable message and meaning...; **t24** at first a wall of friendly phenols but only when you stand back and see the overall picture you can get an idea just how mammoth that wall is; there are intense sugary grassy notes, then this cuts away slightly towards something more mouth-fillingly smoky but now with a hickory sweetness; a light oil captures the long, rhythmic waves, a pulse almost; **f24** gentle, sweetening cocoa notes evolve while the peat pulses... again...and again... **b24.5** apparently this was called "Supernova" in tribute of how I once described a very highly peated Ardbeg. This major beast, carrying a phenol level in excess of 100ppm, isn't quite a Supernova...much more of a Black Hole. Because once you get dragged into this one, there really is no escaping... *58.9%*

Ardbeg Supernova SN2010 db **(93.5) n24** youthful, punchy and spicy; vanillas and bananas add a sweetness to the molten peat; **t23.5** an explosion of sharp citrus and grassy malt. Not quite what was expected but the smoke and spices cause mayhem as they crash around the palate: eye-watering, safety harness-wearing stuff; **f23** the oak has a bitter-ish surprise but soft sugars compensate. Elsewhere the smoke and spice continues its rampage; **b23** there are Supernovas and there are Supernovas. Some have been going on a bit and have formed a shape and indescribable beauty with the aid of time; others are just starting off and though full of unquantifiable energy and wonder have a distance to travel. By comparison to last year's blockbusting Whisky Bible award winner, this is very much in the latter category. *60.1%*

Ardbeg Ardbog The Ultimate db ex-Manzanilla sherry cask **(78.5) n20 t22 f17.5 b19**. The best advice one can be given about bogs is to avoid them. *52.1%. Glenmorangie PLC.*

Ardbeg Uigeadail db **(97.5) n25 t24.5 f23.5 b24.5**. Massive yet tiny. Loud yet whispering. Seemingly ordinary from the bottle, yet unforgettable. It is snowing outside my hotel room in Calgary, yet the sun, in my soul at least, is shining. I came across this bottling while lecturing the Liquor Board of British Columbia in Vancouver on May 6th 2008, so one assumes it is a Canadian market bottling. It was one of those great moments in my whisky life on a par with tasting for the first time the Old Malt Cask 1975 at a tasting in Denmark. There is no masking genius.The only Scotch to come close to this one is another from Ardbeg, Corryvreckan. That has more oomph and lays the beauty and complexity on thick...it could easily have been top dog. But this particular Uigeadail (for I have tasted another bottling this year, without pen or computer to hand and therefore unofficially, which was a couple of points down) offers something far more restrained and cerebral. Believe me: this bottling will be going for thousands at auction in the very near future, I wager. *54.2%*

Ardbeg Uigeadail db **(89) n25 t22 f20 b22**. A curious Ardbeg with a nose to die for. Some tinkering - please guys, as the re-taste is not better - regarding the finish may lift this to being a true classic *54.1%*

⠿ **Cadenhead's Authentic Collection Ardbeg Aged 20 Years** bourbon barrel, dist 93, bott Jun 14 **(95.5) n24.5** dry peat soot; lavender and cloves assert the age; a hint of citrus tries to lighten matters but with very limited success, especially when the cow sheds kick in; the complexity levels defy belief... **t24** soft oils ensure a friendly delivery, mainly of lightly molassed smoke. Then a much more expansive development of gently peated tannins - cue spices - but the sugars dig deep and ramp up the toasty feel: how can something so enormous be quite so gentle and refined? **f23** a little old Allied barrel bitterness accompanies the slowly fading smoked grist; **b24** as this was the 666th new Scottish malt tasted for the Bible 2015, I chose an Ardbeg from one of the most consistently excellent bottlers: I just knew it would be devilishly good.... *55.9%. 186 bottles. WB15/274*

⠿ **Dun Bheagan Ardberg 15 Year Old** dist Jun 98 **(96) n24** classic Ardbeg ambiguity: smoky yet light, a hint of citrus yet dry, peaty yet complex; confident yet non-threatening...; **t24** a delivery every Islayphile dreams of: pounding peat, a volley of spice, a spoonful or two of Demerara, creamy and chewy without it clogging the complexity; **f24** sweetens just the right degree as an almost bourbon liquorice depth forms. The peat remains ashy and spiced...; **b24** when's the next plane to Tokyo...? *57.5%. Bottled for 3 Rivers Tokyo.*

Master of Malt Ardbeg Aged 18 Years, bott 29 Aug 12 **(97) n24** lack of space prevents me from giving this the full treatment. Probably lack of time, too: it would take a good two hours to get to the bottom of this. The peat is diffused evenly with primroses, nutmeg and walnut oil all playing leading roles. It is the salt which seems to lift everything above a secretive whisper and the citrus which creates the third dimension; **t23.5** the nose in fluid form and minus the primroses...; **f24.5** so, so long. The sugars are now flanked by some serious spices, but in keeping with the genteel nature of this malt, they somehow refuse to upset the balance. A sub layer of ulmo honey also keeps tabs on the neo bourbon characteristics of liquorice, hickory and toasted honeycomb; **b25** a thing of outstanding natural beauty...and probably one of the finest single casks ever commercially bottled. *56.3%. ncf sc. 252 bottles.*

Scotch Malt Whisky Society Cask 33.120 Aged 8 Years 1st fill barrel, ex bourbon dist 16 Sept 03 **(97.5) n24.5** because it is still young enough, the gristiness hangs around the glass limp and glowing like someone prostrate having just experienced the greatest sex of their life; and because the cask is top quality there is also a maturity and depth which offers a counter to the sweet malt and slightly rancid smoke, which is a cross between a beach bonfire and an old crofter's hearth; **t24.5** if you didn't think it possible for a nose to completely come alive and be translated in the glass, then try this. Except there is unquestionably more. The relative youth offers a salivating juiciness after which appears the drier embers and charred malt husk; the mid ground really emphasises the youngest aspect, but by underlining the purity and trueness of the malt, which leaks out independently of the smoke; above all though, the sugars: layer upon layer of toasty Demerara and muscovado **f24** long, at last tapering in sweetness, with a little liquorice and mocha to add to the sugars and, finally, tip-of-the-tongue spices; **b24.5** a very simple question begs to be asked: why isn't something this quintessentially Ardbeg, a single cask which points a bright beam on the distillery's greatness, not bottled under the distillery's own label? This is about as complex as any single cask is able to be. Confirmation that the argument for an 8-year-old Ardbeg at 100 per cent ex-bourbon is not as much compelling as unanswerable. For it is time to stop mucking around with the low quality wine cask nonsense and get back to the magnificent and truly unique basics. *58.5%*

Scotch Malt Whisky Society Cask 33.121 Aged 8 Years 1st fill barrel, dist 1 Jul 04 **(94.5) n24** adorable gristy smoke. Hard to better the balance between salt, malt, smoke and sugar. The phenols are probably lower than the norm, but the complexity is right up there...; **t23.5** as expected, it is sweet, juicy, gristy barley first to cross the threshold; the spices appear to radiate from the centre outwards, the sugars solidifying in their wake; the mid-ground has some fascinating coppery moments lubricated by the softest of oils; **f23** the copper theme continues, with the spices pinging off the metallic firmness; **b24** very unusual Ardbeg which appears to be showing some recent work to a still. The smoke, though constantly heard, is merely a spectator. *59%. nc ncf sc. 243 bottles.*

Scotch Malt Whisky Society Cask 33.123 Aged 7 Years 2nd fill barrel, dist 1 Apr 05 **(84.5) n21 t22 f20.5 b21.** Unhelpful wood interferes on the nose and the finish hits the buffers with an unwelcome late tang, too. The peat is shunted off into an unusual cough sweet siding. *59%. nc ncf sc. 234 bottles.*

Scotch Malt Whisky Society Cask 33.128 Aged 7 Years 1st fill barrel, dist 9 May 05 **(89) n22.5 t22.5 f22.5 b21.5.** One of the most unsubtle Ardbegs I've seen in a while. But you have to admire the effect. *64.6%. nc ncf sc. 242 bottles.*

That Boutique-y Whisky Company Ardbeg batch 4 **(86) n21.5 t22 f21 b21.5.** Surprisingly oily, overly sweet and the smoke appears to be infused with some strange and surprising botanicals. *52.4%. Master Of Malt. 427 bottles.*

ARDMORE

Speyside, 1899. Beam Inc. Working.

⊰⊱ **Ardmore 1996** db **(87) n22 t22 f21 b22**. Very curious Ardmore, showing little of its usual dexterity. Perhaps slightly more heavily peated than the norm, but there is also much more intense heavy caramel extracted from the wood. Soft, very pleasant and easy drinking it is almost obsequious. *43%.*

Ardmore 100th Anniversary 12 Years Old dist 1986, bott 1999 db **(94) n24 t23.5 f22.5 b24**. Brilliant. Absolutely stunning, with the peat almost playing games on the palate. Had they not put caramel in this bottling, it most likely would have been an award winner. So, by this time next year, I fully expect to see every last bottle accounted for... *40%*

Ardmore 25 Years Old db **(89.5) n21 t23.5 f22.5 b22.5** a 25-y-o box of chocolates: coffee creams, fudge, orange cream...they are all in there. The nose maybe ordinary: what follows is anything but. *51.4%. ncf.*

Ardmore 30 Years Old Cask Strength db **(94) n23.5** the first time I have encountered a cough-sweetish aroma on an Ardmore but, like every aspect, it is played down and delicate. Melting sugar on porridge. Citrus notes of varying intensity. Fascinating for its apparent metal hand in velvet glove approach; **t23.5** sweet, gristy delivery even after all these years. And a squeeze of sharp lime, too, and no shortage of spices. Does all in its power to appear half its age. This includes blocking the oaks from over development and satisfying itself with a smoky, mocha middle; the muscovado sugars are, with the smoke, spread evenly; **f23** busy spices and a lazy build up of vanillas; **b24** I remember when the present owners of Ardmore launched their first ever distillery bottling. Over a lunch with the hierarchy there I told them, with a passion, to ease off with the caramel so the world can see just how complex this whisky can be. This brilliant, technically faultless, bottling is far more eloquent and persuasive than I was that or any other day... *53.7%. nc ncf. 1428 bottles.*

Ardmore Fully Peated Quarter Casks db **(89) n21 t23 f23 b22**. This is an astonishingly brave attempt by the new owners of Ardmore who, joy of all joys, are committed to putting this distillery in the public domain. Anyone with a 2004 copy of the Whisky Bible will see that my prayers have at last been answered. However, this bottling is for Duty Free and, due to the enormous learning curve associated with this technique, a work in progress. They have used the Quarter Cask process which has been such a spectacular success at its sister distillery Laphroaig. Here I think they have had the odd slight teething problem. Firstly, Ardmore has rarely been filled in ex-bourbon and that oak type is having an effect on the balance and smoke weight; also they have unwisely added caramel, which has flattened things further. I don't expect the caramel to be in later bottlings and, likewise, I think the bourbon edge might be purposely blunted a little. But for a first attempt this is seriously big whisky that shows enormous promise. When they get this right, it could – and should – be a superstar. Now I await the more traditional vintage bottlings... *46%. ncf.*

Ardmore Traditional Cask db **(88.5) n21.5 t22 f23 b22**. Not quite what I expected. "Jim. Any ideas on improving the flavour profile?" asked the nice man from Ardmore distillery when they were originally launching the thing. "Yes. Cut out the caramel." "Ah, right..." So what do I find when the next bottling comes along? More caramel. It's good to have influence... Actually, I can't quite tell if this is a result of natural caramelization from the quarter casking or just an extra dollop of the stuff in the bottling hall. The result is pretty similar: some of the finer complexity is lost. My guess, due to an extra fraction of sweetness and spice, is that it is the former. All that said, the overall experience remains quite beautiful. And this remains one of my top ten distilleries in the world. *46%. ncf.*

Teacher's Highland Single Malt quarter cask finish db **(89) n22.5 t23 f21.5 b22**. This is Ardmore at its very peatiest. And had not the colouring levels been heavily tweaked to meet the flawed perceptions of what some markets believe makes a good whisky, this malt would have been better still. As it is: superb. With the potential of achieving greatness if only they have the confidence and courage... *40%. India/Far East Travel Retail exclusive.*

Cadenhead Ardmore 15 Years Old (88.5) **n22 t22 f22.5 b22**. A malt which whispers its way through life. *46%. sc. WM Cadenhead Ltd. 366 bottles.*

⊰⊱ **Gordan & Macphail Distillery Label Ardmore 1996** (87) **n22 t22 f22 b22**. Very curious Ardmore, showing little of its usual dexterity. Perhaps slightly more heavily peated than the norm, but there is also much more intense heavy caramel extracted from the wood. Soft, very pleasant and easy drinking it is almost obsequious. *43%.*

Malts of Scotland Ardmore 1991 (87) **n21 t23 f21 b22**. An occasional problem with rum casks is that the sugary element they offer can sometimes enclose the malt it is supposedly helping to enrich. Here is a good example, though the delivery is far from lacking. *53.8%*

Old Malt Cask Ardmore Aged 16 Years refill hogshead, cask no. 8020, dist Feb 96, bott Feb 12 (84.5) **n21 t21.5 f21 b21**. Mild brown sugar stirred into a spiced, cocoa-rich smoky oily dram. Perhaps a little too warming. *50%. nc ncf sc. Douglas Laing & Co. 315 bottles.*

⸙ **Old Masters Ardmore 14 Years Old** cask no. 217, dist 2000, bott 2014 **(89.5) n23** lightly minted smoke: it really doesn't come more delicate than this...; **t23.5** the peat arrives early, though plays second fiddle to the combination of mouth-watering grist and sharper crystalised sugars; **f21** good spice but shame about the "Allied bitterness"...; **b22** without the cask blemish – common amongst casks from its previous owners – this really would have been a gem. 58.3%. James MacArthur & Co. Ltd.

⸙ **Old Particular Highland Ardmore 14 Years Old** refill barrel, cask no. 10359, dist May 00, bott May 14 **(89) n22** a high peat register on this; displays a Love Heart candy fizziness, with the barley showing an unsuspected fruity quality; **t22** light oils travel far taking some major sugars and even a degree of delicate tannin with it. The smoke quietly celebrates its powers; **f23** at first a whisper, a highly attractive touch of everything...and nothing. Even the peat has backed off, but retains an elegant presence as a charming degree of mocha grows; **b22** from a barrel made from the same oak from which The Ark was probably built from, this near colourless Ardmore shows certain properties at this age perhaps never before commercially seen... 48.4%. nc ncf sc. 176 bottles.

Provenance Ardmore Over 9 Years refill barrel, cask no. 9341, dist Autumn 2003, bott Winter 13 **(88.5) n21.5 t22.5 f22 b22.5.** Even when in a lazy, sleepy old cask like this, a high quality malt which refuses to let you down. 46%. nc ncf sc. Douglas Laing & Co.

⸙ **Provenance Ardmore 'Young & Feisty'** cask no. 9879, bott summer 2013 **(84) n22 t20 f21.5 b20.5** Anyone who knows this distillery will half expect what they get here from a spirit so young it is virtually unborn. Rock hard on the palate and no shortage of dry, sooty smoke on the finale. 46%. nc ncf sc. Douglas Laing & Co.

Scotch Malt Whisky Society Cask 66.36 Aged 9 Years refill butt, dist 17 Jul 02 **(83.5) n22.5 t21 f19 b21.** Smoke and sherry rarely works. Here, there is a poor (lightly sulphured) cask at work but the hickory and ersatz coffee combine with thick molasses to make for an interesting few moments. 58.2%. nc ncf sc. 702 bottles.

Scotch Malt Whisky Society Cask 66.40 Aged 10 Years refill barrel, dist 9 Oct 02 **(87.5) n21.5 t22.5 f21 b22.5.** A bit lumpy and, for all its attractiveness, fails to find the usual distillery rhythm. 58.9%. nc ncf sc.

Scotch Malt Whisky Society Cask 66.41 Aged 9 Years refill barrel, dist 17 Nov 03 **(91.5) n23 t23 f23 b22.5.** Unbelievably light: molten grist. An essay on understatement. 60.2%. nc ncf sc. 130 bottles.

⸙ **Scotch Malt Whisky Society Cask 66.46 Aged 11 Years** refill butt, dist 17 Jul 02 **(72.5) n21 t22 f12.5 b17.** In my book Ardmore is one of the best distilleries in Scotland, and probably the most unsung. And I adore non-sulphured sherry. So why doesn't this work, then? Well, apart from the fact it is not entirely free of the venomous S word (the fuzzy finale confirms that), this is just too gloopy and gungy, meaning the sugars really are sickly and over the top. An intermittently pleasant exp/erience. But a poor substitute for the old butts of a generation back. 56.7%. nc ncf sc. 440 bottles.

⸙ **The Pearls of Scotland Ardmore 1988 25 Year Old** cask no. 2455, dist Apr 88, bott Feb 14 **(95.5) n23.5** they were running low on peat the day this was made...some beautiful floral, citrus and earthy notes nonetheless; **t24.5** ah-ha! The delivery, at first swirling in a rich whirlpool of salty barley, reveals its truer, smokier self. It remains a gentle phenol attack, though it intensifies to enormous satisfaction. The lighter, more lemon-clad elements, appear to have been discarded for a busier spicier sub plot. It perhaps the weight and sublime balance, though, which sets this apart as something a little special; **f23.5** long, with some buzzing, peat-stained spices homing in on the vanilla; **b24** superb, near faultless, whisky. Takes a long time before the Ardmore make up is applied. 45%.

⸙ **The Whisky Cask Ardmore Aged 13 Years** peated, bourbon cask, dist 2000, bott 2013 **(86.5) n22 t23 f20 b21.5** Sweet and malty, undone slightly by the not uncommon "Allied Bitterness" at the death. Most remarkable, though, is the lightness of touch of the smoke: barely discernable on the nose and though found on the finish, not in force to overcome the fault lines. 57%. nc ncf.

Wemyss Ardmore 1992 Single Speyside "Mellow Mariner" barrel **(95.5) n24** I think if I was asked to show exactly how an Ardmore should "sniff", then this would be just about it. Slightly above the usual peating level to start with, the smoke has reduced just enough over time to form the perfect frame for the charming butterscotch tart and chocolate caramel mix. Gorgeous weight, profound barley and not a single flaw; **t24** off we go again: the nose but in liquid form. The delicate peat entirely envelopes the palate but it is the differing sugary tones, varying in intensity, style and weight which really press the buttons, especially as they are so in tune with the busy spices. Muscovado and liquorice are the front runners but some toasted caramel also has a telling input; **f23** all the slightly drier, toastier notes converge with the sugars now more of a drier New Zealand style and the phenols now take on a more weighty smokiness; **b24.5** as I write this, Grimsby Town have just been knocked out of the play offs for a place in the Football league – so this will be the only Mellow Mariner in the UK right now. Mind you, after a couple of glasses of this even the most ardent Grimsby supporter - Mariner – will have a smile on his face, and the loss to Newport will seem little more than one of life's oft dwelt deuces. Easily one of the finest whiskies unveiled by Wemyss. *46%. sc. 213 bottles.*

AUCHENTOSHAN
Lowlands, 1800. Morrison Bowmore. Working.

Auchentoshan 10 Years Old db **(81)** n22 t21 f19 b19. Much better, maltier, cleaner nose than before. But after the initial barley surge on the palate it shows a much thinner character. *40%*

Auchentoshan 12 Years Old db **(91.5)** n22.5 sexy fruit element – citrus and apples in particular – perfectly lightens the rich, oily barley; **t23.5** oily and buttery; intense barley carrying delicate marzipan and vanilla; **f22.5** simplistic, but the oils keep matters lush and the delicate sugars do the rest; **b23** a delicious malt very much happier with itself than it has been for a while. *40%*

Auchentoshan 14 Years Old Cooper's Reserve db **(83.5)** n20 t21.5 f21 b21. Malty, a little nutty and juicy in part. *46%. ncf.*

Auchentoshan 21 Years Old db **(93)** n23.5 a sprig of mint buried in barely warmed peat, all with an undercoat of the most delicate honeys; **t23** velvety and waif-like, the barley-honey theme is played out is hushed tones and unspoiled elegance; **f23** the smoke deftly returns as the vanillas and citrus slowly rise but the gentle honey-barley plays to the end, despite the shy introduction of cocoa; **b23.5** one of the finest Lowland distillery bottlings of our time. A near faultless masterpiece of astonishing complexity to be cherished and discussed with deserved reverence. So delicate, you fear that sniffing too hard will break the poor thing...! *43%.*

Auchentoshan 1975 db **(88)** n22.5 a soft, pliable nose: no bites or nibbles. Just orange and caramel...; only as the glass dries does the enormity of the oak begin to reveal itself; **t22.5** takes time before the age begins to tell: after a silky, if slightly untaxing, start the tannins and spices begin to roll over the palate; sharp sugars spike here and there; **f21** back to sleep with the caramel, though a little spice does pulse; **b22** goes heavy on the natural caramels. Does not even remotely show its enormous age for this distillery. I detest the word "smooth". But for those who prefer that kind of malt...well, your dreams have come true...; *45.6%*

Auchentoshan 1977 Sherry Cask Matured oloroso sherry cask db **(89)** n23 t22 f22 b22. Rich, creamy and spicy. Almost a digestive biscuit mealiness with a sharp marmalade spread. *49%. sc. Morrison Bowmore. 240 bottles.*

Auchentoshan 1978 Bourbon Cask Matured Limited Edition db **(96)** n24.5 a nose which stops you in your tracks: Taiwanese green tea sweetened with a brave and enthralling mix of muscovado sugar and manuka honey. There is essence of Kentucky, too, with a bourbony-liquorice trait while the vanillas head at you with two or three different degrees of intensity. How subtle. How complex. So beguiling, you almost forget to drink the stuff... **t24** wonderful strands of sweetness of varying types and levels, from the lighter, fragile citrus notes to something sturdier and more honeyed; the middle ground has a few oily moments which allow all the elements to mix without bias or domination: a near perfectly balanced harmony; **f23.5** long, lush with the barley now having the confidence to reveal itself while the toasted fudge ensures an attractive and fitting bitter-sweet finale; **b24** if there was a Lowlander of the Year, this'd probably wipe the floor with the rest. It's as though someone was in a warehouse, stumbled across this gem and protected it with his life to ensure it was not lost in some blend or other. Whoever is responsible should be given a gold medal, and a Dumbarton season ticket. Ensure you taste this one at body temperature for full blow-away results. *53.4%. 480 bottles.*

Auchentoshan 1979 db **(94)** n23.5 very well aged Christmas fruit cake. With an extra thick layer of top quality marzipan; **t24** sumptuous delivery with the burnt raisin biting deep; bursting with juicy barley; **f23** long with the emphasis on the dryness of the sherry; **b23.5** it's amazing what a near faultless sherry butt can do. *50.1%*

Auchentoshan 1998 Sherry Cask Matured fino sherry cask db **(81.5)** n21 t22 f18.5 b20. A genuine shame. Before these casks were treated in Jerez, I imagine they were spectacular. Even with the obvious faults apparent, the nuttiness is profound and milks every last atom of the oils at work to maximum effect. The sugars, also, are delicate and gorgeously weighted. There is still much which is excellent to concentrate on here. *54.6%. ncf. 6000 bottles.*

Auchentoshan American Oak db **(85.5)** n21.5 t22 f20.5 b21.5. Very curious: reminds me very much of Penderyn Welsh whisky before it hits the Madeira casks. Quite creamy with some toasted honeycomb making a brief cameo appearance. *40%*

Auchentoshan Classic db **(80)** n19 t20 f21 b20. Classic what exactly...? Some really decent barley, but goes little further. *40%*

Auchentoshan Select db **(85)** n20 t21.5 f22 b21.5. Has changed shape of late, if not quality. Much more emphasis on the enjoyable juicy barley sharpness these days. *40%*

Auchentoshan Silveroak 1990 Limited Release db **(94.5)** n23.5 the softest fruit: dates and greengages suggest oloroso at its finest. Not a single off note: these are pristine butts enlivened by some of the most butterfly-minded spices you'll find this year. Love the milky-chocolate sub-plot; **t23** a whispering delivery: pithy fruit here, a light burst of intense, salivating barley there, a crisp and crunchy muscovado/Demerara mix of sugars pottering about...; **f24** enters into complexity overdrive as the few oils there are gather and up the varying flavours and textures, allowing them to cling...how satisfying! **b24** okay...tasting pretty blind on this: have only the sample bottle, showing the name of the brand and the strength, but no accompanying production notes. Appears to have good age, probably above 17, and the sherry butts used here (and I don't think it is exclusively wine oak at work) are of rare high quality for these days. Appears to have the imprint of outstanding blender Rachael Barry. *50.9%. Exclusive for Global Travel Retail.*

Auchentoshan Solera db **(88)** n23 t22 f22 b21. Enormous grape input and enjoyable for all its single mindedness. Will benefit when a better balance with the malt is struck. *48%. ncf.*

Auchentoshan Three Wood db **(76)** n20 t18 f20 b18. Takes you directly into the rough. Refuses to harmonise, except maybe for some late molassed sugar. *43%*

Auchentoshan Virgin Oak db **(92)** n23.5 like a busy bourbon with the accent on the buzzing small grains: all the regulation manuka honey and liquorice there in respectful amounts; **t23** big, sugary delivery, but a cushion of hickory and vanilla keeps the sweetness under control; a little molasses adds extra weight to the middle; **f22.5** pretty dry, with a bit of a coppery sheen, as though some work had recently been done to a still; **b23** not quite how I've seen 'Toshan perform before: but would love to see it again! *46%*

⸪ **Cadenhead's Authentic Collection Auchentoshan Aged 24 Years** bourbon barrel, dist 90, bott Jun 14 **(88)** n22 t24.5 f20 b21.5. The high point is the delivery: fabulously juicy and defying the years. But here we have the unusual case of an Auchentoshan being let down by the cask, rather than the other way round as the slight milkiness on the nose develops into a minor fault on the finale as the cask tires beyond endurance. *52.3%. 150 bottles. WB15/273*

⸪ **Hepburn's Choice Auchentoshan 2001 Aged 12 Years** refill hogshead, bott 2014 **(88)** n22 still some youth to be found: thin, fruity with barely an oaky breeze to be felt; **t23** clean, refreshing, gorgeously salivating barley; **f21** thins out to the vanilla-clad bone; **b22** almost certainly a third fill cask. Yet no signs of tiredness causing damage and a lovely study of an unusual distillery virtually disrobed. *46%. nc ncf sc. 372 bottles. WB15/063*

⸪ **Hepburn's Choice Auchentoshan 2002 Aged 11 Years** refill hogshead, dist 2002, bott 2014 **(86)** n22 t22 f20.5 b21.5. The oak has barely scratched the surface of this blond bombshell. Has the build and personality of a malt half its age so there can be no surprise that the barley dominates from beginning to end. *46%. nc ncf sc. 182 bottles.*

Malts of Scotland Auchentoshan 1991 bourbon barrel, cask no. MoS 13016, dist May 91, bott Mar 13 **(91.5)** n22 t23.5 f22.5 b23.5. Another malt distilled by bees. And much sturdier than you normally find from this distillery. A classic of its kind. *52.3%. nc ncf sc. 96 bottles.*

Master of Malt Auchentoshan Aged 27 Years bourbon barrel, dist 11 Dec 84, bott 20 Nov 12 **(89)** n23 t22 f22 b22. Warming to the point of running slightly hot, the juicy, malty blast is a treat. *58%. sc. 209 bottles.*

Old Malt Cask Auchentoshan Aged 15 Years refill hogshead, cask no. 9807, dist Dec 97, bott May 13 **(89)** n22 t22.5 f22 b22.5. simple, on the sweet side but rather adorable. *50%. nc ncf sc. 211 bottles.*

⸪ **Old Malt Cask Auchentoshan Aged 16 Years** refill hogshead, cask no. 10739, dist Oct 97, bott Jul 14 **(84.5)** n21 t21.5 f21 b21. Malty to an almost ridiculous degree but a little bit thin and incendiary. *50%. nc ncf sc. 299 bottles.*

⸪ **Old Masters Auchentoshan 15 Year Old** cask no. 102339, dist 1998, bott 2014 **(87.5)** n21.5 t22 f21 b22. Clean lemon-zesty but equally hot and thin. Salivation levels are raised but austere oak counters any complexity build. Pleasant enough, though. *60.5%.*

⸪ **Old Particular Lowland Auhentoshan 16 Years Old** refill hogshead, cask no. 10201, dist Nov 1997, bott Jan 2014 **(90.5)** n22 bubbling nose, spikey and sparky with excellent malt-oak integration; **t23.5** launches on the palate with a big malty flourish; **f22.5** thins but now the lemon sherbet kicks in; **b22.5** effervescent but with a light touch *48.4%. nc ncf sc. 357 bottles. Douglas Laing & Co.*

Provenance Auchentoshan Over 11 Years refill hogshead, cask no. 8690, dist Autumn 00, bott Summer 12 **(72)** n18 t19 f17 b18. Fair distillate in a less than fair cask. *46% nc ncf sc.*

Provenance Auchentoshan Over 12 Years refill hogshead, cask no. 9311, dist Autumn 00, bott Winter 12 **(85.5)** n20.5 t22 f21.5 b21.5. The kind of whisky every Chancellor hates: untaxing. Clean, grassy, mouth-watering. *46%. nc ncf sc. Douglas Laing & Co.*

Provenance Auchentoshan Over 12 Years hoghshead, cask no. 9755, dist Autumn 00, bott Spring 13 **(87.5) n21.5 t23 f21 b22.** Clearly from the same stable as cask 9311. Except this has a little more oomph and much better use of sugars. 46%. nc ncf sc.

⠿ **Single Cask Collection 1995 Auchentoshan 17 Year Old** sherry butt, dist 1995 **(91) n22.5** heady grape outweighs the half-hearted malt; **t23** a chewy delivery- not the norm for this distillery! The spices attached to the sultana is some treat; **f22.5** dries towards fruit and custard; **b23** that rarest of beasts in Scotland: the sherry butt entirely free of sulphur. Congratulations on producing a real whisky... 53.5%. sc. Single Cask Collection.

⠿ **Signatory Vintage Un-Chillfiltered Collection Auchentoshan 1997 Aged 15 Years** bourbon barrels, cask no. 101832+101833, dist 17 Dec 97, bott 26 Feb 13 **(91.5) n22.5** a little celery and vanilla combine well; **t23** unusually oily for a 'Toshan: fat malt carries the muscovado easily; **f22.5** traces of citrus on the broad vanilla; dries, but with aplomb; **b23.5** a quite lovely pairing of barrels gives a rarely-found sheen to this Lowlander. Almost perfect spice involvement. Quality. 46%. nc ncf. 654 bottles. WB15/028

That Boutique-y Whisky Company Auchentoshan batch 2 **(86.5) n20 t22.5 f22 b22.** Big perfumed guy giving it large with orange blossom honey. For all the dry, sherry character evident, a hint of hickory-style bourbon slips in, too. 46.6%. Master Of Malt. 295 bottles.

Wemyss 1998 Single Lowland Auchentoshan "Candied Fruit" bott 13 **(94) n23** impressively sweetened, high intensity tannin; **t23.5** a stick of rock solid muscovado melts slowly to leave rock solid barley sugar; the spices make an early entry and stay; **f24** inevitable butterscotch, but works well with the toasted fudge and continuing spice; **b23.5** 'Toshan at its most spiced and most barley intense. A bit of a coup for this distillery as this is a genuinely classy piece. 46%. sc. Wemyss Malts. 294 bottles.

⠿ **Wemyss Malts 1998 Single Lowland Auchentoshan "Lemon Zest"** bott 2013 **(78.5) n19 t20 f19 b19.5.** I for one very much enjoy Wemyss' contribution to the whisky world. But am left more than confused by many of their bizarre descriptors of their whisky. This, with their "Lemon Zest" is like so many others in being not even close to the actual character of the malt they have bottled. Not a single atom of citrus to be found anywhere and the unwelcome earthiness of the cask is countered only by some thin sugars. 46%. sc. 342 bottles.

⠿ **Wemyss Malts 1998 Single Lowland Auchentoshan "Summer Fruit Cup"** barrel, dist 98, bott 14 **(88) n22** a tube of fruit pastilles; **t22.5** salivating, deliciously malty but a little fiery nip; **f21.5** thins out as vanilla moves in; **b22** a bottling where the triple distillation is very apparent. 46%. sc. 295 bottles.

⠿ **Wemyss Malts 1998 Single Lowland Auchentoshan "Tarte Au Citron"** dist 1998 bott 2013 **(96) n23.5** delicate and multi complex with clever layering of vanilla – almost to ice cream proportions – complete with the drier wafer cone; **t24** stunning texture and weight. Oiler than to be expected with some tangerine cutting through the gristy butterscotch; **f24** a marvellous display of controlled oak, at times almost on a bourbon liquorice level; **b24.5** a distillery classic with neither a false step nor the vaguest hint of a weakness: simply a complex delight...! 46%. Sc. 342 bottles.

AUCHROISK
Speyside, 1974. Diageo. Working.

Auchroisk Aged 10 Years db **(84) n20 t22 f21 b21.** Tangy orange on the nose, the malt amplified by a curious saltiness on the palate. 43%. Flora and Fauna.

Auchroisk 30 Years Old Special Release 2012 American and European Oak refill casks, dist 1982, bott 2012 db **(91.5) n22** borderline bourbon with a wonderful hickory and liquorice edge to the duller fruit; **t23** outstanding delivery with a mouth feel to die for; the spices buzz busily and with intent, but can never get the better of the soft oils, layered hickory and dried molasses; **f23** the oils intensify, even with a degree of rum-like esters allowing the oak to surge without causing damage; **b23.5** a hugely – and surprisingly - impressive singleton of tannins. 54.7%. nc ncf. Diageo.

Auchroisk Special Release 2010 20 Years Old American and European oak db **(89) n22.5 t22 f22.5 b22.** Can't say I have ever seen Auchroisk quite in this mood before. Some excellent cask selection here. 58.1%. nc ncf. Diageo. Fewer than 6000 bottles.

⠿ **Berry's Own Selection Auchroisk 1991 Aged 21 Years** cask no. 7476, bott 2013 **(87.5) n21.5 t22.5 f21.5 b22.** A juicy, attractive and very simple ensemble of malt and toffee. 52.1%. ncf ncf. WB15/240

⠿ **Berry's Own Selection Auchroisk 2000 Aged 14 Years** cask no. 20, bott 2014 **(85.5) n21.5 t22 f21 b21.** A light, clean run of the mill Speyside-style dram with all the emphasis on the barley and, though pleasant and without fault, very timid and has little of interest to say. 46%. ncf ncf. WB15/251

⠿ **Cadenhead's Small Batch Auchroisk Aged 24 Years** butts, dist 1989, bott 2014 **(71)** n19 t19 f16 b17. Spicy. Lush. And fatally furry. A crying shame as the grapey intensity of the butts is something to genuinely behold. 57.5%. 1140 bottles. WB15/086

⠿ **Càrn Mòr Strictly Limited Edition Auchroisk Aged 13 Years** hogshead, dist 2000, bott 2014 **(88.5)** n21 rather too light for greatness with thin Lincoln biscuit and a hint of mallow; t23 just doesn't cleaner on delivery: crystalline barley which multiply in intensity. Something alluringly gristy about the sweetness; f22.5 simple vanilla; b22 blenders' delight being so clean and graceful. Stands up well as a singleton, too... 46%. nc ncf. WB15/064

Gordon & MacPhail Connoisseurs Choice Auchroisk 1996 (84.5) n21 t21 f21.5 b21 At its most ethereal, naturally toffeed and blendiest. 46%.

⠿ **Hepburn's Choice Auchroisk Aged 12 Years** refill hogshead, dist 01, bott 14 **(87)** n21.5 t22 f22 b21.5. One of the lightest of all Scotland's malts. The singular fresh barley theme is pretty attractive. 46%. 367 bottles.

Kingsbury Auchroisk Aged 21 Years sherry cask, cask no. 2554, dist 91 **(91.5)** n22.5 t23.5 f22.5 b23. The man who would have ordered this into sherry butt, J&B blender Jim Milne, would have been as surprised as he would delighted with this. He found the spirit just too thin in its standard bourbon cask incarnation and looked for excellent sherry butts to give extra lift....he didn't see it surviving to 21 otherwise. A cracker of a cask. 46%. nc ncf.

Master Of Malt Auchroisk 23 Years Old sherry cask, cask no. 3669, bott 2013 **(90)** n22 t23 f22.5 b22.5. Silky, but just enough spice to shake up the taste buds. 44%. sc.

⠿ **Old Malt Cask Auchroisk Aged 18 Years** refill hogshead, cask no. 9877, bott Oct 94, dist Jun 13 **(76)** n20 t19 f18 b19. After all these years the malt has little to thank the cask for... 50%. nc ncf sc. 311 bottles.

⠿ **Old Particular Speyside Auchroisk 18 Years Old** refill hogshead, cask no. 9899, dist Oct 94 bott Aug 13 **(85.5)** n22.5 t22 f20 b21. Makes little effort other than to maximise the maltiness on the nose and delivery. Thins rather a little too quickly, as is this distillery's wont. But the citrusy elegance of the nose is some compensation. 48.4%. nc ncf sc. 335 bottles. Douglas Laing & Co.

⠿ **Old Particular Speyside Auchroisk 20 Years Old** refill hogshead, cask no. 10341, dist Apr 94, bott May 14 **(84)** n21.5 t21 f20.5 b21. A malt which struggles to handle the tannins... 50.1%. nc ncf sc. 312 bottles.

⠿ **Robert Graham 17 Year Old Speyside Malts** cask no. 1977, bott Nov 2013 **(83)** n19 t22 f21 b21. Possibly a third fill cask containing one of Speyside's thinnest whiskies. And though there is a genuine sense of a malt undercooked, you cannot but enjoy the freshness of the barley. 49.8%. ncf sc. Cask strength, 252 bottles.

That Boutique-y Whisky Company Auchroisk batch 1 **(84)** n21 t22 f20.5 b20.5. Soft, run of the still stuff. Pretty taken aback by the nose, though, which threw me back to the Stockholm restaurants of the early '90s, when each one would offer their own aquavit. This nose is not entirely dissimilar to something found there. 44.7%. Master Of Malt. 127 bottles.

AULTMORE
Speyside, 1896. John Dewar & Sons. Working.

Aultmore 12 Years Old db **(86)** n22 t22 f20 b22. Do any of you remember the old DCL distillery bottling of this from, what, 25 years ago? Well, this is nothing like it. 40%

⠿ **Cadenhead's Small Batch Aultmore-Glenlivet Aged 17 Years** bourbon hogsheads, dist 97, bott 14 **(88)** n22 lemon sherbet...and hints of coal; t22.5 lively delivery: eye-watering barley with an off-centre bitter note from the oak; f21 a little too bitter but the toffee-vanilla works well; b22.5 most whiskies would succumb to the tightness of the bitter oak. But this is so well endowed with explosive barley and lightly sugared citrus, it gets away with it. Some great moments. 54.9%. 450 bottles. WB15/261

⠿ **Darkness! Aultmore Aged 16 Years Oloroso Cask Finish (94)** n23 a nose from the old school of faultless oloroso: spiced, dripping in molasses yet a malty sub strata is there for enjoyment; t24 truly magnificent delivery: over ripe plums, thinned a little by greengages. Juicy dates and scorched raisins abound. Meanwhile spices buzz, while a little sherry trifle hits the mark; f23.5 malty, a tad salty and now vanilla joins the fruity fray; b23.5 once I might have called this top heavy with sherry. But after the nightmare of the last decade it would be churlish to find too much fault with this new cask from the past.... 53.6%. 81 bottles. WB15/203

⠿ **Gordon & MacPhail Connoisseurs Choice Aultmore** dist 2000, bott 2013 **(91)** n22 gooseberries and grass; t24 fabulous weight: juicy fresh barley in golden syrup. Back to gooseberries again – uncooked and bursting at the seams; f22 just bitters a little at the fade as some unfriendly oak gets a small foothold; b23 the kind of malt I can drink all day and every day. Just so wonderfully refreshing and alive. 46%. nc ncf. WB15/145

Master Of Malt Aultmore Aged 5 Years first fill sherry puncheon, dist 12 May 07, bott May 12 **(88)** n22 t22.5 f22 b21.5. Exceptionally well hung and ballsy. The oak has an enormous amount to say and the sherry virtually nothing. Solid stuff with not a hint of an off note. *66.8%. ncf sc. 628 bottles.*

Master Of Malt Aultmore 15 Years Old hogshead, cask no. 3560, dist 15 May 97, bott 1 Apr 13 **(95)** n24 adorable. Like the girl next door: pretty and seemingly unremarkable. But look closer and you will see how the mood shifts and brightens, throwing up irresistible traits, especially the spiced chocolate orange; **t24** just so much orange blossom honey, sharpened by apple and pear juice and some gorgeous spiced red liquorice as the oak gets to serious work; **f23** molasses and beech honey still show glimpses of citrus here and there while the spices are like a Rottweiler with a ragdoll; **b24** an amazing degree of apple and orange to this. Really one turn-on of a dram. *55.8%. sc.*

⸭ **Master of Malt Single Cask Aultmore 20 Years Old** refill, dist 10 Oct 91, bott 1 Jun 12 **(92)** n21.5 sawdust-dry oak; sharp malt; **t24** massively pleasing delivery with the palate being washed by magnificently intense barley, some of it salivating. Pepped by spice and oak. Simple, but gloriously effective; **f23** an elegant and now intrinsically complex fade, long and with the malt and vanilla on equal terms; **b23.5** only 20 bottles of this stuff, so hardly surprising it took us two years to track one down. Worth the search. *54.4%. sc. WB15/211*

⸭ **Old Malt Cask Aultmore Aged 21 Years** refill hogshead, cask no. 9869, dist Sept 91, bott Jul 13 **(81)** n19 t22 f19 b20. 50% A bit of a shame: the delivery shows just how up for it the barley is, so fresh, clean and salivating is it. However, the nose and finish are clear indicators of a cask with just a little too much extracted in previous lives. *50%. nc ncf sc.*

Provenance Aultmore Over 11 Years sherry butt, cask no. 8188, dist Autumn 00, bott Winter 12 **(89)** n22.5 t22.5 f22 b22. A beautifully clean malt fest. Don't expect complexity: just enjoy the delicious simplicity. *46% nc ncf sc.*

⸭ **Provenance Aultmore 'Commemorative 1,000 Bottlings' Over 5 Years** dark sherry casks **(77)** n19 t21 f18 b19 A young sherry cask, presumably. A good try, but hmmm... *50%. nc ncf sc. Douglas Laing & Co.*

⸭ **Scotch Malt Whisky Society Cask 73.61 Aged 24 Years** refill butt, dist 31 May 89 **(95.5)** n23.5 both rugged and relaxing within the same sniff: the light fruits mingle with ease in the company of a craftman's sawdust and a batsman's linseed; the toasted hazelnuts tops off the experience; **t24.5** truly masterful delivery. The barley is in its most concentrated form, yet softened and encrusted in a toasted raisin case...almost a hint of Eccles cake about this. Crisp, chunky, mind-blowingly intense...yet with an elegant softness; **f23.5** long, spiced and immensely satisfying; **b24** the kind of malt which makes you purr... Truly superb. *57.1%. nc ncf sc. 521 bottles.*

⸭ **Scotch Malt Whisky Society Cask 73.62 Aged 24 Years** dist 31 May 89 **(83.5)** n21 t22 f19 b21.5. Superficially very similar to 73.61. But look closely and the cracks appear, especially with the light yet tight, furry, finale. Excellent spice, though. *57.8%. nc ncf sc. 386 bottles.*

That Boutique-y Whisky Company Aultmore batch 1 **(94.5)** n23 intense, heavy duty fruit, dates especially. Spices threaten but are kept under control by the thick, almost impenetrable dollops of mixed fruit...; **t23.5** massive delivery – as expected. Again syrupy dates control the early moments, though now with those busy spices which try to be heard on the nose; **f24** softens now for a more red-liquorice, bourbon-style fade, though the oak plays a big part offering both custard and spice in equal measures. The muscovado sugars melt slowly; **b24** one of those rare malts which so often appears to be heading way over the top...but then throttles back so the balance is maintained. A real treat...probably at its best last thing before heading for bed, as the finish is truly fabulous. *53.4%. Master of Malt. 422 Bottles.*

That Boutique-y Whisky Company Aultmore batch 2 **(85)** n21 t22 f21 b21. Big, thumping almost barley wine intensity to the malt. But not the first Boutique-y whisky to have a strange juniper-gin trace element to it. A coincidence? *56%. Master Of Malt. 226 bottles.*

⸭ **That Boutique-y Whisky Aultmore** batch 3 **(88)** n21.5 dry: sandalwood and malt; **t23** resounding barley with a Malteser candy feel; **f21.5** reverts to the nose in style; **b22** understated and malty. *53.2%. 175 bottles. WB15/194*

⸭ **That Boutique-y Whisky Aultmore** batch 4 **(89)** n21.5 t23 f22.5 b22.5. Very similar in style to Batch 4 but with a little extra spice and mid-ground gristy sugar. *473%. WB15/232*

⸭ **The Single Malts of Scotland Aultmore 15 Years Old** hogshead, cask no. 2619, dist 19 Mar 98, bott 29 Oct 13 **(87.5)** n21 t22 f22.5 b22. Huge natural caramels fill in the gaps where the complexity should be. Salivating and excellently chewy. *51.3%. 220 bottles. WB15/317*

The Warehouse Collection Aultmore Aged 16 Years bourbon barrel, cask no. 3565, dist 15 May 97, bott 17 May 13 db **(88.5)** n21.5 t23 f22 b22. Just enough honey to see off the energetic oak. *56.4%. nc ncf sc. Whisky Warehouse No. 8. 186 bottles.*

Wemyss 1982 Single Speyside Aultmore "Sugared Almonds" hogshead, bott 2012 (87.5) n23 t22 f21 b21.5. Starts outstandingly on both nose and palate but fades very quickly 46%. sc. 272 bottles.

⬩ **Wemyss Malts 1991 Single Speyside Aultmore "Sweet Mint Infusion"** dist 1991 bott 2013 (90) n22 delicately floral and earthy; something of dank Spring forest floors; t23 gorgeous firmness to the malt- almost Glen Grant in style. The barley sings proudly and with the cleanest of voices; a gentle sugary breeze while a soft smoke strums almost imperceptibly at the rear; f22.5 back to the earthiness, now intermingling with toasty ice cream cones; b22.5 solid and quite beautifully constructed; makes outstanding use of the small degree of smoke at its disposal. 46%. sc. 354 bottles.

BALBLAIR

Highlands (Northern), 1872. Inver House Distillers. Working.

Balblair 10 Years Old db (86) n21 t22 f22 b21. Such an improved dram away from the clutches of caramel. 40%

Balblair Aged 16 Years db (84) n22 t22 f20 b20. Definitely gone up a notch in the last year. The lime on the nose has been replaced by dim Seville oranges; the once boring finish reveals elements of fruit and spice. It's the barley- rich middle that shines, though, and some more work will belt this up into the high 90s where this great distillery belongs. 40%

Balblair 1965 db (96.5) n23 any more Kentuckian and I do declare that I'd swear this'd been matured in a log cabin with racoons for guards...; a lovely procession of manicured bourbon notes, with semi-peeled kumquats at the van; t24.5 you will not find a more superbly complex delivery, with this seemingly possessing two bodies in one: the first is a little oily and soft but carrying the darker oaky notes, while simultaneously the mouth fills with juices from both barley and fruit; f24.5 a mix of peach and melon yogurt mixed in with chocolate mousse, a rare but delightful concoction; light liquorice and hickory dusted with muscovado sugars reminds one of Kentucky again; b24.5 many malts of this age have the spirit hanging on in there for grim life. This is an exception: the malt is in joint control and never for a moment allows the oak to dominate. It is almost too beautiful for words. 52.3%

Balblair 1969 db (94.5) n22.5 marmalade and pencil shavings; t23.5 just so salivating as sugared orange juice intermingles with a glorious array of delicate caramel and vanilla tones, rounding off with honey; f24 honey still, now stirred into a bowl of rice pudding; b24.5 a charmer. Don't even think about touching this until it has stood in the glass for ten minutes. And if you are not prepared to give each glass a minimum half hour of your time (and absolutely no water), then don't bother getting it for, to be honest, you don't deserve it... 41.4%

Balblair 1975 db (94.5) n24.5 one of the most complex noses in the Highlands with just about everything you can think of making a starring, or at least guest, appearance at some time. That's not a taster's get-out. Nose it and then defy me...For starters, watch the clever bourbon edge alongside the crème brulee and ground cherry topping...hunt the smoke down, also... t23.5 the barley descends in the most gentle manner possible but this does not detract from the intensity: wave upon wave of barley melts upon the tastebuds, varying only in their degree of sweetness; f23 a few more bitter oak noises, but it remains barley all the way, even at this age. Amazing...; b23.5 essential Balblair. 46%

Balblair 1978 db (94) n24 evidence of great antiquity hangs all over this nose, not least in the exotic fruit so typical of such vast aging; there is smoke, too: a delicate peat more common at the distillery in those days is evident and most welcome; t24 the lush delivery offers up an improbably malty juiciness. But this is almost immediately countered by a spicy oakiness which offsets with great charm the salivating barley chorus and layers of delicate fruit and almost nutty vanilla: not for a second is elegance compromised; f23 those of you with a passion for older Ballantine's will not be much surprised that this was, in its Allied days, once a vital ingredient: such is the clarity of the vanilla-led silkiness. Again, great age is never in doubt. Towards the very death the wisps of smoke found on the nose make a lingering reappearance; b23 just one of those drams that exudes greatness and charm in equal measures. Some malts fall apart when hitting thirty: this one is totally intact and in command. A glorious malt underlining the greatness of this mostly under-appreciated distillery. 46%

⬩ **Balblair 1983 Vintage 1st Release** dist 1983 bott 2013. db (96.5) n24.5 the weight has been touched by a wand: Demerara enriched Dundee cake without a trace of dissention in the ranks. The gentle grapey, sultana notes are almost ghostlike and happy to enjoy top billing with the candy store barley sugar and chocolate coconut. Almost impossible to describe the full story, as the changes with the temperature can be as startling as they beautiful. Touches greatness...; t24 an almost exact carbon copy of the nose on the palate, except here the mouth feel tallies exactly with the weight. The sugars dissolve disarmingly and the fruitiness is little more than the odd breeze. A little more spice, though, than can be detected nasally though this reveals a nimbleness of Ali in his pomp. **f23.5** like lengthening shadows on a summer's evening, the oak begins to make itself slightly better known. The barley recedes, though leaving behind a gristiness enhanced by syrup-dank coconut flakes; meanwhile, like bees going about their daily chores, the spices buzz and hum; **b24.5** very few malts are this comfortable, or vibrant, by the time they reach their third decade in the cask. A Highland gathering of sensational casks resulting in a celebration of what great Scotch whisky is really all about. Magnificent. *46%. nc ncf. Inverhouse Distilleries.*

Balblair 1989 db **(91)** n23 t23 f22.5 b22.5. Don't expect gymnastics on the palate or the pyrotechnics of the Cadenhead 18: in many a ways a simple malt, but one beautifully told. Almost Cardhu-esque in the barley department. *43%*

Balblair 1989 db **(88)** n21.5 t22 f22.5 b22. A clean, pleasing malt, though hardly one that will induce anyone to plan a night raid on any shop stocking it... *46%*

Balblair 1990 db **(92.5)** n24 t23.5 f22 b23. Tangy in the great Balblair tradition. Except here this is warts and all with the complexity and greatness of the distillery left in no doubt. *46%*

⁙ **Balblair 1990 Vintage 2nd Release** dist 1990 bott 2013. db **(83.5)** n22 t21 f20 b20.5. Full bodied yet tight and tangy. *46%. nc ncf. Inverhouse Distilleries.*

Balblair 1997 2nd Release db **(94)** n23.5 gooseberry tart with a curious salt and sugar seasoning; a shaving of ginger and a little physalis adds no end of complexity; **t23.5** sharp, tangy, pulsing barley both salivating and showing verve and a complex drier side: quintessential Balblair...; **f23** the vanillas walk hand-in-hand with the barley towards a cocoa-rich, late-spiced finale; **b24** a very relaxed well-made and matured malt, comfortable in its own skin, bursting with complexity and showing an exemplary barley-oak ratio. A minor classic. *46%. nc ncf.*

⁙ **Balblair 1999 Vintage 1st Release dist 1999** bott 2014. db **(92.5)** n23 an apparent diaspora of mixed casks at times singing together; at others happy to knock each other about. Weighty, fruity but with a sharp malt theme, too; **t23.5** fabulous mouth feel: lush without cloying and despite the apparent grape, more than happy for the barley to weild its full juicy might; **f23** a little tangy, perhaps, but nothing too serious. Some lovely marmalade to enrich the toast; **b23** the same colour as the cockerel which wakes me each morning...and crows as loudly. Gorgeous. *46%. nc ncf. Inverhouse Distilleries.*

Balblair 2000 db **(87.5)** n21.5 t22.5 f21.5 b22. No toffee yet still a clever degree of chewy weight for all the apparent lightness. *43%*

Balblair 2001 db **(90.5)** n23.5 gooseberries at varying stages of ripeness; barley so clean it must be freshly scrubbed; the kind of delicate spice prickle that is a must; **t23.5** majestic delivery: hard to imagine barley making a more clean, intense and profound entrance than that. The malt forms many layers, each one sugar accompanied but taking on a little more oak; **f21.5** dries, spices up but bitters a little; **b22.5** a typically high quality whisky from this outrageously underestimated distillery. *46%*

Balblair 2002 1st release bott 2012 db **(90.5)** n22 lively barley dominates, though some first fill bourbons are evident, also; **t23** absolutely brilliant delivery showing the distillery in a playful mood, yet with a deeper, earthier strata. Natural caramels abound in fudgy form, with those creamy sugars thickening the feel of the barley; **f22.5** light banana and custard notes, plus barley sugar, vanilla and yet more fudge; **b23** a malt which reminds you how cold it is during Scottish winters...there is a lot of fresh-faced youth to this. But just so beautiful thanks to its understated complexity and honesty. *46%. nc ncf.*

⁙ **Balblair 2003 Vintage 1st Release** dist 2003 bott 2013. db **(88.5)** n20 strangely tart, at times off key. Not Balblair's nose showing by any means its greatest profile...; **t23.5** ...yet the delivery is an absolute treat, churning out a succession of confident barley themes in classic Balblair style, from eyewateringly salivating and rich to crisp and precise. The sugars are crunchy and follow a gristy route; **f22** a rather lovely succession of vanilla and butterscotch notes, always with a barley theme; **b23** the nose maybe a bit odd, even unattractively flawed. But this a tale with a happy ending. *46%. nc ncf. Inverhouse distilleries.*

⁙ **Balblair 2004 Vintage 1st Release** bourbon matured, dist 2004, bott 2014. db **(88)** n22 a busy chap full of ginger and liquorice; **t22.5** stoked-up sugars find an early release and show a maple syrup edge. The oak is pretty well charged too and reveals a bitter marmalade counter; **f21.5** after the punchy delivery a more pithy finale, again with the oak holding sway; **b22** maybe could have done with a higher percentage of 2nd fill casks to soften the experience and magnify the complexity. *46%. nc ncf. Inverhouse Distilleries.*

⁙ **Balblair 2004 Vintage 1st Release Sherry Matured** dist 2004 bott 2014. db **(68)** n16 t19 f16 b17. The sadness, of course, is that there are some pretty decent sherry butts amongst duds. *46%. nc ncf. Inverhouse Distillers.*

⁙ **Cadenhead's Small Batch Balblair Aged 23 Years** bourbon barrels, dist 1990, bott 2013 **(95.5)** n23.5 tangy orange...and malt concentrate; **t24.5** tangy orange sweetened by muscovado sugar and a vanilla-butterscotch oak edge; the spices are all embracing...; **f23.5** creamy vanilla...and spiced tangy orange; **b24** the thing about Cadenhead is that they rarely get it wrong when it comes to bottling a cask: for the last 25 years they have been probably the most consistently good of all the independents. And the thing about Balblair is that the house style for those of us who blend with it also, is a sweetness suffused with a tangy orange note. So trust Cadenhead to choose a cask which nails it to perfection. *51.7%. 318 bottles. WB15/070*

Master of Malt Balblair 35 Years Old Lost Bottlings Series dist 1964, bott Aug 99 **(96) n24** so rare to find a nose so polished. The seasoning of the American oak hits the high spots with the spices just strong enough without prodding at the nose. The bitter-sweet balance, sharpened by a vague citrus and plum note, could not be better; **t24** silk, as to be expected on delivery. A procession of melt-in-the mouth sugars, with molassed at the vanguard, counter those inevitable spices; a hint of Parkin cake and walnut oil; **f24** I'm sure the toasty raisin is from char, not sherry. But sits so well with that constantly rumbling spice; a touch of late hickory; **b24** despite an outwardly fruity character, I'm pretty sure this is from a supremely high quality bourbon cask which received absolutely Rolls Royce seasoning. No idea what they are charging. Whatever it is, it's not enough...!! *43.1%*

BALMENACH
Speyside, 1824. Inver House Distillers. Working.
Balmenach Aged 25 Years Golden Jubilee db **(89) n21 t23 f22 b23.** What a glorious old charmer this is! An essay in balance despite the bludgeoning nature of the beast early on. Takes a little time to get to know and appreciate: persevere with this belter because it is classic stuff for its age. *58%. Around 800 decanters.*

᠅ **Adelphi Selection Balmenach 11 Years Old** dist 2001, bott 2013 **(91) n22** resounding malt. The grist is doused in citrus; **t24** the delivery fairly rockets into life with a juicy barley intro to die for; the grist, like the nose, enters a little later; **f22.5** much drier. Anyone who can remember a Micky chocolate milk that used to be delivered to the door in the early 60s will recognise this fade; **b22.5** eye-wateringly bright and lively. And lovely... *58.7%. ncf sc. 200 bottles. WB15/411*

Gordon and MacPhail Connoisseurs Choice Balmenach 2004 (78) n20.5 t21 f17.5 b19. Attractive mix of cereal and sultana notes on nose and delivery. But falls to the near inevitable consequence of the modern sherry butt at the very last. *46%. ncf.*

The Whisky Agency Balmenach 1979 ex-bourbon hogshead, dist 79, bott 12 **(95.5) n23.5** for all the upfront oak, the equalising sugars and barley defy the years; smoke...at first shy... more confident as the temperature raises; **t23.5** sumptuous delivery: the barley is ridiculously fresh for the age. The mid-ground moves into a gorgeous heather-honey mode, aided by a languid smokiness; **f24** fabulous finale with such charm to the peek-a-boo peat muscling in, pathetically, to the manuka honey and overdone toast; **b24.5** a must-get malt. Stunning. One of the most delicate and complex this year. *52.8%*

᠅ **Scotch Malt Whisky Society Cask 48.41 Aged 25 Years** refill hogshead, dist 30 Mar 88 **(87) n21.5 t23 f21 b21.5** A really lovely malt full of highly revved barley but diminished slightly by an oaky charge which gets a little out of hand. *48.2%. nc ncf sc. 239 bottles.*

᠅ **Signatory Cask Strength Collection Balmenach 1988 Aged 25 Years** hogshead, cask no. 1132, dist 4 Apr 88, bott 23 Sep 13 **(89.5) n22** a tad OTT oak but balanced by Manor House cake sweetness and a series of vanilla notes of varying sweetness; **t23** the sugars get in before the eye-watering tannin takes too great a grip, ensuring a relatively delicate delivery. A fair amount of natural caramel is swashing about; **f22** caramel and toasty tannin all the way...and don't forget to spit out the splinters; **b22.5** a very sturdy malt which makes the most of its big oak signature. *55.6%. sc nc. Cask handpicked by The Whisky Exchange. WB15/325*

᠅ **Speyside Single Malt Balmenach 30 Years Old** refill hogshead, cask no. 10162, dist Sep 83 bott Dec 13 **(88) n22.5** borderline OTT oak but hangs on to offer just enough sugars to make for an attractive experience, though leaving the antiquity in no doubt; **t22.5** the egg custard nose shows little evidence here as the drier oak notes take an early grip. Just enough malt, some juicy, hangs on...; **f21** pretty austere toward the end; **b22** at times threatens to overload on the oak with the malt body not quite broad enough to carry the oaky burden. The whole, though, has a noble presence. *52.8%. nc ncf sc. 111 bottles.*

THE BALVENIE
Speyside, 1892. William Grant & Sons. Working.
The Balvenie Aged 10 Years Founders Reserve db **(90) n23** astonishing complexity: the fruit is relaxed, crushed sultanas and malty suet. A sliver of smoke and no more: everything is hinted and nudged at rather than stated. Superb; **t24** here we go again: threads of malt

binding together barely detectable nuances. Thin liquorice here, grape there, smoke and vanilla somewhere else; **f20** Light muscovado-toffee flattens out the earlier complexity. The bitter-sweet balance remains brilliant to the end; **b23** just one of those all-time-great standard 10-year-olds from a great distillery – pity they've decided to kill it off. 40%

The Balvenie Double Wood Aged 12 Years db (80.5) **n22 t20.5 f19 b19**. OK. So here's the score: Balvenie is one of my favourite distilleries in the world, I confess. I admit it. The original Balvenie 10 is a whisky I would go to war for. It is what Scotch malt whisky is all about. It invented complexity; or at least properly introduced me to it. But I knew that it was going to die, sacrificed on the altar of ageism. So I have tried to get to love Double Wood. And I have tasted and/or drunk it every month for the last couple of years to get to know it and, hopefully fall in love. But still I find it rather boring company. We may have kissed and canoodled. But still there is no spark. No romance whatsoever. 40%

The Balvenie 14 Years Old Cuban Selection db (86) **n20 t22 f22.5 b21.5**. Unusual malt. No great fan of the nose but the roughness of the delivery grows on you; there is a jarring, tongue-drying quality which actually works quite well and the development of the inherent sweetness is almost in slow motion. Some sophistication here, but also the odd note which, on the nose especially, is a little out of tune. 43%

The Balvenie 14 Years Old Golden Cask db (91) **n23.5** mildly tart: rhubarb and custard, with a vague sprinkling of brown sugar; bourbon notes, too; **t23** mouth-watering and zingy spice offer up a big delivery, but settles towards the middle towards a more metallic barley-rich sharpness; **f22** soft spices peddle towards the finish and a wave or three of gathering oak links well with the sweetened barley strands; **b22.5** a confident, elegant malt which doesn't stint one iota on complexity. Worth raiding the Duty Free shops for this little gem alone. 47.5%

The Balvenie Double Wood Aged 17 Years db (84) **n22 t21 f20 b21**. Balvenie does like 17 years as an age to show off its malt at its most complex, & understandably so as it is an important stage in its development before its usual premature over maturity: the last years or two when it remains full of zest and vigour. Here, though, the oak from the bourbon cask has offered a little too much of its milkier, older side while the sherry is a fraction overzealous and a shade too tangy. Enjoyable, but like a top of the range Mercedes engine which refuses to run evenly. 43%.

The Balvenie Double Wood Aged 17 Years bott 2012 db (91) **n22.5** the sherry does a good job injecting a controlled softness to the experience, perhaps at the expense of some of the higher bourbon cask notes; **t23.5** the softness on the nose is transformed into silkiness on delivery, followed by a really outstanding layering of spice; a few apple notes thins the grape and bourbon style liquorice which piles in with early gusto; **f22** a more restrained and relaxed fade with the higher oak notes playing us out, helped by delicate muscovado sugars; **b23** a far friskier date than the 12-year-old. Here, maturity equals a degree of sophistication. Still not as outrageously sexy as a straightforward high grade bourbon cask offering from the distillery. But easily enough to get you hot under the collar. Lip smacking, high quality entertainment. 43%

The Balvenie Roasted Malt Aged 14 Years db (90) **n21 t23 f22 b24**. Balvenie very much as you've never seen it before. An absolute, mouth-filling cracker! 47.1%

The Balvenie Rum Wood Aged 14 Years db (88) **n22 t23 f21 b22**. Tasted blind I would never have recognized the distillery: I'm not sure if that's a good thing. 47.1%

Balvenie 17 Years Old Rum Cask db (88.5) **n22 t22.5 f22 b22**. For all the best attentions of the rum cask at times this feels all its 17 years, and perhaps a few Summers more. Impossible not to love, however. 43%

Balvenie New Wood Aged 17 Years db (85) **n23 t22 f19 b21**. A naturally good age for Balvenie; the nose is lucid and exciting, the early delivery is thick with rich malt. This, though, has sucked out lots of caramel from the wood to leave an annoyingly flat finish. 40%

The Balvenie Aged 17 Years Old Madeira Cask Madeira finish, bott 2009 db (93.5) **n24** classically two-toned, with a pair of contrasting tales being told simultaneously yet in complete harmony. One is fruity (especially apple) and ripe and blended with the weighty oak; the other is barley-sweet and refreshing; **t23.5** the juicy grape takes the higher ground, joining forces with the juicier barley; some distance below the oak throbs contentedly; **f23** an oak prickle and a hint of sweet mocha on the vanilla; **b23** an essay in deportment. Every aspect appears to have been measured and weighed. Hurry this imperious whisky at your peril. 43%

The Balvenie 17 Year Old Sherry Oak db (88) **n23 t22.5 f21 b21.5**. Clean as a nut. High-class sherry it may be but the price to pay is a flattening out of the astonishing complexity one normally finds from this distillery. Bitter-sweet in every respect. 43%

The Balvenie Aged 21 Years Port Wood db (94.5) **n24** chocolate marzipan with a soft sugar-plum centre; deft, clean and delicate; **t24** hard to imagine a delivery more perfectly weighted: a rich tapestry of fruit and nut plus malt melts on the palate with a welter of drier, pithy, grape skin balancing the vanillas and barley oils; **f23** delicately dry with the vanilla and buttered fruitcake ensuring balance; **b23.5** what a magnificently improved malt. Last time out I struggled to detect the fruit. Here, there's no escaping. 40%

⸭⸭ **The Balvenie Single Barrel Aged 12 Years** 1st fill ex bourbon, cask no. 12755 db **(96.5) n24.5** bananas to roast yam; lime marmalade to honeysuckle; golden syrup to malt grist... keep on looking. They are all there with much else besides...; **t24.5** just about perfect weight on delivery: soft without being gooey, a firm sub-strata without being aggressive. The most delicate honeys are put into play: mainly acacia, though ulmo comes through later on as the vanillas mount; **f23.5** a vague bitterness but absorbed by the welcoming sweetness of the butterscotch tart, ulmo honey and chocolate caramel; **b24** about as close to perfection as a single cask may get. David Stewart, the finest blender of the last decade, may have half retired. But a cask like this shows he has lost none of his magic touch. Sublime. 47.8%. sc ncf. WB15/283

⸭⸭ **The Balvenie Single Barrel Aged 15 Years** sherry cask, cask no. 609 db **(95) n24** huge, faultless sherry: clean, confident and muscling in with wonderful spices and burnt raisin. Enormous...but how is the body going to cope with this little lot..? **t24** a complete sherry fest from first to last. Melton Hunt cake at its moistest, with as many burnt raisins as they could throw into the mix and a few extra dollops of molasses for good measure; **f23.5** some bitterness was bound to catch up at some stage....it cannot with this kind of cask as toastiness abounds. But long and satisfying all the way...; **b23.5** a faultless cask – not a shadow of sulphur anywhere. But a case of where the grape has overwhelmed the barley, meaning balance has been compromised: and on the palate it feels as though you have been mugged by an oloroso butt. That said, this is still a stunning experience - a silky delight to be savoured. 47.8%. sc ncf. No more than 650 bottles. WB15/334

The Balvenie Thirty Aged 30 Years db **(92) n24** has kept its character wonderfully, with a real mixture of varied fruits. Again the smoke similar is apparent, as is the panting oak. Astonishing thet the style should have been kept so similar to previous bottlings; **t23** big, full delivery first of enigmatic, thick barley, then a gentle eruption of controlled, warming spices; **f22** much more oaky involvement but such is the steadiness of the barley, its extraordinary confidence, no damage is done and the harmony remains; **b23** rarely have I come across a bottling of a whisky of these advanced years which is so true to previous ones. Amazing. 47.3%

The Balvenie 1993 Port Wood db **(89) n21 t23 f22 b23.** Oozes class without getting too flash about it: the secret is in the balance. 40%

The Balvenie TUN 1401 batch 1 db **(91) n22.5** one of the crispier Balvenie aromas from over the years: as though the barley has a new sugary husk; **t23** indeed, it is those sugars which arrive first on delivery, and they don't even try to be cute about it. The barley trails in behind almost as an afterthought; **f22.5** now a more composed and relaxed period, though there is a weak residual (presumably sherry butt) buzz; **b23** I have experienced Balvenie a lot more complex than this. But there is no faulting the feel good factor... 48.3%. nc ncf.

The Balvenie TUN 1401 batch 2 db **(89.5) n23 t23 f21.5 b22.** The odd moment here hits high notes from this distillery I only ever before experienced with the old 10-years-old some quarter of a century ago. 50.6%. nc ncf.

The Balvenie TUN 1401 batch 3 db **(91) n22** perhaps a little tight on the nose in part, but there is also a big Kentucky feel to this, too: some of the casks have bitten deep into the American oak and extracted a chunk of toasted honeycomb and Demerara; lots of creamy toffee and raisin; **t23.5** stunning delivery: unlikely you will encounter many better mouth feels for a Speysider this year. Again, that big bourbon oak resonance makes no attempt to hide its macho character. A procession of liquorice and ulmo/manuka honey blend; **f22** some bitter marmalade takes a vaguely furry turn; **b23.5** one of those bottlings which again hits some magnificent heights; it is as though David Stewart is taking his beloved distillery through its repertoire. Still much prefer if he'd keep sherry off the programme, though. 50.3%. nc ncf.

The Balvenie TUN 1401 batch 4 db **(80.5) n21.5 t23 f17 b19.** The finish has all the quality of an Andy Murray line call challenge. In this case it is unacceptably bitter, nowhere near matching up with the utter brilliance of the delivery. 50.4%. nc ncf.

The Balvenie TUN 1401 batch 5 db **(87.5) n22 t22 f21.5 b22.** About as heavy duty a Balvenie as I can remember. Hardly surprising as the bourbon barrels appear to have had all their natural caramels dredged from them and this makes it a double whammy with the sherry. 50.1%. nc ncf.

The Balvenie TUN 1401 batch 6 db **(90) n22.5** about as thick as grapes growing in an oak forest; **t23** huge. Massive. Absolutely fills the mouth. The oak is definitely OTT, but there is something entertaining and intriguing in the way the sugars try to blast a way through with almost laser beam intensity; **f22** still too much oak, but the excesses are deflected into a disarming chocolate mousse finale; **b22.5** I'm amazed my stemmed nosing glass hasn't cracked under the weight of this Speyside monster of a dram. With the mix of fruit and big oak, probably distilled in lead stills... 49.8%. nc ncf.

The Balvenie TUN 1401 batch 7 db **(87) n22.5** jam doughnut but a massive oak spice buzz, too; **t23** sugars arrive early with a lovely ulmo honey sub current; good juice until the raisin becomes increasingly burnt; **f20** slightly bitter, fuzzy finish; **b21.5** more juiciness to the fruit and sugar allows more clarity than the previous batch. *49.2%. William Grant & Sons.*

BANFF
Speyside, 1863–1983. Diageo. Demolished.

Cadenhead Banff 34 Years Old bourbon cask, dist 76, bott 10 **(96)** **n23.5** some serious breakfast cereal notes here (especially those which have honey involved), mixing comfortably with salt and creamy, orangey tannin; **t24.5** the delivery borders perfection: all kinds of tangerine notes here, mixing easily with fresh barley, for all its years, which meld with lime and watered-down orange blossom honey; **f23.5** even the arrival of tannin and leather-style oak seems only to hit the right chord with the sugars and honey notes which linger to the end; **b24.5** I wrote long ago that it is likely that during the mid '70s Banff was making some of the best malt in the world. Don't believe me? Taste this... *53.8%. sc. 232 bottles.*

BEN NEVIS
Highlands (Western), 1825. Nikka. Working.

Ben Nevis 10 Years Old db **(88)** **n21 t22 f23 b22.** A massive malt that has steadied itself in recent bottlings, but keep those knives and forks to hand! *46%*

Ben Nevis 15 Years Old 1996 sherry cask, cask no. 1654, dist Oct 96, bott Sept 12 db **(91)** **n23** clean as a whistle, ultra juicy grape sitting prettily with greengage and vanilla; a lot younger than its age; **t23** crisp and crunchy delivery with the barley at first forming a brittle guard of honour for the developing fruit. Then spices run amok.... **f22** the lightness of age on the nose is underlined as the oak does little more than offer a continued frame for the grape and grain; **b23** doesn't the heart sing when you find a good whisky matured in an unsullied sherry butt...? *51.7%. nc ncf sc. 523 bottles.*

Ben Nevis Synergy 13 Years Old db **(88)** **n22** firm, crisp brown sugars; **t22** intense: all the emphasis on broad muscavado sugars with a degree of a taste of marmalade; **f21.5** long, dries, just a little fuzzy; **b22.5** one of the sweetest Ben Nevis's for a long time, but as chewy as ever! A bit of a lady's dram to be honest. *46%*

⁘ **Berry's Own Selection Ben Nevis 1998 Aged 15 Years** cask no. 1351, bott 2014 **(86)** **n19 t22.5 f22.5 b22.** From the elephantine school of Ben Nevis. A soupy mass of melted fudge, sticky toffee and molasses with a few over-ripe plums tossed in: delicious...especially with that spice. The ugly nose, though, is less kind. *46%. ncf ncf. WB15/238*

⁘ **Càrn Mòr Strictly Limited Edition Ben Nevis Aged 17 Years** dist 1997, bott 2014 **(86.5)** **n20.5 t22.5 f21.5 b22** Pleasant-ish if unremarkable. Unhappy oak on the nose, but there is no denying the freshness of the grape on delivery. Some butterscotch and ulmo honey make contributions to an otherwise simplistic dram. *46%. nc ncf. 747 bottles from 1 cask. WB15/054*

Chieftain's Ben Nevis Aged 13 Years hogshead, cask no. 240, dist May 99, bott Aug 12 **(93)** **n23** occasionally Ben Nevis takes off its heavy duffle coat and dons something of an altogether sleeker cut: here the barley, figs and blackberries are of the lightest hue imaginable; **t23.5** dulcet barley get the juices flowing; the vanilla sub plot is ridiculously polite; initially younger than its years, but revealing a depth beyond; **f23** superbly trimmed with an attractive chalky dryness to the oak, but seasoned with tingling spices; **b23.5** Ben Nevis in its Sunday finest. Immaculate. *46%. nc ncf sc. Ian Macleod Distillers. 354 bottles.*

The Coopers Choice Ben Nevis 1996 15 Years Old sherry cask, cask no. 1478, dist 96, bott 12 **(90.5)** **n22 t22 f23.5 b23.** Complex and deeply satisfying malt. *56%. 300 bottles.*

⁘ **The Coopers Choice Ben Nevis 1996 Aged 17 Years** hogshead, cask no. 1317, bott 2014 **(86.5)** **n21 t22 f22 b21.5.** A chunky, steady dram. Heavy handed on both nose and delivery it settles into an easy going, well spiced fellow content to allow the sharp, toasted barley sugar have its own way. *46%. 320 bottles. WB15/292*

McDonald's Celebrated Ben Nevis (95) **n23.5** a smoky broil drifts and teases. Young yet ever so light honey in every sniff; **t24** superb, youthful body which holds both the malt and smoke so satisfyingly; just enough oil to spread the message far and wide; **f23.5** smoked chocolate ensures a rich finale. **b24** Admirable young whisky with surprising panache and not carrying the usual Ben Nevis weight. Very different - and absolutely top class. There is, indeed, much to celebrate. Wish I saw more whiskies on the market today where the young malt was given free reign - reminds me of the old five year old Bowmores bottled by Oddbins back in the very early 1990s. *46%*

⁘ **The Maltman Ben Nevis Aged 15 Years** oloroso sherry cask **(67)** **n16 t18 f16 b17.** Would have been as sweet as a nut. But the dreaded 's' word has decreed otherwise. *49.1%*

Malts Of Scotland Ben Nevis 1996 sherry hogshead, cask no. MoS 12054, dist Jun 96, bott Nov 12 **(78.5)** **n18 t21.5 f19 b19.** Some decent sherry trifle moments, but never seems to find its balance – pretty dodgy when on Ben Nevis. *53.1%. nc ncf sc. 96 bottles.*

Old Malt Cask Ben Nevis Aged 16 Years sherry butt, cask no. 8228, dist Oct 96, bott Oct 12 (**86**) **n20 t22 f22 b22**. Pleasingly bright and sharp. The intensity of the malt impresses. *50%. sc. Douglas Laing & Co. 512 bottles.*

⁘ **Old Malt Cask Ben Nevis Aged 16 Years** sherry butt, cask no. 9639, dist Nov 96, bott Mar 13 (**80**) **n17 t22 f20 b21**. Once you get past the uncomfortably tight nose things aren't as bad as might be feared. Indeed, the delivery is just dripping with fresh fruit, aided by light muscovado sugar and some compelling heather honey. Would love to have seen this guy had it not been treated in Jerez. The finish is also tight, but could be a lot worse. For those immune to relatively minor sulphurous incursions, go for it. *50%. nc ncf sc. 299 bottles. WB15/133*

⁘ **Old Malt Cask Ben Nevis Aged 18 Years** refill hogshead, cask no. 10503, dist May 96, bott May 14 (**87**) **n21 t22 f21.5 b22**. There are no claims to greatness here or pretensions regarding complexity. An old cask means an insipid colour for 18 years and a malt looking at all the barley-driven angles. Pleasant enough delivery, though, with an attractive sharpness of phrase and sugars which sit comfortably. *50%. nc ncf sc. 305 bottles.*

Old Malt Cask Ben Nevis Aged 46 Years refill hogshead, cask no. 9511, dist Jun 66, bott Feb 13 (**91**) **n23 t23 f22.5 b22.5**. About as close to a pot still rum you'll ever find a whisky! Though this is bottled as a single malt, this appears to have much more of the character of the Coffey still grain distillery which was around at the time. *43.1%. sc. 184 bottles.*

Old Masters Ben Nevis 14 Years Old cask no. 1499, dist 98, bott Nov 12 (**84.5**) **n20 t22.5 f21 b21**. A malt which appears to take delight in rolling up its sleeves and giving the taste buds a bit of a biff. A rough-house dram at its best early on when the barley is in full sparkle. *54.7%. sc. James MacArthur & Co Ltd.*

⁘ **The Pearls of Scotland 1997 16 Year Old** cask no. 45, dist Jan 97, bott Nov 13 (**92**) **n22.5** huge, mountainous nose: thick with coconut and maple-syrup-lightened tannin; **t23.5** spitting splinters from the off, the oils are voluptuous but again it is the sugars really pulling the string: molassed and a little crunchy they make for a stunning mouth feel; **f23** spices are in full swing, with a little molassed liquorice for company; **b23** a Ben Nevis living up to its name...superb! *51.8%*

⁘ **The Pearls of Scotland Ben Nevis 1997** cask no. 612, bott Jun 14 (**93**) **n23.5** a trifle and blancmange dessert, though the depth of citrusy oak present suggests this will not be a malt to be trifled with... **t23**...sure enough the oak is out first and with a rugged, bitting early detachment; the malt catches up a few beats later, showing superb richness; myriad layers of malt and oak intertwining; **f23** now moves into spicy mode, though the oak and malt throb beautifully; **b23.5** a massive Ben Nevis scaling the heights... *50.6%. sc.*

⁘ **Provenance Ben Nevis Over 8 Years** refill hogshead, cask no. 10328, dist Summer 06, bott Summer 14 (**82**) **n20 t21 f21 b20**. Woe! Hasn't really moved in eight years...as close to new make as you can possibly get at this age. Certainly malty! *46%. nc ncf sc.*

⁘ **Signatory Vintage Cask Strength Collection Ben Nevis 1992 Aged 20 Years** sherry butt, cask no. 2310, dist 03 Jul 92, bott 02 Jul 13 (**92.5**) **n22.5** steaming suet pudding with the accent on the sultanas; **t24** the first note or two on delivery is wobbly and unsure. Then piles in with sumptuous grape in the grandest old fruit cake style. The fruit clarifies for a short juicy burst; **f23** a fruitcake which seems to have acquired a chocolatey lid; **b23** by far from textbook, but wonderfully sulphur free and somehow encapsulates the quirkiness of the distillery. *55.5%. nc sc. 623 bottles. WB15/005*

⁘ **Signatory Vintage Un-chillfiltered Collection Ben Nevis 1991 Aged 22 Years** sherry butt, cask no. 2910, dist 16 Aug 91, bott 10 Apr 14 (**81**) **n19 t22 f20 b20**. Curiously, not a great whisky...and has absolutely nothing to do with sulphur as this has none on show. Just lacks quality on the oak front in general and even after 22 years the malt has not been able to find a way to engineer a harmonious relationship. Tangy and disjointed, though the delivery does offer a few moments of juicy respite. *46%. nc ncf sc. 819 bottles. WB15/029*

⁘ **That Boutique-y Whisky Ben Nevis** batch 1 (**89**) **n22** rich, fulsome, treacly sugars and biscuity malt; **t23** massively chunky delivery. All kinds of fruit in play, as well as barley sugar concentrate: chew this until your jaws ache; **f22** a little honey on the fade, but plenty of copper, too; **b22** a malt to match the mountain: just...big! *49.7%. 161 bottles. WB15/205*

The Warehouse Collection Ben Nevis Aged 16 Years bourbon hogshead, cask no. 1739, dist 1 Jan 96, bott 29 Apr 13 (**86.5**) **n21 t23 f21 b21.5**. No shortage of delicious, clear honey on this. But for a 16-year-old, has more in common with a malt half that age; the cask must have been third fill sitting at the very bottom of a very cold warehouse. *53.6%. nc ncf sc. 321 bottles.*

The Whisky Cask Ben Nevis Aged 16 Years hogshead, dist 96, bott 12 (**94**) **n23** the usual chunky barley. But cleaner than the norm with crispier sugars; **t24** excellent dual-toned weight balance. On one hand, big, bustling, thick-cut barley, brimming with oils; the secondary plot is a much juicier barley-sugar little theme; the spices are deft; **f23** chocolate with barley sugar filling; **b24** another quite stunning Ben Nevis to hit the market in the last year – an absolute must find for those looking for the best from each distillery. *53%. nc ncf sc.*

BENRIACH

Speyside, 1898. The BenRiach Distillery Co. Working.

The BenRiach db (86) n21 t22 f21.5 b21.5. The kind of soft malt you could wean nippers on, as opposed to Curiositas, which would be kippers. Unusually for a BenRiach there is a distinct toffee-fudge air to this one late on, but not enough to spoil that butterscotch-malt charm. No colouring added, so a case of the oak being a bit naughty. *40%*

The BenRiach Curiositas Aged 10 Years Single Peated Malt db (90.5) n23 the thin smoke is losing out to the honey-fudge; t23 the peat takes a little time to gather its speech, but when it comes it is fine and softly delivered. In the meantime soft barley and that delicious but curiously dampening sweet fudge struts its stuff; f22 chalky vanillas and a squirt of chocolate like that found on ice cream cones; b22.5 "Hmmmm. Why have my research team marked this down as a 'new' whisky" I wondered to myself. Then immediately on nosing and tasting I discovered the reason without having to ask: the pulse was weaker, the smoke more apologetic...it had been watered down from the original 46% to 40%. This is excellent malt. But can we have our truly great whisky back, please? As lovely as it is, this is a bit of an imposter. As Emperor Hadrian might once have said: "ifus itus aintus brokus..." *40%*

The BenRiach Aged 12 Years db (82.5) n21 t20 f21 b20.5. More enjoyable than the 43% I last tasted. But still an entirely inoffensive malt determined to offer minimal complexity. *40%*

The BenRiach Aged 12 Years db (78.5) n21.5 t20 f18 b19. White peppers on the nose, then goes uncharacteristically quiet and shapeless. *43%*

The BenRiach Aged 12 Years Dark Rum Wood Finish db (85.5) n21 t22 f21 b21.5. More than a decade ago, long before it ever became fashionable, I carried out an extensive programme of whisky maturation in old dark rum casks. So, if someone asked me now what would happen if you rounded off a decently peated whisky in a rum cask, I'd say – depending on time given for the finish and type of rum – the smoke would be contained and there would be a ramrod straight, steel-hard sweetness ensuring the most clipped whisky you possibly can imagine. And this here is exactly what we have... *46%*

The BenRiach Aged 12 Years Matured In Sherry Wood db (95.5) n23.5 big, juicy, compelling grape. Absolutely clean and stupendous in its multi-layering; t24 quite magnificent! How I pray whiskies to be on delivery, but find they so rarely are. Some caramels are caught up in the genteel squabble between the grape juice and the rich barley; f24 long, faultless and ushering in a chocolate raisin depth; late vanilla and any amount of spice; b24 since I last tasted this the number of instances of sampling a sherry wood whisky and not finding my taste buds caked in sulphur has nosedived dramatically. Therefore, to start my tasting day at 7am with something as honest as this propels one with myriad reasons to continue the day. A celebration of a malt whisky in more ways than you could believe. *46%. nc ncf.*

The BenRiach Aged Over 12 Years "Arumaticus Fumosus" richly peated style, ex-dark rum barrels db (91) n23 t23 f22 b23. Very often finishing in rum can sharpen the mouthfeel yet at the same time add a sugary sheen. This little gem is no exception. *46%*

The BenRiach Aged Over 12 Years "Heredotus Fumosus" peated PX finish db (92.5) n23 the peat is so thick you could grow a grape vine in it; t23 the sweetness of the grape arrives in spicy waves, comfortably supported by the thick, oily peat; f23 long, more sugared smoke and cocoa; b23.5 at last a PX-peat marriage not on the rocks. What an improvement on the last bottling. Smokograpus Miracalus. *46%. nc ncf.*

The BenRiach Aged Over 12 Years "Importanticus Fumosus" richly peated style, ex-port hogshead db (87) n22 t22 f21 b22. Hardicus asius Nailsus. *46%*

The BenRiach Aged 12 Years "Importanticus Fumosus" Tawny port wood finish db (91.5) n23 no matter here had it been finished in Short-eared, Long-eared, Little, Barn or Tawny Port, the peat would have come out tops. The smoke is enormous: owl do they do it...? t22.5 a peaty custard pie in the mush: enormous impact with more early vanilla than fruit; f23.5 now the grape begins to get its head above the smoky parapet; a beautiful balance with the smoke, vanilla and minor spices; b22.5 you'd be a twit not to buy two of 'em. *46%*

The BenRiach Aged 13 Years "Maderensis Fumosus" peated madeira finish db (85.5) n20 t23.5 f21 b21. Never a shrinking violet, this still enjoys some pretty off the wall moments. But for a brief success on delivery where the richness of the sugars and smoke work in astonishing harmony, the remainder of the journey is one of vivid disagreement. *46%. nc ncf.*

The BenRiach Aged 15 Years Dark Rum Finish db (86) n20 t22 f22 b22. Drier, spicier than before. Old Jamaica chocolate candy. *46%. nc ncf.*

The BenRiach Aged 15 Years Madeira Wood Finish db (89.5) n22.5 t21.5 f23 b22.5. Very much drier than most Madeira finishes you will find around. Once the scramble on delivery is over, this bottling simply exudes excellence. A collector's must have. *46%*

The BenRiach Aged 15 Years Pedro Ximénez Sherry Wood Finish db **(94.5) n25** astonishing layering, each one delicate and fragile: vanilla and lime; gooseberry; barley; grape...a buzz of spice. Not a single bitter or off note. This is one of the world whisky noses of the year: absolute perfection; **t23.5** mouth-filling barley then a spreading of a sugary but fruity theme, especially to the roof of the mouth where it sticks on a light oil; in the meantime there is a slow burn of increasing spice; **f22.5** long, absolutely thick with butterscotch barley, framed by a constant drone of spicy, sugared grape; **b23.5** some of the strangest Scotch malts I have tasted in the last decade have been fashioned in PX casks. And few have been particularly enjoyable creations. This one, though, bucks the trend thanks principally to the most subtle of spice imprints. All the hallmarks of some kind of award-winner. 46%

The BenRiach Aged 15 Years Tawny Port Wood Finish db **(89.5) n21.5 t23 f22.5 b22.5.** Now that really is the perfect late night dram. 46%

The BenRiach Aged 16 Years db **(83.5) n21.5 t21 f20 b21.** Although maltily enjoyable, if over dependent on caramel flavours, you get the feeling that a full works 46% version would offer something more gripping and true to this great distillery. 40%

The BenRiach Aged 16 Years db **(83.5) n21.5 t21 f20 b21.** Pleasant malt but now without the dab of peat which gave it weight; also a marked reduction of the complexity that once gave this such a commanding presence. 43%. nc ncf.

The BenRiach Aged 16 Years Sauternes Wood Finish db **(85) n19.5 t23 f21.5 b21.** One of the problems with cask finishing is that there is nothing like an exact science of knowing when the matured whisky and introduced wood gel to their fullest potential. BenRiach enjoy a reputation of getting it right more often than most other distillers and bottlers. But here it hasn't come off to quite the same effect as previous, quite sensational, versions I have tasted of the 16-y-o Sauternes finish. No denying the sheer joy of the carpet bombing of the taste buds on delivery, though, so rich is the combination of fresh grape and delicate smoke. 46%

The BenRiach Aged 17 Years "Septendecim" Peated Malt db **(93.5) n24** easily one of the most complex of all the new peaty noses of the year. Both sweet and dry, with an ashy feel to the peat fire mingling with dangerous complexity. Almost perfectly weighted and balanced; **t24.5** the delivery reveals a light oiliness which is entirely absent from the nose. This in turn maximises the intensity of both the sugars and smoke. When the spices arrive, the harmony is just about complete; **f23** just a dash of oaky bitterness reveals a degree of discord. But the Demerara sugars are so crisp and painstaking in their efforts to ensure balance that all can be forgiven....; **b24** proof, not that it is now needed, that Islay is not alone in producing phenomenal phenols... 46%. nc ncf.

The BenRiach "Solstice" 17 Years Old 2nd Edition port finish, heavily peated db **(94) n23.5** a touch of the Bowmores with this: definitely a hint of Fisherman's Friend, but also creamy celery soup; **t23** big and thick, coating the palate superbly, first with peat and then with a rich molassed fruitiness, especially with juicy dates to the fore; **f23.5** reverts back to a Fisherman's Friend stance with the fruit now vanished and some half-hearted spices enlivening the delicate late sugars; **b24** well, it's the 21st June 2012, the summer solstice. And, naturally, pouring down with rain outside. So what better time to taste this whisky? With all that heart-warming, comforting peat as thick as a woolly jumper, this is the perfect dram for a bitterly cold winter's day the world over. Or midsummer's day in England... 50%. nc ncf.

The BenRiach 1995 Aged 17 Years virgin American oak finish, dist 4 May 95 db **(88) n23** not joking, folks: acorns!! Don't know if you've ever roasted them...but it's a bit like this! **t22** a soft shuffling of power between the maple syrup and vanilla concentrate; **f21** ye gods...the tannins!!! **b22** from little acorns and all that.... 53.1%. Whisky Shop Exclusive.

The BenRiach Aged 18 Years Gaja Barolo Wood Finish db **(89) n22 t23 f21.5 b22.5.** The delivery gives one of the most salivating experiences of the year. 46%

The BenRiach Aged 18 Years Moscatel Wood Finish db **(92.5) n23.5** one of those sublime noses where everything is understated: the fresh apples and grape, the most delicate of smoke, the jam on toast, the vanilla...; **t23.5** textbook delivery: every note clean and clear, especially the juicy fruits melting into the lush barley. A buzz of distant background smoke all helped along by the most subtle of oils; **f22** leans towards the vanilla; **b23.5** one of those rare whiskies which renews and upholds any belief I have for cask finishing. Superb. 46%

The BenRiach Aged 20 Years db **(85.5) n21.5 t23 f19 b22.** A much more attractive version than the American Release 46%. The barley offers a disarming intensity and sweetness which makes the most of the light oils. Only a bittering finish shuts the gate on excellence. 43%. nc ncf.

The BenRiach Aged 20 Years db **(78) n19 t20 f19 b20.** This is big, but not necessarily for the right reasons or in the right places. A big cut of oiliness combines with some surging sugars for a most un-BenRiachy ride. US Market.

The BenRiach Aged 21 Years "Authenticus" Peated Malt db **(85.5) n22 t21.5 f21 b21.** A heavy malt, though the smoke only adds a small degree to its weight. The barley is thick and chewy but the oak has a very big say. 46%

The BenRiach 25 Years Old db **(87.5)** n21.5 t23 f21 b22. The tranquillity and excellent balance of the middle is the highlight by far. *50%*

The BenRiach 30 Years Old db **(94.5)** n24 the fruit, though very ripe and rich, remains uncluttered and clean and is helped along the way by a superb injection of sweetened cloves and Parma Violets; the oak is present and correct offering an egg custard sub-plot; t24 how ridiculously deft is that? There is total equilibrium in the barley and fruit as it massages the palate in one of the softest deliveries of a 30-y-o around; the middle ground is creamy and leans towards the vanilla; even so, there are some amazingly juicy moments to savour; f23 very lightly oiled and mixing light grist and rich vanilla; b23.5 it's spent 30 years in the cask: give one glass of this at least half an hour of your time: seal the room, no sounds, no distractions. It's worth it...for as hard as I try, I can barely find a single fault with this. *50%*

⋰ **BenRiach Batch 11 1976 37 Years Old** sherry cask matured, bourbon finish, cask no. 529 db **(92)** n22.5 shuddering monoliths of oak. Trees, in fact. But the nipping spice, poppy seed and floor polish certainly bring the brain into focus...; t23.5 waxy, oily and thicker than a butt of molasses. The oaks are at forest level, but somehow the barley and dates keep the game going; f23 pulsing spices somehow overcome the excesses of the oak – and there are many. Still the barley delivers, as well as a plum pudding and custard; b23 when tasted live, I gave this a similar knee-jerk appraisal to the 1978 version. But on analysing countless replays I found I was wrong and the goal not only good but quite spectatular. Goooooooooooallllllllllll!!!!! Bennnn-Reeeee-Ack!!!!!! Blimey. And this is even before the 2014 World Cup has started....! *44.2%. sc.*

⋰ **BenRiach Batch 11 1976 37 Years Old** peated, sherry cask finish, bourbon finish, cask no. 5463 db **(95)** n24.5 bold and allowing the oak only limited dominance. This must have been a supreme sherry butt in its day as the spices rock, not least for their understated beauty and the lightness of touch to the honeys, despite the relative great weight of the nose; t23 where the nose shows no age at all, the first few waves here are sent crashing onto the taste buds by the great god Quercus himself; slowly recovers as the grape establishes a foothold: a kind of toasty fruitcake at first and then a topping of Demerara; f23.5 quite sublime with the oils gliding the spicier Genoa cake into place; b24 with the bourbon finish on the original sherry butt, a reversal of the norm. And with so much sulphur around these days, thank heavens for that! No sulphur here. Interesting to compare the vitality on this bottling to the flagging cask 529 sister bottling. A joy of a dram. *51.9%. sc.*

⋰ **BenRiach Batch 11 1977 37 Years Old** hogshead, cask no. 7114 db **(92.5)** n24 delicate, lime encrusted and even a touch of kiwi fruit. Indeed, that exotic fruit says all you need to know about its age...; t23,5 just so gentle. The rich barley flavours glide onto the palate, most of them of a sugary disposition and all with an oaky fingerprint; the oils are graceful and kind; f22 pretty oaky, but enough maple syrup for damage limitation; b23 I was hitch-hiking through the Sahara Desert with my life before me when this was filled into cask, most likely to end up as a three year old blend somewhere. Fate decreed otherwise. Now this beautiful, graceful old dram is in a place where the oak the is now casting a long shadow in the setting sun... *48.3%. sc.*

⋰ **BenRiach Batch 11 1977 37 Years Old** dark rum finish, cask no. 1891 db **(96.5)** n25 the gooseberry, the marzipan, the citrus-edged creamy fudge, the astonishing deftness to the maple syrup and ulmo honey, the patient restraint of the oak-laden spice: quiet, unassuming perfection. One of the great whisky noses of the year...; t24.5 a soft delivery with the vanilla out in force but happy to take the vanilla route. Elsewhere the malt drifts in with a barley-sugar opus while the spices plant little oaky flags around the palate; f23 dries and thins in typical rum cask style: short but with a lovely chocolate biscuit flourish; b24 if you tip your whisky into a rum cask then you have to expect its wings to be clipped. It's what rum does to a whisky, almost without exception. Now, Benriach was not designed for long term maturation: certainly not 39 years. So although there may be a degree of frustration regarding the tightness of the mid-term and finish, there is no doubt this has improved a tiring whisky beyond measure, perhaps beyond comprehension. The nose, a beauty creature to be adored and cherished, generates the suspicion that it has. *43.2%. sc.*

⋰ **BenRiach Batch 11 1978 36 Years Old** sherry cask matured. bourbon finish cask no. 5469 db **(85.5)** n22 t21.5 f21 b21. I know some people will probably beat their bare chests until they bleed, declaring this the greatest thing they have ever tasted. But I have to say the oak has just marginally crossed the line here, like a football might before being centred for a headed goal. So much beauty on the grape and fruit and chocolate, not to mention stem ginger-tinged spice. But the flag is up....and, like the referee ruling out a winning gal for Rangers again Celtic, doubtless I'll take dog's abuse...*41.7%. sc.*

⠴ **BenRiach Batch 11 1984 29 Years Old** peated, cask no. 488 db **(77)** n19 t20 f19 b19. Sweet, massively smoked. But just doesn't do it for me at all. Too tangy, agricultural and incapable of finding a cord. 51.1%. sc.

⠴ **BenRiach Batch 11 1984 29 Years Old** peated, Tawny port finish, cask no. 4051 db **(85.5)** n21 t21.5 f22 b21. A must have for the warts-and-all peatophiles. And there are some memorable moments. But too often just a little awkward and fruit pie in the face as the two main constituents haven't really found their range together. 50.3%. sc.

⠴ **BenRiach Batch 11 1994 20 Years Old** Tawny port finish, cask no. 1703 db **(94)** n23.5 the grape is so thick your nose has to blast a course through it to get to the underlying bourbon notes; **t23** sharp, medium sweetness but with a surprising degree of oil. Thick, chewy and wine-glazed. Some jammy, Bakewell tart notes in the mid ground; **f23.5** dries, then a steady build up of cocoa...with the a single toasted raisin tossed in for good measure; **b24** has one of the chunkiest and most overt displays of port I have seen in any Port Finish since the first was launched over 20 years ago. As ports go, about Rotterdam in size...55.6%. sc.

⠴ **BenRiach Batch 11 1994 20 Years Old** peated, Madeira hogshead, cask no. 5626 db **(93)** n22.5 peat. Smoke. More peat. A little more peat. Plenty more smoke. And finally a dose of peat concentrate...oh, with a raisin perched pathetically on top as an afterthought... **t24** a surprisingly non-hostile beginning with molten muscovado mingling with hickory. Then the peat gains a slightly oily foothold after which all smoky hell breaks loose.... **f23.5** guess.... Oh, and a tranquil squeeze of grape juice very late in the show; **b23** for a whisky to show this much peat after 20 years, this must have been one of the smokiest Benriach's ever distilled. For it to be this peaty after 20 years, during which its latter ones have been spent being tamed in a Madeira cask...then it probably ranks as one the smokiest Speysiders in history. Massive is an understatement. 53.2%. sc.

⠴ **BenRiach Batch 11 1996 18 Years Old** Pedro Ximenez sherry puncheon finish, cask no. 7176 db **(90)** n23 the grape takes a step backwards to allow the sweet, gentle smoke centre stage; **t22** soft and oily beginnings, then a plethora of crisp sugars cushioned in smoky velvet; **f23** complex finale with a the spices adding a tingle to chewey procedings; the peat becomes almost sooty and dry; the fruits move towards apricot....engulfed in butterscotch; **b22** OK, OK...I admit it...: I actually like this PX peat mix. Now I've said it! 52.4%. sc.

⠴ **BenRiach Batch 11 1997 16 Years Old** Marsala finish, cask no. 4435 db **(93)** n23 borderline shy with the clean, nut and clove-enriched fruit holding both map and the steering wheel; pretty creamy; **t23.5** a finish which works brilliantly on delivery, the grape enjoying a piquancy which salivates, an intensity which ethralls; the creaminess on the nose translates perfectly while a pithy elements comes through; **f23** soft with the sugars slowly panning out, perhaps aided by a smidgeon of molasses; **b23.5** people say I like neither finishes nor whisky matured in wine casks, whatever they may be. Show me something a delicious as this and I'll show you its greatest supporter... 56.1%. sc.

⠴ **BenRiach Batch 11 1998 16 Years Old** triple distilled, Pedro Ximenez sherry finish, cask no. 5171 db **(82.5)** n19 t21.5 f21 b21. One of the most uncompromising drams of the year. I have actually spent an hour trying to fathom this one, but it sticks in the glass as an opaque mass of peat and grape. Nowhere near as unpleasant as the nose suggested it might be. It is just that it is an indecipherable wall of taste... 57.9%. sc.

⠴ **BenRiach Batch 11 2000 14 Years Old** bourbon barrel, cask no. 38131 db **(87)** n21.5 t23 f21 b21.5. Sugars dominate and the fruit revolves around a gooseberry style, while salt intensifies....so much is right about this. Shame, then, that the actual cask itself adds only limited positivity... 59.3%. sc.

⠴ **BenRiach Batch 11 2005 9 Years Old** peated, virgin American oak finish, cask no. 3781 db **(94.5)** n23 a strange cross between a honeyed breakfast cereal and very smoky bacon...; **t24** gosh...so sweet! Any sweeter and you'd want to kiss it and ask its father for permission to marry it rather than drink the thing! The oaky sugars have rushed headlong into the gristy sugars of the smoky malt...that is some phenolic explosion...; **f23.5** long, pulsing, with the spices now at least on a par with the sugar and **b24** peat, America and virgins. Oh, and Benriach distillery. What is there not to like...? Brilliant! 58.7%. sc.

The BenRiach Single Cask 1976 Aged 37 Years batch 10, hogshead, cask no. 2013, dist 19 Mar 76, bott Jun 13 db **(82)** n20 t24 f18 b20. What can you say? The delivery, absolutely brimming with maple syrup and the lime filling which dissects the better chocolate cakes, is just so exotically right. The nose and the finish in particular are just so wrong. 49.6%. nc ncf sc.

The BenRiach Single Cask 1977 Aged 36 Years batch 10, Muscatel hogshead, cask no. 1031, dist 15 Apr 77, bott Jun 13 db **(87)** n21 heavily perfumed with herb-laden grape; **t24** not just juicy, but multi-juiced. Ranging from sultana, through prunes and pear, the toasted raisin is given a helping hand with beech honey; **f20** bitters out; **b22** when the grape kicks in with all its glory, it really does hit the heights. *54.9%. nc ncf sc.*

The BenRiach Single Cask 1983 Aged 30 Years batch 10, hogshead, cask no. 296, dist 20 Apr 83, bott Jun 13 db **(96) n24** not sure you can ask more of a cask than this: there is no telling which wins, the oak or barley. Neither, really, as the interplay glazed ginger and ulmo and manuka honey, all carried out in whispers, almost makes the mind explode. There is the faintest sliver of smoke which seems to introduce the spices. Some thin cucumber tops it off; **t24** soft, caressing…like a siren calling in the distance, the delivery is barley sugar enlivened with sterner oak which is overtaken by lilting spice and honey in the middle; **f24** long, back on to ulmo honey and still with a spicy tail; **b24** that, to me, is how a great Speyside malt of three decades maturation should taste. Classic doesn't do it justice. *43.9%. nc ncf sc.*

The BenRiach Single Cask 1984 Aged 28 Years batch 10, peated/PX sherry finish, cask no. 1051, dist 19 Sep 84, bott Jun 13 db **(94) n23** raisins pitched onto a peat-rich bonfire; **t23.5** massive delivery: a surprising amount of dried molasses and treacle at work; the peat appears to be trying to fight the fruit rather than talking to the palate; a real bite to this, part spice, part sheer violence from the warring factions; **f24** at last settles into something we can make sense of: a few buttery vanilla notes pop their head timidly above the smoky firing line; a little mocha and hickory is soothed by Demerara sugar; **b23.5** my palate just raised a white flag. My jaw literally ached from chewing this, my brain hurt trying to work out the shake and direction. Still, the cask is unusually clean for sherry, faultless in fact, and the entertainment offered cannot be matched elsewhere. One of the best peat/PX combos I've seen worldwide so far. Amazing what a difference a non-spoiled cask can make. *49.9%. nc ncf sc.*

The BenRiach Single Cask 1985 Aged 27 Years batch 10, peated/virgin American oak finish, cask no. 7188, dist 13 Nov 85, bott Jun 13 db **(85) n22 t22 f20 b21.** Even the more sugary elements has a battle to cope with the late bitterness. At times on nose and delivery it is less of a malt than a battle plan – none of the participants too happy with the other. Nothing, if not intriguing. Save the overly bitter finale. *48.9%. nc ncf sc.*

The BenRiach Single Cask 1988 Aged 24 Years batch 10, tawny port hogshead, cask no. 4000, dist 12 Oct 88, bott Jun 13 db **(95.5) n23.5** thicker than a1970 Vintage; oakier and spicier than even a '35 Cockburn. Pulsing with orange peel; **t24.5** no let up on the delivery. Zesty with sublime spiced Dominican cocoa while the sugars never veer very far away from light molasses; **f23.5** dries but towards dates and fudge; **b24** why can't all wine cask matured whisky be like this? Hardly a single telling off note. Sublime. *52.6%. nc ncf sc.*

The BenRiach Single Cask 1992 Aged 21 Years batch 10, Pedro Ximenez sherry finish, cask no. 986, dist 19 Feb 92, bott Jun 13 db **(91.5) n24** any sign of malt has vanished under the incoming tide of sweet, spiced grape juice; **t24** and there goes that grape again off on full juice and treacle alert; **f21** bitters out as it becomes pithy; **b22.5** a top rate PX butt displays its sugary charms without being shrouded in a peaty smog. Even so, the malt is nowhere to be seen… *53.3%. nc ncf sc.*

The BenRiach Single Cask 1994 Aged 18 Years batch 10, virgin American oak hogshead, cask no. 4385, dist 27 Jul 94, bott Jun 13 db **(93) n23** distinctly Kentuckian in feel, especially with the ping-ponging of manuka honeys and hickory all over the show; **t24** oh, what a to-die-for delivery. The complexity levels have rattled the roof in the sugar types alone, though the pre-dominant ones are crisp and toasty. There is a buttery sub-plot, though the big spice tries to cover this; **f22** some of the older oak dives in to add a bit of a tang, but only after the last of the sugars have done their duty with something akin to a meringue and custard sign off; **b24** the weight of the malt means that this distillery is absolutely ideal to take on virgin oak. Quite lovely. *55.5%. nc ncf sc.*

The BenRiach Single Cask 1996 Aged 17 Years batch 10, Marsala hogshead, cask no. 10306, dist 2 Apr 96, bott Jun 13 db **(96) n23.5** dried dates, juicier figs and Maryland cookie mix bigging it up on the spices; **t24.5** that spice on the nose turns up on delivery en masse from the first second, as does countering acacia honey; despite the delicious grape and kumquat intervention malt comes through loud and clear; astoundingly beautiful…; **f23.5** enters complexity overdrive. The muscovado sugar and manuka honey mix is matched by deep liquorice and pulsing spice. The fruit here is restrained but still manages to hint of old fruit cake, sans nuts; **b24.5** a very high quality cask, entirely free of faults, ensures an exceptionally spicy and endearingly complex Benriach. A distillery landmark malt. *56%. nc cnf sc.*

The BenRiach Single Cask 1998 Aged 15 Years batch 10, Pedro Ximenez sherry puncheon, cask no. 7633, dist 27 May 98, bott Jun 13 db **(71) n17 t18 f18 b18.** I have to admit, despite the low score, I love the sugars involved here. But overall… it just doesn't do it for me. *56.1%. nc ncf sc.*

The BenRiach Single Cask 2005 Aged 8 Years batch 10, peated virgin American oak hogshead, cask no. 3782, dist 23 Feb 05, bott Jun 13 db **(94.5) n22.5** shovels full of peat here: outmuscling the thudding oak; **t24.5** absolutely typical sugars as leeched from bourbon ensuring an almost eye-watering delivery; if that isn't enough, massive phenols attack from every direction. This bizarre Kentucky meets Islay format continues with the intense muscovado sugars and hickory pitching tent for the long haul; **f23.5** sizzling smoky spice with a crisp sugary accompaniment; **b24** this is hairy, bare-chested macho, peck-thumping stuff.... the ladies will love it! *58.1%. nc ncf sc.*

The BenRiach Vestige 1966 hogshead, cask no. 2381, bott Nov 12 db **(89.5) n23** as though the tide has gone out, leaving concentrated oloroso...and oak; **t22** massive tannin intro then, thankfully, those grape notes re-form with treacle and a sliver of manuka honey to sweeten and balance; **f23** vivid vanilla, bountiful butterscotch....and oceans of oak; **b22.5** you should be able to find this in the Last Legs saloon. But enough fruit and sugar hang around to see us through this dark forest of a dram. *44.1%. 62 bottles.*

⋰⋱ **The BenRiach Vintage 1999 Bottling Aged 13 Years** finished in virgin American oak casks, dist 12 Aug 99 db **(91) n24.5** like dipping into Trumper's off Jermyn Street for my three monthly supply of virtually odourless soap: an amalgamation of attractively scented notes, though here they all seem to be tannin related. Particularly love the dark cherry, the moist Lubek marzipan (perhaps over a layer of Jaffa Cake)...and then a succession of delicate bourbony toasted honey-rich tones. Wow! **t22.5** all kinds of natural caramel fills in any gap on the palate from which the barley has retreated – which makes a lot of them; incredibly soft mouthfeel ...almost sticky; **f22** a dry-ish though pleasant toffee and vanilla finale; **b22** doesn't quite live up to the billing on the nose...but then not much would. *46%. ncf nc. WB15/330*

The BenRiach "Heart of Speyside" db **(85.5) n21.5 t22 f21 b21.** A decent, non-fussy malt where the emphasis is on biscuity barley. At times juicy and sharp. Just a tease of very distant smoke here and there adds weight. *40%*

The BenRiach "Horizons" db **(87) n22 t22.5 f21 b21.5.** Few mountains or even hills on this horizon. But the view is still an agreeable one. *50%. nc ncf.*

The BenRiach "Solstice" db **(94) n23.5** gorgeous non-coastal peat. By which I mean, intense smoke, but none of the brine and rock pools which sometimes accompanies it. This is simply clean, lumbering phenols, thickened still further by a good dollop of lascivious fruit...; **t24** a barrage of firm brown sugars are first to show, followed soon after by a cream sundae fruitiness. The smoke is all pervasive and intensifies as the flavours play out; there is also a decent showing of peppery spice pulsing in its intensity; **f23** an enormously long fade, a bit like a midsummer sunset. No surprises, bitterness or off notes whatsoever. Just a slow dimming of all that has gone on before; **b23.5** on midsummer's day 2011, the summer solstice, I took a rare day off from writing this book. With the maximum light available in my part of the world for the day I set off at daybreak to see how many miles I could walk along remote country paths stopping, naturally, only at a few remote pubs on the way. It was a fraction under 28 miles. Had this spellbinding whisky been waiting for me just a little further down the road, I am sure, despite my troubled left knee and blistered right foot, I would have made it 30... *50%. nc ncf.*

Birnie Moss Intensely Peated db **(90) n22** youthful, full of fresh barley and lively, clean smoke; **t23.5** juicy, fabulously smoked, wet-behind the ears gristy sugars; **f22** some vanillas try to enter a degree of complexity; **b22.5** before Birnie Moss started shaving... or even possibly toddling. Young and stunning. *48%. nc ncf.*

Gordon and MacPhail Connoisseurs Choice BenRiach 1997 (88.5) n22 t23 f21.5 b22. A toffee-nut straight down the line Speysider designed for blending, but polishing up very pleasantly, indeed. *46%. ncf.*

Liquid Library BenRiach 1996 ex-bourbon hogshead, dist 96, bott 12 **(90) n21.5 t22.5 f23 b23.** Though patently made for blending, this bottling shows just how effortlessly good the distillery can be. *51.1%.*

That Boutique-y Whisky Company BenRiach batch 1 **(90.5) n23 t23 f22 b22.5.** As though some acacia honey has been burnt with the toast. So much sugar, yet so much balancing bitters: a fascinating, delicious whisky of extremes. *48.2%. 140 Bottles.*

That Boutique-y Whisky Company BenRiach batch 2 **(94) n23.5** impressive light peat, slightly unusual for not dragging any gristy sugars with it; **t23.5** here we go: determined to whisper its way around the palate. Listen hard and you can just hear the smoke cloaking the tannin-rich honey; **f23** smoke signals pass the silent message that the butterscotch is clean and offering a graceful sweetness; **b24** elegant, graceful and understated from first to last. A little gem that's easy to overlook. *48.1%. Master Of Malt. 58 bottles.*

⋰⋱ **That Boutique-y Whisky Benriach** batch 3 **(66) n16 t17 f16 b17.** The two previous batches had either been hit by sulphur, or a triumph of clean sherry. Guess which camp this falls into. *48.9%. 103 bottles. WB15/192*

BENRINNES

Speyside, 1826. Diageo. Working.

Benrinnes Aged 15 Years db **(70)** n16 t19 f17 b18. What a shame that in the year the independent bottlers at last get it right for Benrinnes, the actual owners of the distillery make such a pig's ear of it. Sulphured and sicklysweet, this bottling has little to do with the very good whisky made there day in day out by its talented team. Depressing. 43%. Flora and Fauna.

⁙ **A.D.Rattray Stronachie 10 Years Old** oak **(94)** n23 thin, nippy, malty but with a grainy harshness; **t24** rips into the throat, claws at the taste buds with a vicious maltiness; **f23** long, a slight malty tang, some vague fruity notes but still bites and kicks and reaches its conclusion anything but sedately...; **b24** curiously, utterly bizarrely, has the fizz and bite of an old fashioned standard thin, if decently malted, blend of three decades ago. Complex, brain-explodingly busy...and I absolutely love it...! 43% WB15/338

⁙ **A.D.Rattray Stronachie 18 Years Old** oak **(88.5)** n22.5 heavy duty fruit with some pretty ancient apple and pear in play; **t22.5** one of the more fuller bodied Benrinnes you are likely to find with a spiced fruitcake feel; someone forgot to say 'whoa!' When the golden syrup was being poured; **f21.5** slightly tangy, earthy, toffeed residue; **b22** not how Benrinnes normally pans out. Rather love this opulent feel: a real chewer. 46% WB15/310

⁙ **Cadenhead's Authentic Collection Benrinnes Cask Strength Aged 25 Years** bourbon hogshead, bott Jul 13 **(84)** n20.5 t21 f21.5 b21. You'll do well to find a thinner 25-year-old all year. Warming, at times aggressive with crisp barley sugar. 53%. 270 bottles. WB15/095

⁙ **Darkness! Benrinnes Aged 15 Years Oloroso Cask Finish (85)** n21 t21 f22 b21. Had a few reservations about this fellow even before I tasted it. If you are going to have big sherry, then that fruity muscle needs a backbone. And this distillery provides little at the best of times. Pleasant, thanks to being sulphur-free, and spicy. But otherwise devoid of complexity and structure. 52.9%. 96 bottles. WB15/202

⁙ **Darkness! Benrinnes Aged 15 Years Pedro Ximenez Cask Finish (86)** n21.5 t22 f21 b21.5. Very much the same can be said for this as the oloroso version. The PX cranks up the sugars as well as the spice big time, though. 53.3%. 94 bottles. WB15/235

Gordon and MacPhail Connoisseurs Choice Benrinnes 1997 (85) n20.5 t23 f20 b21.5. Attractive, entertaining whisky in its own sweet and unencumbered way. A busy small grains feel and plentiful sugars. The quality of the oak contributes positives and negatives. But the caramel and pinging spices star. 46%. ncf.

⁙ **Hepburn's Choice Benrinnes Aged 11 Years** sherry butt, dist 02, bott 14 **(87)** n21 t22 f22 b22. Thin, but makes its malty, banana and custard statement very well. Enjoyably refreshing and sales should get their just desserts... 46%. nc ncf sc. 672 bottles.

Liquid Library Benrinnes 1984 refill sherry hogshead, dist 84, bott 12 **(91.5)** n22.5 t23.5 f22.5 b23. Even in a softer, lightly graped, incarnation than normal there is something about the way the malts jar into the taste buds which makes the style recognisable. But being so clean and with no off notes, this is way above the distillery's norm. 46.9%.

⁙ **The Maltman Benrinnes Aged 17 Years (83)** n20 t21.5 f21 b20.5. Surprisingly dull and passionless. A soft caramel and milk chocolate softness engulfs frustrated flames. 43% WB15/216

Master of Malt Benrinnes 14 Years Old (82.5) n20 t20.5 f21 b21. Uncompromisingly Raw and ready. Expect your taste buds to be napalmed. If you like a bit of rough on the side, this is the stuff for you. Some redeeming barley juice, though. 57.8%

Master Of Malt Benrinnes 14 Years Old sherry butt, cask no. 6841, dist 2 Sep 98, bott 1 Apr 13 **(90)** n22 t22.5 f22.5 b23. A high quality sherry butt which allows the barley to play. But enough spice to guarantee complexity. 55%. sc. 570 bottles.

⁙ **Montgomerie's Single Cask Collection Benrinnes** cask no. 2835, dist 5 Oct 88, bott Mar 13 **(86.5)** n21.5 t21.5 f22 b21.5. Typically light, simplistic and warming, this has an attractive profile in which the barley is highlighted well. Is it because it is 6.30am and my first sample of the day, but is that a little sugared instant coffee I taste at the death.....? 46%. nc ncf sc. WB15/124

Old Malt Cask Benrinnes Aged 14 Years sherry butt, cask no. 9631, dist Dec 98, bott Mar 13 **(89)** n21 t22.5 f23 b22. Curiously, a cleaner cask than its Provenance twin, 9632, technically better by far but fewer twists and turns. 50%. sc. Hunter Laing & Co. 302 bottle.

Old Malt Cask Benrinnes Aged 17 Years sherry butt, cask no. 7437, dist May 94, bott Jul 11 **(87)** n22 t23 f20 b22. Flawed genius: the delivery is worth the investment alone. 55.1%. Douglas Laing and Co. nc ncf sc. 300 bottles. The Whisky Shop Dufftown.

⁙ **Old Malt Cask Benrinnes Aged 19 Years** bourbon barrel, cask no. 10577, dist May 95, bott Jun 14 **(88)** n22.5 much bigger and more to say than normal: a vague hint of (not unpleasant) boiled carrot amid the earthier oak; **t22** usually barnstorming, hot-as-hell delivery, this time a little salty but settles into an immediate chorus of cocoa; **f21.5** malt re-emerges and remains salivating until the death; **b22** a distillery not over-given to complexity of surprises, this entertains with more force and consistence than normal. *50%. nc ncf sc. 221 bottles.*

Provenance Benrinnes Over 12 Years sherry butt, cask no. 8571, dist Summer 99, bott Summer 12 **(86) n20 t22.5 f21.5 b22.** Rattles the teeth and taste buds with a bludgeoning maltiness which displays impressive sugars. Even a surprising and beguiling hint of smoke. *46%. nc ncf sc. Douglas Laing & Co.*

Provenance Benrinnes Over 14 Years sherry butt, cask no. 9632, dist Winter 98, bott Spring 13 **(90) n22 t23.5 f21 b23.5.** Rare to find a crisp sherry, but this is one. And fabulously backed by a shell of sugar. *46%. nc ncf. Douglas Laing & Co.*

Provenance Benrinnes Over 18 Years sherry butt, cask no. 9765, dist Winter 95, bott Spring 13 **(96.5) n23.5** the grape is so thick, the spice hanging from it so deft, the sharper greengage notes so clean, you almost forget to drink the stuff....; **t24.5** luscious delivery: the grape appears to have had its sugars rationed early on leaving a concentrated mass. A light molassed note begins to filter through, though not before the spices get to work; **f24** reverts to a quiet sweetness with a spicy buzz working pleasantly on the chocolate raisin finale; **b24.5** this uncommonly good year for Benrinnes bottlings also includes an absolutely spotless sherry edition. A masterpiece from the leftfield. Superb! *46%. nc ncf sc.*

꙰꙰꙰ **Scotch Malt Whisky Society Cask 36.74 Aged 9 Years** 1st fill barrel, dist 17 Jun 04 **(81.5) n21 t21.5 f19 b20** As ever, too thin to be an effective single malt, though the barley has some attractive moments early on. From the bubble gum school of whisky. *59.9%. nc ncf sc. 235 bottles.*

꙰꙰꙰ **Signatory Vintage Single Malt Benrinnes 1999 Aged 14 Years**, bourbon barrels, cask no. 9919+9921, dist 18 Oct 99, bott 06 Feb 14 **(85) n21 t22.5 f20 b21.** Sweet and syrupy with very little structure. Not unpleasant, and quite well spiced, but you find yourself shouting at the glass to do something else... *43%. nc. 723 bottles. WB15/017*

Stronachie Aged 12 Years Small Batch 2012 (83.5) n21 t21 f21.5 b20. A warming – actually, slightly hot – malt which relies on the intensity of the youthful barley to fill in the gaps left by the fragility of the spirit. Decent barley sugar residue. *43%.*

That Boutique-y Whisky Company Benrinnes batch 1 **(93) n23** something of the sherry trifles about this...; **t23.5** ....and even more about a limited single malt thriving in a beautifully rich grape and Demerara environment: just so thick yet juicy! **f22.5** dries with an agreeable degree of spice for company; the sweet sultanas work long hours...; **b23.5** the near (though not quite) faultless sherry has polished this malt up rather impressively. *48.9%.*

That Boutique-y Whisky Company Benrinnes batch 2 **(85) n21 t22 f21 b21.** Heavy caramel and a little sulphur dulls an otherwise pleasant bottling. *49.5%. 420 bottles.*

BENROMACH
Speyside, 1898. Gordon & MacPhail. Working.

Benromach 10 Years Old matured in hand selected oak casks db **(87.5) n22 t22 f21.5 b22.** For a relatively small still using peat, the experience is an unexpected and delicately light one. *43%*

Benromach 21 Years Old db **(91.5) n22** some exotic fruit and green banana is topped off with a splodge of maple syrup; **t23.5** excellent interplay between the sweeter, barley-rich components and the elegant, spiced oaky backbone; virtually no bite and softened further by an unfurling of vanilla on the middle; **f23** long, oak-edged with a slow, tapering dryness which does nothing to confront the sugared backnotes or even the suggesting of the most delicate smoke; **b23** an entirely different, indeed lost, style of malt from the old, now gone, big stills. The result is an airier whisky which has embraced such good age with a touch of panache and grace. *43%*

Benromach 22 Years Old Finished in Port Pipes db **(86) n22 t23 f20 b21.** Slightly Jekyll and Hyde. *45%. 3500 bottles.*

Benromach 25 Years Old db **(92) n24** seriously sexy with spices interplaying with tactile malt: the bitter-sweet balance is just so. There is even the faintest flicker of peat-smoke to underscore the pedigree; **t22** an early, surprising, delivery of caramel amongst the juicy barley; **f23** lots of gentle spices warm the enriched barley and ice-creamy vanilla; **b23** a classic old-age Speysider, showing all the quality you'd hope for. *43%*

Benromach 30 Years Old db **(95.5) n23.5** spiced sultana, walnuts and polished bookcases; **t24** no malt has the right to be anything near so silky. The sugars are a cunning mix of molasses and muscovado; the honey is thinned manuka. Still the barley gets through, though the vanilla is right behind; **f24** drier, but never fully dries and has enough spotted dog in reserve to make for a moist, lightly spiced finish. And finally a thin strata of sweet, Venezualan cocoa; **b24** you will struggle to find a 30-year-old with less wrinkles than this.. Magnificent: one of the outstanding malts of the year. *43%*

Benromach Cask Strength 1981 db (91) n21.5 t23 f23.5 b23. Really unusual with that seaweedy aroma awash with salt: stunningly delicious stuff. *54.2%*

Benromach Cask Strength 2001 db (89) n21.5 t23 f22 b22.5. Just fun whisky which has been very well made and matured with total sympathy to the style. Go get. *59.9%*

Benromach 2002 Cask Strength db (88.5) n22 t22.5 f22 b22. Most peaty malts frighten those who aren't turned on by smoky whisky. This might be an exception: they just don't come any friendlier. *60.3%*

⫶⫶⫶ **Benromach Cask Strength 2003** db (92) n22.5 the smoke is elusive and registers little more than the outline of your previous night's dream. Dry, with a little earthy nip and pinch; t23.5 it takes a long time for the peat to finally arrive. But when it gets there it stays, though little more than a shadow to the rampant muscovado sugar; f23 long, a little fizz and spice to the smoke now, but those sugars make light work of the gathering vanilla; b23.5 hats off to the most subtle and sophisticated Benromach I have tasted in a while. *59.4%.*

Benromach 2002 Sassicaia Wood Finish db (86) n21 t22 f21 b22. Again this entirely idiosyncratic wood-type comes crashing head to head with the smoke to form a whisky style like nothing else. Dense, breathless and crushed, there is little room for much else to get a word in, other than some oak-extracted sugars. A must experience dram. *45%*

Benromach 2005 Sassicaia Finish db (92.5) n22.5 lightly smoked, well weighted and boasting a delicate degree of Turkish Delight; t24 the delivery is just a little special with a silky texture to die for and phenols and fruit that dissolve like candy; f23 an injection of vanillas stiffens things up. But the weight remains impressive; b23 a sassy dram in every way... *45%*

Benromach Madeira Wood db (92) n22 some rolling smoke and chunky dried fruits almost cancel each other out; t24 voluptuous body displaying soft oils which coat the mouth with a spot on peat which is at once full and chewy yet light enough to allow the layered fruits full reign; the bitter-sweet balance just couldn't be better; f23 some touches of almost Jack Daniel hickory amid the circling smoke and juiced up fruit; mind-boggling complexity to this for so long; b23 if you want a boring, safe, timid malt, stay well away from this one. Fabulous: you are getting the feeling that the real Benromach is now beginning to stand up. *45%*

Benromach Marsala Wood db (86.5) n21.5 t22 f22 b21. Solid, well made, enjoyable malt, which in some ways is too solid: the imperviousness of both the peat and grape appears not to allow much else get through. Not a dram to say no to, however, and the spices in particular are a delight. *45%*

Benromach Organic db (91) n23 massive oak input and the freshest oak imaginable. But sits comfortably with the young pulsing malts. Wow!!; t23 oak arrives first again, but has enough deftness of touch to allow the rich, mouthwatering malts to prosper; f22 plenty of vanillins and natural, sweet toffee; b23 young and matured in possibly first fill bourbon or, more likely, European (even Scottish) oak; you cannot do other than sit up and take notice of this guns-blazing big 'un. An absolute treat! *43%. nc ncf.*

Benromach Organic Special Edition db (85.5) n22 t21 f21.5 b21. The smoky bacon crisp aroma underscores the obvious youth. Also, one of the driest malts of the year. Overall, pretty. But pretty pre-pubescent, too... *43%*

Benromach Origins db (84.5) n20 t22 f21 b21.5. You'd think after tasting over 1,250 whiskies in the space of a few months you'd have nosed and tasted it all. But no: here is something very different. Discordant noises from nose to finish, it is saved by the extraordinary richness of the coppery input and a vague smoky richness finishing with cold latte. *50%*

Benromach Origins Batch 1 "Golden Promise" dist 1999 db (69.5) n17 t17.5 f17.5 b17.5. The nose is less than promising. And with good reason. *50%*

Benromach Origins Batch 2 "Port Pipe" dist 1999 db (86) n22 t20.5 f23 b20.5. Dense whisky with huge spice. But it is as if in concentrate form with little room for complexity to develop into its full potential. Some charming chocolate and toffee on the finish. *50%*

Benromach Origins Batch 3 "Optic" dist 2000 db (83.5) n21 t20 f21.5 b21. Another chunky, tight malt from the new Benromach. Some serious chewing, but a few feints on which to chew... *50%*

Benromach Peat Smoke Batch 3 db (90.5) n22 excellent nose: pretty decent levels of peak reek evident but dried, rather than cured...; t23 the dry peat builds in intensity, though not after the clean and powering barley makes the first speech; f22.5 dry, chalky and compact; damn it – this is very good, indeed! b23 an excellent malt that has been beautifully made. Had it been bottled at 46 we would have seen it offer an extra degree of richness. *40%*

⫶⫶⫶ **Benromach Peat Smoke 2005** 67ppm db (88.5) n22 dry, peat soot; t22.5 light oils and slightly over sugared barley. The smoke, surprisingly, takes a bit of a back seat while gentle oak calm the over zealous maple syrup; a fair chunk of marmalade in there; f21.5 falls away rather too quickly with lightly smoked butterscotch; b22.5 this may be 67 parts per million phenols when it started. But size, so I have been told, is not important. Stamina and finesse both are. And while this may enjoy a degree of the latter, it has little of the former. 46%.

Benromach Traditional db (86) n22 t21 f21.5 b21.5. Deliciously clean and smoky. But very raw and simplistic, too. 40%

Benromach Wood Finish Hermitage dist 2001 db (84) n19 t23 f21 b21. A sweet, tight dram with all the shape crushed out of it. It does have its moment of greatness, though: about three or four seconds after arrival when it zooms into the stratosphere on a massively fruity, sensuously spiced rocket. Then it just fades away... 45%

Benromach Wood Finish Pedro Ximénez dist 2002 db (85.5) n21 t22.5 f21 b21. Combining PX with peated whisky is still probably the hardest ask in the maturation lexicon. Lagavulin are still to get it right. And they have not quite managed it here, either. It's a bumpy old ride, though some of the early chewing moments are fun. Not a bad attempt, at all. Just the learning curve is still on the rise... 45%

Benromach Vintage 1968 db (94.5) n23 theoretically way over the top oak. But the sherry acts as a sponge...or, to be more precise, a very well aged fruit cake; some mega juicy plums and figs; t23 can't fault the marbling with the fruit running thickly into the spicier, almost bourbony meat. Again the oak is over the top, yet, thanks to the depth of the cocoa and juicy grape, somehow gets away with some outrageous splinters; f24.5 now completely dazzles as all the more militant elements of the oak have been pacified and we are left with not only a sherry trifle/fruitcake mix, but chocolate cream/raspberry roll for good measure... b24 a 40 year plus whisky of astonishing quality...? A piece of cake... 45.4%

Benromach Vintage 1969 db (92) n22 a slightly tired, sappy aroma; honeycomb offers the perfect antidote; t24 the sugars are queuing to deliver and do so with a barley-rich gentleness. Some milk chocolate arrives, and then a succession of much drier, more assertive oak; f23 hangs on well and the seasoning is at times both complex and challenging; finishes with coconut shreds dunked in Golden Syrup; b23 the odd branch of the old oak too many. But still has many magical mahogany moments. 42.6%

⁙ **Benromach Vintage 1976** db (89.5) n23 exotic fruit is expected...and doesn't disappoint; yawns a little from tiredness here and there; t23.5 silky, mouth-watering though attractively tart. Any blender looking to ensure the malty but exotic frame to an old blend would be searching in his arsenal for a series of Speysiders just like this; f21 mainly vanilla and cocoa milkshake; bitters out slightly as the oak bites; b22 hardly complex and shows all the old age attributes to be expected. That said...a very comfortable and satisfying ride. 46%

Gordon & MacPhail Benromach Vintage 1976 db (89) n22.5 t22 f22 b22.5. For all the massive oak which shapes every inch of this dram, the degree of ulmo honey at work is extraordinary. 46%. ncf.

Gordon & MacPhail Benromach Port Wood finish 2000 db (86.5) n22 t21 f22 b21.5. A pleasant experience with a distinctive chocolate liqueur feel to it. Just a little too heavily laden with grape (though thankfully clean and entirely sulphur-free) for greatness as the malt is all but obliterated, though the spices rack up the complexity levels. 45%. ncf.

BLADNOCH
Lowlands, 1817. Armstrong Brothers. Working.

Bladnoch Aged 6 Years Bourbon Matured db (91) n21.5 young, yes. But the soft feints have nothing to do with that; t22.5 a youthful, oily delivery, not exactly a picture of harmony, gives way to a brutal coup d'etat of ultra intense prisoner-slaughtering barley; f24 intense barley-concentrate oils offer a perplexing array of sweet, grassy tones; you simply chew and chew until the jaw aches. Cocoa at last arrives, all with a spiced buzz and a smearing of vanillas. Meanwhile your tongue explores the mouth, wondering what the hell is going on; b23 the fun starts with the late middle, where those extra oils congregate and the taste buds are sent rocking. Great to see a Lowlander bottled at an age nearer its natural best and even the smaller cut, in a roundabout way, ensures a mind-blowing dram. 573%

Bladnoch Aged 6 Years Lightly Peated db (93) n23 a peat fire just bursting into life; t23 firm, bitter-sweet; the layering of the peat is awesome, with the youth of the malt adding an extra dimension; some citrus notes help lighten the load; f23.5 smoky hickory; the vanillas make a feeble entry, a gentle oiliness persists; b23.5 the peat has nothing to do with the overall score here: this is a much better-made whisky with not a single off-note and the cut is spot on. And although it claims to be lightly peated, that is not exactly true: such is the gentle nature of the distillate, the smoke comes through imperiously and on several levels. "Spirit of the Lowlands" drones the label. Since when has outstanding peated malt been associated with that part of the whisky world...?? 58.5%

Bladnoch Aged 6 Years Sherry Matured db (73.5) n18 t19 f18.5 b18. A sticky, lop-sided malt where something, or a group of somethings, conjures up a very unattractive overture. Feints on the palate but no excellent bourbon cask to the rescue here. 56.9%

Bladnoch Aged 10 Years db **(94)** n23 lemon and lime, marmalade on fresh-sliced flour-topped crusty bread; t24 immensely fruity and chewy, lush and mouthwatering and then the most beguiling build-up of spices: the mouthfeel is full and faultless; f23 long, remains mildly peppery and then a dryer advance of oak. The line between bitter and sweet is not once crossed; b24 this is probably the ultimate Bladnoch, certainly the best I have tasted in over 25 years. This Flora and Fauna bottling by then owners United Distillers should be regarded as the must-get-at-all-costs Bladnoch. If the new owner can create something even to hang on to this one's coat-tails then he has excelled himself. For those few of us lucky enough to experience this, this dram is nothing short of a piece of Lowland legend and folklore. 43%.

Bladnoch Aged 15 Years db **(91)** n22.5 remnants of zest and barley sit comfortably with the gentle oaks; t22.5 excellent delivery and soon gets into classic Bladnoch citric stride; f23 wonderfully clean barley belies the age and lowers the curtain so delicately you hardly notice; b23 quite outstanding Lowland whisky which, I must admit, is far better than I would have thought possible at this age. 55%

Bladnoch Aged 16 Years "Spirit of the Lowlands" db **(88)** n22 t22 f22 b22. Really lovely whisky and unusual to see a Lowlander quite this comfortable at such advanced age. 46%. ncf.

Bladnoch 18 Years Old db **(88.5)** n21 t23.5 f22 b22. The juiciness and clarity to the barley, and especially the big gooseberry kick, early on makes this a dram well worth finding. 55%

⊙ **Adelphi Selection Bladnoch 23 Years Old** cask no. 30043, dist 90, bott 13 **(89)** n22.5 weighty and nutty: marzipan with low sugar content...slightly Aberfeldy-ish in style; t23 superb delivery: magnificent weight to the oil which carries a wonderful maple syrup and acacia honey blend; f21.5 at first profound butterscotch tart, then bitters slightly as the oak grabs hold; b22 Bladnoch at its most full bodied. Remarkably fit for its age. 49.2%. ncf sc. 74 bottles. WB15/412

⊙ **Cadenhead's Small Batch Bladnoch Aged 21 Years** bourbon hogsheads, dist 1992, bott 2014 **(92)** n22 lively barley on all levels – from grassy to malty and embraces the Black Jacks easily; t24 one of the most eye-watering and stunningly clean deliveries you could imagine: like watching a five-year-old with a grey beard...; the sugars stay gristy and bounce beautifully alongside the peppers; f23 long, at last some vanilla, but that malt won't stop chasing...; b23 a fizzing little malt-concentrated beauty which defies the years! 54.9%. 510 bottles. WB15/091

⊙ **Cadenhead's Authentic Collection Bladnoch Cask Strength Aged 23 Years** bourbon hogshead, dist 1990, bott Jul 13 **(87)** n21 t22 f22 b22. A real softie of a dram which doesn't really want to cover much more than the basics. Very sweet malt is at its heart. And with the creamy Ovaltine at the finish, a good one as a night cap. 48.5%. 282 bottles. WB15/094

Gordon and MacPhail Connoisseurs Choice Bladnoch 1993 (84.5) n21 t21 f22 b20.5. We have reached a point here where the oak and barley are not on speaking terms. Perhaps not the greatest spirit to start off with, as the nose testifies, it certainly lacks sufficient muscle to see off the more vivid embraces of the oak. Some attractive muscovado-topped butterscotch from time to time, but all too much of a mishmash. 46%. ncf.

Old Malt Cask Bladnoch Aged 20 Years refill hogshead, cask no. 9431, dist Nov 92, bott Feb 13 **(71)** n18 t18 f17 b18. A malt some Germans will adore while those of us not immune to the dreaded "s" word can only weep. Some decent chocolate notes, though. 50%. sc.

⊙ **Old Malt Cask Bladnoch Aged 21 Years** refill hogshead, cask no. 10418, dist Nov 92, bott May 14 **(86)** n21.5 t23 f20.5 b21. Beautifully malty on delivery. But has the sharpness of a lemon drop at times – a malt certainly not behaving its age. 50%. nc ncf sc. 322 bottles.

⊙ **Signatory Vintage Single Malt Bladnoch 1993 Aged 20 Years** hogsheads, cask no. 767+773, dist 08 Mar 93, bott 25 Apr 13 **(88)** n20 messy: the two casks have not gelled. All kinds of in-fighting going on. Off key; t23.5 makes amends on the eye-watering delivery which appears to be barley concentrate infiltrated by heather and orange blossom honey; f22 reverts to a theme noticeable on the nose, but now enough spices and mocha to add to the complexity; b22.5 you get the feeling you have dodged a bullet here. The nose puts you on your guard as some of the oak used isn't what it might be. But it ends up working a treat, especially on the brilliant delivery. 43%. nc. 798 bottles. WB15/016

BLAIR ATHOL

Highlands (Perthshire), 1798. Diageo. Working.

Blair Athol Aged 12 Years db **(77)** n18 t19 f21 b19. Thick, fruity, syrupy and a little sulphury and heavy. The finish has some attractive complexity among the chunkyness. 43%. Flora and Fauna.

⊙ **Berry's Own Selection Blair Athol 1989 Aged 23 Years** cask no. 6333, bott 2013 **(87.5)** n21.5 t22 f21.5 b22. Bold, full bodied and fat. Slightly puckering and a little greasy. 46%. ncf. WB15/243

⋰ **Cadenhead's Authentic Colleection Blair Athol Cask Strength Aged 24 Years** bourbon hogsheads, dist 1989, bott Jul 13 **(92) n23** kind of similar to this year's G&M bottling, only here the buttery honey is sharper and three dimensional; **t23.5** suerb delivery with the creamy, intense malt bursting out with a wonderful gristy barley starburst; **f22.5** creamy butterscotch; **b23** great to see the distillery at full throttle taste and quality-wise. *50.8%. 186 bottles. WB15/093*

⋰ **Càrn Mòr Strictly Limited Edition Blair Athol Aged 15 Years** hogshead, dist 1998, bott 2013 **(67) n17 t19 f16 b17**. Furry and woefully off key. *46%. nc ncf. 736 bottles. WB15/159*

⋰ **Gordon & MacPhail Connoisseurs Choice Blair Athol** dist 1997, bott 2013 **(87) n22 t22 f21 b22**. How soft and friendly is the honey on this? At other times like distilled Worther's Originals candy. A little late oak bitterness. *46%. nc ncf. WB15/110*

⋰ **Hepburn's Choice Blair Athol 2002 Aged 11 Years** refill hogshead, dist 2002, bott 2014 **(80.5) n19.5 t22 f19 b21**. The delivery works fine and the entire piece falls within a malty framework. But the nose and finish reveals enough weaknesses to make this an uphill battle. *46%. nc ncf sc. 421 bottles.*

⋰ **Hepburn's Choice Blair Athol 2002 Aged 11 Years** refill hogsead, dist 02, bott 14 **(87.5) n21.5 t22 f22 b22**. A robust dram absolutely bursting with all kinds of malty life. Lively, fresh, clean and naughtily warming. *46%. nc ncf sc. 394 bottles.*

Old Malt Cask Blair Athol Aged 15 Years sherry butt, cask no. 9759, dist Aug 97, May 13 **(92) n23.5** the sprinkle of cinnamon and kiwi fruit makes all the difference to an already faultless butt; **t23** the sugars arrive first, second and fourth, with a few mixed barley ale and spice notes intervening; **f22.5** the toasted raisins make their mark, settling neatly into the spotted dog finale; **b23** don't see many Blair Athols in this kind of nick. Especially from sherry. *50%. nc ncf sc. Hunter Laing & Co Ltd. 271 bottles.*

⋰ **Old Malt Cask Blair Athol Aged 16 Years** sherry butt, cask no. 10127, dist May 97, bott Oct 13 **(85.5) n21.5 t22 f21 b21.5**. A pretty enough picture, thanks mainly to the muscovado sugars. But a bit like a jigsaw with some of the pieces in the wrong place... *50%. sc. 545 bottles.*

⋰ **Old Particular Highland Blair Athol 20 Year Old** 1st fill sherry butt, cask no. DL9908, dist Apr 93, bott Aug 13 **(81) n20 t21 f20 b20**. Malty, clean and a little sharp. But among this flight of drams, this is the one which stubbornly refused to take off. *51.5%. nc ncf sc. 477 bottles. Douglas Laing & Co.*

Provenance Blair Athol Over 12 Years sherry butt, cask no. 8767, dist Winter 99, bott Summer 12 **(86.5) n21 t22 f21.5 b22**. Malty, juicy, spicy though it is the lightest hint of smoke which throws up the biggest surprise. *46%. nc ncf sc. Douglas Laing & Co.*

Provenance Blair Athol Over 15 Years sherry butt, cask no. 9757, dist summer 97, bott spring 13 **(93) n22** pear drops and hot cross buns; **t23.5** deft delivery with the spices up early. The malt has almost as big a say as the fruit; a surprising juicy volley hits the mid ground; **f24** mocha rules supreme, though the vanilla surges late and strong; **b23.5** clearly a twin butt to the OMC 15, it is seemingly flatter in most areas, but pulls together with more complexity from the mid ground onwards. *46%. nc ncf sc. Douglas Laing & Co.*

Wemyss 1986 Single Highland Blair Athol "Autumn Berries" hogshead, bott 2012 **(86.5) n22 t22 f21 b21.5**. A light malt always going out of its way to tip-toe over the taste buds. The delivery is adorable, though, with more than a nod, on the nose too, to the venerable sweetshop, with all kinds of boiled candy of varying fruits. The finish, though clean and vanilla vibrant, is a little austere by comparison. *46%. sc. 268 bottles.*

⋰ **Wemyss Malts 1991 Single Highland Blair Athol "Blackcurrant Coulis"** barrel, dist 91, bott 14 **(86.5) n21.5 t22 f21.5 b21.5**. A very pleasant whisky intent to do simple, juicy things without really thinking much about complexity. A malty blending dram on the lightweight side for this distillery. *46%. sc. 338 bottles.*

⋰ **The Whisky Agency Blair Athol 1989** dist 1989 **(88) n22** a fizzing mix of stout, bourbonesque tannin, all peppery and rich. A baser, thinner note on the malt gives shrill warning to original state of the spirit; **t22.5** an intrigueing mix of dark sugars and resounding spice ensure a dapper delivery hardly short of character. But the body is woefully thin...; **f21.5** disappears quickly, leaving a few oaky, sugary tide marks; **b22** all the hallmarks of a whisky run fast through the stills, that near quarter of a century ago. But good oak has helped integrate it back into polite quaffing society. *50.8%.*

BOWMORE
Islay, 1779. Morrison Bowmore. Working.

Bowmore Aged 12 Years db **(91) n22.5** light peats, the air of a room with a man sucking cough sweets; sweet pipe smoke; **t23.5** soft, beautiful delivery of multi-layered peats; lots of effervescent spices and molassed sugars; spices abound; **f22.5** much drier with sharper berries and barley; the peat still rumbles onwards, but has no problems with the light, sawdusty oaks; **b23.5** this new bottling still proudly carries the Fisherman's Friend cough sweet character, but the coastal, saline properties here are a notch or three up: far more representative of Islay and the old distillery style. Easily by far the truest Bowmore I have tasted in a long while with myriad complexity. Even going back more than a quarter of a century, the malt at this age rarely showed such relaxed elegance. Most enjoyable. *40%*

⠶⠶ **Bowmore Black Rock** oak casks db **(87.5) n22.5 t22 f21 b22.** A friendly, full bodied dram whose bark is worse than its bite. Smoked toasted fudge is the main theme. But that would not work too well without the aid of a vague backdrop cinnamon and marmalade. If you are looking for a gentle giant, they don't come more wimpish than this. *40% WB15/336*

Bowmore "Enigma" Aged 12 Years db **(82) n19 t22 f20 b21.** Sweet, molassed and with that tell-tale Fisherman's Friend tang representing the light smoke. This Enigma hasn't quite cracked it, though. *40%. Duty Free.*

Bowmore "Darkest" Aged 15 Years db **(83) n20 t23 f19 b21.** In recent years a dram you tasted with glass in one hand and a revolver in the other. No more. But for the sulphur present, this would have been a much higher score. *43%*

⠶⠶ **Bowmore Gold Reef** oak casks db **(79) n19.5 t21 f19 b19.5.** Simple, standard (and rather boring and safe) fare for the masses gagged by toffee. *43% WB15/280*

Bowmore "Mariner" Aged 15 Years db **(79) n19 t21 f19 b20.** There are two ways of looking at this. As a Bowmore. Which is how I have marked it. Or a something to throw down your neck for pure fun. Which is probably worth another seven or eight points. Either way, there is something not entirely right here. *43%. Duty Free.*

Bowmore Aged 17 Years db **(77) n18 t22 f18 b19.** For all the attractiveness of the sweet fruit on delivery, the combination of butt and cough sweet makes for pretty hard going. *43%*

Bowmore Aged 18 Years db **(79) n20 t21 f19 b19.** Pleasant, drinkable Fisherman's Friend style – like every Bowmore it appears around this age. But why so toffee-dull? *43%*

Bowmore Aged 23 Years Port Matured db **(86) n22 t22 f21 b21.** Have you ever sucked Fisherman's Friends and fruit pastels at the same time, and thrown in the odd Palma Violet for good measure...? *50.8%*

Bowmore Aged 25 Years db **(86) n21 t22 f21 b22.** Not the big, chunky guy of yore: the age would surprise you if tasted blind. *43%*

Bowmore Aged 30 Years db **(94) n23** intense burnt raisin amid the intense burnt peat; a deft rummy sweetness strikes an improbable chord with the sweetened lime; the oak is backward coming forward but binds beautifully with both peat and fruit; **t24** near flawless delivery showing a glimpse of Bowmore in a form similar to how I remember it some 25 years ago. The peat, though intense does have a hint of the Fisherman's Friend about it, but not so upfront as today. For all the peat, this is clean whisky, moulded by a craftsman into how a truly great Islay should be; **f23** dries sublimely as the oak contains the peat and adds a touch of coffee to it in unsugared form. Gentle oils cling tightly to the roof of the mouth; **b24** a Bowmore that no Islay scholar should be without. Shows the distillery at its most intense yet delicate; an essay in balance and how great oak, peat and fruit can combine for those special moments in life. Unquestionably one of the best Bowmores bottled this century. *43%*

Bowmore 1985 db **(89) n21.5 t24 f22 b21.5.** I may have tasted a sweeter Islay. Just not sure when. This whisky is so wrong..it's fantastically right...! *52.6%*

Bowmore 100 Degrees Proof db **(90.5) n22** low key smoke. Anyone who has been to Arbroath looking for where the Smokies are cured and homed in on the spot by nose alone will recognise this aroma...; **t23** delicate in all departments, including the peat. The barley is sweet but it is the tenderness of the oils which stars; **f22.5** long with a tapering muscovado finale; **b23** proof positive! A real charmer. *57.1%. ncf.*

Bowmore Devil's Cask db **(87.5) n22** a p-souper of a nose...peaty, that is. Just so dense, it is really a little too much; **t23** there's no smoke without fire and the flames lick around a fruity Hades; **f21** hints of brimstone; **b21.5** not really my style of whisky, for all its obvious fun...and this little devil doesn't really even to try and balance itself out. *56.9%*

Bowmore Laimrig III db **(92) n23.5** so delicate is the ultra clean grape, I am assuming this is a sherry cask finish. Not usually a fan of smoke and grape, but when it is this delicate, what isn't there to like?; **t23.5** the softness found on the nose is continued on the palate. The sweetness is cleverly controlled and when the Fisherman's Friend personality arrives, it is quietly muffled, if not smothered to death, by a combination of silky grape, teasing spice and melting muscovado sugars; **f22.5** the oak now raises its profile, the deep vanillas and hint of honeycomb underlining a reasonable age; **b23** I must ask my research team: where the hell are Laimrigs I and II....? *53.7%*

Bowmore Legend db **(88) n22 t22.5 f22 b22.5.** Not sure what has happened here, but it has gone through the gears dramatically to offer a substantial dram with both big peat and excellent balancing molasses. Major stuff. *40%*

⫶⫶ **Bowmore Small Batch "Bourbon Cask Matured"** db (86) n22 t22 f21 b21. A big improvement on the underwhelming previous Small Batch from this distillery, then called "Reserve", though there appears to be a naievity to the proceeding which both charm and frustrate. The smoke, hanging on the grist, is very low key. 40%.

Bowmore Small Batch Reserve db (80.5) n20 t21 f19 b20.5. With a name like "Small Batch Reserve" I was expecting a marriage between intense Kentucky and Islay. Alas, this falls well short of the mark. 40%

Bowmore Tempest Aged 10 Years Small Batch Release No.1 db first fill bourbon, bott 2009 (87) n22.5 t22 f21 b21.5. Perhaps too dependent on the fudgy character. When given a chance, its coastal attributes are set off to excellent effect. 55.3%

Bowmore Tempest Aged 10 Years Small Batch Release No.2 1st fill bourbon, bott 2010 db (93) n23.5 a rousing and strangely subtle mixture of dusty, bone-dry phenols not uncommon to non-island peated malts and a sweeter, tangier smoke, much more reminiscent of lums reeking their winter warmth; all this charged and emboldened by sly degrees of golden syrup and juicy figs; t23.5 sturdy delivery. Just a light introduction of oils help the easy passage of a more fulsome earthiness, like the nose assisted by sugars, much more gristy this time. There is also a youthful citrus tone to this, though the dissolving vanilla and icing sugars do much good work; f23 a hint of bitterness from the oak, but the smoke and spices bombard the taste buds. Some muscovado sugars and even the most playful hint of molasses ensures the salty, coastal notes don't take too great a hold...; b23.5 just turned the bottle round to find some tasting notes banging on about "lemon pepper" here there and everywhere. That is only part of the tale: this is one of the better distillery bottlings to be found at Bowmore in recent years and does much to restore a slightly jaded reputation. Less a tempest than a glide across the Sound of Islay on a sunny day, cheese and tomato sandwich in hand.. But a massive statement by Bowmore, nonetheless. 56%. ncf.

Bowmore Tempest Aged 10 Years Small Batch Release No. 4 db (89) n22 t23 f22 b22. A much tamer version than the last Tempest I tasted. Then, there was a crescendo. This one sweeps gently across the palate without kicking up anything like a storm. 55.1%. ncf.

⫶⫶ **Bowmore Tempest Aged 10 Years Small Batch Release V** db (90.5) n23 where Kildalton meets Kentucky...soft, some might say puny, smoke swept almost contemptuously aside as confident honey-bourbon notes claims lordship; t23 at least the barley gets a brief look in as a wave of gristy sugars erupt for a salivating opening; the light smoke drifts aimlessly while red liquorice and thin ulmo honey coats the palate; f21.5 vaguely smoked vanilla; bitters out; b23 if you like your Islays on the subtle side but with a bold undercurrent, here you go..! 55.9%. ncf. WB15/279

⫶⫶ **A.D. Rattray Bowmore 1999** butt, cask no. 2262, dist 16 Sep 99, bott Nov 12 (87) n22 t22.5 f21 b21.5. Not quite a flawless butt, but the outstanding points outweigh the blemishes. 59%. sc. A.D. Rattray. DRCC Japan and Holland markets.

⫶⫶ **Alexander Weine&distillate Bowmore 16 Year Old** refill bourbon hogshead, cask no. 9646, dist 1996, bott 2013 (84.5) n21.5 t22 f20 b21. The intense sugars shape much of the mouth feel. But, ultimately, we are in pure Fisherman's Friend territory... 57.1%. sc. Cask strength.

⫶⫶ **Blackadder Raw Cask 1997 16 Years Old Bowmore** single oak hogshead, cask no. 1896, dist 13 Jun 97, bott Oct 13 (85.5) n21 t22.5 f21 b21. Bitty and shapeless, there is a lot to commend the salivating delivery. But not much else stacks up. Busy and rather hot. 57.5%. nc ncf sc. 284 bottles, cask strength. WB15/058

⫶⫶ **Blackadder Raw Cask 2001 12 Years Old Bowmore** single oak hogshead, cask no. 20063, dist 13 Mar 01, bott Oct 13 (94) n23 punchy smoke: some mocha seasoned with ginger and allspice; t24 stunning oils ensure the depth of the muscovado sugars reaches where they have best effect; the smoke appears to be part of the sugars and flying a little higher, too; f23.5 smoked butterscotch; b24 the old distillery back on top of its game. 58.5%. nc ncf sc. 312 bottles, cask strength. WB15/059

The Coopers Choice Bowmore 2001 10 Years Old refill butt, cask no. 9074, dist 01, bott 11 (91) n22.5 t22.5 f23 b23. Bowmore at its most relaxed and effortlessly enjoyable. Without question above the normal peating levels. 46%. The Vintage Malt Whisky Co Ltd. 360 bottles.

Fine Malt Selection Bowmore 12 Years Old cask no. 800252, dist 00, bott Apr 13 (85.5) n21.5 t22 f20.5 b21.5. A beauty of Bowmore is that the peating level can vary by intriguing degrees. Chewy and malty and less encumbered with salt than usual. But even the higher than normal phenols fails to fully overcome the late oak bitterness. 46%. sc.

Kingsbury Bowmore Aged 14 Years barrel, cask no. 800194, dist 98 (86.5) n22 t22 f21 b21.5. A delicate Bowmore which never quite hits the heights, but the gristy sweetness is soothing and pleasant. 46%. nc ncf. Japan Import System. 273 bottles.

Kingsbury Bowmore Aged 17 Years butt, cask no. 14, dist 95 (88.5) n21.5 t23 f22.5 b21.5. Typically disjointed yet enormous and somehow works. 53.6%. nc ncf. 545 bottles.

Malts of Scotland Bowmore 2001 bourbon hogshead, cask no. MoS 12060, dist Oct 01, bott Nov 12 **(87.5) n21.5 t22 f22 b22.** Never low key and makes the most of its youthful anarchy. 58.2%. nc ncf sc. 96 bottles.

⁕ **Montgomerie's Single Cask Collection Bowmore** cask no. 085078, dist 24 Apr 90, bott Mar 13 **(92) n23** relaxed smoke but by no means horizontal. A lovely salty twang gives this a rock pool feel; a little marmalade, too; **t24** sublime texture has a near perfect meeting of smoke and sugar; most remarkably, the barley is still intact and readable; **f22** slow smoke fade; a tad bitter late on; **b23** resplendent in its deft smoke and refined sugars, an impressive Bowmore. 46%. nc ncf sc. WB15/125

⁕ **Old Malt Cask Bowmore Aged 14 Years** refill hogshead, cask no. 10146, dist Sep 99, bott Oct 13 **(87.5) n21.5 t22 f22 b22.** Pleasant enough. But never really has much to say or a point to make and gets lost in its on sugary, phenolic fug. 50%. nc ncf sc. 563 bottles.

Old Master Bowmore 16 Years Old cask no. 800203 **(94) n23** pungent from so many angles: a massive saline kick to this, which fully accentuates not just the otherwise lazy phenols but the citrus curve to the vanilla; **t23.5** outrageously salivating for its age: now the lemon is in free flow, ensuring the taste buds see the barley before the smoke begins to make a noise, though not a very loud one; **f24** the sherbet lemon fizz continues, the delicate smoke and light cocoa coating in its wake: the best part of the experience! **b23.5** love it! 57%. sc.

⁕ **Old Particular Islay Bowmore Aged 12 Years** refill hogshead, cask no. 10284, dist Dec 01, bott Mar 14 **(86) n22 t21 f21.5 b21.5.** Curiously metallic, as if a new still or maybe condenser had been recently put in place. The gristy element and fudgy smoke remains untarnished, though. 48.4%. nc ncf sc. 421 bottles.

⁕ **Old Particular Islay Bowmore 17 Years Old** refill hogshead, dist Mar 96, bott Aug 13 **(88) n21** a typically askew aroma, totally in keeping with the distillery's profile for this period; **t23** compensates more than adequately with the type of delivery which could give you a toothache, so all encompassing are the sugars. A little liquorice and hickory sets up the smoky complexity deliciously; **f21.5** the final fade is a bit too jagged for comfort but the lead up is entertaining enough; **b22.5** one of those quirks of whisky where someone appears to have tipped a bag of sugar into some peat...and ended up with a malt which works! 48.4%. nc ncf sc. 312 bottles. Douglas Laing & Co.

⁕ **Old Particular Islay Bowmore 25 Year Old** refill hogshead, cask no 9906, dist Dec 87, bott Aug 13 **(80) n20 t21 f19 b20.** Indubitably from the unforgiving "Fisherman's Friend" period of Bowmore's production history. 50.2%. nc ncf sc. 234 bottles.

Old & Rare Bowmore Aged 25 Years refill butt, dist Feb 87, bott Apr 12 **(91.5) n23 t23 f22.5 b23.** Shows some imperfections and eccentricities reminiscent of a certain colourful period in the distillery's history. But this has moved on from the simple Fisherman's Friend of old to something altogether more complex and almost erotically enjoyable. 56.1%. nc ncf sc.

Provenance Bowmore Over 10 Years refill hogshead, cask no. 9325, dist Autumn 02, bott winter 12 **(84.5) n20 t22 f21 b21.5.** A sweet, warming dram perfect for a cold day. Shows impressive malt-peat complexity despite the dull oak. 46%. nc, ncf, sc. Douglas Laing & Co.

Provenance Bowmore Over 10 Years refill hogshead, cask no. 9574, dist winter 02, bott spring 13 **(89.5) n22 t23 f22 b22.5.** Simplistic, yet the most complete Bowmore of this age I've seen bottled for a while. Evidence the quality is on the way back. Beautiful. 46%. nc ncf sc.

⁕ **Riverstown Bowmore Aged 16 Years** oak hogshead, cask 2013-205, dist 13 Jun 97, bott Aug 13 **(94) n23.5** complex Bowmore making the most of its slightly above average peating level. A degree of Fisherman's Friend, but this has been checked, allowing the muscovado sugars a free hand; **t23.5** wow! And do those sugars let rip! A seriously full on degree of sugars, some in heather honey form, appears to somehow intensify the peat further; **f23.5** settles for a degree of complexity and sanity: a little mocha uses the muscovado well while strands of barley and Digestive biscuit can also be picked out; **b23.5** I think this is what is known by some as a honey cask...and for good reason. 56.1%. nc ncf sc. 251 bottles. WB15/123

Scotch Malt Whisky Society Cask 3.192 Aged 24 Years 2nd fill sherry butt, dist 8 Dec 87 **(94.5) n23** the peat and fruit are good mates: this is one very clean sherry butt and delicate smoke takes full advantage to blossom; **t24** about as good a sherry delivery as you are likely to find with this distillery. The submissive nature of the peat allows the rich fruitcake to thrive and even show a nutty nature; **f23.5** must be oloroso at work as there is a rich sheen to the grape which carries the light (and spice-free) smoke effortlessly; **b24** unusually creamy and just sweet enough. Absolutely exceptional and quite fruitless sherry butt at work. Sublime. 51.8%. nc ncf sc. 145 bottles.

Scotch Malt Whisky Society Cask 3.195 Aged 14 Years 2nd fill sherry butt, dist 25 Sep 97 **(76.5) n18 t20 f18.5 b19.** Sweet, but cuts up rough. About as unbalanced as 3.192 is textbook. 58.5%. nc ncf sc. 609 bottles.

⠿ **Scotch Malt Whisky Society Cask 3.212 Aged 19 Years** refill butt, dist 19 Apr 94 **(91.5) n22.5** dry, a little over-simplistic but showing some intense, dusty phenols to most un-Bowmore effect; **t24** absolutely rocking peat delivery! A Hell's Angle of a delivery, riding up to you with some ill-disguised age, rage and no little threat...; **f22** sharp, sweetly smoked but comparitively slightly off the pace; **b23** not the usual Bowmore style...someone has ramped up the phenols big time...!! *55.7%. nc ncf sc. 534 bottles.*

⠿ **Scotch Malt Whisky Society Cask 3.216 Aged 18 Years** refill hogshead, dist 06 Apr 95 **(90.5) n23** just down the lane from me is a pigstye. Some the more agricultural aromas here are what may greet me on an evening stroll...; **t23** intense sugars on delivery: a kind of smoked Demerara; **f22** dry and spiced; **b22.5** a whisky which will you can stand your mucking out shovel up in... *56.1%. nc ncf sc. 266 bottles.*

⠿ **Scotch Malt Whisky Society Cask 3.220 Aged 13 Years** 1st fill barrel, dist 13 Oct 00 **(87.5) n21.5 t22.5 f21.5 b22.** Juicy, effervescent and lusty. *55.4%. nc ncf sc. 235 bottles.*

⠿ **Signatory Vintage Cask Strength Collection Bowmore 1997 Aged 16 Years** hogshead, cask no. 1911, dist 13 Jun 97, bott 07 Jul 13 **(93.5) n22.5** unassuming and polite to a fault, the smoke drifts in through the back door but has some presence once it has wiped its feet; **t24** astonishingly sweet, as though every atom of sugar from the grist has been stored up and allowed to tumble on to the taste buds; the smoke takes up a dual role of comforter and backbone; **f23** long, with the emphasis on crisp muscovado sugars sooted by peat smoke; the spices grow, glow, rumble and stay...; **b24** does the heart good to see a Bowmore offer this degree of top quality entertainment. Smoked a little over the norm, one suspects. *55.4%. nc sc. 276 bottles. WB15/02*

⠿ **Signatory Vintage Un-chillfiltered Collection Bowmore 2001 Aged 12 Years** refill butt, cask no. 1365, dist 25 Sep 01, bott 06 Mar 14 **(77) n20 t22 f17 b18.** The usual gathering of suspects: Fisherman's Friends, molasses, Parma Violets. But despite the best attempts of decent spice and hickory, with its off-key fruit absolutely fails to make a coherent noise. *46%. nc ncf sc. 777 bottles. WB15/027*

That Boutique-y Whisky Company Bowmore batch 1 **(84.5) n20 t21 f22.5 b21.** Pleasant. Sweet. Very lightly smoked. Even more lightly fruited. Yet seems to struggle for a pulse. The delicate spices are the star turn. *48.7%. Master of Malt. 263 bottles.*

That Boutique-y Whisky Company Bowmore batch 2 **(91) n21.5 t23.5 f23 b23.** Bowmore in a very good form, indeed, with the smokiness decidedly enigmatic. *49%.*

⠿ **Wemyss Malts 1982 Single Islay Bowmore "Loch Indaal Catch"** hogshead, dist 82, bott 14 **(85.5) n21 t22 f21 b21.5.** Could have done with this liquid Fisherman's Friend when I had a cold a couple of months back.... *46%. sc. 165 bottles.*

⠿ **Wemyss Malts 1987 Single Islay Bowmore "Sweet Peat Posy"** hogshead, dist 87, bott 14 **(89.5) n23** charmingly floral signature to the decent smoke; **t22** distinctive Fisherman's Friend tang; **f22.5** salty, spicy sharp finish. More FF and an extra shake of salt to wring out all the delicate fruit notes from the vanilla; **b22** Bowmore's old Fisherman's Friend style could be hit and miss. This one hits... *46%. sc. 231 bottles.*

⠿ **Wemyss Malts 1996 Single Islay Bowmore "Aniseed Pastille"** hogshead, dist 96, bott 14 **(90) n21.5** lazy, remarkably peat-free. High vanilla dependency; **t23** unlike the nose, this takes off with a prodigious leap of juicy barley and grabs the attention. Mouth-watering and refreshing, the fudgy sugars and shy spice work well; **f22.5** still no smoke to mention. Dries as the vanilla grips; **b23** more or less an unpeated Bowmore which shows its malty teeth in a rare display. Always fascinating to see what lurks beneath the phenols. Quite lovely. *46%. sc. 344 bottles.*

⠿ **Wemyss Malts 2001 Single Islay Bowmore "Peat Smoked Herring"** hogshead, dist 01, bott 13 **(87) n21.5 t22 f21 b21.5.** Call me a stick-in-the-peat but I would have much rather seen this do its business in a blend than as a single malt. Know what I could have done with this to give some body. As a singleton, enjoyable for the smoke-encrusted grist but rathers lacks development other than some pleasing spice. Alays enjoyable, though, and worth the experience. But as for "Peat Smoked Herring" on the label. FFS, as they say... As a man who eats herring at least twice a week and tastes one helluva lot of peated whisky, possibly as much as anyone else on this planet, and grew up on kippers and Arbroath Smokies...I could honestly weep for the poor bemused punter...*46%. sc. 460 bottles.*

⠿ **The Whisky Agency Bowmore 1998** dist 1998 **(87.5) n21.5 t22 f22 b22.** Harmony is something deeply hoped for but rarely attained thanks to both the egotistical grape and peat being at loggerheads; the anthracite side story is a pleasant one, though. Even so, a spotless sherry butt with not a hint of sulphur. But the entanglement between grape and smoke sometimes becomes a little too much of a test. *52.1%.*

BRAEVAL

Speyside, 1974. Chivas Brothers. Working.

❀ **Càrn Mòr Strictly Limited Edition Braes of Glenlivet Aged 19 Years** bourbon barrel, dist 1994, bott 2014 **(86.5) n21.5 t23 f20.5 b21.5.** When this distillery is good it is very good. The quality punctured only by residual oak bitterness. The delivery, though, offers a malty-citrus mix of the highest quality. *46%. nc ncf. 486 bottles. WB15/156*

❀ **Directors' Cut Braes of Glenlivet Aged 25 Years** refill hogshead, cask no. 10350, dist May 89, bott Jun 14 **(91.5) n22.5** complex and weighty: mainly toasty but some milky mocha softens; **t23** surprisingly salivating as an early malt blast catches the toasty tannins off guard; liberal burnt treacle tart and spices; **f23** fabulous chocolate mousse; **b23** a malt which knows how to go all with a spring in its step. *60.3%. nc ncf sc. 174 bottles.*

Dun Bheagan Braeval Aged 16 Years hogshead, cask no. 85163, 85165, 85166, dist May 96, bott 13 **(89) n21.5 t23 f22 b22.5.** A cheery, high quality dram full of happy, uncomplicated malty notes. *43%. nc ncf. Ian Macleod Distillers. 1050 bottles.*

❀ **Gordon & MacPhail Connoisseurs Choice Braeval** dist 1995, bott 2013 **(85) n21 t22 f21 b21** From the intensely grassy school of Speyside. Despite a short juicy phase, not quite as perky as you'd like from this distillery and fails to find a different groove. *46%. nc ncf. WB15/144*

❀ **Hepburn's Choice Braeval 2001 Aged 12 Years** sherry, dist 2013 **(89) n22** barley, the whole barley and nothing but the barley...; **t23.5** clean, juicy malt intensifies into full Malteser mode; **f21.5** after an injection of tannin, a tired oak tang takes a little polish from the previous charming moments; **b22** the type of cask which allows the barley an unhindered life. *46%. nc ncf sc. 807 bottles. WB15/062*

❀ **Hepburn's Choice 2001 Aged 12 Years** sherry butt, dist 2001, bott 2014 **(84) n22 t21.5 f20 b20.5.** A bit like the coffee served to you in First Class on the 08:07am Wellingborough to London St Pancras. You thank them on being handed it, appreciate the first mouthful but on realising how insipid it is you decline their offer for a refill...*46%. nc ncf sc. 523 bottles.*

Master of Malt Braes O'Glenlivet Aged 21 Years ex-bourbon cask, dist 23 Aug 92, bott 28 Nov 12 **(94) n23.5** much more Buffalo Trace than Braeval: the tannins leap from the glass like Nureyev from the stage floor with a wonderful accompaniment of muscavado sugars and liquorice; sharp rhubarb and gooseberry preserve on mildly burned toast; **t24** malts of this age rarely arrive on the palate so saturated in barley juice...it just drips with the stuff. With it comes a supreme sweet-sharp barley balance, then a slow introduction of vanilla and butterscotch.; **f23** the finish reverts back to the bourbon style with toasted honeycomb walnuts in abundance; **b23.5** when Braes is good it can be, like this, bloody marvellous...!! *47.4%. sc. 251 bottles.*

❀ **Old Particular Speyside Braeval 15 Year Old** refill hogshead, cask no. 9989, dist Feb 98 bott Aug 13 **(85) n21 t22 f20.5 b21.5.** An interesting one: though the cask has a few wobbly moments, especially on the nose and finish, the malt compensates with some extra barley sugar intensity. *48.4%. nc ncf sc. 329 bottles. Douglas Laing & Co.*

❀ **The Pearls of Scotland Braeval 1991 22 Year Old** cask no. 95119, dist Aug 91, bott Nov 13 **(92.5) n23.5** an irrepressible thread of ginger on no less confident field of tannin; superb malt which has blossomed in first fill ex-bourbon; **t22.5** some zinging spice as the oak holds all the aces; **f23.5** settles into intense cocoa backed handsomely by deft molasses; **b23** a high value oldie, no little thanks to a top quality cask. *52.9%.*

❀ **Signatory Vintage Single Malt Braeval 1998 Aged 14 Years** bourbon barrels, cask no. 168894+168895, dist 12 Nov 98, bott 22 Mar 13 **(94.5) n23.5** gorgeous apples and pears beefs up the barley; **t24** a delivery from some kind of Speyside heaven: faultless barley which is at once firm yet yielding. The layering of the sugars, topped with soft ulmo honey is a joy; **f23** beautifully even oak input, allowing the barley and feint fruit safe passage; faultlessly clean to the very death; **b24** quintessential Speyside malt. Not overly complex. Just does what it does very beautifully helped by some exceptional oak. If you see it, grab it and be seduced... *43%. nc ncf. 668 bottles. WB15/014*

That Boutique-y Whisky Company Braes O'Glenlivet batch 1 **(78) n21 t20 f18 b19.** Flat, toffeed, bitter and very disappointing for this distillery. *47.2%. 210 bottles.*

❀ **The Whisky Agency Braeval 1994** dist 1994 **(86.5) n21.5 t22.5 f21 b21.5** Absolutely prime blending malt where the barley performs cartwheels, but little other excitement besides gentle spices. *52.9%.*

BRORA

Highlands (Northern), 1819–1983. Diageo. Closed.

Brora 25 Year Old 7th Release bott 2008 db **(96) n24** even with the lowest peating levels you ever have nosed from this distillery, the aura of beauty is unmistakable: the soft phenol molecules appears to be perfectly matched with the oak ones. Meanwhile fragile citrus ensures a youthful charm; somewhere there is a hint of bourbon; **t24.5** superb barley kick off, absolute waves of juices running about the palate, and still the smoke holds back, no more than a background murmur; as the middle fills, that bourbon on the nose become more pronounced with shades of honeyed liquorice; **f23.5** long, with the sugars hanging in there allowing the vanillas to form very slowly; **b24** as the distillery closed in March 1983, if memory serves me correctly, this must be coming to the end of the road for the true 25-year-old. Those looking for the usual big peat show might be disappointed. Others, in search of majesty, sophistication and timeless grace, will be blown away. 56.3%

Brora 30 Years Old db **(97) n24 t25 f24 b24.** Here we go again! Just like last year's bottling, we have something of near unbelievable beauty with the weight perfectly pitched and the barley-oak interaction the stuff of dreams. And as for the peat: an entirely unique species, a giant that is so gentle. Last year's bottling was one of the whiskies of the year. This even better version is the perfect follow-up. 56.4%

Brora 30 Years Old Special Release refill American and European oak db **(89) n22 t23.5 f21.5 b22.** Seeing as I was the guy who proudly discovered this whisky over 20 years ago, I take more than a keen interest. But like a loved and cherished old relative, you can still adore its personality and unique independence but be aware that it is slowly fading away... 54.3%. nc ncf. Diageo. 2958 bottles.

Brora 32 Years Old Special Release 2011 db **(89) n22 t23 f22 b22.** A strange bottling containing more natural caramels from a Brora than I have ever before seen. Obviously a dumbing down effect is inevitable but enough of the original beauty remains to enthral. 54.7%. nc ncf.

Brora 35 Years Old Special Release 2012 Refill American Oak, dist 1976 & 1977, bott 2012 db **(90.5) n24.5** got a spare day or two...? This is Brora in transformation: the peat levels have dropped now to a whisper while the exotic fruit delegation, often present in very old whisky, though more normally found in Speyside, have turned up in full force. The oak notes dominate over the peat at a rate of about three to one. But, some of those vanilla and guava notes in particular are exceptionally complex; **t22.5** eye-watering oak on delivery. The oils prevent too much damage and the kumquats retain a degree of juiciness; predictable cocoa in mid-ground; the smoke has thinned like the hair on an old man's pate; **f21** there is a buzz, less of spice and more of exhausted oak. But, again, those cocoa oils fill and sooth; just enough sugars around to guarantee balance; **b22.5** perhaps 90% of other Scottish malts would have failed under such an oaky onslaught. However, the pedigree of this distillery sees it through against the odd and the nose rewards a good hour's study. Not sure how much longer this guy can hold out for, though. 48.1%. nc ncf. Diageo.

BRUICHLADDICH

Islay, 1881. Rémy Cointreau. Working.

Bruichladdich 10 Years Old db **(90) n22** beautifully clean and zesty, the malt is almost juvenile; **t23** sweet, fruity then malty charge along the tastebuds that geets the mouth salivating; **f23** the usual soft vanilla and custard but a bigger barley kick in the latter stages; **b22** more oomph than previous bottlings, yet still retaining its fragile personality. Truly great stuff for a standard bottling. 46%

Bruichladdich 12 Years Old 2nd Edition db **(88) n23 t22 f22 b21.** A similar type of wine involvement to "Waves", but this is oilier in the old-fashioned 'Laddie style and lacks a little of the sparkle. The fruit on the finish is outstanding, though, and I don't think you or I would turn down a third glass... 46%

Bruichladdich 15 Years Old 2nd Edition db **(86) n22 t23 f20 b21.** Delicious, as usual, but something, possibly fruity, appears to be holding back the show. 46%

Bruichladdich 16 Years Old bourbon cask db **(89) n22.5 t22.5 f22 b22.** Plucked from the cask in the nick of time. In this state rather charming, but another Summer or two might have seen the oak take a more sinister turn. 46%

Bruichladdich 16 Years Old bourbon/Chateau d'Yquem cask db **(95) n24** if you've got a good half an hour to spend, try using it intelligently by sticking your nose in this for a while: the grape is sweet and sultana juicy; the understated spices somehow hit just the right point to satisfy grape, oak and barley in one hit: some achievement... **t23.5** sweet, as the nose suggests, but the arrival is not all about grape. That sweetness also contains pristine barley... **f23.5** just so soft and subtle with the vanillas offering a discreet escort to the barley-grape marriage; **b24** possibly the most delicate and understated of all the truly great whiskies of the year. Not one for the ice and water brigade. 46%

Bruichladdich 16 Years Old bourbon/Chateau Haut Brion cask db **(81.5) n21 t21.5 f19 b20.** fruity and busy for sure. But just not the kind of wine barrel effect that does much for me, I'm afraid, not least because of the background buzz on the palate. 46%

Bruichladdich 16 Years Old bourbon/Chateau Lafite cask db **(89)** n24 t22.5 f21.5 b21.5. Ridiculously soft. Could just do with an injection of something to propel it into greatness. *46%*

Bruichladdich 16 Years Old bourbon/Chateau Lafleur cask db **(92.5)** n23 t23.5 f23 b23. So luminous on the palate, it's positively Lafleurescent... *46%*

Bruichladdich 16 Years Old bourbon/Chateau Latour cask db **(84.5)** n21 t21.5 f21 b21. Enjoyable. But there is a strange aggression to the spice which doesn't altogether sit as comfortably as it might. The fruit heads off into not just grapey but citrus territory, but there is a always a but about the direction it takes... *46%*

Bruichladdich 16 Years Old bourbon/Chateau Margaux cask db **(78.5)** n20.5 t20 f19 b19. Not 1st Cru Bruichladdich, I'm afraid. *46%*

Bruichladdich XVII Aged 17 Years bourbon/renegade rum db **(92)** n23 typical rum "clipped" nose; this one with just a shade of soft, dry rubber typical of certain Guyana (especially Enmore) or Barbados marks; a rather lovely lemon tint to the vanilla works a treat; t23.5 super dry delivery, too, with the sugars taking time to arrive. When they do, they weld with the barley attractively; formidable balance between the barley and spices while a light sprinkling of salt seems to up the spicy oak input to counter the sugars; f22 mainly dry and attractively layered with short, sweet bands; b23.5 always good to see the casks of drier, more complexly structured rums being put to such intelligent use. My sample doesn't tell me which rum casks were used, but I was getting vivid flashbacks here of Ruby-Topaz Hummingbirds flitting from flower to flower in the gardens of the now closed Eigflucht distillery in Guyana in the long gone days when I used to scramble around the warehouses there. That distinctive dryness though is pure Enmore, though some Barbadian rum can offer a similar effect. Something very different and a top quality experience. *46%. nc ncf.*

Bruichladdich 18 Years Old bourbon/cognac cask db **(84.5)** n23.5 t21 f20 b20. Big oak-spice buzz but thin. Sublime grapey nose, for sure, but pays a certain price, ultimately, for associating with such an inferior spirit... *46%*

Bruichladdich 18 Years Old bourbon/opitz cask db **(80.5)** n19 t22 f19.5 b20. Dry, complex; at times oak-stretched. *46%*

Bruichladdich 18 Years Old 2nd Edition bourbon/jurancon db **(86)** n22 t21.5 f21 b21.5. Plenty of fruit, including medium ripe greengages and slightly under-ripe grape. Juicy and sweet in the right places. *46%*

Bruichladdich Flirtation Aged 20 Years 2nd Edition db **(86)** n21 t22 f22 b21. Hi sugar! A Laddie for those with a sweet tooth. *46%*

Bruichladdich 21 Years Old oloroso cask db **(76.5)** n18.5 t21 f18 b19. Oops! *46%*

Bruichladdich Black Art 3rd Edition Aged 22 Years db **(83)** n22 t21.5 f20 b20.5. Where last year' Black Art II managed to get away with the odd slight off note due to its brain-exploding enormity, this year it just hasn't got what it takes to get over the hurdles. Some sumptuous fruit through the middle, but it just ain't enough... *48.7%. nc ncf.*

Bruichladdich 32 Years Old DNA 1977 bourbon cask db **(94.5)** n23 there are so many bourbon tags on this, especially the waxiness to the honey, that just for a fleeting, off-guard moment I thought I was back nosing Kentucky whisky again. Then a giveaway salty tang coupled with a delicate hint of barley reminded me that I was in the land where the bagpipe abounds...; t24 ridiculous! I mean, bloody outrageous! No whisky has the right to a delivery that perfect with the lightly oiled texture seemingly holding both oak and grain in equal measures. Buttery and rich, it then pans out back towards Kentucky with some liquorice and threads of honey. Then propels back to Scotland with a uniquely salty toffee middle; f23.5 relatively easy going and simplistic. But the cream toffee hangs in there and then a late breakdown of almost clichéd bourbon notes from honey to hickory...; b24 absolutely top of the range, profound and virtually faultless whisky which makes you remember the reason why you fell so deeply in love with this stuff all those many years ago. How fitting that when this was made Laddie was the Scotch distillery closest to America. For this is as much a bourbon in style as Scotch. But who cares? It doesn't matter: great whisky is great whisky. Full stop. *474%*

Bruichladdich 37 Years Old DNA 80% bourbon/20% sherry cask, aged in Le Pin wine casks db **(87)** n23.5 t22 f20.5 b21. Balance..? What balance...? Actually, somehow, this crazy thing does find some kind of equilibrium... *41%*

Bruichladdich 1984 Golder Still bourbon cask, db **(88.5)** n22 t23 f22 b21.5. A huge amount of natural caramels leached from the oak does the joint job of ensuring extraordinary softness and eroding the higher notes. Still, there is enough eye-rolling honey and spice to keep anyone happy and the rich bourbony character on delivery really is dreamy stuff. *51%*

Bruichladdich 1984 Redder Still db **(95.5)** n23.5 t24 f23.5 b24.5. Now it's finding whiskies like this that I became the world's first-full time whisky for. I dreamed of discovering drams which stretched my tastebuds & spoke to me with eloquence, charisma & unmistakable class. This is one such whisky: the style is highly unusual; the cleverness of the layering almost unique. This is the kind of near flawless whisky for which we were given tastebuds. Oh, & a nose... *50.4%*

Bruichladdich 1989 db (75.5) n20 t19 f17.5 b19. Ouch! 52.9%. Special bottling for Alberta.

Bruichladdich 1989 Black Art 2nd Edition bourbon cask db (95) n24 a thick fruit composite of probably the juiciest dates you'll find south of the Sahara and a dense hickory and honey strain of bourbon... Not just compelling. But absolutely magnificent...and just so right!!! Sulphur? Can it be? Yes, no...? Can't quite make it out...; t24 how many deliveries allow the spice ahead of the main thrust? Perhaps more accurately, alongside. Still pretty rare and the way in which the chocolate fruit and nut melts in with the honey and liquorice bourbon notes, you feel anything can happen; f23 some wonderful oils helping those dates and now walnuts, too, all embedded in light cocoa, to their final spicy farewell; b24 Bourbon cask, it says. Right. But how did those lush dates get in there? Also, there even appears to be the very faintest (and I mean the odd molecule) of sulphur. But so miniscule it does no damage whatsoever. This is a whisky that asks ten times more questions than it answers. Time, though, not to wonder why, but just bloody well enjoy, for this is one of the great whiskies of the year. 49.7%

Bruichladdich Black Art 1990 Aged 23 Years 4th Edition cask no. 13/161 db (79) n20 t21 f18 b20. The same wobbly weaknesses found in the 3rd edition are back here in force once again. Big, juicy fruit notes will form a degree of compensation for some. 49.2%. nc ncf sc.

Bruichladdich 1990 Aged 18 Years db (85.5) n22.5 t21 f21 b21. Enlivened by citrus and emboldened by soft salt. 46%

Bruichladdich 1990 Aged 18 Years cognac cask db (81.5) n20.5 t21 f20 b20. Wouldn't be a far greater benefit to the spirit world if Cognac was matured in a Bruichladdich cask...? 46%

Bruichladdich 1991 Aged 16 Years Chat Margaux finish db (94) n23 t25 f22.5 b23.5. A true Premier Cru malt...I have been almost certainly the most outspoken critic of whisky finishes: trust me, if they were all like this, you would never hear the merest clack of a dissenting typing key from me again... 46%

Bruichladdich 1991 Valinch Anaerobic Digestion 19 Years Old bourbon & madeira casks db (96.5) n24.5 huge, yet cleverly weighted fruit with spiced boiled greengages oozing from the glass but very happy to allow golden syrup to share some of its limelight; t24 if the nose was excellent, the delivery is of no less quality. A light, oily bed allows the grape and sugars to land gently, then a light spicy layer forms another level entirely. All the hallmarks of a juicy first fill Madeira cask at work here...and working well; f24 perhaps drier than all else before with the spices chipping away and a burnt raisin sharpness mingling with the latent honey; virtually a never ending tale...; b24 about 20 minutes ago I could name you 250 excellent reasons to go and visit this distillery. I can now name you 251...A potential world whisky of the year that manages to do just about everything right...!!! 52.5% ncf sc. Only available at distillery.

Bruichladdich 1992 Sherry Edition "Fino" Aged 17 Years bourbon/fino sherry db (94) n23.5 dry, suety, spotted dick; in the background, dried dates lurk deliciously; wonderful balance; t24 fabulously subtle malt-generated sweetness sits comfortably with a much drier, juicier sub-plot; the mouthfeel hovers around perfection with just enough light oil to grease the roof of the mouth and keep the barley in the ascendancy; f23 lots to chew here as the vanillas offer a custardy edge, though sugars – whilst present - are at a premium. Again we are back to the dregs of dried dates; b23.5 exceptionally good: a rare showing of Fino at its most sophisticated and unblemished. 46%. nc ncf.

Bruichladdich 1992 Sherry Edition Pedro Ximénez Aged 17 Years bourbon/PX db (83) n22 t22 f18.5 b20.5. My word, that grape really does fly relentlessly at the taste buds. Probably the hardest sherry type to get right and here it works pretty well for the most part. 46%. nc ncf.

Bruichladdich 1993 14 Years Old Bolgheri French oak db (85.5) n23 t21 f21.5 b20. The fabulous nose doesn't quite translate once on the palate. The natural caramels and barley combo never quite gets it together with the grape. Now the nose: that's a different matter! 46%

Bruichladdich 1993 14 Years Old Sassicaia French oak db (83) n20 t21 f20.5 b21. From a too tight nose to a too limp body. Just not my sac... 46%

Bruichladdich 1994 Valinch Blandola bourbon/Chateau d'Yquem casks, dist Sep 94 db (87) n21.5 t22.5 f21 b22. A bit muddled here and there but, like the distillery and staff, no shortage of personality. 55.3%. Available only from Bruichladdich's distillery shop.

Bruichladdich 1994 "Kosher" Aged 12 Years db (85.5) n22 t21 f21 b21.5. Clean. What else, my dear? 46%

Bruichladdich 1998 db (89) n22 t22.5 f22.5 b22. A truly unique signature to this but absolute class in a glass. 46%

Bruichladdich 1998 bourbon/oloroso cask, dist 1998 db (87.5) n22.5 t22.5 f21 b21.5. Surprisingly conservative. But, joy of joys, not an atom of sulphur to be found...!! 46%

Bruichladdich 1998 bourbon/Manzanilla cask, dist 1998 db (82.5) n21 t21 f20 b20.5. Fruity. But bitter where it should be sweet. 46%

Bruichladdich 1998 Ancien Regime db (84.5) n22 t21.5 f20 b21 An easy, slightly plodding celebration of all things malty, caramelly, oily and vanillay... 46%

Bruichladdich 2001 Renaissance db **(91)** n23 lively with the smoke and oak in particular going hammer and tongs; **t23** brilliant delivery! Varying fruit tones hit the palate running but there is a bit of barley reinforcement flexing some considerable muscle. But the star is the ubiquitous smoke which shows a gentle iron fist; **f22.5** a big surge of natural caramels but the spices make a scene; **b22.5** a Big Laddie. 46%

Bruichladdich 2001 The Resurrection Dram 23.10.01 bourbon cask, dist 2001, bott 2009 db **(90.5)** n23 so subtle! Spiced sultana on malt, laced with golden syrup; **t23** grist dissolves in the mouth: molten (fruitless) barley again with a sugary sheen. Simplistic, but beautifully effective; **f21.5** long, vanilla-led, spiced and a little bitter; **b23** now, be honest. How can you not have a first class Resurrection in the Bible...? 46%. 24,000 bottles.

Bruichladdich 2004 Islay Barley Valinch fresh sherry butt db **(89.5)** n22.5 t24 f21 b22. Yet another quite fabulous bottling form Bruichladdich, this one really cranking up the flavours to maximum effect. Having said all that, call me mad if you will...but seeing as this is Islay barley, would it not have been a good idea to shove it into a bourbon barrel, so we could see exactly what it tastes like? Hopefully that is on its way... 57.5%

Bruichladdich Infinity Second Edition bourbon/rioja db **(94)** n24 t24 f23 b23. Wasn't it Daffy Duck who used to put on his cape and shout: "Infinity and Beyond" ? Oh, no... it was Buzz Lightyear. Anyways, he must have been thinking of this. And there's certainly nothing dethspicable about this one... 52.5%

Bruichladdich Infinity Third Edition refill sherry tempranillo db **(94.5)** n24 the smokiness appears to have a life of its own: still cured bacon, as in previous Infinities (actually can there be such a thing...?) but perhaps a touch of Bavarian smoked cheese, perhaps, as a side dish, next to a freshly diced apple? I adore the lack of oils on the nose; the teasing dryness compensated by a distant fruit freshness; **t24** and its more of the same: just so dry, the palate is parched in seconds. The smoke is ashy, the vanilla is powdery, the malt gristy...just flakes of flavour wafting into every crevice like snow falling on a silent day; **f23** long, with the inevitable build up of dry, powdery spices which match the vanilla for weight and impact; **b23.5** I dare anybody who says they don't like smoky whisky not to be blown away by this. Go on...I dare you... 50%

Bruichladdich Islay Barley Aged 5 Years db **(86)** n21 t22.5 f21.5 b21. The nose suggests a trainee has been let loose at the stills. But it makes amends with an almost debauched degree of barley on delivery which lasts the entirety of the experience. Heavens! This is different. But I have to say: it's bloody fun, too! 50%. nc ncf.

Bruichladdich Islay Barley Rockside Farm 2007 bourbon, cask no. 13/159 db **(88)** n22 so, so young! Maybe Islay barley, but it is still pretty green; very odd molecule of smoke here and there; **t22** juicy youthful barley; the final echoes of new make but otherwise absolutely pure, uncomplicated malt. Spices litter the palate, as do some hardening sugars and softer caramel; **f22** a few cocoa, mildly minty notes, though this seems more like the remnants of new make than cask; **b22** clean and chirpy. Great fun. 50%. nc ncf.

Bruichladdich Laddie Classic Edition 1 db **(89.5)** n23 t23 f21 b22.5. You probably have to be a certain vintage yourself to fully appreciate this one. Hard to believe, but I can remember the days when the most popular malt among those actually living on Islay was the Laddie 10. That was a staunchly unpeated dram offering a breezy complexity. Not sure of the age on this Retroladdich, but the similarities almost bring a lump to the throat... 46%

Bruichladdich Legacy Series 3 Aged 35 Years db **(91)** n22 t22.5 f23.5 b23. So they managed to find a whisky exactly the same age as Ladie distiller Jim. 40.7%

Bruichladdich Links "Carnoustie" 14 Years Old db **(78)** n19 t20 f19 b20. Hits some unexpected rough. 46%

Bruichladdich Links K Club Ireland "16th Hole" 14 Years Old bourbon/syrah, dist 1992, bott 2007 db **(93)** n23 t23 f23 b24. I quite like this, though as hard as I try I can't quite love it. The spices offer great entertainment value and the juiciness on delivery is astonishing, but... My tongue is investigating every crevice in my mouth with some urgency, so I know it's complex – and very unusual, but... It's gossamer light. It kind of teases you. It's playful. But it's not beautiful. Is it...? Third mouthful in and I'm getting hooked. Oh, sod it! I've just upped it from a 86 to 93. What can I do? I'm in love... 46%. nc ncf. 12,000 bottles.

Bruichladdich Links "Torrey Pines" 15 Years Old db **(89.5)** n23 t22.5 f22 b22. As clean as the perfect tee shot from the 15th... 46%

Bruichladdich Organic 2003 Anns An T-Seann Doigh bourbon db **(84.5)** n22 t22 f20 b20.5. Thick barley carrying a soft smoke. A slight bitterness threads in and out of the proceedings. 46%. nc ncf. 100% Scottish barley.

Bruichladdich Organic Multi Vintage bourbon db **(87.5)** n22 t22 f20.5 b22. Genteel. 46%
Bruichladdich Peat db **(89.5)** n23 peat; t22.5 peat; f22 peat; b22 peaty. 46%

Bruichladdich Rocks db **(82)** n19 t22 f20 b21. Perhaps softer than you'd imagine something called "rocks"! Beautiful little malty charge on entry. 46%

Bruichladdich Scottish Barley The Classic Laddie db (78.5) n20 t21.5 f18 b19. Not often a Laddie fluffs its lines. But despite some obviously complex and promising moves, the unusual infiltration of some sub-standard casks has undone the good of the local barley. If you manage to tune out of the off-notes, some sublime moments can still be had. 50%. nc ncf sc.

Bruichladdich Sherry Classic Fusion: Fernando de Castilla bourbon/Jerez de la Frontera db (91) n23 t23 f22 b23. What a fantastically stylish piece of work! I had an overwhelming urge to sing Noel Coward songs while tasting this: for the Dry Martini drinkers out there who have never thought of moving on to Scotch... 46%

Bruichladdich Waves db (81.5) n20.5 t21.5 f19.5 b20. Not sure if the tide is coming in or out on this one. Got various sugar and spice aspects which appeals, but there is something lurking in the depth that makes me a little uneasy... 46%

Bruichladdich WMD II - The Yellow Submarine 1991 db (75) n20 t19 f18 b18. This one just doesn't have the balance and sinks. 46%

Bruichladdich X4 db (82) n18 t22 f21 b21. Frankly, like no new make I have ever come across in Scotland before. Thankfully, the taste is sweet, malty and compact: far, far better than the grim, cabbage water nose. Doesn't really have the X-Factor yet, though. 50%

Bruichladdich X4 +3 Quadruple Distilled 3 Aged Years bourbon db (86) n21.5 t22 f21 b21.5. It is as if the sugars in the barley have been reduced to their most intense form: this is all about huge barley of eye-watering intensity. A novel and not unattractive experience. 63.5%. nc ncf. 15,000 bottles.

The Laddie Ten American oak db (94.5) n24 a stunning balance between sea spray, the most delicate liquorice and hickory imaginable and blemish-free barley; t23.5 no let down on delivery with the barley and delicate sugars hand in hand for the first three or four very big flavour waves; the middle has an oaky richness but not a single hint of weary dryness: gorgeously weighted and rich without over sweetening; f23 at last the salts form, as do the vanillins and slightly coarser oaky notes. Retains that distinctly coastal feel; b24 this, I assume, is the 2012 full strength version of an Islay classic which was the preferred choice of the people of Islay throughout the 70s, 80s and early 90s. And I have to say that this is already a classic in its own right.... 46%. nc ncf.

Octomore 5 Years Old db (96) n23.5 seeing how Octomore is actually a farm on Islay, it is rather fitting that the massive peat here yields a distinctly farm-yardy aroma. Yet this is curiously low on peat reek for a dram boasting phenomenal phenols at 131 parts per million – Ardbeg is about 50; the much smokier PC7 is just 40. That said, obviously peaty, yet an age-related lemon lightness, too...and a herd of cattle...; t24.5 the oils are absolutely perfect, as is the slow unfurling of the myriad strata of peat; those youthful, zesty, citrus notes have been enriched with a perfect degree of golden syrup; a near-perfect sprinkling of spice enriches further...; f24 a wonderful array of vanillas lighten not just the peat but the sweetened mocha which is now making its mark. Long, relaxed and very assured for a malt so young... b24 forget about the age. Don't be frightened by the phenol levels. Great whisky is not about numbers. It is about excellent distillation and careful maturation. And here you have a memorable combination of both... 63.5%

Octomore Edition 2.1 Aged 5 Years (140 ppm) bourbon cask, bott Jun 09 db (94) n23 a snug nose of tight, thick peat: needs a chainsaw to cut through it; t24 surprisingly sweet delivery with more than a hint of citrus: a massive gristy surge which is about as mouth-watering as heavily peated malt ever gets; the smoke is all enveloping; f23 long with some vanilla at last getting into the act; some excellent late mocha and marzipan thins the smoke; b23 talk about a gentle giant: as though your taste buds are being clubbed to death by a ton of smoky feathers. 62.5%. nc ncf. 15,000 bottles.

Octomore Edition 2.2 "Orpheus" Aged 5 Years (140 ppm) bourbon/chateau Petrus, bott 2009 db (96.5) n24 when you clean out the ashes of fire that had been fed 100% by peat, that morning after the night before task, this is what you get. Well, partially. You will have to have one hand in the grate, the other around a glass of Petrus...; t24.5 let's get this right: 140ppm phenols? Check. 61% abv? Check. How then, can the landing on the palate be like jumping onto a bed of feathers? The Demerara-gristy sweetness helps. So does the smoke, which envelopes the mouth. But the peat is also dry and that means a magnificent balance with those gristy sugars, so all seems to be in harmony. Brilliant! f23.5 long, and just a gentle wind down of all before. Maybe a bit of extra fruit visible later on, as well as some Liquorice Allsorts; b24.5 a standing ovation for this massive performance...the quite perfect way to bring up my 900th new whisky for the 2011 Bible. Everything works; the age and freshness of the barley, the controlled enormity of the smoke...even the entirely sulphur-free wine barrel. For those with a lot of hair on their chest...and want even more. 61%. 15,000 bottles.

Octomore Edition 5.1 db (91.5) n23 sooty peat with a sprig of mint; t22.5 the youth is immediately apparent – more than usual – with the fresh gristy malt soon being lost under the sugars; f23 after last year I was waiting for the cocoa...for a long time. A vague mocha note does appear, sweetened by several spoonfuls of smoky Demerara; **b23** a slightly less complex version, probably because of the obvious lack of years. Great fun, though. 59.9%

Octomore Edition 6.1 Aged 5 Years bourbon cask db **(91.5) n24** acrid smoke. Bonfires at my Dad's old allotment back in Surrey, it's leafy sweetness mixing with the chunkier peak reek; beyond that is a mix of Fisherman's Friend and cherry cough sweet. Also detectable, if you can spot it, is very young grist...the aroma of grist mashing...; **t23** a brief new make opening amid the big sugary delivery: concentrated Demerara concentrated again. The smoke is both chewy and also acts as a counter for the staggering grist sweetness; **f22** some late coconut cake carries the smoke and mocha; **b22.5** a slightly different Octomore, a little more tart than usual and wears its youth with pride. 57%

⠿ **Octomore Edition 6.1 Aged 5 Years Scottish Barley** (167 ppm) db **(94) n23.5** peat so dense, at first appears as a wall of smoked hickory and burnt cocoa: it takes a while for a layer of smoke to drift off lightly enough for the peat to come across as...well, peat...! **t24** a one-off delivery which absolutely grips the palate: the peat is beyond concentrated. Some molasses filter through to reduce the singularity of the impact, but hardly diverts it from its course of feeling that you are engulfed in the dense smoke of a peaty bonfire...from which there is no escaping; **f24** now the peat reveals a lighter touch and a degree of layering. But it is all part of the same relentless story: balance here hardly comes into play....; **b22.5** talk about can't see the wood for the trees: here you can't see the peat for the moss. It appears that when you get to a certain degree of phenol saturation, the smokiness suggests less rather than more. On the nose that is. Then you taste it...and you are then in for the peatiest experience of your life... 57% WB15/314

Octomore Edition 6.2 Aged 5 Years Cognac cask db **(90) n22.5** the peat is already crushed, the fruit strangles any possible movement; **t23.5** hard to imagine the smoke playing second fiddle, but it does: the sugars are so intense and the barley so salivating, for a few moments you even forget it is there; **f22** even tighter oak and crisp enough to break all your teeth; **b22** one of the sweetest bottlings from this distillery of all time. Some warming late spice, too; 58.2%. Travel Retail Exclusive Limited Edition Release. 18,000 bottles.

Octomore 3rd Edition Aged 5 Years db **(95) n24.5** as someone who grew up in the countryside and, to this day, spends as much of what little spare time I get traipsing around fields and farmsteads, this is an aroma I know too well... cowsheds! Except here there is that extra element of peat, but that intense sweetness is unmistakable: It may only be a young 'un, and the youth is noticeable, but it remains one of the most distinguished and most flawless of all Scotland's whisky aromas...; **t24** as soft to the palate as a view of the sea from Port Charlotte is to the eye... The peat does not compromise, yet nor does it bully, allowing any amount of Demerara sugars to form and intensify with the vanilla and natural caramels from, I suspect, from first fill oak; **f23** much quieter than you might expect from the nose, but there is a touch of the Horlicks about the finale; **b23.5** I usually taste this late on in the Bible writing cycle: it is so important to be rewarded at the end of a long journey. This hasn't let me down and here's the rub: how something which looms so large be made from so many traits so small...? 59%

Octomore 4th Edition Aged 5 Years (167 ppm) db **(92) n21.5** hardly believable as an Octomore: the smoke appears locked in a caramel bubble...; **t23.5** sheer power seems to allow the smoke to burst away from its shackles, but it has to work hard. But there is none of the normal peaty dryness. Instead we are directed towards a delicious praline thread with the nut oils building and a non-specific fruitiness offering little more than a hint; **f23.5** 80% cocoa smoked chocolate...outrageous! **b23.5** Choctomore, surely? 62.5%

Octomore 10 db **(95) n24** have I ever mentioned cowsheds? This is David and Ruth Archer's threatened milking parlour...but without the milk...awww nawooo..! **t24** as ever, smoke...like someone's set fire to the barn...awww nawooo!; **f23** the most intense of all finishes, as though the excess of the cowshed has been drained by marauding badgers... awww nawoooo! **b24** when I am tasting an Octomore, it means I am in the home straight inside the stadium after running (or should I say nosing and tasting) a marathon. After this, there is barely another 20 more Scotch malts to go and I am closing in on completing my 1,200 new whiskies for the year. So how does this fair? It is Octomore. It is what I expect and demand. It gives me the sustenance and willpower to get to that crossing line. For to tell you guys about a whisky like this is always worth it...whatever the pain and price. Because honesty and doing the right thing is beyond value. Just ask David Archer... 50%. nc ncf.

Port Charlotte An Turas Mor Multi Vintage bourbon cask db **(85.5) n23 t22 f20 b20.5** Does much right, especially the intriguing bullying of the colossal peat over what probably passes for grape. But bitters out and struggles to find a balance or plot line to keep you wanting to discover more. 46%

Port Charlotte Heavily Peated db **(94.5) n23** smoke comes scudding into the nose, vigorously, giving the joint effect of death by peat and acrid burnt toast; **t24** a youthful livewire delivery with a pretty surprising degree of maple syrup and treacle latching onto the phenols: the effect and balance is wonderful; pay attention and you'll spot some juicy fruit notes popping up here and there, too; **f23.5** the lack of major oak means the finish is fractionally lighter than it might be, but the smoke is now even and pretty soft despite the late spice; **b24** rearrange the following two words: "giant" and "gentle". 50%

Port Charlotte PC6 db (96.5) **n24.5** ohhhhhh... arrrrrrrrhh... mmmmmmmmmmm... oh, the peat, the peat... yesssssss... oh my god... mmmmmmmm... ohhhhhhh... **t24** first you get the smoky... oooooohhhhhhh... arrrrrrrrrr... then the sweeter... mmmmmmmmm... arrrrooooohhhh... **f24** it finishes with a more gentle arghoooo... mmmmmmmm... oooophhhhhh... arrrrrrrrrr... **24** not many whiskies have a truly unmistakable nose... and... but this is, this... is... this... mmmmmmmm..., arrrrrhh. Ohhhhhhh... 61.6%

Port Charlotte PC7 dist 2001 db (93.5) **n24** dry. The most profound peat fire ashes: not for peaty amateurs... **t24** a few drops of sweetness added; a liquorice/molassed melt to the massive smoke: the phenols seems a lot higher than the 40ppm they talk about; **f22** drops down a gear or two as some bitterness creeps in, as does a secondary fizz to the spice; **b22.5** not quite as orgasmic as last year, sadly. But should still be pretty stimulating... 60.5%

Port Charlotte PC8 bourbon, dist 2001, bott 2009 db (88) **n22 t23 f21 b22**. Enjoyable, but muted by PC standards... 60.5%. 30,000 bottles.

Port Charlotte PC10 db (96) **n24** promises to be the best PC for a few years! There is a vague kumquat undercoat that does well having itself heard amid the formidable phenols. But the weight is just so enormous, yet somehow crushes nothing; **t24.5** stunning! You know the peat is omnipotent yet, miraculously, it is the sugar-honey mix which dictates play, especially the pace of flavour development. Some oils and caramels ensure excellent shape and body; **f23.5** the smoke works hard to re-establish itself but the oak still has much to say; **b24** just so right....!!! 59.8%

Port Charlotte The Peat Project db (93.5) **n23.5** rhubarb and custard with an outrageous dollop of manuka honey. And a lot of soft, sweet smoke...so sweet it could be from a tobacconists; **t24** so intriguingly sweet I tried to re-create it: the closest I got was orange-blossom honey, muscovado sugar, treacle and maple syrup. Pretty close. What I couldn't copy was the enigmatic peat: one moment seeming massive, another barely noticeable; **f22.5** surprisingly low key; all kinds of butterscotch and lemon curd tart but, like the peat, only hinted at; **b23.5** a very curious, odd even, PC when much is said in the nose and glass, but few speeches are made. 46%

⁘ **Port Charlotte The Peat Project** db (95.5) **n24.5** the smoke drifts through in varying degrees of intensity and types of mood. Whenever it darkens, a burst of citrus appears to brighten its countenance; **t24** soft sugars form a guard of honour as the smoke tip-toes into the arena. The peat does not seem so prominent here as it does on the nose, a light vanilla infusion also detracting from the smoke; **f23** dries slowly, allowing in a delicate cocoa oil intensity to the smoke; **b24** this is not peat for peat's sake. This appears to be crafted and layered, offering a pleasing timbre and unusual gracefulness. 46% WB15/339

The Laddie Sixteen American oak db (88) **n22** huge natural caramels dipped in brine; **t22.5** very even and gentle with a degree of citrus perking it up; **f21.5** reverts to caramels before the tannins strike hard; **b22** oak 'n' salt all the way... 46%

The Laddie Twenty Two db (90.5) **n24** a breakfast plate of three pieces of toast: one with salted butter, another with ulmo honey and the last one with marmalade; light spices, too. Busy yet understated; **t23** silky salted butters again on delivery immediately backed by intense barley sugar; **f21.5** the oak cranks up significantly; **b22** fabulous coastal malt, though the oak is a presence always felt. 46%

⁘ **Alexander Weine & Destillate Port Charlotte 10 Year Old** fresh port wine cask, cask no. 646, dist 07 Jul 03 bott 06 Sep 13 (95.5) **n24** one of those noses which stops you dead in your tracks. First you have to comprehend the enormity of the peat, then the intensity and clarity of the grape...and then the ease in which they combine. You know this s major piece of phenols when the peat comes across so dry and dusty; **t24** the fabulous port is so juicy and fresh for a few moments the peat doesn't get a look in. When it goes it exacts revenge by sending in spices as intense as the dry smoke; the fruity sugars simply carry on regardless; **f23.5** majors in spice. Very long with the dry, slight cocoa-shrouded peat always in play; **b24** you know that I am no fan of big peat and big wine. But when something arrives in your glass this enormous, this magnificent...you will not hear a dissenting word from me. 60%. sc. cask strength.

Berry's Own Selection Bruichladdich 1991 cask no. 2998, bott 2013 (94) **n23** a field of grass freshly mown; gooseberry tart with limited sugars; **t23.5** you expect salivating, you get salivating. In fact you get advanced salivating, for as well as the pure juiciness of it all, you also get a degree of salt and spice to zap up the sharpness; **f24.5** amid the zipping, seriously warming spice, we somehow return to those gooseberries; naturally, a little custard arrives at the end, as well as some chocolate mousse; **b24** classic Bruichladdich for those of us of a certain vintage...! Few malts over 20 are this alive. Spectacular. *51.6%. nc ncf sc.*

⠿ **The Coopers Choice Bruichladdich 1992 Aged 20 Years** hogshead, cask no. 3685, bott 2013 **(89.5) n22** salted bananas; old garden sheds; **t23.5** gorgeous juicy malt: salivation cannot be prevented; **f22** several thick layers of caramel; **b22** the early threat of over-aged oak is swept away by the juicy malt and toffee. Satisfying whisky. *46%. 365 bottles. WB15/303*

⠿ **The Coopers Choice Port Charlotte 2004 Aged 9 Years** hogshead, cask no. 1032, bott 2014 **(92) n23.5 t23 f22.5 b23.** Description is pointless: it's Port Charlotte.! That said, there is an extra injection of lime. And this cask appears to have brought the most out of the caramel because there are deadening toffee notes I have never seen in this make before. A dozing giant. *46%. 330 bottles. WB15/302*

Director's Cut Bruichladdich Aged 21 Years refill sherry butt, cask no. 8937, dist Oct 90, bott Sep 12 **(96) n24** it doesn't happen often these days, but a 20-y-o malt sitting in a 100% untarnished, truly perfect, sherry butt. The meeting between the prickly spiced grape and malt is something to savour for as long as you possible can...; **t24.5** absolute silk on delivery, and then all kinds of rampant spices biting and exploding, yet such is the almost barley wine thickness to the malt the impact is contained with ease; a distinctive chocolate fruit and nut bar forms in the middle ground; **f23.5** more scope for the oak as the vanillas seize control from the fruit; **b24** a couple of years ago a whisky "expert" (he has/had a web page or something in Canada, so he must be one) took me to task for saying that Bruichladdich made outstandingly good unpeated whisky during the days when they had no smoked output at all. Apparently I was wrong on both counts. They always made peated, I was lectured, and, secondly, when they made unpeated it was due to running out of peated malt and was of inferior quality. Don't remember the name of the fool, but if he is reading this...just get your kisser around this and learn....For not only is this unpeated, but it comes from a perfect sherry butt. Sensational! *57.1%. sc. Douglas Laing & Co. 255 bottles.*

Gordon and MacPhail Connoisseurs Choice Bruichladdich 1991 (92) n23.5 the oaks are mildly over enthusiastic but vanilla ice cream with a generous dollop of lime sauce bumps up the sweetness; **t3** superb delivery - spices abound; the tannins boast bourbon-style liquorice and hickory but enough juicy barley to balance matters out; **f22.5** consistent vanilla and spice; **b23** old school Laddie which has passed its Highers. *46%.*

⠿ **The Maltman Port Charlotte Aged 12 Years** bourbon cask **(94) n23** the driest known peat soot known to mankind...; **t23.5** yet sweetens dramatically on delivery as the big phenolic grist takes hold. From then on its melt in the mouth smoke, bolstered by an extra degree of golden syrup; **f23.5** returns to a more even balance between sweet and dry. The smoke, though, is big and constant...; **b24** with PC you know what you are going to get. Only the cask type impacts and here we have a lethargic bourbon cask happy for the peat to get on with it. *52.4%*

Malts of Scotland Bruichladdich 1988 sherry hogshead, cask no. MoS 12040, dist Apr 88, bott Sep 12 **(80) n21.5 t21.5 f18 b19.** Sharp on delivery with a good spice blast. But bitters out at finish. *54.3%. nc ncf sc. 96 bottles. Bottled exclusively for Islay Whisky Dinner 2012.*

Malts of Scotland Bruichladdich 2002 cask no. MoS 13026, dist May 02, bott Apr 13 **(88.5) n22 t22 f22.5 b22.** Creamy, sugary, buttery....and smoky! *55.2%. nc ncf sc. 96 bottles.*

Malts of Scotland Port Charlotte 2001 sherry hogshead, cask no. MoS 12039, dist Nov 2001, bott Sep 2012 **(83.5) n20.5 t22 f20 b21.** Smoked raisin soup. The sherry furriness at the finish confirms suspicions on the nose... *63.3%. nc ncf sc. 96 bottles. Bottled exclusively for Islay Whisky Dinner 2012.*

Malts of Scotland Port Charlotte 2001 sherry hogshead, cask no. MoS 13013, dist 01, bott 13 **(87.5) n21.5 t22 f22 b22.** I know there are those out there who will sell their children into slavery for this, despite the modest flaw. *62.4%. nc ncf sc. 48 bottles.*

Old Malt Cask Bruichladdich Aged 20 Years refilled sherry butt, cask no. 9037, dist Feb 92, bott Nov 12 **(95) n23.5** do you remember that luscious moment when you get to the bottom of the sherry trifle...? **t23.5** mouth-filling, fruity beyond measure...a Richter Scale for fruitiness would probably explode at this point. Some barley makes the odd noise, as does the oak but that grape is all consuming; **f24** complexity begins to really kick in now as some cocoa filters through, then mocha. But someone is stirring some sherry into it, too; **b24** restores one's faith in whisky kind when sherry butts like this turn up. Flawless and a fabulous exhibition of how a great sherry cask can do enough to influence, but leave room for the other elements to play. *50%. nc ncf sc. Douglas Laing & Co. 363 bottles.*

Old Malt Cask Bruichladdich Aged 25 Years refill hogshead, cask no. 9810, dist Feb 88, May 13 **(94) n22.5** marzipan with raspberry jam; **t24** the distillery's old fashioned silk delivery brimming with concentrated barley soon loses out to a much more aggressive oakiness, though the ulmo honey soothes the spat; the balance between sugar and tannin is something to be experienced; **f23.5** loads more ulmo honey and now the oak has been tamed and only purrs a butterscotch and crème brûlée finale; **b24** just starting to vanish under the oak. All that is left is pure magnificence...! 48.3%. nc ncf sc. 328 bottles.

Scotch Malt Whisky Society Cask 127.28 Aged 9 Years refill butt, dist 21 Jun 02 **(94.5) n23.5** thick and heady: you could stand a spoon in the aroma alone...; **t24.5** it is not the delivery, it is not the moment after the delivery: it is from about the sixth flavour pulse...then, even after the smoggy beauty of before, it becomes a work of compelling, eye-rolling beauty with the fruity sugars meeting the phenols on even ground and at equal weight; **f23** long, with soft oils helping lift the mocha; brown sugars abound; a little off key and tangy at the very death; **b24** engrossing and unmissable. 65.1%. nc ncf sc. 217 bottles.

Scotch Malt Whisky Society Cask 127.29 Aged 10 Years refill butt, dist 14 Dec 01 **(73.5) n19 t19.5 f17 b18.** Ever wondered what a fumarole in the middle of an Islay peat bog might nose and taste like....? 63.8%. nc ncf sc. 73 bottles.

Scotch Malt Whisky Society Cask 127.30 Aged 10 Years refill barrel, dist 21 Jun 02 **(91) n22.5 t23.5 f22 b23.** Should be the preferred dram of the Scottish Union of Chimney Sweeps... 66.8%. nc ncf sc. .

⁘ **That Boutique-y Whisky Bruichladdich** batch 1 **(88.5) n22** dried pickled cucumber, sundried tomato and must; **t22.5** again a series of odd, slightly sharp notes to back up the intense juicy barley and salt; **f22** malty and straightforward on one level, curiously dry on another; **b22** it's Bruichladdich, Jim (McEwan). But not as we know it... 49.6%. 94 bottles. WB15/191

BUNNAHABHAIN
Islay, 1881. Burn Stewart Distillers. Working.

Bunnahabhain 12 Years Old (Older Bottling) db **(80) n19 t21 f20 b20.** Pleasant in its own clumsily sweet, smoky way. But unrecognisable to the masterful, salty Bunna 12 of old. 43.3%. nc ncf.

Bunnahabhain Aged 12 Years db **(85.5) n20 t23 f21 b21.5.** Lovers of Cadbury's Fruit and Nut will adore this. There is, incongruously, a big bourbony kick alongside some smoke, too. A lusty fellow who is perhaps a bit too much of a bruiser for his own good. Some outstanding moments, though. But, as before, still a long way removed from the magnificent Bunna 12 of old... 46.3%. nc ncf.

Bunnahabhain Aged 16 Years Manzanilla Sherry Wood Finish db **(87) n20.5 t23 f21.5 b22.** The kind of undisciplined but fun malt which just makes it up as it goes along... 53.2%

Bunnahabhain Aged 18 Years (Older Bottling) db **(94) n24.5** chestnut colour and, fittingly, roast chestnut on the fruitcake nose: the health-conscious might say there is too much salt in the mix, but it works perfectly here...; **t24** outstanding oloroso with the clean, faultless grape dripping of the salty barley; the oak again offers a nutty background, while Demerara sugars form a crisp counter to the invading salt; burnt raisin underscores the fruitcake character; **f22.5** light mocha, as a very slight bitterness steels its way in; **b23** a triumph for the sherry cask and a reminder of just how good this distillery can be. It's been a long time since I've enjoyed a distillery bottling to this extent. 43%

Bunnahabhain Aged 18 Years db **(93.5) n24** a sumptuous amalgam of lightly salted roasted hazelnut shimmering within its own oil. Oloroso bulging with toasted, slightly singed currants, a sliver of kumquat and topped by thick vanilla. Irresistible... **t24.5** almost impossible to fault: the oloroso grandly, almost pompously, leads the way exuding thick, Christmas pudding depth; a light muscovado sugar top dressing counters the deeper, lightly salted vanillas which begin to emerge; **f22** a very slight sulphury note sullies the tone somewhat, but there is still enough rich vanilla and spotted dick for some enjoyable afters; **b23** only an odd cask has dropped this from being a potential award winner to something that is merely magnificent... 46.3%. nc ncf.

Bunnahabhain XXV Aged 25 Years (Older Bottling) db **(91.5) n23** hard to imagine a more coastal aroma than this: the grape tries to get a word in edgeways but the salt has formed a crusty doorway; what fruit does get through is top quality; **t23** excellent arrival, the grape forcing the pace but with a tell-tale tang of saltiness; busy with a sneaky arrival of malt through the middle; **f22.5** chocolate fruit and nut... and salt; **b23** an intense and fun-packed malt for those who like a fine sherry and a sea breeze. 43%

Bunnahabhain XXV Aged 25 Years db **(94) n23** you almost need a blow torch to cut through the oloroso, so thick is it. A little tight thanks to a minor distortion to a butt, but I am being picky. Salty and seaweedy, the ocean hangs in the air...; **t24** glorious weight and sheen to the delivery. The early balance is nearly perfect as the thick fruit is thinned by the proud barley. The early, contemplative sweetness, buttressed by a wonderful mixture of sultana and Demerara, gives way to the drier oaks and the tingly, chalky signs of a mildly treated butt; **f23** despite the winding down of the sugars the residual fruit manages to overcome the small obstacles placed before it; **b24** no major blemishes here at all. Carefully selected sherry butts of the highest quality (well, except maybe one) and a malt with enough personality to still gets its character across after 25 years. Who could ask for more...? *46.3%. nc ncf.*

Bunnahabhain Cruach-Mhòna batch no.1 db **(83) n17.5 t24.5 f21 b20.** It appears that there is a new house style of being strangely off balance and less than brilliantly made, but making amends by offering a blistering maltiness which leaves one almost speechless. The delivery alone, with its light smokiness mixing in with the Demerara sugars and Grenadine spices, is the stuff of Islay legend. All else is skewed and out of sync. Unique, for sure. *50% nc ncf.*

Bunnahabhain Darach Ùr Batch no. 1 db **(87) n21.5 t22.5 f21 b22.** Almost milkshake thick. Not exactly a technical triumph but high marks for entertainment value! *46.3%*

Bunnahabhain Darach Ùr Batch no. 4 db **(95) n24** good grief; as though matured in a barrel full of plump sultanas... but from the depth of sweetness, rather than the fruit...if you get my drift. Just a hint of spice as well as coconut and honey. Fabulous in a bourbon kind of salty, Hebridean way...; **t24.5** as thick and richly-textured as any malt you'll find this year. Intense, lightly salted barley is a match for the brimming, fruit-like sweetness; with a salivation factor which disappears through the roof, wonderful bourbon over- and under-tones link wonderfully to the mega sugars attached to the vanilla; **f23** much drier with a tangy, kumquat fade but plenty of vigorous spice; **b23.5** because of my deep love for this distillery, with my association with it spanning some 30 years, I have been its harshest critic in recent times. This, though, is a stunner. *46.3%. nc ncf.*

Bunnahabhain Toiteach db **(78) n19 t21 f19 b19.** Cloying, sweet, oily, disjointedly smoky. Had you put me in a time capsule at the distillery 30 years ago, whizzed me forward to the present day and given me this, it would have needed some serious convincing for me to believe this to be a Bunna. *46%*

Bunnahabhain Toiteach Un-Chillfiltered db **(75.5) n18 t21 f17.5 b19.** A big gristy, peaty confrontation on the palate doesn't hide the technical fault lines of the actual whisky. *46%. ncf.*

Abbey Whisky Bunnahabhain Aged 23 Years The Rare Casks refill bourbon cask, dist 89, bott 13 **(86) n21.5 t23 f20 b21.5.** Any amount of complex honey and sea-salt makes for some riveting early dramming. But the eye-watering oak takes few prisoners. *44%. nc ncf sc. 96 bottles.*

⋰ **Berry's Own Selection Bunnahabhain 1987 Aged 26 Years** cask no. 2451, bott 2014 **(96.5) n23.5** not a distillery naturally suited to great age, this is very comfortable in its fruity clothes, loose fitting and, despite the odd patch here and there, mildly exotic; **t25** quite literally faultless: perhaps the softest delivery of the year with lush, understated exotic fruit and molasses and maple syrup. The oak is pretty ingrained but only the spices make a stand out contribution: you cannot find anything more completely balanced than this; **f23.5** naturally falls away a little but only as the oak takes the upper hand from the spent sugars; **b24.5** for my 900th new whisky for the 2015 Bible, a malt from a distillery I stayed at in the year this was distilled. It appears to have fared infinitely better over the years than me.... *49.8%. ncf ncf. WB15/242*

Berry's Own Selection Bunnahabhain 1989 cask no. 5756, bott 2013 **(89) n22.5 t23 f21.5 b22.** From a distillery which rarely ages too happily an oldie which creaks a bit but can still put on a show. *44%. nc ncf sc.*

⋰ **Berry's Own Selection Bunnahabhain 2006 Aged 7 Years** cask no. 800092, bott 2014 **(91.5) n23.5** not for the ageists: luckily I am from a generation brought up on young smoky whisky rather than the geriatrics you see bottled today. So how can you not adore that lively, lemon-tinged smoky grist...? **t23.5** firm with more of that fabulous grist sensually caressing the palate; **f21.5** it is inevitable that a little imbalance should kick in, and it does towards the end, as a bitterness strikes; **b23** a handsome youth promising good things for the future. Oh, and on the subject of young 'uns, whilst writing these notes at 11.46pm on 28th July discovered fledgling willow warbler in my garden for the very first time, which for five minutes from my vantage point from under the apple tree where I am tasting today (shielded from the sun my trusty Panama and only my parrot Percy for company) I watched spellbound as it learned how to hunt solo. I shall raise a fitting toast with this fledgling Bunna...*56.1%. ncf ncf. WB15/247*

Chieftain's Bunnahabhain Aged 10 Years sherry butt, cask no. 466, dist Sep 01, bott Aug 12 **(71) n16 t19 f18 b18.** Another example of what might have been. If you don't pick up sulphur on the palate, the richness of the fruit will blow you away. *46%. nc ncf sc. 778 bottles.*

⋰ **The Coopers Choice Bunnahabhain 1990 Aged 23 Years** hogshead, cask no. 8944, bott 2013 **(87) n21 t22.5 f22 b21.5.** A well mannered gentleman of a dram. But got to the stage in its life where the suits are frayed and ill-fitting and the comb-over detracts rather than adds. Some pretty tired oak intruding where not wanted. No denying the excellent toasted honeycomb, though. *46%. 345 bottles. WB15/304*

The Coopers Choice Bunnahabhain 2001 9 Years Old cask no. 1269 **(90)** n23.5 t23 f21.5 b22. Always great to see a sherry butt in near unsullied condition. And a malt reminding everyone that complexity abounds in many malts before the 10th birthday is reached. 46%. nc ncf sc.

⁖ **Directors' Cut Bunnahabhain Aged 35 Years** refill hogshead, cask no. 10348, dist Dec 78, bott Jun 14 **(89)** n23.5 exotic fruit of the most emboldened kind: kumquat and salty Tunnock's wafer give it some desirable depth; t22.5 soft, melt-in-the-mouth milk chocolate then a steady increase of the oak; f21.5 much drier, with remaining sugars holding the tannins at bay; b21.5 never a relaxed dram, as the oak uses a tad too much force in making itself known. But the soft chocolate malt shake is a delight. 45.2%. nc ncf sc. 129 bottles.

Duncan Taylor Octave Bunnahabhain 33 Years Old oak cask, cask no. 383401, dist 1979, bott 2012 **(91)** n24 t21 f23.5 b22.5. Even an injection of massive oak which might have killed off lesser malts cannot entirely dent the enormity of this ancient beauty which finishes with surprising aplomb and dexterity. That said, a malt taken as far as it can go. 52.4%. sc.

⁖ **Fine Malt Selection Bunnahabhain 33 Years Old** cask no. 84, dist 1980, bott 2013 **(92)** n23.5 weighty oak. But a kind of salty chocolate raisin and fudge cake sees it beautifully through what might have been a crisis; t22 much lighter delivery, first offering saline-soaked barley. Then a forest of splinters leaves you in no dout of its vintage. Minty chocolate revives the spirit(s); f23.5 returns to a major fruit chocolate assault, aided by salty treacle; b23 Bunna has rarely been a distillery given to old age: for me it reaches its peak in average casks in standard maturation conditions at 12 years. So I feared the worst. And although this has more than its fair share of splinters, it still retains enough class to warrant investigation. A genuine surprise package. 45%. James MacArthur & Co. Ltd.

Gordon & MacPhail MacPhail's Collection Bunnahabhain Peated 8 Years Old (88) n22 t22.5 f21.5 b22. No pages on complexity could ever be written about a bottling like this. But no faulting its overall enjoyment. 43%

Gordon and MacPhail Collection Bunnahabhain 2004 **(87)** n22 t22 f21.5 b21.5. The oak is an unreconstructed fogey: an 8-y-o going on 80...!! 43%

Kingsbury Bunnahabhain Aged 14 Years hogshead, cask no. 5384, dist 97 **(86)** n21 t22 f21.5 b21.5. Smoky and surprisingly oily – almost with a Caol Ila style weight. Light sugars make for an easy and enjoyable journey, but don't look for any complex views. 46%. nc ncf. Japan Import System. 321 bottles.

⁖ **Liquid Sun Bunnah abhain 1989 Aged 23 Year**s dist 1989 **(87.5)** n23 t22 f21 b21.5. The usual Bunna wilting towards the end under the onslaught of a good time in the cask. But a salty, dreamy – even distantly smoky – nose to cherish and with just enough butterscotch on delivery to see off the more rampant tannin. Boiled yam sweetness also offers a shield. 44.2%.

⁖ **The Maltman Bunnahabhain Aged 10 Years** sherry cask, cask no. 1003710, dist Dec 02, bott Apr 13 **(80)** n20 t21 f19 b20. Not sure this was a classic period for Bunna. An overly sweet soup of a dram which bitters out with a degree of meanness and aggression. 46%. sc ncf nc. 229 bottles. WB15/227

Malts of Scotland Bunnahabhain 1980 bourbon hogshead, cask no. MoS 12038, dist Apr 80, bott Jun 12 **(88.5)** n23 t23 f21 b21.5. Just about stands the test of time and where it is good, it is magnificent. 46.8%. nc ncf sc. 96 bottles.

Master of Malt Bunnahabhain Aged 23 Years refill hogshead, dist 20 Oct 89, bott 28 Nov 12 **(93)** n23 tangy malt, helped along by red liquorice and lightly salted cold vegetable stew... busy stuff! t23 the barley pitches up in a surprisingly juicy uniform for its age. It takes time for the oak to filter through, but does so alongside lazy, warming spices and even a touch of coriander. The sweet-dry ratio is exemplary; f23.5 long, and the continuing, controlled, dryness – despite the obvious barley – lends towards a degree of sophistication. But even at the end, it is a sugar-light Malteser sign off which accentuates the vitality of the barley; b23.5 old style Bunna up to its full malty max. 46%. sc. 253 bottles.

Master Of Malt Bunnahabhain 23 Years Old Lost Bottlings Series dist 1979, bott 2002 **(71.5)** n16.5 t20 f17 b18. Bit of a shame this cask was ever found again. 49.7%

Old Malt Cask Bunnahabhain Aged 10 Years sherry butt, cask no. 8215, dist Dec 01, bott Mar 12 **(94.5)** n23.5 wonderfully clean aroma with the grape taking varying forms between lightly burnt raisins and under-ripe ones from the vine. The lightness of touch from the spice makes one purr...; t24 a fantastic delivery of very rare quality these days. The sherry influence is absolutely clean cut and embraces not just (very!) juicy grape but almost a chocolate sherry truffle of limited sweetness; the sugars are decidedly of the Demerara style; f23.5 beautiful mocha and a mix of pith and barley; b23.5 a phenomenal sherry butt for its era. Always heart-warming to see this one truly great distillery being shown in its brighter colours. 50%. nc ncf sc. Douglas Laing & Co. 342 bottles.

Old Malt Cask Bunnahabhain Aged 11 Years cask no. 9428, dist Dec 01, bott Jan 13 **(88)** n21.5 t23 f21.5 b22. Can hardly have been presented with a better weight. 50%. sc.

⸫ **Old Malt Cask Bunnahabhain Aged 16 Years** refill hogshead, cask no. 10128, dist Aug 97, bott Oct 13 **(91)** n22 sweet chestnuts and smoke; t23 the sugars arrive as clearly and unhurried on the palate as the sweet waters tumbling down a highland stream; the smoke is demure and accentuates the muscovado; f23 vanilla and gristy smoked barley play us out; b23 how many of us are left, I wonder, who still do a bit of a mental double take every time we nose a smoked Bunna – so used were we for this distillery to be unsmoked. This chap is one of the better examples of recent years, showing an impressive clarity to the phenolic proceedings. *50%. nc ncf sc. 348 bottles.*

Old Malt Cask Bunnahabhain Aged 21 Years refill hogshead, cask no. 9819, dist Nov 91, bott May 13 **(77)** n19 t21 f18 b19. The predictable tang arrives in all the predictable places. *48.3%. nc ncf sc. Hunter Laing & Co Ltd. 256 bottles.*

Old Malt Cask Bunnahabhain Aged 25 Years refill hogshead, cask no. 9516, dist Nov 87, bott Feb 13 **(67)** n17 t17 f16 b17. Time for some cheese and tomato...my poor ol' taste buds! *50%. sc. Douglas Laing & Co. 271 bottles.*

⸫ **Old Malt Cask Bunnahabhain Aged 25 Years** refill hogshead, cask no. 9516, dist Nov 87, bott Feb 13 **(69)** n18 t19 f15 b17. Furry. Off key. Grim. *50%. nc ncf sc. 271 bottles. WB15/135*

⸫ **Provenance Bunahabhain Over 12 Years** sherry butt, cask no. 10330, dist Winter 01, bott Spring 14 **(87.5)** n21.5 t22.5 f22 b21.5. Soft and easy going, this is a Bunna from the old non-peated school which leaks a fair bit of oak for its age but works charmingly especially when the salt and malt remain in tandem. *46%. nc ncf sc.*

Provenance Bunnahabhain Young & Feisty two refill hogsheads, cask nos. 8672 & 8673, bott Summer 12 **(85.5)** n20 t22 f22 b21.5. Young and Peaty, more like. Not sure of the age, but has the feel of a five year old in very average wood: Bambi-like in its ability to steer an even course. Juicy, too, early on, as you might expect. *46%. nc ncf. Douglas Laing & Co.*

⸫ **Provenance Bunnahabain ' Young & Feisty'** refill hogshead, cask no. 10175, bott Winter 2014 **(85)** n21 t21.5 f21.5 b21. Refreshing and almost puckeringly juicy. Well made and clean with some lovely oils helping the un-peated malt travel further. *Nc ncf sc. Douglas Laing & Co.*

⸫ **Scotch Malt Whisky Society Cask 10.77 Aged 6 Years** refill hogshead, dist 03 Oct 07 **(76.5)** n19 t19.5 f19 b19. Not that there is anything technically wrong with this dram: you are unlikely to find malts on such a stampede for the remainder of the year. It is just that young whiskies are like Bambi: they take a little time to find their feet. From one month to the next they could be looking OK one minute, then flat on their arse the next. This is a cask picked at entirely the wrong time either through ignorance or genius. Other than a learning curve for whisky students, there is not much point to it... *61.4%. nc ncf sc. 196 bottles.*

⸫ **Signatory Vintage Cask Strength Collection Bunnahabhain 1997 Heavily Peated Aged 18 Years** hogsheads, cask no. 5513+5514, dist 11 Dec 97, bott 08 Nov 13 **(94)** n23 good saline edge to the powdery peat. A little chocolate Swiss roll alongside the smoky Blackjack; t24 silky delivery. Fabulous sugars: seemingly a heather honey sweetness to the increasingly intense smoke, like a lightly oiled Highand Park on peaty overdrive; f23 carries on without a hint of bitterness or tiredness. The vanillas do stack up, but so do the spices which buzz by the finale; b24 curious how this was filled into cask on the same day as the Signatory UCF version. Yet this offers lustre and complexity. Because of the oils being broken up by reducing to 46? Or was the other one unlucky by simply having inferior wood? Probably a bit of both. *51.3%. nc. 527 bottles. WB15/001*

⸫ **Signatory Vintage Un-chillfiltered Collection Bunnahabhain 1997 Heavily Peated Aged 15 Years** hogsheads, cask no.5578+5579, dist 11 Dec 97, bott 05 Jul 13 **(87)** n21 t22 f22 b22 Chocolate mint amid some smoky barley oil. The nose is problematic but saved by subtle citrus. *46%. nc ncf. 798 bottles. WB15/026*

Single Cask Collection Bunnahabhain Aged 21 Years bourbon hogshead, cask no. 5468, dist 2 Dec 91, bott 22 Aug 12 **(92.5)** n22.5 the oak has no hesitation in taking the lead but there is a playful sweetness, too...those of us old enough to remember packs of candy cigarettes will be taken back to another world...; t23.5 a fabulously sophisticated landing: can barley be so gorgeously juicy and sweet yet held in check by firm, unblemished tannin...? f23 a slight hint of salt brings out the oakiness to a greater degree but liquorice and manuka honey thinned by barley water allows the finale to show excellent poise; b23.5 when Bunna shines, it really does sparkle. *49.1%. nc ncf sc. 290 bottles.*

⸫ **That Boutique-y Whisky Bunnahabhain** batch 2 **(78)** n20 t21 f18 b19. A bit of a train wreck: hard to see what this is trying to be or achieve. There appears to be smoke, some kind of fruit, all kinds of oils, treacle-type sugars and much else besides. Absolutely no structure or balance, other than the odd fleeting accidental moment. Tasted blind, would not have recognised this as my beloved Bunna in a million years. *45.3%. 156 bottles. WB15/198*

The Warehouse Collection Bunnahabhain Aged 21 Years bourbon hogshead, cask no. 5477, dist 2 Dec 91, bott 6 Feb 13 (95) n23 beech and ulmo honey beautifully mixed and salt-seasoned; a little dank pine forest floor; earthy, at times vaguely peaty; t24 quite superb delivery: the oak, as with most Bunnas over 12, has a big, sharp impact, but the countering weaving of the honey into the broad barley theme is stunning; a light saltiness enriches; f24 long with the oak just staying honest, though it is the red liquorice, maple syrup, molten salted butters and fabulous late introduction of black pepper to the butterscotch that keeps the pot bubbling; b24 not a distillery naturally given to good age, this is about as you'll find for the age. You'd find me Westering Home for this any day.... 49.6%. nc ncf sc. 261 bottles.

⁘ **Wemyss Malts 1991 Single Islay Bunnahabhain "A Thread of Smoke"** bott 14 (88.5) n22 thumping oak washes over every aspect of the nose. Briny, sharp and fading, like an old wooden rowing boat, the remains of which are sinking after many years into the silt of an estuary; t22 it needed some muscovado sugars on the delivery – at least – to make this work... and they arrive quite plentifully. The tannins work prodigiously hard to drag the experience off the edge, but fail; f22.5 lovely butterscotch tart softens the edges of the worst of the oak, as does some chocolate fudge; salty to the very end; b22 a distillery which struggles uncommonly with age and this cask comes from the Ancient Order of Bunnas. Just enough sweetness left in the tank to make this an elegant dram...but it is a close run thing. 46%. sc. 302 bottles.

⁘ **Wemyss Malts 1991 Single Islay Bunnahabhain "Oysters With Lemon Pearls"** bott 14 (87) n21 t23 f21 b22. Bunna struggles with age like England batsman Robson struggles with the ball outside his off stump. This, had it been bottled just maybe three years back, would probably have been memorable. But the tannin on the nose is too assertive and the rich, briny malt and toffee has to work too hard to keep it under control on the palate. An enjoyable dram, not least because of the mocha...but all a bit too stretched and frantic. 46%. sc. 265 bottles.

⁘ **Wemyss Malts 1991 Single Islay Bunnahabhain "Seaweed On The Rocks"** dist 1991 bott 2013 (91.5) n23.5 sumptuous diced fruit with tinned pears to the fore. The vaguest (and surprising) smoke thickens over the sugary barley; t23 lively from the off with enough salt to underline the coastal credentials. The smoke has vanished but plenty of spices amid the vivid sugars; f22.5 medium length with a thinning crispness accentuating the oak; b23 a fruity cove. Almost literally... sc. 294 bottles.

⁘ **Wemyss Malts 1997 Single Islay Bunnahabhain "The Bosun's Dram"** hogshead, dist 97, bott 13 (88) n22 one of the peated crop showing some impressive salt and sea spray...; t22.5 blisteringly sweet delivery but thin enough to avoid any cloying, though thickens with peat in a spicy fashion; f22 salted spiced smoky vanilla; b22 "Westering home with some Peat In the Air..." 46%. sc. 380 bottles.

⁘ **Wemyss Malts 1997 Single Islay Bunnahabhain "A Peaty Punch!"** bott 2013 (86.5) n21.5 t23 f21 b21. Very pleasant if simple whisky. But there is a fascinating – and revealing – contrast between this and the Wemyss Bunna 1991 which starkly shows the strengths and weaknesses of the old and new style Bunnahabhain. Here we have just another peaty malt with an attractive gristy sweetness but not quite of the eminence or complexity of an Ardbeg or Lagavulin coasting in neutral. And a long way behind the classic un-peated style where the salt and delicate fruits can truly weave pictures of beauty. 46%. sc. 348 bottles.

The Whisky Agency Bunnahabhain 'Sea Life' 1968 refill sherry butt, dist 68, bott 12 (87) n21.5 t22.5 f21.5 b21.5. Bunna is not a distillery that clings to great age without casualties. Plenty of salt and honey delights but the oak gouges just a little deep for its own good. Ten years ago this would have been truly Premiership stuff. 47%

Wemyss 1989 Single Islay "Maritime Embrace" hogshead, dist 89, bott 13 (93) n22 the oak comes out as if wishing to brain you. The big saline counter, softened by Dundee cake, rescues a tricky situation; t24 no surprises when the oak is first over the hurdles. But the way the light molasses cushion the blow, then Sao Tome cocoa and hickory fill the middle ground; f23 bitter marmalade...with a shake of salt, of course! b24 an oaky embrace for sure. The tannins squeeze a little too tight at times, though the salt and chocolate-orange combination ensures a memorable, multi-complex performance. 46%. sc. 265 bottles.

Wemyss Bunnhabhain 1997 Single Islay "Billowing Embers" hogshead (76) n18 t19 f20 b19. Awkward, ill-balanced and, at times, overly sweet, this is not one for the Bunna Hall of Fame. 46%. 331 bottles.

Wemyss 2001 Single Islay Bunnahabhain "Chocolate Honeycomb" puncheon, bott 13 (86) n21 t22.5 f21 b21.5. Tasted many a Bunna over the last three decades...and I mean many! But never before found one with these kinds of fingerprints. Thick to the point of being glutinous spices intervene late on to give some roughage to the otherwise ultra-silky experience. Don't get the chocolate, do get a little toasted honeycomb, but the spirit does not seem overly comfortable to begin with. Enjoyable...but a head scratcher. 46%. sc. 812 bottles.

CAOL ILA

Islay, 1846. Diageo. Working.

Caol Ila Aged 8 Years Unpeated Style dist 1999, bott 2007 db (**93.5**) **n23 t24 f23 b23.5.** Oh well, here goes my reputation...honest opinion: on this evidence (backed by other samples over the years) Caol Ila makes better straight malt than it does the peated stuff. Sorry, peat lovers. This should be a, if not the, mainstay of the official Caol Ila portfolio. *64.9%*

Caol Ila Aged 8 Years Unpeated Style 1st fill bourbon, dist 2000, bott 2008 db (**91.5**) **n23** a touch maltier than the previous bottling; salty digestive biscuit; **t23** beautifully refreshing with a real puckering, salty tartness to the barley; I seem to remember citrus here last year. But this time we have butterscotch and toffee; **f22.5** long, very delicately oiled with the vanillas and toffee in decent harmony; **b23** a bit more of a pudding than last year's offering, but delicious dramming all the way. *64.2%*

Caol Ila Aged 10 Years "Unpeated Style" bott Aug 09 db (**93.5**) **n24** a beautiful medley of pear and lime with a thin spread of peanut butter for good measure...not exactly what one might expect...!!! **t23.5** the barley is just so juicy from the kickoff: the citrus on the nose reappears, though any hopes of pear vanishes; the barley, so rarely heard in a Caol-Ila grows in confidence and intensity as the delivery develops; **f23** not as oily as you might expect, allowing extra oak to emerge; **b23** always fascinating to see a traditional peaty Islay stripped bare and in full naked form. Shapely and very high class indeed. *65.4%. Only available at the Distillery.*

Caol Ila Aged 12 Years db (**89**) **n23 t23 f21 b22.** A telling improvement on the old 12-y-o with much greater expression and width. *43%*

Caol Ila 12 Years Old Special Release 2010 1st fill bourbon oak cask, dist 1997 db (**95.5**) **n23** the smoke is almost an afterthought to the red liquorice lead. Bracing, tangy, full of energy...; **t24** to die for. The trademark oils arrive only as an apologetic afterthought to the delivery which takes at least six mouthfuls to get the measure of. Uniquely, the lead characteristic is sweetened cocoa, something of a bourbon front which is further backed by toasted honeycomb. The smoke offers no more than ballast and refuses to assert any authority on the salivating malt; **f24** now the limited oils have arrived they are put to excellent use by lengthening the finale. The vanillas are sweetened; the barley is galvanised by a curiously fruity earthiness and the most delicate spices imaginable tiptoe across the taste buds...; finally, a discreet muscavado sugar fanfare pipes the experience to its majestic close... **b24.5** the peat more or less takes a back seat in what is a masterful display of finesse and diplomacy on the palate. Most probably the best Caol Ila I have tasted in recent years. And this in a year of magnificent Caol Ilas. *57.6%. nc ncf. Diageo. Unpeated, fewer than 6000 bottles.*

Caol Ila 12 Years Old Special Release 2011 db (**89**) **n21.5 t23.5 f22 b22.** A sideways look at a big distillery allowing the casks to have the loudest say over the malt: not at all common with this Islay. *64%. nc ncf.*

Caol Ila 14 Years Old Unpeated Style First fill ex-bodega European Oak Casks, dist 1997, bott 2012 db (**95.5**) **n22.5** unusual for it to happen, but the tannins from the oak outgun the fruit! The vaguest hint of something smoky – perhaps from the air breathed in by the cask. But salty in a bacon sandwich kind of way...and as though it is slightly smoky bacon...and bacon that has been smeared with sugar, too...; **t24** at first the tannins explode and advance with an intensity which doesn't bode too well. Then, half way in, the malt relaxes to allow those sugars caught on the nose a freer hand while the tannins re-emerge but now with delicate spices...and that vaguest hint of smoke, though there is nothing so subtle about the hickory; **f23** dries like oak in the Spanish sun. Big burned fudge, embittered slightly by the crumbs of lightly burnt toast; the barley now rises but that too is pretty singed; **b24** what a night's entertainment to battle your way through this. In normal circumstances the astonishing machinations of this malt would be lost under a sea of peat. But the malt here – 14 going on 40 – never ceases to amaze. A whisky grey and hunched way beyond its years...but what a story it tells...! A malt that lives long on the palate...and in the memory... *59.3%. nc ncf.*

Caol Ila Aged 18 Years db (**80**) **n21 t20 f19 b20.** Another improvement on the last bottling, especially with the comfortable integration of citrus. But still too much oil spoils the dram, particularly at the death. *43%*

Caol Ila 1979 db (**74**) **n20 t19 f17 b18.** Disappointing. I could go on about tropical fruit yada, yada, yada. Truth is, it just conks out under the weight of the oak. Too old. Simple as that. *58.6%*

Caol Ila 1997 The Manager's Choice db (**93.5**) **n24** dry, ashy peat sweetened less by grist but mango chutney; **t23.5** the grist arrives and sharpens up quickly: a barley juiciness sets in as Lincoln biscuit/garibaldi dunked in peat hogs the middle ground; hickory and liquorice begin to form; **f23** dusty, but the liquorice and smoke hold sway; **b23** when this malt is not enveloped in taste bud-clogging oil, it really can be a little special. Here's further proof. *58%*

⋅⋅⋅ **Caol Ila Distillers Edition** dist 00, bott 12 db (**95**) **n23** any more oil from the nose and people will start fracking it ....; the smoke is largely untroubled by fruit, as is the visible malt; **t24** usual oily delivery...about the fifth or sixth flavour wave in some gentle, sweet grape can be found; the spices form more quickly and, as modest as they are, last the course; **f24** a beautiful smoked trifle and caramelised wafer washed down with milky mocha; **b24** an accomplished, delicate malt where the grape and smoke harmonise with uncommon good will. Fabulous. *43% WB15/281*

Caol Ila 'Distillery Only' bott 2007 db **(95.5) n24 t24 f23.5 b24.** Caol Ila is the third hardest distillery to get to in Scotland: however should you do so some time soon you can reward yourself by picking up a bottle of this. I can say honestly that the journey will be very much worthwhile... *58.4%. 5,000 bottles. Available only from the Caol Ila Distillery shop.*

Caol Ila Moch db **(87) n22 t22 f21 b22.** Easy drinking Islay. Though I think they mean "Mocha"... *43%*

⁘ **Caol Ila Stitchell Reserve "Unpeated Style"** bott 2013 db **(89) n23** breezy salt and spices lighten the fruity load; a rare pinch of allspice; **t24** so confident – possibly thanks to the backing of a near 60% abv leg up – the intense fruit enjoys a rare balance of silky sultana and drier grape skins; **f20** dries a little too vigorously; **b22** not really a patch on the 2012 bottling, mainly due to inferior sherry butts, any smoke which does appear is like a half-imagined movement in the shadows. The delivery, though, is superb! *59.6% WB15/344*

⁘ **Cooper's Choice for Limburg Fair Caol Ila 1982** dist 1982 db **(84.5) n21 t22.5 f20 b21.** Tangy and tight, the smoke plays a supporting role to the slightly muddled oak and sugars. *52%.*

The Coopers Choice Caol Ila 1992 18 Years Old hogshead, cask no. 4511, dist 92, bott 10. **(78.5) n19 t21 f19 b19.5.** Tangy and off key. Not the greatest help from the oak. *46%. nc ncf sc. The Vintage Malt Whisky Co Ltd. 330 bottles.*

The Coopers Choice Caol Ila 1990 20 Years Old hogshead, cask no. 4171, dist 90, bott 12 **(89) n22 t23 f22 b23.** Wonderfully elegant and almost glassy in its mouth feel. *53%. nc ncf sc. The Vintage Malt Whisky Co Ltd. 250 bottles.*

Fine Old Islay Single Malt Aged 19 Years ex-bourbon cask **(90) n22 t23.5 f22 b22.5.** A pleasing complexity and a fruitiness which sits comfortably with the smoke. *55.9%. Caol Ila.*

⁘ **Gordon & MacPhail Cask Strength Caol Ila** refill sherry butts, cask no. 308843 & 308845, dist 29 Aug 01, bott 07 Mar 14 **(90.5) n23** a dry, wonderfully powdery, peat sooty offering; **t23** the usual early grassy release of sugars then a return to charmingly smokier ways; **f22** just a little bitter oak bite. Much the smoked dried date sweetness is impressively underplayed; **b22.5** always fascinating to see this distillery immerge from its usual oily cloak. In part a much drier, grittier dram than normal, though more than enough balancing sweetness to please.. *59.2%.*

Gordon and MacPhail Connoisseurs Choice Caol Ila 1999 **(88) n22 t22.5 f21.5 b22.** Cannot be mistaken for any other distiller: Caol Ila nutshelled. *46%. ncf.*

⁘ **Gordan & Macphail Connoisseurs Choice Caol Ila 2001 (91.5) n22** dry, slightly minty phenols; **t23.5** sharp grassy, salivating barley, as though a crisp Speysider has been blended into the peaty mix. The spices lead the counter attack while the smoke slowly envelopes, builds and intensifies...; **f23** lightly molassed peat, then vanilla; **b23** simple but very effective. *46%. WB15/112*

Gordon and MacPhail Private Collection Caol Ila Sassicaia 1994 **(83) n21 t21.5 f20 b20.5.** A thin warble of a dram in which the fruit tries to sing but never raises enough puff to get past the smoke or make even a balancing contribution. Pleasant, but neither fish nor fowl. *45%. ncf.*

Gordon and MacPhail Private Collection Caol Ila Madeira 1995 (94) n22.5 so heavy with grape and smoke (most of it anthracite), little else gets through; **t24** Lordy, me! Just how many fronts does this work on? First, the texture on delivery is nigh perfect: the usual Caol Ila oils have been tamed by the richness of the grape, the sweetness of the fruit matching the gristy contours of the smoke perfectly; elsewhere the spices sting with just the right degree of venom; **f23.5** long, with a gorgeous spiced chocolate fruit and nut theme; **b24** well, you know by now my feelings about grape and peat...so welcome to rare exception. This is a stunner, in anyone's money...! *45%. ncf.*

⁘ **Hepburn's Choice Caol Ila Aged 5 Years** refill hogshead, dist 08, bott 14 **(92.5) n22.5** new make but with the new born nip strained out. The smoke is nothing more than pure grist. Rather lovely; **t24** and like highly peated grist, the sugars have the big say on the juicy delivery, but the smoke forms the framework; **f23.5** more of the same, with a little spice arriving late; **b22.5** when little things like oak aren't about to interfere with new make Caol Ila for five years, what isn't there to like? *46%. nc ncf sc. 414 bottles.*

⁘ **Islay Single Malt Caol Ila 33 Years** refill hogshead, cask no. 10159, dist Sept 1980, bott Dec 2013 **(95.5) n24** anthracite mixed in with peak reek. Almost a mix of a south Wales mining village from 30 years ago, or a winter (and summer!) cottage on Islay. Predominantly dry for all the ground muscovado sugars and hickory; **t24** a Catherine wheel of a delivery, with sparks and smoke flying in all directions. Helped by a bizarre lack of oils for this distillery, the shape and layering forms unhindered; chewey and no shortage of burnt fudge mixing with the weighty peat; **f23.5** long with a more toasty finale than normal. Again the sugars have much to say, but do so with quiet assertiveness though never speaking above the rumbling phenols; **b24** you will do well to find a Caol Ila in better nick than this over the next year or so. Absolutely tip top form and showing an unusual vibrancy thanks to some restraint with the oils and oak at its very best. Simply glorious. *58.8%. nc ncf sc. 136 bottles. Douglas Laing & Co.*

Kingsbury Caol Ila Aged 16 Years hogshead, cask no. 793, dist 96 **(88) n22 t22 f22 b22.** Well rounded and quicksand soft. *46%. nc ncf. 359 bottles.*

⠿ **Kingsbury Gold Caol Ila 28 Year Old** cask no. 2749, dist 1984 **(88.5) n22** egg and cress sandwich...but the bun is very dry and smoky; **t23** huge grist ensures a stunning salivatory signature...the smoke does its own thing; **f21.5** pretty dull and oily but with a dry, bitter smokiness; **b22** the sharpness on delivery more than compensates for the all-round oiliness. *51.5%. nc ncf sc. 235 bottles.*

Liquid Sun Caol Ila 1979 ex-bourbon hogshead, dist 79, bott 12 **(86) n22 t22 f20.5 b21.5.** The buttery smokiness does its best to fill some of the oaky, slightly off beam cracks. Pretty rigorous stuff – a surprise package and impressively virile for its age. *52.9%.*

Malts of Scotland Caol Ila 1990 bourbon hogshead, cask no. MoS 12042, dist Apr 90, bott Sep 12 **(91) n22 t23.5 f22.5 b23.5.** Always great to see Caol Ila in this kind of complex yet relaxed form. *55.6%. nc ncf sc. 96 bottles.*

⠿ **Montgomerie's Single Cask Collection Caol Ila** cask no. 1477, dist 08 Feb 90, bott Mar 13 **(95) n23** minted chocolate...in smoke, of course...; **t24** mouth-watering and gorgeously refreshing; all kinds of spices fizz but softened by creamy butter milk plus a little liquorice, fudge and mocha; **f24** more of the same, with a slow fade; **b24** sharp, yet easy going, charming and totally moreish. An understated gem. *46%. nc ncf sc. WB15/126*

Old Masters Caol Ila 12 Years Old cask no. 3309908, dist 00, bott Nov 12 **(91) n22.5 t23 f22.5 b23.** Anyone with a sweet tooth and a penchant for smoky whisky will be in their element. *56.8%. sc. James MacArthur & Co Ltd.*

Old Malt Cask Caol Ila Aged 16 Years refill hogshead, cask no. 9512, dist Sep 96, bott Feb 13 **(95) n23.5** dry: the hearth being cleaned of the previous night's burnt peats; **t24** outstanding citrus attack on delivery – fresh and salivating. The peat arrives by the squadron load but the light oils carry some serious barley sugar; **f23.5** more like the drier nose now as diced coconut and fudge make for a chewy finish; the confident peat makes all the right noise; **b24** never one of Caol Ila's greatest fans (well, since it was rebuilt), I have to say this is a dram I could drink all day any day, simply because it is so subtle and understated....and without a single distilling or maturation blemish. Truly sublime. *50%. sc. 156 bottles.*

Old Malt Cask Caol Ila Aged 16 Years refill hogshead, cask no. 9823, dist 1996, bott 2013 **(92) n22.5** slightly estery, though the peat shines; **t23.5** juicy, citrus and grist in a lovely oily base; smoked chocolate in muscovado sugars through the middle; **f23** long, with a gorgeous smoked custard fade; **b23.5** excellent distillate in good oak which both supports and allows the malt, and complex sugars in particular, a full view. Superb. *50%. nc ncf sc. 145 bottles.*

Old Malt Cask Caol Ila Aged 16 Years refill hogshead, cask no. 9057, dist Sep 96, bott Sep 12 **(86) n21 t22.5 f21 b21.5.** Competent, gristy malt with the smoke subdued but eventually makes its mark. The delivery enjoys a juicy peak. *50%. sc. 213 bottles.*

⠿ **Old Malt Cask Caol Ila Aged 17 Years** refill hogshead, cask no. 10123, dist Sep 96, bott Oct 13 **(86.5) n21.5 t21.5 f22 b21.5** Pleasant, decently smoked, attractively spiced but the big natural caramels and vanillas blunt the experience. *50%. nc ncf sc. 324 bottles. WB15/132*

⠿ **Old Malt Cask Caol Ila Aged 17 Years** refill hogshead, cask no. 10229, dist Sep 96, bott Jan 14 **(91) n23** anthracite and drying bombarding peat reek appear to take this above the normal 35ppm phenols. Dry and challenging; **t22** the sugars absent on the nose appear on the delivery, but soon spices enter the fray. The peat also appears to have a chocolate orange persona; **f23** long, drying, complex with the smoke appearing in all kinds of degrees of intensity; **b23** bare knuckle Caol Ila, with all the punches unencumbered by oil. *50%. nc ncf sc. 271 bottles.*

⠿ **Old Malt Cask Caol Ila Aged 17 Years** refill hogshead, cask no. 10446, dist Sep 96, bott Apr 14 **(95.5) n23.5** some sizzling spice is calmed by the soft smoke; **t23.5** textbook Islay: the peat waits a moment or two before revealing the full intensity of its hand, allowing a few vital seconds of sugared barley to sparkle. The oak offers an attractive mocha sub plot; **f23.5** a few saline notes hoist the coastal flag while the smoke drifts on in more layers than you'll ever be able to count; **b24** hats off to a bottling which shows the distillery in the most positive light possible. There is less oils than normal for here, allowing the peat to show a much more guile than is the norm. Not to be missed! And gentle and complex enough to convert the unbelievers... *50%.nc ncf sc. 354 bottles.*

⫶⫶ **Old Malt Cask Caol Ila Aged 18 Years** refill hogshead, cask no. 9913, dist Sep 94, bott Aug 13 **(88) n22.5** some decent citrus cuts through the smoke; **t21.5** only the midland spices pep up some standard malt; **f22** better finale with the smoke now layering, the spices persisting and the sugars softening; **b22** enjoyable. But could have been better...and a lot worse. *50%. nc ncf sc. 328 bottles.*

⫶⫶ **Old Malt Cask Caol Ila Aged 29 Years** refill hogshead, cask no.10069, dist Jan 84, bott Oct 13 **(96.5) n24** dry smoke meets its light orange and minty match; **t24** the softest of oils hoist the phenols aloft, but it dries quickly to let in a wonderful minty mocha middle; **f24** dispenses with the coffee and concentrates fully on the chocolate; elegant, well balanced and allows that citrus to show through at the finish; **b24.5** one of the most chocolate-rich smokies you'll ever come across. Rare to find a whisky of this age so beautifully weighted and balanced: shows absolutely no signs of wear. Sublime. *50%. nc ncf sc. 131 bottles. WB15/136*

Port Sgioba Private Cask Caol Ila Aged 12 Years bourbon barrel, dist 3 Nov 12, bott 5 Nov 12 **(89.5) n22 t23 f22 b22.5.** A spot on barrel, above average in complexity thanks probably to the lighter than the norm oils. *55.5%. nc ncf sc. 205 bottles.*

Provenance Caol Ila Young and Feisty two refill hogshead, cask no. 9278 & 9279, bott Winter 12 **(85.5) n21 t22 f21 b21.5.** Uncomplicated blending malt where the peat and early sugars would have done the job intended. The finish is a little undercooked. *46%. nc ncf sc.*

⫶⫶ **Provenance Caol Ila 'Young & Feisty'** refill hogshead, cask no. 10178 **(77) n20 t19 f20 b18.** Young for sure. But not even remotely feisty. Fails to work on so many levels, though lack of body and balance are the main stumbling blocks. *46%. nc ncf sc.*

Scotch Malt Whisky Society Cask 53.170 Aged 22 Years refill hogshead, dist 19 dec 89 **(86.5) n21 t22.5 f21 b22.** A chewy, toasty dram which doesn't over beef up on the smoke. This allows in a period of outstanding cocoa and Demerara sugar, but ultimately just a little too frenzied oak for its own good. *55.1%. nc ncf sc. 183 bottles.*

Scotch Malt Whisky Society Cask 53.174 Aged 12 Years refill hogshead, dist 18 Nov 99 **(81.5) n22 t21 f19 b19.5.** Ye gods! Celtic must have been playing Rangers live on TV when this was made. This has been fair ripped through the stills as this is as thin and hot a Caol Ila as you'll ever encounter. *64.2%. nc ncf sc. 297 bottles.*

⫶⫶ **Scotch Malt Whisky Society Cask 53.197 Aged 18 Years** refill hogshead, dist 24 Aug 95 **(91) n22** simplistic but very effective gristy peat reek; **t23** abounds with crisp sugars on delivery, then a beguiling degree of interwoven spice. The smoke is omnipresent; **f23** some tangy citrus among the embers; **b23** sweet and beautifully made. *57.4%. nc ncf sc. 253 bottles.*

⫶⫶ **Scotch Malt Whisky Society Cask 53.198 Aged 18 Years** refill butt, dist 29 Aug 95 **(85) n21 t21.5 f21.5 b21** Less giving oak ensures the barley and peat show a degree of enforced astringency. *59%. nc ncf sc. 510 bottles.*

⫶⫶ **Scotch Malt Whisky Society Cask 53.201 Aged 18 Years** refill butt, dist 29 Aug 95 **(86.5) n22 t22 f21 b21.5.** Some biting spices make this a Caol Ila to remember. The oils play a stranger role than usual, thickening things at the beginning but dying at the finale to allow the drier peat notes and some more bitter tanins to filter through. *60%. nc ncf sc. 575 bottles.*

⫶⫶ **Scotch Malt Whisky Society Cask 53.203 Aged 17 Years** refill hogshead, dist 03 Sep 96 **(89) n22.5** quintessential Caol Ila: oily and pugnaciously smoky...; **t22** gristy and full of peaty resolve. Some mocha and hickory notes enrich; **f22.5** some searing spices at the death; **b22** some lovely complexity to this guy. *57.8%. nc ncf sc. 271 bottles.*

⫶⫶ **Scotch Malt Whisky Society Cask 53.205 Aged 22 Years** refill hogshead, dist 17 Jan 92 **(95.5) n23.5** superb oak sets up the pea for a sweet, bluebell wood earthiness; a sublime drier sub-strata balances matters; **t23.5** for all the obvious oils, the oak, juicy barley and smoke puncture the sugary bubble easily...; **f24.5** a chewy, smoky finish with a slow development of dark sugars, fudge and cocoa; meanwhile the spices buzz laudibly; **b24** straight as a dye truly great whisky! *52.9%. nc ncf sc. 229 bottles.*

⫶⫶ **Scotch Malt Whisky Society Cask 53.206 Aged 18 Years** refill hogshead, dist 24 Aug 95 **(85.5) n21.5 t21.5 f21 b21.5.** They've gone very easy on the smoke, rendering this lively but rather tart. *56.6%. nc ncf sc. 233 bottles.*

⫶⫶ **Signatory Vintage Un-chillfiltered Collection Caol Ila 1996 Aged 17 Years** hogsheads, cask no. 5572+5573, dist 04 Apr 96, bott 05 Jul 13 **(95) n23.5** dry, slightly sooty and toast slightly burned an hour ago. A little salt add piquancy so, naturally, matching pepper is around somewhere; **t24** very high quality delivery. The oak is already up and running and helps keep the smoke in order. Spices pound from early on and even a dab of hickory offers a brief glimpse of something bourbony The high point, though, is the mid ground when the ulmo honey softens, caresses and ensures complexity and balance; **f23.5** lovely spice tingle and low level smoke on the butter shortcake; **b24** there is something irresistible – and sadly rare – about a Caol Ila that is sparing on the oil and big on complexity. Sublime spirit in a top hole cask. Superb. *46%. nc ncf. 729 bottles. WB15/024*

That Boutique-y Whisky Company Caol Ila batch 1 **(84.5)** n20.5 t22 f21 b21. Excellent use of a salt and sugar combination. Not so sure about the juniper, though, as this has a distinct gin-like quality... *45.8%. Master Of Malt. 732 bottles.*

Wemyss 1980 Single Islay Caol Ila "The Smokery" hogshead, dist 80, bott 13 **(94)** n23.5 more lime than lemon in the citrus; the smoke has been weathered by time and clings to the vanilla for dear life; **t23.5** silky delivery with a slow but ever-growing punctuation of oaky spice; lovely hickory middle with smoky ulmo honey glaze; **f23** slightly more lightly oiled than an average Caol Ila, just enough hangs around to ensure the drier smoke elements balance against the late maple syrup and butterscotch; **b24** fabulous, understated elegance. *46%. sc. 322 bottles.*

 Wemyss Malts 1982 Single Islay Caol Ila "Smoke on the Water" hogshead, dist 82, bott 14 **(91)** n22.5 minted weak peat reek; **t22.5** lively delivery, though some cracks show early from the big age. Enough oil around to gloss them over and allow the smoke and spice to build; **f23** hit genuine complexity: the smoke dissolves into a delicious mocha finale sweetened by surprising heather honey; **b23** a little touch of the Highland Parks on the finish helps this become a venerable and enjoyable dram. *46%. sc. 255 bottles.*

Wemyss 1987 Single Speyside Tamdhu "The Hay Bale" hogshead, dist 87, bott 13 **(88)** n22 t23 f21 b22. A solid malt making few apologies for its one-dimensional maltiness. Not the greatest oak input, but the original richness of the spirit makes for an enjoyable digestive biscuit style dram. *46%. sc. 330 bottles.*

Wemyss 1996 Single Islay Caol Ila "Lemon Smoke" hogshead, bott 2012 **(95)** n23.5 astonishingly dry and oil-less for a Caol Ila with the accent on a salty, sea-breezy smokiness and crammed with rock pools and other coastline clichés; **t24.5** absolutely top-notch. Again the lack of oil is evident, allowing both the peat and impressively deft oak full reign. The sugars are pure grist, though after the smoke drifts in and out it is backed by a heavier muscovado style; the growing oak again displays a light salty seasoning; **f23** dries to allow the vanilla a much bigger (though still dry) say, almost like a smoky ice cream cone; late spices tingle and mingle with the little sugars which thrive; a light cocoa coating forms at the finish; **b24** Caol Ila at by far its most delicate and in single malt rather than blending mode. Another breath-taking connoisseur's must have from a distillery which doesn't always hit the heights, but when it does.... *46%. sc. 380 bottles.*

Wemyss 1996 Single Islay Caol Ila "The Tobacconist" hogshead, dist 96, bott 13 **(81.5)** n20.5 t22 f19 b20. Never having as much as put an unlit cigarette to my lips, let alone smoked (a reason some specialist doctors in the field have told me as to why my palate is so sensitive), I know little of what goes on in tobacconists, other than that their hovercrafts are full of eels. Bouncy, bouncy! I assume whoever picked this cask goes quite often, otherwise he or she might have spotted the bitter oak flaw. *46%. sc. Wemyss Malts. 381 bottles. Exclusive for France.*

The Whisky Agency Caol Ila 1982 bott 12 **(91.5)** n23.5 t23 f22 b23. A delightfully full of character; a high quality dram which makes no secret of its age and home turf; *51.2%*

The Whisky Agency Caol Ila 'Sea Life' 1984 ex-bourbon hogshead, dist 1984, bott 2012 **(89.5)** n22 t23 f22 b22.5. The distillery at its groveiest, as opposed to grooviest as the citrus plays a massive role. *53.5%*

 The Whisky Agency Perfect Dram Caol Ila 1995 dist 1995 **(94.5)** n23 sultry, gentle, delightfully sweet and above the norm degree of smoke for a Caol Ila; **t24** the usual C I oils have been limited here, allowing the smokiness full reign. Just so gentle and elegant, the vanillas and spices are in total harmony with the mouth-filling smoke; **f23.5** the spices intensify, as does the brittleness of the sugars; **b24** whoever was working out their 35ppm phenols must have been a little numerically dyslexic...some whopping peat here. *50.6%.*

CAPERDONICH

Speyside, 1898. Chivas Brothers. Closed.

Abbey Whisky Caperdonich Aged 17 Years The Rare Casks refill bourbon barrel, dist 95, bott 12 **(86.5)** n21.5 t22.5 f21 b21.5. The ulmo honey and spices work overtime to see off the over-enthusiasm of the oak. Never less than entertaining, but the tannins win the day a little too convincingly. *57.8%. nc ncf. 96 bottles.*

 Alexander Weine&distillate Caperdonich 20 Year Old refill bourbon hogshead, cask no. 121120, dist 1992, bott 2013 **(86.5)** n23 t22 f20 b21.5. I remember back in 1992 wandering around this distillery and being told by its manager that, no matter how they tried, they had problems guaranteeing the quality of the distillate. The distillery has gone now, a victim of its own quirkiness and uneven temperament. This bottling gives some clues as to why, with a hotness which has nothing to do with spice. But there is a charismatic charm to the barley too. The oak, though, is all embracing. *54.7%.sc. Cask Strength.*

⁙ **Berry's Own Selection Caperdonich 1995 Aged 18 Years** cask no. 95076, bott 2014 (86) n22 t22 f20 b21. While tasting this, I have just been presented by my partner, Judy, a massive toad found in the garden minding its own business under a bush. This splendid fellow was a fat, rather ugly thing but brimming with personality. By contrast, this has its moments of beauty – with the barley sugar delivery for instance – but is rather devoid of character. I know which of the two kept my attention longer.... *46%. ncf ncf. WB15/241*

Duncan Taylor Octave Caperdonich 20 Years Old cask no. 413904, dist 92 (96) n23.5 the oak makes for a overtly dry experience, but it doesn't take too much work to locate the delicate ulmo honey and spiced peach melba; t22.5 dry delivery but enough sugars from the barley to soften things beautifully; f25 heads into overdrive as we come up with one of the most complex and beautifully weighted finishes of the year. The barley has now absorbed enough tannin to pulse a sweet sharpness and the weight and feel has altered from bone dry and heavy to semi ethereal and dusted with gentle sugars including, astonishingly, grist. Playful lemon drop notes also hint of a bygone youth: a bit like an old man still with the profile of the child he once was...; b24 just about the complete Speyside for its type and age. A finish to be revered. Superb. *54.6%. sc. Duncan Taylor & Co.*

Gordon & MacPhail Connoisseurs Choice Caperdonich 1999 (91.5) n22.5 t23.5 f22.5 b23. Irresistible! *46%. ncf.*

Liquid Sun Caperdonich 1992 bott 12 (92.5) n22 freshly diced Granny Smith freshens up the oak; t24 exceptional texture: just enough oils brought home by the big malt to ensure serious weight; eye-watering pears instead of apples and so much spice...; f23 long and, though thinning out to a gruel at the finish, the deft maple syrup ensures balance is maintained; b23.5 the distillery may now be dead, but this is so alive on the palate...*51.9%.*

Old Malt Cask Caperdonich Aged 18 Years refill hogshead, cask no. 8475, dist Jun 94, bott Jun 12 (89) n23 t22 f23.5 b22.5. Oscillates between excellence and very good. *50%. nc ncf sc. Douglas Laing & Co. 297 bottles.*

Old Malt Cask Caperdonich Aged 20 Years cask no. 9321, bott Jan 13 (92.5) n24 almost perfumed in its fruitiness: wine gums melting in the sun. A hint of hot cross bun does for the spice and sherbet for tartness; t23 with the sherbet on the nose, the fizzing delivery seems a natural way for the barley to hit home on the palate; delicate spices pop around, as does a light creamed mocha-butterscotch middle; f22.5 much drier now and something for vanilla fans to enjoy; b23 never seen a Caperdonich perform like this before: come to think of it, its style is a first in a couple of decades of tastings. Inventive and pure fun. *50%. sc.*

That Boutique-y Whisky Company Caperdonich batch 3 (94) n24 wild mint dissolves into a subtle honey and herbal mix; t23 steady oak from delivery offers maple syrup alongside the zingy, citrusy edge; f23.5 egg custard tart with spice; very late ulmo honey; b23.5 a quality malt which is not only complex but displays a near perfect weight. *45.7%.*

⁙ **That Boutique-y Whisky Caperdonich** batch 4 (85) n21.5 t22 f20 b21.5. Not a distillery to raise its head high above the parapet before it reaches at least 25, this shows good form – and no little banana - until the mean, limited finish. *48.1%. 79 bottles. WB15/197*

The Warehouse Collection Caperdonich Aged 18 Years bourbon hogshead, cask no. 88853, dist 23 Jun 94, bott 28 Oct 12 (82) n20 t20 f21.5 b20.5. A seriously weird one. In over three decades, I have tasted Caper in all shapes, forms, ages and sizes. This is the first, though, that smells more like cider brandy and tastes something akin to slivovitz. Impossible not to enjoy in its own right, though. *62.8%. nc ncf sc. Whisky Warehouse No. 8. 278 bottles.*

⁙ **The Whisky Agency Caperdonich 1992** dist 1992 (89.5) n21.5 thin, rather strained, uninspiring oak; t24 one dimensional, ultra intense malt with a near faultless body you really want to explore: amazing and really quite beautiful...; f21.5 thins out once more, though a few warming spices filter through; b22.5 the whisky equivalent of getting a malty custard pie in the kisser.... *60.9%.*

⁙ **The Whisky Cask Caperdonich Aged 20 Years** bourbon hogshead, dist 1994, bott 2014 (87) n22 t22 f21 b22. Malty and salivating with plenty of barley sugar candy. A little bite but simplistic stuff. *54.7%. nc ncf.*

CARDHU
Speyside, 1824. Diageo. Working.

Cardhu 12 Years Old db (83) n22 t22 f18 b21. What appears to be a small change in the wood profile has resulted in a big shift in personality. What was once a guaranteed malt love-in is now a drier, oakier, fruitier affair. Sadly, though, with more than a touch of something furry. *40%*

⁃ **Cardhu Amber Rock** db **(87.5)** n22 t23 f21 b21.5. Amber is the right colour for this: it appears stuck between green and red, not sure whether to go or not. The delivery, in which the tangerine cream is in full flow reflects the better elements of the nose. But the finish is all about being stuck in neutral. Not helped by the useless 40% abv, you get the feeling that a great whisky is trying to get out. The odd tweak and we'll have a winner. That said, very enjoyable indeed. Just even more frustrating! 40%. Diageo.

Duncan Taylor Octave Cardhu 27 Years Old cask no. 863289, dist 84 **(93.5)** n24 while virtually every aroma somehow stems from the oak, it is achieved with such effortless sophistication that there is not a hint of tired or laboured tannin; perhaps there is a hint of malt on the ulmo honey, while the spice carries the fruitiness found in rye or pure pot Irish. Really complex stuff; t23 translates onto the palate perfectly; the sugars lead the way, all of a silky disposition, before a few tannins hit home, as do the spices. But there is a slightly overcooked jam tart darkness to this, too: quite lovely; f23 the spices keep up the pace and intensity while the custard pie intended target; b23.5 uber-high quality and shows its grey hairs in only a distinguished manner. Cardhu is one of the few delicate Speysiders which can translate to older ages with such grace. 51.1%. sc. Duncan Taylor & Co.

CLYNELISH
Highlands (Northern), 1968. Diageo. Working.

Clynelish Aged 15 Years "The Distillers Edition" double matured in oloroso-seco casks Cl-Br: 169-1f, bott code L6264CM000 03847665, dist 1991, bott 2006 db **(79)** n20 t20 f19 b20. Big in places, distinctly oily in others but the overall feel is of a potentially brilliant whisky matured in unsympathetic barrels. 46%

⁃ **Adelphi Selection Clynelish Aged 17 Years** dist 96, bott 14 **(92)** n22.5 oak through a loudhailer...good creamy Swiss roll filling keeps down the noise; t24 for the muscle on the tannin, the red liquorice and treacle mixing with the major spice makes this something to savour; f22.5 as the sugars wear thin, the slight over eagerness of the dry, toasty oak is again revealed...as is a big helping of powering cocoa; b23 gargantuan, relatively brawny for a Clynelish but, as usual, just exploding with character. Slightly over aged but gets away with it with aplomb. 57.1%. ncf. 264 bottles. WB15/335

⁃ **Alexander Weine & Destillate Clynelish 24 Years Old** refill bourbon hogshead, cask no. 4550, dist 1988, bott 2013 **(89)** n23 remember when the icecream man used to pour some of that green sweet stuff on your vanilla cornet...? t22 buzzing spices take no time to delve into the gathering, multi-layered sugars, most of a dark, smouldering variety; f21.5 the tannins take few prisoners; the spices keep on buzzing...and a puff of smoke appears on the most distant horizon...; b22.5 another malt caught in the tailwind of the oak. But the steering sugars see this oldie home. 48.8%. sc. Cask strength.

⁃ **Berry's Own Selection Clynelish 1997 Aged 16 Years** cask no. 6871, bott 2014 **(94)** n22.5 a salty, unsure nose. Directionless and half-hearted but enough lively malt and marmalade in there to offer hope...; t24 which is soon rewarded: fabulous oils and spice combine for a seriously complex delivery, which only gets better as the ulmo honey and chocolate wafer gets to work; f23.5 custard creams and raisin shortcake biscuits mix it with the ulmo honey; b24 this poor thing had to follow the two Balvenie Single Barrels I reviewed...a very hard act to follow. The nose suggested it might bomb, but excellence will out in the end. 55.4%. ncf ncf. WB15/246

⁃ **Cadenhead's Clynelish 2014 Aged 24 Years** dist 1990, bott Apr 14 **(92)** n23.5 the volume is set on low: the ulmo honey, red liquorice, molasses just audible above the vanilla chatter; t23 salivating barley – so fresh it mocks its 24 years in barrel; the sugars are constantly at arms against the encroaching oak, but attacks with a feather duster, merely tickling the intruder; excellent spices add some varoom; honey returns for the late mid-ground going into the finale; f22.5 spiced Tunnock's wafers...; b23 an exclusive to one shop. Lucky London: Millwall and this shy little charmer... 47.5%. 228 bottles. London exclusive. WB15/079

The Coopers Choice Clynelish 1998 13 Years Old hogshead, cask no. 7733, dist 98, bott 11 **(80)** n19 t22.5 f18 b20.5. Moist ginger cake, anyone? Proof, though, that a sub-standard cask will do damage to, or at best restrict, even arguably Scotland's finest mainland spirit. 46%. po ncf sc. The Vintage Malt Whisky Co Ltd. 350 bottles.

⁃ **Darkness! Clynelish Aged 16 Years Oloroso Cask Finish** **(90.5)** n22.5 errr...oloroso...; t22.5 errr....oloroso...with lots of spice. And I mean lots...; f23 errr...oloroso. With a massive date and walnut swirl to the finish plus the inevitable spiced cocoa; b22.5 no off notes from the sherry butt whatsoever. But a good example of more being less: far too much fruit completely overwhelms the usual Clynelish complexity. Still, brilliant chewiness to the fruit and the spice is uncompromising. Soothing, rich but overly simple – especially on the finish - so far as this distillery is concerned....yet still just so bloody delicious...! *54.9%. 94 bottles. WB15/200*

Dun Bheagan Clynelish Aged 22 Years Port Hogshead Finish, cask no. 93781, 93783, dist Dec 90, bott 13 **(87.5) n21.5 t22 f22 b22.** A surprising lack of oak; the port pipes have taken years off this malt, though the balance has suffered a little. *46%*

Fine Malt Selection Clynelish 15 Years Old cask no. 4711, dist 97, bott Apr 13 **(92) n22.5** no getting away from a coastal saltiness...like Tyrrell crisps on a seaside picnic where Tunnock's caramel wafers are the main course; **t23** a sharp, juicy barley and salt bite at first, then a surprise custardy back up...with the vaguest hint of smoke; **f23** the saline sharpness lasts the entire tale and even merges with the Toffo finish; just a little glassy at the death, suggesting even greater age; **b23.5** more natural caramels and vanillas than normal for this distillery. But a stunner is a stunner... *46%. sc. James MacArthur & Co Ltd.*

Gordon and MacPhail Connoisseurs Choice Clynelish 1996 (95) n24.5 you never need to buy a ticket to travel with a Clynelish of this era in the glass: one is transported, Business Class at least, to a world where ulmo honey drips from greengage trees and orange blossom honey fills any gaps. Something so Mediterranean about this: time after time this distillery comes up with soft, pliable aromas which near perfection; **t24** slightly more oak adorns the delivery than is noticeable on the nose. A wave of toffee fudge is interspersed with raisin and kumquats; the spices are teasing and ticklish, the balance always in tune; **f22.5** buttery barley and butterscotch fence off the advancing oak; **b24** in recent years I have been coming to the conclusion that Clynelish is probably the greatest of all the mainland Scotch distilleries. This bottling does little to dissuade me. *46%. ncf.*

᠅ **Gordan & MacPhail Cask Strength Clynelish 1997 (89.5) n22** there is a rumble of sherry in this glass like there is a rumble of thunder outside my tasting room. Only there, there is far more water...this nose is also earthy as though mixing manuka honey with ginger, allspice and freshly trimmed beans: definitely unusual; **t23** massive delivery with several layers of jam amid the honey. Again the spices are at full throttle; thought I caught a furry off note...; **f21.5** and indeed I have, as confirmation is received that this has been matured in sherry butts, though the damage by the sulphur is pretty limited. **b23** almost a brilliant whisky. For Clynelish, certainly an oddball. *57.9%.*

᠅ **The Maltman Clynelish Aged 15 Years** bourbon cask **(96.5) n24.5** fabulous display of oak-based spice and dried orange peel: cedar and sandalwood sweetened by molassed liquorice: magnificent...and worth a good ten minutes' study before tasting...; **t24.5** the spices zing through from the first moment again with that sublime backdrop of distant, dark sugars: a malt which claims at first on the palate to be dry but then broadcasts the most astonishing degree of spice and subtle sugar complexity with deeper complexity offered by the high cocoa chocolate orange; **f23** long, long, long and enjoyed a slightly oily depth to that superb spiced chocolate orange; **b24.5** near perfect weight and layering, especially with the spices. An essay in poise and sophistication, the secret being the persistent, dry undertone: the fact so much has happened in just a single cask borders the incredible. *46%. WB15/215*

Master of Malt Clynelish Aged 15 Years refill hogshead, dist 3 Apr 97, bott 28 Nov 12 **(94.5) n23.5** swoon time! Massive oak, more than a usual 15-y-o Clynelish, but the tannins are so beautifully buttressed by the buttery, gently honeyed malt you could almost shed a tear of delight; **t23.5** the little honey on the nose now unleashes unexpected intensity and depth; the malt gains in juiciness; **f23.5** now the drier flip side. But true to the distillery's magnificent character, where the delicate sugars cannot be denied, wins through; **b24** hard to go wrong with Clynelish. And here you won't...at all. Another malt of thundering, yet somehow coy beauty. *56.1%. sc. 255 bottles.*

Master Of Malt Clynelish 16 Years Old sherry, cask no. 4033, dist 3 Apr 97, bott 1 Apr 13 **(94) n22.5** powerful cinnamon-specked grape, kumquat and greengage; **t24** for all the fruit influence, it is the concentrated honey notes which dominate and to a satisfaction which makes one purr...; the early spice makes you grip your seat with pleasure; **f23.5** surprising degree of vanilla; tangy; **b24** at times the grape looks as though it might strange the malt, but so virile are the sugars, there is just no holding this malt down. Just another astonishing whisky from what is probably Scotland's finest mainland malt. *56.7%. sc.*

᠅ **Old Malt Cask Clynelish Aged 15 Years** refill hogshead, cask no. 9881, dist Jul 1997, bott Jun 2013 **(94) n23** the citrus prods the vanilla awake; **t24** now your taste buds get a wake up call as the muscovado and lemon sherbet dusted barley makes its stunning opening salvo; powdered custard cream biscuits fill the mid ground; **f23** a slow denouement of those astonishing barley and matching oak notes. Perhaps the most subtle spice attack of the year gets under way late on... **b24** just can't always trust a nose, can you? This one is dul by Clynelish's normally mesmeric standards. But the delivery....wow!!! *50%. nc ncf sc. 315 bottles.*

Old Malt Cask Clynelish Aged 16 Years refill hogshead, cask no. 8253, dist Jun 95, bott Mar 12 (**92**) n23 from the banana and custard side of the Clynelish family; t23 tangy malt coated in lightly oiled maple syrup; a grassier side is revealed at midpoint before the oak gathers; f23 much drier oaks now. Toasty with vanilla and just a late hint of hazel nut; b23 unerringly gorgeous. 50%. sc. Douglas Laing & Co. 319 bottles.

⚜ **Old Malt Cask Clynelish Aged 16 Years** refill hogshead, cask no. 10227, dist May 97, bott Dec 13 (**85**) n20 t22 f20.5 b21. Some usually limited oak for this distillery ensures a Clynelish a long way from its normal mark. Oddly enough, the smoke and spices are accentuated here, but the remainder is an off target mish-mash. 50%. nc ncf sc. 154 bottles.

⚜ **Old Malt Cask Clynelish Aged 16 Years** refill hogshead, cask no. 10298, dist May 97, bott Feb 14 (**92**) n22 beautiful suet pudding with salted acacia honey spread all over it; t23.5 after a series of uninspiring malts, great to at last receive a delivery which makes the hairs stand on end: classic Clynelish, even if slightly understated. Elegant barley gets things off to a juicy start; the spices enter with aplomb and purpose; pear juice thins honey; f23 more pear juice..and even that crunchy texture to match. A lovely swirl of muscovado; b23.5 the annual OMC Clynelish 16 has become a fixture of excellence in this Bible: if memory serves, this is bang on course with the others. 50%. nc ncf sc. 318 bottles.

Provenance Clynelish Over 15 Years refill hogshead, cask no. 9660, dist Summer 97, bott Spring 13 (**94**) n23.5 buttery vanilla, with a clear and ulmo honey blend; t24 deliveries on the palate rarely come softer or more beautiful: the malt is in silky, concentrate form, while light liquorice and even lighter clove are coated with a thin layer of molasses; somehow enough barley escapes to guarantee a juicy mouthful; f23 liquorice and butterscotch, though the oak gathers peacefully; b23.5 this really has to be the most consistent malt distillery in Scotland. Another angle-kissed dram. 46%. nc ncf. Douglas Laing & Co.

Scotch Malt Whisky Society Cask 26.92 Aged 28 Years refill butt, dist 13 dec 84 (**88**) n23 t22 f21 b22. Just a little too old to ensure the usual Clynelish genius. 58.2%. nc ncf sc. 491 bottles. Ian Macleod Distillers.

⚜ **Scotch Malt Whisky Society Cask 26.95 Aged 10 Years** 1st fill barrel, dist 16 Jun 03 (**92.5**) n23 unusually intense and busy for a Clynelish...even some hints of lobster and paprika here; t24 wow...!!! Takes more time than there is in the day to understand the nature of this fruity-spicy beast. Mangoes and honeydew melon dominate early on. Really has absorbed some major tannin but the fruit is volumised by deft ulmo honey; f22.5 could be a little too much oak, but soft smoke cushions the blows; the sugars are eaked out cleverly; b23.5 has become a greybeard ahead of its time. But the fruity structure is compelling. 61.3%. nc ncf sc. 157 bottles.

⚜ **Scotch Malt Whisky Society Cask 26.101 Aged 9 Years** 1st fill barrel, dist 03 Jun 04 (**94**) n22 unusually mono syllabic with the tannins far too in control; t24.5 ye gods!!! Nobody could expect that! The delivery rocks you off your chair and blows your socks off as the spices combust on impact. The depth charge stirs up some sedimentary sugars and the resulting soup is a spicy treat; f23.5 the fade is a delicious run through of many of the tangier notes found in older bourbons; b24 the dullness of the nose is a good decoy for the rampaging spice which follows....! 59.3%. nc ncf sc. 247 bottles.

⚜ **Signatory Cask Strength Collection Clynelish 1995 Aged 17 Years** refill sherry butt, cask no. 12794, dist 12 Dec 95, bott 23 Sep 13 (**91**) n22.5 curious subtle smoke and gentle grape mix. Clean sherry butt at work...so even a bourbon-style edge from the oak is detected; t23 two-toned spice – presumably two types, one from the oak, the other from the grape – dominate early on before a Cadbury's Fruit and Nut middle even apes its cotton wool texture; f22.5 delicate fruit but mainly tannins which rather over dominate despite the Demerara; b23 probably peaked two years earlier. Great to see a magnificent sherry butt offering zero negativity and allowing the character of the distillate to come through. 56.2%. sc nc. Cask hand picked by The Whisky Exchange. WB15/322

⚜ **Signatory Vintage Un-chillfiltered Collection Clynelish 1997 Aged 16 Years** dist 29 Oct 97, bott 19 Feb 14, hogsheads, cask no. 12375+12376 (85.5) n23 t21.5 f20 b21. Even one of the world's great distilleries, such as Clynelish, struggles to hit the heights after spending 16 years in oak coming to the end of its useful life. But at least the nose is allowed to give a virtuoso display of sublimely subtle citrus and barley, enriched further by floral honey. 46%. nc ncf. 787 bottles. WB15/025

⚜ **The Single Malts of Scotland Clynelish Aged 18 Years** hogshead, cask no. 10193, dist 31 Oct 95, bott 25 Mar 14 (**88.5**) n22 a little light peat mingles with the silky vanillas; t22.5 juicy with a few malty thrusts early on, then the expected spice which arrives in abundance; some boiled cooking apple tries to penetrate the tannins; f22 dries, though retains that vaguely sweet oiliness. The tang of the tannins surrounds the malt and sugars like Indians around a waggon train of settlers; **b22** just a little too bold with the oak for true greatness. But plenty to see along the way. *57.5%. 265 bottles. WB15/294*

That Boutique-y Whisky Company Clynelish batch 2 **(85) n21.5 t22 f20.5 b21.** May be wrong, but this has all the hallmarks of a sherry-treated barrel from the distillery's United Distillers days. The soft sulphur mixing with the trademark honey really is a very unusual combination. *56.6%. Master Of Malt. 319 bottles.*

⁘ **The First Editions Clynelish 1996 Aged 17 Years** refill hogshead, dist 1996, bott 2014 **(96.5) n24.5** this is all about complexity and deftness. Just hints here, murmurs there...and the odd whisper, sometimes bolstered by a caress. Honey is at the vanguard, though in varying forms, most light and flickering, the odd shard of honeycomb momentarily adding a touch of weight before vanishing again...; citrus flickers, a sprinkling of salt amplifies; **t24.5** a delivery crafted by the gods: the spices arrive early and in force to show this is going to be no namby-pamby honeyfest. They buzz and spit, often truculently, yet do so without breaking the spell of the honey, in its myriad manifestations, being broken. Sublime oils help the honey-lemon sub strata flourish; salty with a butterscotch middle; **f23.5** only some late bitterness detracts vaguely from the elegance of the ever-drying finale, though the spices which started entirely unobtrusively now take on a more commanding roll; **b24** not sure if they should rename this distillery "Old Faithful". Just never, ever seems to let you down. Another beautifully, almost perfectly, crafted essay. *58.2%. nc ncf sc. 265 bottles.*

The Warehouse Collection Clynelish Aged 15 Years bourbon barrel, cask no. 5740, dist 21 May 97, bott 5 May 13 **(95.5) n23.5** salty bite to the spiced honey; **t24.5** immediate complexity: varying honey style from beech to ulmo; the salt really does up the sharpness and intensity as hickory and liquorice finds a place; some juicy barley pulses in and out; **f23** much drier with creamy fudge and cocoa layered with molassed sugar; **b24.5** effortless brilliance from Clynelish: this is how malt whisky should be..! *55.5%. nc ncf sc. 157 bottles.*

Wemyss Clynelish 1997 Single Highland "Spiced Chocolate Cup" bott 13 **(91.5) n23 t23 f22.5 b23.** Hard to go wrong with this distillery. And this doesn't... *46%. sc. 302 bottles.*

⁘ **Wemyss Clynelish Malts 1997 Single Highland "Apple Basket"** bott 2013. **(88) n22.5** under-ripe conference Pear and vanilla; **t23** charming and salivating in the first instant, thins rather too quickly though a dose of spices are welcome; **f20.5** dry, flaky oak; **b22** one of those casks which has been damaged by being reduced to 46%. The oils, so essential for the finish, have been split and the oak takes on too chalky a style as a result. *46%. Sc. 339 bottles.*

⁘ **Wemyss Clynelish Malts 1997 Single Highland "Beach with a Sea View"** hogshead, dist 97, bott 14 **(95) n23** coconut water and milky mocha; **t24** magnificent delivery – comes from nowhere as the nose doesn't hint at this. Outstanding weight, an early spice eruption then the ulmo honey coming thick and confidently. Malt is also intense, lightened by just a touch of citrus; **f24** a gentle saltiness gives a nod towards the oak but also helps highlight the long malt and bourbon biscuit dunked in coffee fade; **b24** probably the only distillery on this planet which can surprise like this does. Another gem of a malt from this distillery which, for my money, is now in the world's top three... *46%. sc. 371 bottles.*

⁘ **Wemyss Clynelish Malts 1997 Single Highland "Cayenne Cocoa Bean" (91) n22** coconut water & pineapple; **t23** sweet citrusy kick off: Jaffa orange tamed by ulmo honey & butterscotch; **f23** a sugary fade and the coconut water returns as spices build; **b23** shows a bit more age than you might expect but still has that effortless Clynelish panache. *46%. sc.*

⁘ **Wemyss Clynelish Malts 1997 Single Highland "Toffee Glaze"** bott 13 **(95) n23.5** surging tannin. But is met with no shortage of red liquorice and, tellingly, light ulmo honey; **t24** a majestic delivery where the soft oils and molten golden sugars and spices counter the confident oak to a tee; the ulmo honey continues its impressive repair job; **f23.5** mocha towards the finish but the estery finale is almost more in keeping with a fine pot still rum; **b24** another gorgeous little essay from this most expressive of distilleries. *46%. sc. 258 bottles.*

The Whisky Cask Clynelish Aged 15 Years *(see Warehouse Collection Clynelish)*

⁘ **The Whisky Cask Clynelish** bourbon cask, dist 1997, bott 2014 **(88.5) n23** earthy and oaky, the malt is working at full stretch to keep out the tannins. A soft honey undercurrent helps; **t22.5** for a few seconds on delivery we are treated to a malty brilliance: the unidentifiable honey, grist and oak are in perfect harmony; dries out rapidly; **f21.5** warming spices and hovering oak; **b21.5** creamy for a Clynelish with no shortage of oaky aggression. *52.5%.*

COLEBURN
Speyside, 1897–1985. Diageo. Closed.

The Whisky Agency Coleburn 26 Year Old dist 1983, bott 2009 **(88.5) n22 t23 f21.5 b22.** Coleburn is a rare whisky. A thoroughly enjoyable Coleburn is rarer still. So here's one you've just got to go and track down... *49.5%. The Whisky Agency, Germany.*

CONVALMORE

Speyside, 1894–1985. William Grant & Sons. Closed.

Convalmore 1977 bott 2005 db **(91)** n23 t23 f22 b23. Must be blended with Botox, as there is no detrimental ageing to either nose or delivery. A quite lovely and charming whisky to remember this lost – and extremely rare - distillery by. 57.9%. 3900 bottles.

CRAGGANMORE

Speyside, 1870. Diageo. Working.

Cragganmore Aged 12 Years db **(81.5)** n20 t21 f20 b20.5. I have a dozen bottles of Cragganmore in my personal cellar dating from the early 90s when the distillery was first bottled as a Classic Malt. Their astonishing dexterity and charm, their naked celebration of all things Speyside, casts a sad shadow over this drinkable but drab and instantly forgettable expression. 40%

Cragganmore Aged 14 Years The Distillers Edition finished in port casks, dist 1993, bott 2007 db **(85)** n22 t21 f21 b21. The tightly closed fruit on the palate doesn't quite match the more expansive and complex nose. 40%

⋰ **Cragganmore Distillers Edition** double matured, dist 00, bott 13 db **(82.5)** n21 t21.5 f20 b20. Matured in toffee, one presumes. Hard to imagine a flatter, less inspiring malt from a great distillery if you tried. 40% WB15/313

Cragganmore Special Release 2010 21 Years Old refill American oak, dist 1989 db **(95.5)** n23.5 huge age, but the close knitted nature of the clean barley ensures all the strength required to keep the oak in check; the odd pine-laden tannin and even a touch of pineapple and honeydew melon gives the nod towards something a little exotic; t24 you can ask little more from a Speyside-style delivery at this age and from bourbon. The barley is so wholesome and well integrated that the palate goes into immediate barley-juice overdrive; the oaks offer up some half-hearted cocoa but some full blown molasses. The result is a single malt of unstinting enormity, yet unambiguous magnificence; f23.5 some light liquorice joins forces with the cocoa and molasses to underline the bourbon credentials. Massive age, the odd creak here and there. But never for a second is the quality breeched; b24.5 what a fascinating, awe-inspiring dram. More or less at the very time this malt was being made, I remember talking to the manager at the then barely known Speyside distillery. He told me that the new Classic Malt 12-year-old was selected at that age because it was felt that, as a singleton (though not for blending), Cragganmore did not give its best over that age. I still tend to agree, in general. But here is a bottling which is making me look at this distillery is a new light...and that light is a beacon. I think the manager and I would have stood in amazement if we knew just how fine that young spirit would be when entering its 21st year. 112 per cent proof that you should never say never... 56%. nc ncf. Diageo. Fewer than 6000 bottles.

⋰ **Cadenhead's Authentic Collection Cragganmore-Glenlivet Cask Strength Aged 13 Years** bourbon hogshead, dist 1999, bott Oct 13 **(85)** n21 t23 f20 b21. Tangy and intense, here's a fine example of excellent malt battling against sub-standard oak and almost winning the battle. Reveals a citrusy side. And the spices also helps paper over the cracks. Built for blending. 54.5%. 276 bottles. WB15/092

⋰ **Cadenhead's Wine Cask Cragganmore-Glenlivet Aged 21 Years** Chateau Lafitte cask, dist 93, bott Jul 14 **(74)** n17 t20 f18 b19. I have had many bottles of Chateau Lafitte in my life of all kinds of vintages. In my cellar are many more. But I have never had one that shows the sulphur on this. Presumably a sulphur stick at work... 56.1%. 198 bottles. WB15/253

⋰ **Old Malt Cask Cragganmore Aged 16 Years** refill hogshead, cask no. 9931, dist Mar 97, bott Aug 13 **(89)** n23 lemon curd tart; t22.5 another tyoe of tart: thi time eye-watering and salivatingly grassy; f21.5 custard cram biscuits (as opposed to the lemon puffs on the nose); b22 doesn't really try when it comes to complexity. Just does the simple things well. 50%. nc ncf sc. 204 bottles.

⋰ **Old Malt Cask Cragganmore Aged 24 Years** refill hogshead, cask no. 10375, dist Nov 89, bott Mar 14 **(87.5)** n22.5 t23 f20.5 b21.5. Those still around who remember the bracing sea-salty old Bunnas of three decades back will give this one a curious, sideway look. Inland Speysiders don't come more coastal and salty than this in style...so not sure where it has been matured. The oak has left little space for much else to breath. An early-morning malt to wake you up, much like a sea-front wave direct into the kisser. 50%. sc. 169 bottles.

Scotch Malt Whisky Society Cask 37.52 refill hogshead, dist 11 Jun 02 **(87.5)** n21 t22.5 f22 b22. Recovers adroitly from a lazy nose. 58.9%. nc ncf sc. 286 bottles.

Scotch Malt Whisky Society Cask 37.54 Aged 27 Years refill hogshead, dist 24 Apr 85 **(93)** n22 at first the muscle on the vanilla signals over-age. Slowly, delicate exotic fruits begin to escape from the cracks; t24 yep: just about perfect weight on delivery. By the time the second phase of heavy artillery oak arrives, the ground has been perfectly prepared by the light, fruity but always lush malt concentrate on delivery. The mid-ground is unashamed mocha, with a sprig of mint; **f23** any threat of over oaking has receded and the vanilla is now pleasantly topped by a thin layer of orange blossom honey; **b24** stupendous whisky which gives a master class as to why blenders love this beauty to add such subtle flavour pyrotechnics to their blends... *52.4%. nc ncf sc. 215 bottles.*

Wemyss 1989 Single Speyside "Evergreen Forest" hogshead, dist 89, bott 13 **(85.5) n21.5 t22 f20 b21.** As though a light, intensely malty dram has been infused with lemon sherbet. *46%. sc. 326 bottles.*

CRAIGELLACHIE
Speyside, 1891. John Dewar & Sons. Working.

Chieftain's Craigellachie Aged 21 Years hogshead, cask no. 2713, dist Mar 91, bott Apr 12 **(75.5) n19 t19 f18.5 b19.** As hot and aggressive as a tanked up imbiber of the same age falling out of a highland hostelry in the wee hours and looking for a punch up. *50%. nc ncf sc. Ian Macleod Distillers. 292 bottles.*

Gordon and MacPhail Connoisseurs Choice Craigellachie 1997 (91) n23 t23 f22 b23. Captures this distillery at its most polite yet lively. Really lovely. *46%. ncf.*

Old Malt Cask Craigellachie Aged 13 Years sherry butt, cask no. 9730, dist 00, bott 13 **(77) n18 t21 f19 b19.** Malty; sweet but off key during the vital movements. *50%. sc. 338 bottles.*

Old Malt Cask Craigellachie Aged 15 Years refill hogshead, cask no. 9344, dist Dec 97, bott Jan 13 **(89) n22 t22.5 f22 b22.5.** Sometimes this distillery can really sparkle on the palate and wow you. Here is one such juicy, yet gloriously subtle, example. *50%. sc. 293 bottles.*

⁛ **Old Malt Cask Craigellachie Aged 18 Years** sherry butt, cask no. 10589, dist Nov 95, Jun 14 **(85) n21 t22.5 f20 b21.5.** A silky, rather quagmire-ish moist fruitcake number. After the dates and walnut on delivery, and the rather cloying treacle follow through, the finale shows a slight furry quality. *50%. nc ncf sc. 730 bottles.*

Old Masters Craigellachie 11 Years Old cask no. 150, dist 00, bott Oct 12 **(86) n21.5 t22 f21 b21.5.** A competent Speysider with few party tricks. Concentrates almost exclusively on keeping the barley on an even keel. A little citrus zestiness provides the jazz. *57.3%. sc.*

Provenance Craigellachie Over 10 Years sherry refill butt, cask no. 9421, dist 2002, bott 2012 **(74.5) n17.5 t19 f19 b19.** It's 7am. First whisky of my 12 hour tasting day and...bugger! Where's my bed? Despite the attractive smoked mint finish, woefully off key. *46%. nc, ncf, sc.*

Scotch Malt Whisky Society Cask 44.57 Aged 22 Years refill hogshead, dist 13 Aug 90 **(86) n22 t22 f21 b21.** Hardly surprising that a distillery set at the very centre of Speyside should produce a malt which so ably summarises the region's style. Only a less than helpful old bourbon barrel detracts as the spirit is bustling with fresh malty intent and makes for a lively and busy chew. *52.9%. nc ncf sc. 305 bottles.*

⁛ **Signatory Vintage Single Malt Craigellachie 1999 Aged 14 Years**, bourbon barrels, cask no. 148+149, dist 30 Aug 99, bott 26 Nov 13 **(88) n22.5** over-ripe, seasoned gooseberries; **t22.5** beautifully refreshing malt, though it is the mouth feel which steels the show; **f21** dries lopsidedly with some bitterness from the oak; **b22** a decnt malt mostly in fine shape. *43%. nc. 614 bottles. WB15/018*

⁛ **Single Cask Collection 10 Year Old Craigellachie Rum Cask Finish** bourbon barrel, finished in a rum cask, cask no. 162, dist 26 Jun 03, bott 08 Jul 13 **(87.5) n22 t22 f21 b21.5.** A pleasant, inoffensive whisky right enough. But a danger of finishing in rum is that a cask is left open to being sealed in a crisp sugary wrapping, which is what has happened here. Limited development results, especially on the finish. *54.4%. sc. 267 bottles.*

⁛ **The Single Malts of Scotland Craigellachie 16 Years Old** hogshead, cask no. 7286, dist 14 Nov 96, bott 11 Nov 13 **(90.5) n22.5** a moment of smoke heralds a slightly salty maltiness; **t23.5** not sure if the light smoke on delivery is my imagination triggered by my nose. But excellent weight, not least from the treacle pudding; **f22** salty fudge; mint chocolate lolly; **b22.5** even before I looked to see what I was tasting next, that curious, quite unique puff of near invisible smoke told me this was a Craigellachie. A jolly, expansive dram from a usually neat and tidy distillery. *52.7%. 312 bottles. WB15/308*

DAILUAINE
Speyside, 1854. Diageo. Working.

Dailuaine 1997 The Manager's Choice db **(87.5) n21.5 t23 f21 b22.** One of the most enjoyable (unpeated!!) Dailuaines I've come across in an age. There is the usual distillery biff to this, but not without a honeyed safety net. Great fun. *58.6%*

Dailuaine Aged 16 Years bott lot no. L4334 db **(79) n19 t21 f20 b19.** Syrupy, almost grotesquely heavy at times; the lighter notes of previous bottlings have been lost under an avalanche of sugary, over-ripe tomatoes. One for those who want a massive dram. *43%*

⫶ **Càrn Mòr Strictly Limited Edition Dailuaine Aged 14 Years** hogshead, dist 1999, bott 2013 **(90)** n22.5 beautifully clean spirit with a real sparkle to the barley; the slightly tangy oak may prove problematic later; **t23.5** superb delivery: a gorgeous coconut in golden syrup thread breaking down into an umo honey and grist middle, helped along by clever, delicate spices; **f21.5** vanilla then bitters somewhat; **b22.5** this usually run of the still distillery offers little to get too excited about. But here is a rare exception. *46%. nc ncf. 653 bottles. WB15/158*

Chieftain's Dailuaine Aged 30 Years hogshead, cask no. 3893, dist Oct 82, bott Jan 13 **(83.5)** n21 t21 f21 b20.5. Even after all this time, remains a malt confined by its own lack of character despite offering an attractive if brief mouth-watering quality. Interesting how some distillates which offer little when young, such as Caperdonich, blossom into grandee malts as the whiskers grey. Not this guy, which perhaps would have served an old blend in more telling effect. *52%. nc ncf sc. Ian Macleod Distillers. 282 bottles.*

⫶ **Darkness! Dailuaine Aged 15 Years** Pedro Ximenez Cask Finish **(73)** n19 t19 f16 b18. Dull-uaine more like. Not just flat and lifeless but even sports a suspect furriness on the finish. *53.9%. 96 bottles. WB15/220*

⫶ **Hepburn's Choice Dailuaine 2005 Aged 8 Years** sherry butt **(83)** n19 t22.5 f21.5 b20. Designed to be shoved into a three year old blend, only the dazzling malt delivery, with its profound searchlit-starring barley, is up to true single malt billing. *46%. 393 bottles.*

Master of Malt Dailuaine 15 Years Old hogshead, cask no. 15562, dist 25 Nov 97, bott 1 Apr 13 **(94.5)** n23.5 complex and busy with the vanillas skipping between barley and citrus; **t24** salivating at first, but the lightest of oils ensures fabulous depth to the barley sugar. There is a fabulous spice sub structure and a touch of ulmo honey strengthened with toasted honeycomb; **f23** Maryland cookie, nuts, spice and light chocolate; **b24** Dailuine in the kind of nick and showing a complexity very rarely seen for this distillery. This you must experience..! *55.7%. sc. 282 bottles.*

⫶ **Old Masters Dailuaine 13 Year Old** dist 2001, bott 2014 **(88.5)** n20 a touch of the sweaty armpits...; **t24** ...but makes up for it with a sensationally vibrant delivery of punchy barley. How explosively juicy was that!?! **f22.5** lovely chocolate mousse overcomes the more ambiguous oak notes; **b22** absolutely nothing simple or straightforward about this one. *61.3%. James MacArthur & Co. Ltd.*

⫶ **Old Particular Speyside Dailuaine 16 Years Old** bourbon barrel, cask no. 10207, dist Apr 1997, bott Jan 2014 **(88.5)** n22 a little earthy, with an intriguing mix of freshly dug greens, lettuce and pastry baking in the background; **t23** a serious barley fest with the sugars mixing with a little acacia and ulmo honey; **f21** a little tangy, but some decent vanilla; **b22** my glasses overfloweth with impressive Dailuaines. Not often that has happened over the last 25 years...*55.2%. nc ncf sc. 91 bottles. Douglas Laing & Co.*

⫶ **The Pearls of Scotland Dailuaine 1997 15 Year Old** cask no. 15561, dist Dec 97, bott Nov 13 **(88)** n21.5 rhubarb and custard with a major tannin injection; **t23.5** absolutely enormous and gob-smackingly beautiful delivery with just-so oils. The barley is on steroids and punches through the massive, well spiked and spicy oak; **f21** reverts to type with a thin, sugary underwhelming finale; **b22** a top dollar Dailuaine which sparkles quite dazzlingly early on. *55.9%. WB15/006*

Provenance Dailuaine Over 10 Years sherry cask, cask no. 9195, dist Autumn 02, bott Autumn 12 **(88)** n22 t22 f22 b22. Though it sticks to its oft repeated style of hefty oils and sugars, enough barley gushes through to make for an enjoyable if obvious malt. Helped along the way by an above average cask. *46%. nc ncf sc. Douglas Laing & Co.*

Provenance Dailuaine Over 15 Years refill hogshead, cask no. 9641, dist Summer 97, bott Spring 13 **(83)** n20 t21 f21 b21. Malty, salty and sugary. And thin enough to be on whisky weight watchers. *46%. nc ncf. Douglas Laing & Co.*

Scotch Malt Whisky Society Cask 41.54 Aged 8 Years 1st fill barrel, 11 May 04 **(81)** n22 t19 f20 b20. Despite the gooseberry and lime dust, robust to the point of aggressive in its malty single-mindedness. *58.7%. nc ncf sc. 217 bottles.*

Scotch Malt Whisky Society Cask 41.56 Aged 24 Years refill hogshead, 28 Aug 88 **(84)** n22.5 t21.5 f20.5 b20.5. Frantic sugars cool down the fiery-thin spirit. For the odd moment, it seems more like the spirit from an over-excited German column still. Attractive grapefruit and pineapple nose, though. *51.9%. nc ncf sc. 280 bottles.*

⫶ **Scotch Malt Whisky Society Cask 41.59 Aged 10 Years** 1st fill barrel, dist 14 Jul 03 **(94.5)** n23.5 gloriously uplifting barley with a major under-ripe Cox's apple freshness; **t24** stupendous delivery absolutely bursting with rich, salivating barley. There are some wonderful oak-induced spices (this has matured in an absolutely top-grade bourbon cask, by the way) with red liquorice delving into the rich esters; **f23** long with a wonderful "Nice" coconut biscuit signature...; **b24** always good to see a younger bottling from the SWMS.

Especially when, as is the case here, it helps show a distillery in its very best light... A surprise dram which seems to be a liquid form of the sunny spring morning outside the sample room windows... *61.9%. 233 bottles.*

That Boutique-y Whisky Company Dailuaine batch 1 **(83.5) n22.5 t22 f19 b20.** Great that Dailuaine offers a bit of sheen to its normal dose of sugar-barley. Pity about the bitter oak, though. *51.5%. Master Of Malt. 201 bottles.*

That Boutique-y Whisky Dailuaine 15 Year Old (94.5) n23.5 complex and busy with the vanillas skipping between barley and citrus; **t24** salivating at first, but the lightest of oils ensures fabulous depth and to the barley sugar. There is a fabulous spice sub structure and a touch of ulmo honey strengthened with toasted honeycomb; **f23** Maryland cookie, nuts, spice and light chocolate; **b24** Dailuine in the kind of nick and showing a complexity very rarely seen for this distillery. This you must experience..! *55.7%*

DALLAS DHU
Speyside, 1899–1983. Closed. Now a museum.

Gordon & MacPhail Rare Vintage Dallas Dhu 1979 (94.5) n23 marginally earthy but probably only there for the fruit and nuts to grow in; green banana and toasted yam lead, pecan pie follows behind; **t23.5** How can barley melt in the mouth after 32 years? It defies logic and description. What makes it work so well, is that the base and baritone sugars from the oak never for a moment attempt to drown the tenor from the grist. Often that is the key to a whisky's success and here it is demonstrated perfectly: it means the complexity levels remain high at all times and the depth of oak controlled; **f23.5** long, with the vanilla enjoying a nutty depth, moving into a more deliciously praline oiliness. The tannins are firm enough to remind us that 1979 was a long time ago now but not a single hint of oaky degradation. Clear, confident, strident notes from first to last; **b24** I can hardly recall the last time a bottling from this distillery popped along – depressing to think I am old enough to remember when they were so relatively common they were being sold on special offer! It was always a class act; it's closure an act of whisky vandalism, whether it be preserved as a museum or not. This, even after all these years, shows the extraordinary quality we are missing day in, day out. *43%*

DALMORE
Highands (Northern), 1839. Whyte and Mackay. Working.

The Dalmore 12 Years Old db **(90) n22** mixed dates: both dry and juicy; **t23** fat, rich delivery with a wonderful dovetailing of juicy barley and thick, rumbling fruit; **t22.5** lots of toffee on the finish, but gets away with it thanks to the sheer depth to the barley and the busy sherry sub-plot; **b22.5** has changed character of late yet remains underpowered and with a shade too much toffee. But such is the quality of the malt in its own right it can overcome any hurdles placed before it to ensure a real mouth-filling, rumbustious dram. *40%*

The Dalmore Dee Dram 12 Years Old db **(63.5) n15.5 t17 f14 b16.** Words fail me...*40%*

The Dalmore 15 Years Old db **(83.5) n21 t21 f20.5 b21.** Another pleasant Dalmore that coasts along the runway but simply fails to get off the ground. The odd off note here and there, but it's the blood orange which shines brightest. *40%*

The Dalmore 18 Years Old db **(76.5) n19 t21 f18 b18.5.** Heaps of caramel and the cask choice might have been better. *43%*

The Dalmore 21 Years Old db **(87) n22 t23 f20 b22.** Bottled elegance. *43%*

The Dalmore 25 db **(88) n23.5** hugely attractive with a sherry-trifle signature; **t22.5** a glossy delivery with the accent very much on fruit, plums in particular; an attractive degree of sharpness throughout; **f20** just a little dry with a tell-tale tang towards the end; **b22** the kind of neat and tidy, if imperfect, whisky which, were it in human form, would sport a carefully trimmed and possibly darkened little moustache, a pin-striped suit, matching tie and square and shiny black shoes. *42%. Whyte & Mackay Ltd.*

The Dalmore Forty Years Old db **(82) n23 t20 f19 b20.** Doubtless my dear friend Richard Paterson will question whether I have the ability to spot a good whisky if it ran me over in a ten ton truck. But I have to say here that we have a disappointing malt: I had left this too late on in writing this year's (2008) Bible as a treat. But it wasn't to be. A soft delivery: but of what? Hard to exactly pin down what's going on here as there is so much toffee and fruit that the oak and barley have been overwhelmed. Pleasant, perhaps, but it's all rather dull and passionless. Like going through the motions with an old lover. Adore the sherry-trifle/toffee mousse nose, though... *40%*

The Dalmore Astrum Aged 40 Years db **(89) n23.5 t21 f22 b22.5.** This guy is all about the nose. The oak is too big for the overall framework and the balance hangs by a thread. Yet somehow the overall effect is impressive. Another summer and you suspect the whole thing would have snapped... *42%*

The Dalmore Aurora Aged 45 Years db **(90.5) n25** unquestionably an intriguing and engaging nose, full of subtleties and quirky side streets. Initially, all these sub plots and intrigues are to do with oak and very little else. However, the spices once located are a treat and open the door to the delicate boiled fruit which, after making a tentative entrance, begins to inject the required sweetness; give ten minutes in the glass to discover something quite sublime and faultless... **t22** rounded on delivery but again it's all about the oak which piles up untidily on the palate, though the odd exotic fruit note can be detected. Salt dovetails with that fruit but it is heading downhill... **f21.5** some vaguely malty vanilla but the oak is now dominating though some mocha does come to the rescue; **b22** sophisticated for sure. But so huge is the oak on the palate, it cannot hope to match the freakish brilliance of the nose. 45%

The Dalmore 50 Years Old db **(88) n21 t19 f25 b23.** Takes a while to warm up, but when it does becomes a genuinely classy and memorable dram befitting one of the world's great and undervalued distilleries. 52%

The Dalmore Candela Aged 50 Years db **(96) n25** there you go: that's the next half hour to 45 minutes taken up...trying to unravel this one. Fresh fruity frame, but the picture in the middle is far more difficult to understand. Dates – both dried and juicy – mingle with finest quality Lubec marzipan paste (sans chocolate) while a few spices nip in to say 'hullo'; clean, relaxed... and very sprightly for its age; **t24** immediate onrush of oaks, offset by a cherry sauce and later plain chocolate fondant to ensure any bitterness is kept in check; elsewhere an improbable layering of barley juice and fruit again makes a mockery of the age; **f23.5** for a whisky reaching half a century, curiously reserved with the oaks now really starting to get a degree of bitterness generated; a thin line of chocolate and raisin helps keep that bitterness at acceptable levels; **b23.5** just one of those whiskies which you come across only a handful of times in your life. All because a malt makes it to 50 does not mean it will automatically be great. This, however, is a masterpiece, the end of which seemingly has never been written. 50% (bottled at 45%).

The Dalmore Eos Aged 59 Years db **(95) n24.5** extraordinary pulsing of rich, dry sherry notes: nutty and polished oak in one of the finer Mayfair antique shops or clubs. The moistest, choicest Lubeck marzipan with a thread of Jaffa jam and, as the whisky settles into its stride, this moves to Jaffa cakes with heavy dark chocolate; very limited spice, but the salt levels grow..; **t24** ultra dry delivery despite the juices flowing from the very first moment: the grape is beautifully firm and holds together light oils and burgeoning oak which threaten to inject a weighty toastiness; the mid ground though is a triumph of glorious lightly molassed vanilla notes with strands of barley; spices buzz and fizz and add even further life; **f22.5** a light off-key bitterness knocks off a mark or two, but the cocoa and burnt raisin charge to the rescue; **b24** for those of you who thought this was a camera, let me put you in the picture. This is one well developed whisky, but by no means over exposed, as it would have every right to be after nearly 60 years. Indeed: it is one of those drams which utterly confounds and amazes. I specially chose this as the 1001st new whisky for the 2012 Bible, and those of us old enough to be young when most of its sister casks were hauled off for blending, there was an advert in the '60s which said: "1,001 cleans a big, big carpet...for less than half a crown." Well this 1001 cleans a big, big palate. But I can't see a bottle of this majestic malt going for as little as that... 44%

The Dalmore 62 Years Old db **(95) n23** PM or REV marked demerara potstill rum, surely? Massive coffee presence, clean and enormous, stunning, topdrawer peat just to round things off; **t25** this is brilliant: pure silk wrapping fabulous moist fruitcake soaked in finest oloroso sherry and then weighed with peat which somehow has defied nature and survived in cask all these years. I really cannot fault this: I sit here stunned and in awe; **f24** perfect spices with flecks of ginger and lemon rind; **b24** if I am just half as beautiful, elegant and fascinating as this by the time I reach 62, I'll be a happy man. Somehow I doubt it. A once-in-a-lifetime whisky – something that comes around every 62 years, in fact. Forget Dalmore Cigar Malt – even I might be tempted to start smoking just to get a full bottle of this. 40.5%

The Dalmore 1263 King Alexander III db **(86) n22 t22.5 f20 b21.5.** Starts brightly with all kinds of barley sugar, fruit and decent age and oak combinations, plus some excellent spice prickle. So far, so good...and obviously thoughtfully and complexly structured. But then vanishes without trace on finish. 40%

The Dalmore 1978 db **(89.5) n23.5 t22 f21.5 b22.5.** A seriously lovely old dram which is much weightier on the palate than nose. 471%. 477 bottles.

The Dalmore 1979 db **(84) n21 t21.5 f20 b21.5.** Hard to find a more rounded malt. Strangely earthy, though. 42%. 487 bottles.

The Dalmore 1980 db **(81.5) n19 t21 f20.5 b21.** Wonderful barley intensity on delivery does its best to overcome the so-so nose and finale. 40%

The Dalmore Matusalem 1981 db **(91.5) n23** muscular and beautifully primed with soft herbs amid the fruit; marmalade at the bottom of an old jar; **t23.5** now, do I love that delivery! Waxy and thick in a uniquely Whyte and Mackay style, there is a clever muscovado-molasses mix which not just ramps up the sugars but the weight and depth, also; **f22.5** some tangy notes while the sugars fight a rearguard action with the bittering oak; **b22.5** had someone tied me to a rack and kept pulling until I said this could be something other than a W&M production, I would have defied them to the bitter end... 44%. 497 bottles.

The Dalmore 1981 Amoroso Sherry Finesse amoroso sherry wood cask db (85.5) **n21 t22 f21.5 b21.** A very tight, fruity, dram which gives away its secrets with all the enthusiasm of an agent under torture. Enjoyable to a degree... but bloody hard work. 42%

The Dalmore Mackenzie 1992 American oak/port pipes, bott 2009 db (88.5) **n23 t22 f21 b22.5.** I suppose you could say that such is the influence of the grape that this is a tad one dimensional. But such is the grim state of wine casks in the industry today, one is forgiven for falling on bended knee and kissing the bottle. Though even this isn't without its sulphury failings... 46%

Dalmore 1995 Vintage Distillery Manager Exclusive db (87) **n22** soft, mildly spiced dates and yam; **t22** soft, mildly spiced milk fudge with some lovely malt undertones; **f21.5** more milk fudge...sans spice; **b21.5** pleasant. But seems stuck in a single gear. 40%. Whisky Shop Exclusive. 1800 bottles.

The Dalmore Vintage 2001 Limited Edition db (84.5) **n21 t22 f20.5 b21.** Ah... a Dalmore of straw colour displaying such delicate intricacies with the barley...complex, especially with the varying degrees of malt to the oils... What???? I was asleep? I was dreaming...? What do we have here? Oh. Yet another mahogany-coloured Dalmore. Another Dalmore so thick, nutty-toffeed and chewy you can hardly tell when the story starts and ends. Or exactly what the story is that differs from the others... Yes, overall a generally pleasant experience but the feeling of déjà vu and underachievement is depressingly overwhelming. 48%

The Dalmore Rivers Collection Dee Dram Season 2011 db (81.5) **n20 t22.5 f19 b20.** Where the previous bottling was a complete disaster, this one is friendly and approachable. Still don't expect anything two dimensional on the finish as the caramel attack and a strand of bitterness dries your taste buds to squeaking point. But the delivery is a very pleasant, chewy affair for sure. 40%

The Dalmore Rivers Collection Tweed Dram Season 2011 db (86) **n21 t22 f21.5 b21.5.** Silky and slinky, a real soup of a malt in which the barley occasionally rises high to deliciously juicy effect. 40%

The Dalmore Rivers Collection Tay Dram Season 2011 db (86.5) **n22.5 t23 f20 b21.** Despite the house toffee-neutered finale and the odd but obvious cask-related off note, there is still plenty to enjoy here. 40%

The Dalmore Cabernet Sauvignon db (79) **n22 t19 f19 b19.** Too intense and soupy for its own good. 45%

The Dalmore Castle Leod db (77) **n18.5 t21 f18.5 b19.** Thumpingly big and soupy. More fruit than you can wave a wasp at. But, sadly, the sting comes with the slightly obvious off note. 46%

The Dalmore Ceti db (91.5) **n24** a nose for fruitcake lovers everywhere: ripe cherries and blood orange abound and work most attractively with the slightly suety, muscovado enriched body...; **t23.5** the nose demands a silky delivery and that's exactly what you get. Rich fruit notes form the principle flavour profile but the backing salivating barley and spice is spot on; the mid ground becomes a little saltier and more coastal...; **f21.5** a vague bitterness to the rapidly thinning finale, almost a pithy element, which is slightly out of sync with the joys of before; **b22.5** a Ceti which warbles rather well... 44.7%

The Dalmore Cigar Malt Reserve Limited Edition db (73.5) **n19 t19.5 f17 b18.** One assumes this off key sugarfest is for the cigar that explodes in your face... 44%

The Dalmore Cromartie dist 1996 db (78.5) **n20 t22 f17.5 b19.** Always hard to forecast what these type of bottlings may be like. Sadly there is a sulphur-induced bitterness and tightness to this guy which undermines the more attractive marmalade notes. 45%

The Dalmore Gran Reserva sherry wood and American white oak casks db (82.5) **n22 t21.5 f19 b20.** An improvement on the near nonentity this once was. But still the middle and finish are basic and lacking sophistication or substance outside a broad sweet of oaky chocolate toffee. Delightful mixture of blood orange and nuts on the approach, though. 40%

The Dalmore Valour db (85.5) **n21 t22 f21 b21.5.** Not often you get the words "Valour" and "fudge" in the same sentence. 40%. Whyte and Mackay. Travel Retail Exclusive.

The Dalmore Visitor Centre Exclusive db (95.5) **n25** this isn't just about fruit: this is a lesson in a nosing glass in how the marriage and equilibrium between salt, sugars, barley and delicate fruit juices should be arranged. There is not an off note; no party dominates; the complexity is beguiling as the picture shifts and changes in the glass every few seconds. Also, how the weight of the whisky is essential to balance. It is, frankly, the perfect malt whisky nose... **t24** so off we go on a journey around about fifteen fruit levels, half that number of sugar intensities and a fabulous salty counter. Close your eyes and be seduced...; **f22.5** a minor blemish as a vaguely bitter note from the oak interjects. Luckily, the thick barley sugar is in there to repair the damage; remains salty to the very end; **b24** not exactly the easiest distillery to find but a bottle of this is worth the journey alone. I have tasted some sumptuous Dalmores over the last 30-odd years. But this one stands among the very finest. 46%

⫶ **Cadenhead's Single Cask Dalmore Aged 37 Years** butt, dist 1976, bott 2014 **(94) n24.5** nosed blind I would have sworn that was corn oil coming at me; certainly a bourbony stance in the way the oak has threaded tannin, kumquats, mocha and liquorice into the narrative; a little suet pudding and raisin, too, thinned slightly by a little fresh fruit salad: seriously wonderful; **t24** busy with mocha and spice soon thrown into action, both genuinely getting a firm hold by the middle; still oily and the sugars help a little glazed ginger mix with the half-hearted fruit; **f22** huge degree of natural caramels make for a low key, slightly oily finish; **b23.5** a heaven-sent nose sending you on all kinds of wild goose chases. And but for the mildly lazy finale, this might well have been a Bible a category ward winner. 46.2%. 150 bottles. WB15/106

⫶ **Cadenhead's Small Batch Dalmore Aged 24 Years** bourbon barrels, dist 1989, bott 2013, **(87.5) n23.5 t22 f21 b22.** Starts beautifully both on nose and delivery but the bite and bitterness of the oak wins out towards the end. Some lovely sharp navel orange and custard delights. 46.6%. 312 bottles. WB15/068

⫶ **The Maltman Dalmore Aged 16 Years** sherry finish, cask no. 3221, dist Oct 96, bott Apr 13 **(87.5) n21.5 t23.5 f21.5 b21.** The good news: despite a sherry finish, this is clean and 100% untroubled by sulphur. The bad news: from the slight sweaty armpit nose to the surprisingly fruit toffee finale, it is easy to see that, when bottled, the marrying process was in a state of slight imbalance. Even so, enjoy the spiced dates and the molasses – and all-round, unspoiled moist fruitcakiness: it does have some excellent moments. 46%. sc ncf nc. 298 bottles. WB15/218

⫶ **Montgomerie's Single Cask Collection Dalmore** cask no. 3093, dist 19 Jun 1986, bott Sep 13 **(87.5) n22 t23 f20.5 b22.** A silky-soft offering, with superb citrus on the nose and a wonderfully salivating burst of juicy malt on delivery, backed by toasted fudge. Just a little too bitter at the death, though. 46%. nc ncf sc. WB15/129

Old Malt Cask Dalmore Aged 16 Years refill hogshead, cask no. 9816, dist Oct 96, bott May 2013 **(89) n21.5 t23 f22 b22.5.** Deliciously neat and tidy despite the odd nose. Superb! 50%. nc ncf sc. 371 bottles.

⫶ **Old Particular Highland Dalmore 17 Years Old** refill hogshead, cask no. 10206, dist Oct 1996, bott Jan 2014 **(90) n22** lemon tart with a dash of custard; **t23.5** kerpow...!!! Dalmore denuded at last. A spanking array of top drawer barley notes, all fresh and sparkling allowing full juiciness and depth to show. The barley steals the the show, but the supporting cast of playful, custard cream vanilla are also worthy of a standing ovation; **f22** gentle waves of light spices and citrus; **b22.5** when one finally comes across a Dalmore matured in a decent cask and neither hindered, hidden nor bullied by the opaque fug of caramel, one could almost weep with joy...54.8%. nc ncf sc. 139 bottles. Douglas Laing & Co.

Provenance Dalmore Over 11 Years refill hogshead, cask no. 6879, dist Spring 99, bott Winter 11 **(86) n21.5 t22 f21 b21.5.** From the sweaty armpit nose, you know this is going to be interesting without hitting the heights. Revels in a rich digestive biscuit graininess but the bitter orange finish dashes hopes of further complexity. 46%. nc ncf sc. Douglas Laing & Co.

Provenance Dalmore Over 12 Years refill hogshead, cask no. 9501, dist Summer 2000, bott Spring 2013 **(86) n21 t21.5 f22 b21.5.** Glutinous, tangy and with the intensity of the malt and barley sugar growing attractively along the road. 46%. nc ncf sc. Douglas Laing & Co.

⫶ **Single Cask Collection 1996 Dalmore 17 Year Old** bourbon hogshead/sherry cask finish, dist 1996 **(89.5) n22.5** from the suet pudding school of malt; **t23** superb barley explosion on impact. Gentle gristy tones slowly bend into the vanilla; **f22** much duller, but the oak has a gentle late message; **b22** very little, if any, evidence of the sherry cask finish. And for that we can be truly thankful.... 53.5%. sc. Single Cask Collection.

⫶ **Single Cask Collection 2000 Dalmore 13 Year Old** Bourbon Hogshead/ HOMOK (Willi Opitz) finish, dist 2000 **(90) n23** fizzes and zips with various, though mainly kumquat-style, citrus notes; some attractive salt-buttered toast, too; **t23** deep and pungent delivery, again erring towards light citrus with maybe a touch of delicate, wild strawberry; **f22** spices begin to mount as it dries; **b22** never less than fresh and salivating. Almost like a chewy fruit pastel. 56.3%. sc. Single Cask Collection.

Wemyss 1997 Single Highland "Gooseberry Marmalade" hogshead, dist 1997, bott 2013 **(90) n22 t22.5 f22.5 b23.** A lovely dram for sure. But what on earth is "gooseberry marmalade"? Marmalade, in the English language, is made from citrus, including the peel. The huge Surrey garden in which I spent my formative summers had a great number of gooseberry bushes and I grew up on gooseberry jam made by my mother. And my fridge or larder is seldom out of a commercially made jar of it. Either way, no gooseberries here – jam or "marmalade" - or citrus, either! Apricot and under-ripe greengage...now you're talking...!! 46%. sc. 372 bottles.

DALWHINNIE
Highlands (Central), 1898. Diageo. Working.

Dalwhinnie 15 Years Old db **(95) n24** sublime stuff: a curious mixture of coke smoke and peat-reek wafts teasingly over the gently honied malt. A hint of melon offers some fruit but the caressing malt stars; **t24** that rarest of combinations: at once silky and malt intense, yet at the same time peppery and tin-hat time for the tastebuds, but the silk wins out and a sheen of barley sugar coats everything, soft peat included; **f23** some cocoa and coffee notes, yet the pervading slightly honied sweetness means that there is no bitterness that cannot be controlled; **b24** a malt it is hard to decide whether to drink or bath in: I suggest you do both. One of the most complete mainland malts of them all. Know anyone who reckons they don't like whisky? Give them a glass of this – that's them cured. Oh, if only the average masterpiece could be this good. 43%

Dalwhinnie 25 Years Old Special Release 2012 Rejuvenated American oak hogshead, dist 1987, bott 2012 db **(92) n23.5** toasty with lashings of hickory and maple syrup. A little sappy but the busy saltiness lifts the barley; **t23.5** a busy delivery of light sugars and spice; red liquorice and acacia honey combine beautifully. The spice rises as the oiliness increases; **f22** thins as the impact of the oak lessens. Just the vaguest hint of smoke drifts in; **b23** more from the mountains of Kentucky than central Scotland. Anyone with a bourbon bent and a sweet tooth will adore this. As will bee keepers. 52.1 %. nc ncf. Diageo.

DEANSTON
Highlands (Perthshire), 1966. Burn Stewart Distillers. Working.

Deanston 6 Years Old db **(83) n20 t21 f22 b20.** Great news for those who remember how good Deanston was a decade or two ago: it's on its way back. A delightfully clean dram with its trademark honey character restored. A little beauty slightly undermined by caramel. 40%

Deanston 12 Years Old db **(74) n18 t19 f18.5 b18.5.** It is quite bizarre how you can interchange this with Tobermory in style; or, rather, at least the faults are the same. 46%. ncf.

Deanston Aged 12 Years db **(75) n18 t21.5 f17.5 b18.** The delivery is, for a brief moment, a malty/orangey delight. But the nose is painfully out of sync and finish is full of bitter, undesirable elements. A lot of work still required to get this up to a second grade malt, let alone a top flight one. 46.3%. ncf. Burn Stewart.

Deanston Virgin Oak db **(90) n22.5** does exactly what it says on the tin: absolutely brimming with virgin oak. To the cost of all other characteristics. And don't expect a bourbon style for a second: this is sharp-end tannins where the sugars have their own syrupy point of entry; **t23** now those sugars dissolve with some major oak attached: many years back, I tasted a paste made from roasted acorns and brown sugar...not entirely dissimilar; **f22.5** continues to rumble contentedly in the oakiest possible manner...but now with some fizzy spice; **b22** quirky. Don't expect this to taste anything like Scotch... 46.3%

⁙ **Cadenhead's Small Batch Deanston Aged 19 Years** butts, dist 1994, bott 2014 **(83) n20.5 t21.5 f20 b21.** A syrupy, unsubtle malt which paints on the sugar-coated barley with a spray gun. The odd fruit note, especially some diced, crunchy French apple. But counts for little when the jigsaw has been mis-printed. 56.4%. 846 bottles. WB15/067

Kingsbury Deanston Aged 14 Years hogshead, cask no. 1989, dist 97 **(88) n21 t22.5 f22.5 b22.** A very decent Deanston experience. 55.1%. nc ncf. 281 bottles.

Marks & Spencer Deanston Aged 12 Years db **(84.5) n20.5 t22 f21 b21.** It's been a while since I found so much honeyed malt in a Deanston. Echoes of 20 years ago. 40%. UK.

Marks & Spencer Deanston Aged 17 Years Limited Edition db **(88.5) n20 t23.5 f22.5 b22.5.** Overcomes a taught, off-key nose to open into something full of juice, fruity intrigue. Really enjoyed this one. 46.3%. ncf. 979 bottles.

Master of Malt Deanston Aged 19 Years refill hogshead, dist 16 Dec 92, bott 20 Nov 12 **(86.5) n21.5 t22 f21.5 b21.5.** Technically on the thin side on delivery and finish and possessing a degree of burn. But very hard not to thoroughly enjoy the creamy barley middle and the gamut of sugars surrounding it. A little charmer. 53.4%. sc. 260 Bottles.

⁙ **Old Malt Cask Deanston Aged 18 Years** refill butt, cask no. 10428, dist Apr 96, bott Apr 14, **(73) n19 t19 f17 b18.** Tart and tangy, this was produced some of Deanston's grimmer production days. This, alas, seems to celebrate the fact. 50%. sc. 628 bottles.

⁙ **Robert Graham Deanstown 19 Year Old Highland Malt** hogshead, cask no. 3139, dist 24 Jun 94, bott 13 Nov 13 **(92.5) n23** vague strawberry thinly spread on toast while sugared shredded wheat buckles in the warm milk; **t23.5** a touch of class to the delivery: just so oils really do crank up the massive malt; f22.5 residual muscovado sugars and maple syrup embattle the slight bitterness to the oak; b23.5 warms the heart to see a Deanston showing as well as this. It seems like a very long time ago... 46%. 201 bottles.

⁘ **Signatory Vintage Un-chillfiltered Collection Deanston 1997 Aged 16 Years** refill sherry butt, cask no. 1347, dist 18 Jun 97, bott 05 Nov 13 (89.5) n21 a little weak on the oak front. But devoid of the dreaded S word and some half decent fruit gurgles contentedly; t24 now I didn't expect that! The fruit has combined rather beautifully with a light maple syrup muscovado mix and thrown in some Nice coconut biscuit for good measure. The spices rise with aplomb; f22 the spice carries on its good work as tasted mallows and fruit cake ends mingle with vanilla; b22.5 I'll be honest. I had marked this as an end-of-session potential dud, the last before a meal in order to restore my palate after twinning a less than auspicious distillery with a sherry butt: usually a sure-fire recipe for disaster. But it has twitted me. For both the butt and spirit are above average on both counts and make for enjoyable dramming. I do so love these little surprises! Breakfast is delayed... 46%. nc ncf sc. 786 bottles. WB15/022

That Boutique-y Whisky Company Deanston batch 1 (94) n23 Deanston-by-the-Sea! Where on earth has this salt come from? Sits comfortably with the more usual Perthshire honey....and even a touch of seaweed for the bees to pollinate; t24 massive honey but what works is the complex oak strata which absorbs the silky barley with aplomb; the middle is a very thick dose of malt...gosh! f23 a top-notch cask reverberates with tangy salt and a light butterscotch and honey fade! b24 wow! Not seen Deanston in this kind of nick for about 15 years! I am quite taken aback. Just grab some of that honey...!! 50.8%. 218 bottles.

⁘ **That Boutique-y Whisky Deanston** batch 2 (88) n22 intense malt attractively balanced with chalky oak; t22.5 barley still dominates, even more so now, and bolstered by a surprising degree of oiliness; just after delivery, a brief burst of barley sugar offers the only sweetness on show; f22 oil-lengthened and keeps to the malty but oak-dusty path; b22 something of an oily soul, this. No faulting the crisp and sparkling barley which glistens most notable on delivery but could do with its old honey injection of three decades back — and now seemingly lost — which would have added so much more. 49.6%. 248 bottles. WB15/223

DUFFTOWN
Speyside, 1898. Diageo. Working.

⁘ **Cadenhead's Single Cask Dufftown-Glenlivet Aged 34 Years** sherry butt, dist 1979, bott 2014 (92.5) n22.5 so, after three decades the weightiest spirit of Speyside emerges from a presumably still wet when filled sherry butt. It is a mess: a thick, undecipherable puddin' of a malt. Yet, you know what? With those juicy dates fighting against the grimy oils and the sugars being shovelled in to keep the bitterness out...I rather like it...; t23 massive: filthy on the palate...but those sugars and plums...; f24 and now a soup made mainly of molasses and spice....outrageous! b23 since it arrived in my tasting lab yesterday, this bottle and I have been staring at each other like distrusting old foes wondering who was going to blink first. I remember being at the distillery about 30 years ago and tasting some three- and four- year old and saying "Christ!" to the warehouseman as I sampled the unbelievably oily, dirty whisky which had been placed into my nosing glass. It was then part of Bell's and it had been a long time since any money had been spent on the stills, which were being run into the ground... producing pretty poor distillate. The thing I have learned over the years, though, is that the worse the distillate when young, the better it can be after time has played all kinds of tricks on it. Just look at some of those ancient Fettercairns, for instance. So I give you at the end my preamble...and now I get to work... And, as I suspected, for its myriad faults, its coarseness and whisky depravity...I'd queue for a second glass. Must appeal to the whisky Neanderthal in me. Or maybe we all like a bit of rough now and then... 48%. 216 bottles. WB15/107

Gordon and MacPhail Connoisseurs Choice Dufftown 2002 (84.5) n21 t22 f20.5 b21. Dufftown at its very cleanest. The sugars are full on and spices dip in usefully. Hardly inspirational but will attract barley freaks. 46%. ncf.

⁘ **Gordan & MacPhail Connoisseurs Choice Dufftown 2004** (82.5) n20 t21.5 f20 b21. Srypy thick sugars at first but a dullard by nature. 46%.

⁘ **Old Malt Cask Dufftown Aged 18 Years** refill butt, cask no. 10378, dist Aug 95, bott Mar 14 (83.5) n21 t21.5 f20 b21. Bludgeons the taste buds into submission. Malty to the point of being almost opaque. 50%. sc. 589 bottles.

Old Malt Cask Dufftown Aged 30 Years refill hogshead, cask no. 9272, dist Nov 82, bott Nov 12 (73) n19 t19 f17 b18. Sweet, thick, hot and unimpressive. The house style, in fact. 50%. sc. Douglas Laing & Co. 174 bottles.

Provenance Dufftown Over 13 Years refill hogshead, cask no. 9659, dist Autumn 99. Bott Spring 13 (85) n22 t21.5 f20 b21.5. Typically syrupy and one dimensional for the distillery with only the spices giving the profound molassed malt an alternative vibe. 46%. nc ncf. Douglas Laing & Co.

⁖ **Signatory Cask Strength Collection Dufftown 1997 Aged 15 Years** hogshead, cask no. 19488, dist 09 Dec 97, bott 30 Apr 13 **(83)** n20.5 t21.5 f20 b21. At times you actually feel you are spitting out splinters. Massive oak, but the usual sugary soup offers some kind of counter. 56.1%. nc sc. 309 bottles. WB15/142

Singleton of Dufftown 12 Years Old db **(71)** n18 t18 f17 b18. A roughhouse malt that's finesse-free. For those who like their tastebuds Dufft up a bit... 40%

⁖ **The Singleton of Dufftown "Sunray"** **(77)** n20 t20 f18 b19. One can assume only that the sun has gone in behind a big toffeed cloud. Apparently, according to the label, this is "intense". Yeah: about as intense as a ham sandwich. Only not as enjoyable. db 40%. WB15/121

⁖ **The Singleton of Dufftown "Tailfire"** db **(79)** n20 t20 f19 b20. Tailspin, more like. 40%. WB15/122

EDRADOUR

Highlands (Perthshire), 1837. Signatory Vintage. Working.

Edradour Aged 10 Years db **(79)** n18 t20 f22 b19. A dense, fat malt that tries offer something along the sherry front but succeeds mainly in producing a whisky cloyingly sweet and unfathomable. Some complexity to the finish compensates. 43%

Edradour Ballachin #1 The Burgundy Casks db **(63)** n17 t16 f15 b15. A bitter disappointment in every sense. Were the Burgundy casks sulphur treated? I'd say so. Something completely off-key here. A shocker. 46%

Edradour Ballachin #2 Madeira Matured db **(89)** n22 t22 f23 b22. On the nose and entry I didn't quite get the point here: putting a massively peated malt like this in a Madeira cask is a bit like putting Stan Laural into bed with Marylyn Munro. Thankfully doesn't come out a fine mess and the Madeira certainly has a vital say towards the beautifully structured finale. It works! I feel the hand of a former Laphroaig man at work here. 46%

⁖ **Edradour Ballechin The Discovery Series #3** Port Cask Matured Heavily Peated, First fill port casks db **(88)** n21 a little bit of a smoky-fruit shambles; the peat, as phenolic as anything I've ever encountered, is actually aggressive; t23 eye-watering delivery as the fruit appears to have a chiselled countenance. Mind you, it needs to: the smoke is borderline opaque; f22 the taste buds are beaten into smoky submission...; b22 for Peat Freaks and masochists only... 46%. nc ncf. 6,000 bottles. WB15/033

⁖ **Edradour Ballechin The Discovery Series #4** Oloroso Sherry Cask Matured Heavily Peated, First fill oloroso sherry butts db **(87)** n22.5 simply huge smoke – a peat refinery on fire; t23.5 you cannot but be taken aback by this entirely unique experience: the delivery begins smokily enough, then a wave of phenolic oils grab command; f20 bitter and furry; b21 one of the fattest malts of all time. Just trips with tarry oil... 46%. nc ncf. 6,000 bottles. WB15/034

⁖ **Edradour Ballechin The Discovery Series #5** Marsala Cask Matured Heavily Peated, First fill Marsala hogsheads db **(92)** n23 usual big, soot-dry phenols – almost acidic. The fruit hardly gets a look in...; t23.5 works superbly, with the sugars, phenols and grape sugars working in tandem; f22.5 long with Demerara sugar working hard on the peat; moves into smoked Black Forest Gateaux mode – very Bavarian; b23 challenging at first, not least because the oily spirit takes some navigating, but once you dip your shoulders under the peat, you are in...!!! Complex, well weighted and beautifully formulated. 46%. nc ncf. 6,000 bottles. WB15/035

⁖ **Edradour Ballechin The Discovery Series #6** Bourbon Cask Matured Heavily Peated, First fill bourbon barrels db **(90.5)** n23 seriously dry: substantial peat presence given a pretty clear run other than a light floral sub note; t23 big coppery charge to the smoke: the oils really carry weight and purpose – much more kippers than Arbroath Smokies; f22 smoked cocoa butter; b22.5 Edradour's tiny still give this ultra smoky malt a truly unique fingerprint. 46%. nc ncf. 6,000 bottles. WB15/036

⁖ **Edradour Ballechin The Discovery Series #7** Bordeaux Cask Matured Heavily Peated, First fill Bordeaux hogsheads db **(74)** n20 t21 f16 b17. A sweet, phenolic start...but goes horribly downhill from there... 46%. nc ncf. 6,000 bottles. WB15/037

⁖ **Edradour Ballechin The Discovery Series #8** Sauternes Cask Matured Heavily Peated, First fill sauternes hogsheads db **(82)** n21 t22 f19 b20. A bit like looking at the Mona Lisa through cracked glass. There is something so right with it, yet so very wrong. Massive peat enshrined in what might have been a truly stunning cask. But hardly for a moment do the two twains meet. 46%. nc ncf. 6,000 bottles. WB15/038

⫶⫶· **Edradour Barolo Cask Matured** Barolo hogsheads, dist March/April 06, bott Apr 14 db **(79.5) n19 t21.5 f19 b20.** Never entirely at ease at spirit or maturation level. The wide cut doesn't suit the indisciplined grape 46%. nc ncf. batch number: One, 2450 bottles. WB15/041

⫶⫶· **Edradour Chardonnay Cask Matured** chardonnay hogsheads, dist Dec 2003, bott Sep 2011 db db **(72) n18 t19 f17 b18.** Crushingly dry. Grim. 46%. nc ncf. batch number: One, 1600 bottles. WB15/043

⫶⫶· **Edradour Dougie Maclean's Caledonia Selection Aged 12 Years** db **(91) n23** about as thick as it gets: nose this and fruit is soon dripping off your proboscis. A clean cask, but not sure the initial spirit was entirely spot on. Just can' get enough of those juicy, syrupy dates, though; **t23** genuine intensity now with the tannin matching the fruit blow for blow. Nothing sugars other than molasses could live with this company...and it doesn't; **f22** the lingering oils confirm a wide cut was made those dozen years back; **b23** gosh! Hold on to your hats. This is some ride.... 46%. nc ncf. WB15/044

⫶⫶· **Edradour Port Cask Matured** port hogsheads, dist June/July 2003, bott Mar 14 db **(91.5) n23** wonderful liveliness: the grape is fresh with trace sweetness embracing its more natural dry side; old sweet shops, of the jars of boiled candy variety; **t23.5** one of the lightest delivery I can remember in 30 years of tasting Edradour. Rarely have I seen the sugars so disentangled from the grain and grape; **f22** a little bitterness; slightly pithy as it dries; short; **b23** wonderful malt, make no mistake. Hardly any small still trace, allowing for a more expansive whisky. 46%. nc ncf. batch number: One, 2400 bottles. WB15/042

⫶⫶· **Edradour Sauternes Cask Matured** Sauternes hogsheads, dist Dec 03, bott Feb 13 db **(81) n19 t24 f18 b20.** For a few brief, glorious moments this malt soars to the heights obtained only by great Sauternes casks and looks imperiously down at everything else around. But to get there you have to go through a dodgy take off and an even bumpier landing... 46%. nc ncf. batch number: Three, 2150 bottles. WB15/039

⫶⫶· **Edradour Straight From The Cask Aged 10 Years** sherry butt, cask no. 530, dist 06 Dec 01, bott 21 Nov 12 db **(88.5) n22.5** nutty – a bit like an Harvey's Bristol Cream...only with the kick of a Scottish rather than Spanish mule. Intriguingly, the spice appears more oak – almost bourbon type – than fruit related; **t23** myriad sugars, and no shortage of intense grapey ones, hit early but it is the texture and overall mouth feel which wins the heart; vanillas creep in slowly; **f21** a little furry; **b22** some you know what. But otherwise sweet as a nut... 57.3%. sc. 984 bottles. WB15/051

⫶⫶· **Edradour Straight From The Cask Barolo Cask Finish Aged 10 Years** dist 28 May 02 in hogsheads, disgorged 28 Feb 11, finished in a Barolo hogshead, bott 15 Apr 13 db **(88) n22** between the grape and chunky original spirit, a nose dense enough to create its own gravitational pull... **t22.5** a series of thick, nondescript fruit notes clutter he taste buds; at last a juicy, spice-riddled, blast is detectable; **f22** some Columbian cocoa dulls any last chance of fruity sharpness; **b22** it packs a presence, that's for sure. 58.3%. 423 bottles. WB15/050

⫶⫶· **Edradour Straight From The Cask Burgundy Cask Finish Aged 11 Years** dist 08 May 02 in hogsheads, disgorged 24 Mar 11, finished in a Burgundy hogshead, bott 09 Dec 13 db **(89.5) n23.5** for those who like a little fruit in their spice...; **t22** hits you like a fruity custard tart in the face. The heftiness of the original spirit is never far from the surface...but those spices...! **f22.5** raisins dipped in cocoa; **b21.5** lurches around the palate like Ron Burgundy on a bender. Great fun, though. 58.6%. 429 bottles. WB15/048

⫶⫶· **Edradour Straight From The Cask Chardonnay Cask Finish Aged 12 Years** dist 30 Jun 00 in hogsheads, disgorged 22 Nov 08, finished in a Chardonnay hogshead, bott 11 Apr 13 db **(82.5) n20 t22 f20 b20.5.** Massive grape statement and no shortage of cocoa on the furry finish. But not my type of whisky, I'm afraid, and leaves me cold. 56.3%. 451 bottles. WB15/045

⫶⫶· **Edradour Straight From The Cask Chateauneuf Du Pape Cask Finish Aged 11 Years** dist 28 May 13 in hogsheads, disgorged 28 Feb 11, finished in a Chateauneuf Du Pape hogshead, bott 28 Nov 13 db **(94) n24** a dense nose, a bit like a bag of soft-centred fruit bon bons where one has broken allowing the sticky stuff inside to escape; some delicate salt and pepper raises the game further; **t24** hang on: these are fruit bon bons! A really jammy edge to this, some strawberry and greengage dives into the mix; **f22** forcefully dries as the spices rise and the vanilla gathers; a hint of cocoa and hickory challenges the dying fruit; **b24** had no idea Chateauneuf Du Papa 2002 was this good a vintage.... 57.6%. 440 bottles. WB15/049

⫶⫶· **Edradour Straight From The Cask Marsala Cask Finish Aged 11 Years** dist 28 May 02 in hogsheads, disgorged 28 Feb 11, finished in a Marsala hogshead, bott 04 Oct 13 db **(93.5) n23.5** deep, dry fruit. Seasoned dates and crushed grape seeds; **t24** enormously salivating delivery, tinged with juicy malt as well as the more obvious grape; maple syrup brushes the edges before those more austere grape notes return; **f22.5** remains juicy but doesn't quite live up to the delivery thanks to a late uncompromising bitterness; **b23.5** good to see another sulphur-free wine cask. At its very height, quite stupendous. *58.6%. 603 bottles. WB15/047*

⠿ **Edradour Straight From The Cask Port Wood Finish Aged 13 Years** dist 23 Jan 2001 in hogsheads, disgorged 10 Dec 2010, finished in a port pipe, bott 20 Feb 2014 db **(95) n24** hard to imagine the grape being any more intense, yet opens out slowly. Like an unfurling petal, to reveal not just scalding peppers but soft ribbons of orange-caressed marzipan and Melton Hunt Cake at its most moist; **t24** a posse of sugars round up the heavier fruit notes and keep them quiet, allowing the spices and even barley to infiltrate the juicier elements. Slowly the oils and cocoa arrive...; **f23** undone slightly by the fatness of the spirit, the grape battles on manfully; **b24** one of the greatest Port Finishes for a very long time. *56.3%. 1010 bottles. WB15/046*

⠿ **Edradour Super Tuscan Cask Matured** Super Tuscan hogsheads, dist March/April 06, bott Apr 14 db **(81) n20.5 t23 f18 b19.5**. Not sure what a non-Super cask would have been like. Imbalanced from nose to finish, at least it boasts a rousing chocolate fruit and nut middle. *46%. nc ncf. Batch number: One, 2450 bottles. WB15/040*

⠿ **Edradour Vintage 2006** oloroso sherry cask matured, cask no. 240, dist 1 Jun 06, bott 3 Sep 13 db **(91.5) n24** errrr...oloroso...and about as grapey and cherry fruitcakey as it gets...; no shortage of plum jam and spice, too; **t23** sharp, quivering effect on the palate as a mix of fruit and molasses get to work in earnest; **f21.5** just a little over bitter and toasty: things not quite tickety-boo; **b23** a big malt still dripping with the fresh contents of the handsome sherry butt. *59.2%. sc nc. Cask hand picked by The Whisky Exchange. WB15/282*

Master Of Malt Edradour 27 Years Old Lost Bottlings Series dist 68, bott 95 **(61) n13 t18 f15 b16**. A shocker. Very similar in character to some Littlemill and Glenora I have encountered over the years where way too much soap was stuffed into the still or washback as a calming exercise. Not saying that happened here, of course...*45.8%*

⠿ **Signatory Vintage Un-chillfiltered Collection Edradour 2002 Aged 10 Years** cask no. 464, dist 13 Dec 02, bott 17 Jul 13 **(88.5) n22** moist fruitcake. No shortage of orange peel and dates have been pitched in; **t23** sensuous arrival with a big toasted fudge and raisin back up. Spices are bitty and warming; the dates hinted on the nose arrive in mid stream; **f21** thins quickly; late minor furriness; **b22.5** a much better than average butt for its day. A real small still intensity throughout. *46%. nc ncf sc. 774 bottles. WB15/021*

FETTERCAIRN
Highland (Eastern), 1824. Whyte and Mackay. Working.

Fettercairn 12 Year Old db **(66) n14 t19 f16 b17**. If the nose doesn't get you, what follows probably will...Grim doesn't quite cover it. *40%*

Fettercairn 30 Years Old db **(73) n19 t18 f18 b18**. A bitter disappointment. Literally. *46.3%*

Fettercairn 40 Years Old db **(92) n23** technically, not exactly how you want a 40-y-o to be: a bit like your old silver-haired granny knitting in her rocking chair...and sporting tattoos. But I also have to say there is no shortage of charm, too...and like some old tattooed granny, you know it is full of personality and has a tale to tell... **t24** I was expecting dates and walnuts... and I have not been let down. A veritable date and walnut pie you can chew on until your jaw is numb; the sharp raisiny notes, too, plus a metallic sheen which reminds you of its provenance...; **f22** those burned raisins get just a little more burned...; **b23** yes, everyone knows my views on this distillery. But I'll have to call this spade a wonderfully big, old shovel you can't help loving...just like the memory of me tattooed ol' granny... *40%. 463 bottles.*

Fettercairn 1824 db **(69) n17 t19 f16 b17**. By Fettercairn standards, not a bad offering. Relatively free from its inherent sulphury and rubbery qualities, this displays a sweet nutty character not altogther unattractive – though caramel plays a calming role here. Need my arm twisting for a second glass, though. *40%*

⠿ **Gordon & MacPhail Connoisseurs Choice Fettercairn** dist 1997 , bott 2013 **(83) n21 t21.5 f19.5 b21**. Nutty, milky sweet (a little cloyingly at times, surprise, surprise...) and malty. A bit hot and a little oak bitterness at the death, as well as its usual house tang. That apart, perfectly drinkable. *46%. nc ncf. WB15/143*

⠿ **Hepburn's Choice Fettercairn 2005 Aged 8 Years** refill hogshead, bott 2014 **(79) n19 t21.5 f19 b19.5**. Goodness gracious... I have just been flung back nearly 30 years and I have returned to a Glasgow hotel room, my evening sanctuary while being seconded to Scotland for a national newspaper. I had invested in a bottle of Fettercairn of perhaps this very age in order to try and understand a cloying whisky argument I little agreed with...and here it seems to be again, like a ghost from the past, determined to haunt me and have the last, nagging word. I'll give it credit for its nutty, lopsided consistency over the passing three decades. Thing is: I was no fan of it then. I am still perhaps even less so today. *46%. nc ncf sc. 377 bottles.*

⫶⫶ **Hepburn's Choice Fettercairn Aged 11 Years** refill hogshead, dist 2002, bott 2014 **(79) n19 t20 f20 b20.** Nutty, malty and more rubber than a school pencil case. *46%. nc ncf sc. 384 bottles.*

Malts Of Scotland Fettercairn 1990 bourbon hogshead, cask no. 13004, dist May 90, bott Jan 13 **(69) n16 t18 f17 b18.** I am trying to think of something positive to say about this sickly sweet, off-key mess of a pot still malt. I admit defeat. *51.5%. nc ncf sc. 96 bottles.*

⫶⫶ **Master of Malt Single Cask Fettercairn 17 Years Old** hogshead, dist 30 Oct 95, bott Jul 13 **(85) n22 t23 f19 b21.** By no means the Fettercairn horror show one always fears, despite the trademark rubbery qualities to the tail. The nose and delivery certainly come up trumps with an, at times, malty elegance which is able to make full use of the light molasses on offer. The oak also pitches in with a very acceptable, countering dryness. The finale, though, gives the game away... *57.9%. sc. 294 bottles. WB15/212*

⫶⫶ **Old Malt Cask Fettercairn Aged 18 Years** refill hogshead, cask no. 10314, dist Nov 95, bott Feb 14 **(86) n21 t21.5 f22 b21.5.** Acceptably pleasant. The intense, cloying barley and sugar has been granted a spicy butterscotch and custard pardon by some very decent oak. *50%. sc. 268 bottles.*

Provenance Fettercairn Over 10 Years refill hogshead, cask no. 9307, dist Autumn 02, bott Autumn 12 **(73) n18 t19 f18 b18.** Syrupy sweet, rubbery, heavy duty. About as delicate and sophisticated as dropping a brick on your enemy's toe. *46%. nc ncf sc.*

⫶⫶ **Provenance Fettercairn Over 10 Years** one refill hogshead, cask no. 9653, dist Autumn 2000, bott Spring 2013 **(76) n20 t20 f17.5 b18.5.** Not unpleasant. But nutty, thin and varnish-like particularly towards the finish. For most distilleries, hardly one to write home about. For Fettercairn, a triumph. *46%. nc ncf sc. Douglas Laing & Co.*

⫶⫶ **Provenance Fettercairn Over 10 Years** refill hogshead, cask no. 10329, dist Winter 04, bott Spring 14 **(72) n17 t19 f18 b18.** As I feared: strip all the oak out of a Fettercairn and you can see it in all its naked, rubbery, cloying ugliness. *46%. nc ncf sc.*

⫶⫶ **Signatory Cask Strength Collection Fettercairn 1995 Aged 18 Years** bourbon barrel, cask no. 419, dist 22 Mar 95, bott 24 Oct 13 **(74.5) n21.5 t18.5 f17.5 b18.** The nose offers false hope (a false nose...?) as a genuinely attractive degree of relatively uncluttered barley comes across. But those hopes are dashed the moment the palate is struck and we are thrown back into familiar rubbery, over cloyingly sweet, sticky-bitter territory. Can't blame the bottlers: they tell it as it is. *58%. nc sc. 208 bottles. WB15/139*

GLEN ALBYN
Highlands (Northern) 1846–1983. Diageo. Demolished.

Gordon & MacPhail Rare Vintage Glen Albyn 1976 (96) n22.5 salty and nippy. And the theme thunders into an early Kentuckian drawl, with red liquorice and hickory prominent; **t24.5** I am shaking my head in disbelief. Not through disappointment, but wonder! How can something of this antiquity still fill your mouth with so much juice? The barley still offers a degree of grassiness, though this is camouflaged by the softest bourbon characters I have seen in a long time. The honeycomb is in molten form, as is the vanilla which appears to carry with it a fabulous blend of avocado pear and ulmo honey; **f24.5** a pathetic degree of oaky bitterness tries to interrupt, but it is swept aside by the residual and very complex sugars. There remains some spicy activity and even some Kentuckian red liquorice and hickory, but that South American honey really does the business **b24.5** wow! My eyes nearly popped out of my head when I spotted this in my sample room. Glen Albyns come round as rarely as Scotsman winning Wimbledon. Well, almost. When I used to buy this (from Gordon and MacPhail in their early Connoisseur's Choice range, as it happens) when the distillery was still alive (just) I always found it an interesting if occasionally aggressive dram. This masterpiece, though, is something else entirely. And the delivery really does take us to places where only the truly great whiskies go... *43%*

GLENALLACHIE
Speyside, 1968. Chivas Brothers. Working.

Glenallachie 15 Years Old Distillery Edition db **(81) n20 t21 f19 b19.** Real battle between nature and nurture: an exceptional sherry butt has silk gloves and honied marzipan, while a hot-tempered bruiser lurks beneath. *58%*

⫶⫶ **Hepburn's Choice Glenallachie 2005 Aged 9 Years** sherry butt **(71) n17 t18 f18 b18.** An ample, hideously off-key indicator as to why you'll find this distillery on no true blender's top dressing list. *46%. 299 bottles.*

Provenance Glenallachie Over 11 Years refill hogshead, cask no. 8689, dist Winter 00, bott Autumn 12 **(74) n19 t19.5 f18 b18.5.** Thin, one-dimensional and aggressive: seen more fat on a chip. *46%. nc ncf sc. Douglas Laing & Co.*

GLENBURGIE

Speyside, 1810. Chivas Brothers. Working.

Glenburgie Aged 15 Years bott code L00/129 db (84) n22 t23 f19 b20. Doing so well until the spectacularly flat, bitter finish. Orangey citrus and liquorice had abounded. 46%

Chieftain's Glenburgie 14 Years (86) n21.5 t22.5 f20.5 b21.5. Solid single malt. And the backbone is pure oak. 59.6%

⁘ **Old Malt Cask Glenburgie Aged 16 Years** sherry butt, cask no. 10222, dist Jun 97, bott Dec 13 (68) n16 t18 f16 b18. You know that neighbour whose cat keeps crapping on your lawn? I think I've just found his Christmas present for you... Just awful oak. What more can you say? 50%. nc ncf sc. 449 Bottles.

⁘ **Old Particular Speyside Glenburgie Aged 18 Years** refill hogshead, cask no. 10277, dist Jun 95, bott Mar 14 (86.5) n21.5 t23 f21 b21. An oily, intense beastie at its best shortly after delivery when the malt is piled on thick and with syrupy intent. Elsewhere, though, fails to develop as it might. 48.4%. nc ncf sc. 318 bottles.

⁘ **The Pearls of Scotland Glenburgie 1995 17 Year Old** cask no. 6281, dist Dec 95, bott Nov 13 (92) n22 a few apples in the straw; t23.5 how can a whisky show such intensity, yet hardly stretches itself? The delivery is a little juicy but the coconut-biscuit oakiness comes all the way from Nice; the sugars settle early, as do some pounding spices; f23 really lovely oils stay on the biscuit theme, but now a style from Brazil...; b23.5 nonchalantly superb. 54.1%

Provenance Glenburgie Over 12 Years refill hogshead, cask no. 8015, dist Spring 99, bott Winter 12 (82.5) n20 t21.5 f20.5 b20.5. Fizzes and frolics on the palate, though it is the simplistic barley doing all the work. 46%. nc ncf sc. Douglas Laing & Co.

⁘ **Signatory Cask Strength Collection Glenburgie 1983 Aged 29 Years** hogshead, cask no. 9820, dist 23 Oct 83, bott 10 Jul 13 (96.5) n24 gorgeously estery with all kinds of honeyed apple notes drifting about the glass with chunkier spiced muscovado, It is as if ulmo and manuka honey has been mixed and then set solid...; t24.5 give yourself about twenty minutes for this one to pan out on the palate: the first half dozen notes almost defy description as nothing appears to want to take the lead; the mouth feel is luxurious to the point of eroticism, the weight of the sugars are just about perfect with a hypnotic alternation between toasty liquorice and lighter acacia honey; the mid ground is a see-sawing of sugars (and even a degree of grist!) and oak, with a slow introduction of spice; f24 a little tangy at first, but this is checked as a spiced ulmo honey note hoves into view and the oiles congregate to block out anything negative; a little pineapple juice and few other semi wxotic fruit notes announce that great age is on display here...; b24 seriously asks the question: why has Glenburgie, like Clynelish, never been made into a mainstream malt. Here is a classic example as to why as it is the first commercial bottling of its matured spirit I have seen in a while which properly reflects the quality of the blending samples I see in my lab. If you see one of these guys, don't leave the shop without it... 53.4%. nc sc. 197 bottles. WB15/141

⁘ **Signatory Vintage Single Malt Glenallachie 1996 Aged 16 Years** hogsheads, cask no. 5235+5244, dist 17 Oct 96, bott 22 Feb 13 (89) n22 polished barley; t23 barley sugar with a real twinkle; f22 gisty even towards the finish; good late butterscotch; b22 Glenallachie this ship shape is a collectors' item. As clean as it gets. 43%. nc. 827 bottles. WB15/009

⁘ **Signatory Vintage Single Malt Glenallachie 1995 Aged 17 Years** hogsheads, cask no. 6452+6453, dist 13 Jun 95, bott 05 Mar 13 (87.5) n22 t22 f21 b21.5. A little extra oil diminishes the more telling aspects of the barley. The nose may suggest some kind of peppery celery, but the delivery never moves far from simple malt. Good spices but needs to escape the vanilla skirt tails. 43%. nc. 882 bottles. WB15/008

⁘ **The Single Malts of Scotland Glenallachie 21 Years Old** bourbon barrel, cask no. 588, dist 20 Feb 92, bott 13 Sep 13 (91.5) n22.5 a touch of exotic fruit mixing with more prosaic diced pear; t23.5 big kick to the delivery (as in the tradition of the distillery) but fascinating blend of heather and ulmo honey; red liquorice and a hint of hickory: well balanced and complex; f22.5 an outstanding malt finale despite the oaky attention; b23 good example of a malt that's a bit rubbish when young showing what's for in old age. 47.9%. 235 bottles. WB15/342

⁘ **That Boutique-y Whisky Glenburgie** batch 1 (90.5) n22 green barley; fresh with apple and barley water; t24 fabulously salivating delivery when the malt is juicy and pitch-perfect. The sugars are refined – in both senses of the word – and play second fiddle to the ultra-intense malt; f22 a slow movement towards oak-induced butterscotch tart – with the emphasis on the tart...; b22.5 always a bit of a lucky dip with bottled versions of this distillery: very rarely match the consistency experienced in the blending lab. This one shows all its malty cards. 49%. 183 bottles. WB15/222

GLENCADAM

Highlands (Eastern), 1825. Angus Dundee. Working.

Glencadam Aged 10 Years db **(95) n24** crystal clarity to the sharp, ultra fresh barley. Clean, uncluttered by excessive oak, the apparent lightness is deceptive; the intensity of the malt carries its own impressive weight and the citrus note compliments rather than thins. Enticing; **t24** immediately zingy and eye-wateringly salivating with a fabulous layering of sweet barley. Equally delicate oak chimes in to ensure a lightly spiced balance and a degree of attitude; **f23** longer than the early barley freshness would have you expecting, with soft oils ensuring an extended, tapering, malty edge to the gentle, clean oak; **b24** sophisticated, sensual, salivating and seemingly serene, this malt is all about juicy barley and balance. Just bristles with character and about as puckeringly elegant as single malt gets...and even thirst-quenching. My God: the guy who put this one together must be a genius, or something... 46%

Glencadam Aged 12 Years Portwood Finish db **(89.5) n22.5 t22.5 f22 b22.5.** After coming across a few disappointing Port finishes in recent weeks, just wonderful to experience one as you would hope and expect it to be. 46%

Glencadam Aged 14 Years Oloroso Sherry Cask Finish bott May 10 db **(95) n24** pinch me: I'm dreaming. Oloroso exactly how it should be: classically clean with a dovetailing of dry and sweeter grape notes which are weighty, but not heavy enough to crush the lighter barley and vanillas from adding to the sumptuous and elegant mix; **t23.5** mouth-filling with firstly fat grape then a second flavour round of spices and custardy vanillas; **f24** much drier now with the accent on the barley but still that light spice persists, actually increasing in weight and effect as it goes along; **b23.5** what a total treat. Restores one's faith in Oloroso whilst offering more than a glimpse of the most charming infusion of fruit imaginable. 46%

Glencadam Aged 15 Years db **(90.5) n22.5** soft kumquats mingle with the even softer barley. A trace of drier mint and chalk dust points towards the shy oak. Harmonious and dovetails beautifully; **t23** sharp, juicy barley - almost fruity - fuses with sharper oak. The mouth-watering house style appears to fatten out as gentle oils emerge and then give way for a spicy middle; **f22** long, with those teasing, playful spices pepping up the continued barley theme. Dries as a 15 year old ought but the usual bitterness is kept in check by the prevailing malt; **b23** the spices keep the taste buds on full alert but the richness and depth of the barley defies the years. Another exhibition of Glencadam's understated elegance. Some more genius malt creation... 46%

Glencadam Aged 21 Years "The Exceptional" bott May 10 db **(81) n21.5 t22 f17.5 b20.** For a little distillery with a reputation for producing a more delicate malt this is one big whisky. Sadly, the finish is out of kilter, for the delivery is a knife and fork job, offering some extraordinary variations on a fudgy-maple syrup theme which promises much. 46%

Glencadam Aged 21 Years "The Exceptional" bott 2011 db **(94) n23.5** just so sexy! The sugars have a sparkle in their eye while the malt carries a lemon sharpness which breaks up the heavier aromas. A nose to take a good 10-15 minutes with, as the clarity allows you to see a long way; **t24** the sugars show first. But here there is more complexity: almost a step ladder of intensity. As it climbs, it gets a little heavier in oils, eventually taking on a barley-themed fudge; the whole show is in slow motion, with the odd, short-lived burst of spice, and a very lightweight fruitcake richness; **f23** long, now surprising spice-free and sugar-softened with the accent very much on the vanilla; **b23.5** this distillery is emerging out of the shadows from its bad old Allied days as one of the great Scottish single malt distilleries. So good is some of their whisky, this "exceptional" bottling is almost becoming the norm. 46%. nc ncf.

Glencadam 30 Years Old Single Cask 1982 Limited Edition cask no. 730, dist 10 Jun 82, bott Oct 12 db **(96) n25** try finding the nose of a Glencadam — or any Highland malt - in better shape. Even after three decades, the oak is content to share equal status with the still lemon-fresh barley and pitches in with quiet hints of eucalyptus, kumquat, the mist of distant smoke and exotic fruit. Impossible to find a nose more stable or subtle showing magnificent balance and poise throughout: perfection. **t24** the oak is a little more upfront on delivery, but there is also a wave of delicate peat of surprising, if brief, intensity bursting onto the scene before vanishing under the still juicy barley and richer cocoa tones; **f23** the expected vanillas surface, with the cocoa dust upping in percentages; a few late oils develop to ensure a lubricated, longer finale than first seemed possible; **b24** a rare bottling from a country at war. This was distilled in the very final days of the Falklands War when the conflict was at its most ferocious. Anyone finding a bottle of this can raise a glass to honour the memory to the gallant who are no longer with us. On both sides. 46%. nc ncf sc.

⋅⋅⋅ **Abbey Whisky Glencadam Aged 22 Years Limited Edition Release** dist 1991, bott 2014 **(92) n22.5** a pretty old but unspoiled cask at work allows the barley maximum freedom at least cost to its freshness. A little toasted yam is on offer to represent age, but the grassy gristiness remains intact; **t24** absolutely sublime delivery with the barley offering a sharpness which is as eye-watering as it is vivid; the spices which follow are the perfect counter point; the maple syrup appears to crystallise; **f22** a little glassy with a big sheen to the mouth feel; a little bitterness creeps in, but there is enough barley sugar about to do the job; **b23.5** in the right conditions this is one of the most salivating malts in the world. This sparkling little gem is a wonderful exponent. Fresh-faced and adorable. 55.3%.

Berry's Own Selection Glencadam 1991 cask no. 4762, bott 2012 **(95.5) n24** it is a warm summer's day outside, and inside, in the cool, I have a glass of fruit salad: freshly diced Somerset apples and Worcestershire pears, fully ripened and dripping with juice; to set them off, a little nutmeg and allspice have given them a dry spiciness...; **t24.5** one of the deliveries of the year! The eye-closingly, low-sighingly impact is an explosion of livewire, juicy fruit. Still with pears, maybe now some cherry and yellow plum. A thick custardy vanilla tops the lot while the spices quiver...; **f23** dark sugars fend off the hickory thrust of the oak; buttery caramels try to soften things. But those warming spices will have their way; **b24** just startlingly beautiful. 53.9%. nc ncf sc.

⋰ **Berry's Own Selection Glencadam 1991 Aged 22 Years** cask no. 4765, bott 2014 **(95) n23** delicate barley with a hint of gooseberry; a distant hint of Trebor mints; **t24** gorgeously refreshing, outrageously sharp yet still a gooseberry theme, though the barley and, later, chocolate limes offer complexity; **f23.5** the oak has spoken and speaks as dry as dust; **b24.5** oh, if only Brechin City could play football as well as its next door neighbour, Glencadam, makes whisky....Champions League: bring it on...! 53.3%. ncf ncf. WB15/249

⋰ **Gordon & MacPhail Connoisseurs Choice Glencadam** dist 1991, bott 2013 **(88) n21.5** just a little over reliant on vanilla and natural caramel; **t23** much more life on delivery: a mix of citrus and crisp sugars sets the tone; soft but with excellent spice; **f21.5** the spices overcome the Allied bitterness; **b22** the limitations of the oak prevent you from see Glencadam at full throttle. Some lovely moments, though. 46%. nc ncf. WB15/150

⋰ **Hepburn's Choice Glencadam 2004 Aged 10 Years** refill hogshead, dist 2004, bott 2014 **(87.5) n21.5 t22 f22 b22.** As one dimensional whiskies go, this is up there with the best of them: in being both delicious...and one dimensional. Actually, I suppose the big spice kick late on is a second dimension. Otherwise, it's the house style juicy barley at its new-make juiciest as the oak from this third fill cask barely registers at all. 46%. nc ncf sc. 177 bottles.

Old Malt Cask Glencadam Aged 14 Years refill butt, cask no. 9633, dist Dec 98, bott Mar 13 **(86.5) n20 t22.5 f22 b22.** The nose is hardly a turn on but there is enough energy in both the cask and barley to make for a mouth-watering interlude. Good body and delicate spice, too. 50%. sc. Hunter Laing & Co Ltd. 256 bottles.

⋰ **Old Malt Cask Aged 18 Years** refill hogshead, cask no. 4581, dist Nov 95, bott Feb 14 **(90) n22.5** apples and pears....with the accent on the pears; **t23** gets the sugars in early and, better still, makes them of a gristy type. Which means that the ever-growing oak is comfortably contained and the complexity increases...; the barley is juicy despite the years and the spices busiest early on; **f22** some very clever oils ensure a dessert feel to the finale, which includes some sugary diced coconut; **b22.5** creamy, complex and luxurious. Both well made and matured. 50%. sc. 162 bottles.

Provenance Glencadam Over 8 Years refill hogshead, cask no. 9484, dist Spring 2004, bott Winter 2013 **(80) n20 t21 f19 b20.** Decent barley versus under par cask. 46%. nc ncf.

Provenance Glencadam Over 14 Years refill butt, cask no. 9634, dist Winter 98, bott Spring 13 **(89.5) n22 t23 f22 b22.5.** Impossible to fault. 46%. nc ncf sc.

GLENCRAIG

Speyside, 1958. Chivas Brothers. Silent.

Cadenhead Glencraig 31 Years Old bourbon, dist 81, bott 12 **(89) n23 t22 f22 b22.** Time warp whisky. The last time I tasted Glencraig like this was probably in the late 1980s or very early 1990s. It is a whisky from a dead distillery which appears frozen in time: a ghostly spirit in your glass. 50.8%. sc. 186 bottles.

GLENDRONACH

Highlands, 1826. The BenRiach Distillery Co. Working.

The GlenDronach Aged 8 Years "Octarine" db **(86.5) n23.5 t23 f19 b21.** Juicy yet bitter: a bipolar malt offering two contrasting characters in one glass. 46%. nc ncf.

The GlenDronach 12 Years Old db **(92) n22** some pretty juicy grape in there; **t24** silky delivery with the grape teaming with the barley to produce the sharpest delivery and follow through you can imagine: exceptionally good weight with just enough oils to make full use of the delicate sweetness and the build towards spices and cocoa in the middle ground is a wonderful tease; **f22.5** dries and heads into bitter marmalade country; **b23.5** an astonishingly beautiful malt despite the fact that a rogue sherry butt has come in under the radar. But for that, this would have been a mega scorer: potentially an award-winner. Fault or no fault, seriously worth discovering this bottling of this too long undiscovered great distillery 43%

The GlenDronach Aged 12 Years "Original" db (86.5) n21 t22 f22 b21.5. One of the more bizarre moments of the year: thought I'd got this one mixed up with a German malt whisky I had tasted earlier in the day. There is a light drying tobacco feel to this and the exact same corresponding delivery on the palate. That German version is distilled in a different type of still; this is made in probably the most classic stillhouse on mainland Scotland. Good, enjoyable whisky. But I see a long debate with distillery owner Billy Walker on the near horizon, though it was in Allied's hands when this was produced. 43%

The GlenDronach Aged 12 Years db (83) n20 t21 f20.5 b20. Glendronach at 12 is a whisky which has long intrigued me...for the last three decades, in fact. Always felt Allied had problems dealing with it, though when it was right it was sumptuous. Here it is a distance from being right: odd tobacco notes creeping into the fray, though that rings a bell with this distillery as I'm sure the old "Original" showed a similar trait. A very decent malty middle but elsewhere it flounders somewhat. 43%. nc ncf.

The GlenDronach Original Aged 12 Years Double Matured db (88) n23 t21 f22 b22. Vastly improved from the sulphur-tainted bottling of last year. In fact, their most enjoyable standard distillery bottling I've had for many years. But forget about the whisky: the blurb on the back is among the most interesting you are likely to find anywhere. And I quote: "Founder James Allardice called the original Glendronach, 'The Guid Glendronach'. But there's no need to imitate his marketing methods. The first converts to his malt were the 'ladies of the night' in Edinburgh's Canongate!" Fascinating. And as a professional whisky taster I am left wondering: did they swallow or spit... 40%

The GlenDronach 14 Years Old Sauternes Finish db (78.5) n18 t22 f19 b19.5. That unique Sauternes three dimensional spiced fruit is there sure enough...and some awesome oils. But, with so much out of key bitterness around, not quite I had hoped for. 46%. nc ncf.

The GlenDronach 14 Years Old Virgin Oak db (87) n22.5 t22 f21 b21.5. Charming, pretty, but perhaps lacking in passion... 46%. nc ncf.

The GlenDronach 15 Years Old db (77.5) n19 t18.5 f20 b20. The really frustrating thing is, you can hear those amazingly brilliant sherry butts screaming to be heard in their purest voice. Those alone, and you could, like the 12-y-o, have a score cruising over the 95 mark. I can't wait for the next bottling. 46%

The GlenDronach 15 Years Old db (83) n20 t22 f20 b21. Chocolate fudge and grape juice to start then tails off towards a slightly bitter, dry finish. 40%

The GlenDronach 15 Years Old Moscatel Finish db (84) n19 t22.5 f21.5 b21. Such is the intensity of the grape, its force of life, it makes a truly remarkable recovery from such a limited start. But it is hard to be yourself when shackled... 46%. nc ncf.

The GlenDronach 15 Years Old Tawny Port Finish db (84.5) n21 t22 f20.5 b21.5. Quite a tight fit for the most part. But when it does relax, especially a few beats after delivery, the clean fruit fairly drips onto the palate. 46%. nc ncf.

The GlenDronach Aged 15 Years "Revival" db (88.5) n22 t23 f21.5 b22. Unambiguously Scottish... A fantastically malty dram. 46%

The GlenDronach 18 Years Old db (96.5) n24 groaning under the weight of sublime, faultless sherry and peppers; t24 puckering enormity as the saltiness thumps home. Black forest Gateaux complete with cherries and blended with sherry trifle. The spices have to be tasted to be believed. The sugars range from Demerara to light molasses; f24 again the sugars are in perfect position to ramp up the sweetness, but the grape, vanilla and spices are the perfect foil; b24.5 the ultimate sherry cask whisky. Faultless and truly astounding! 46%. nc ncf.

The GlenDronach Aged 18 Years "Allardice" db (83.5) n19 t22 f21 b21.5. Huge fruit. But a long-running bitter edge to the toffee and raisin sits awkwardly on the palate. 46%

⸭ **GlenDronach Batch 10 1995 18 Years Old** Pedro Ximenez sherry puncheon, cask no. 3025, dist 25 Oct 95 db (88.5) n22.5 tight, but somewhat sweeter, more gentle and prune-like than its sister PX bottlings; t22 some disquiet on delivery as the sugars and oak seem ill-at-ease. A brief dose of spice and caressing fruit calm matters; f22 dries, though mainly in a vanilla direction; b22 yippee for the sulphur-free sherry butt. But PX whisky can labour a point somewhat... 51.1%. sc.

⸭ **GlenDronach Batch 10 1996 18 Years Old** Pedro Ximenez sherry puncheon, cask no. 1487, dist 16 Feb 96 db (94) n23 oddly enough, this displays both youth and unusual old age in equal measures: definitely a strand of eucalyptus amid the vibrant, juicy grape; t23.5 having been worn down by the deathly plod of dryness marching from one end of a PX whisky to the other, rather taken aback by the vitality of the grape, the confidence of the sugars – some surprisingly gristy – and the complexity of the layering of the fruit...; f23.5 dries, but well within its own structure and with oak-induced spice and mocha really taking up important position; **b24** I hold my hand up and admit I am surprised by the excellence of this whisky. An exercise in layering and elegance. For once the sugars are soft enough to allow the whisky to breathe. 54.1%. sc.

⁘ **GlenDronach Batch 10 1994 19 Years Old** Pedro Ximenez sherry puncheon, cask no. 326, dist 16 Dec 94 db (**92.5**) **n21** typically tight and non-expansive...the PX calling card on the nose. As you have guessed, I am not a fan, though it is the nature of the beast...; **t23.5** among the most sharp, salivating deliveries you'll find this year; for once there appears to be a malty element to this and maybe it is this which really makes the complexity levels almost jump off the scale. The mid ground is a touch nutty with good vanilla and clean, even interplay between malt and fruit; spices buzz contendedly; **f24** a light spiced throbbing does no harm. Genuine sophistication here with a dry peachy tone slightly lightening the hefty grape mood while the sugars dovetail between light grist and thinned muscovado; **b24** if only the nose could be a little less unforgiving and expansive we'd have a stunning all rounder of a sherry butt. Again, absolutely sulphur-free. 53.5%. sc.

⁘ **GlenDronach Batch 10 1994 19 Years Old** Pedro Ximenez sherry puncheon, cask no. 3397 dist 23 Sep 1994 db (**89.5**) **n21** astonishingly estery and a bit of the dunder pit about this...; **t23** a kind of thicker version of cask 326, but with a less relaxed attitude towards the sugars; **f23** dry: almost hickory infused grape; **b22.5** more than a single element of this had me whizzing back to Jamaica. A degree of high ester rum here and there. But one wnders: how can such a sweet wine create such a dry whisky? 53.8%. sc.

The GlenDronach 21 Years Old db (**91.5**) **n23.5** thumping sherry of the old fruitcake school; a serious number of toasty notes including hickory of a bourbon style; **t23.5** no less lush delivery than the nose portends; the follow up layerings of burnt raisin and cremated fudge are pretty entertaining; **f22** like burnt toast, a touch of bitterness at the death; **b22.5** a quite unique slant on a 21-year-old malt: some aspects appear very much older, but some elements of the grape occasionally reveal a welcome youth. Memorable stuff. 48%. nc ncf.

⁘ **GlenDronach Batch 10 1993 21 Years Old** Oloroso sherry butt, cask no. 494, dist 19 Feb 93 db (**96.5**) **n23.5** a nose I used to enjoy in the warehouses of Macallan back in the early '90s. The grape is intense and clear, soft and pulling its finger towards itself, indicating that you must follow...how can you not...? **t24.5** this is where you come close to swooning: the butt is, indeed, faultless. No sulphur ambush here: instead just a complex and, frankly, mind-blowing procession of fruit notes of varying intensity and sweetness, seekigly topped with spiced butterscotch; **f24** the chewiness continues...the spice continues...the grape still offers both depth and juice...and a little vanilla remds you of its age...; **b24.5** yet another faultless sherry butt from Glendronach with not an atom of sulphur. I must be dreaming, or, miraculously, I have found myself back amongst the great sherried whiskies of 25 years ago... Now, compare this to the 1992 cask 199 Glendronach and you will see how far Scotch whisky has descended in a single generation. And why I am at war with the SWA and the apologist self-styled "whisky writers" and publishers and know-nothing, worthless, egocentric bloggers who cover up this shocking decline. 55.8%. sc.

⁘ **GlenDronach Batch 10 1992 22 Years Old** Oloroso sherry butt, cask no. 199, dist 29 May 92 db (**68.5**) **n17.5 t19 f15 b17.** A sherry butt of its time, alas... 59.4%. sc.

⁘ **GlenDronach Batch 10 1991 22 Years Old** PedroXimenez sherry puncheon, cask no. 1346, dist 02/11/1991db (**91.5**) **n22** held in a molassed sugar and dry, pip-infested grape concentrate embrace, the malt is nowhere to be seen...; **t23** much softer delivery with an intense under-ripe greengage tartness blending in well with the more expansive molasses; grape juice begins to spill freely while the sugars lighten in tone; **f23.5** as the grape wears off a Danish marzipan in dark chocolate mask is worn; **b23** a delicious clean sherry butt with no sulphury hanky-panky whatsoever. 52.1%. sc.

⁘ **GlenDronach Batch 10 1990 24 Years Old** PX sherry puncheon, cask no. 2970, dist 13/06/90 db (**94**) **n23** low key. A kind of toffee and raisin thing going on; also, a bag of those liquorice allsorts with the coffee-coloured sugar bits; the vaguest hint of something smoky, too; **t23.5** the oak strikes first and pretty hard. Enough grape and spice is around to cushion the blow. There is also a controlled explosion of sugars, plus – surprisingly - a little ulmo and heather honey. Vanilla dominates the middle; even a tad earthy; **f23.5** slightly angled and skew, not least because of the unexpected earthiness. The usual tight sugars are refusing to straighten the picture but the praline-lined caramel wafer works wonders; **b24** faultless sherry butt and a whisky which never quite works out the direction it is headed. Which kind of equals complexity. And makes for a very enjoyable experience....and a top rate malt. 51.3%. sc.

The GlenDronach Grandeur Aged 31 Years db (**94.5**) **n23.5** dry, mildly peppery vanilla; crushed golden raisin counter-plot; **t24** spice-dusted grapes explode on the palate on entry;

the mouth-feel plays a key role as the early lushness carries the fruit only so far before it begins to break up, allowing a fabulous spicy complexity to develop; **f23.5** beautiful intertwining between those golden raisins and coffee. The spices are never far away...; **b23.5** just one hell of an alpha sherry butt. 45.8%

The GlenDronach Aged 33 Years oloroso db **(95) n24 t24 f23 b24.** Want to know what sherry should really taste like: invest in a bottle of this. This is a vivid malt boasting spellbinding clarity and charm. A golden nugget of a dram, which would have been better still at 46%. 40%

⁙ **GlenDronach Batch 10 2002 12 Years Old** Pedro Ximenez sherry puncheon, cask no. 1500, dist 11 Jun 02 db **(94.5) n23** another clean butt and a less than dogmatic insistence on tight, humourless sugar-crushed lines. Instead there is enticing plum jam, the vaguest hint of malt and a spreading of molten muscovado sugar; the roast horse (not sweet) chestnut is an interesting addition; **t24** yea gods! A sweat PX Glendronach!!! And beautifully so: with fingers of lightly molassed muscovado caressing in all directions, the spices massaging teasingly and the oak proferring red liquorice; the fruit takes a back seat, but you are aware in the rear view mirror; **f23** dries but now towards dark liquorice and Black Jacks; **b24** confirmation, were it required that PX usually feels far more at home alongside younger malt that the old stuff. Quite brilliant. 56.7%. sc.

The GlenDronach Cask Strength batch 2 Oloroso & Pedro Ximenez sherry casks db **(94) n23** nosing this without aid of any info on this bottling. But this is a very strange maturation combination, as it appears to have had more than a single life; a tightness suggest some possible PX involvement but the over-ripe greengage and burnt sultana is profound; about heavy ester, coffee style not uncommon in rums (another PX nod); **t24.5** definitely PX (he says, not overly sure at all). Again there is a crispness to the sugars unique to that kind of maturation; but really it is the mix of pure Panama coffee and the milky mocha which knocks you backwards: this really is some mouthful, for the grape contains pips, skin the lot....a bit like a Valpolicella Ripasso on steroids...; **f23** the vaguest hint of something furry from a slightly flawed cask. But even so, such is the intensity to the dried grape skins, enclosed in a light cocoa case, that the damage is minimal; **b23.5** for those who like their sherried malts to take not a single prisoner. Immense, magnificent and quite unique in flavour profile. 55.2%. nc ncf.

⁙ **GlenDronach Cask Strength Batch 3** db **(90) n21.5** very tight and not exactly finding the balance it sought. Dry for all the obvious fruitiness, with a distinctly crushed pip edge...in some ways closer to a Cognac style than whisky; improves and opens a little after about 20 minutes airing; **t23** again, tight on delivery. When it does relax, it is too slowly allowing only a gradual release of juice and welcome sugars. The spices do pulse attractively throughout and man mark the sugars; **f22.5** so dry. Again back to a pithy countenance with the brief flirtation with Nicuaguan [spelling?] coffee. The sugars have been soundly defeated; **b23** after last year's Batch 2, I had laid a knife and fork out in my lab for this and tucked a napkin into my shirt. However, this proved just a little more aloof, austere and sophisticated. 54.9%.

⁙ **GlenDronach Grandeur 24 Year Old Batch 5** db **(93.5) n23** a busybody nose: fussing around the oak one moment, some traces of toasted malt the next....; **t24** a lush delivery, as soft as you like. Thick, almost syrupy malt and then a constant pulse of spice which warms by the moment; **f23** spiced butterscotch tart; and rather tart towards the finale, too...; **b23.5** one to stand your spoon up in. Enormous whisky. 48.9%.

The GlenDronach Single Cask 1971 Aged 42 Years batch 8, Pedro Ximenez sherry puncheon, cask no. 1246, dist 15 Feb 71, bott May 13 db **(92.5) n22** spiced toffee apple; creosote drying next door; **t23.5** the oak doesn't wipe its feet before entering. But the wall of robust fudgy sugar and treacle is up to absorbing any excess. Busy and chewy; **f23.5** much more settled and last some distance. A light build up of spice turns this even more into a fruity boiled cough sweet; **b23.5** the PX cask leaves so little room for the malt to get a word in. The spices, though, make this when it could so easily have just tipped over the oaky edge. Curiously delicious and different. 44.6%. nc ncf sc.

The GlenDronach Single Cask 1990 Aged 22 Years batch 8, Pedro Ximenez sherry puncheon, cask no. 2971, dist 13 Jun 90, bott May 13 db **(86) n21 t22.5 f21 b21.5.** Although a relatively healthy puncheon, there is tightness here where the sugars, for all their intense fruit and fudginess, strangle other development. Enjoyable. But... 50.8%. nc ncf sc.

The GlenDronach Single Cask 1991 Aged 21 Years batch 8, Pedro Ximenez sherry puncheon, cask no. 5409, dist 22 Nov 91, bott May 13 db **(81) n20 t21 f20 b20.** A steady stream of treacle. 49.8%. nc ncf sc.

The GlenDronach Single Cask 1992 Aged 19 Years batch 7, Oloroso sherry butt, dist 92, bott 12 db **(85) n22 t21.5 f20 b21.5.** Distinctly nutty, with walnuts shining on the nose. Very dry and oaky throughout with the grape helped along with some busy spice. 57.8%. nc ncf sc.

The GlenDronach Single Cask 1992 Aged 21 Years batch 8, oloroso sherry butt, cask no. 145, dist 22 May 92, bott May 13 db **(96) n23.5** excellent balance between the lightweight spice and the grape; citrus darts in and out to ensure subtlety while the heavier oak offer ballast; **t24.5** the delivery of dreams: as near as damn it perfect weight with the grape as juicy as you like and the balancing oils full of malty intent. The sugars are molassed but thin enough for the buttery vanillas to make it to the middle; **f24** much lighter, with a sultana-laced butterscotch sign off; **b24** call me old fashioned, but I really do think there is a vast difference in the quality between whisky matured in good oloroso and PX. The trouble with PX is that it is so intense it often snuffs out the complexity which can make a good whisky great. Here, you can see so many aspects of the malt which has been lost in previous vintages: this is sherried Highland malt of the very highest calibre. 58.1%. nc ncf sc.

The GlenDronach Single Cask 1993 Aged 20 Years batch 8, oloroso sherry butt, cask no. 3, dist 15 Jan 93, bott May 13 db (**90.5**) **n22** pretty heavy and tight. But at its best, a fruitcake on steroids; **t24** melt in the mouth – while your mouth melts into the malt thanks to the spices; sublime range of sugars, topped with manuka honey and dates; **f21.5** a little furry and dull towards the end; **b23** a very slight blemish on the butt, but there are enough stunning moments to make this one to savour. 52.9%. nc ncf sc.

The GlenDronach Single Cask 1994 Aged 19 Years batch 8, oloroso sherry butt, cask no. 101, bott May 13 db (**96**) **n24** a half hour nosing job, this. Apart from the crisp toffee apple and pepper and steamed ginger spice, just look out for the interaction of the bourbon-style liquorice and carrot juice; ulmo honey is on the prowl, also; **t24.5** that is perfect weight and an equally perfect match between the silky fruit and the spice and vanilla led oak; heather honey and molasses thicken the fruitcake; **f23.5** back to ulmo honey and butterscotch, with a confident sultana thread and continuing spice; **b24** proof that great, unspoiled sherry butts were getting into Scotland during this period. And what proof! Magnificent. 58.4%. nc ncf sc.

The GlenDronach Single Cask 1996 Aged 17 Years batch 8, Pedro Ximenez sherry puncheon, cask no. 1490, dist 16 feb 96, bott May 13 db (**76**) **n19 t20 f18 b19**. Syrupy and too many spent matches. 53.1%. nc ncf sc.

The GlenDronach Single Cask 2002 Aged 10 Years batch 8, Pedro Ximenez sherry puncheon, cask no. 1988, dist 3 Jul 02, bott May 13 db (**94.5**) **n23.5** probably the cleanest PX puncheon I have ever nosed that's available commercially. Dense, of course. But sufficiently light enough to allow a little coffee and spice to wander in and out; **t23** quite feminine? Sugars and spice and all things nice...; **f24** where the delivery jars sensationally for a moment, this is probably the highlight: the toasted sugars come through in varying degrees of intensity, as does the pulsing spice. Is there even a hint of malt in there...? My imagination, surely...; **b24** a superior PX cask in that it is not so heavy as to blot out some of the more quixotic elements of the whisky and is as clean as a whistle and as spicy as a poppadom. The best PX puncheon I have found on the market in my lifetime. 55.6%. nc ncf sc.

The GlenDronach Recherché 1968 oloroso sherry butt, cask no. 5, bott 12 db (**97**) **n24** unsubtle with in-your-face grape, so thick you can hardly breathe; the sugars are no less loutish and the spices are pure thugs. And you know what? I bloody love it...!!! **t24** the most ridiculously clumsy start to a whisky of all time with the grape notes tripping over each other to get out first. However, they are beaten back into second place by rip-roaring plum treacle and molasses; the degree of oils border on perfect, but then so, too, does the balance between oaky toast and the jammy fruit spread all over it; **f24** you expect spices...and you get spices. Here, though, the fruit is more temperate and even a little ulmo honey kisses and seduces; **b25** once, I admit, I found this kind of cask OTT. And it is a style that was often found with the obsolete Glendronach 12-year-old sherry edition, which compared to other oloroso styles around lacked a little couth. However, with good sherry butts these days being rarer than a Millwall goal at home, I have come to look at this style of malt beyond fondly. In fact this is love. A 44-year-old malt and not one atom of over age: truly incredible. A real once in a lifetime treat for most. And a throwback. 48.6%. 1968 Vintage aged 44 years.

⫶⫶⫶ **Abbey Whisky GlenDronach Aged 20 Years** cask no. 33, dist 1993, bott 2013 (**96.5**) **n24** not a single atom of sulphur means a treat in store: spiced, vaguely erfumed with lavender and clove and intense oloroso of your dreams proffering a near Guyana pot still rum heaviness and intensity; **t24.5** one of the few whiskies this year I really struggled to spit. That sticky molasses Demerera rum style hits hard and early: something akin to concentrated Melton Hunt Cake but with twice the number of toasted raisin; a wonderful nip and bite ensures this is no sherried softy; **f24** toasty...a mix of high percentage cocoa chocolate liberally dotted with burnt raisins; a last minute sign of some S-word treatment...but little or no damage done; **b24** faultless sherry butt. Glendronach at full throttle....and very few whiskies can come close to that! Those into heavy Demerera pot still rum will make be drawn like a moth to a flame to this gorgeous beast! 59.1%. sc.

⫶⫶⫶ **Cadenhead's Small Batch Glendronach Aged 23 Years** bourbon hogsheads, dist 90, bott 13 (**86**) **n21.5 t22.5 f20 b22**. Nothing wrong with the heather-honey, viscous distillate.

The oak has a few niggles, though, and detracts rather than spoils. Nothing wrong with the intensity of the malt content though. *49.5%. 534 bottles. WB15/260*

GLENDULLAN *(see also below)*
Speyside, 1972. Diageo. Working.

Glendullan Aged 8 Years db (89) n20 t22 f24 b23. This is just how I like my Speysiders: young fresh and uplifting. A truly charming malt. *40%*

Singleton of Glendullan 12 Years Old db (87) n22 t22 f21 b22. Much more age than is comfortable for a 12-y-o. *40%*

Gordon and MacPhail Connoisseurs Choice Glendullan 1999 (84.5) n21.5 t22 f20 b21. Nutty, full bodied and unfailingly pleasant, it is a tad too dependent on crystalline sugars for impact. Better oak might have helped here. *46%. ncf.*

⋆ **Old Malt Cask Glendullan Aged 14 Years** refill hogshead, cask no. 10124, dist Oct 99, bott Oct 13 (93) n23.5 what a beautiful mix between clean, alluring barley and citrus, mainly clementines; a little lavender freshens it up even further; t24 just about a perfect impact on delivery: the malts are salivating, the sugars are crisp and clean, the vanilla unembittered... wow!!! f22 here's the dull bit in Glendullan...the oak injects a little natural caramel but a few spices compensate; b23.5 at last! A Glendullan how I normally see it in the blending lab, rather than when tasting bottlings for the Bible. Of late they have been pretty ordinary and hardly representative. This one is much truer to its known quality among the pros, mainly due to this crisp malt being presented in decent oak for a change. *50%. nc ncf sc.336 bottles.*

GLENDULLAN *(see also above)*
Speyside, 1898–1985. Closed.

Glendullan 1978 Rare Malt db (88) n23 t22 f21 b22. Sherlock Holmes would have loved this one: he would have found it lemon-entry. *56.8%*

GLEN ELGIN
Speyside, 1900. Diageo. Working.

Glen Elgin Aged 12 Years db (89) n23 t24 f20 b22. Absolutely murders Cragganmore as Diageo's top dog bottled Speysider. The marks would be several points further north if one didn't get the feeling that some caramel was weaving a derogatory spell. Brilliant stuff nonetheless. States Pot Still on label – not to be confused with Irish Pot Still. This is 100% malt... and it shows! *43%*

⋆ **Cadenhead's Glen Elgin-Glenlivet Aged 22 Years** dist 1991, bott Oct 13 (94) n23.5 does whisky come any more molassed than this...? Under-ripe greengages and over-ripe should add weight, but here they lighten...; t24 every bit as massive as on the nose: the sugars, a mix of molasses and treacle, arrive as a thick wall, guarded along the top by spikey spices. When you do surmount it a thick field of ulmo honey mingles with the typical Glen Elgin high intensity barley comes into view; f22.5 big, if relatively quiet. But an excellent cask means the tannins offer a degree of butterscotch...with glazed sugar and spices, of course...! b24 a bit more than a must for those with a sweet tooth: I thinking we are entering new territory so far continuous intensity goes. There is a vague hint of fruit but it is blasted from insignificance into irrelevance... *56.8%. 498 bottles. WB15/078*

⋆ **The Coopers Choice Glen Elgin 1995 Aged 17 Years** sherry finish, cask no. 9043, bott 2013 (93.5) n22 a black cherry pie straight in the kisser...; t24 fabulously silky but unravels into something a lot more interesting as honeydew melon and heather honey gets involved in the Dundee cake and toasted honeycomb: big....! f23.5 the spices and honeycomb work well; b24 a blemish-free sherry butt, thankfully. And the malt has enough character to see off its slightly smothering presence. A dram to end an exhausting day with...as I am doing now, having just tasted the 950th new whisky of the 2015 Bible... *46%. 360 bottles. WB15/299*

Dun Bheagan Glen Elgin Aged 21 Years sherry butt, cask no. 8294, dist Dec 91, bott 13 (90.5) n23.5 t23 f21.5 b22.5. Clean sherry influence for a typical Glen Elgin picture book malt. *52.5%. nc ncf sc. Ian Macleod Distillers. 558 bottles.*

Milroy's of Soho Glen Elgin Aged 17 Years hogshead, cask no. 1669, dist Nov 95, bott 15 Apr 13 (89) n22.5 t23.5 f21 b22. A delicious distillery here at its most silky and creamy. *46%.*

Old Masters Glen Elgin 16 Years Old cask no. 1660, dist 95, bott Oct 12 (92) n23 that gorgeous aroma you sometimes find in antique restoration workshops: a sweet resin mixing with sugared almonds; t23.5 so sensuously silky. The malt leads in both a rich barley ale style (almost complete with slightly bitter hops) and in a juicier, semi-gristy incarnation; f22.5 a butterscotch finale beacons from early on and arrives. A hint of lemon curd tart and bittering oak are also present; b23 a distillery which, in the lab, rarely disappoints. And in bottled form is more likely than not to offer a treat. *56.4%. sc. James MacArthur & Co Ltd.*

⠋ **Old Particular Speyside Glen Elgin 21 Year Old** 2nd fill sherry butt, cask no. 10185, dist Jun 92, bott Dec 13 **(94) n23.5** mmmm!! Glazed ginger and fudgy tannin. Beautifully weighted and then brought to life with a sprinkling of pepper; **t23** both voluptuous and eruptuous... the ginger and spice combine to make a massive statement, all the more remarkable when the juicy barley is taken into account; **f24** lingers and fizzes. One of the great controlled spice explosions of the year is a class act to the end; **b23.5** what a way to start the day...!! *51.5%. nc ncf sc. 219 bottles. Douglas Laing & Co.*

⠋ **Wemyss Malts 1995 Single Speyside Glen Elgin "Eastern Promise"** bott 2013 **(84) n21.5 t21.5 f20 b21.** After a Douglas Laing Glen Elgin which is perfect as morning's first dram, this oaky incarnation is one to take to bed.... for it is all rather over-tired. *46%. sc. 363 bottles.*

The Whisky Agency Glen Elgin 1975 dist 75, bott 12 **(88) n23 t20 f23 b22.** Proof that a whisky, as it develops, goes through an unsettled period not just around its birth. *48.4%*

GLENESK
Highlands (Eastern), 1897–1985. Diageo. Demolished.
Duncan Taylor Collection Glenesk 1983 cask no. 4930 **(89.5) n22 t23 f22 b22.5.** By far the best Glen Esk I've tasted in years. Perhaps not the most complex, but the liveliness and clarity are a treat. *52.1%*

GLENFARCLAS
Speyside, 1836. J&G Grant. Working.
Glenfarclas 8 Years Old db **(86) n21 t22 f22 b21.** Less intense sherry allows the youth of this malt to stand out. Mildly quirky as a Glenfarclas and enormous entertainment. *40%*

Glenfarclas 10 Years Old db **(80) n19 t20 f22 b19.** Always an enjoyable malt, but for some reason this version never seems to fire on all cylinders. There is a vague honey sheen which works well with the barley, but struggles for balance and the nose is a bit sweaty. Still has distinctly impressive elements but an odd fish. *40%*

Glenfarclas 12 Years Old db **(94) n23.5** a wonderfully fresh mix of grape and mint; **t24** light, youthful, playful, mouthwatering. Less plodding honey, more vibrant Demerara and juiced-up butterscotch; **f23** long, with soft almost ice-cream style vanillas with a grapey topping; **b23.5** a superb re-working of an always trustworthy malt. This dramatic change in shape works a treat and suits the malt perfectly. What a sensational success!! *43%*

Glenfarclas 15 Years Old db **(85.5) n21.5 t23 f20 b21.** One thing is for certain: working with sherry butts these days is a bit like working with ACME dynamite....you are never sure when it is about to blow up in your face. There is only minimal sulphur here, but enough to take the edge off a normally magnificent whisky, at the death. Instead it is now merely, in part, quite lovely. The talent at Glenfarclas is unquestionably among the highest in the industry: I'll be surprised to see the same weaknesses with the next bottling. *46%*

Glenfarclas 17 Years Old db **(93) n23** just so light and playful: custard powder lightens and sweetens, sultana softens, barley moistens, spice threatens...; **t23** the relaxed sherry influence really lets the honey deliver; delightfully roasty and well spiced towards the middle; **f23** when I was a kid there was a candy – pretend tobacco, no less! – made from strands of coconut and sweetened with a Demerara syrup. My, this takes me back...; **b24** an excellent age for this distillery, allowing just enough oak in to stir up the complexity. A stupendous addition to the range. *40%*

Glenfarclas 18 Years Old db **(84) n21 t22 f20 b21.** Tight, nutty and full of crisp muscovado sugar. *43%. Travel Retail Exclusive.*

Glenfarclas 21 Years Old db **(83) n20 t23 f19 b21.** A chorus of sweet, honied malt and mildly spiced, teasing fruit on the fabulous mouth arrival and middle compensates for the few blips. *43%*

Glenfarclas 25 Years Old db **(84) n20 t22 f20 b22.** A curious old bat: by no means free from imperfect sherry but compensating with some staggering age – seemingly way beyond the 25-year statement. Enjoys the deportment of a doddering old classics master from a family of good means and breeding. *43%*

Glenfarclas 30 Years Old db **(85) n20 t22 f21 b22.** Flawed yet juicy. *43%*

Glenfarclas 40 Years Old db **(94) n23** old Demerara rum laced with well aged oloroso. Spicy, deep though checked by vanilla; **t23** toasty fruitcake with just the right degree of burnt raisin; again the spices are central to the plot though now a Jamaican Blue Mountain/Mysore medium roast mix makes an impressive entrance; **f24** long, with the oak not just ticking every box, but doing so with a flourish. The Melton Hunt cake finale is divine... **b24** couldn't help me laugh: this sample was sent by the guys at Glenfarclas after they spotted that I had last year called their disappointing 40-year-old a "freak". I think we have both proved a point... *46%*

Glenfarclas 40 Years Old Millennium Edition db **(92) n23 t23 f23 b23.** An almost immaculate portrayal of an old-fashioned, high-quality malt with unblemished sherry freshness and depth. The hallmark of quality is the sherry's refusal to dominate the spicy, softly peated malt. The oak offers a bourbony sweetness but ensures a rich depth throughout. Quite outstanding for its age. 54.7%. nc ncf.

Glenfarclas 50 Years Old db **(92)** n24 Unique. Almost a marriage between 20-y-o bourbon and intense, old-fashioned sherry. Earthy, weighty stuff that repays time in the glass and oxidization because only then does the subtlety become apparent and a soft peat-reek reveal itself; **t23** an unexpected sweet – even mouthwatering - arrival, again with a touch of peat to add counter ballast to the intense richness of the sherry. The oak is intense from the middle onwards, but of such high quality that it merely accompanies rather then dominates; **f22** warming black peppers ping around the palate; some lovely cocoa oils coat the mouth for a bitter-sweet, warming and very long finish; **b23** Most whiskies cannot survive such great age. This one really does bloom in the glass and the earthy, peaty aspect makes it all the more memorable. It has taken 50 years to reach this state. Give a glass of this at least an hour's inquisition, as I have. Your patience will be rewarded many times over. 44.4%

Glenfarclas 105 db **(95.5)** n23.5 the youthful grape comes in clean, juicy bunches; the herbs and spices on a rack on the kitchen wall; **t24** any lovers of the old Jennings books will here do a Mr Wilkins explosive snort as the magnificent barley-grape mix is propelled with the force of dynamite into the taste buds; survivors of this experience still able to speak may mention something about cocoa notes forming; **f24** long, luxurious, with a pulsing vanilla-grape mix and a build up of spices; light oils intensify and elongate; **b24** I doubt if any restorative on the planet works quite as well as this one does. Or if any sherry cask whisky is so clean and full of the joys of Jerez. A classic malt which has upped a gear or two and has become exactly what it is: a whisky of pure brilliance... 60%

Glenfarclas 1995 45° The Heritage Malt Collection sherry cask, dist Nov 95, bott Sep 06 db **(94.5)** n24 t23.5 f23.5 b23.5. Exceptional. Absolutely everything you could demand from a sherried malt of this age. Not a single off note and the freshness of comparative youth and complexity of years in the cask are in perfect harmony. 45%. Spain.

⠿ **Glenfarclas 2000 Vintage** bott 2014 db **(76)** n18.5 t22.5 f17 b18. Surprisingly youthful in part. Wonderful early coffee and spice before the dull, bitter furriness kicks in... 43%. Exclusive to The Whisky Shop.

Glenfarclas 2003 db **(83)** n21.5 t23 f18 b20.5. Some classic oloroso moments here, bounding with rich grape and walnuts. Alas, a little tight and furry. 46%. Whisky Shop Exclusive.

Glenfarclas 175th Anniversary 2011 db **(94)** n23.5 crisp and precise fruit: clean and hedging towards bon bons. The very vaguest hint of smoke adds extra depth; vanilla and spice fly the other way; **t24** fabulous delivery: every aspect dissolves on impact. The fruits are again subtle yet lush, the sweetness initially from gristy icing sugar, though towards the middle more muscovado. Again, the lightest imaginable wisps of smoke and more profound spices; **f23** cream toffee; burnt raisin; **b23.5** hard to imagine an experience more gentle than this where alcohol is concerned. No slam bam stuff here. Every moment is about whispers and brushes of the nerve endings. Sensual whisky. 43%. nc. J&G Grant. 6000 bottles.

⠿ **Cadenhead's Authentic Collection Glenfarclas Aged 25 Years** bourbon hogshead, dist 1988, bott Oct 2013 **(95)** n24 so complex – love it. A mild mocha element adds weight: gooseberries, glazed cherries and lemon cream Swiss roll ensures the fun; the barley is concentrated barley concentrate...; **t24** buttery malt is swathed in lightly fizzing, gorgeously spiced barley sugar; the intensity is almost beyond description; **f23** here comes the cream to the Swiss roll, very sticky and jammy; **b24** just adore the way Cadenhead gets out to the world a wonderful side of the incomparable Glenfarclas distillery we would not otherwise often see. Probably the liveliest 25-year-old I will taste this year! 53.7%. 222 bottles. WB15/275

⠿ **Cadenhead's Authentic Collection Glenfarclas Aged 41 Years** bourbon hogshead, dist 73, bott July 14 **(94.5)** n22.5 the tannins have taken over the asylum: oak, intense to the point of paranoia, dictate shape and form. Even the marmalade is tannin-based and slowly sweetens to soften all the edges; **t24.5** the sugary marmalade arrives immediately but it is the malt which opens up. Coconut cake mix has Demerara mixed into it, then a butter cream which also offers soft oils; a little bourbon biscuit chocolate cream is added to the mix; **f23.5** dries as the tannin returns. But enough cake mix survives to ensure a comfortable finale; lovely late spices tingle; **b24** thankfully, the dreamy palate makes a lie of the nose which suggests we have one overly tired dram. However, it appears it was the strength of the whisky which suggested it was time to bottle, not the zealous oak. One important suggestion: leave it in the glass for 25-30 mins before tasting to allow it to open to its fullest potential. 40.7%. 186 bottles. WB15/270

Director's Cut Glenfarclas Aged 46 Years refill butt, cask no. 9176, dist Jun 66, bott Sep 12 **(90.5)** n24 t22.5 f22 b22. If you can take full on oak, you'll marvel at this. 49.7%.

Malts Of Scotland 1836 - 2001 cask no. MoS 12062, dist Jun 2001, bott Nov 2012 **(81.5)** n20 t23 f18.5 b20 Interesting. Laden with fruit. Yet still very tight. *57.8%. nc ncf sc. 96 bottles.*

Riegger's Selection Eagle of Spey Glenfarclas 1993 (96.5) n24.5 hard to imagine a Glenfarclas more sexy and alluring than this: carries a gorgeous gooseberry and lemon tart aroma with panache; so delicate: the degree of salt is sublime and uplifting; the sharpness is in equal measure to the shy coconut and thin beech honey sweetness; there are times I actually forget about going on to taste it! One of the great Speyside aromas of the year...; t24.5 the impact would be extraordinary had not the nose told you of the complexity to come: myriad mini flavour explosions on delivery – perhaps the small grains attack found on six-year-old bourbon from the Tom Moore distillery is the closest relation sensation-wise. Here, there is a bit more honey from the barley, which lets itself be heard by the juiciness which develops at slow-motion pace; f23 a little tangy as some of the more exhausted tannins get a slight foot-hold. You crave cocoa to compensate. And, inevitably, it is cocoa you get...; b24.5 you will have to pass a few bottlings to find one from this distillery so fruity yet not from a sherry butt. An absolute masterpiece from this outstanding distillery. *53.6%.*

Scotch Malt Whisky Society Cask 1.166 Aged 25 Years refill hogshead, 3 Dec 86 **(93)** n23.5 surprising amounts of fresh barley even after all this time: almost like moist hay; a touch of citrus to the sawdusty oak; t23 big, punchy intense oak carries attractive light spice and burnt toast qualities; the sugars are even and happy to drive from the back seat; f23 long, chewy barley once more with a light ulmo honey topping to the butterscotch; b23.5 sound and steady malt where the sum is much bigger than all the subtle parts. *48.3%. nc ncf sc.*

Scotch Malt Whisky Society Cask 1.172 Aged 19 Years 23 Sep 93 **(89.5)** n22.5 t22.5 f22 b23. Something so stylishly Speyside about this one. *55.7%. nc ncf sc. 230 bottles.*

⋰ **Scotch Malt Whisky Society Cask 1.178 Aged 11 Years** 1st fill barrel, dist 07 Jun 02 **(92.5)** n23 hefty malt revels in the barley fest; t23 salivates like a bottled Glenfarclas has rarely salivated before. Fresh grist which refuses to let up; just adore the developing spices; f23 impressive spiced cocoa; b23.5 this is the flip side of Glenfarclas: relatively young and showing its malty rather than fruity plumage. A bit of a treat. *56.8%. nc ncf sc. 232 bottles.*

⋰ **Scotch Malt Whisky Society Cask 1.179 Aged 27 Years** refill hogshead, dist 03 Dec 86 **(89.5)** n23 a thin layering of ulmo honey on toast; t23 the delivery pings with voluptuous barley at times tantalising, others tangy; f21 dries as oak gains hold; b22.5 another superb blending malt slightly highjacked by oak. *47.2%. nc ncf sc. 201 bottles.*

The Whisky Shop Dufftown Glenfarclas The Family Casks 40 Years Old oloroso sherry cask, cask no. 152, dist 8 Jan 71, bott 14 Feb 11 **(89)** n24 t23 f20 b22. A mottled malt where the toasted raisins turn up here and there but never quite run true. Some serious entertainment and quality early on, though. *51.6%. nc ncf sc. 496 bottles.*

GLENFIDDICH
Speyside, 1887. William Grant & Sons. Working.

Glenfiddich 12 Years Old db **(85.5)** n21 t22 f21 b21.5. A malt now showing a bit of zap and spark. Even displays a flicker of attractive muscovado sugars. Simple, untaxing and safe. *40%*

Glenfiddich 12 Years Old Toasted Oak Reserve db **(92.5)** n22.5 t23.5 f22.5 b24. Another bottling to confound the critics of Glenfiddich. This is as fine an essay in balance, charm and sophistication as you are likely to find in the whole of Speyside this year. Crack open a bottle... but only when you have a good hour to spend. *40%*

Glenfiddich Caoran Reserve Aged 12 Years db **(89)** n22.5 t22 f21.5 b23. Has fizzed up a little in the last year or so with some salivating charm from the barley and a touch of cocoa from the oak. A complex little number. *40%*

Glenfiddich Rich Oak Over 14 Years Old new American & new Spanish oak finish db **(90.5)** n23 fascinating: there is a nod towards Japanese oak in the naked wood profile here. Toned down, though, by a huge pithy kumquat presence. That this is virgin oak there can be no doubt, so don't expect an easy ride; t22 soft oils help for a quiet landing: like lonely oaks falling in a forest...there is a brief sensation of passing barley. Then it returns again to a number of oak-laden notes, especially the spices which move towards a creamy mocha territory; f23.5 possibly the best phase of the experience. The vivid, surging oak has cooled and some barley oils mingle in a relaxed fashion with the sweetening, very mildly sugared mocha; b22 from the moment you nose this, there is absolutely no doubting its virgin oak background. It pulls towards bourbon, but never gets there. Apparently European oak is used, too. The result is something curiously hinting at Japanese, but without the crushing intensity. Delicious, thoughtful whisky and one to tick off on your journey of malt whisky discovery. Though a pity we don't see it at 46% and in full voluptuous nudity: you get the feeling that this would have been something really exceptional to conjure with. *40%. William Grant.*

Glenfiddich 15 Years Old db **(94.5)** n23 such a deft intermingling of the softer fruits and bourbon notes...with barley in there to remind you of the distillery; t23 intense and big yet all the time appearing delicate and light; the most apologetic of spices help spotlight the barley sweetness and delicate fruits; **f24.5** just so long and complex; something of the old fashioned fruit salad candy about this but with a small degree of toffee just rounding off the edges; **b24** if an award were to be given for the most consistently beautiful dram in Scotland, this would win more often than not. This under-rated distillery has won more friends with this masterpiece than probably any other brand. *40%*

Glenfiddich Aged 15 Years Cask Strength db (85.5) **n20 t23 f21 b21.**5. Improved upon the surprisingly bland bottlings of old, especially on the fabulously juicy delivery. Still off the pace due to an annoying toffee-ness towards the middle and at the death. *51%*

Glenfiddich Distillery Edition 15 Years Old db (93.5) **n24.5** banana skins, but there is no slip up here as the aroma spectrum moves from ultra fat sultanas on one side to dried coconut on the other. You'll find countless other reference points, including lightly salted celery and even molten candle wax. Quite astonishing and, even with its spice nip, one of the great whisky noses of 2010; **t24** my word!! Just so lively...enormous complexity from the very first mouthful. The mouthfeel is two-toned with heavier fruit not quite outstripping the flightier barley. All kinds of vanilla – both dry and sweet – and a dusty spiciness, too; **f22** tones down rather too dramatically, hedging much more towards the more docile banana-vanilla elements; **b23** had this exceptional whisky been able to maintain the pace through to the finish, this would have been a single malt of the year contender - at least. *51%. ncf.*

Glenfiddich Aged 15 Years Solera Reserve *(see Glenfiddich 15 Years Old)*

Glenfiddich 18 Years Old db (95) **n23.5** the smoke, which for long marked this aroma, appears to have vanished. But the usual suspects of blood orange and various other fruit appear to thrive in the lightly salted complexity; **t24.5** how long are you allowed to actually keep the whisky held on the palate before you damage your teeth? One to really close your eyes and study because here we have one of the most complex deliveries Speyside can conjour: the peat may have gone, but there is coal smoke around as the juicy barley embeds with big fat sultanas, plums, dates and grapes. Despite the distinct lack of oil, the mouthfeel is entirely yielding to present one of the softest and most complete essays on the palate you can imagine, especially when you take the bitter-sweet ratio and spice into balance; **f23** long, despite the miserly 40% offered, with plenty of banana-custard and a touch of pear; **b24** at the moment, the ace in the Glenfiddich pack. If this was bottled at 46%, unchilfiltered etc, I dread to think what the score might be... *40%*

Glenfiddich Age Of Discovery Aged 19 Years Bourbon Cask Reserve db (92) **n23.5** not just complex, but so delicate one is almost afraid to nose too deeply incase you break the poor thing into a million pieces. The barley skits around like a highly strung actress on the edge of a breakdown; **t24** of such butterfly qualities, it wanders at random around the palate, touching down here and there to offer a barely legible malty weight; the sugars are no less constrained, a thin heather honey style feebly patting away the encroaching oak: the whole thing, like the nose, is wonderfully neurotic; **f22** melts away with limited grace and tact for far too short a finale; **b22.5** for my money Glenfiddich turns from something quite workaday to a malt extraordinaire between the ages of 15 and 18. So, depending on the casks chosen, a year the other side of that golden age shouldn't make too much difference. The jury is still out on whether it was helped by being at 40%, which means the natural oils have been broken down somewhat, allowing the intensity and richness only an outside chance of fully forming. *40%*

Glenfiddich Age Of Discovery Aged 19 Years Madeira Cask Finish db (88.5) **n22.5 t22.5 f21 b22.5.** Oddly enough, almost a breakfast malt: it is uncommonly soft and light yet carries a real jam and marmalade character. *40%*

Glenfiddich 21 Years Old db (86) **n21 t23 f21 b21.** A much more uninhibited bottling with loads of fun as the mouth-watering barley comes rolling in. But still falls short on taking the hair-raisingly rich delivery forward and simply peters out. *40%*

Glenfiddich 30 Years Old db (93.5) **n23** always expect sherry trifle with this: here is some sherry not to be trifled with... salty, too; **t23.5** the juiciest 30-y-o I can remember from this distillery for a while: both the grape and barley are contributing to the salivation factor...; the mid ground if filled with light cocoa, soft oils and a delicate hickory-demerara bourbon-style sweetness; **f23.5** here usually the malt ends all too briefly. Not this time: chunky grape carries on its chattering with the ever-increasing bourbon-honeycomb notes; a vague furry finale...; **b23.5** a 'Fiddich which has changed its spots. Much more voluptuous than of old and happy to mine a grapey seam while digging at the sweeter bourbon elements for all it is worth. Just one less than magnificent butt away from near perfection and a certain Bible Award... *40%*

Glenfiddich 40 Years Old batch 7 db (96) **n24** it's the spices which win hands down here. Yes, there is all kinds of juicy, voluptuous fruit...this nose is dripping with it. But the spices are the rudder steering a path through spectacular scenery...; **t24** ...so no surprises it is the eloquent spices which speak first on delivery. Nothing brash. No violence. Just considered and balanced, bringing the most from the oak and allowing a juicy degree of salt to enliven things further; to work properly sugars are required and sublime traces of muscovado sugars appear to bring the fat sultanas to bursting; **f23.5** now we get to the burnt raisin bit of the fruit cake effect. That's just how it should be...; oh, and did I mention the spices...? **b24.5** for the 750th New Whisky for the 2012 Bible, I decided to select a distillery close to my heart... and the age I'll be next birthday... Believe me: this guy didn't let me down. Full frontal fruit and spice. Perfectly toned and all the curves in the right places. Rrrrr!!! 45.8%. 600 bottles.

Glenfiddich Rare Collection 40 Years Old db (86.5) **n22.5 t23 f20 b21.** A quite different version to the last with the smoke having all but vanished, allowing the finish to show the full weight of its considerable age. The nose and delivery are superb, though. The barley sheen on arrival really deserves better support. 43.5%

Glenfiddich 50 Years Old db (97) **n25** we are talking 50 years, and yet we are still talking fresh barley, freshly peeled grape and honey. Not ordinary honey. Not the stuff you find in jars. But the pollen that attracts the bees to the petunia; and not any old petunia: not the white or the red or pink or yellow. But the two-toned purple ones. For on the nose at least this is perfection; this is nectar... **t24** a silky delivery: silky barley with silky, watered down maple syrup. The middle ground, in some previous Glenfiddich 50-year-olds a forest of pine and oak, is this time filled with soft, grassy barley and the vaguest hint of a distant smoke spice; **f24** long, long, long, with the very faintest snatch of something most delicately smoked: a distant puff of peat reek carried off on the persistent Speyside winds, then a winding-down of vanillas, dropping through the gears of sweetness until the very last traces are chalky dry; **b24** for the record, my actual words, after tasting my first significant mouthful, were: "fuck! This is brilliant." It was an ejaculation of genuine surprise, as any fly on the wall of my Tasting Room at 1:17am on Tuesday 4th August would testify. Because I have tasted many 50-year-old whiskies over the years, quite possibly as many as anyone currently drawing breath. For not only have I tasted those which have made it onto the whisky shelves, but, privately, or as a consultant, an untold number which didn't: the heroic but doomed oak-laden failures. This, however, is a quite different animal. We were on the cusp of going to press when this was released, so we hung back. William Grant blender David Stewart, whom I rank above all other blenders on this planet, has known me long and well enough to realise that the surrounding hype, with this being the most expensive whisky ever bottled at £10,000 a go or a sobering £360 a pour, would bounce off me like a pebble from a boulder. "Honestly, David," he told my chief researcher with a timorous insistence, "please tell Jim I really think this isn't too oaky." He offered almost an apology for bringing into the world this 50-year-old babe. Well, as usual David Stewart, doyen of the blending lab and Ayr United season ticket holders, was absolutely spot on. And, as is his want, he was rather understating his case. For the record, David, next time someone asks you how good this whisky is, just for once do away with the Ayeshire niceness installed by generations of very nice members of the Stewart family and tell them: "Actually, it's bloody brilliant if I say so myself! And I don't give a rat's bollocks what Murray thinks." 46.1%

Glenfiddich Malt Master's Edition double matured in oak and sherry butts db (84) **n21 t22 f20 b21.** I would have preferred to have seen this double matured in bourbon barrels and bourbon barrels... The sherry has done this no great favours. 43%

Glenfiddich Millennium Vintage dist 2000, bott 2012 db (83.5) **n21.5 t22 f20 b20.** Short and not very sweet. Good juicy delivery though, reminiscent of the much missed original old bottling. 40%

Glenfiddich Snow Phoenix bott 2010 db (95) **n23.5** graceful and delicate, there is obviously some age lurking, lord-like, in the background. But it is the younger malts, reminiscent of the long-lost, original, no-age statement version that steals the show, imprinting the unique grassy, tingly signature into the glass; **t24** a time machine has taken me back 25 years: it is like the original Glenfiddich at its juicy, ultra-salivating youthful finest but now with a honey enriched backbone and some real belief in the oaky spices, where they were once half-hearted a generation ago; **f23** long, with that honeyed sheen remaining impressively attached to the dynamic barley; **b24.5** it is no easy task for blender Brian Kinsman to emerge from the considerable shadow of the now retired David Stewart, the world's finest blender of the last 20 years. But here he has stepped up to the plate to create something which captures the very essence of the distillery. It is almost a deluxe version of the original Glenfiddich: something that is so far advanced of the dull 12-year-old, it is scary. This is sophisticated whisky, have no doubt. And the first clear, impressive statement declaring that Glenfiddich appears to remain in very safe hands. Whatever Brian did from those casks, exposed to the bleak Speyside winter, he should do again. But to a far wider audience. 476%. ncf.

GLEN GARIOCH
Highlands (Eastern), 1798. Morrison Bowmore. Working.

Glen Garioch 8 Years Old db (85.5) **n21 t22 f21 b21.5.** A soft, gummy, malt – not something one would often write about a dram of this or any age from Geary! However, this may have something to do with the copious toffee which swamps the light fruits which try to emerge. 40%

Glen Garioch 10 Years Old db (80) n19 t22 f19 b20. Chunky and charming, this is a malt that once would have ripped your tonsils out. Much more sedate and even a touch of honey to the rich body. Toffeed at the finish. 40%

Glen Garioch 12 Years Old db (88.5) n22 t23 f21.5 b22. A significant improvement on the complexity front. The return of the smoke after a while away was a surprise and treat. 43%

Glen Garioch 12 Years Old db (88) n22.5 t22.5 f21.5 b22. Sticks, broadly, to the winning course of the original 43% version, though here there is a fraction more toffee at the expense of the smoke. 48%. ncf.

Glen Garioch 15 Years Old db (86.5) n20.5 t22 f22 b22. In the bottling I sampled last year the peat definitely vanished. Now it's back again, though in tiny, if entertaining, amounts. 43%

Glen Garioch 21 Years Old db (91) n21 a few wood shavings interrupt the toasty barley; t23 really good bitter-sweet balance with honeycomb and butterscotch leading the line; pretty juicy, busy stuff; f24 dries as it should with some vague spices adding to the vanilla and hickory; b23 an entirely re-worked, now smokeless, malt that has little in common with its predecessors. Quite lovely, though. 43%

Glen Garioch 1797 Founders Reserve db (87.5) n21 t22 f22.5 b22. Impressively fruity and chewy: some serious flavour profiles in there. 48%

Glen Garioch 1958 db (90) n24 t21 f23 b22. The distillery in its old smoky clothes: and quite splendid it looks! 43%. 328 bottles.

Glen Garioch 1995 db (86) n21 t22 f21.5 b21.5. Typically noisy on the palate, even though the malty core is quite thin. Some big natural caramels, though. 55.3%. ncf.

Glen Garioch 1997 db (89) n22 unusually salty, dry and subtle; t22.5 just a few semi-gristy sugars make a minor noise while the barley appears in intense bursts but happy to duck behind the oak; some early barley wine oils early on; f22 a charming fade of caramelised barley; b22.5 had you tasted this malt as a 15-year-old back in 1997, you would have tasted something far removed from this, with a peaty bite ripping into the palate. To say this malt has evolved is an understatement. 56.5%. Whisky Shop Exclusive. 204 bottles.

Glen Garioch 1997 db (89.5) n22 t23 f22 b22.5. I have to say: I have long been a bit of a voice in the wilderness among whisky professionals as regards this distillery. This not so subtly muscled malt does my case no harm whatsoever. 56.7%. ncf.

Glen Garioch 1999 db (64) n16 t17 f15 b16. Massively sulphured. 56.3%. ncf.

⟶ **Glen Garioch Sherry Cask Matured** Oloroso sherry casks, batch no. 30, dist 1999, bott 2013 db (79) n19 t23 f18 b19. The usual sherry problems arise. Which is enough to make you weep, because for a few glorious seconds on delivery (about the third to the fifth taste beats in) the impact and beauty of the oloroso matches anything experienced in Scotland this year. But the s-word wins, as it so often does, in the end. 56.3%. ncf. WB15/157

Glen Garioch Virgin Oak db (93) n22 a salty, unsmoked bacon feel to this with quietly controlled tannins and hickory; t23.5 a series of complex sugar notes are first to arrive. Then come in second, third and fourth, the complexity levels rising by the second; grated coconut and Brazilian biscuit works well with the maple syrup; f24 now the complexity peaks with modest spices cranking up the vanilla and countering the light layer of ulmo and manuka honey blend; b23.5 Glen Garioch as probably never seen before and at its most beautifully complex. 48%

Berry's Own Selection 1992 cask no. 3464, bott 2013 (87) n23 t23 f19.5 b21.5. A distillery with the propensity to make gorgeous whisky without seemingly breaking sweat is at it again...just not helped by a indifferent piece of wood. 46%. nc ncf sc.

⟶ **Berry's Own Selection Glen Garioch 1989 Aged 24 Years** cask no. 7854, bott 2014 (89.5) n22.5 understated smoke and passion fruit; t23 fabulous delivery: muscovado sugar and deft smoke make a malty soup interesting; salivating sweet juicy barley; f21.5 thins and warms but the sugars continue; b22.5 fascinating bottling which captures the spirit of that period, with the smoke apparent but reduced from what it once was. And a little bite from the lively spirit. 53.8%. ncf ncf. WB15/250

⟶ **Directors' Cut Glen Garioch Aged 21 Years** refill hogshead, cask no. 10353, dist Apr 93, bott Jun 14 (84.5) n21.5 t21 f21 b21. Expected some smoke on this. Instead, got the malty, fireball version of that era...and some pretty full on oak, too. 57.4%. nc ncf sc. 213 bottles.

⟶ **The First Editions Glen Garioch 1993 Aged 20 Years** (95.5) n23.5 a Fisherman's Friend-Worther's Original cross...; t24.5 that is how I like to see a Geery on to the palate: like a fast bowler's ball on to my bat...true, fast, clean and with no little zip. Absolutely creams the taste buds with a gorgeous barley-sugar-butterscotch mix while other sugars, mainly maple syrup, giving a delicate, cleansing effect despite the bite and spice....just so fantastically malty and juicy...to the nth degree; f23.5 still some fizz, but settles into a more medium-paced vanilla-textured finale; b24 could drink this all day and every day. If you know what I mean. A stunner. 58.2%. nc ncf sc.

⁘ **Kingsbury Silver Glen Garioch 19 Year Old** cask no. 345, dist 1993 **(84) n20 t22 f21 b21.** A good example of decent though not entirely convincing malt being filled into a decent though not entirely convincing cask. The mottled effect on the taste buds results, though when the barley sparkles it makes the duller moments bearable. *46%. nc ncf sc. 284 bottles.*

⁘ **The Last Drop Glen Garioch 47 Year Old** hogshead, cask no. 662 dist 23 Mar 67 **(96) n24** you will do well to find a another nose like this over the next year or five: profound, chunky oak thinned and tamed by sharp kumquat notes and finally defused by the friendliest – slightly cocoa-softened – peat reek. For it to be this confident now, it must have been a peaty monster some half a century ago...; in its lighter, relaxed mode the oak pulses out soft liquorice and hickory; **t23.5** a slight eye-watering moment as the tannins bite with intent on delivery. But again the smoke and citrus come rushing to the rescue and now we go from salvation into salivation mode as even remnants of barley make an impact; now creamy, fudgy and liquorice bourbony and helped further by the thinnest layer of smoked molasses; **f24** so long...and a delightful tangle of oaky roots and peaty off-shoots make way first for the citrus then a fabulous pounding spiciness; **b24.5** when this distillery produced the whisky in the bottle before me it was making probably the smokiest malt on mainland Scotland. Which is just as well for this grizzled old greybeard. Because this preserve rather well in peat – and this Glen Garioch is no exception. Just a standard low- or non-peated malt would have vanished behind the layers of tannins which have formed a crust around some of the lighter components of the dram. But here the smoke softens the oaky blows until they become only caresses. It is a quite extraordinary - and in many ways lucky – experience. *45.4%. Morrison Bowmore.*

Liquid Library Glen Garioch 1991 ex-bourbon hogshead, dist 91, bott 12 **(93.5) n23** an irresistible blend of boiled gooseberries and cordite (non-boiled); **t24** the delicate smoke adds minor ballast to the evocative light fruit and barley mix: just so many mind-blowing layers; **f23** long with a few late oils offering a cocoa bitterness and ever thickening vanilla; **b23.5** an all day any, day dram showing wonderful sleight of hand. *52.5%. The Whisky Agency.*

Master of Malt Glen Garioch Aged 21 Years bourbon cask, dist 16 May 90, bott 8 Feb 12 **(86) n22 t23 f20 b21.** Anyone remember the original 21-y-o produced by the distillery? Not exactly like this one...none of the bite (or even smoke), though that didn't offer the gorgeous fresh malt and gooseberries available here. *48.8%. ncf sc.*

⁘ **Master of Malt Single Cask Glen Garioch 20 Year Old** (87.5) **n21 t23 f21.5 b22.** Magnificent delivery of concentrated barley. A minor oak niggle prevents development. But for those into intense malt...you'll be pouring a second glass! *58.8%. sc.*

⁘ **Montgomerie's Single Cask Collection Glen Garioch** cask no. 8555, dist 12 Nov 90, bott Mar 13 **(87) n21 t22 f22 b22.** Made at an interesting period in the distillery's period when they were just trying to work out who they were. Once, I had been a peaty malt which added not just smoke to a blend but a degree of ruggedness. Here it is undergoing a makeover. The smoke has vanished. And rather rip at the throat as of yore, is rather too tame and vanishes, albeit pleasantly, behind the skirts of fudgy toffee. *46%. nc ncf sc. WB15/128*

Old Malt Cask Glen Garioch Aged 21 Years refill hogshead, cask no. 9809, dist Nov 91, bott May 13 **(85.5) n21.5 t22 f20.5 b21.5.** A sweet, nutty number where the sugars at times seem a little out of control because of the lack of body. Enjoyable, if characteristically thin. *50%. nc ncf sc. 251 bottles.*

⁘ **Old Particular Highland Glen Garioch 21 Years Old** refill hogshead, cask no. 9901, dist May 92, bott Aug 13 **(88) n21.5** a little gingerbread amid the toasty barley; **t23** quietly aggressive delivery with a beautiful and salivating build up of oily barley; **f21.5** returns to the toasty nose with a lovely pulse of spice lingering; **b22** at times quite irresistible for all its rough edges. *51.5%. nc ncf sc. 122 bottles. Douglas Laing & Co.*

⁘ **The Pearls of Scotland Glen Garioch 1989** cask no. 7855, bott Jun 14 **(83.5) n20 t21.5 f21 b21.** From that razor-blade-hot-as-Hades-slap-on-the-wallpaper-paste school of Geery. Still, plenty to enjoy with its intense maltiness and Demerara input. *56%. sc.*

Provenance Glen Garioch Over 17 Years refill hogshead, cask no. 9767, dist Spring 95, bott Spring 13 **(87.5) n21.5 t22 f22 b22.** Glen Garioch in this mood can win the hearts of anyone. *46%. nc ncf sc.*

⁘ **Single Cask Collection 1993 Glen Garioch 20 Year Old** bourbon hogshead, dist 1993 **(87) n21 t23 f21 b22.** An infuriating "Geery". Flips with alarming and confusing regularity between a juicy, malty big boy and a thin, austere wimp of a dram. It is a bit of a distillery character trait. Finally settles on wimpy alternative. *55.1%. sc. Single Cask Collection.*

⁘ **That Boutique-y Whisky Glen Garioch** batch 1 **(85) n21 t22 f21 b21.** Very straight up and down blending malt. Pleasant barley which shows brief vitality before the natural caramels take hold. *50.6%. 284 bottles. WB15/225*

⁘ **Wemyss Glen Garioch Malts 1989 Single Highland "Brandy Casket"** bott 13 **(86)** n22 t22 f20.5 b21.5. A curious remnant from a lost Geery style. The smoke hammers its phenolic point home hard and the spices nip and nibble delightfully. But there is also an underlying austerity to this, too, which prevents it from entering the next level. 46%. Sc.

Wemyss Glen Garioch 1989 Single Highland "Fruit Bonbons" hogshead **(91.5)** n22 t23.5 f23 b23. The spirit from the stills at this time had a "fire water" reputation which now, as is so often the case, means we have a malt which is wilful and complex and able to take the two decades of maturation comfortably in its stride. 46%. sc. 325 bottles.

⁘ **Wemyss Glen Garioch Malts 1989 Single Highland "Peaches and Cream"** hogshead, dist 89, bott 14 **(92)** n22 pretty tired but just enough smoke and vanilla to paper over the cracks; t23.5 mouth-filling, oily and attractively sharp. Deft peat ensures both substance and gristy sweetness to make for a chewy experience; f23 smoked mocha with a lovely piece of Battenberg cake; b23.5 improves as it goes along, helped by the peaty remnants. Ends up as a delicious whole. 46%. sc. 357 bottles.

GLENGLASSAUGH
Speyside, 1875. The BenRiach Distillery Co. Working.

Glenglassaugh 21 Year Old db **(94)** n23.5 elegant and adroit, the lightness of touch between the citrus and barley is nigh on mesmeric: conflicting messages of age in that it appears younger and yet you feel something has to be this kind of vintage to hit this degree of aloofness. Delicate and charming...; t24.5 again we have all kinds of messages on delivery: the spices fizz around announcing oaky intentions and then the barley sooths and sweetens even with a degree of youthful juiciness. The tastebuds are never more than caressed, the sugar-sweetened citrus ensuring neither the barley or oak form any kind of advantage; impeccably weighted, a near perfect treat for the palate; f22.5 white chocolate and vanilla lead the way as the oak begins to offer a degree of comparative austerity; b23.5 a malt which simply sings on the palate and a fabulous benchmark for the new owners to try to achieve in 2030...!! 46%

Glenglassaugh 26 Years Old db **(78.5)** n19 t21.5 f18.5 b19.5. Industrial amounts of cream toffee here. Also some odd and off key fruit notes winging in from somewhere. Not quite the gem I had hoped for. 46%

⁘ **Glenglassaugh Batch 1 1986 28 Years Old** hogshead, cask no. 2101, dist 19 Feb 86, db **(93)** n23.5 sublime fruit intervention on the rampant honey. Moist cherry fruit cake and vanilla also show well; t24 and off goes those honey tones again. A fabulous marriage between soothing ulmo and grittier manuka. A little maple syrup says hello; f22.5 bitter marmalade as the tannins begin to show form; b23 a spotless cask which has more grey hairs than you might expect for its age. Superb, though. 43.7%. sc.

Glenglassaugh Master Distillers' Selection Aged 28 Years dist 1983 db **(93)** n23 seville orange and vanilla. But not quite that simple...don't get me started on the antique leather...; t24 the body is of the type you might see on a Scandinavian beach in high summer: beautiful tone and delicate curves in all the right places. The barley myriad juices; the oak conjures several layers of vanillas, including a light covering of ulmo honey; f22.5 just bitters out slightly, though remains busy; b23.5 knowing Norway as I do, glad to see these lovely people are getting their money's worth! 49.8%. nc ncf sc. Norway exclusive. 400 bottles.

Glenglassaugh 30 Year Old db **(89)** n23 t23 f21 b22. Sheer poetry. Or not... 43.1%

⁘ **Glenglassaugh 30 Year Old** db **(87)** n22.5 t23 f20 b21.5. A gentle perambulation around soft fruitcake. Moist and nutty it still has a major job on its hands overcoming the enormity of the oak. The buzzing spices underline the oak involvement. Meek, charming though a touch furry on the finish. 44.8%.

Glenglassaugh Rare Casks Aged Over 30 Years db **(86)** n22 t21 f21.5 b21.5. Nearly four decades in an oak cask has resulted in a huge eruption of caramels. Soft oils and citrus abounds but it is the oak which dominates. 43%. nc ncf sc. Actual age 36 years. 280 bottles.

⁘ **Glenglassaugh 1963 51 Years Old** cask no. 3301 db **(88)** n23.5 cherry cough sweets: a dram that should help you breathe more easily...; t22.5 oddly enough it remains medicinal as the intensity of the tannins almost carve out a creosote-ish bite; some sugars – again something akin to black cherry juice – does all it can to stem the oaky tide; steady weight and pace to development; f20 burnt toast meets burnt coffee: slowly, all meaningful sweetness is consumed by the rampant oak; b22 a shame this wasn't bottled a few years back: there are some magnificent phases here. The nose and delivery possess their own morbid beauty and the battle of the fruity sugars against the passage of time is of heroic status. The final moments, though, are a little painful. 41.7%

⁘ **Glenglassaugh Batch 1 1978 35 Years Old** sherry hogshead, cask no. 1803, dist 06 Oct 78 db **(95.5)** n23.5 a light brushing of kumquat but vanilla dominates. Slightly milky nougat. Elegant, clean and some delightful hints of moist fruitcake; t24 its age beats it chest on entry with a distinctive oaky yodel. But the marzipan and ulmo honey mix really does make you purr...; **f24** so, so gentle. A vague hint of something fruity. A gentle statement of spice, more deft vanilla and again a fruitiness which slips through your grasp...; **b24** truly exceptional. *41.6%. sc.*

⁘ **Glenglassaugh Batch 1 1978 35 Years Old** port hogshead, cask no. 1810, dist 06 Oct 78 db (**93**) **n23** a slightly feminine perfume, decidedly tangerine and celery-based; **t23.5** so soft on delivery. The oak is old enough to possess a sheen; the barley confident enough to still generate a degree of salivation; **f23** long with the complexity levels rising. The main theme now, though, revolves around cocoa..with a little coconut grated into the mix. The vanilla is strictly Walnut Whip fondant...complete with walnut; **b23.5** one of those quiet, unassuming chaps who takes about half an hour to fully fathom. Worth the effort, though. *42.9%. sc.*

⁘ **Glenglassaugh Batch 1 1975 38 Years Old** Oloroso sherry hogshead, cask no. 7301, dist 03 Sep 75 db (**94.5**) **n23.5** entirely intact: the dry, sophisticated grape remains firm and allows only limited passages of oak to intervene. Very gentle; **t23.5** good sugar presence to cap that inherent dryness. The fruits are simple, clean, occasionally salivating and rarely make any effort to steer away from a grape effect; **f23.5** remains dry but spices now buzz in to elongate the finale; **b24** a classy, understated little malt, one that does all it can to pass under the radar,. Sorry – but you've been outed! Also, at its best after being allowed to breathe in glass for a good half hour. *40.7%. sc.*

⁘ **Glenglassaugh Batch 1 1975 38 Years Old** Moscatel hogshead, cask no. 7801, dist 18 Jun 75, db (**89**) **n21.5** the grape works hard to polish up some uncomfortable old oak; **t21.5** still lacks shape on delivery and we are several layers in before a milky chocolate embrace comes to its rescue; **f22.5** now comfortable with soft tannins meeting the fruit in the eye; **b22.5** a more voluptuous, expansive version of cask 7301. But in being so, has somewhere lost its finesse and complexity down the line. Oh, not the similarity of the cask numbers: probably from being tucked away in an inaccessible part of an old warehouse... *42.4%. sc.*

Glenglassaugh The Chosen Few 1st Edition "Ronnie Routledge" 35 Years Old sherry butt, dist May 76 db (**95**) **n24** lacking the over enthusiastic oak which might have been expected, it enjoys the freedom with a wonderful display of its trademark orange blossom honey but with extra butterscotch, red liquorice and glace cherries. Very bourbony, but this time with a distinctive barley lilt; **t24** the strength is almost perfect for the degree of intensity proffered by the complex early sugars. The natural caramel forms a medium-depthed layer, but one easily penetrated by myriad further bourbon signatures, the spiced liquorice not being the least of them; **f23.5** long with a near perfect weight to the oil and oaky background. Busy spices and busier sugars, all done with panache; egg custard tart, improbably sprinkled with a little hickory and allspice; **b23.5** I had no idea Ronnie Routledge was 35 years old. Thought he was much younger... *49.6%. 654 bottles.*

Glenglassaugh Aged 37 Years db (**92**) **n23.5** honeycomb and hickory; burnt (or with the vaguest hint of smoke, is that burning?) date and walnut cake with liberal helpings of Demerara sugar; a hint of spice on the ever thickening vanilla. Not a single off note, or hint of over exertion...; **t23** excellent honey and spice delivery. First-class oils and beeswax ensure the sugars glide around the palate as if on skates; a curious subplot of glazed cherry ups the salivation factor even further; **f22** more vanillas and a little (smoky?) praline for a finale flourish; **b23.5** after all those years, dementia has set in: it thinks it's a bourbon... And not any old bourbon, believe me... *54.8%. nc ncf.*

Glenglassaugh Master Distillers' Selection Aged 37 Years dist 1974 db (**90.5**) **n23** a complex smattering of oaky tones, almost all of them recognisable in well matured bourbon: the most attractive is the interplay between the orange blossom honey and much drier hickory; **t23** the honey tries to carry on from the nose. But brought to a halt a far more aggressive toasty oak, though a brief early kumquat injection restores balance; **f22** sugar-free mocha; **b22.5** for the US market only, one assumes it was sent to Oakland. And I have just spotted the tasting notes I did for their 37-year-old bottled last year...the characteristics almost identical! Oh well, it is personally reassuring that even with over 1,000 tasting notes completed for the next Bible, my poor old palate is still registering! *56%. nc ncf sc. USA exclusive. 470 bottles.*

Glenglassaugh Massandra Collection Aleatico Aged 39 Years db (**96.5**) **n24.5** when you have grape in a malt, you really want it to do something and not either ruin it or swamp the barley into silence. Here is that rarest of beasts of a grape which has so much to say, especially in its deep Sumatra and Blue Mountain mix of coffee. The sharpness of the tannin works against the brilliance of the thick barley, yet does so with a soft, always alluring, voice; **t25** this appears to be an old malt (again, I don't have details with the sample) for the layering of the oak is truly exceptional. But where this truly excels is with both the weight, intensity and vivacity of the barley coupling so seamlessly with the much richer grape which, like the nose, is intent on displaying a fabulous coffeed edge, though here much more milky and of a mocha style. We are talking, in short, perfection...; **f23** more vanilla at play, and some courser sugars plus a furry buzz which may be more of a marmalade character than anything more sinister; **b24** if you are looking for something very different, and truly exceptional quality wise, you could do a lot worse. One of the few whiskies this year which has made me sit bolt upright in my seat. A whisky of the very rarest beauty and one of the finest scotch whiskies to land on my tasting desk for a great many years... *50.7%.*

Glenglassaugh 40 Year Old db **(96) n24.5** the kind of oak you'd expect at this age – if you are uncommonly lucky or have access to some of the most glorious-nosing ancient casks in all Scotland - but there is so much else on the fruity front besides: grape, over-ripe yam, fat cherries...And then there is a bourbony element with molassed hickory and sweetened vanilla: wake me, I must be dreaming...on second thoughts, don't; **t24.5** pure silk on delivery. All the flavours arrive in one rich wave of consummate sweetness, a tapestry celebrating the enormity of both the fruit and oak, yet condensed into a few inches rather than feet; plenty of soft medium roast Jamaican Blue Mountain and then at times mocha; on the fruity front there is juicy dates mulched with burned raisin; **f23** the relative Achilles heel as the more bitter, nutty parts of the oak gather; **b24** it is as if this malt has gone through a 40-year marrying process: the interlinking of flavours and styles is truly beyond belief. *44.6%*

⁖ **Glenglassaugh 40 Year Old** db **(87.5) n21.5 t23.5 f21 b21.5.** Not entirely sure what it is with this one. I wasn't too happy about my 40th birthday, I remember, and this appears to have had the same mind-set. Hasn't quite extracted some of the better qualities of the oak, so never entirely gets its game together. A few flashy clothes (mainly in the form of a brief outbreak of stunning exotic fruit) and bling. But, underneath, for all its occasionally exotic patter a bit of a dullard, really. And then, maybe late of an evening, when less analytical, I see this in a slightly different light and home in on its good points, jettisoning the bad – then it is worth half a dozen points more. Entirely a mood and/or moment thing. *42.5%.*

⁖ **Glenglassaugh Batch 1 1973 40 Years Old** Manzanilla sherry puncheon, cask no. 6801, dist 05 Dec 73 db **(74) n22 t20 f15 b17.** A particularly lingering and unwanted drying note has gone traipsing over what looks like fabulous sherry. Some lovely fleeting moments, but will be tarnished for some. I was caught off guard on this one due to the overt richness of the nose. *52.1%. sc.*

⁖ **Glenglassaugh Batch 1 1972 41 Years Old** refill sherry butt, cask no. 2114, dist 25 Oct 72 db **(87.5) n23 t23 f20 b21.5.** The nose has the malt's age tattooed in oak across it. But there is big grape with no intention of yielding on delivery and for a while is an essay on style. Sad, then, that it should bitter out on the finish with no less single mindedness. *50.6%. sc.*

Glenglassaugh Aged 43 Years db **(91) n23.5** a nose of rare clarity for its age. Or it is once it has been in the glass for a good 15 minutes. Then the wrinkles vanish and we are left with a vibrant, juicy nose offering a sweetness that runs the full gamut from fruit to biscuit... Not surprisingly there is a death by chocolate feel to this one, too. And even a little smoke; not entire free of the odd gremlin, but not too much damage done; **t24** you really don't spit this kind of whisky, however professional you are. Not sure if the silkworm has been bred yet that can produce something as silky as this guy. A few random spices here, a splash of walnut oil there; **f21** a slight Achilles heel: some weaknesses show as a mild bitterness leaks in. But I am not quibbling; **b22.5** another ludicrously magnificent malt from a distillery which should never have been closed in the first place... *48.7%. nc ncf.*

⁖ **Glenglassaugh Batch 1 1968 45 Years Old** sherry hogshead, cask no. 1601, dist 07 May 68 db **(96) n23.5** intense orange peel, almost like that you might find in a gin. Slight spotted dog puddin', though the full blown fruitcake effect slowly grows...with a bit of extra tannin where you hope the Demerara might be...; **t23.5**....and, likewise, the oak rams a few splinters home early on. But as the oils settle and some sugar does slowly start to sooth, the true story and elegance of this malt can at last be recognised and told... **f24.5** what a finish! This is nigh on perfection. Not an off note; barely an atom of detectable sulphur (if it has been touched up in a new cask it, miraculously, got away with it): just outstanding, as it how seems, very lightly smoked, spirit maturing for 45 years in a sherry butt the way they once were and we can only hope against hope will be again one day. Look, and it is there somewhere: a little liquorice and marzipan; black cherries, a squirt of sweetening ulmo honey, Melton Hunt Cake kept in the larder for a good four or five years; vanilla snd butterscotch in small spoon fulls...on and on and on it goes....all the way back to 1968! **b24.5** it may be hanging on for grim death at times against the oak, but what emerges is something you'll remember forever. *44.3%. sc.*

Glenglassaugh Andrea Cammineci 1972 refill butt db **(92.5) n23.5** spiced bonbons, with some black cherry for good measure; the sweetness is dull, of the liquorice variety as well as toasty raisin; **t24** those looking for a big sherry statement are in for a shock: the delivery is nearer Kentucky with tidal waves of waxy honeycomb and natural caramels; the odd piece of fruitcake can be spotted bobbing around; **f22** enters a no-man's-land for a while where there is a lack of anything much. Then, slowly, a fruitcake toasty dryness emerges, along with walnut oil; **b23** one of those rare hybrids that manages to get the best of both worlds; will appeal to high quality bourbon lovers every bit as those looking for sumptuous sherried drams... *59.1%. nc ncf sc. For German distribution.*

Glenglassaugh 1973 Family Silver db (95) n23 t24 f24 b24. From first to last this whisky caresses and teases. It is old but shows no over-ageing. It offers what appears a malt veneer but is complexity itself. Brilliant. And now, sadly, almost impossible to find. Except, possibly, at the Mansefield Hotel, Elgin. *40%*

Glenglassaugh The Chosen Few 1978 db (94) n24 the nose of a malt which has seen probably more summers than it should have done. But it has picked up a creamy, orange blossom honey tan along the way; the multiple vanilla tones are seasoned beautifully with a soft saltiness. Enough to make one swoon...; **t23** despite the early sugars, the delivery is dominated with over-aged oak: punchy tannins which creak around the palate. Thankfully there is enough spotted dog pudding encased in sugar – and coconut cream – to see off the aged excess; **f23.5** settles now with a few spices adding to the sweetened Carnation evaporated milk; **b23.5** hate to say it, and almost impossible to believe: but Mhairi McDonald has not seen off the years quite as well as Ronnie Routledge. Even so, still some looker! *46.5%.*

Glenglassaugh Evolution Ex-Tennessee Cask db (87) n22 crème brule; **t22.5** an ever increasing intensifying degree of muscovado sugars stirred into the vanilla; **f21** the fondant of a Walnut Whip battling with some random barley and oak notes; **b21.5** a Bambi of a dram, youthfully stumbling around seeking balance with limited success. Interesting: the 10cl sample bottle here tells me only it is ex-Tennessee cask. I'd be willing to bet a wad of this is Dickel over Daniel any day. The giveaway is the fact that the punchier tannins are not in evidence – suggesting older maturation in the US. Nor is the residual oiliness which usually makes its mark. Having said all that, I'm sure someone will now tell me this is a JD cask! *57.2%.*

⁙ **Glenglassaugh Evolution** db (85) n21 t22 f21 b21. Cumbersome, oily and sweet, this youngster is still evolving. *50%.*

Glenglassaugh Madeira db (93) n23.5 spices rarely come sexier: busy, pulsing and of varying tone and heat; mainly appear to be oak led, though the sultana concentrate makes its mark, also; **t23.5** thick grape dulls the expected spice kick; the sugars, at first beaming, are also quickly subdued, though of a lightly molassed style; supremely chewy, though, with just so sugar impact; **f22.5** a gorgeous creamy mocha with a tea spoon of molasses; a slightly muffled, furry finale; **b23.5** a deliciously rich but surprising malt in that the spices fanfared on the nose never quite arrive. Love it, warts and all. *44.8% nc ncf sc. 437 bottles.*

Glenglassaugh The Manager's Legacy No.1 Jim Cryle 1974 db (90.5) n21.5 citrus and various salty, herbal notes try to prop up a crumbling castle as an incoming tide of oak begins to wash it away...; **t23.5** where did that come from? Early oak, but then a magnificent recovery in the form of sharp old orange peel and a salty, mega malty thrust. Some dried fruit, mainly old dates and plums, build further bridges and as the saline quality intensifies, the juicier it all becomes; **f22.5** long with spices and plenty of cream toffee; **b23** talk about blowing away the cobwebs! The nose trumpets all the hallmarks of a tired old malt in decline. What follows on the palate could not be more opposite. Don't you just love a surprise! *52.9%. nc ncf sc.*

Glenglassaugh The Manager's Legacy No.2 Dod Cameron 1986 refill sherry butt, dist Dec 86 db (92) n23.5 the sherry residue must have been as thick as tar when they billed this butt: an enormous welter of pithy and juicy grape married with the aroma one might expect at a Fruitcake Fest. The odd roasty bitter note counters the sweeter Demerara tones. Wow! **t24** a near perfect delivery with that thick grape arriving hand-in-hand with sublime spices; again a burnt toast bitterness battles it out with some macho sugars; **f22** back to a more Dundee cake style, with a few natural caramels thrown in; **b22.5** did anyone mention this was from a sherry butt...? A vague, mildly out of kilter, bitterness knocks the odd mark off here and there, but a dram to kick the shoes off to and savour. *45.3%. nc ncf sc. 500 bottles.*

Glenglassaugh The Manager's Legacy No.3 Bert Forsyth 1968 db (89) n22 t23 f22 b22. A kind of upside down whisky: usually the big oaks arrive at the death. Here they are all upfront... An excellent whisky that, by rights, should never be... *44.9%. nc ncf sc. 300 bottles.*

Glenglassaugh The Manager's Legacy No.4 Walter Grant 1967 refill sherry hogshead, dist May 67 db (86.5) n19.5 t22 f23 b22. Despite the oaky wounds to the nose, the palate is far more open and somehow reaches a degree of depth and complexity which makes for an excellent and unexpected experience. *40.4%. nc ncf sc. 200 bottles.*

⁙ **Glenglassaugh Massandra Connection 1978 35 Years Old** Madeira Finish db (94.5) n24.5 the softest and most silky aroma it is possible to imagine. A whisper of buzzing spice reminds you this is a living thing, otherwise you are likely to drift off with the sultry, juicy spices into a happy oblivion; **t24** and a delivery to match. The rarest of styles: both velvety on delivery yet broadcasting enough fresh juiciness to leave you in no doubt it means business as far as complexity is concerned. The spices rattle apologetically, the sugars drift towards molasses. Then...a little bitterness...; **f22.5** ah, an unwelcome tang on the long, soft finish...; **b23.5** last year's Massandra created a rod for its own back, so beguilingly beautiful was it. This one has done all it can, very quietly, though somewhat suavely to live up to the expectation. A marginally less clean-cut cask this time, though. *41.7%.*

⁘ **Glenglassaugh Massandra Connection 1973 41 Years Old** Sherry Finish db (**86.5**) **n20.5 t22 f22 b22.** Plenty of nibble on this for such a relatively weak cask strength malt. The grape appears to have such a hard time overcoming the obvious tiredness of the cask, it has little scope to draw pretty pictures. Pleasant but borderline austere. *44.5%.*

Glenglassaugh Muscat Finish db (**94**) **n23** the nose appears to be hit continuously with an oak stave. The blows are softened only by a thick layer of boiled plums and under-ripe dates; **t23.5** salivating to the point of near incontrollable dribbling...as juicy as any malt you'll taste this year. But, unusually, oak-weighted, too, with that sucked back of pencil unmistakable in its sheer woodiness. Even so, it works..beautifully! And not least because of a fabulous mocha, rum and raisin middle; **f24** at last softens, though the fruits, aided by lemon-topped marzipan, rumble on; the butterscotch fade is truly classic; **b23.5** you'd expect any Muscat finish to be over the top...and it is. Great to see a whisky named after a former Millwall hardman...wasn't it...? *44.1% nc ncf sc. 308 bottles.*

Glenglassaugh Red Port db (**85**) **n22 t22 f20 b21**. Loads of homemade redcurrant jam on toast here. Excellent texture, good age but an off key finish. *50.2%. nc ncf sc.*

Glenglassaugh Revival new, refill and Oloroso sherry casks db (**75**) **n19 t20 f17 b19**. Rule number one: if you are going to spend a lot of money to rebuild a distillery and make great whisky, then ensure you put the spirit into excellent oak. Which is why it is best avoiding present day sherry butts at all costs as the chances of running into sulphur is high. There is some stonkingly good malt included in this bottling, and the fabulous chocolate raisin is there to see. But I look forward to seeing a bottling from 100% ex-bourbon. *46%. nc ncf.*

Glenglassaugh Sherry db (**87**) **n21.5** pure sherry trifle...with an extra dollop of custard; **t22.5** rampant tannins are impressively quelled by a viscous layer of clean, unambiguous sherry which, after untangling, offers greengage and spice; **f21** long, with those oak notes calming down into gentler cocoa tones; no shortage of raisin, too...; **b22** at first the sherry is over dominant, but once it relaxes the complexity and enjoyment levels rise. Technically, a bit of a nightmare. But the impact of the sherry is compelling. *53.3% nc ncf sc. 328 bottles.*

Glenglassaugh The Spirit Drink db (**85**) **n20 t22 f21.5 b21.5**. A pretty wide margin taken on the cut here, it seems, so there is plenty to chew over. Richly flavoured and a tad oily, as is to be expected, which helps the barley to assert itself in midstream. The usual new make chocolaty element at work here, too, late on. Just great to see this distillery back in harness after all these years. And a great idea to get the new spirit out to the public, something I have been encouraging distilleries to do since my beard was still blue. Look forward to seeing another version where a narrower cut was made. *50%. 8,160 bottles.*

Glenglassaugh The Spirit Drink Fledgling XB db (**91**) **n22 t23.5 f22.5 b23**. The barley arrives unblemished and makes a proud, juicy stand. A surprising degree of early natural caramel. Prefer this over the peat, to be honest, and augers well for the distillery's future. *50%*

Glenglassaugh The Spirit Drink Peated db (**89.5**) **n22 t23 f22 b22.5**. Enjoyable and doesn't appear close to its 50%abv. But it's not about the bite, for there is a welcome citrus freshness to this, helped along the way by a peatiness which is big but by no means out to be the only important voice. *50%*

Glenglassaugh The Spirit Drink That Blushes to Speak Its Name db (**85**) **n22 t21.5 f21 b21**. Not whisky, of course. New make matured for a few months in wine barrels. The result is a Rose-looking spirit. Actually takes me back to my early childhood – no, not the tasting of new make spirit. But the redcurrant aroma which does its best to calm the new make ruggedness. Tasty and fascinating, though the wine tries to minimalise the usual sweetness you find in malt spirit. *50%*

⁘ **Glenglassaugh Torfa** db (**90**) **n23.5** not stinting on the phenols: the peat appears to have been shovelled into the furnace like a fireman feeding coals to the Flying Scotsman; **t22.5** crisp, sugary delivery with some meaningful smoke layering. Some Parma Violet candy nuzzles alongside the treacle-cocnut; **f22** good phenolic grist fade; **b22** appears happy and well suited in its new smoky incarnation. *50%.*

GLENGOYNE
Highlands (Southwest), 1833. Ian Macleod Distillers. Working.

Glengoyne 10 Years Old db (**90**) **n22** beautifully clean despite coal-gas bite. The barley is almost in concentrate form with a marmalade sweetness adding richness; **t23** crisp, firm arrival with massive barley surge, seriously chewy and textbook bitter-sweet balance; but now some oils have tucked in to intensify and lengthen; **f22** incredibly long and refined for such a light malt. The oak, which made soft noises in the middle now intensifies, but harmonises with the intense barley; an added touch of coffee signals some extra oak in recent bottlings; **b23** proof that to create balance you do not have to have peat at work. The secret is the intensity of barley intermingling with oak. Not a single negative note from first to last and now a touch of oil and coffee has upped the intensity further. *40%*

Glengoyne 12 Years Old db **(91.5)** n22.5 salty, sweet, lightly fruity; **t23** one of the softest deliveries on the market: the fruit, gristy sugars and malt combine to melt in the mouth: there is not a single hint of firmness; **f23** a graduation of spices and vanilla. Delicate and delightful...; **b23** the nose has a curiously intimate feel but the tasting experience is a wonderful surprise. *43%*

Glengoyne 12 Years Old Cask Strength db **(79)** n18 t22 f19 b20. Not quite the happiest Glengoyne I've ever come across with the better notes compromised. *57.2%. nc ncf.*

Glengoyne Aged 14 Years Limited Edition oloroso cask db **(77)** n19 t20 f19 b19. A vague sulphur taint. But rather underpowered anyway. *40%. nc. Marks & Spencer UK.*

Glengoyne 15 Years Old db **(73.5)** n18 t19 f18 b18.5. Some sub-standard, left-out-in-the-rain oak crept in from somewhere. Ouch. *40%. Travel Retail exclusive.*

Glengoyne 15 Years sherry casks db **(81)** n19 t20 f21 b21. Brain-numbingly dull and heavily toffeed in style. Just don't get what is trying to be created here. Some late spices remind me I'm awake, but still the perfect dram to have before bed – simply to send you to sleep. Or maybe I just need to see a Doctor... *43%. nc. Ian Macleod Distillers.*

Glengoyne 17 Years Old db **(86)** n21 t23 f21 b21. Some of the guys at Glengoyne think I'm nuts. They couldn't get their head around the 79 I gave it last time. And they will be shaking my neck not my hand when they see the score here...Vastly improved but there is an off sherry tang which points to a naughty butt or two somewhere. Elsewhere mouth-watering and at times fabulously intense. *43%*

Glengoyne 18 Years first-fill sherry casks db **(82)** n22 t22 f18 b20. Bunches of lush grape on nose and delivery, where there is no shortage of caramel. But things go downhill once the dreaded "s" word kicks in. *43%. nc. Ian Macleod Distillers.*

Glengoyne 21 Years Old db **(90)** n21 closed and tight for the most part as Glengoyne sometimes has a tendency to be nose-wise, with the emphasis very much on coal gas; **t22** slow to start with a few barley heads popping up to be seen; then spices arrive with the oak for a slightly bourbony feel. Gentle butterscotch and honey add a mouth-watering edge to the drier oaks; **f24** a stupendous honey thread is cross-stitched through the developing oak to deliver near perfect poise and balance at finish; **b23** a vastly improved dram where the caramel has vanished and the tastebuds are constantly assailed and questioned. A malt which builds in pace and passion to delivery a final, wonderful coup-de-grace. Moments of being quite cerebral stuff. *43%*

Glengoyne 21 Years Old Sherry Edition db **(93)** n22 t24 f23 b24. The nose at first is not overly promising, but it settles at it warms and what follows on the palate is at times glorious. Few whiskies will match this for its bitter-sweet depth which is pure textbook. Glengoyne as few will have seen it before. *43%*

Glengoyne 40 Years Old db **(83)** n23 t21 f19 b20. Thick fruit intermittently pads around the nose and palate but the oak is pretty colossal. Apparent attempts to reinvigorate it appear to have backfired. *45.9%*

Glengoyne Cask Strength db **(86)** n21.5 t23 f20 b21.5. The grape is nailed to the nose and palate with minimum subtlety. Initial flavour explosion packed with eye-glisteningly intense grape. But a furriness to the finish also plays a part, though not quite so upbeat. *58.7%. nc ncf. Ian Macleod Distillers. batch no. 001.*

⫶⫶⫶ **Glengoyne Cask Strength** batch no. 002 db **(85.5)** n20 t23.5 f20.5 b21.5. Perhaps only the single slightly off-key cask has found its way into this. But it plays out far better on the palate than it does the nose, though you get the feeling that there is a grinding in the gears as it tries to run through its set-pieces. Love the lilting richness of the delivery, though, with its honey concentrate and bubbling, jammy fruit. A spicy chap, too. So close to a classic. *58.9%. nc. WB15/119*

Glengoyne Port Cask Finish 1996 db **(74)** n17 t20 f18.5 b18.5. Decent fruit on delivery, but elsewhere proof that in whisky there is no such thing as any port cask in a storm... *46%*

Glengoyne Teapot Dram db **(86.5)** n23 t22 f20.5 b21. The nose, for its obvious fault, still has a truly classic oloroso-style depth. However, the light sulphur stain is not so easily covered up once tasted. A slightly cracked teapot, I'm afraid. *58.8%. nc ncf. Distillery exclusive.*

Glengoyne Vintage 1996 db **(70)** n16 t18 f18 b18. Creamy, but off key. *43%. nc ncf. USA.*

Glengoyne Vintage 1997 db **(68)** n16 t18 f17 b17. The "S" word strikes. And with a vengeance. *43%. nc ncf. German release.*

Glengoyne 'Glen Guin' 16 Year Old Shiraz Finish db (79) n18.5 t20 f19.5 b20. Some oily depth here. 48%

Glengoyne Burnfoot db (84) n21 t21 f21.5 b21. A clodhopping bruiser of a malt. Good honey, though. 40%. Duty Free Market.

A.D. Rattray Glengoyne 2001 sherry butt, cask no. 388, dist 8 Mar 2001, bott Apr 2013 (68) n18 t18 f16 b16. Whenever "sherry butt" and "Glengoyne" are mentioned in the same sentence, I give an involuntary shudder. Here you can see why. 58.4%. sc.

⋙ **Hepburn's Choice Glengoyne Aged 7 Years** sherry butt, dist 07, bott 14 (84.5) n21 t22.5 f21 b20. Less new make and more embryo malt. This must have been not only filled into a third fill cask but kept for seven years at the bottom of the warehouse. But apart from the wobbly nose, this youngest-ever seven-year-old ever bottled still charms with its Nesquik banana milkshake sweetness and the vivid beauty of its all-round maltiness. 46%. nc ncf sc. 774 bottles.

⋙ **Ian Macleod Glengoyne 25 Years Old** db (94.5) n23 the grape may be a little tight but the marmalade really comes into its own: bursting with hints of spice and no more, as well as ground toasted hazelnuts; t24 sumptuous delivery which gets increasingly more salivating as the grape plot thickens; some toasty depth, but only for a little more marmalade to be spread over it...just so beautifully weighted...; f23.5 now really upping the spiciness, but also a late butterscotch and crème brule signature...showing the oaks have more to say than just something spicy; light oils keep the elegance levels on a high; b24 by far and away the best Glengoyne sherry butts I have come across for a very, very long time. One worth tracking down. 48%.

Malts Of Scotland Glengoyne 1997 bourbon hogshead, cask no. MoS 13020, dist Mar 97, bott Apr 13 (86) n21.5 t22.5 f21 b21. Outstanding weight and texture to the body, with the malt offering a gorgeously honeyed sheen. Oak of only fair quality limits further development. 54.6%. nc ncf sc. 96 bottles.

Malts Of Scotland Glengoyne 1998 sherry hogshead, cask no. MoS 12050, dist Apr 98, bott Oct 12 (72.5) n21 t20 f15 b16.5. What could have been an orange fest to remember turns into a sulphury lemon. 54.2%. nc ncf sc. 96 bottles. Exclusive bottling for Aquavitae Die Messe.

⋙ **Old Malt Cask Glengoyne Aged 16 Years** refill hogshead, cask no. 10302, dist Sep 97, bott Feb 14 (86) n21 t22 f21 b22. Doesn't even try to tax you with matters regarding complexity and shape. Simply dolls out gristy, sugar-coated malt by the cask-load with rich intensity, but in a cask which offers scant support. 50%. sc. 285 bottles.

Provenance Glengoyne Over 12 Years refill hogshead, cask no. 8567, dist Winter 99, bott Summer 12 (84) n21 t21.5 f20.5 b21. Crispy barley sugar. 46%. nc ncf sc.

Provenance Glengoyne Over 13 Years refill hogshead, cask no. 9517, dist Winter 1999, bott Winter 2013 (91.5) n22.5 t23 f23 b23. Simple yet ridiculously charming. 46%. nc ncf.

GLEN GRANT
Speyside, 1840. Campari. Working.

Glen Grant db (87) n21.5 t23 f21 b21.5. This is a collector's malt for the back label alone: truly one of the most bizarre I have ever seen. "James Grant, 'The Major'" it cheerfully chirrups, "was only 25 when he set about achieving his vision of a single malt with a clear colour. The unique flavour and appearance was due to the purifiers and the tall slender stills he designed and the decision to retain its natural colour..." Then underneath is written: "Farven Justeter Med Karamel/Mit Farbstoff"" Doh! Or, as they say in German: "Doh!" Need any more be said about the nonsense, the pure insanity, of adding colouring to whisky. 40%

Glen Grant 5 Years Old db (89) n22.5 t22 f21.5 b23. Elegant malt which has noticeably grown in stature and complexity of late. 40%

Glen Grant Aged 10 Years db (96) n23.5 OK: let's take turns in counting the rungs on the barley ladder here....the usual crisp aroma, but softened by deft, if unspecific fruitiness (maybe the distant aroma of a very old orange and by no means unpleasant!), myriad vanilla and butterscotch notes can do without the toffee one; t24 magnificent! A malty delivery which simultaneously melts in the mouth, yet offers granite-like barley that crashes into your teeth; the star, perhaps are the sugars which vary from caster, through golden syrup and pans out somewhere in the muscovado range – curiously honey-free, though; f23.5 a tad tangy, though the caramel returns to turn out the lights after the butterscotch and marzipan say goodnight..; b24 unquestionably the best official 10-y-o distillery bottling I have tasted from this distillery. Absolutely nails it! Oh, and had they bottled this at 46% abv and without the trimmings...my word! Might well have been a contender for Scotch of the Year. It won't be long before word finally gets around about just how bloody good this distillery is. 40% ⊙ ⊙

Glen Grant Aged 16 Years bott Mar 10 db (91.5) n23 a lovely under-ripe banana sharpness to this while the malt snuggles up to the crunchy green apple; a playful molecule of smoke wafts around; t23.5 salivating, fresh, slightly green ...and that's just the first few nano-seconds of the delivery! Next comes a lengthy, relaxed wave of oilier barley, with a coppery, honeyed depth; tangy vanilla fills the middle ground; **f21.5** medium length, more oils and barley but with a degree of bitterness; **b22** again the finish doesn't do justice to the earlier jousting on the nose and palate. The label talks about orchard fruits, and they are absolutely spot on. Apples are order of the day, but not sure about the ripe bit: they appear slightly green to me... and that suits the nature of the crisp malt. A gorgeous whisky I fully expect to see improve over coming batches: it's one that has potential to hit superstar status. 43%

Glen Grant Distillery Edition Cask Strength Aged 20 Years cask no. 17165, dist 12 Feb 92, bott 14 Aug 12 db **(95.5) n23.5** oranges and roasted hazelnuts...and distant peat...?; **t24** busy delivery but the improbable smoke on the nose is confirmed on the palate, the peats clinging to the oils on which barley, as usual, abounds. More marmalade which works well with the buttery element. Amazing shape and complexity, all helped by the usual, unique clarity of this glorious distillery; **f23.5** so, so long, with the spices picking up where the smoke leaves off; cream jam doughnuts come to mind late on; **b24.5** I can only assume that this was matured in a cask which once held a high phenol Islay. The underlying peat is as intriguing as it is delicious! Glen Grant as you may never have seen it before...and will definitely want to see again. 55.7%. ncf. sc. 360 bottles.

⫶⫶⫶ **Glen Grant 40 Year Old** db **(83.5) n22.5 t21 f20 b20.** Probably about ten summers too may. The nose threatens an oakfest, though there are enough peripheral sugars for balance and hope. Sadly, on the palate the cavalry never quite gets there. 40%.

Glen Grant Cellar Reserve 1992 bottled 2008 db **(94.5) n23** a beguiling array of crisp barley and crystalised sugary notes; if a nose can be crunchy and brittle, then this really is it; **t24** the tastebuds virtually swoon under this glorious bathing of barley and sugar; unbelievably juicy and mouth-watering for its age, the oak is there to ensure backbone and fair play and does nothing to subtract from the most graceful notes, except perhaps to pep up slightly with a teasing spiciness; **f24** more playful spices and a chocolate fudge lending weight to the glassy barley edge; one to close the eyes to and be consumed by; **b23.5** one of the great world distilleries being revealed to the us in its very finest colours. They tend to be natural, with no colourings added, therefore allowing the extraordinary kaleidoscope of subtle sweetnesses to be deployed and enjoyed to their fullest. I defy you not to be blown away by this one, especially when you realise there is not a single big base note to be heard... 46%. nc ncf.

⫶⫶⫶ **Glen Grant 50 Year Old** db **(96.5) n24** heavyweight malt: toasted hazelnut and fruit combine with ridiculous ease; the spryness of the spice is amazing; a few old black cherries bob around on the breeze; **t24** silky delivery with early oak signs, but these are little more than polite enquiries. Delicate molasses and black cherry combine to match the drier elements of the oak; half way through, a surprising blast of juicy malt pierces the darkness; **f24** like on delivery, the weight of the piece is extraordinary: near-perfect, in fact. Just a slight hint of smoke for the first time and this sits well with the chocolate and cherry pie served up with cream on the finish. Naturally, a little treacle is mixed in for effect; **b24.5** I really don't know how G&M keep coming up with these golden oldies. The quality of the oak must have been pretty exceptional. Sexier than any 50-year-old has the right to be. For those celebrating their 50th birthday or wedding...well you'd only regret it if you missed out. 40%

Glen Grant 170th Anniversary db **(89) n23.5 t23.5 f20 b22.** The odd mildly sulphured cask has slipped through the net here to reduce what was shaping to be something magnificent. Still enjoyable, though. 46%

Glen Grant Five Decades bott 2013 db **(92) n24** the kind of aroma which leaves you transfixed: the trademark crisp, juicy barley is there in force, but the darker, deeper tones rumble with a spiced orange lead: sublimely complex; **t23.5** the delivery is full of the usual malty zest for life. There is a unique clarity to the barley of Glen Grant and here, on delivery and for a few a few moments after, this goes into overdrive. The mid ground is more muddled with tannin and burnt raisin making their presence felt; **f21.5** tangy marmalade; **b23** a nose and delivery of astonishing complexity. Hardly surprising the fade cannot keep up the pace. 46%

Glen Grant The Major's Reserve bott Mar 10 db **(85.5) n21.5 t23 f20 b21.** Forget about the so-so nose and finish. This is one of those drams that demands you melt into your chair on delivery, such is the fresh beauty of the malt and stunning honeycomb threads which tie themselves around every taste bud. Pity about the ultra dry, caramel-rich finish, but apparently nearly all the sherry butts have now been used up at the distillery. Thank gawd for that. 40%

⫶⫶⫶ **Cadenhead's Small Batch Glen Grant-Glenlivet Aged 15 Years** bourbon hogsheads, dist 97, bott 13 **(88) n23** unusually oily. Fresh malt, still with a hint of green grassiness; **t22.5** oils apparent early on delivery; malt and icing sugar evolve at equal rate; Madeira cake oakiness hits mid-ground; **f21** bitters and dries slightly; **b21.5** usually a crisp, brittle malt, this is the oiliest from this distillery I've seen for at least a decade. 46%. 924 bottles. WB15/265

⫶⫶⫶ **Cadenhead's Authentic Collection Glen Grant Cask Strength Aged 24 Years** bourbon barrel, dist 1989, bott Oct 13 **(83.5)** n21.5 t21.5 f20.5 b20. Glen Grant, as Gordon & MacPhail have shown continuously for the last three decades, can be bottled at very great age with very great success. Sometimes, though, a mixing of casks is required to keep the bolder oak influences at bay. Here we have a cask that was probably too good for long termism. The degree of tannin has thrown out of kilter all else and balance has vanished from the map. There are some major marmalade moments as well as some sugar-spice interplay. But this is a tweezers whisky... *58%. 156 bottles. WB15/084*

Duncan Taylor Dimensions Glen Grant 17 Years Old cask no. 85116, dist May 95, bott May 12 **(84.5)** n21 t21 f21.5 b21. The usual chunky barley at play. But rather workmanlike and urbane by Glen Grant standards, concentrating on its fiery element rather than its usual deft complexity. *54.2%. nc ncf sc. Duncan Taylor & Co. 226 bottles.*

Duncan Taylor Dimensions Glen Grant 19 Years Old cask no. 142040, dist 1992, bott 2012 **(88.5)** n22 t22 f22.5 b22. A blenders' delight of a malt possessing just enough tricks and turns to make for an entertainer. *52.7%. nc ncf sc. 242 bottles.*

⫶⫶⫶ **The First Editions Glen Grant 1994 Aged 19 Years** refill hogshead, dist 1994, bott 2014 **(93.5)** n23 oak plays a deft hand here, merely offering a drying chain to shackle the lively barley; **t24** hard to imagine a Speysider being more Speyside-like at this age. So clean you can almost polish your teeth with it. How the sugars and barley appear to be in such perfect harmony is a wonder to behold; **f23.5** much more inclined to vanilla; **b23.5** a malty study in crunchy sugars. Adorable. *55.5%. nc ncf sc. 256 bottles.*

⫶⫶⫶ **Gordan & Macphail Distillery Label Glen Grant 40 Year Old** (83.5) n22.5 t21 f20 **b20.** Probably about ten summers too many. The nose threatens an oakfest, though there are enough peripheral sugars for balance and hope. Sadly, on the palate the cavalry never quite gets there. *40%*

⫶⫶⫶ **Gordan & MacPhail Distillery Label Glen Grant 50 Year Old** (96.5) **n24** heavyweight malt: toasted hazelnut and fruit combine with ridiculous ease; the spryness of the spice is amazing; a few old black cherries bob around on the breeze; **t24** silky delivery with early oak signs, but these are little more than polite enquiries. Delicate molasses and black cherry combine to match the drier elements of the oak; half way through, a surprising blast of juicy malt pierces the darkness; **f24** like on delivery, the weight of the piece is extraordinary: near perfect, in fact. Just a slight hint of smoke for the first time and this sits well with the chocolate and cherry pie served up with cream on the finish. Naturally, a little treacle is mixed in for effect; **b24.5** I really don't know how G&M keep coming up with these golden oldies. The quality of the oak must have been pretty exceptional. Sexier than any 50-year-old has the right to be. For those celebrating their 50th birthday or wedding...well you'd only regret it if you missed out. *40%*

⫶⫶⫶ **Gordon & MacPhail Glen Grant 1948 66 Year Old** cask no. 1369 **(96)** n24 improbably charming and delicate after all this time: a light caress of smoke helps you to forgive any over eagerness by the oak – the tannin is confident but softened not just by the smoke but a gentle marmalade sharpness; **t24** an immediate puff of smoke on delivery is a fabulous time machine to take you back to a day when Speyside malts were smokier and more fuller bodied than they are today. Aping the nose, the tannins are next through, and for a few moments are sharp, aggressive almost, and threaten to spoil the party. But, like on the nose, they are reigned back, this time by a delicious milk chocolate, though only after there has been a telling burst of molasses to ensure there will be enough sweetness for the duration; **f23.5** long, with the oak threat now falling silent thanks to a spent, rounded feel one often finds in very old rum casks in South America. The compensation is a delicate, gently sweetened mocha which leaves a gorgeous, tang-less and clean last impression; **b24.5** when this was being made, my parents were getting married (they had me late!), Millwall were in the process of being relegated from the second tier under the auspices of manager Jack Cock and the Ealing classic, Whisky Galore, was being filmed on Barra. So what better whisky to choose as my 1,111 new dram for the 2015 Bible? Hearty congratulations to Gordon and MacPhail – and the extraordinary Glen Grant distillery, and those hardy, war-bitten souls who made this malt two generations ago – on somehow defying the odds and logic and, 66 years on, giving us a whisky experience which leaves you cooing with delight. My last little taste shall be to those lost men of Glen Grant distillery, 1948. I salute your memories, sirs, fittingly with your very own magnificent craftwork. *46.6%. sc.*

Gordon & MacPhail Distillery Label Glen Grant 1960 (96) n24.5 oh my word! Spices with mufflers attached, oloroso with a few brush strokes of prune juice and molasses. And for all the obvious Spanish influence, we have echoes of Kentucky with liquorice and honey in delicate proportions and pastel shades; **t23** the oak makes an early impact, as you might expect. But that is soon buried under layers of melt-in-the-mouth fruit, then a more bitter burnt raisin; f24.5 fabulously long. And the most extraordinary bisection of an ancient, slightly over cooked fruitcake. Which consisted of about 76% raisin; b24 the kind of nose which makes it difficult to get to the next stage. But when you make that next, tentative step, you are so glad you did! Just about perfect oloroso which alone these days makes this a national treasure. 40%

⠶ **Hepburn's Choice Glen Grant 2004 Aged 10 Years** refill hogshead, dist 2004, bott 2014 **(88)** n22.5 sound barley enlivened by citrus; t22.5 young and youthful – a few years below its actual age. But the barley is crisp, profound, clean and just so enjoyable... f21 just a little tangy from the half-hearted oak; b22 a distillery which rarely disappoints....even in probably a third-fill cask. 46%. nc ncf sc. 390 bottles.

⠶ **The Maltman Glen Grant Aged 17 Years** bourbon cask **(95)** n23 fabulous: crisp and flinty as type, yet somehow radiates the malt beautifully, allowing the fresh greenness to intermingle with both the drier, chalkier oak and a more cereal-rich maltiness: just so understated! t24.5 salivating barley appears rampant on three or four different levels of intensity and sweetness. Seemingly simple, yet for a Speysider just about all you can ask of it...; f23.5 the malt pulses with a little salt taking the sharpness of the grains higher than the delicate oak; b24 can't help wondering if this distillery provides the perfect Speyside malt... 46% WB15/219

Master Of Malt Glen Grant 31 Years Old Lost Bottlings Series dist 64, bott 95 **(97)** n24.5 near perfect. Spices, fruit, mocha and, one fancies, a touch of barley-carrying apple, in all the right places. Not a single atom of sulphur...anywhere...; t24 you laugh as it delivers: the weight is as it should be, the treacle sugars and burnt raisin understand each other completely; the oils seem to have been weighted to sub-particle exactitude...ohhh, bliss; f24 lingering, spiced up and suave. The raisin and sultana could not be better matched, with just so toastiness leading to a subtle chocolate fade; b24.5 by 'eck! Sherry butts like this haven't been seen in Scotland for quite a while, believe me. If you wonder why I'm on the warpath with the modern day rubbish which passes for sherry-matured malt, get a gander at this...and welcome back to the lost world in which I used to belong and the majority of those working in today's industry have never seen, or even have the faintest idea ever existed. 45.8%

⠶ **Old Malt Cask Glen Grant Aged 18 Years** refill hogshead, cask no.9920, dist Apr 95, bott Aug 13 **(94.5)** n24.5 wow...so subtle and sexy. This could charm its way into the stoniest heart. Perhas by being both more flinty with the barley and more delicate with the citrus than nearly any other malt you might find this year. One to dab behind the ears, if not drink...; t23.5 simplistically sexy and salivating. The barley really has much to say; f23 a slow realisation of spices; b23.5 now, find any whisky refusenik who condemns whisky out of hand and if, after a mouthful or three of this, they cannot be shewn the error of their misguided ways then they deserve a life of Cognac and vodka... 50%. nc ncf sc. 178 bottles.

⠶ **Old Particular Speyside Glen Grant Aged 18 Years** refill hogshead, cask no. 10283, dist Apr 95, bott Mar 14 **(94)** n23.5 deft smoke, rather unlike a Glen Grant, may be the ghostly echoes from an old Islay cask. But the firmness of the grain and crispness of sugars confirms, indubitably, from which distillery this hails from; t24.5 a truly textbook delivery. The clarity of the malt, oak and oiling sugars cannot be truer, reflected in the extraordinary salivating qualities it displays. The barley appears to be polished and cleaned to a startling degree; meanwhile the crunchiness of the sugars presents the oaks in their most dignified light; f22.5 medium length but always precise and crisp, with a late vaguely smoky fade; b23.5 a scary malt: quite beautiful – yet without ever seeming to try. 48.4%. nc ncf sc. 282 bottles.

⠶ **Scotch Malt Whisky Society Cask 9.77 Aged 25 Years** refill butt, dist 25 May 88 **(79)** n19 t20 f20 b20. Off key, tangy and a little hot. 56.9%. nc ncf sc.

⠶ **Scotch Malt Whisky Society Cask 9.85 Aged 16 Years** dist 03 May 97 **(94.5)** n23.5 defies the years with oak-repellent barley. Fresh, clean and crisp; t24 the delivering sugars boast an almost bourbon quality, though the barley which engulfs slams home the pedigree; spices fill the mid-ground; f23.5 one of the better finishes of any Speyside of this age. There are enough sugars in the bank to let in the oak, sluice-like, for a tapering, high quality finale; b23.5 a deceptively complex malt very at home at this good age. 55.3%. nc ncf sc. 290 bottles.

⠶ **The Single Malts of Scotland Glen Grant Aged 22 Years** bourbon barrel, cask no. 35936, dist 13 Mar 92, bott 25 Mar 14 **(94)** n22 bit of a slovenly nose: lazy malt with a half-hearted attempt to generate spice and complexity; t24.5 yes...!!! That's more like it: pure Glen Grant! The mixed sugars explode simultaneously with the barley on impact. The usual firmness is rammed home, making the sensation almost unique to this delivery. As the spices settle a vague hint of smoke forms, then a succession of treacle and spiced liquorice; f23.5 long with a fabulous singed feel: treacle on overdone toast. Some oils surface from somewhere and spread an ulmo and manuka honey mix to the finish; **b24** talk about mixed messages! The nose gives no hint of the magic to be unleashed on the palate. A true stunner. 5/78%. WB15/295

⫶ **That Boutique-y Whisky Glen Grant** batch 1 (**91**) **n21.5** rather un Glen Grant-y kind of nose: uncharacteristically yielding in part, though the mix of green malt and butterscotch is familiar to the blending lab; **t24** delivery of the day so far: a starburst of ultra clean salivating malt, seemingly intensified by the unusual oils and icing sugar; **f22.5** slightly tangy as the oak make inroads but the barley pulses; **b23** has loosened its belt and nowhere near as starched as normal. But that delivery...wow!! 50.1%. 138 bottles. WB15/210

⫶ **Wemyss Malts 1995 Single Speyside Glen Grant "In a Bluebell Wood"** bott 14 (**88.5**) **n22** surprisingly hefty oak. A few toasted almond, marmalade on toast and fudge notes offer balance; **t23** eye-watering impact. The oak really does come at you. But a concentrated gristy sweetness counters, getting the ol' saliva glands going; **f21.5** dries a tad too austerely; decent late spice; **b22** such a good distillery that, even when a cask struggles to live up to its normal standards, still has enough quality and surprises in the locker to make for a lovely dram. 46%. sc.

GLENGYLE
Campbeltown, 2004. J&A Mitchell & Co. Working.

Kilkerran Single Malt db (**80**) **n19 t20 f21 b20**. Glyngyle's first offering doesn't rip up any trees. And maybe the odd flaw to its character that you won't see when the distillery is fine-tuned. But this is the first-ever bottling from this brand new Campbeltown distillery and therefore its chances of being a worldbeater as an untried and untested 3-y-o were pretty slim. I will be watching its development with relish. And with heart pounding... 46%.

Kilkerran Single Malt bott 22 May 07 db (**84**) **n20 t21 f22 b21**. Sadly, I was out of the country and couldn't attend the Coming of Age of Kilkerran, when its first casks turned three and became whisky. Very kindly, they sent me a bottle as if I was there and, therefore, these are the notes of the very first bottling handed out to visitors. Interestingly, there is a marked similarity in distillery style to the 46% bottling in that the malt offers a crescendo of quality. This is only three year old whisky, of course, and its fingerprints will alter as it spends longer in the cask. 62%. nc ncf.

Kilkerran 'Work in Progress' db (**88**) **n22.5 t22 f21.5 b22** doing very well. 46%

⫶ **Kilkerran Work In Progress 5 Bourbon Wood** db (**90.5**) **n22.5** dry, toasty phenols sweetened by a smattering of smoky grist; **t23.5** takes a few waves, but finally the sugars are unleashed and rain down as crisp Demarara; the smoke swirls around placidly, though there is a slightly acidic bite to the peat; **f22** medium length, delicately smoked with a milky mocha fade; **b22.5** that ever-decreasing number of us who were around when Port Ellen could be tasted as a bit of a youngster will immediately spot more than the odd passing similarity. 46%. WB15/098

⫶ **Kilkerran Work In Progress 5 Sherry Wood** db (**86**) **n21 t22.5 f21 b21.5**. Sometimes you can have too much of a good thing. Almost a form of smoke and grape cancelling the other up, leaving the path for some powerful sugars to look pretty but do little for the balance. 46%. WB15/097

⫶ **Kilkerran Work In Progress 6 Bourbon Wood** db (**92.5**) **n23.5** the peat is more astringent and demanding: tighter with less will to share the limelight with the sweeter elements, though it does allow a firm and clean fruit note entry; **t23** mouth filling with both soft oils and then puffs of peat reek; sharp and angular on the palate despite the oil, it is obvious the peat is both of a high phenol content but of a singular bent; the muscovado sugars slowly leak into the plot, but they seem controlled; **f22.5** pulsing spices as the smoke keeps its foot on the throat of the sugars; **b23.5** an intriguing dram offering a style of peated malt like nowhere else in Scotland. Where WIP 5 had something of the Port Ellen about it, this has no such pretentions. Austere and disciplined, the precision of the sugar and fruit is a thing at which to marvel. 46%. WB15/100

⫶ **Kilkerran Work In Progress 6 Sherry Wood** db (**88.5**) **n21.5** whoosh!!! The peat is slapped on over the undercoat of grape; **t23** the phenols must be nearing record level for Campbeltown because the poor old sherry is a-hollorin'-an'-a-shoutin'...and you can barely hear a thing; **f22** busy spice amid the smoke; **b22** less lugubrious than WIP5, and though things here are painted with a wallpaper brush, there is some fun to be had for sure. 46%. WB15/099

GLEN KEITH
Speyside, 1957. Chivas Brothers. Working (re-opened 14th June 2013).

Glen Keith 10 Years Old db (**80**) **n22 t21 f18 b19**. A malty if thin dram that finishes with a whimper after an impressively refreshing, grassy start. 43%

⫶⫶⫶ **Cadenhead's Single Cask Glen Keith-Glenlivet Aged 29 Years** bourbon hogshead, dist 85, bott 14 **(93.5) n24** lightly salted ginger beer and sandalwood; even a light hint of smoke; a stratum of peach, lychee and over-ripe papaya underscores the big age; **t24** a yummy delivery full of oaky vim of a mainly herbal kind. The tannins bite hard but cannot get further than the treacle and maple syrup which accompanies the barley sugar; a soft, vaguely smoky buzz of spice; **f22** long, a little bitter but the toffee plays out attractively; **b23.5** offers great age for a GK but without too many recriminations. So complex... 47.5%. 108 bottles. WB15/257

⫶⫶⫶ **Gordon & MacPhail Connoisseurs Choice Glen Keith** dist 1996, bott 2013 **(86) n21 t21.5 f22 b21.5.** Puckering, juicy malt and lemon zest. A well used cask means Keith just never grew up... 46%. nc ncf. WB15/148

Kingsbury Glen Keith Aged 15 Years hogshead, cask no. 72621, dist 97 **(80.5) n20.5 t21 f19 b20.** A good example of a second class blending malt struggling to find another gear beyond some basic barley and icing sugar. 46%. nc ncf. Japan Import System. 378 bottles.

⫶⫶⫶ **Old Malt Cask Glen Keith Aged 20 Years** refill hogshead, cask no. 10147, diss Sept 93, bott Oct 13 **(89) n21.5** grassy and about as lightweight as any 20-y-o you'll nose this year. Clean and malty, though...; **t23** and that clarity on the nose transfers perfectly on the palate with a stunning injection of grassy, zesty, salivating malt...; **f22** thin, vanilla clad but lightly spiced, too; **b22.5** good to see this unfashionable distillery show itself in such a good light. 50%. nc ncf sc. 318 bottles.

⫶⫶⫶ **Old Particluar Speyside Glen Keith 20 Year Old** refill hogshead, cask no. 9953, dist Jul 93, bott 2013 **(87) n21 t23 f21 b22.** One of those classic drams which should, with half a dozen similar casks, be used in a 21-y-o blend to add the zip and malty sparkle to the weightier complexity. On its own a tasty, juicy, highly intense and well-made malt but lacking depth and desired deviation. 51.5%. nc ncf sc. 274 bottles. Douglas Laing & Co.

⫶⫶⫶ **The Pearls of Scotland Glen Keith 1995 18 Year Old** cask no. 171224, dist Nov 95, bott Nov 13 **(88) n22** adroitly complex with vague puff of smoke add some bllast to the citrusy lead; **t22.5** promises citrus on the nose and juicy lemon obliges early on; a surprising degree of oil; **f21.5** oak casks a heavy shadow over the more delicate elements; **b22** a satisfying dram for a malt of such age from this distillery. 56%.

Provenance Glen Keith Over 15 Years refill hogshead, cask no. 9655, dist Winter 97, bott Spring 13 **(84) n19 t22 f21.5 b21.5.** Glen Keith was once regarded the lightest of all the Chivas Speysiders. With minimal oak interference here, and with the barley at its most sparkling, you can see exactly why. 46%. nc ncf.

⫶⫶⫶ **That Boutique-y Whisky Glen Keith** batch 1 **(90) n22** freshly-made paper with a gristy overtone; **t23.5** superb delivery with rare clarity to the malt delivery. Light sugars and a little ulmo honey spreads the sweetness and ups the complexity; **f22** a simple but beautifully clean oak-barley fade; **b22.5** concentrates on doing the little it does exceptionally well. 51.2%. 176 bottles. WB15/234

⫶⫶⫶ **The Whisky Agency Perfect Dram Glen Keith 1992** dist 1992 **(90) n22.5** attractively malty and delicate; some tangy citrus and promise of complex bourbon notes to come further down the line; **t24** the highlight by some way: a superb lift off of intense malt followed by a plethora of a gorgeously well- defined sugars and ever-intensifying vanilla-led bourbon-oak notes. A little citrus leaks into the ongoing malt; biscuit, chewy middle. The weight and pace is truly wonderful; **f21** typically thin, pasty finale; **b22.5** hmmm! Dangerous to flaunt yourself as "perfect" anything. But as far as a Glen Keith goes from this particular era, this ain't half bad. 46.6%.

The Whisky Cask Glen Keith Aged 17 Years bourbon hogshead, dist 95, bott 12 **(85.5) n20 t23 f21 b21.5.** Lightly smoked Love Heart candy fizzes on the palate for a charming, low key malt which overcomes its slightly too underwhelming nose and finish. Anyone who remembers mint chocolate Merlin's Brew lollies from the late 1970s and early '80s will appreciate the mid ground of this malt. 52.9%. nc ncf sc.

GLENKINCHIE
Lowlands, 1837. Diageo. Working.

Glenkinchie 12 Years Old db **(85) n19 t22.5 f21.5 b22.** The last 'Kinchie 12 I encountered was beyond woeful. This is anything but. Still not firing on all cylinders and can definitely do better. But there is a fabulous vibrancy to this which nearly all the bottlings I have tasted in the last few years have sadly lacked. Impressive. 43%

⫶⫶⫶ **Glenkinchie The Distillers Edition** dist 99, bott 12 db **(80.5) n20 t23 f18.5 b19.** A bitter-sweet experience, though never for a moment finds its equilibrium. Attractively creamy and nutty. But, ultimately the furry tanginess of the wine cask wins, alas. 43% WB15/284

Glenkinchie Aged 15 Years The Distillers Edition Amontillado finished, dist 1992, bott 2007 db (94) n23.5 t24 f23 b23.5. Now this is absolutely top class wine cask finishing. One of my last whiskies of the night, and one to take home with me. Sophisticated, intelligent and classy. 46%

Glenkinchie 20 Years Old db (85.5) n21 t22 f21.5 b21. When I sampled this, I thought: "hang on, haven't I tasted this one before?" When I checked with my tasting notes for one or two independents who bottled around this age a year or two ago, I found they were nigh identical to what I was going to say here. Well, you can't say its not a consistent dram. The battle of the citrus-barley against the welling oak is a rich and entertaining one. 58.4%

Glenkinchie 1992 The Manager's Choice db (78) n19 t22 f18 b19. Has a lot going for it on delivery with a barley explosion which rocks you back in your chair and has you salivating like a rabies victim. But the rest of it is just too off key. 58.1%. Diageo.

THE GLENLIVET
Speyside, 1824. Chivas Brothers. Working.

The Glenlivet Aged 12 Years db (79.5) n22 t21 f18 b18.5. Wonderful nose and very early development but then flattens out towards the kind of caramel finish you just wouldn't traditionally associate with this malt, and further weakened by a bitter, furry finale. 40%

The Glenlivet Aged 12 Years Old First Fill Matured db (91) n22.5 t22.5 f23 b23. A quite wonderful whisky, far truer to The Glenlivet than the standard 12 and one which every malt whisky lover should try once in their journey through the amber stuff. Forget the tasting notes on the bottle, which bear little relation to what is inside. A gem of a dram. 40%

The Glenlivet Excellence 12 Year Old db (87) n22 t21.5 f22 b21.5. Low key but very clean. The emphasis is on delicate. 40%. Visitor Centre and Asian exclusive.

⬧ **The Glenlivet The Gaurdians' Chapter** db (81.5) n20 t21 f20 b20.5. Read the chapter – but can make neither head nor tail of it. A brief moment of honeyed enjoyment. But nothing else really adds up. Just doesn't gel. 48.7%. WB15/120

The Glenlivet 15 Years of Age db (80) n19 t21 f20 b20. Undeniable charm to the countless waves of malt and oak. But don't expect much in the way of complexity or charisma. 40%

Glenlivet Quercus 17 Years Old db (93.5) n23.5 Brazilian coconut biscuit and Victoria sponge cake drizzled with lemon...and just love that faintest trail of smoke...; t23.5 a little more viscous than your average Glenlivet. The barley offers both maltshake and sugar barley candy; again the citrus peps all around it; f23 more custardy vanilla; the expected spices arrive; b23.5 someone has cherry-picked a cracker of a cask... 52.1%. Whisky Shop Exclusive. 250 bottles.

The Glenlivet Alpha db (92) n23.5 a clever use of counter weights here with good aged oak – enter delicate exotic fruit – harmonising with an orange blossom/ulmo honey blend, a sweet sultana fruitiness and marmalade; t24 just love that delivery! The texture is sublime, boasting a crisp muscovado sugar sheen, with juicy barley being just below the surface: really doesn't get more Speyside than that! The intensity also dazzles, as does the glazed ginger guest appearance, though the exotic fruit makes only a surprisingly brief appearance before a light dusting of spices and Kit Kat milky chocolate-vanilla mix moves in; f21.5 short and slightly disappointing with a definite furriness to the marmalade; b23 you get the feeling some people have worked very hard at creating a multi-toned, complex creature celebrating the distillery's position at the centre of Speyside. They have succeeded. Just a cask selection or two away from a potential major Bible award. Maybe for the next bottling.... 50%

The Glenlivet French Oak Reserve 15 Years of Age Limousin oak casks db (91) n22.5 oo la la citrus; avec spice; t23 comme ci comme ca caramels rescued by an uplifting injection of sweet barley; the juicy, salivating qualities are quite startling if not profound; f22.5 long, with a fabulous butterscotch fade and a slow dissolving of dark sugars; b23 I have to say that after tasting nearly 800 cask strength whiskies, to come across something at the ancient 40% is a shock to the system. My taste buds say merci... And, what is more, a bottle of this shall remain in my dining room for guests. Having, a lifetime ago, lived with a wonderful French girl for three years I suspect I know how her country folk will regard that... Oh, and forgive a personal message to a literary friend: Bobby-Ann...keep a bottle of this beside the Ancient Age... 40%

⬧ **The Glenlivet Nadurra Aged 16 Years** batch no. 0712U, bott 07/12 db (95.5) n24 a half-hour nosing job, this. Just about everything at the right weight and density and in near perfect order. At any varying moment you will spot apple crumble (with custard, of course), butter shortbread, a cup of coffee-flavoured mocha, rhubarb with a squeeze of kumquat, a light layer of peppery spice and maple syrup...and probably the odd rather delicious thing besides; t24 and it purrs, a massive delivery of gently spiced, generously endowed sugar-laden essay in age-defying gristiness; f23.5 more oily now, but so rare to find oak so sympathetic to the complexity and weight of the malt...a light saltiness to the malty, vanilla-gathering fade; b24 so rare to find a big corporate dram like this showing every sign of grey-bearded cherry picking. A wise whisky, where care has been taken to wring every last drop of complexity from this great malt. 55.5%.

⁙ **The Glenlivet Nadurra Aged 16 Years** batch no. 0313W, bott 03/13 db (**88.5**) **n21.5** a simple mix of vanilla and barley; **t23** oily (maybe too oily) delivery of tart barley and spice; the malt expands out in ever-increasing circles until a familiar mocha character is found; **f22** spiced butterscotch; **b22** an enjoyable enough whisky which would be more than acceptable to most distilleries. But palls by comparison with other Nadurras. 54.8%.

⁙ **The Glenlivet Nadurra Aged 16 Years** batch no. 0114A, bott 01/14 db (**94.5**) **n23** huge barley sugar statement; **t24.5** wow! Some delivery as the intense ulmo honey and most concentrated form of grassy barley combine to make the eyes water: glorious in its enormity; **f23** coconut biscuit speckled with salt; **b24** confident, rich, full-bodied and clean: exactly how a Nadurra should be. And as though this is a distilled, concentrated definition of Speyside whisky. Fabulous. 55.3% WB15/312

⁙ **The Glenlivet Nadurra Oloroso Matured** batch no. 0LO314, first fill sherry casks, bott 03/14 db (**73**) **n19 t21 f16 b17**. Present generation first fill sherry butts at work here...so I'll let you guess. Meanwhile, those immune to sulphur will find this this rich and many a fruity dream come true. 48%.

The Glenlivet Aged 18 Years bott Feb 10 db (**91**) **n22** attractive mixture of honeycombed bourbon and fruitcake; **t23.5** oh...just didn't expect that...!! Fabulous, honey-sweet and slightly sharp edge to the barley: excellent weight and mouthfeel with the honeycomb on the nose making slow but decisive incursions; **f23** a very slight technical flaw drops it half a point, but there is no taking away from the improbable length of the dissolving honey and barley...some gentle chewing is required, especially with the late juices and vanilla arriving; **b23** a hugely improved bottling seriously worth discovering in this form. Appears to have thrown off its old shackles and offers up an intensity that leaves you giving a little groan of pleasure. 43%

⁙ **The Glenlivet Archive 21 Years of Age** batch 1012L db (**95.5**) **n24** so soft, so teasing, you might have to go to a local university and pick up some kind of aroma detector to aid your nose: Turkish delight and distant banana lead the sweeter elements while lime chews and lemon-drizzled lychee leads the fruit; even the drier vanilla tones are only half-hearted, as this entire scene is played out in whispers and innuendo; **t24** the delivery is so soft, you can hardly detect its landing: I could give a plethora of varying tones, some being barely audible to the taste buds. But, really, it is the understated effect which counts so importantly; **f23** it took me three hours to confirm a slight degree of sulphur. That is because I nosed and tasted alongside the XXV for comparison, and that, too, had creeping sulphur: it is not immediately detectable, as it is in relatively low amounts. A shame – this might have been one of the top three whiskies of the year...; **b24.5** possibly the most delicate whisky of this and many years: a kind o' Ballantine's 17, but in single malt form... 43%.

The Glenlivet Founder's Reserve 21 Years Old db (**95.5**) **n23.5** initially tight and, even after 20 minutes in the glass, allows the grape to unfurl in the most niggardly fashion. Thing is: the few notes, in tandem with some gorgeous Columbian cocoa, spices, orange peel and rich dates, reveals that much is to come on the palate... **t24.5** those spices are the first to flee the confines of the thick grape, but so many layers of grape skin and mocha follow that you can sit there for a good five minutes and still not entirely work out what is going on; the spices are not just persistent but simply magnificent; **f23.5** long, with (milky) cocoa and dates (of the juicy rather than dried variety) leading the way; a light sulphur note detracts half a mark, but it is testament to the malt that it barely detracts from the moment; **b24** on this evidence, one of the whiskies of the year for sure. I really don't think my 800th new single malt of the year could have been a more inspired – or lucky - choice. 55.6%. ncf. 1824 bottles.

⁙ **The Glenlivet XXV Twenty Five Years of Age** Batch No. 0913A, finished in first fill OLOROSO sherry casks db (**93.5**) **n24** nutty, sassy, elegant but showing just a little smirk and attitude. Dried dates and cock-a-snook spice. Yet all set within walls of quiet reflection; **t24** mouth-filling, soft with fruit and malt in equal measures; the oils and spices border perfection; **f22** some cocoa and butter cream. But, alas, late on a little sulphur niggle, too; **b23.5** probably one dodgy sherry butt away from immortality: some of the passages here are lifetime memorable. 43%.

The Glenlivet 1973 Cellar Collection bott Oct 09 db (**94.5**) **n24** luxurious stewed sultanas in a custard tart; yet for a malt heading towards 40, improbable grist, too: clean, complex, thick and simply spellbinding... **t24** just melts into the taste buds with the freshest, cleanest, juiciest charm you could possibly imagine, yet always with a nibbling spice darting around the side of the tongue; **f23** a touch of oaky bitterness, but a mere detail: the late oils are sympathetic and contain a surprising degree of vanilla; **b23.5** for Glenlivet lovers, I point you towards something a little special... 49%. Chivas.

The Glenlivet Cellar Collection 1980 bott Aug 11 db **(94.5) n23** no shortage of chalky oak creating almost a bloom to the fruit. There is citrus, but that fruit has slightly more tropical shades, especially green banana; **t24** one of those deliveries where the mouth-feel actually outpoints the flavours – not that there is anything wrong there. Soft and yielding, even with an early puff of distant smoke, but just enough fibre to ensure a chewy element to those fruits which are now extolling the virtues of grassy barley; **f23.5** it would be easy just to concentrate on the big peppery spices. But then you would be missing the mocha, not to mention the vanilla ice cream with a physalis topping; **b24** some of you in the know will have been expecting exotic fruit from this...and you won't be disappointed! *43.3%. ncf. 500 bottles.*

The Glenlivet Master Distiller's Reserve db **(86.5) n22.5 t22 f20.5 b21.5**. I chose this as my 800th whisky to taste for the 2012 Bible against the Founder's Reserve on the strength of the nose over the first 30 seconds. Oh, well. Shows you the pricelessness of time when evaluating a whisky... *40%*

The Glenlivet Single Cask Inveravon Aged 21 Years cask no. 10667, bott 25 Oct 11 db **(96.5) n24** sophisticated: obviously bourbon cask, but the malt still somehow conjures up a number of fruit notes, including salted cucumber and lime. Delicate, hushed liquorice and hazelnut tones and polite spice. Everything is so understated; **t24** no disappointment on delivery. The weight is sublime: just enough oil to carry the more powerful fruit notes towards the growing cocoa without there being a gap; the spices are equal and busy; **f24** happy to sign off with a simple Neapolitan ice cream vanilla and chocolate finish; **b24.5** this was a single cask for the Taiwanese market I think. Time to get a flight to Taipei...this is Glenlivet at its absolute best. *54.6%*

Cadenhead Glenlivet 24 Years Old claret, dist 88, bott 13 **(94.5) n23** classic sweaty armpit saltiness; vague fruit of the plummy school; **t24** the juices are in explosive mood thanks to some energetic spice; again the salts are up to all kinds of tricks; the malt is of Malteser-sweet intensity; **f23.5** the spices continue to glow, though the milk chocolate finale settles things; **b24** how good is that! A wine cask with not a single off note: a real collector's item! Another masterpiece for what is a vintage year for Glenlivet lovers. *53.9%. sc. 258 bottles.*

⠿ **Cadenhead's Glenlivet (Minmore) Wine Cask Aged 24 Years** Claret cask, dist 1988, bott Feb 2013 **(93) n22.5** attractive balance between spice and firm, almost non-porous oak; **t23.5** juicy barley lead; spiced fruit follows not too far behind. The middle is softly toffee; **f23.5** the spices now really hammer the point home; a light Venezuelan cocoa assists the fade; **b23.5** how good is that? A cask from France without a trace of sulphur! A genuine – and rather delicious – collectors' item. *53.9%. 258 bottles. WB15/075*

⠿ **Cadenhead's Single Cask Glenlivet (Minmore) Aged 25 Years** bourbon hogshead, dist 88, bott 14 **(89) n22.5** toffee apple, which was bitten into half an hour ago...; **t22** succulent fudge and treacle tart; and tart barley, too; **f22** all about the molasses and warming, busy spice. Oh...and the toffee...; **b22.5** every last atom of natural caramel appears to have been extracted from the cask. *54.5%. 252 bottles. WB15/258*

⠿ **Montgomerie's Single Cask Collection Glenlivet** cask no. 13643, dist 12/06/89, bott Sep 13 **(91.5) n23.5** a beauty! Myriad deft sweet notes, some borderline Muscat grape mixes with a marzipan; a rising degree of eucalyptus highlights the age; **t23** sugars up and running fast, solidly ensuring against the lurking oak; attractive bite despite the natural caramels; **f22.5** plenty of vanilla, but those deft sugars keep on working; **b22.5** a complex malt which embraces it age lines comfortably. *46%. nc ncf sc. WB15/127*

Old Malt Cask Glenlivet Aged 11 Years sherry butt, cask no. 9210, dist Sep 01, bott Oct 23 2012 **(90) n23.5 t23.5 f20 b23**. As fruity as a nut cake. *50%. sc. 374 bottles.*

Old Malt Cask Glenlivet Aged 11 Years sherry butt, cask no. 9637, dist Sep 01, bott May 13 **(86.5) n21.5 t22.5 f21 b21.5**. An odd one, this. Works on certain delicious fruitcake levels, especially with the extra molasses, but a good example of how the grape and natural caramels from the oak can combine to restrict complexity. *50%. nc ncf sc. 382 bottles.*

Provenance Glenlivet Over 11 Years sherry butt, cask no. 0000, dist 2001, bott 2013 **(94) n23.5** a once common aroma of crushed hazelnut and medium baked raisin; a slightly salty, seasoned edge to the barley; **t24** lush in the traditional and present-day meaning of the word: the grape engulfs the palate, even forming a slightly oily layer before a truly to-die-for succession of flavour mechanisms with subtly varying weights and intensity begin to lap against the taste buds. The sugars are restrained, allowing the drier notes of the oloroso and oak to caress with a distinct degree of sophistication; **f23** a delicate furriness confirms the butt did not entirely escape brutal Spanish hands, but the salty, sugar-deprived old farmhouse cake feel continues; **b23.5** what the Scotch whisky industry would give to have all its sherry butts in this wonderful, (nearly) unspoiled form. Thirty years ago, this was pretty close to how 11-year-old sherry matured whisky nosed and tasted. Now it is almost a freak. *46%. nc ncf.*

Scotch Malt Whisky Society Cask 2.83 Aged 19 Years (94.5) n23.5 the exotic fruit, diced pear, orange blossom honey, all underscored by a chalky dryness, suggests a malt a whole lot older; t24 a two-toned delivery. Simultaneously, you are treated to massive juicy barley & spiced tropical fruits; the middle pans out towards superb mocha with a playful, alluring smokiness; f23 long, and reverts back to the nose; drier with over-ripe banana; b24 about as spick and span as you could pray for. When this distillery produces good whisky...wow! 55.2%. nc ncf sc.

⁑ **Scotch Malt Whisky Society Cask 2.84 Aged 20 Years** dist 11 May 93 (89) n22 sweet grape. Soft yet almost unbearably intense; clean but clammy also; t23.5 the palate vanishes under a tidal wave of concentrated grape. Spices begin to sparkle through the murk and some big crystalline Demerara sugar notes chizzle through, too; a sub strata of honeycomb does no harm at all; f21 a degree of tanginess attached to the fruit but slightly over-dries; b22.5 a clean sherry butt by today's poor standards. But really full on with the fruit giving way to little else. Like being slapped in the face with a spicy ten pound grape. 53.2%. nc ncf sc. 77 bottles.

Wemyss Glenlivet 1977 Single Speyside "Dark Chocolate Orange" hogshead, bott 13 (92.5) n23 some serious grey hairs here: a good deal of marmalade and vanilla, no shortage of ulmo honey but weighed down by oak increasing in weight with each sniff; t23.5 a fabulously salivating start with the remnants of the barley making an early salvo. Varying degree of cocoa arrive with both the ever-thickening oils and the tangy spiced citrus; f22.5 thinner now, with the accent back on the vanilla. But that tangy marmalade takes a long time to fade; b23.5 yep. I think Dark Chocolate Orange is a good call for this oldie. 46%. sc. 149 bottles.

GLENLOCHY
Highlands (Western), 1898–1983. Diageo. Closed.

Gordon & MacPhail Rare Old Glenlochy 1979 (95) n23.5 proudly displays its age with major, but entirely acceptable, oak involvement. A pretty salty affair, lifted by delicate kumquat & wild strawberry (two fruits usually associated with oak) though the natural caramel & nibbling spice also balance beautifully; t24 ridiculously soft delivery, even though the oak insists on at least a dual starring role. The deft & fleeting malt moments are really quite monumental & with the milky chocolate gathering in intensity, the entire piece seems to become like a Malteser liqueur; f23.5 the spices which had a little attitude early on now drift serenely about the melted Malteser. A hint of late butterscotch, but the malt holds firm. Or should that be soft? b24 it has been many years since a bottle from this long lost distillery turned up and that was such a classic, I can remember every nuance of it even now. This shows far greater age, but the way with which the malt takes it in its stride will become the stuff of legend. I held back on tasting this until today, August 2nd 2013, because my lad David this afternoon moved into the first home he has bought, with new wife Rachael and little Abi. It is near Fort William, the remote west coast Highland town in which this whisky was made, and where David will be teaching next year. His first job after moving in, though, will be to continue editing this book, for he worked on the Whisky Bible for a number of editions as researcher and editor over the years. So I can think of no better way of wishing David a happy life in his new home than by toasting him with what turned out to be a stunningly beautiful malt from one of the rarest of all the lost distilleries which, by strange coincidence, was first put up for sale exactly 100 years ago. So, to David, Rachael & little Abigail... your new home! And this time I swallowed.. 46%. ncf.

GLENLOSSIE
Speyside, 1876. Diageo. Working.

A.D. Rattray Glenlossie 1992 hogshead, cask no. 3440, dist 18 Nov 92, bott Jun 11 (93) n23 no peat, yet a compelling earthiness to this perhaps helped by freshly diced vegetable mixed with molassed tannin; t23.5 perfect weight on delivery and spices which know just how to get maximum effect with minimum effort. The sugars drive the barley, mainly darkened but lightening as the butterscotch arrives; f23 classic vanilla and spice finish with the oak sturdy and steadfast even after two decades: superb! b23.5 oh, I so love this distillery! And remains so faithful to you, too! 56.6%. sc. Dewar Rattray Cask Collection.

Berry's Glenlossie 1992 (87) n23 t23 f19.5 b21.5. A distillery with the propensity to make gorgeous whisky without seemingly breaking sweat is at it again...just not helped by a indifferent piece of wood. 46%

⁑ **Cadenhead's Authentic Collection Glenlossie-Glenlivet Cask Strength Aged 20 Years** bourbon hogsheads, dist 1993, bott Feb 14 (94.5) n23 an astonishing lucidity to the barley even after all these years; fruit salad with a stick of celery; t24.5 three dimensional malt: any cleaner and your teeth would sparkle. Incredibly sharp, crisp and salivating, the sugars are crunchy and of a crystalline quality. The spices positively hiss and singe the palate; f23 returns to a softer barley sugar countenance, but a little pear juice helps...; b24 fruitier than a barrow boy down East Lane.... Magnificent! 53.3%. 252 bottles. WB15/083

⁘ **Cadenhead's Single Cask Glenlossie-Glenlivet Aged 48 Years** bourbon hogsheads, dist 66, bott 14 (**91**) **n**22.5 a little oxidisation and warming takes the edge off the sharper end of the tannin attack: even a little ulmo honey comes out to play; **t**23.5 again, the tannins are crawling over every inch of this. But the light liquorice and treacle teams with the creamy fudge to repair the time damage; **f**22 salty, spicy...and just generally bloody old! But the sugars keep it breathing...; **b**23 When you consider this was distilled in the year Harold Wilson was prime minister of Great Britain, England won the World Cup (no, we did.... honestly...I remember it!), when virtually all of Scotland's dual carriageways of today were simple, ambling roads offering a bottleneck from town to town, I saw Millwall play for the very first time...and I was still two years short of tasting my first whisky, and you realise we are approaching something close to pre-history. So the fact a malt like Glenlossie, not renowned for its propensity to last overly long in the cask, can still come up with the goods, even if a little tarnished and dented, really does make this worth a good 45 minutes in the glass before drinking. A dram that deserves as much time as you've got...and a little more besides. 43.5%. 168 bottles. WB15/254

⁘ **Gordon & MacPhail Connoisseurs Choice Glenlossie** dist 1995, bott 2013 (**96**) **n**24 cucumbers and celery get this off to an unusual but complex start with spice, naturally, in the mix; as the nose opens the complexity of the varied honeys becomes apparent, as does the delicate smoke; **t**24 mouth-watering delivery, but quickly thickens as the honey takes hold. A mix of heather and acacia grip and then mingles with the growing maple syrup; a soft earthiness begins to add weight; **f**24 a deft touch of smoke appears to be the crowning glory to the delicate vanillas and walnut cake; **b**24 getting harder and harder to find a dud Lossie these days: glad people are getting a chance to be in on one of the best kept secrets in Scotland... This one is truly glorious: absolutely exceptional even by the distillery' very high standards. 46%. nc ncf. WB15/149

Gordon and MacPhail Connoisseurs Choice Glenlossie 1993 (**94**) **n**23.5 the cleanest sherry I have nosed this year; the grape is rampant and full of spiced juice, dates and greengages. And not a single off not...not even a murmur...; **t**23.5 silky, oily and fabulous fusion of fruitcake and sherry trifle with heady use of molassed sugars...waiting for the off note...there isn't one; **f**23 the oak begins to make a noise of its own beyond the fruit with a gorgeous chocolate pudding contribution...dries, a distant furry mumble but nothing at all to worry about; **b**24 the first green shoots of heavy sherry cask involvement but (virtually) no sulphur...? I could almost weep. A whisky to rejoice about...for so many reasons! 46%. ncf.

⁘ **Gordan & Macphail Connoisseurs Choice Glenlossie 1997** (**74**) **n**17 **t**21 **f**18 **b**18. I had put this to one side, earmarked as a special treat. But what a disappointment. The nose and finish are off key in such a way, one has no difficulty recognising the culprit. 46%.

⁘ **Scotch Malt Whisky Society Cask 46.24 aged 20 Years** refill hogshead, dist 30 Sep 93 (**92.5**) **n**23 interesting and unusual mix of green barley, green tea and minted liquorice; **t**23.5 lively, salivating delivery at first hints at youth. But a few waves of controlled tannin re-focuses the mind...: just love the layered structure...; **f**23 the semi-lush body carries the darker sugars onward to meet the developing natural caramels and drier toast; **b**23 Lossies from the SMWS are a bit thin on the ground...but this is worth waiting for! Has no problems taking off... 53.8%. nc ncf sc. 260 bottles.

⁘ **Signatory Vintage Un-chillfiltered Collection Glenlossie 1992 Aged 16 Years** hogshead, cask no. 3439, dist 18 Nov 92, bott 17 Jan 13 (**94.5**) **n**24 despite the school room plasticine, it is the massive and magnificent Lubek marzipan which dominates, creaking under the weight of diced almond. Spices are required for balance and oblige; honey is represented by a blend of ulmo and heather; **t**23.5 you'd expect one of the above to come out top on delivery. Instead, it is the barley. Carries a degree of oak bitterness (less when you taste at body temp) but any excesses there are dealt with by the rampant sugars; **f**23 reverts to a more conservative creamy fudge finale; **b**24 puts the Glossie in Genlossie. Masterful stuff. 46%. nc ncf sc. 378 bottles. WB15/023

⁘ **Signatory Cask Strength Collection Glenlossie 1992 Aged 20 Years** hogshead, cask no. 3443, dist 18 Nov 92, bott 03 Apr 13 (**94**) **n**23.5 busy, waxy, weighty: a malt making a big statement. The oak has an old, been round the block feel, even to the point you are sure you can pick up dank, lichen-crusted walls. There is evidence of apple and barley, but this is so enormously muddled and complex; **t**24 the honey, notable by its absence on the nose, arrives by the jar full here. But it does not have a clear run in goal and even some gristy sugars and rich vanilla manage to make their mark. Chewey..; **f**23 quite a salty finale. Remains heavy, oily and dense to the far from bitter end; **b**23.5 a marathon of a malt. Enormous and seemingly goes on forever. 57.1%. nc sc. 274 bottles. WB15/140

The Whisky Agency Glenlossie 1975 bott 13 **(91.5) n22 t22 f24 b23.5.** Put your ear to the glass and you can hear the timber creaking....comes through though with a fine mocha polish. 46.6%. The Whisky Agency.

GLEN MHOR
Highlands (Northern), 1892–1983. Diageo. Demolished.

Glen Mhor 1976 Rare Malt db **(92.5) n23 t24 f22 b23.5.** You just dream of truly great whisky sitting in your glass from time to time. But you don't expect it, especially from such an old cask. This was the best example from this distillery I've tasted in 30 years...until the Glenkeir version was unleashed! If you ever want to see a scotch that has stretched the use of oak as far it will go without detriment, here it is. What a pity the distillery has gone because the Mhor the merrier... 52.2%

⋰ **Cadenhead's Single Malt Glen Mhor Aged 31 Years** hogshead, dist 82, bott Jul 14 **(94.5) n24** an exotic blast of pineapple cube candy, grapefruit and dried lychee topped, surprisingly, with a delicate puff of smoke; tannins issue a constant hum; **t23** a thick stick of oak beats the taste buds on delivery, but that calms sufficiently to allow amazing spices to launch beautifully; indeed, there is even a mouth-watering maltiness still to be found – astonishing! Early on, a degree of cocoa takes hold and, thanks to some treacle and oil, sits comfortably on the palate; **f24** more well balanced milky, lightly sweetened cocoa with that hint of smoke returning to accompany the spice; **b23.5** a malt which pushes itself about in an oak constructed Zimmer frame, reaching its destination in ungainly fashion but always well groomed and dressed elegantly. This charming ghost of this long lost distillery is about as good as you could hope for. 52.9%. 186 bottles. WB15/267

Old Malt Cask Glen Mhor Aged 30 Years refill hogshead, cask no. 9183, dist Aug 82, bott Oct 12 **(89.5) n23 t23 f21.5 b22.** What a fascinating malt! Yes, it is too old for true greatness, but what a wonderful battle between time and structure. Every glass needs a good 20 minutes (and at body temperature, remember) to realise its full potential. 50%. sc. Douglas Laing & Co. 228 bottles.

GLENMORANGIE
Highlands (Northern), 1843. Glenmorangie Plc. Working.

Glenmorangie 10 Years Old db **(94) n24** perhaps the most enigmatic aroma of them all: delicate yet assertive, sweet yet dry, young yet oaky: a malty tone poem; **t22** flaky oakiness throughout but there is an impossibly complex toastiness to the barley which seems to suggest the lightest hint of smoke; **f24** amazingly long for such a light dram, drying from the initial sweetness but with flaked almonds amid the oakier, rich cocoa notes; **b24** you might find the occasional "orange variant", where the extra degree of oak, usually from a few too many first-fill casks, has flattened out the more extreme peaks and toughs of complexity (scores about 89). But these are pretty rare – almost a collector's item – and overall this remains one of the great single malts: a whisky of uncompromising aesthetic beauty from the first enigmatic whiff to the last teasing and tantalising gulp. Complexity at its most complex. 40%

Glenmorangie 15 Years Old db **(90.5) n23** chunky and fruity: something distinctly sugar candy about this one; the barley's no slouch, either; and, just to raise the eyebrows, just the faintest waft of something smoky...; **t23** silky, a tad sultry, and serious interplay between oak and barley; a real, satisfying juiciness to this one; **f22** dries towards the oaky side of things, but just a faint squeeze of liquorice adds extra weight; **b22.5** exudes quality. 43%

Glenmorangie 15 Years Old Sauternes Wood Finish db **(68) n16 t18 f17 b17.** I had hoped – and expected – an improvement on the sulphured version I came across last time. Oh, whisky! Why are you such a cruel mistress...? 46%

Glenmorangie 18 Years Old db **(91) n22** pleasant if unconvincing spotted dick; **t23** sharp, eye-watering mix of fruit and mainly honeyed barley; nutty and, with the confident vanillas, forming a breakfast cereal completeness; **f23** Cocoa Krispies; **b23** having thrown off some previous gremlins, now a perfect start to the day whisky... 43%

Glenmorangie 25 Years Old db **(95.5) n24** it's strap yourself in time: this is a massive nose with more layers, twists and turns than you can shake a thief at. Soft, mildly lush Lubec marzipan is sandwiched between fruit bonbons and myriad barley tones. Worth taking half an hour over this one, and no kidding... **t24** the clarity on the nose is matched here. Every single wave of flavour is there in crystal form, starting, naturally, with the barley but this is soon paired with various unidentified fruits. The result is salivation. Towards the middle the oak shows form and does so in various cocoa-tinged ways; every nuance is delicately carved, almost fragile, but the overall picture is one of strength; **f23.5** medium length with the cocoa heading towards medium roast Java **b24** every bit as statesmanlike and elegant as a whisky of this age from such a blinding distillery should be. Ticks every single box for a 25-year-old and is Morangie's most improved malt by the distance of Tain to Wellingborough. There is a hint of genius with each unfolding wave of flavours with this one: a whisky that will go in 99/100 whisky lover's top 50 malts of all time. And that includes the Peatheads. 43%

Glenmorangie 30 Years Old db **(72) n17 t18 f19 b18.** From the evidence in the glass the jury is out on whether it has been spruced up a little in a poor sherry cask – and spruce is the operative word: lots of pine on this wrinkly. 44.1%

Glenmorangie Vintage 1975 db **(89) n23 t23 f21 b22.** A charming, fruity and beautifully spiced oldie. 43%

Glenmorangie 1977 db **(92) n24 t23 f22 b23.** Excellent, but a trifle underpowered...what would this have been like at 46%...??? Shows little of its great age as the oak is always subservient to the sweet barley and citrus. 43%. *Exclusively at Harrods.*

Glenmorangie Pride 1981 dist Oct 81, bott 2010, Sauternes barrique db **(77.5) n18 t22 f18 b19.5.** The Pride before a fall...? I know that gifted blender Bill Lumsden feels that a touch of sulphur can sometimes bring good to a dram. He and I share many similar views on whisky. But here we very much part company. For me, sulphur is a fault. Nothing more. Nothing less. The entire reason for stills to be made from copper is so sulphur compounds are removed. So by adding them back in, as they obviously have here via the barriques, can be nothing other than a negative step. Perhaps I am at fault for having a zero tolerance on sulphur. But when, for me, it spoils the nose, muddies the middle and bitters the finish, how can I do anything other than judge accordingly? The tragedy here is that it is obvious that some astonishing elements are at play. Even through the bitter haze I could detect some gorgeous honey and glazed fruits and stems; so excellent, in fact, that for a few brief moments the faults are silenced. But that is only a respite. Those unable to spot sulphur, through smoking or their DNA, will doubtless find much to enjoy and wonder why I have marked this down. But I cannot join the general back-slapping on this whisky. I have been told that someone has suggested the sulphur on this soon goes away. It doesn't: it never does – that is absolutely ridiculous. And why some whisky critics can't nose sulphur is beyond me. About as useful as a wine writer unable to spot a corked wine; or a music critic unable to hear the cello playing in entirely the wrong key. Sorry. But I have to be the sole dissenting voice on this one. 56.7%

Glenmorangie Artein Private Edition db **(94) n24** it's the spices that get you: at first you don't quite notice them. Then you realise there is a background buzz, like peppers slyly added to a gazpacho soup, and there is a slight tomato fruitiness, too; the sweetness is a subtle combination of maple syrup and molten Mars Bars; **t23.5** that sweetness arrives early but in very diluted form and refuses to overtake the barley sugar and chocolate raisin; **f23** the spices on the nose return for the finale which sit deliciously with the malt-nougat fade; **b23.5** if someone has gone out of their way to create probably the softest Scotch single malt of the year, then they have succeeded. 46%. ncf.

Glenmorangie Artein Private Edition 15 Years Old db **(91) n23** a beautiful mix of fruit pastilles and coconut lime cake; **t23.5** sensual delivery: soft with a few spices to mix with the developing mocha and raisin; **f21.5** lovely buttery oils to the fade but bitters out slightly; **b23** a truly sensual and complex dram, gorgeously weighted underplaying the fruit and wine aspect to a disarming degree. 46%. ncf.

Glenmorangie Artisan Casks db **(93) n23 t23.5 f23 b23.5.** If whisky could be sexed, this would be a woman. Every time I encounter Morangie Artisan, it pops up with a new look, a different perfume. And mood. It appears not to be able to make up its mind. But does it know how to pout, seduce and win your heart...? Oh yes. 46%

Glenmorangie Astar db **(88) n21 t23 f22.5 b22.** Decidedly strange malt: for quite a while it is as if someone has extracted the barley and left everything else behind. A star is born? Not yet, perhaps. But perhaps a new breed of single malt. 57.1%

Glenmorangie Burgundy Wood Finish db **(72) n17.5 t19.5 f18 b18.** Sulphured whisky de table. 43%

Glenmorangie Burr Oak Reserve db **(92) n24 t24 f22 b22.** Fades on the finish as a slightly spent force, but nose and arrival are simply breathtaking. Wouldn't be out of place in Kentucky. 56.3%

Glenmorangie Cellar 13 Ten Years Old db **(88.5) n22 t22.5 f22 b22** oh, if only I could lose weight as efficiently as this appears to have done... oh, I have! My love and thanks to Nancy, Nigel and Ann Marie. 43%

⋰ **Glenmorangie Companta** Clos de Tart & Rasteau casks, dist 27 Jan 99, bott 14 Nov 13 db **(74) n17 t20 f18 b19.** "I don't think you'll be a fan of this one, Jim" said the Glenmorangie blender to me, letting me know the sample was on its way. How right he was. Have to say there is some breath-taking fruit to be had before the sulphur does its worst. 46%. ncf.

⋰ **Glenmorangie Dornoch** db **(94) n23.5** light and sea breezy: grist on a coastal wing. The gristiness extends to the sugars which stick to a simple but effective path. The secret to its charm, though, is the clarity and layering... **t23** even on delivery the malt arrives on all levels and in different hues, ranging from sweet and fresh to a duller, oak-dried digestive biscuit – but quite tightly bound; **f23.5** a beautiful unravelling: those tighter notes relax offering a procession of further biscuity, malty themes – not without a light sprinkling of salt – and then a denser malt extract feel; **b24** a rare Glenmorangie which this time does not put the emphasis on fruit or oak influence. But this appears to concentrate on the malt itself, taking it through a routine which reveals as many angles and facets as it can possibly conjure. Even if the casks are from a central warehouse, at times a seascape has been created by a light salty influence – so befitting the whisky's name. A real treat. 43%

Glenmorangie Ealanta 1993 Vintage db **(97.5) n24** a near faultless nose, as one might expect from ultra high quality oak and supremely well-made distillate. A kind of elite Stranahan's nose, all black tie and wing collars and without the oils. Here, a mesmerising mix of dried orange peel and lychee flips for the leading role with gristy barley sugar and butterscotch seasoned with drying allspice and a few shavings of hickory: monumental...! **t24** the delivery, tasted blind, is bourbon! The nose whispers it, the palate sings it proudly! A gorgeous intertwining of black and red liquorice leaves no doubt. Most amazing is the weight: just an astonishing degree of oils and sugars with the grist seemingly mixed with an 80% Venezuelan cocoa and molassed and muscovado sugar mix (actually, leaning more towards the muscovado); **f24.5** one of the longest finishes to any Scotch this year and borderline perfection. The sugars are supremely weighted, their trick being not to interfere with the complex permutation of vanilla and barley. I cannot remember a fade so wonderfully orchestrated – like the final dying notes of a Vaughan Williams masterpiece – and so entirely free of distracting side issues of weakness and interference. Assisted perfectly by the lightest but most welcome degree of oil; **b25** when is a bourbon not a bourbon? When it is a Scotch single malt...And here we have potentially the World Whisky of the Year. Free from the embarrassing nonsense which passes for today's sherry butt, and undamaged by less than careful after use care of second-hand bourbon casks, we see what happens when the more telling aspects of oak, the business end which gives bourbon that extra edge, blends with the some of the very finest malt made in Scotland. Something approaching one of the best whiskies of my lifetime is the result... 46%

Glenmorangie Elegance db **(92) n22** quite herbal and soothing; **t24** the thinnest layer of icing sugar coats the silk-soft malt; every bit as gentle as the nose suggests; **f22** medium to short with some attractive rolling vanilla; **b24** a surprise package that is not entirely dissimilar to the Golden Rum, only a tad sweeter. 43%

Glemorangie Finealta db **(84.5) n21 t22 f20.5 b21**. Plump and thick, one of the creamiest malts around. For what it lacks in fine detail it makes up for in effect, especially the perky oaky spices. 46%

Glenmorangie Lasanta sherry casks db **(68.5) n16 t19 f16 b17.5**. The sherry problem has increased dramatically rather than being solved. 46%

⠁⠁ **Glenmorangie Lasanta Aged 12 Years** sherry cask finish db **(93) n23.5** a dry exhibition of fruit – or perhaps an exhibition of dry fruit. Either way, quietly rich and showing the range of old fruit cake depths I had hoped to find on the original Lasanta; really love the stewed plums and spotted dick; **t24** wonderfully soft delivery, backed handsomely by a two-toned sherry fruitiness, with dry and cream being just about on equal terms. The sugars appear both fruit and cask borne, though it is the deeper Eccles cake and treacle notes which carry furthest; **f22** a fluffy dryness and numbing to the tip of the tongue reveals that not every sherry butt used here was faultless, but there is enough of a chocolate and walnut butter cream sideshow to distract; **b23.5** a delightful surprise: every bottling of Lasanta I'd ever tasted had been sulphur ruined. But this new 12-y-o incarnation has got off to a flying start. Although a little bit of a niggle on the finish, I can live with that in the present climate. Here's to a faultless second bottling... 43%

Glenmorangie Madeira Wood Finish db **(78) n19.5 t20.5 f19 b19**. One of the real problems with wine finishes is getting the point of balance right when the fruit, barley and oak are in harmony. Here it is on a par with me singing in the shower, though frankly my aroma would be a notch or two up. 43%

Glenmorangie Margaux Cask Finish db **(88) n22 t22 f22 b22**. Even taking every whisky with an open mind, I admit this was better than my subconscious might have considered. Certainly better than the near undrinkable Ch. Margaux '57 I used to bring out for my birthday each year some 20-odd years ago... 46%

Glenmorangie Nectar D'or Sauternes Finish db **(94) n23** delicate cinnamon on toast and a drizzle of greengage and sultana; **t24** refreshing and dense on the palate as the bitter-sweet battle goes into overdrive; excellent weight and body; **f23** remains clean and precise, allowing some custard onto the apple strudel finale; **b24** great to see French casks that actually complement a whisky – so rare! This has replaced the Madeira finish. But there are some similar sweet-fruit characteristics. An exercise in outrageously good sweet-dry balancing. 46%

Glenmorangie Quinta Ruban Port Finish db (92) n24 typical Morangie complexity, but the grape notes added act almost like a prism to show their varied hues; t23 fruit and spice about as the oak goes in search of glory: barley stands in its way; f22 light, deftly sweetened and juicy to the end; b23 this replacement of the original Port finish shows a genuine understanding of the importance of grape-oak balance. Both are portrayed with clarity and confidence. This is a form of cask finishing that has progressed from experimentation to certainty. 46%

Glenmorangie Sherry Wood Finish db (84) n23 t21 f20 b20. Stupendous clean sherry nose, then disappoints with a somewhat bland display on the palate. 43%

Glenmorangie Signet db (80.5) n20 t21.5 f19 b20. A great whisky holed below the waterline by oak of unsatisfactory quality. Tragic. 46%

Glenmorangie Sonnalta PX db (96.5) n24 now this works: has that heavy-handed feel of a sweet sherry butt (or five) at work here, usually the kiss of death for so many whiskies. But an adroit praline sub-plot really does the trick. So with the malt evident, too, we have a three-pronged attack which somehow meshes in to one. And not even the merest hint of an off-note...goodness gracious: a new experience...!!! t24 Neanderthal grape drags its knuckles along the big vanilla floor before a really subtle light Columbian coffee kick puts us back on course; sharper vanillas from some awkward oak threatens to send us off course again but somehow it finds a settled, common ground; f24.5 now goes into orgasmic overdrive as Demerara sugar is tipped into some gorgeous, cream-lightened mocha. This is obviously to wash down the Melton Hunt cake which is resplendent in its grape and roast nut finery. It is the perfect whisky finish... b24 remains a giant among the tall stills. A mesmeric whisky... 46%

⋯ **Glenmorangie Taghta** db (92) n23 a soft infusion of dates and chocolate; t23 fresh and salivating: a barley juiciness gives way to a slow amplification of oak; the sugars are of a lightly molassed bent, helping to inject life into a pithy sub-current; f23 there have been hints of chocolate throughout and here it offers a more precise outline of a fruit and chocolate theme. Remains soft and deft to the last...; b23 a curious Glenmorangie which, unusually, appears not to be trying to make a statement or force a point. This is an old Sunday afternoon film of a dram: an old-fashioned black and whitie, (home grown and not an Ealing, or Bogie or Edward G Robinson) where, whether we have seen it before or not, we know pretty much what is going to happen, in a reassuring kind of way... 46%

Glenmorangie Traditional db (90.5) n22 orange blossom, barley sugar and chalk dust; t23 delicate delivery revelling in gentle complexity: really playful young-ish malt makes for a clean start and middle; f22.5 soft mocha notes play out a quiet finish; b23 an improved dram with much more to say, but does so quietly. 571%

Glenmorangie Truffle Oak db (96) n24 t24 f25 b23. The Glenmorangie of all Glenmorangies. I really have to work hard and deep into the night to find fault with it. If I am going to be hyper-critical, I'll dock it a mark for being so constantly sweet, though in its defence I have to say that the degree of sweetness alters with astonishing dexterity. Go on, it's Truffle oak: make a pig of yourself...!! 60.5%

GLEN MORAY
Speyside, 1897. La Martiniquaise. Working.

Glen Moray Classic 8 Years Old db (86) n20 t22 f21 b23. A vast improvement on previous bottlings with the sluggish fatness replaced by a thinner, barley-rich, slightly sweeter and more precise mouthfeel. 40%

Glen Moray 10 Years Old Chardonnay Matured db (73.5) n18.5 t19 f18 b18. Tighter than a wine cork. 40%

Glen Moray 12 Years Old db (90) n22.5 gentle malt of varying pitch and intensity; t22 a duller start than it should be with the vanilla diving in almost before the barley but the juicy, grassy notes arrive in good time; f23 long, back on track with intense malt and the custardy oak is almost apologetic but enlivened with a dash of lime: mmmmm... pure Glen Moray! b22.5 I have always regarded this as the measuring stick by which all other malty and clean Speysiders should be tried and tested. It is still a fabulous whisky, full of malty intricacies. Something has fallen off the edge, perhaps, but minutely so. Still think a trick or two is being missed by bottling this at 40%: the natural timbre of this malt demands 46% and no less.... 40%

Glen Moray 16 Years Old db (74) n19 t19 f18 b19. A serious dip in form. Drab. 40%

Glen Moray 16 Years Old Chenin Blanc Mellowed in Wine Barrels db (85) n20 t22 f22 b21. A fruity, oak-shaded dram just brimming with complexity. 40%

Glen Moray 20 Years Old db (80) n22 t22 f18 b18. With so much natural cream toffee, it is hard to believe that this has so many years on it. After a quick, refreshing start it pans out, if anything, a little dull. 40%

Glen Moray Aged 25 Years Portwood Finish Rare Vintage Limited Edition bott code. 3153, dist 1986 db (87.5) n22.5 very unusual signature: the fruit is tight though spicy, even if it does limit the obvious excesses of the oak; **t22** both spice and fruit spring immediately into action but the sugars are subdued due to a wine-must dryness; at least the juices flow, complete with muscovado sugars, for a few magical moments; **f21** still a little tight and refuses to open as you might expect. A touch of chocolate raisin for sure, but also a furry bitterness; **b22** just get the feeling that the Port pipe has not quite added what was desired. 43%

Glen Moray 30 Years Old db (92.5) **n23.5** it's probably the deftness of the old-fashioned Speyside smoke in tandem with the structured fruits that makes this so special; **t23.5** for a light Speysider, the degree of barley to oak is remarkable: soft, oil-gilde d barley is met by a wonderful, if brief, spice prickle; **f22.5** deft layering of vanilla and cocoa; a sprinkle of muscovado sugar repels any darker oak notes; **b23** for all its years, this is comfortable malt, untroubled by time. There is no mistaking quality. 43%

Glen Moray Peated Spirit Batch #1 cask 141 db (88.5) **n21 t23.5 f22 b22**. A gorgeously jazzed up kindergarten Glen Moray, not so wet behind the ears as it might be thanks to what appears to be a very fresh bourbon cask. Imbalance on nose and finish for sure, but with a mega-delivery of smoked French toast washed down with cocoa and tannin concentrate, who cares whether this is strictly whisky or not? 60.6%. phenol content 18ppm

Glen Moray 1959 Rare Vintage db (91) **n25 t23 f21 b22**. They must have been keeping their eyes on this one for a long time: a stunning malt that just about defies nature. The nose reaches absolute perfection. 50.9%

Glen Moray 1962 Very Rare Vintage Aged 42 Years db (94) **n23 t24 f23 b24**. The first temptation is to think that this has succumbed to age, but a second and a third tasting reveal that there is much more complexity, integrity and balance to this than first meets the tastebuds. The last cask chosen by the legendary Ed Dodson before his retirement from the distillery: a pretty perceptive choice. A corker! 50.9%. sc.

Glen Moray 1984 db (83) **n20 t22 f20 b21**. Mouthwatering and incredibly refreshing malt for its age. 40%

Glen Moray 1989 db (86) **n23 t22 f20 b21**. Doesn't quite live up to the fruit smoothie nose but I'm being a little picky here. 40%

Glen Moray 1992 Single Cask No 1441 sherry butt db (74) **n17 t21 f18 b18**. Oops! Didn't anyone spot the sulphur...? 59.6%

Glen Moray 1995 Port Wood Finish bott Dec 2009 db (95.5) **n23** a surprising liquorice base to the healthy spiced fruit; **t24** vivid grape: clean, intense and, for a while, dominant. The oak surges back with a few tricks of its own, the most impressive being a liquorice-hickory thrust and a soothing custardy topping. Meanwhile, the grape offers spice and a sheen; **f24.5** a wonderful array of spicy chocolate and raisin notes that appear to continue indefinitely. Needs to be tasted to be believed. **b24** possibly the most satisfying wine finish of the year. 56.7%

Glen Moray 1995 Single Sherry Cask sherry butt db (56) **n15 t14 f13 b14**. So stunned was I about the abject quality of this bottling, I even looked on the Glen Moray website to see if they had said anything about it. Apparently, if you add water you find on the nose "the lingering soft sulphury smoke of a struck match." Well, here's the news: you don't need water. Just open the bottle and there's Rotorua in all it's stink bomb finery. And errr...hullo, guys... some further news: that means it's a bloody faulty, useless cask. And has no right to be put anywhere near a bottling hall let alone set loose in a single bottling. This, quite frankly, is absolutely rank whisky, the type of which makes my blood boil. I mean, is this really the best cask that could be found in the entire and considerable estate of Glen Moray..???? Am I, or is it the whisky world going mad...? 59.6%

Glen Moray Classic db (86.5) **n22 t21.5 f21.5 b21.5**. The nose is the star with a wonderful, clean barley-fruit tandem, but what follows cannot quite match its sure-footed wit. 40%

Glen Moray Wine Cask Edition bott Sep 09 db (83.5) **n20 t23 f20 b20.5**. When in full flow this is just bursting with some of the juiciest fruit you are likely to encounter. But a familiar bitter buzz brings down the value. How sad. 59.7%

⋰⋰ **Adelphi Selection Glen Moray 27 Years Old** cask no. 1931, dist 86, bott 13 (87) **n21.5 t21 f22.5 b21.5**. A brave and, at times, nuclear battle against old age, mainly using molasses in the front line. But when you are fighting time there can be only one winner. Some of the early spice and later cocoa notes are an absolute treat, though. 56.8%. ncf sc. WB15/413

⋰⋰ **Blackadder Raw Cask Glen Moray 1995 18 Years Old** single oak hogshead, cask no. 2510, dist 21 Mar 95, bott Apr 13 (92) **n22** a real oaky buzz , but enough sugars for balance; **t24** oily from the off, allowing some pretty major citrus and banana notes to develop. A little golden syrup helps master the intense tannin; **f23** long, oil-deendent with the oak straining at the least but just about muzzled; **b23** not a distillery naturally given to passing this many summers. But this is rather lovely, at times wonderful, despite the obvious oak encroachment. 54.9%. nc ncf sc. 211 bottles. WB15/162

⁙ **Cadenhead's Small Batch Glen Moray-Glenlivet Aged 15 Years** bourbon hogsheads, dist 1998, bott 2013 **(84) n20 t21.5 f21 b21.5.** Both citrus and barley is working flat out to get results. Certainly manages to get the juices flowing, but a less than magnificent cask means an underlying bitterness knocks things a little off key. 46%. 684 bottles. WB15/087

⁙ **Cadenhead's Glen Moray Wine Cask Aged 21 Years** Claret cask, dist 1992, bott Feb 14 **(95) n23.5** elegant mix between lightly spiced greengage and more basic boiled fruit sweets, with a lemon drop thrown in for extra bite; **t24** one of the cleanest deliveries of the year: the oak may be present, but the fruit and sugar is crisp and linear, the spices confident and clear; **f23.5** really good age showing now, but the quality of the oak is faultless. This means the fruits can still trill their top notes, while the spices rumble and the cocoa builds; **b24** highly unusual example of Glen Moray, the least oak-damaged I have ever encountered at this age. Brilliant. Literally. 55.4%. 216 bottles. WB15/077

⁙ **Darkness! Glen Moray Aged 22 Years** Oloroso Cask Finish **(85.5) n22 t22.5 f21 b20.** One can only presume that there is some malt in there somewhere...The nose takes me right back to my Fleet Street days when a famous old wine bar there served up the most outrageously OTT oloroso sherry matured whisky I had ever come across. Until now... 57.8%. 88 bottles. WB15/201

⁙ **Hepburn's Choice Glen Moray 2001 Aged 12 Years** refill hogshead, dist 01, bott 14 **(91) n22.5** fresh, lively maltiness boasting a citrus-vanilla backdrop; **t23** massive malt: clean, salivating, gristy. The sugars are understated and light; **f22** heavier finale as the vanilla returns; **b23** absolutely classic for the distillery at this age: a case where simplicity can be quietly beautiful. 46%. nc ncf sc. 193 bottles.

Master Of Malt Glen Moray 21 Years Old cask no. 5661, dist 91, bott 13 **(89) n21.5 t23 f22 b22.5.** A fast talking Glen Moray with an unusually vast amount to say for itself about spice. 60.7%. 260 bottles.

⁙ **Old Malt Cask Glen Moray Aged 21 Years** refill hogshead, cask no. 9935, dist Oct 91, bott Aug 13 **(85) n21 t22 f21 b21.** I can see why it's the Glen Moray 21....! Pleasant enough, but the oak has injected some major natural caramels which have rubbed out the usual juicy aspects of this malt. 50%. nc ncf sc. 165 bottles.

Provenance Glen Moray Over 12 Years refill hogshead, cask no. 8435, dist Autumn 99, bott Spring 12 **(88.5) n22 t22 f22.5 b22.** A gentle malt from one of the gentler distilleries, but just enough attitude to make it interesting. 46%. nc ncf sc. Douglas Laing & Co.

Scotch Malt Whisky Society Cask 35.68 Aged 25 Years refill hogshead, dist 15 May 87 **(94.5) n23.5** at first the sandpaper bites and threatens; fortunately there is more to the oak with dank, mossy north-facing gardens, bluebells and mint perfectly embracing the Lubek marzipan and sweeter barley sugar; **t24** exceptional delivery. The barley forms a thick layer under which bourbony liquorice and thin molasses sit. Spices strike early and persistently, the mint rising with the developing cocoa; **f23** back to a slightly oily vanilla, but a barley trail can be followed; **b24** the oak shows little sign of compromise; fortunately the barley has more than enough in the tank to match it. A malt of stunning complexity and brinkmanship ensues. 54.2%. nc ncf sc. 92 bottles.

Scotch Malt Whisky Society Cask 35.79 Aged 28 Years refill butt, dist 22 Dec 83 **(70) n17 t18 f17 b18.** Scarred, sadly, by sulphur. 57.7%. nc ncf sc. 167 bottles.

Scotch Malt Whisky Society Cask 35.85 Aged 17 Years 1st fill barrel, 27 Oct 95 **(88) n21.5 t22.5 f22 b22.** An Elgin gristfest... 56.7%. nc ncf sc. 233 bottles.

Scotch Malt Whisky Society Cask 35.89 Aged 17 Years dist 27 Oct 95 **(91) n22 t23.5 f22.5 b23.** Beautifully made and matured whisky. Technically top notch. 59.7%. nc ncf sc.

⁙ **Scotch Malt Whisky Society Cask 35.102 Aged 39 Years** refill hogshead, dist 19 Feb 74 **(85.5) n22 t22 f20 b21.5.** Never a distillery designed for such great age, the oak ultimately proves all-conquering. But there are some pretty skirmishes along the way and I admit to being somewhat enthralled between the battle between the golden syrup and highly toasted tannin, with some pungent marmalade (and, later, chocolate-orange) notes, like me, looking on from a distance. Another cask which could have served so much better in a blend but at least a couple of hundred whisky lovers will get the chance see what happens when a lightweight malt pulls out all the stops to survive 30 years against the odds. 52.1% 180 bottles.

⁙ **Scotch Malt Whisky Society Cask 35.107 Aged 19 Years** 1st fill toasted oak hogshead, dist 11 Nov 94 **(87.5) n22** some serious prickle from the big oak; **t22.5** very good mouth feel, helped at first by a mix of kumquat and maple syrup. Spices built but the tannins thicken...; **f21** just a tad too dry, though some oils spread the remaining sugars attractively; **b22** probably from a first fill cask, the tannins have taken just too big grip. Compelling, but ultimately limited as a single cask. 58.7%. nc ncf sc. 204 bottles.

⁕ **Scotch Malt Whisky Society Cask 35.108 Aged 12 Years** 1st fill butt, dist 17 May 01 **(85.5) n22.5 t22 f20 b21.** A surprising bottling, this, with the oak really cutting up rough against the trademark charming, gentle and elegant barley and grapey fruit. A shame after such a pleasing deft nose. *60.5%. nc ncf sc. 230 bottles.*

⁕ **Scotch Malt Whisky Society Cask 35.109 Aged 28 Years** refill hogshead, dist 19 Mar 85 **(88.5) n23** bananas and custard, suet pudding base; **t22.5** a bit like dipping your shoulders under the tepid water, the oak doesn't appear half as bad as it seems on initial impact; the barley holds its position impressively against the oaky advance and even manages to fight back and regain ground; a vague gristiness appears to be even throughout; **f21** some deft spice enriches the sugar-tannin fade; **b22** a complex whisky, though this is more through luck than judgement. *46.8%. nc ncf sc. 128 bottles.*

⁕ **Scotch Malt Whisky Society Cask 35.110 Aged 17 Years** 1st fill designer barrel, dist 17 Dec 96 **(95) n24** very high class: all is softness and whispers with a crème brule and butterscotch tart mix topped with a squeeze of tangerine; a serious nod towards top grade bourbon here; **t23** gorgeously salivating with the barley gliding around on the lush, spiced acacia honey; **f24** the spices pulse while the citrus-honey sweetness embraces the coconut milk and other sign of high quality oak; **b24** a demure and spellbinding essay in balance. A truly must have bottling for this distillery. *49.6%. nc ncf sc. 97 bottles.*

⁕ **Scotch Malt Whisky Society Cask 35.111 Aged 12 Years** refill chardonnay hogshead, dist 27 Nov 01 **(83) n20 t22 f20 b21.** A dumpy, off-key fruitiness has the odd bright moment but it's just all too discordant. *59.4%. nc ncf sc. 256 bottles.*

That Boutique-y Whisky Company Glen Moray batch 1 **(86.5) n20.5 t23 f21.5 b21.5.** Rowntree Toffo with a juicy injection of concentrated malt and glazed cherry. Undone slightly by an indifferent nose. *49.1%. Master Of Malt. 176 bottles.*

⁕ **That Boutique-y Whisky Glen Moray** batch 1 **(84.5) n21 t22 f21 b21.5.** Kind of a near 50%abv chocolate toffee bar. *49.1%. 176 bottles. WB15/208*

The Whisky Agency Glen Moray 1977 bott 12 **(87.5) n22.5 t22 f21.5 b21.5.** A splintery white knuckle ride. *51.8%*

GLEN ORD
Highlands (Northern), 1838. Diageo. Working.

Glen Ord Aged 12 Years db **(81) n20 t23 f18 b20.** Just when you thought it safe to go back...for a while Diageo ditched the sherry-style Ord. It has returned. Better than some years ago, when it was an unhappy shadow of its once-great self, but without the sparkle of the vaguely-smoked bottling of a year or two back. Nothing wrong with the rich arrival, but the finish is a mess. I'll open the next bottling with trepidation... *43%*

Glen Ord 25 Years Old dist 1978 db **(95) n24 t24 f23 b24.** Some stupendous vatting here: cask selection at its very highest to display Ord in all its far too rarely seen magnificence. *58.3%*

Glen Ord 28 Years Old db **(90) n22 t23 f22 b23.** This is mega whisky showing slight traces of sap, especially on the nose, but otherwise a concentrate of many of the qualities I remember from this distillery before it was bottled in a much ruined form. Blisteringly beautiful. *58.3%*

Glen Ord 30 Years Old db **(87) n22 t21 f23 b21.** Creaking with oak, but such is the polish to the barley some serious class is on show. *58.8%*

Glen Ord 1997 The Manager's Choice db **(93.5) n24** oh my word...what have we here...? Just the most enticing little fruit pastel number you could ask for, and all played out on the softest malty field imaginable. Genuinely complex and enticing with the nose being teasingly caressed; **t23.5** then, just to shock, a real injection of bite and nip on delivery with a tangy blood orange thread which follows from the nose; **f23** custard powder oakiness with some late hickory and toffee; **b23** when given the chance, Glen Ord offers one of the fruitiest drams on the market. Here it is in its full blood orange element. A beauty! *59.2%*

Singleton of Glen Ord 12 Years Old db **(89) n22.5 t22.5 f22 b22** a fabulous improvement on the last bottling I encountered. Still possesses blood oranges to die for, but greatly enhanced by some sublime spices and a magnificent juiciness. *40%*

Singleton of Glen Ord 32 Year Old db **(91) n23.5 t23 f22 b22.5.** Delicious. But if ever a malt has screamed out to be at 46%, this is it. *40%*

Liquid Library Glen Ord 1997 ex-bourbon hogshead, dist 97, bott 11 **(84) n22 t21 f20 b21.** A pretty tired cask even before it was filled back in 1997, the oak involvement here is virtually trace. *50.4%. The Whisky Agency.*

Liquid Sun Glen Ord 1997 ex-bourbon hogshead, dist 97, bott 12 **(86) n21 t21.5 f22 b21.5.** Wow! Some of the oldest new make on the market! Like the Liquid Library 50.4% we have what appears to be a third fill cask in play here. The result is a juicy, ultra malty beast. But the oak should be injecting so much extra complexity by now. *49.9%. The Whisky Agency.*

⁖ **Old Particular Highland Glen Ord 16 Years Old** refill hogshead, cask no. 9954, dist Apr 1997, bott Aug 2013 **(94) n23.5** one of those teasing noses which keeps you spellbound and in its thrall for seemingly hours A near perfect marriage of ridiculously light peat and green and over-ripe banana. At once chunky...yet light. How does it do that....? **t24** juicy delivery with the malt entering on many levels of intensity and complexity. A string of oak offers both backbone and further density; the mid-ground retains its pulsing, fresh malt and the lightest layer of smoke; **f22.5** some light esters hang on creating almost a Jamaican rum style; **b24** staggeringly beautiful, effortlessly complex whisky. 48.4%. nc ncf sc. 396 bottles.

Provenance Glen Ord Over 8 Years refill hogshead, cask no. 9034, dist Autumn 04, bott Autumn 12 **(81.5) n19 t21.5 f20.5 b20.5.** A third fill barrel which makes no attempt to interfere with the development of the malt. For those with a penchant for lightweight mega juicy barley fests. 46%. nc ncf sc.

Provenance Glen Ord Over 14 Years refill hogshead, cask no. 9652, dist Spring 99, bott Spring 13 **(87) n22.5 t23 f20 b21.5.** Even the thin, pasty finish cannot fully detract from the vitality of the nose and delivery. Early on its barley, barley everywhere! 46%. nc ncf.

Scotch Malt Whisky Society Cask 77.28 Aged 25 Years 2nd fill hogshead, charred oak, dist 13 Aug 87 **(97) n24** someone has quietly poured some paprika a jar of beech honey and topped it off with oak shavings. The result is enticingly formidable; **t24.5** just ridiculous. No delivery should have quite so many things going on at once. In 20 minutes I have identified four different honey types at work, perhaps the most telling of them all being a light manuka, but blended in with ulmo thinned with clear: probably the most complex set of honey notes I've encountered in the last five or six years. The serious age means the oak injects a dryness which counters any honey-led excess of sweetness; **f24** at last something other than honey holds sway: the oak pitches in late with an almost tarry character, though, in essence, we are feeling the drying strains of spent honey and barley with a half-hearted spiciness seeing in the much broader cocoa; **b24.5** truly amazing. Make a bee-line for this one. No idea of the price, but impossible to get stung here. For this is, as sure as bee eggs are bee eggs, an award winner of some sort this year! You cannot ask for any more from any single malt, as this is a thing of the very rarest beauty. 54.9%. nc ncf sc. 236 bottles.

GLENROTHES
Speyside, 1878. Edrington. Working.

The Glenrothes 1978 dist Nov 78, bott 2008 db **(90.5) n23** over-ripe gooseberries mixed with dry tobacco; suet pudding and vanilla pods: attractively intriguing; **t23** relaxed, lush barley coats the mouth with a muscovado sugar edge; **f22** mushy sultana and toasty oak; **b22.5** sheer – and delicious – entertainment. 43%

The Glenrothes 1988 Vintage dist 16 Dec 88, bott 04 Nov 08 db **(93) n22** stunning toasted honeycomb **t24.5** exceptional delivery. Not only is the mouth feel quite perfect, the deft marriage of honey, honeycomb, treacle and maple syrup has to be tasted to be believed...; **f23** dries and spices up as the oaks grab hold; **b23.5** a gorgeous bottling still doing the rounds... and should be hunted down and polished off. 43%

The Glenrothes 1988 Vintage bott 2010 db **(74) n18.5 t19 f18 b18.5.** For all the obvious high quality sugars present, it still can't overcome the Spanish imposition. 43%

The Glenrothes 1994 dist Oct 94, bott 2007 db **(77) n19 t20 f19 b19.** The citrus appears as promised on the label, but sadly a few unadvertised sulphured butt-related gremlins are present also. 43%

The Glenrothes 1995 Vintage dist 26 Oct 95, bott 06 Sep 10 db **(87.5) n20 t22 f23 b22.5.** Like an old grump that takes its time to wake and finally has to be kicked out of bed. Once up, certainly does the biz. 43%

The Glenrothes 1998 Vintage dist Dec 98, bott Feb 09 db **(66) n16 t20 f14 b16.** Really would have thought they would have got the hang of this sulphur lark by now... 43%

The Glenrothes 1998 Vintage bott 2010 db **(73.5) n20 t19 f16 b18.5.** Talk about bitter-sweet...!!! 43%

⁖ **Glenrothes 2001** dist 25 May 01, bott 13 db **(72) n16 t21 f17 b18.** The sulphur in Spain makes this whisky very plain. 43% WB15/297

The Glenrothes Alba Reserve db **(87.5) n22 t22 f21.5 b22.** You know that smartly groomed, polite but rather dull chap you invariable get at dinner parties? 40%

The Glenrothes John Ramsay bott 2009 db **(89.5) n22.5 t23.5 f21.5 b22.** Elegant and charming. What else did you expect...? 46.7%. 1400 bottles.

The Glenrothes Robur Reserve db **(81.5) n20.5 t22 f19 b20.** With the youthful barley prominent early on, one of the sweetest distillery bottling from Glenrothes I've come across. Bitter cask fade, though. 40%

The Glenrothes Select Reserve db **(80) n17.5 t22 f20.5 b21.** Flawed in the usual Glenrothes sherry places, but the brilliance of the sharp barley wins your heart. 40%

The Glenrothes Three Decades bott 2009 db **(90.5)** n23.5 t24 f21.5 b22.5. Not without a minor blemish here and there, but the overall magnitude of this allows you to forgive quite easily. The distant sulphur apart, a stunner. *43%. Duty Free exclusive.*

⠿ **Cadenhead's Small Batch Glenrothes-Glenlivet Aged 24 Years** bourbon barrels, dist 1989, bott 2013 **(96.5)** n23.5 toasted hazelnuts, natural caramels...a kind of Topic candy but with spice taking the place of milk chocolate; a little kumquat...not unlike what might be found at Four Roses; **t23.5** superb delivery: a wide range of sugars, from juicy icing sugar to muscovado adding real depth to the intense grist and breath-taking spice; ridiculously and quite staggering fresh; the ulmo honey builds early on, revealing itself into a more earthy, heather-honey style later; **f25** long, with evidence of a high copper content (maybe a new part of a still or condenser at work) which gives a certain polish to the cocoa. But it doesn't end there: we are seemingly whisked away to Kentucky, for the late honey, liquorice and hickory gives a distinctly top-notch bourbon feel: no bad thing; **b24.5** always thought Glenrothes to be a little over-rated (though obviously not helped by its sherry butt regime of the last two decades), but this is unreconstituted quality. The tasting notes attached to the bottle bangs on about fruit, I have just noticed (I never read anything like that until mine are done and dusted). I haven't a clue as to what they are going on about...if this hasn't all the hallmarks of a ultra-high quality bourbon cask or probably two, taking into account the degree of complexity, I really don't know what does. *56.9%. 360 bottles. WB15/071*

⠿ **Cheiftain's Glenrothes Aged 13 Years** sherry butt, cask no. 3400/3401, dist Mar 99, bott Feb 13 **(68)** n17 t19 f16 b17. Absolutely standard of its cask type from this period from this distillery. Alas. *46%. 1896 bottles. WB15/163*

⠿ **The Coopers Choice Glenrothes 1997 Aged 16 Years** hogshead, cask no. 15715, bott 2014 **(85.5)** n22.5 t22 f20 b21. Par for the course Glenrothes: starts well with a big malty proclamation...and fades almost without trace. Still, if you like a bit of blood orange and boot polish to your nose. Go for it. *46%. 300 bottles. WB15/300*

Director's Cut Glenrothes Aged 18 Years refill hogshead, cask no. 7958, dist Mar 93, bott Jan 12 **(87)** n22.5 t23 f19.5 b22. A blemish for sure, but an excellent delivery. *54.2%. sc. Douglas Laing & Co. 127 bottles.*

Gordon and MacPhail Collection Glenrothes 8 Years Old (91) n22 t23.5 f22.5 b23. A malt which confirms, with impressive gait, and no little gaiety, that unspoiled Glenrothes really is top class fare, even at this tender age. *43%*

Malts Of Scotland Glenrothes 1982 bourbon hogshead, cask no. MoS 12065, dist Apr 82, bott Nov 12 **(85)** n21 t23.5 f19 b21.5. An unfriendly bourbon cask picks at and undoes the tangled honey and salt. In a better wood this would have been something a little special. *53.2%. nc ncf sc. 96 bottles.*

⠿ **Master of Malt Single Cask Glenrothes 25 Years Old** refill, dist 20 Jun 88, bott 18 Feb 14 **(87)** n23 t22.5 f20 b21.5. An old chap with no major faults to speak of and, in many ways, a remarkably unscathed dram for its age. However , while the Digestive biscuit note adds a morish roughage, it is a little too toffee dependent. *54.2%. sc. 50 bottles. WB15/213*

⠿ **Old Malt Cask Glenrothes Aged 16 Years** refill hogshead, cask no. 10435, dist Dec 97, bott Apr 14 **(92.5)** n23 clean with a proud butterscotch tart theme. The barley is still fresh and at times concentrated; **t23.5** I defy you to count how many different style of natural toffee you can find on this...; a thin layering of ulmo honey sits well with the maple syrup and persistent malt; **f23** a little spiced cocoa on the fading barley sugar; **b23** given the right cask, shows what a lovely malt this distillery is capable of producing. Engaging and irresistible. *50%. sc. 361 bottles.*

Old and Rare Glenrothes Aged 21 Years sherry hogshead, dist Jun 90, bott Jan 12 **(77)** n18.5 t22 f17.5 b19. One of those drams you could weep for. The grape has great richness and integrity. Sadly the furry, bitter notes reveal its Achilles heel: a problem not uncommon with this distillery. *56.1%. nc ncf sc. Douglas Laing & Co. 94 bottles.*

Provenance Glenrothes Over 8 Years sherry butt, cask no. 9212, dist Spring 04, bott Autumn 12 **(72)** n17 t19 f18 b18. For a brief second the grape glistens on the palate. But for the remainder...oh, sulphury dear...! *46%. nc ncf sc. Douglas Laing & Co.*

⠿ **Provenance Glenrothes 'Over 9 Years** sherry butt, cask no. 10191, dist Spring 2004, bott Winter 2014 **(76)** n19 t22 f16.5 b18.5. Mildly sulphured, and for a Glenrothes very mildly early on. Good to see a youngster at play here and the unmistakable oloroso has some blisteringly good moments early on. But the lack of sophistication to be offered by slow maturation added to the eventual uncomfortable powderiness of the treated butt leads to a disappointing, though inevitable, decline. *61.2%. nc ncf sc. Douglas Laing & Co.*

Scotch Malt Whisky Society Cask 30.74 Aged 11 Years refill port pipe, dist 27 Mar **(86.5)** n21.5 t23 f20.5 b21.5. Despite the obvious and almost inevitable flaws from the sherry butt, there are some spiced sultana and greengage notes to die for. Close your taste buds to the faults and you have a real spicy treat at work. 60.3%. nc ncf sc. 767 bottles.

⁘ **The Single Malts of Scotland Glenrothes Aged 23 Years** bourbon barrels, cask no. 35484, dist 12 Nov 90, bott 25 Mar 14 **(80.5) n21.5 t21.5 f18.5 b18**. While the barley is thick enough to chisel through, the slight milkiness and bitterness present suggests the cask failed to make it through the 23 years... 494%. 210 bottles. WB15/291

⁘ **Speyside Single Malt Glenrothes 26 Years** 2nd fill sherry butt, dist Jun 1987, bott Dec 2013 **(89) n22** massive barley sugar signature; some sherbet lemons rather undermine the age but the overall experience is invigorating; **t23** barley at its most pumped up, fresh and salivating – hard to believe it has spent over quarter of a century in the barrel; **f22** slightly tart and tired oak but again the freshness of the barley, coupled with some fizzy candy-like properties, make this something to behold! **b22** by no means a run of the distillery Glenrothes. Not sure if this has been distilled or made in a sweet shop... 53.3%. nc ncf sc. 288 bottles. Douglas Laing & Co.

⁘ **That Boutique-y Whisky Glenrothes** batch 1 **(89) n22.5** charming lemon curd tart and custard; clean malt; **t22.5** viscous, lightly sweetened malt on delivery, a vanilla and barley mix follows; **f22** diced Nice coconut biscuit; **b22** well mannered, non-taxing...and very attractive. 479%. 235 bottles. WB15/189

⁘ **Wemyss Malts 1988 Single Speyside Glenrothes "Aromatic Orange Tobacco"** butt, dist 1988, bott 2013 **(71) n18 t20 f15 b18**. Just...grim. 46%. sc. 730 bottles.

Wemyss 1988 Single Speyside Glenrothes "Ginger Spice" butt, bott 13 **(88) n22 t22.5 f21 b22.5**. Only the slight blemish on the cask prevents this score from being a whole lot higher. Excellent, all the same. 46%. sc. Wemyss Malts. 660 bottles.

⁘ **The Whisky Cask Glenrothes Aged 22 Years** sherry butt, dist 1990, bott 2012 **(91.5) n22** nutty, dry, vague spice; a little salty; **t23** rich delivery with the first half dozen waves displaying an oloroso-style bent...and in no half-hearted manner. Still nutty, still salty and now with a decent degree of muscovado and treacle leaking into the mix; **f22.5** more treacle and slightly burned fudge; a little bitter as the effect of the cask takes a grip; **b23** just so great to enjoy the unusual experience of savouring an unspoiled sherried Glenrothes. 53.8%. nc ncf.

The Whisky Shop Dufftown Glenrothes Aged 41 Years oak octave casks, cask no. 491630, dist 6 Jul 70, bott 21 Sep 11 **(92) n23** lavender and fizzing spice points towards big age; lots of bourbon traits; **t22.5** aggressive oak at first, but slowly relents as, miraculously, juicy malt and even some dark sugars, liquorice and ulmo honey begin to make their presence felt; **f23.5** massive spice and still the crunchy sugars crystallize; **b23** does nothing to hide its age. Luckily the sugars and honey are powerful enough to ensure parity. After 41 years it deserves the extra time in the glass to show itself as the mini star it actually is. 43.5%. nc ncf sc. 69 bottles.

GLEN SCOTIA
Campbeltown, 1832. Loch Lomond Distillers. Working

⁘ **Glen Scotia 2005 9 Year Old Heavily Peated** cask no. 136, bourbon cask db **(92.5) n23 t23.5 f23 b23**. Peaty malts which nose like a farmyard can go either way...and usually to extremes. This settles into a beautifully compact, fabulously distilled dram where the barley gets an equal airing to the massive smoke. The sugars are on song from first to last and help bring out the best of the late cocoa. Brilliant stuff helped by the lack of aggressive oak. 57.7%. nc ncf. Taiwan exclusive.

Glen Scotia Aged 10 Years bourbon cask, bott Dec 12 db **(90.5) n22.5** soft salty edge to the brittle, clean barley; **t23.5** one of the cleanest deliveries of the year: the barley is tinged with muscovado sugar and oak plays a back seat role; **f22** such a pleasing mix of spice and sugar; just a pinch of ginger reminds you of the oak; **b22.5** fabulous to see Scotia back in this excellent nick again. 46%. nc ncf.

Glen Scotia 12 Years Old db **(73.5) n18 t19 f18 b18.5**. Ooops! I once said you could write a book about this called "Murder by Caramel." Now it would be a short story called "Murder by Flavours Unknown." What is happening here? Well, a dozen years ago Glen Scotia was not quite the place to be for consistent whisky, unlike now. Here, the caramel is the only constant as the constituent parts disintegrate. 40%

Glen Scotia Aged 12 Years bourbon cask, bott Dec 12 db **(89) n22 t22 f23 b22**. Simplistic but delicious. 46%. nc ncf.

⁘ **Glen Scotia 1999 14 Year Old Heavily Peated** cask 528, bourbon cask db **(89) n22.5 t22 f22.5 b22**. Elegant peat and showing excellent sugars a third of the way in. At times a little thin and on the fierce side with fast still spirit burn rather than spice. But genuinely pleasing overall. 55.9% nc ncf. Taiwan exclusive.

Glen Scotia 14 Year Old Peated bourbon cask db **(87)** n21.5 t22 f21.5 b22. A very straight bat played by this one: a malty up and downer with few frills others than a slow though ineffective build up of smoke. 50%. nc ncf.

Glen Scotia Aged 16 Years bourbon cask, bott Dec 12 db **(87)** n22 t22 f21 b22. Signs of a less than brilliant distillate which has been ironed out to some good effect in the cask. 46%. nc ncf.

Glen Scotia Aged 18 Years bourbon cask, bott Dec 12 db **(77)** n20 t21 f17 b19. Malty but hot as Hades: a reminder of a less than glorious period in the distillery's history. 46%. nc ncf.

Glen Scotia Aged 21 Years bourbon cask, bott Dec 12 db **(86.5)** n21.5 t22.5 f21 b21.5. Appears nothing like its age: the very vaguely smoked malt is entirely on top and offers little deviation. A playful spice reminds you oak is involved somewhere. 46%. nc ncf.

Glen Scotia 1989 23 Years Old cask 310, bourbon cask db **(96)** n24 t24 f24 b24. Obviously a cherry-picked cask, as this is stunning. A riot of delicate honey notes trying to outdo each other. Majestic ulmo honey leads the way with heather honey not far behind. Light spice flickers like a butterfly on a lavender bush. Off note free and about as good a Glen Scotia I have ever seen. Like the other new Glen Scotias, arrived too late for full tasting notes. 55.6% nc ncf. Taiwan exclusive.

Glen Scotia Legends of Scotia 1st Release "Picture House" 10 Year Old Heavily Peated bourbon cask db **(85.5)** n21 t21 f22 b21.5. Not exactly a B Movie. But doesn't have you on the edge of your seat, either. Some smoke meanders along the thin plot line with little to say while weight takes on only a walk on part. Occasionally complex, but you'll be asleep before the lights come on... 50%. nc ncf. 6,000 bottles.

Glen Scotia Legends of Scotia 2nd Release "Murfield" Heavily Peated bourbon cask db **(94.5)** n23 t24 f23.5 b24. The nose has about as much smoky power as me teeing off from the 5th: virtually none. But it apologetically creaks into action on the palate and actually plays a delicate and intriguing game with the peat no more than shadowing the muscovado and liquorice. Again, a little ulmo honey shows to add understated sweetness and body. With such genius at play less Muirfeld, more Tynecastle, I'd say... 50%. nc ncf. 6,000 bottles.

The Pearls of Scotland Glen Scotia 1992 22 Year Old cask no. 35, dist Jan 92, bott Feb 14, **(91)** n22.5 the malt is still evident, if a little surly; the oak is layered and sweetened with yam; t23.5 an indulgent but enjoyable lift off with the sugars showing early, like molten sugar on porridge. But the chewy, creamier fudge is sublime; the barey is unmolested and intense; f22.5 the oaks reappear on a custardy ticket, though doing nothing to reduce the barley effect; b23 a few clues here that that spirit may have been a bit of a tough guy when first distilled. But over 20 years in a top quality cask has set it on a blameless path...48.7%.

Scotch Malt Whisky Society Cask 93.53 Aged 10 Years refill barrel, dist 30 Apr 02 **(86.5)** n21 t22.5 f20.5 b21.5. Firm almost to the point of being solid. The shimmering saltiness of the juicy barley is underscored, but there are a few scorch marks, especially to the thin finale. 58.7%. nc ncf sc. 233 bottles.

Scotch Malt Whisky Society Cask 93.55 Aged 13 Years refill barrel, dist 31 Jul 99 **(88)** n22 t22 f22 b22. An attractive, steady-as-she-goes merchant offering mild peat. 61.4%. nc ncf sc. 217 bottles.

Scotch Malt Whisky Society Cask 93.59 Aged 14 Years refill barrel, dist 31 Jul 99 **(94.5)** n24 uncommonly delicate and dry, and charms its way around the nose with its well-mannered, lightly salted smokiness; t23.5 probably more heavily smoked than you might first think. First on the scene are gorgeous gristy sugars while the smoke builds quietly and unobtrusively. Some cocoa residue arrives with the pinging spices; f23 delicate vanilla and smoke entwines; b24 an understatedly attractive smoky Scotia which disarms more than overpowers with peat. A semi-silent classic... 60.8%. nc ncf sc. 193 bottles.

Wemyss Malts 1991 Single Campbletown Glen Scotia "At Anchor in a Cave" butt, dist 91, bott 14 **(85.5)** n21 t22 f21 b21.5. The threat of big oak hinted on the nose is not really carried out, just a cartload of natural caramels. 46%. sc. 304 bottles.

Wemyss Malts 1991 Single Cambeltown Glen Scotia "Merchant's Mahogany Chest" dist 1991 bott 2013 **(87)** n22 t22 f21 b22. From a strange period in this distillery's production history, it is stranger still to see a sherry butt coming to the aid of some average and pretty thin distillate. The nutty, fizzy-spiced riches of a delightfully unsullied cask dominate and embolden. 46%. sc. 807 bottles.

Wemyss 1991 Single Campbeltown "Salted Caramels" barrel, dist 91, bott 13 **(85)** n22 t21 f21 b21. Can't argue with the title this time: a malt swimming in brine and with toffee aplenty. Like the celery on the nose, though. 46%. sc. 279 bottles.

The Whisky Cask Glen Scotia Aged 20 Years dist 92, bott 12 **(74)** n18 t19 f18.5 b18.5. Not particularly well made spirit though the oak has made a valiant effort to reduce the deficit. Those into sweaty armpits might find this a turn on, though. 50.6%. sc.

GLEN SPEY

Speyside, 1885. Diageo. Working.

Glen Spey Aged 12 Years db (90) n23 the kind of firm, busy malt you expect from this distillery plus some lovely spice; t22 mouthwatering and fresh, a layer of honey makes for an easy three or four minutes; f22 drier vanilla, but the pulsing oak is controlled and stylish; b23 very similar to the first Glen Spey I can remember in this range, the one before the over-toffeed effort of two years ago. Great to see it back to its more natural, stunningly beautiful self. 43%

Glen Spey Special Release 2010 21 Years Old sherry American oak cask, dist 1988 db (94.5) n23 a huge nose by this distillery's standards. There are elements of fruit, but more delicious are the controlled oaky bourbony offerings. Honeydew melon, vanilla and red liquorice abounds...telling you something about the variation of weight; t24 the delivery is silky and positively melts into the taste buds, making a mockery of the strength. The honey is stupendously well proportioned and carries spices which prickle as much as the sugars sparkle; f23.5 long, with a wonderful butterscotch/lemon curd tart ensemble. There is a distant fruitiness, burned raisin more associated with aging oak than grape; b24 Glen Speys of this age tended to find their way into blends where they would beef up the sweeter malt content. Sometimes they were used to impart clean sherry or at least fruit, but otherwise give nothing of themselves. This bottling tends to take both strands and then ties them up in a complex and compelling fashion. Wonderful. 50.4%. nc ncf. Diageo.

⁙ **Cadenhead's Small Batch Glen Spey-Glenlivet Aged 17 Years** bourbon hogsheads, dist 1995, bott 2013 (90) n23 the lightest trace of smoke — probably due to the history of a pre-used hogshead — adds surprising extra weight to the perky tannin and usual floral earthiness. The gooseberries show the barley in good form, though; t22.5 salivating as the sharp, tangy barley cuts through the soft oils; both gristy and pithy in equal measures, it doesn't take long for the spices to say "hi"; f22 tangy oak but the firm barley retains control; b22.5 a few decades back this was not a difficult malt to locate, either as a proprietary-bottled youngster or among the independents. By no means the case today, which is a shame: few do light but fruity and juicy Speyside quite like this distillery. 46%. 948 bottles. WB15/088

⁙ **Hepburn's Choice Glen Spey Aged 11 Years** sherry butt, dist 02, bott 14 (85.5) n21 t22 f21 b21.5. Another of those juicy, somewhat oak-free malts Hunter Laing specialise in, where you see the whisky naked, warts and all. Just a light citric tang to this, but there is no tannin to disguise the minor butyric, either. Still, salivating and lively with a curious grappa finale. 46%. nc ncf sc. 816 bottles.

⁙ **Old Particular Speyside Glen Spey Aged 15 Years** refill hogshead, cask no. 10286, dist Apr 99, bott Apr 14 (85.5) n21 t23 f20.5 b21. Pleasantly clean, though strictly limited malt thanks to the old cask employed. But the after-delivery, a combination gristy malt and concentrated, unhindered sugars, is sheer joy. 48.4%. nc ncf sc. 324 bottles.

Provenance Glen Spey Over 9 Years refill hogshead, cask no. 8468, dist Summer 00, bott Spring 12 (77) n20 t19 f19 b19. Docile even by third fill cask standards. Virtually colourless, the barley is untroubled by oak or the passing years so the new make style remains intact. 46%. nc ncf sc. Douglas Laing & Co.

GLENTAUCHERS

Speyside, 1898. Chivas Brothers. Working.

⁙ **Càrn Mòr Strictly Limited Edition Glentauchers Aged 18 Years** bourbon barrels, dist 1996, bott 2014 (91) n23 soft William pear serenaded by vanilla; t23.5 a juicy quasi-fruity sprint off the gun before settling into an intensely malty theme; f22 slight oak bitterness, but good spice, too; b22.5 the type which makes you sigh thanks to its delicious simplicity. 46%. nc ncf. 443 bottles from 2 casks. WB15/052

Chieftain's Glentaughers Aged 20 Years hogshead, cask no. 6016, dist Sep 92, bott Mar 13 (95) n23.5 older 'Tauchers are not unknown to throw up enticing banana notes amid the usual cereal stuff, and this is no exception; slightly salty porridge; distant peat embers... surely not...; t24 I am not particularly fond of cats, I admit. But I cannot help but purr with this near perfect concoction of barley, spice, ulmo honey and marzipan. The delicate oils are not thick enough to interfere with the natural interplay. Just a light vaguely bizarre coastal sea-breeze of salt and peat stir towards the middle; f23.5 all the previous notes scaled down with more accent on grapefruit and cocoa; b24 one of the most consistent distilleries in not just Speyside but Scotland. Yet another treat of a dram: technically flawless. 59.5%. nc ncf sc. Ian Macleod Distillers. 265 bottles.

⁙ **Gordan & Macphail Cask Strength Glentauchers 1995** (76) n17 t20 f19 b20. I have been banging the gong longest of all for Gentauchers being one of the greatest yet-to-be-discovered distilleries of the world. But not even this distillery's brilliance can fully overcome the curse of lightly sulphured sherry butts... 58.3%.

Gordon and MacPhail Distillery Label Glentauchers 1994 (96.5) n23.5 impossible to imagine a nose more subtle or intrinsic: the barley is so delicate you expect it to shatter if you sniff too hard; **t24.5** oh my word! The barley melts on the palate, yet at the same time has enough firmness to crash land into the taste buds...but with the aid of a parachute. Hard to imagine a barley where the flavours are so pronounced, the use of muscovado sugar so well judged. The oak, all buttress and little show, could be knighted for its services to diplomacy; **f23.5** relies on the slow burn of egg custard tart and melting muscovado; a little diced coconut is added to the mix, as is citrus; **b25** one day someone else who matters in the industry will wake up to just how good this malt is...probably the finest of the G&M Distillery Label fleet. Certainly find a bottle or two for myself...the perfect early evening accompaniment to life...and a good read... 43%

❖ **Hepburn's Choice Glentauchers Aged 8 Years** sherry butt, bott 2014 **(74.5) n20 t19 f17.5 b18.** Usually hard to go wrong with a Glentauchers, one of the world's most consistent spirits. Unless the oak has a personality disorder, of course... 46%. nc ncf sc. 310 bottles.

❖ **The Maltman Glentauchers Aged 15 Years** bourbon cask, cask no. 3854, dist Jul 97, bott Apr 13 **(90.5) n22.5** sliced green banana and gooseberry; **t23** fresh barley, of the barley sugar variety; **f22.5** vanilla and crisp, gristy barley: simple but effective...; **b22.5** after a day of tasting finishes of every shape and hue, oh! the sheer unalloyed joy of finding excellent distillate having grown up in a respectable bourbon cask... 46%. sc ncf nc. 298 bottles. WB15/214

❖ **Master of Malt Single Cask Glentauchers 15 Year Old (96) n23** egg custard tart... with a gristy layering; **t25** one of the deliveries of the year: mouth-watering explosion of barley at its gristiest — and fortified with a citrus-muscovado sugar mix; **f24** elegant oak in slight sherbet-fizzing form. Of course, the barley has the final word; **b24** a great distillery, magnificently and truly faultlessly portrayed. Not a weakness nor off note: hard to see this distillery in a better light. 55.1%. sc.

Old Malt Cask Glentauchers Aged 16 Years refill hogshead, cask no. 8902, dist Jul 96, bott Sep 12 **(88) n22 t21.5 f22.5 b22.** They were skimping on the cask paste slightly when this one was made. Delightfully layered, though. 50%. sc. Douglas Laing & Co. 229 bottles.

❖ **The Pearls of Scotland Glentauchers 1996 17 Year Old** cask no. 3616, dist Jun 96, bott Nov 13 **(94) n23.5** such a relaxed Speyside-style nose: the balance between the oak and crisp barley is nigh spot on, with neither determined to overpower the other. Simple, but effective...; **t23.5** just the right kind of bite — the kind of bite which every bender worth his salt is looking for in a blended scotch. So it is no coincidence that this is a malt truly prized by the grey beards of the lab. This manifests itself in a rushing wave of sprightly barley, at once jagged and soft with salivates, and continues to do so as a light mocha on the oak begins to shape; **f23** like the nose, but in pulses and now with soft oils rather than celery...; **b24** even when as a relaxed as this, a 'Tauchers is just such balm for the soul. A true little gem. 47.7%.

Single Cask Collection Glentauchers 17 Years Old bourbon hogshead, cask no. 1155, dist 1 Feb 96, bott 13 Feb 13 **(95.5) n23.5** really beautiful gooseberry and greengage mash; plenty of barley apparent. So clean, with the sweetness restricted to the delicate fruit notes; high tannin, but rounded by those stunning, delicate fruits; **t24** just as salivating as the nose promises, though far more in the way of spice which comes through at its own ambling pace as the tannins begin to bite; the evenness of the brown sugars is truly textbook; **f23.5** a light pulsing of spice works beautifully with the increasing depth of the Venezuelan Criollo cocoa; **b24.5** this distillery is one of the unknown gems of Speyside and rarely does it come better polished than this... 55.2%. nc ncf sc. 167 bottles.

❖ **That Boutique-y Whisky Glentauchers** batch 1 **(91.5) n22** apple tart...with custard... and maybe a little hay thrown in on top; **t23.5** intense malt from the off with crystallised muscovado sugars adding extra crunch; **f23** firm and flinty; the light malty oil gather a little spice; **b23** shouts "top grade Speyside blending fodder" at every opportunity. 50.7%. 185 bottles. WB15/224

❖ **Wemyss Malts 1992 Single Speyside Glentauchers "Liquorice Spiral"** bott 13 **(92) n24** sensual and soft, this just has to be just about the epitome of high grade blending Speyside, so far as a nose is concerned. The barley is ripe and sugar coated and anyone old enough to remember Black Jack and Fruit Salad candy in its pomp will be cheerfully transported back to their childhood; **t23** the nose suggests "salivating". And salivating it is...to a dribblesome degree. The citrus notes are also evident as well as the tangy barley. Vanilla begins to fill the middle ground; **f22** biscuity and dries as the oak shows some puny muscle; **b23** another minor gem from one of the most trustworthy malts in the business. 46%. sc. 339 bottles.

GLENTURRET
Highlands (Perthshire), 1775. Edrington. Working.

Glenturret Aged 8 Years db **(88) n21 t22 f23 b22.** Technically no prizewinner. But the dexterity of the honey is charming, as this distillery has a tendency sometimes to be. *40%*

The Glenturret Aged 10 Years db **(76) n19 t18 f20 b19.** Lots of trademark honey but some less than impressive contributions from both cask and the stillman. *40%*

The Glenturret Aged 15 Years db **(87) n21 t22 f22 b22.** A beautifully clean, small-still style dram that would have benefitted from being bottled at a fuller strength. A discontinued bottling now: if you see it, it is worth the small investment. *40%*

⁘ **The Famous Grouse 1986 Glenturret Glasgow 2014 Limited Edition** dist 86, bott 14 db **(95) n24** about as chunky a Glenturret as I can remember: chocolate fudge in tandem with apricot and kumquat. The sugars are no less heavy with treacle and pears in close proximity; **t24** every bit as rounded and chewy as the nose suggests. This distillery always has honey somewhere and it arrives as a blend of manuka and – ensuring the depth and mouth feel – ulmo honeys make a huge impact and add even thicker layers of complexity; **f23** maybe a slight tang to the finish from some kind of wine cask. It was expected but nowhere near as damaging as I had feared. Again, the chocolate fudge is back on the menu doing all it can to see off the late but prevailing furry bitterness; **b24** I honestly can't remember the last time I experienced a Glenturret this good – even taking into account its blemish. A PB and Gold medal performance... *46.4%. 1,800 bottles. WB15/409*

Gordon and MacPhail Collection Glenturret 1999 (84.5) n20.5 t22.5 f20.5 b21.5. Lots of small still coppery action, all sharp and angular. Some powdery, gristy sweetness, too, amid the tartness. Yet, curiously, though pleasant, never quite falls together as one might hope or expect. One for those looking for a very different dram. *43%*

Liquid Sun Glenturret 1980 bott 12 **(92.5) n23** major sma' still coppery edge to this, with the usual Perthshire heather- depth; some curious earthiness, too; **t23** rounded delivery and follow through. Again, heather-honey leads the way with a lavender and spice back up; **f23.5** soft oils and a return of the coppery edge. Crisp sugars sign off; **b23.5** 'Turret's classic style. *42.4%. The Whisky Agency.*

Master Of Malt Glenturret Aged 34 Years refill sherry hogshead, dist 77, bott 12 **(87) n21 t22.5 f21.5 b22.** A breakfast malt if ever there was one. *47.9%. ncf nc. 247 bottles.*

Old Malt Cask Glenturret Aged 18 Years sherry cask, cask no. 9037, dist Sep 94, bott Sep 12 **(83.5) n19 t23 f20.5 b21.** One of those heartbreak casks. The delivery lights up in neon the original beauty of the butt, but the nose and finish reveal its Achilles heel. Some, though, may find this a stunningly beautiful oloroso-influenced malt. *50%. sc. 288 bottles.*

⁘ **Signatory Vintage Single Malt Glenturret 1993 Aged 20 Years** hogsheads, cask no. 173, dist 19 Apr 93, 07 Feb 14 **(81) n20.5 t21 f19 b20.5.** Borderline feinty with the cut adding a few extra oils offering kumquats in nougat. Big whisky from a tiny distillery, but struggles beyond the early barley-honey mix. *43%. nc sc. 376 bottles. WB15/019*

GLENUGIE
Highlands (Eastern). 1834–1983. Whitbread. Closed.

Deoch an Doras Glenugie 30 Years Old dist 1980, bott 2011 db **(87) n22 t23.5 f19.5 b22.** Now there's something I didn't expect to see again: a distillery bottling of Glenugie. Well, technically, anyway, as Glenugie was part of the Chivas group when it died in the 1980s. As far as I can remember they only brought it out once, either as a seven- or five-year-old. I think that went to Italy, so when I walked around the old site just after it closed, it was a Gordon and MacPhail bottling I drank from and it tasted nothing like this! Just a shame there is a very slight flaw in the sherry butt, but just great to see it in bottle again. *52.13%. nc ncf. Chivas Brothers.*

GLENURY ROYAL
Highlands (Eastern), 1868–1985. Diageo. Demolished.

Glenury Royal 36 Years Old db **(89) n22 t23.5 f21.5 b22** With so much dark, threatening oak around, the delivery defies belief or logic. Cracking stuff!! *57.9%*

Glenury Royal 36 Years Old db **(89) n21 t23 f22 b23.** An undulating dram, hitting highs and lows. The finish, in particular, is impressive: just when it looks on its last legs, it revives delightfully. The whole package, though far from perfect, is pretty astounding. *50.2%*

Glenury Royal 40 Year Old Limited Edition dist 1970, bott 2011 db **(84) n20.5 t20 f22 b21.5.** Glenury is these days so rare I kept this back as a treat to savour as I neared the end of the book. The finale throws up a number of interesting citrus equations. But the oak, for the most part, is too rampant here and makes for a puckering experience. *59.4%. 1,500 bottles.*

Glenury Royal 50 Years Old dist 1953 db **(91) n23** marvellous freshness to the sherry butt; this had obviously been a high quality cask in its day and the intensity of the fruit sweetened slightly by the most delicate marzipan and old leather oozes class; a little mint reveals some worry lines; **t24** the early arrival is sweet and nimble with the barley, against the odds, still having the major say after all these years. The oak is waiting in the wings and with a burst of soft liquorice and velvety, understated spice beginning to make an impression; the sweetness is very similar to a traditional British child's candy of "tobacco" made from strands of coconut and sugar; **f22** masses of oak yet, somehow, refuses to go over the top and that slightly molassed sweetness sits very comfortably with the mildly oily body; **b22** I am always touched when sampling a whisky like this from a now departed distillery. *42.8%*

HAZELBURN *(see Springbank)*

HIGHLAND PARK
Highlands (Island–Orkney), 1795. Edrington. Working.

⁘ **Highland Park Dark Origins** db (80) **n19 t23 f18 b20**. Part of that Dark Origin must be cocoa, as there is an abundance of delicious high grade chocolate here. But the other part is not so much dark as yellow, as sulphur is around on the nose and finish in particular - and does plenty of damage. Genuinely disappointing to see one of the world's greatest distilleries refusing to play to its strengths and putting so much of its weight on its Achilles heel. *46.8%. ncf.*

⁘ **Highland Park Einar** db (90.5) **n23** soft, warmingly smoky, toffee apple; **t23** fresh, salivating delivery but bordered by tannin and imbued with spice; vague heather honey; **f22** dry with the tannins and spices buzzing to the end; **b22.5** a curious style of HP which shows most of its usual traits but possesses an extra sharpness. *40% WB15/328*

⁘ **Highland Park Freya** 1st fill ex-bourbon casks db (88.5) **n22** a peculiar nose by HP standards: a kind of smoky nougat and salted smoky bacon mix; the odd off-key note, too; **t23** the distillery honey maybe absent on the nose. But it is first off the blocks here; **f21.5** a slightly uncomfortable finish rescued by the chocolate sauce on the vanilla ice cream; **b22** the majestic honey on delivery makes up for some of the untidier moments. *52.10%.*

⁘ **Highland Park Harald** db (74.5) **n19 t20 f17 b18.5**. Warrior Harald has been wounded by sulphur. Fatally. *40% WB15/337*

⁘ **Highland Park Sigurd** db (96) **n23.5** clever, delicate layering of exotic fruit lurking behind gentle smoke, all heightened by a shake of salt; **t24.5** truly beautiful delivery which nutshells HP at its most intense: the smoke is rounded and only marginally intense, the heather-honey forms the centre point and is equally as circular in its shape and motion around the palate. Yet all along, there is that exotic fruit, omnipresent, but so easy to miss. And, if that is not enough, the mouth feel is simply perfection...; **f23.5** just when you need spice, you really get it...; **b24.5** breath-taking, star-studded and ridiculously complex reminder that this distillery is capable of serving up some of the best whisky the world can enjoy. *43%*

⁘ **Highland Park Svein** db (87) **n22 t22 f21.5 b21.5**. A soft, friendly dram with good spice pick up. But rather too dependent on a tannin-toffee theme. *40% WB15/318*

Highland Park 8 Years Old db (87) **n22 t22 f22 b21**. A journey back in time for some of us: this is the orginal distillery bottling of the 70s and 80s, bottles of which are still doing the rounds in obscure Japanese bars and specialist outlets such as the Whisky Exchange. *40%*

Highland Park Aged 12 Years db (78) **n19 t21 f19 b19**. Let's just hope that the choice of casks for this bottling was a freak. To be honest, this was one of my favourite whiskies of all time, one of my desert island drams, and I could weep. *40%*

Highland Park Saint Magnus Aged 12 Years 2nd edition db (76.5) **n18.5 t21 f19 b19**. Tight and bitter 2nd edition. *55%*

Highland Park 15 Years db (85) **n21 t22 f21 b21**. Had to re-taste this several times, surprised as I was by just how relatively flat this was. A hill of honey forms the early delivery, but then... *40%*

Highland Park Earl Magnus Aged 15 Years 1st edition db (76.5) **n20 t21 f17.5 b18**. Tight and bitter. *52.6%. 5976 bottles.*

Highland Park Loki Aged 15 Years db (96) **n24** heather honey milling around in a confident, but soft, plume of smoke – but a curious different type of lighter heather! Usual stewed apples at play, but sweetened by the honey rather than sugar; a little stem ginger amid the hickory and vanilla, too; **t24** wonderful HP silkiness, a rasping snort of barley is captured and enwrapped by the heather-ish-honey while those ginger-led spices are pitched at the smouldering smoke; **f23.5** tangy marmalade changes the fruity dimension, but the comforting oils continue to ensure a gentle mouth feel, despite the best efforts of some late herbal interaction. The smoke continues on its cheery but quietly deep way...; **b24.5** the weirdness of the heather apart, a bit of a trip back in time. A higher smoke ratio than the bottlings of more recent years which new converts to the distillery will be unfamiliar with, but reverting to the levels regularly found in the 1970s and 80s, probably right through to about 1993/94. Which is a very good thing because the secret of the peat at HP was that, as puffed out as it could be in the old days, it never interfered with the overall complexity, other than adding to it. Which is exactly the case here. Beyond excellent! 48.7%. Edrington.

Highland Park 16 Years Old db (88) n23 t23 f20 b22. I tasted this the day it first came out at one of the Heathrow whisky shops. I thought it a bit flat and uninspiring. This sample, maybe from another bottling, is more impressive and showing true Highland Park colours, the finish apart. 40%. Exclusively available in Duty Free/Travel Retail.

Highland Park Thor Aged 16 Years db (87.5) n22.5 t23.5 f19 b22.5. Now, from what I remember of my Norse gods, Thor was the God of Thunder. Which is a bit spooky seeing as hailstones are crashing down outside as I write this and lightning is striking overhead. Certainly a whisky built on power. Even taking into account the glitch in one or two of the casks, a dram to be savoured on delivery. 52.1%. 23,000 bottles.

Highland Park Aged 18 Years db (95.5) n23.5 a thick dollop of honey spread across a layer of salted butter; in the background the ashes of a peat fire are emptied; t24 eye closing beauty: immediate glossy impact of rich, vaguely metallic honey but upped in the complexity stakes by the subtle intense marbling of peat; the muscular richness, aided by the softness of the oil ensures that maximum intensity is not only reached but maintained; f24 long continuation of those elements found in the delivery but now radiating soft spices and hints of marzipan; b24 if familiarity breeds contempt, then it has yet to happen between myself and HP 18. This is a must-have dram. I show it to ladies the world over to win their hearts, minds and tastebuds when it comes to whisky. And the more time I spend with it, the more I become aware and appreciative of its extraordinary consistency. The very latest bottlings have been astonishing, possibly because colouring has now been dropped, and wisely so. Why in any way reduce what is one of the world's great whisky experiences? Such has been the staggering consistency of this dram I have thought of late of promoting the distillery into the world's top three: only Ardbeg and Buffalo Trace have been bottling whisk(e)y of such quality over a wide range of ages in such metronomic fashion. Anyway, enough: a glass of something honeyed and dazzling calls... 43%

Highland Park Aged 21 Years db (82.5) n20.5 t22 f19 b21. Good news and bad news. The good news is that they appear to have done away with the insane notion of reducing this to 40% abv. The bad news: a sulphured sherry butt has found its way into this bottling. 47.5%

Highland Park Aged 25 Years db (96) n24 big aged oak amid the smoke and honey: it appears something a lot older has got in here...; uniquely complex and back to its very best; t24 silky and confident, every usual box is ticked – or even double ticked. Much more honey and smoke than I have seen here for a while and it's not all about quantity. What quality! f24 long with amazing degrees of oil, almost of the bourbony-corn variety! Helps keep those mind-bending honeys coming! b24 I am a relieved man: the finest HP 25 for a number of years which displays the distillery's unmistakable fingerprints with a pride bordering on arrogance. One of the most improved bottlings of the year: an emperor of a dram. 48.1%

Highland Park Aged 30 Years db (90) n22 a fascinating balancing act between juicy fruit and very tired, splintered oak; t22.5 the age waters the eye, so powerful is the oak. But it settles into an oily sweetness displaying both a lazy smokiness and burnt raisin; f23 some real complexity here with oils filling in the drier vanilla moments; b22.5 a very dramatic shift from the last bottling I tasted; this has taken a fruitier route. Sheer quality, though. 48.1%

Highland Park 40 Years Old db (90.5) n20.5 tired and over-oaked but the usual HP traits are there in just enough force to save it from failing with an extra puff of something smoky diving in to be on the safe side; t22.5 even after 40 years, pure silk. Like a 40-year-old woman who has kept her figure and looks, and now only satin stands in the way between you and so much beauty and experience...and believe me: she's spicy...; f24 amazing layering of peat caresses you at every level; the oak has receded and now barley and traces of golden syrup balance things; b23.5 I have to admit to picking splinters from my nose with this one. Some of the casks used here have obviously choked on oak, and I feared the worst. But such is the brilliance of the resilience by being on the money with the honey, you can say only that it has pulled off an amazing feat with the peat. Sheer poetry... 48.3%

⋰ **Highland Park 40 Year Old** re-fill American oak sherry casks cask db (92.5) n21 yes, enormous amount of tannins and spice from the oak. Some will love it. I'm not convinced; t24 ah...that's better. Much better! The sugars have found their voice and arrive early but are instantly outmuscled by scalding spices. The oak is less a splinter and more a log. Yet enough soft smoke and molasses is on hand to soften the thrusts and blows; and a dribble of honey for this busy little bee..; f23.5 long, with plenty of plenty of oak and even sweetened pine. Yet, astonishingly, it retains balance throughout and avoids the OTT splinter effect b24 many years ago – long before even this whisky was distilled – there used to be a BBC television programme called Juke Box Jury. It was on early Saturday evenings directly after Grandstand and learning of Millwall's latest victory. The presenter of this was David Jacobs, a bit part actor turned DJ and more suave than any Highland Park yet bottled. We are talking so long back I remember that they had Penny Lane and Strawberry Fields Forever by The Beatles both listened, one after the other, to by the panel of guests, who voted "Hit" or "Miss". The idea was that they had to decide, on this occasion, which should be the A side of their next single. I can't remember the outcome in the show, but I do know it was released as a double A-side. I mention all this because this whisky was bottled to mark the 40th anniversary of legendary Scottish record dec makers Linn, who have been known to use HP casks in their making of their prized equipment. So, "hit" or "miss"? The nose, so overly oaked, or decked as we might now say, was a miss. But, overall, a resounding "hit". 48.3%. *Paired with the Sondek LP12 turntable.*

Highland Park 50 Years Old dist Jan 60 db (**96.5**) **n24.5** mint, cloves and a thin coat of creosote usurp the usual deft heather and smoke to loudly announce this whisky's enormous age. Don't bother looking for heather, either. Well, not at first... However, there is a growling sweetness from the start: deep and giving up its part molten Demerara-part treacle character with miserly contempt, as though outraged by being awoken from a 50-year slumber. Of course, as the whisky oxidises there is a shift in pattern. And after about ten minutes a wine effect – and we are talking something much more akin to a First Growth Bordeaux than sherry - begins to make a statement. Then the sugars transmogrify from treacle to molasses to manuka honey; **t24** certain sugars present on the delivery, though at first hard to quite make out which. Some surprising oil ensures suppleness to the oak; there is also a wonderful marriage, or perhaps it is a threesome, between old nutty fruitcake, tangy orange-enriched high quality north European marzipan, and ancient bourbon...; **f24** silky with some wonderful caramels and toasted fudge forming a really chewy finale. As well as ensuring any possible old-age holes are plugged; **b24** old whiskies tend to react to unchartered territory as far as time in the oak is concerned in quite different ways. This grey beard has certainly given us a new slant. Nothing unique about the nose. But when one is usually confronted with those characteristics on the nose, what follows on the palate moves towards a reasonably predictable path. Not here. Truly unique – as it should be after all this time. 44.8%. sc. 275 bottles.

Highland Park 1964 Orcadian Vintage refill hogshead, bott 2009 db (**90.5**) **n23 t22 f23 b22.5**. At times you think the old oak is going to sink without trace, taking the whisky with it. But such is the pedigree of the HP make, that it not only fights back but regains control. An honour to experience. 42.2%. 290 bottles.

Highland Park 1968 Orcadian Vintage refill casks, bott 2009 db (**88.5**) **n20 t23.5 f23 b22.** The spicy oak has taken too firm a grip for true greatness. But some of the passages offer wonderful moments of contemplation. 45.6%. 1550 bottles.

Highland Park 1970 Orcadian Vintage db (**94.5**) **n23.5** much smokier than present day HP..would love to have nosed the new make 40 years ago: it would have been massive; helped along here with a squeeze of blood orange; **t24** splinters on delivery – in both senses - but the silky malt-honey body is able to absorb everything thrown at it; the degrees of sweetness run from honey, through light sugars to subtle Lubec marzipan: sublime; **f23.5** long, again with a distinctive orangey note clinging to the sweet, lightly smoked barley: elegant...; **b23.5** most other malts would have disintegrated under the weight of the oak. This takes it in its stride, and actually uses the extra vanilla to excellent effect. Memorable. 48%

Highland Park 1973 bott 2010 db (**96**) **n24** what could be better than a standard HP nose, complete with all that delicate smoke and honey? An HP nose with a decent smidgeon of high quality bourbon! Well that's what those extra years in the cask has gone and given you; **t25** mouth-watering barley enters the arena hand-in-hand with pristine acacia honey. Directly behind is two-tone smoke: one firm, lightly peated and spiced, the other a softer, billowing safety net; the middle ground concerns molten manuka honey and muscovado sugar thickened with vanilla and then the lightest hint of mocha. Frankly, perfect...; **f23** lighter, lengthy with toffee and liquorice; **b24** now that, folks, is Highland Park and make no mistake! 50.6%

Highland Park Vintage 1978 db (**95.5**) **n24** some thumping oak is of such high quality it only adds to the mix, rather than detracts. The smoke level is pretty high considering it's had so long in the cask and this helps fend off any oaky excess. Elsewhere tangy kumquats mix with physalis and greengages. The usual honey has given way to soft molasses; **t24** I hope the flight is a long one if you have bought this Duty Free: you really need a good hour alone with this guy to begin to understand its foibles and complexities. The delivery offers a surprising degree of sharpness and life, in which those citrus notes formulate. Then a gentle mixing of delicate, vaguely weary smoke and an almost bourbony red liquorice and light honeycomb mix...; **f23.5** a very light oiliness has formed and provides all that is required to give an extra polish to those soft oaky tones. An equally understated mocha and molasses creamy sweetness ties up the loose ends; **b24** if you are buying this in Duty Free, a tip:

get it for yourself...it's too good for a gift!! This purrs quality from first to last. And is quite unmistakably Highland Park. A noble malt. *47.8%. Available in Global Travel Retail.*

Highland Park 1990 bott 2010 db **(90) n23** a sprig of lavender (probably in lieu of standard heather) dovetails jauntily with ubiquitous honey and a puff of smoke; **t23** sublime delivery: an almost perfect degree of oil to help the honey slither into its rightful place at the head of the flavour queue with some toffee vanilla not far behind. Just a hint of soapiness; **f22** long, with a buzzing smokiness...and late toffee pudding; **b22** much more like it...!! *40%*

Highland Park 1994 bott 2010 db **(87) n23 t22 f20.5 b21.5.** I am not sure what is happening here. HPs of this vintage should be soaring into the comfortable 90s. But again the finish is dull and the usual complexity of the malt is vanishing behind a murky veil. *40%*

Highland Park 1997 "The Sword" db **(79.5) n19 t23 f18 b19.5.** Shows its cutting edge for only a brief while on delivery – when it is quite spectacular. Otherwise, painfully blunted. *43%. Available in Taiwan.*

Highland Park 1998 bott 2010 db **(85) n22 t22 f20 b21.** They must have special Orcadian spiders to spin a silk this fine. But, though pleasant, disappointing by HP standards as it never gets to spread its wings. The whisky, that is: not the spider. *40%*

Highland Park Earl Haakon db **(92) n22.5** the smoke is unusually fishy – something of the Arbroath Smokie. But there are massive tracts of oak waiting in the wings – fresh, red-blooded and happy to keep the honey company; **t24** even by HP's extraordinary standards, the mouth feel on this guy makes the knees tremble. Aided by spices which shimmy and contort all over the palate, the first five or six waves are as good as any malt I have tasted this year; heads towards a surprisingly lightweight butterscotch middle; **f22.5** caramels are happy to lead the fade; **b23** a fabulous malt offering some of the best individual moments of the year. But appears to run out of steam about two thirds in. *54.9%. 3,300 bottles.*

Highland Park Hjärta db **(79.5) n18.5 t22 f19 b20.** In part, really does celebrate the honeycomb character of Highland Park to the full. But obviously a major blemish or two in there as well. *58.1%. 3924 bottles.*

Highland Park Leif Eriksson bourbon and American oak db **(86) n22 t22 f21 b21.** The usual distillery traits have gone AWOL while all kinds of caramel notes have usurped them. That said, this has to be one of the softest drams you'll find. *40%. Edrington.*

Highland Park New Make Spirit Drink dist Feb 10, bott Mar 10 db **(85.5) n21 t22 f21 b21.5.** Doesn't boast the usual degree of ultra rich texture of new make HP – even when reduced – and though sweet, malty and enjoyable, with its few extra metallic molecules not exactly how I recently tasted new make HP in a blending lab. A curious choice. *50%. Venture Whisky Ltd.*

⁙ **Adelphi Selection Highland Park 26 Years Old** cask no. 10112, dist 86, bott 13 **(95.5) n23.5** HP in that delightful form when you can actually pick up pollen...; **t24** some people say they can't find heather honey on HP. No? Give this a go...; **f23.5** just so long...and it's a fair way in before the very first puff of smoke is detected. By then your taste buds have already weaved their way through myriad minor flavour hints and statements, the delicate spices having the greatest amount to say and gaining confidence from the late smoke; a full mark docked for a slightly tangy but persistent, tongue-tingling finale; **b24.5** one of the most complex bottlings of the year showing HP's ability to mesmerise the taste buds and blow the mind. *44%. ncf sc. 240 bottles. WB15/414*

A.D. Rattray Highland Park 1990 butt, cask no. 577, dist 3 Dec 90, bott Apr 13 **(68.5) n17 t20 f14.5 b17.** Reminiscent of being On the Beach. For, amid the sulphury radiation the salty honey and peat taps out its proud, elegant and ultimately heartbreaking farewell... *58.1%. sc. A.D. Rattray. Dewar Rattray Cask Collection.*

Director's Cut Highland Park Aged 21 Years refill butt, cask no. 9200, dist Feb 91, bott Oct 12 **(87) n21 t23 f21 b22** a two-toned malt which errs on the dry side. *53.6%. sc.*

Douglas Laing Premier Barrel Highland Park Aged 15 Years (91) n22.5 t22.5 f23 b23. Classic HP ticking every required box with a flourish! *46%. nc ncf sc. 483 bottles.*

⁙ **Gordon & MacPhail Cask Strength Highland Park** first fill Bourbon barrels, cask no. 2809, 2810, 2811 & 2812, dist 18 Apr 05, bott 07 Mar 14 **(95.5) n23.5** the presence of the heather honey makes you smile: it is a cliché come true. But there it is, though without its usual lightly smoked accompaniment. Thought eh delicate spice might well be peat induced; **t25** OK. That's it...I might as well pack it in for the week. I am not likely to find a better delivery and follow through between now and the ending of writing this Bible...and seeing as this is the 624th new whisky of the 2015 edition (and so far the best), I am unofficially one short of being halfway through. This is the sweetest a whisky can get without being cloying, the smokiest without being heavy, the spiciest without being aggressive: it is, truly...perfection; **f23.5** long, with toasted honeycomb; the spices massage and warm and even so far in the malt filters through, a little smoked, still with those traces of heather honey....it is like all your dreams and fantasies in a 70cl bottle...; **b23.5** I think the first HP I ever tasted was an 8-y-o from Gordon and MacPhail. That was something in the region of 40 years ago. It wasn't even half way to being this good, though. As it was at 40% and the added caramel filled in and homogenised all the interesting features. This 8-year-old, seemingly distilled by bees and matured in a hive might be the perfect whisky for Brentford supporters to celebrate their return to the second tier of English football after a very long time. And one for the blending lab at HP, as here is proof that sherry butts are not remotely required to impart greatness in their core brands. Just care. This is a whisky of a lifetime. *591%. WB15/111*

Gordon and MacPhail Cask Strength Highland Park 2003 (96.5) n23.5 no other distillery on the planet holds a thumbprint quite this recognisable or is able to stroke the heart with such gentle grace: heather-honey and trace peat reek **t24.5** the delivery is pretty near perfection: the degree of oils mix with unbelievable aplomb and a light coppery sheen (had they just done some repair work to a still, I wonder?) and then layer upon layer of spice and heather-honey tinged tannin and smoke...; **f24** long, with the smoke now radiating with unusual weight and confidence for an HP but still it is that chocolate caramel tart, criss-crossed with honey that just makes you want to curl up and hug this glass to death...; **b24.5** oh...my.....gawd....!!!! *578%. ncf.*

Gordon & MacPhail MacPhail's Collection Highland Park 8 Years Old (74) n18 t20 f17 b19. Completely off the pace for all its groin-fumbling sweetness, with the odd dodgy cask involved here. *43%*

⠶ **The MacPhail's Collection from Highland Park 1988 (88)** n23 ginger and Turkish delight make a change from the usual honeyed offering, but emphasises the age. Spices, naturally; **t22.5** after a bright display of barley pretty rabid caramels soften the texture by overshadowing the usual complexity; again honey absent, but some toasty fudge instead; **f21** soft, dry and toasty but essentially flat-lining; **b21.5** pleasant, but drab. Very flat for a HP with the usual signature smoke and heather honey conspicuous by their absence...and an absence which doesn't make the hard grow fonder. *43%.*

Malts Of Scotland Highland Park 1998 sherry hogshead, cask no. MoS 12058, dist Mar 98, bott Nov 12 **(92.5)** n23.5 spiced coffee – sweetened by a big dollop of Harvey's Bristol Cream; **t23.5** for the most part you are drinking high strength sherry, but about two-thirds in, juicy barley does make an impudent entrance; **f23** tart marmalade, as opposed to marmalade tart; **b22** one of the old-fashioned types of sherry casks which three decades ago would have been regarded as slightly inferior quality for overwhelming and bullying the malt, but is today of a higher class for being generally clean of sulphur. *574%. nc ncf sc. 96 bottles.*

⠶ **Old Malt Cask Highland Park Aged 17 Years** cask no. 9903, dist Sep 96, bott Sept 13 **(94)** n23.5 Ok, so it doesn't have the usual heather-honey. But that lurking hint of smoke? Those deftly layered barley tones? The neat and tidy, liquorice-leaning tannins? Don't tell me what Highland Park has done for us...; **t24** well, no doubting the honey now. The ulmo variety is up there loud and clear with the peat offering a low rumble in the background; the barley also has a delicious input; **f23** citrus drizzled, delicately smoked vanilla, enlivened with peek-a-boo, spice; **b23.5** simple genius cannot be denied. *50%. nc ncf sc. 206 bottles.*

⠶ **Old Malt Cask Highland Park Aged 17 Years** refill hogshead, cask no. 10313, dist Sep 96, bott Feb 14 **(90)** n23 the feeble but compelling smoke locked into the heather honey can mean only one distillery....; **t23.5** gorgeous medium weight honeyed barley given a little extra depth by the spiced smoke and minty cocoa; **f21** spicy; just a little lingering bitterness; **b22.5** the distillery more or less nut-shelled... *50%. sc. 296 bottles.*

⠶ **Old Particular Highland Park Aged 17 Years** refill hogshead, cask no. 10230, dist Sep 96, bott Apr 14 **(92.5)** n22 here we go: heather honey spread on light, golden toast; **t24** more emphasis on the barley on delivery, then a light honeyed footfall. The smoke drifts in as an afterthought; **f23** roasty, almost like a Guinness but without the hops; the smoke lingers awhile; **b23.5** that heather honey really isn't a cliché. But it is the deftness of the smoke which steals the show. *48.4%. nc ncf sc. 324 bottles.*

⠶ **Old Particular Highland Park 18 Years Old** refill hogshead, cask no. 10161, dist Nov 95, bott Dec 13 **(92)** n22 the sugars are suppressed by tight smoky citrus; **t22.5** opens up to better effect on delivery as the barley offers both juiciness and depth; a light smokiness flickers around; **f24** its finest hour for the malt Churchill loved. At last all the boxes are ticked, especially the peaty one, with aplomb and even the lengthening oak is weighted perfectly with the juicier elements; **b23.5** HP lovers will not be disappointed. *48.4%. nc ncf sc. 332 bottles. Douglas Laing & Co.*

Provenance Highland Park Over 14 Years sherry cask, cask no. 9630, dist Summer 98, bott Spring 13 **(75)** n16 t21 f19 b19. A Lazarus of a dram: from a dreadful nose which is dead in the glass, it rises with eerie aplomb for a heather-honey fanfare which really does treat the palate despite the obvious flaws! *46%. nc ncf. Douglas Laing & Co.*

Scotch Malt Whisky Society Cask 4.173 Aged 23 Years refill hogshead, dist 19 May 89 (94.5) n23.5 a bowl of honey Cheerios for breakfast, though someone has tipped on a little salt: tangy tannins point at the year of distillation with glee; t24 the weave of the honeyed thread is intricate, yet bold. Aided and abetted by the weightier smoke and spice, the honey moves between manuka and beech with a beguiling deftness; the age is underscored by a cocoa-hickory mix; f23 long, lightly oiled, a hint now of pith but with the spices ensuring a vigorous fade; b24 in this kind of cask, nonchalantly shows why this is one of the best distilleries in the world... 52%. nc ncf sc. 210 bottles.

⸖ Scotch Malt Whisky Society Cask 4.186 Aged 22 Years dist 31 May 91 (96.5) n24 ever nosed heather honey? Here's your chance. But please take the smouldering toast from the cask into account, please; oh, and the peat is found in degrees not often seen in latter day casks; t24 one distillery and one distillery only offers this citric tartness to the honey and soft smoke which embrace so charmingly; f24 the smoke drifts, the oak thickens and engrosses, spices assemble, the honey flirts...all is well in this sublime bottling; b24.5 absolutely had to laugh when nosing this. Among of group of whiskies waiting inspection, I nosed without studying the source of the sample: "Bloody hell," I thought. "This is a old Highland Park impersonating an old Highland Park at a old Highland Park gathering" You will be hard pressed to find a bottling so true to the distillery's nature as this... 52.2%. nc ncf sc. 250 bottles.

⸖ Scotch Malt Whisky Society Cask 4.189 Aged 13 Years 1st fill barrel, dist 24 Aug 00 (88.5) n22 a quiet HP skimping on the smoke and focussing on the vanilla; t23 tangy and boisterous, a wave of citrus breaks over the saltier malt; f21.5 a spicy oak reprise; b22 coastal but short of the required smoke. 59.5%. nc ncf sc. 278 bottles.

That Boutique-y Whisky Company Highland Park Batch 1 (87.5) n23 t22 f21 b21.5. Pleasant, but sometimes doesn't seem to have the will to get the wheels off the ground. 44.7%.

⸖ That Boutique-y Whisky Highland Park batch 2 (90.5) n22.5 some serious oak at work muffles the smoke; almost an estery, pot still rum-like sweetness; t23 again the oak really does come charging at you. And, again, an estery mouth feel saves the day, helped along by some building spice; f22.5 a lovely spice glow works well with the late arriving malt...but the oak never goes away; b22.5 top heavy with oak and missing its trademark honey accompaniment. Lovely, though! 46%. 386 bottles. WB15/207

IMPERIAL

Speyside, 1897. Chivas Brothers. Silent.

Imperial Aged 15 Years "Special Distillery Bottling" db (69) n17 t18 f17 b17. At least one very poor cask, hot spirit and overly sweet. Apart from that it's wonderful. 46%

⸖ Imperial 1995 db (87.5) n21.5 t23 f21 b22. Ipressively sweet with more grist than you might believe possible for a malt this old. Good spice involvement, too. Light, limited but delicious. 46%

Gordon and MacPhail Distillery Label Imperial 1994 (94) n22.5 an unusual example of exact equal input from both barley (some still a little green) and oak: beautifully even and weighted; t24 resplendent barley on delivery, both at its thickest and with lighter, crispier notes which carry delicate hints of salivating, under-ripe greengage and busy spice; f23.5 pure American malt shake to the last embers, though with extra, gentle spice; b24 if anyone can get the best out of this distillery it is G&M. Really is an endearing bottling. 43%

⸖ Gordan & Macphail Imperial 1995 (87.5) n21.5 t23 f21 b22. Impressively sweet, with more grist than you might believe possible for a malt this old. Good spice involvement, too. Light, limited but delicious. 43%

Liquid Sun Imperial 1995 bott 12 (84) n21.5 t22.5 f19 b21. Fabulous delivery shows Speyside at its maltiest. The helping hand required by the oak doesn't really happen. 50.3%

Old Malt Cask Imperial Aged 18 Years refill hogshead, cask no. 9815, dist May 95, bott May 13 (86.5) n21.5 t22 f21.5 b21.5. A firm, compact malt, with a major vanilla theme, very much of the classical Imperial style which refuses to open out too far even with gentle coaxing. But what it does, it does with pleasing aplomb. 50%. nc ncf sc. 346 bottles.

⸖ Signatory Vintage Cask Strength Collection Imperial 1995 Aged 18 Years hogsheads, cask no. 50143+50144, dist 21 Aug 95, bott 07 Jan 14 (84.5) n21 t21.5 f21 b21. Not sure Imperial was being filled into the world's greatest oak by this stage of its declining life when its spirit was already not what it once was. The result is an ultra malty dram trying to say much but being gagged at every turn. 51.9%. nc. 573 bottles. WB15/003

⸖ Signatory Vintage Un-chillfiltered Collection Imperial 1995 Aged 18 Years hogsheads, cask no. 50280+50281, dist, 18 Sep 95, bott 27 Nov 13 (86) n21 t22 f21.5 b21.5. A lively, tangy Imperial, though by no means at its most imperious. Only sweet-toothed grist lovers need apply... 46%. nc ncf. 692 bottles. WB15/020

The Whisky Shop Dufftown Imperial 16 Years Old remade refill hogshead. Cask no. 7300, dist 28 Sep 94, bott Aug 11 (87) n22 t22.5 f21 b21.5. Typically stretched and tight for the distillery. 57.4%. nc ncf sc. 267 bottles.

INCHGOWER

Speyside, 1872. Diageo. Working.

Inchgower 1993 The Manager's Choice db (84.5) n21 t21.5 f21 b21. Like your malts subtle, delicate, clean and sophisticated? Don't bother with this one if you do. This has all the feel of a malt that's been spray painted onto the taste buds: thick, chewy and resilient. Can't help but like that mix of hazelnut and Demerara, though. You can stand a spoon in it. 61.9%

Cadenhead Inchgower 22 Years Old bourbon cask, bott 12 (85) n23 t22 f19 b21. There is a lovely mix of raspberry jam and bourbon-style clear honey on the nose. The palate, though initially lush and malty, fails to quite match the early magic. 56.5%. sc. 246 bottles.

⸪ Gordan & MacPhail Connoisseurs Choice Inchgower 1998 (85.5) n21 t22.5 f21 b21. Flavoursome if one dimensional. Soupy and syrupy with a big juicy barley kick at first. Tangy finish. 46%.

⸪ Montgomerie's Single Cask Collection Inchgower cask no. 31032, dist 11 Oct 90, bott Mar 13 (94) n23.5 someone has spilled a tin of molasses in a liquorice factory...; elsewhere a lovely pollen attack; t24 massive delivery: pounding spice cuts through the usual distillery oils. A fabulous mix of treacle and maple syrup is toned down by dry coconut shavings and vanilla; f23.5 a long line of ulmo honey, liquorice and those outstanding spices; b24 impressively above the norm for an Inchgower. Inching towards excellence all the way through - pretty damn delicious. 46%. nc ncf sc. WB15/131

Old Malt Cask Inchgower Aged 16 Years sherry butt, cask no. 8827, dist Dec 95, bott Aug 12 (95) n23.5 something of the Harvey's Bristol Cream to this one, except enough barley and egg custard tart get through to confirm the whisky identity; t24 a mixture of silk and barb as the spices cut through the oily grape with style. Salivating at first with plump grape, then morphs into barley. The oak dig deep into the middle ground; f23.5 complex and layered with the vanillas and butterscotch playing a more telling role by the second; b24 one of the better sherry butt bottlings of recent times: clean as a whistle and complex. 50%. nc ncf sc. 642 bottles.

⸪ Old Malt Cask Inchgower Aged 18 Years refill hogshead, cask no. 9983, dist Jan 95, bott Aug 13 (85.5) n21.5 t21.5 f21.5 b21. Typically soupy and dense. But the Demerara sugars come out loud and clear. 50%. nc ncf sc. 242 bottles.

Old Malt Cask Inchgower Aged 30 Years refill hogshead, cask no. 8258, dist Jun 82, bott Jun 12 (84.5) n21.5 t20 f22 b21. Showing Inchgower at its most exhausted when the distillery was run into the ground to produce Bell's. Hot and thin at first, the almost concentrated intensity of the barley doesn't just save the day but makes for an, ultimately, attractive experience. 50%. nc ncf sc. Douglas Laing & Co. 260 bottles.

Wemyss Inchgower 1982 Single Highland "Pears and Almonds" hogshead, bott 13 (88.5) n22.5 t22 f22 b22. A malt which doesn't just rage against its age...it just rages. A real warts and all character. 46%. sc. 315 bottles.

The Whisky Agency Inchgower 'Sea Life' 1980 refill sherry butt, dist 80, bott 12 (67) n17 t18 f15 b17. The only Sea Life I see here is a squid setting off a dozen box of matches... 52%

⸪ The Whisky Agency Inchgower 1985 dist 1985 (81) n21 t21 f19 b20. Typical Inchgower in sludgy, shapeless form showing big malt intent but a slovenly attitude. 50.8%.

⸪ The Whisky Cask Inchgower Aged 14 Years bourbon cask, dist 1999, bott 2013 (90) n22 a slight creosote bite amid the molasses; t23 no prisoners taken here: the spices and spirit nip in equal measure but those intense sugars, helped by manuka honey, bathe the wounds deliciously; f22.5 stays rough and basic all the way...with warming liquorice for a final, growling flourish; b22.5 full on fighting whisky: not even the vaguest attempt at subtlety...but it works fabulously well in its own way. 56.1%. nc ncf.

INVERLEVEN

Lowland, 1938–1991. Demolished.

Deoch an Doras Inverleven 36 Years Old dist 1973 (94.5) n24 just one of those noses where you think twice about tasting: not because it is bad, but quite the opposite...you really don't want the experience to end. Exotic fruit sitting comfortably with bigger oak notes and the juiciest of grassy malt; t23.5 a slightly ungainly delivery but after the first three or four flavour waves settles into a more rhythmic pulsing of light golden syrup, fresh barley, cocoa and spices; a bourbon sub text is deliciously fascinating; f23 exemplary dovetailing of the finer details of the malt, with the spices now showing a little more keenly; b24 as light on the palate as a morning mist. This distillery just wasn't designed to make a malt of this antiquity, yet this is to the manor born. 48.85%. nc ncf. Chivas Brothers. 500 bottles.

ISLE OF ARRAN

Highlands (Island–Arran), 1995. Isle of Arran Distillers. Working.

The Arran Malt 8 Years Old Pinot Noir Finish db (79.5) n19 t21 f19.5 b20. Pleasant enough. But just seems to lack the trademark Arran balance and has a few lopsided moments to boot, especially at the death. 50%. Isle of Arran Distillers.

The Arran Malt 8 Years Old Pomerol Wine Finish db (87) n19 t23.5 f22 b22.5. Full bodied and lush. 50%. Isle of Arran Distillers.

The Arran Malt Under 10 Years Old db (89) n22 t23 f22 b22. This one's kicked its shoes and socks off... 43%

The Arran Malt 10 Year Old db (87) n22.5 t22.5 f20 b22. It has been a while since I last officially tasted this. If they are willing to accept some friendly advice, I think the blenders should tone down on raising any fruit profile and concentrate on the malt, which is amongst the best in the business. 46%. nc ncf.

The Arran Malt 12 Years Old db (85) n21.5 t22 f20.5 b21 Hmmmm. Surprise one, this. There must be more than one bottling already of this. The first I tasted was perhaps slightly on the oaky side but otherwise intact and salt-honeyed where need be. This one has a bit of a tang: very drinkable, but definitely a less than brilliant cask around. 46%

The Arran Malt 12 Years Old Cask Strength Batch 1 bott Sep 11 db (78) n21 t22 f17 b18. There is no questioning that Arran is now one of Scotland's Premier League quality malts. But the strength of their whisky is in their bourbon casks, not so much their sherry. And to create a batch like this was tempting fate. The sulphur present is by no means huge, but it takes only a single off butt to spoil the party. 54.1%. nc ncf. 12,000 bottles.

⠿ **The Arran Malt Aged 12 Years Cask Strength** batch no. 2, bott 09/12 db (80) n21 t22 f18 b19. A better dram than their 2011 bottling with a little extra depth, nuttiness and sweetness and small degree less sulphur. But there is still enough on the finish in particular to make the difference between the great whisky it should be, and this essay in off-key ordinariness it actually is. 53.6%. nc ncf. 13,200 bottles. WB15/114

The Arran Malt Aged 14 Years db (89.5) n22 t23.5 f21.5 b22.5. A superb whisky, but the evidence that there has been a subtle shift in emphasis, with the oak now taking too keen an interest, is easily attained. 46%. ncf.

The Arran Malt 15 Years Old sherry hogshead, dist 21 Jul 97, bott 30 Apr 13 db (90) n22 banana and custard; oak marauds everywhere...quietly; t23 gorgeous, silky delivery with a major oaky statement but glazed with barley sugar; f22 chocolate mint; b23 a truly lovely whisky which, as is often the case from this distillery, has somewhat become prematurely grey as the oak has made its mark. But enough light fruit and sugar abound to make for a treat. 50.7%. 230 bottles. Whisky Shop Exclusive.

⠿ **The Arran Malt Aged 17 Years** db (91.5) n23.5 the grape assumes a non-aggressive stance, allowing the sweeter elements to flourish. Freshly bitten toffee apple and vaguely salty barley dust make for a delightful and understated signature; t23.5 the sharpness on delivery is helped by the crisp sugars which crunch about a bit before melting into the grist. The fruit, mainly dates and dry, over-ripened plums, is subdued and makes way for the more intense pollen-honey middle; f21.5 only a very minor furry notes reminds you sherry is at work here but a late salty vanilla helps; b23 "matured in the finest ex-Sherry casks" trills the back label. And, by and large, they are right. Maybe a single less than finest imparts the light furriness to the finish. But by present day sherry butt standards, a pretty outstanding effort. 46%. nc ncf. 9000 bottles. WB15/152

⠿ **The Arran Malt 1996 Single Cask** ex-sherry puncheon, cask no. 96/1327, dist 1996, (89) n21 strangely disjointed. Nothing wrong with the sherry for once. But the oak, grape and malt have problems finding a comfortable rhythm with a bit of nip here and there; t23.5 a marvellously sweet and soft delivery; two types of honey on song: mainly heather with a light drizzle of ulmo. The malt appears to have a metallic kick; f22 tangy, metallic but redeemed by excellent, grape-induced spice – a bit like a seasoned Genoa cake; b22 Arran showing a very different face here. The early copper of the young stills is still apparently evident as there is a metallic kick to this. Slightly knocks the decent sherry influence off kilter. 55.8%. sc.

The Arran Malt 1996 'The Peacock' Icons of Arran bott 2009 db (96) n24.5 oh my word: what a shame I have only three or four months to write this book: the degree of complexity will take that time to unravel. Both floral and fruity in almost perfect doses, the white pepper perfectly balances the light saltiness. The big weight is deceptive as the delicate sultana and perry sub plot appears to give more air and space to the overall picture. Outstanding...; t24.5 what a delicate creature this is: the juicy grape appears to be apparent on a couple of levels, sandwiching the honey and hickory bourbon notes between them; f23 long, now with that hint of pear on the nose re-surfacing as the finish nestles somewhere between butterscotch tart and buttered toast; b24 yet again this outstanding distillery delivers the goods: one of the most outstanding malts of the year and certainly one of the most complex. I've not yet spoken to the Arran guys about this, but would happily bet my house that this is a sublime mix of top bourbon cask and faultless sherry. As fabulous as this distillery unquestionably is, they will be hard pressed to keep this standard going... 46%

The Arran Malt 1997 'The Rown Tree' Icons of Arran bott 2010 db (77.5) **n18.5 t22 f18 b19.** The key here is balance and harmony. And this, unusually for an Arran, possesses little of either. The bitter finish confirms the unhappiness hinted at on the nose. Someone was barking up the wrong tree when putting this one together and the malt, in this form, even for all the sweet, bright moments on delivery, is ready for the chop. 46% Isle of Arran Distillers

The Arran Malt 1999 "The Eagle" Icons Of Arran bourbon barrels & sherry hogsheads, bott 2012 db (77) **n19.5 t20.5 f18 b19.** Don't know about the eagle having landed: this one never took off...the wings have been clipped by sulphur. 46%. nc ncf. 6,000 bottles.

The Arran Malt 1999 Vintage 15th Anniversary Edition finished in amontillado, bott 2010 db (92.5) **n24** sherry as you demand its shows on the nose. Clean, confident, a hint of sultana only as this is dry, yet always with enough finesse for the barley to come through loud and clear: an absolute treat...; **t23.5** salivating from the off with a glittering delivery of fresh grape and spice. Waves of vanilla punch through and there is a fabulous malty flourish towards the middle. But those spices continue to pulse...; **f22.5** drier, with vanilla pods and a buttery residue; **b22.5** there is no mistaking excellence. And here it appears to flow freely. 54.6%

The Arran Malt Open Day Single Bourbon Cask Bottling 2011 db (94) **n23.5** unbelievable degree of fruit sitting alongside the rich barley and muscovado-enriched bourbon notes; **t24** a match of spice and sugared barley made in heaven; **f23.5** the earlier juiciness evaporates as the vanillas lay claim. But enough spices – and fruit – remain for the finale to be anything but standard; **b23.5** to me, Arran in a high class bourbon cask shows the distillery to its very finest advantage: my case rests... 52%. nc ncf sc. Sold at distillery during 2011 Open Day.

The Arran Malt Ambassador's Choice db (87.5) **n22 t22 f21.5 b22.** So heavy with oak I was amazed I could pick the nosing glass up... 46%

The Arran Malt Amarone Cask Finish db (94.5) **n23** the buzzing black peppers leave you in no doubt what is to follow. As does the stunning clarity of the grape and crisp, business-like manner of the barley: stirring! **t24** and so it is played out on the palate: the grape is juicy and sweet, the barley is firm and forms the perfect skeleton, the spices pop busily around the palate. No great age evident, but the oak also chimes in with a few choice cocoa notes; **f23** a shard of bitterness, but nothing which subtracts from the gloss; **b23.5** as cask finishes go, this one is just about perfect. 50%. nc ncf.

The Arran Malt Bourgogne Finish db (74) **n18 t19 f18 b19.** Arran Malt Vinegar more like... 56.4%

The Arran Malt Chianti Classico Riserva Cask Finish db (85) **n19 t23 f21 b22.** Mamma mia: there eeza poco zolfo ina mia malto!! Butta chicco d'uva, ee eez eccellente! 55%

The Arran Malt Devil's Punch Bowl Chapter No. 1 db (72) **n17.5 t22.5 f15 b17.** For a few brief moments the delivery shows why Arran can rightly be considered one of the best distilleries in Scotland. But the finish, following on from the faulty nose, suggests they are in danger of blowing their reputation. I don't know what's happened in the last year but there appears to be a new policy of involving sherry butts at every turn. Sadly, they are not weeding out the sulphured ones and the result here is ruinous brimstone for the Devil's Punch Bowl. If you are going to dance with the devil – present era sherry butts – you had better know exactly what you are doing. Otherwise you're be playing with fire 52.3%. nc ncf. 6,600 bottles.

⁙ **The Arran Malt Devil's Punch Bowl Chapter No. 2 Angels & Devils** db (87.5) **n22 t24 f20 b21.5.** When Chapter I was launched, the whisky was what it said on the tin...for it offered little more than brimstone. I gave the devil a poke in the eye for going to the trouble of undermining one of the world's greatest distilleries with contemptuous sulphur. And it appears someone has taken heed. For this is an almost unimaginable improvement over the previous bottling. Is this entirely without blemish? The finish suggests not. But, clearly, much greater diligence has been taken in cask selection. To the extent that those lucky ones who do not possess the genetic make up to detect sulphur will have a hell of a time. Even those of us who do cannot be but astonished by the beauty of the intense, mollassed fruit. With even more judicious care in the cherry picking of casks next time round, this could be a monster whisky that will give any devil a run for his money. 52.3%. 6,660 bottles. WB15/153

The Arran Malt Fino Sherry Cask Finish db (82.5) **n21 t20 f21 b20.5.** Pretty tight with the bitterness not being properly compensated for. 50%

The Arran Malt Fontalloro Wine Cask Finish db (84.5) **n20 t22 f21.5 b21.** For a wine cask, the malt really does sing. 55%

The Arran Malt Lepanto PX Brandy Finish db (85) **n22 t22 f20 b21.** Tight, unusually thin for an Arran, but some lovely sweet fruit amid the confusion. Pretty oaky, too. 59%

The Arran Malt Madeira Wine Cask Finish db (77.5) n19 t21 f18.5 b19. The odd exultant moment but generally flat, flaky and bitter. *50%*

⁘ **The Arran Malt Millenium Casks** db (94) n23.5 the nutty, honeyed overture has as much in common with bourbon as it does a single malt scotch; there is a soft Turkish Delight fruitiness, too as well as fruit pastel candy. As I nose this a female great spotted woodpecker is tucking into the feeder outside my tasting room window: had I the window open she might have come in attracted by the sweet oak wafting from the glass... t24 absolutely beautiful delivery with the malt leading healthily and though all is seemingly soft and controlled, has a bite like Lois Suarez. A mix of heather honey and thin manuka works a treat; f23 more nuttiness, now of a marzipan type, a pinch of salt plus a little unwelcome furriness from a renegade sherry cask; b23.5 at times hits some dizzying heights. Superbly complex the late fault line. *53.5%. nc ncf. 7,800 bottles.* WB15/154

The Arran Malt Moscatel Cask Finish db (87) n22 t21.5 f22 b21.5. Arran is pretty full bodied stuff when just left to its own devices. In this kind of finish it heads towards an almost syrupy texture. Luckily, the grape effect works fine. *55%*

The Arran Malt 'Original' db (80.5) n19 t22 f19.5 b20. Not the greatest bourbon casks used here. *43%*

The Arran Malt Pineau des Charentes Cask Finish db (94) n22.5 wispy barley clouds in a bright, sweet-grapey sky; t24 succulent and spicy. Delivery is first class, allowing full weight to the grassy barley before those fuller, fruitier notes close in. The spices are fabulously subtle and mildly puckering; f23.5 a real chocolate dessert helped by the slow build up of soft oils; b24 I may not be the greatest fan of cask finishes, but when one comes along like this, exhibiting such excellence, I'll be the first to doff my hat. *55%*

The Arran Malt Pinot Noir Cask Finish db (73.5) n18 t19 f18 b18.5. A less than efficient cask from the Germans who produced it. Plenty of off key moments on nose and taste, but it does enjoy a too brief, barely redeeming Bird's Angel Delight chocolatey moment. *50%*

The Arran Malt Pomerol Cask Finish Bordeux wine casks db (86.5) n20 t23 f22 b21.5. Although the cask is very marginally flawed, the relentlessness of the sweet, juicy grape and barley is a sheer delight. The odd cocoa note does no harm either. *50%*

The Arran Malt Port Cask Finish db (85.5) n21 t22.5 f22 b20. One of the real problems with cask finishes is that there is no real or straightforward reference point to knowing exactly when the host flavours and the guest ones are in maximum alignment. For all this one's obvious charms, I get the feeling it was bottled when the balance was pretty low on the graph... *58.3%. nc ncf.*

The Arran Malt Premier Cru Bourgogne Cask Finish db (86) n21 t22 f21 b22. An entertaining dram which some would do somersaults for, but marks docked because we have lost the unique Arran character. *56.4%*

The Arran Malt Robert Burns 250 Years Anniversary Edition db (91.5) n22.5 mainly floral with just a light touch from the barley; t23.5 unusually light and flighty in body. A dusting of caster sugar softens the vanilla even further: juicy, a touch spicy and quite wonderful; f22.5 a few oils had formed towards the middle and follow through to the end. Again it is barley dominant with a squeeze of something citrussy; b23 curiously, not that far away from the light Lowland style of malt produced in the 60s and 70s in Burns' native Lowlands. Not the usual Arran, but shows that it can change personality now and again and still be a total charmer. *43%*

The Arran Malt St. Emilion Cask Finish Grand Cru Classé wine casks db (89) n24 t22 f21.5 b21.5. Not the best balanced whisky you'll ever pour. But such is the sheer force of flavours, you have to doff your beret... *50%*

The Arran Malt Sassicaia Wine Cask Finish db (92.5) n22.5 t23.5 f23 b23.5. Unquestionably one of Arran's better wine finishes. *55%*

The Arran Malt Sauternes Cask Finish db (86) n21 t23 f21 b21. Plenty of sugars and allure. But natural caramels bring an abrupt halt to the complexity. *50%. nc ncf.*

The Arran Malt Sauternes Finish db (84) n21 t22 f20 b21. Strap yourself in for this one: eye-watering sultana and 240 volts of spice. Choked with oak, though. *56%*

The Arran Malt "The Sleeping Warrior" bott 2011 db (84.5) n19 t22.5 f21.5 b21.5. Zzzzzzzz. *54.9%. nc ncf. 6000 bottles.*

The Arran Malt Tokaji Aszu Wine Cask Finish db (83) n20 t21.5 f21 b20.5. Pleasant enough, but the wine dulls the more interesting edges. *55%*

Isle of Arran 'Jons Utvalgte' Aged 7 Years db (87) n22 t21.5 f22 b21.5. The clean intensity of the malt is soup-like. *46%. Norway.*

The Peated Arran "Machrie Moor" 1st release db (86.5) n22 t22 f21 b21.5. A bit of a surprise package: I have tasted many peated Arrans over recent years, the majority voluptuous and generous in their giving. Yet this one is strangely aloof. The flavours and nuances have to be sought rather than presented for inspection and there is a hardness throughout which makes for a very solid dram. That said, it has many fine qualities, too. And the mouth-watering unravelling of its slightly cough-sweetish intensity is great entertainment. A fascinating, mixed bag. 46%. nc ncf. 9000 bottles.

⁖ **The Peated Arran "Machrie Moor" Fourth Edition** 14 ppm, bott 2013 db **(95.5) n23** delicate rape seed honey and powder-puff peat; **t23.5** playful oil, nor polite smoke cannot curtail the sharpness of the mouth-watering malt; **f24.5** slow spice buzz moves towards a wonderful light molasses and chocolate finale. Ridiculously long...and so much happening... so many whispering layers even so late on; **b24.5** a masterful, gentle but wonderfully complex whisky. A complete gem. 46%. nc ncf. 12,000 bottles. WB15/343

⁖ **Berry's Own Selection Arran 1997 Aged 16 Years** cask no. 5, bott 2014 **(75) n19.5** **t22 f16 b17.5.** Dry, nutty with an exceptionally rich delivery. But sulphur tainted. 56.9%. ncf ncf. WB15/237

⁖ **Cadenhead's Small Batch Arran Aged 16 Years** 1 Hogshead and 1 butt, dist 1997, bott 2013 **(92) n23** sharp lemon softened by orange blossom honey; complex earthy, salted celery and vanilla; **t23.5** big, full-bodied delivery. Oil and what seems (however unlikely) as a brief flicker of smoke adds further weight; spices and mocha on one level, more orange blossom honey on another; **f22.5** the cocoa is now very intense as it dries; just a slight furriness; **b23** a busy tapestry of salt and honey. 46%. 792 bottles. WB15/089

⁖ **Càrn Mòr Strictly Limited Edition Arran Aged 16 Years** hogsheads, dist 1997, bott 2014 **(92.5) n23** probably what you get when you stir marmalade into honey...and then add a pinch of salt; **t24** succulent, soothing and quietly rich delivery. Citrus early on. Peaks, though, on about the fourth to seventh waves when the sugars hot perfect pitch and in total harmony with the tannin; a short blast of Worther's Originals; **f22.5** long, soft with a slow build up of salt 'n' spice; **b23** a very simple joy... 46%. nc ncf. 568 bottles from 2 casks. WB15/053

Chieftain's Isle of Arran Aged 15 Years butt, cask no. 935, dist Jun 97, bott Jan 13 **(83.5) n20 t21.5 f21 b21.** Disappointingly dull for an Arran. Shows virtually no coastal flair with both saline and layering conspicuous by their absence. Pleasant and malty enough, but a bit of a one-trick pony. 46%. nc ncf sc. Ian Macleod Distillers. 786 bottles.

⁖ **Gordon & MacPhail Connoisseurs Choice Arran** dist 2000, bott 2013 **(89) n22** malty; light layer of honey; **t23** identical to nose, except more juicy than might be expected and an excellent burst of barley sugar; **f22** hangs on to the vanilla; **b22** simplistic by Arran standards but attractive. 46%. nc ncf. WB15/146

Malts Of Scotland Isle of Arran 1996 sherry hogshead, cask no. MoS 13002, dist Dec 96, bott Jan 13 **(96) n24** fantastic array of salted gooseberries and boiled greengages; hint of exotic fruit cocktail; grated Cadbury's milk chocolate; first shoots of high quality bourbon with red liquorice and vague molasses; **t24** near perfect weight and mouth feel with the barley radiating from the palate and its sugary juiciness contrasting with the background noise of big aged malt; the mid ground hurtles towards Chinese gooseberries with a growing degree of butterscotch; **f23.5** much drier now, but this must have been one high quality cask because the bourbon notes, just like on the nose, take time to form but are unmistakable on arrival with thinned down liquorice and hickory and a thin degree of maple syrup; **b24.5** almost premature aging: lots of exotic fruit seeping through: a Speyside style of twice the age...and the result is as mesmerising as it is magnificent. One of the greatest-ever bottlings from this brilliant distillery. 56.3%. nc ncf sc. 96 bottles.

Master of Malt Arran Aged 16 Years refill sherry hogshead, dist 13 Jun 96, bott 21 Nov 12 **(89) n21.5 t22 f23.5 b22.** Quite tight and sometimes aggressive. Massively enjoyable, though. 55.4%. sc. 218 bottles.

⁖ **Master of Malt Single Cask Arran 17 Years Old** refill, dist 5 Aug 1995, bott 4 Feb 2014 **(94) n23.5** a delicate citrus sheen to the slightly salt-breezed barley; the spiced oak nips attractively; **t23.5** intense, salivating and sound. Excellent muscovado sugar development; the saltiness is now rather Digestive biscuit in style; **f23** dries quickly as a little spice moves in; a light coating of oil patches up the cracks; **b24** lovely, composed malt and, though the passing years are beginning to stretch its finer points, this is still a work of whisky art. 53.6%. 100 bottles. WB15/231

Old Malt Cask Arran Aged 15 Years refill hogshead, cask no. 9273, dist Jan 97, bott Nov 12 **(95.5) n23.5** good grief! A mix of cloves, dates and walnuts go into one of the thickest noses I have ever encountered from this distillery: beautiful! **t24.5** delivery nears perfection with a massive deployment of spiced fruit on a gloriously thick and silky bed. Even so, the barley peels as distinctly as a church bell, allowing a pleasing degree of salivating. Some soft high roast Papua coffee notes drift through; it is the sultanas, though, which abound and make the most telling contribution; **f23.5** longer than it first appears because the sugars, mildly molassed and deft, linger longer than you think. The wonderful clarity allows the gentle spices and vanilla to thrive; **b24** if you find a better refill hoggy than this over the next year you will have tasted thousands to get there. A major malt whisky. Just sorry that it is not a distillery bottling... 50%. sc. Douglas Laing & Co. 282 bottles.

⋄⋄⋄ **Old Malt Cask Arran Aged 16 Years** port finished puncheon, cask no. 9901, dist Sep 98, bott Jul 13 **(82) n19 t22 f20 b21.** The tangy nose points accusingly to an off-key cask. Which is a shame: there is enough salty acacia and ulmo honey to have made for a dram of purely memorable proportions. Does have some symphonic early moments all the same. 50%. sc. 330 bottles.

⋄⋄⋄ **Old Particular Highland Arran 17 Years Old** refill hogshead, cask no. 9983, dist Feb 96, Aug 13 **(89) n22** moody in its old age (old for Arran, that is). Only at body temperature does its nature sweeten; **t22** trimmed and clipped delivery by Arran standards with only some of the usual small still body which normally serves it so well. Still, the malts are neat, crisp and almost crunchy; **f22.5** expands in complexity as the vanillas gather momentum; **b22.5** a malt which begrudgingly fills the bottle – and palate - at this age. Enjoyable and high quality, but not quite the complex charmer it would have been half a dozen years before. 48.4%. nc ncf sc. 318 bottles. Douglas Laing & Co.

Provenance Arran Over 12 Years cask no. 9237, dist Spring 00, bott Autumn 12 **(88) n21.5 t22 f22.5 b22.** A delightful malt without even really trying... 46%. nc ncf sc.

Provenance Arran Over 12 Years refill hogshead, cask no. 8575, dist Winter 00, bott Summer 12 **(82) n20 t21 f20.5 b20.5.** Malty, if monosyllabic. 46%. nc ncf sc.

Provenance Arran Over 16 Years sherry butt, cask no. 9753, dist Summer 96, bott Spring 13 **(88.5) n22.5 t22.5 f21.5 b22.** Probably from a first fill bourbon cask, here is one of the first examples of an Arran showing signs of wear and tear having absorbed a little too much oak. That said, what a delight it still is and the honey-barley tandem delights throughout. 46%. nc ncf sc.

Riegger's Selection Arran 1997 bourbon cask, cask no. 1073, dist 21 Jul 97, bott 21 Dec 12 **(94.5) n23.5** a lovely hint of sandpaper being worked on an old piece of oak: sawdusty but brought to life by a squeeze of lemon and lime and sweetened by a gentle sprinkling of icing sugar; **t24** a magnificent delivery: has to be a first fill bourbon cask for this amount of tannin to be balanced by an orange blossom-ulmo honey mix of such magnitude; red and black liquorice combine to add a lightly sweetened weight; **f23** dries out impressively to give a feeling of controlled age and sophistication; **b24** Arran at absolutely the top of its game – and in a top notch bourbon cask, so it doesn't get any better! 55.5%. nc ncf sc. Viktor-Riegger GmbH. 396 bottles.

Scotch Malt Whisky Society Cask 121.54 Aged 9 Years refill barrel, dist 15 Jul 2002 **(92) n22** tannins start pushing towards a bourbon course but the barley is steadfast, if paradoxically youthful; **t23.5** oh my word! If you find a more malty delivery than this this year, you'll obviously just have fallen into a vat of malt. Maltesers on speed yet still juicy and absolutely full of vim; **f23** now even the chocolate to complete the Malteser effect; **b23.5** Arran as it was intended! Actually, if you had asked my dear recently departed friend, Gordon Mitchell , the start up manager of Arran if he would have accepted this as standard make as the place was being built, he would have shaken your bloody hand off...58.9%. nc ncf sc. 192 bottles.

Scotch Malt Whisky Society Cask 121.56 Aged 9 Years refill barrel, dist 15 Jul 02 **(88) n22 t22 f22 b22.** An attractive, more simplistic and low key version of 121.54. 58.5%

Scotch Malt Whisky Society Cask 121.58 Aged 10 Years refill barrel, dist 15 Jul 2002 **(86) n21.5 t21 f22 b21.5.** Curious how an off beam cask can completely alter the direction of a malt. It is obvious the spirit is of the same quality as 121.54/56. But the niggardly character of the oak makes for a more aggressive (though still ultra malty) child. 57.8%. nc ncf sc. 131 bottles.

⋄⋄⋄ **Scotch Malt Whisky Society Cask 121.66 Aged 15 Years** refill barrel, dist 07 Sep 98 **(93) n23.5** maple syrup and a slice of lime brushed with salt; **t23.5** spectacular mouth feel: the softest of oils allows the salivating butterscotch and barley to do its thing; **f23** the oak cranks up a little; **b23** the way in which it keeps is sweetness in such delicate voice is a thing of wonder. 55.5%. nc ncf sc. 273 bottles.

⋄⋄⋄ **Scotch Malt Whisky Society Cask 121.68 Aged 14 Years** refill hogshead, dist 02 Dec 99 **(89) n23** suety and rich; **t22** the oak bite early and hard but there is enough gristy sugar to absorb the wounds; **f22** a little citrus still goes a long way...and needs to; **b22** great whisky on its way down as the tannins don the captain's armband. 55.1%. nc ncf sc. 273 bottles.

⋄⋄⋄ **Scotch Malt Whisky Society Cask 121.70 Aged 13 Years** refill hogshead, dist 01 Jan 2000 **(94.5) n23.5** controlled oak; a hint of Kellogg's Cornflakes in heavily sugared gold top milk; **t24** crisp Demerara sugars encrust toasted barley; the salivation factor rises sharply; **f23.5** despite the close attention of the oak, the spices and toasted almond flakes leave you purring; **b23.5** such a delicate, complex malt: someone will one day wake up to the fact that it peaks at around twelve. This is still pulsing with brilliance though I suspect had it been bottled two or three years ago it would have enjoyed legendary status. *54.7%. nc ncf sc. 307 bottles.*

⫶⫶⫶ **Scotch Malt Whisky Society Cask 121.71 Aged 14 Years** refill hogshead, dist 02 Dec 99 **(92.5) n23** suet and blood orange; **t23** a spectacular delivery which hits you like some kind of full-frontal celebration of bourbon but soon calms to offer a more malty, saline crusted coastal picture; **f23** a light, vaguely zesty citrus fleeting moment which you must look out for is probably the highlight; late on the oak gathers; **b23.5** a busy number which just never stops working the palate. *54.9%. nc ncf sc. 224 bottles.*

That Boutique-y Whisky Company Arran batch 1 **(74) n19 t19 f18 b18**. A clumsy, off key whisky at best. *49.1%. Master Of Malt. 211 bottles.*

That Boutique-y Whisky Company Arran batch 2 **(95) n23.5** crushed poppy seeds, diced apple and salted tannin star; **t23.5** massive malt on delivery, pepped up by manuka honey in a hurry and a peppery glow taking it slow; **f24** long, with the persistent barley as well as the vanilla being coated in muscovado sugar; and still those spices sing...; **b24** shimmers like the sun reflecting off the Sound of Bute...from the right cask, one of the truly great distilleries of the world. *49.4% Master of Malt. 459 bottles.*

⫶⫶⫶ **That Boutique-y Whisky Arran** batch 3 **(74.5) n18.5 t19 f18.5 b18.5**. Unusually cumbersome for an Arran with a little too much oil and feint. Malty, a touch salty but a distinct lack of sweetness and charisma. Now just checking back, I see Batch 1 was of the same ilk... *51.5%. 728 bottles. WB15/221*

ISLE OF JURA
Highlands (Island–Jura), 1810. Whyte and Mackay. Working.

Isle of Jura 5 Years Old 1999 db **(83) n19 t23 f21 b20**. Absolutely enormously peated, but has reached that awkward time in its life when it is massively sweet and as well balanced as a two-hour-old foal. *46% The Whisky Exchange*

Isle of Jura Aged 10 Years db **(79.5) n19 t22 f19 b19.5**. Perhaps a little livelier than before, but still miles short of where you might hope it to be. *40%*

Jura Elixir Aged 12 Years Fruity & Spicy db **(77) n18 t21 f18 b20**. Fruity, spicy and a little sulphury, I'm afraid. Those who can't spot sulphur will love the caramel-fruitcake enormity. *40%*

Isle of Jura Mountain of Gold 15 Years Old Pinot Noir cask finish db **(67.5) n15 t18 f17 b17.5**. Not for the first time a Jura seriously hamstrung by sulphur - for all its honeyed sweetness and promise: there are some amazingly brilliant casks in there tragically wasted. And my tastebuds partially crocked because of it. Depressing. *46%. 1366 bottles.*

Isle of Jura Mountain of Sound 15 Years Old Cabernet Sauvignon finish db **(81) n20 t21.5 f19.5 b20**. Pretty quiet. *43%*

Isle of Jura The Sacred Mountain 15 Years Old Barolo finish db **(89.5) n21.5 t24 f21.5 b22.5** Hoo-bloody-rah! One of the three from this series has actually managed to raise my pulse. Not, it must be said, without the odd fault here and there. But there really is a stunning interaction between grape and barley that sets the nerves twitching: at its height this is about as entertaining a malt as I've come across for some time and should be on everyone's list for a jolly jaunt for the taste buds. Just when I was beginning to lose faith in this distillery... *43%*

Isle Of Jura Aged 16 Years db **(90.5) n21.5** salty, coastal, seaweedy, but with an injection of honey; **t23.5** carries on from the nose perfectly and then ups the stakes. The delivery is malt dependent and rich, the salty tang a true delight; **f23** all kinds of vanillas and honeys carried on a salty wind; **b23** a massive improvement, this time celebrating its salty, earthy heritage to good effect. The odd strange, less than harmonious note. But by far and away the most improved Jura for a long, long while. *40%*

Isle of Jura Aged 21 Years 200th Anniversary db **(74) n19 t19 f18 b18**. Don't know what to say. Actually, I do. But what's the point...? *44%*

Isle of Jura 21 Years Old Cask Strength db **(92) n22 t24 f23 b23**. Every mouthful exudes class and quality. A must-have for Scottish Island collector... or those who know how to appreciate a damn fine malt *58.1%*

Isle of Jura 30 Years Old db **(89) n22.5 t22.5 f22 b22**. A relaxed dram with the caramel dousing the higher notes just as they started to get very interesting. If there is a way of bringing down these presumably natural caramels – it is a 30 years old, so who in their right mind would add colouring? – this would score very highly, indeed. *40%*

Isle of Jura 40 Years Old finished in oloroso wood db **(90) n23** a different species of Jura from anything you are likely to have seen before: swamped in sherry, there is a vague, rather odd smokiness to this. Not to mention salty, sea-side rockpools. As a pairing (sherry and smoke), the odd couple... which works and doesn't work at the same time. Strange... **t22** syrupy sweet delivery with thick waves of fruit and then an apologetic 'ahem' from the smoke, which drifts in nervously. Again, everything is awkward... f22 remains soft and velvety, though now strands of bitter, salty oak and molasses drift in and out; b23 throw the Jura textbooks away. This is something very different. Completely out of sync in so many ways, but... 40%

Isle of Jura 1974 db (87.5) n23 t22.5 f20.5 b21.5. Stick your nose in this and enjoy those very first outstanding moments on delivery. 42%

Isle Of Jura 1974 db (85.5) n22 t23 f18.5 b22. A case where the unhappy, bitter ending is broadcast on the nose. Talk about warts 'n all...!! 44.5%

Isle of Jura 1976 db (94.5) n24.5 a fascinating wisp of smoke acts almost like a thread which stitches together myriad complex, barely discernable facets which make for a nose to be treasured. We are talking pastel shades here, nothing brash or vivid. Vanilla shapes the background but the light herbal notes, marrying with the deft, crushed between the fingers berries makes for the most teasing of experiences. Look out for gooseberries and a butterscotch/honey mix in particular; t24 works with rare magnificence from the go simply because the barley leads the way with such ease and there is neither OTT oils or oaks to blur the picture; varying types of sugars follow behind and spices are also in close attendance, again with a marvellous hint of smoke lingering; f22.5 shows an acceptable and understandable degree of oaky bitterness but the spices and barley still ride high; b23.5 absolutely beautiful whisky which carries its age with unfeigned elegance. 46.1%

Isle of Jura 1977 first fill bourbon casks finished in Ruby Port pipe db (94.5) n24 pretty classy: greengages about to explode while soft marzipan and spices form the spine; t23.5 melt-in-the-mouth delivery with a really impressive meeting of heather-honey, Demerara sugars and sherry trifle, or maybe that should be Port trifle...; f23 the vaguest hint of spiced praline as the silky essay draws to a close; b24 now and again something rather special and significant emerges from this distillery. 46%. Whyte and Mackay. 498 bottles.

Jura Boutique Barrels Vintage 1995 bourbon Jo finish db (89.5) n24.5 t23.5 f20 b21.5. There are moments when you wonder if you have a possible malt of the year on your hands. Then the slip shows... Even so, one of the more memorable whiskies of the 2011 Bible. 56.5%

Jura Boutique Barrels 1996 db (78) n21 t21.5 f17.5 b18. A clumsy whisky in which the fruit fits the malt in the same way a size 46 jacket fits a guy with a 40 inch chest. Either too cloyingly sweet or just too viciously bitter. 54%. 493 bottles.

Jura Boutique Barrels Vintage 1999 heavily peated, bourbon Xu finish db (84) n21.5 t21 f20.5 b21. Pretty peat. But not in the same league as the Prophecy, simply because the base spirit is nowhere near as good. 55%

Jura Elements "Air" db (76) n19.5 t19 f18.5 b19. Initially, I thought this was earth: there is something strangely dirty and flat about both nose and delivery. Plenty of fruits here and there but just doesn't get the pulse racing at all. 45%

Jura Elements "Earth" db (89) n23.5 t22 f21.5 b22. I haven't spoken to blender Richard Paterson about these whiskies yet. No doubt I'll be greeted with a knee on the nuts for declaring two as duds. My guess is that this is the youngest of the quartet by a distance and that is probably why it is the best. The peat profile is very different and challenging. I'd still love to see this in its natural plumage as the caramel really does put the brakes on the complexity and development. Otherwise we could have had an elementary classic. 45%

Jura Elements "Fire" db (86.5) n22.5 t21.5 f21 b21.5. Pleasant fare, the highlight coming with the vaguely Canadian-style nose thanks to a classic toffee-oak mix well known east of the Rockies. Some botanicals also there to be sniffed at while a few busy oaky notes pep up the barley-juiced delivery, too. Sadly, just a shade too toffee dependent. 45%

Jura Elements "Water" db (73.5) n18.5 t19 f18 b18. Oranges by the box-full trying to get out but the mouth is sent into puckering spasm by the same sulphur which spoils the nose. 50%

Jura Prophecy profoundly peated db (90.5) n23.5 something almost akin to birchwood in there with the peat and salt; there is a wonderful natural floral note as well as coastal elements to this one; t23 impressively two-toned: on one side is the sharper, active barley and peat offering an almost puckering youthfulness and zest; on the other, a sweeter, lightly oiled buzz...a treat; f22 thins as the vanillas enter; b22 youthful, well made and I prophesize this will be one of Jura's top scorers of 2011... 46%

Jura Superstition db (73.5) n17 t19 f18 b18.5. I thought this could only improve. I was wrong. One to superstitiously avoid. 43%

⁖ **Jura Tastival** (79) n20 t22 f18 b19. Light, complex, multi-layered, varying strata of subtle....oh...oh! Sorry, dozed off and had a dream about being let loose in a Jura warehouse and lab. Sorry where was I? Oh yes; Jura Tastival. Thick, black, impenetrably sweet raisin fudge and dates. Otherwise furry and characterless...indeed, a clone of so many other previous Juras, alas. Zzzzzz. 44%. 3000 bottles. Whisky Festival Exclusive 2014. WB15/285

Jura Turas-Mara db (82.5) n20.5 t22 f19 b21. Some irresistible Jaffa Cake moments. But the oils are rather too severe and tangy. 42%. Travel Retail Exclusive.

Gordon & MacPhail Connoisseurs Choice Jura 1997 (84.5) n20 t23 f20.5 b21. Drink plenty before tasting this: few whiskies work on your saliva glands as does the delivery of this guy. Juicy doesn't even begin to half cover it. *46%. ncf.*

⠿ **Hepburn's Choice Jura 2006 Aged 8 Years** refill butt (80) n19 t21.5 f19.5 b20. Fat, malty but lacking couth. *46%. sc. 598 bottles.*

Malts Of Scotland Isle of Jura 1992 bourbon hogshead, cask no. MoS 12064, dist 92, dist 12 (78) n18 t21 f19 b20. A thick, syrupy, overly sweet and, finally, tangy addition to the Jura cannon. Though one which, by and large, fails to hit the target. *50.3%. nc ncf sc. 96 bottles.*

Old Malt Cask Jura Aged 21 Years refill hogshead, cask no. 9806, dist Mar 92, bott May 13 (93) n23 wow! Delicate and so complex: steamed pears lead the considerable fruit interest; the merest hint of lychee and ginger underscores the oak; t23.5 fabulous mouth feel with near perfect oil involvement; the tannins have the greater clout, with buttered toast and a shaving of hickory. A brief barley sugar surge, then immediate dry toast and spice; f23 long, and benefitting from a really top quality barrel, with the oak drying to an excellent pitch; b23 oh, if only all Juras were this stunning: as refreshing as the wind blowing in from the sound directly into your face.... *48%. nc ncf sc. 239 bottles.*

Scotch Malt Whisky Society Cask 31.24 Aged 24 Years refill hogshead, dist 27 Sep 88 (85.5) n19 t22 f22.5 b22. Relentlessly coastal with brine hitting the taste buds from every direction. Once past the strangely fishy nose the malt has a big, juicy say before the sea spray takes hold. A little mocha makes a pleasant late flourish. *54%. nc ncf sc. 255 bottles.*

⠿ **Signatory Cask Strength Collection Jura 1989 Heavily Peated Aged 23 Years** bourbon barrel, cask no. 30708, dist 17 Dec 89, bott 10 May 13 (87.5) n22 t21.5 f22 b22. Pleasant enough, and at times thoroughly enjoyable, but this must go down as one of the least heavily peated "heavily peated" whiskies in history. The fact that the tannin has just as much to say as the smoke speaks volumes.Perhaps a bit too heavy on the oak, in fact, but the soft oil does stir the sugars in attractively. *57.6%. nc sc. 196 bottles. WB15/137*

The Whisky Agency Joint Bottling Bresser & Timmer Isle Of Jura 1988 ex-bourbon hogshead, dist 88, bott 12 (88) n22 t22 f22 b22. Shows the distillery off in a better light than many. *50.8%*

KILCHOMAN
Islay, 2005. Kilchoman Distillery Co. Working.

Kilchoman Autumn 09 Release db (85) n21 t22.5 f20 b21.5. Still to completely find it's legs: a youthful malt is trying desperately hard to hit the high notes, but falling short. Or perhaps I should say flat as the fruit here is acting like caramel in dumbing down the more complex notes you know are in there somewhere...especially in the final third. Like the Inaugeral Release there is a feinty element to this, not all of it bad, but certainly marks the nose and finish. Also a charming gristiness: you feel as though you are standing there watching the barley being dried. But as yet doesn't quite have the early excellence that Arran, for instance, boasted. But these are early days in the distillery's life. And, for me, anything drinkable at all is a bonus... *46%*

⠿ **Kilchoman 2007 Vintage** dist 2007, bott 2013 db (95.5) n24.5 surely one of the great peat noses of the world now. This is like grist in the palm of your hand: sweet, dripping with coastal air, salty and dank....yet at the same time tuning into another band width astringent, dry and sooty. The balance is truly exceptional...; t24 stunning hazelnut crème wafer ensures the sugars are out in force early, the majority of them muscovado based. The drier, sooty peat can add so much acidity and dust, but no more; f23 citrus joins the fun as the peats now fizz with light spice and the vanilla appears from under a smoky hood; b24 credit where credit is due. This malt has moved on in quality expedientially from one vintage to the next since its first unsteady, Bambiesque, feinty bottlings. Not hint of feints now. But excellence is writ large... *46%. nc ncf. WB15/116*

Kilchoman 2008 first fill bourbon cask db (92.5) n23 someone has put some green apples amid the peat; t23.5 like the nose, sensationally clean and so crystal clear you can even pick out the barley sugar notes quite separately from the phenols; pretty youthful; f23 dry now the majority of the muscovado sugars are spent with cocoa powder moving in; b23 as fresh as an autumnal Islay wind on your cheeks... *61%. sc. Whisky Shop Exclusive. 260 bottles.*

Kilchoman Winter 2010 Release db (88) n23 t22 f21 b22. Size doesn't really matter, apparently. Well that is certainly the case here. This may be a big boy, displaying a stonking 50ppm phenols, but its fails to match the overall elegance of the Kilchoman Inaugural 100% Islay...which is a p-challenged 15ppm. The Inaugural showed great purpose throughout. This is a big crash, bang wallop merchant. That said, fully enjoyable stuff! *46%. nc ncf.*

Kilchoman Spring 2011 Release oloroso finish db (93.5) n23.5 there is no doubting the enormity of the smoke, but that is matched by the deftness of the lightly molassed grape. What a surprisingly well suited marriage; t24 and there we go again: juicy yet dry at the same time. The delivery offers outstanding early balance and control. Also, very hard to believe this is just three years old: behaves something nearer ten or twelve. Excellent soft oils which act as a reservoir for the melting muscovado sugar; **f22.5** garibaldi biscuit and coffee; the smoke does not act much like a 50ppm giant; **b23.5** have to admit: when I this was a 50ppm phenol malt finished in oloroso, my head was in my hands and my heart was filled with trepidation. This is a story that normally ends in tears... But what a surprise! A faultlessly clean butt helped, but the grape is by no means overplayed and its main function, apart from balance, appears to be to generate a feeling of extra age and tranquillity in the glass. A lovely and genuinely unexpected Islay experience. On this evidence, Kilchoman has well and truly arrived and can hold its head as high as the other Islay distilleries... *46%. nc ncf.*

Kilchoman Inaugural Release db (87.5) **n21 t23 f21.5 b22**. Not by any means perfect but what could have been something of a bumpy ride has been helped along by some very good casks: like an excellent football referee, you don't notice it, but not only is it there, it makes the best of what is on offer. Not a great whisky. But a very promising start. *46%. nc ncf.*

Kilchoman Inaugural 100% Islay 1st fill bourbon db (91.5) **n23.5** a superb nose which takes full advantage of some excellent oak to give weight to the soft gristiness. Young, but no hint of a Bambi here: this has found its feet already...; **t24** fabulous delivery. Soft, genteel peats melt into a light citrus sweetness and then several waves of red-liquorice oak add just the right anchor; **f21.5** pleasant and vanilla-driven though slightly untidy, as one might reasonably expect; **b22.5** in a quite different world to the first two bottlings. Those, falteringly, gave reason for hope. But a slight degree of concern, too. This is unerringly fine: clean and purposeful and making a very clear and eloquent statement. *50%. nc ncf.*

Kilchoman 100% Islay The 2nd Edition db (93) **n23** tannins have kicked in already to create a redcurrant and liquorice dais to the smoke; **t23.5** a pup of a dram, the juices from the barley cascade onto the palate. The sugars are uncomplicated and dripping in phenols before custard cream biscuits take charge; **f23** the custard cream is dunked into milky, muscovado-rich Panama coffee; smoky praline is a side dish; **b23.5** the first edition of this sent out, I remember, a clear statement as to regards the quality of the spirit being produced at Kilchomen. This doesn't just endorse it, but actually takes us further down the line. Less storms and drama than the previous bottling, but this is far better controlled and weighted with the praline and coffee liqueur mix making for one of the best three-year-olds ever bottled in Scotland. *50%. nc ncf.*

Kilchoman Loch Gorm sherry cask, dist 07, bott 13 db (92.5) **n23.5** anyone who has squelched through the blackest peat bog on a stormy Islay day will recognise parts of this earthy aroma; fruit has tightened the smoky, slightly coal tar creosote aspect; **t23.5** ridiculously soft landing on the palate with those now familiar oils soon aboard and to all parts of the palate; one of the oiliest middles I have tasted in a Scotch; **f22.5** big smoked raisin fudge; **b23** it is never a good idea to be Gorm-less...especially when a whisky is quite this scarily enormous. On this and other evidence, it could be that Kilchomen is not just challenging Caol Ila as the oiliest malt on Islay, but may well have surpassed it. *46%. nc ncf.*

Kilchoman Machir Bay bott 2012 db (93) **n23** fireside peat ash wrapped in sherry; **t23.5** beautifully distilled barley and grist – both youthful and some weighed down with a little vanilla – tapping out some major peaty notes; just a little bitter as it appears the oak has been forced slightly. The sultana fruit maximises the juiciness; **f23** long with a wonderful ulmo honey depth and the now restrained peat taking a support role rather than the lead; **b23.5** it is over 30 years since I first tried to play football on the sands of Machir Bay. I did it because with the winds never ceasing, it was, like a latter day Canute, an attempt at the impossible. A bit like trying to get to the bottom of this malt, in fact. In some respects it works, in others I feel a degree of sherry may just have knocked out some of the more complex characters in an attempt to soften. It is, however, much more successful than my failed attempts at playing "Keepie Uppie" against the perennial winds of Machir Bay... *46%. nc ncf.*

Kilchoman Machir Bay oloroso sherry butt finish, bott 13 db (90.5) **n23** as fat as an Islay goose with the wine helping to turn this chunky; **t22.5** how sweet it is: to be loved by those who want their palate caked Caol Ila style in thick oil with the phenols subdued and trying to get out from under the weight of the juicy sultanas; **f22** the oiliest coffee ever; **b23** I think this was more honeyed last time, but the sultanas ring a bell. Another very different but high quality offering from Kilchomen. *46%. nc ncf.*

⠿ **Kilchoman Machir Bay** bott 2014 db (92) **n23** soft, teasing, engulfing smoke lightened further by grapefruit; **t24** pleasing grist offers bold sugars which melt in the mouth and an intensifying peat which gathers like storm clouds on the horizon; **f22** the storm wanders in another direction leaving a slightly bitter oakiness washed up on the beach alongside some sugar and spice; **b23** some 25 years ago, Machir Bay would be where my children and I tried to play blow football: it was us against the impossible, relentless winds which howled off the sea with a will and singularity of mind that could not be tamed. There was only ever one winner. So, interesting to see that they have created a malt to reflect those very rare days when you can explore the length of it untroubled by nature. As lovely as this whisky is, I think I would have enjoyed it more had it reflected the Bay in all its fury... 46%. ncf nc. WB15/27

Kilchoman Sherry Cask Release bott 2011 db **(83)** n21.5 t21.5 f19 b21. The thumping peat at times almost syrupy sherry is just too much of a good thing. 46%. nc ncf.

❊ **Kilchoman Single Cask Release** bourbon, cask no.473/2008, dist 25 Sep 08, bott 16 Sep 13 db **(95.5)** n23.5 a hint of Fisherman's Friend adds a menacing sharpness to the otherwise serenely sweet peat; **t24** quite outstanding mouth feel on delivery: the palate is a blur of smoke and dark sugars, though midway in, ash and coal dust bites; **f24** as long as demanded for a malt this big; the peat now layering in both intensity and sweetness. The spices buzz cleverly and almost below the taste buds' radar; **b24** most of the whiskies I have tasted from this distillery this year have been truly exceptional. Here is another one. 61%. ncf nc. Bottled in celebration of the 5th year of The Whisky Show. The Whisky Exchange. WB15/278

Kilchoman Vintage 2006 bott 2012 db **(93.5)** n24 I close my eyes and allow myself to be consumed by the aroma which takes me away from a freezing, rain-soaked summer in England, to a freezing, rain-soaked summer on Islay, with gulls screeching from a distance, peat on the wind from Port Ellen and midges biting hard with an uncanny accuracy for the most sensitive nerve endings. You are unlikely to find an aroma which so perfectly embodies maritime Islay; **t23.5** the sugars seemingly so tied up with the phenols on the nose appear to have momentarily escaped the smoky masters to make the delivery a sweet one. But the smoke is on its trail and soon has the caster sugar and maple syrup back in custody allowing vanilla to make its presence felt; **f22.5** bitters very slightly; the peat now has the density of an Arbroath smoky while spice rattles in late on; **b23** a sweetly peated triumph. 46%. nc ncf.

❊ **Master of Malt Single Cask Kilchoman 5 Years Old (96)** n24 delicate smoke and marmalade: that's basic. Where this works is in the complexity lurking behind the phenols: minor dabs of ginger and allspice keeping things warm and dry; **t24.5** the smoke is up there but again happy to play second fiddle to the much more integrated grain and oak notes which dovetail sugar and spice and all things nice...a feminine whisky one might say...; **f23.5** light oils towards the end...; **b24** the smoke keeps a lower than usual profile. No bad thing: the intricacy of the oak in particular takes some believing. A wonder malt. 59.6%. sc.

Scotch Malt Whisky Society Cask 129.1 Aged 5 Years dist 28 Jun 06 **(89)** n22.5 t22.5 f21.5 b22.5. A delicious, if different, experience not to be missed. 60.2%. nc ncf sc.

Scotch Malt Whisky Society Cask 129.2 Aged 4 Years 1st fill barrel, dist 13 Dec 07 **(92.5)** n23 a smashed bottle of TCP... which happens to have conveniently landed in a bowl of grist and freshly squeezed lemon; **t23.5** at first the delivery concentrates on the ashy aspect of the peat, being dry and dusty. The spices fizz like fuse wire for a few seconds but the way in which the oils form to create an entirely different character in mid act is some trick...; **f22.5** continues along its young smoky path but there is a short burst of Demerara sugars to reinvigorate the complexity; **b23.5** probably because of its comparative youth, a malt which somehow bypasses the coastal feel other Kilchomens have conjured in previous bottlings and instead decided to flaunt its peaty charms shamelessly. 61.6%. nc ncf sc. 250 bottles.

❊ **That Boutique-y Whisky Kilchoman** batch 1 **(95)** n24 if you want to know what just about faultless heavily peat grist is like, try this: a wonderful mix of salty sea spray and peat reek on the wind; **t24** the sweetness promised on the nose arrives immediately; the sugars play out from gristy melt-in-the-mouth icing sugar through to muscovado. Always, though, it is handcuffed to smoke; **f23.5** much drier with the sugars seemingly spent and a little nudge towards light vanilla; **b24** sublimely made and maturing comfortably. When whisky is this good, age matters not a jot. 55.5%. 272 bottles.

KINCLAITH
Lowlands, 1957–1975. Closed / Dismantled.

Mo Ôr Collection Kinclaith 1969 41 Years Old first fill bourbon hogshead, cask no. 301453A, dist 28 May 69, bott 29 Oct 10 **(85.5)** n22 t22 f20.5 b21. Hangs on gamely to the last vestiges of life, though the oak, without being overtly aggressive, is squeezing all the breath of out of it. 46%. nc ncf sc. Release No. 2. The Whisky Talker. 164 bottles.

KNOCKANDO
Speyside, 1898. Diageo. Working.

Knockando Aged 12 Years dist 94 db **(86)** n22 t22 f21 b21. An unusually light bottling. Here you get full exploration of the attractive, malty skeleton. But Knockando has a tendency towards dryness and the casks here oblige rather too well. A delicate dram all the same. 43%

Knockando Aged 12 Years dist 1995 db **(71.5)** n16 t19 f18 b18.5. If there was an award for Worst Nose of the Year, this must be somewhere in the running. 43%

Knockando Aged 12 Years dist 1996 db (76) n18 t20.5 f18.5 b19. Disappointing. As someone who knows this distillery perhaps as well as anyone working for its current owners, I had hoped for a dry, sophisticated dram to send me into various degrees of ecstasy. Instead, I am left lamenting a few poor casks which have distorted what this distillery stands for. 43%

Knockando Aged 18 Years sherry casks, dist 1987 db (77) n19 t21 f18 b19. Bland and docile. Someone wake me up. 43%

Knockando 25 Years Old Special Release 2011 db (77) n20 t22 f16 b19. One or two renegade sherry butts away from what would have been a memorable whisky. 43%. nc ncf.

Knockando 1990 db (83) n21 t22 f20 b20. The most fruity Knockando I've come across with some attractive salty notes. Dry, but a little extra malty sweetness these days. 40%

KNOCKDHU
Speyside, 1894. Inver House Distillers. Working.

AnCnoc 12 Year Old db (94.5) n24 so complex it is frightening: delicate barley; delicate spices; delicate butterscotch-vanilla, delicate citrus... and all the while the lightest discernible sugars melt into the malt; t23 it had to be salivating... and is! Yet there is enough oaky-vanilla roughage to ensure the citrus and barley don't get their own way; f23.5 a slow but telling arrival of spices fit hand in glove with the complex cocoa-barley tones; b24.5 a more complete or confident Speyside-style malt you are unlikely to find. Shimmers with everything that is great about Scotch whisky... always a reliable dram, but this is stupendous. 40%

AnCnoc 13 Year Old Highland Selection db (85) n21 t23 f20 b21. A big Knockdhu, but something is dulling the complexity. 46%

AnCnoc 16 Years Old db (91.5) n22 sharp, pithy, salty, busy...; t23.5 those salts crash headlong into the taste buds and then give way to massive spice and barley; soft sugars and vanilla follow at a distance; f23 salted mocha and spice; b23 unquestionably the spiciest AnCnoc of all time. Has this distillery been moved to the coast..? 46%

AnCnoc 22 Year Old db (87) n22 a classic case of polished oak floor; t21.5 the tingle on delivery is oak concentrate. The sweeter barley recovers and battles to keep it in check, but there are casualties; f22 settles gently towards a cocoa and butterscotch finish. The oaks seem less militant; b21.5 often a malt which blossoms before being a teenager, as does the fruits of Knockdhu; struggles to cope comfortably with the inevitable oakiness of old age. Here is such a case. 46%. Inverhouse Distillers.

AnCnoc 26 Years Old Highland Selection db (89) n23 t22 f23 b21. There is a little flat moment between the middle and finish for which I have chipped off a point or two. That apart, superb. 48.2%

AnCnoc 30 Years Old db (85) n21 t23 f19 b22. Seat-of-the-pants whisky that is just on the turn. Still has a twinkle in the eye, though. 49%

AnCnoc 35 Years Old db (86) n21 t21 f22.5 b21.5. Tries to take the exotic fruit route to antiquity but headed off at the pass by a massive dollop of natural caramels. The slow burn on the spice is an unexpected extra treat, though. 43%

AnCnoc 35 Years Old bourbon and sherry casks db (88) n22.5 t22 f21.5 b22. The usual big barley sheen has dulled with time here. Some attractive cocoa notes do compensate. 44.3%. nc ncf.

An Cnoc 1993 db (89) n22 t21 f24 b22. Quite an odd one this. I have tasted it a couple of times with different samples and there is a variance. This one takes an oakier path and then invites the barley to do its stuff. Delicious, but underscores the deft touch of the standard 12-year-old. 46%

AnCnoc 1994 db (88.5) n22.5 t22.5 f21.5 b22. Coasts through effortlessly, showing the odd flash of brilliance here and there. Just get the feeling that it never quite gets out of third gear... 46%. ncf.

AnCnoc 1995 db (84.5) n21 t22 f20.5 b21. Very plump for a Knockdhu with caramel notes on a par with the citrus and burgeoning bourbon. Some barley juice escapes on delivery but the finish is peculiarly dry for the distillery. 46%

⠿ **AnCnoc 1999** db (95.5) n24 ridiculously delicate with a heather honey backbone from which certain light liquorice and citrus notes hang. Rarely is good age so cleverly revealed, or disguised, or spices so polite; even a hint of light smoke for goodness sake; t24 both firm yet silky delivery, the two contrasting tones continuing throughout. The spices buzz while a little maple syrup thins that prominent heather honey; a decent puff of vanilla; f23.5 pretty lengthy, helped by the spice and the muscovado-topped butterscotch; a late milky chocolate flourish does no harm; b24 I noticed as I was putting the bottle away that on their back label their description includes "Colour: soft, very aromatic with a hint of honey and lemon in the foreground" and "Nose: amber with a slight yellow hue." Which would make this malt pretty unique. But this is worth getting for far more than just the collectors' item typo: this is brilliant whisky – one of their best vintage malts for a very long time. In fact, one of their best ever bottlings...period. *46%. nc ncf. WB15/160*

⫶⫶ **AnCnoc Flaughter** 14.8 ppm db **(88.5) n23** dense malt with something of distant kippers; **t22** soft oils, several layers of malt of varying intensity. But a quite piquant smokiness; **f21.5** surprisingly hard smoke and even harder sugars. Something to break your teeth on; **b22** interesting to compare the relative heavy handedness of this against the Rutter. A lovely whisky this may be, but has nothing like the poise or balance. *46%. ncf nc. WB15/345*

AnCnoc Peter Arkle first fill sherry casks db **(67) n17 t17.5 f16.5 b17.** Unattractive and grimly off key. *46%. nc ncf.*

⫶⫶ **AnCnoc Peter Arkle Limited Edition** db (87.5) **n22.5 t22.5 f20.5 b22.** A floral nose, with lavender and honeysuckle in abundance. Also offers dried orange peel. But the malt doesn't move on from there as one might hope, becoming just a little too sugary and caramel stodgy for the malt to do itself justice. All that said, a great dram to chew on for a few minutes! *46%. ncf nc. WB15/321*

⫶⫶ **AnCnoc Rutter** 11 ppm phenols db **(96.5) n24.5** citrus with a twist of peat...; the most delicately yet meaningfully smoked nose on the market today **t24.5** a delivery from heaven: melt-in-the mouth sugary grist continues with its lemony dress. While all around smoke plays, at times hardly audibly, in the background; **f23.5** fabulous finale: no bitterness, no angst or mess. Just the most elegant and charming fade of grist and smoke, perhaps with a dusting of honeyed cocoa on the way down; **b24** I remember vividly, at this great distillery's Centenary party exactly 20 years ago this summer, mentioning to the then distillery manager that I thought that the style of the malt produced at Knockdhu was perfectly geared to make a lightly malted peat along the lines of its neighbour, Ardmore. Only for a few weeks of the year I ventured. I'm pretty certain this malt was not a result of that observation, but it is heartening to see that my instincts were right: it's a sensation! *46%. ncf nc. WB15/320*

Knockdhu 23 Years Old db **(94) n23 t24 f23 b24.** Pass the smelling salts. This is whisky to knock you out. A malt that confirms Knockdhu as not simply one of the great Speysiders, but unquestionably among the world's elite. *57.4%.*

LADYBURN
Lowlands, 1966–2000. William Grant & Sons. Closed.

Mo Ór Collection Rare Ayrshire 1974 36 Years Old first fill bourbon barrel, cask no. 2608, dist 10 May 74, bott 1 Nov 11 **(89.5) n22 t23.5 f22 b22.5.** I had a feeling it'd be this distillery when I saw the title on the label... it couldn't be much else! Fascinating to think that I was in final countdown for my 'O' levels when this was made. It appears to have dealt with the passing years better than I have. Even so, I had not been prepared for this. For years during the very early 1990s Grant's blender David Stewart sent me samples of this stuff and it was, to put it mildly, not great. Some were the oakiest malt I ever tasted in my life. And, to compound matters further, the distillery's own bottling was truly awful. But this cask has re-written history. *46%. nc ncf sc. Release No. 4. The Whisky Talker. 261 bottles.*

LAGAVULIN
Islay, 1816. Diageo. Working.

Lagavulin 12 Years Old 7th releasedb **(92.5) n23 t23 f23 b23.5.** Brooding, enigmatic and just pulsing with quiet sophistication. A dram to drink quietly so all can be heard in the glass... *56.4%*

Lagavulin 12 Years Old 8th release, bott 2008 db **(94.5) n24** heady mixture of coal dust and peat reek, quite dry but not without some fried banana sweetness in the most delicate terms possible; **t24.5** a lightly oiled landing allows the peats to glide around the palate with minimal friction; a light dusting of hickory powder works well with the big, but by no means brooding phenols; the sweetness levels are just about perfect; **f22.5** surprisingly short with a dull toffee flourish to the smoke; **b23.5** sensational malt: simply by doing all the simple things rather brilliantly. *56.4%*

Lagavulin 12 Years Old 10th release, bott 2010 db **(94.5) n23.5** a dusty, gristy combination. As though someone has swept up the remnants of an anthracite pile and mixed it in with powdered peat and grist. And then sprinkled liberally with hickory. Dry with sugars at a premium; **t24** the arrival offers a surprising amount of juice: still enough rich barley still not under the influence of oak. The sugars, so shy on the nose, show all the bashfulness of a teenage wannabe on a TV talent show. Except these sugars do have talent...; all the while the smoke hangs around like reek on a windless winter morn; **f23.5** long with a touch of melted molasses spread over a butterscotch tart; the peat could hardly be more gentile; **b23.5** keeps on track with previous Releases. Though this is the first where the lowering of the ppms from 50 to 35 really do seem noticeable. Quite beautiful, nonetheless. *56.5%*

Lagavulin 12 Years Old Special Release 2011 db (96.5) n24.5 the kind of perfectly weighted aroma which makes your hairs stand on end and your taste buds salivate. The peat takes neither ashy nor oily form, or maybe it takes both....you decide. And the light mintiness to the lemon....extraordinary! t24 the oils form with limited density on delivery. Not only do they usher in the controlled peat, but also a milky mocha thread which perfectly absorbs the percussion of most explosive spices; f23.5 softens out with the deft sugars now in command over the vanilla; the thin, creamy mocha continues; b24.5 so the peat may not pound as it did when the Whisky Bible began life in 2003: the phenols are noticeably lighter here. But it is not all about size: balance and complexity still reign supreme. 57.5%. nc ncf.

Lagavulin 12 Years Old Special Release 2012 Refill American oak casks, bott 2012 db (95) n23 firm peat, firm gristy barley, firm sugar. Yet the subtle oils and underlying vanillas ensure a soft centre; t24 big and juicy delivery with major barley sparking on delivery. The peat is sublime, appearing on varying waves of intensity and depth: a delivery and follow through which always appears fresh and on the move; f24 more vanilla and butterscotch; buttery, too – of the salted variety. Like the nose and delivery a fluid finale, with the sugar melting, solidifying and melting again and a mild, smoky manuka honey fade; b24 truly wonderful. A very clever, sympathetic and professional choice of casks from this superstar distillery. 56.1%. nc ncf. Diageo.

Lagavulin 16 Years Old db (95) n24 morning cinders of peat from the fire of the night before: dry, ashy, improbably delicate. Just a hint of Demerara sweetness caught on the edge; t24 that dryness is perfectly encapsulated on the delivery with the light sugars eclipsed by those countless waves of ash. A tame spiciness generates a degree of hostility on the palate, but the mid-ground sticks to a smoky, coffee-vanilla theme; f23 light spicy waves in a gentle sea of smoke; b24 although i have enjoyed this whisky countless times socially, it is the first time for a while I have dragged it into the Tasting Room for professional analysis for the Bible. If anyone has noticed a slight change in Lagavulin, they would be right. The peat remains profound but much more delicate than before, while the oils appear to have receded. A different shape and weight dispersal for sure. But the sky-high quality remains just the same. 43%

⋅⋅⋅ **Lagavulin The Distillers Edition** batch lgv.4/502, dist 97, bott 13 db (94.5) n25 two toned peat with Arbroath Smokies battling buttery kippers for supremacy; salty, soft and seemingly with some kind of indecipherable fruit number lurking in the near opaque background; t23.5 probably the silkiest delivery you'll come across this year. Voluptuous, moist date drowned in smoke descends into a molassed mass; f22 fades a little too fast as the vanilla bring matters to a surprisingly tangy conclusion; b24 hugely enjoyable. In some ways simply too dense to maximise the distillery's enormous complexity. The nose, however, deserves legendary status and its presence on the palate offers something exceptional, even if the flavours have been daubed on, rather than finely painted. 43% WB15/309

Lagavulin Aged 16 Years The Distillers Edition PX cask, dist 1991, bott 2007 db (83) n22 t21 f20 b20. I have oft stated that peat and sherry are uncomfortable bed-fellows. Here, the two, both obviously from fine stock and not without some individual attraction, manage to successfully cancel each other out. One is hard pressed to imagine any Lagavulin this dull. 43%

Lagavulin 21 Years Old bott 2007 db (96) n24.5 t24 f23 b24.5. Big peat and grape rarely work comfortably together and here we a have malt which struggles from the nose to finish to make some kind of sense of itself. There will be some Islayphiles who will doubtless drool at this and while certain aspects of the finish are quite excellent the balance never appears to come into focus. 56.5%

Lagavulin 21 Years Old Special Release 2012 dist 1991, bott 2012 db (92.5) n23.5 fruity and fresh: toffee raisin meets Rupp cheese; salty and seaside, too...and rather sweet; t23.5 thick, smoky, juicy fruitcake...and rather sweet; f23 exceptionally clean fruit and a slow, sweet pulsing smokiness...and rather sweet; b22.5 the impact of the fruit is truly delicious in its sweet juiciness, but the smoke means complexity is slightly subdued. Fantastic whisky, though...and rather sweet. 52%. nc ncf. Diageo.

Lagavulin Special Release 2010 12 Years Old db (94) n24.5 unambiguously Lagavulin: the mixture of chalkiness to the gristy peat, all ringed by light oil, is unmistakable. Clean, wonderfully shaped and disciplined in its use of spice; t24 the same can be said here as the nose: it absolutely screams Lagavulin and is bolstered by a clever injection of muscovado sugars which actually boosts rather than relieves the intensity. The oils are so soft, they could come from Leeds...; f22 just a shade of disappointing bitterness as tired cask cocks a snook at the continuing spices and forming cocoa; b23.5 Bloody hell! This is some whisky...! 56.5%. nc ncf.

LAPHROAIG

Islay, 1815. Beam Inc. Working.

Laphroaig 10 Years Old db (90) n24 impossible not to nose this and think of Islay: no other aroma so perfectly encapsulates the island – clean despite the rampaging peat-reek and soft oak, raggy coast-scapes and screeching gulls – all in a glass; **t23** one of the crispiest peaty malts of them all, the barley standing out alone, brittle and unbowed, before the peat comes rushing in like the tide: iodine and soft salty tones; **f20.5** the nagging bitterness of many ex-Allied bourbon casks filled during this period is annoyingly apparent here... **b22.5** has reverted back slightly towards a heavier style in more recent bottling, though I would like to see that old oomph at the very death. Even so, this is, indisputably, a classic whisky. The favourite of Prince Charles apparently: he will make a wise king... 40%

Laphroaig 10 Years Old Cask Strength batch no. 001 bott Feb 09 db (**91.5**) **n22.5** like a throbbing 6 litre engine below a still bonnet, you are aware of the peaty power waiting to be unleashed; **t23.5** a stunningly sublime, slightly watered muscovado sugar coating ensures the dry, phenolic explosion conjures myriad variances on a theme; **f23** a quite beautiful milk chocolate quality dovetails to excellent effect with the smoke; **b22.5** a Groundhog Day of a malt with the waves of smoke starting identically but always panning out a little differently each time. Fascinating and fun. 57.8%

Laphroaig 10 Years Old Original Cask Strength db (**92**) **n22** a duller nose than usual: caramel reducing the normal iodine kick; **t24** recovers supremely for the early delivery with some stunning black peppers exploding all over the palate leaving behind a trail of peat smoke; the controlled sweetness to the barley is sublime; **f23** again there is a caramel edge to the finish, but this does not entirely prevent a fizzing finale; **b23** caramel apart, this is much truer to form than one or two or more recent bottlings, aided by the fresh, gristy sweetness and explosive spices. Wonderful! 55.7%

Laphroaig Aged 15 Years db (**79**) **n20 t20 f19 b20.** A hugely disappointing, lacklustre dram that is oily and woefully short on complexity. Not what one comes to expect either from this distillery or age. 43%

Laphroaig 18 Years Old db (**94**) **n24** multi-layered smokiness: there are soft, flightier, sweeter notes and a duller, earthier peat ingrained with salt and leather; **t23.5** perhaps it's the big leg-up from the rampant hickory, but the peat here offers a vague Fisherman's Friend cough sweet quality far more usually associated with Bowmore, except here it comes in a milder, Demerara-sweetened form with a few strands of liquorice helping that hickory to a gentler level; **f23** soft oils help keep some late, slightly juicy barley notes on track while the peat dances off with some spices to niggle the roof of the mouth and a few odd areas of the tongue; **b23.5** this is Laphroaig's replacement to the woefully inadequate and gutless 15-year-old. And talk about taking a giant step in the right direction. Absolutely brimming with character and panache, from the first molecules escaping the bottle as you pour to the very final ember dying on the middle of your tongue. 48%

Laphroaig Aged 25 Years db (**94**) **n23** the clean - almost prim and proper - fruit appears to have somehow given a lift to the iodine character and accentuated it to maximum effect. The result is something much younger than the label demands and not immediately recognisable as Islay, either. But no less dangerously enticing... **t24** the grapes ensure the peat is met by a salivating palate; particularly impressive is the way the sweet peat slowly finds its footing and spreads beautifully; **f23.5** no shortage of cocoa: a kind of peaty fruit and nut chocolate bar... **b23.5** like the 27-y-o, an Islay which doesn't suffer for sherry involvement. Very different from a standard, bourbon barrel-aged Laphroaig with much of the usually complexity reined in, though its development is first class. This one's all about effect - and it works a treat! 40%

Laphroaig Aged 25 Years Cask Strength 2011 Edition oloroso and American oak casks db (**96.5**) **n24** an immense nose with fruit and smoke dished out in equal measure: rarely have I located so much marmalade on a Laphroaig nose. An extraordinary degree of black pepper, too. The smoke, though intense, enjoys a wonderful degree of layering; **t24.5** the peat is, as is so often the case with this distillery, the first to show. But it does so with such a suave sophistication that one is tempted to bow at its majesty. The backdrop to this is a molassed cocoa depth. But it is the light oils bringing in the distinctive vanilla followed by the Jaffa cake orange...; **f24** lengthened by those most delicate oils, the vanilla still has a presence while the smoke forms circular patterns of almost feather-like substance; **b24** quite possibly the finest bottling of Laphroaig I have ever encountered. And over the last 35 years there have been a great many bottles... 48.6%

Laphroaig Aged 30 Years db (**94**) **n24 t23 f23 b24.** The best Laphroaig of all time? Nope, because the 40-y-o is perhaps better still... just. However, Laphroaig of this subtlety and charm gives even the very finest Ardbeg a run for its money. A sheer treat that should be bottled at greater strength. 43%

Laphroaig Aged 40 Years db (**94**) **n23 t24 f23 b24.** Mind-blowing. A malt that defies all logic and theory to be in this kind of shape at such age. The Jane Fonda of Islay whisky. 43%

⁙ **Laphroaig Cairdeas** bourbon barrels and Amontillado seasoned traditional hogsheads, bott 2014 db (**92.5**) **n22.5** ashy...with a few dabs of TCP; **t23** something seemingly youthful bites and bites hard: the light muscovado sugars melt; a little lavender creeps up from nowhere; f23.5 now pretty dry with the lavender and peat on equal terms; b23.5 as dry as Laphroaig gets. Rather beautifully made and so delicate you feel it might simply crumble in your mouth. *51.4%.*

Laphroaig Càirdeas Ileach Edition ex bourbon Maker's Mark casks, bott 2011 db **(90)** n23 a beautiful grist theme with spice and floral tones; t22.5 lounges around the palate as though it owns the place. Just stretches out, brings a few brown sugar notes absent-mindedly into play and dozes off into a toffee-enriched land of nod; f22 a few bitter oak notes, but the natural caramels and peaty spices tip toe around determined not to cause a scene; b22.5 the name of the whisky means "friendship". And it is unlikely you will ever find a Laphraoig 101 any friendlier than this... *50.5%*

Laphroaig Càirdeas Origin quarter casks, bott 2012 db **(89)** n24 t22.5 f20.5 b22. Started like a train and hit the buffers for the finish. Still, early on it is quite superb. *51.2%. ncf.*

Laphroaig PX Cask bourbon, quarter and Pedro Ximenez casks db **(96)** n23.5 a strangely coal dusty element to this: anthracite, to be precise. The grape effect is a little blunt and monosyllabic. But there is an extra sturdiness to the oak which injects the required complexity and helps identify the figs and physalis against the clearer red liquorice-bourbon background; t24.5 the delivery is at first muddled, though the texture and shape of the body is never less than superb; the smoke bounces contentedly around the firmer oaks; even a touch of lightly smoked mocha here and there. A harder sugar edge from the PX tries to quieten matters a little too forcefully, but there is enough left in the peaty tank to allow spices to quash any chance of that; f24 long, perhaps restricted by some uncompromisingly firm sugars, but there is both barley and smoke enough for a satisfying finale which includes some high quality cocoa; b24 I get the feeling that this is a breathtaking success despite the inclusion of Pedro Ximenez casks. This ultra sweet wine is often paired with smoky malt, often with disastrous consequences. Here it has worked, but only because the PX has been controlled itself by absolutely outstanding oak. And the ability of the smoke to take on several roles and personas simultaneously. A quite beautiful whisky and unquestionably one of the great malts of the year...in spite of itself. *48%. Travel Retail exclusive.*

Laphroaig Quarter Cask db **(96)** n23 burning embers of peat in a crofter's fireplace; sweet intense malt and lovely, refreshing citrus as well; t24 mouthwatering, mouth-filling and mouth-astounding: the perfect weight of the smoke has no problems filling every crevice of the palate; builds towards a sensationally sweet maltiness at the middle; f24 really long, and dries appropriately with smoke and spice. Classic Laphroaig; b25 a great distillery back to its awesome, if a little sweet, self. Layer upon layer of sexed-up peatiness. The previous bottling just needed a little extra complexity on the nose for this to hit mega malt status. Now it has been achieved... *48%*

⫶ **Laphroaig Select** db **(89)** n22 not just full of smoke, but vitality, too. Certain aspects of the sweetness are slightly more aligned to bourbon with a red liquorice flourish to the gristy smoke; t22 soft – almost too soft – as the smoked toffee becomes decidedly fudgy; f23 more of the same, only a hint of cocoa and Demerara plus some late oil and spice; b22 missed a trick by not being unchillfiltered at 46%. An apre-taste squint at the back label revealed some virgin oak casks had been used here, which explains much! *40%. WB15/117*

Laphroaig Triple Wood ex-bourbon, quarter and European oak casks db **(86)** n21 t21.5 f21.5 b21. A pleasing and formidable dram. But one where the peat takes perhaps just too much of a back seat. Or, rather, is somewhat neutralised to the point of directional loss. The sugars, driven home by the heavy weight of oak, help give the whisky a gloss almost unrecognisable for this distillery. Even so, an attractive whisky in many ways. *48%. ncf.*

Dr Jekyll's Laphroaig Aged 7 Years Pedro Ximenez cask, bott 12 **(78.5)** n21.5 t22 f17 b18. Loads of attitude and has much to say. A giveaway furriness on the tongue reveals an unwanted secret about the cask...and it sticks; the final notes are not at all helpful. *54.5%*

Chieftain's Laphroaig Aged 14 Years cask no. 8601,8604, dist Sep 98, bott Feb 13 **(87.5)** n23 t23 f19.5 b22. A very decent dram until the Allied bitter cask curse hits. *44.3%. nc ncf.*

⫶ **Cheiftain's Laphroaig Aged 14 Years** hogshead, cask no. 8601/8604, dist Sep 98, bott Feb 13 **(90)** n23 dry, powdery...like sticking your head up a peat sooted chimney (and believe me, I've done it often enough...); t22.5 an early burst of typical gristy smoke, then a move towards mocha; f22 quiet: returns to a smoky powdery dryness; b22.5 curious, as there is hardly a bite of spice to be had. Intriguing, as you feel the malt is operating very much within its capabilities. *44.3%. 1518 bottles. WB15/164*

Dun Bheagan Laphroaig Aged 17 Years hogshead, cask no. 5035,5037, dist May 94, bott 12 **(89)** n22 t23 f22 b22. Pleasant, sweet but never abandons cruise control. *49.2%. nc ncf.*

⫶ **Hepburn's Choice Laphroaig Aged 11 Years** refill hogshead, dist 02, bott 2014 **(90)** n22.5 soot dry, with matching attractively acrid phenols; t22 every atom of the 35ppm phenols arrives on delivery or very soon after. Light oil blends well with the light ulmo honey; f23 gorgeous build up of smoked chocolate; b23 does the simple things exceedingly well. Clean and helped by an impeccably behaved cask. *46%. nc ncf sc. 151 bottles.*

Kingsbury Laphroaig Aged 13 Years hogshead, cask no. 4145, dist 99 **(89.5) n21.5 t23 f23 b22.** Nippy and, at times, with some serious bite. But acclimatise for a fabulous experience. *46%. nc ncf. Japan Import System. 314 bottles.*

Kingsbury Laphroaig Aged 22 Years hogshead, cask no. 2234, dist 90 **(91) n21.5 t22.5 f24 b23.** Takes time to get going. But it is the lightness of touch which astounds. *53.7%. nc ncf. Japan Import System. 242 bottles.*

Malts Of Scotland Laphroaig 1996 sherry hogshead, cask no. MoS 12041, dist Jun 96, bott Sep 12 **(83.5) n23 t21.5 f19 b20.** The quality of the superb nose and early delivery cannot be maintained. *56.1%. nc ncf sc. 96 bottles.*

Malts Of Scotland Laphroaig 1996 bourbon hogshead, cask no. MoS 13028, dist Jul 96, bott Apr 13 **(89.5) n22.5 t23 f22 b22.** A very curious, head-scratching bottling. Amazing delivery. *56.2%. nc ncf sc. 96 bottles.*

Malts Of Scotland Laphroaig 1998 sherry **(69) n17 t19 f15 b18.** All you'll ever need of the four Ss: sugar, sherry, smoke...and sulphur. *56.8%.*

Malts Of Scotland Laphroaig 2000 sherry hogshead, cask no. MoS 13010, dist Feb 00, bott Feb 13 **(85.5) n22 t22 f20 b21.5.** One of the oiliest Laphroaigs I have encountered in years: like a dollop of cream sherry in every glass. A tell-tale fuzziness to the finish, but a fulsome, medium-sweet, toffee-ish chew. *57.8%. nc ncf sc. 96 bottles.*

Old Malt Cask Laphroaig Aged 12 Years refill hogshead, cask no. 8677, dist Jun 2000, bott Aug 12 **(88) n22 t22 f22 b22.** Lower than the usual 35ppm phenols, this is light, sugar dependent and an easy, clean and non-taxing ride all the way. *50%. nc ncf sc. 387 bottles.*

Old Malt Cask Laphroaig Aged 14 Years refill hogshead, cask no. 9227, dist Oct 98, bott Dec 12 **(86.5) n21.5 t22 f21.5 b21.5.** Not the most complex Laphroaig you'll encounter. But if you are a Peat Freak there are enough phenols here to keep you happy for an hour or two. *50%. nc ncf sc. Douglas Laing & Co. 311 bottles.*

Old Malt Cask Laphroaig Aged 14 Years refill hogshead, cask no. 9222, dist Oct 98, bott Oct 12 **(89.5) n22 t23 f22 b22.5.** Just works on so many levels better than its close relation, cask 9227: great example of how oak makes all the difference. *50%. sc. 322 bottles.*

⬥ **Old Malt Cask Aged 14 Years** refill butt, cask no. 10432, dis Apr 00, bott Apr 14 **(81.5) n20.5 t21 f20 b20.** A trademark old Allied bitter barrel des for this, its signature legible on the nose. Never happy, there are still plenty of sugars among the smoke. *50%. sc. 731 bottles.*

⬥ **Old Malt Cask Laphroaig Aged 15 Years** refill hogshead, cask no. 9932, dist Apr 98, bott Aug 13 **(95) n24** classically coastal with all kinds of saline rock pools mixing with the peat reek; a bit of a stunner... **t23.5** melt-in-the-mouth Demerara sugars gells sublimely with the slightly lighter than expected smoke; **f23.5** now the spices begins to orbit the late hickory, all played out on a smoky bed; **b24** intense and comfortably lives up to the distillery's reputation, throwing in the odd surprise for good measure. *50%. nc ncf sc. 212 bottles.*

⬥ **Old Malt Cask Laphroaig Aged 15 Years** refill butt, cask no. 10167, dist Mar 99, bott Jun 14 **(80.5) n21 t21.5 f19 b19.** An untidy mish-mash of a malt which boasts smoke aplenty. But another agent causes annoying disharmony. *50%. nc ncf sc. 292 bottles.*

Old Malt Cask Laphroaig Aged 16 Years refill hogshead, cask no. 9736, dist Oct 96, bott May 13 **(93) n23.5** a few violets and salty crushed green olives amid the usual smoke; **t23.5** well behaved peat which shows just enough muscle you hope for from a Laphroaig but no more. German coffee biscuit, and half-hearted hint of spice; outstandingly well-balanced oils; **f23** cinders and molasses; long and chewy all the way with late hickory; **b23** these peaty ashes don't come with a straighter bat than this, or are played with such effortless grace. What a difference a high quality piece of oak can make.... *50%. nc ncf sc. 168 bottles.*

⬥ **Old Malt Cask Laphroaig Aged 16 Years** refill hogshead, cask no. 10260, dist Oct 97, bott Dec 13 **(77) n19 t21 f18 b19.** Welcome to an old-fashioned Allied Domecq dud bourbon cask. Perhaps the slightly Fisherman's Friend-style distillate is not helping, but this is a pretty rough ride. *50%. nc ncf sc. 322 bottles.*

⬥ **Old Malt Cask Laphroaig Aged 17 Years** refill hogshead, cask no. 10125, dist Oct 96, bott Oct 13 **(86.5) n22 t21.5 f21.5 b21.5.** The smoke is a little dull and though plenty to chew at, liquorice in particular, this is rather hotter whisky than it should be. *50%. nc ncf sc.*

⬥ **Old Particular Islay Laphroaig Aged 15 Years** refill hogshead, cask no. 10273, dist Mar 99, bott Mar 14 **(95) n23.5** firm in both its gristiness and oak involvement. Clean and almost chiselled in its smoky profile; **t24** spot on delivery with a fabulous interplay between the liquorice and Demerara bourbon notes and the forthright, unerring smoke; **f23.5** long, with a biscuit edge to the tapering smoke and moist ginger cake finale; **b24** beautifully disciplined and attractively sweet. *48.4%. nc ncf sc. 288 bottles.*

Provenance Laphroaig Over 12 Years bourbon hogshead, cask no. 475 **(88)** n22.5 t22 f21.5 b22. A steady-as-she-goes bottling; 46%.

Riegger's Selection Laphroaig 2000 bourbon-sherry cask, cask no. 4121, dist 2000, bott 2013 **(90.5)** n23 t23 f21.5 b23. It is pretty well known that I'm not the greatest fan of big peat and sherry together. And this is rougher than three day old stubble. But you know what? This works...and is a magnificent journey - a bit like driving a Land Rover over some rocky terrain. 55.2%. ncf sc. Viktor-Riegger GmbH.

Scotch Malt Whisky Society Cask 29.125 Aged 17 Years refill barrel, dist 95 **(89)** n21.5 t23 f22 b22.5. No shortage of sugars outflanking the peat. 60.6%. nc ncf sc. 205 bottles.

Scotch Malt Whisky Society Cask 29.128 Aged 21 Years refill butt, dist 12 Oct 90 **(79)** n20 t20 f19 b20. A big brown sugar bonanza which, with a clean cask, would have been a sherried belter of the very top order. 58.8%. nc ncf sc. 601 bottles.

Scotch Malt Whisky Society Cask 29.136 Aged 17 Years refill barrel, dist 4 Apr 95 **(86)** n22.5 t22 f20.5 b21. Disappointingly bitter cask influence undermines the sweet charms of the smoke and spice. 59.2%. nc cf sc. 128 bottles.

⸬ **Scotch Malt Whisky Society Cask 29.148 Aged 18 Years** refill barrel, dist 04 Apr 95 **(90.5)** n22 smoke-charged with the peat having that morning after in the Highland hearth feel; t22.5 harp delivery with the sugars almost combustable; tangy melon fills the midground; f23 long, lightly oiled and surprisingly delicate; b23 quietly goes about its subtly citrusy business. 60.6%. nc ncf sc. 206 bottles.

⸬ **Scotch Malt Whisky Society Cask 29.151 Aged 24 Years** refill butt, dist 09 Nov 89 **(85.5)** n21.5 t22 f21 b21. Top heavy with oak, giving the smoke a restricted space to work its magic. 50.7%. nc ncf sc. 311 bottles.

⸬ **Scotch Malt Whisky Society Cask 29.154 Aged 23 Years** refill hogshead, dist 12 Oct 90 **(89)** n23 a sprig of mint amid the smoke underlines the age; t22 a short burst of younf gristiness holding on for grim death, then an avalanche of smoky oak; f22 soft oils preserve the sugars...thankfully; b22 a big, proud malt trying not to vanish under the oak. 49.9%. nc ncf sc. 253 bottles

⸬ **Signatory Cask Strength Collection Laphroaig Aged 15 Years** refill sherry butt, cask no. 700393, dist 22 Sep 98, bott 23 Sep 13 **(96.5)** n24 so farmyardy...with allotment bonfires thrown in for stunning effect; t24.5 a truly exceptional clean sherry butt offers a fruity gloss to the smoky gristy sugars and spices. With a light oil to hand, the mouth feel and weight are spot on, as ulmo honey and treacle combine; f23.5 minty chocolate as well as chocolate raisin. But all this couched in wonderfully dry peat ash...; b24.5 if I have ever tasted a better sherry-peat combination, it escapes my mind. Look what happens when you have a sulphur free cask: magic and malty miracles... 60.8%. sc nc. 551 bottles. WB15/298

⸬ **Signatory Cask Strength Collection Laphroaig Aged 17 Years** hogshead, cask no. 8519, dist 26 Nov 96, bott 07 Jan 14 **(88)** n22.5 light clan peat; citrus fresh; t22 sweet, thin acacia honey, a little marzipan...and the remainder is peaty grist; f21.5 drier, smokey; b22 a cask which has done the rounds makes only a marginal contribution. So this is fresh stuff, but not quite so complex or heavy as it might be. 50.7%. nc sc. 271 bottles. WB15/138

Wemyss 1998 Single Islay Laphroaig "Beach Bonfires" hogshead, bott 2012 **(92.5)** n23 beautiful mix of dry peat and sweeter barley and peach notes; t23 gorgeously juicy, again, like the nose having a distinctive barley edge to this with the smoke playing second fiddle, if slightly loudly; f23 the vanilla and late honey is so clear, only a top quality cask can be at work here. The smoke continues to drink lazily and, finally, some spices can be heard; b23.5 this great distillery has been cursed a little by having technically outstanding spirit maturing in indifferent wood. This beauty, however, is not so constrained. 46%. sc. 357 bottles.

The Whisky Cask Laphroaig Aged 21 Years bourbon cask, dist 1990, bott 2011 **(86.5)** n21.5 t22 f21.5 b21.5. One of the more sugar-saturated versions of Laphroaig. It needs to be, with the typical Allied cask bitterness coming through long before the death. But impossible not to love these heavily smoked, chocolatey brown and black Liquorice Allsorts... 52.5%. sc.

LINKWOOD

Speyside, 1820. Diageo. Working.

Linkwood 12 Years Old db **(94.5)** n23.5 gorgeous malt absolutely bursting at the seems with barley-rich vitality; citrus and anthracite abound; t24 a quite stunning delivery with some of the clearest, cleanest, most crystalline malt on the market. The sugars are angular and decidedly Demerara; f23 a long play out of sharp barley which refuses to be embattled by the oaky vanillas; light spices compliment the persistent sugars; b24 possibly the most improved distillery bottling in recent times. Having gone through a period of dreadful casks, it appears to have come through to the other side very much on top and close to how some of us remember it a quarter of a century ago. Sublime malt: one of the most glittering gems in the Diageo crown. 43%

Linkwood 26 Year Old port finish dist 1981, bott 2008 db **(85)** n20 t24 f20.5 b20.5. Can't say that either nose or finish do it for me. But the delivery is brilliant: the enormity and luxurious sweetness of the grape leaves you simply purring and rolling your eyes in delight. 56.9%

Linkwood 26 Year Old rum finish, dist 1981, bott 2008 db **(89.5)** n23.5 t23.5 f21 b21.5. A real touch of the rum toffee raisin candy to this one. 56.5%

Linkwood 26 Year Old sweet red wine, dist 1981, bott 2008 db **(89)** n22.5 t23 f21 b22. Juicy, spicy: doesn't stint on complexity. 56.5%

Linkwood 1974 Rare Malt db **(79)** n20 t21 f19 b19. Wobbles about the palate in search of a story and balance. Finds neither but some of the early moments, though warming, offer very decent malt. The best bit follows a couple of seconds after – and lasts as long. 55%

⠿ **Berry's Own Selection Linkwood 1999 Aged 14 Years** cask no. 11971, bott 2014 **(93)** n23 wickedly sharp! t23.5 oh my word...! The barley is so lively and puckering: enough oil and lemon-soaked sugar to deeply satisfy; f23 a little bitterness to the tang, but that barley just keeps on coming, now with zesty flourish; b23.5 a wonderful malt brimming with character. Speyside nutshelled. 46%. ncf ncf. WB15/244

⠿ **Berry's Own Selection Linkwood 1987 Aged 26 Years** cask no. 1043, bott 2013 **(96.5)** n24.5 a nose I could nose all day, had I the time: fabulous blood orange meeting moist Lubec marzipan head on; a fiendishly clever layering of delicate herbs; the fruitiness reforms into a wonderful exotic mush, caressing, cajoling, teasing, reminding you of its past, whispering about the delights yet to come...; t24 the weight, the pace of flavour development, the degree of malt, its juiciness, of residual sugar of vanilla and natural caramel from the oak, the spices...all just about perfect for its age; f23.5 concentrates on the vanillas, allowing any tanginess from the cask to filter through; b24 there is not a competent professional blender in the world who might not resort to murder to get a parcel of malt like this in his 25-year-old blend. This would be the apex of the top dressing, the cherry on the cake, the box of subtle delights that could tip a creation from excellence to magnificence. 46%. ncf ncf. WB15/239

⠿ **Cadenhead's Authentic Collection Linkwood-Glenlivet Cask Strength Aged 12 Years** bourbon hogsheads, dist 2001, bott Oct 13 **(89.5)** n22 fresh, clean and faultless. The barley sparkles while the vanilla and spice does its thing quietly; t23 salivating delivery with beautiful oscillation between the sharp barley, lingering sugars and spice; f22 yet more barley, with a little late fudge and marzipan; some late bitterness; b22.5 exemplary Linkwood at it most –Glenlivetish...! 57%. 246 bottles. WB15/082

⠿ **Cadenhead's Authentic Collection Linkwood-Glenlivet Cask Strength Aged 12 Years** bourbon hogsheads, dist 2001, bott Feb 14 **(90)** n22.5 a few apples amid the tannins; t23 light oils close ranks to keep in and magnify the enormity of the barley and spice; the mid ground is surrpsiignly juicy and offering over-ripe pear; f22 late muscovado shadows the tannins; b22.5 leave in glass a good half hour to unfold. Complex and surprisingly big. 57.8%. 294 bottles. WB15/085

⠿ **Cadenhead's Small Batch Linkwood-Glenlivet Aged 26 Years** dist 1987, bott 2014 **(95.5)** n24 one of the cleanest amalgamations of delicate fruit and barley you'll encounter for a while; t25 one of the best deliveries this year: the barley is three dimensional and lit by a laser-sharp spotlight. For about ten seconds, oak, sugar, fruit and malt, all brought to the height of their flavour profiles by a liberal dose of salt, come together for an orgasmic blast which leaves the head spinning in delight...; f22.5 the afterglow seems a little tame by comparison; the vanillas bob and weave but a slight tang shows the oaks are beginning to wither; b24 when Linkwood is on top form, few Speysiders comes close. 56.8%. 972 bottles. WB15/259

The Coopers Choice Linkwood 1995 15 Years Old hogshead, cask no. 9140, dist 95, bott 10 **(88)** n22 t22 f22 b22. Anyone searching for a typical Speyside clean "grassy" style can end their search here. 46%. nc ncf sc. The Vintage Malt Whisky Co Ltd. 360 bottles.

Duncan Taylor Octave Linkwood 22 Years Old cask no. 764147, dist 89 **(88)** n22.5 t21.5 f22 b22. A blender would enjoy this in a 21-year-old creation for the confident barley and controlled spice. 48.9%. sc. Duncan Taylor & Co.

⠿ **Duncan Taylor Dimensions Linkwood Aged 22 Years** oak casks, cask no. 8326, dist 10/90, bott 04/13 **(94)** n24 an astonishing nose in which my daily uncooked vegetable salad has been chopped up and mixed with Melton Hunt fruit cake at its most ridiculously moist and rich. With a little pepper added, of course...hang on, this kind of reminds me....(see summary)...; t23.5 a plethora of dark sugars mingle with thick fruit and juicy barley. Still the spices buzz...; f23 more spiced moist fruitcake; b23.5 had to say, this got me scrambling to my 2014 Bible checking up Linkwood. And there was a DT bottling from a sister cask showing a very similar nonconventionalist style. Only this goes off on a different, fruitier tangent altogether. Staggeringly lovely. 48.7%. nc ncf sc. 237 bottles. WB15/115

⸬ **Gordan & MacPhail Exclusive Single Malt Linkwood** refill sherry hogshead, cask no. 5018, dist 08 Dec 88 **(97.5) n25** dry lead thanks to some well-muscled tannins. Lovely spices inject extra life into the sharp pineapple candy; some moist parkin cake underlines the age; even deeper notes babble underneath...; **t24** good weight of early, surprising, barley alongside a sturdier volley of spices. A procession of exotic fruits is topped off by custard and a few volts of tannin; the odd atom of smoke drifts around deliciously; **f24** the smoke persists and give extra life and depth, as well as captures the darker sugars to ensure the oak remains contented and positive; the late mocha tops it off magnificently; **b24.5** just like the proprietor of SWC, has aged with sophistication, elegance...and a touch of spice. Also, surrounded by smoke... A tip or two. Allow to sit in the glass for at least ten minutes to breathe. Nose and taste only at body temperature. Not a degree below. And do not add water. That way you will experience one of the most complete single casks ever bottled. *55.3%. nc ncf sc. 229 Bottles. WB15/066*

⸬ **Kingsbury Silver Linkwood 24 Year Old** cask no. 568, dist 1989 **(85) n20.5 t23.5 f20.5 b21.** What seems like a thumping heavyweight oloroso butt has its weaknesses on both nose and finish. But there is no denying the delivery which is of the Harvey's Bristol Cream variety and is stashed with some serious grapey treasures. A flawed diamond, indeed... *46%. nc ncf sc. 568 bottles.*

⸬ **Montgomerie's Single Cask Collection Linkwood** cask no. 6713, dist 05 Dec 89, bott Mar 13 **(89.5) n22.5** just dig the diced apple and over-ripe pear; **t23** beautifully clean and busy delivery with the sugar and spice at the vanguard. Most of the sugars are gristy but the pear returns...even with that curious grittiness you get from the fruit...; **f22** tangy and heading towards a vanilla and Walnut Whip fondant finale; **b22** in many ways a modest whisky. But what it does right can be breath-taking. *46%. nc ncf sc. WB15/130*

⸬ **Old Malt Cask Linkwood Aged 16 Years** sherry butt, cask no. 10068, dist Nov 96, bott Oct 13 **(91.5) n22.5** fresh, almost gristy but weighted by excellent vanilla and the lightest (and most surprising) smoke; **t23** mouth-watering with an alloy of fresh barley and crisp sugars; **f23** long, heading down the vanilla route but some late Manuka honey and liquorice intervene; **b23** an understated little gem. *50%. nc ncf sc.407 bottles.*

Old Malt Cask Linkwood Aged 21 Years refill hogshead, cask no. 9218, dist Sep 91, bott Oct 12 **(88.5) n21.5 t22 f22.5 b22.5.** Standard Linkwood without frills, though with the odd spicy thrill. *50%. sc. 252 bottles.*

⸬ **Old Masters Linkwood 14 Years Old** cask no. 11980, dist 2001, bott 2014 **(77) n20 t20 f18 b19.** Never gets into step, let alone stride. Tart and as hot as Hades as the stills were obviously full steam ahead when this cut was taken. Then, to add insult to injury, it was then filled into a poor cask which bitters out unpleasantly at the end. Not even remotely up to usual Old Masters high standard. *58.1%. James MacArthur & Co. Ltd.*

Provenance Linkwood Over 15 Years refill hogshead, cask no. 9661, dist Summer 97, bott Spring 13 **(84) n22 t21 f20 b21.** Built as a blending malt and refuses to stray from the simple barley-intense script. The heat on the finish suggests the stills were at one stage a little too over excited. *46%. nc ncf. Douglas Laing & Co.*

Scotch Malt Whisky Society Cask 39.88 Aged 22 Years refill hogshead, dist 29 Oct 90 **(84.5) n22 t22 f19.5 b21.** After the initial delivery, the oak takes too firm a grasp. But for a few brief moments there is a lively fruit and fudge entrance which borders on burnt raisin. *47.8%. nc ncf sc. 231 bottles.*

⸬ **Scotch Malt Whisky Society Cask 39.91 Aged 22 Years** refill hogshead, dist 29 Oct 90 **(88.5) n21.5** clammy and tight, the oak punches hard; **t22** surprisingly crisp delivery with some early esters and barley sugar. A vague fruitiness rumbles amid the oak; **f22.5** chocolate orange; tangy; **b22** a little fruit here goes a long, long way... *48.5%. nc ncf sc. 226 bottles.*

⸬ **Scotch Malt Whisky Society Cask 39.92 Aged 23 Years** refill hogshead, dist 29 Oct 90 **(82) n20 t22 f19.5 b20.5.** Tasting this absent-mindedly (a nuthatch had just descended on to a tree in my garden), the first words to form in my mind was: "United Distillers." Absolutely typical of their cask policy at the time. Showing some oaky strain but a vague fruitiness somehow proffers an alarmingly discordant note. *49.4%. nc ncf sc. 226 bottles.*

⸬ **Scotch Malt Whisky Society Cask 39.93 Aged 29 Years** refill hogshead, dist 04 Sep 84 **(83) n21.5 t21 f20 b20.5.** There are times when oak can be a little too sturdy...and here is one. The odd bitterness, too, where you hope the sugars would play. *57.9%. nc ncf sc.*

⸬ **Scotch Malt Whisky Society Cask 39.94 Aged 23 Years** refill hogshead, dist 29 Oct 90 **(88.5) n22** spotted dog, suet pudding; **t23** vibrant raisins team well initially with the barley but the oak has a grumpy demeanor; **f21.5** dries as the oak surge continues; **b22** shows the odd scar of passing time but not half bad. *44.7%. nc ncf sc. 196 bottles.*

⸬ **Scotch Malt Whisky Society Cask 39.96 Aged 29 Years** refill hogshead,dist 04 Sep 84 **(87.5) n22 t22.5 f21 b22.** Outwardly, a close relation to 39.93. Except this one works on many more levels. Including a more luxuriant, estery mouth feel countering the purposeful oak plus some charming spices which punctuate at every opportunity. 55%. nc ncf sc. 131 bottles.

⫶ **Scotch Malt Whisky Society Cask 39.97 Aged 23 Years** refill hogshead, dist 29 Oct 90 (87.5) n21.5 t23 f21.5 b22. Though clearly designed as a blending malt this cask has its moments in the sun. Especially on delivery when, for about fifteen mercurial seconds, all the elements - including the slight but welcome ulmo honey - combine beautifully. Spice on the finish, but a little tangy too. 45.9%. nc ncf sc. 228 bottles.

⫶ **Scotch Malt Whisky Society Cask 39.99 Aged 23 Years** refill hogshead, dist 30 Apr 90 **(94) n23** here you get a compelling sense of the passing years with the oak, though wilting slightly, being supported by an attractive boiled sweet fruitiness and playful spice. A really good balance...; **t24** a sublime mouth feel is matched by the most charming combination of intense, salivating barley, light muscovado sugars, liquorice and fresh black peppers; good esters and fabulous weight; **f23.5** there was something inevitable that butterscotch tart develops, but this is heftily spiced, with the odd sultana dropped in for good measure! **b23.5** this one operates on an entirely different level to the other SWMS Linkwoods I have tasted this year. This, uniquely, is very high class. 58.9%. nc ncf sc. 222 bottles.

⫶ **Signatory Vintage Single Malt Linkwood 1995 Aged 18 Years** cask no. 652+653, bott 13 **(95.5) n24.5** all bells and whistles at full blast as we enter a delicately fruity world. Cox's apples and Williams pears make for a great combination, especially alongside gooseberries fit to burst. But there is also a succession of cake and pudding notes...walnut plus spotted dog and sticky toffee. Glorious. **t24** silky delivery, with the suet from the spotted dog pudding prevalent. The barley is grassy, juicy and fresh; the spices nibble rather than bite; natural caramels thicken and sweeten; **f23** long, with the buttery barley spreading further. The sugars are molten and a little nutty; the tannins offer up further spices; **b24** great whisky. Simple as. 43%. nc. WB15/013

⫶ **Speyside Single Malt Linkwood Aged 30 Years** hogshead, cask no. 8250, dist Jan 84, bott Mar 14 **(92) n23.5** even after such a long time the oak ad barley appear to be holding hands in unison. All is understated yet quietly confident, with soft ground cashews mixing beautifully with the deft bluebell and primrose floral tones; **t23.5** the underlying sweetness of the nose is quickly apparent: gentle sugars with a gristy hue make way for sparkier, spicier, oak-stained depth; **f22** tires a little and dries, but the big tannins stay alive thanks to a sprinkling of Demerara; **b23** just so attractive in so many way. 52.7%. sc. 69 bottles.

Wemyss 1991 Single Speyside "Apple Pastry" hogshead, dist 91, bott 13 **(83.5) n21.5 t21.5 f19.5 b20.5**. Starts off as boiled pears under a blanket of custard but the aggressive, bitter oak turns this more into a pear-drop...I coughed!! A prickly pear, indeed. 46%. sc. 320 bottles.

⫶ **Wemyss Malts 1997 Single Speyside Linkwood "Citrus Burst"** bott 13 **(88) n22.5** an old oak chair sandpapered down; a squeeze of lime from somewhere; **t22.5** almost a lemon sherbet explosion on delivery....; **f21** ....and here's the liquorice. Plus mega dry oak for good measure; **b22** those looking for a fizzy Speysider will be in their element. 46%. sc. 363 bottles.

Wemyss Linkwood 2000 Single Speyside "Summer Orchard" butt **(84.5) n20 t21.5 f22 b21**. Less Summer Orchard and maybe more Early Spring: underdeveloped and very green. Little to report beyond the massive barley. 46%. sc. 762 bottles.

LITTLEMILL

Lowland, 1772. Loch Lomond Distillers. Demolished.

Littlemill Aged 8 Years db **(84) n20 t22 f21 b21**. Aged 8 Years, claims the neck of the dumpy bottle, which shows a drawing of a distillery that no longer exists, as it has done for the last quarter of a century. Well, double that and you'll be a lot closer to the real age of this deliciously sweet, chewy and increasingly spicy chap. And it is about as far removed from the original 8-y-o fire-water it once was as is imaginable. 40%.

Littlemill Aged 21 Years bourbon cask, bott Dec 12 db **(88) n21.5** hard not to miss the nail varnish element to this, but now softened enough to act as a sharpening tool for the barley; **t22** simple, salivating barley which warms as expected....; **f22** the usual raging fire is now a pleasant glow; **b22.5** Littlemill again enjoying an Indian Summer of a dram...after many years of grim rain. 46%. nc ncf. Glen Catrine Bonded Warehouse Ltd.

⫶ **Littlemill 21 Year Old 2nd Release** bourbon cask db **(87) n22 t21.5 f21.5 b22**. So thin you expect it to fragment into a zillion pieces on the palate. But the improvement on this as a new make almost defies belief. The sugars are crisp enough to shatter on your teeth, the malt is stone hard and fractured and, on the finish, does show some definite charm before showing its less attractive teeth....and its roots... Overall, though, more than enjoyable. 47%. nc ncf.

Littlemill 1964 db **(82) n21 t20 f21 b20**. A soft-natured, bourbony chap that shows little of the manic tendencies that made this one of Scotland's most-feared malts. Talk about mellowing with age... 40%

Littlemill 1990 Vintage Aged 22 Years bott 2013 db (**91**) **n23** despite a light flame licking at the nose there is enough honey and sugar on the barley to persuade you to dive in head first; **t23** peppered barley attacks the taste buds with gusto, leaving behind a trail of tannins and honey; **f22.5** butterscotch and watered-down napalm in equal measures; **b22.5** a very tasty bit of rough. 50.6%. nc ncf. Glen Contrine Bonded Warehouse Ltd.

Berry's Own Selection Littlemill 1992 cask no. 10, bott 2013 (**86**) **n21.5 t23 f20 b21.5**. Plenty of synthetic raspberry cream a la Swiss role. Bit of a malty belter but the original paint stripper burn is still there. Bless it! 54.9%. nc ncf sc.

The Coopers Choice Littlemill 1985 25 Years Old refill butt, cask no. 105, dist 1985, bott 2011 (**75**) **n19 t19 f18 b19**. Big barley and very drinkable. But the clarity of the malt also helps accentuate the whisky's technical problems. 46%. nc ncf sc. The Vintage Malt Whisky Co Ltd. 480 bottles.

The Coopers Choice Littlemill 1985 26 Years Old hogshead, cask no. 99, dist 85, bott 11 (**87.5**) **n22.5 t22.5 f20.5 b22**. If you find a fudge with more fudge characteristics than this, I'll buy you a box of the finest fudge I can find. And I won't fudge the issue...53%. nc ncf sc. The Vintage Malt Whisky Co Ltd. 270 bottles.

⫶⫶ **Gordan & Macphail Rare Old Littlemill 1985** (**89**) **n22** slightly gluey in the grand tradition of Littlemill but some exotic fruit sticks, too; **t23.5** so ridiculously soft on delivery with sme kind of non-specific fruit curling up cosily with the barley. Juicy and surprisingly fresh; **f21.5** diminishes as it thins out like Dr Jekyll returning to be Mr Hyde....; **b23** this is so soft in part, you cannot help but laugh when you know exactly what brand of firewater this would have been in the cask 25 years ago. A lovely treat. 46%.

Liquid Library Littlemill 1992 ex-bourbon hogshead, bott 12 (**84**) **n21 t22 f20 b21**. A few apples in the offing. As well as the standard bug malt kick. But the flames lick just a little too hard on the palate. 51.6%

⫶⫶ **Lowland Single Malt Littlemill Aged 25 Years** refill hogshead, cask no. 10349, dist Nov 88, bott Jun 14 (**87.5**) **n21.5 t23 f21 b22**. Good to see a Littlemill celebrate its quarter century in style. The obvious limitations are more than made up for by the odd elaborate and/ or elegant flourish. But it is the texture plus the biting intensity of the barley, coupled with the happy link between the brown sugars and vanilla-rich oak which makes this a winner. 56.2%. sc. 225 bottles.

Old Malt Cask Littlemill Aged 21 Years refill hogshead, cask no. 9443, dist Nov 91, bott Feb 13 (**84.5**) **n21 t21 f21.5 b21**. Something of a minor juicy treat. Has much more the feel of east European slivovitz than a single malt. 50%. sc. Douglas Laing & Co. 262 bottles.

Old Malt Cask Littlemill Aged 21 Years refill hogshead, dist Nov 91, bott May 13 (**87.5**) **n22.5 t22.5 f21 b21.5**. Despite its obvious charms and sophistication of middle age, the tattoos and scars of a wild childhood are still clearly visible. 50%. nc ncf sc. 315 bottles.

⫶⫶ **The Pearls of Scotland Littlemill 1991** bott Jun 14, cask no. 112 (**83.5**) **n20 t22 f20.5 b21**. More than most, alas, this has retained many of the aspects which made this distillery an impossible one to continue as a commercial concern. However, among the obvious chinks and cracks there can be found a few attractive pieces of mosaic, especially when the crisp muscovado sugars enter into play. 52.9%. sc.

⫶⫶ **The Pearls of Scotland 1988 25 Year Old** cask no. 132, dist Oct 88, bott Feb 14 (**87**) **n22 t23 f20.5 b21.5**. This is like a shuffling old man walking with a stoop and telling the guys in the pub of his former hell-fire days. For when he was young he would have thought nothing of grasping your throat and ripping out your tonsils and setting a flame-thrower to the remainder of your mouth. Now, just a quiet, malt-and-gooseberry sort of guy who will do nothing to offend. 43.5%.

⫶⫶ **The Pearls of Scotland 1988 25 Year Old** cask no. 134, dist Oct 88, bott Feb 14 (**85**) **n21.5 t22 f20.5 b21**. Some gentle oils bathe where the last remnants of the scalding spirit bites. Some attractive barley, but all a little too brusque. 47.6%.

Riegger's Selection Littlemill 1992 bourbon cask, dist 27 Feb 1092, bott 2 Nov 2012 (**94.5**) **n23.5** talk about moist fruitcake: all kinds of burnt raisin and molasses at work. Only the remnants of an initially indifferent spirit drops this a point; **t24** what a delivery! Again that little technical blip, pulsing like the distant beat of an extinct star, is evident. But so too is the controlled enormity of a fabulous sherry butt which allows the grape and spice to intermingle with the barley on equal terms; naturally, the molassed sugars play an important part; even a degree of Demerara rum to this; **f23** a mix of sherry trifle and butterscotch; the vanilla has both the tang of the old spirit; **b24** shows you what's possible with a 100% unblemished, clean-as-a-whistle, entirely sulphur-free sherry butt. These guys do this whisky so magnificently well!! Some in the industry – and a few commentators – would do well to find a bottle of this – and learn. 54.5%. nc ncf. Viktor-Riegger GmbH. 629 bottles.

Single Cask Collection Littlemill 21 Years Old bourbon hogshead, cask no. 20, dist 27 Feb 92, bott 28 Feb 13 **(95) n23** a belter of a bourbon influence: a pinch of drying allspice and cloves accentuate the oak without taking it past a point of no return; some stunning marmalade as the whisky warms; **t24** a volley of sugars on delivery, some containing barley, but most dark and seasoned; the spices towards the middle are worth awards on their own; **f23.5** a slow injection of ulmo and manuka honey underlines the butterscotch and spice; the weight and oil involvement is just about perfect; **b24.5** a tamed bruiser which has many similarities to the Scott's 1992 bottling of last year, though this boasts the odd extra gear. World class malt from a failed distillery. 55.6%. nc ncf sc. 318 bottles.

The Whisky Agency Littlemill 1989 bott 12 **(82.5) n21 t21 f20 b20.5.** When distilled, Littlemill was virtually undrinkable: it was more likely to be the fuel to take rockets to Mars than be a decent malt. But years of maturation calmed it and brought out the best of the intense malt. And a number of casks which have surfaced have been top-notch: truly out of this world. However, this one is re-entering earth's orbit...and is hot and burning up... 52.1%

⠿ **The Whisky Agency Littlemill 1990 (90) n22** soft cardboard containing a pithy fruitiness and malty, nutty mix; **t24** gorgeously salivating opening movement followed by a procession of malty notes, all of varying intensity but always superb; **f22** much thinner with its signature pastiness; **b22** you have to doff your cap to this old fellow: undrinkable when in its youth and prime; unmissable in its dotage. 52.4%

The Whisky Agency Littlemill 'Sea Life' 1990 refill sherry butt, dist 90, bott 12 **(85.5) n22 t22 f20.5 b21.** A little bit of the old trademark wallpaper glue. And the heat cannot be denied. But the barley content will impress anyone who can hone in on the buffering marzipan. 52.2%

⠿ **The Whisky Cask Littlemill** 1st fill sherry butt, cask no. 601 **(90.5) n23.5** ultra-attractive fruitiness appears to mingle the apple and pear house style with the juicy grape from the sherry butt. Beautiful, yet unassuming; **t23** crisp and salivating. Again the fruits enjoy star status, but there is room enough for the malt to shine; **f21.5** just a little grunting from the more negative aspects of the initial spirit. But can be forgiven; **b22.5** amazing; you get probably the worst-made spirit of 1992, put it into a first fill sherry butt at a time they were arriving from Spain in hideously sub-standard condition and what so you get? A quietly delicious whisky. 53%.

⠿ **The Whisky Cask Littlemill Aged 21 Years** bourbon hogshead, dist 1992, bott 2013 **(88.5) n22** fruity, apples especially and topped with over-ripe pear; **t22** juicy chewing gum, Some of the wallpaper paste of old can just about be detected but icing sugars compensate attractively; **f22.5** some genuine complexity here with a malty blast catching the light oak-led vanilla full on; **b22** odd how a malt once undrinkable in its youth can offer such charm as a greybeard... 49.9%. nc ncf.

LOCH LOMOND
Highlands (Southwestern), 1966. Loch Lomond Distillers. Working.

Inchmurrin 12 Years Old db **(86.5) n21.5 t22 f21.5 b21.5.** A significantly improved dram which is a bit of a malt soup. Love the Demerara injection. 40%

Inchmurrin Aged 12 Years bourbon cask, bott Dec 12 db **(88) n22** surprising oak visible; some citrus **t22** Malteser-like maltiness with lovely cocoa thread; **f22** yet more malt, with a vanilla veneer; **b22** a superior dosage of simple, intense malt. 46%. nc ncf.

⠿ **Loch Lomond Organic 12 Year Old** bourbon cask db **(83.5) n19 t20 f23 b21.5.** A malty beast. But in some respects has more in common with a German still than a traditional pot. Definite traces of feint. 48%. nc ncf.

⠿ **Loch Lomond 14 Year Old Peated** bourbon cask db **(83) n21 t21.5 f20.5 b20.** Lomond can do a lot, lot better than this. Huge malts but entirely out of sync and never comfortable with the oils present. This isn't the Loch Lomond I know and love. 46% nc ncf.

Inchmurrin Aged 15 Years bourbon cask, bott Dec 12 db **(86) n22 t21.5 f21 b21.5.** Slightly tangy with an edge to the cask which interferes with the usual malty procession. 46%. nc ncf. Glen Catrine Bonded Warehouse Ltd.

Loch Lomond 18 Years Old db **(78.5) n19 t21 f19 b19.5.** A demanding, oily malt which is a long way from technical excellence but is no slouch on the chocolate nougat front. 43%

Inchmurrin Aged 18 Years bourbon cask, bott Dec 12 db **(92.5) n22.5** something of the old-fashioned hop-less Barley Wine about this, spiked by warming, vivid white pepper; **t23.5** a fascinating Rowntree Fruit Pastille citrus kick to this. But only after the usual mega-malt delivery; **f23.5** now rambles around the palate with hands in pockets – just so relaxed. Mainly malt at varying levels; natural caramels and two or three different honey tones, orange-blossom the most prevalent. Outstanding late spice, too; **b23** Loch Lomond distillery in its brightest colours. 46%. nc ncf. Glen Catrine Bonded Warehouse Ltd.

Loch Lomond 21 Years Old db (89.5) n22.5 t23 f22 b22. A little while since I last tasted this, and pretty close to exactly how I remember it. Seems to revel in its own enormity! 43%

Inchmurrin Aged 21 Years bourbon cask, bott Dec 12 db (90) n22 big vanilla injection; t23 profound juice radiating from the barley; the sugars are kept in reserve as the hickory holds court; f22.5 back to the vanilla again, though now some muscovado turns up to ensure a delicate finale; b22.5 this has spent 21 years in a very exceptional cask. Not exactly breathtaking complexity, but what it does is completed with aplomb. 46%. nc ncf. Glen Catrine Bonded Warehouse Ltd.

Loch Lomond Copper Pot Still 1966 db (92) n23 t23.5 f23 b22.5. Shows remarkably little wear and tear for its great age. A gentleman of a whisky. 45%

Loch Lomond Gavin's Single Highland Malt dist 1996, bott 2007 db (90.5) n23 t23 f22.5 b22. Ester-fuelled and fabulous. 45%. nc ncf.

Loch Lomond No Age Statement db (74.5) n18 t20 f18 b18.5. Still feinty and out of sync, though the lively sugars try to compensate. 40%

Loch Lomond Single Highland Peated Malt db (74) n16.5 t20 f19 b18.5. Feints and peat simultaneously: not something you happen upon very often. Thankfully. 46%

⠴ **That Boutique-y Whisky Inchmurrin** batch 1 (83) n21 t21 f20 b21. The label calls it about right: for despite the trace manuka honey and blood orange, this is a bit of a soup. 54.7%. 543 bottles. WB15/195

LOCHSIDE
Highlands (Eastern), 1957–1992. Chivas Brothers. Demolished.

The Cooper's Choice Lochside 1967 Aged 44 Years cask no. 807 (96.5) n24.5 yep. Pretty close to perfection. At first it is the softest of smoke which gets you primed. Then the pastel-shaded fruit begins to take shape, perhaps drawing from the honey blossom honey which is weighted by the butterscotch oak and Nice biscuits; t24.5 again the smoke makes a very early foray, but it is a ghostly one and does a masterful job of keeping anchored the lighter fruit tones. Astonishingly after all these years the barley is still capable of a big juicy volley. While the oak, though arriving early, is of the most benign type offering a seemingly impossible layering of delicate tannins which emboldens and enriches; f23.5 just a little thinner here with the oat now showing a slightly more austere trait. However, that priceless and ultra-complex smoke ensures the finale is one of quiet dignity; b24 it is amazing that I had to travel 6,000 miles to find this in British Columbia. But, this is the kind of whisky you would travel four times that kind of distance to experience. Easily one of the top ten single casks I have tasted in the last five years. 41.5%. 354 bottles.

LONGMORN
Speyside, 1895. Chivas Brothers. Working.

Longmorn 15 Years Old db (93) n23 curiously salty and coastal for a Speysider, really beautifully structured oak but the malt offers both African violets and barley sugar; t24 your mouth aches from the enormity of the complexity, while your tongue wipes grooves into the roof of your mouth. Just about flawless bitter-sweet balance, the intensity of the malt is enormous, yet – even after 15 years – it maintains a cut-grass Speyside character; f22 long, acceptably sappy and salty with chewy malt and oak. Just refuses to end; b24 these latest bottlings are the best yet: previous ones had shown just a little too much oak but this has hit a perfect compromise. An all-time Speyside great. 45%

Longmorn 16 Years Old db (84.5) n20.5 t22 f21 b21. This was one of the disappointments of the 2008 edition, thanks to the lacklustre nose and finish. This time we see a cautious nudge in the right direction: the colour has been dropped fractionally and the nose celebrates with a sharper barley kick with a peppery accompaniment. The non-existent (caramel apart) finale of yore now offers a distinct wave of butterscotch and thinned honey...and still some spice. Only the delivery has dropped a tad...but a price worth paying for the overall improvement. Still a way to go before the real Longmorn 16 shines in our glasses for all to see and fall deeply in love with. Come on lads in the Chivas lab: we know you can do it... 48%

⠴ **Adelphi Selection Longmorn 28 Years Old** cask no. 9907, dist 85, bott 14 (94.5) n23.5 ridiculously elegant for its age: the tannins have made no meaningful incursions other than a citrus butterscotch note and half-hearted spice. Elsewhere the barley enjoys sharing the spotlight with angel cake; t24 a Longmorn...at nearly 30...? Wow! One of the first never to grind my taste buds down with over excited oak. It's the barley which still sings clearly and trills sweetly and without falter; f23 after the cake and tart notes earlier, I had anticipated chocolate sponge on the very finish...... and what do you know...! b24 not normally a distillery that raises my pulse once the years pile on. This, though, is exceptional for its age. A must get Longmorn. 50.6%. ncf sc. 247 bottles. WB15/415

⫶⫶ **Alexander Weine & Destillate Longmorn 22 Years Old** refill bourbon hogshead, cask no. 8646, dist 90, bott 13 **(93)** n23.5 very high quality mix diced glazed fruit and Bakewell pudding; t24 best Longmorn delivery for some time! Textbook mouth feel carrying confident barley sugar, some rampant oak but controlled by maple syrup and liquorice; f22.5 elegant with a fine spice fade and toasty, creamy fudge; b23 nectar... 55.1%. sc. cask strength.

⫶⫶ **Berry's Own Selection Longmorn 1988 Aged 24 Years** cask no. 14385, bott 2013 **(94)** n24 a wonderful array of ultra-delicate mixed fruit notes, all so well married that you can barely pick one from another. But some old conference pear mixes seamlessly with Sharon fruit skin, backed by a banana paste and manuka honey; t24 hardly seems possible, but more silky on delivery than nose. Less fruit apparent now, but a wide selection of medium to dark sugars; f22.5 bitters slightly as the oak tires; b23.5 a malt which evolved on to regal status. And the kind of malt which is the mainstay for the more imperious Ballantine's and Royal Salute brands. 46%. ncf ncf. WB15/245

⫶⫶ **Berry's Own Selection Longmorn 1992** cask no. 71775, bott 2013 **(94.5)** n23.5 for those who love their fruitcake dripping with toasted almonds; decently spiced and even slightly salted; t24 sultry delivery with the treacle and manuka honey arm-wrestling the burnt raisins to the death; surprisingly mouth-watering, showing how lively that salt 'n' spice is, and that, amazingly, the barley is able to be heard amid the fruity din; f23 sticky toffee pudding with thick molasses oozing from every pore. A dusting of cocoa tops it off; few finishes come any chewier...; b24 at times the oak reminds you that here is a distillery uneasy about the passing years. But the enormity of the principal players overcomes any doubts. 58.6%. nc ncf sc.

⫶⫶ **Berry's Own Selection Longmorn 1992 Aged 20 Years** cask no. 149091, bott 2013 **(86)** n22 t22.5 f20 b21.5. Something of a curate's egg, this. Starts its journey on the palate as an essay of sweet, friendly, gently oiled benignity and ends its trek as a rock hard, slightly bitter figure of malevolence. But the good moments are very good... 50.9%. ncf ncf. WB15/248

⫶⫶ **Best Dram Longmorn 21 Years Old** refill sherry, dist 92, bott 13 **(87.5)** n21 you'll get a splintered nose; t23.5 oak threatens but the outbreak of spices and molasses gets things off to a juicy start; lighter golden syrup and mocha make for a big mouthful; f22.5 a long honey and oak fade; b23 tries to fight off its age like a nudist flings off its clothes. But in the end, an arthritic joint means the oaky coat is a little too heavy. Bottled two years earlier this would have been an astonishing malt... 48.8%. ncf. 121 bottles.

⫶⫶ **Chivas Brothers Cask Strength Edition Longmorn Aged 18 Years** batch no. LM 18 009, dist 95, bott 13 **(85.5)** n20 t22.5 f21 b21.5. Disappointing when you think about what they must have available. The dull nose is not much more exciting on the toffee-thick finale. Lacks complexity but at least the delivery affords a jazzed up spicy maltiness. 53.1%. sc ncf. WB15/319

The Coopers Choice Longmorn 1992 19 Years Old hogshead, cask no. 71779, dist 92, bott 12 **(89.5)** n23 t22.5 f22 b22. Straight-as-a-die, no nonsense Speysider with an extra malty edge. 58.2%. nc ncf sc. The Vintage Malt Whisky Co Ltd.

The Coopers Choice Longmorn 1992 19 Years Old hogshead, cask no. 48461, dist 92, bott 2011 **(88.5)** n22.5 t22 f22 b22. Big and flooded with natural caramel. 46%. nc ncf sc.

Duncan Taylor Octave Longmorn 15 Years Old oak cask, cask no. 923352, dist 96 **(96)** n23.5 some bourbon elements full of red liquorice and ulmo honey with the tannins showing the right degree of muscovado; t24 this distillery can offer one of the most complex deliveries in all Speyside. And that's what happens here as the oak churn up the barley-rich procession. Malteser candy mingles with almost eye-watering barley juice; f24.5 after the pizzazz we now have the sophistication. All the previous qualities, but now drier and in seeming slow motion; the butterscotch is astonishing and the varying shades of controlled oak almost beyond belief; b24 gosh, I wish Chivas would take note: Longmorn at 15, in an excellent cask with no caramel...my word: you have to go a long way to beat it! One of the single casks of the year. 53.4%. sc. Duncan Taylor & Co.

⫶⫶ **Hepburn's Choice Longmorn Aged 11 Years** bourbon barrel, dist 03, bott 14 **(87)** n22 t22.5 f20.5 b22. Malty, zesty and vibrant, the barley gives an impressive one-man show in this production until the tanginess of a weary cask intervenes. 46%. nc ncf sc. 351 bottles.

Liquid Library Longmorn 1992 ex-bourbon hogshead, dist 92, bott 12 **(86)** n22 t21.5 f21 b21.5. Despite the house style of bruising, biscuit barley, Longmorn does have a tendency to show puckering oak at the first opportunity. Here is a classic example – could pass for a 30-year-old with no problems. 52.7%

Malts Of Scotland Longmorn 1992 cask no. MoS 13014 **(95)** n23 dry 'n' spicy; t24.5 much sweeter, though the spices live up to the nose's expectation; beautiful mix of molasses and clear honey for the big sugary thread, though the barley still plays a big, juicy part; the middle dries quickly and covers butterscotch ground; f23.5 more butterscotch, though with a thin muscavado layer; the spices provide the backing to the very end; b24 outwardly a classic honey on toast effort. Further investigation reveals a gem. 54.2%. nc ncf sc.

⋊⋉ **Old Malt Cask Longmorn Aged 18 Years** refill hogshead, cask no. 9885, dist Dec 94, bott Jun 13 **(95) n23.5** hard to know which is the firmer: the barley or the vanilla. The subtle tannin-led spices are a dream; **t24** magnificent! The delivery ticks every box you can think of, and a few more besides. Gorgeous weight, yet never too lofty or threatening. Very much in the hands of the oak – the spices ensure that – but complexity is the key word here. Just above dexterity....; **f23.5** a wonderful spectrum of dark sugars...and teasing spice; **b24** the kind of bottle which will keep you good company on the coldest of winter nights... 50%. nc ncf sc. 321 bottles.

Old Masters Longmorn 16 Years Old cask no. 156778, dist 96, bott 13 **(91) n22 t23.5 f22.5 b23.** Anyone with a love for malt shakes or Malteser candy will probably take no prisoners to get their hands on this one. Truly idiosyncratic. 56.3%. sc.

⋊⋉ **Old Masters Longmorn 17 Years** Old dist 96, bott 14, cask no. 156779 **(94.5) n23** the vaguest of smoke mingles with the oak but thinned slightly by the more conventional citrus and honey; **t24** excellent delivery: spot-on weight and the timing by the oak to intervene in the sugar and malt fest; the mid ground is a "Milky Way" candy mix of milk chocolate and delicate malty nougat; light ulmo honey arrives at the midpoint; **f23.5** gentle oak returns to lead the way back home, but the malt and honey still have delicate, understated parts to play; **b24** Longmorn in its most classic pose. 57.1%. James MacArthur & Co. Ltd.

⋊⋉ **Old Particular Speyside Longmorn 21 Years Old** refill hogshead, cask no. 10264, dist May 93, bott May 14 **(91.5) n22.5** light, vaguely floral with a busy barley-vanilla interplay; **t23** amazingly clean for its age, a little young, too; the barley is juicy and bristling with life: the sugars are of a gristy nature; **f23** oil develops and allows the malt full weight; **b23** the type of malt a blender rubs his hands about: here is a perfect insight into how a whisky like Ballantine's can feel so demure at such a great age. 51.5%. nc ncf sc. 246 bottles.

Scotch Malt Whisky Society Cask 7.75 Aged 27 Years 2nd fill sherry butt, dist 26 Oct 84 **(95.5) n23.5** dry from both the oloroso and huge oak input. Probably a second fill sherry butt which escaped a sulphury death in Jerez and emptied at three or five years first time around as the oaky fingerprints are massive and unusual; **t24.5** bliss! That ultra-rare experience of taking the full value of high quality, untarnished oloroso on board, complete with big spiced sultana, then layer upon layer of cream chocolate wafer, all with a magnificent dusting of grist and Danish marzipan; **f23.5** slightly shorter finish than might be expected, but the fade is both elegant and boisterous: the spices warm the ulmo honey and coconut water mix; **b24** a clean butt, so to speak, and though there are too many rings in the oak, this is a sherry cask not to be trifled with.....If you can get one, buy two...! 51.7%. nc ncf sc. 54 bottles.

Scotch Malt Whisky Society Cask 7.84 Aged 27 Years refill hogshead, dist 24 Sep 85 **(92) n23** shouldn't be having coffee at this time of the evening, but here it is...no shortage of tannin and hickory, too; **t23** excellent body; the barley and muscavado sugars form a crisp, almost biscuity, alternative to the oilier theme; **f23** butterscotch and hazelnut conclude an in impressive experience, with the dark sugars rumbling on and on; **b23** Longmorn at its most confident at an age when it can sometimes become oak-soaked and a little jittery. 56.3%. nc ncf sc. 173 bottles.

Scotch Malt Whisky Society Cask 7.86 Aged 27 Years refill hogshead, dist 24 Sep 85 **(83) n21.5 t20 f21 b20.5.** Disappointing considering the all-round might of the distillery. Hot and at no stage of the proceedings does it ever look remotely in control. 56.7%. nc ncf sc.

⋊⋉ **Signatory Vintage Single Malt Longmorn 1996 Aged 17 Years** 1st fill sherry butts, cask no. 72325, dist 01 May 96, bott 06 Aug 13 **(77) n19 t21 f18 b19**. Fails to find any form of meaningful harmony, though there are a brief few intriguing moments post-delivery when the background salivatory sharpness cannot be attributed to either grape or grain. Furry. But above all, dull. 43%. nc sc. 869 bottles. WB15/010

⋊⋉ **The Single Malts of Scotland Longmorn Aged 21 Years** hogshead, cask no. 110979, dist 11 Sep 92, bott 25 Mar 14 **(95) n23.5** dusty sweet shops of the early '60s! Boiled candy in jars; oak floor polish; Demerara-sweetened high value cocoa; **t24** silky delivery of malt. Below stairs, the mocha-enriched dark sugars play while the spices strike up; **f23.5** spiced creamy fudge and toasted honeycomb; **b24** absolutely beautiful, evocative malt. A rare treat of a dram. 49.7%. 293 bottles. WB15/293

⋊⋉ **The Single Malts of Scotland Longmorn 22 Years Old** cask no. 12289, dist 90, bott 14 Sep 13 **(89.5) n22.5** a puff of smoke heralds an otherwise malty nose; **t23** good fresh, mouth-watering properties: the barley takes up all the leading positions. Slowly drier vanillas begin to emerge; **f22** just a hint of coconut biscuit and marzipan bolsters the finale; **b22** a very decent Longmorn which does the simple things attractively. 48.1%. 199 bottles. WB15/305

⋊⋉ **Speyside Single Malt Longmorn Aged 25 Years** refill hogshead, cask no. 10368, dist Apr 89, bott Jun 14 **(94) n23** diced hazelnut, polished oak floors, Shredded Wheat (though shouldn't it be barley...?); **t24** a two-tiered experience: first, young malt gushes into view, complete with gristy sugars and full salivating impact...then the oak arrives...; **f23.5**...and it's the oak all the way on the finish, though the Digestive Biscuit and retained sugars ensures balance is preserved; **b23.5** the degree of control throughout is breath-taking. It is like the marathon runner who has times his use of energy to the second to maximise everything available. Simple. But superb. *54.2%. sc. 183 bottles.*

⁖ **Wemyss Malts 1992 Single Speyside Longmorn "Coconut and Sandalwood"** dist 1992 bott 2013 **(74)** **n19** the light citrus notes which normally heralds a particular style of Bardstown bourbon gets lost slightly in a light milk-creamy, oaky nose – not always a good sign. Some fine moments but this has quite a few danger signals... **t23** too early to tell if problems arrive yet as we are happily swamped in a deluge of intense and beautifully complex barley and even more telling vanilla; **f15** there is a busy early finish; again with a slight bourbon edge, but that problem hinted on the nose is confirmed and promptly reduces the quality of the finale....and your ability to taste and the tongue goes fuzzy and furry... **b17** "Coconut and Sandalwood" says the label, presumably listing about the only two things you can't find in what would minor classic had it not been for a flaw in the cask. When at its best, in some ways more like a busy small-grain bourbon than a scotch with the oak playing all kinds of delicious tricks. What a shame, though. *46%. sc. 330 bottles.*

Wemyss 1996 Single Speyside Longmorn "Toasted Hazelnuts" hogshead, bott 13 **(84)** **n21 t21.5 f20.5 b21.** Elements of chocolate orange and some major oils for a Speysider. But the oak is a little too loud for comfort. *46%. sc. Wemyss Malts. 234 bottles.*

THE MACALLAN
Speyside, 1824. Edrington. Working.
The Macallan 7 Years Old db **(89)** **n23 t23 f21 b22.** An outstanding dram that underlines just how good young malts can be. Fun, fabulous and in recent bottlings has upped the clarity of the sherry intensity to profound new heights. *40%*

The Macallan Fine Oak 8 Years Old db **(82.5)** **n20.5 t22 f20 b20.** A slight flaw has entered the mix here. Even so, the barley fights to create a distinctive sharpness. However, a rogue sherry butt has put paid to any hopes the honey and spice normally found in this brand. *40%*

The Macallan 10 Years Old db **(91)** **n23** oloroso appears to be the big noise here, but clever, almost meaty, incursions of spice offer an extra dimension; fruity, yet bitter-sweet: dense yet teasingly light in places; **t23** chewy fruit and the old Macallan silk is back: creamy cherries and mildly under-ripe plum ensures a sweet-sour style; **f21.5** traces of vanilla and barley remind us of the oak and barley, but the fruit reverberates for some while, as does some annoying caramel; **b23.5** for a great many of us, it is with the Mac 10 our great Speyside odyssey began. It has to be said that in recent years it has been something of a shadow of its former great self. However, this is the best version I have come across for a while. Not perhaps in the same league as those bottlings in the 1970s which made us re-evaluate the possibilities of single malt. But fine enough to show just how great this whisky can be when the butts have not been tainted and, towards the end, the balance between barley and grape is a relatively equal one. *40%*

The Macallan 10 Years Old Cask Strength db **(85)** **n20 t22 f22 b21.** Enjoyable and a would give chewing gum a run for its money. But over-egged the sherry here and not a patch on the previous bottling. *58.8%. Duty Free.*

The Macallan Fine Oak 10 Years Old db **(90)** **n23** finely tuned and balanced: everything on a nudge-nudge basis with neither fruit nor barley willing to come out and lead: really take your time over this to maximise the entertainment; **t22.5** brimming with tiny, delicate oak notes which just brush gently, almost erotically, against the clean barley; **f21.5** drier, chewier and no less laid-back; **b22** much more on the ball than the last bottling of this I came across. Malts really come as understated or clever than this. *40%*

The Macallan Sherry Oak 12 Years Old db **(93)** **n24** thick, almost concentrated grape with a stunning degree of light spices. Topped with boiled greengage; **t23.5** clean sherry is heralded not just by vanilla-thickened grape but a deft muscovado sweetening and a light seasoning of spice; **f22.5** cocoa, vanilla and fudge. Remains clean and beautifully layered; **b23** I have to say that some Macallan 12 I have tasted on the road has let me down in the last year or so. This is virtually faultless. Virtually a time machine back to another era... *40%*

The Macallan 12 Years Old Sherry Oak Elegancia db **(86)** **n23 t22 f20 b21.** Promises, but delivers only to an extent. *40%*

The Macallan Fine Oak 12 Years Old db **(95.5)** **n24** faultless, intense sherry light enough to allow the fabulous apple and cinnamon to blend in with the greengage and grape; **t24** a near perfect entry: firm, rummy sugars are thinned by a barley-grape double act; juicy yet enough vanilla to ensure structure and layering; **f23.5** delicate spice keeps the finish going and refuses to let the muscovado-grape take control; **b24** a whisky whose quality has hit the stratosphere since I last tasted it. I encountered a disappointing one early in the year. This has restored my faith to the point of being a disciple... 40%

Macallan Gran Reserva Aged 12 Years db (92) **n23** massive cream sherry background with well matured fruit cake to the fore: big, clean, luxurious in a wonderfully old-fashioned way. Oh, and a sprinkling of crushed sultana just in case the grapey message didn't get across... **t24** a startlingly unusual combination on delivery: dry yet juicy! The ultra fruity lushness is dappled with soft spices; oak arriving early-ish does little to alter the path of the sweetening fruit; just a hint of hickory reveals the oak's handiwork towards the middle; **f22** dry, as oloroso does, with a vaguely sweeter edge sparked by notes of dried date; the delicate but busy spices battle through to the toffeed end; **b23** well, you don't get many of these to the pound. A real throwback. The oloroso threatens to overwhelm but there is enough intrigue to make for a quite lovely dram which, as all good whiskies should, never quite tells the story the same way twice. Not entirely without blemish, but I'm being picky. A Macallan soaked in oloroso which traditionalists will swoon over. 45.6%

The Macallan Fine Oak 15 Years Old db (79.5) **n19 t21.5 f19 b20.** As the stock of the Fine oak 12 rises, so its 15-y-o brother, once one of my Favourite drams, falls. Plenty to enjoy, but a few sulphur stains remove the gloss. 43%

The Macallan Fine Oak 17 Years Old db (82) **n19.5 t22 f19.5 b21.** Where once it couldn't quite make up its mind on just where to sit, it has now gone across to the sherry benches. Sadly, there are a few dissenters. 43%

The Macallan Sherry Oak 18 Years Old db (87) **n24 t22 f20 b21.** Underpowered. The body doesn't even come close to matching the nose which builds up the expectancy to enormous levels and, by comparison to the Independents, this at 43% appears weak and unrepresentative. Why this isn't at 46% at the very least and unambiguously uncoloured, I have no idea. 43%

The Macallan 18 Years Old dist 1991 db (87) **n22 t22.5 f21 b21.5** Honestly: I could weep. Some of the sherry notes aren't just textbook...they go back to the Macallan manuals of the early 1970s. But the achievable greatness is thwarted by the odd butt of you know what... 43%

The Macallan Fine Oak 18 Years Old db (94.5) **n23.5** classic cream sherry aroma: thick, sweet but enlivened by a distinct barley sharpness; **t24** juicy, chewy, clean and intense delivery. Strands of honey and syrup help pave the way for vanillas and spices to get a grip; the complexity levels are startling and the weight just about spot on; **f23** a degree of blood orange bitterness amid the cocoa and raisin; the spices remain lazy, the texture creamy; **b24** is this the new Fine Oak 15 in terms of complexity? That original bottling thrived on the balance between casks types. This is much more accentuated on a cream sherry persona. But this sample is sulphur-free and quite fabulous. 43%

The Macallan Masters Of Photography Albert Watson 20 Years Old db (94.5) **n24** if there is such a thing as a seismograph for measuring sherry, this would be bouncing from wall to wall. Concentrated noble rot, with a few roasted almonds and spices tossed in; **t24.5** as soft as a 20-year-old sherry... without the whisky. It works beautifully as the required balance between sugars and spice is there in bundles; and as well as sherry trifle, there is blackcurrant on butterscotch, too; **f22.5** just a hint of bitterness but plenty of over-ripe greengage and toasty vanilla to see you off; **b23.5** it's one of those! (Bizarrely, as I wrote that, Milton Jones said exactly the same words on the radio...spooky!) Once I would have marked this down as being simply too sherry drowned. But since clean sherry butts are now at a premium, I am seeing whiskies like this in a very different light: certainly not in the negative... It can still be argued that this is far too sherry driven, with too much else overpowered. And maybe just a little too bitter on the finish. But of its once thought extinct type, staggering. 46.5%. Edrington.

The Macallan Fine Oak 21 Years Old db (84) **n21 t22 f20 b21.** An improvement on the characterless dullard I last encountered. But the peaks aren't quite high enough to counter the sulphur notes and make this a great malt. 43%

The Macallan 25 Years Old db (84.5) **n22 t21 f20.5 b21.** Dry with an even drier oloroso residue; blood orange adds to the fruity mix. Something, though, is not entirely right about this and one fears from the bitter tang at the death that a rogue butt has gained entry to what should be the most hallowed of dumping troughs. 43%

The Macallan Fine Oak 25 Years Old db (90) **n22** coal dusty: the plate of old steam engines; a speckle of raisin and fruitcake; **t23.5** despite the early signs of juicy grape, it takes only a nanosecond or two for a much drier oak-spiced spine to take shape; the weight is never less than ounce perfect, however; **f22** puckering, aged oak leaves little doubt that this is a malt of advanced years, but a few liquorice notes ensure a degree of balance; **b22.5** the first time I tasted this brand a few years back I was knocked off my perch by the peat reek which wafted about with cheerful abandon. Here the smoke is tighter, more shy and of a distinctly more anthracitic quality. Even so, the sweet juiciness of the grape juxtaposes gamely with the obvious age to create a malt of obvious class. 43%

The Macallan Fine Oak 25 Years Old db (89) n23 t23 f21 b22. Very similar to the Fine Oak 18. However, the signature smoke has vanished, as I suppose over time it must. Not entirely clean sherry, but much remains to enjoy. 43%

The Macallan Fine Oak 30 Years Old db (81.5) n22 t22 f18 b19.5. For all its many riches on delivery, especially those moments of great bourbon-honey glory, it has been comprehensively bowled middle stump by the sherry. Gutted. 43%

The Macallan 40 Years Old dist 10 May 61, bott 09 Sep 05 db (90) n23 no shortage of oak, as you might expect. But nutty, too (chestnut pure, to be precise). The scope is broadened with a distracted smokiness while oak maximizes the longer it stays in the glass; t23 soft and yielding, with a lovely dovetailing of vanillins and delicate sherry. The grape appears to gain control with a sweet barley sidekick before the oak recovers; f22 soft oils formulate with some laite and slightly salted, Digestive-style biscuit. Gentle spices delight; b22 very well-rounded dram that sees off advancing years with a touch of grace and humour. So often you think the oak will take control, but each time an element intervenes to win back the balance. It is as if the dram is teasing you. Wonderful entertainment. 43%

The Macallan 50 Years Old dist 29 Mar 52, bott 21 Sep 05 db (90) n25 we all have pictures in our minds of the perfect grandmother: perhaps grey-haired and knitting in her rocking-chair. Or grandfather: kindly, gentle, quietly wise, pottering about in the shed with some gadget he has just made for you. This, then, is the cliched nose of the perfect 50-year-old malt: time-defying intensity and clarity; attractive demerara (rum and sugar!) sweetened coffee, a tantalizing glimpse at something smoky and sensationally rich grape and old fruit cake. So that the sweetness and dryness don't cancel each other out, but complement each other and between them tell a thousand tales. Basically, there's not much missing here... and absolutely all you could wish to find in such an ancient Speysider...; t23 dry delivery with the oak making the early running. But slowly the grape and grain fights back to gain more than just a foothold; again telling wisps of smoke appear to lay down a sound base and some oily barley; f19 now the oak has taken over. There is a burnt-toast and burnt raisin bitterness, lessened in effect marginally by a sweeter vanilla add-on; b23 loses it at the end, which is entirely excusable. But until then, a fabulous experience full of passion and complexity. I nosed and tasted this for over an hour. It was one very rewarding, almost touching, experience. 46%

The Macallan Millennium 50 Years Old (1949) db (90) n23 t22 f22 b23. Magnificent finesse and charm despite some big oak makes this another Macallan to die for. 40%

The Macallan Lalique III 57 Years Old db (95) n24.5 coffee and walnut cake. That's the simple way of looking at this one: but give yourself maybe half an hour and a slightly more detailed picture forms. The fruit conjures dates and walnuts – so walnuts and walnut oil is a pretty common thread here. And truffle oil, amazingly. The oak is toasty liquorice and overcooked fudge. But the delicate smoke I was expecting is conspicuous by its absence... until very late on. Only after a major degree of oxidisation does it add that extra delicate dimension; t23 a soft landing in the canopy of the oaky trees with those coffee notes noticeable on the nose now really making a stir. Most beautiful, perhaps, is the lightness of touch of the Demerara and muscovado sugar blend, damped in intensity by a sprinkling of vanilla. Some surprising oils form and make for a silky middle ground; f23.5 some late spices, no more than a smattering, underline the oak without overstating the case while the sugars do their almost invisible job of keeping the dryer notes under control; like on the nose, a little smoke drifts in from seemingly nowhere; b24 I chose this as my 1,000th new whisky tasted for the 2012 Bible not just because of my long-standing deep love affair with this distillery, but also because I honestly felt it had perhaps the best chance to offer not just a glimpse at the past but also the possibility of a whisky experience that sets the hairs on the back of my neck on end. I really wasn't disappointed. It is almost scary to think that this was from a vintage that would have supplied the whiskies I tasted when getting to first discover their 21-year-old. Then, I remember, I thought the malt almost too comfortable for its age. I expected a bit more of a struggle in the glass. No less than 36 years on, the same thing crosses the mind: how does this whisky find it so easy to fit into such enormous shoes? No experience with this whisky under an hour pays sufficient tribute to what it is all about. Checking my watch, I am writing this just two minutes under two hours after first nosing this malt. The score started at 88.5. With time, warmth, oxidation and understanding that score has risen to 95. It has spent 57 years in the cask; it deserves two hours to be heard. It takes that time, at least, to not just hear what it has to say to interpret it, but to put it into context. And for certain notes, once locked away and forgotten, to be slowly released. The last Lalique was good. But simply not this good. 48.5%

The Macallan 1824 db (88) n24 t23.5 f19 b21.5. Absolutely magnificent whisky, in part. But there are times my job is depressing...and this is one of them.. 48%

The Macallan 1824 Estate Reserve db (90.5) n22 excellent clean grape with an intriguing dusting of mint; t23 almost a Jamaican pot still rum sheen and sweetness; beautiful weight and even some barley present; **f22.5** satisfying, gorgeously clean with very good vanilla-grape balance; **b23** don't know about Reserve: definitely good enough for the First Team. *45.7%*

The Macallan 1824 Select Oak db **(82) n19 t22 f20 b21.** Soft, silky, sometimes sugary... and tangy. Not convinced every oak selected was quite the right one. *40%*

The Macallan 1851 Inspiration db **(77) n19.5 t19.5 f19 b19.** Flat and uninspirational in 2008. *41%*

The Macallan 1937 bott 1969 db **(92) n23** an outline of barley can eventually be made in the oaky mist; more defined as a honeyed sweetness cuts in. Fingers of smoke tease. When nosing in the glass hours later the fresh, smoky gristiness is to die for ... and takes you back to the mill room 67 years ago; **t22** pleasantly sweet start as the barley piles in – even a touch of melon in there; this time the oak takes second place and acts as a perfect counter; **f24** excellent weight with soft peat softening the oak; **b23** subtle if not overly complex whisky where there are few characters but each play its part exceptionally well. One to get out with a DVD of Will Hay's sublime Oh Mr Porter which was being made in Britain at the same time as this whisky and as Laurel and Hardy were singing about a Lonesome Pine on the other side of the pond; or any Pathe film of Millwall's FA Cup semi-final with Sunderland. *43%*

The Macallan Gran Reserva 1981 db **(90) n23 t22 f22 b23.** Macallan in a nutshell. Brilliant. But could do with being at 46% for full effect. *40%*

The Macallan Gran Reserva 1982 db **(82) n21 t22 f20 b19.** Big, clean, sweet sherry influence from first to last but doesn't open up and sing like the '81 vintage. *40%*

Macallan Cask Strength db **(94) n22 t24 f24 b24.** One of those big sherry babies; it's like surfacing a massive wave of barley-sweetened sherry. Go for the ride. *58.6%. USA.*

The Macallan Easter Elchies Seasonal Cask Selection Winter Choice 14 Years Old db **(94) n24 t24 f23 b23.** From a faultless cask and one big enough to have its own Postcode... *54%. Exclusive to visitor centre.*

The Macallan Amber sherry oak cask db **(78) n19 t22 f18 b19.** The texture alone shows this should be something truly special. The first few moments of the delivery likewise, with its astonishing Locket's honey filling; honey is the unambiguous theme throughout. But the tangy presence of a few sub-standard sherry butts undermine some great work in the lab. I suspect the next bottling might be a corker. *40%*

The Macallan Estate Reserve db **(84) n22 t22 f20 b20.** Doh! So much juice lurking about, but so much bitterness, too. ...grrrrr!!!! *45.7%*

The Macallan Fine Oak Master's Edition db **(91) n23** one of the most delicate of all Macallan's house noses, depending on a floral scented theme with a sweetish malty tinge to the dank bracken and bluebells; **t23** so salivating and sensual! The tastebuds are caressed with sugar-coated oaky notes that have a devilish buzz about them; **f22** more malt and now vanilla with a bitter cocoa death... **b23** adorable. *42.8%*

The Macallan Fine Oak Whisky Maker's Selection db **(92) n22 t23 f23 b24.** This is a dram of exquisite sophistication. Coy, mildly cocoaed dryness, set against just enough barley and fruit sweetness here and there to see off any hints of austerity. Some great work has gone on in the lab to make this happen: fabulous stuff! *42.8%. Duty Free.*

The Macallan Gold sherry oak cask db **(89.5) n22** the accent is on a fabulous blend of clear and ulmo honey; creamed rice; **t23.5** like Macallan Amber, the texture makes great play of the smallness of the copper stills, with a slightly metallic, rich theme; it is the (chocolate) biscuity barley laced with honey and maple syrup which blows you away though...; **f21.5** ulmo honey still, this time spread over farmhouse bread; a late tang; **b22.5** no Macallan I have tasted since my first in 1975 has been sculpted to show the distillery in such delicate form. *40%*

The Macallan Oscuro db **(95.5) n24.5** the cleanest, most juicy grape dripping into a puddle of molten muscovado sugar: amazed I have not been attacked by wasps while nosing this; it would be too much on its own, but there is a sprinkling of spice to balance things beautifully; **t24** golden sultanas, ripe fig, exploding greengages and that muscovado sugar and spice again...unreal...; **f23** a little bitter, probably from the oak which until now had hardly got a look in; some toasty vanilla makes a late entry but that juicy, lightly spiced fruit just keeps on going; **b24** oh, if all sherried whiskies could be that kind - and taste bud-blowingly fabulous! *46.5%*

The Macallan Ruby sherry oak cask db **(92.5) n23** classic Macallan super-soft cream sherry nose, incorporating rose petals and other Turkish delight traits, such as powdered sugar; **t24** sumptuous and just sweet enough to remind one of noble rot grapes before heavier tannins and cream coffee begins to gain the middle ground; **f22** layering of grape and vanilla coffee; the vaguest hint of a treated sherry butt can just be found; **b23.5** those longer in the tooth who remember the Macallan 10 of 30 years ago will nod approvingly at this chap. Perhaps one butt away from a gong! *43%*

The Macallan Sienna sherry cask db **(94.5) n23** another Macallan with honey in its sights: simplistic clear honey this time, though enriched by grated desiccated coconut and vanilla; **t24** soothing texture with the barley bringing forward enough juice to the soft oil to give extra complexity; easy going to the point of falling backwards off its chair, the barley gives way eventually to a gorgeous ulmo honey, vanilla and butterscotch middle; **f23.5** buttery and not unlike uncooked cake mix you scrape from the bowl; **b24** the pre-bottling sample presented to me was much more vibrant than this early on, but lacked the overall easy charm and readily flowing general complexity of the finished article. A huge and pleasing improvement. *43%.*

The Macallan The Queen's Diamond Jubilee db sherry cask matured **(94) n23.5** heavy duty grape, but clean as a whistle. Damsons and dates abound; **t23** it's one of those amazingly full, slightly uncouth, types of sherry malts, where the grape is piled on thick and only the fittest barley and oak notes manage to make their way through – and there are few. Tasty, though! **f24.5** now it moves into overdrive. The overbearing grape on delivery has vanished and we are left with a really complex fade, full of massive chocolate which sits atop a plum pudding sweetened by molasses; **b23** a wonderful, high quality sulphur-free zone where Macallan unashamedly nails its sherried credentials to the union flag. *52%. 2012 bottles. UK exclusive.*

The Macallan Royal Marriage db **(89) n23.5 t22.5 f21 b22.** Some amazing moments to remember. *46.8%*

The Macallan Select Oak db **(83) n23 t21 f19 b20.** Exceptionally dry and tight; and a little furry despite the early fruitiness. *40%*

The Macallan Whisky Makers Edition db **(76) n19 t20 f18 b19.** Distorted and embittered by the horrific "S" element... *42.8%*

The Macallan Woodlands Limited Edition Estate Bottling db **(86) n21 t23 f21 b21.** Toffee towards the finish brings a premature halt to a wonderfully mollased early delivery. *40%*

⁘ **Darkness! Macallan Aged 15 Years Pedro Ximenez Cask Finish** (85.5) **n21.5 t22 f21.5 b20.5.** Mixed feelings here. A clean sherry influence, which is great. But the PX is so tightly bound with thick sugar that expression, complexity and balance all take a right pounding. Good spices, though. And I'm sure some will regard this as some kind of Macallan orgasm. Whatever turns you on... *52.3%*

⁘ **Gordan & MacPhail Speymalt Macallan 1972** (93) **n23** heady, heavy-duty stuff with the oak furthest up the flagpole. The tannins may be hefty but there is enough Spotted Dog pudding and molten sugar on porridge to form a salute; **t23.5** a fabulous example of the small still syndrome enjoyed by Macallan, as this is tight and intense, sharp and punchy despite the gentle rounding polishing of the last 40-odd years. A lovely mix of intense malt and juicy non-specific fruitiness; a layer of muscovado sugar stands guard and charges in when required; **f23** a little oak buzz but the late mocha charms; **b23.5** the astonishing sugar reserves bring this old timer back from the dead on more than one occasion. *43%.*

Gordon and MacPhail Speymalt Macallan 1991 (89) **n22.5 t23.5 f20.5 b22.5.** Wobbles and bitters out towards the end, but some lovely fruit and nut moments up until then. *43%*

⁘ **Gordan & Macphail Speymalt Macallan 1994** (91.5) **n23** banana cake is crumbled into concentrated, lightly oiled barley; **t24** you expect intense...and you get intense. The malt, as the nose suggests, is in concentrated form but he sugars and spice fix around to give a colourful third dimension; there are layers of citrus, too, each of varying depth and sweetness; **f22** tangy; **b22.5** a busy malt which never quite decides the path it wishes to take, but lets you in for an enjoyable journey nonetheless. *43%.*

Gordon and MacPhail Speymalt Macallan 2003 (68.5) **n16 t19 f16.5 b17.** One to throw back into the river... *43%*

⁘ **Gordan & Macphail Speymalt Macallan 2005** (84.5) **n20.5 t22 f21 b21.5.** Sweet, malty, sharp in places. But the nose and finish reveals a distinct tang. Kind of OK, but I expect a lot better. *43%.*

Heiko Thieme's 1974 Macallan 65th Birthday Bottling cask no. 16807 dist 25 Nov 74 bott Jul 08 **(94) n23** the clarity of the sherry takes some believing: this malt has obviously been in a good clean home for the last 34 years: not a single off note and the balance between grape, oak, spice and sweetened tomato puree is exceptional...; **t23** the arrival is sharp, both in terms of barley and grape. At first it looks shocked to have escaped the cask, or is hunting around for the alcohol to tie it together. But soon it finds harmony, helped along the way by a stunning chocolate and raisin middle which leads to some sweetening molasses; **f24** now enters into a class of its own. We all know about the fruitcake cliché: well here it is in glorious roasted raisin brilliance. Melton Hunt cake and trifle combined; the length makes a mockery of the strength. And it looks as though someone forgot to go easy on the burnt cherry. The vanillas are deft, the coffees are medium roast; **b24** this is not whisky because it is 38%abv. It is Scottish spirit. However, this is more of a whisky than a great many samples I have tasted this year. Ageism is outlawed. So is sexism. But alcoholism isn't....!! Try and become a friend of Herr Thieme and grab hold of something a little special. *38% 238 bottles.*

Old Malt Cask Macallan Aged 15 Years refill hogshead, cask no. 9458, dist Oct 97, bott Feb 13 **(92) n23** thick barley seems as though it is stuck fast to the red liquorice. High quality oak at play...and the pedigree of the initial spirit is pretty impressive, too; t23.5 classic small still intensity here with the oils tight and copper giving both a lustre and sharpness to the barley. As intense as Speyside malt gets; f22.5 thins out as the vanilla arrives, though the copper lingers; b23 Macallan at its most malty and muscular. Really beautiful, if simplistic. 50%. sc. Douglas Laing & Co. 329 bottles.

⁘ **Old Malt Cask Macallan Aged 15 Years** refill hogshead, cask no. 991, dist Oct 97, bott Sep 13 (90) n21.5 pretty one dimensional, with the barley at full throttle; t23 strap yourself in for this one: the malt starts of gently enough, but then bursts through the gears until you have barley concentrate impacting on every taste bud! Wowww....!!! f22.5 settles down somewhat to allow the tad salty vanillas back into the match; b23 this mac shows its small still muscle to full effect. Impressive. 50%. nc ncf sc. 210 bottles.

Old Malt Cask Macallan Aged 16 Years refill butt, cask no. 8815, dist Mar 96, bott Jul 12 (84) n22 t21 f20 b21. A tangy offering from what appears to be a slightly tired cask. 50%. nc ncf sc. Douglas Laing & Co. 189 bottles.

Old Malt Cask Macallan Aged 18 Years refill hogshead, cask no. 8678, dist Sep 93, bott Jun 12 (93) n23 pretty salty, which tends to crank up the oaky side. Plenty of fruitcake, too, complete with nuts..; t24 now that is one impressive delivery: the grape arrives in bunches but the malt will not be outdone and vies for equal juiciness; f22.5 perhaps fades in stature as a little bitterness creeps in, but the weight remains exemplary; b23.5 a treat of a malt. Even the most hard to please Macallan lover will be charmed off his Winchester... 50%. nc ncf sc. Douglas Laing & Co. 349 bottles.

Old Malt Cask Macallan Aged 18 Years refill hogshead, cask no. 9127, dist Nov 93, bott Sep 12 (92) n22.5 curiously creamy and a touch spicy; t23 silky, voluptuously bodied with the malt intensity stoked up to the full; f23.5 an intriguing hint of late smoke raise the complexity levels – and weight; b23 blending Macallan in its best single malt suit. 50%. sc. Douglas Laing & Co. 265 bottles.

Old Malt Cask Macallan Aged 18 Years refill hogshead, cask no. 9202, dist Dec 93, bott Nov 12 (86.5) n21 t22.5 f21 b22. Very drinkable with an attractive hyper-malty fizz. But a lazy cask which refuses to stump up on the complexity. 50%. nc ncf sc. 273 bottles.

Old Malt Cask Macallan Aged 20 Years refill hogshead, cask no. 9449, dist Oct 92, bott Mar 13 (93) n23 gorgeous cream sherry and intense sultana; t23.5 slick and thick, the sultana and marzipan dominates; f23 long and aided by a flawless cask which pulses spice and ginger nut biscuits for quite a while; b23.5 a crackerjack of a cask. 50%. sc. 131 bottles.

Old Malt Cask Macallan Aged 20 Years refill hogshead, cask no. 9853, dist Jun 93, bott Jun 13 (88.5) n22 t22.5 f22 b22. A dry, sophisticated Macallan showing a side it rarely reveals. 50%. nc ncf sc. 285 bottles.

⁘ **Old Malt Cask Macallan Aged 20 Years** bourbon barrel, cask no. 10290, dist Jun 93, bott Feb 14 (93) n23 apples and pears freshly diced, topped with a squeeze of lemon. The tannins look on seemingly bemused and powerless...; t23.5....though they don't hang around on delivery. Red liquorice to the fore, though soon swamped by salivating barley and muscovado sugar. A little orange hangs about; f23 long, softy oiled and not a degree of light molasses and toffee as the tannins begin to make their mark; b23.5 ironically, a Macallan not from a wine cask, yet turns out to be as fruity as you'll find! A real treat. 50%. nc ncf sc. 263 bottles. WB15/134

⁘ **The Pearls of Scotland Macallan 1989 24 Year Old** cask no. 17895, dist Sep 89, bott Feb 14 (94.5) n23 a little bit of a fruit salad thing going on here...and they haven't spared the pears; t24 just massive intensity to the malt. There are some coppery sub-plots here, but it is hard to get away from the salivating qualities of the barley; f23.5 long, with those barley tones stretching and stretching until they are sure to break. The spice is remarkably calm, the texture remains a little like the pear juice apparent: bitty refreshing and sweet; b24 a fine example of small style syndrome... dense, vaguely metallic and delightful! 46.5%.

Provenance Macallan Over 15 Years refill hogshead, cask no. 9657, dist 97, bott 13 (85.5) n22 t22 f20 b21.5. Unusually firm barley for a Macallan with a crisp sugar shell. 46%. nc ncf.

That Boutique-y Whisky Company Macallan batch 3 (77) n18 t21 f19 b19. Sweet, malty but dismally underwhelming. 43.4%. Master Of Malt. 245 bottles.

MACDUFF

Speyside, 1963. John Dewar & Sons. Working.

Glen Deveron Aged 10 Years dist 1995 db (86) n19 t23 f23 b21. The enormity of the third and fourth waves on delivery give some idea of the greatness this distillery could achieve perhaps with a little more care with cask selection, upping the strength to 46% and banning caramel. We'd have a malt scoring in the low to mid 90s every time. At the moment we must remain frustrated. 40%

Glen Deveron Aged 15 Years db **(88.5)** n22 t22.5 f22 b22. For those who like whisky to caress rather than attack their taste buds. *40%*

A.D. Rattray Macduff 1984 sherry butt, cask no. 3149, dist 18 May 84, bott Apr 13 **(88.5)** n23.5 t22 f21.5 b21.5. Some aspects of this malt are breathtaking. *51.4%. sc.*

⁕ **Gordan & MacPhail Connoisseurs Choice Macduff 2000 (95.5)** n23.5 n23.5 a blend of praline and Jaffa Cake....almost impossible to extract your nose from; **t24** oooh....!!! That is one erotic delivery: near perfect texture which glides around the palate. Where it touches a fabulous hazelnut cream cake (yes, they do exist...though, sadly not common enough!) mingles with lustrous barley. Heather honey and muscovado sugar do the rest...; **f24** now drifts into ulmo honey topped with praline. Then more chopped hazelnuts. Simply sublime...; **b24** you'll go nuts for this. But, then, it is the nuttiest dram you'll encounter this year. Stunningly made and matured. *46%.*

Kingsbury Macduff Aged 15 Years hogshead, cask no. 4129, dist 97 **(86.5)** n21.5 t22 f21.5 b21.5. Compact, barley intense and unusually dependent on the malt rather than the usual little honeyed flourishes. *46%. nc ncf. Japan Import System. 354 bottles.*

⁕ **Master of Malt Single Cask Macduff 15 Year Old (90.5)** n23 surprisingly salty malt; **t23** the saline feel kicks in immediately: very sharp, slightly tangy barley. A little banana and citrus adds depth; **f22** stays on the malty theme, but that tang goes up an extra notch; **b22.5** not remotely complex. And the oak might be better. But the malty acrobatics are something else. *56.9%. sc.*

⁕ **Old Malt Cask Macduff Aged 21 Years** refill hogshead, cask no. 9909, dist Dec 91, bott Aug 13 **(87)** n22 t21.5 f22 b21.5. As a blending malt, invaluable. The tartness of the barley would add some malty punch; the finish would be enriched by a light, glossy honey. *50%. nc ncf sc. 262 bottles.*

⁕ **Old Particular Speyside Macduff 14 Years Old** refill butt, cask no. 10358, dist Dec 99, bott May 14 **(81.5)** n20 t22 f19.5 b20. MacRough. *48.4%. nc ncf sc. 587 bottles.*

⁕ **The Pearls of Scotland Macduff 1997 24 Year Old** cask no. 5232, dist Sep 97, bott Nov 13 **(89)** n22 the accent firmly on the barley, but a little peach, too; **t22** early acacia honey is dwarfed by the spice attack; the barley displays some youthful traits; **f22.5** reverts to a softer honeyed, juicy barley style before drying with a vanilla flourish; **b22.5** a bit of a honeyed carry on... *54.4%. WB15/007*

⁕ **Signatory Vintage Un-chillfiltered Collection Macduff 1997 Aged 16 Years** hogsheads, cask no. 4077+4078, dist 12 Jun 97, bott 13 Nov 13 **(88.5)** n22 some nagging tired oak tries to disrupt the honey ceremony; **t23** superb delivery of wonderful weight and thinned acacia honey. A little spice advances and retreats...; **f21.5** standard, and annoying, oak-induced bitterness; **b22** possibly distilled by bees...with the odd wasp. *46%. nc ncf. 692 bottles. WB15/030*

Single Cask Collection Macduff Aged 31 Years sherry hogshead, cask no. 6900, dist 28 Nov 80, bott 7 Mar 12 **(91.5)** n23 t24 f21.5 b23. When a treated sherry butt comes close to pulling off greatness...; *50%. nc ncf sc. 191 bottles.*

⁕ **That Boutique-y Whisky Macduff** batch 1 **(93)** n23.5 the clarity of the vanilla and butterscotch suggests the oak is top notch. The squeeze of lime amid the barley water suggests unsullied youth; **t23.5** mouth-watering barley – literally of the thirst quenching variety. Thinned maple syrup has a little ulmo stirred in for extra depth; **f22.5** perfect oaky footprints offer extra weight and depth but with no bitter recrimination. At last the spices begin to throb; **b23.5** youthful, fresh and brimming with all kinds of citrus and sugars. Delightful. *52%. 340 bottles. WB15/190*

⁕ **Wemyss Malts 2002 Single Speyside Macduff "Lead On Macduff!"** dist 2002 bott 2013 **(61)** n15 t16 f15 b16. Thanks to the hideously rank sulphur, a duff Macduff, Macduff... *46%. sc. 46%. 854 bottles.*

MANNOCHMORE

Speyside, 1971. Diageo. Working.

Mannochmore Aged 12 Years db **(84)** n22 t21 f20 b21. As usual the mouth arrival fails to live up to the great nose. Quite a greasy dram with sweet malt and bitter oak. *43%.*

Mannochmore 1998 The Manager's Choice db **(71.5)** n18 t18 f17.5 b18. A very bad cask day... *59.1%*

⁕ **Cadenhead's Authentic Collection Mannochmore Aged 17 Years** bourbon hogshead, dist 96, bott Jul 14 **(91)** n23 lemon and lime in equal measure; the barley positively sparkles; **t23.5** the nose points to clean, intense, salivating barley and that's what you get: in droves; **f22** a little allspice cuts down the gristy sugars; a little tang from the wearying oak; **b22.5** yet another lovely, high quality cask from Cadenhead. *52.5%. 174 bottles. WB15/255*

⁛ **Gordan & MacPhail Connoisseurs Choice Mannochmore 1994 (95.5) n24** quietly enormous. The oak puffs out its chest to offer marzipan lined with a little orange filling – most cake like! But the barley counters with a juicy grassiness which makes you purr, as this is both clean yet complex; **t24** if you locate a more spotless exhibition of intense yet clean and sugary barley this year, give me a call...; the lilting poise of the oils beggars belief; **f23.5** the oaks return to add spice and coconut macaroon. Naturally, golden syrup accompanies it; **b24** full of vitality, charm and class. Quite irresistible. 46%.

Old Malt Cask Mannochmore Aged 13 Years refill hogshead, cask no. 9230, dist Apr 99, bott Oct 12 **(91.5) n22.5** a dreamy aroma: just the right degree of icing sugar to put a gloss to the sultana, vanilla, barley and tannin; **t23** how crisp and juicy is that?! The barley crackles on the palate and melts into the comfortable vanilla; **f23** just the degree of spice required, as well as the most distant apple and barley; **b23** class at its most simple. Beautiful stuff! 50%. sc. Douglas Laing & Co. 182 bottles.

Provenance Mannochmore Over 14 Years bourbon barrel, cask no. 9766, dist Spring 1999, bott Spring 2013 **(89) n22 t23 f21.5 b22.5.** Thumbs up for a thumping barley monster. 46%. nc ncf sc.

Scotch Malt Whisky Society Cask 64.42 Aged 22 Years refill barrel, dist 14 Feb 90 **(96) n24** tasting this on a Sunday (yes, I really do taste seven days a week...!), which is rather fitting as this has all the hallmarks of a gorgeous, creamy Victoria sponge, though rather than powdered sugar being sprinkled on top, there appears to be grist; **t25** faultless: the weight is exactly where a mix of beautifully intense, yet gristilly-sweetened barley should be, plus butterscotch oak. The oils are again, like the nose, on the creamy side and the mid ground also hosts diced pistachio and almonds; **f23** a late tinge of ulmo honey does the required as the oak dries to a chalky conclusion; **b24** finding Mannochmores of this vintage is becoming one of my favourite aspects of my work. Another truly memorable, sensational dram. 55.6%. nc ncf sc. 198 bottles.

MILLBURN
Highlands (Northern), 1807–1985. Diageo. Demolished.

Millburn 1969 Rare Malt db **(77) n19 t21 f18 b19.** Some lovely bourbon-honey touches but sadly over the hill and declining fast. Nothing like as interesting or entertaining as the massage parlour that was firebombed a few yards from my office twenty minutes ago. Or as smoky... 51.3%

MILTONDUFF
Speyside, 1824. Chivas Brothers. Working.

Miltonduff Aged 15 Years bott code L00/123 db **(86) n23 t22 f20 b21.** Some casks beyond their years have crept in and unsettled this one. But some real big salty moments to savour, too. 46%

⁛ **Cadenhead's Single Malt Miltonduff-Glenlivet Aged 20 Years** dist 1994, bott Jun 2014 **(82) n21 t22 f19 b20.** An "Allied Distillers" trait cask with more residual bitterness than is good for it. An untidy dram that hits the ground limping... 50.4%. 246 bottles. London exclusive. WB15/272

Cadenhead Miltonduff 22 years Old claret, dist 90, bott 12 **(96) n23** manuka honey points to the age, as does the delicate clove and primrose. Gloriously floral; t24.5 here we go...we are entering superstar malt land. The delivery carries no shortage of oak. But there is so much honey and treacle to hand, it makes no kind of negative impact at all. The mid ground is a sea of rich barley with a slow mocha growth of Ghana chocolate and Sumatra coffee; **f24** classic ulmo honey fade...with magnificent spices guaranteeing maximum balance and complexity; **b24.5** a great distillery...being truly great... 56.8%. sc. 252 bottles.

⁛ **Cadenhead's Small Batch Miltonduff-Glenlivet Aged 24 Years** bourbon hogheads, dist 90, bott 14 **(95) n23.5** Ok, this must be Miltonduff in Franklin County, Kentucky. Every part of this nose screams bourbon from the honeycomb to the liquorice. Wonderful...; **t24** maybe a fleeting trace of malt just after the big sugar delivery. But blink and you'll miss it because the spices are there in number, gentle yet determined and accentuating those muscovado honey and treacle notes; **f23.5** well, ya'll all be enjoying this elegant sweetened tannin finish. The malt has thrown in the white flag and scarpered leaving all those toasty sugar notes to be on their lonesome; **b24** probably a first fill bourbon at play as there is more 'ye-harr' to this than 'och-eye'. Bit of a Kentucky belle. 55.3%. 474 bottles. WB15/256

⁛ **Gordan & MacPhail Rare Vintage Miltonduff 1984 (85) n21.5 t21.5 f21 b21.** Overcooked on the oak, alas. Even the spikey nose is a bourbon, sniffed blind. Has a few moments of brilliance when the barley shines and the spices bite. But would have done a way better job in a blend than as a singleton. 43%.

⫶⫶⫶ **Hepburn's Choice Miltonduff Aged 7 Years** sherry butt, dist 07, bott 14 **(75) n18 t20 f18 b19.** More duff than Milton for the nose, finish and balance. Paradise has certainly been lost. *46%. nc ncf sc. 805 bottles.*

⫶⫶⫶ **Kingsbury Silver Miltonduff 18 Year Old** cask no. 2796, dist 1995 **(89.5) n22** some overcooked oak but the lemon-drizzled barley is divine; **t23** impeccably salivating and clean; **f22** toasty with a butterscotch topping; **b22.5** a distillery in its usual effortless sumptuous mood. *46%. nc ncf sc. 166 bottles.*

Liquid Sun Miltonduff 1980 ex-bourbon hogshead, dist 80, bott 12 **(85) n22 t21 f21 b21.** Attractive malt in need of a stairlift to hit the heights. The oak creeks from start to finish, but just enough honey and natural caramel filters through to blunt the sharper splinters. *41.9%*

⫶⫶⫶ **Old Malt Cask Miltonduff Aged 18 Years** refill barrel, cask no. 10120, dist Feb 95, bott Oct 13 **(91) n22** peat! What on earth, literally, is that doing there...? **t23** clean, gristy, citrus enhanced barley which fair pings about the palate and enjoys full salivations levels; **f23** smoked mocha; a bit of a Cornish cream tea finish....but with a dollop of smoke, too; the residual spices tingle; **b23** a fully fledged peated Miltonduff. With the parent distillery owning nothing on Islay, they did get their Speyside distilleries to produce a peaty whisky for bending purposes. Can't remember finding a Miltonduff of this type, however. As intriguing as it is delicious! *50%. nc ncf sc.228 bottles.*

⫶⫶⫶ **Old Particular Speyside Miltonduff 17 Years Old 2013** refill hogshead, cask no. 9904 dist Mar 1996 bott Aug **(81.5) n20 t21 f20.5 b20.** A staple of the all-conquering Ballantine's 17 has been housed in some under-performing oak thus allowing almost unfettered access to a youthfulness rarely seen in usually thicker, more cerebral malt than this. Lightweight and juicy, save some very late cocoa. *48.4%. nc ncf sc. 319 bottles. Douglas Laing & Co.*

Premier Barrel Miltonduff Aged 7 Years (86.5) n21 t22.5 f21.5 b21.5. A veritable fruit bomb which explodes on impact. Youthful and not dissimilar to sucking a fruit pastille. The dark ones in particular. *46%. nc ncf sc.*

Provenance Miltonduff Over 7 Years sherry butt, cask no. 9239, dist Autumn 05, bott Autumn 12 **(83.5) n19.5 t21.5 f22 b20.5.** Not a bad butt, in that there are no off notes. But here we have an example where the wine and barley are at an awkward stage of their lives. Plenty to enjoy, though, and no shortage of juicy grape. *46%. nc ncf sc. Douglas Laing & Co.*

Scotch Malt Whisky Society Cask 72.25 Aged 29 Years refill hogshead, dist 15 dec 83 **(94) n23.5** what a bag of tricks: fabulously earthy and with a teasing fruit and veg mix, with crushed watercress and under-ripe greengages and cape gooseberries at the vanguard; **t24** sumptuous, multi-layered and faceted from the very first rumblings on the taste buds. Again, the spices, like on the nose, go into overdrive, yet are never for a moment aggressive – they sit happily with the oily, syrupy mix which keeps the lid on the big oak; **f22.5** much drier with the emphasis now on the cocoa and, much later on, gorgeous and unmistakable Panama high roast coffee; **b24** another of the great undiscovered distilleries of Scotland showing exactly why it should be not just better known but actually revered. This rare bottling from the SMWS for this distillery was more than worth waiting for. *499%. nc ncf sc. 174 bottles.*

⫶⫶⫶ **Scotch Malt Whisky Society Cask 72.38 Aged 28 Years** refill hogshead, dist 27 Nov 84 **(94) n23.5** a little bit of glue has got into the attractive vanilla and barley scene; elsewhere some bourbon notes play around with the lavender honey; **t23** sumptuous delivery with the accent always in the salivating barley...even after all these years...!! **f24** elegant, complex finale with the barley proferring a clean crispness, rounded by delicate maple syrup and a vanilla/butterscotch finale; **b23.5** the kind of bottling which leaves you in no doubt why this malt is sought after for being at the heart of the very finest bended scotch. *50.1%. nc ncf sc.*

⫶⫶⫶ **Scotch Malt Whisky Society Cask 72.39** refill hogshead, dist 03 Nov 81 **(95) n23.5** myriad barley notes range from pristine and untouched to those engulfed in rich oaky depth; **t24** lush yet lively the barley doesn't just explode on the palate but brings with it a host of vanilla tones which reverberate around the palate with delightful abandon; **f23.5** tangy, but only from the barley pulsing in a big tannin afterglow **b24** like Noel Cowerd in The Italian Job a whisky which positively glows in its age and veneration. *51.1%. nc ncf sc. 185 bottles.*

⫶⫶⫶ **Scotch Malt Whisky Society Cask 72.40 Aged 31 Years** refill hogshead, dist 03 Nov 81 **(90) n21.5** massive oak but a Horlicks maltiness attracts; **t23.5** enormous delivery with thick oils combining with extraordinary barley and beefsteak tannin; some kumquats not just fill the middle ground but positively give it the kiss of life; **f22** a memorable and enthralling essay in spiced tannin and vanilla; **b23** delightful whisky but one slightly in danger of being over engrossed in its own oaky dominance. The saving grace is a sublime citrus tones which steers an orangey path to greatness. *50.7%. nc ncf sc. 239 bottles.*

⫶⫶⫶ **Scotch Malt Whisky Society Cask 72.41 Aged 9 Years** 1st fill white wine hogshead, dist 23 Sep 04 **(86) n21.5 t22 f21 b21.5.** Now this is the thing about single cask youngish malts: to get the best job out of a whisky of this age you need a squadron of casks, not just the lone flyer. In total a competent, attractively spiced and lively cove. But perhaps lacking in depth, weight and overall complexity. *59.8%. nc ncf sc. 199 bottles.*

⁙ **Signatory Vintage Un-chillfiltered Collection Miltonduff 1995 Aged 18 Years** bourbon barrels, cask no. 4112+4113+4114, dist 23 Feb 95, bott 18 Mar 13 **(89) n22** those who have travelled out to enjoy the World Cup in Brazil, though presumably very few will be Scots, might happen across a local coconut-based biscuit with an almost identical aroma; **t23** magnificent early barley, helped along by butterscotch and ulmo honey; red liquorice - then warms...; **f22** a light spice perks up the finish by numbers; **b22** very good blending fodder unleashed upon a lucky public. *46%. nc ncf. 870 bottles. WB15/031*

⁙ **That Boutique-y Whisky Miltonduff** batch 1 **(86) n21 t22 f21.5 b21.5.** Funny how, as generously malty as this dram is, if I get a speck of botanical where it shouldn't, my nose and taste buds focus on that to the cost of all else. A bit like the tongue on a chipped tooth. *51.4%. 122 bottles. WB15/226*

⁙ **The Whisky Cask Miltonduff Aged 21 Years** first fill sherry butt, dist 1992, bott 2013 **(76.5) n19 t22.5 f17 b18.** A shame: no shortage of honey and fruit from this great distillery. But the S word rears its ugly head just enough to spoil the party. Those immune will find this an outstanding dram. *56.7%. nc ncf.*

MORTLACH
Speyside, 1824. Diageo. Working.

Mortlach Aged 16 Years db **(87) n20 t23 f22 b22.** Once it gets past the bold if very mildly sulphured nose, the rest of the journey is superb. Earlier Mortlachs in this range had a slightly unclean feel to them and the nose here doesn't inspire confidence. But from arrival on the palate onwards, it's sure-footed, fruity and even refreshing... and always delicious. *43%*

⁙ **Mortlach 18 Year Old** db **(75) n19 t19 f18 b19.** When I first tasted Mortlach, probably over 30 years ago now, it really wasn't even close to this. Something went very wrong in the late '80s, I can tell you...*43.4%. Diageo.*

⁙ **Mortlach 25 Year Old** db **(91.5) n23** just love the lemon grass alongside the liquorice and hickory; **t23.5** thick and palate-encompassing. The sugars are pretty toasty with a light mocha element in play; **f22.5** crisp finale with a return of the citrus, sitting confidently with the late spice; **b22.5** much more like it. The sugars may be pretty full on, but there is enough depth and complexity for a narrative to be told. Very much a better Mortlach on so many levels. *43.4%. Diageo.*

Mortlach 32 Years Old dist 1971 db **(88) n22 t22 f22 b22.** Big and with attitude... *50.1%*

⁙ **Mortlach Rare Old** db **(79) n20 t21 f19 b19.** Not rare enough... *43.4%. Diageo.*

⁙ **Mortlach Special Strength** db **(79.5) n20 t21.5 f19 b19.** Does whisky come any more cloyingly sweet than Mortlach...? Not in my experience.... *49%. Diageo.*

⁙ **Cadenhead's Sherry Cask Mortlach Aged 25 Years** sherrywood, dist 88, bott July 14 **(68) n16 t19 f16 b17.** Huge grape and the 'S' word in equal measure battle it out. But there is only one loser. *56.8%. 576 bottles. WB15/269*

Chieftain's Mortlach Aged 22 Years sherry butt, cask no. 5159, dist Aug 90, bott Feb 13 **(92) n23** virtually Guyanese pot still rum in its almost impenetrable density and big molassed sweetness. We see also have the enormity of a super-rich sherry, spattered, burned raisin-infested Melton Hunt cake complete with over-ripe figs, the most lush dates in syrup imaginable and plums to contend with; not entirely clean, but good enough...; **t24** not sure if you are supposed to drink or eat this: just keep chewing until your jaw aches and a wonderful intermingling of melted sugars, French toast and a blend of maple syrup and mollasses; **f22** just a little bitter but the toasty oak is now poking through; **b23** funny how a type of whisky I used to thoroughly dislike as OTT, I now truly enjoy. Because this shows a form of sherry butt matured once more common in Scotland, but now lost under the onslaught of sherry. Here there are only traces of an off note. It is still OTT....but, oh, thank you for that...!!! *50%. nc ncf sc.*

Chieftain's Mortlach Aged 22 Years sherry butt, cask no. 5160, dist Aug 90, bott Mar 13 **(95.5) n23.5** just like the 50% abv version, but cleaner and distinctly nuttier; **t24** again, very similar in style to the 50% abv bottling. Here, however, we have a more compact nutty element which fits beautifully with the mocha middle, while the sugars have sharper teeth; **f24** again, so similar to the other bottling but cleaner on the finish, with the molasses and raisins taking far longer to drift away; **b24** there are going to be some very lucky Americans: they will be tasting an almost extinct Scotch whisky style... *58.1%. For USA nc ncf sc.*

⁙ **Gordan & MacPhail Rare Vintage Mortlach 1981 (90) n23.5** various exotic fruit with Chinese gooseberry at the vanguard; **t23** slightly papery start with the broken down oak getting in first. But then we return to fruity normal service and the barley juices up to a serious degree as the sugars begin to dissolve; diluted honeycomb moves into the mid-ground; **f21.5** slightly bitty, with the oak becoming papery and a little too dry; **b22** really don't even begin to understand why this is at 43%abv rather than at least 46 and preferably at cask strength. Reducing to this strength after so many years has broken down the vital oils holding the aged elements together and subtracted from what might have been a great experience. *43%.*

⫶⫶ **Gordan & MacPhail Rare Vintage Mortlach 1984 (89) n23** slightly dirty, almost coal dust-like, or the aromas from a burning anthracite. But it is sweetened by a syrup including outrageously over-ripe figs and plums; **t22** silky delivery and then an avalanche of some the most eye-watering sugars and fruits you can imagine. Curiously, never hits liqueur mode and the malt positively sparkles; **f22** long, back to those over-ripe fruit and now some serious spice; **b22** ridiculously sweet and soupy in typical Mortlach fashion. But, against the odd, this one works rather well! *43%.*

⫶⫶ **Hepburn's Choice Mortlach Aged 9 Years** refill hogshead, dist 04, bott 14 **(88) n22** young, expansive malt; slight bubble gum; lemon zest; **t23** fresh-faced but builds into barley sugar intensity; juicy grist throughout; **f21** citrus and flaky vanilla; **b22** a fascinating and juicy insight into a malt which has changed style in the last decade. *46%. nc ncf sc. 380 bottles.*

⫶⫶ **The Maltman Mortlach Aged 14 Years** bourbon cask, cask no. 10998, dist Oct 98, bott Apr 13 **(84.5) n22 t23 f19.5 b20.** Ticks all the boxes for those looking for a big malty Speysider. But suffers from a lack of complexity and guile, unspiced heat and a thin finale. *46%. sc ncf nc. 376 bottles. WB15/228*

Malts Of Scotland Mortlach 1994 sherry hogshead, cask no. MoS 12059, dist Aug 94, bott Nov 12 **(76.5) n18.5 t20 f19 b19.** There's a rare beast these days: a sherry butt which doesn't work...and not an atom of sulphur in sight. *55.2%. nc ncf sc. 96 bottles.*

⫶⫶ **Old Malt Cask Mortlach Aged 13 Years** refill hogshead, cask no. 10200, bott Dec 13 **(94) n23.5** delicate peat reek on the breeze; **t23** juicy, lively barley dashes haphazardly around the palate; **f23.5** more vanilla and citrus now...and a return to a lightly spiced smoke; some late praline adds to the puzzlement; **b24** effervescent, fresh and works the palate continually. A surprise treat with massive entertainment value.. *50%. nc ncf sc. 319 bottles.*

⫶⫶ **Old Malt Cask Mortlach Aged 18 Years** refill hogshead, dist Jun 95, bott Jun 13 **(86) n22 t22.5 f20.5 b21.** Juicy, honest, majorly malty and very simple Speysider. *50%. nc ncf sc. 279 bottles.*

Old Malt Cask Mortlach Aged 21 Years refill hogshead, cask no. 9432, dist Sep 91, bott Feb 13 **(86) n21 t22 f21.5 b21.5.** Typically chunky and glutinous, full of thick brown sugars, liquorice and spice. *50%. sc. Douglas Laing & Co. 259 bottles.*

Provenance Mortlach Over 10 Years refill hogshead, cask no. 9520, dist Winter 2002, bott Winter 2013 **(79.5) n20 t20.5 f19 b20.** No shortage of barley sugar but complexity is at a premium. *46%. nc ncf sc. Douglas Laing & Co.*

Scotch Malt Whisky Society Cask 76.100 Aged 19 Years refill sherry butt, dist 1 Jun 93 **(68.5) n16.5 t18 f17 b17.5.** I have no notes in front of me today. Just the sample. I assume this is from a sherry butt. Because guess what's spoiling the party... *58.1%. nc ncf sc.*

Scotch Malt Whisky Society Cask 76.101 Aged 24 Years refill hogshead, dist 12 Apr 88 **(86) n21.5 t22 f21 b21.5.** Puckering, eye-wateringly tart fare which enjoys some good moments, especially when the concentrated molasses drive, with deranged viciousness, into the oak concentrate. *55.7%. nc ncf sc. 194 bottles.*

⫶⫶ **Scotch Malt Whisky Society Cask 76.112 Aged 27 Years** refill hogshead, dist 24 Apr 86 **(85) n21.5 t22 f20.5 b21.** Astonishingly dense and sweet....almost sickly so: similar to an over the top Bakewell tart. Without the late spices it would flounder. Almost like walking through a sugar plantation without a map...*58.2%. nc ncf sc. 284 bottles.*

⫶⫶ **Scotch Malt Whisky Society Cask 76.115 Aged 18 Years** refill butt, dist 19 Jul 95 **(85.5) n21 t22 f21 b21.5.** Massively sweet and about as subtle as being biffed over the head with a stick of sugar cane. *56.7%. nc ncf sc. 535 bottles.*

⫶⫶ **Scotch Malt Whisky Society Cask 76.116 Aged 26 Years** refill hogshead, dist 07 Apr 87 **(84.5) n20.5 t22 f21 b21.** A slightly sub-standard cask ensures a tartness to the experience As is the wont with Mortlach the sugars are way out of control, though the intensity if the malt and some late spices tries to save the day... *48.4%. nc ncf sc. 239 bottles.*

⫶⫶ **Signatory Vintage Single Malt Mortlach Aged 13 Years** hogsheads, cask no. 7900+7901, dist 28 May 99, bott 05 Mar 13 **(90) n22.5** gentle, gristy malt; a little maple syrup adds weight; **t23** the juiciest barley delivery imaginable. Limited complexity back up so the squeeze of citrus is welcome; **f22.5** keeps right on that juicy malt road; **b22.5** absolutely middle of the road Speysider. But it does it all rather well. One of the most lightweight Mortachs I have encountered for a very long while. *43%. nc. 851 bottles. WB15/011*

∴ **Signatory Vintage Un-chillfiltered Collection Mortlach Aged 17 Years** cask no. 4092+4093, bott Apr 13 **(86)** **n21.5 t22 f21.5 b22.** Mortlach in its usual syrupy mode. Just a little too cloying for its own good, though it does have a few juicy moments. *46%. nc ncf. WB15/032*

∴ **Wemyss Malts 1998 Mortlach Single Speyside "Pastille Bouquet"** dist 1998 bott 2013 **(88.5)** **n22** light sawdust sprinkled on vanilla; **t22.5** massive barley thrust with a slow unravelling of sugars; **f22** thickens as the grist intensifies; **b22.5** well constructed, unmistakable Speysider. Some serious weight towards the finish, too. *46%. sc. 325 bottles.*

Wemyss 1998 Mortlach Single Speyside "Tarte aux Pommes" hogshead, dist 98, bott 13 **(84.5)** **n21 t22.5 f20 b21.** Some appeasing chocolate mint arrives down the line. But by and large about as subtle as being hit around the head with a malt shovel....full of malt. A tart for dirty malt Johnnies more like. *46%. sc. 337 bottles.*

The Whisky Cask Mortlach Aged 17 Years hogshead, dist 95, bott 12 **(84.5)** **n22 t21 f21.5 b20.** It is as though your taste buds are being crushed under the weight of a runaway tank made entirely of sugar. In some way, more of a liqueur than a malt. *56.4%. nc ncf sc.*

MOSSTOWIE
Speyside, 1964–1981. Chivas Brothers. Closed.

Rare Old Mosstowie 1979 (84.5) **n21.5 t21 f21 b21.** Edging inextricably well beyond its sell by date. But there is a lovely walnut cream cake (topped off with brown sugar and spices) to this which warms the cockles. Bless... *43%. Gordon & MacPhail.*

NORTH PORT
Highlands (Eastern), 1820–1983. Diageo. Demolished.

Brechin 1977 db **(78)** **n19 t21 f18 b20.** Fire and brimstone was never an unknown quantity with the whisky from this doomed distillery. Some soothing oils are poured on this troubled – and sometimes attractively honeyed – water of life. *54.2%*

OBAN
Highlands (Western), 1794. Diageo. Working.

Oban 14 Years Old db **(79)** **n19 t22 f18 b20.** Absolutely all over the place. The cask selection sits very uncomfortably with the malt. I look forward to the resumption of normality to this great but ill-served distillery. *43%*

Oban Aged 15 Years The Distiller's Edition db finished in Montilla Fino casks, dist 1992, bott 2007 **(90)** **n22.5 t23 f22.5 b22.** This isn't all about complexity and layering. It's about style and effect. And it pulls it off brilliantly. *43%*

Oban Aged 15 Years The Distiller's Edition db finished in Montilla Fino casks, dist 1993, bott 2008 **(91.5)** **n22** nutty, tight, a little musty; **t24** much more assured: the dryness of the grape sports beautifully against the obviously more outgoing and sweeter barley: excellent balance between the two; **f22.5** perhaps the Fino wins, as it dries and embraces the oak quite happily; **b23** delicate and sophisticated whisky. *43%*

PITTYVAICH
Speyside, 1975–1993. Diageo. Demolished.

Pittyvaich Aged 12 Years db **(64)** **n16 t18 f15 b15.** It was hard to imagine this whisky getting worse. But somehow it has achieved it. From fire-water to cloying undrinkability. What amazes me is not that this is such bad whisky: we have long known that Pittyvaich can be as grim as it gets. It's the fact they bother bottling it and inflicting it on the public. Vat this with malt from Fettercairn and neighbouring Dufftown and you'll have the perfect dram for masochists. Or those who have entirely lost the will to live. Jesus... *43%. Flora and Fauna.*

PORT ELLEN
Islay, 1825–1983. Diageo. Closed.

Port Ellen 1979 db **(93)** **n22** mousy and retiring; a degree of oak fade and fruit on the delicate smoke **t23** non-committal delivery but bursts into stride with a series of sublime, peat-licorice waves and a few rounds of spices; **f22** a surprising gathering of oils rounds up the last traces of sweet barley and ensures an improbably long – and refined – finish; **b24** takes so long to get out of the traps, you wonder if anything is going to happen. But when it does, my word...it's glorious! *57.5%*

Port Ellen 29 Year Old 8th Release, dist 1978, bott 2008 db **(90.5)** **n23 t22.5 f22.5 b22.5.** The glory and charisma is still there to cast you under its spell, but some high notes are missed, the timing not quite what it was; yet still we stand and applaud because we recognise it exactly for what it is: beauty and genius still, but fading beauty; receding genius. Something which only those of us of a certain vintage, can remember as being that unique, almost naked, celebration of Islay malt whisky it once so beautifully and so gloriously was. *55.3%*

Port Ellen 31 Years Old Special Release refill American & European oak, dist 1978, bott 2010 db **(88.5) n22 t23 f22 b21.5** shows some serious cracks now, though that can't be helped; this whisky was never made for this type of age. Still some moments to close the eyes to and simply cherish, however; 54.6%. nc ncf. Diageo. Fewer than 3000 bottles.

Port Ellen 32 Years Old Special Release 2011 db **(88.5) n22.5 t22.5 f22 b22**. Really feeling its age, though there are many superb passages of play. 53.9%. nc ncf.

Port Ellen 32 Years Old Special Release 2012 Refill American and European oak casks, dist 1979, bott 2012 db **(88.5) n23** presumably the use of sherry casks has dampened the fire. The smoke is hard to spot, other than a slightly acrid burned toast bite; **t23.5** comes together gorgeously on delivery with a sharp, salty whip to the arrival of both the big malt and feathered grape; pretty mouthwatering and now the smoke really does grab hold...with silk gloves; **f20** furry and most un-Port Ellenly off key; **b22** some mesmerising moments. Not sure what the finish is all about, though. 52.5 %. nc ncf. Diageo.

Chieftain's Port Ellen Aged 30 Years hogshead, cask no. 1518, dist May 82, bott Sep 12 **(96.5) n24** exceptional nose: a few strands of citrus and banana delicately sweeten the dry, sooty peat and oak-rich hickory; **t25** the delivery amazes: even after 30 years of tasting the rare fruits of this distillery, I was still taken aback by the beautifully fragile nature of the fruit which is first to show. Both tangerine and ordinary oranges show immediately, then a brief cherry note before the honey arrives in both ulmo and heather form. And the peat. At first politely allows the fruit and sugars to lead the way, then slowly takes command first as a base phenol note, then by taking off in smoke form across the palate; **f23** thins and tires quite quickly, though the oak is good enough never to detract; **b24.5** when you consider first the quality of this malt and then that with each new bottling of Port Ellen the remaining reserves of its whisky shrinks like a puddle in the noonday sun, one is not sure whether to laugh or cry. But like all great whiskies of near perfect balance, it is a bitter-sweet experience. 50.1%. nc ncf sc. Ian Macleod Distillers. 308 bottles.

⋅≎⋅ **Directors' Cut Port Ellen Aged 35 Years** refill hogshead, cask no. 10355, dist May 79, bott Jun 14 **(94) n22.5** the trademark gristy nose has given way over the decades to a minty one, though here infused with lemon tea and hickory where once the smoke might have been; **t23** sharp delivery full of fired-up, juicy malt. The oak really does hound and pound but the teamwork between first, the apologetic muscovado then the more confident smoke ensures there's plenty of life and complexity in the slightly salty old dog; **f24** only on about the third tasting does the minty mocha begin to make enough noise to drown out the tannin. Ends up as a genuinely classy fade where balance, somehow, has been clawed back; **b24.5** a great distillery whose few remaining casks are now, sadly, coming to the end of their life. But this one just hangs in their enough to show that greatness and genius is still to be found in abundance. You'll find it only on about the third or fourth taste, as this is a dram the palate must acclimatise to. Ensure your tastebuds are in top notch nick before you take this one on... and no smoking, water or strong food. It is a dram which deserves and demands you to be at the top of your game. 51.1%. nc ncf sc. 162 bottles.

Gordon and MacPhail rare Old Port Ellen 1979 (96) n24 what can you say? Looking at the negative points...a touch of oak-faulted bitterness. But it is a side issue, far, far outweighed by the peat which appears to begin as a single, lonely atom but slowly multiplies hand in hand with the kumquats. Even now, after all these years, the trademark gristy barley can still be detected....truly astonishing...; **t23.5** just as on the nose, the smoke begins with little more than a shadow but with a touch of buttercream and muscovado sugar, climbs in weight and depth; immediate spices underline the oak and age; **f23** the nose suggested a bitter landing; it was a false call. This is in keeping with all before, concentrating mainly on a soft fondant (Walnut whip-type) with a light degree of cocoa and what little weight there is created by that sophisticated, understated smoke and balanced by that thin thread of ulmo honey; **b24.5** a fascinating dram. This is what happens when peat diminishes over the decades. It begins on both nose and palate like a small tattoo, a mark you can see but is indistinguishable. Then, with each sniff and mouthful, that tattoo is added to and is formed into a dragon. But not one breathing fire... just soft, elegant smoke. And a dragon with green, mossy, earthy eyes with flecksof golden honey which draws you in further, deeper...An erotic, beautiful whisky which displays charm and depth in equal measures. And, here's the rub: does so without seemingly knowing. 46%

Old & Rare Port Ellen Aged 30 Years refill hogshead, dist 82, bott 12 **(95) n24.5** almost perfect: the signature delicate PE gristiness, the peat in butterfly mode, revealing just the odd sprig of mint as a nod towards age; **t23.5** can a whisky be both delicate and intense? This seems to manage it with the muscovado sugars having as much to say as the phenols; **f23** playful smoky butterscotch....little oil, so dry but always elegant; **b24** what can you say? How much longer will we be able to enjoy masterpieces like these? 51.8%. nc ncf sc. 154 bottles.

Old & Rare Port Ellen Aged 32 Years refill butt, dist 79, bott 12 **(93.5) n24** lots of tannins but the spice and smoke balance with ease. Lovely sweet-dry interplay; **t23** sweet barley shows first then, like distant smoke signals the phenols send their message; **f23** lots of vanilla and the sugars bite deep as the tannins return; **b23.5** the oak is doing its best to spoil the party but the sheer mastery of the peat foils that plan. Superb. *54.8%. nc ncf sc. 145 bottles.*

PULTENEY
Highlands (Northern), 1826. Inver House Distillers. Working.

Old Pulteney Aged 12 Years db **(90.5) n22** pungent, busy and full of zesty zap. Enough salt to get your blood pressure up; **t23** beautifully clean barley, again showing little shortage of saltiness, but thriving in its zesty environment; **f22.5** the vanillas and cocoa carry out an excellent drying operation. The sea-breeze saltiness continues to hang on the taste buds...; **b23** a cleaner, zestier more joyous composition than the old 43%, though that has less to do with strength than overall construction. A dramatic whisky which, with further care, could get even closer to the truth of this distillery. *40%*

Old Pulteney Aged 12 Years db **(85) n22 t23 f19 b21.** There are few malts whose finish dies as spectacularly as this. The nose and delivery are spot on with a real buzz and panache. The delivery in particular just bowls you over with its sharp barley integrity: real pulse-racing stuff! Then... toffee...!!! Grrrr!!! If it is caramel causing this, then it can be easily remedied. And in the process we'd have a malt absolutely basking in the low 90s...! *43%*

Old Pulteney Aged 15 Years db **(91) n21** pretty harsh and thin at first but some defter barley notes can be detected; **t24** an attention-grabbing, eye-wateringly sharp delivery with the barley in roasty mood and biting immediately with a salty incision; the barley-sugar effect is mesmerising and the clarity astonishing for its age; **f23** long, with those barley sugars working overtime; a slight salty edge there but the oak behaves impeccably; **b23** only on about the fourth or fifth mouthful do you start getting the picture here: enormously complex with a genuine coastal edge to this. The complexity is awesome. *54.9%*

Old Pulteney Aged 17 Years db **(95) n22** tight but does all that is possible to reveal its salty, fruity complexity with pears and lemons to the fore; **t25** one of the softest, most beautifully crafted deliveries in the whisky world. Absolutely faultless as it picks the most fabulous course among the honeyed vanilla and barley which is so delicate words simply cannot do justice; **f24** near perfect balance between the vanillas and delicate honeys; **b24** the nose confirms that some of the casks at work here are not A1. Even so, the whisky performs to the kind of levels some distillers could only dream of. *46%*

Old Pulteney Aged 21 Years db **(97.5) n25** if you had the formula to perfectly transform salt, citrus, the most delicate smoke imaginable, sharp barley, more gristy barley, light vanilla, toasty vanilla, roasted hazelnut, thinned manuka honey, lavender honey, arbutus blossom and cherry blossom, light hickory, liquorice, and the softest demerara sugar into the aroma of a whisky, you still wouldn't quite be able to recreate this perfection...; **t24** the sugars arrive: first gristy and malt-laden, then Demerara. This is followed by a salty, nerve-tingling journey of barley at varying intensity and then a slow but magnificently complete delivery of spice...; **f24** those spices continue to buzz, the vanillas dovetail with the malt and the fruit displaying a puckering, lively intensity. Ridiculously long fade for a malt so seemingly light, the salts and spices kiss the taste buds goodnight...; **b24.5** by far and away one of the great whiskies of 2012, absolutely exploding from the glass with vitality, charisma and class. One of Scotland's great undiscovered distilleries about to become discovered, I think... and rightly so! *46%*

Old Pulteney Aged 30 Years db **(93.5) n23** magnificent spectrum of exotic fruits leave no doubts about its age: plenty of mango, especially, while the odd tinned peach appears to have been tossed into the dainty salad; **t24** melts-in-the-mouth, aided by the strength. But that means the richer flavours grab only half a hold and soon slip away; the mid-ground has the feel of a chocolate fruit liqueur, except the liqueur might have more attitude; **f23** medium length but we are back into exotic fruits territory: an unusual development for a malt. Maybe it is a mixture of the subtle salt and delicate, semi-drowned orange blossom honey which is raising the fruity profile; **b23.5** I know there is not too much of this north Scottish nectar, but they would have been better to have brought this out at 46%...if they were able, that is. *40.1%*

Old Pulteney 30 Years Old db **(92) n23.5** fabulous mix of Jaffa cake and bourbon, seasoned by a pinch of salt; **t23.5** an early, unexpected, wave of light smoke and silkier oak gives immediate depth. But stunning, ultra-juicy citrus and barley ensures this doesn't get all big and brooding; **f22** thinner and oakier with a playful oak-spice tingle; plenty of vanilla controls the drier aspects; **b23** I had to laugh when I tasted this: indeed, it had me scrambling for a copy of the 2009 Bible to check for sure what I had written. And there it was: after bemoaning the over oaking I conjectured, "As Pulteney has the fascinating tendency to radically shift style over not too long a period, I can't wait for the next instalment." And barely a year on, here it is. Pretty far removed from last year's offering and an absolute peach of a dram that laughs in the face of its 30 years... *45%*

⠿ **Old Pulteney 35 Year Old** db **(89)** n23 the dry ginger doesn't do anything to make this feel younger than its 35 years; a meeting place of various forms of tannin, some sweeter than others. But it is those delicate muscovado sugars alongside the manuka honey, alongside the ginger, which are key; t21.5 much harder to keep it together on the palate:th attractive mouth feel is undermined by the drier oa elements, some of which are very dry; f22.5 some lovely mint chocolate does offer great charm; b22 a malt on the perimeter of its comfort zone. But there are enough gold nuggets included to make this work. Just. 46%. Inverhouse Distilleries.

Old Pulteney Aged 40 Years db **(95)** n23.5 gosh! That's pretty aged stuff with the exotic fruit hanging on by a fingernail. Some major bourbon notes now evident – and lip-smacking; t23.5 massive delivery, again with tannins coming from every angle. But a mix of liquorice, dates, burnt raisin and honey cope well while spices tingle; f24 settles for a long essay of happy old bourbon-style led whisky; b24 this malt still flies as close to the sun as possible. But some extra fruit, honey and spice now grasps the tannins by the throat to ensure a whisky of enormous magnitude and complexity 51.3%

⠿ **Old Pulteney 1990 Vintage** American oak ex bourbon & Spanish oak ex sherry butts. db **(85)** n21 t23 f21 b20. As you know, anything which mentions sherry butts gets me nervous – and for good reason. Even with a World Great distillery like Pulteney. Oddly enough, this bottling is, as near a dammit, free of sulphur. Yee-hah! The bad news, though, is that it is also untroubled by complexity as well. It reminded me of some heavily sherried peaty jobs...and then I learned that that ex Islay casks were involved. That may or may not be it. But have to say, beyond the first big, salivating, lightly spiced moments on delivery you wait for the story to unfurl...and it all turns out to be dull rumours. 46%. Inverhouse Distilleries.

⠿ **Old Pulteney Clipper American** ex bourbon and ex sherry casks db **(93)** n23 slightly less salty than you might expect, but enough to tease the more complex tones from the delicate oak and raise the spice profile; citrus-soaked grist give the malt a big platform; t24 fabulous delivery: so light yet salivating and packed with many layers of sugar, including acacia and ulmo honey; f22.5 extra weight as the oak kicks in, mainly of a toffee-fudge style; and as the salt returns, a little manuka honey now, of course...; b23.5 looks like honey, tastes like honey. Most un-Pulteney like. The most delicate and disarming bottling from this distillery I can remember. 46%. ncf nc. 2013-14 commemorative bottling. WB15/276

⠿ **Old Pulteney Duncansby Head Lighthouse** bourbon and sherry casks db **(90.5)** n23 Manor House cake; blood oranges; t23 stunning weight: the malt is weighed down by a toffee sponge pudding with the odd toasted raisin thrown in here and there; f22 toasted fudge and raisin; b22.5 beginning to wonder if Pulteney is into making whisky or cakes. And malt straight from the oven. 46% WB15/329

⠿ **Old Pulteney Isabella Fourtuna WK499 2nd Release** db **(89)** n23 coconut cake, anyone? Or moist Battenburg? t23 a brilliant delivery of Madeira cake with an extra dollop of malty icing sugar; f21.5 bread pudding – but someone forgot to add the sugar; b22 this sailing lark...a piece of cake! 46%. Travel retail exclusive. WB15/324

⠿ **Old Pulteney Noss Head Lighthouse** bourbon casks db **(84)** n22.5 t22 f19 b20.5. If Noss Head was as light as this dram, it'd be gone half way through its first half decent storm. An apparent slight overuse of third and less sturdy second fill casks means the finale bitters out considerably. A shame, as the nose and delivery is about as fine a display of citrus maltiness as you'll find. 46%. Travel retail exclusive. WB15/327

⠿ **Old Pulteney Pentland Skerries Lighthouse** db **(85)** n21 t22 f20.5 b21.5. A chewy dram with an emphasis on the fruit. Sound, evens enjoys the odd chocolate-toffee moment. But a little sulphur, apparent on the nose, creeps in to take the gloss off. 46%. WB15/323

Old Pulteney WK209 db **(71)** n68.5 t18 f16.5 b17. Could well be liked by the Germans. 46%

Old Pulteney WK217 db **(88.5)** n21 t22 f23 b22.5. The WK series is named after the old fishing vessels which used to be based in the town's harbour. I suspect old WK217 rarely had a day at sea in waters as calm as this softy of a malt. 46%

⠿ **Gordan & Macphail Rare Vintage Old Pulteney 1982** (87.5) n21 t22.5 f22 b22. So oak-soaked there is even a degree of creosote on the nose. The oak involvement makes for a tart experience to the very death, but I adore the battle put up by the barley and banana to keep this alive and kicking. 43%.

ROSEBANK

Lowlands, 1840–1993. Diageo. Closed. (But if there is a God will surely one day re-open)
Rosebank Aged 12 Years db **(95)** n24 t24 f23 b24. Infinately better than the last bottling, this is quite legendary stuff, even better than the old 8-y-o version, though probably a point or two down regarding complexity. The kind of whisky that brings a tear to the eye... for many a reason... 43%. Flora and Fauna.

Rosebank 21 Years Old Special Release db (94) n24 fabulous interplay between apple and berry fruits, though it's the pear juice which acts as the sweetening agent; a nose to spend a good 20 minutes over; t23.5 at once fizzing and busy while soft and caressing; natural caramels combine with coconut oil to offer the weightier sheen; f23 dries but never bitters; healthy vanilla all the way b23.5 can any Lowland be compared to a fully blossomed Rosebank? This is whisky to both savour and worship for this is nectar in a Rose... 53.8%. nc ncf.

Rosebank 22 Years Old Rare Malts 2004 db (85) n22 t23 f19 b21. One or two Rosebank moments of joyous complexity but, hand on heart, this is simply too old. 61.1%

Rosebank 25 Years Old db (96) n24.5 t23.5 f24 b24. I had to sit back, take a deep breath and get my head around this. It was like Highland Park but with a huge injection of sweetened chocolate on the finale and weight – and even smoke – from a Rosebank I had never quite seen before. And believe me, as this distillery's greatest champion, I've tasted a few hundred, possibly thousands, of casks of this stuff over the last 25 years. Is this the greatest of all time? I am beginning to wonder. Is it the most extraordinary since the single malt revolution took off? Certainly. Do I endorse it? My god, yes! 61.4%

⁖ **Gordan & Macphail Rare Old Rosebank 1989** (85.5) n21 t22 f21 b21.5. The once dazzling greatness of this malt has been sacrificed on the alter of time. Enjoyable whisky, but significantly limited by the degree of involvement from the vanilla and natural caramels which dominate completely. Eye-watering at times, but the juicy moments are a plus. 46%.

⁖ **Scotch Malt Whisky Society Cask 25.65 Aged 22 Years** refill barrel, dist 01 Jul 91 (89.5) n23.5 some sharp rhubarb crumble with exotic fruit on a side plate.. The custard is extra thick...; t23 the oak lets rip from the first moment, like a cry of despair and lament for a lost soul.... The layerings of muscovado sugars sooth and comfort, though; f21 bitters out; b22 the odd spell of magic, but a malt now on the way down. 50%. nc ncf sc. 220 bottles.

⁖ **Scotch Malt Whisky Society Cask 25.66 Aged 23 Years** refill hogshead, dist 14 Nov 90 (96) n23.5 red liquorice abounds - perhaps a little nearer bourbon these days... t24 a stunner: literally! You are stopped in your tracks as the beaty of this malt first grips you, then seduces. The early spices help. Ripping into the tastebuds but immediately undoing any damage with intimate caresses of muscovado and Demerara sugars f24 now enters in mocha territory, with a toasty sugar fade which last seemingly forever...; b24.5 you'll be hard-pressed to find a spicier, sweeter single malt than this all year. Wat a way for this distillery to bid its farewells. A world classic. 57.9%. nc ncf sc. 206 bottles.

ROYAL BRACKLA
Speyside, 1812. John Dewar & Sons. Working.

Royal Brackla Aged 10 Years db (73) n18 t20 f17 b18. A distinct lowering of the colours since I last tasted this. What on earth is going on? 40%

⁖ **Adelphi Selection Royal Brackla 16 Years Old** dist 97, bott 14 (94) n24 you feel like applauding at the near perfect marriage between grassy-fresh barley, freshly squeezed lime and the slice of kumquat which tops it off. A delicate spice prickle underlines just how fragile this fabulous nose is; t23 as mouth-watering as the nose announces. Barley holds court and a succession of light sugars see off the rising oak; f23.5 a little ulmo honey seeps into the proceedings, ensuring a controlled gentle sweetness to match the vanilla; b23.5 uncommonly superb! 56.8%. ncf. 268 bottles. WB15/315

Gordon and MacPhail Connoisseurs Choice Royal Brackla 1997 (84.5) n20.5 t22 f21 b21. An intriguing battle between good, sprightly spirit and so-so oak which offers little and detracts some. 46%. ncf.

⁖ **Gordan & MacPhail Connoisseurs Choice Royal Brackla 1998** (87) n22 t22 f21.5 b21.5. A slightly more adventurous bottling than their '97 version thanks to the three-way dogfight between abrasive oak, the attractively honeyed barley and the coppery sheen at the death. 46%.

ROYAL LOCHNAGAR
Highlands (Eastern), 1826. Diageo. Working.

Royal Lochnagar Aged 12 Years db (84) n21 t22 f20 b21. More care has been taken with this than some other bottlings from this wonderful distillery. But I still can't understand why it never quite manages to get out of third gear...or is the caramel on the finish the giveaway...? 40%

Royal Lochnagar 1994 The Manager's Choice db (89.5) n23 t23.5 f21.5 b21.5. Much more intense and heavyweight than the norm. Also a bit of toffee on the finish brings down the marks slightly. Great stuff, even so. 59.3%

Royal Lochnagar Selected Reserve db (89) n23 t23 f21 b22. Quite brilliant sherry influence. The spices are a treat. 43%

⋰⋱ **Cadenhead's Royal Lochnagar Rum Cask Aged 17 Years** dist 1996, bott Oct 13 **(89.5)** **n23** ethereal and translucent, you know what you are nosing is good but it is hard to pin the tail on the donkey: crisp muscovado sugars, for certain, spices pinging around like a bat after moths – for sure. But it is earthy, too, with a slight vegetable note, like the smell of the stem of a freshly cut tulip. It is all these things...and sometimes none...; **t23.5** no doubts about the delivery: a cascade of molten sugary grist with even bigger spices, at tis with the nip of a midge, directly behind; acacia honey and maple syrup sooths the pain; **f21** tails off through a little cask bitterness; **b22**. little Royal Lochnager like you have never quite seen her before... *57.4%. 606 bottles. WB15/076*

Old Malt Cask Royal Lochnagar Aged 15 Years refill butt, cask no. 9818, dist Jun 97, bott May 13 **(86)** **n22 t21 f21.5 b21.5**. Pretty even but when the flavours spike, especially with the lemon attached to the heather honey, Queen Victoria – the distillery's greatest advocate – would have been amused. *50%. nc ncf sc. Hunter Laing & Co Ltd. 329 bottles.*

⋰⋱ **Old Malt Cask Royal Lochnagar Aged 16 Years** cask no. 10588, dist Aug 97, bott Jun 14 **(94)** **n24** now there's a nose...! Wonderful shifting pattern of interwoven marzipan, ulmo honey, barley sugar, lemon zest, Blackjack candy and diced macadamia nuts; **t23.5** the delivery is superbly executed and evolves with the same complexity as the nose, though here the oak add a controlling dryness and spice; the weight, oils and slight copper tang is sublime; **f23** some barley, zesty citrus and milky mocha; **b23.5** it is some 30 years since I spotted a ring ouzel half way up a hill very near the Lochnagar distillery, the only time I have ever seen one. Unlike that elusive bird, there is nothing black and white about this. Absolutely champions its small stills by offering here a malt of regal depth and virtuosity. *50%. nc ncf sc.*

ST. MAGDALENE
Lowlands, 1798–1983. Diageo. Demolished.
Linlithgow 30 Years Old dist 1973 db **(70)** **n18 t18 f16 b18**. A brave but ultimately futile effort from a malt that is way past its sell-by date. *59.6%*

SCAPA
Highlands (Island–Orkney), 1885. Chivas Brothers. Working.
Scapa 12 Years Old db **(88)** **n23 t22 f21 b22**. Always a joy. *40%*
Scapa 14 Years Old db **(88)** **n22 t22.5 f21.5 b22**. Enormous variation from bottling to bottling. In Canada I have tasted one that I gave 94 to: but don't have notes or sample here. This one is a bit of dis-service due to the over-the-top caramel added which appears to douse the usual honeyed balance. Usually, this is one of the truly great malts of the Chivas empire and a classic islander. *40%*
Scapa 16 Years Old db **(81)** **n21 t20.5 f19.5 b20**. For it to be so tamed and toothless is a crime against a truly great whisky which, handled correctly, would be easily among the finest the world has to offer. *40%*
Scapa 'the' Orcadian 16 Years Old db **(87.5)** **n22 t22 f21.5 b22**. A thin wisp of honey is key to the weight and balance of this malt. *40%. For the Swiss market.*
Gordon and MacPhail Distillery Label Scapa 2001 (94.5) **n23** the fresh, slightly fruity aromas of a high class bakery on first opening its doors; the barley is so, so young...but equally unblemished; **t24** the delivery is near perfect: a light oil helps spread the juiciest of salty barley notes, young and chock-a-bloc with gristy sugars; a very light, cooling mintiness to the vanilla; **f23.5** more of the same, the oils ensuring a long fade and high quality oak offering weight and keeping things on track; **b24** showing Scapa exactly as it should be. One of the easiest drinking malts currently in the market place, and quite probably the most moreish. Genius. And dangerous... *43%*

SPEYBURN
Speyside, 1897. Inver House Distillers. Working.
Speyburn 10 Year Old db **(82)** **n20 t21 f20.5 b20.5**. A tight, sharp dram with slightly more emphasis on the citric. A bit of toffee on the finale. *40%*
Speyside 12 Years Old db **(85)** **n22 t22 f20.5 b21.5** Copious honey and malt on delivery. Simplistic, effective but a tad bitter on finish. *40%*
Speyburn Aged 25 Years db **(92)** **n22 t24 f23 b23**. Either they have re-bottled very quickly or I got the diagnosis dreadfully wrong first time round. Previously I wasn't overly impressed; now I'm taken aback by its beauty. Some change. *46%*
Speyburn Bradan Orach db **(76.5)** **n19 t20 f19.5 b18**. Fresh, young, but struggles to find a balance. *40%*
Gordon and MacPhail Connoisseurs Choice Speyburn 1989 (82.5) **n21 t21.5 f20 b20**. A kind of Speyside version of malt gruel. *46%. ncf.*

Provenance Speyburn Over 8 Years sherry butt, cask no. 9435, dist Autumn 04, bott Winter 13 **(88) n21.5 t22.5 f22 b22.** Muscles up on the barley. Simple, but effective. *46%. nc, ncf, sc. Douglas Laing & Co.*

THE SPEYSIDE DISTILLERY
Speyside, 1990. Speyside Distillers. Working.

The Speyside 10 Years Old db **(81) n19 t21 f20 b21.** Plenty of sharp oranges around; the malt is towering and the bite is deep. A weighty Speysider with no shortage of mouth prickle. *40%*

The Speyside Aged 12 Years db **(81) n19 t22 f19.5 b20.5.** Unusual to find feints to this degree after twelve years. Some short-lived honey...but it's hard work! *40%*

⋰⋱ **Spey 12 Years Old** limited edition, finished in new oak casks db **(85.5) n21.5 t23 f19.5 b21.5.** One of the hardest whiskies I have had to define this year: it is a curious mixture of niggling faults and charming positives which come together to create a truly unique scotch. The crescendo is reached early after the delivery with an amalgamation of acacia honey, barley sugar and butter notes interlocking with something bordering classicism. However, the nose and finish, despite the chalky oak, reveals that something was lacking in the original distillate or, to be more precise, was rather more than it should have been. Still, some hard work has obviously gone into maximising the strengths of a distillery that had hitherto failed to raise the pulse and impresses for that alone. *40%. nc. 8,000 bottles.*

The Speyside Aged 15 Years db **(75) n19 t20 f18 b18.** A case of quantity of flavours over quality. *40%*

⋰⋱ **Spey 18 Years Old** ltd edition, fresh sherry casks db **(82.5) n19 t23.5 f19 b21.** What a shame this malt has been brushed with sulphur. Apparent on nose and finish, it still can't diminish from the joy of the juicy grape on delivery and the excellent weight as the liquorice and treacle add their gentle treasures and pleasures. So close to a true classic. *46%. nc.*

⋰⋱ **Spey Chairman's Choice** db **(77) n19 t21 f18 b19.** Their Chairman's Choice, maybe. But not mine... *40%*

⋰⋱ **Spey Royal Choice** db **(87) n21 t23 f21 b22.** "I'll have the slightly feinty one, Fortescue." "Of course, Your Highness. Would that be the slightly feinty one which has a surprising softness on the palate, a bit like a moist date and walnut cake? But with a touch too much oil on the finish?" "That's the blighter! No ice, Fortescue!" "Perish the thought, Sir." Or water, Forters. One must drink according to the Murray Method, don't you know!" "Very wise, Sir." *46%*

⋰⋱ **Spey Tenné** finished in Tawny Port casks db **(90) n22.5** the usual Spey character, but made short work of by a crisp, boiled sweet fruitiness; **t23** softer than marshmallow, which is odd as it has a kind of mallow quality about it: creamy, sugary and melt-in-the-mouth; the cherry-grape fruits are omnipresent; **f22** long, rings out every last drop of sweetness before entering a lightly oiled, bitter phase; **b22.5** upon pouring, the handsome pink blush tells you one of three things: i) someone has swiped the whisky and filled the bottle with Matheus Rose instead; ii) I have just located where I put the pink paraffin or iii) this whisky has been matured in brand spanking new port casks. Far from a technical paragon of virtue so far as distilling is concerned. But those Tawny Port casks have brought something rather magical to the table. And glass. *46%. nc. 18,000 bottles.*

Cú Dhub db **(88) n22 t22.5 f21.5 b22.** Not exactly a thoroughbred and you won't find it winning any prizes at Cruft's. But a malt which has improved beyond recognition in recent years and now even boasts a degree of enjoyable complexity. And you know something else...not a single sulphur note in sight... *40%*

Drumguish db **(87) n18 t22 f19 b19.** Historically, not one of my favourite drams. But I have to say that this has improved by a considerable degree. Still feinty, and the delivery is not promising. But once it settles, there is a very acceptable degree of honey-led complexity before the feints bite back. *40%*

⋰⋱ **Cadenhead's Small Batch Speyside-Glenlivet Aged 18 Years** 1 sherry butt & 1 hogshead, dist 95, bott 14 **(95.5) n23.5** I am as bowled over as I am nonplussed: thick, juicy dates, a pinch on the nose of anthracite gas, succulent grape and Turkish delight in a high cocoa chocolate casing: this is Speyside distillery...???? **t24.5** the workings of a faultless sherry butt, entirely untroubled by brainless ruination by sulphur, allows the distillery's usual generous width of cut a free hand to add a light nougat and toasted honeycomb; **f23.5** back to the kind of dates plus Cadbury fruit and nut chocolate which makes you check your waistline after each mouthful; **b24** unquestionably the best bottle of Speyside distillery whisky I have ever encountered. Having a sublime sherry butt at work has done it no harm at all. Whatever you do, find this whisky and add to your collection. Gawd knows when you might find another like it! *62.8%. 738 bottles. WB15/262*

⠿ **Old Particular Highland The Speyside Distillery 17 Years Old** sherry butt, cask no. 10097, dist Nov 96, bott Jan 14 **(91.5) n22** an apple surprise; **t23** massively rich with the pomanian theme being stepped up and even chivvied along as the spices arrive with apple pie panache; **f23** superb oils help meld the fruits with the Demerara sugars. The spices hold firm...; **b23** so rare to find Speyside in this kind of nick. It fair warms the cockles... 48.4%. nc ncf sc. 413 bottles. Douglas Laing & Co.

Provenance Speyside Over 13 Years refill hogshead, cask no. 9215, dist Winter 99, bott Autumn 12 **(75) n18 t19 f18 b18.** Very big injection of malt and quite brusque sugar; and even a touch of Weetabix on the fade. But, quite patently, poorly distilled spirit. 46%. nc ncf sc.

Riegger's Selection The Speyside 1999 bourbon cask no. 190, bott 2013 **(86) n22 t21.5 f21 b21.5.** A very acceptable rendition of the distillery from this period. A few clumsy notes still can't entirely disrupt the integrity of the intense barley sugar. 45%. sc.

⠿ **The Single Malts of Scotland Speyside 18 Years Old** sherry butt, cask no. 0018, dist 02 May 95, bott 29 Oct 13 **(94) n24** sweet, intense sultana; a little ginger and pepper, too. Fabulous; **t23** thick, glutinous malt enriched by that outrageously fresh and bright sherry; **f23.5** long: sherry trifle and chocolate cup cake happily united. Oh, with an extra dollop of treacle; **b23.5** a sherry butt that hasn't been within ten miles of a sulphur candle...and just look at the spectacular results! Beautiful... 52.3%. 600 bottles. WB15/316

The Warehouse Collection The Speyside Aged 16 Years bourbon barrel, cask no. 928, dist 28 Aug 96, bott 30 Apr 13 **(92.5) n23** lemon curd spread generously over barley sugar. Lashings of tannins; **t23.5** a fizzy start with light muscovado sugars accompany the unusually clean and concentrated barley for The Speyside; the oaks are firm and a little earthy: ersatz coffee and hickory lead; **f23** latte coffee sweetened with barley grist; **b23** had to look twice at the label here. Rarely does this distillery come across with such easy charm. No great complexity. But everything it does is done with a swagger. 52.7%. nc ncf sc. 171 bottles.

SPRINGBANK
Campbeltown, 1828. J&A Mitchell & Co. Working.

Hazelburn Aged 8 Years bourbon cask, bott 2011 db **(94.5) n23** green apple represents the more dashing aspect of the very young barley; **t24** fabulously solid barley; intense and complete. The youth shimmers on the palate, the malt mixing contentedly with pleasing early butterscotch; elsewhere there is a real richness seemingly imparted from the stills themselves; **f23.5** confirmation of an excellent cask in use here as the lightly spiced vanilla enjoys the odd strand of honey; more light metals breaking into the lengthy barley; **b24** a very curious coppery sheen adds extra lustre and does no harm to a very well made spirit filled into top grade oak. For an eight year old malt, something extra special. 46%

Hazelburn Aged 8 Years 3rd Edition (triple distilled) bott 2007 db **(89) n22 t22.5 f22 b22.5.** Somewhat effete by comparison to last year's big malty number. Here there is a shade more accent on fruit. Very light, indeed. 46%

Longrow Aged 10 Years db **(78) n19 t20 f19 b20.** This has completely bemused me: bereft not only of the usual to-die-for smoke, its warts are exposed badly, as this is way too young. Sweet and malty, perhaps, and technically better than the marks I'm giving it – but this is Longrow, dammit! I am astonished. 46%

Longrow Aged 10 Years 100 Proof db **(86) n20 t23 f22 b21.** Still bizarrely smokeless – well, maybe a flicker of smoke as you may find the involuntary twitching of a leg of a dying fly – but the mouthfeel is much better here and although a bit too oily and dense for complexity to get going, a genuinely decent ride heading towards Hazelburn-esque barley intensity. Love it, because this oozes class. But where's the ruddy peat...?! 57%

⠿ **Longrow Red 11 Year Old** Port cask db **(85.5) n21.5 t21 f22 b21.** I know some people will take a bottle of this to bed with them...to cuddle rather than drink. But, for me, this is just too astringent with a coal gas fierceness to both nose and delivery which doesn't quite sit with the fruit. Passages to enjoy, especially at the end when some kind of compromise is reached. But otherwise just too in your face. 51.8%. 9,000 bottles.

⠿ **Longrow Red Aged 11 Years** Australian Shiraz Cask Peated six years in refill bourbon hogsheads & five years in fresh Shiraz casks db **(91) n23** an airless blockbuster: all done by smoke and shiraz; **t23** thick, almost impenetrable delivery: blackcurrant jam in a smoke chamber; **f22.5** tangy, still dense though fair dinkum honey seeps out at the end; **b22.5** strewth! No surprise that a combination of peat and shiraz has biffed out the complexity. But enough goodies to go round. Just. 53.7%. ncf. 9000 bottles. WB15/252

Hazelburn Aged 12 Years fresh sherrywood, bott 2012 db **(85.5) n22 t21 f21.5 b21.** At times nutty. At others, oily. And is that the vaguest hint of phenol I spot bouncing around at one stage...? But overall a malt which does not, at this juncture in its life, seem entirely at ease with either itself or the cask. Some lovely moments of lucidity but for the most part it's an interrupted work in progress. Still, this is the 666th new whisky I have tasted for the 2013 Bible, so it was likely to have a little bit of devil in it... 46%

‑❖‑ **Hazelburn Rundlets & Kilderkins Aged 10 Years** dist Nov 03, bott Jan 14 db **(95.5)** n24 firm and oak-enriched there is a fascinating halfway house between light coconut cake, moistened in syrup, and walnut bread. Further sweetness is provided by a gentle orange blossom honey; t24 the delivery is just as intense as the nose gives hope for. Except the honey is more up front than expected and arrives abreast of the spiced tannin; wonderfully dry in part, with a soft cocoa powder edge, but golden syrup returns delicately and deliciously; f23.5 the tannins try to get a charge going but those fabulous sugars stand fast; b24 Rundlets. Kilderkins. There's a blast from the past: a name I had seen now and then from my vast library of 19th and early 20th century literature on whisky and distilling, and only a handful of times in warehouses in nearly 40 years of distillery hopping. But here we have a malt matured in these tiny casks. And though the barrels may be small, the whisky they are responsible for really is quite huge. The kind of multi-faceted whisky I could so easily drink all day every day, if you know what I mean... 50.1%. 12,000 bottles. WB15/101

‑❖‑ **Hazelburn Rundlets & Kilderkins Aged 11 Years** dist Nov 01, bott Jan 13 db **(95.5)** n23.5 dry and farm-yardy there is a lovely interplay between peat fire and byre; the sub plot is salty and citrusy but the whole ensemble is quite harsh and austere; t24.5 hells bells! Where did that come from? Much juicier and sweeter on delivery with early spice and then more extended oak and smoke: at times borderline perfection; oils out simplifies towards the middle; f23.5 dries again and moves towards a slightly citrusy edge; cocoa, and spicy peat account for the fade; b24 a fascinating comparison with the Hazelburn sister bottling. Doubtless the Peat Freaks will have this down as a clear winner. But, to me, the smoke in giving so much also subtracts some of the more intricate moments found on the non-peated version, even allowing for a ten second purple patch which is as good as whisky can get. A battle which goes the full 15 rounds, but the Hazelburn, just a little lighter on its feet and with a devastating jab, wins narrowly on points. But, if you have the opportunity, grab both bottlings and compare. It will be one of the best whisky moments you'll have this year. 51.7%. nc ncf. 9,000 bottles. WB15/118

Longrow 14 Years Old refill bourbon and sherry casks db **(89)** n24 t23.5 f19 b22.5. Again, a sherry butt proves the Achilles heel. But until then, a charmer. 46%

Longrow Aged 18 Years (94.5) n25 my work for the day has stopped: I will not nose a better whisky today, this week, this month, this year... The playfulness, the disarmingly relaxed state of the smoke, even in the face of some pretty major tannins, is something you might regret never experiencing. The heather honey offers a slight Highland Park outlook to this, except no HP has ever been so deep, so meaningful, so absolutely perfect to nose...; t23 the sugars dissolve on impact, some seemingly extracted from manuka honey, others from molasses. The smoke swirls around the palate, and tunnels down onto the taste buds now and again, creating a light but busy spice back drop; f23 now ulmo honey stretches the sweetness as the drier elements of the oak begin to bite a tad, mixing with the peat to u the spices further...; b23.5 if you gently peat a blend of ulmo, manuka and heather honey you might end up with something as breathtakingly stunning as this. But you probably won't... 46%. WB15/103 ⊙ ⊙

Longrow CV bott 2012 db **(91)** n24 nippy spices infuse with the dry date; the smoke is delicate with an almost dry tobacco edge; the harder peat teams up with the gentle Demerara; t24.5 soft and silky, again the fruit notes intermingle and add a banana and mango juiciness to the oils; the smoke again keeps a low profile, happy to accompany the more telling sugars; f19.5 dries quickly as the furry bitterness from a sherry butt take hold; b23 for a few moments this is heading onto the shortlist of potential Whisky Bible award winners, but a familiar furry rumble – a bit like the distant thunder currently heard from my tasting room – means vital points are lost. Even so, the nose and delivery are something very special, indeed. 46%

Longrow Gaja Barola Wood Expression Aged 7 Years db **(91.5)** n23.5 t22.5 f23 b22.5. Taking this on is like running around an asylum claiming you're Napoleon. But I have to admit; it's fun! An accidental classic that is unlikely to be repeated...even if they tried..!! 55.8%

‑❖‑ **Longrow Limited Edition 18 Years Old** db **(82)** n21 t22 f19 b20. Spicy. Smoky. But a long way from its usual brilliant self. A cask, presumably a sherry one, has done it no favours at all. 46%. WB15/104

Springbank Society Aged 9 Years Rum Wood bott Mar 07 db **(93.5)** n23 t23.5 f23 b24. A mere pup by Springbank standards. For once its comes through as a real winner in these tender years, doubtless aided by the mercurial charms of the rum and even an unexpected touch of smoke to make for a most complex and entertaining dram. 60.2%

⁖ **Springbank Aged 9 Years** dist Feb 04, bott Oct 13 db **(94) n24** a smoky Springbank? Looks like it, though the message is confused by the spiced fruit. Somewhere in the tumult Cape Gooseberry puree calls. But still surprisingly sooty; **t24.5** good grief...!!! The taste buds are impaled by the enormity of the delivery. Again we have a sooty start, but while your head is getting around that you are overwhelmed by dynamite-laced spice and a kind of concentrated apple and pear juice-barley sugar thingy. Pretty much unique and by the fifth mouthful, delicious...; **f22** bitters slightly but the rumble of spice is very noisy; **b23.5** can you have too much of a good thing? When you combine an undercooked malt like Springbank at half the age it is usually comfortable at being with the intense impact of these very fresh Barolo casks, then the onrush of flavours is almost too much. Certainly harmony takes a bit of a ding. Still, if you are looking for something different and quite memorable... and after a while confusion makes way for awe...! 54.7%. 11,000 bottles. WB15/074

Springbank Aged 10 Years db **(89.5) n22 t23 f22 b22.5**. Although the inherent youthfulness of the 10-y-o has not changed, the depth of body around it has. Keeps the taste buds on full alert. 46%

Springbank Aged 10 Years (100 Proof) db **(86) n21.5 t22 f21 b21.5**. Trying to map a Springbank demands all the skills required of a young 18th century British naval officer attempting to record the exact form and shape of a newly discovered land just after his sextant had fallen into the sea. There is no exact point on which you can fix...and so it is here. A shifting dram that never quite tastes the same twice, but one constant, sadly, is the bitterness towards the finale. Elsewhere, it's one hell of a journey...! 57%

Springbank 11 Years Old Madeira Wood Expression db **(88) n23 t22.5 f21.5 b21**. Madeira perhaps as you've never seen it before: don't go thinking Glenmorangie or Penderyn with this one. As big as the fruit is, the smoke outguns it. 55.8%

⁖ **Springbank Aged 12 Years Cask Strength** db **(89) n21.5** tangy fruit; **t24** superb delivery: rather thick and almost overwhelming, but enough mocha escapes to lighten the load; the sugar and treacle mix takes some believing; **f22** Cadbury's dairy fruit...with an injection of spice and tannin; just a little too bitter for greatness; **b22** does well to untangle itself at critical times to make for an OTT but wonderfully intense superheavyweight whisky. 50.3%. WB15/073

⁖ **Springbank Aged 12 Years Cask Strength** db **(87) n21.5 t23.5 f21 b21**. Springbank is such an enormous whisky that for decades the 12 has usually struggled to cope with successfully making sense of all it has to offer. This is borderline going under its own weight, with so much fruit, oil and toffee-tannin to disperse on the palate. Best just to sit back and role with the delivery which offers more different types of sugar than you probably knew existed. Have a white flag at the ready, though.... 52.3%. WB15/072

Springbank Aged 15 Years db **(88.5) n22.5 t22 f22 b22**. Last time I had one of these, sulphur spoiled the party. Not this time. But the combination of oil and caramel does detract from the complexity a little. 46%

⁖ **Springbank Aged 16 Years** 10 years in refill bourbon, 6 years in fresh Madeira, cask no. 07/178-3, dist Jun 97, bott Oct 13 db **(93) n23** liquorice laced with honeycomb; **t23** an eye-watering spice attack is a dramatic contra to the gushing barley sugar; **f23.5** settles into a more sober and satisfying treacle tart finish; **b23.5** a superb malt which, early on, does little quietly, but is at its best when in sedate contemplation. 56%. sc ncf nc. WB15/266

Springbank Aged 18 Years db **(90.5) n23** busy in the wonderful Springbank way; delicate greengage and date; nippy; **t23** yummy, mouthwatering barley and green banana. Fresh with excellent light acacia honey; **f21.5** fabulous oak layering, including chocolate. A little off-key furriness from a sherry butt late on; **b23** just one so-so butt away from bliss... 46%

⁖ **Springbank Aged 21 Years** db **(90) n22** vague, un-Springbank-like smoke adds more weight than the oak; a few berries doing the rounds; **t23** silky delivery where the barley momentarily dominates the gristy malt and accompanying maple syrup goes into overdrive; the spices are compact and confident; **f22.5** long, a surprising trace of tapering and very distant smoke, all enlivened by ripe gooseberries; the spice carries on growling; **b22.5** a few years ago I was at Springbank when they were bottling a very dark, old-fashioned style 21-year-old. I asked if I could take a 10cl sample with me for inclusion in the Bible; they said they would send it on, though I tasted a glass there and then just for enjoyment's sake. They never did send it, which was a shame. For had they, they most probably would have carried off World Whisky of the Year. This, though very good, is not quite in the same class. But just to mark how special this brand has always been to me, I have made this the 500th new single malt scotch and 700th new whisky in all of the 2015 Whisky Bible. 46%. WB15/096

⁖ **Cadenhead's Authentic Collection Hazelburn Aged 12 Years** bourbon hogshead, dist 02, bott July 14 **(89) n23** a poke in the eye and up the nose with a tannin stick: toasted mallows and, though from a bourbon cask, a hefty degree of fruitcake, too; **t22** tigerish oak claws at you while piranha-esque spice nips and nibbles; only juicy malt concentrate bathes the wounds; **f22** in some ways, too oaky. But allow the butterscotch and molasses to drift across you and the minty mocha finale makes sense; **b22** chunky, dense whisky with a dazzling number of oaky layers for a mere 12-year-old... 54.1%. 294 bottles. WB15/271

Duthies Springbank 11 Years Old (80) n20.5 t21 f19 b20.5. Malty, fruity and sugary. But never finds the semblance of a rhythm, bitters out and seems about as harmonious and happy as the Australian batting line up. 46%. sc. WM Cadenhead Ltd. 528 bottles.

⁘ **Kingsbury Gold Springbank 20 Year Old** cask no. 381, dist 93 **(92) n22.5** the oak creaks like the door to a mansion but some red liquorice and redcurrants join the vaguest hint of smoke to ensure balance; **t23.5** a stunning delivery with a slow dissolving of heather honey alongside the spice: quite outstanding body; **f22.5** a slow, gently spiced, butterscotch and (natural!) caramel fade; **b23.5** tip your cap to understated, gentle genius. 53.6%. nc ncf sc.

⁘ **The Maltman Springbank Aged 16 Years** first fill port, cask no. 212 **(88) n23.5** a curious Fisherman's Friend phenol appears to marry beautifully with very fresh fruit: big but never awkward; **t23.5** bizarre delivery with the fruit, that strange smokiness, thick molasses and intense butterscotch all melding together harmoniously...somehow; **f19.5** tangy, metallic: not right; **b21.5** a very curious malt: it's as if some iron has got into the system somehow, though the whisky is not black enough. A faulty whisky which is rather delicious. 51.2%

⁘ **The Maltman Springbank Aged 17 Years** sherry cask **(88.5) n23** cream sherry overlay; **t23.5** massive head-on clash between a bold oloroso style and Malteasers on speed; **f20** a slight bitter furiness creeps in from the oak – remarkable it can make itself heard above the din of the grape and malt; **b22.5** a profound malt to get sherry lovers smacking their lips. 50.1%

Master of Malt Springbank Aged 19 Years hogshead, cask no. 129, dist 7 May 93, bott 27 Nov 12 **(96) n24** beautiful whole-hearted aroma: fills the glass with a thick, digestive biscuit concentrate with extra salt sprinkled in. A hint of kumquat helps lighten the load. Few malts are quite this intense yet intact; **t24.5** the delivery is near perfect: malt concentrate cascades onto the palate with a brown sugar-sweetened mocha hanging on to its coat tails; fabulous black liquorice and hickory middle, sweetened by butterscotch and an ulmo honey trace; **f23.5** long, with a slow degree of building oils which seems only to amplify the barley; spiced French toast drips with late sugars...; **b24** world class whisky. End of... 57.8%. sc. 221 bottles.

Master of Malt Springbank Aged 19 Years hogshead, cask no. 482, dist 26 Nov 93, bott 27 Nov 12 **(88.5) n22 t23 f21.5 b22.** Thoroughly enjoyable and packed with character. But very much the poor relation of the three Master of Malt bottlings. 55.2%. sc. 250 bottles.

Master Of Malt Springbank 30 Years Old Lost Bottlings Series dist 65, bott 95 **(77.5) n18 t22 f18.5 b19.** A real weirdo for a Springbank. Sign on nose and finish that we are in exhausted oak territory. Big sugars and even a hint of something smoky on palate saves the day...or part of it. 45.6%

Scotch Malt Whisky Society Cask 27.100 Aged 12 Years refill barrel, dist 31 Mar 00 **(86.5) n22 t22 f21 b21.5.** A beautifully constructed spirit plucked from the cask far too ahead of time. The oak makes an impression but it is an unclear one. The youthful nuttiness always charms, though. 52.4%. nc ncf sc. 176 bottles.

Scotch Malt Whisky Society Cask 27.102 Aged 12 Years 1st fill sherry hogshead, dist 31 Mar 00 **(85) n21 t22 f21 b21.** Another Springbank which lurches uncontrolled around the palate. The toasted fudge is fun and the quality of the cloth is fine. But it is all a little too anarchic and shapeless. 52%. nc ncf sc. 301 bottles.

⁘ **Scotch Malt Whisky Society Cask 27.105 Aged 13 Years** refill sherry hogshead, dist 31/03/2000 **(73.5) n19 t20.5 f16 b18.** Too young and cramped. And a butt which offers no help at all. 53.9%. Nc ncf sc. 288 bottles.

That Boutique-y Whisky Company Springbank batch 1 **(93) n23** serious big oak brinkmanship: this spirit has got wood; **t23** the delivery is deceptively silky and soft with the malt at almost barley wine intensity. But soon the oak is biting hard and deep adding a far more aggressive and old-bourbon bitterness; **f23.5** settles now for a much more contented bourbon-style fade with red liquorice and manuka honey trying to blunt the more jagged oaky edges; **b23.5** the taste buds are battered by oak notes which gang up like marauding thugs. Never less than delicious...but not for the squeamish. 54.6%. 252 bottles.

That Boutique-y Whisky Company Springbank batch 2 **(91) n22 t23 f23 b23.** A very soft Springbank body-wise, but still pulls no punches. 53.1%. 450 bottles.

STRATHISLA

Speyside, 1786. Chivas Brothers. Working.

Strathisla 12 Years Old db **(87.5) n22.5 t23.5 f20 b21.5.** Still a big, chewy dram which is about as heavy in body as you are likely to find anywhere in Speyside. Very enjoyable, though you know deep down that some fine tuning could take this guy easily into the 90s. 43%

⫶ **Strathisla 12 Years Old** db (85.5) n21.5 t22 f21 b21. A slight reduction in strength from the old bottling and a significant ramping up of toffee notes means this is a malt which will do little to exert your taste buds. Only a profusion of spice is able to cut through the monotonous style. Always sad to see such a lovely distillery so comprehensively gagged. *40%*.

Strathisla Distillery Edition 15 Years Old db (94) n23 flawlessly clean and enriched by that silky intensity of fruity malt unique to this distillery; t23 the malt is lush, sweet and every bit as intense as the nose; a touch of toffeespice does it no harm; f24 just so long and lingering, again with the malt being of extraordinary enormity: these is simply wave upon wave of pure delight; b24 what a belter! The distillery is beautiful enough to visit: to take away a bottle of this as well would just be too good to be true! *53.7%*

⫶ **Gordon & MacPhail Strathisla 1999** bott 2013 (83.5) n22 t21 f20 b20.5. Odd that a bottling which for many years you could showcase as a "that's the way to do it" malt has been off the boil for a while now. There is a charming honey-pollen element to the nose, but beyond that balance is at a premium as the cask types clash. *43%. WB15/109*

Gordon & MacPhail Distillery Label Strathisla 1965 (94.5) n23.5 punchy old oloroso: nutty and big roast raisin; a few dried dates thrown in; the spices are of the old kitchen larder variety; t23 a big jolting oakiness is immediately soothed by the united front of molasses and toasted raisin; f24 some light manuka honey bathed by ulmo honey. Then in comes the several years matured Melton Hunt cake; b24 needs to be left in the glass for a little while for it to open and reveal its secrets. Gorgeous. *43%*

Gordon and MacPhail Distillery Label Strathisla 1993 (83.5) n21.5 t22 f19 b21. Honey, oils and fruit combine for a juicy and lively opening but this is a malt which fails to build on its early promise. A bit like a film which starts brightly but within a few minutes you can predict exactly where it is going to go...especially with the fruit influence... *43%*.

Old Malt Cask Strathisla Aged 21 Years refill hogshead, cask no. 9519, dist Jun 91, bott Feb 13 (86.5) n21 t22 f22 b21.5. A typically silky Strathisla which, despite some early floral notes, tends to over rely on the big barley for effect. Impossible not to enjoy, though. *50%. sc. Douglas Laing & Co. 155 bottles.*

Scotch Malt Whisky Society Cask 58.14 Aged 23 Years refill barrel, dist 5 Jan 89 (85.5) n22.5 t22 f20 b21. A very curious Strathisla which deliciously blasts off all guns blazing down the malt and muscovado sugar road. But after a strangely sugary middle, tails off with surprising rapidity and is positively anorexic by the finish. *57.8%. nc ncf sc. 222 bottles.*

STRATHMILL

Speyside, 1891. Diageo. Working.

⫶ **Cadenhead's Authentic Collection Cask Strength Strathmill Aged 18 Years** bourbon hogshead, dist 1995, bott Feb 14 (87.5) n22 t23 f21 b21.5. Crusty barley offers good gristiness and ultra juiciness. Really lovely malt, as you'd expect from Strathmill, with excellent spice kick, too. But the oak tires slightly injects a late bitterness. Just revere the delivery, though! *54.4%. 282 bottles. WB15/080*

Duncan Taylor Dimensions Strathmill 21 Years cask no. 4248, dist Aug 90, bott Jun 12 (90) n22 t24 f22 b22. Oh, but for the briefest insertion of a sulphur candle 21 years ago – and I mean for a few seconds – we would have had a contender for Malt Whisky of the Year here... *54.4%. nc ncf sc. Duncan Taylor & Co. 280 bottles.*

⫶ **Gordon & MacPhail Connoisseurs Choice Strathmill 1999** bott 2013 (94.5) n23.5 slowly roasting yams, a splodge of custard and a quite a few half-hearted bourbon notes, especially the diluted molasses; t24 soft delivery, with the light, malty oils rolling over the palate on a cushion of light maple syrup; delicate shades of mandarin and Jammy Dodger biscuits; f23 superb oak means there is no bitterness, allowing the vanillas and sugars to continue the friendly glide towards the fade; b24 there is no substitute for good old-fashioned simple complexity...if you know what I mean...! *46%. nc ncf. WB15/147*

⫶ **Gordan & Macphail Connoisseurs Choice Strathmill 2000** (89) n22 grassy barley; t22.5 fresh, concentrated barley juice; gristy with a twist of citrus; f22 a simple play out of sugar barley and butterscotch; b22.5 un-taxing but the kind of clean, intense barley-rich malt any blender worth his salt would be licking his lips at...*46%*.

Master Of Malt Strathmill 21 Years Old cask no. 2534, bott 13 (89) n22.5 t22 f22.5 b22. A malt taken out of its usual comfort zone, age-wise. But gets through the oaky ordeal. *57.7%. sc.*

⫶ **Old Malt Cask Strathmill Aged 21 Years** refill hogshead, cask no. 10122, dist Dec 91, bott Oct 13 (91) n22 plenty of Kentucky at work here with the liquorice and hickory giving depth to the vanilla. The barley is not outdone, though...; t23 the oak yoke is discarded on delivery and the barley is at full blast; f23 just adore those gristy sugars which have somehow survived all these years; some lemon to the late vanilla; b23 simple, but so elegant with it! *50%. nc ncf sc. 294 bottles.*

∷ **Robert Graham Strathmill 22 Year Old Speyside Malt** hogshead, cask no. 3795, dist 09 Sep 91 bott Oct 2013 (82.5) n20 t22 f20 b20.5. Strathmill is a wilting flower of a malt which bruises easily. When kept for this number of years, the cask has to be spot on. The oak here makes too many of its flaws apparent to be a force for good. 46%. 232 bottles.

∷ **Single Cask Collection 23 Year Old Strathmill Sherry Butt** sherry butt, cask no. 2258, dist 07 May 90, bott 04 Jul 13 (96) n24.5 elegant dry sherry, entirely free from both sulphur or oloroso weightiness; beautiful nuttiness, the only sweetness maybe from some top notch Lubek marzipan; a real gem of a nose which takes me back to a previous distilling era in Scotland; t23.5 the delivery is both firm yet somehow rounded with the grape again nothing other than sophistication. The weight is in keeping with the dexterity of the malt, which somehow allows the juicier elements of the barley through while keeping them under control with a crisp fruitiness; spice begins to pulse, though in a typically understated style; f23.5 rounding off one of the casks of the year is a dull, throbbing spice meeting perfectly the covert sweetness and drying vanillas; b24.5 in the Spring of 1990, J&B blender Jim Milne and I nosed some sherry butts just prior to them being filled at Strathmill. They were clean and fresh, like this one. I wonder.... 51.3%. sc. 470 bottles.

∷ **That Boutique-y Whisky Strathmill** batch 1 (86.5) n21.5 t22.5 f21 b21.5. Not a Strathmill style I am particularly familiar with (and I'd thought I'd seen the lot!): beyond the intense barley, there is, on the nose especially, a drier, vegetable note. Not unpleasant. But just seems out of place. Still, deliciously juicy and malty in part. 48.2%. 167 bottles. WB15/206

The Warehouse Collection Strathmill Aged 22 Years bourbon hogshead, cask no. 5349, dist 1990, bott 2013 (91) n22.5 t23 f22.5 b23. A gorgeous cocoa g-spot for all to enjoy. Rrrrrrr....! 52.8%. nc ncf sc. 219 bottles.

∷ **The Whisky Agency Strathmill 1976** dist 1976 (95) n23.5 the oak throbs gently, offering a nutty – and sometimes coconutty – depth, lightened by seemingly being dipped into maple syrup. Elsewhere a little malt and vaguest of smoky notes stirs...; t24.5 a ridiculously sweet and caressing delivery with no effort to make any kind of oaky statement or claim. Again the coconut has a big say, still serenaded by delicate sugars; the spices are at the vanguard of the symphony and remain, though in lesser intensity, throughout; f23 the dryness which slowly assembles is in perfect keeping with the delicate sugars. But the ace is the light puff of smoke which offers just the right amount of lingering ballast; b24 this was the year my beloved Millwall, helped in no small part by my dear old friends Barry Kitchener and John Seasman, completed a run of 15 unbeaten games – and conceding only four goals in the process - to somehow claw promotion back to the second tier from the mid-table invisibility. Later that year we walloped Chelsea 3-0, with my dad standing proudly beside me as another great mate, Terry Brisley, sent the most lethal of all bullet headers past Peter Bonetti to complete the route. It was also the year when I played a game of cricket in which I could hardly see the ball bowled at me through a blizzard of ladybirds during a blistering heat wave that rendered England's green and pleasant land brown. And it was, above all, the year an unassuming Speyside distillery filled into cask a malt destined for a blend at four years old, most probably J&B, yet somehow – against every odd possible - lived on into antiquity with charming good grace. 47%.

TALISKER

Highlands (Island–Skye), 1832. Diageo. Working.

Talisker Aged 10 Years db (93) n23 Cumberland sausage and kipper side by side; t23 early wisps of smoke that develop into something a little spicier; lively barley that feels a little oak-dried but sweetens out wonderfully; f24 still not at full throttle with the signature ka-boom spice, but never less than enlivening. Some wonderful chocolate adds to the smoke; b23 the deadening caramel that had crept into recent bottlings of the 10-y-o has retreated, and although that extraordinary, that wholly unique finale has still to be re-found in its unblemished, explosive entirety, this is much, much closer to the mark and a quite stupendous malt to be enjoyed at any time. But at night especially. 45.8%

Talisker 12 Years Old Friends of the Classic Malts db (86) n22 t21.5 f21 b21.5. Decent, sweet, lightly smoked...but the explosion which made this distillery unique - the old kerpow! - appears kaput. 45.8%

Talisker Aged 14 Years The Distillers Edition Jerez Amoroso cask, dist 1993, bott 2007 db (90.5) n23 t23 f22 b22.5. Certainly on the nose, one of the more old-fashioned peppery Taliskers I've come across for a while. Still I mourn the loss of the nuclear effect it once had, but the sheer quality of this compensates. 45.8%

Talisker Aged 20 Years db (95) n24 t24 f23 b24. I have been tasting Talisker for 28 years. This is the best bottling ever. Miss this and your life will be incomplete. 62%

Talisker 25 Years Old db (88) n22.5 t22 f21.5 b22. Pretty taken aback by this one: it has taken a fancy to being a bit of a Bowmore, complete with a bountiful supply of Fisherman's Friends. 45.8%

Talisker 25 Year Old bott 2008 db (92) n23 lazy smoke drifts over a scene of light citrus and slowly forming ancient oaks; t23.5 soft vanillas arrive first, then a wave of muted peppers stinging only playfully as the sweet barley unfolds just so charmingly; f22.5 the oaks really are revving up, but the sweet barley provides the balance; peat and citrus provide an unlikely fade; b23 busy and creaking but a glass or two of this offers some classy entertainment for the evening. 54.2%

Talisker 25 Years Old db (88.5) n23 t22 f21.5 b22. Another Talisker almost choked with natural caramels. Chewy and undoubtedly charming. 54.8%

Talisker 25 Years Old db (92) n23.5 t24 f22.5 b22.5. Fabulous stuff, even though the finish in particular is strangely well behaved. 58.1%

Talisker 30 Years Old db (93.5) n23 complex and slightly bitty, lemon-lightened phenols, sitting comfortably atop a pile of buttery egg custard tart. A lot sexier than it sounds...! t24 the citrus leads the way here, too. It helps intensify the juiciness of the barley, though a countering liquorice and crunchy Demerara sugar sweetness amplifies the age. The smoke is restrained though not beyond offering a spice throb; f23 just a few shuddering oaky passes, but the smoke, sugar, spice and even a little salted butter ensure the fade is long and satisfying; b23.5 much fresher and more infinitely entertaining than the 25 year old...!!! 45.8%

Talisker 30 Year Old bott 2008 db (89) n21 t23.5 f22 b22.5. This malt seriously defies the nose, which gives every indication of a whisky about to peg it. The softness of the experience is memorable. 49%

Talisker 30 Years Old db (84.5) n21 t21.5 f21 b21. Toffee-rich and pretty one dimensional. Did I ever expect to say that about a Talisker at 30...? 53.1%

Talisker Special Release 2010 30 Years Old refill American & European oak db (93) n23 shards of honeycomb pierce the thin cloud of smoke; some bristling spice suggests daddy may be home; t24 superb delivery: an explosion of rabid spices tear at the taste buds, though some astonishingly refined honey does its best to hold it back; there is a melt-in-the-mouth barley sub plot and the natural caramels one comes to expect from this guy; a late burst of garibaldi biscuit rounds things off efficiently; f23 relatively docile by comparison and perhaps over dependent on the caramel. But at least the spice keeps buzzing...; b23 a Talisker with some snap, grunt and attitude. 573%. nc ncf. Diageo. Fewer than 3000 bottles.

Talisker 1977 Special Release 2012 American and European oak refill casks, bott 2012 db (86.5) n22 t21 f22.5 b21 Distilled just two years after I first visited the distillery, I remember being told that they bottled their whisky at 8-years-old as they felt it was the optimum age of the maturing malt. The manager pointed to some very old casks in a warehouse there but said they were for blending, as it tastes better that way rather than as a singleton. Interesting to hear those works echo around my head now. Certainly this is a malt of character, but over the time the majority of the peat has vanished and huge oak has taken its place. The highlight is somewhere near the end, when the sugars have at last come to terms with the tannins and a gorgeous, vaguely smoky mocha theme strikes up. 54.6%. nc ncf.

Talisker 57 Degrees North db (95) n24 salty, smoky, coastal, breezy. The distillery's location in a nose... t24.5 peat encased in a muscovado sugar, in the same way a fly might be enveloped in amber, melts to allow the slow blossoming of a quite beautiful and peaty thing...; f23 some welcome whip and bite; the smoke and vanillas hang in there and even the odd hint of mocha puffs around a bit; b23.5 a glowing tribute, I hope, for a glowing whisky... 57%

Talisker Dark Storm charred oak db (92) n22 some pretty chunky peat and spice is blown around the glass, certainly big enough to take the muscovado sugars and red liquorice head on...; t23.5 the sugars on the nose appear to multiply on delivery, as does the bourbon-style tannin-led liquorice and hickory. The smoke takes a bit of time to get back into the game, as if hiding behind the sofa until safe to come out again but mildly reasserts itself; f23 even the sugars buckle under the oaky strain. But all is fresh and balanced enough to come good, even with some very late spices; b23.5 much more like it! Unlike the Storm, which appeared to labour under some indifferent American oak, this is just brimming with vitality and purpose. 45.8%

Talisker Port Ruighe db (88) n22 earthy, boiled tomato and chives; t22 now pretty soupy. The delivery offers that thick, airless delivery which peat and wine uniquely conjour up; the sugars are pretty profound....and very dark; f22 a little saline note enters the fray as well as an inevitable chocolate raisin touch; b22 sails into port without changing course 45.8%.

Talisker Storm db (85.5) n20 t23 f21 b21.5 The nose didn't exactly go down a storm in my tasting room. There are some deft seashore touches, but the odd poor cask –evident on the finish, also - has undone the good. But it does recover on the palate early on with an even, undemanding and attractively sweet display showing malt to a higher degree than I have seen any Talksker before. 45.8%.

⁘ **Hepburn's Choice Talisker Aged 6 Years** refill hogshead, dist 08, bott 14 **(92.5) n22.5** a little tame compared to days of yore with the smoke noticeable by its half-heartedness with the emphasis now on vanilla and butterscotch; **t23.5** certainly a bite on delivery. But where a decade or two ago those spices would have roared into your throat, rendering you speechless for a minute or two, now they buzz with intent. Malty, juicily so, with a lovely muscovado sugar backdrop; **f23** at last the smoke builds enough to register but, ironically softens as it does so; cocoa and smoke fill the last moments; **b23.5** sadly, I am one of those long enough in the tooth to remember the only Talisker you could find was an 8-year-old distillery bottling (unless you were lucky enough to happen upon a Gordon and MacPhail 1950s vintage). So seeing this at such a seemingly young age in bottled form is nothing new. But it also confirms that the peat from this distillery is nowhere near as telling as it once was. All that said, still a very classy act. *46%. nc ncf sc. 410 bottles.*

⁘ **Provenance Talisker Young & Feisty** refill hogshead, cask no. 10227 & 10229, bott Spring 14 **(87) n22 t22.5 f21 b21.5**. Should actually be called Young, Sweet, Smoky and slightly Fiesty... *46%.*

TAMDHU
Speyside, 1897. Ian Macleod Distillers. Working (re-opened 3rd March 2013).

Tamdhu db **(84.5) n20 t22.5 f21 b21.** So-so nose, but there is no disputing the fabulous, stylistic honey on delivery. The silkiest Speyside delivery of them all. *40%*

Tamdhu Aged 10 Years oak sherry cask db **(69.5) n17 t18.5 f17 b17.** A much better malt when they stick exclusively to ex-bourbon casks, as used to be the case. *40%*

Tamdhu Aged 18 Years bott code L0602G L12 20/08 db **(74.5) n19 t19 f18 b18.5**. Bitterly disappointing. Literally. *43%.*

Tamdhu 25 Years Old db **(88) n22 t22 f21 b23**. Radiates quality. *43%*

⁘ **Cadenhead's Tamdhu-Glenlivet Port Cask Aged 22 Years** dist 1991, bott Feb 2014 **(95.5) n24** lively, gripping, fruity, perky, fresh, clean and about a clear in its Port signals as any whisky you'll find; **t24.5** a fabulous delivery, ripping into your taste buds with determination and clarity of purpose which fair – and literally – takes the breath away. The spices are extraordinary, as they are profound, bite in throat like a great whisky of yesteryear, but never uncouth or over dominating. However, it is the early sugar-grape mix on delivery which, for a few moments, offers one of the great whisky experiences of the year; **f23** much more oak oriented, so a big chunk of cocoa compliments rather well; **b24** can't remember the last time I tasted a Tamdhu this stunningly dressed up and with so many places to go. A belter! *57%. 258 bottles. WB15/081*

⁘ **Cadenhead's Small Batch Tamdhu-Glenlivet Aged 22 Years** bourbon hogsheads, dist 91, bott 14 **(87.5) n21.5 t22.5 f22 b21.5**. Hangs its very large hat on punchy sugars, but complexity is lost to the big toffee-coffee element. Pleasant, chewy and one for those who have a sweet tooth while liking a bit of bite to their dram. *56%. 522 bottles. WB15/264*

Gordon & MacPhail Cask Strength Tamdhu 2001 (75) n19 t19 f17 b18. Sweet and fruity but slightly off key. *58%. Gordon & MacPhail.*

Gordon & MacPhail MacPhail's Collection Tamdhu 8 Years old (84.5) n21 t22.5 f20 b21. Quintessential Speyside in its simplistic juicy broadside and light vanilla backing. *43%.*

⁘ **Hepburn's Choice Tamdhu 2005 Aged 8 Years** refill hogshead, dist 05, bott 14 **(80) n20 t21 f19 b20.** As young whiskies mature, they tend to peak and trough. This is not peaking. The sweaty armpit nose is interesting... *46%. nc ncf sc. 381 bottles.*

⁘ **The Macphail's Collection from Tamdhu 1971 (91.5) n22** Nice coconut biscuits dunked in weakish milky tea, but gripping on for dear life against the oaky scars; some citrus does offer some alleviation; **t23** now that is classy! Somehow the oils have survived the last 40-odd years to smear citrus-tinged maple syrup all over the palate. Astonishing...; **f23** not a single hint of bitterness or over indulgent oak. Just more vanilla and citrus...and ths delicate sugars, of course; **b23.5** must admit: been a little let down by some of the older whiskies this year. But this unassuming guy has stepped u to the plate and done Speyside proud. *43%.*

Malts Of Scotland Tamdhu 1988 sherry hogshead, cask no. MoS 12029, dist 88, bott 12 **(78.5) n19 t22.5 f18 b19**. One of the myriad heartbreakers we see in Scotland these days. The nose and finish tell a sad story of suicidal sulphur candles, the delivery speaks of a sherry butt that was once made by the hands of Dionysus himself. *52.3%. nc ncf sc. 96 bottles.*

Old Malt Cask Tamdhu Aged 14 Years refill hogshead, cask no. 9076, dist Mar 98, bott Sep 12 **(90) n22 t23.5 f22 b22.5.** Great to see a blending malt step up to the plate and puff out its chest as a singleton. *50%. nc ncf sc. Douglas Laing & Co. 262 bottles.*

⁘ **Old Malt Cask Tamdhu Aged 23 Years** refill hogshead, cask no. 10585, dist May 91, bott Jun 14 **(90) n22.5** apples. With a hint of apples, with a heavy apple undercurrent, lightened slightly with...apples...; **t23**...juicy....ummmm...apples? **f22.5** the oak arrives to offer some lovely crusty late notes...apple pie...? **b22** cor(e)! Not dissimilar to some whiskies I have seen matured in cider brandy warehouses. Must leave some of this out for the great spotted woodpecker in my garden. *50%. nc ncf sc. 215 bottles.*

⋯ **Provenance Tamdhu Over 8 Years** refill hogshead, cask no. 10293, dist Summer 05, bott Spring 2013 **(87.5) n22 t22.5 f21 b22.** Spiffing stuff, chaps. A deliciously juicy, malty ball bowled directly on the middle stump but with too little deviation to cause the taste buds any trouble. *46%. nc ncf sc.*

⋯ **Speyside Single Malt Tamdhu Aged 25 Years** sherry butt, cask no. 10297, dist Sep 88, bott Mar 14 **(68.5) n18 t19 f15 b16.5.** A sherry butt from a distillery once owned by Highland Distillers. You don't have to be Sherlock Holmes to work out what has gone wrong here... *50.1%. sc. 288 bottles.*

TAMNAVULIN
Speyside. 1966. Whyte and Mackay. Working.

Tamnavulin 1966 Aged 35 Years cream sherry butt db **(91) n24 t22 f23 b22.** For those who love great old sherry, this is an absolute. Perhaps too much sherry to ever make it a true great, but there is no denying such quality. *52.6%*

⋯ **Cadenhead's Small Batch Tamnavulin-Glenlivet Aged 22 Years** bourbon hogsheads, dist 1992, bott 2014 **(85) n21.5 t22 f20.5 b21.** Very good malt in part but a distinct feel of sugared porridge, too. The oak has obvious limitations, though the metallic feel to the Crunchie bar candy is rather attractive. *52.9%. 432 bottles. WB15/263*

⋯ **Directors' Cut Tamnavulin Aged 25 Years** refill hogshead, cask no. 10352, dist May 89, bott Jun 14 **(90.5) n22** a puff of smoke sweetens the minty tannin; **t22.5** silky again, with a light smokiness softening the oak; **f23** Love Heart candy adds a slightly sweet fizz to the coffee-hued vanilla. Still that vague smokiness persists, aided now by a late but busy spice; **b23** a delightful dram where lots of little things make a much bigger whole. Satisfying. *48.8%. nc ncf sc. 78 bottles.*

⋯ **The Single Malts of Scotland Tamnavulin 21 Years Old** hogshead, cask no. 5849, dist 06 Dec 91, bott 14 Sep 13 **(85) n22.5 t21.5 f20 b21.** Promises much on the nose with its surprisingly fresh maltiness. But after rubbing your hands for what is to come next, the palate is met by a juicy delivery, then an uncompromising cask tang. *48.2%. 328 bottles. WB15/340*

TEANINICH
Highlands (Northern), 1817. Diageo. Working.

Director's Cut Teaninich Aged 30 Years refill butt, cask no. 9323, dist Dec 82, bott Dec 12 **(89) n22 t22.5 f22 b22.5.** Charming and complex to the point of never tasting the same twice. *478%. sc. Douglas Laing & Co. 201 bottles.*

Dun Bheagan Teaninich Aged 30 Years butt, cask no. 4453, dist May 82, bott 13 **(81.5) n20.5 t21 f20 b20.** Harsh and hot, the butt, though entirely free from sulphur, has done little to add lustre. *475%. nc ncf sc. Ian Macleod Distillers. 576 bottles.*

Gordon & MacPhail Connoisseurs Choice Teaninich 2004 (84) n21 t22 f20 b21. Sharp and at times feisty, the barley rolls up its sleeves to give some pretty unsympathetic oak a good bashing. Not for the first time, a sugary sheen helps soften the blows. *46%. ncf.*

⋯ **Gordan & MacPhail Connoisseurs Choice Teaninich 2006 (86.5) n22 t22 f21 b21.5.** Sugary and unsophisticated, has all the bells and whistles required for a very decent blending malt, though one from a decent cask. Lots of spice and busyness, though thins out a little too quickly. *46%.*

⋯ **Highland Single Malt Teaninich Aged 40 Years** refill hogshead, cask no. 10234, dist Dec 73, bott Mar 14 **(91) n23** has the brooding, quasi creosote quality of a whisky which has seen a dozen summers too many. But a dense, liquorice-crusted Demerara tarriness appears to offer balance...and hope...; **t21** sugary, but yep...too oaky...; **f24** the most extraordinary thing: after a bout of semi-excrutiating tannin, it suddenly relaxes and bursts out into a series of chocolate fruit creams in the style of Quality Street or Roses, the orange centres in particular; **b22** the whisky which came back from the dead. *48.9%. sc. 156 bottles.*

Malts Of Scotland Teaninich 1973 bourbon hogshead, cask no. MoS 13011, bott 13 **(84.5) n21.5 t22 f20 b21.** Sugared almonds followed by blood orange on the delivery is the highlight. But this is a malt on the way down and was plummeting fast when bottled: the sawdusty oak is just a little too rabid. *41.8%. nc ncf sc. 96 bottles.*

⋯ **Old Particular Highland Teaninich 30 Years Old** refill hogshead, cask no. 9900, dist Dec 82, Bott Aug 13 **(95.5) n24** gosh! A malt which stops you in your tracks: three styles of whisk(e)y are all in evidence here – single malt, Irish pot still and bourbon. Just love the glorious cumquat and peat topping; **t24** spectacular weight to this. Light oils fill the mouth and allow a spiced maltyness to infiltrate the layered, intense yet charming oak, all the while a playful smokiness cranking up the weight; some sublime hickory and maple syrup champions the late middle ground; **f23** dries as rich chocolate builds; **b24.5** some people in the industry give this distillery a bit of a hard time. A couple of mouthfuls of this will makes them understand why, 30 years ago, I rated this distillery so highly. Magnificent! *49.3%. nc ncf sc. 198 bottles. Douglas Laing & Co.*

Scotch Malt Whisky Society Cask 59.43 Aged 29 Years refill hogshead, dist 8 Nov 83 **(92.5) n23** gorgeous gooseberry and butterscotch tart: mega yummy; **t24** a rare example of a truly faultless delivery. The weight, the sugar levels, the tartness and compelling intensity of the barley meld together to create a seamless beauty; the first 15 seconds offers all you'll ever need from a Highland malt; **f22** altogether more austere with the thin vanillas lording it over the retreating malt; **b23.5** goes to town on the complexity. *56.4%. nc ncf sc. 252 bottles.*

⋰ **Scotch Malt Whisky Society Cask 59.48 Aged 30 Years** refill hogshead, dist 08 Nov 83 **(90) n23** the exotic fruit draws attention to the 30-plus years in the cask; **t22.5** impressive fruit – including pears and rhubarb – compliments the buttery vanilla; **f22** thinks about over-drying but enough sugars hang on; **b22.5** a malt at the end of its age range but enjoys this last hurrah of excellence. *51.3%. nc ncf sc. 158 bottles.*

⋰ **Scotch Malt Whisky Society Cask 59.49 Aged 30 Years** refill hogshead, dist 08 Nov 83 **(87) n22 t22 f21.5 b21.5.** A very similar animal to 59.48, except here the oak has gained just too austere a control of matters with a resulting decrease in complexity and balance, despite the best efforts of the esters. Enjoyable as a pre-prandial moment, though. *49.3%. nc ncf sc. 196 bottles.*

The Whisky Agency Teaninich 1973 bott 12 **(84.5) n22 t21 f20.5 b21.** Excellent kumquat and cocoa. But I just need to find the tweezers for those splinters.... *42%*

The Whisky Cask Teaninich Aged 39 Years bourbon cask, cask no. 6068, dist 1973, bott 2013 **(85) n21 t22.5 f20.5 b21.** Sultry and at times shimmering on the palate, but this has been left in the cask a few years too many as the oak input is just is too overzealous. Even so, a decent layering of heather honey repairs some damage. *40.1%. nc ncf sc.*

TOBERMORY
Highlands (Island–Mull), 1795. Burn Stewart Distillers. Working.

Ledaig 10 Years Old db **(85) n21.5 t22 f20 b21.5.** Some gorgeous and beautifully weighted peat at play here, showcased in full glory on the nose and delivery. Has to paper over some cracks towards the finish, though. *46.3%*

Ledaig Aged 10 Years db **(85.5) n20 t22.5 f21.5 b21.5.** Almost a Bowmore in disguise, such are its distinctive cough sweet qualities. Massive peat: easily one of the highest phenol Ledaigs of all time. But, as usual, a slight hiccup on the technical front. Hard work not to enjoy it, though. *46.3%. nc ncf.*

Ledaig Aged 10 Years db **(63) n14 t17 f15 b17.** What the hell is going on? Butyric and peat in a ghoulish harmony on nose and palate that is not for the squeamish. *43%*

Ledaig Aged 12 Years db **(90) n23** serious farmyard aromas – and as someone who spent three years living on one, believe me...borderline butyric, but somehow gets away with it, or at least turns it to an advantage; **t23.5** the staggering peat on the nose is no less remarkable here: chunky, clunking, entirely lacking poise and posture. And it obviously doesn't give a damn...; **f21.5** strange gin-type juniper amid the smoke; **b22** it has ever been known that there is the finest of lines between genius and madness. A side-by-side comparison of the Ledaig 10 and 12 will probably be one of whisky's best examples of this of all time... *43%*

Tobermory Aged 10 Years db **(67.5) n16 t17 f17.5 b17.** A less than brilliantly made malt totally bereft of character or charm. I have no idea what has happened here. I must investigate. Frankly, I'm gutted. *40%*

Tobermory 10 Years Old db **(73.5) n17.5 t19 f18 b19.** The last time I tasted an official Tobermory 10 for the Bible, I was aghast with what I found. So I prodded this sample I had before me of the new 46.3% version with all the confidence Wile E Coyote might have with a failed stick of Acme dynamite. No explosions in the glass or on my palate to report. And though this is still a long way short, and I'm talking light years here, of the technical excellence of the old days, the uncomplicated sweet maltiness has a very basic charm. The nose and finish, though, are still very hard going. *46.3%*

Tobermory Aged 10 Years db **(85) n20 t22.5 f21 b21.5** Bracing, nutty and malty the oils perhaps overdo it a little but there are enough sugars on hand to steer this one home for an enjoyable experience overall. *46.3%. nc ncf.*

Tobermory Aged 15 Years db **(93) n23.5** dripping with fresh, clean, ultra high quality oloroso there remains enough tangy malt to underscore the island location; **t23.5** a fabulous marriage of juicy grape and thick, uncompromising malt. It is an arm wrestle for supremacy between the two...but it is the delicate spices which win; **f23** salty chocolate raisin; **b23** a tang to the oils on both nose and finish suggests an over widened middle. But such is the quality of the sherry butts and the intensity of the salt-stained malt, all is forgiven. *46.3%. nc ncf.*

Tobermory Aged 15 Years Limited Edition db (72.5) **n17 t18 f19 b18.5.** Another poorly made whisky: the nose and delivery tells you all you need to know. *46.3%*

A.D. Rattray Ledaig 2004 butt, cask no. 900161, dist 24 Nov 04, bott 25 Nov 12 **(94) n23.5** there is possibly some barley amid all that smoke... even the influence of the sherry struggles to get a note in edgeways; **t23** the delivery is so thick and intense it takes a little while for things to be distinguished amid the smoke. A real pea-souper, an old fashioned smog of a dram, where the grape does now have an input, though it battles tigerishly to make itself heard. When the spirit is located it is obvious that, technically, it is not Premier league. But such is the hurly burly of the smoke, it doesn't very much matter; **f24** long with the grape having a chocolate coating. The smoke, though, refuses to stop molesting it; **b23.5** easily one of the most heavily peated Ledaigs I have encountered in the last two decades. Must be well over the 50ppm of the Ardbegs of this world...one for those who prefer the insane Bruichladdichs. *60.5%. sc. A.D. Rattray. DRCC German and Denmark Markets.*

Best Dram Ledaig 9 Years Old bourbon barrel, dist 05, bott 14 **(89) n22.5** unsophisticated, pile-it-high peat; youthful gristiness lurks at every corner; **t22** yet even bigger peat than the nose, though that seems hardly possible; the sugars take a while to register; **f22.5** dry, ultimately ashy; **b22** one of the most heavily peated Ledaigs I've found in a while, though younger than its years. *52.2%. ncf. 182 bottles.*

Cadenhead Ledaig 16 Years Old (77.5) **n19 t20 f19 b19.5.** Sweet and smoky. But hardly textbook distillate. *46%. WM Cadenhead Ltd. 360 bottles.*

Cadenhead's Sherry Cask Tobermory Aged 19 Years sherrywood, dist 95, bott July 14 **(67) n15 t20 f16 b16.** Riddled with sulphur. *54.2%. 498 bottles. WB15/268*

Caermory Aged 20 Years cask 246 **(94) n23.5** lively malt both offers a jaunty juice grain element and a balancing barley sugar counter. The oak is ridiculously well-behaved for its age and ensures just enough vanilla for depth without reducing the crispier, crunchier notes; **t24** I adore this type of malt: the barley is both eye-wateringly fresh, sharp and salivating. Yet there is also enough spice fizz and, eventually, oil creating a secondary personality – almost a parallel whisky universe in the glass; **f23** the very faintest tang from the bourbon cask is the only thing which contradicts the startling clarity of this 20-y-o, and so minor it hardly detracts. Especially when there is enough cocoa and salt around to makes for a lip-smacking finale; **b23.5** Tobermory at its very sprightliest: a malt to get you off to a breezy start to the day, or end it on an up-note. *49.6%*

Càrn Mòr Strictly Limited Edition Ledaig Aged 7 Years hogshead, dist 2005, bott 2013 **(89) n22.5** a citrusy smokiness which never shakes off its youth but the peat intensifies; **t22.5** lightly oiled, rather beautifully made ad still offering major citrus notes on the juicy malt; **f22** thinly slightly, but the smoke remains intact and quietly delicious, having sweetened slightly; **b22** oh, for the promise of youth... So lovely to for once see this malt uncluttered by oak. *46%. nc ncf. 785 bottles. WB15/155*

The Coopers Choice Ledaig 2005 Aged 8 Years hogshead, cask no. 0062, bott 2014 **(91.5) n23** sharp, pungest, acidic, rather acrid peak reek....love it! **t23** softer on delivery than nose thanks to a big oil surge. The gristy sugars have a field day as the smoke envelops; **f22.5** more accent on vanilla and a little citrus; **b23** I really do adore young Ledaigs which allow the grist to do its thing. Oily enough to woo Caol Ila fans. *46%. 400 bottles. WB15/301*

Dramboree 2014 Ledaig 8 Years Old sherry butt, cask no. 900173 **(87) n22 t21 f22 b22** Says this is from the Ledaig distillery. I think they mean Tobermory. Don't mind the strength, but there is some heat coming from elsewhere other than the alcohol. No sulphur on the sherry – hurrah! But the big peat and grape are in a bit of a grapple which blasts balance and complexity out of the window. Still, great fun and the perfect dram to sort out any plaque. *58.8%. WB15/410*

Gordon and MacPhail Connoisseurs Choice Ledaig 1994 **(90) n21.5 t23.5 f22 b23.** Probably the most miserly peated Ledaig of all time. But don't let that worry you: the chocolate chip mint is a stunner...! *46%. ncf.*

Gordan & MacPhail Connoisseurs Choice Ledaig 1996 **(82) n20 t21 f20.5 b20.5.** Occasionally the Ledaig from Tobermory became a smoky renegade. Here is such an example: thin and seemingly missing some copper from the system. Even the peat fails to make any kind of a positive impact save, perhaps, for its contribution towards a degree of soft mocha. Astringent and underwhelming. *46%.*

Gordan & MacPhail Exclusive Single Malt Ledaig sherry hogshead, cask no. 469, dist 23 Oct 97, bott Oct 13 **(86.5) n21 t23.5 f21 b21.** Has you gripping your seat...not in excitement but trying to hold on tight. Hardly brilliant distillate here and the peat is thrust at you like clods of turf and anthracite eggs hitting you slap on the nose: it is all rather austere, brutal and distinctly farmyardy. Peaks on delivery when a bevvy of sugars, mainly molasses and maple syrup combined, overcome the covert bitterness and soften the peaty blows. The finish is mildly less brutal, and even offers black cherries to counter the bittering oak. For peat freaks, you'll find this a hard-faced, icy-hearted lover. But you'll probably return to her for more...*58.6%. nc ncf sc. 263 bottles, bottled exclusively for The Vintage House. WB15/065*

⠿ **The Maltman Tobermory Aged 16 Years** sherry cask, cask no. 5010, dist Jun 96, bott Apr 13 **(71.5) n16.5 t19 f18 b18**. More distilling faults in this than you can wave a whisky thief at. Feinty though sweet. *43%. sc ncf nc. 233 bottles. WB15/217*

⠿ **Master of Malt Single Cask Ledaig 7 Year Old (94) n23.5** fresh, citrusy, medium-peated grist. And...that's all folks...! **t24** wonderful buttery quality to the intense gristy sweetness. A little lemon lightens and sharpens; **f23** the oak cannot resist adding a touch of bitterness, but is kind about it. A spice buzz is kept to a barely audible hum by the low blanket of smoke; **b23.5** a distillery style beautifully captured. *61.9%. sc.*

⠿ **Master of Malt Single Cask Tobermory 18 Years Old** refill, dist 22 Nov 95, bott 4 Feb 14 **(88.5) n21** intense malt compensates the odd blemish on the distillate; **t22.5** unusually flinty for a Tobermory, but the degree of muscovado-sugared malt rises to impressive proportions; **f22** a little salt raises the sharpness of the grain while the oak offers a buttery touch; **b22** a better than expected malt given the nose. For its obvious technical faults it is impossible not to enjoy the overall richness of the picture. *53.9%. 100 bottles. WB15/230*

Master of Malt Tobermory Aged 17 Years refill hogshead, dist 26 Apr 95, bott 26 Nov 12 **(84.5) n21 t20.5 f22 b21**. A raucous dram which heaves and pitches on delivery but sails home to safety as the barley and spice take hold. *57%. sc. 274 bottles.*

⠿ **Old Malt Cask Tobermory Aged 19 Years** refill hogshead, cask no. 9910, dist Apr 94, bott Aug 13 **(81.5) n20 t21.5 f20 b20**. Smoky, but stringent and eye-watering, too. Those stills were running at a lick when this was made... *50%. nc ncf sc. 170 bottles.*

⠿ **Old Malt Cask Ledaig Aged 20 Years** refill hogshead, cask no. 9858, dist Mar 93, bott Jun 13 **(89) n22** an usually sweet nose for a Ledaig, the delicate honey tones holding sway over the crushed Digestive biscuits and earthier floral notes; **t22** mild hint of glazed ginger amid the tannin; **f22.5** a lovely ginger buzz, crystalline sugars and the vaguest of phenolic fades; **b22.5** a juicy little trip with an almost apologetic degree of smoke. *50%. nc ncf sc.*

⠿ **Old Particular Highland Tobermory 18 Years Old** refill butt, cask no. 10361, dist Feb 96, bott May 14 **(84.5) n21 t22 f21.5 b21**. Salted celery nose and profound malt throughout on the palate. But never quite raises its game high enough. *48.4%. nc ncf sc. 314 bottles.*

⠿ **Old Particular Highland Leidag Aged 21 Years** refill hogshead, cask no. 10263, dist Mar 1993, bott Mar 2014 **(95.5) n24** the astonishing complexity signals a whisky of importance and no little greatness: perfect fruit and spices commensurate with age, mainly of a kumquat theme but heightened in effect by the gorgeous coastal saltiness; **t24** wonderful...truly wonderful. That coastal effect is not lost on delivery, though plays its hand quietly, content in allowing the delicate fruit to intermingle with the rich barley and multi-layered oakiness; the sugars purr gentle...; **f23.5** gentle vanillas and ever-intensifying cocoa tones, some distinctly Cuban; **b24** one of the best fruit plucked from Tobermory for many a year. Sublime. *50.9%. nc ncf sc.288 bottles.*

Provenance Tobermory Over 6 Years sherry butt, cask no. 8760, dist Summer 06, bott Summer 12 **(81) n18 t20 f22 b21**. Decidedly odd. The nose is best ignored and doesn't bode well. But on the palate a malt which intrigues, not least with its marzipan, cocoa and cough sweet finale. *46%. nc ncf sc. Douglas Laing & Co.*

Provenance Ledaig Over 7 Years refill hogshead, cask no. 9654, dist Autumn 05, bott Spring 13 **(92) n22.5** youthful – not uncommon for a nose like this on a five-year-old – with the peat sharpened by the crispness of the barley and acrid intensity of the soot; **t24** beautifully salivating: exactly as it should be with the peat acting almost like lead weights to stop the juicier barley from flying off; superb gristy sugars pound the mid ground: magnificently wild! **f22.5** the light oils noticeable throughout cling to the death and help accentuate the little oak present; **b23** feisty, flighty and fun. *46%. nc ncf. Douglas Laing & Co.*

Single Cask Collection Tobermory 17 Years Old bourbon hogshead, cask no. 699, dist 6 Jun 95, bott 5 Feb 13 **(80.5) n19 t21.5 f20 b20**. The astonishingly intense barley on delivery is the star of the show here. But don't look for harmony as it is obvious the original spirit was never in tune. *54.9%. nc ncf sc. 251 bottles.*

⠿ **The Single Malts of Scotland Tobermory Aged 19 Years** hogshead, cask no. 5174, dist 14 Dec 1994, bott 25 Mar 2014 **(74) n18 t19 f18 b19**. Furry, sweet but off key. *55.8%. 279 bottles. WB15/311*

That Boutique-y Whisky Company Tobermory batch 1 **(75.5) n18 t20 f18.5 b19.** Occasionally you come across a magnificent whisky which absolutely makes your day. This isn't one of them. Badly made and good maturation offers only damage limitation. *53.8%.*

⫶⫶⫶ **That Boutique-y Whisky Ledaig** batch 1 **(91.5) n24** pure smoked grist: astonishing. Ignore the soft feint niggle and breathe in something remarkable...; **t23.5** decently peated grist with the sugars dissolving on the tongue. A little golden syrup adds lustre to the sweetness; **f21.5** bitters slightly and the oils mount; **b22.5** technically, not the most gifted malt. But blunders along beautifully, helped by its disarming peat profile. *57.1%.* 217 bottles. WB15/209

⫶⫶⫶ **That Boutique-y Whisky Tobermory** batch 2 **(76) n18 t19 f20 b19.** Follows pretty much in the same footsteps as Batch 1, except the finish enjoys an extra smudge of decent barley. *53.9%.* 73 bottles. WB15/196

⫶⫶⫶ **That Boutique-y Whisky Tobermory** batch 3 **(76.5) n18.5 t20 f19 b19.** Malty, hot but another one that sinks without trace like the wrecks off Tobermory... *48.1%.* WB15/233

The Whisky Agency Ledaig 2005 bott 12 **(86) n21 t22 f21.5 b21.5** No shortage of hazel nuts in toffee to soften the peppery peat. *52.1%.*

TOMATIN

Speyside, 1897. Takara, Shuzo and Okura & Co. Working.

Cù Bòcan Highland Single Malt virgin oak, bourbon & sherry casks db **(85.5) n21 t21 f22 b21.5.** An old fashioned dram: the type Pitt the Younger, or Pitt the Embryo might remember... and appreciate. Appears to be nearer new make than fully matured Scotch: the big player is the oak which, almost, bourbon-like, shovels cart loads of caramel and muscovado into the mix. Green...and engrossing. *46%*

⫶⫶⫶ **Cù Bòcan Highland Single Malt 1989 Vintage** db **(95.5) n23** what the....??? A peaty Tomatin! And classy, too...; **t24** sure, the peat is first to show...and glistens as it does so. But where the hell has all that juicy fruit come from. Fruit and peat...not usually happy marriage. But here it is bliss...; **f24.5** now dries slightly to allow the smoke to have a slightly sharp tang,as though the phenls have risen to surprisingly high levels. Still the fruit is on song, like the citrus jelly which accompanies some of the better marzipans....; **b24** the last Cu Bocan I got my nose around, I likened to Pitt the Younger. Well, the only pit here would be a peat one... This is not only absolutely superb whisky, but a bit of a shock, too...Indeed, I am stunned! *53.2%. ncf.*

Tomatin 12 Years Old db **(85.5) n21 t21.5 f22 b21.** Reverted back to a delicately sherried style, or at least shows signs of a touch of fruit, as opposed to the single-minded maltfest it had recently been. So, nudge or two closer to the 18-y-o as a style and shows nothing other than good grace and no shortage of barley, either. *40%*

⫶⫶⫶ **Tomatin 14 Year Old** Port Finish db **(92.5) n23** under-ripe greengage shows some nip and spice; **t24** salivating, as a Tomatin delivery so ften is. But here we get all juiced up by succulent fruit, helped along by glazed muscvado; **f22.5** the fruit tails off allowing the vanilla and spice an easy ride; **b23** allows the top notch port a clear road. *46%. ncf.*

Tomatin Aged 15 Years ex bourbon cask, bott 2010 db **(86) n21 t22 f21.5 b21.5.** One of the most malty drams on the market today. Perhaps suffers a little from the 43% strength as some of the lesser oak notes get a slightly disruptive foothold. But the intense, juicy barley trademark remains clear and delicious. *43% Tomatin Distillery*

Tomatin 15 Years Old bourbon barrels and Spanish Tempranillo wine casks db **(88.5) n22 t23 f21 b22.5.** Not free from the odd problem with the Spanish wine casks but gets away with it as the overall complexity and enjoyment levels are high. *52%*

Tomatin Aged 18 Years db **(85) n22 t21 f21 b21.** I have always held a torch for this distillery and it is good to see some of the official older stuff being released. This one has some serious zing to it, leaving your tastebuds to pucker up - especially as the oak hits. *40%*

Tomatin 18 Years Old db **(88) n22.5 t22 f21.5 b22.** What a well-mannered malt. As though it grew up in a loving, caring family and behaves itself impeccably from first nose to last whimpering finale; *43%*

Tomatin Aged 18 Years sherry finish, bott 2010 db **(92.5) n22.5** busy, thick milkshake maltiness with a touch of fruitcake; **t23.5** cream sherry: creamy + sweet barley + fruity = cream sherry...; **f23** very long with a touch of controlled spicy fizz to the proceedings. But that indomitable barley signature sings to the end; **b23.5** finished in quite superior sherry butts. A malt brimming with character and quality. What a treat! *46%. ncf. Tomatin Distillery.*

Tomatin Aged 21 Years created using 6 refill American oak casks and the 7th an ex sherry butt, bott 2009 db **(81) n22 t22.5 f18.5 b19.** A clattering, chattering, cluttering malt never once getting into rhythm to tell a coherent story. The sherry-pitched nose is jumbled but attractive; the delivery is at first rampant and entertaining but the middle and finale fall away, with the odd negative note at the death. A good one to pour your friends while they are blindfolded: this will confuse them. *52% Tomatin Distillery. 2400 bottles.*

Tomatin 25 Years Old db **(89)** n22 t23 f21.5 b22.5. Not a nasty bone in its body: understated but significant. 43%

Tomatin 30 Years Old db **(91)** n22 if there was a hint of the exotics in the 25-y-o, it's here, five years on, by the barrel load. Evidence of grape, but the malt won't be outdone, either; **t23** silky and sultry, there is every suggestion that the oak is thinking of going too far. Yet such is the purity and intensity of the malt, damage has been repaired and/or prevented and even at this age one can only salivate as the soft oils kick in; **f23.5** probably my favourite part of the experience because the sheer deliciousness of the chocolaty finale is awesome; **b22.5** malts of this age rarely maintain such a level of viscosity. Soft oils can often be damaging to a whisky, because they often refuse to allow character to flourish. Yet here we have a whisky that has come to terms with its age with great grace. And no little class. 49.3%

Tomatin 30 Year Old European & American oak casks db **(85.5)** n21 t21 f22.5 b21. Unusually for an ancient malt, the whisky becomes more comfortable as it wears its aged shoes. The delivery is just a bit too enthusiastic on the oaky front, but the natural caramels soften the journey rather delightfully. 46%. ncf.

Tomatin 40 Years Old db **(89.5)** n21.5 t22 f23 b23. Not quite sure how it's done it, but somehow it has made it through all those oaky scares to make for one very impressive 40-y-o!! Often it shows the character of a bourbon on a Zimmer. 42.9%

⫶⫶⫶⫶ **Tomatin 1981 Single Cask** db **(93.5)** n24 classic nutty old sherry; dried dates and burnt raisin...the label really doesn't need to mention the type of cask...; **t23.5** further indelible hallmarks of an eye-watering dry oloroso, the oak offering a degree of bitter orange but only after the clipped, spiced delivery; **f22.5** brooding molasses offering stingy amounts of sweetness to counter that late bitterness; **b23.5** a hand-picked beautifully rip cherry from Tomatin, one that essentially has to be tasted at body temperature for very best results. Even then, still one of the driest sherry butts you'll find this year. 43.2%.

⫶⫶⫶⫶ **Tomatin Highland 1988 Vintage** db **(86.5)** n22 t22 f21 b21.5. Few whiskies in the world shows off its malty muscle like Tomatin and here, briefly, it goes into overdrive. For the most part, a happy meeting of slightly salty malt and oak. 46%. ncf.

Tomatin 1997 1st fill bourbon, bott 2009 db **(93.5)** n23.5 t24 f23 b23. Another outlandishly beautiful malt from this underrated distillery. Had they mixed in a few second fill casks into this, the complexity would have been fearsome and the stuff of legend. 57.1%. 244 bottles.

Tomatin 1999 refill American oak, Tempranillo finish, bott 2009 db **(92)** n22 t23.5 f23 b23.5. Looking for something different? Give this a whirl around the palate. Fabulous. 57.1%. 302 bottles.

Tomatin Decades European & American oak casks db **(91)** n23 floral and earthy yet equally fruity and vivid: as if nosing in a greenhouse.. **t23** big malt but the strands of toffee become chewier as the oaky theme develops; light, vaguely peaty, spices open out on an increasingly vanilla landscape; **f22.5** big age as the oak, in curiously diverse forms, take control. Just love the sugars of the cream toffee; **b22.5** an intriguing onion of a malt, of which the layers can, with concentration, be stripped away. The light smoke does its job immaculately. A malt for those with an hour to spare... 46%. ncf. Marriage of 1967, 1976, 1984, 1990 and peated 2005 Tomatins.

Tomatin Legacy bourbon barrels & virgin oak cask db **(94.5)** n22.5 an even blend of young barley and confidently sugared oak; **t24** some of the honey and tannin notes here more easily relate to bourbon than Scotch: there must be exceptionally fresh casks at work! The result is a dram of rare mouth-watering quality, ably assisted by layered cocoa and hickory; the mix of molassed and muscovado sugars is something which makes you want to gasp with pleasure; the spices are almost too much of a good thing...; **f23.5** long, with a wonderful fade of clear honey and crystalline barley; **b24.5** again, just working here with the sample, I don't have the label to hand. But this screams new oak to me, as the sugars and spice are almost identical to those found in bourbon. Mix that with probably the maltiest distillate in Scotland and the result is something to truly savour. No great age evident, for all the oak input. But as they say: if you are good enough, you are old enough... 43%

⫶⫶⫶⫶ **Cadenhead's Small Batch Tomatin Aged 19 Years** bourbon hogshead, dist 1994, bott 2014 **(89)** n22 dry, borderline austere with a grainy barley and spice outer shell: a bender's delight; **t22.5** honeycombed, juicy barley **f22.5** impressively clean oak but still that simple gristiness presses home; **b22** malt at the max. The complexity is down to the kind oak rather than any magic within the spirit. A simple, very decent quality Tomatin nutshelled, really. 46%. 534 bottles. WB15/090

Director's Cut Tomatin Aged 45 Years refill butt, cask no. 9315, dist Nov 67, bott Dec 12 **(73)** n18 t19 f17 b19. Will someone please tell me that this wasn't "freshened" in a present day sherry butt.... 51.6%. sc. Douglas Laing & Co. 175 bottles.

⫶⫶⫶⫶ **Gordon & MacPhail Connoisseurs Choice Tomatin 1996** **(82)** n19 t22 f20 b21. Undone somewhat by a hint of butyric and an oak-bitter finish. But you might love the gooseberry and lychee combination. 46%.

⋅⋅⋅∷⋅ **Old Masters Tomatin 16 Years Old** cask no. 5969, dist 1997, bott 2014 **(92.5) n24** a zesty fruit salad, including raw rhubarb. Estery and sharpened with fresh spring grass: one of the brightest noses you'll fine! **t23.5** from the nose you expect max salivation...and you get it. Fabulously grassy, sugar-coated malt; **f22** quietens as vanilla and butterscotch find a home; very late cocoa; **b23** a cut glass malt. 56.4%. James MacArthur & Co. Ltd.

⋅⋅⋅∷⋅ **Old Particular Speyside Tomatin 20 Years Old** refill hogshead cask no. 9984, dist Jan 93, bott Aug 13 **(84.5) n21 t22 f20.5 b21.** Concentrates on the house big malt theme. But a few spices tag along to enliven procedings. 51.5%. nc ncf sc. 211 Bottles. OLP0037.

⋅⋅⋅∷⋅ **The Pearls of Scotland Tomatin 1998** cask no. 3667, bott Jun 14 **(88) n22.5** refreshing, despite a stodgy spotted dog pudding touch. The sugars are like molten Demerera on lightly salted porridge; **t23** wonderfully clean and intense barley which becomes more concentrated as it continues; the salt begins to open up the tannins as the spices arrive; **f20.5** more excellent malt which takes an age to wither away; beware the mild "milky" fault at the end which suggests the cask had reached the end of its useful life in the final year or two of maturation; **b22** a dram which splashes malt about it like an artist may throw paint at his canvas. 52.4%. sc.

The Warehouse Collection Tomatin Aged 19 Years bourbon hogshead, cask no. 7116, dist 17 Jun 93, bott 6 Feb 13 **(94) n23** a few old tangerine peels inject a crusty citrus note to the heather-honey barley; **t24.5** fabulous spiced honey of the very highest order gives way to wave upon wave of clean, juicy barley. That, in turn makes way for a second coming of honey, this time of light ulmo: simple...but so beautifully effective! **f22.5** big vanilla fade, but again no off notes or bitterness from the cask...just a light barley flourish; **b24** Tomatin is one of those few malts which has enough about its barley-intense single mindedness to be able to absorb good oak with alacrity. A good example as to why there is no need to display this malt (ever!) in ex-sherry, as those casks, even those free of sulphur, are invariably inferior to how well it works with ex-bourbon. Indeed, this is always a distillery my pulse rate rises to when confronted with ex-bourbon cask samples on my desk. Again, I have not been let down. For though this is in many ways a simply dram, it is truly stunning. 46.4%. nc ncf sc.

⋅⋅⋅∷⋅ **The Whisky Cask Tomatin Aged 8 Years** sherry cask, dist 2004, bott 2013 **(77) n19 t23 f17 b18.** Extra marks for the incredible intensity of the malt and sweet grape on delivery. Stunning. But this is from a contemporary sherry butt. So I'll let you guess what happens next... 58.6%. nc ncf.

TOMINTOUL
Speyside, 1965. Angus Dundee. Working.

Tomintoul Aged 10 Years db **(83.5) n21 t20 f21.5 b21**. Has bucked up recently to offer a juicy, salivating barley thrust. Yet still a little on the thin side, despite some late oak. 40%

Tomintoul Aged 12 Years Oloroso Sherry Cask Finish db **(73.5) n18.5 t19 f18 b18**. Tomintoul, with good reason, styles itself as "The Gentle Dram" and you'll hear no argument from me about that one. However, the sherry influence here offers a rough ride. 40%

Tomintoul Aged 12 Years Portwood Finish db **(87.5) n22 t22 f21.5 b22**. As Portwood finishes go, a real lightweight allowing the barley plenty of room to flex its juicier muscles. 46%. nc ncf.

Tomintoul Aged 14 Years db **(91) n23.5 t23 f21.5**. This guy has shortened its breath somewhat: with the distinct thinness to the barley and oak arriving a little flustered and half-hearted rather than with a confident stride; **b23** remains a beautiful whisky full of vitality and displaying the malt in its most naked and vulnerable state. But I get the feeling that perhaps a few too many third fills, or under-performing seconds, has resulted in the intensity and hair-raising harmony of the truly great previous bottlings just being slightly undercooked. That said, still a worthy and delicious dram! 46%. nc ncf.

Tomintoul Aged 16 Years db **(94.5) n24.5** a fruity concoction of apples and pears topped with vanilla ice cream; even the vaguest hint of something smoky...one of the noses of the year; **t23.5** every bit as gentle as the label promises, as the light oils coat the palate with a fabulously intense and delicately sweetened barley skin. The skeleton is playful oak; **f23** a wonderful, multi-layered interplay between malt and oak-vanillas. Long, curiously spice-free, increasingly dry but hugely sophisticated; **b23.5** confirms Tomintoul's ability to dice with greatness. 40%

Tomintoul Aged 21 Years db **(94) n24** has all the hallmarks of a malt which contains casks a lot older than the stated age: the fruit is of the exotic variety and the manner in which those fruit and defter floral notes effortlessly intertwine confirms not just the magnificence of quality but also familiarity between oak and malt **t24** silky and soft with the balance of the light sugars to barley almost perfect; the vanillas grow, as they should, but the freshness to the barley never diminishes **f22.5** a beautiful butterscotch and custard confection **b23.5** just how good this whisky would have been at cask strength or even at 46 absolutely terrifies me. 40%.

Tomintoul Aged 27 Years db **(87)** n22 t22.5 21.5 b21. The last time I saw a colour like this was on antique expert David Dickinson's face. Still, lots of charm and character to go round… and on the whisky, too. 40%

Tomintoul Aged 33 Years db **(95.5)** n24.5 just about textbook aged high quality malt: exotic fruit at every turn…and displaying extraordinary depth and intensity into the bargain. The level of fruit sweetness against the more lush semi-bourbony brown sugars is an experience to savour. The spices twinkle endearingly; t24.5 the weight on the palate defies belief. Just about perfection in that department while there is almost a sheen to the oaky input. The sugars dissolve readily allowing the spices a controlled lift off. Somehow, after all these years, a salivating element is preserved…virtually faultless; f23 just loses its way a little as a light, tight furriness burrows into the crisp sugars and silky oaks; even so, some stunning moments in the oaky sunset; b24 the point about whiskies of this age is that sometimes you have to deal with what you are given. Some 33 years ago a blender didn't decide to put these to one side for a single malt; this was made to be blended away and have arrived at this point with a pleasing randomness: the casks used here escaped the call of the warehouse foreman. Which means this breathtakingly beautiful 33 Year Old Tomintoul bares virtually no resemblance to the last one I tasted. Which is what makes this job of mine, at times, so bloody fascinating. 43%.

Tomintoul With A Peaty Tang db **(94)** n23 t24 f23 b24. A bit more than a tang, believe me! Faultlessly clean distillate that revels in its unaccustomed peaty role. The age is confusing and appears mixed, with both young and older traits being evident. 40%

⁙ **Darkness! Tomintoul Aged 18 Years Oloroso Cask Finish (91.5)** n23 huge fruitcake: Melton Hunt Cake at its moistest, though with separate layers of Sumatra coffee and Venezuelan cocoa…intriguing; t23 a mixed, noisy bag on delivery but settles towards a spiced, high cocoa chocolate raisin treat…; f22.5 more of the same, but with extra oils and vanilla; b23 luscious sherry with not a sulphur of atom in sight…! 52.7%. 95 bottles. WB15/204

Gordon & MacPhail Private Collection Tomintoul 1972 refill sherry hogshead, cask no. 1974 **(86.5)** n23 t20 f22 b21.5. Such a great nose and, eventually, complex finish. Wonderful. But the senses are elsewhere bombarded and sometimes overwhelmed with just too many oak fundamentalists. 45.1%. ncf.

Master Of Malt Tomintoul 17 Years Old cask no. 2175, dist 1 May 95, bott 1 Apr 95 **(89)** n22.5 t22 f22 b22.5. Shares many similar elements as the Boutique-y batch 1…but better tooled up on the oil and barley front. 54.5%. sc.

Old Ballantruan The Peated Malt Aged 10 Years (86.5) n21.5 t22 f21.5 b21.5. A busy youngster of a malt whose peaty sweetness nibbles at the taste buds than swamps them. Delicious and well made, with only a surprising lack of complexity development keeping the score down. 50%. ncf. Tomintoul

That Boutique-y Whisky Company Tomintoul batch 1 **(88.5)** n22.5 t22 f21.5 b22.5. A lovely distillery showing a somewhat brooding side to its nature. 47.8%. 172 bottles.

The Whisky Agency Tomintoul 1967 bott 12 **(84)** n24 t21 f19 b20. Fantastic spices, all of them oak-derived. But it is all about the nose which is an essay of poise and complexity. There is even a brief malt moment in there somewhere. Don't bother drinking. Just sniff..and preferably after it has been in the glass for at least 20 minutes. 44.6%

The Whisky Cask Tomintoul Aged 43 Years bourbon hogshead, dist 69, bott 12 **(86)** n20.5 t21.5 f22.5 b21.5. Tired, limping whisky. But enough muscular sugars – helped by an unusual degree of oil for its age – allows the more subtle oak notes to come through as well. 42.7%. sc.

TORMORE
Speyside, 1960. Chivas Brothers. Working.

Tormore 12 Years Old db **(75)** n19 t19 f19 b18. For those who like whisky in their caramel. 40%

⁙ **Tormore Aged 14 Years** batch no. A1308, bott 2013 db **(83.5)** n21 t21.5 f20.5 b20.5. Toffeed, flat and inoffensive. Good dram to have last thing at night: chances are you'll be asleep before you finish the glass… 43% WB15/326

Tormore Aged 15 Years "Special Distillery Bottling" db **(71)** n17 t18 f19 b17. Even a supposed pick of choice casks can't save this from its fiery fate. 46%

⁙ **Gordon & MacPhail Connoisseurs Choice Tormore 1996**, bott 2011 **(86)** n22 gooseberry and butterscotch; Bakewell pudding; t21 a tad hot and hostile; becalmed by soft malt; f22 lovely malty fade; b21 can't say this is an example of how scotch should be distilled, but pans out well thanks to decent oak. 46%. nc ncf. WB15/151

Gordon & MacPhail Connoisseurs Choice Tormore 1997 (86) n21.5 t22 f21 b21.5. Easy going malt with a big lemon curd kick early on but soon reverts to simple, clean barley throughout. 46%. ncf.

⊱ **Gordan & MacPhail Cask Strength Tormore 1999** (90.5) n22 custard cream tart meets lemon merengue pie; t23.5 hugely intense eye-watering barley, crunchy sugar with a lovely gooseberry edge; f22 bitters out a tad, but the barley sugar remains on top; b23 lays it on thick with the barley. Attractive. *58%.*

Malts Of Scotland Tormore 1988 sherry butt, cask no. MoS 12043, dist Sept 1999, bott Sept 2012 (92.5) n23 black peppers rubbed into thin creosote and raisin-soaked tannin; t23.5 great body; some real oloroso-cream sherry style oiliness at play, and it gets creamier by the moment; a short burst of juicy barley then the cocoa in the fore- and middle-ground becomes also Cadbury-like; f23 more creamy chocolate, though some spices offer an edge. The fruit is now more date-like; b23 Tormore does not offer the greatest spirit known to Scotland. But when in a top grade, almost (though not quite) faultless sherry butt like this, there is just sufficient juiciness to make the most of the grape. *55.4%. nc ncf sc. 96 bottles.*

Master of Malt Tormore Aged 28 Years ex-bourbon cask, dist 24 Feb 84, bott 21 Nov 12 (83.5) n21 t20 f21.5 b21. The intense malt and concentrated sugars save it. But it is as hot as Hades...and that has nothing to do with the strength. *60.2%. sc. 182 bottles.*

Old Malt Cask Tormore Aged 17 Years refill hogshead, cask no. 9036, dist Jun 95, bott Sep 12 (77.5) n19 t20 f19 b19.5. You can count on this distillery to rarely satisfy you, and this off beam (if very malty) offering is no disappointment...if you see what I mean... *50%. sc. Douglas Laing & Co. 340 bottles.*

⊱ **The Pearls of Scotland Tormore 1995 17 Year Old** cask no. 20097, dist Dec 95, bott Nov 13 (86.5) n21.5 t22 f20.5 b22. Quite well made, malty, sweet, fruity, spicy, technically OK. Wholly likeable. Yet, for some reason (maybe because there appears to be no spine), somehow fails to get the adrenalin going... *476%.*

⊱ **Signatory Vintage Single Malt Tormore 1995 Aged 18 Years** hogsheads, cask no. 3885+3886, dist 27 Apr 95, bott 07 Feb 14 (85.5) n21.5 t22 f21 b21. Clean, sweet, unchallenging malt. Perfectly acceptable. Easily drinkable. Safe. Just give me a nudge if it starts to do something. *43%. nc. 779 bottles. WB15/012*

⊱ **The Single Malts of Scotland Tormore 25 Years Old** bourbon barrel, cask no. 603, dist 03 Feb 8, bott 14 Feb 13 (94.5) n23 freshly toasted hazelnut embedded in chocolate mousse; someone is burning the toast in the kitchen next door; t23.5 yep; burnt toast. On delivery. Or, rather burnt French toast as there is plenty of sugar to compensate. Under all this noise, malt throbs away contentedly; f24 long with the most profound toasted fudge you'll ever find; the spices carry on merrily, the oils thicken and the general feel of excellent bourbon accentuates; b24 from the colour and strength, you'd be thinking this had been matured in Kentucky. And as for the flavour profile...OK, what have you done with the real Tormore...that guys nothing like as handsome as you! Never seen anything like it from this distillery in 30 years! A fabulous freak of a dram. *64.2%. 194 bottles. WB15/306*

That Boutique-y Whisky Company Tormore batch 1 (88) n22 t22 f22 b22. Easy going Tormore with enough zest to the barley to make for an interesting and pleasant experience. *50%. Master Of Malt. 226 bottles.*

⊱ **Wemyss Malts 1988 Single Speyside Tormore "Floral Trellis"** barrel, dist 1988, bott 2014 (85) n21 t22 f21 b21. Pleasant though thin, malty, and too simplistically toffee dependent for greatness. *46%. sc. 286 bottles.*

Wemyss 1988 Single Speyside Tormore "White Chocolate Torte" barrel, bott 2012 (91) n22.5 t23 f22.5 b23.5. Not my favourite distillery, but here the elements work together like a charm. An absolute little beauty cluttered with surprising nooks and crannies. *46%. sc.*

TULLIBARDINE

Highlands (Perthshire), 1949. Tullibardine Ltd. Working.

Tullibardine 1988 John Black Edition 4 bott 2008 db (91.5) n23.5 gosh!! How about this for ultra ripe figs and greengages? Wonderfully spiced, honeyed - in an intriguingly understated style - and clean for good measure. One of those you leave the empty glass to give any room's aroma a touch of class to for a few days... t23 the grape cascades onto the taste buds in a thick, dizzying regiment of fruitiness, by no means all sugar, either. The spices hinted at on the nose are here ramrod hard and unyielding; f22.5 the intensity on delivery fades quite dramatically to leave an almost new-makey cocoa residue. Surprising... and delicious...; b22.5 An altogether superior and much more complex animal to J B's disappointing No 3 Selection. *46%*

Tullibardine 1992 Rum Finish bott 2009 db (89.5) n22 t23 f22.5 b22. Cracking stuff! *46%*

Tullibardine 1993 bott 2009 db (91.5) n22 t23.5 f23 b23. Intrinsically sweet barley. But spellbindingly charming all the way. *40%*

Tullibardine 1993 Moscatel Finish bott 2007 db (92.5) n23.5 t23.5 f23 b22.5. This really is how wine casks should integrate. A minor stunner. *46%*

Tullibardine 1993 Oloroso Sherry Finish bott 2008 db **(89)** n23 t23 f21 b22. Almost a trip down Memory Lane: once a pretty standard sherry butt, but now a treat. *46%*

Tullibardine 1993 Pedro Ximénez Sherry Finish bott 2009 db **(87)** n21 t23 f20.5 b22.5. Sticky and enjoyable. *46%*

Tullibardine 1993 Port Finish bott 2008 db **(83.5)** n21.5 t21 f20 b21. A bumbling, weighty kind of dram with indistinct shape and purpose, even to the extent of displaying a more bourbony gait than a fruity one. Enjoyable, decently spiced but limited in scope. *46%*

Tullibardine 1993 Sauternes Finish bott 2008 db **(84.5)** n22 t22 f20 b20.5. Sleepy and soft with the expected major grape input. Yet rather flattens out too early and to too great a degree. Pleasant, but a little disappointing, too. *46%*

Tullibardine Aged 20 Years db **(92.5)** n22.5 busy and can't decide which weight to adopt; ethereal hazelnut and citrus rise above the languid tannins; t24 no doubting the richness of body and the exceptional weight: first it is scorched yet juicy barley by the cartload, then thudding oak with just enough ulmo honey to oil the wheels. And then rampaging spice; f22.5 settles for more prosaic butterscotch but the spices continue to bristle; b23.5 while there are whiskies like this in the world, there is a point to this book... *43%*

Tullibardine Aged 25 Years db **(86.5)** n22 t22 f21 b21.5. There can be too much of a good thing. And although the intricacies of the honey makes you sigh inwardly with pleasure, the overall rigidity and fundamentalism of the oak goes a little too far. *43%*

Tullibardine 225 sauternes cask finish db **(85)** n20 t22.5 f21 b21.5. Hits the heights early on in the delivery when the honey and Lubeck marzipan are at full throttle. *43%*

Tullibardine 228 Burgundy cask finish db **(82)** n21 t22 f18 b21. No shortage of bitter chocolate. Flawed but a wow for those looking for mega dry malt. *43%*

Tullibardine 500 sherry cask finish db **(79.5)** n19 t21 f19 b20.5. The usual problems from Jerez, but the grape ensures maximum chewability. *43%*

Tullibardine Aged Oak bott 2009 db **(86)** n21.5 t21 f22 b21.5. Aged oak maybe. But early on this is all about the malt which is faultless. Major oaky buzz later. *40%*

Tullibardine Aged Oak Edition bott 2010 db **(88)** n21 t22 f22.5 b22.5. Beautifully made malt which is full of life. *40%. nc.*

Tullibardine Banyuls Finish bott 2011 db **(68)** n16 t18 f17 b17. I saw the sulphur coming on this. A steaming mug of intense black coffee and a cool glass of taste bud restorative coconut water wait in the wings. *46%. nc ncf.*

Tullibardine Banyuls Finish bott 2012 db **(71)** n17 t19 f17 b18. A minor tragedy: take away the sulphur and you have what would have been a serious juicefest. Not for the first time with a banyuls cask, I could cry! *46%. nc ncf.*

Tullibardine John Black db **(84.5)** n20 t21.5 f22 b21. Young, clean and bursting with all kinds of delicious maltiness. An almost perfect first dram of the day. *40%. nc.*

Tullibardine Pure Pot new make db **(90.5)** n24 t23 f21.5 b22. Pure delight! Not whisky, of course, but a great example of how new make malt should be. *69%*

Tullibardine PX Finish dist 1993, bott 2008 db **(85)** n23 t22 f20 b20. A big, at times bone-hard, whisky which, like many which have spent time in Pedro Ximénez casks, have found it difficult to acquire the kind of balance hoped. The nose offers great promise with a real old-fashioned fruitcake flourish but after the melt-in-the-mouth delivery gets past the barley lead, the degree of bitterness outweighs the growing soft fig notes. For equilibrium, needed less – or more – time in cask: we'll never know. *46%*

Tullibardine Sauternes Finish bott 2012 db **(90.5)** n22 quite tight with fruit and barley bound together; a mild spearmint sweetness lightens things; t23 the balance between the juicier grape, diced apple and the keynote light sugars is excellent, as is the soft oils and ever buzzing spices; f22.5 butterscotch tart with a light chocolate topping; b23 the spices attached to the richness of the body makes for a very satisfying and quite intriguing malt. *46%. nc ncf.*

Tullibardine Sovereign bourbon barrel db **(89.5)** n22 t22.5 a kind of 'what's what' of bourbon aromas: an entire regiment of delicate oaky tones from the standard butterscotch through to polished oak floors. But all tinged with a green-ish barley note. Always light and a little chalky; t23 the nose is transferred almost in identical form to the delivery: more light sugars at play here and a little nutty, too; f21.5 a slight tang to the fading milky Sugar Puffs; b22.5 beautifully salivating despite the intricate oak notes. *43%*

Tullibardine Vintage Edition Aged 20 Years dist 1988, bott 2008 db **(86)** n22 t22 f21 b21. The malt sparkles on the nose and delivery. Fades as caramels kick in. *46%*

Cadenhead Tullibardine 19 Years Old Chateau Lafitte dist 93, bott 13 **(89)** n23 t22.5 f21.5 b22. Sometimes these wine finishes can anything other than to pop your cork for. This, though, has enough depth to handle the majority of the massive grape. *48.3%. 210 bottles.*

⁖ **Old Malt Cask Tullibardine Aged 23 Years** cask no. 10453, bott 14 **(95)** n23.5 beautiful structure and weight: a little toasty, but welcomes the nutty spread. Excellent salt to sugar ratio; t24 sublime delivery with near perfect weight and poise and some ramped up barley. The oils are delicate, the sugars playful and the quasi-bourbon style liquorice adding just the right degree of tostesterone; **f23.5** a late settling of some sugary scores as the light muscovado overpowers the fudgy oak; **b24** an early morning reminder why I can really love this job. *50%. sc.*

⠿ **The Pearls of Scotland Tullibardine 1990** cask no. 6115, bott Jun 14 **(94) n23.5** borderline bourbon in style with nut and toasted honeycomb amid the red liquorice; **t24** superb delivery: the mouth feel, approach and realisation of the soft molassed sugars. Their intermingling with the liquorice and light hickory; the weight...and pace of change....the stamp of rich malt to remind you this is Scotch...classy! **f23** more bourbon-style notes hang in there, especially the sugar-oak and red liquorice; **b23.5** top drawer whisky which embraces the oak like a Kentuckian. *51.7%. sc.*

UNSPECIFIED SINGLE MALTS (Campbeltown)

Cadenhead's Campbeltown Malt (92) n22 t24 f23 b23. On their home turf you'd expect them to get it right... and, my word, so they do!! *59.5%*

Cadenhead's Classic Campbeltown (92) n23 t24 f22 b23. What a dram! Must be what they gave Lazarus... *50%*

UNSPECIFIED SINGLE MALTS (Highland)

Fortnum and Mason Highland Aged 10 Years (88.5) n23 t22 f21.5 b22. A very soft ride around the Highlands. Dangerously easy drinking in Mayfair. *43%*

Glen Marnoch Aged 18 Years Limited Edition Release Cask Reserve (88.5) n23 t22.5 f21 b22. Quite beautiful. Distilled hot cross bun. *40%. Aldi.*

Glen Turner Aged 12 Years Exclusive Reserve bott code. L206557A **(87) n22 t22 f21 b22.** Charming and showing delicate complexity in all the right places. *40%*

Maxwell 33 Year Old Highland Single Malt (95) n24.5 t24 f22.5 b24. Last year Lidl unearthed a couple of stunning whiskies to be sold at an improbably economic price to the consumer. They have done it again for Christmas 2012 with a malt destined to be another collectors' item. At times towards the end the age is apparent. But no less so is a malt which has on the nose and delivery a marriage between oak and barley matured in heaven. A very softly smoked, delightfully fruity gem. *40%. sc. Lidl. 5280 bottles.*

Wemyss Aged 16 Years Highland "Beachcomber" hogshead, bott 11 **(90) n23 t23.5 f21.5 b22.** The honey elements are to die for. Not sure where the beach comes in, though; such fanciful and, frankly, pretentious names does the brand no favours whatsoever and imbues a degree of amateurism which does the brand and whisky a disservice... *46%. sc.*

Wemyss Glen Garioch 1989 Single Highland "Fruit Bonbons" hogshead **(91.5) n22 t23.5 f23 b23.** The spirit from the stills at this time had a "fire water" reputation which now, as is so often the case, means we have a malt which is wilful and complex and able to take the two decades of maturation comfortably in its stride. *46%. sc. 325 bottles.*

UNSPECIFIED SINGLE MALTS (Island)

Master Of Malt Island Single Malt (91.5) n22.5 t23 f22.5 b23.5. Don't know about Lord of the Isles. More like Lord of the Flies...Fruit flies, that is...! They would be hard pressed to find even an over-ripe mango any juicier than this gorgeous malt... *40%*

UNSPECIFIED SINGLE MALTS (Islay)

⠿ **Blackadder Peat Reek Raw Cask Islay** single oak hogshead, bott Jul 13 **(88.5) n23** rich in phenols and sugar cane juice. Oily, too; **t23** big and chewy arrival, but still allows the sugars a pretty full hand. The oak is bit niggardly but banana and vanilla still hold out; **f21** finally bitters out on the oak; **b21.5** a more sympathetic hoggy and this would have scored very highly. *60.6%. nc ncf sc. 216 bottles. WB15/060*

⠿ **Blackadder Smoking Islay** cask. BA2013/450, bott Jun 13 **(88) n22** on the nose, more like Fighting Islay: the peat is pretty spiced up and gives the old schnoz a sharp biff; **t23** the palate becomes a playground for energetic young sugars; **f21** slightly overly aggressive on the bitterness front; spice tries to compensate; **b22** attractive, but not quite up to the usual very high standards for this bottling. *55%. nc ncf sc. 386 bottles. WB15/161*

⠿ **Blackadder Smoking Islay Raw Cask** cask no. BA2013/449 **(92.5) n24** brilliant nose. Very high phenols offering Parma violets (flowers, not candy), celery and accompanying pepper, salted liquorice, hickory and, cleverly hidden, smoked treacle; **t23.5** the more sugary elements have enough power to hold off the creeping, drying smoke for a while. It is the massive spice which really focusses the attention; **f22** dries and bitters. But the dark, buttery, cake-mix, sugars combine with the smoke to see off the worst; **b23** almost a curious re-run of Blackadder's Peat Reek, with the fun threatening to end as the bitterness of the cask bites, adder-like. But just many good points compensate. Really lovely. *59.9%. nc ncf sc. 318 bottles. WB15/061*

⫶⫶ **Celtique Connexion Origine Islay Affine Sauternes Cask** dist 1999, bott 2013 **(95.5)** n23 huge smoke is somehow contained in a creamy, sultana studded crust; t24 soft and voluptuous, the peat arrives confidently, spices in hand; silky fruit soon takes command displaying a fine array of varied sugars; f24 a finish marginally longer than the Channel Tunnel...an offering an even more comfortable ride; dries into a sooty peat finale; b24.5 that rarest of beasts: a heavily peated malt happy to mature in a wine cask. Not surprised it required a spotless Sauternes cask to do the job. Mind-blowingly glorious. 46%

⫶⫶ **Elements of Islay AR4 (93.5)** n23.5 t23.5 f23 b23.5. Massive oak infusion: the slow burn of smoke leaves no doubt to distillery. Clever oily-dry interplay plus hickory and cocoa-orange. 58.1% WB15/341

⫶⫶ **Elements of Islay BN6 (80)** n20 t22 f19 b19. Simply too sweet and cloying for its own good. Zero complexity as the molasses, golden syrup and manuka honey go ballistic. Off key finale. 56.9% WB15/346

Elements of Islay BR4 (93) n22.5 t24 f23 b23.5. Non-peated Islay at is most deliciously coastal. 54.7%.

⫶⫶ **Elements of Islay BR5 (96)** n24 t24.5 f23.5 b24. An unpeated masterpiece of the Laddie old school. Possibly the most complete and harmonious alloy of honeys bottled this year. Genius. 53.8% WB15/296

Elements of Islay BW1 (89) n22 t22 f22 b23. Pretty regulation oily peat, but with helpful oak. 52.9%. Speciality Drinks Ltd.

⫶⫶ **Elements of Islay BW3 (90.5)** n22.5 t23.5 f22 b22.5. A playful Bowmore showing a copper sharpness amid the more languid smoke. Fabulous delivery: acacia and ulmo honey starring. 51.6% WB15/289

Elements of Islay CL4 (92.5) n23.5 t23.5 f22.5 b23. Astonishing. If you are looking for a soft, easy going peat job with polite smoke, go somewhere else. This is bold as brass. Massive and magnificent. 58.7% Speciality Drinks Ltd.

⫶⫶ **Elements of Islay CL6 (94)** n23 t24 f23 b24. Less oil means more balance for this stunning Caol Ila. The major citrus element cuts through the peat; light sugar and malt salivates. 61.2% WB15/290

⫶⫶ **Elements of Islay LG4 (87.5)** n22 t23 f21 b21.5. Typical huge Lagavulin but untypical sharpness on delivery & sweet finish. The phenols are of a smoked mackerel variety. 55.7% WB15/287

⫶⫶ **Elements of Islay LP4 (89)** n22.5 t22.5 f22 b22. Profound peat at its earthiest. A tangy delivery but then soothing, as muscovado sugars & vanillas arrive. A gentle giant. 54.8% WB15/286

⫶⫶ **Elements of Islay LP5 (92)** n23.5 t22.5 f22 b22. Elements is right for this Laphroaig: what we are getting here is the malt at its gristiest with the sugars releasing the smoke beautifully. 52.4% WB15/288

Finlaggan Old Reserve Cask Strength (94) n23 t23.5 f23.5 b24. I can imagine even people who proclaim not to like peaty whisky slowly falling in love with this...it is so enormous, that it would be a case of kill or cure. 58%. The Vintage Malt Whisky Co Ltd.

Fortnum and Mason Islay Aged 10 Years (90.5) n23 t23 f22 b22.5. it is nearly 20 years since I began giving whisky tastings at Fortnum and Mason. And I remember when I unleashed the first big Islay malt the majority of the veritable patrons of Mayfair had ever tasted. It was not unlike this, though less oily. The shock in the room could be felt all the way to my hat suppliers, Bates, about 250 yards away. And not all were convinced. Amazing how the same clientele, or at least their heirs, demand that a malt like this should be available to them. Times have changed drastically over two decades... 43%

Milroy's of Soho Peated Single Malt hogshead, cask no. 8099, dist 4 Dec 08, bott 13 Apr 13 **(84)** n22 t21 f21 b20. Semi new-makey on nose and delivery, this enormous whisky positively flops around the palate with little discernible balance. Some thick sugar battles out the bitter oak and ash influence. Very different. 40%. 497 bottles.

Mystery Lochside (95) n24.5 t24 f22.5 b24. The kind of malt that deserves all the time you can afford it. It will repay you handsomely, especially on the nose and delivery and will never come at you at the same speed or angle. Subtle and sublime.

Port Askaig Harbour Aged 12 Years (84.5) n21.5 t22 f20 b21. Perfect if you are looking for a peaty fix. But the quality of the bittering oak doesn't do the malt many favours. 45.8%

Port Askaig Harbour Aged 19 Years (94) n23.5 t23.5 f23 b24. One of those gorgeous offerings which basks in its simplicity, but takes what it does to the max. 50.4%.

Port Askaig Harbour Aged 30 Years (89) n22 t23 f22 b22. A barrel of brinkmanship: the oak influence is immense, but the quality of the spirit and profound sugars make relatively light work of it. 51.1%.

Wemyss Aged 14 Years Islay "Smoke on the Rocks" (87) hogshead, bott Aug 11 **(87)** n22 t22.5 f20 b22.5. Laphroaig-style smoke dispersal...and even complete with late cask bitterness. 46%. sc. 338 bottles. USA exclusive.

Wemyss Aged 30 Years Islay "Heathery Smoke" hogshead, bott Aug 11 (95.5) n24 t24 f23.5 b24. One of those magical malts which never noses or tastes the same twice and always offers a different perspective and new facets each time it is sampled. A true gem. 46%. sc. 272 bottles. USA exclusive.

Wemyss 1997 Single Islay "Seaspray", bott 11 (74) n18 t21 f17 b18. The furry bitterness on the finish tells you all you need to know: a reject cask has got through. 46%. sc.

UNSPECIFIED SINGLE MALTS (Lowland)

Master of Malt Lowland Single Malt 2nd Edition (87) n23 t22.5 f20.5 b21. For a malt seemingly light in body, it appears to put on weight like a pie shop regular. 40%. ncf.

McClelland's Lowland (87.5) n22 t22.5 f21 b22. A lovely, relaxed Lowlander which doesn't claim greatness but offers modest distinction. 40%

⁖ **Tweeddale Single Lowland Malt Scotch Whisky 14 Years** db (89) n21.5 sharp citrus and basic vanilla; t23.5 lively, clean and salivating, the grist positively pulses; f22 back to simple vanilla basics...but attractively done; b22 busy, bustling, elegant and old-fashioned... like a small borders town. 62%. nc ncf sc. Stonedean Ltd.

UNSPECIFIED SINGLE MALTS (Speyside)

Master of Malt Speyside 30 Years Old 5th Edition (89) n22.5 t21.5 f23 b22. A whisky moving in and out of acceptable oak like a how patient might drift in and out of consciousness. 43%.

⁖ **Master of Malt Speyside 30 Years Old 6th edition** (95) n24.5 textbook balance and dexterity to the oak. Like opening up an old herb and spice cupboard and the last reverberations of a hundred cakes and stews made many years ago come quietly drifting back...; t24 no less delicate on delivery. Probably made in a big still as there is little oil or metallic residue, leaving the oak to, again, lead the way, both in weight and depth of layering; the sweetness is confined to a light mintiness and a vague grist presence, but after the brief initial barley juice outpouring, it is the drying oak which dominates; f22.5 so light, the fade is over quickly but not without delicate spice and overall elegance; b24 Hmmmm. My 13th whisky of the day...and this comes from bottle number 13 of 238. The omens may be bad but in fact it has proved to be the best of the session so far. From the understated school of Speysiders where subtlety is key. 43.7%. 238 bottles. WB15/229

Master Of Malt Speyside 40 Years Old 2nd Edition (95) n23.5 t24 f23.5 b24. Magnificent. has no problem mastering the years. 43%.

Master of Malt Speyside 50 Years Old 3rd Edition (96.5) n24 t23.5 f24.5 b24.5. Like many an old 'un, it seems to forget where it's going for a while. But when it reaches its destination, it just charms you to death. 43%.

⁖ **Old Malt Cask Probably Speyside's Finest Distillery** wine finished refill hogshead, cask no. 10376, dist Nov 92, bott Mar 14 (74) n18 t20 f17 b19. Tart, furry, woefully off key: I think Speyside can do a little better than this. 50%. sc. 152 bottles.

⁖ **Old Masters Queen of Spey 12 Year Old** dist 2001, bott 2013 (89.5) n22 an attractive thread of anthracite smoke weaves in and out of the fresh ear and gristy malt; t23 much, much younger on delivery than its 14 years, with a hint of new make. But the mix of intense juicy barley and spice is gorgeous; f22 a little oak bite and nibble but vanilla dominates; b22.5 an unspecified single malt of very specified freshness and beauty. 56.8%.

That Boutique-y Whisky Company Secret Distillery Number One batch 1 (92.5) n23 t24 f22.5 b23. A pretty satisfying experience for those with an oloroso bent. 55.4%.

The Whisky Agency Speyside House Malt 1995 refill sherry wood, bott 12 (88) n22.5 t23.5 f20 b22. Sublime fruit early on. 50.8%

UNSPECIFIED SINGLE MALTS (General)

⁖ **Blackadder Black Smoke Vat No. 2 First Venom** bott Sept 13 (95) n23.5 fudge with juicy raisin; slight hint of greengage; t23.5 superb delivery: the barley is in full concentrated mode and after a toffee-laden interlude returns, alongside a wave of grape to make for a delightful, mouth-watering juiciness; f24 spiced grape..which can't entirely escape the toffee encasement; some attractive praline and mocha mix to finish; b24 great to find a malt finished in sherry and has not paid the price...pure entertainment. 56.9%. nc ncf. 474 bottles.

⁖ **Blackadder The Legendary Cask Strength** (93) n23 delicate, (non-salted) buttery tones link with boiled pear and creamy custard....yummy! t24 if there are awards for the softest cask strength deliveries, this would be up there. A playfully light oil adds lustre to the intense barley and toffee tones which dominate; a gorgeous layer or two of ulmo honey absorbs and punches the spices try to give; f23 very light tannin adds depth, but it is a slow fade of all that has gone before...; **b23** if the legendary Blackadder, complete with trusted sword, reappeared through the "swirling mists of time" and came back as a whisky, I think he'd prefer to be something a little more butch than this essay of gentility bordering on femininity. *58.1%. nc ncf sc. WB15/055*

⋯ **Blackadder The Legendary 20 Years Old** cask no. LT132013-02 (87.5) **n22 t22 f21.5 b22.** Appears to have spent a significant part of the passing 20 years trapping all the soft caramel notes it can find. This overcomes the more stark oakiness, but at the cost of complexity. Hardly challenging but very pleasant, though. *46%. nc ncf sc. WB15/057*

Chieftain's The Cigar Malt Aged 15 Years hogshead, dist Apr 95, bott 2011 (94) **n24 t22.5 f23.5 b24.** Must be one of those chocolate cigars I used to eat when I was a kid. Seemingly distilled from 100% malted cocoa and matured in a cask coopered by the gods. A gun to the head would never induce me to smoke a cigar or even cigarette (I did once have one put to my head by a weirdo to force me to smoke dope, and I turned that down, too — but that's another story). But just try and stop me drinking this stuff... *46%. nc ncf. USA release.*

⋯ **Chieftain's The Cigar Malt Aged 20 Years** sherry butt, dist May 93, bott Sept 13 (86.5) **n21 t23 f21 b21.5** From a 90% clean sherry butt (the finish gives the game away a bit), a whisky you can puff on, apparently. Not being a smoker — and never having ever been one — I have no idea what this is about. But as a single malt, a pleasant enough experience, though strictly limited in its scope and desires and the real fun bit revolves around the impressively rich delivery. *51.8%. ncf nc. Ian Macleod Distillers Ltd.*

Scottish Vatted Malts
(also Pure Malts/Blended Malt Scotch)

100 Pipers Aged 8 Years Blended Malt (74) **n19 t20 f17 b18.** A better nose, perhaps, and some spice on arrival. But when you consider the Speysiders at their disposal, all those mouth-wateringly grassy possibilities, it is such a shame to find something as bland as this. *40%*

Ballantine's Pure Malt Aged 12 Years bott code. LKAC1538 (88.5) **n22.5 t23 f21 b22.** No sign of the peat being reintroduced to major effect, although the orange is a welcome addition. Remains a charmer. *40%. Chivas.*

Bally Delicious 23 Year Old refill hogshead, cask no. 288, dist 10 Mar 89, bott 26 Nov 12 (86) **n22 t21 f22 b21.** A vatted malt in that this comes from one distillery (probably Balvenie) and has a minute amount of its sister malt (Glenfiddich) entered into the cask — thus making it impossible for the single cask Balvenie to enter into the market place as this is made for other blending companies. And, somewhat typically for the distillery, the oak plays too grand a part in affairs when it gets to this kind of advanced age. That said, there are some majestic honey and marmalade moments amid the barley. But the oak is simply far too loud for a malt so delicate. *54%. sc. Master of Malt. 288 bottles.*

Barrogill (90) **n22.5 t23 f22.5 b22.** Prince Charles, who allows the name to be used for this whisky, is said to enjoy this dram. Hardly surprising, as its pretty hard not to: this is wonderful fun. Curiously, I have just read the back label and noticed they use the word "robust". I have employed "lusty". Either way, I think you might get the message. *40%*

Barrogill North Highland Blended Malt Mey Selections bott code P012630 (79) **n18 t21 f20 b20.** Recovers attractively — helped by a mighty dose of concentrated maltiness - from the disappointing nose. *40%. Inver House Distillers for North Highland.*

Bell's Signature Blend Limited Edition (83.5) **n19 t22 f21 b21.5.** The front label makes large that this vatted malt has Blair Athol and Inchgower at the heart of it as they are "two fine malts selected for their exceptionally rich character". Kind of like saying you have invited the Kray twins to your knees up as they might liven it up a bit. Well those two distilleries were both part of the original Bell's empire, so fair dos. But to call them both fine malts is perhaps stretching the imagination somewhat. A robust vatting to say the least. And, to be honest, once you get past the nose, good back-slapping fun. *40%. 90,000 bottles.*

Berrys' Best Islay Vatted Malt Aged 8 Years (82) **n20 t21 f20 b21.** Smoky, raw, sweet, clean and massive fun! *43%. Berry Bros & Rudd.*

Berry's Own Selection Blue Hanger 5th Release bott 2010 (81) **n20 t21 f20 b20.** Not a lot — but enough — sulphur has crept in to take the edge of this one. *45.6%. nc ncf.*

Berry's Own Selection Islay Reserve 2nd Edition (86.5) **n22 t22 f21 b21.5.** Maybe an Islay reserve but has enough smoky weight and hickory/chocolate charisma to be pushing for the first team squad. *46%. nc ncf. Berry Bros & Rudd.*

Berry's Own Selection Speyside Reserve 2nd Edition (79.5) **n21 t21.5 f18 b19.** Some excellent early sharpness and honey depth but falters. *46%. nc ncf. Berry Bros & Rudd.*

Big Peat (96) **n25 t24 f23.5 b23.5.** I suppose if you put Ardbeg and Port Ellen together there is a chance you might get something rather special. Not guaranteed, but achieved here with the kind of panache that leaves you spellbound. The complexity and balance are virtually off the charts, though had the Caol Ila been reduced slightly, and with it the oils, this might well have been World Whisky of the Year. *46%. ncf Douglas Laing & Co.*

Big Peat Batch 20 Xmas 2011 (96) n24 t23.5 f24.5 b24. I haven't got a television these days as my life is simply too busy. And with entertainment like this in the glass to keep you occupied, who needs one...? I doubt if any Christmas Special on the box came remotely close to matching this...! *57.8%. nc ncf.*

Big Peat Batch 26 (83.5) n21.5 t21.5 f20 b21. Not quite as big a peat as some, suffering from over-active oils and a bitter rear-guard. Still has a the odd powerful puff. *46%. nc ncf.*

Big Peat Batch 27 (88) n22 t22 f22 b22. Well weighted sugars and just the right degree of smoked vanilla fade. Just spotted that this, the 888th new whisky for the Bible 2013 scored...88. It had to be ...!! *46%. nc ncf. Douglas Laing & Co.*

Big Peat Batch 28 (84.5) n22 t22 f20 b20.5. Pleasant. But appears to possess a bit too much Caol Ila style oiliness to set the peaty pulse racing. *46%. nc ncf. Douglas Laing & Co.*

Big Peat Batch 29 (89.5) n22.5 t23 f22 b22. A peaty massage. *46%. nc ncf.*

Big Peat Batch 30 (92) n23 t22 f23.5 b23.5. That's much more like it! This is far more how I expect this dram to be. *46%. nc ncf. Douglas Laing & Co.*

Big Peat Batch 31 (90.5) n23 love it: superb mix of allotment bonfire and peat reek. Some young spirit offering great energy; t22 gristy sweet delivery pounded by spicy attitude; a blast of hickory and cocoa; f22.5 the smoke rumbles along, but there is no letting up in intensity of peat or spice; b23 good to see it has maintained its cheery high standard. Youthful, boisterous and challenging throughout. *46%. nc ncf. Douglas Laing & Co.*

The Big Smoke 40 (83) n22 t21 f20 b20. Pure grist. *40%*

The Big Smoke 60 (92) n23 t23.5 f22.5 b23. Much more delicate and in touch with its more feminine self than was once the case. A real beauty. *60%. Duncan Taylor & Co.*

Black Face 8 Years Old (78.5) n18.5 t22 f19 b19. A huge malt explosion in the kisser on delivery, but otherwise not that pretty to behold. *46%. The Vintage Malt Whisky Co Ltd.*

Burns Nectar (89.5) n22 t22 f23 b22.5. A delight of a dram and with all that honey around, "Nectar" is about right. *40%*

Carme 10 Years Old (79) n21.5 t20 f18.5 b19. On paper Ardmore and Clynelish should work well together. But vatting is not done on paper and here you have two malts cancelling each other out and some less than great wood sticking its oar in. *43%*

Cask Islay Vatting No. 1 (89) n23 t22 f22 b22. Those looking for a soft, smoky, inoffensive little Islay to keep them company had better look elsewhere... *46%. ncf. A.D. Rattray Ltd.*

Castle Rock Aged 12 Years Blended Malt (87) n22.5 t23 f19.5 b22. Stupendously refreshing: the finish apart, I just love this style of malt. *40%*

Cearban (79.5) n18 t21.5 f20 b19. The label shows a shark. It should be a whale: this is massive. Sweet with the malts not quite on the same wavelength. *40%. Robert Graham Ltd.*

Celtique Connexion Sauternes 16 Years Old dist 1995, bott 2012 **(95)** n24 t24 f23 b24. Not many whiskies make me cough, and hardly any at all at just 46%abv. But this, though only because the intensity caught me by surprise. And what a pleasant one! This horse chestnut-coloured malt is one you are unlikely to forget in a hurry. As sweetly balanced and beautiful to enjoy as Josh Wright's stunning volley for Millwall at Burnley in February 2012.... *46%. nc ncf.*

Clan Campbell 8 Years Old Pure Malt (82) n20 t22 f20 b20. Enjoyable, extremely safe whisky that tries to offend nobody. The star quality is all on the complex delivery, then it's toffee. *40%. Chivas Brothers.*

Clan Denny (Bowmore, Bunnahabhain, Caol Ila and Laphroaig) **(94)** n24 t23 f23 b24. A very different note on Islay with heavy peats somehow having a floating quality. Unique *40%*

Clan Denny Islay (86.5) n21.5 t23 f21 b21. A curiously bipolar malt with the sweetness and bitterness at times going to extremes. Some niggardly oak has taken the edge of what might have been a sublime malt as the peat and spices at times positively glistens with honey. *46.5%. nc ncf sc. Douglas Laing & Co.*

Clan Denny Speyside (87) n22 t22 f21 b22. A Tamdhu-esque oiliness pervades here and slightly detracts from the complexity. That said, the early freshness is rather lovely. *46%*

Compass Box Canto Cask 10 bott Jul 07 **(86.5)** n20.5 t21 f23.5 b21.5. One the Canto collection which slipped through my net a few years back, but is still around, I understand. Typical of the race, this one has perhaps an extra dollop of honey which helps keep the over vigorous oaks under some degree of control. Sublime finish. *54.2%. nc ncf. 200-250 bottles.*

Compass Box Eleuthera Marriage married for nine months in an American oak Hogshead **(86)** n22 t22 f20 b22. I'm not sure if it's the name that gets me on edge here, but as big and robust as it is I still can't help feeling that the oak has bitten too deep. Any chance of a Compass Box Divorce...? *49.2%. Compass Box for La Maison du Whisky.*

Compass Box Flaming Heart second batch, bottling no. FH16MMVII **(95.5)** n23.5 t24.5 f23 b24.5. The Canto range was, I admit, a huge over-oaked disappointment. This, though, fully underlines Compass Box's ability to come up with something approaching genius. This is a whisky that will be remembered by anyone who drinks it for the rest of their lives as just about the perfect study of full-bodied balance and sophistication. And that is not cheap hyperbole. *48.9%. nc ncf. 4,302 bottles.*

Compass Box Flaming Heart 4th Edition bott Aug 12 **(95) n23.5 t24.5 f23 b24.** Vatted malt at its very best. A genuine celebration of great Scotch malt whisky. 48.9%. *9,147 bottles.*

Compass Box Flaming Heart 10th Anniversary bott Sep 10 **(92) n24 t23 f22 b23.** This one, as Flaming Heart so often is, is about counterweight and mouth feel. Everything appears just where it should be... *48.9%. nc ncf. 4186 bottles.*

Compass Box Lady Luck bott Sep 09 **(91) n22 t24 f23 b22.** Just a shade too sweet for mega greatness like The Spice Tree, but quite an endearing box of tricks. *46%.*

Compass Box Oak Cross bott May 10 **(92.5) n23 t24 f22.5 b23.** The oak often threatens to be just too big a cross to bear. But such is the degree of complexity, and cleverness of weight, the overall brilliance is never dimmed. Overall, a bit of a tart of a whisky... *43%. nc ncf.*

Compass Box The Peat Monster bott May 10 **(82) n21.5 t21.5 f19 b20.** It is as though Victor Frankenstein's creation has met Bambi. Monsters don't come much stranger or more sanitised than this... *46%. nc ncf.*

Compass Box The Peat Monster first fill and refill American Oak Casks, bott 18 Aug 12 **(94) n23.5 t23.5 f23 b24.** Wonderful to see peat working on so many levels. The sugars are perhaps more judicially used this time around. *46%. nc ncf.*

Compass Box The Peat Monster Reserve **(92) n23 t23.5 f22.5 b23.** At times a bit of a Sweet Monster...beautiful stuff! *48.9%*

⠿ **Compass Box The Peat Monster Tenth Anniversary Release** bott Sept 13 **(95) n24** it has retained its sooty style from last year, though has bent at the knee to allow a little extra light brown sugar to soften the more eye-watering, sharper elements of the peat; **t24** a very clever delivery: both muscovado sugar and thick smoke are battling for early supremacy with neither having the heart for the kill. The oils enter and side with the muscovado, spreading around the palate, aided with a cocoa-bitter edge, while the smoke patrols and watches; **f23** a little bitter now, with a slight return to an acrid bite; slight sootiness foils attempts by the vanilla to gain a foothold; **b24** here we appear to see a mix, or compromise, between the sweeter bottling of two years ago and last year's searing dryness. And, unlike most compromises, this one works... *48.9%. 5,700 bottles.*

Compass Box The Spice Tree first-fill and refill American oak. Secondary maturation: heavily toasted new French oak **(95.5) n24.5 t24.5 f23 b23.5.** Having initially been chopped down by the SWA, who were indignant that extra staves had been inserted into the casks, The Spice Tree is not only back but in full bloom. Indeed, the blossom on this, created by the use of fresh oak barrel heads, is more intoxicating than its predecessor – mainly because there is a more even and less dramatic personality to this. Not just a great malt, but a serious contender for Jim Murray Whisky Bible 2011 World Whisky of the Year. *46%*

Compass Box The Spice Tree Inaugural Batch (93) n23 t23 f23 b24. The map for flavour distribution had to be drawn for the first time here: an entirely different whisky in shape and flavour emphasis. And it is a map that takes a long time to draw... *46%. 4150 bottles.*

Co-operative Group (CWS) Blended Malt Aged 8 Years (86.5) n22 t22 f21 b21.5. Much, much better! Still a little on the sticky and sweet side, but there is some real body and pace to the changes on the palate. Quite rich, complex and charming. *40%*

Cutty Sark Blended Malt (92.5) n22 t24 f23 b23.5. Sheer quality: as if two styles have been placed in the bottle and told to fight it out between them. What a treat! *40%.*

⠿ **Douglas Laing's Double Barrel Ardbeg & Aultmore (85) n21.5 t22.5 f20 b21.** Fruity, juicy and fulsome, the smoke has an adroit presence. But, ultimately, a little too tangy for its own good. *46%.*

⠿ **Douglas Laing's Double Barrel Ardbeg & Craigellachie (94.5) n24** the peat appears on so many levels and in so many different hues, it is mind-blowing. The most telling, though, involves a stratum of lavender lightened with linseed oil; muscovado sugars ensure things don't get too heavy; **t23** a sweeter more salivating delivery than expected. Lighter, too, with malt and mocha at play early on and also while the oaks build up steam. The smoke is subdued; **f23.5** the peat builds as does the oak, making this a much more hefty finish. The mocha returns but requires sturdier molasses to keep the toastiness in check; **b24** magnificent complexity. *46%*

Douglas Laing's Double Barrel Ardbeg & Glenrothes (91) n23 t23 f22 b23. A feather-light whisky offering subtlety throughout; *46%*

Douglas Laing's Double Barrel Ardbeg & Glenrothes 8th Release (85.5) n22.5 t22 f20 b21. Nothing like as perky as the bottling I tasted last year: the Glenrothes appears to blunt the more intricate machinations of the Ardbeg after a beautifully choreographed nose and very early delivery. *46%*

Douglas Laing's Double Barrel Ardbeg & Glenrothes Aged 10 Years product no. MSW2685 **(92)** n22 t24 f23 b23. Not what I was expecting. But a lovely experience nonetheless. 46%

Douglas Laing's Double Barrel Ardbeg & Glenrothes Aged 10 Years product no. DBS0003 **(88.5)** n23 t22 f21.5 b22. An uncompromising but fun way to bring up New Whisky no. 750 for Bible 2011... 46%. Douglas Laing.

❖ **Douglas Laing's Double Barrel Ben Nevis & Caol Ila (87.5)** n22.5 t22 f21 b22. One of the lightest coloured malt whiskies I have ever seen bottled so, unsurprisingly, oak appears to play no part in either nose or flavour profile other than a very late tang at the finish. The Ben Nevis has thinned both the oils and smoky intensity if the Islay, which shows a delicate charm on both nose and delivery in particular. 46%

Douglas Laing's Double Barrel Braeval & Caol Ila Aged 10 Years (78) n18 t21 f20 b19. The Mike and Bernie Winters of double barrelled whisky. 46%. Douglas Laing & Co Ltd.

Douglas Laing's Double Barrel Caol Ila & Braeval 4th Release (92.5) n23 t23.5 f22.5 b23.5. After a few failures with this combination, a hit. A real egg and bacon of a vatted malt with the two personalities this time complimenting each other beautifully. 46%

Douglas Laing's Double Barrel Caol Ila & Braeval Aged 10 Years (84.5) n21 t22 f20.5 b21. It is probably impossible to find a malt which is more friendly and inoffensive. Or two malts which have done such a first class job of cancelling each other's personalities out. 46%

Douglas Laing's Double Barrel Caol Ila & Tamdhu (89) n22 t23 f22 b22. Put two oily malts together and you get...an oily whisky... 46%

❖ **Douglas Laing's Double Barrel Caol Ila & Tamdhu (86.5)** n22 t22.5 f21 b21. Positivly shimmers on the palate while the smoke blasts its way through any encumberences. But there is something a little too youthful about the malt and too inhibited about the oak to make the most of the occasion. 46%.

Douglas Laing's Double Barrel Glenallachie & Bowmore 1st Release (89) n22 t22.5 f22 b22.5. The delicate smoke of the Bowmore has tamed the wilder elements of the Glenallachie. A good mix. 46%

Douglas Laing's Double Barrel Glenrothes & Ardbeg Aged 10 Years 4th Release (89.5) n21.5 t23 f22.5 b22.5. Despite the average nose the charmingly effete palate is another matter entirely. 46%. Douglas Laing.

Douglas Laing's Double Barrel Highland Park & Bowmore (95) n23 t24.5 f24 b23.5. The vital spark of fury to this one keeps the palate ignited. A standing ovation for such a magnificent performance on the palate. 46%. Douglas Laing & Co Ltd.

Douglas Laing's Double Barrel Ledaig & Bowmore (87) n22.5 t22 f21.5 b21. About as sweet a marriage as you are likely to find. For some, it may be too sweet! 46%

Douglas Laing's Double Barrel Macallan & Laphroaig 5th Release (93) n23.5 t24 f22.5 b23. As if born to be together. 46%

Douglas Laing's Double Barrel Macallan & Laphroaig Aged 9 Years (83.5) n21 t22 f20 b20.5. Curiously muted. Sweet with the natural caramels outweighing the smoke. 46%

Douglas Laing's Double Barrel Mortlach & Laphroaig 2nd Release **(83.5)** n20 t22 f20.5 b21. Compared to the Ardbeg/Glenrothes match, about as subtle and delicate as a smoky custard pie in the face. Hot and snarling fare. 46%

Douglas Laing's Double Barrel Mortlach & Laphroaig 3rd Release (82.5) n22.5 t21 f19 b20. Its sweet nose and soft touch in the opening seconds promises so much, but fails to deliver – especially on the finish. 46%

Douglas Laing's Double Barrel Mortlach & Laphroaig 4th Release (85.5) n21.5 t21.5 f21 b21.5. All kinds of sugars heading off every which way. Juicy and punchy, interests and entertains without harmonising. 46%

Douglas Laing's Double Barrel Talisker & Craigellachie (73) n19 t19 f17 b18. Should be divorced on the grounds of adultery with a poor cask. 46%

Douglas Laing's Double Barrel Talisker & Craigellachie 2nd Release (94.5) n23 t24 f23.5 b24. These two malts go together like bacon & eggs. And very smoky bacon at that... 46%

Duncan Taylor Regional Malt Collection Islay 10 Years Old (81) n21 t22 f19 b19. Soft citrus cleanses the palate, while gentle peats muddies it up again. 40%

❖ **Duthies Campbeltown Region Blended Malt Scotch Whisky (76)** n18 t21 f18 b19. Off key and furry: one suspects the hand of a naughty butt...Those not troubled by such things will lap up the rich delivery in particular. 46%. WB15/360

❖ **Duthies Highland Region Blended Malt Scotch Whisky (85)** n22.5 t22 f20 b21. Nose stars with its sweet; untoasted marshmallow. Delivery has attractive nip to the barley; accent on the malt; exceptionally creamy but then bitters out. Competent and pleasant other than an unforgiving bourbon cask. 46% WB15/361

❖ **Duthies Islay Region Blended Malt Scotch Whisky (94)** n23.5 mid-range peat....top range oil; a few gorgeous dry sooty moments; **t23.5** sweet delivery with the sugars, Demerara topping the bill, arriving before the smoke. Though only just, for that makes quite a noise, like thunder after a flash of sugary lightning; **f23** the oils unravel and coat the palate with a smoky top dressing...which lasts a fair while; **b24** has no great pretentions to enormity of complexity. But just displays a decent degree of peat in a thoroughly enjoyable and classical Islay manner. *46% WB15/359*

⫶⫶⫶ **Duthies Lowland Region Blended Malt Scotch Whisky (89.5) n22** lovely citrus freshens up the barley; **t22** the barley jags into the palate from various, unsatisfied angles until settling on a light massaging style full of lightly sugared, soothing oils; **f23** happier now, reverts to citrus and simple, caressing vanilla; **b22.5** a classic gentle pre-prandial top up. *46% WB15/356*

The Famous Grouse 10 Years Old Malt (77) n19 t20 f19 b19. The nose and finish headed south in the last Winter and landed in the sulphur marshes of Jerez. *40%. Edrington Group.*

The Famous Grouse 15 Years Old Malt (86) n21 t22 f21.5 b21.5. Salty and smoky with a real sharp twang. *43%. Edrington Group.*

The Famous Grouse 15 Years Old Malt (86) n19 t24 f22 b21. There had been a hint of the "s" word on the nose, but it got away with it. Now it has crossed that fine – and fatal – line where the petulance of the sulphur has thrown all else slightly out of kilter. All, that is, apart from the delivery which is a pure symphony of fruit and spice deserving a far better introduction and final movement. Some moving, beautiful moments. Flawed genius or what...? *40%*

The Famous Grouse 18 Years Old Malt (82) n19 t21.5 f21 b20.5. Some highly attractive honey outweighs the odd uncomfortable moment. *43%. Edrington Group.*

The Famous Grouse Malt 21 Years Old (91) n22 t24 f22 b23. A very dangerous dram: the sort where the third or fourth would slip down without noticing. Wonderful scotch! *43%.*

The Famous Grouse 30 Years Old Malt (94) n23.5 t24 f23 b23.5. Whisky of this sky-high quality is exactly what vatted malt should be all about. Outrageously good. *43%*

Glenalmond 2001 Vintage (82.5) n22 t21.5 f19 b20. Glenkumquat, more like: the most citrusy malt I have tasted in a very long time. *40%. The Vintage Malt Whisky Co Ltd.*

Glenalmond "Everyday" (89.5) n21.5 t23.5 f22 b22.5. They are not joking; this really is an everyday whisky. Glorious malt which is so dangerously easy to drink. *40%*

Glen Brynth Aged 12 Years Blended Malt (87) n22.5 t23 f19.5 b22. Deja vu...! Thought I was going mad: identical to the Castle Rock I tasted this morning, right down to the (very) bitter end ..!!! *40%. Quality Spirits International.*

Glenbrynth Blended Malt 12 Years (87.5) n22.5 t22.5 f21 b21.5. Heavyweight malt which gets off to a rip-roaring start on the delivery but falls away somewhat from the mid ground onwards. *43%. OTI Africa.*

Glenbrynth Ruby 40 Year Old Limited Edition (94) n23.5 t24 f23 b23.5. Has all the hallmarks of a completely OTT, far too old sherry butt being brought back to life with the aid of a livelier barrel. A magnificent experience, full of fun and evidence of some top quality vatting at work, too. *43%. OTI Africa.*

Glendower 8 Years Old (84) n21.5 t21 f20.5 b21 Nutty and spicy. *43%*

The Glenfohry Aged 8 Years Special Reserve (73) n19 t19 f17 b18. Some of the malt used here appears to have come from a still where the safe has not so much been broken into, but just broken! Oily and feinty, to say the least. Normally I would glower at anyone who even thought of putting a coke into their malt. Here, I think it might be for the best.. *40%*

Glen Turner Heritage Double Wood Bourbon & Madeira casks, bott code. L311657A **(85.5) n21.5 t22 f21 b21.** A very curious amalgamation of flavours. The oak appears to be in shock with the way the fruit is coming on to it and offers a bitter backlash. No faulting the crisp delivery with busy sugar and spice for a few moments brightening the palate. *40%.*

Glen Turner Pure Malt Aged 8 Years L525956A **(84) n20 t22 f22 b20.** A lush and lively vatting annoyingly over dependent on thick toffee but simply brimming with fabulously mouth-watering barley and over-ripe blood oranges. To those who bottle this, I say: let me into your lab. I can help you bring out something sublime!! *40%*

Glen Orchy (80.5) n19.5 t21.5 f19.5 b20. Not exactly the most subtle of vatted malts though when the juicy barley briefly pours through on delivery, enjoyable. *40%. Lidl.*

Glen Orchy 5 Year Old Blended Malt Scotch Whisky (88.5) n22 t22.5 f22 b22. Excellent malt plus very decent casks equals light-bodied fun. *40%. Lidl.*

Glen Orrin (68) n16.5 t17.5 f17 b17. In its favour, it doesn't appear to be troubled by caramel. Which means the nose and palate are exposed to the full force of this quite dreadful whisky. *40%.*

Glen Orrin Six Year Old (88) n22 t23 f21 b22. A vatting that has improved in the short time it has been around, now displaying some lovely orangey notes on the nose and a genuinely lushness to the body and spice on the finish. You can almost forgive the caramel, this being such a well balanced, full-bodied ride. A quality show for the price. *40%*

Hedges and Butler Special Pure Malt (83) n20 t21 f22 b21. Just so laid back: nosed and tasted blind I'd swear this was a blend (you know, a real blend with grains and stuff) because of the biting lightness and youth. Just love the citrus theme and, err...graininess...!! *40%*

⋰ **Highland Harvest Organic Blended Malt 7 Casks** batch 002 **(86.5)** n21.5 grassy, single-minded maltiness; **t22.5** juicy, clean barley; muscovado sugar; **f21** some late citrus; **b21.5** not even remotely complex. But pleaant enough. 40% WB15/371

Imperial Tribute (83) n19.5 t21.5 f21 b21. I am sure – and sincerely hope – the next bottling will be cleaned up and the true Imperial Tribute can be nosed and tasted. Because this is what should be a very fine malt... but just isn't. 46%. Spencer Collings.

Islay Trilogy 1969 (Bruichladdich 1966, Bunnahabhain 1968, Bowmore 1969) Bourbon/ Sherry **(91)** n23 t23 f22 b23. Decided to mark the 700th tasting for the 2007 edition with this highly unusual vatting. And no bad choice. The smoke is as elusive as the Paps of Jura on a dark November morning, but the silky fruits and salty tang tells a story as good as anything you'll hear by a peat fire. Take your time...the whiskies have. 40.3%. Murray McDavid.

J & B Exception Aged 12 Years (80) n20 t23 f18 b19. Very pleasant in so many ways. A charming sweetness develops quickly, with excellent soft honeycomb. But the nose and finish are just so...so...dull...!! For the last 30 years J&B has meant, to me, (and probably within that old company) exceptionally clean, fresh Speysiders offering a crisp, mouth-watering treat. I feel this is off target. 40%. Diageo/Justerini & Brooks.

J & B Nox (89) n23 t23 f21 b22. A teasing, pleasing little number that is unmistakably from the J&B stable. 40%. Diageo.

John Black 8 Years Old Honey (88) n21 t22.5 f22.5 b22. A charming vatting. 40%

John Black 10 Years Old Peaty (91) n23 salty and peaty; **t23** soft and peaty; **f22** delicate and peaty; **b23** classy and er...peaty. 40%. Tullibardine Distillery.

John McDougall's Selection Islay Malt 1993 (94.5) n23.5 t24.5 f22.5 b24. Complex, superbly weighted and balanced malt which just keeps you wondering what will happen next. 54.7%.

Johnnie Walker Green Label 15 Years Old (95) n24 t23.5 f23.5 b24. God, I love this stuff...this is exactly how a vatted malt should be and one of the best samples I've come across since its launch. 43%. Diageo.

Jon, Mark and Robbo's The Rich Spicy One (89) n22 t23 f22 b22. So much better without the dodgy casks: a real late night dram of distinction though the spices perhaps a little on the subtle side... 40%. Edrington.

Jon, Mark and Robbo's The Smoky Peaty One (92) n23 t22 f23 b24. Genuinely high-class whisky where the peat is full-on yet allows impressive complexity and malt development. A malt for those who appreciate the better, more elegant things in life. 40%. Edrington.

The Last Vatted Malt bott Nov 11 **(96.5)** n24 t25 f23.5 b24. Being an American, Compass Box founder and blender, John Glaser, knows a thing or two about pouring two fingers of whisky. So I join John in raising two fingers to the SWA and toast them in the spirit they deserve to thank them for their single-minded and successful quest to outlaw this ancient whisky term. 53.7%. nc ncf. 1,323 bottles.

Mackinlay's Rare Old Highland Malt (89) n22 t22 f22 b23. Possibly the most delicate malt whisky I can remember coming from the labs of Whyte and Mackay. Thought it still, on the palate, must rank as heavy medium. This is designed as an approximation of the whisky found at Shackleton's camp in the Antarctic. And as a life-long Mackinlay drinker myself, it is great to find a whisky baring its name that, on the nose only, briefly reminds me of the defter touches which won my heart over 30 years ago. That was with a blend: this is a vatted malt. And a delicious one. In case you wondered: I did resist the temptation to use ice. 47.3%

⋰ **Master of Malt Reference Series I (82)** n19.5 t23 f19 b20.5. Not quite the happiest of bunnies at times, as it occasionally struggles to find a balance in the face of big, not entirely desired, oils. That said, nothing to stop you embracing the enormity of the date & sugar-drizzled barley soon after delivery & during the period it has escaped a certain feintiness. 47.5% WB15/349

⋰ **Master of Malt Reference Series II (84.5)** n20 t22 f21.5 b21. The oils have been toned down for this one, though the sugars have reached shrieking point. Malty, but perhaps a tad too cloying for its own good. 47.5% WB15/350

⋰ **Master of Malt Reference Series III (88)** n22 fruit and nut...in abundance; **t23** salty beginnings on delivery then sugary shockwaves with the malt riding the surf; **f21** calms at last for the spices to form and the fruit/oak/malt elements to gel quite impressively before the warming fade; a slight fuzziness on the finale; **b22** still one for the sweet toothed, but you don't need a diagram at the back to tell you some decent age has been added to this vatting. The odd blemish, but great fun. 47.5% WB15/351

Matisse 12 Year Old Blended Malt (93) n23.5 t23 f22.5 b23. Succulent, clean-as-a-whistle mixture of malts with zero bitterness and not even a whisper of an off note: easily the best form I have ever seen this brand in. Superb. 40%. Matisse Spirits Co Ltd.

Matisse Aged 12 Years (79) n17 t21 f20 b21. Not sure if some finishing or re-casking has been going on here to liven it up. Has some genuine buzz on the palate, but intriguing weirdness, too. Don't bother nosing this one. 40%. The Matisse Spirits Co Ltd.

Milroy's of Soho Finest Blended Malt (76) n18 t19 f20 b19. Full flavoured, nutty, malty but hardly textbook. 40%. Milroy's of Soho.

⁙ **Moidart Aged 10 Years** (89.5) n23 wonderfully clean and blends malty promise with youth; t23 superb! The delivery is rich in oils which makes the light, gristy-citrus notes just a little heavier; salivating and satisfying; f21.5 some of the more well-used casks radiating a degree of tiredness which slightly detracts from the delicate malts; b22 just love the fresh, crystal clarity of this whisky. 46% WB15/358

Mo'land (82) n21 t22 f19 b20. Extra malty but lumbering and on the bitter side. 40%.

Monkey Shoulder batch 27 (79.5) n21 t21.5 f18 b19. Been a while since I lasted tasted this one. Though its claims to be Batch 27, I assume all bottlings are Batch 27 seeing as they are from 27 casks. This one, whichever it is, has a distinctive fault found especially at the finale, which is disappointing. Even before hitting that point a big toffeed personality makes for a pleasant if limited experience. 40%. William Grant & Sons.

"No Age Declared" The Unique Pure Malt Very Limited Edition 16-49 Years (85) n22.5 t19.5 f22 b21. Very drinkable. But this is odd stuff: as the ages are as they are, and as it tastes as it does, I can surmise only that the casks were added together as a matter of necessity rather than any great blending thought or planning. Certainly the malt never finds a rhythm but maybe it's the eclectic style on the finish that finally wins through. 45%. Samaroli.

Norse Cask Selection Vatted Islay 1992 Aged 16 Years hogshead cask no. QWVIM3, dist 92, bott 09 (95) n24 t24 f23 b24. The recipe of 60/35/5 Ardbeg/Laphroaig/Bowmore new make matured in one cask is a surprise: the oiliness here suggests a squirt of Caol Ila somewhere. This hybrid is certainly different, showing that the DNA of Ardbeg is unrecognisable when mixed, like The Fly, with others. Drinkable...? Oh, yes...!! Because this, without a single negative note to its name, is easily one of the whiskies of the year and a collector's and/or Islayphile's absolute must have. 56.7%

Norse Cask Selection Vatted Islay 1991 Aged 12 Years (89) n24 t23 f21 b21. Fabulous, but not much going in the way of complexity. But if you're a peat freak, I don't think you either notice...or much care...!! 59.5%. Quality World, Denmark.

Old St Andrews Fireside (88.5) n22 t22.5 f21.5 b22.5. Beautifully driven... 40%.

Old St Andrews Nightcap (89) n21.5 t24 f21 b22.5. Some delightful weight and mass but perhaps a bit too much toffee takes its toll. 40%. Old St Andrews Ltd.

Old St Andrews Twilight (94.5) n24 t23.5 f23 b24. Less Twilight as Sunrise as this is full of invigorating freshness which fills the heart with hope and joy: Lip-smacking Scotch malt whisky as it should be. Anyone who thinks the vatted malt served up for golf lovers in these novelty bottles is a load of old balls are a fair way off target... 40%. Old St Andrews Ltd.

⁙ **The Pearls of Scotland Burnside 1992 20 Year Old** cask no. 7350, dist Dec 92, bott Nov 13 (85) n22 t22 f20 b21. You can tell this is 99% Balvenie: it just has real problems handling the oak at this age. Nothing too much wrong with the nose for those into over-ripe banana. And the delivery boasts excellent mouth feel and early sugars until the merciless tannin bites deep. 55.8%.

Poit Dhubh 8 Bliadhna (90) n22.5 t23.5 f21.5 b22.5. Though the smoke which marked this vatting has vanished, it has more than compensated with a complex beefing up of the core barley tones. Cracking whisky. 43%. ncf. Pràban na Linne.

Poit Dhubh 12 Bliadhna (77) n20 t20 f18 b19. Toffee-apples. Without the apples. 43%. ncf. Pràban na Linne.

Poit Dhubh 21 Bliadhna (86) n22 t22.5 f21 b20.5. Over generous toffee has robbed us of what would have been a very classy malt. 43%. ncf. Pràban na Linne.

The Pot Still Scotch Vatted Malt Over 8 Years Old (90) n22 t24 f22 b22. Such sophistication: the Charlotte Rampling of Scotch. 43.5%. ncf. Celtic Whisky Compagnie, France.

Prime Blue Pure Malt (83) n21 t21 f21 b20. Steady, with a real chewy toffee middle. Friendly stuff. 40%

Prime Blue 12 Years Old Pure Malt (78) n20 t20 f19 b19. A touch of fruit but tart. 40%

Prime Blue 17 Years Old Pure Malt (88) n23 t21 f22 b22. Lovely, lively vatting: something to get your teeth into! 40%

Prime Blue 21 Years Old Pure Malt (77) n21 t20 f18 b18. After the teasing, bourbony nose the remainder disappoints with a caramel-rich flatness. The reprise of a style of whisky I thought had vanished about four of five years ago 40%

Rattray's Selection Blended Malt 19 Years Old Batch 1 Benrinnes sherry hogsheads (89.5) n22 t23.5 f21.5 b22.5. Absolutely love it! Offers just the right degree of mouth-watering complexity. not a malt for those looking for the sit-on-the-fence wishy-washy type. 55.8%. Auchentoshan, Bowmore, Balblair & BenRiach. A.D. Rattray Ltd.

Sainsbury's Malt Whisky Finished in Sherry Casks (70) n18 t19 f16 b17. Never the greatest of the Sainsbury range, it's somehow managed to get worse. Actually, not too difficult when it comes to finishing in sherry, and the odd sulphur butt or three has done its worst here. 40%. UK.

Scottish Collie (86.5) n22 t23 f20.5 b21. A really young pup of a vatting. Full of life and fun but muzzled by toffee at the death. 40%. *Quality Spirits International.*

Scottish Collie 5 Years Old (90.5) n22.5 t23 f22 b23. Fabulous mixing here showing just what malt whisky can do at this brilliant and under-rated age. Lively and complex with the malts wonderfully herded and penned. Without colouring and at 50% abv I bet this would have been given a right wolf-whistle. Perfect for one man and his grog. 40%.

Scottish Collie 8 Years Old (85.5) n22 t21.5 f21 b21. A good boy. But just wants to sleep rather than play. 40%. *Quality Spirits International.*

Scottish Collie 12 Years Old (82) n20 t22 f20 b20. For a malt that's aged 84 in Collie years, it understandably smells a bit funny and refuses to do many tricks. If you want some fun you'll need a younger version. 40%. *Quality Spirits International.*

Scottish Leader Imperial Blended Malt (77) n20 t20 f18 b19. Now don't be confused here: this isn't Imperial malt from Speyside. And although it says Blended, it is 100% malt. What is clear, though, is that this is pretty average stuff. 40%. *Burn Stewart.*

Scottish Leader Aged 14 Years (80) n21 t21 f19 b19. A cleaner, less peaty version than the no-age statement vatting, but still fails to entirely ignite the tastebuds 40%. *Burn Stewart.*

Scott's Selection Burnside 1994 (93) n23.5 t24 f22.5 b23.5. I may well be wrong. But I think this is the first time I have seen a Burnside, which is a cask of Balvenie spoiled as a single malt by having a spoonful of same age Glenfiddich added to it, in a commercial bottling rather than as a sample in my blending lab! Believe me: it was well worth waiting for...! 56.7%.

Sheep Dip (84) n19 t22 f22 b21. Young and sprightly like a new-born lamb, this enjoys a fresh, mouthwatering grassy style wth a touch of spice. Maligned by some, but to me a clever, accomplished vatting of alluring complexity. 40%

Sheep Dip 'Old Hebridean' 1990 dist in or before 1990 (94) n23 t24 f23.5 b23.5. You honey!! Now, that's what I call a whisky...!! 40%. *The Spencerfield Spirit Co.*

The Six Isles Pomerol Finish Limited Edition French oak Pomerol wine cask no. 90631-90638, dist 03, bott 10 (85.5) n19 t23 f21.5 b22. What makes the standard Six Isles work as a vatted malt is its freshness and complexity. With these attributes, plus the distinctive distilleries used, we consistently have one the world's great and truly entertaining whiskies. With this version we have just a decent malt. The wine finish has levelled the mountains and valleys and restricted the finish dramatically, while the nose doesn't work at all. Perfectly drinkable and the delivery is extremely enjoyable. But as a Six Isles, delighted it's a Limited Edition. 46%.

The Six Isles St Etienne Rum Cask Finish American oak & Caribbean rum casks, cask no. 92011/920110, bott 12 (96.5) n24 t24 f24 b24.5. Six Isles rarely lets you down; these rum casks are distilled sugar icing on the cake. Most probably the best use of rum casks I have ever encountered in the Scotch whisky industry. Bloody well done, chaps! 46%. nc ncf. *Ian Macleod Distillers.* 3161 bottles.

S'Mokey (88) n22.5 t22 f21.5 b22. Delicate, sweet and more lightly smoked than the nose advertises. 40%.

Smokey Joe Islay Malt (87) n21.5 t22 f21.5 b22. A soft, soporific version of a smoky Islay. No thumping of waves here: the tide is out. 46%. ncf *Angus Dundee Distillers.*

⁖ **Speyside Mysteria 24 Years Old Blended Malt** bourbon cask, dist 90, bott 14 (90) n22.5 hangs on against the advancing years with gritty determination...and a dollop of gooseberry jam; t23.5 fruity delivery: black cherry preserve and strawberry jam and cream Swiss roll, aided by delicate ulmo honey; f21.5 just a little too much oak, perhaps; b22.5 a malt which has lived a long and rich life...and has plenty of wrinkles to show for it. 54.2%. ncf.

⁖ **Sweet Wee Scallywag** Sherry butts & bourbon hogsheads (72) n17 t20 f17 b18. And a sulphured Scallywag at that...! 46%. ncf. *Douglas Laing & co.*

Tambowie (84.5) n21.5 t21.5 f20.5 b21. A decent improvement on the nondescript bottling of yore. I have re-included this to both celebrate its newly acquired lightly fruited attractiveness...and to celebrate the 125th anniversary of the long departed Tambowie Distillery whose whisky, I am sure, tasted nothing like this. 40%. *The Vintage Malt Whisky Co Ltd.*

Treasurer 1874 Reserve Cask (90.5) n23 t23 f22.5 b22. Some judicious adding has been carried out here in the Robert Graham shop. Amazing for a living cask that I detect no major sulphur faultlines. Excellent! 51%. *Live casks available in all Robert Graham shops.*

Triple Wood Blended Malt Scotch Whisky (77) n17.5 t22 f18.5 b19. At least one wood too many. Tangy...for all the wrong reasons. 42%. *Lidl.*

Vintner's Choice Speyside 10 Years Old (84) n21.5 t22 f20 b20.5. Pleasant. But considering the quality of the Speysiders Grants have to play with, the dullness is a bit hard to fathom. 40%. *Quality Spirits International.*

Waitrose Pure Highland Malt (86.5) n22 t22 f20.5 b22. Blood orange by the cartload: amazingly tangy and fresh; bitters out at the finish. This is one highly improved malt and great to see a supermarket bottling showing some serious attitude...as well as taste!! Fun, refreshing and enjoyable. 40%

Wemyss Malts "The Hive" Aged 8 Years bott Nov 11 **(85.5) n21 t23 f20 b21.5.** You may get stung on the nose but the delivery is pure nectar. Sadly, the bitter finish lives up to the nose's prediction. 40%. Wemyss Malts.

Wemyss Malts "The Hive" Aged 12 Years (93) n23 t24 f22.5 b23.5. Mixing different malt whiskies is an art form – one that is prone to going horribly wrong. Here, though, whoever is responsible really is the bees-knees... 40%

Wemyss Malts "Peat Chimney" 5 Years Old (82.5) n20.5 t21 f20 b21. Rougher than the tongue of a smoking cat. 40%. Wemyss Malts Ltd.

Wemyss Malts "Peat Chimney" 8 Years Old (85) n21.5 t21.5 f21 b21. Delightful chocolate amid the attractively course peat. 40%. Wemyss Malts Ltd.

Wemyss Malts "Peat Chimney" Aged 12 Years bott Oct 10 **(90.5) n22.5 t23 f22.5 b22.5.** Gorgeous: does what it says on the tin... 40%. Wemyss Malts.

Wemyss Malts "Smooth Gentleman" 5 Years Old (80) n20 t21 f19 b20. A bit of a schoolkid with an affectation. 40%. Wemyss Malts Ltd.

Wemyss Malts "Smooth Gentleman" 8 Years Old (89) n21 t23.5 f22 b22.5. More of a Kentuckian George Clooney than a Bristolian Cary Grant. 40%. Wemyss Malts Ltd.

Wemyss Malts "Smooth Gentleman" Aged 12 Years 1st fill bourbon cask, bott Oct 10 **(88.5) n23 t22 f21.5 b22.** A very attractive and competent, vaguely spicy gentleman who has a bit of a penchant for butterscotch and chocolate. 40%. Wemyss Malts.

Wemyss Malts "Spice King" 5 Years Old (76) n18.5 t20 f18.5 b19. A little on the mucky, tangy side. 40%. Wemyss Malts Ltd.

Wemyss Malts "Spice King" 8 Years Old (87) n22 t22 f21.5 b21.5. Hard to believe this lush malt is in any way related to the 5-y-o...!! 40%. Wemyss Malts Ltd.

Wemyss Malts "Spice King" Aged 12 Years bott Oct 10 **(85) n22.5 t21 f21 b21.** Thoroughly enjoyable sugar edge to the decent smoke. A bit thin on the complexity front, though. 40%. Wemyss Malts.

⋰⋱⋰ **Wemyss Velvet Fig (64) n15 t19 f15 b15.** Either vatted by someone who smokes 20 a day minimum or on purpose for the German and Chinese market which appears to enjoy this sort of thing. I eat a lot of figs which, on song, are sweet and spicy. This isn't. Although another "S" word plays a very big, debilitating, part... 46%. ncf.

Wemyss Vintage Malt The Peat Chimney Hand Crafted Blended Malt Whisky (80) n19 t22 f20 b19. The balance is askew here, especially on the bone-dry wallpapery finish. Does have some excellent spicy/coffee moments, though. 43%. Wemyss Vintage Malts Ltd.

Wemyss Vintage Malt The Smooth Gentleman Hand Crafted Blended Malt Whisky (83) n19 t22 f21 b21. Not sure about the nose: curiously fishy (very gently smoked). But the malts tuck into the tastebuds with aplomb showing some sticky barley sugar along the way. 43%

Wemyss Vintage Malt The Spice King Hand Crafted Blended Malt Whisky (84) n22 t22 f20 b20. Funnily enough, I've not a great fan of the word "smooth" when it comes to whisky. But the introduction of oily Caol Ila-style peat here makes it a more of a smooth gentleman than the "Smooth Gentleman." Excellent spices very late on. 43%. Wemyss Vintage Malts.

Wholly Smoke Aged 10 Years (86.5) n22.5 t22.5 f20 b21.5. A big, peaty, sweat, rumbustuous number with absolutely no nod towards sophistication or balance and the finish virtually disintegrates. The smoke is slapped on and the whole appears seemingly younger than its 10 years. Massive fun, all the same. 40%. Macdonald & Muir Ltd for Oddbins.

Whyte & Mackay Blended Malt Scotch Whisky (78) n19 t22 f18 b19. You know when the engine to your car is sort of misfiring and feels a bit sluggish and rough...? 40%. Waitrose.

Wild Scotsman Scotch Malt Whisky (Black Label) batch no. CBV001 **(91) n23.5 t23.5 f21 b23.** The type of dram you drink from a dirty glass. Formidable and entertaining. 47%

Wild Scotsman Aged 15 Years Vatted Malt (95) n23 t24 f24 b24. If anyone wants an object lesson as to why you don't screw your whisky with caramel, here it is. Jeff Topping can feel a justifiable sense of pride in his new whisky: for its age, it is an unreconstituted masterpiece... 46% (92 proof). nc ncf. USA.

⋰⋱⋰ **William Grant & Sons Rare Cask Reserves 25 Years Old Blended Malt Scotch Whisky (82) n21 t22 f19 b20.** Mouth-filling, chewy and mildly fruity, doesn't quite grow into the decent start offered and finishes untidily. 47%. Exclusive to The Whisky Shop.

Mystery Malts

Chieftain's Limited Edition Aged 40 Years hogshead **(78) n22 t22 f16 b18.** Oak-ravaged and predictably bitter on the death (those of you who enjoy Continental bitters might go for this..!) But the lead up does offer a short, though sublime and intense honey kick. The finish, though... 48.5%. Ian Macleod.

Cu Dhub (see Speyside Distillery)

Scottish Grain

It's a bit weird, really. Many whisky lovers stay clear of blended Scotch, preferring instead single malts. The reason, I am often told, is that the grain included in a blend makes it rough and ready. Yet I wish I had a twenty pound note for each time I have been told in recent years how much someone enjoys a single grain. The ones that the connoisseurs die for are the older versions, usually special independent bottlings displaying great age and more often than not brandishing a lavish Canadian or bourbon style.

Like single malts, grain distilleries produce whisky bearing their own style and signature. And, also, some display characteristics and a richness that can surprise and delight. Most of the grains available in (usually specialist) whisky outlets are pretty elderly. Being made from maize and wheat helps give them either that Canadian or, depending on the freshness of the cask, an unmistakable bourbony style. So older grains display far greater body than is commonly anticipated.

Light whiskies, including some Speysiders, tend to adopt this north American stance when the spirit has absorbed so much oak that the balance has been tipped. So overtly Kentuckian can they be, I once playfully introduced an old single grain Scotch whisky into a bourbon tasting I was conducting and nobody spotted that it was the cuckoo in the nest ... until I revealed all at the end of the evening. And even had to display the bottle to satisfy the disbelievers. Younger grains may give a hint of oncoming bourbon-ness. But, rather, they tend to celebrate either a softness in taste or, in the case of North British, a certain rigidity. Where many malts have a tendency to pulverise the taste-buds and announce their intent and character at the top of their voice, younger grains are content to stroke and whisper.

Scotch whisky companies had a relaxed attitude to marketing their grains. William Grant had made some inroads with Black Barrel, though with nothing like the enthusiasm they unleash upon us with their blends and malts. But Diageo have raised the bar and the grain whisky temperature by spending probably more than my beloved Millwall have in their history forked out for players by signing up David Beckham to be the face of their new Haig Club grain brand. If his fee did not trump Millwall's historical spend, then the massive budget they appear to have set aside for a glamorous advertising campaign probably will have. Hopefully younger grains, rather than the massive-impact pensioner ones that can normally be found kicking about, will be accepted for being the quality product they unquestionably are. Even if other companies follow suit, I cannot see them trying to make quite the same impact as Diageo are trying with Beckham. For many distillers, trying to find enough grain whisky for their existing blend portfolio is proving challenging enough.

In Ireland, Cooley have in the past forged a healthy following with their introduction of grain whiskies at various ages. They have shown that the interest is there and some fresh thinking and boldness in a marketing department can create niche and often profitable markets. Edrington entered the market with a vatted grain called Snow Grouse, designed to be consumed chilled and obviously a tilt at the vodka market. The first bottling I received, though, was disappointingly poor and I hope future vattings will be more carefully attended to. All round, then, the news for Scottish grain lovers has not been good of late with the demolition of mighty Dumbarton and, controversially, closure of Port Dundas itself. With the expansion of Cameronbridge and a 50% stake in North British, Diageo obviously believe they have all the grain capacity they require.

The tastings notes here for grains cover only a few pages, disappointingly, due to their scarcity. However, it is a whisky style growing in stature, helped along the way not just by Cooley but also by more Independent bottlers bringing out a succession of high quality ancient casks. There has even been an organic grain on the market, distilled at the unfashionable Loch Lomond Distillery. Why, though, it has to be asked does it take the relatively little guys to lead the way? Perhaps the answer is in the growing markets in the east: the big distillers are very likely holding on to their stocks to facilitate their expansion there.

At last the message is getting through that the reaction to oak of this relatively lightweight spirit - and please don't for one moment regard it as neutral, for it is most certainly anything but - can throw up some fascinating and sometimes delicious possibilities. Blenders have known that for a long time. Now public interest is growing. And people are willing to admit that they can enjoy an ancient Cambus, Caledonian or Dumbarton in very much the way they might celebrate a single malt. Even if it does go against the grain...

Single Grain Scotch
CALEDONIAN

Clan Denny Caledonian 45 Years Old bourbon barrel, cask no. HH6294, dist 1965 **(89)** n22 t23.5 f21.5 b22. For all its obvious tiredness, there is plenty of rich character. 46.1%. nc ncf sc.

Clan Denny Caledonian 45 Years Old refill hogshead, cask no. HH6228, dist 1965 **(96)** n23.5 t25 f23.5 b24. Super Caley...my prayers have been answered... 476%. nc ncf sc.

Clan Denny Caledonian Aged 45 Years bourbon barrel, cask no. HH7501, dist 1965 **(94)** n23.5 t24 f23 b23.5. Anyone who managed to get their hands on the very oldest maturing stocks of Barton bourbon from twenty years ago (and there were very few of us who managed it) would recognise it immediately. The similarities are uncanny. 473%. nc ncf sc.

Scotch Malt Whisky Society Cask G3.3 Aged 26 Years refill barrel, dist 29 Apr 86 **(87)** n21.5 t22 f21.5 b22. A straight up and downer other than the unusual coastal twang. 56%.

Scott's Selection Caledonian 1965 bott 2011 **(89.5)** n24 t22.5 f20.5 b22.5. How about that? The nose belongs to Kentucky, the flavours carry a Maple Leaf flag. Aaah, pure Scotch! 45%

CAMBUS

Clan Denny Cambus Vintage Aged 25 Years refill hogshead, cask no. HH9320 **(96.5)** n24 t24.5 f23.5 b24.5. Nosed blind, this would be mistaken for absolutely top notch Canadian, and in particular the finer output from the now entirely lost LaSalle Distillery. But that rarely engaged its sugars in such a breathtakingly, almost outrageously, attractive way. One of the grain bottlings that will be remember among those in the know until the last one amongst us follow the Path of LaSalle...and, no less tragically, Cambus. 53.1%. ncf sc. DEN0093.

Clan Denny Cambus Aged 36 Years bourbon barrel, cask no. HH7252, dist 1975 **(89.5)** n22 t23.5 f22 b22. Flawless grain limited only by its simplicity. 52.1%. nc ncf sc.

Clan Denny Cambus 45 Years Old refill bourbon barrel, cask no. HH5638, dist 1965 **(88.5)** n22 t23 f21.5 b22. A grain which has learned to deal with the impact of age in its very own, sweet way... 45.9%. nc ncf sc. Douglas Laing & Co.

Clan Denny Cambus 47 Years Old bourbon barrel, cask no. HH7029, dist 1963 **(97)** n24.5 a mesmeric blending of classic liquorice-bourbony tones, the vivid vanilla of a great Canadian and the sharp, lively precision of a massive scotch... **t25** if you spent a dozen years of your life trying to create a whisky with absolutely perfect weight on delivery, you'd still fail to match the natural genius of this. The oils have just enough body to coat the palate with a delicate fretwork of the finest light liquorice and honeycomb lustre, but whose fragility is exposed by the orange-citrus sharpness which etches its own, impressive course; the sugars mingle with the spices with 47 years of understanding...; **f23** after almost 50 years in the barrel, there is no surprise that a degree of bitter tightness comes into play. But the compactness of the vanilla keeps damage to a minimum; **b24.5** if this wasn't a Scotch single grain, it might just qualify as Bourbon of the Year. Proof that where a whisky is made, matured, or from makes absolutely no difference: it is the quality which counts. And there will be very few whiskies I taste this year that will outgun this one in the quality stakes... 49.7%. nc ncf sc. Douglas Laing & Co.

Clan Denny Cambus Aged 48 Years bourbon barrel, cask no. HH 7863, dist 1963 **(93)** n24 t23 f22.5 b23.5. No wonder they closed down the Cambus distillery; they must've plain gone and shipped it to Kentucky... 49.5%. nc ncf sc. Douglas Laing & Co.

Scotch Malt Whisky Society Cask G8.1 Aged 21 Years refill hogshead, cask no. 41759, dist 1989 **(85.5)** n22.5 t22 f20 b21. Decent enough, but a relatively underwhelming way to kick off the Society's account with this legendary grain distillery. A less than endearing piece of oak keeps any chance of the distillery's usual ability to tantalise with clever use of weight and complexity. A few kumquat and delicate clove notes do shake up the caramels on the nose, though. 61.2%. sc. 272 bottles.

Scotch Malt Whisky Society Cask G8.2 Aged 23 Years refill hogshead, dist 12 Jun 89 **(94.5)** n24 t23 f23.5 b24. Not as complex as some Cambus you'll find but just ridiculously pleasing and steady, while the attitude and bite is a turn on.. Wow! 62.4%. sc. 252 bottles.

CAMERONBRIDGE

⸭ **Cadenhead's Small Batch Cameronbridge Aged 24 Years** bourbon hogsheads, dist 1989, bott 2013 **(92)** n21.5 slightly aggressive oak becalmed by vanilla; **t23.5** weighty delivery for a grain: indeed, more malt-like with decent oils and a delicious dollop of ulmo honey and butterscotch; **f23** a little busier as the tannins rev up the spices; **b23.5** a pleasing grain with idea above its supposedly lowly station. Kicks the crap out ofa great many single malts it is supposed to kow-tow to. 46%. 618 bottles. WB15/167

Clan Denny Cameronbridge Aged 21 Years refill butt, cask no. HH7541, dist 1990 **(85.5)** n21.5 t22 f20.5 b21.5. Creamy textured and sweet. Possibly filled into an old – and tired - Islay cask as there is the odd strand of smoke. 58.2%. nc ncf sc. Douglas Laing & Co.

Clan Denny Cameronbridge Aged 38 Years refill barrel, cask no. HH9488 **(94)** n23.5 t24 f22.5 b24. Some kind of Canadian and corn whiskey orgy. And a bit of a turn on it is, too...52.4%. sc. Douglas Laing & Co.

Clan Denny Cameronbridge 45 Years Old bourbon, cask no. HH6805, dist 1965 **(78)** n21 t20 f18 b19. Even grains can feel the cold hand of Father Time on their shoulder... 40.5%. nc ncf sc.

Rare Auld Grain Cameronbridge 32 Years Old cask no. 3597, dist 1979 **(92)** n23 t23.5 f22.5 b23. Anything but the norm. 48.8%. sc. Duncan Taylor & Co.

Scott's Selection Cameron Bridge 1973 bott 2010 **(77)** n19 t21 f18 b19. Good grain + poor cask = 77. 41.4%. Speyside Distillers.

Scott's Selection Cameron Bridge 1973 bott 2010 **(85)** n23.5 t21 f20 b20.5. Worth getting just for the nose alone, which is top rate Canadian with the corn leaping from the glass. A disappointing bitterness from the oak creeps in to spoil the party somewhat. 44.9%

⸬ **Signatory Single Grain Collection Cameronbridge 1995** dist 31 Jan 95, bott 18 Mar 14 **(87)** n22 t22 f21.5 b21.5. Although with nearly 20 years on the clock, living nearly two decades in presumably a third fill cask has done little for colour or complexity: it has the demeanour of a grain very much younger. The good news is that this is still high quality oak, so although a simple dram the mix of sugars and light vanilla is a pleasing one. 43%. WB15/170

⸬ **The Sovereign Single Cask Cameronbridge 1990** cask no. 9860, dist 1990, bott Jun 13, **(88)** n22 soft natural caramels with just a squeeze of lemon; t22 an outpouring of sugary butterscotch; f22 the accent is purely on the clean vanilla; b22 pretty monosyllabic but joyous ride for all that. 59.2%. sc. Hunter Laing & Co.

CARSEBRIDGE

Clan Denny Carsebridge 29 Years Old 1st fill hogshead, cask no. HH6609, dist 1981 **(82)** n22 t22 f18 b20. The intensity of the corn is profound. So too, alas, is the bitter retribution of the tired cask. 53.1%. nc ncf sc. Douglas Laing & Co.

Clan Denny Carsebridge Aged 30 Years refill hogshead, cask no. HH7780, dist 1981 **(91.5)** n21.5 t23.5 f23 b23.5. Is there such a thing as a juicy 30-year-old grain? On this evidence, indubitably. 59.1%. nc ncf sc. Douglas Laing & Co.

Clan Denny Carsebridge Aged 45 Years bourbon barrel, cask no. HH7500, dist 1965 **(95)** n24 t24 f23 b24. As we have so often seen in Kentucky and Canada, old grains maturing in high quality casks rank among the best whiskies in the world: here is a stunning example. 44.7%. nc ncf sc.

Clan Denny Carsebridge Aged 47 Years refill barrel, cask no. HH9489 **(91)** n23.5 t23.5 f22 b22. A simple grain, despite the antiquity, doing the easy things attractively. 45.3%. sc.

DUMBARTON

Cadenhead Dumbarton 24 Years Old bourbon, dist 87, bott 12 **(93)** n24 t22.5 f23 b23.5. For those of you who adore the older Ballantine's, you can certainly see the square root of some of the complex flavour profiles. Dumbarton grain was, to me, the best of the industrial-sized grain plants by a distance. Try this for proof. 49.5%. sc. 210 bottles.

Clan Denny Dumbarton 45 Years Old refill hogshead, cask no. HH7001, dist 1965 **(89.5)** n23 t23 f21.5 b22. A lovely grain bottled in the nick of time and happy to display the remnants of its zesty vigour. 49.5%. nc ncf sc. Douglas Laing & Co.

Clan Denny Dumbarton Aged 46 Years refill hogshead, cask no. HH7542, dist 1964 **(86.5)** n22 t23 f20 b21.5. The tiredness on the finish, confirming the big oaks on the nose, still cannot entirely overcome the beauty of the honey and golden syrup delivery: some of the early moments in the mouth are akin to the soaring strings of John Barry score. The finish is pure Bay City Rollers. 47.4%. nc ncf sc. Douglas Laing & Co.

Clan Denny Dumbarton Aged 48 Years refill hogshead, cask no. HH9345 **(96.5)** n25 t24 f23.5 b24. Truly great whisky. Forget this being a grain: excellence is excellence. Full stop. 50.1%. sc.

Scott's Selection Dumbarton 1986 bott 11 **(94)** n24.5 t24 f22 b23.5. When this distillery was closed I was almost beside myself with disappointment...and rage. Following the closure of Cambus, this left Dumbarton as the brightest star in the collapsing grain whisky galaxy. This bottle will give you some insight into just why I treasured it so greatly; certainly more so than the bead counters at Allied who saw its potential as prime real estate over its ability to keep making arguably the best blended Scotch whiskies in the world. My main point of surprise now is why so few bottlings from this giant of a distillery ever see the shelves. 51.5%.

GARNHEATH

Clan Denny Garnheath 43 Years Old refill hogshead, cask no. HH6642, dist 1967 **(94)** n24.5 t23.5 f22.5 b23.5. What a treat: not just a whisky as rare as budgie teeth, but one in tip-top nick for its age. A rare delight. 44.4%. nc ncf sc. Douglas Laing & Co.

The Coopers Choice Golden Grains Garnheath 1967 45 Years Old (94.5) n23.5 t24 f23.5 b24. I remember the last time I tasted Garneath it was Atlanta corn whiskey coming back at me from the glass. Now we have top grade bourbon... *42%. nc ncf sc.*

GIRVAN

⫶⫶⫶ **The Girvan Patent Still No. 4 Apps** db **(87) n21.5 t22 f21.5 b22.** A first look at probably the lightest of all Scotland grain whiskies. A little cream soda sweetens a soft, rather sweet, but spineless affair. The vanillas get a good, unmolested outing too. *42% WB15/369*

Girvan Single Grain 22 Years Old cask no. 110633, dist 89, bott Oct 11 **(88) n21.5 t22.5 f22 b22.** Safe and conservative. *63%. sc.*

Berry's Own Selection Girvan Aged 46 Years cask no. 37532, bott 2011 **(94.5) n24 t23.5 f23 b24.** If you have not yet crossed the divide and got into grain whisky, here really is your chance. What a stunner! *46%. nc ncf sc.*

Berry's Own Selection Girvan 1989 cask no. 37530/1, bott 2010 **(82.5) n21 t22 f19.5 b20.** Thick, sweet but a little on the tardy side... *45.1%. nc ncf sc. Berry Bros & Rudd.*

⫶⫶⫶ **Cadenhead's Small Batch Girvan Aged 33 Years** bourbon barrels, dist 1979 bott 2013 **(85) n22 t23 f19 b21.** Some parts of this are light and citrusy enough to be a gin or flavoured rum. The fact this is 33 years old at times defies belief. But where it does work is on delivery when the citrus notes are under control thanks to the butterscotch tart. Then the sugars go on a rampage. *46% 222 bottles. WB15/165*

Clan Denny Girvan Aged 21 Years refill barrel, cask no. HH9451 **(92) n23 t23.5 f22.5 b23.** Complex, busy and compelling. *59.6%. sc.*

Clan Denny Girvan 45 Years Old refill hogshead, cask no. HH6276, dist 1965 **(90) n23 t23.5 f21.5 b22.5.** Laid on with a golden trowel. *47.3%. nc ncf sc.*

Clan Denny Girvan 45 Years Old refill hogshead, cask no. HH6923, dist 1965 **(88.5) n23 t23 f20.5 b22.** Simplistic, certainly. But as you get older, you learn to appreciate the more simple things in life... *45.3%. nc ncf sc. Douglas Laing & Co.*

Clan Denny Girvan Aged 46 Years refill hogshead, cask no. HH7669, dist 1965 **(94.5) n23 t24 f23.5 b24.** Sublime. *49.7%. nc ncf sc. Douglas Laing & Co.*

Riegger's Selection Girvan 1964 bourbon cask, cask no. 86, dist 64, bott Feb 11 **(87) n22.5 t22.5 f20 b22.** Lovers of corn whisky will enjoy many aspects of this oldie. *48.7%. nc ncf sc.*

Scotch Malt Whisky Society Cask G7.5 Aged 28 Years refill hogshead, dist 84 **(91) n23.5 t23.5 f22 b22.** Keep bottling gems like this and they'll have to form the Grain Whisky Society. *58.9%. sc. 275 bottles.*

Scott's Selection Girvan 1964 bott 2011 **(92.5) n23.5 t24 f22 b23.** Girvan, like Invergordon, is grain which takes full advantage of its sumptuous persona. Here, though, it adds some controlled sharpness. But it's the lordly sugars which really win the day. Superb. *48.8%*

The Whisky Agency Girvan Aged 48 Years ex-sherry butt, dist 64, bott 12 **(87.5) n23 t22.5 f20 b22.** Outwardly like a Macallan from the early 1980s. Except with a bourbon rather than malt background...the oak is just leaking a little bitterness, though. *49.5%. ncf. 487 bottles.*

INVERGORDON

Berry's Own Selection Invergordon 1971 cask no. 2, bott 2011 **(91.5) n24 t23 f22 b22.5.** A beautiful experience. *46.7%. nc ncf sc. Berry Bros & Rudd.*

⫶⫶⫶ **The Clan Denny Invergordon Aged 26 Years** North American Oak, cask no. 10250, dist 1998 **(92) n22** the gangly oak interrupts a charming interchange between corn oils and light, toast fudge sugars; **t24** superb delivery with oils at full throttle, but unable to eclipse the sugar-spice interplay or the depth of the lemon-edged sugars; **f22.5** soft, subtle and more lightly oiled complexity; some spices try to take off but don't quite get off the ground; **b23.5** perhaps should be exported to Canada. True Canadian lovers will swoon at this: so similar to the now lost La Salles distillery in its final days. *50.6%. Douglas Laing & Co.*

Clan Denny Invergordon 44 Years Old refill barrel, cask no. HH4995, dist 1966 **(95.5) n23.5 t24 f23.5 b24.5.** Almost quicksand-ish in its softness. But an amazing degree of complexity, too. A true gem of a whisky. *46.8%. nc ncf sc. Douglas Laing & Co.*

Clan Denny Invergordon 45 Years Old bourbon barrel, cask no. HH7254, dist 1966 **(88) n22 t22 f22 b22.** Played with an absolutely straight bat: over 45 years every kink appears to have been ironed out. *47.1%. nc ncf sc. Douglas Laing & Co.*

Clan Denny Invergordon Aged 45 Years bourbon barrel, cask no. HH7864, dist 1966 **(88.5) n22.5 t22 f22 b22.** An unspectacular, well-made and matured grain offering quiet gracefulness. *47.5%. nc ncf sc. Douglas Laing & Co.*

Clan Denny Invergordon Vintage Aged 46 Years barrel, cask no. HH9077 **(91.5) n24 t23 f22 b22.5.** About a quiet a dram you could wish to bring into your house. Open late at night... it will disturb nobody. *44.2%. sc. Douglas Laing & Co.*

Duncan Taylor Octave Invergordon 38 Years Old cask no. 520883, dist 1972 **(86.5) n24** t21 f20 b21.5. Some serious Demerara sugars knit tightly into the intense vanilla. A few bitter notes amid the booming spice. The nose, however, excels and conjures myriad bourbon images. 47.8%. sc. Duncan Taylor & Co.

First Cask Invergordon 37 Years Old American oak, cask no. 63641, dist 1 Jul 72, bott 3 Jul 09 **(85) n23.5 t21 f20 b20.5.** A dram which conjures up clearer pictures of ice cracking on the Great Lakes than it does water coursing through the Scottish glens. The corn works beautifully on the nose in particular but the oak bitters from delivery onwards. 44%. nc ncf sc. 135 bottles.

Malts Of Scotland Invergordon 1973 bourbon hogshead, cask no. MoS 12063, dist 1973, bott 2012 **(90) n22 t22 f23 b23.** A grain which makes you groan with pleasure. How soft is that! 42%. 96 bottles.

⠐⠶ **The Pearls of Scotland Invergordan 1972** bott May 14 **(96) n23.5** a kind of Canadian with corn to the fore and evolving into a complex pattern of oak-spiked honeys, hardened further by treacle; **t24** huge, seemingly much bigger that its meagre alcohol strength. The sugars are out early, even handed with the vanilla and butterscotch which reveals the oak's friendly nature. Again light honey tones, mainly ulmo, drift in...; **f24.5** now at its most complex. A little bit of welcome niggle and bite yet matched by a soothing lime-drizzled maple syrup softness, helped with a little corn oil. The fade reveals some of the most delicate vanillas you can imagine; **b24** really don't quite understand why the distillery is not bringing out its own bottlings when it has gems of drams like this to choose from. This, for its age, is astonishing. 43.4%.

Rare Auld Grain Invergordon 38 Years Old cask no. 96251, dist 1972 **(88.5) n22.5 t22.5 f21.5 b22.** Ramrod straight and beyond the nose eschews any grand design of complexity. 44%. sc. Duncan Taylor & Co.

Scotch Malt Whisky Society Cask G5.2 Aged 17 Years virgin toasted oak hogshead, cask no. 53285, dist 1993 **(90.5) n23 t23 f21.5 b23.** Oils apart, barely representative of the distillery at this age but bourbon lovers will be thrilled. 65.3%. sc. 248 bottles.

Scotch Malt Whisky Society Cask G5.3 Aged 18 Years virgin toasted oak, cask no. 53289, dist 1993 **(95.5) n23.5 t24.5 f23.5 b24.** There aren't many grain whiskies so gorgeously influenced by oak to the dozen. Invergordon as you have probably never seen before...and are unlikely to see again... 65.6%. sc.

Scotch Malt Whisky Society Cask G5.4 Aged 18 Years virgin toasted oak, cask no. 53288, dist 1993 **(92) n23 t23 f22.5 b23.5.** I must admit I gave the whisky a bit of a quizzical look after both clapping my eyes on its rich colour and breathing in that intense marmalade nose. Only on reading the small print did it all make sense. 65.6%. Scotch Malt Whisky Society.

Scotch Malt Whisky Society Cask G5.5 Aged 18 Years virgin toasted oak hogshead, cask no. 53286, dist 1993 **(94.5) n24 t24 f23 b23.5.** A whisky I've had to taste to hit deadline without being supplied with cask details. From the way this is behaving it must be some kind of super first fill or even virgin oak: it is much nearer bourbon than Scotch! 65.3%. sc.

Scotch Malt Whisky Society Cask G5.7 Aged 19 Years refill hogshead, dist 20 May 93 **(92) n24 t23 f22 b23.** For those who like a little whisky in their oak....Outrageous. But somehow works! 64.6%. sc. 234 bottles.

Scott's Selection Invergordon 1964 bott 2011 **(92) n24 t24 f21 b23.** Another which keeps faithfully to the distillery's yielding, melt-in-the-mouth style. But here we have a deep Kentucky drawl and a nose from heaven... 43.8%. Speyside Distillers.

Scott's Selection Invergordon 1964 bott 2012 **(94) n22.5 t24 f23.5 b24.** When I first nosed this, my instinct was that it would have been better off propping up an ancient old blend. Having now fully tasted it, I am not so sure... 42.3%.

Single Cask Collection Ivergordon Aged 24 Years bourbon barrel, cask no. 18589, dist 22 Feb 1988, bott 22 Aug 2012 **(89.5) n21.5 t23.5 f22 b22.5.** Softly, softly all the way. 55.5%. nc ncf sc. 188 bottles.

⠐⠶ **The Sovereign Single Cask Invergordon 1964** cask no. 9861, dist 1964, bott Jun 13 **(92.5) n23.5** dank corn bread. Coconut drowned in maple syrup; chunky tannins, but the age is controlled beautifully; **t23** so massively lush thanks to the heavyweight corn oils. At times sharp with the accent on the marauding sugars; **f22.5** it was inevitable the oak would catch up and there is a little mocha at work when it does; **b23.5** high voltage Canadian style whisky of yesteryear... 43.7%. sc. Hunter Laing & Co.

⠐⠶ **The Sovereign Single Cask Invergordon 1992** cask no. 10155, dist 1992, bott Nov 13 **(87) n22 t22 f21.5 b22.** Very quiet: as though trained for a silent part in a blend. Some spice does make a noise, though. 60.4%. sc.

⠐⠶ **The Sovereign Single Cask Invergordon Aged 25 Years** cask no. 10699 dist 1988, bott Jul 14 **(94.5) n23** rich with spiced sultana and butterscotch concentrate; **t24** fabulous delivery: arrives silky and soft and immediately explodes into an unbelievable cauldron on spices and fruit; **f23.5** more moreish magnificence on a vague fruit and rape seed honey theme; **b24** ignore the fact this is grain and not malt. Just grab yourself a bottle of something rather beautiful... 58.1%. sc.

That Boutique-y Whisky Company Invergordon Batch 1 **(93)** n23 t23.5 f23 b23.5. An ancient old bourbon in all but name. 41.6%. 252 bottles.

⋯ **That Boutique-y Whisky Invergordan** batch 2 **(88.5)** n22 lightly spiced toffee; t23 a Demerara-treacle mix melts as the spices evolve; **f21.5** vanilla and toffee; **b22** unassuming, easy going and just-so spiced. 58.3%. 160 bottles. WB15/347

⋯ **Wemyss Malts 1988 Single Grain "Lemon Cheesecake"** barrel, dist 88, bott 14 **(90)** n22.5 just like the butterscotch tart I had at junior school...; t23 silky delivery with an array of sugars ranging from golden syrup to...golden syrup; **f22** slight oak bitterness as it reverts back to butterscotch tart; **b22.5** classic Invergordon pudding-type grain. 46%. sc. 220 bottles.

⋯ **Wemyss Malts 1988 Single Grain "Vintage Strawberry Punnet"** barrel, dist 88, bott 14 **(92.5)** n22 quiet, soft and lightly oiled in the Invergordon way..; t24 whoosh....!! The taste buds are awash with sexily oiled, Canadian-style maple syrup and vanilla-drenched sugars – almost takes your breath away...! **f23** calms impressively to allow a few spices a gig. Remains rich, slightly butter-biscuity and chewy for a long time; **b23.5** from a non-committal nose to a delivery which speaks volumes. Fabulous! 46%. sc. 242 bottles.

The Whisky Agency Invergordon 1965 bott 2010 **(90)** n23.5 t23 f21 b22.5. A glorious old timer, showing some quality Canadian-style manoeuvres. 44.7%. The Whisky Agency.

LOCH LOMOND

⋯ **Master of Malt Single Cask Loch Lomond 16 Year Old (89)** n22 malt; t23 mouthwatering gristy malt; **f21.5** bitters out a shade but the malt, and now spice as well, keeps on coming; **b22.5** on this evidence, Loch Lomond is filled with malt and malt alone.... 62.7%. sc.

Rhosdhu 2008 Cask No. 2483 re-char bourbon, dist 17/03/08, bott 27/07/11 **(86.5)** n22 t22 f21 b21.5. Delicately clean barley with a touch of lemon and, though engagingly soft, is not beyond showing some sugary teeth. 45%. nc ncf sc.

Rhosdhu 2008 Cask No. 2484 bourbon barrel, dist 17/03/08, bott 27/07/11 **(84)** n21.5 t21.5 f20.5 b21. The barley battles with some aggressive oak, even at this tender age. The spice count is pretty high. 45%. nc ncf sc.

⋯ **That Boutique-y Whisky Loch Lomond** batch 1 **(89.5)** n22 glorious but delicate citrus; soft toffee; **t23.5** the salivation index goes flying off the page as the citrus and malt combine beautifully before a heavier treacle toffee trait moves in; **f22** tangy toffee; **b22** a sometimes unloved and often misunderstood distillery, shown here to excellent fruity effect with the yeast ensuring the citrus is working at full blast. 52.4%. 191 bottles. WB15/348

LOCHSIDE

The Coopers Choice Lochside 1964 47 Years Old sherry, bott 12 **(95.5)** n24.5 t24 f23.5 **b23.5**. There are still some around who remember 1964 as a very special year in Montrose. First, their distillery, Lochside, was working. Secondly, they were receiving top quality sherry butts, long before the days they were ruined by reckless, unforgivable – and unforgiving - sulphur treatment. And, thirdly, for a while their football team enjoyed rare success on the park. In fact, in 1964 the guys at the distillery would have seen their blue-hooped heroes thrash neighbours Forfar 5-0 (having already murdered them 8-2 earlier in the season), would have made the short journey to next door Brechin for victory there as well as seen their lads annihilate Raith 8-3 and Stenhousemuir 7-1 back on home soil. The only thing they were denied was victory over the upstarts down the coast at Arbroath. But you can't have everything. Obviously happy workers make happy whisky. Amazing how those goals – and sound sherry butts - of 1964 can come back and heighten our enjoyment now. 41.5%. ncf sc.

NORTH BRITISH

Berry's Own Selection North British 2000 cask no. 4312, bott 2011 **(87.7)** n22 t22.5 f21. Bitters thanks to some indifferent oak; **b22** neutral whisky....? I don't think so. 46%. nc ncf sc.

⋯ **Cadenhead's Small Batch North British Aged 24 Years** bourbon barrel, dist 1989, bott 2014 **(94)** n23.5 molten honeycomb, coconut and golden syrup...wow!! All on top of usual spices and butterscotch. Kind of Canadian on stilts; t24 the nose...in pure fluidity; f23 more of the same...with extra spice, including Canadian Ginger Ale; **b23.5** made on another continent, as it so easily could have been, and we might have had Canadian Whisky of the Year.. 46%. 240 bottles. WB15/168

⋯ **Darkness! North British Aged 18 Years** Oloroso Cask Finish **(89.5)** n22 clean, uninterrupted olosoro waves a thick, fruity flag; **t22.5** sweet, thick on the fruit and pith; a slow arrival of spice; developing juiciness; **f23.5** at last some complexity as the spices layer superbly with the sherry trifle; **b21.5** a rule of thumb is that putting grain into fresh sherry tells you far more about the cask than the distillate. And it hangs true here. Very good cask, by the way... 50.4%. 94 bottles. WB15/352

Director's Cut North British Aged 50 Years refill butt, cask no. 8228, dist 1962 **(82.5) n22 t21 f19 b20.5**. How truly bizarre that the whisky waits 50 years to be tasted. And on the day I get round to it, the distillery is closed in the national gaze during a Legionaire's disease outbreak: certainly not what the distiller who made this would have expected two generations ago. I don't think he would have expected this whisky either. Now I may be completely wrong. But I suspect this has been finished in a pretty fresh sherry butt to spruce the dear old thing up before bottling. Sadly, the sherry cask has a light sulphur taint, so the bitterness creeps in. Leave these whiskies well alone, is my motto... 57.1%. nc ncf sc. 222 bottles.

Director's Cut North British Aged 52 Years first fill hogshead, cask no. 10356, dist 1962 **(85) n23** fruity and surprisingly fresh for a grain so old with little oak impacting; **t22.5** firm and juicy, though somewhat bitter, with again a fruity theme: mainly plummy; **f19.5** some mocha makes a move but a furry bitterness begins to take command; **b20** as you can see from the strength, this oldie was bottled just in the nick of time. Hard to imagine that when this was made, just the other side of the distillery walls, Hearts were sitting top of the Scottish League, their Tynecastle ground packed every other week, and that year won the League Cup. Now as I taste this, they are acclimatising to life in a lower league being watched by only a fraction of that once solid support. Curiously, in 1962 they got off to a bright start and then faded badly at the end. Odd that 52 years on a cask of whisky filled just a few yards away did exactly the same thing... 41.1%. sc. 195 bottles.

Malts Of Scotland North British 1962 bourbon hogshead, cask no. MoS 13017, dist May 62, bott Mar 13 **(95.5) n23.5 t24 f24 b24**. A faultless whisky for rum lovers. Tasted blind, no difference. Fabulous grain, breathtaking, continuous and still Demerara in style. Who cares? Hang on: come to think of it, both come from Coffey stills...interesting... 41.5%. 48 bottles.

Master of Malt North British 18 Years Old bourbon, cask no. 309896, dist 23 Dec 94, bott 1 Apr 13 **(77) n17.5 t22 f18 b19.5**. From around this time a number of blenders were bemoaning the sulphurous qualities of North British. Even taking into account the oily, sugary charge on the palate, you can see why. This, I have just discovered, is the 777th new whisky for the 2014 Bible. And it scores 77...how weird is that! But this 777, a very lopsided grain, never takes off. 52.3%. 240 bottles.

Master Of Malt North British 20 Year Old cask no. 3228, dist 1991 **(85.5) n22 t22 f20.5 b21**. Some decent, slightly syrupy sugars but bitter at death. 54.1%. sc. Master Of Malt.

The Pearls of Scotland North British 1994 18 Year Old cask no. 309880, dist Dec 94, bott Nov 13 **(89) n22** reverberating butterscotch and creamy Worther's originals; **t22.5** a surprising little nip on delivery, then settles for an ulmo honey symphony, but with the volume turned down very low; **f22** a little attitude returns...as does the butterscotch; **b22.5** simple fayre, but enough honey to make a single malt, let alone grain, proud. 52.6%.

Scotch Malt Whisky Society Cask G1.10 Aged 21 Years refill hogshead, dist 14 dec 90 **(85) n22 t22 f20 b21**. Absolutely standard and non-spectacular without enough grain character to see off the massive caramels dragged from the oak. Pleasant and easy going, though the finish is on the bitter side. 61.1%. sc. 137 bottles.

Scott's Selection North British 1989 bott 2011 **(86) n21.5 t22.5 f20.5 b21.5**. Threatens to break out and expand on its vanilla-led theme but remains pretty tight throughout. Some puckering saltiness early on. 54%. Speyside Distillers.

Signatory Single Grain Collection North British 1997 dist 14 May 97, bott 28 Nov 13 **(92.5) n22.5** surprisingly hefty: looks like an ex Islay cask has been involved somewhere along the line. The mocha certainly has a puff of smoke in there; **t23** beautiful delivery aided by the softest of oils coating the palate with a thin layer of ulmo honey and vanilla; **f23** yet more ulmo honey (could have been distilled in Chile!) weighted by the hint of smoke and spreading of molasses; **b24** the vague, distant smokiness adds further intrigue to a fine grain whisky. 43%. WB15/169

The Sovereign Single Cask North British 1962 cask no. 9930, dist 1962, bott Aug 13 **(94.5) n24** the grape is clean and a caress; the oak is firm yet friendly; the spices are delicate yet determined. Can this really be a 50 year old...? **t23** much livelier on the palate. And, to be honest, I am astonished by the alcoholic strength after all these years. Somehow it remains mouthwatering, the corn bristling amid the sherry...; **f24** there is a buzz, but not the sort you normally from sherry butts these days. It is the spice still working overtime to ensure the pep is maintained. The vanillas try to form some kind of backbone, but it is the nutty (toasted almonds coated in honey) counterweight which works so well; a little mocha and the softest oils compliment the fade; **b23.5** another grain of legend from Hunter Laing. Bottlings such as these really do re-draw the map of truly great whisky...And as for this: one of the most gentle rides you will ever enjoy around a whisky bottle, entirely sans bumps; indeed, a 50-year-old without a single wrinkle...*57.2%. sc. Hunter Laing & Co.*

That Boutique-y Whisky Company North British Batch 1 (73.5) n18 t19 f18 b18.5. Really didn't know they were making gin at North British. What the bloody hell is this...? *51.1%. 117 bottles.*

The Whisky Agency North British 1962 (93) n24 t23.5 f22.5 b23. Full of traits and characteristics as rare as this type of whisky. But, above all, absolutely refuses to admit its age. This grain is an inspiration to us all... *479% The Whisky Agency.*

NORTH OF SCOTLAND

Clan Denny North Of Scotland Vintage Aged 38 Years barrel, cask no. HH9078 **(94.5) n23 t24 f23.5 b24.** Fascinating how some grains, like the Cambus, head in a Canadian style of direction, while this is pure Kentucky. And superb Kentucky at that... *52%. sc. DEN0030*

Late Lamented North of Scotland 37 Years Old (94.5) n23.5 t23.5 f23.5 b24. An astonishing whisky completely devoid of the bitterness often found in a whisky of such antiquity, or over the top oakiness. One of the great Scottish Single Grains of recent years and a bottling that Canadian whisky devotees of a near lost style of half a century ago will relish. Monumentally magnificent and, of its type, almost flawless. *44.2%*

⁙ **The Pearls of Scotland North of Scotland 1971** bott May 14 **(94.5) n23** oak dominates, but the corn oils and light molasses keep things friendly; **t24.5** a fabulous nip to the delivery with busy, scurrying dark sugars met head on by hickory and spice with mocha pouncing when possible; incredibly lush and intense; **f23** long, seamless vanilla with vague spice buzz and clean sugars; **b24** how can a whisky of this enormous age have such great weight yet still enjoy a rich simplicity. A bourbon in all but name. *43.3%*

Scott's Selection North Of Scotland 1971 bott 2012 **(87) n21 t22 f22 b22.** What a weirdo. If grain is filled into an old Islay cask, over 40 years the phenols will vanish. What they are still doing here, though in minor quantities, is open to debate...! *45.1%*

Scott's Selection North Of Scotland 1973 bott 2012 **(92) n23.5 t23 f22.5 b23.** You just know you've had one hell of a big whisky... *48.5%*

PORT DUNDAS

Port Dundas 20 Years Old Special Release 2011 db **(90) n21.5 t22 f23.5 b23.** Can a whisky be a little too silky. This one tries, especially on the non-committal nose and over friendly delivery. But once the spices rise, things get very interesting... *574%. nc ncf sc.*

⁙ **Cadenhead's Small Batch Port Dundas Aged 25 Years** bourbon hogshead, dist 88, bott 14 **(96) n24.5** presumably distilled from corn as this is like an ultra high quality Canadian: red liquorice, sweetened tannin, a mix of over-ripe greengage and kiwifruit, but, above all, lightly peppered corn oil; **t24** the oils sit and balance on the palate like a tightrope walker above the Grand Canyon; the sugars are barely believable varying from ulmo honey to muscovado; just so refined...; **f23.5** the oak performs somersaults, balancing a little bitterness with a further array of sugars which now head towards lighter manuka honey and maple syrup; the corn oil never relents for a moment; **b24** as grain whisky goes, and Port Dundas in particular, just about perfect. Certainly represents one of the best three nose and delivery combinations of the year. *46%. 246 bottles. WB15/363*

Clan Denny Port Dundas Aged 21 Years refill hogshead, cask no. HH9452 **(93) n23 t23.5 f23 b23.5.** Astonishingly invigorating. Leaps from the glass with intent and purpose. Wonderful! *55.7%. sc. Douglas Laing & Co.*

Clan Denny Port Dundas Vintage Aged 24 Years hogshead, cask no. HH9079 **(94.5) n23 t24 f23.5 b24.** A typical Coffey still heavyweight which never thinks of stinting on the dark sugars. *52.2%. sc. Douglas Laing & Co. DEN0091*

Clan Denny Port Dundas Aged 34 Years refill hogshead, cask no. HH7543, dist 1978 **(92) n22 t23 f23.5 b23.5.** One of those deliciously rare beasts that just gets better and better as it goes along. *54.2%. nc ncf sc.*

Clan Denny Port Dundas Aged 34 Years refill hogshead, cask no. HH7543, dist 1978 **(94.5) n23.5 t24 f23.5 b23.5.** Not many single malts can match this for sheer deliciousness. *58.6%. nc ncf sc. Douglas Laing & Co.*

Director's Cut Port Dundas Aged 30 Years refill hogshead, cask no. 8416, dist 1982 **(87) n21 t23.5 f20 b22.5.** No shortage of action...but, oh! for a better cask!! *58.7%. nc ncf sc. Douglas Laing & Co. 207 bottles.*

Duncan Taylor Octave Port Dundas 38 Years Old cask no. 600952, dist 1973 **(86) n23 t21.5 f20.5 b21.5.** One very strange grain whisky. An equal tugging between fruit and bourbon which ensures a fascinating nose. But it never quite gels after the initial rich, biscuity delivery, though always enjoyable and even occasionally juicy, tails off a little. *55.6%. sc.*

Scotch Malt Whisky Society Cask G6.2 Aged 18 Years refill barrel, cask no. 20061, dist 1993 **(82)** n22 t21 f19 b20. For all the early sweetness, never quite succeeds in shrugging off an ultimately debilitating bitterness. *55.2%. sc. Scotch Malt Whisky Society.*

Scott's Selection Port Dundas 1965 bott 2011 **(91)** n24 t23 f21.5 b22.5. If you ever see a witch's chest in Holland...this is even flatter than that... No peaks or troughs. Just one flavour rolling, seemingly without a second glance, hesitation or join into the next... Not sure whether to adore this incredibly delicate whisky or try to thrash some life into it. Certainly, as I come up to tasting my 1,000th whisky of the year (this is no. 972) I can safely say there has been no other one quite like it. Which must be a good thing. So, upon reflection, one to get to know and love. For it is a thing of rare beauty. Flat chest or not... *43.3%. Speyside Distillers.*

⁘ **The Sovereign Single Cask Port Dundas 1978** cask no. 9864, dist 1978, bott Jun 13 **(96.5)** n24 good lord! A distant whiff of smoke...how far is Port Dundas from Port Ellen...? Very distant...Elsewhere, newly baked bread and the single-cell depth of ulmo honey spread...; t24 the ulmo honey s here far more dominant, helped along delicate tannins and even an intertwined thread of hickory and liquorice; the soft beat of the spices does no harm at all; f24 gentle spices remain while the mocha is topped off with the most alluring puff of smoke; b24.5 one can assume only that this matured in an old Islay cask. For phenolic fingerprints are all over this, but so subtly and fleeting that this is one hell of a turn on. Intriguing, entertaining, beautifully made and matured. A grainy dream... *58.1%. sc. Hunter Laing & Co.*

⁘ **The Sovereign Single Cask Port Dundas 1978** cask no. 10431, dist 1978, bott Apr 14 **(94.5)** n23.5 bitty, busy spice keeps the nose well tweaked. No shortage of tannin and even confident citrus, too; t24 salivating, sensuous and caressing, this is delivery to die for. The sugars are very lightly softened by what seems to be corn oil and very at home with the concentrated vanilla...tasted blind I would have sworn this was from La Salle Distillery about 3,000 miles west...; f23 a little toastiness; and toasted yam too; b24 the Mounted Police are probably tracking this down: it appears to have escaped from Canada...And he's big enough to spot from miles away. A grain which puts so many malts to shame. *58.7%. sc.*

STRATHCLYDE

⁘ **Cadenhead's Small Batch Strathclyde Aged 24 Years** bourbon barrels, dist 1989, bott 2013 **(79.5)** n20.5 t22 f18 b19. Quaffable enough – providing you don't concentrate too hard on what's going on on your palate. Two dozen years ago there wasn't enough copper in the distilling system by half. And even all these years on, it shows! A bit of an Allied bitter cask doesn't help, either. *46%. 504 bottles. WB15/166*

⁘ **Chivas Brothers Cask Strength Edition Strathclyde Aged 12 Years** batch no. ST 12 001, dist 01, bott 13 **(88.5)** n22 creamy toffee... t23 ahhh..Rolos...in concentrated form; f21.5 burnt fudge; b22 the back label informs us: "You may notice a slight natural haze for when you add water or ice. This is perfectly natural." I am sorry but there is nothing natural about adding ice... *62.1%. ncf nc. WB15/370*

Clan Denny Strathclyde 33 Years Old refill butt, cask no. HH6144, dist 1977, bott 2010 **(94.5)** n23.5 t23.5 f24 b23.5. I am not told it has been, but imagine an old grain finished in a lively, fresh and very clean wine cask... A stunner! *57.2%. nc ncf sc.*

Clan Denny Strathclyde Aged 38 Years refill barrel, cask no. HH9486 **(88)** n23.5 t22 f20.5 b22. Appears to be wheated grain as opposed to corn. Very early if so. *55.5%. sc.*

Scotch Malt Whisky Society Cask G10.1 Aged 23 Years refill hogshead, dist 31 Aug 89 **(94)** n24 t23 f23.5 b23.5. Oh, if only the majority of malts could offer such clarity from the cask! *59.6%. sc. 280 bottles. Scotch Malt Whisky Society.*

⁘ **The Sovereign Single Cask Strathclyde 1977** cask no. 9912, dist 1977, bott Aug 13 **(95)** n23 just about enough thickening grain – and alcohol to make this into a whisky. Otherwise the nose is pure cream oloroso, of the fruitiest variety possible; t24 the delivery is one mouth-coating homage to the gods of sherry, slightly sticky, gently sweetened...and dripping in sharp grape and emboldened by a vague but busy spiciness; And so it continues...; f24 the finish is all about offering balance as the grape at last punches itself out. The oak comes into its own now, a kind of spiced Cadbury's fruit and nut candy bar...; b24 those who fell in love with Macallan all those years back because of its faultlessly silky sherry influence are about to have their hearts won again. It'll be love at first flight... *58.1%. sc. Hunter Laing & Co.*

UNSPECIFIED SINGLE GRAIN

⁘ **Haig Club** toasted oak casks **(89)** n21.5 soft, non-commital, medium aged, medium oaked...safe...; t23 attractive degree of sharpness early on but soon reverts to full supine mode once the oils begin to gather. The vanilla on the oak infuses enough to ensure the levels of sweetness are contained; **f22.5** gentle cream fudge and vanilla with a pleasant spice fade; **b22** when I first saw this, wasn't quite sure whether to laugh or cry. Because 25 years ago bottles of single grain whisky was the unique domain of the flat cap brigade, the miners and other working class in the Kirkcaldy area of Scotland. Their grain, Cameron Brig, would be drunk with a splash, mixed with Coke or ginger, even occasionally with Irn Bru, or straight and unmolested as a chaser to the ubiquitous kegged heavy, McEwan's lager or a bottle of Sweetheart stout. When I suggested to the hierarchy at United Distillers, the forerunners of Diageo, that in their finer grains they had a product which could conquer the world, the looks I got ranged from sympathy for my lack of understanding in matters whisky to downright concern about my mental wellbeing. I had suggested the exquisite Cambus, now lost to us like so many other grain distilleries in those passing years, should be brought out as a high class singleton. It was pointed out to me that single grain was, always had been and always will be, the preferred choice of the less sophisticated; those not wishing to pay too much for their dram. Fast forward a quarter of a century and here sits a gorgeously expensive bottle in a deep cobalt blue normally associated with Ballantine's and a very classy, heavyweight stopper. In it is a grain which, if the advertising is to be believed, is the preferred choice not of the back street bar room idlers carefully counting their pennies but of its major ambassador David Beckham: it is the drop to be savoured by the moneyed, jet-set sophisticates. My, oh my. Let's not call this hype. Let's just say it has taken some genius exec in a suit half a lifetime – and probably most of his or hers - to come around to my way of thinking and convince those in the offices on the floor above to go for it. Wonder if I qualify for 10 percent of profit for suggesting it all those years back...or, preferably, five percent of their advertising budget. Meanwhile, I look forward to watching David pouring this into some of his Clynelish and Talisker. After all, no-one can Blend it like Beckham... 40%. WB15/408

Lady of the Glen Twenty Four Year Old (89.5) n21.5 t23 f22.5 b22.5. Squelchy-sift Invergordon at its sugary best. 56%. Hannah Whisky Merchants.

The Last Vatted Grain bott Nov 11 (88.5) n23 t22 f21.5 b22. Not just sad that the term "vatted" is now pointlessly outlawed on the bottle. But also that half of the four grain distilleries used in this vatting are equally consigned to history. 46%. nc ncf. Compass Box.

Scottish Spirits Single Grain 3 Years Old (Canned) (82.5) n21 t21.5 f20 b20. An absolutely standard, decent quality grain whisky with an attractive sweetness and latent youthful zesty fizz. Ill-served, however, by what I presume is caramel to give it a clichéd scotch look which dulls the finish in particular. In its natural form, this would have scored a lot higher. 40% (80 Proof).

⫶⫶ **Tweeddale Single Lowland Grain Scotch Whisky Aged 16 Years** (88) n23 alluring: a touch earthy with some boiling root veg. But sprinkled liberally with muscovado sugars as opposed to salt; **t22** a midway mouth feel in firmness, with enough oils to make the most of the delicate spice warming the acacia honey; **f21** a tad oak tangy; **b22** a quiet speech of understatement. 46%. nc ncf sc. Stonedean.

Vatted Grain

Compass Box Hedonism first fill American oak cask, bott 20 Feb 13 (84) n22 t22 f19 b20. Just too fat, too sweet and too bitter at the finale to work to great effect. Some decent oak on both nose and delivery, though. 43%. nc ncf. Compass Box Whisky Company.

Compass Box Hedonism Maximus (93.5) n25 t22.5 f23 b23. Bourbon Maximus... 46%

Compass Box The Entertainer Limited Edition bott Aug 12 (88.5) n21.5 t22.5 f22 b22. A pleasant blend, though the tanginess is perhaps a little too sharp. 46%. Compass Box Whisky Company. 1000 bottles. Commissioned by Selfridges.

⫶⫶ **William Grant & Sons Rare Cask Reserves 25 Years Old Blended Grain Scotch Whisky** (92.5) n23 creamy aroma – almost cream soda-ish – vanilla and very lazy spice; **t23.5** just as yielding on the palate as the nose promises with some spices blasting life into the supine grains. The oak battles with a light, fudgy dullness to break through this quagmire, though it is a ponderous battle. Tasty and, best of all, never overly sweet...; **f23** a little tart as the bourbon cask kicks in, but absolutely massive vanilla; **b23** a really interesting one, this. In the old days, blenders always spent as much time vatting the grains together as they did the malts, for if they did not work well as a unit it was unlikely harmony would be found in their blend. A long time ago I was taught to, whenever possible, use a soft grain to counter a firmer one, and vica versa. Today, there are far fewer blends to choose from, though 25 years ago the choice was wider. So interesting to see that this grain is soft-dominated with very little backbone at all. Delicious. But screams for some backbone. 47%. Exclusive to The Whisky Shop.

Scottish Blends

For the first time in my career, I got a bit of an ear-bashing from a dissatisfied customer at one of my blind whisky tastings. And, of all things, it was because I had not included a blended Scotch in the line-up. My-oh-my! How times change.

Actually the guy was good natured about it, especially when I told him it was because the samples had been lost in transit, but his sense of loss was real. Apparently, he had attended one of my tastings a few years before, arriving as a self-confessed malt snob. He left converted to the blended whisky cause... to the extent it was now his favourite whisky style. As much as it is annoying when things go slightly wrong at an event, I still felt a thrill that more hardcore whisky lovers find experimenting in blends every bit as enjoyable as finding new malts. This implies blended scotch is as good as single malt. And, for my money, that is entirely the case; and if the blender is really doing his or her job, it should often be better. However, that job is getting a little harder each year. Once it was the standard joke that a sulphured sherry butt that had once been marked for a single malt brand would be dumped into a large blend where it would work on BP Chief executive Tony Hayward's "drop in the ocean" principle. However, there is now a lot more than just the odd off sherry butt finding their way in and blenders have to take guard that their blends are not being negatively affected. Certainly, during the course of writing the Whisky Bible I discovered this was becoming a much more common occurrence from the 2010 edition onwards. Indeed, one or two brands which a few years back I would have expected to pick up awards on a regular basis have been hit badly: disappointing and a great loss to whisky lovers.

As if to drive home this point, this year's Blend of the Year, from the irrepressable Last Drop Company, consisted of malt and grain from the year 1965. It had not, thankfully, been rounded off in new sherry to "freshen it up". Had they done, it probably wouldn't have been top Scotch.

Over 90 out of every 100 bottles of Scotch consumed is a blend, and therefore rather common. That has brought about some cold-shouldering from certain elitist whisky lovers who convince themselves a blend must be inferior. Well, not in my books. In fact, perhaps the opposite is true. Until you get to grips with blends you may well be entitled to regard yourself knowledgeable in single malts, but not in Scotch as a whole. Blends should be the best that Scotland can offer, because with a blend you have the ability to create any degree of complexity. And surely balance and complexity are the cornerstones of any great whisky, irrespective of type.

Of course there are some pretty awful blends created simply as a commodity with little thought going into their structure – just young whiskies, sometimes consisting of stock that is of dubious quality and then coloured up to give some impression of age. Yes, you are more likely to find that among blends than malts and for this reason the poorest blends can be pretty nasty. And, yes, they contain grain. Too often, though, grain is regarded as a kind of whisky leper – not to be touched under any circumstances. Some writers dismiss grain as "neutral" and "cheap", thus putting into the minds of the uninitiated the perception of inferiority.

But there really is nothing inferior about blends. In fact, whilst researching The Bible, I have to say that my heart misses more than one beat usually when I received a sample of a blend I have never found before. Why? Well, with single malts each distillery produces a style that can be found within known parameters. With a blend, anything is possible. There are myriad styles of malts to choose from and they will react slightly differently with certain grains.

For that reason, perhaps, I have marked blends a little more strictly and tighter than I have single malts. Because blends, by definition, should offer more.

The most exciting blends, like White Horse 12 (why, oh, why is that, like Old Parr 18, restricted mainly to Japan?) Grant's and the perennially glorious Ballantine's show bite, character and attitude. Silk and charm are to be appreciated. But after a long, hard day is anything better than a blend that is young and confident enough to nip and nibble at your throat on its way down and then throw up an array of flavours and shapes to get your taste-buds round? Certainly, I have always found blends ultimately more satisfying than malts. Especially when the balance, like this year's Scotch Blend of the Year, The Last drop 1965, simply caresses your soul. They do more: they paint pictures on the palate, flavour-scapes of extraordinary subtlety and texture. No two bottles are ever exactly the same, but they are usually close enough and further illustrate the fascination of a beautifully orchestrated variation on a theme.

With Blended Scotch the range and possibilities are limitless. All it takes is for the drinker not just to use his or her nose and taste-buds. But also an open mind.

Scottish Blends

"10 Years and a Bit" Blended Scotch (84) n21.5 t22 f20 b20.5. Matured in oloroso and finished in a Cognac quartercask. Explains why this blend lurches drunkenly all over the palate. Enough honeycomb, though, for a pleasant few minutes *42%. Qualityworld, Denmark.*

100 Pipers (74) n18.5 t18 f19 b18.5. An improved blend, even with a touch of spice to the finish. I get the feeling the grains are a bit less aggressive than they for so long were. I'd let you know for sure, if only I could get through the caramel. *40%. Chivas.*

Aberdour Piper (88.5) n22 t23 f21.5 b22. Always great to find a blend that appears to have upped the stakes in the quality department. Clean, refreshing with juicy young Speysiders at times simply showing off. *40%. Hayman Distillers.*

Adelphi Private Stock Loyal Old Mature (88) n21 t23 f22 b22. A very attractive number, especially for those with a slightly sweet tooth. *40%*

Antiquary 12 Years Old (92) n23.5 t23.5 f22 b23 A staggering about turn for a blend which, for a very long time, has flown the Speyside flag. *40%. Tomatin Distillery.*

Antiquary 21 Years Old (93) n23.5 t23.5 f23 b23 A huge blend, scoring a magnificent 93 points. But I have tasted better, and another sample, direct from the blending lab, came with even greater complexity and less apparent caramel. A top-notch blend of rare distinction. *43%*

Antiquary 30 Years Old (86) n22 t23 f20 b21. Decidedly odd fare but the eccentric nose and early delivery are sublime, with silky complexity tumbling over the palate. *46%*

Antiquary Finest (79.5) n20 t21 f19 b19.5. Pleasantly sweet and plump with the accent on the quick early malt delivery. *40%. Tomatin Distillery.*

Arden House Scotch Whisky (86) n19.5 t22 f22.5 b22. Another great bit of fun from the Co-op. Very closely related to their Finest Blend, though this has, for some reason or other, a trace of a slightly fatter, mildly more earthy style. If only they would ditch the caramel and let those sweet malts and grains breathe! *40%. Co-Operative Group.*

Asda Blended Scotch Whisky (76.5) n19 t21 f17.5 b19. A scattergun approach with sweet, syrupy notes hitting the palate early and hard. Beware the rather bitter finish, though. *40%*

Asda Extra Special 12 Years Old (78) n19 t21 f19 b19. Pleasantish but dragged down by the dreaded S word. *40%. Glenmorangie for Asda.*

The Bailie Nicol Jarvie (B.N.J) (95) n24 t24 f23 b24. I know my criticism of BNJ, historically one of my favourite blends, over the last year or two has been taken to heart by Glenmorangie. Delighted to report that they have responded: the blend has been fixed and is back to its blisteringly brilliant, ultra-mouth-watering self. Someone's sharpened their ideas up. *40%*

Ballantine's Aged 12 Years (84.5) n22.5 t22 f19 b21. Attractive but odd fellow, this, with a touch of juniper to the nose and furry bitter marmalade on the finish. But some excellent barley-cocoa moments, too. *43%. Chivas.*

Ballantine's 12 Years Old (87) n21 t22 f21 b23. The kind of old-fashioned, mildly moody blend Colonel Farquharson-Smythe (retired) might have recognised when relaxing at the 19th hole back in the early '50s. Too good for a squirt of soda, mind. *40%. Chivas Bros.*

Ballantine's 17 Years Old (97.5) n24.5 deft grain and honey plus teasing salty peat; ultra high quality with bourbon and pear drops offering the thrust; a near unbelievable integration with gooseberry juice offering a touch of sharpness muted by watered golden syrup; t24 immediately mouthwatering with maltier tones clambering over the graceful cocoa-enriched grain; the degrees of sweetness are varied but near perfection; just hints of smoke here and there; f24 lashings of vanilla and cocoa on the fade; drier with a faint spicey, vaguely smoky buzz; has become longer with more recent bottlings with the most subtle oiliness imaginable; b25 now only slightly less weighty than of old. After a change of style it has comfortably reverted back to its sophisticated, mildly erotic old self. One of the most beautiful, complex and stunningly structured whiskies ever created. Truly the epitome of great Scotch. *43%.* ⊙

Ballantine's Aged 17 Years Limited Edition Miltonduff Signature Distillery (91.5) n22.5 t24 f21.5 b23.5. The usual alto libretto of the Ballantine's 17 has been replaced here by a much weightier composition, even though the usual subtle smoke is missing. Using sherry butts is to enter a minefield in this day and age, one I'm afraid, there is no clear path through. The ones here are of mixed quality, but the overall effect is pleasing. *43%*

Ballantine's Aged 21 Years (93) n24 t24 f22 b23 One of the reasons I think I have loved the Ballantine's range over the years is because it is a blenders' blend. In other words, you get the feeling that they have made as much, and probably more, as possible from the stocks available and made complexity and balance the keystones to the whisky. That is still the case, except you find now that somehow, although part of a larger concern, it appears that the spectrum of flavours is less wide, though what has been achieved with those available remains absolutely top drawer. This is truly great whisky, but it has changed in style as blends, especially of this age, cannot help but doing. *43%*

Ballantine's Aged 30 Years (94) n23.5 t24 f23.5 b23.5. Quite a different animal to that which I tasted last year...and the year before. Having come across it in three different markets,

I each time noted a richer, more balanced product: less a bunch of old casks being brought together but more a sculpted piece from preferred materials. That said, I still get the feeling that this is a work in progress: a Kenny Jackett-style building of a team bit by bit, so that each compartment is improved when it is possible, but not to the detriment of another and, vitally, balance is maintained. *43%*

Ballantine's Christmas Reserve (72) n18 t19 f17 b18. Not quite what I asked from Santa. A rare sulphury slip up in the Christmas day snow from the Ballantine's stable. *40%*

Ballantine's Finest (96) n24 a playful balance and counter-balance between grains, lighter malts and a gentle smokiness. The upped peat of recent years has given an extra weight and charm that had been missing; **t24** sublime delivery: the mouthfeel couldn't be better had your prayers been answered; velvety and brittle grains combine to get the most out of the juicy malts: a lot of chewing to get through here; **f23.5** soft, gentle, yet retains its weight and shape with a re-emergence of smoke and a gristy sweetness to counter the gentle vanillas and cocoa from the oak **b24.5** as a standard blend this is coming through as a major work of art. Each time I taste this the weight has gone up a notch or two more and the sweetness has increased to balance out with the drier grain elements. Take a mouthful of this and experience the work of a blender very much at the top of his game. *40%. Chivas Bros.* ☉

Ballantine's Limited brown bottle, bott code D03518 **(94.5) n23.5 t24 f23 b24.** When it comes to Ballantine's I am beginning to run out of superlatives. The last time I tasted Limited, I remember being disappointed by the un-Ballantine's-like bitter finish. Well, from nose to finale, there is a barely perceptible trace of a rogue cask costing half a point from each stage: indeed, it may have cost it World Whisky of the Year. But so magnificent are all those keeping it company there has been no such falling at the last hurdle here. This bottle, rather than finding its way back into my warehouse library, will be living at my home for offering an ethereal quality unmatched by any other whisky in the world. *43%. Chivas.*

Ballantine's Limited 75cl royal blue bottle **(89) n22 t24 f21 b22.** Hadn't tasted this for a little while but maintains its early style and quite glorious delivery. *43%*

⠿ **Ballantine's Limited Release no. J13295 (95.5) n24.5** just so soft...ridiculously so. You have to listen hard to what is happening here...only perfect silence will do. Then you will pick up fluting fruit calls which are absorbed by the delicate smoke. The sugars and honey mix shyly but effectively, all this seemingly glazed. A hint of spice wakes you if you are being caressed to sleep; **t25** there is no point in trying to describe the indescribable. Just about the best delivery I have experienced from a blended whisky with the fruit and grains seemingly having a telepathic understanding of each other's movements; **f22** annoying bitters out and a slight furriness attaches to the late smoke; **b24** I absolutely take my hat off to the blender. When it comes to the weight, complexity, subtlety, suaveness, balance, pace of flavour development, charm and just all-round yessss!!!!ness, I am not sure how the delivery can be bettered. A slight mix of exhausted bourbon cask (allowing some bitterness) and a degree of perhaps sherry-induced furriness means the finish can't quite reach those heights of seemingly effortless perfection and rob this of the World Whisky of the Year for this Bible it most likely would have picked up. But for the combination of nose and delivery I will take those losses. Yet again a Ballantine's which just makes me purr and celebrate the greatness some whiskies can reach. *43%.*

Ballantine's Master's (82) n21 t22 f19 b20. Excellent lively grain and chewy malt, but the always suspect, grain-drizzled finish has become even more nondescript in recent bottlings. *40%*

Ballantine's Rare Limited (89.5) n23.5 t22.5 f21.5 b22 A heavier, more mouth watering blend than the "Bluebottle" version. *43%. ncf. Chivas.*

Barley Barony (83) n21.5 t21 f20 b20.5. A faintly furry finish follows from a firm, fruity front. *40%. Quality Spirits International.*

Bell's Original (91) n23 t22.5 f22.5 b23 Your whisky sleuth came across the new version for the first time in the bar of a London theatre back in December 2009 during the interval of "The 39 Steps". To say I was impressed and pleasantly surprised is putting it mildly. And with the whisky, too, which is a massive improvement on the relatively stagnant 8-year-old especially with the subtle extra smoky weight. If the blender asks me: "Did I get it right, Sir?" then the answer has to be a resounding "yes". *40%*

Bells 8 Years Old (85) n21.5 t22.5 f20 b21. Some mixed messages here: on one hand it is telling me that it has been faithful to some of the old Bells distilleries – hence a slight dirty note, especially on the finish. On the other, there are some sublime specks of complexity and weight. Quite literally the rough and the smooth. *40%. Diageo.*

Benmore (74) n19 t19 f18 b18. Underwhelming to the point of being nondescript. *40%*

Berrys' Blue Hanger 30 Years Old 3rd Release bott 2007 **(90.5) n23 t22.5 f22.5 b22.5** Much improved version on the last, closer to the original in every respect. Excellent. *45.6%. Berry Bros & Rudd.*

Big "T" 5 Years Old (75) n19 t20 f18 b18. Still doesn't have the finesse of old and clatters about the tastebuds charmlessly. 40%. *Tomatin Distillery.*

Black & White (91) n22 t23 f22.5 b23.5 This one hasn't gone to the dogs: quite the opposite. I always go a bit misty-eyed when I taste something this traditional: the crisp grains work to maximum effect in reflecting the malts. A classic of its type. 40%. *Diageo.*

Black Bottle (74.5) n18 t20.5 f17 b18. Barely a shadow of its once masterful, great self. 40%.

Black Bottle 10 Years Old (89) n22 t23 f22 b23 A stupendous blend of weight and poise, but possessing little of the all-round steaming, rampaging sexuality of the younger version... but like the younger version showing a degree less peat: here perhaps even two. Not, I hope, the start of a new trend under the new owners. 40%

Black Dog 12 Years Old (92) n21 t23 f24 b24. Offering genuine sophistication and élan. This minor classic will probably require two or three glass-fulls before you take the bait... 42.8%

Black Dog Century (89) n21 t23 f23 b22. I adore this style of no-nonsense, full bodied bruising blend which amid the muscle offers exemplary dexterity and finesse. What entertainment in every glass!! 42.8%. *McDowell & Co Ltd. Blended in Scotland/Bottled in India.*

The Black Douglas bott code 340/06/183 **(84)** n19 t20 f23 b22. Don't expect raptures of mind-bending complexity. But on the other hand, enough chewability and spice buzz here to make for a genuinely decent whisky, especially on the excellent finish. Not dissimilar to a bunch of blends you might have found in the 1950s. 40%. *Foster's Group, Australia.*

The Black Douglas Aged 8 Years bott code 348/06/187 **(79)** n20 t21 f19 b19. Slightly lacking for an 8-y-o: probably duller than its non-age-statement brother because of an extra dollop of caramel. 40%. *Foster's Group, Australia.*

The Black Douglas Aged 12 Years "The Black Reserve" bott code 347/06/188 **(87)** n21 t21 f23 b22. The toffee does its best to wreck the show – but there are simply too many good things going on to succeed. The slight smoke to the nose delights and the honeycomb middle really does star. 40%. *Foster's Group, Australia.*

Black Grouse (94) n23 t24 f23 b24. A superb return to a peaty blend for Edrington for the first time since they sold Black Bottle. Not entirely different from that brand, either, from the Highland Distillers days with the smokiness being superbly couched by sweet malts. A real treasure. 40%

The Black Grouse Alpha Edition (72.5) n17 t19.5 f17 b18. Dreadfully sulphured. 40%

Black Knight (85.5) n21 t22 f21 b21.5. More of a White Knight as it peacefully goes about its business. Not many taste buds slain, but just love the juicy charge. 43%. *Quality Spirits Int.*

Black Ram Aged 12 Years (85) n21 t23 f21 b20. An upfront blend that gives its all in the chewy delivery. Some major oak in there but it's all ultra soft toffee and molasses towards the finish. 40%. *Vinprom Peshtera, Bulgaria.*

Blend No. 888 (86.5) n20 t21.5 f23 b22. A good old-fashioned, rip-roaring, nippy blend with a fudge-honey style many of a certain age will fondly remember from the 60s and 70s. Love it! 40%. *The House of MacDuff.*

Boxes Blend (90) n22.5 t23.5 f21 b23. A box which gets plenty of ticks. 40.9%. *ncf.*

Broadford (78.5) n19 t19.5 f20 b20. Boringly inoffensive. Toffee anyone? 40%. *Burn Stewart.*

Buchanan's De Luxe 12 Years Old (82) n18 t21 f22 b21. The nose shows more than just a single fault and the character simply refuses to get out of second gear. Certainly pleasant, and some of the chocolate notes towards the end are gorgeous. But just not the normal brilliant show-stopper! 40%. *Diageo.*

Buchanan's Red Seal (90) n22 t23 f22 b23 Exceptional, no-frills blend whose apparent simplicity paradoxically celebrates its complexity. 40%. *Diageo.*

Budgen's Scotch Whisky Finely Blended (85) n21 t22 f21 b21. A sweet, chunky blend offering no shortage of dates, walnuts, spice and toffee. A decent one to mull over. 40%

⁘ **Cadenhead's Putachieside Aged 12 Years (91)** n23 no shortage of citrus and vanilla: fresh, and the flaky, puff-pastry topping is fitting; t23 the sugars and oils make an early assault. A little bitterness from the oak creeps in; f22 malty-lemon sawdust; b23 not tasted for a while and delighted to re-discover this understated little gem. Also, has to be one of the best labels of any scotch going... 40% WB15/357

⁘ **Cadenhead's Creations Light Creamy Vanilla Aged 17 Years** batch no. 1, bott 2014 **(91)** n22 mainly oranges and lemons, the only weight coming from the faintest echo of smoke; t23 a miniature painting of subtlety and, though a blend, a powerful juicy barley theme, with digestive biscuit and Tunnock's teacake filling also playing a major role; f23 the grain gets to work, though the backdrop is caramelised biscuit and sugar cubes; the fade brings together all the natural caramels on show...and late spice; b23 just adore clean, refreshing blends like this: says so much while appearing to do so little. For the record: Ardmore, Auchroisk, Caperdonich, and Clynelish are the malts involved, while Invergordon represents the grain. 46%. *ncf nc.* WB15/362

Callander 12 Years Old (86) n21 t22 f21.5 b21.5. No shortage of malt sparkle and even a touch of tangy salt. Very attractive and enjoyable without ripping up trees. *46.3%. Burn Stewart.*

⁙ **Campbeltown Loch** (94) n23 soft, creamy vanilla: Jammy Dodger biscuit; t24 rousingly salivating with some extraordinary young malt allowing the grain in only by degree. The grain is no less lush and the creaminess apparent on the nose shows here, too; f23.5 wonderful sugars enjoy a light vanilla and lemon glow; b23.5 over 30 years ago, this blend was one of my preferred drams at home. Not seen it for a while, so disappeared from The Bible. Found again and though it has changed a little in structure, its overall excellence takes me back to when I was a young man. *40% WB15/355*

Campbeltown Loch Aged 15 Years (88) n22.5 t22.5 f21 b22 Well weighted with the age in no hurry to arrive. *40%. Springbank Distillers.*

⁙ **Cambletown Loch 21 Years Old** db (83) n21 t23 f19 b20 Neither the nose or finish are much to write home about, the latter being a little tangy and bitter. But the delivery is rich and comforting: like a Digestive biscuit dunked in coffee. A seemingly decent malt content and a bit of toffee before the furry finale. *46%. WB15/102*

Castle Rock (81) n20 t20.5 f20 b20.5. Clean and juicy entertainment. *40%*

Catto's Aged 25 Years (87.5) n23 t22.5 f20.5 b21.5. A hugely enjoyable yet immensely frustrating dram. The higher fruit and spice notes are a delight, but it all appears to be played out in a padded cell of cream caramel. One assumes the natural oak caramels have gone into overdrive. Had they not, we would have had a supreme blend scoring well into the 90s. *40%*

Catto's Deluxe 12 Years Old (79.5) n20 t21.5 f18 b20. Refreshing and spicy in part, but still a note in there which doesn't quite work. *40%. Inverhouse Distillers.*

Catto's Rare Old Scottish (92) n23.5 t23.5 f22 b23 Currently one of my regular blends to drink at home. Astonishingly old-fashioned with a perfect accent on clean Speyside and crisp grain. In the last year or so it has taken on a sublime sparkle on the nose and palate. An absolutely masterful whisky which both refreshes and relaxes. *40%. James Catto & Co.*

Chequers Deluxe (78.5) n19.5 t20 f19 b20. Charm, elegance, sophistication...not a single sign of any of them. Still if you want a bit of rough and tumble, just the job. *40%. Diageo.*

Chivas Regal Aged 12 Years (83.5) n20.5 t22.5 f20 b20.5. Chewy fruit toffee. Silky grain mouth-feel with a toasty, oaky presence. *40%. Chivas.*

Chivas Regal Aged 18 Years (73.5) n17.5 t20 f17.5 b18.5. The nose is dulled by a whiff of sulphur and confirmation that all is not well comes with the disagreeably dry, bitter finish. Early on in the delivery some apples and spices show promise but it is an unequal battle against the caramel and off notes. *40%*

Chivas Regal 25 Years Old (95) n23 t23.5 f24 b24.5. Unadulterated class where the grain-malt balance is exemplary and the deft intertwining of well-mannered oak and elegant barley leaves you demanding another glass. Brilliant! *40%*

Clan Campbell (86.5) n21.5 t22.5 f21 b21.5. I'll wager that if I could taste this whisky before the colouring is added it would be scoring into the 90s. Not a single off note; a sublime early array of Speyside freshness but dulls at the end. *40%. Chivas.*

Clan Gold 3 Year Old (95) n23.5 t24 f23.5 b24. A blend-drinkers blend which will also slay the hearts of Speyside single malt lovers. For me, this is love at first sip... *40%*

Clan Gold Blended 15 Years Old (91) n21.5 t23 f23.5 b23 An unusual blend for the 21st century, which steadfastly refuses to blast you away with over the top flavour and/or aroma profiles and instead depends on subtlety and poise despite the obvious richness of flavour. The grains make an impact but only by creating the frame in which the more complex notes can be admired. *40%*

Clan Gold Blended 18 Years Old (94.5) n23 t24 f23.5 b24. Almost the ultimate preprandial whisky with its at once robust yet delicate working over of the taste buds by the carefully muzzled juiciness of the malt. This is the real deal: a truly classy act which at first appears to wallow in a sea of simplicity but then bursts out into something very much more complex and alluring. About as clean and charming an 18-year-old blend as you are likely to find. *40%*

Clan MacGregor (92) n22 t24 f23 b23 Just gets better and better. Now a true classic and getting up there with Grant's. *43%*

Clan Murray Rare Old (84) n18 t23 f21 b22. The wonderful malt delivery on the palate is totally incongruous with the weak, nondescript nose. Glorious, mouth-watering complexity on the arrival, though. Maybe it needs a Murray to bring to perfection... *40%. Benriach Distillery.*

Clansman (80.5) n20.5 t21 f19 b20. Sweet, grainy and soft. *40%. Loch Lomond.*

Clansman (78.5) n20 t21.5 f18 b19. Plenty of weight, oil and honey-ginger. Some bitterness, too. *43%. Loch Lomond Distillers.*

The Claymore (85) n19 t22 f22 b22. These days you are run through by spices. The blend is pure Paterson in style with guts etc, which is not something you always like to associate with a Claymore; some delightful muscovado sugar at the death. Get the nose sorted and a very decent and complex whisky is there to be had. 40%. Whyte & Mackay Distillers Ltd.

Compass Box Asyla 1st fill American oak ex-bourbon, bott May 10 (93) n24 t24 f22.5 b23.5 If you can hear a purring noise, it is me tasting this... 40%. nc ncf.

Compass Box Asyla Marriage nine months in an American oak barrel (88) n22 t23 f21 b22 A lovely blend, but can't help feeling that this was one marriage that lasted too long. 43.6%. Compass Box Whisky for La Maison du Whisky in commemoration of their 50th Anniversary.

Compass Box Delilah's Limited Release American oak, bott Jul 13 (89.5) n23 t22 f22 b22.5. A clean and satisfying blend which ramps up the sugars when need be. I'll be surprised if you get to the point where you couldn't take any more... 40%. 6400 bottles.

⠶ **Compass Box Delilah's Limited Release Small Batch** American oak (92.5) n23 the tannins arrive early, offering a delicate spice, but it is the weak acacia honey whisky dominates; but all hush-hush and understated; t23.5 this time the hney shoulders the tannins to one side. The grain is of the soft, yielding variety offering succour and comfort... like a soft pillow or gentle breast at the end of a hard day's tasting...; f23 tangy as the tannins begin to bite...and much warmer now thanks to busier spice. The bourbn effect I had been waiting for fails to materialise...though the is the odd Canadian strain here and there...; b23 blends rarely come more honeyed, or even sweeter, than this with every last sugary element seemingly extracted from the oak. My only sorrow for this whisky, given its American theme, was that it wasn't bottled as a 101 (ie 50.5% abv) instead of the rather underpowered 80 proof – because you have the feeling this would have become pretty three dimensional and leapt from the glass. And then down your throat with serious effect. 40%. nc ncf. WB15/171

Compass Box The Entertainer Limited Edition bott Aug 12 (88.5) n21.5 t22.5 f22 b22. A pleasant blend, though the tanginess is perhaps a little too sharp. 46%. Compass Box Whisky Company. 1000 bottles. Commissioned by Selfridges.

⠶ **Compass Box The General** bott Nov 13 (95) n24 for a blend. This is the closest nose to a Macallan 10 year old of three decades ago I have ever encountered: the fruit is compact, assured, spiced yet open enough to offer lighter morsels, such as toffee apple and, neatly completing that fruitcake feel, marzipan; t24 those spices step up early and with commendable enthusiasm. The fruit, plummy but lightened by an attractive thread of washy treacle pudding, is not content to take a back seat. Some liquorice and cocoa get in on the act, too; f23 now thins to allow the vanillas a say; b24 I have never encountered a bend quite like this one. The grain's part in the act appears only to give breathing space to the more delicate notes: a pretty worthy cause. Commanding and unambiguously brilliant. 53.4%. ncf nc. 1,698 bottles.

Compass Box Great King St. Artist's Blend (93) n24 t23 f22.5 b23.5. The nose of this uncoloured and non-chill filtered whisky is not dissimilar to some better known blends before they have colouring added to do its worst. A beautiful young thing this blend: nubile, naked and dangerously come hither. Compass Box's founder John Glaser has done some memorable work in recent years, though one has always had the feeling that he has still been learning his trade, sometimes forcing the issue a little too enthusiastically. Here, there is absolutely no doubting that he has come of age as a blender. 43%. nc ncf.

⠶ **Compass Box Great King Street Experimental Batch #00-V4** bott Sep 13 (93) n22.5 the slightly over-bittered out marmalade sends a clear oak message, especially seeing how it has its breakfast colleague, honey, on hand; t24 for a moment you are left mentally speechless: for a 43%-er this delivery has some serious bite and kick and again the oak is pumped and displaying its muscle. But the grain does a fabulous job in first soothing then allowing the sugars to slowly infiltrate; f23 the calm after the storm with light ulmo honey disturbed only by the quietly seething oak; b23.5 a blend combining astonishing vibrancy with oaky Russian roulette. Not a dram to do things by halves... 43%. 3,439 bottles.

⠶ **Compass Box Great King Street Experimental Batch #TR-06** bott Sep 13 (92) n22 the most dense of all the GKS I have yet tasted. All, including batch 00-V4 have shewn signs of younger malts offering a bright outlet. This, though, is a distant rumble, like highway traffic a mile off, of tannin, toast and smoke; t23.5 unlike on the nose, the first to display is a sweet, buttery maltiness, mixed with the gentle elements of the grain. And there is sweet smoke, too which holds the middle until the tannins return; f23 long, oily, with a smoked Demerara theme. The oak, though, rumbles and grumbles on; b23.5 I think this one's been rumbled... 43%. 3,805 bottles.

Compass Box Great King St. New York Blend bott Aug 12 (89.5) n22.5 t23.5 f21.5 b22. Another thoughtful blend with Compass Box making good use of Caol Ila-style oiliness. 46%. nc ncf. 1,840 bottles. USA exclusive.

Consulate (89) n22 t22 f22.5 b22.5. One assumes this beautifully balanced dram was designed to accompany Passport in the drinks cabinet. I suggest if buying them, use Visa. 40%

Co-operative Finest Blend (92.5) n23.5 t23 f22.5 b23.5 A fabulous and fascinating blend which has divested itself of its peaty backbone and instead packed the core with honey. Not the same heavyweight blend of old, but still one which is to be taken seriously – and straight – by those looking for a classic whisky of the old school. 40%

Co-operative Premium Scotch 5 Years Old (91.5) n22 t24 f22.5 b23 From the nose I thought this blend had nosedived emphatically from when I last tasted it. However the delivery remains the stuff of legend. And though it has shifted emphasis and style to marked degree, there is no disputing its overall clout and entertainment value remains very high. 40%

Craigellachie Hotel Quaich Bar Range (81) n20 t21 f20 b20. A delightful malt delivery early on, but doesn't push on with complexity as perhaps it might. 40%

Crawford's (83.5) n19 t21 f22 b21.5. A lovely spice display helps overcome the caramel. 40%.

Cutty Black (83) n20 t23 f19 b21. Both nose and finish are dwarfed and flung into the realms of ordinariness by the magnificently substantial delivery. Whilst there is a taint to the nose, its richness augers well for what is to follow; and you won't be disappointed. At times it behaves like a Highland Park with a toffeed spine, such is the richness and depth of the honey and dates and complexity of the grain-vanilla background. But those warning notes on the nose are there for good reason and the finish tells you why. Would not be surprised to see this score into the 90s on a different bottling day. 40%. Edrington.

Cutty Sark (78) n19 t21 f19 b19. Crisp and juicy. But a nipping furriness, too. 40%

Cutty Sark Aged 12 Years (92) n22 t24 f23 b23 At last! Cutty 12 at full sail...and blended whisky rarely looks any more beautiful! 40%. Edrington.

Cutty Sark Aged 15 Years (82) n19 t22 f20 b21. Attempts to take the honey route. But seriously dulled by toffee and the odd sulphured cask. 40%. Edrington.

Cutty Sark Aged 18 Years (88) n22 t22 f22 b22 Lost the subtle fruitiness which worked so well. Easy-going and attractive. 43%

Cutty Sark Aged 25 Years (91) n21 t23.5 f22.5 b23 Magnificent, though not quite flawless, this whisky is as elegant and effortlessly powerful as the ship after which the brand was named... 45.7%. Berry Bros & Rudd.

Cutty Sark Storm (81.5) n18 t23.5 f19.5 b20.5. When the wind is set fair, which is mainly on delivery and for the first six or seven flavour waves which follow, we really do have an astonishingly beautiful blend, seemingly high in malt content and really putting the accent on ulmo honey and marzipan: a breath-taking combination. This is assisted by a gorgeous weight to the silky body and a light raspberry jam moment to the late arriving Ecuadorian cocoa. All magnificent. However, the blend, as Cutty sadly tends to, sails into sulphurous seas. 40%. Edrington.

Demijohn's Finest Blended Scotch Whisky (88) n21 t22 f23 b22 A fun, characterful blend that appears to have above the norm malt. Enjoy. 40%. Adelphi.

Dew of Ben Nevis Blue Label (82) n19 t22 f20 b21. The odd off-key note is handsomely outnumbered by deliciously complex mocha and demerara tones. Ditch the caramel and you'd have a sizzler! 40%. Ben Nevis Distillery. Replacement for Dew of Ben Nevis Millennium Blend.

Dew of Ben Nevis Special Reserve (85) n19 t21 f23 b22. A much juicier blend than of old, still sporting some bruising and rough patches. But that kind of makes this all the more attractive, with the caramel mixing with some fuller malts to provide a date and nuts effect which makes for a grand finale. 40%. Ben Nevis Distillery.

Dew of Ben Nevis Supreme Selection (77) n18 t20 f20 b19. Some lovely raspberry jam swiss roll moments here. But the grain could be friendlier, especially on the nose. 40%

Dewar House Experimental Batch No. A39 Age 17 Years sherry finish, cask no. 001, bott 17 Jul 12 (96) n24 faultless grape, but not overly heavy or too sweet. Instead a busy procession of spices, some of them quite peppery and nippy, binds rather beautifully with a delicate vanilla, date and walnut base; t24 you feel you have been flung to the bed and your hands tied while wave upon wave of sensual flavours wash over you, one moment juicy and soft, the next attacking with as much controlled aggression as you can withstand... and all the times the plums and dates and walnuts continue on their ultra-rich fruitcake way; f23.5 you'd expect – demand – a long finish after all that. And you get it thanks to a sublime mix of all those delicate fruits. Alas, a minor build up of sulphur has accumulated, knocking off half a point or so. But if you keep on drinking this stuff, you don't get to the point of noticing...; b24.5 like old Tommy Dewar himself, a unique and classy, classy act. To be honest, when I saw "finished in sherry" on the label I had got to the point this year where I was terrified of opening the bottle. But this shows how it should be done: I'd like to shake the blender by the hand! This was exactly the whisky the scotch industry needed at this precise moment, well that vague residue on the finish apart...(one that probably robbed it of World Whisky of the Year). Even so, unforgettable and truly magnificent. And as experiments go, it knocks the relatively unimportant goings on at Cern into a cocked hat... 58.9%. sc. 30 bottles.

Dewar's Special Reserve 12 Years Old (84) n20 t23 f19 b22. Some s... you know what... has crept onboard here and duffed up the nose and finish. A shame because elements of the delivery and background balance shows some serious blending went on here. 40%

Dewar's 18 Years Old (93) n23 t24 f22.5 b23.5 Here is a classic case of where great blends are not all about the malt. The grain plays in many ways the most significant role here, as it is the perfect backdrop to see the complexity of the malt at its clearest. Simply magnificent blending with the use of flawless whisky. 43%. John Dewar & Sons.

Dewar's 18 Year Old Founders Reserve (86.5) n22.5 t22 f20.5 b21.5. A big, blustering dram which doesn't stint on the fruit. A lovely, thin seam of golden syrup runs through the piece, but the dull, aching finale is somewhat out of character. 40%. John Dewar & Sons.

Dewar's Signature (93) n24 t23.5 f22 b23.5. A slight departure in style, with the fruit becoming just a little sharper and juicier. Top range blending and if the odd butt could be weeded out, this'd be an award winner for sure. 43%

Dewar's White Label (78.5) n19 t21.5 f19 b19. When on song, one of my preferred daily blends. But not when like this, with its accentuated bitter-sweet polarisation. 40%

Dhoon Glen (85.5) n21 t22 f21 b21.5 Full of big flavours, broad grainy strokes and copious amounts of dark sugar including toffee. 40%. Lombard Brands Ltd.

Dimple 12 Years Old (86.5) n22 t22 f21.5 b21. Lots of sultana; the spice adds aggression. 40%.

Dimple 15 Years Old (87.5) n20 t21 f24 b22.5. Only on the late middle and finish does this particular flower unfurl and to magnificently complex effect. The texture of the grains in particular delight while the strands of barley entwine. A type of treat for the more technically minded of the serious blend drinkers among you. 40%. Diageo.

Drummer (81) n20 t21 f20 b20. Big toffee. Rolos...? 40%. Inver House Distillers.

Drummer Aged 5 Years (83) n19 t22.5 f20.5 b21. The nose may beat a retreat but it certainly gets on a roll when those fabulous sharp notes hit the palate. However, it deserves some stick as the boring fudge finishes in a cymbal of too much toffee. 40%. Inver House.

Duncan Taylor Auld Blended Aged 35 Years dist pre 70 (93) n23 t24 f22 b24 An infinitely better dram than previous bottlings, due mainly to the fact that the dangers of old oak appear to have been compensated for. 46%. 131 bottles.

Duncan Taylor Collection Black Bull 12 Year Old (88.5) n22.5 t22.5 f21.5 b22 Black Bulls enjoy a reputation for being dangerous. So does this: once you pour yourself a glass, it is difficult not to have another...and another... 50%. Duncan Taylor & Co Ltd.

Duncan Taylor Collection Black Bull Deluxe Blend Aged 30 Years (93) n24 t24 f22 b23. This pedigree Black Bull doesn't pull its horns in... 50%. Duncan Taylor.

Duncan Taylor Collection Rarest of the Rare Deluxe Blend 33 Years Old (94) n24 t24 f22 b23. Outstanding and astounding blended whisky. An absolute must for blend lovers... especially those with a bourbony bent. 43.4%

Duncan Taylor Collection Black Bull 40 Year Old batch 1 (86.5) n23 t21 f21.5 b21. Almost certainly whisky which had dipped below 40%abv in the cask has been included in this blend. That would account for the occasional spasm of ultra intense natural caramels, a kind of tell-tale fingerprint indicating this is likely to have been done. The nose is exotic fruit; the delivery is a battle to keep the oak at bay. One which is happily won. 40.2%

Duncan Taylor Collection Black Bull 40 Years Old batch 2 (94) n23 t24 f23 b24. Just sit back and marvel at something so old...yet so young at heart. 41.9%. Duncan Taylor & Co.

Duncan Taylor Collection Black Bull Special Reserve batch 1 (86) n21 t22.5 f21 b21.5. Juicy in just the right areas. Some charming spice and vanilla, too. 46.6%

Duncan Taylor Black Bull Special Reserve batch 2 (87.5) n23 t23.5 f19 b22. Has seriously upped the fruit and spice from the original version to make for a compelling blend. 50%

Duncan Taylor Smokin' (85) n21 t22 f21 b21. On one hand phenolic, on the other surprisingly lightweight. Attractively sweet and friendly, though. 40%. Duncan Taylor.

The Famous Grouse (89) n22 t23 f21.5 b22.5 It almost seems that Grouse is, by degrees, moving from its traditional position of a light blend to something much closer to Grant's as a middle-weighted dram. Again the colouring has been raised a fraction and now the body and depth have been adjusted to follow suit. Have to say that this is one very complex whisky these days: I had spotted slight changes when drinking it socially, but this was the first time I had a chance to sit down and professionally analyse what was happening in the glass. A fascinating and tasty bird, indeed. 40%. Edrington Group.

The Famous Grouse Aged 16 Years Special 2013 Edition (84) n22 t22 f19 b21. A completely different type of Grouse which on one hand offers a pretty comprehensive guide of the sugar shelves, yet somehow manages, for all its apparent esters, to bitter out violently at the finish. Intriguing, to put it mildly. 40%. Edrington Group.

The Famous Grouse Gold Reserve (90) n23.5 t23 f21.5 b22 Great to know the value of the Gold Reserve is going up...as should the strength of this blend. The old-fashioned 40% just ain't enough carats. 40%. Edrington Group.

The Famous Jubilee (83.5) n21.5 t22.5 f18.5 b21. A heavyweight, stodgy, toffee-laden kind of blend a long way from the Grouse tradition. With its ham-fisted date and walnut middle I would have sworn this was the work of another blender entirely. There are redeeming rich honey tones that are a joy. But the dull, pulsing sulphur on the finish has almost an air of inevitability. I promise you this: go back 60 years, and there would have been no blend created with this signature...not only did the style not exist, but it would have been impossible to accomplish. 40%. Edrington.

The Formidable Jock of Bennachie (82) n19 t22 f21 b20. "Scotland's best kept secret" claims the label. Hardly. But the silky delivery on the palate is worth investigating. Impressive roastiness to the malt and oak, but the caramel needs thinning. 40%. Bennachie Scotch Whisky.

Fort Glen The Blender's Reserve Aged 12 Years (88.5) n21.5 t23 f21.5 b22.5 An entirely enjoyable blend which is clean and boasting decent complexity and weight. 40%

Fort Glen The Distiller's Reserve (78) n18 t22 f19 b19. Juicy, salivating delivery as it storms the ramparts. Draws down the portcullis elsewhere. 40%. The Fort Glen Whisky Company.

Fraser MacDonald (85) n21 t21.5 f21 b21.5. Some fudge towards the middle and end but the journey there is an enjoyable one. 40%. Loch Lomond Distillers.

Gairloch (79) n19 t20 f20 b20. For those who like their butterscotch at 40% abv. 40%

Glen Brynth (70.5) n18 t19 f16 b17.5. Bitter and awkward. 43%

Glenbrynth 8 Year Old (88) n21.5 t22 f22.5 b22. An impressive blend which improves second by second on the palate. 40%. OTI Africa.

Glenbrynth Pearl 30 Year Old Limited Edition (90.5) n22.5 t23.5 f21.5 b23 Attractive, beautifully weighted, no off notes...though perhaps quietened by toffee. Still a treat of a blend. 43%. OTI Africa.

Glen Gray (84.5) n20 t22.5 f21 b21. A knife and fork blend you can stand your spoon in. Plain going for most of the way, but the area between delivery and middle enjoys several waves of rich chocolate honeycomb...and some of the cocoa resurfaces at the finale. 43%

Glen Lyon (85) n19 t22.5 f22 b21.5. Works a lot better than the nose suggests: seriously chewy with a rabid spice attack and lots of juices. For those who have just retired as dynamite testers. Unpretentious fun. 43%. Diageo.

Glen Orrin Aged 5 Years (77) n19 t21 f18 b19. Glen Orrible more like. A step up from the no age statement version, thanks mainly to a very delicate underlying smokiness. But the core malt is still of that ilk that will drive people to bourbon. 40%. Aldi.

Glen Orin 30 Years old Blend (95) n24 the grains have made a first-class job of drawing out the most lively vanillas and when fully warmed in the hand the delightfully sharp marmalade is at its zenith. The malt is no less graceful and dovetails majestically and at times almost covertly, injecting a delicate maple syrup sweetness to soften the richer elements of the grassy barley; t24 crisp, firm grain ensures a cracking delivery and a very old-fashioned style. Despite its early ramrod rigidity, it softens slowly – almost tantalizingly - with first mouth-watering barley then a volley of the vanillas promised on the nose. The sugars are delicate, still offering a degree of maple but more inclined now towards a thin layer of acacia honey; f23 the same grainy crispness which makes the delivery so strident ensures a less dramatic, more peaceful finale. Here, the influence of the oak is underlined with a drier, chalkier feel to the persistent vanillas. A light barley frame ensures that drier oak, patiently sculpted over three decades, is seen to its fullest advantage; b24 a clean, charming blend from the old school and of a style too rarely seen today, alas. The accent, as it should be, is on the grain, and its very brittleness accentuates just how delicate this whisky is. A perfect pre-prandial dram to be taken straight and at body temperature, without water or ice, so its astonishing complexity can be fully explored. Or very late at night when you might find time for all its mysteries to unravel. Top notch Scotch where subtlety is the watchword. Delicacy and understatement is the key; yet with enough life and juiciness to entertain even the most fatigued taste buds. Truly outstanding. 40%. Aldi

⁂ **Glory Leading Blended Scotch Whisky 30 Years Old** American oak casks (93) n22.5 apple; some grain bite shows that all is not fully aligned; t23 more relaxed on delivery, though concentrates on treacle tart (with custard) and spice; f23.5 now makes much more sense as a little smoke and spice adds to the mix yet allows the malt a good platform and the grains a much clearer voice; b24 a big, clever, satisfying blend which just gets better and better... though not too sure about the Crystal Palace style eagle on the label. Even so, love it! 43%

Golden Piper (86.5) n22 t21 f22 b21.5. A firm, clean blend with a steady flush through of diverse sugars. The grain does all the steering and therefore complexity is limited. But the overall freshness is a delight. 43%. Whisky Shack.

Grand Sail (87) n21 t22 f22 b22 A sweet, attractive blend with enough bite to really matter. 40%

Grand Sail Aged 10 Years (79) n20 t22 f18 b19. Pleasant and at times fascinating but with a tang that perhaps the next vatting will benefit from losing. 40%. China market.

Grand Sail Rare Reserve Aged 18 Years (94) n23 t24 f23 b24. A truly beautiful whisky which cuts effortlessly and elegantly through the taste buds. 40% Angus Dundee. China market.

Glenross Blended (83) n20 t22 f20 b21. Decent, easy-drinking whisky with a much sharper delivery than the nose suggests. 40%. Speyside Distillers.

Glen Simon (77) n20 t19 f19 b19. Simple. Lots of caramel. 40%. Quality Spirits International.

The Gordon Highlanders (86) n21 t22 f21 b22. Lush and juicy, there is a distinctive Speysidey feel to this one with the grains doing their best to accentuate the developing spice. Plenty of feel good factor here. 40%. William Grant & Sons.

Grand Macnish (79) n19 t21 f19 b20. Welcome back to an old friend...but the years have caught up with it. Still on the feral side, but has exchanged its robust good looks for an unwashed and unkempt appearance on the palate. Will do a great job to bring some life back to you, though. 43%. MacDuff International Ltd.

Grand Macnish 12 Years Old (86) n21 t22 f21.5 b21.5. A grander Grand Macnich than of old with the wonderful feather pillow delivery maintained and a greater harmonisation of the malt, especially those which contain a honey-copper sheen. 40%. MacDuff.

Grant's Aged 12 Years bott 30/09/10 (89.5) n23 t23 f21.5 b22 Can't argue too much with the tasting notes on the label (although I contend that "full, rich and rounded" has more to do with its body than taste, but that is by the by). Beautiful whisky, as can be reasonably expected from a Grant's blend. If only the sharpness could last the distance. 40%.

Grant's Cask Edition No.1 Ale Cask Finish Edinburgh ale casks (88.5) n22 t23 f21.5 b22. always loved this concept: a whisky and chaser in one bottle. This was has plenty of cheer in the complex opening, but gets maudlin towards the end. 40%. William Grant & Sons.

Great MacCauley (81) n20 t20.5 f20 b20.5. Reminds me of another whisky I tasted earlier: Castle Rock, I think. Identical profile with toffee & spice adding to the juicy & youthful fun. 40%.

Green Plaid 12 Years Old (89) n22 t23 f22 b22 Beautifully constructed; juicy. 40%.

Guneagal Aged 12 Years (85.5) n21 t22.5 f20.5 b21.5. The salty, sweaty armpit nose gives way to an even saltier delivery, helped along by sweet glycerine and a boiled candy fruity sweetness. The finish is a little roughhouse by comparison. 40%. William Grant & Sons.

Haddington House (85.5) n21 t21.5 f22 b21. Mouth-watering and delicate. 40%

Haig Gold Label (88) n21 t23 f22 b22 What had before been pretty standard stuff has upped the complexity by an impressive distance. 40%. Diageo.

Hankey Bannister (84.5) n20.5 t22 f21 b21. Lots of early life and even a malt kick early on. Toffee later. 40%. Inverhouse Distillers.

Hankey Bannister 12 Years Old (86.5) n22 t21.5 f21 b22. A much improved blend with a nose and early delivery which makes full play of the blending company's Speyside malts. Plenty of toffee on the finish. 40%. Inverhouse Distillers.

Hankey Bannister Regency 12 Year Old (84.5) n22.5 t22 f19 b21 Plenty of honey and some fine, silky structuring. Just a tad too bitter and furry on the finish, though. 40%.

Hankey Bannister 21 Years Old (95) n23.5 a fruity ensemble, clean, vibrant and loath to show its age t24 as juicy as the nose suggests, except for the odd rumble of distant smoke; a firm, barley-sugar hardness as the grains keep control; f23.5 the arrival of the oak adds further weight and for the first time begins to behave like a 21-y-o; long, now with decent spice and with some crusty dryness at the very death; b24 with top dressing like this and some obviously complex secondary malts, too, how can it fail? 43%.

Hankey Bannister 25 Years Old (91) n22.5 t24 f21.5 b23 Follows on in style and quality to 21-year-old. Gorgeous. 40%

Hankey Bannister 40 Years Old (89.5) n23.5 t24 f19.5 b22.5 Not sure where the finish came from. But the fruit symphony leading up to it is a thing of beauty. 43.3%.

Hankey Bannister 40 Years Old (89) n22 t23 f22 b22. This blend has been put together to mark the 250th anniversary of the forging of the business relations between Messrs. Hankey and Bannister. And although the oak creaks like a ship of its day, there is enough verve and viscosity to ensure a rather delicious toast to the gentlemen. Love it! 44%. Inverhouse.

Hankey Bannister 40 Year Old (94) n23.5 t23.5 f23 b24. Pure quality. The attention to detail is sublime. 44.3%. Inverhouse Distillers.

Hankey Bannister Heritage (84.5) n21 t22 f20.5 b21. So softly spoken sometimes you struggle to hear it. Makes a juicy, malty chuntering mid-way through, though. 46%.

⠐⠂ **Hankey Bannister Heritage Blend** (92) n23 despite the evidence of sherry the spiced chocolate fudge keeps you spellbound; t24 at moments like this, one's taste buds are purely in love. They are being caressed, serenaded and kisses by the most glorious of old grains, encrusted with a Speyside-syle maltiness which makes you purr with pleasure; f22 the weakness on the nose returns, though sparingly. Outstanding late Malteser candy style confirms a very decent malt depth; b23 just so soft and sensual... 46%. Inverhouse Distillers.

⠐⠂ **Harveys Lewes Blend Eight Year Old** (89.5) n23 a tightness to the grape cannot entirely outdo the beauty of the soft fruit and delicate smoke combining; t23.5 excellent grain choice ensures a velvety delivery on the palate, helped along by dates and nuts and a marvellous succession of dark sugar notes, Demerara leading the way. The malt content is evident beyond the fruit and delivers a Brazilian-style biscuit sweetness; sublimely chewy; f20.5 only a single dodgy (sulphured) sherry butt, most probably – but that's all it takes! - within the malt content of the blend plus some enthusiastic caramelling detracts from a superb experience...; **b22.5** when a blend is this good you can forgive them the missing apostrophe... A superb whisky, despite its unfortunate hiccup, from a gem of a British brewery. 40%.

Hedges & Butler Royal (92) n22.5 t23.5 f23 b23 Massively improved to become a juicy and charming blend of the very highest order. 40%

High Commissioner (88.5) n22.5 t22.5 f20.5 b22.5 Now I admit I had a hand in cleaning this brand up a couple of years back, giving it a good polish and much needed balance complexity. But I don't remember leaving it in quite this good a shape. Just a bitter semi-off note on the finish, otherwise this guy would have been in the 90s. What a great fun, three-course dram this is... 40%. Loch Lomond Distillers.

Highland Baron (85.5) n21 t22 f21 b21.5. A very clean, sweet and competent young blend showing admirable weight and depth. 40%. Loch Lomond Distillers.

Highland Bird (77) n19 t19 f19 b20. I've has a few of these over the years, I admit. But I can't remember one quite as rough and ready as this... 40%. Quality Spirits International.

Highland Black 8 Years Old Special Reserve (85.5) n22 t22.5 f20 b21. A lovely blend which has significantly improved since my last encounter with it. A touch too much grain on the finish for greatness, perhaps. But the nose and delivery both prosper from a honey-roast almond sweetness. 40%. Aldi.

Highland Dream 12 Years Old bott Jan 05 **(94.5)** n23.5 t24 f23 b24. Now that is what I call a blend! How comes it has taken me two years to find it? A wet dream, if ever there was one... 43%. J & G Grant. 9000 bottles.

Highland Dream 18 Years Old bott May 07 **(88.5)** n22.5 t22.5 f21.5 b22. Perhaps doesn't get the marks on balance that a whisky of this quality might expect. This is due to the slight over egging of the sherry which, while offering a beautiful delivery, masks the complexities one might expect. Lovely whisky, and make no mistake. But, technically, doesn't match the 12-year-old for balance and brilliance. 43%. J & G Grant. 3000 bottles.

Highland Earl (77) n19 t20 f19 b19. Might have marked it higher had it called itself a grain: the malt is silent. 40%. Aldi.

Highland Gathering Blended Scotch Whisky (78) n19 t20 f19 b20. Attractive, juicy stuff, though caramel wins in the end. 40%. Lombards Brands.

Highland Glendon (87.5) n21.5 t22.5 f21.5 b22 An honest, simple but effectively attractive blend. 43%. Quality Spirits International.

Highland Harvest Organic Scotch Whisky (76) n18 t21 f19 b18. A very interesting blend. Great try, but a little bit of a lost opportunity here as I don't think the balance is quite right. But at least I now know what organic caramel tastes like... 40%

Highland Mist (88.5) n20.5 t23 f22.5 b22.5 Fabulously fun whisky bursting from the bottle with character and mischief. Had to admit, broke all my own rules and just had to have a glass of this after doing the notes... 40%. Loch Lomond Distillers.

Highland Piper (79) n20 t20 f19 b20. Good quaffing blend – if sweet - of sticky toffee and dates. Some gin on the nose – and finish. 40%

Highland Pride (86) n21 t22 f21.5 b21.5. A beefy, weighty thick dram with plenty to chew on. The developing sweetness is a joy. 40%. Whyte & Mackay Distillers Ltd.

Highland Queen Blended Scotch Whisky (86.5) n22 t21 f21.5 b22. Lots of grains at play here. But what grains?! Clean and crisp with a superb bite which balances the softening mouth feel attractively. Old fashioned and delicious. 40%

Highland Queen Aged 8 Years Blended Scotch Whisky (90) n22.5 t23.5 f21.5 b22.5. Lots of entertainment value from a high quality whisky. The blender has done a great job in the lab. 43%

Highland Queen Aged 12 Years Blended Scotch Whisky (87) n22 t22 f21 b22. A polite, slightly more sophisticated version of the 8-year-old...but without the passion and drama! 40%

Highland Reserve (82) n20 t21 f20 b21. You'll probably find this just off the Highland Way and incorporating Highland Bird and Monarch of the Glen. Floral and muddy. 40%

Highland Reserve Aged 12 Years (87) n21 t22 f22 b22 Anyone who has tasted Monarch of the Glen 12 will appreciate this. Maybe a bit more fizz here, though, despite the big caramel. 43%. Quality Spirits International.

Highland Warrior (77.8) n19 t19 f19.5 b20. Just like his Scottish Chief, he's on the attack armed with some Dufftown, methinks... 40%. Quality Spirits International.

Highland Way (84) n19 t20.5 f22.5 b22. This lovely little number takes the High Road with some beautiful light scenery along the way. The finish takes a charming Speyside path. 40%

Inverarity Limited Edition cask no. 698, dist 1997, bott 2009 **(84.5) n**20.5 **t**22 **f**21 **b**21. A heady, heavy-duty blend where honeycomb rules on the palate and thick dates offer a more intense sweetness. But don't go looking for subtlety or guile: those whose palates have been educated at the Whyte and Mackay school of delicate sophistication will have a ball. 40%

Islay Mist 8 Years Old (84) n20 **t**22 **f**21 **b**21. Turned into one heavy dusty dram since last tasting a couple of years back. This appears to absorb everything it touches leaving one chewy, smoky hombre. Just a little tangy at the end. 40%. MacDuff International Ltd.

Islay Mist 12 Years Old (90) n22 **t**23 **f**22 **b**23 Adore it: classic bad cop - good cop stuff with an apparent high malt content. 40%

Islay Mist 17 Years Old (92.5) n22.5 **t**23.5 **f**23 **b**23.5 Always a cracking blend, this has improved of late into a genuine must have. 40%. MacDuff International Ltd.

Islay Mist Delux (85) n21.5 **t**22 **f**21.5 **b**20. Remains a highly unusual blend with the youthful peat now more brilliant than before, though the sugar levels appear to have risen markedly. 40%

Isle of Skye 8 Years Old (94) n23 **t**24 **f**23.5 **b**23.5. Where once peat ruled and with its grain ally formed a smoky iron fist, now honey and subtlety reigns. A change of character and pace which may disappoint gung-ho peat freaks but will intrigue and delight those looking for a more sophisticated dram. 40%. Ian Macleod.

Isle of Skye 21 years Old (91) n21 **t**23.5 **f**23 **b**23.5 What an absolute charmer! The malt content appears pretty high, but the overall balance is wonderful. 40%. Ian Macleod.

Isle of Skye 50 Years Old (82.5) n21.5 **t**21 **f**20 **b**20. Drier incarnation than the 50% version. But still the age has yet to be balanced out, towards the end in particular. Early on some distinguished moments involving something vaguely smoked and a sweetened spice. 41.6%

The Jacobite (78.5) n18 **t**18.5 **f**22 **b**20. Neither the nose or delivery are of the cleanest style. But comes into its own towards the finish when the thick soup of a whisky thins to allow an attractive degree of complexity. Not for those with catholic tastes. 40%. Booker.

Jackson McCloud Premium Blended Scotch Whisky (81) n20 **t**21 **f**20 **b**20. Absolutely standard fare, full of grainy bite and caramel. 40%. Galleon Liqueurs.

Jackson McCloud Rare Batch Blended Scotch Whisky (85.5) n20 **t**22.5 **f**22 **b**21. Pleasant, but with little or no effort to overcome the dominating grain. As it happens, it turns out to be pretty decent silky grain with some attractive fruit notes. 40%. Galleon Liqueurs.

James Alexander (85.5) n21 **t**21.5 **f**21.5 **b**21.5. Some lovely spices link the grassier Speysiders to the earthier elements. 40%. Quality Spirits International.

James King (76.5) n20 **t**18 **f**20 **b**18.5. Young whiskies of a certain rank take their time to find their feet. The finish, though, does generate some pleasant complexity. 43%

James King Aged 5 Years (85) n21 **t**21.5 **f**21 **b**21.5. Very attractive, old fashioned and well weighted with a pleasing degree of fat and chewy sweetness and chocolate fudge. Refreshingly good quality distillate and oak have been used in this: I'd drink it any day. 40%

James King 8 Years Old (78.5) n18.5 **t**21.5 **f**19 **b**19.5. Charming spices grip at the delivery and fine malt-grain interplay through the middle, even showing a touch of vanilla. But such a delicate blend can't fully survive the caramel. 43%. Quality Spirits International.

James King 12 Years Old (81) n19 **t**23 **f**19 **b**20. Caramel dulls the nose and finish. But for some time a quite beautiful blend soars about the taste buds offering exemplary complexity and weight. 40%. Quality Spirits International.

James King 15 Years Old (89) n22 **t**23 **f**21.5 **b**22.5. Now offers extra spice and zip. 43%

James King 21 Years Old (87.5) n20.5 **t**23.5 **f**22 **b**22. Attractive blend, but one that could do with the strength upped to 46% and the caramel reduced if not entirely got rid of. One of those potentially excellent yet underperforming guys I'd love to be let loose on! 43%

James Martin 20 Years Old (93) n21 **t**23.5 **f**24.5 **b**24. I had always regarded this as something of an untamed beast. No longer: still something of a beast, but a beautiful one that is among the most complex found on today's market. 43%. Glenmorangie.

James Martin 30 Years Old (86) n21.5 **t**22 **f**21 **b**21.5. Enjoyable for all its exotic fruitiness. But with just too many creaking joints to take it to the same level as the sublime 20-y-o. Even so, a blend worth treating with a touch of respect and allowing time for it to tell some pretty ancient tales... 43%. Glenmorangie.

J&B Jet (79.5) n19 **t**20 **f**20.5 **b**20. Never quite gets off the ground due to carrying too heavy a load. Unrecognisable to its pomp in the old J&B days: this one is far too weighty and never properly finds either balance or thrust. 40%. Diageo.

J&B Reserve Aged 15 Years (78) n23 **t**19 **f**18 **b**18. What a crying shame. The sophisticated and demure nose is just so wonderfully seductive but what follows is an open-eyed, passionless embrace. Coarsely grain-dominant and unbalanced, this is frustrating beyond words and not worthy to be mentioned in the same breath as the old, original J&B 15 which, by vivid contrast, was a malty, salivating fruit-fest and minor classic. 40%. Diageo.

J&B Rare (88.5) n21.5 **t**22.5 **f**22 **b**22.5 I have been drinking a lot of J&B from a previous time of late, due to the death of their former blender Jim Milne. I think he would have been pretty taken aback by the youthful zip offered here: whether it is down to a decrease in age or the use of slightly more tired casks – or both – is hard to say. 40%. *Diageo.*

Jim McEwan's Blended Whisky (86.5) n20 t22 f22.5 b22. Juicy and eye-watering with clever late spices. 46%. *Bruichladdich.*

John Barr (85.5) n20 t22 f21.5 b22. I assume from the big juicy dates to be found that Fettercairn is at work. Outwardly a big bruiser; given time to state its case and it's a bit of a gentle giant. 40%. *Whyte & Mackay Distillers Ltd.*

Johnnie Walker Black Label 12 Years Old (95.5) n23.5 pretty sharp grain: hard and buffeting the nose; a buffer of yielding smoke, apple pie and delicate spice cushions the encounter; **t24.5** if there is a silkier delivery on the market today, I have not seen it: this is sublime stuff with the grains singing the sweetest hymns as they go down, taking with them a near perfection of weighty smoke lightened by brilliantly balanced barley which leans towards both soft apple and crème broulee; **f23.5** those reassuringly rigid grains re-emerge and with them the most juicy Speysidey malts imaginable; the lovely sheen to the finish underlines the good age of the whiskies used; **b24** here it is: one of the world's most masterful whiskies back in all its complex glory. A bottle like this is like being visited by an old lover. It just warms the heart and excites. 40%. *Diageo.*

Johnnie Walker Blue Label (88) n21 t24 f21 b22 What a frustrating blend! Just so close to brilliance but the nose and finish are slightly out of kilter. Worth the experience of the mouth arrival alone. 43%. *Diageo.*

Johnnie Walker Blue Label The Casks Edition (97) n24.5 now that is a nose: absolutely brimming with intent and character, this obviously has no designs to just sit there and look pretty. A blend where the malts have a far bigger say than the grains, especially the honeydew melon and red berries. The phenols are surprisingly laconic, but that gives more scope for the duskier notes from the oak to come through, especially the more bourbon-style liquorice and hickory. There is also something there which would be appreciated by lovers of high ester Jamaican pot still rum; **t24.5** the great blends have, traditionally, offered a little nip and bite...and the delivery here shows as many teeth as it does soothing fingers of honey. Wonderful walnut oil and marzipan offer the nuts to go with the delicate fruit and chocolate; the mid range carries on with this high ester, slightly oily sweetness which coats the mouth with kumquats and liquorice; the spices are shallow but offer excellent variance to the vanilla; **f23.5** long, languid, delicately oiled and bowing out with a stunning display of spiced heather honey, mocha, dates, walnuts and the lightest of smoky fades...; **b24.5** this is a triumph of scotch whisky blending. With not as much as a hint of a single off note to be traced from the tip of the nose to tail, this shameless exhibition of complexity and brilliance is the star turn in the Diageo portfolio right now. Indeed, it is the type of blend that every person who genuinely adores whisky must experience for the good of their soul....if only once in their life. 55.8%.

Johnnie Walker Double Black (94.5) n23 t23.5 f24 b24. Double tops! Rolling along the taste buds like distant thunder, this is a welcome and impressive addition to the Johnnie Walker stable. Perhaps not as complete and rounded as the original Johnnie Walker Black... but, then, what is? 40%.

Johnnie Walker Explorers' Club Collection The Gold Route (89) n23.5 t24 f19.5 b22. Much of this blend is truly the stuff of golden dreams. Like its Explorer's Club stable mate, some attention has to be paid to the disappointing finish. Worth sending out an expedition, though, just for the beautiful nose and delivery... 40%. *Diageo.*

⁘ **Johnnie Walker Explorer's Club Collection 'The Royal Route' (93) n24.5** that's just how a blended whisky's nose should be: understated, clever, complex without being showy, multi-faceted and ambiguous enough to have to constantly changing your mind as to whether it is the lightly smoked mocha or the more ethereal citrus and jasmine which is leading the way. I'll let you decide...; **t24** soft to the point of surrender, the grains allow the malts to melt into them in the sexiest way imaginable; the accomodating smoke drifts and swirls, light Demerara sharpens, a thin layer of ulmo honey fattens and enriches; **f21.5** just the odd injudicious use of cask results in an unwelcome late bitterness which has robbed this of a gong: otherwise this would have been challenging for a spot in the world's top three. So, eye-wateringly bitter marmalade and furry...such a shame....; **b23** a fabulous journey, travelling first Class most of the way. But to have discovered more, could have been bottled at 46% for a much more panoramic view of the great whiskies on show. 40%. *Diageo*

Johnnie Walker Explorers' Club Collection The Spice Road (84.5) n22 t23.5 f18 b21. Sublime delivery of exceptionally intense juiciness: in fact, probably the juiciest blend released this year. But the bitter, fuzzy finish reveals certain casks haven't helped. 40%.

Johnnie Walker Gold Label Reserve (91.5) n23 t24 f22 b23. Moments of true star quality here, but the finish could do with a polish. 40%. *Diageo.*

Johnnie Walker King George V db (88) n23 t22 f21 b22 One assumes that King George V is no relation to George IV. This has genuine style and breeding, if a tad too much caramel. *43%*

Johnnie Walker Platinum Label Aged 18 Years (88) n22 t23 f21 b22. This blend might sound like some kind of Airmiles card. Which wouldn't be too inappropriate, though this is more Business than First... *40%. Diageo.*

Johnnie Walker Red Label (87.5) n22 t22 f21.5 b22. The ongoing move through the scales quality-wise appears to suggest we have a work still in progress here. This sample has skimped on the smoke, though not quality. Yet a few months back when I was in the BA Business Lounge at Heathrow's new Terminal Five, I nearly keeled from almost being overcome by peat in the earthiest JW Red I had tasted in decades. I found another bottle and I'm still not sure which represents the real Striding Man. *40%. Diageo.*

Johnnie Walker X.R Aged 21 Years (94) n23.5 t24 f23 b23.5. How weird: I nosed this blind before seeing what the brand was. My first thought was: "mmm, same structure of Crown Royal XR. Canadian??? No, there's smoke!" Then looked at what was before me and spotted it was its sister whisky from the Johnnie Walker stable. A coincidence? I don't think so... *40%. Diageo.*

Kenmore Special Reserve Aged 5 Years bott code L07285 (75) n18 t20 f19 b18. Recovers to a degree from the poor nose. A must-have for those who prefer their Scotch big-flavoured and gawky. *40%*

⋅⋛⋅ **Kingsbury Gold Mhain Baraille 1980 32 Year Old** diss 1980 (92) n23 soft, though displaying that old syrupy coconut that used to be so prevalent in British candy 50 years ago... t23.5 a little honey and honeycomb underline the years but still there is a riveting freshness to the barley which is grassy and salivating; f22.5 aged as drier vanilla notes are introduced. The sugars, though, cannot be extinguished; b23 a distinguished blend with just a little grey around the temples... A rathere brilliant first bending attempt by Kingsbury after all these years. *473%. nc ncf. Cask Strength. 424 bottles.*

King Robert II (77) n19 t19 f20 b19. A bustier, more bruising batch than the last 40 per cent version. Handles the OTT caramel much better. Agreeably weighty slugging whisky. *43%.*

Kings Blended 3 Years Old (83) n21 t21.5 f20 b20.5. A young, chunky blend that you can chew forever. *40%. Speyside Distillers.*

King's Crest Scotch Whisky 25 Years Old (83) n22 t22 f19 b20. A silky middle weight. The toffee-flat finish needs some attention because the softly estered nose and delivery is a honey-rich treat and deserves better. *40%. Speyside Distillers.*

Label 5 Aged 18 Years (84.5) n20.5 t22 f21 b21. A big mouthful and mouth-feel. Has changed course since I last had this one. Almost a feel of rum to this with its estery sheen. Sweet, simple, easy dramming. *40%. La Martiniquaise, France.*

Label 5 Classic Black (75) n18 t20 f18 b19. The off-key nose needs some serious re-working. Drop the caramel, though, and you would have a lot more character. Needs some buffing. *40%. The First Blending for La Martiniquaise, France.*

Label 5 Classic Black bott code L3060 (84.5) n20.5 t22 f21 b21. A better whisky than when last tasted with more even use of the date and walnut theme. Caramel still substantial, but complexity levels are higher. *40%. La Martiniquaise, France.*

Label 5 Classic Black bott code L3084 (83.5) n20 t21.5 f21 b21. Like L3060. Except the nose is even harsher and here the grain have a much more jarring effect. *40%.*

Label 5 Classic Black bott code L3144 (85) n20.5 t22 f21 b21.5. Stays in the same areas as the two previous bottlings, but slightly better use of spices. Still needs a nose job, though... *40%. Glen Turner.*

Label 5 Reserve No. 55 sherry cask finish, bott code B-3695 (89) n22 t23 f21.5 b22.5. The last one of these I had a couple of years back was a sulphur-damaged disaster. This is anything but. A real bold treat. *43%. La Martiniquaise, France.*

Label 5 Reserve No. 55 sherry cask finish, bott code F-4482 (87) n20.5 t22.5 f22 b22. Lacking the suave sweetness of the B-3695 bottling, but excellent spice. *43%.*

Label 5 Reserve No. 55 Single Cask sherry cask finish, bott code no. E-1067 (75) n19 t20 f18 b18. The cordite on the nose suggests fireworks. But somehow we end up with a damp squib. *43%. La Martiniquaise, France.*

Label 5 Aged 12 Years bott code L307157A (82) n21 t20 f21 b20. Heavy duty date and walnut. Loads of caramel, too. For those looking for a weighty and chewy, rather complex dram. *40%. Glen Turner.*

Lang's Supreme Aged 5 Years (93.5) n23.5 t23.5 f23 b23.5. Every time I taste this the shape and structure has altered slightly. Here there is a fraction more smoke, installing a deeper confidence all round. This is blended whisky as it should be: Supreme in its ability to create shape and harmony. *40%. Ian Macleod Distillers Ltd.*

The Last Drop (96.5) n24 t25 f23.5 b24. How do you mark a whisky like this? It is scotch. Yet every molecule of flavour and aroma is pure bourbon. I think I'll have to mark for quality, principally, which simply flies off the graph. I'll dock it a point for not being Scotch-like but I feel a pang of guilt for doing so. This, by the way, is a blend that was discovered by accident. It had been put away many years ago for marrying – and then forgotten about in a warehouse. The chances of finding another whisky quite of this ilk are remote, though I'm sure the hunters are now out. It is a one off and anyone who misses this one will kick themselves forever. Astonishing. A freak whisky at its very peak. *52%. The Last Drop Distillers Ltd.*

⠿ **The Last Drop 1965** American Standard Barrel (96.5) n24 ridiculously pliable nose: the grain used is clearly made from corn which, with the great age, means a distinct Canadian/bourbon trait impresses; the spices are playful and occasionally an apologetic puff of smoke reminds you this is a blend, not a grain...; t24.5 the corn oils pave the way for a fabulous delivery – not entirely unlike a breakfast cereal with a dollop of honey to sweeten things up. The oak offers a precision to the weight and spice; f23.5 again, a hint of smoke takes you away from the North American feel to this. The honey remains perfectly measures to ensure the encroaching oaky vanilla never dominates; b24.5 almost impossible to imagine a blended whisky to be better balanced than this. If there is a cleverer use of honey or less intrusive oak in any blended whisky bottled in the last year, I have yet to taste it. An award winner if ever I tasted one. Magnificent doesn't quite cover it... *48.6%. Morrison Bowmore. The Last Drop Distillers Ltd.*

The Last Drop 50 Years Old (96.5) n25 where once there was bourbon only, now we have a cross fertilisation of aromas. Certainly, once you allow it to breathe, the grape engulfs most else. It is as if the whisky has undergone a fruity polish and shine. On first pouring, the oak has the ability to cause splinters; allow to settle for a while and we are talking a much softer, less senile Drop; t24.5 perhaps what is so astounding about this, is the way that the balance does not, even for a second, waiver under the occasional oaky onslaught: as it bites, from somewhere a grapey honeycomb flies in to the rescue offering just-so compensatory sugars which perfectly match the most delicate spices imaginable...; f22.5 now we edge towards a drier finale than before. The original was remarkable for not having a degree of bitterness, though it had every right to be there. Now, alas, there is. The bitterness is slightly furry and dusty, but to make amends we are treated to one very old Melton Hunt cake, indeed; b24.5 I tend to stick to the old adage: if it isn't broke, don't fix it. However, I do admire what has been done here. Because it was a gamble for the right reasons, which has paid handsomely in many ways, yet has just fallen short in others. Here, they took a magnificent whisky which for no other reason than pure serendipity, like Adam Adament, had awoken in another age but instead of, like our Victorian hero, being lost in a strange new world, found itself in one ready to appreciate and embrace its manifold beauty. This whisky was thrown back for a few extra summers in oak to take it to 50 years. A bold move. And it remains a quite astonishing, for life-remembering dram of labyrinthine complexity. *52%. 198 bottles.*

Lauder's (74) n18 t21 f17 b18. Well, it's consistent: you can say that for it! As usual, fabulous delivery, but as for the rest...oh dear. *40%. MacDuff International Ltd.*

Lauder's Aged 12 Years (93.5) n23 t24 f23 b23.5 This is every bit as magnificent as the standard Lauder's isn't. *43%*

⠿ **The Loch Fyne** (89.5) n22 the grains and toffee notes call like a siren; t23 so, so soft on impact...ohhhh! Less a caress, more a series of soft kisses on the palate. There is a slight sharpness to the citrus but it pricks just as the toffees build; f21.5 fudgy and dreamy... an amazing degree of chewability to the vanilla and butterscotch clad end; some very late furriness and nibbling of the throat; b23 not seen this fellow for a while, so a warm welcome back to The Whisky Bible. When I first visited Loch Fyne whiskies in Inverary well over 20 years ago I came across my first ever Spotted Flycatcher as I parked my car close to some old canons. By strange coincidence I have this year had a pair of Spotteds breeding in my garden...at a time when they are very much rarer. Maybe an omen this whisky was on its way...By the way: this is an adorable old-style blend....a bit of a throwback. But no ruinous sherry notes...just clean and delicious. Well, mainly... *40%*

Loch Lomond Blended Scotch (89) n22 t22.5 f22 b22.5 A fabulously improved blend: clean and precise and though malt is seemingly at a premium, a fine interplay. *40%*

Lochranza (83.5) n21 t21.5 f21 b20. Pleasant, clean, but, thanks to the caramel, goes easy on the complexity. *40%. Isle of Arran.*

Lochside 1964 Rare Old Single Blend (94.5) n24 t23.5 f23 b24. A unique and entirely fitting tribute to a distillery which should never have been lost. *42.1%. nc ncf.*

Logan (78.5) n19 t19 f20 b19.5. Entirely drinkable but a bit heavy-handed with the grains and caramel. *40%. Diageo.*

Lombard's Gold Label (85) n21 t22 f21 b21. Big and chewy, not as complex as of old but those who like chunky toffee will be in for a treat. *40%. Lombard Brands Ltd.*

⸫ **Lord Elcho (76) n**19 t20 f18 b19. Oh, Lord...! *40%. Wemyss Malts.*

Lord Elcho Aged 15 Years (84) n21 t21 f21 b21. A straight wicket with no turn at all. A degree of coppery sharpness and caramel, but low key. *40%. Wemyss Malts.*

Lord Hynett (88.5) n21.5 t23 f22 b22 Just perfect after a shitty day. *40%.*

Lord Hynett (87) n22 t22 f21.5 b21.5. An honest, beautifully made blend with a welcome degree of attitude. *43%. Loch Lomond Distillers.*

Lord Scot (77.5) n18.5 t20 f19.5 b19.5. A touch cloying but the mocha fudge ensures a friendly enough ride. *40%. Loch Lomond Distillers.*

Lord Scot (86.5) n20 t22 f22.5 b22. A gorgeously lush honey and liquorice middle. *43%*

The Lost Distilleries batch 2 **(94) n**22.5 t24 f23.5 b24. Whoever lost it better find it again: this is how you dream every whisky should be. *53.2%.*

Mackessack Premium Aged 8 Years (87.5) n21.5 t23 f21.5 b21.5. Claims a high Speyside content and the early character confirms it. Shoots itself in the foot, rather, by overdoing the caramel and flattening the finish. *40%. Mackessack Giovenetti. Italian Market.*

Mac Na Mara (83) n20 t22.5 f20 b20.5. Absolutely brimming with salty, fruity character. But just a little more toffee and furriness than it needs. Enjoyable, though. *40%*

Mac Na Mara Rum Finish (93) n22 t24 f23 b24. High quality blending, and the usage of the rum appears to have retained the old Mac Na Mara style. *40%. Praban na Linne.*

MacQueens (89) n21.5 t22.5 f22.5 b22.5. I am long enough in the tooth now to remember blends like this found in quiet country hotels in the furthest-flung reaches of the Highlands beyond a generation ago. A wonderfully old-fashioned, traditional one might say, blend of a type that is getting harder and harder to find. *40%. Quality Spirits International.*

Master of Malt 8 Years Old (88) n22.5 t22.5 f21 b22. Understated and refined. *40%*

Master Of Malt 8 Year Old Blended Whisky (83.5) n21 t22 f20.5 b20. Never quite makes up its mind what it wants to do, or where it wants to go. A few intriguing vaguely Irish Pot Still-style moments on delivery, though. *40%*

⸫ **Master of Malt Blended 10 Years Old 1st Edition (84.5) n**21.5 t22.5 f20 b20.5. A pleasant enough, though hardly complex, blend benefitting from the lovely malty, then silky pick-up from delivery and a brief juicy barley sharpness. But unsettled elsewhere due, mainly, to using the wrong fit of grain: too firm when a little give was needed. *47.5%. ncf. 819 bottles. WB15/353*

Master Of Malt St Isidore (84) n21 t22 f20 b21. Sweet, lightly smoked but really struggles to put together a coherent story. Something, somewhere, is not quite right. *41.4%*

Master Of Malt World Whisky Day Blend (86) n21.5 t22 f21 b21.5. Limited complexity and depth but it gets the Orange Aero bit right.... *40.18%. Master Of Malt.*

Matisse 12 Years Old (90.5) n23 t23 f22 b22.5 Moved up yet another notch as this brand continues its development. Much more clean-malt oriented with a Speyside-style to the fore. Majestic and charming. *40%. Matisse Spirits Co Ltd.*

Matisse 21 Years Old (86) n23 t22 f20 b21. Begins breathtakingly on the nose, with a full array of exotic fruit showing the older bourbon casks up to max effect. Nothing wrong with the early delivery, which offers a touch of honeycomb on the grain. But the caramel effect on the finish stops everything in its tracks. Soft and alluring, all the same. *40%*

Matisse Old (85.5) n20 t23 f21 b21.5. Appears to improve each time I come across it. The nose is a bit on the grimy side and the finish disappears under a sea of caramel. But the delivery works deliciously, with a chewy weight which highlights the sweeter malts. *40%*

Matisse Royal (81) n19 t22 f20 b20. Pleasant, if a little clumsy. Extra caramel appears to have scuppered the spice. *40%. Matisse Spirits Co Ltd.*

McArthurs (89.5) n22 t22.5 f22 b23 One of the most improved blends on the market. The clever use of the peat is exceptional. *40%. Inverhouse Distillers.*

Michael Jackson Special Memorial Blend bott 2009 **(89) n**24 t22.5 f20.5 b22. Whenever Michael and I had a dram together, his would either be massively sherried or equally well endowed with smoke. This is neither, so an odd tribute. Even so, there is more than enough here for him to savour. *43%. Berry Bros & Rudd. 1000 bottles.*

Mitchell's Glengyle Blend (86.5) n21.5 t22 f21.5 b21.5. A taste of history here, as this is the first blend ever to contain malt from the new Campbeltown distillery, Glengyle. Something of a departure in style which, though tended to put the accent on a crisper grain. Interestingly, here they have chosen one at least that is soft and voluptuous enough to absorb the sharper malt notes. *40%. Springbank Distillers.*

Monarch Of The Glen Connoisseurs Choice (80) n20 t21 f19 b20. Has changed shape a little. Positively wallows in its fat and sweet personality. *40%. Quality Spirits International.*

Monarch Of The Glen Connoisseurs Choice Aged 8 Years (76.5) n19 t20.5 f18 b19. Leaves no doubt that there are some malts in there... *40%. Quality Spirits International.*

Monarch Of The Glen Connoisseurs Choice Aged 12 Years (88) n21.5 t22.5 f22 b22 Charming, fruity and a blend to put your feet up with. *40%. Quality Spirits International.*

Monarch Of The Glen Connoisseurs Choice Aged 15 Years (83) n21 t22 f19 b21. Starts off on the very same footing as the 12-y-o, especially with the sumptuous delivery. But fails to build on that due to toffee and bitters at the death. 40%. *Quality Spirits International.*

Montrose (74.5) n18 t20 f18 b18.5. A battling performance but bitter defeat in the end. 40%. *Burn Stewart.*

Morrisons The Best 8 Years Old (87) n21 t23 f22 b21. Some of the traces of its excellence are still there, it remains highly drinkable, but that greatness has been lost in a tide of caramel. When, oh when, are people going to understand that you can't just tip this stuff into whisky to up the colour without causing a detrimental effect on the product? Is anybody listening? Does anyone care??? Someone has gone to great lengths to create a sublime blend – to see it wasted. Natural colour and this'd be an experience to die for. 40% *Wm Morrison Supermarket.*

Morrisons Fine Blended Whisky (77) n18.5 t21 f18.5 b19. Sweet, chewy but a few rough edges. 40%. *Wm Morrison Supermarket.*

Muirhead's (83) n19 t22 f23 b21. A beautifully compartmentalised dram that integrates superbly, if that makes sense. 40%. *MacDonald & Muir.*

Muirhead's Blue Seal (83) n21 t21 f20.5 b20.5. Goes to town quite heavily on the grain. If this is the new version of the old McDonald and Muir brand, then this is a lot oilier, with a silkier mouthfeel. 40%. *Highland Queen Scotch Whisky Company.*

The Naked Grouse (76.5) n19 t21 f17.5 b19. Sweet. But reveals too many sulphur tattoos. 40%. *Edrington.*

Northern Scot (68) n16 t18 f17 b17. Heading South bigtime. 40%. *Bruce and Co. for Tesco.*

Old Crofter Special Old Scotch Whisky (83) n18 t22 f21 b22. A very decent blend, much better than the nose suggests thanks to some outstanding, velvety grain and wonderfully controlled sweetness. 40%. *Smith & Henderson for London & Scottish International.*

Old Masters "Freemason Whisky" (92) n24 t23 f22 b23. A high quality blend that doesn't stint on the malt. The nose, in particular, is sublime. 40%. *Supplied online. Lombard Brands*

Old McDonald (83.5) n20 t22 f20.5 b21. Attractively tart and bracing where it needs to be with lovely grain bite. Lots of toffee, though. 43.%. *The Last Drop Distillers. For India.*

Old Mull (84.5) n22 t21 f20.5 b21. With dates and walnuts clambering all over the nose, very much in the house style. But this one is a shade oilier than most – and certainly on how it used to be – and has dropped a degree or two of complexity. That said, enjoyable stuff with the spices performing well, as does the lingering sweetness. 40%

Old Parr 12 Years Old (91.5) n21.5 t23.5 f23 b23.5 Perhaps on about the fourth of fifth mouthful, the penny drops that this is not just exceptionally good whisky: it is blending Parr excellence.... 40%. *Diageo.*

Old Parr Aged 15 Years (84) n19 t22 f21 b22. Absolutely massive sherry input here. Some of it is of the highest order. The nose, reveals, however, that some isn't... 43%

Old Parr Classic 18 Years Old (84.5) n21 t21.5 f21 b21. A real jumbled, mixed bag with fruit and barley falling over each other and the grains offering little sympathy. Enough to enjoy, but with Old Parr, one expects a little more... 46%. *Diageo.*

Old Parr Superior 18 Years Old batch no. L5171 (97) n25 a nose with just about a touch of everything: especially clever smoke which gives weight but allows apples and bourbon to filter through at will. Perfect weight and harmony while the complexity goes off the scales; t25 voluptuous body, at times silky but the grains offer enough jagged edges for a degree of bite and bourbon; mouthwatering and spicey with the peats remaining on a slow burner. Toasty and so, so chewy; f23 the vanilla is gentle and a counter to the firmness of the combined oak and grain. A flinty, almost reedy finish with spices and cocoa very much in evidence; b24 year in, year out, this blend just gets better and better. This bottling struck me as a possible Whisky of the Year, but perhaps only an outsider. Familiarity, though, bred anything but contempt and over the passing months I have tried to get to the bottom of this truly great whisky. Blended whisky has long needed a champion. This grand old man looks just the chap. This is a worthy, if unexpected (even to me), Jim Murray' Whisky Bible 2007 World Whisky of the Year. 43%.

Old Smuggler (85.5) n21 t22 f21 b21.5. A much sharper act than its Allied days with a new honeyed-maple syrup thread which is rather delightful. Could still do with toning down the caramel, though, to brighten the picture further. 40%. *Campari, France.*

Old St Andrews Clubhouse (82) n18 t22 f21 b21. Not quite the clean, bright young thing it was many years back. But great to see back in my nosing glass after such a long while and though the nose hits the rough, the delivery is as sweetly struck as you might hope for. 40%

Old Stag (75.5) n18.5 t20 f18.5 b18.5. Wants shooting. 40%. *Loch Lomond Distillers.*

The Original Lochlan Aged 8 Years (80.5) n19 t21 f20 b20.5. Doused in caramel. So much so it's like a toffee and nut bar. One to chew on until your fillings fall out, though the spices compensate on the finish to a degree. Pleasant and sweet, but don't expect great refinement. 40%. *Tesco.*

The Original Mackinlay (83) n19 t21 f22 b21. A hard nose to overcome and the toffee remains in force for those addicted to fudge. But now a degree of bite and ballast appears to have been added, giving more of a story to the experience. 40%. *Whyte & Mackay Distillers Ltd.*

Passport (83) n22 t19 f21 b21. It looks as though Chivas have decided to take the blend away from its original sophisticated, Business Class J&B/Cutty Sark, style for good now, as they have continued this decently quaffable but steerage quality blend with its big caramel kick and chewy, rather than lithe, body. 40%. *Chivas.*

Passport v (91) n23 23.5 f22 b22.5. Easily one of the better versions I have come across for a long time and impressively true to its original style. 40%. *Bottled in Brazil.*

Passport v (91) n22.5 t22 f23.5 b23.5. A lovely version closer to original style with markedly less caramel impact and grittier grain. An old-fashioned treat. 40%. *Ecuador.*

Parkers (78) n17 t22 f20 b19. The nose has regressed, disappearing into ever more caramel, yet the mouth-watering lushness on the palate remains and the finish now holds greater complexity and interest. 40%. *Angus Dundee.*

Prince Charlie Special Reserve (73) n17 t20 f18 b18. Thankfully not as cloyingly sweet as of old, but remains pretty basic. 40%. *Somerfield, UK.*

Prince Charlie Special Reserve 8 Years Old (81) n18 t20 f22 b21. A lumbering bruiser of a dram; keeps its trademark shapelessness but the spices and lush malt ensure an enjoyable experience. 40%. *Somerfield, UK.*

Queen Margot (86) n21 t22 f21.5 b21.5. A lovely blend which makes no effort to skimp on a spicy depth. Plenty of cocoa from the grain late on but no shortage of good whiskies put to work. 40%. *Wallace and Young for Lidl.*

Queen Margot v (83.5) n20.5 t22 f20 b21. Same brand, but a different name on the back label. And certainly a different feel to the whisky with the grains having harsher words than before. 40%. *Clydesdale Scotch Whisky Co for Lidl.*

Queen Margot Aged 8 Years (89) n22 t22.5 f22 b22.5. A satisfying blend with a delicious clarity to the light malts and high class grains. Just the right touch of sweetness, too. 40%. *Wallace and Young for Lidl.*

Queen Margot Aged 8 Years (84) n20.5 t21 f21.5 b21. Here's the variant. Darker in colour I notice and a bit of a dullard and simpleton by comparison, though not without an acceptable degree of charm. Much weightier. 40%. *Clydesdale Scotch Whisky Co for Lidl.*

Real Mackenzie (80) n17 t21 f21 b21. As ever, try and ignore the dreadful nose and get cracking with the unsubtle, big bruising delivery. A thug in a glass. 40%. *Diageo.*

Real Mackenzie Extra Smooth (81) n18 t22 f20 b21. Once, the only time the terms "Real Mackenzie" and "Extra Smooth" were ever uttered in the same sentence was if someone was talking about the barman. Now it is a genuine descriptor. Which is odd, because when Diageo sent me a sample of their blend last year it was a snarling beast ripping at the leash. This, by contrast, is a whimpering sop. "Killer? Where are you...???" 40%. *Diageo.*

Red Seal 12 Years Old (82) n19 t22 f20 b21. Charming, mouthwatering. But toffee numbs it down towards the finish. 40%. *Charles Wells UK.*

Reliance PL (76) n18 t20 f19 b19. Some of the old spiciness evident. But has flattened out noticeably. 43%. *Diageo.*

Robert Burns (85) n20 t22.5 f21 b21.5. Skeletal and juicy: very little fat and gets to the mouthwatering point pretty quickly. Genuine fun. 40%. *Isle of Arran.*

Robertson's of Pitlochry Rare Old Blended (83) n21 t20 f21 b21. Handsome grain bite with a late malty flourish. Classic light blend available only from Pitlochry's landmark whisky shop. 40%

The Royal & Ancient (80.5) n20 t21.5 f19 b20. Has thinned out dramatically in the last year or so. Now clean, untaxing, briefly mouth-watering and radiating young grain throughout. 40%

Royal Castle (84.5) n20 t22 f21 b21.5. From Quality Street, or Quality Spirits? Sweet and very well toffeed! 43%. *Quality Spirits International.*

Royal Castle 12 Years Old (84.5) n22 t22 f20 b20.5. Busy nose and delivery with much to chew over. Entirely enjoyable, and seems better each time you taste it. Even so, the finish crumbles a bit. 40%. *Quality Spirits International.*

Royal Clan Aged 18 Years (85) n21.5 t21 f21.5 b21. For those giving up gum, here's something to really chew on. Huge degree of cream toffee and toasted fudge which makes for a satin-soft blend, but also one which ensures any big moves towards complexity are nipped in the bud. Very enjoyable, all the same. 40%. *Quality Spirits International.*

Royal Household (90.5) n21.5 t23 f23 b23 We are amused. 43%. *Diageo.*

Royal Park (85) n21.5 t22.5 f20 b21. Pretty generic with an attractive silky sheen, Demerara sugars and decent late spice swim around in an ocean of caramel. 40%

Royal Salute 21 Years Old (92.5) n23 t23.5 f23 b23.5 If you are looking for the velvety character of yore, forget it. This one comes with some real character and is much the better for it. The grain, in particular, excels. 40%. *Chivas.*

Royal Salute 62 Gun Salute (95.5) n24.5 prunes and apples plus a little cinnamon. And grapes, of course. All this in a bed of seemingly natural caramels. It is a smoke-free environment where every oak note is rounded and friendly, where you fancy you can still find the odd mark of barley and yet although being a blend, the grain is refusing to take it down a bourbon path, despite the peek-a-boo honeycomb; **t24** the oak is relatively full on, but early on adds a toasty quality to the marmalade and plum jam. The mid ground casts off any sherry-like clothes and heads for a more honey-rich, vaguely bourbon style without ever reaching Kentucky; **f23** the fade is on the gentle side with sugars dissolving against a slightly bittering background as some of the oak rebels, as you might expect at least one or two of these old timers to do. At the very death comes the one and only sign of smoke...that is some parting shot; **b24** how do you get a bunch of varying whiskies in style, but each obviously growing a grey beard and probably cantankerous to boot, to settle in and harmonise with the others? A kind of Old People's Home for whisky, if you like. Well, here's how...*43%. Chivas.*

Royal Salute The Diamond Tribute (91) n23.5 t23 f21.5 b23. Ironic that a diamond is probably the hardest natural creation, yet this whisky is one of man's softest... *40%. Chivas.*

Royal Salute The Hundred Cask Selection Limited Release No. 7 (92) n22 t23.5 f23 b23.5 As blends go, its entire countenance talks about great age and elegance. And does so with a clipped accent. *40%. Chivas.*

Royal Silk Reserve (93) n22 t24 f24 b23 I named this the best newcomer of 2001 and it hasn't let me down. A session blend for any time of the day, this just proves that you don't need piles of peat to create a blend of genuine stature. A must have. *40%*

Sainsbury's Basics Blended Scotch Whisky (78.5) n19 t20.5 f19.5 b19.5. "A little less refined, great for mixing," says the label. Frankly, there are a lot of malts out there far less enjoyable than this. Don't be scared to have straight: it's more than decent enough. *40%*

Sainsbury's Scotch Whisky (84.5) n20 t22 f21 b21.5. A surprisingly full bodied, chewy blend allowing a pleasing degree of sweetness to develop. No shortage of toffee at the finish – a marked improvement on recent years. *40%. UK.*

Sainsbury's Finest Old Matured Aged 8 Years (86) n21.5 t21 f22 b21.5. A sweet blend enjoying a melt-in-the-mouth delivery, a silky body and toffee-vanilla character. The spices arriving towards the end are exceptionally pleasing and welcome. *40%. UK.*

Sandy Mac (76) n18 t20 f19 b19. Basic, decent blend that's chunky and raw. *40%. Diageo.*

Scots Earl (76.5) n18 t20 f19 b19.5. It's name is Earl. And it must have upset someone in a previous life. Always thrived on its engaging disharmony. But just a tad too syrupy now. *40%. Loch Lomond Distillers.*

Scottish Chief (77) n19 t19 f19 b20. This is one big-bodied chief, and not given to taking prisoners. *40%. Quality Spirits International.*

Scottish Collie (77) n19 t19 f19 b20. Caramel still, but a Collie with a bit more bite. *40%*

Scottish Collie 12 Years Old (85) n22 t22 f20 b21. On the cusp of a really classy blend here but the bitterness on the finish loses serious Brownie points. *40%. Quality Spirits Int, UK.*

Scottish Collie 18 Years Old (92) n24 t23 f22 b23. This, honey-led beaut would be a winner even at Crufts: an absolute master class of how an old, yet light and unpeated blend should be. No discord whatsoever between the major elements and not a single hint of over-aging. Superb. *40%. Quality Spirits International, UK.*

Scottish Glory dist 2002, bott 2005 **(85) n21 t21 f22 b21.** An improved blend now bursting with vitality. The ability of the grain to lift the barley is very pleasing. *40%. Duncan Taylor.*

Scottish Leader Original (83.5) n17.5 t22.5 f21 b22.5. About as subtle as a poke in the eye with a spirit thief. The nose, it must be said, is not great. But I have to admit I thoroughly enjoy the almost indulgent coarseness from the moment it invades the palate. A real chewathon of a spicy blend with a wicked, in-yer-face attitude. Among all the rough-'n-tumble and slap-'n-tickle, the overall depth, weight, balance and molassed charm ain't half bad. *40%. Burn Stewart.*

Scottish Leader Aged 12 Years (91) n22.5 t23 f22 b22.5 Absolutely unrecognisable from the Leader 12 I last tasted. This has taken a plumy, fruity route with the weight of a cannonball but the texture of mallow. Big and quite beautiful. *40%. Burn Stewart.*

Scottish Leader 30 Years Old (87) n23.5 t21.5 f20.5 b21.5 A little too docile ever to be a great whisky, but the nose is something rather special. A bit of attention on the finish and this could be a real corker. *40%. Burn Stewart.*

Scottish Leader Select (91.5) n23 t23.5 f22.5 b22.5 Don't make the mistake of thinking this is just the 40% with three extra percentage points of alcohol. This appears to be an entirely different bottling with an entirely different personality. A delight. *43%. Burn Stewart. For the South African Market.*

Scottish Leader Select (74) n18.5 t19 f18 b18.5. I assume the leader is Major Disharmony. *40%. Burn Stewart.*

Scottish Leader Supreme (72.5) n17 t19 f18 b18.5. Jings! It's like an old-fashioned Gorbals punch-up in the glass – and palate. *40%. Burn Stewart.*

Scottish Piper (80) n20 t20 f20 b20. A light, mildly- raw, sweet blend with lovely late vanilla intonation. *40%*

Scottish Prince (83.5) n21 t22 f20 b20.5. Muscular, but agreeably juicy. *40%*

Scottish Reel (78.5) n19 t19 f20 b19.5. Non fussy with an attractive bite, as all such blends should boast. *40%. London & Scottish International.*

Scottish Rill (85) n20 t20.5 f22.5 b22. Refreshing yet earthy. *40%. Quality Spirits Int.*

Sheep Dip Amoroso Oloroso 1999 Oloroso sherry casks, bott Mar 12 (92) n23.5 t24 f21 b23.5. More like Sherry Dip than Sheep Dip. Actually, chocolate dip wouldn't be too far off the mark, either. To create this, malt which had spent three years maturing in bourbon cask was then shipped to Jerez where it spent a further nine years in presumably fresh sherry. It was worth the trouble... *41.8%. Spencerfield Spirits.*

Something Special (85) n21.5 t22 f20.5 b21. Mollycoddled by toffee, any murderous tendencies seem to have been fudged away, leaving just the odd moment of attractive complexity. You suspect there is a hit man in there somewhere trying to get out. *40%. Chivas.*

Something Special Premium Aged 15 Years (89) n22 t23 f21 b23 Fabulous malt thread and some curious raisiny/sultana fruitiness, too. A blend-lover's blend. *40%.*

Spar Finest Reserve (90.5) n21.5 t22.5 f23.5 b23 One of Britain's best value for money blends with an honest charm which revels in the clean high quality grain and earthier malts which work so well together. *40%*

⦂⦂ **Spirit of Freedom Aged 30 Years** (91) n23.5 though the age says 30, you get the feeling something a hell of a lot older is in there! A ripe aroma on every front from ancient oak to passion fruit just about on the turn; t22.5 yet: it's old!! Silky, vaguely coppery and crisp, crystalline Demerara sugar; f22 dry, flaky almost sawdusty oak; b23 a blend created to mark the 700th anniversary of Bannockburn has a battle of its own against so many aging casks. Somehow, it just about wins. *46%. 2014 bottles. WB15/364*

Stewart's Old Blended (93) n22.5 t24 f23 b23.5 Really lovely whisky for those who like to close their eyes, contemplate and have a damned good chew. *40%*

Storm (94) n23 t23.5 f24 b23.5. A little gem of a blend that really will take you by storm. *43%. Whisky Shack.*

Swords (78) n20 t21 f18 b19. Beefed up somewhat with some early smoke thrusting through and rapier grains to follow. *40%. Morrison Bowmore.*

Talisman 5 Years Old (85.5) n22 t22 f20.5 b21. Unquestionably an earthier, weightier version of what was once a Speyside romp. Soft peats also add extra sweetness. *40%*

Teacher's 50 - 12 Years Old batch 2-16, bott Sep 11 (85.5) n20.5 t22.5 f21.5 b21. Once, before entering the Indian bottling hall, this must have been a strutting peacock of a Scotch blend. But after being doused in a far too liberal amount of caramels it has been reduced to a house sparrow: outwardly common and dull but at least with an engaging personality. The usual Teacher's smoke shows itself only at the death, alas. And all else is a silky honeyed sweetness pleading for an extra degree of complexity. The very complexity, indeed, which was almost certainly there before being coloured to death. If they could sort out the caramel levels in the bottling hall, this would be a blend that would put on a spectacular display.... *42.8%*

Teacher's Aged 25 Years batch 1 (96.5) n24 at first this Teacher's lectures malt to you; not any old malt, but delicately smoked and as light with citrus as it is heavy with phenol. Then slowly the grains emerge, offering weighted consistency to the sweeter, maple syrup elements, until there is a satisfying fusion between the two....; t24.5 not sure one can quite nose silk, though that's what it appeared to be. But you can certainly spot it on the palate, and that's exactly what we have on delivery: every atom, be it smoky or marmalade orangey, simply melts in the mouth though unusually for a 25-y-o, it does not leave an oaky residue; f23.5 long, spicy, a little tangy; b24.5 only 1300 bottles means they will be hard pushed to create this exact style again. Worth a go, chaps: considering this is India bound, it is the karma sutra of blended scotch. *46%. Beam Inc. 1300 bottles. India & Far East Travel Retail exclusive.*

Teacher's Highland Cream (90) n23 t23 f22 b22 Not yet back to its best but a massive improvement on the 2005 bottlings. Harder grains to accentuate the malt will bring it closer to the classic of old. *40%*

Teacher's Highland Cream v (90) n23 t22.5 f22 b22.5 A very curious, seriously high grade, variant. Although the Ardmore distillery is on the label, it is the only place it can really be seen. Certainly - the least smoky Teacher's I've come across in 35 years of drinking the stuff: the smoke is there, but adds only ballast rather than taking any form of lead. But the grain is soft and knits with the malts with ease to make for a sweeter, much more lush version than the rest of the world may recognize. *40%*

Teacher's Origin (88.5) n22 t23.5 f21 b22 A fascinating blend which probably ranks as the softest on the market today. That is aided and abetted by the exceptionally high malt content, 65%, which makes this something of an inverted blend, as that, for most established brands, is the average grain content. What appears to be a high level of caramel also makes for a rounding of the edges, as well as evidence of sherry butts. The bad news is that that has resulted in a duller finish than perhaps might have been intended, which is even more pronounced given the impressive speech made on delivery. Lovely whisky, yes. But something, I feel, of a work in progress. Bringing the caramel down by the percentage points of the malt would be a very positive start... *42.8%. ncf. Beam Global.*

Té Bheag (86) n22 t21 f21.5 b21.5. Classic style of rich caramels and bite. *40%. ncf. Pràban na Linne.*

Tesco Finest Reserve Aged 12 Years (74) n18.5 t19 f18 b18.5. The most astonishing thing about this, apart from the fact it is a 12 year-old, is that it won a Gold "Best in Class" in a 2010 international whisky competition: it surely could not have been from the same batch as the one before me. Frankly, you have to go a long way to find a whisky as bland as this and for a 12-y-o it is monumentally disappointing. *40%.*

Tesco Special Reserve Minimum 3 Years Old (78) n18.5 t21.5 f19 b19. Decent early spice on delivery but otherwise anonymous. *40%. Tesco.*

Tesco Value Scotch Whisky (83) n19 t21 f22 b21. Young and genuinely refreshing whisky. Without the caramel this really would be a little darling. *40%*

Traquair (78) n19 t21 f19 b19. Young, but offering a substantial mouthful including attractive smoke. *46%. Burn Stewart.*

⠿ **That Boutique-y Whisky Blended Whisky #1** batch 1 (72) n18 t19 f17 b18. Fuzzy, furry and generally out of sorts. *50.3%. 148 bottles. WB15/354*

The Tweeddale Blend Aged 10 Years (89.5) n22 t23.5 f21.5 b22.5 The first bottling of this blend since World War 2, it has been well worth waiting for. *46%. ncf. 50% malt. Stonedean.*

The Tweeddale Blend Aged 12 Years bott Jun 11 (94.5) n23.5 t24 f23 b24. Bravo! A blend which sets out to maximise the (in this case) high quality whiskies used. An engrossing and massively enjoyable celebration of blended scotch. A minor classic, in fact. And not entirely dissimilar, curiously, to a blend I occasionally concoct for my own enjoyment... *46%. ncf.*

The Tweeddale Blend Aged 12 Years bott code 28, Feb 13 (95) n23.5 t24 f23 b24.5 For the tasting notes see the 2011 bottling above. Very, very similar, except more crisp grain on the nose and a slightly more clever use of citrus throughout. How heart-warming to see a blend not just keep faithfully to its style, but appears to somehow up the quality a fraction. A treat of a whisky experience. *46%. nc ncf. Stonedean. 3rd release.*

⠿ **Tweeddale Blended Scotch Whisky Aged 14 Years** Batch 4 db (94) n23 fresh as a daisy with the emphasis on th malt rather than the grain. More of a heavy duty malt of a Lowland/Speyside variety, though the grains are crisp; t24 charming, vaguely effervescent and again the malt and grains appear to arm wrestle over control: the clean malt wins...; f23 now deftly spiced, with both grain and malt still having a say. Some citrus makes a late intervention; b24 now, that is very good whisky. And one of the maltiest blends around... Simple. But quite beautiful. *46%. nc ncf. bottle No. 373.*

Ushers Green Stripe (85) n19 t22.5 f21.5 b22. Upped a notch or two in all-round quality. The juicy theme and clever weight is highly impressive and enjoyable. *43%. Diageo.*

VAT 69 (84.5) n20 t22 f21 b21.5. Has thickened up in style: weightier, more macho, much more to say and a long way off that old lightweight. A little cleaning up wouldn't go amiss. *40%*

White Horse (90.5) n22 t23 f22.5 b23 A malt which has subtlety changed shape. Not just the smoke which gives it weight, but you get the feeling that some of Diageo's less delicate malts have been sent in to pack a punch. As long as they are kept in line, as is the case here – just – we can all enjoy a very big blend. *40%. Diageo.*

White Horse Aged 12 Years (86) n21 t23 f21 b21. enjoyable, complex if not always entirely harmonious. For instance, the apples and grapes on the nose appear on a limb from the grain and caramel and nothing like the thoroughbred of old. Lighter, more flaccid and caramel dominated. *40%. Diageo.*

Whyte & Mackay 'The Thirteen' 13 Year Old (92) n22.5 t23.5 f23 b23. Try this and your luck'll be in...easily the pick of the W&M blended range. *40%. Whyte & Mackay Distillers Ltd.*

Whyte & Mackay Luxury 19 Year Old (84.5) n21 t22 f20 b21.5. A pleasant house style chewathon. Nutty, biting but with a tang. *40%. Whyte & Mackay Distillers Ltd.*

Whyte & Mackay Supreme 22 Year Old (87) n21 t23 f20.5 b22.5. Ignore the nose and finish and just enjoy the early ride. *43%*

Whyte & Mackay Oldest 30 Year Old (87.5) n23 t23 f20 b21.5. What exasperating whisky this is. So many good things about it, but... *45%*

Whyte & Mackay Original Aged Blended 40 Years Old (93) n23 t24 f22 b24. I admit, when I nosed and tasted this at room temp, not a lot happened. Pretty, but closed. But once warmed in the hand up to full body temperature, it was obvious that Richard Paterson had created a quite wonderful monster of a blend offering so many avenues to explore that the mind almost explodes. Well done RP for creating something that further proves, and in such magnitude, just how warmth can make an apparently ordinary whisky something bordering genius. *45%*

Whyte & Mackay Special (84.5) n20 t23 f20 b21.5. If you are looking for a big-flavoured dram and with something approaching a vicious left uppercut, this might be a useful bottle to have on hand. The nose, I'm afraid, has not improved over the years but there appears to be compensation with the enormity and complexity of the delivery, a veritable orgy of big, oily, juicy, murky flavours and tones if ever there was one. You cannot but like it, in the same way as you may occasionally like rough sex. But if you are looking for a delicate dram to gently kiss you and caress your fevered brow, then leave well alone. 40%

William Grant's 12 Years Old Bourbon Cask (90.5) n23 t22.5 f22 b23. Very clever blending where balance is the key. 40%

William Grant's 15 Years Old (85) n21 t23 f20 b21. Grain and, later, caramel dominates but the initial delivery reveals the odd moment of sheer genius and complexity on max revs. 43%

William Grant's 25 Years Old (95.5) n23.5 some serious oak, but chaperoned by top quality oloroso, itself thinned by firm and graceful grain; t24 sheer quality: complexity as the shovel-load as juicy fruits interact with darting, crisp barley; again the grain shows elegance both sharpening increasingly mouth-watering malt and softening the oak; f24 medium length, but not a single sign of fatigue: the sweet barley runs and runs and some jammy fruits charm. Just to cap it all, some wonderful spices dazzle and a touch of low roast Java enriches; b24 absolutely top-rank blending that appears to maximize every last degree of complexity. Most astonishing, though, is its sprightly countenance: even Scottish footballing genius Ally MacLeod struggled to send out Ayr Utd. sides with this kind of brio. And that's saying something! A gem. 40%

William Grant's 100 US Proof Superior Strength (92) n23 t24 f22 b23. A fruitier drop now than it was in previous years but no less supremely constructed. 50% (100 US proof)

William Grant's Ale Cask Reserve (89) n21 t23 f22 b23. A real fun blend that is just jam-packed with jagged malty notes. The hops were around more on earlier bottlings, but watch out for them. Nothing pint-sized about this: this is a big blend and very true in flavour/ shape to the original with just a delicious shading of grain to really up the complexity. 40%

William Grant's Family Reserve (94) n25 t23 f22 b24. There are those puzzled by my obvious love affair with blended whisky - both Scotch and Japanese - at a time when malts are all the rage. But take a glass of this and carefully nurture and savour it for the best part of half an hour and you may begin to see why I believe this to be the finest art form of whisky. For my money, this brand - brilliantly kept in tip-top shape by probably the world's most naturally gifted blender - is the closest thing to the blends of old and, considering it is pretty ubiquitous, it defies the odds for quality. It is a dram with which you can start the day and end it: one to keep you going at low points in between, or to celebrate the victories. It is the daily dram that has everything. 40%

⋰ **William Grant's Rare Cask Reserves 25 Years Old Blended Scotch Whisky** (88) n22.5 busy without offering a narrative. Punchy, salty notes, dried dates and a vague fruitiness; t23 confident delivery: silky textured and mouth-filling; a little ulmo honey mingles with dull fruit and butterscotch; f20.5 fudgy and furry; b22 an appealing blend that appears to be designed to come at you as a concept rather than allowing the different instrumentalists to have the odd solo. Not helped by what appear to be some less than perfect casks. 47%.

William Grant's Sherry Cask Reserve (82) n20 t22 f20 b20. Raspberry jam and cream from time to time. Attractive, but somewhat plodding dram that's content in second gear. 40%

William Lawson's Finest (85) n18.5 t22.5 f22 b22. Not only has the label become more colourful, but so, too, has the whisky. However that has not interfered with the joyous old-fashioned grainy bite. A complex and busy blend from the old charm school. 40%

William Lawson's Scottish Gold Aged 12 Years (89) n22 t23 f22 b22. For years Lawson's 12 was the best example of the combined wizardry of clean grain, unpeated barley and good bourbon cask that you could find anywhere in the world: a last-request dram before the firing squad. Today it is still excellent, but just another sherried blend. What's that saying about if it's not being broke...? 40%

Windsor 12 Years Old (81) n20 t21 f20 b20. Thick, walloped-on blend that you can stand a spoon in. Hard at times to get past the caramel. 40%. Diageo.

Windsor Aged 17 Years Super Premium (89) n23 t22 f22 b22. Still on the safe side for all its charm and quality. An extra dose of complexity would lift this onto another level. 40%

Windsor 21 Years Old (90) n20 t23 f24 b23. Recovers fabulously from the broken nose and envelopes the palate with a silky-sweet style unique to the Windsor scotch brand. Excellent. 40%. Diageo.

Ye Monks (86) n20 t23 f21.5 b21.5. Just hope they are praying for less caramel to maximize the complexity. Still, a decent spicy chew and outstanding bite which is great fun and worth finding when in South America. 40%. Diageo.

Yokozuna Blended 3 Years Old (79.5) n18.5 t20.5 f20 b20.5. It appears the Mongols are gaining a passion for thick, sweet, toffeed, oily, slightly feinty whisky. For a nation breastfed on airag, this'll be a doddle... 40%. Speyside Distillers. Mongolian market.

Irish Whiskey

Of all the whiskies in the world, it is Irish which probably causes most confusion amongst both established whisk(e)y lovers and the novices.

Ask anyone to define what is unique to Irish Whiskey – apart from it being made in Ireland – and the answers, if my audiences around the world at my tastings are anything to go by, are in this order: i) It is triple distilled; ii) It is never, ever made from peat; iii) They exclusively use sherry casks; iv) It comes from the oldest distillery in the world; v) It is made from a mixture of malted and unmalted barley.

Only one of those answers is true: the fifth. And it is usually the final answer extracted from the audience when the last hand raised sticks to his guns after the previous four responses have been shot down.

There was no shortage of Blarney when the Irish were trying to market their whiskey back in the 1950s and early 60s. Hence the triple distilled/non-peated myth was born. The Irish had had a thin time of it since the 1920s and seen their industry decimated. So the marketing guys got to work.

As much of Ireland is covered in peat, it is hardly surprising that in the 19th century smoky whiskey from inland distilleries was not uncommon. Like Scotland. Some distilleries used two stills, others three. Like Scotland. Sherry butts were ubiquitous in Ireland before World War 2. Just as they were in Scotland. And there are distilleries in Scotland older than Bushmills, which dates from 1784 (and certainly not 1608 as some still rabidly believe). However, the practice of using malted and unmalted barley, begun so less tax had to be paid on malted grain, had died out in the Lowlands of Scotland, leaving it for Ireland to carry on alone.

It is hard to believe, then, that when I was researching my Irish Whiskey Almanac way back in 1993, Redbreast had just been discontinued as a brand leaving Green Spot, an ancient gem of a bottling from Mitchell and Son, Dublin's legendary high class wine and spirit merchants, as the sole surviving Pure Irish Pot Still Whiskey. At first Redbreast's owners refused to send me a bottle as they regarded it as a pointless exercise, seeing as the brand had gone. After I wrote about it, first in my Almanac and then in newspapers and magazines elsewhere, they had no option other than to reverse their decision: interest had been whetted and people were asking for it once more.

When it was relaunched, the Pot Still came from Midleton. The Redbreast they were discontinuing was Pure Pot Still from the long defunct original Jameson Distillery in Dublin. Jameson may once have been locked in commercial battle with their neighbouring Power's distillery, but they united in the late 19th century when they brought out a book called: "The Truth About Irish Whiskey" in which they together, along with other Dublin distillers, fought against blended and other types of what they considered adulterated whiskey to tell the world that the only true Irish whiskey was Pure Pot Still. The last direct descendent of the true Irish distilling DNA from that era is Barry Crockett. We first met over 20 years ago when he took me around the very Midleton Distillery in whose grounds he had been born long before the present plant of 1975 had been as much as a glint in an accountant's eye. Barry, myself, Irish Distillers blender Barry Walsh and Green Spot owners Mitchell and Son were then the only people in the entire industry who knew just how great true Irish pot still whiskey was and the deadly threat it was under with Redbreast having been discontinued.

The two Barrys had their hands tied: one had to blend in a certain way and for set markets, the other to produce to order. But I was more than aware of the sorrow in both men that they could not produce more pot still (there was simply not enough capacity), or make extra available to be tasted in its own unmolested glory. So when I met up with Barry Crockett in Stockholm a year or two back and we posed for photos with the new Pot Still range, there was a quiet sense of achievement between us. He had been granted his wish and produced more of the world's most esoteric whiskey style, and my long campaign to see it back on the shelves (begun with a flaming row with the directors of Irish Distillers) had born fruit.

In March 2013 Barry retired, ending nearly 50 years in Irish whisky production, more than 30 of them as distillery manager at Midleton. A nation's loss is a Nation's gain – his deputy Brian Nation takes over after a decade's mentoring. But Barry, who will be now found burrowing into the distillery's archives, will be able to look back proudly at a lifetime's work quite magnificently done. And doubtless, he will be accompanied by a glass of his quite beautiful Redbreast 21 pure pot still: a World Whiskey of the Year just waiting to happen.

Pure Pot Still
MIDLETON (old distillery)

Midleton 25 Years Old Pot Still db (92) n24 t24 f21 b23. A really enormous whiskey that is in the truest classic Irish style. The un-malted barley really does make the tastebuds hum and the oak has added fabulous depth. Interesting when tasted against an American rye – the closeness of the character is there to be experienced, but also the differences. A subtle mature whiskey of unquestionable quality. Superb. *43%*

Midleton 30 Years Old Pot Still db (85) n19 t22 f22 b22. A typically brittle, crunchy Irish pot still where the un-malted grains have a telling say. The oak has travelled as far as it can without having an adverse effect. A chewy whiskey which revels in its bitter-sweet balance. An impressively tasty and fascinating insight into yesteryear. *45%*

Midleton 1973 Pure Pot Still db (95) n24 t24 f23 b24. The enormous character of true Irish pot still whiskey (a mixture of malted and unmalted barley) appears to absorb age better than most other grain spirits. This one is in its element. But drink at full strength and at body temp (it is pretty closed when cool) for the most startling – and memorable effects. I have no idea how much this costs. But if you can find one and afford it... then buy it!! *56%*

MIDLETON (new distillery)

⁃ **Master Distiller's Selection Single Pot** db (94) n23.5 something of the cake shop about this: sweet with random honey, apples, citrus and flour notes mixing together eloquently and enticingly; t23.5 the first two waves are soft and welcoming. What follows is a ram-rod firm thwack of barley, which is as crunchy as it is chewy. Slowly, some fruit notes unravel, mainly of the plummy type, though the odd pear shows its hand. The spices are beginning to warm; f23 maybe some sherry at work as there is a vague furriness now. But the spices and the crisp barley remain on course to the end; b24 at the sweeter end of the Pot Still spectrum. The use of fruit as a background noise, rather than a lead, is a masterstroke. *46%. 500 bottles. ncf.*

Midleton Single Pot Still Single Cask 1991 cask no. 48750, dist Nov 91, bott Oct 12 db (96.5) n23.5 usual mix of beech honey, manuka honey and an indistinguishable fruit-like sweetness, somewhere between pear and strawberry; a fascinating blend of bourbon and rye styles; t24 just one of those deliveries you pray for: magnificent mouth feel and weight, just about perfect in fact. Then that unique iron rod of sweet barley couched in velvet. The salivation levels are off the scale, while the hard-nosed unmalted barley offers up their standard crisp honey tones. The enormous age is supported by a crypto-bourbon attack of liquorice and hickory; f23.5 softens, elongates and really kicks in with more bourbon/rye-style molasses, though this only adds weight to the strawberry and chocolate mousse towards the very death; b24.5 like the majority of Pot Still whiskeys, takes a little time to settle in the glass: always give it time to breath and come alive. When it finally does...just....wow!! 54.1%. ncf. Irish Distillers. Warehouse No. M09, exclusive to The Whisky Exchange.

Midleton Single Pot Still Single Cask 1994 cask no. 74060, dist 15 Nov 94 db (93) n23 t23 f23.5 b23.5. Probably a mod pot as opposed to a heavy one. A charming bottling, though if only they had been braver and gone for full cask strength... 46%. ncf. Irish Distillers. Exclusive to the Celtic Whiskey Shop.

Midleton Barry Crockett Legacy db (94) n23.5 t24.5 f22.5 b23.5. Another fabulous Pot Still, very unusual for its clever use of the varied ages of the oak to form strata of intensity. One very sophisticated whiskey. 46%. ncf.

Paddy Centenary Edition db (93) n22 t23.5 f24 b23.5. This 7-year-old Pure Pot Still whiskey really is a throwback. All Paddy's original whiskey from this era would have been from the old Midleton distillery which sits, in aspic, beside the one opened in 1975. Even with the likelihood of oats being in the mash in those days, still can't believe the original would have been quite as sweet on the palate – and soul – as this. 43%

Powers John's Lane Release Aged 12 Years db (96.5) n24 unmistakable. Unique. Utopian. Irish pure pot still at its most embracing and magnificent. That bizarre bipolar character of rock hard grain so at home in the company of silky, molten honey. Some light, non-specific fruit – a bit like boiled sweets in a candy shop. But a vague menthol note, too...; t25 as Irish whiskey goes: perfection! The delivery can come only from Irish Pot still – I have encountered it nowhere else. And it is a replay of the nose: soft, dissolve-on-the-palate honey and elsewhere strands of something much firmer – hardening more and more as it moves to the middle ground; f23.5 wonderful fade: a distant medium roast Java, the Lubec marzipan which you just knew would be coming; a little caramel; some orangey notes... b24 this is a style of Irish Pot Still I have rarely seen outside the blending lab. I had many times thought of trying to find some of this and bottling it myself. No need now. I think I have just tasted Irish Whiskey of the Year, and certainly one of the top five world whiskies of the year. 46%

Powers John's Lane Release Aged 12 Years bott 13 Nov 12 db (91) n24 t23.5 f21 b22.5. Researchers some time ago discovered the American accent is derived from an Irish one (and the Canadian from Scots). As pure Irish pot still is the foundation stone of all Irish whiskey, there is no little irony that so many aspects of this bottling is more recognisable as Kentuckian than it is from Cork. Only a slightly off beam cask undermines the finish a tad. Otherwise, superb. 46%. Irish Distillers.

Powers Signature Release bott code. L3065 db (91) n23.5 t22.5 f22 b23. When I first tasted pure pot still over three decades ago, virtually all that I came across was maturing in oloroso butts. Often, the quality of the casks was better than the spirit from the dilapidated distilleries which produced it. Here again sherry butts are of the highest quality. Maybe one is below par and this is evidenced, very vaguely, on the finish. But, overall, superb! 46%

Redbreast 12 Years Old db (96) n23.5 lively and firm, this one offering a gentle fruity swetness not too dissimilar to a rye, ironic as there is light bourbony kick off the oak, too; t24.5 wonderfully clipped and correct in delivery: firm at first - very firm!!! - but slowly the barley melts and light muscovado sugars dovetail with a flinty fruitiness and pillow-soft vanilla; incorrigibly mouthwatering and the build up of spices is just showing off; f24 remains spicy but clean, allowing a clear view of those varying barley tones drifting away; b24 Yess...!!! Back to its classically classy, brilliant best. No sulphur casks this time (unlike last year). Just juicy pot still all the way. An old loved one has returned... more gorgeous than ever. 40%. Irish Distillers.

Redbreast Aged 12 Years bott 7 Jan 13, bott code: L3007 db (89) n22 t23.5 f21.5 b22. This one took me aback. One of the softest Irish pot stills I have encountered, in or outside a lab. Delicious, but displaying very little of the trademark steel which sets this whiskey apart. 40%. Irish Distillers.

Redbreast Aged 12 Years Cask Strength batch B1/11 db (96) n24.5 just about the ultimate in Irish whiskey noses. Absolutely rock hard: you feel you could cut diamonds with an aroma like this. It is curiously fruity in that unique Irish Pot Still way, and not just from the obvious sherry involvement, yet shows clearly it's a relation to another whiskey style: American rye. A little hint of mint and lavender goes a long way and offers the only softness in this glorious bitter-sweet aroma; t24.5 my, oh my, oh my, oh my...one of those deliveries which takes your breath away and it is a few moments before you can compose yourself to think. Or, in my case, to compose myself to compose. The first thing is the sweetness which is never apparent on the nose: here we have the crunchiest Demerara sugar meeting even crunchier muscovado;

then a litany of varied fruit and quasi-rye juicy bits...mmmmmm; **f23** majestically long and moves in fabulously mysterious chocolatey ways - chocolate and raisin to be more precise - generating even more salivating moments right until the big chocolate sponge/sherry trifle finale. Late spices, even the faintest possible bitterness of a rogue treated sherry butt, though for once it does no serious damage, other than costing it a possible place in the world's top three. The vanillas come into action for the first time here, too...; **b24** this is Irish pot still on steroids. And sporting an Irish brogue as thick as my great great grandfather John Murray's. To think, had I not included Redbreast in Jim Murray's Irish Whiskey Almanac back in 1994, after it had already been unceremoniously scrapped and discontinued, while championing the then entirely unknown Irish Pot Still cause this brand would no longer have been with us. If I get run over by a bus tomorrow, at least I have that as a tick when St Peter is totting up the plusses and minuses... And with the cask strength, he might even give me two... *57.7%. ncf. Irish Distillers.*

Redbreast Aged 12 Years Cask Strength Edition batch B1/12 bott 4 Apr 12, bott code: L2095 db **(97)** n24.5 t24 f24 b24.5. For the sake of space, it is best I refer you to the tasting notes for Batch B1/11. Except here there is less fruit and absolutely no off notes. It is, as Irish whiskey is concerned, nigh-on perfection. *58.6%. ncf. Irish Distillers.*

Redbreast 15 Years Old db **(94)** n23 t24 f23 b24. For years I have been pleading for Irish Distillers to launch a pot still at 46%, natural colour and unchillfiltered. Well, I've got two out of three wishes. And what we have here is a truly great Irish whiskey and my pulse races in the certain knowledge it can get better still... *46%. ncf. France.*

Redbreast Aged 15 Years bott 12 Nov 12, bott code: L2317 db **(96)** n23.5 soft fruits from peaches to strawberry with boiled yam and molasses as back up. Rich, intense, vaguely spiced yet so, so gentle...; **t25** how does this happen...? Take all of the following ingredients but in their most delicate individual form: treacle, banana (or is it yam again?), liquorice, molasses, manuka honey, ulmo honey, maltshake, raisin, dates, vanilla....and stir until your arm drops off; **f23.5** just a thinner, less oily version of the delivery and middle; the vaguest hint of furriness; **b24** just so far better than the original 15-year-old it is hard to know where to start. You get the feeling there is wider stock to choose from and the casks are peaking, showing no sign of regressive traits. The delivery, though, is something you are unlikely ever to forget. *46%. ncf. Irish Distillers.*

⋰⋱ **Redbreast Aged 21 Years** db **(96)** n24 so rare to find age so obvious on a nose, yet so positive in all it does. The pot still is easily recognised with its unique firmness and playful bite, surrounded by a vague fruitiness and encrusted muscovado. But the honey astonishes: so deft and calming, offering acacia in sweetness and heather in floral weight; a half mark is lost though for a light dustiness revealing, surely, added caramel; **t25** perfection: at once the palate is met by a two-toned delivery - a voluptuous silkiness enwrapping steel-hard spine which a great pot still whiskey demands. The sugars melt first, then the malt and this opens the way for a delicate spice to throw a deft contrast against the cough-sweet style mentholated citrus and honey; **f23** concentrates now on the more simple aspects; the vanilla-honey balance, the fading malt, the chalkiness of the cask against the buzzing spice....though, sadly that buzzing goes on to reveal the weakest of sulphur inputs, and all the standard off-key bitterness which follows; **b24** I have tasted no shortage of 21-year-old pot still before in my career, but that was some time back when the whiskey in question was usually from the original Jameson distillery in Dublin, or Power's. I also managed to get my hands on some old stuff from the original Midleton as well as Tullamore Dew and few others. That old spirit had been made at a time when those distilleries were in the process of being closed down and the quality was nothing like it once was. This, I admit, is the first I can remember from Midleton's rebuilt distillery and it knocks the spots of the Jameson and Power's. Those did not have the balance or the insouciance so far as the honey involvement was concerned or the all-round world-class star quality which positively radiates from the glass. Hopefully this gentle giant amongst the world's truly great whiskies and near blue print for the perfect pot still Irish is here to stay. Only for the next bottling absolutely no need for the pointless caramel and the damaging sherry, both which contribute in tarnishing the dazzling sheen. There are times when less is so significantly more. *46%. ncf. WB15/417*

Green Spot (94.5) n23.5 t24 f23.5 b23.5. This honeyed state has remained a few years, and its shar ness has now been regained. Complex throughout. Unquestionably one of the world's greatest branded whiskies. *40%. Irish Distillers for Mitchell & Son, Dublin.*

Green Spot 10 Year Old Single Pot Still dist 1993 **(92)** n23 t22 f24 b23. Launched to celebrate the 200th anniversary of this wonderful Dublin landmark, this is bottled from three mixed bourbon casks of Irish Pot Still. The extra age has detracted slightly from the usual vitality of the standard Green Spot (an 8-y-o) but its quality still must be experienced. *40%*

Green Spot 12 Year Old Single Pot Still dist 1991 **(93)** n24 t24 f22 b23. A single cask restricted to exactly 200 bottles to mark the 200th anniversary of the grand old man of

Kildare Street, this is the first Middleton pot still I have seen at this strength outside of a lab. A one-off in every sense. *58%*

Irish Whiskey Society Single Cask Aged 17 Years cask no. 1038, dist 13 Jan 1995, bott 12 Jul 2012 **(91.5) n22 t23.5 f23 b23**. Even in the lab, I have encountered very few pure pot still whiskies of this age. The degree the sugars take over is a bit of a surprise. Delicious, to be sure. *55.2%. sc. Irish Distillers.*

Yellow Spot Aged 12 Years bourbon, sherry and Malaga casks db **(88.5) n23.5 t22.5 f20 b22.5**. If anything, just a shade too many wine casks used which somewhat drowns out the unique IP character. Reminds me of when Barry Walsh was working on the triple maturation theme of the Bushmills 16, probably about 15 years ago. Not until the very last days did all the components click. Just before then, it went through a phase like this (though obviously with malt, not IPS). Knowing current blender Billy Leighton as I do, I can see this whiskey improving in future batches as lessons are learned. not that there isn't already much to enjoy... *46%.*

OLD COMBER

Old Comber 30 Years Old Pure Pot Still (88) n23 t24 f20 b21. A classic example of a whiskey spending a few Summers too many in wood: increasing age doesn't equal excellence. That said, always very drinkable and early on positively sparkles with a stunning mouthfeel. Out of respect for the old I have made the markings for taste cover the first seven or eight seconds... *40%*

Single Malt
COOLEY

Connemara bott code L9042 db **(88) n23 t22.5 f20.5 b22**. One of the softest smoked whiskies in the world which though quite lovely gives the impression it can't make its mind up about what it wants to be. *40%*

Connemara Aged 8 Years db **(85) n22.5 t21.5 f20 b21**. Another Connemara lacking teeth. The peat charms, especially on the nose, but the complexity needs working on. *46%*

Connemara Aged 12 Years bott code L9024 db **(85.5) n23 t21.5 f20 b21**. The nose, with its beautiful orange, fruity lilt, puts the shy smoke in the shade. *40%*

Connemara Bog Oak bott 26 July 2011, batch V11/07 db **(93) n24 t24 f22.5 b22.5**. I guessed with the hand of Cooley blender Noel "Nosher" Sweeney (the man who can put away a roast dinner more quickly than most of us can successfully open a bar of Nutri Grain) behind this it would be anything other than bog standard...And Noel: well done on successfully getting your ancient ends away... *57.5%*

Connemara Cask Strength bott code L9041 db **(90) n21.5 t23 f22 b22.5**. A juicy negative of the standard bottling: does its talking on the palate rather than nose. Maybe an absence of caramel notes might have something to do with that. *57.9%*

Connemara Distillers Edition db **(86) n22 t22.5 f20 b21.5**. When I give whisk(e)y tastings around the world, I love to include Connemara. Firstly, people don't expect peated Irish. Secondly, their smoked whisky stock is eclectic and you never quite know what is going to come out of the bottle. This is a particularly tight, sharp style. No prisoners survived... *43%*

Connemara Single Cask 18 Years Old Amontillado Sherry Finish Solera Amontillado sherry cask, cask no. 155, dist 31 Aug 92, bott 12 May 92 db **(70) n18 t19 f16 b17**. Blast! I hoped to finally get through an entire day without sulphur for once. Failed! *46%. sc.*

Connemara Turf Mór Limited Edition Small Batch Collection bott code L10215 db **(94) n23.5 t23.5 f23.5 b23.5**. At Burnley FC, the wine served in their boardroom is The Claret's Claret, naturally. I will not be surprised to find this the whiskey on offer... The tasting notes to this just about perfectly match the ones above. *58.2%*

Cooley Poitín Origin Edition dist 26 July 2011, rotation 232/11 db **(92.5) n23.5 t23 f23 b23**. Full bloodied and rumbustious, this is high quality new make Irish that absolutely thumps the salivation button on palate. And, apparently, a mix of malted and unmalted barley in the traditional Irish Pot Still style....though this neither noses nor tastes anything like the new spirit from Middleton. The label waffles on about 1,000 years of Irish tradition. But the use of unmalted barley came into use only when distillers found a way of avoiding tax on the malted stuff. Were there taxes on alcohol in Ireland 1,000 years ago...? *65%*

Inish Turk Beg Maiden Voyage db **(91.5) n22 t23.5 f22.5 b22.5** Brooding and quite delicious. *44%*

Locke's Aged 8 Years bott code L9005 db **(88) n22.5 t22 f22 b21.5**. A beautiful malt at probably this distillery's optimum age. *40%*

Locke's Aged 8 Years Crock (92) n23 t24 f22 b23. Much, much better cask selection than of old: some real honey casks here. A crock of gold...! *40%*

Locke's Aged 9 Years Grand Crew cask no. 700, bott Sep 09 db **(91.5) n23 t23.5 f22.5 b22.5**. This took me back a few years. Having the three new Locke's lined up was like the days when I went through the Cooley warehouses looking for casks to put into Knappogue. This wasn't far off the style I was searching for. The right age, too. *58.9%. 233 bottles.*

Locke's Aged 10 Years Premier Crew cask no. 713, dist Feb 00, bott Jul 10 db **(88)** n22 t23 f21 b22. The cask does its best to try and spoil the barley fun. Here's a tip: stick to younger malts. Cooley is brilliant and relatively undiscovered at between seven and nine years. And there is less time for cask to bite back... *46%. Cooley for The Irish Whisky Society. 292 bottles.*

Tullamore Dew Single Malt 10 Years Old db **(91.5)** n23 t23 f22.5 b23. The best whiskey I have ever encountered with a Tullamore label. Furtively complex and daringly delicate. If only they could find a way to minimise the toffee... *40%. William Grant & Sons.*

The Tyrconnell bott code L9074 db **(86)** n21 t22 f22 b21. Sweet, soft, chunky and with a finely spice finale. *40%*

The Tyrconnell Aged 10 Years Madeira Finish bott code L8136 db **(91)** n23 t23 f22 b23. Not quite the award-winning effort of a few years back, as those lilting high notes which so complimented the baser fruit tones haven't turned up here. But remains in the top echelon and still much here to delight the palate. *46%*

The Tyrconnell Aged 10 Years Port Finish bott code L8167 db **(81.5)** n21.5 t21 f19 b20. Toffee all the way. *46%*

The Tyrconnell Aged 10 Years Sherry Finish bott code L8168 db **(84)** n22 t21 f21 b20. Like the Port Cask in this present series we have a thick malt that is friendly, toffeed and generally flat. This one, though, does have the odd peak of grapey richness, but you have to travel through a few plateaux to reach them. *46%*

Tyrconnell Aged 11 Years sherry cask finish, cask no. V09-10 #336 db **(95)** n23.5 my word! This bodes very well! Black pepper notes ginger up the intense marmalade and honey. Clean and brimming with undisguised intent; **t24** magnificent. The palate is left salivating and, if you are not careful, you are left dribbling as a glorious delivery of rich grape and sweetened orange paste offers the juicy introduction while a slow rumbling of ever-increasing spice shakes you to the core; **f23.5** long with a slow build up of oils and further fruit. Very late on a succession of bourbon-style honeycomb and molassed notes begin to make their mark; **b24** a thrilling virtuoso performance. Those who bought a bottle of this when they had the chance are unlikely to have regretted it. *58.5%. Bottled for Whisky Live 2011.*

The Tyrconnell Aged 14 Years cask no. 3179, rotation K92/25 db **(93)** n23 t23 f23 b24. By rotation, K92 means it was distilled in 1992. Which just proves this distillery really has come of age, because, make no mistake, this is a belter... *46%*

The Tyrconnell Single Cask 11 Year Old db **(95.5)** n23.5 sings the house style with a voice of rare clarity. The thin orange blossom honey is divine; **t25** of the great Irish whiskey malt deliveries for this and many years: perfection. The weight of the barley and oak cannot be bettered while the clarity of the malt and pink grapefruit is faultless; **f23** long, but concentrates purely on winding down the charming complexity of all that has gone before. And not an atom of bitterness from the oak...; **b24** well, if there weren't enough reasons to go to Dublin, you now have this... *46%. sc. Exclusive to the Celtic Whiskey Shop.*

The Tyrconnell Single Cask 11 Year Old Anima Negra Mallorcan Wine Cask Finish db **(86)** n21.5 t22 f21 b21.5. Loads going on here and those who like a boiled fruit candy feel to their malt will appreciate this one. *46%. sc. Exclusive to the Celtic Whiskey Shop.*

The Tyrconnell Aged 15 Years Single Cask cask no. 1854/92 db **(92.5)** n24 t23 f22.5 b23. Infinitely more comfortable in its aging skin a similar malt I tasted in Canada last year. *46%*

The Tyrconnell Aged 17 Years Single Cask cask no. 5306/92 db **(87)** n22 t22 f21.5 b21.5. Attractive barley all the way but barely deviates. *46%*

The Tyrconnell Aged 18 Years Single Cask cask no. 592/93 db **(94.5)** n24 wow! What a nose! A half hour aroma, with the myriad variances in the shades of honey and marmalade taking an age to unravel; **t23.5** melt-in-the-mouth delivery, but there is a superb sharpness which really allows the barley to stand out after all these years and those kumquat notes to positively fizz; the complexity quotient increases as the vanilla joins to the spices in beating out an oaky tattoo; **f23** lemon curd tart and marmalade mix now works alongside the spice; **b24** "beautiful in its simplicity" trills the label. Guys: are you kidding? Don't undersell yourselves. This is a very complex dram, indeed! And a fitting swan song to this wonderful distillery's final days of independence... *46%. sc.*

The Tyrconnell Single Cask cask no. 9571/1992 db **(85.5)** n23 t21 f20.5 b21. The wonderful citrus notes on the nose are swamped by the oak further down the line. There is no doubting the age of this Cooley! *46%*

Clonmel Peated Aged 8 Years (86) n22 t23 f20 b21. Take the toffee away and you would have one hell of an Irish. Claims to be "Pure Pot Still". It isn't (in Irish terms): it's malt. *40%*

Craoi na Mona Irish Malt Whiskey (68) n16 t18 f17 b17. I'm afraid my Gaelic is slipping these days: I assume Craoi na Mona means "Feinty, badly made smoky malt"... (that's the end of my tasting for the day...) *40%*

Glen Dimplex (88) n23 t22 f21 b22. Overall, clean and classically Cooley. 40%

Knappogue Castle 1990 (91) n22 t23 f22 b24. For a light whiskey this shows enormous complexity and depth. Genuine balance from nose to finish; refreshing and dangerously more-ish. Entirely from bourbon cask and personally selected and vatted by a certain Jim Murray. 40%. nc. Great Spirits.

Knappogue Castle 1991 (90) n22 t23 f22 b23. Offers rare complexity for such a youthful malt especially in the subtle battles that rage on the palate between sweet and dry, malt and oak and so on. The spiciness is a great foil for the malt. Each cask picked and vatted by the author. 40%. nc. Great Spirits.

Knappogue Castle 1992 (94) n23 t23 f24 b24. A different Knappogue altogether from the delicate, ultra-refined type. This expression positively revels in its handsome ruggedness and muscular body: a surprisingly bruising yet complex malt that always remains balanced and fresh – the alter-ego of the '90 and '91 vintages. I mean, as the guy who put this whiskey together, what do you expect? But it's not bad if I say so myself and was voted the USA's No. 1 Spirit. Virtually all vanished, but worth getting a bottle if you can find it (I don't receive a penny – I was paid as a consultant!). 40%. nc. Great Spirits.

Knappogue Castle 1993 (see Bushmills)

Knappogue Castle 1994 (see Bushmills)

Liquid Sun Cooley 1999 bott 2012 **(87)** n22 t22 f21.5 b21.5 awash with natural caramels and enjoyable in a horrible way...without the horrible. 53.2%. nc ncf sc. The Whisky Agency.

Magilligan Cooley Pure Pot Still Single Malt (91) n22 t22 f24 b23. A touch of honey for good measure ...or maybe not..!! 43%. Ian MacLeod Distillers.

Magilligan Irish Whiskey Peated Malt 8 Years Old (89) n21 t23 f22 b23. Such a different animal from the docile creature that formally passed as Magilligan peated. Quite lovely...and very classy. 43%. Ian MacLeod Distillers.

Merry's Single Malt (83) n20 t22 f20 b21. Ultra-clean barley rich nose is found on the early palate. The finish is flat, though. 40%

Michael Collins Irish Whiskey Single Malt db **(68)** n17 t18 f17 b16. Bloody hell, I thought. Didn't anyone get my message from last year? Apparently not – and it's our fault as the tasting notes above were accidentally edited out before they went in. Sorry. But the caramel in the latest bottling has been upped to take the whisky from deep gold to bronze. Making this among the most over-coloured single malt I have tasted in years. Please guys. For the love of whiskey. Please let us taste exactly what a great malt this could be. 40% (80 proof)

Milroy's of Soho Single Malt Cooley Aged 11 Years first fill bourbon, cask no. 3442, dist 22 Oct 01, bott 5 Nov 12 **(91)** n23.5 t23 f22.5 b23. Seriously enjoyable. Just what the doctor ordered...! 46%

Sainsbury's Single Malt Irish Whiskey bott code L10083/16 **(87.5)** n22 t22 f21.5 b22. Classic Cooley showing its big, malty depth. 40%

Sainsbury's Dún Léire Aged 8 Years Single Malt (95.5) n24 the score for this crept upwards as I investigated the aroma like the thermometer in my back garden on a bright Summer's day. The first thing to throw itself at you is Seville blood orange, backed up by a clever layering of barley at varying intensity and sweetness; the delicate oak acts as no more than a buffer in between; **t24** just about the perfect mouth feel: silky and melting on the palate. Again, it was an orangey citrus first to show, then again followed by some stunning malt. Everything dissolves: you don't have to do anything but close your eyes and enjoy, indeed: marvel...but it is hard work to stop yourself chewing; **f23.5** dries slightly, but the bitterness threatened on the label fails to materialise...thankfully. The fruit and barley ride off into the sunset in tandem; **b24** when I read "notes of bitter orange" on the label I feared the worst and expected a sulphurous whiskey. Well maybe there is a molecule or two hanging around, but so minor is so, it is impossible to tell exactly where it comes from. This is one of the great whiskeys from Cooley, ever. And as a supermarket Irish... unsurpassed. One of the surprise packages of world whisky for 2010. Magnificent. 40%. Cooley for Sainsbury's Supermarket.

Shannahan's (92) n23 t22 f24 b23. Cooley natural and unplugged: quite adorable. 40%

Slieve Foy Single Malt Aged 8 Years bott code L9108 **(88)** n23 t22.5 f21 b21.5. Never deviates from its delicate touch. 40%. Cooley for Marks & Spencer.

Vom Fass Cooley Irish Single Malt 8 Years Old (88) n22 t22.5 f21.5 b22. A very decent, if undemonstrative, example of the distillery at an age which well suits. 40%

The Wild Geese Single Malt (85.5) n21.5 t21 f22 b21. "A Rare Blend of Pure Aged Irish Malt Whiskies" says the front label. Yet it is a single malt. Confusing. And very unhelpful to a whisky public already being totally bamboozled by the bizarre and misguided antics of the Scotch Whisky Association. It is not a blend. It is a mixing of Cooley malt whiskey, as I understand it. The back label's "Smoother Because We Distil it Longer" is also a bit of a blarney. It's made in a pot still and whilst it is true that if you distil faster (by higher temperatures) you could well end up with "hot" whiskey, I am not aware of this being distilled at a significantly slower rate than at either Bushmills or Midleton. Or do they mean the cut of the run from the spirit still is longer, which would impart more oils – not all of them great? Just ignore the Wild Goose chase the labels send you on and enjoy the malt, with all its failings, for what it is (and this is pretty enjoyable in an agreeably rough and ready manner, though not exactly the stiff of Irish whiskey purists): which in this case for all its malt, toffee and delicate smoke, also appears to have more than a slight touch of feints - so maybe they were right all along...!!! 43%. *Cooley for Avalon.*

OLD KILBEGGAN

Kilbeggan Distillery Reserve Malt matured in quarter casks, batch no. 1, bott Jun 10 db **(89) n22.5 t22.5 b22.** An endearingly soft malt to see Kilbeggan distillery back into the whiskey world. Shame it has been reduced to 40%, as this one demanded to be at least 46% - indeed, preferably naked - and allowing those delicate, elegant but marginalised characters a chance to bloom. But welcome back...and I look forward to many an evening with me tasting you as you blossom, as I am sure you will. It has been nearly 20 years since I first discovered the beauty of Kilbeggan Distillery and I have countless times since dreamed of that moment. *40%. 1500 bottles. Available only in the distillery gift shop.*

The Spirit of Kilbeggan 1 Month (90.5) n22 t23 f23 b22.5. Wow!! They are really getting to grips with the apparatus. Full bodied and lush small still feel to this but radiating complexity, depth, barley and cocoa in equal measures. The development of the oils really does give this excellent length. Impressed! *65.5%*

The Spirit of Kilbeggan 1 Year (85) n20.5 t21 f22 b21.5. A veritable Bambi of a spirit: a typical one year old malt which, as hard as it tries, just can't locate its centre of gravity. Even so, the richness is impressive and some highly sugared chocolate mousse near the end is a treat. *62.7%*

The Spirit of Kilbeggan 2 Years (84) n20 t21 f22 b21. A tad raw and a little thin. There is some decent balance between oak and malt, but the overall feeling is that the still has not yet been quite mastered. *60.3%*

OLD BUSHMILLS

Bushmills Aged 10 Years matured in two woods db **(92.5) n23 t23 f23 b23.5.** Absolutely superb whiskey showing great balance and the usual Antrim 19th century pace with its favour development. The odd bottle of this I have come across over the last couple of years has been spoiled by the sherry involvement. But, this, as is usually the case, is absolutely spot on. 40%

Bushmills Select Casks Aged 12 Years married with Caribbean rum cask db **(95) n23** unusual moist rum and raisin cake effect: effective and just enough spice to deliver extra complexity. Just the very slightest hint of bourbon, too; **t24** adorable malt richness; biscuity and stupendously seasoned yet always remains fresh and mouthwatering. The sweetness is very cleverly controlled; **f24** there are just so many layers to this: the oak is a growing force, but restricts itself to a vanilla topping; **b24** one of the most complex Bushmills in living memory, and probably since it was established in 1784. 40%

Bushmills Aged 16 Years db **(71) n18 t21 f15 b17.** In my days as a consultant Irish whiskey blender, going through the Bushmills warehouses I found only one or two sulphur-treated butts. Alas, there are many more than that at play here. 40%

Bushmills Aged 21 Years db **(95.5) n24.5** this remains something of a Chinese puzzle on the nose: just how do all those different notes , sometimes soft and rounded, sometimes hard and angular, many of them fruity, manage to intertwine...yet never clash? And why can you never detach one without another clinging on to it. If Sherlock Holmes tried to solve it, this would be a three pipe conundrum...except the use of tobacco would ruin the experience. Just marvel at the greengage and physalis, the flaked vanilla and liquorice, the ulmo honey and hickory...so much else besides; **t24** as melt-in-the-mouth as a whiskey can be: amazingly juicy barley offers the cutting edge and lead while a plethora of delicate sugars dissolve on impact; the fruit is served as a perpetual mixed salad; **f23.5** this is where I am really impressed. Despite all the complexity of the nose and delivery, at the finish the Bushmills trademark flaky vanilla and delicate barley comes through...a signature unique to one distillery in the world; **b24** an Irish journey as beautiful as the dramatic landscape which borders the distillery. Magnificent. 40%

Clontarf Single Malt (90.5) n23 t23 f22 b22.5. Beautiful in its simplicity, this has eschewed complexity for delicious minimalism; *40%. Clontarf Irish Whiskey Co.*

⠿ **Connemara Original Peated Single Malt** db **(81.5) n21 t21.5 f19 b20.** It's been about a week since I last tasted a whisk(e)y at 40% abv...a shock to the system! Also a bit of a while since the first thing I got off the nose and last thing on the finish was caramel. Not the

Connemara I witnessed being launched in a blaze of defiant glory those decades back. This rather meek, pleasant, safe, lightly smoked version appears to have been sanitised. Today's Connemara it may sadly be. Original Connemara it is most certainly NOT...! 40%

The Irishman Single Malt bottle no. E2496 **(83) n20 t21 f21 b21.** Highly pleasant malt but the coffee and toffee on the finish underline a caramel-style whiskey which may, potentially, offer so much more. 40%. *Hot Irishman Ltd.*

The Irishman Single Malt 12 Years Old 1st fill bourbon barrels, casks no. 70691 & 70692, bott Nov 2012 **(88) n22 t22.5 f21.5 b22.** Very pleasant but, ultimately, docile thanks to the caramels at work. Putting my Irish blender's hat on for a moment, I think the whiskey would had offered a lot more had it been carefully selected first and second fill bourbon casks at play, rather than two very similar B1s. 43%. *ncf. Hot Irishman Ltd.*

⸪ **The Irishman Small Batch Single Malt** batch no. 1703/2013, sherry and bourbon casks **(86.5) n22 t22 f21 b21.5.** A pleasant, sticky malt with early fudge and raisin sweetness and then an over dependence on a single caramel note. 40% *WB15/403*

Knappogue Castle Aged 12 Years bourbon cask matured **(90) n23.5 t23 f21 b22.5.** The massive toffee influence deflects from the huge character elsewhere which springs a few surprises. 40%. *Castle Brands Group.*

Knappogue Castle Aged 16 Years sherry finished, dist 1994, bott 2010 **(84) n23 t23 f18 b20.** The nose: love it! Beautifully spiced, windfall apples piled into a barrow...just wonderful! The delivery: soft, chewy, deftly spiced again, even a sexy touch of Turkish Delight, with the malt having so much to say still....then, the finish. The finish...Oh dear, oh dear. Let's just say, the perfect malt to have before bedtime, because if this doesn't send you to sleep, nothing will. As flat and lifeless as the nose and delivery are rich with invention. And, to make matters worse, a sulphury sub plot bites with bitterness. What a shame. Someone took their eye off the ball, and a potential award has gone begging... 40%. *ncf.*

Knappogue Castle 1990 *(see Cooley)*
Knappogue Castle 1991 *(see Cooley)*
Knappogue Castle 1992 *(see Cooley)*

Knappogue Castle 1993 (91) n22 b22 f23 b24. A malt of exceptional character and charisma. Almost squeaky clean but proudly contains enormous depth and intensity. The chocolate finish is an absolute delight. Quite different and darker than any previous Knappogue but not dwarfed in stature to any of the previous three vintages. Created by yours truly. 40%. *nc. Great Spirits.*

Knappogue Castle 1994 lot no. L6 **(89) n23 t24 f20 b22.** A wonderful whiskey in the Knappogue tradition, although this one was not done by its creator. That said, it does have an Achilles heel: the finish. This is the most important bit to get right, especially as this is the oldest Knappogue yet. But not enough attention has been paid to getting rid of the oak-induced bitterness. 40%. *Castle Brands.*

Knappogue Castle 1995 bott 2007 **(88) n23 t22 f21 b22.** A charming malt showing Old Bushmills in very unusual colours. Lacking the charisma, clarity and complexity of the first Knappogues simply because they were designed to extol the virtues of young (8-year-old) malt. Naturally, extra oak has crept in here, forcing out – as it must – the sharpness and vitality of the barley. A decent effort, but perhaps more should have been done to keep out the aggressive bitterness. 40%

Single Grain
COOLEY

Greenore 6 Year Old bott code L9015 db **(89) n23.5 t22.5 f21 b22.** Very enjoyable whiskey. But two points: cut the caramel and really see the baby sing. And secondly, as a "Small Batch" bottling, how about putting a batch number on the label...? 40%. *Cooley.*

Greenore 8 Year Old bott code L8190 db **(86.5) n20 t22 f23 b21.5.** The vague hint of butyric on the nose is more than amply compensated by the gradual build up to something rather larger on the palate than you might have expected (and don't be surprised if the two events are linked). The corn oil is almost a meal in itself and the degree of accompanying sugar and corn flour is a treat. 40%. *Cooley.*

Greenore 10 Years Old dist 1997, bott 2007 db **(87.5) n22 f21.5 b22.** Well made grain and always enjoyable but perhaps not brought to its fullest potential due to some less than inspired oak. 40%

Greenore 15 Years Old bott code L8044 **(90) n23 t22.5 f22 b22.5.** The advent of the Kilbeggan 15 reminded us that there must be some grain of that age around, and here to prove it is a superb bottling of the stuff which, weirdly, is a lot better than the blend. Beautiful. 43%

Greenore 18 Years Old db **(91) n22.5 t22.5 f23 b23.** This continuous still at Cooley should be marked by the State as an Irish national treasure. One of the most complex grains you'll ever find, even when heading into uncharted territory like this one. 46%. *ncf. 4000 bottles.*

Blends

Bushmills 12 Years Old Distillery Reserve db **(86) n22.5 t22.5 f20 b21**. This version has gone straight for the ultra lush feel. For those who want to take home some 40% abv fruit fudge from the distillery. *40%*

Bushmills 1608 anniversary edition **(94) n23.5 t23.5 f23 b24**. This whiskey is talking an entirely different language to any Irish blend I have come across before, or any blend come to that. Indeed, nosed blind you'd not even regard it a blend: the malt calls to you like a Siren. But perhaps it is the crystal malt they have used here which is sending out such unique signals, helping the whiskey to form a thick cloak of roasty, toasty, burnt toffeed, bitter-sweetness which takes your breath away. What a fabulous whiskey! And whether it be a malt or blend, who cares? Genius whiskey is genius whiskey. *40%*

Bushmills 1608 400th Anniversary (83) n21 t21.5 f20 b20.5. Thin-bodied, hard as nails and sports a peculiarly Canadian feel. *46%. Diageo.*

⋅⋰⋅ **Bushmills 1608** db **(87) n22 t23 f20 b22**. A blend which, through accident, evolution or design, has moved a long way in style from when it was first launched. More accent on fruit though, predictably, the casks aren't quite what they once were. Ignoring the furriness on the finish, there is much to enjoy on the grape-must nose and how the fruit bounces off the rigid grain on delivery. *46%*

Bushmills Black Bush (91) n23 t23 f21.5 b23.5. This famous old blend may be under new management and even blender. But still the high quality, top-notch complexity rolls around the glass and your palate. As beautiful as ever. *40%*

Bushmills Original (80) n19 t21 f20 b20. Remains one of the hardest whiskeys on the circuit with the Midleton grain at its most unflinching. There is a sweeter, faintly maltier edge to this now while the toffee and biscuits qualities remain. *40%*

Cassidy's Distiller's Reserve bott code L8067 **(84.5) n21.5 t22 f20 b21**. Some salivating malt on flavour-exploding delivery, but all else tame and gentle. *40%. Cooley.*

Clancey's bott code L8025 **(87) n22 t21 f22 b22**. Remains an excellent blend for all the toffee. The spice balance excels. *40%. Cooley for Wm Morrison.*

Clontarf Classic Blend (81) n20 t22 f19.5 b19.5. A hard as nails blend softened only by the heavy use of caramel which, though chewy, tends to obliterate any complexity from elsewhere. Ouch! 40%. Castle Brands Group.

Delaney's (85.5) n20 t21.5 f22 b22. Young, clean, citrusy, refreshing and proud. Thoroughly enjoyable and dangerously moreish. *40%. Cooley for Co-operative UK.*

Delaney's Special Reserve (84) n21.5 t20.5 f22 b21. An attractive blend with a big late spicy blast. The toffee dominates for long periods. *40%. Cooley for Co-operative Group.*

Feckin Irish Whiskey (81) n20 t21 f20 b20. Tastes just about exactly the feckin same as the Feckin Strangford Gold... *40%. The Feckin Drinks Co.*

Golden Irish bott code L7064 **(93) n23 t23 f23.5 b23.5**. By far one of the most enjoyable Irish blends around. Simple, but what it does, it does deliciously well. *40%. Cooley.*

The Irishman Rare Cask Strength bott 10 **(81.5) n20 t22.5 f19 b20**. Fabulous crescendo of weighty malt on delivery. But just too much bitterness and toffee hits this one. *53%.*

The Irishman Rare Cask Strength bott 2011 **(94.5) n23 t24 f23.5 b24**. The back labels of Hot Irishman whiskeys are always entertaining, not least for their unique use of the English language. A free Jim Murray's Whisky Bible 2012 for the first person to e-mail in and tell us what the cock-up is on this label. Back to the whiskey: this blend of malt whisky and Pure Irish Pot still, is a mildly more lilting, more lightly coloured, version of Writer's Tears. And, just like the first bottling, a must-have stunner. *53%. Hot Irishman. 2400 bottles.*

The Irishman Superior Irish Whiskey bott code L6299L059 **(93) n23 t23 f23 b24**. What a quite wonderful blend: not of the norm for those that have recently come onto the market and there is much more of the Irish Distillers about this than most. Forget about the smoke promised in the tasting notes on the label...it gives you everything else but. And that is one hell of a lot!! *40%. Hot Irishman Ltd.*

Jameson (95) n24.5 Swoon...bizarrely shows even more Pot Still character than the Redbreast I tasted yesterday. Flinty to the point of cracking. The sherry is there but on reduced terms, allowing the firm grain to amplify the unmalted barley: truly brilliant; **t24** mouth-watering delivery and then wave upon wave of diamond-hard barley and grain; the odd eclectic layer of something sweetish and honeyed, but this is eye-watering stuff; **f22.5** an annoying touch of caramel creeps in, costing points, but even beyond that you still cannot other than be charmed by the layering of cocoa, barley and light grape; **b24** I thought I had detected in bottlings I had found around the world a very slight reduction in the Pot Still character that defines this truly classic whiskey. So I sat down with a fresh bottle in more controlled conditions...and was blown away as usual. The sharpness of the PS is vivid and unique; the supporting grain of the required crispness. Fear not: this very special whiskey remains in stunning, truly wondrous form. *40%*

Jameson 12 Years Old Special Reserve (88) n22 t23 f21 b22. Much more sherry than of late and the pot still makes inroads, too. Just needs to lose some of the caramel effect; *40%*

Jameson 18 Years Old Limited Reserve eighth batch bott code JJ18-8 (91) n23 t22.5 f22.5 b22.5. The astonishing degree of bourbon on the nose thankfully doesn't make it to the palate where Ireland rather than Kentucky rules. *40%*

Jameson 18 Years Old Limited Reserve bott 13.07.12 (89.5) n22 t23.5 f22 b22. This guy has changed shape since the last time I tasted it. Toffee has a far bigger say these days. *40%.*

Jameson Black Barrel (91.5) n23 t23 f22.5 b23. Here's the problem faced by any Jameson blender: the column still grain from Midleton is the hardest on the palate made anywhere in the world. So how do you get it to mould into what you want? Usually you can't, so you have to make the whiskeys around it reflect and deflect for maximum effect. And that's what's going on here: a brittle whisky where the pot still element is magnified very cleverly indeed. Lovely stuff: New Yorkers are a lucky bunch! *40%. NY exclusive.*

Jameson Gold Reserve (88) n22 t23 f20 b22. Enjoyable, but so very different: an absolute re-working with all the lighter, more definitively sweeter elements shaved mercilessly while the thicker oak is on a roll. Some distance from the masterpiece it once was. *40%*

Jameson Rarest 2007 Vintage Reserve (96) n24.5 the crispest, cleanest, most beautifully defined of all the Jameson family: orange peel, hickory, spotted dog pudding, lavender – they're all there mushed around and in near-perfect proportions; t24 ditto the arrival with the mouth puckering under the onslaught of very old Pot Still: the bitter-sweet sharpness one would expect from this is there in spades; oak present and correct and edged in thin muscovado layer; f23.5 vanilla by the barrel-load, pithy fruit and softly spiced barley b24 is this the whiskey where we see a blender truly come of age. Tall green hats off to Billy Leighton who has, as all the better blenders did in the past, worked his way from quality-testing barrels on the dumping room floor to the lab. With this stupendous offering we have a blender in clover for he has earned his Golden Shamrocks. If the blending alone wasn't stellar enough, then making this a 46%, non chill-filtered offering really does put the tin hat on it (so Billy: you really have been listening to me over the years...!!!) This is truly great whiskey, among the pantheon of the world's finest. *46%*

Jameson Signature Reserve (93) n23.5 t23.5 f22.5 b23.5. Be assured that Signature, with its clever structuring of delicate and inter-weaving flavours, says far more about the blender, Billy Leighton, than it does John Jameson. *40%. Irish Distillers.*

Kellan American oak cask (84) n21 t22 f20 b21. Safe whisky which is clean, sweet and showing many toffeed attributes. Decent spices, too. *40% (80 Proof). Cooley.*

Kilbeggan bott code L7091 (86) n21 t22 f21.5 b21.5. A much more confident blend by comparison with that faltering one of the last few years. Here, the malts make a significant drive towards increasing the overall complexity and gentle citrus style. *40%. Cooley.*

Kilbeggan 15 Years Old bott code L7048 (85.5) n21.5 t22 f21 b21. My word! 15 years, eh? How time flies! And on the subject of flying, surely I have winged my way back to Canada and am tasting a native blend. No, this is Irish albeit in sweet, deliciously rounded form. However, one cannot help feeling that the dark arts have been performed, as in an injection of caramel, which, as well as giving that Canadian feel has also probably shaved off some of the more complex notes to middle and finish. Even so, a sweet, silky experience. *40%. Cooley.*

Kilbeggan 18 Year Old db (89) n23 t21.5 f22.5 b22. Although the impressive bottle lavishly claims "From the World's Oldest Distillery" I think one can take this as so much Blarney. It certainly had my researcher going, who lined this up for me under the Old Kilbeggan distillery, a forgivable mistake and one I think he will not be alone in making. This, so it appears on the palate, is a blend. From the quite excellent Cooley distillery, and it could be that whiskey used in this matured at Kilbeggan... which is another thing entirely. As for the whiskey: apart from some heavy handedness on the toffee, it really is quite a beautiful and delicate thing. *40%*

Kilgeary bott code L8063 (79) n20 t20 f19 b20. There has always, and still proudly is, something strange about this blend. Cold tea on the nose and a bitter bite to the finish, sandwiches a brief flirtation with something sweet. *40%. Cooley.*

Locke's bott code L8056 (85.5) n21 t22 f21.5 b21. Now, there you go!! Since I last really got round to analysing this one it has grown from a half-hearted kind of a waif to something altogether more gutsy and muscular. Sweeter, too, as the malts and grains combine harmoniously. A clean and pleasant experience with some decent malt fingerprints. *40%. Cooley.*

Michael Collins A Blend (77) n19 t20 f19 b19. Michael Collins was known as the "big fellow". This pleasant, impressively spiced dram, might have enjoyed the same epithet had it not surrendered to and then been strangled by caramel on the finish. *40% (80 proof). Cooley.*

Midleton Distillery Reserve (85) n22 t22 f20 b21. A whiskey which, for all its muscovado sweetness offers some memorable barley moments. *40%. Irish Distillers Midleton Distillery only. Changes character slightly with each new vatting. This one is some departure.*

Midleton Very Rare 1984 (70) n19 t18 f17 b16. Disappointing with little backbone or balance. *40%. Irish Distillers.*

Midleton Very Rare 1985 (77) n20 t20 f18 b19. Medium-bodied and oily, this is a big improvement on the initial vintage. *40%. Irish Distillers.*

Midleton Very Rare 1986 (79) n21 t20 f18 b20. A very malty Midleton richer in character than previous vintages. *40%. Irish Distillers.*

Midleton Very Rare 1987 (77) n20 t19 f19 b19. Quite oaky at first until a late surge of excellent pot still. *40%. Irish Distillers.*

Midleton Very Rare 1988 (86) n23 t21 f21 b21. A landmark MVR as it is the first vintage to celebrate the Irish pot-still style. *40%. Irish Distillers.*

Midleton Very Rare 1989 (87) n22 t22 f22 b21. A real mouthful but has lost balance to achieve the effect. *40%. Irish Distillers.*

Midleton Very Rare 1990 (93) n23 t23 f24 b23. Astounding whiskey: one of the vintages every true Irish whiskey lover should hunt for. *40%. Irish Distillers.*

Midleton Very Rare 1991 (76) n19 t20 f19 b18. After the Lord Mayor's Show, relatively dull and uninspiring. *40%. Irish Distillers.*

Midleton Very Rare 1992 (84) n20 t20 f23 b21. Superb finish with outstanding use of feisty grain. *40%. Irish Distillers.*

Midleton Very Rare 1993 (88) n21 t22 f23 b22. big, brash and beautiful – the perfect way to celebrate the 10th-ever bottling of MVR. *40%. Irish Distillers.*

Midleton Very Rare 1994 (87) n22 t22 f21 b22. Another different style of MVR, one of amazing lushness. *40%. Irish Distillers.*

Midleton Very Rare 1995 (90) n23 t24 b21 b22. They don't come much bigger than this. Prepare a knife and fork to battle through this one. Fabulous. *40%. Irish Distillers.*

Midleton Very Rare 1996 (82) n21 t22 f19 b20. The grains lead a soft course, hardened by subtle pot still. Just missing a beat on the finish, though. *40%. Irish Distillers.*

Midleton Very Rare 1997 (83) n22 t21 f19 b21. The piercing pot still fruitiness of the nose is met by a countering grain of rare softness on the palate. Just dies on the finish when you want it to make a little speech. Very drinkable. *40%. Irish Distillers.*

Midleton Very Rare 1999 (89) n21 t23 f22 b23. One of the maltiest Midletons of all time: a superb blend. *40%. Irish Distillers.*

Midleton Very Rare 2000 (85) n22 t21 f21 b21. An extraordinary departure even by Midleton's eclectic standards. The pot still is like a distant church spire in an hypnotic Fen landscape. *40%. Irish Distillers.*

Midleton Very Rare 2001 (79) n21 t20 f18 b20. Extremely light but the finish is slightly on the bitter side. *40%. Irish Distillers.*

Midleton Very Rare 2002 (79) n20 t22 f18 b19. The nose is rather subdued and the finish is likewise toffee-quiet and shy. There are some fabulous middle moments, some of flashing genius, when the pot still and grain combine for a spicy kick, but the finish really is lacklustre and disappointing. *40%. Irish Distillers.*

Midleton Very Rare 2003 (84) n22 t22 f19 b21. Beautifully fruity on both nose and palate (even some orange blossom on aroma). But the delicious spicy richness that is in mid launch on the tastebuds is cut short by caramel on the middle and finish. A crying shame, but the best Midleton for a year or two. *40%. Irish Distillers.*

Midleton Very Rare 2004 (82) n21 t21 f19 b21. Yet again caramel is the dominant feature, though some quite wonderful citrus and spice escape the toffeed blitz. *40%.*

Midleton Very Rare 2005 (92) n23 t24 f22 b23. OK, you can take this one only as a rough translation. The sample I have worked from here is from the Irish Distillers blending lab, reduced to 40% in mine but without caramel added. And, as Midleton Very Rares always are at this stage, it's an absolute treat. Never has such a great blend suffered so in the hands of colouring and here the chirpiness of the pot still and élan of the honey (very Jameson Gold Label in part) show just what could be on offer given half the chance. Has wonderful natural colour and surely it is a matter of time before we see this great whiskey in its natural state. *40%*

Midleton Very Rare 2006 (92) n22 t24 f23 b23. As raw as a Dublin rough-house and for once not overly swamped with caramel. An uncut diamond. *40%*

Midleton Very Rare 2007 (83) n20 t22 f20 b21. Annoyingly buffeted from nose to finish by powering caramel. Some sweeter wisps do escape but the aroma suggests Canadian and insufficient Pot Still gets through to make this a Midleton of distinction. *40%. Irish Distillers*

Midleton Very Rare 2008 (88.5) n22 t23 f21.5 b22. A dense bottling which offers considerably more than the 2007 Vintage. Attractive, very drinkable and without the caramel it might really have hit the heights. *40%. Irish Distillers.*

Midleton Very Rare 2009 (95) n24 oh, wow! the best post bottling nose I have ever found on a Midleton, though a few pre-bottlings have exceeded it in grace. Just. This is the fruitiest I can remember, for sure, with a wonderful sherry trifle feel, only with the extra firmness of

Irish pot still. A little avocado pear creaminess also goes a long way; **t24** it is that creaminess which shows first on delivery, alongside a plethora of crisp, dark sugary notes which appear to shadow the pot still character; the star is the contra deal between the soft oils and the rock hard pot still...stunning **f23** remains clean with far more complexity than a Midleton usually retains; the spices are busy and appear to pulse and vary in intensity; **b24** I've been waiting a few years for one like this to come along. One of the most complex, cleanest and least caramel-spoiled bottlings for a good few years and one which makes the pot still character its centre piece. A genuine celebration of all things Midleton and Barry Crockett's excellence as a distiller in particular. 40%. *Irish Distillers.*

Midleton Very Rare 2010 (84) **n21 t22 f20 b21.** A case of after the Lord Mayor's Show. Chewy and some decent sugars. But hard to make out detail through the fog of caramel. 40%

Midleton Very Rare 2011 (81.5) **n22.5 t20 f19 b20** Another disappointing version where the colour of its personality has been compromised for the sake of the colour in the bottle. A dullard of a whiskey, especially after the promising nose. 40%. *Irish Distillers.*

Midleton Very Rare Irish Whisky 2012 db (89.5) **n22 t23 f22 b22.5.** Much more like it! After a couple of dud vintages, here we have a bottling worthy of its great name & heritage. 40%.

⋰ **Midleton Very Rare Irish Whisky 2014** db (78.5) **n20.5 t22 f17 b19.** Hmmm. Somehow we have missed the 2013 Midleton Very Rare...only the second of all the Midleton Rares to get away - ever. We shall try to remedy that for Jim Murray's Whisky Bible 2016. Must say how odd it looks to see Brian Nation's signature scrawled across the label and not Barry Crockett's. Also, I was a bit worried by this one when I saw the depth of orange hue to this whiskey. Sadly, my fears were pretty well founded. Toffee creaks from every corner making for a mainly flat encounter with what should be an uplifting Irish. Some lift at about the midway point when something, probably pot still, throws off the shackles of its jailer and emerges briefly with spice. But all rather too little, especially in the face of a dull, disappointingly flawed, fuzzy finale. Midleton Very Rare should be, as the name implies, a lot, lot better than this safe but flabby, personality bypassed offering. The most frutrating aspect of this is that twice I have tasted MVR in lab form just prior to bottling. And both were quite stunning whiskeys. That was until the colouring was added in the bottling hall. 40% WB15/416

Millars Special Reserve bott code L8069 (86) **n21 t22 f21.5 b21.5.** Now that's some improvement on the last bottling of this I found, with spices back with abandon and grains ensuring a fine mouthfeel. Even the chocolate fudge at the death is a treat. 40%. *Cooley.*

Morrisons Irish Whiskey bott code L10028 (78) **n19 t20 f19 b20.** Sweet, pleasant and inoffensive. 40%. *Wm Morrison Supermarket.*

Paddy (74) **n18.5 t20 f17.5 b18.** Cleaned its act up a little. Even a touch of attractive citrus on the nose and delivery. But where does that cloying sweetness come from? As bland as an Irish peat bog but, sadly, nothing like so potentially tasty. 40%. *Irish Distillers.*

Powers (91) **n23 t24 f22 b22.** Is it any coincidence that in this bottling the influence of the caramel has been significantly reduced and the whiskey is getting back to its old, brilliant self? I think not. Classic stuff. 40%. *Irish Distillers.*

Powers Gold Label (87) **n22 t22 f21 b22.** The solid pot still, the very DNA of what made Powers, well, Powers is vanishing in front of our very noses. Yes, still some pot still around, but nothing like so pronounced in the way that made this, for decades, a truly one-off Irish and one of the world greats. Still delightful and with many charms but the rock hard pot still effect is sadly missed. What is going on here? 40%. *Irish Distillers.*

Powers Gold Label db (93) **n23 t24 f22.5 b23.5.** Now, that's much more like it! The last Gold Label I had was pleasant, but just so not like a Power's in style. This is right back on track. Nothing to do with the extra alcohol. It's to do with the extra pot still, which here acts as backbone and muscle. Cut the caramel down, and it'd be a real world superstar whiskey. 43.2%

Redbreast Blend (88) **n23 t23 f20 b22.** Really impressed with this one-off bottling for Dillons the Irish wine merchants. Must try and get another bottle before they all vanish. 40%.

Sainsbury's Blended Irish Whiskey (86.5) **n22 t22 f21 b21.5.** A beautifully relaxed blend showing pretty clearly – literally, thanks to an admirable lack of colouring - just how good the Cooley grain whiskey is even at no great age. Clean with a deceptively busy and intense flavour profile. Far too good for the cola the back label says this should go with... 40%. *UK.*

St Patrick bott code L030907 (77) **n19 t20 f19 b19.** Good grief! No prisoners here as we have either a bitter oakiness or mildly cloying sweetness, rarely working in tandem. A few gremlins for the Kremlin. 40%. *Cooley for Russia.*

Strangford Gold (81) **n20 t21 f20 b20.** A simplistic, exceptionally easy drinking blend with high quality grain offering silk to the countering spice but caramel flattens any malt involvement. 40%. *The Feckin Drinks Co.*

The Teeling Whiskey Company Poitin (85) **n21 t22 f21 b21.** Intense and makes the eyes water to the required levels. Much cleaner, if not as sweet, though a lot safer than the illegal stuff I've tasted over there for the last 20-odd years! 61.5%

Tesco Special Reserve Irish Whiskey bott code L8061 (89.5) n21.5 t23.5 f22 b22.5. A cracker of a blend which allows the malts full scope to do their juicy bit. Possibly more malt than usual for a Cooley blend, but as they say: every little bit helps. 40%. *Cooley.*

Tullamore Dew (85) n22 t21.5 f20.5 b21. The days of the throat being savaged by this one appear to be over. Much more pot still character from nose to finish and the rough edges remain, attractively, just that. 40%. *Campbell & Cochrane Group.*

Tullamore Dew 10 Years Old (81.5) n21 t21.5 f19 b20. A bright start from this new kid on the Tullamore block. Soft fruit and harder pot still make some kind of complexity, but peters out at the death. 40%. *Campbell & Cochrane Group.*

Tullamore Dew 12 Years Old (84.5) n21.5 t21.5 f20 b21.5. Silky thanks to some excellent Midleton grain: there are mouthwatering qualities here that make the most of the soft spices and gentle fruit. An improved whiskey, if still somewhat meek and shy. 40%. *Campbell & Cochrane Group.*

Tullamore Dew Black 43 (85) n19 t22 f22.5 b21.5. "Black". Now there's an original name for a new whiskey. Don't think it'll catch on, personally: after all, who has ever heard of a whisky being called "This or That" Black...?? But the whiskey might. Once you get past the usual Tullamore granite-like nose, here even more unyielding than usual, some rather engaging and complex (and especially spicy) things happen, though the caramel does its best to neuter them. 43%. *William Grant & Sons.*

Tullamore Dew Heritage (78) n20 t21 f18 b19. Tedious going with the caramel finish a real turn off. 40.0%. *Campbell & Cochrane Group.*

Waitrose Irish Whiskey (86.5) n21.5 t22 f21.5 b21.5. Cooley's grain whiskey, about as good a grain made anywhere in the world, is in fine voice here. Pity some toffee stifles it slightly. 40%

Walker & Scott Irish Whiskey "Copper Pot Distilled" (83) n20 t22 f20 b21. A collectors' item. This charming, if slightly fudgy-finished blend was made by Cooley as the house Irish for one of Britain's finest breweries. Sadly, someone put "Copper Pot Distilled" on the label, which, as it's a blend, can hardly be the case. And even if it wasn't a blend, would still be confusing in terms of Irish whiskey, there not being any traditional Irish Pot Still, that mixture of malted and unmalted barley. So Sam's, being one of the most traditional brewers in Britain, with the next bottling changed the label by dropping all mention of pot still. Top marks, chaps! The next bottling can be seen below. 40%. *Sam Smith's.*

Walker & Scott Irish Whiskey (85) n21 t22 f21 b21. Oddly, sharper grain has helped give his some extra edge through the toffee. A very decent blend. 40%

The Wild Geese Classic Blend (80.5) n20 t21 f19.5 b19. Easy going, pretty neutral and conservative. If you are looking for zip, zest and charisma you've picked the wrong goose (see below). 40%. *Cooley for Avalon.*

The Wild Geese Limited Edition Fourth Centennial (93) n23 t23.5 f23 b23.5. A limited edition of unlimited beauty. One of the lightest, subtle, intriguing and quite simply disarming Irish whiskeys on the market. As a bird and whiskey lover, this is one goose that I shall be looking out for. 43%. *Cooley for Avalon.*

The Wild Geese Rare Irish (89.5) n22 t23 f22 b22.5. Just love this. The Cooley grain is working sublimely and dovetails with the malt in the same effortless way wild geese fly in perfect formation. A treat. 43%. *Cooley for Avalon.*

Writers Tears (93) n23.5 t24 f22 b23.5. Now that really was different. The first mix of pure Pot Still and single malt I have knowingly come across in a commercial bottling, but only because I wasn't aware of the make up of last year's Irishman Blend. The malt, like the Pot Still, is, I understand from proprietor Bernard Walsh, from Midleton, but the two styles mixed shows a remarkably similar character to when I carried out an identical experiment with pure pot still and Bushmills the best part of a decade ago. A success and hopefully not a one off. Which is more than I can say for the label, a whiskey collectors – sorry, collector's – item in its own right. There is a wonderfully Irish irony that a whiskey dedicated to Ireland's extraordinary literary heritage should be represented by a label, even a brand name, so punctually inept; it's almost brilliant. The reason for the Writers (sic) Tears, if from the spirits of James Joyce, Samuel Beckett, George Bernard Shaw, Oscar Wilde and perhaps even Maurice Walsh, author of The Quiet Man whose even quieter grandson, Barry, became a legendary blender at Irish Distillers, will be open to debate: we will never know whether they laughed or cried. As far as the actual whiskey is concerned, though, I am sure they, to a man, would have no hesitation to pen the most luminous and positive critiques possible. 40%. *Writers Tears Whiskey Co.*

Writer's Tears Cask Strength bott 2011 (90.5) n23 t22 f22.5 b23. Sometimes seems a rabble of whiskey, with the flavours and shapes never quite deciding where it wants to go. But the randomness of the style is also a strength as you are entertained from first to last, though the caramels do keep the lid on some of the more honeyed moments. And memo to brand proprietor Bernard Walsh: only one mistake on your back label this time... 53%.

American Whiskey

That green – and slightly blue – baized undulating block of limestone known as Kentucky is not much known for high magnitude earthquakes.

It may get the odd tremor to test the loosest tiles, but they are very few and far between. However, the State's whiskey industry was rocked by a couple of massive jolts just seven weeks apart when two of the all-time giants of bourbon were lost to us.

Between them Elmer T Lee and Lincoln Henderson had clocked up over 100 years' experience in the making and blending of bourbon; and in Linc's case the shockwaves were felt as far as Tennessee where he had worked for decades on Jack Daniels.

Though Elmer was 93 and Lincoln 75, both treated their retirements almost as if they had never happened and continued working to the very end. Elmer kept his hand in by once a week visiting the blending lab at Buffalo Trace which, as the George T Stagg distillery on the banks of the Kentucky River in his home town of Frankfort, he had joined in 1949. There, for the last few years, he would sample the possibles and probables of what had become his signature brand, Elmer T Lee single barrel. Tasting samples was nothing new to Elmer, even though he was a technical guy with an engineering degree who had worked his way from the maintenance department to the stillroom by becoming distillery manager in 1969. He made his last visit a fortnight before his death. But his legacy to the distillery – indeed the industry and whisky lovers everywhere – was bringing out the first regular single barrel brand by a whisky company, as opposed to an independent bottler. In 1985 he officially retired from the distillery, by then known as Ancient Age. But a year earlier he had pioneered the Blanton's brand, a labour-intensive, hand-bottled single barrel bourbon which proved to be the pathfinder for much-needed high quality Kentucky whiskey when the industry was at its nadir.

After his retirement Elmer could often be spotted under his trademark flat cap doing this and that around the distillery, especially in the warehouses and lab. He was as much a part of the historic building's structure as any of the salmon pink bricks which form the eclectic contours of an entire nation's distilling heritage. Indeed, there was something touchingly fitting yet other worldly that just two days after his death on July 16th 2013 Buffalo Trace were at liberty to announce that the distillery had the honour of having been designated a National Historical Landmark, the highest and rarest award for any structure or place in the USA. For we who had spent a long time in the whiskey industry already knew that this funny, warm, articulate, whisky-passionate, highly professional and deeply knowledgeable old gent had been a living National Historical Landmark for a great many years.

Where Elmer was the consummate traditionalist to the last, Lincoln Henderson, by contrast, ended his long and distinguished career blending avant-garde whiskeys for the new family concern, Angel's Envy. Linc and I spent quite a lot of time together in the 1990s where he took me through his work in Kentucky for Brown-Forman's bourbon brands and in Tennessee with Jack Daniels, where I found him to be a blender by instinct, the best type of them all. But we spent many months together as an old pile of limestone bricks on McCracken Pike near Frankfort was miraculously transformed back into the historic Labrot and Graham distillery, later to be renamed Woodford Reserve. And with distillery manager Dave Scheurich we would raid the warehouses at random times during day and night, especially night, to test how the first, embryonic spirit was maturing.

Being in Linc Henderson's company was, for me, the highlight of over two decades in the world whisky industry. A smile and Linc were always in close proximity, his gentle voice never lost its Oklahoma warmness and his charm, wit, one-liners and innate kindness meant you always looked forward to being around him. Linc was even an honorary grand-dad to my son James while I lived in Kentucky for a while; and he treated him like his own.

After his retirement in 2004 Linc was always a little perplexed and disappointed that the bourbon industry did not make use of his vast knowledge and insight. Instead it was the Japanese, through Suntory, who deployed him to spread the word of their whiskies around the globe, a strange situation which was not lost on him. Especially after, back in 1994, I gave him his first-ever taste of a peated whisky... which he instantly loathed. After one judging session at the International Wine and Spirit Competition some years later I took Linc on a drive around my native Surrey and mischievously asked him how he liked Suntory's more heavily peated malts. With trademark Henderson timing he replied without skipping a beat: "What peat?" The crinkled, disguised smile below his manicured moustache said it all.

The pity was that just weeks before his passing I wrote the piece in Bible Thumping criticising the type of whisky he was creating for the Angel's Envy. I had planned to see Linc that November to debate with him his thinking. What was certain, no matter how far apart we may have been in the argument, it would have been one carried out amid a flurry of laughs and smiles.

I make no apology for admitting that I loved that man as he was unquestionably the kindest, most gentle and decent person I have met in the last three decades. And the Angel's Envy now is that there will be none of them up there able to hold a candle to him.

A year on from their loss I still deeply miss Elmer and Linc. Two very special, dearly loved, friends who painstakingly went out of their way to teach me so much. And who between them raised the bar in American whiskey to an extent that has never been fully recorded or appreciated. But in time, that most vital ingredient in all things whiskey, surely will.

Bardstown
  Heaven Hill
  Tom Moore
Frankfort
  Buffalo Trace

Woodford Reserve
Louisville
  Early Times
  Bernheim
  Stitzel Weller

Bourbon Distilleries

Bourbon confuses people. Often they don't even realise it is a whiskey, a situation not helped by leading British pub chains, such as Wetherspoon, whose bar menus list "whiskey" and "bourbon" in separate sections. And if I see the liqueur Southern Comfort listed as a bourbon one more time I may not be responsible for my actions.

Bourbon is a whiskey. It is made from grain and matured in oak, so really it can't be much else. To be legally called bourbon it must have been made with a minimum of 51% corn and matured in virgin oak casks for at least two years. Oh, and no colouring can be added other than that which comes naturally from the barrel.

Where it does differ, from, say Scotch, is that the straight whiskey from the distillery may be called by something other than that distillery name. Indeed, the distillery may change its name which has happened to two this year already and two others in the last three or four. So, to make things easy and reference as quick as possible, I shall list the Kentucky-based distilleries first and then their products in alphabetical order along with their owners and operational status.

BUFFALO TRACE Leestown, Frankfort. Sazerac. Operating.

BROWN-FORMAN Shively, Louisville. Brown-Forman. Operating.

FOUR ROSES Lawrenceburg. Kirin. Operating

HEAVEN HILL BERNHEIM DISTILLERY Louisville. Heaven Hill. Operating.

JIM BEAM Boston and Clermont. Fortune Brands. Operating.

MAKER'S MARK Loretto. Fortune Brands. Operating.

TOM MOORE Bardstown. Sazerac. Operating.

WILD TURKEY Lawrenceburg. Campari Group. Operating.

WOODFORD RESERVE Near Millville. Brown-Forman. Operating.

Bourbon

Ancient Ancient Age 10 Star (94.5) n23 t24 f23.5 b24. A bourbon which has slipped effortlessly through the gears over the last decade. It is now cruising and offers so many nuggets of pure joy this is now a must have for the serious bourbon devotee. Now a truly great bourbon which positively revels in its newfound complexity: a new 10 Star is born... 45%

Ancient Age Bonded (92) n23 t24 f23 b23. Unmistakably Buffalo Trace... with balls. 50%

Ancient Ancient Age 10 Years Old (96) n23.5 t24 f24 b24.5. This whiskey is like shifting sands: same score as last time out, but the shape is quite different again. Somehow underlines the genius of the distillery that a world class whiskey can reach the same point of greatness, but by taking two different routes...However, in this case the bourbon actually finds something a little extra to move it on to a point very few whiskeys very rarely reach... 43%

Benjamin Prichard's Double Barrelled Bourbon 9 Years Old (94.5) n24.5 double chocolate, it appears... as usual a stunning nose from Prichard. Crisp rye and crisper apple teams with equally firm Demerara and liquorice but that chocolate plus corn and vanilla offers the countering softness required; a mega bourbon nose...; **t24.5** like the nose, absolutely breathtaking intensity which spells bourbon with every atom; spellbinding balance between the maple syrup sweetness and the drier vanillas; the corn really does have a major input in flavour **f22** oils and dries out a fraction and some cocoa returns, but remains chewy; **b23.5** if only they could bottle that nose...oh, they have...!!! Just wonderful whiskey. 40%

Big Bottom Straight Bourbon 91 (95) n23 tight, in that small grain dominates over the corn, while making the most of its oils, and the oak is chunky, salty and chocolaty; **t24** again, a big salty tang to this, but this then serves to bring out the enormity of the grains, in which the corn has fought back pole position; the middle is full of honey, liquorice and burgeoning spices; **b24** and now the small grains are back behind the wheel for a tantalisingly complex finale; **b24** stupendous bourbon. 45.5% (91 proof) ncf.

Big Bottom Straight Bourbon 111 (85.5) n21.5 t20.5 f22.5 b21. An aggressive bourbon and that has nothing to do with the strength. The delivery is tart and lopsided. The sharpness recedes towards the middle and, finally, the lights shine as the praline and mocha enter the fray on the spicy finish. 55.5% (111 proof) ncf.

Blanton's (92) n21.5 t24 f23 b23.5. If it were not for the sluggish nose this would be a Whisky Bible Liquid Gold award winner for sure. On the palate it shows just why little can touch Buffalo Trace for quality at the moment... 40%

Blanton's Gold Original Single Barrel (96.5) n24 a thumping barrage of old honey forgotten in a jar with lavender and leather; **t24.5** rarely does a flavour profile follow the nose so faithfully. Here it also confirms the weight and texture; this is pure chewability. One of the most honeyed middles on the circuit with liquorice, usually ballast, here actually thinning things down a little; the spices hit an early crescendo and then buzz contentedly; **f24** long and remains absolutely unblemished and on a steady course. The honey remains intact; soft vanillas joins the liquorice while the spices just carry on...and on... **b24** it is improbable that a whiskey this enormous and with so many star turns can glide so effortlessly over the palate. One of the best Blanton's in years, this is true Gold standard... 46.5% (93 Proof)

Blanton's Takara (91.5) n24.5 t23 f22 b22. Not quite how many people might envisage a bourbon: certainly not butch enough to keep the wild west gunslingers happy. No this is a bourbon which searches for your feminine side. And being so light, leaves itself open for any off-key bitter notes which might just happen along the way. 49% (98 proof)

Blanton's Uncut/Unfiltered (96.5) n25 t24 f23.5 b24. Uncut. Unfiltered. Unbelievable. 65.9%

Booker's 7 Years 0 Months batch C03-1-16 **(92.5)** n22.5 t23 f23 b23.5. The alcohol may be big but it hardly makes an impact against the enormity of the huge ok statement. Big, seriously fascinating whiskey. 63.7% (1274 Proof)

Booker's 7 Years 4 Months batch no. C03-1-17 **(95.5)** n24 t25 f22.5 b24. The best Booker's I have tasted for a very long while, probably ever. Absolutely world class whiskey. 64%

Booker's 7 Years 4 Months batch C04-A-28 **(92.5)** n23 t24 f22 b23.5. You can always guarantee Booker's to entertain and wow you. No exception here. 64.55% (129.1 proof)

Bowman Brother's Virginia Straight Bourbon (90) n21 t23 f23 b23. Quietly confident and complex: a bit of a gem waiting to be discovered. 45% (90 proof)

Buffalo Trace (92.5) n23 t23 f23.5 b23. Easily one of the lightest BTs I have tasted in a very long while. The rye has not just taken a back seat, but has fallen off the bus. 45%

Buffalo Trace Master Distiller Emeritus Elmer T Lee Collector's Edition bott. 06/09/11 **(96)** n24.5 t24 f23.5 b24. Simply spellbinding. One of the best BT bottlings I have ever enjoyed for bourbon rarely comes more understatedly complete and complex than this. This is the bottle with a nickel coin glued to it. And each complex character within this whiskey gets more than its five cents worth... 45%

Buffalo Trace Single Oak Project Barrel #132 (r1yKA1 see key below) db **(95)** n24 t23.5 f23.5 b24. This sample struck me for possessing, among the first batch of bottlings, the classic Buffalo Trace personality. Afterwards they revealed that it was of a profile which perhaps most closely matches their standard 8-year-old BT. Therefore it is this one I shall use as the tasting template. *45% (90 Proof)*

Key to Buffalo Trace Single Oak Project Codes

Mash bill type: r = rye; w = wheat
Tree grain: 1 = course; 2 = average; 3 = tight
Tree cut: x = top half; y = bottom half
Warehouse type: K = rick; L = concrete

Entry strength: A = 125; B = 105
Seasoning: 1 = 6 Months; 2 = 12 Months
Char: All #4 except * = #3

Buffalo Trace Single Oak Project Barrel #1 (r3xKA1*) db (90.5) n22 t23 f23 b22.5. Soft corn oil aroma, buttery, big sugars building, silky texture, long. *45% (90 Proof)*

⠸⠿ **Buffalo Trace Single Oak Project Barrel #2** (r3yKA1*) db (91.5) n23 t23 f22.5 b23. Bright rye on nose and delivery. Juicy red liquorice and soft corn oil to chew on... *45%*

Buffalo Trace Single Oak Project Barrel #3 (r2xKA1) db (90.5) n22.5 t23 f22.5 b22.5. Nutty, dry aroma; apple fruitiness and brown sugars. *45% (90 Proof)*

Buffalo Trace Single Oak Project Barrel #4 (r2yKA1) db (92) n23 t23 f23 b23. Exceptionally crisp; sharp rye, honeycomb, big liquorice. *45% (90 Proof)*

Buffalo Trace Single Oak Project Barrel #5 (r2xLA1*) db (89) n23 t22.5 f21.5 b22. Dullish after a rye-intense and busy nose. Early muscovado followed by vanilla and spice. *45%*

Buffalo Trace Single Oak Project Barrel #6 (r3yLA1*) db (90) n22.5 t23 f22.5 b22.5. Toast with salted butter and maple syrup. Prickly, mildly aggressive spice throughout. *45%*

Buffalo Trace Single Oak Project Barrel #8 (r3yLA1) db (92.5) n23 t23 f23.5 b23. Crisp rye aroma. Fruity, firm, salivating. Spiced toffee and muscovado; toasty. *45% (90 Proof)*

Buffalo Trace Single Oak Project Barrel #9 (r3xKA2*) db (90) n22 t23 f23 b22.5. Marmalade on singed toast. Soft oils: slow release of natural caramels and mocha. *45%*

Buffalo Trace Single Oak Project Barrel #10 (r3yKA2*) db (93) n23.5 t23.5 f22.5 b23.5. Rich, delicate rye. Complex, busy body; rye oils, tannins; slow sugar build. Bitters. *45%*

⠸⠿ **Buffalo Trace Single Oak Project Barrel #11** (r3xKA2) db (94.5) n23 t24 f23.5 b24. Pronounced accent on rye, especially on delivery. Oak nose upfront; good muscovado fade. *45%.*

⠸⠿ **Buffalo Trace Single Oak Project Barrel #12** (r3yKA2) db (90) n24 t23 f22.5 b23. The floral, supremely balanced nose isn't matched on the palate in weight or complexity. *45%*

⠸⠿ **Buffalo Trace Single Oak Project Barrel #13** (r3xLA2*) db (89.5) n22 t23 f22 b22.5. Soft, yielding tactile. Early juicy, rye stance, slow build of duller light vanilla. Late spice. *45%.*

Buffalo Trace Single Oak Project Barrel #14 (r3yLA2*) db (95) n24 t24 f23 b24. Chocolate rye nose and body; silky texture; brown sugar and vanilla; rye-rich sweet finish. *45%*

⠸⠿ **Buffalo Trace Single Oak Project Barrel #15** (r3xLA2) db (90.5) n22.5 t23 f22 b23. Mouth feel concentrates on sugars and spices, which grow well. Fruity on nose and finish. *45%.*

⠸⠿ **Buffalo Trace Single Oak Project Barrel #16** (r3yLA2) db (91.5) n22.5 t23.5 f22.5 b23. Explosive delivery: big spices, juicy, firm rye. Silky middle butterscotch & ulmo honey finish. *45%.*

Buffalo Trace Single Oak Project Barrel #18 (r3yKB1*) db (92.5) n23 t23 f23.5 b23. Full bodied from nose to finish. Cocoa mingles with rye and rich corn oil. Deep, intense, even. *45%*

⠸⠿ **Buffalo Trace Single Oak Project Barrel #19** (r3xKB1) db (93) n23 t23.5 f23 b23.5. Solid, crisp rye hallmark on nose, delivery. Sugars firm and fractured. Precise whiskey. Salivating. *45%*

⠸⠿ **Buffalo Trace Single Oak Project Barrel #23** (r3xLB1) db (89) n21 t22.5 f22.5 b23. Massive spices throughout; juicy, rye-dominated middle. Soft corn oil and rounded. *45%.*

Buffalo Trace Single Oak Project Barrel #25 (r3xKB2*) db (90.5) n22.5 t23 f22.5 b22.5. Much more accent on the rye and a slow revealing of rich caramels and Demerara. *45%*

Buffalo Trace Single Oak Project Barrel #26 (r3yKB2*) db (89.5) n22 t23.5 f22 b22. A sugary volley follows a shy nose. Quietens quickly; small grains add complexity. *45%*

Buffalo Trace Single Oak Project Barrel #27 (r3xKB2) db (95.5) n23 t24 f24.5 b24. Bold timber on nose and delivery; hickory and liquorice evident; a big spiced honey finale. *45%*

Buffalo Trace Single Oak Project Barrel #28 (r3yKB2) db (94.5) n23 t24 f23.5 b24. Sublime balance between sugars and grains on body. Controlled spice; layered cocoa. *45%*

Buffalo Trace Single Oak Project Barrel #29 (r3xLB2) db (91) n23 t22.5 f23 b22.5. Crisp rye nose; more precise grain. Excellent spices. *45% (90 Proof)*

Buffalo Trace Single Oak Project Barrel #30 (r3yLB2*) db (95.5) n23.5 t24 f24 b24. One of the most delicate yet: crisp rye and sugars, minty forthright oak. Clean yet deep. *45%*

Buffalo Trace Single Oak Project Barrel #32 (r3yLB2) db (90.5) n23 t23 f21.5 b22.5. Soft corn oils dominate. Buttery, molten muscovado. Late hickory. Bitterish finish. *45%*

Buffalo Trace Single Oak Project Barrel #33 (w3xKA1*) db (94.5) n24 t23.5 f23 b24. Huge, busy baking spiced cake; muscovado sugar delivery; remains sweet, silky and spicy; *45%*

⠸⠿ **Buffalo Trace Single Oak Project Barrel #34** (w3yKA1*) db (90) n21.5 t23.5 f22.5 b22.5. Lazy nose but big succulent spiced molasses on delivery, with a mint cocoa finale. *45%*

Buffalo Trace Single Oak Project Barrel #36 (w3yKA1) db **(91.5)** n23 t23 f22.5 b23. Vague rum and toffee; bold, salivating, slow spice. 45% (90 Proof)

Buffalo Trace Single Oak Project Barrel #37 (w3xLA1*) db **(90)** n21 t23 f22 b22. Typical big spice beast. Complex, doughy middle with accent on butterscotch and citrus. 45% (90 Proof)

Buffalo Trace Single Oak Project Barrel #38 (w3yLA1*) db **(87.5)** n22 t23.5 f20.5 b21.5. Fizzy, busy nose matched by massive spice attack on delivery. Bitter, thin finish. 45% (90 Proof)

Buffalo Trace Single Oak Project Barrel #40 (w3xLA1) db **(93)** n23 t23 f23.5 b23.5. Soft, spiced cake, big citrus; silky, oily, bananas and golden syrup; late spice, balancing bitters. 45%

Buffalo Trace Single Oak Project Barrel #41 (w3xKA2*) db **(92.5)** n22 t23 f23.5 b24. Less spice than expected. Docile start, builds in intensity. Buttery, big sugars. Balanced. 45%

꞉꞉꞉ **Buffalo Trace Single Oak Project Barrel #43** (w3xKA2) db **(89)** n22 t23 f22 b22. Dates & plum nose; succulent fruit with broad maple syrup & molasses flourish. Big late spice. 45%.

꞉꞉꞉ **Buffalo Trace Single Oak Project Barrel #44** (w3yKA2) db **(89)** n23 t23 f21 b22. Spice rack nose; superb warm liquorice eruption on palate but dull finale. 45%

꞉꞉꞉ **Buffalo Trace Single Oak Project Barrel #45** (w3xLA2*) db **(87)** n23 t22 f21 b21. Ginger and allspice nose; body thick corn oil and toffee. Short finish. 45%.

꞉꞉꞉ **Buffalo Trace Single Oak Project Barrel #47** (w3xLA2) db **(88.5)** n22.5 t22 f22 b22. Floral, waxy aroma; sugars dominate on palate with vanilla-butterscotch-ulmo theme. 45%.

꞉꞉꞉ **Buffalo Trace Single Oak Project Barrel #48** (w3yLA2) db **(90.5)** n22 t23 f22.5 b23. Sound, rounded from first to last. Greater accent on sugar intensity and vanilla inclusion. 45%.

Buffalo Trace Single Oak Project Barrel #49 (w3xKB1) db **(93)** n24 t23 f23 b23. Chocolate spice, apples, oaky aroma; treacle pudding, soft oils; banana and custard; bitters. 45%

Buffalo Trace Single Oak Project Barrel #50 (w3yKB1*) db **(88)** n21.5 t23 f21.5 b22. Flat nose. Muscovado delivery. Slow spices. Late liquorice. Even. Limited depth. 45% (90 Proof)

꞉꞉꞉ **Buffalo Trace Single Oak Project Barrel #51** (w3xKB1) db **(89.5)** n23 t23 f21.5 b22. Firm and well spiced from start. Oils play bigger role as sugar develops. 45%.

꞉꞉꞉ **Buffalo Trace Single Oak Project Barrel #55** (w3xLB1) db **(89)** n22 t22 f23 b22. Mocha nose with sturdy tannin and vanilla early on delivery. Red liquorice and vanilla late on. 45%.

Buffalo Trace Single Oak Project Barrel #56 (w3yLB1) db **(91)** n24 t22.5 f22 b22.5. Chocolate vanilla and tannins; soft, slow build up of spice, oily; bitters. 45% (90 Proof)

Buffalo Trace Single Oak Project Barrel #57 (w3xKB2*) db **(94)** n23 t23.5 f23.5 b24. Immediate spice kick on nose and delivery. Caramels and marmalade. Busy, balanced. 45%

Buffalo Trace Single Oak Project Barrel #58 (w3yKB2*) db **(90.5)** n22.5 t23 f22.5 b22.5. Liquorice and Fisherman's Friend nose; molassed middle and big spice finish. 45%

Buffalo Trace Single Oak Project Barrel #59 (w3xKB2) db **(92)** n22 t23.5 f23 b23.5. Lighter Fisherman's Friend; roasted fudge; busy small grains attack. Mega complex. 45%

Buffalo Trace Single Oak Project Barrel #60 (w3yKB2) db **(89)** n22.5 t22.5 f21 b21.5. Aggression to spice nose; tame delivery and body. Soft corn oil and muscovado. 46%

Buffalo Trace Single Oak Project Barrel #61 (w3xLB2*) db **(94.5)** n24 t23 f23.5 b24. Classic spiced wheat; Demerara sugars and spices abound. Big. 45% (90 Proof)

Buffalo Trace Single Oak Project Barrel #62 (w3yLB2*) db **(88)** n22 t22.5 f21.5 b22. Caramel is leading theme; soft, big wheated spice. Oily. 45% (90 Proof)

Buffalo Trace Single Oak Project Barrel #63 (w3xLB2) db **(95.5)** n24 t23 f24 b24.5. Subtle dates, spice, cocoa; gentle, oily, perfect spice build. Ultra complex. 45% (90 Proof)

Buffalo Trace Single Oak Project Barrel #64 (w3yLB2) db **(91)** n22.5 t23.5 f22.5 b23. Citrus nose. Big oak and spice delivery; treacle tart and liquorice. Softens into caramel. 45%

Buffalo Trace Single Oak Project Barrel #65 (r2xKA1) db **(91)** n23.5 t22 f23 b22.5. Small grain nose; crunchy muscovado, corn oil; liquorice, vanilla; late spice. Complex. 45%

꞉꞉꞉ **Buffalo Trace Single Oak Project Barrel #66** (r2yKA1*) db **(88.5)** n22.5 t22.5 f21.5 b22. Dry tannin dominates on nose and palate; good spice kick and treacle. Short finish. 45%

Buffalo Trace Single Oak Project Barrel #68 (r2yKA1) db **(92)** n22.5 t23 f23.5 b23. Rye depth; deeper, warmer spices, liquorice and light molasses. 45% (90 Proof)

Buffalo Trace Single Oak Project Barrel #69 (r2xLA1*) db **(94.5)** n23 t24 f23.5 b24. Crisp, sharp rye on nose and delivery. Jagged muscovado and spice. Goes down a treat... 45%

Buffalo Trace Single Oak Project Barrel #70 (r2yLA1*) db **(91.5)** n22.5 t23 f23 b23. Yielding caramel and vanilla. Rye and hot spice breaks up the sleepy theme. 45% (90 Proof)

Buffalo Trace Single Oak Project Barrel #73 (r2xKA2*) db **(87.5)** n21.5 t22 f22 b22. Tight, unyielding nose. Initially crisp rye then thick vanilla and baked apple blanket. 45%

꞉꞉꞉ **Buffalo Trace Single Oak Project Barrel #75** (r2xKA2) db **(91.5)** n22 t22.5 f23 b23. Clean with accent firmly on grain throughout. Spiced minty mocha middle and fade. 45%.

꞉꞉꞉ **Buffalo Trace Single Oak Project Barrel #76** (r2yKA2) db **(89)** n22.5 t22.5 f22 b22. Bristling rye on nose and delivery; fruity edge then dullish spiced fudge and mocha. 45%

꞉꞉꞉ **Buffalo Trace Single Oak Project Barrel #77** (r2xLA2*) db **(88)** n22 t23 f21 b22. Busy, bitty nose; sugary blast on delivery; spice follow through then vanilla overload. 45%.

⫶⫶⫶ **Buffalo Trace Single Oak Project Barrel #79** (r2xLA2) db **(93)** n23 t23.5 f23 b23.5. Juicy crisp sugars. Toasty with slow liquorice burn. Creamed spiced hickory fade. Complex. *45%*.

⫶⫶⫶ **Buffalo Trace Single Oak Project Barrel #80** (r2yLA2) db **(91.5)** n23 t22.5 f23 b23. Broad oily strokes on nose, delivery. Simple vanilla tannins and ulmo honey. *45%*.

Buffalo Trace Single Oak Project Barrel #81 (r2yKB1*) db **(94)** n23 t23 f24 b24. Candy shop fruitiness; delicate oils and flavour development; big yet subdued brown sugars. *45%*

Buffalo Trace Single Oak Project Barrel #82 (r2yKB1*) db **(91.5)** n22.5 t23.5 f22.5 b23. Liquoice, manuka honey; lurid rye bite and lychee fruitiness; mocha and Demerara. *45%*

⫶⫶⫶ **Buffalo Trace Single Oak Project Barrel #83** (r2xKB1) db **(92)** n22.5 t23 f23.5 b23. Sharp, angular grain, rye dominant. Softer salty praline fade. *45%*.

⫶⫶⫶ **Buffalo Trace Single Oak Project Barrel #87** (r2xLB1) db **(93.5)** n22.5 t23.5 f23.5 b24. Citrus-led nose; slow, corn oil start then explode grain; rye, liquorice & honey to the fore. *45%*.

Buffalo Trace Single Oak Project Barrel #89 (r2xKB2*) db **(89.5)** n22 t22.5 f22 b22.5. Rye radiates on nose and delivery. Big spice surge to the middle. Late mocha, liquorice. *45%*

Buffalo Trace Single Oak Project Barrel #90 (r2yKB2*) db **(94)** n23.5 t24 f23 b23.5. Big tannin, cocoa and caramel throughout. Major maple spice. Complex. *45% (90 Proof)*

Buffalo Trace Single Oak Project Barrel #91 (r2xKB2) db **(86.5)** n21.5 t22 f21.5 b21.5. Half-cooked: dull caramel throughout. Short spice peak. Sweet, oily, lacking complexity. *45%*

Buffalo Trace Single Oak Project Barrel #92 (r2yKB2) db **(91)** n22 t23 f23 b23. Silky texture. Big corn oil but intense tannin thinned by beech honey. Hickory and maple syrup. *45%*

Buffalo Trace Single Oak Project Barrel #94 (r2yLB2*) db **(92.5)** n22.5 t24 f23 b23. Rich, hefty. Slightly salty, crisp rye. Light caramel, hint of Guyanese rum. Delicate spice. *45%*

Buffalo Trace Single Oak Project Barrel #95 (r2xLB2) db **(94)** n23.5 f23.5 f23.5 b24. Citrus, banana; soft vanilla, profound rye sharpness, spices. Big. *45% (90 Proof)*

Buffalo Trace Single Oak Project Barrel #96 (r2yLB2) db **(89)** n22 t23.5 f21.5 b22. Bright, grainy delivery in contrast to oily nose and finish. Heavy, dry molasses at the death. *45%*

⫶⫶⫶ **Buffalo Trace Single Oak Project Barrel #98** (w2yKA1*) db **(93)** n23 t23.5 f23 b23.5. Peppers on at full blast on nose and delivery; big oily liquorice and treacle counter. *45%*

Buffalo Trace Single Oak Project Barrel #100 (w2yKA1) db **(94)** n23 t23.5 f23.5 b24. Busy, green, fresh; big juicy, vanilla, muscovado, spices. *45% (90 Proof)*

Buffalo Trace Single Oak Project Barrel #101 (w2xLA1) db **(96)** n23.5 t24 f23.5 b25. Unerring chocolate and mint aided by even muscovado, vanilla and spice. Hugely complex. *45%*

Buffalo Trace Single Oak Project Barrel #102 (w2yLA1*) db **(88.5)** n22 t22 f22.5 b22. Insane tannin on nose; overcooked caramel. Massive sugar-spice mix. *45% (90 Proof)*

Buffalo Trace Single Oak Project Barrel #104 (w2xLA1) db **(91)** n23 t23 f22 b22.5. Apple, cinnamon; light spice; corn oil; vanilla and ulmo honey; spices, bitters out. *45%*

Buffalo Trace Single Oak Project Barrel #105 (w2xKA2*) db **(89)** n22.5 t22 f22.5 b22. Spiced, lively nose; hot cross buns; oils and sugars build slowly; spices intensify at end. *45%*

Buffalo Trace Single Oak Project Barrel #106 (w2yKA2*) db **(92.5)** n24 t23 f23 b23.5. Mega complex nose: busy sugars and spices; silky texture; nougat, caramel. *45%*

⫶⫶⫶ **Buffalo Trace Single Oak Project Barrel #107** (w2xKA2) db **(93.5)** n23.5 t23 f23 b24. Bold, rich nose; pepper bite; thick body: maple syrup, molasses, cocoa. Classic wheat recipe. *45%*.

⫶⫶⫶ **Buffalo Trace Single Oak Project Barrel #108** (w2yKA2) db **(94)** n22.5 t24 f23.5 b24. Soft, delicate. Ulmo honey leads the sugars; corn oil but complex liquorice and lavender. *45%*

⫶⫶⫶ **Buffalo Trace Single Oak Project Barrel #109** (w2xLA2*) db **(87.5)** n21.5 t23.5 f21 b21.5. Dull nose and finish. Delivery lush, souped-up spiced caramel-toffee fudge. *45%*

⫶⫶⫶ **Buffalo Trace Single Oak Project Barrel #111** (w2yKB1*) db **(89)** n22.5 t22.5 f22 b22. Intriguing sugar operatic. Vary from castor to muscovado. Countering spices make it work. *45%*.

Buffalo Trace Single Oak Project Barrel #112 (w2yLA2) db **(90)** n21.5 t23 f22.5 b23. Caramel fudge lead. Usual whited spice before heavier, liquorice development. *45%*.

Buffalo Trace Single Oak Project Barrel #114 (w2yKB1*) db **(90)** n22 t23 f22 b23. Elements of citrus. Oily corn. Controlled spice. Earthy and sweet. *45% (90 Proof)*

⫶⫶⫶ **Buffalo Trace Single Oak Project Barrel #115** (w2xKB1) db **(88.5)** n22 t22.5 f22 b22. An even mix of corn oil and persistant light sugars. Low level spice until finish. A tad dull. *45%*.

⫶⫶⫶ **Buffalo Trace Single Oak Project Barrel #119** (w2xLB1) db **(93.5)** n22.5 t24 f23.5 b23.5. Spices from nose to fade, accompanied by chewy burnt fudge. French toast finale. Big. *45%*.

Buffalo Trace Single Oak Project Barrel #121 (w2xKB2*) db **(89)** n22.5 t23 f21.5 b22. Citrusy corn oil apparent and dominates. Sugars rampant, spices shy. Rather flat finale. *45%*

Buffalo Trace Single Oak Project Barrel #122 (w2yKB2*) db **(93)** n22 t23.5 f23.5 b24. Serious wheat-spice with cocoa back up. Demerara sugars evenly spread. Complex. *45%*

Buffalo Trace Single Oak Project Barrel #123 (w2xKB2) db **(85.5)** n21 t22 f21 b21.5. One of the dullest yet: limited sparkle despite light spice. Big caramel. *45% (90 Proof)*

Buffalo Trace Single Oak Project Barrel #124 (w2yKB2) db **(90.5)** n22.5 t22.5 f22 b22.5. The startling, extra sugars over #123 impact hugely. Juicy; oak (liquorice) support. *45%*

Buffalo Trace Single Oak Project Barrel #125 (w2xLB2*) db (93) n24 t22 f22.5 b22.5. Heavy oak, spices; firm, juicy. Softer caramel fade. 45% (90 Proof)

Buffalo Trace Single Oak Project Barrel #126 (w2yLB2*) db (90) n22 t23 f22.5 b22.5. Floral nose (primroses); elaborate delivery of spice and creamed mocha plus molasses. 45%

Buffalo Trace Single Oak Project Barrel #128 (w2yLB2) db (89) n21.5 t22 f22.5 b22.5. Conservative nose, OTT spice on delivery. Molassed dates and walnut. 45% (90 Proof)

⋅⋛⋅ **Buffalo Trace Single Oak Project Barrel #130** (r1yKA1*) db (92.5) n22 t23.5 f23 b24. Macho: cloaked in oak. Kumquats on nose, oily, punchy tannins on sharp, silky delivery. 45%

Buffalo Trace Single Oak Project Barrel #131 (r1xKA1) db (92.5) n23 t23 f23.5 b23. Relaxed vanilla, light tannin; corn oily, icing sugars, marzipan. 45% (90 Proof)

Buffalo Trace Single Oak Project Barrel #133 (r1xLA1*) db (89) n22.5 t23 f21 b22.5. Small grain busyness does the business: rye leads the dark sugar procession. Bitters out. 45%

Buffalo Trace Single Oak Project Barrel #134 (r1yLA1*) db (91.5) n22 t23.5 f23 b23. Velvet delivery: big spice cushioned by muscovado and butterscotch. Mixed honey finale. 45%

Buffalo Trace Single Oak Project Barrel #136 (r1yLA1) db (92) n23.5 t22.5 f23 b23. Liquorice on nose and delivery. Spicy. Richer oils. Demerara. Spice. 45% (90 Proof)

Buffalo Trace Single Oak Project Barrel #137 (r1xKA2*) db (90.5) n22 t23.5 f22 b23. Fruity opening with a hardening rye presence and emphasis on muscovado. Late cocoa. 45%

⋅⋛⋅ **Buffalo Trace Single Oak Project Barrel #139** (r1xKA2) db (88) n22.5 t22 f21.5 b22. More or less flatlines throughout. Big corn oil with limited spice and cocoa. 45%.

⋅⋛⋅ **Buffalo Trace Single Oak Project Barrel #140** (r1xKA2) db (93) n23 t24 f23 b23. Classic bourbon: citrus-rich nose, thumping spicy molassed liquorice-hickory delivery. 45%

⋅⋛⋅ **Buffalo Trace Single Oak Project Barrel #141** (r1xLA2*) db (90) n23.5 t22 f22.5 b22. Busy nose & finish. Corn dominates the mid ground. Sugar, spice growth. Complex finale. 45%.

⋅⋛⋅ **Buffalo Trace Single Oak Project Barrel #143** (r1xLA2) db (88.5) n22.5 t22.5 f21.5 b22. Hickory drifts in and out of narrative. Light rye & vanilla. Very soft – overly gentle. 45%.

⋅⋛⋅ **Buffalo Trace Single Oak Project Barrel #144** (r1yLA2) db (91) n23 t23 f22.5 b22.5. Tannin led. Bristling dark sugars. Oily with comforting vanilla. 45%.

Buffalo Trace Single Oak Project Barrel #145 (r1xKB1*) db (91) n22.5 t22 f23.5 b23. Nougat, cocoa; busy small grains; oily corn; spiced chocolate. 45% (90 Proof)

Buffalo Trace Single Oak Project Barrel #146 (r1yKB1*) db (93) n23 t24 f22 b24. Rye dominates with clarity and aplomb. Crystal clean nose and delivery. Dundee cake. 45%

⋅⋛⋅ **Buffalo Trace Single Oak Project Barrel #147** (r1xKB1) db (93) n23.5 t23 f23.5 b23. Macho rye & tannins. Toasty & dry delivery; liquorice, sugars, soft spice gain ascendency. 45%.

⋅⋛⋅ **Buffalo Trace Single Oak Project Barrel #151** (r1xLB1) db (91.5) n22 t23 f23.5 b23. Diced citrus; light body with busy grains. Powerful dark sugars gain upper hand. 45%.

Buffalo Trace Single Oak Project Barrel #153 (r1xKB2*) db (94) n23.5 t23.5 f23 b24. Complex nose, delivery. Big spice with crisp, juicy rye. Praline, delicate oils. Big but elegant. 45%

Buffalo Trace Single Oak Project Barrel #154 (r1yKB2*) db (92) n22.5 t23 f23.5 b23.5. Rye dominates. Hard on palate; yet burnt raisin, lychee and muscovado soften. 45% (90 Proof)

Buffalo Trace Single Oak Project Barrel #155 (r1xKB2) db (93) n23 t24 f22.5 b23.5. Fierce spice. Dynamic rye shapes all directions. Hickory and manuka honey combine. 45%

Buffalo Trace Single Oak Project Barrel #156 (r1yKB2) db (85.5) n22 t21 f21.5 b21. Doesn't work. Spices too hot. Caramels and oils negate development. 45% (90 Proof)

Buffalo Trace Single Oak Project Barrel #157 (r1xLB2*) db (84.5) n21 t21.5 f20.5 b21. Vague butyric; sharp, juicy corn with slow rye build. Bitter. 45% (90 Proof)

Buffalo Trace Single Oak Project Barrel #158 (r1yLB2*) db (88) n22 t22 f22 b22. Another brawny, corn-oily, oaky effort. Excellent cocoa, citrus and spice development. 45%

Buffalo Trace Single Oak Project Barrel #160 (r1yLB2) db (92.5) n23.5 t23 f22 b23. A salty style with fruity, crisp rye right behind. Steady and firm. 45% (90 Proof)

⋅⋛⋅ **Buffalo Trace Single Oak Project Barrel #162** (w1yKA1*) db (88.5) n22 t22 f22.5 b22. Cream soda and minty fudge. Early treacle kick then settles for simple life. 45%

Buffalo Trace Single Oak Project Barrel #164 (w1yKA1) db (94.5) n23.5 t23 f24 b24. Citrus and vanilla; massive spice, building. Demerara. Warm and complex. 45% (90 Proof)

Buffalo Trace Single oak Project Barrel #165 (w1xLA1*) db (91.5) n22.5 t23 f23 b23. Lively, spice dominated. Ulmo honey offers superb back up. 45% (90 Proof)

Buffalo Trace Single Oak Project Barrel #166 (w1yLA1*) db (91) n22 t23 f23 b23. Heady, leathery. Sublime spice middle; molasses and liquorice enrich the tail. 45% (90 Proof)

Buffalo Trace Single Oak Project Barrel #167 (w1yLB1) db (94) n23.5 t23.5 f23 b24. Demerara, rummy; intense liquorice, hickory; dark sugars and big spice. 45% (90 Proof)

Buffalo Trace Single Oak Project Barrel #169 (w1xKA2*) db (94) n23.5 t23.5 f23 b24. Spice, lavender & leather on delivery; spicy nose. Honey & corn oil follow through. 45% (90 proof)

Buffalo Trace Single Oak Project Barrel #170 (w1yKA2*) db (92.5) n22.5 t23 f23.5 b23.5. Sweet, spiced nose; firm, spicy delivery; Demerara and ulmo honey. 45% (90 Proof)

⠿ **Buffalo Trace Single Oak Project Barrel #171** (w1xKA2) db (88.5) n22 t23 f21.5 b22. Friendly corn oils dominate. Estery. Dry finish after sugar & spice crescendo. 45%.

⠿ **Buffalo Trace Single Oak Project Barrel #172** (w1yKA2) db (90.5) n22.5 t23 f22.5 b22.5. Tannins prevalent on nose and spiced delivery. Good bite, esters and oils. Late mocha. 45%

⠿ **Buffalo Trace Single Oak Project Barrel #173** (w1xLA2*) db (91) n23.5 t23 f22 b22.5. Bold nose & delivery: honeycomb, tannins. Liquorice & vanilla middle; good spice balance. 45%.

⠿ **Buffalo Trace Single Oak Project Barrel #175** (w1xLA2) db (91.5) n21.5 t23 f24 b23. Lazy nose, juicy delivery. Big vanilla profile. Buttery caramel; light honey & spice. Long. 45%.

⠿ **Buffalo Trace Single Oak Project Barrel #176** (w1yLA2) db (89) n21.5 t22.5 f22.5 b22.5. Light caramel aroma; sharp, juicy (rye-esque) delivery with mocha & butter toffee finale. 45%.

Buffalo Trace Single Oak Project Barrel #178 (w1yKB1*) db (88.5) n22.5 t23 f21.5 b21.5. Complex marzipan and Demerara nose and delivery; runs out of things to say. 45%

⠿ **Buffalo Trace Single Oak Project Barrel #179** (w1xKB1) db (88) n21 t22 f22.5 b22.5 Dull caramel nose. Toffee caramel continues on palate. Late fudge sweetness. Growing spice. 45%.

⠿ **Buffalo Trace Single Oak Project Barrel #183** (w1xLB1) db (95.5) n24 t24 f23.5 b24. Intense. Brilliant fudge/honey/molasses delivery; cocoa finish; perfect spices: mini Weller! 45%.

Buffalo Trace Single Oak Project Barrel #184 (w1yLA1) db (93) n23.5 t23 f23 b23.5. Tannins, walnut oil; nutty, corn oils. Light spice, firm Demerara. Late fruity spice. Complex. 45%

Buffalo Trace Single Oak Project Barrel #185 (w1xKB2*) db (92.5) n23 t23.5 f23 b23. Dry, riveting nose; liquorice dominates the palate. Cocoa, hickory enlivened by sugars. 45%

Buffalo Trace Single Oak Project Barrel #186 (w1yKB2*) db (90) n23 t22.5 f22 b22.5. Rampant spice from delivery onwards. Burnt fudge and toasted raisin. 45% (90 Proof)

Buffalo Trace Single Oak Project Barrel #187 (w1xKB2) db (88) n22 t22 f22 b22. Exceptionally even and caramel rich. Unbalanced tannin and lack of spice. 45% (90 Proof)

Buffalo Trace Single Oak Project Barrel #188 (w1yKB2) db (90) n21.5 t23.5 f22.5 b22.5. Lazy nose. Bright delivery; citrusy corn oil and muscovado. Late mocha and liquorice. 45%

Buffalo Trace Single Oak Project Barrel #190 (w1yLB2*) db (94) n23.5 t24 f23 b23.5. Ulmo/manuka honey mix on nose and delivery; silky corn oil; spiced mocha. Complex. 45%

Buffalo Trace Single Oak Project Barrel #191 (w1xLB2) db (94.5) n23 t23.5 f24 b24. Big, spicy, classic; firm wheaty spiciness, juicy, thick caramels. Complex. 45% (90 Proof)

Buffalo Trace Single Oak Project Barrel #192 (w1yLB2) db (94.5) n23 t24 f23.5 b24. Demerara rum nose; heavy, dry liquorice body; late spice; molassed butterscotch finish. 45%

Buffalo Trace Experiment #7 Heavy Char Barrel charred white oak, dist 21 Jan 97, bott Oct 12 db (77) n20 t21.5 f17 b18.5. The very nature of experiments means that, sometimes, they go wrong. Perhaps a bit harsh for this one which, to be more precise, has not gone right. The nose has an almost bizarre sherry feel to it, the fruitiness really striking home on the attractive delivery. From then on, it's downhill, leaving an unattractive tang at the death. 45%

Buffalo Trace Experiment Hot Box Toasted Barrel charred white oak, dist 2 Jun 96, bott 22 Oct 12 db (95.5) n24 very unusual: almost a seaside saltiness to this and the fruit from the rye grains emphasised; sensual and almost too delicate for words; t24 it is probably on about the third mouthful that you begin to realise this is very different: where the small grains can sometime be quite angular when not lost against an oak of this age, and where the tannins are usually just begging to get a little over boisterous, you recognise that all the sharp edges and undulations expected have been worn down like a pebble. This is as soft and rounded as any 16-y-o bourbon you will taste in your lifetime, with not even the hint of a splinter; the sugars and the spices are entirely in sync, the maple syrup just melting around the palate; f23 moves into cocoa and mocha territory. Still the dark sugars fashion the shape, but not the overall outcome...especially when a citric tang is reprised; b24.5 I remember having this experimental barrel-making process explained to me what seems a lifetime ago – so long, I'd actually forgotten all about it. But nearly 17 years on, here it is, whiskey from a barrel where the staves were steamed into shape after undergoing some major roasting. The end product is definitely a different kind of BT, where the accent is on softness and pastel-shaded cocoa: a gentle, slightly erotic massage of a bourbon. 45% (90 proof)

⠿ **Buffalo Trace Experimental Collection 12 Year Old Bourbon From Floor #1** dist 11/29/01, barreled 11/30/01, bott 3/12/14, still proof: 140, entry proof: 125, warehouse/ floor: K/1, rick/row/slot:1/1/1-4, charred white oak, age at bottling, 12 years, 3 months, evaporation: 27% db (91.5) n23.5 alive with small grain bittiness; manuka honey; a tad salty; t23 sweet delivery: soft corn oils and polite spice; German coffee biscuit; f22.5 a slight bitterness as the sugars can't stretch that far; b22.5 delicate bourbon with limited fight. 45%.

⠿ **Buffalo Trace Experimental Collection 12 Year Old Bourbon From Floor #5** dist 11/29/01, barreled 11/30/01, bott 3/12/14, still proof: 140, entry proof: 125, warehouse/ floor: K/5, rick/row/slot:51/1/21-24, charred white oak, age at bottling, 12 years, 3 months, evaporation: 25% db (91) n22 corn oil and citrus; a touch minty with a hint of eucalyptus; t23 quite a heavy delivery: much more rich, molassed tannin than Floor #1, and a greater depth to the natural caramels, too; **f23** pulsing spices; **b23** though heavier, lacks some of the grace and complexity of its lower-matured stablemate. 45%.

⬧⬧⬧ **Buffalo Trace Experimental Collection 12 Year Old Bourbon From Floor #9** dist 11/29/01, barreled 11/30/01, bott 3/12/14, still proof: 140, entry proof: 125, warehouse/floor: K/9, rick/row/slot:44/1/13-16, charred white oak, age at bottling, 12 years, 3 months, evaporation: 49% db **(95.5) n24** big profound bourbon with liquorice softened by molasses; **t24** from the very first moment of delivery, this sings "massive, absolutely top quality bourbon" to you from every one of its countless layers; we are talking various types of liquorice, Fisherman's Friend cough sweets, treacle, dried molasses, dried dates and biting spice...and so much more, including a layering of ulmo honey in tanden with manuka; **f23.5** though quieter, the sugars not only stretch further but remain in harmony with the heavier tannins: the rumble goes on seemingly forever....thankfully! **b24** floorless...and confirms about bourbon maturation what we already know. And this distillery in particular... 45%.

⬧⬧⬧ **Buffalo Trace Experimental Collection 15 Year Old Standard Stave Dry Time** dist 28/01/1998, bott 10/09/2013, charred white oak. Rick 52; Row 1; Slot 5-12 db **(92) n21.5** slightly tight and lazy: big vanilla, gentle tannin; **t23** superb sugar delivery: mainly Demerara with a little molasses to thicken and intensify; all the bourbon-style big guns are out in force; **f24** sublime finish: the sugars keep their shape while the liquorice and caramels from the mid ground retain their stay; **b23.5** wonderful bourbon: far better than the nose heralds. 45%. *Total production 8 barrels; still proof 140; entry proof 125; age at bottling 15 years, 7 months.*

⬧⬧⬧ **Buffalo Trace Experimental Collection 15 Year Old Extended Stave Dry Time** dist 29/01/1998, bott 09/09/201, charred white oak. Rick 48; Row 1; Slot 15-22 db **(92) n23.5** big, deposits sack-fulls of spice, nutty with n little manuka honey thinning the liquorice; **t23.5** the huge delivery fits the nose perfectly: confirming all tht can be found in the aromas; a little corn oil creeps in; **f22.5** fades quickly and the emphasis is now completely on the oily corn; **b22.5** and the result of the experiment: extending the stave drying time gets you off to a wonderful start with the whiskey then fading and the reverse for the standard. Conclusion: do as I did – blend the two for a quite brilliant result... 45%.

⬧⬧⬧ **Buffalo Trace Experimental Collection Entry Proof Rye Bourbon 90** db dist 02/11/2001 bott 20/08/2013 charred white oak. Rick 15/row 2/ slot 10-11. **(90.5) n23** charmingly nutty (very oddly, the type you often get from an old dry oloroso butt!) with enough spice ramp up the interest levels; **t22** somewhat dull delivery by BT standards with the small grains struggling to get a foothold in the swamping corn oil; **f23** as soon as the Demerara arrives things look up. And as soon as the mocha comes into play, we are in serious business. Amazingly long fade; **b22.5** a classy bourbon, though shackled slightly... 45%.

⬧⬧⬧ **Buffalo Trace Experimental Collection Entry Proof Rye Bourbon 105** db dist 02/11/01 bott 20/08/13 charred white oak. Rick 15/row 2/ slot 9-10. **(87.5) n22 t22 f22 b21.5.** Fails to ignite on either the palate or nose in quite the same way the 90 entry achieved. The oils are even more dominant here while the sugars are of a softer more maple syrup variety. 45%.

⬧⬧⬧ **Buffalo Trace Experimental Collection Entry Proof Rye Bourbon 115** db dist 02/11/2001 bott 20/08/2013 charred white oak. Rick 15/row 2/ slot 14-15. **(93) n21.5 t23.5 f24 b24.** Talk about hiding your light... The nose is sound if unspectacular bourbon with a hefty nod towards the tannins. But the delivery and follow through: stunning! Immediate impact is an explosion of Demerara-sweetened spices, but now with the oils much less prevalent and the small grains able to dance a jig. The light, refreshing fruitiness of rye content goes a long way....until a delicate Java coffee note begins to take charge. 45%.

⬧⬧⬧ **Buffalo Trace Experimental Collection Entry Proof Rye Bourbon 125** db dist 02/11/2001 bott 20/08/2013 charred white oak. Rick 15/row 2/ slot 6-7. **(95.5) n23.5 t24 f23.5 b24.5.** Of the four experiments, this one has produced the most profound rye-grain involvement, especially on the nose. A busy whiskey, with spices flickering alongside the small grains. Complex, wonderfully busy, a little more oily than the 115 entry and far more warming towards the end. Perhaps most impressive is being able to keep such excellent balance, even when the flavours and weights within the bourbon are moving apace. And as for the milky Demerara-mocha finale... Quite simply, a bourbon of your dreams. 45%.

Buffalo Trace Experimental Collection Wheat 90 charred white oak, dist 24 Oct 01, bott 15 Jun 13 db **(84.5) n21.5 t22.5 f20.5 b20.** A curious exhibition of wheated BT, where the sugars appear to have been separated at birth from the dryer elements of the oak. Pleasant, but not up to the usual BT greatness and really not bothered about balance. 45% (90 proof)

Buffalo Trace Experimental Collection Wheat 105 charred white oak, dist 24 Oct 01, bott 14 Jun 13 db **(93.5) n24 t22.5 f23.5 b23.5.** Just look at the difference between this and the 90: amazing....!!!! 45% (90 proof)

Buffalo Trace Experimental Collection Wheat 115 charred white oak, dist 24 Oct 01, bott 17 Jun 13 db **(90) n22 t24 f21.5 b22.5.** This is like the 105 in reverse: the nose not working so well, but the delivery showing some impressive muscle. 45% (90 proof)

Buffalo Trace Experimental Collection Wheat 125 charred white oak, dist 01, bott 13 db (94) n23 t23.5 f23.5 b24. Sensationally satisfying. Bourbon with knobs on...!! 45% (90 proof)

-:⁘:- **Cadenhead's World Whiskies Heaven Hill Aged 17 Years** bott 14, (93.5) n24.5 hard to imagine a more complete or classic bourbon aroma at this age: massive tannin toned down and beatified by a dollop of manuka honey, marzipan and toasted fudge....no shortage of corn apparent, too; t23 rich, dripping with corn oil and molasses with a slow burnt toast, thick liquorice growth; f23 a light ulmo honey layering sticks to the corn oil; b23 although it says "distilled at Heaven Hill Bardstown," the distillery was by then a burnt out husk and production had shifted to various other distilleries around Kentucky who were happy to distil to contract, or sell spare parcels of maturing distillate to help plug the huge stock gap. Not sure exactly where this single cask was from but has a certain touch of the Old Forester from Louisville, which often displayed the heavy liquorice and honey character apparent here. 58%. WB15/378

Calhoun Bros Straight Bourbon (84.5) n20.5 t22 f21 b21. Very different! A much wider cut than the norm on straight bourbon whisky results in an oily fellow which you can chew until your jaws ache. Massively toasty, vanilla gorged and intense. 43% (86 proof)

Charter 101 (95.5) n23.5 t24.5 f23.5 b24. Now here is a whiskey which has changed tack dramatically. In many ways it's like the Charter 101 of a year back. But this bottling suggests they have turned a warehouse into a giant beehive. Because few whiskeys offer this degree of honey. You can imagine that after all these years, rarely does a whiskey genuinely surprise me: this one has. No wonder there is such a buzz in the bourbon industry right now... 50.5%

Clarke's Old Kentucky Straight Sour Mash Whisky Bourbon (88.5) n22.5 t22 f22 b22. Honest and hugely impressive bourbon. The rich colour – and remember straight bourbon cannot be falsely coloured – tells its own tale. 40%. Aldi.

Colonel E H Taylor Barrel Proof (91) n23.5 t23 f22 b22.5. A big boy which turns out to be a bit of a softy in the end... 67.25% (134.5 Proof). nc ncf.

Colonel E. H. Taylor Old Fashioned Sour Mash (94) n24 t23.5 f23 b23.5. When they say "old fashioned" they really aren't joking. This is a style which takes me back to my first bourbon tasting days of the mid 1970s. And, at the moment, it is hard to name another bourbon offering this unique, technically brilliant style. Outstanding! 50% (100 Proof)

Colonel E H Taylor Single Barrel (93) n23.5 t23 f23 b23.5. An exceptionally bright barrel that's a bit of a tease. 50% (100 Proof)

Colonel E.H. Taylor Small Batch (94.5) n23 pretty effortlessly classic: a friendly layering of crisp sugars and teasing spice as well as a thin hint of mint and eucalyptus; the natural vanillas are out in force, too; t24 pretty perfect weight: the oils have just enough clout to ensure the sugars remain in check and on the Demerara side of things; the small grains do stir, also, and herald the arrival of the toastier elements; f23.5 long, again with the sweetness in harmony with the butterscotch tart and late peppery bite; b24 from first nose, to last, the exemplary high quality of this bourbon is not for a second in dispute. 50% (100 Proof)

Cougar Bourbon Aged 5 Years (95) n25 t24 f23 b23. If Karl Kennedy of Neighbours really is the whisky buff he reckons he is, I want to see a bottle of this in his home next to Dahl. By the way: where is Dahl these days...? (And by the way, Karl, the guy who married you and Susan in London is a fan of mine. So you had better listen up...!) 37% (74 proof). Foster's Group, Australia.

Daniel Stewart 8 Years Old (92.5) n22 t23 f23.5 b24. Stellar sophistication. Real complexity here, and, as 8-year-olds go, probably among the most complex of them all. A deep notch up on the previous bottling I encountered. 45%

Eagle Rare Aged 10 Years Single Barrel (89) n21.5 t23 f22 b22.5. A surprising trip, this, with some dramatic changes en route. 45%

-:⁘:- **Eagle Rare 17 Years Old** bott Spring 2013 db (94) n23 wonderful chocolate fudge; thick and toasty; t24 ker-pow! By far and away the biggest landing by this rare Eagle for quite some time. Almost aggressive in its bite, which entirely suits the intensity of the spice which sits prettily with the manuka honey and treacle; f23 tones down quite quickly and we are back to the lovely chocolate fudge found on the nose; b24 a much more profound bottling than the 2012 edition with the accent firmly on the heavy, chocolatey sugars. Shows BT to enormous advantage and is, above all, great fun. 45%. Buffalo Trace Antique Collection.

Eagle Rare Kentucky Straight Bourbon 17 Years Old bott Fall 2010 (92.5) n24 t23.5 f22 b23. The corn hardly makes itself heard and oil's at a premium. But for those who love bourbon in their rye...wow!! Oddly enough, while tasting this I am watching, from my sample room, a pair of black vultures circling a bluff at Frankfort, Ky, a short glide from the distillery where this whiskey was made. They are not exactly eagles, I grant you. But, with its eagle-esque deportment and chunkiness, close enough for the moment not to be lost...The Turkey Vultures, meanwhile, are probably waiting until I start on the samples from Lawrenceburg... 45%

Eagle Rare Kentucky Straight Bourbon Whiskey 17 Years Old dist Spring 1993, bott Fall 2011 (94) n23.5 t24 f23 b23.5. A marked improvement on previous bottlings, this goes out of its way to show some macho Kentuckian muscle. 45% (90 Proof)

Eagle Rare Kentucky Straight Bourbon Whiskey 17 Years Old bott Spring 2012 **(92) n23** t24 f22 b23. Eagle Rare is the big BT brand which appears to have the widest range. Hit and miss you might say...but always seeming to hit some part of the bull's-eye. *45% (90 proof)*

Elijah Craig Barrel Proof Bourbon 12 Years of Aging db **(95.5) n23.5** heavy duty and fudgy, the fruits are all about plums fit to burst and the sweetness from molasses and reduced manuka honey; **t24** Batman would love the ker-pow factor to this. Everything so intense and the balancing sugars and the enormity of the liquorice make this one to remember. Spices punctuate at every point...just astonishing...; **f24** slightly overcooked toast with treacle spread and washed down with a sublime Javan coffee; **b24** not sure when I saw a darker bourbon at 12 years commercially available. Remember that in straight bourbon colour represents interaction between spirit and barrel. So expect big oak presence and you will not be disappointed! A bourbon for bourbon lovers with very hairy chests – male or female.. *67.1% (134.2 proof) ncf.*

Elijah Craig 18 Years Old Single Barrel barrel no. 3328, dist 8/9/91 **(94.5) n25 t23.5 f22.5 b23.5.** Masterful. Don't even bother opening the bottle unless you have an hour to spend. *45%*

⸭ **Elijah Craig 21 Year Old Single Barrel** barrelled 26/11/90, barrel no. 41 db **(95.5) n23.5** the busy nose shows no discomfort despite the major age: a real jumble of seasonings ranging from the nonchalantly sweet toasted honeycomb through to the much more abrupt ginger and coriander mix and diced, dried orange peel. A light sprinkling of salt brings everything out to the full; **t24**, and, of course, it is that oak-weighted seasoning which shows first, semi explosively and almost like botanicals of a dry gin. The sugars, flanked by minute amounts of ulmo honey, take their time to evolve and thread their way into the complex tapestry; **f23.5** still mainly dry with the vanillas building alongside the increasingly peppery spices; light corn oil helps spread the limited sugar and honey; **b24.5** even by bourbon's high standards, this is a thing of rare beauty and of a type. One of the most subtle and sophisticated bottlings you'll ever find at this age and one for those who prefer their Martinis and gins dry. And I mean very dry.... *45%.*

Elmer T Lee Single Barrel (91) n22 t23.5 f(22.5) b23. A sturdy, dense bourbon with above average sweetness. So effortless, it is hard to immediately realise that greatness has entered your glass. *45%*

⸭ **Elmer T. Lee Single Barrel Bourbon 1919 - 2013** db **(96.5) n24.5** BT at its most genteel and delicate: an evening breeze of honeysuckle, rain-washed roses and orange blossom. Below that, a darker, earthier depth – a rich aroma from which much might grow; **t24** quite brilliant. A disguised delivery moving your senses in one direction thanks to a rumbling, growling, tannin-rich preamble, then suddenly switches tack and offers a flutier, juicier, more highly charged, spice-ridden essay of small grains and a few kumquats; **f24** perhaps the most chocolate-rich finish of any whisky this year. And we are not talking Hershey but high quality oily cocoa bean of a distinctly South American hue: wow! **b24** I left this as the 1,145th and final new whisk(e)y to be tasted for the 2015 Jim Murray's Whisky Bible. Elmer, once a neighbour of mine, loved his garden and more than once I helped him safely remove squirrels without them being hurt in any way. Which makes this whiskey, seemingly gentle but with a backbone of American steel - yet on the nose flowing with floral notes, a touching and entirely apposite marker to his memory. And it delights me to say that I know, with absolute certainty, he would have been blown away by this barrel of glorious complexity. Elmer: with a glass of this rare genius I salute your memory, my friend. *46.5%*

European Bourbon Rye Association Kentucky Straight Bourbon Whiskey 16 Years hogshead, cask no. 1.1, dist 1994 **(95.5) n24.5** a Kentucky bourbon offering sublime Danish marzipan coated with Venezuelan cocoa and Demerara sugar. If that isn't enough, there is a touch of New Zealand manuka honey and Chilean ulmo honey. Does a nose really get more international than this...? **t24.5** the delivery is nothing as scary as it seems: keep your mouth open while tasting and the alcohol burns off quickly leaving a stunning residue of fabulously concentrated toasted honeycomb and ulmo honey notes. Next a slow deployment of slightly sweetened marmalade tones. Incredible! **f23** finishes like most 16 years olds...quickly! That is once you get past the enormous middle; **b23.5** mind-blowing whisky; the sort of stuff you can trust good ol' Mr Bourbon in Germany to unearth. A stunner..The whiskey ...not Mr Bourbon... *82.7% (165.4 Proof). sc. EBRA. 77 bottles.*

Evan Williams 23 Years Old (94) n22 t23.5 f24.5 b24. Struts his stuff, refusing to allow age to slow him or dim the shine from his glowing grains. Now oak has taken its toll. This seems older than its 23 years... Or so I first thought. Then a light shone in my soul and it occurred to me: hang on...I have wines going back to the last century. For the older ones, do I not allow them to breathe? So I let the whiskey breathe. And, behold, it rose from the dead. This Methuselah of a whiskey had come alive once more...and how!! *53.5%*

Evan Williams Single Barrel Vintage 2002 barrel no 1. barrelled 7 Jun 02 bott 1 Nov 11 **(92.5) n23.5 t23.5 f22.5 b23.** An altogether different animal to the Evan Williams single barrel which came from the original Heaven Hill distillery: that was incapable of making a bourbon as feminine as this... *43.3% (86.6 Proof)*

Evan Williams Single Barrel Vintage 2003 barrel no 1. barrelled 11 Feb 03, bott 28 Nov 12 **(84.5) n22 t22 f20 b20.5.** How curious. When this brand was first launched, the whiskey came from the original Heaven Hill distillery and the big copper content showed through its luxurious complexity. Here we have a great deal of honey and a brash sugary lead on delivery. But the lack of copper is evident further down the line. *43.3% (86.6 Proof)*

⁙ **Evan Williams Single Barrel 2004 Edition** barrel no. 1, dist 19/03/2004, bott 16/11/2013 db **(89.5) n22** relatively simplistic: ulmo honey and vanilla enlivened by a faint dash of tangerine peel; **t24** profound early sugars, mainly of an icing and syrupy variety. The spices are dull, though weighty and plod and prod rather than stimulate; **f21.5** thins and vanillas out with surprising abruptness; **b22** demure: wouldn't say boo to a goose. *43.3%. 19th in the series.*

⁙ **Four Roses 125th Anniversary Small Batch Bourbon** OBSV - 18 years, OBSK - 13years, OESK- 13 years db **(96.5) n24** how can something so big and rich be equally as delicate and complex? Quintessential bourbon aroma with manuka honey, liquorice, treacle, black cherry, coffee and toasted honeycomb all dipping in and out, or forming a whole...; **t24.5** the rye I couldn't find on the nose has saved itself for the crisp, juicy, controlled, sweetened delivery. Corn oils have formed now and hold the dark sugars and magnificent spices beautifully; **f24** toasty, medium roast Java coffee, then a slow fade in which the sugars counter the gathering tannin-led bitterness; **b24** nosing and tasting a whiskey like this and, after a morning of sulphur-ruined horrors, I am reminded why I still do this job. A celebration of bourbon; a triumph of blending. *51.6%. ncf. 12468 bottles. WB15/385*

Four Roses Limited Edition 2012 Small Batch Barrel Strength (96) n24 if someone asked me to show exactly how a rye-included mashbill bourbon should nose, I could do no better than to pour this: it is truly classic with a fascinating, almost bottomless depth to the dark sugars which works in breath-taking tandem with one of the most subtle and disarming citrus and strawberry sub plots you will find; **t24.5** crisp, salivating and bulging with the rye present: clean, yet so amazingly complex; **f23.5** Phase II: ditch the crispness and replace it with a soft toffee finale; **b24** the improvement of Four Roses has been one of the highlights of recent world whisky events. I was curious to see if this 2012 edition could carry on where the sublime 2011 left off. It has. *57.5% (115 Proof). 4000 Bottles approx.*

Four Roses Single Barrel warehouse US cask no. 10-2A **(96.5) n25 t24.5 f23 b24.** If you have ever wondered if Four Roses has the wherewithal to play amongst the super-elite of the whiskey world, then track down this particular bottling and all will be revealed...For me, the finest Four Roses I have ever come across. *50%*

Four Roses Single Barrel barrel 11-3T **(94) n23.5 t23 f23.5 b24.** In so many ways the quintessential delicate bourbon. But one of the most attractive for chocoholics, too.... *50%*

Four Roses Single Barrel barrel no 8-1 Q **(91) n22.5 t23.5 f22 b23.** This bourbon reminds you of how Four Roses was a decade ago when it embraced a lighter style. Except it now has a chunkier depth. *50% (100 proof)*

Four Roses Single Barrel barrelled 11 Apr 01 35% rye mashbill barrel 4-1F **(95) n23.5** bristling rye and barley nibbles, nips and bites in all the right places; **t24.5** textbook – no, make that advanced textbook – delivery with the ryes really punching out the crisp, sugary lead while the sub plot of chocolate malt shake and crème brûlée fill in the spaces with pure joy; **f23** much more even, even slightly tangy with kumquats; very light spice and liquorice; **b24** brims with small grain complexity. A classy act. *61% Binny's, Chicago.*

Four Roses Single Barrel 9 Years 4 Months bott July 13 20% rye mashbill barrel 85-3Q **(94) n23.5 t24 f23 b23.5.** A wonderful bourbon, alternating between full-on and reserved. *58.8% Four Roses Gift Shop.*

Four Roses Single Barrel 11 Years bott July 13 20% rye mashbill barrel 47-4Q **(95) n23** cream wafer biscuits; fig roll cookies; **t24** oh, wow! Same mashbill as the 9-y-o, but very different delivery and personality: fabulously brittle, spiced and salivating delivery with oak interweaving from the very off; creamy textured, toffee-rich and chewy; **f23.5** now we enter cream toffee, a few toasted raisins and high cocoa content chocolate – with Demerara sugars at every corner; **b24.5** a three course bourbon. *61.1% Four Roses Gift Shop.*

Four Roses Single Barrel 11 Years bott July 13 35% rye mashbill barrel 29-3I **(86.5) n21.5 t21 f23 b21.** A serious pea souper of a bourbon. Perhaps a little bit too much of everything. The oak is all pervading, though the mocha and spice firestorms it sets off are lovely. I know some will die for a bourbon like this. But just feel it needs to breathe from time to time. The finish, though, where it gets a chance to stretch, is truly superb. *58.6 %*

Four Roses Single Barrel 12 Years 5 Months bott July 13 35% rye mashbill barrel 22-2F **(96.5) n24** a ridiculous nose for its age. So delicate with citrus, kiwi fruit and steamed yam so soft it could crumble; rhubarb tart offers bite while crisp sugars back off; **t24** just sit back and enjoy the glow...and after glow. The ryes are bursting out from every direction, offering an unspecified fruit, muscovado sugars and spice; the oak does the liquorice thing well; **f24** a gentle fade, but pointing at all the highlights before, with a little extra Bassett's chocolate liquorice for good measure; **b24.5** pretty hard to imagine a single barrel of bourbon outflanking this for all round sex appeal. Majestic and marvellous. *54.6%*

Four Roses 16 Years Old Single Barrel Barrel Strength barrel 78-3B, bott Nov 11 (96.5) **n24.5 t23.5 f24 b24.5**. In all honesty, 17 years ago – based on previous experience – if someone had asked if Four Roses had it in it to produce a top-drawer 16-year-old bourbon, I would have said: "probably not". Their whisky, then, was a little on the sparse side and struggled to add body to the oak. This, though, is not of a type that was around back in those days. The mix of fruit and chocolate is sublime. But above all, it's the silky texture and balance that have you scratching your head in amazement. *55.5%*

Four Roses 2013 Limited Edition Single Barrel #3-4P Aged 13 Years db (97) **n24.5** anyone who knows Fox's Party Rings biscuits from the UK will get this nose immediately. It involves vanilla and rich muscovado sugar and a little molasses for good measure. But then there is the light liquorice, too, and the ulmo honey spread on a thin slice of moist gingerbread. Magnificent. And truly classic...; **t24.5** a Four Roses feminine touch for it is sugar and spice and all things nice on delivery. The molasses ensure a crispness t the manuka honey and liquorice follow through, but then softens as the lightly oiled vanillas ad caramels arrive; the biting spice ensures that the classical aspect of this bourbon is sustained; **f24** long, oily molasses and treacle complicated by a seemingly rye-like crisp fruitiness; **b24** in that great horse racing state of Kentucky, the home of the Derby, only one distillery is seriously threatening Buffalo Trace's position of supreme bourbon maker. Coming fast up on the rails is Four Roses. Here is another truly sensational bottling. In many ways this is the quintessential bourbon displaying just about every character you can as for. The fact that so much has come from just a single barrel is truly astonishing, as usually you require several mixed together to offer such a rich and classic diversity on nose and palate. Indeed, this is probably the best single barrel bourbon I have ever encountered...from anywhere. *63.4%. WB15/173*

Four Roses 2014 Limited Edition Single Barrel Aged 11 Years Recipe OESF db (88.5) **n22** busy small grain plus a touch nougat and eucalyptus to accompany the honeycomb; **t23.5** light delivery though the intensity builds as the manuka honey and liquorice build up a head of steam; developing spice; **f21** unusally thin finale, with a little lime to accompany the vanilla; **b22** a pretty quiet cask refusing to scale the highest peaks. *60%*.

Four Roses Limited Edition Small Batch 2011 Barrel Strength oldest 13-y-o, youngest 11-y-o (95.5) **n23.5 t24 f24 b24**. The bottles of Four Roses I have been working through this year have been one of the most extraordinary treats it has been my privilege to enjoy for a very long time. This, on top of the 16-year-old is simply blowing me away... *55.1%*

George T Stagg dist Winter 1993, bott Fall 2011 (96.5) **n24 t25 f24 b24.5**. Before the bottling of each George T Stagg, the stirring process can shake the dice somewhat, and the scores can be different. Here we see Stagg with fewer oils than normal. This has shifted its stance very slightly. But you have only to ask an astronomer what happens if a planet changes its orbit by only fractions of a degree... *71.3% (142.6 Proof)*

George T. Stagg (97.5) **n24 t25 f24 b24.5**. Astonishing how so much oak can form and yet have such limited negative impact and so few unpleasant side effects. These tasting notes took nearly four hours to compile. Yet they are still in a simplified form to fit into this book... George T Stagg is once again... staggering. *71.5% (143 Proof). ncf.*

George T. Stagg (Barrel Proof) db (95) **n24** a big parade of rye and creamy toffee make a curious juxtaposition; toffee apple against the ever-intensifying spice also make for another big match; **t24** just like on the nose, the delivery is a battle between rye grain and caramel supremacy, only now with no quarter given: salivating, mainly crisp and, again, echoing the nose, spices gather and intensify to startling effect; **f23** an outbreak of vanilla and butterscotch, topped by liquorice and molasses, makes for a relatively supine finale; **b24** quite beautiful bourbon of the top order. But not quite so breathtakingly complex and brain-shatteringly vivid as Staggs of past times. *64.1%. Buffalo Trace Antique Collection.*

George T. Stagg Limited Edition (96.5) **n24** it is as if someone has come up with the quintessential bourbon aroma...and then multiplied it by itself. This is huge, yet the small grains are busy enough to ensure the complexity levels go spinning off the chart. Even a few apples at play. Interestingly low in oils for a Stagg; **t24.5** if you want to know what a big game bourbon should taste like, just take a small mouthful of this. The rye ensures a degree of sharpness present; there are eye-wateringly bright sugars and some serious toasted honeycomb; the tannins nibble; at last the oils form though the spices allow them only so far; **f24** beautifully toasty, all kinds of mocha and hickory and even the outlines of a rather overcooked blackberry tart; **b24** as spectacular as a sunset from the hilltop village of Coldharbour in my beloved Surrey *71.4% (142.8 proof). ncf.*

Hancock's Reserve Single Barrel (92) **n23 t23 f21.5 b22.5**. A slightly quieter example of this consistently fine brand. The nose, though, is the stuff of wet whiskey dreams... *44.45%*

Jefferson's Reserve batch no. 84 **(91)** n23 t23.5 f22 b23. Once a 15-year-old, no age statement here. But this has seen off a few Summers, and sweetened with each passing one. 45.1%. 2400 bottles.

Jim Beam Black Double Age Aged 8 Years (93) n23 t24 f22.5 b23.5. Rather than the big, noisy, thrill-seeking JB Black, here it is in quiet, reflective, sophisticated mode. Quite a shift. But no less enjoyable. 43% (86 proof)

⠿ **Jim Beam Signature Craft Aged 12 Years** db **(92.5)** n23 gorgeous roasted coffee and liquorice. The rye pokes through gamely; **t23.5** soft delivery with a wonderful toasted fudge quality. Takes time for the rye to arrive but it does as the spices mount; **f23** softly spiced with plenty of creamy mocha; **b23** classic Beam: big rye and massive fruit. Quite lovely. 43% WB15/386

John B. Stetson Straight Bourbon Whiskey (92) n23.5 t23.5 f22 b23. Absolutely love it! Quality: I take my hat off to you...42%

John E. Fitzgerald Larceny (94) n23 t23.5 f23.5 b24. If this doesn't win a few converts to wheated bourbon, nothing will. A high quality, stunningly adorable whiskey, pulsing with elegance and personality. Every drinks cabinet should have this wonderful new addition to the bourbon lexicon. 46%

John J Bowman Virginia Straight Bourbon Single Barrel (94) n23 t24 f23 b24. One of the biggest yet most easily relaxed and beautifully balanced bourbons on the market. 50%

Johnny Drum (Black Label) (89.5) n22 t23 f21.5 b23. How often does that happen? The same whiskey, different strength, virtually same quality (though this has a little more depth) but gets there by a slightly different route. 43%

Johnny Drum (Green Label) (89) n22.5 t23 f21 b22.5. Much more honey these days. Worth making a bee-line for. 40%

Johnny Drum Private Stock (90.5) n22.5 t22.5 f23 b22.5. One of those bourbons where a single glass is never quite enough. Great stuff! 50.5% (101 proof)

Kentucky Vintage batch 08-72 **(94.5)** n23.5 delicate to the point of brittle. Playful spice prickles as the small grains dance and tease; beautiful citrus notes are just showing off; **t24.5** the whole thing just melts in the mouth. No grating oak nor rabid spices. No bitter char. Just an intricate and delicate mix of grain and vanilla interweaving...and then melting along with some accompanying butterscotch and muscovado sugar. Quite stunning; **f23** both the bitterness and spices grow. But all is balanced and genteel; **b23.5** staggered! I really didn't quite expect that. Previous bottlings I have enjoyed of this have had hair attached to the muscle. This is a very different Vintage, one that reaches for the feminine side of a macho whiskey. If you want to spend an hour just getting to know how sensitive your taste buds can be, hunt down this batch... 45%

Knob Creek Aged 9 Years (94.5) n23.5 almost arrogantly consistent: you know pretty well what you are going to get...and there it is. In this classic whiskey's case a whole bunch of honeycomb and vanilla, always more delicate than it first appears...; **t24** salivating delivery with rye and barley absolutely hammering on the palate. The corn oil is there not for flavour but effect – it is a fabulous mixture of dates and Demerara rum having the biggest say; **f23.5** wonderfully long with the oak toastiness now really beginning to bite...; **b23.5** no whiskey in the world has a more macho name, and this is not for the faint-hearted. Big, hard in character and expansive, it drives home its point with gusto, celebrating its explosive finish. 50%

Maker's Mark (Red Seal) (91) n22.5 t23.5 f22 b23. The big honey injection has done no harm whatsoever. This sample came from a litre bottle and the whiskey was darker than normal. What you seem to have is the usual steady Maker's with a helping hand of extra weight. In fact this reminds me of the old Maker's Gold wax. 45%

Maker's 46 (95) n23.5 crushed toasted hazelnuts dappled with honeycomb and delicate hickory; beautifully even and well mannered; **t24.5** quite superb: an initially thick, intense delivery which fans out in directions; excellent weight as those honeycomb notes go into overdrive; a dotting of wheaty and oaky spices but it's the way the softest of silky and highly complex flavours crash feather-like into the taste buds which cranks up the points; **f23** surprisingly light and simplistic with the accent firmly on vanilla; **b24** some people have a problem with oak staves. I don't: whisky, after all, is about the interaction of a grain spirit and oak. This guy is all about the nose and, especially, the delivery. With so much controlled honey on show, it cannot be anything other than a show-stopper. Frankly, magnificent. I think I've met my Maker's... 47% (94 proof)

Noah's Mill batch 10-170 **(93)** n23.5 t23.5 f23 b23. This monster of a bourbon just rumbles along on the palate like one of the four thunderstorms I have encountered in Kentucky today... 57.15%

Noah's Mill batch 13-81 **(93.5)** n23 gorgeous glazed almonds; a little citrus & cold coffee; **t23.5** oddly enough, doesn't taste like the nose: much more macho, with the full blooded hickory & Demerara; enormous weight & depth; assorted honey notes begin to form; **f22.5** gentle finale, reverting back to the style of the aroma. Excellent vanilla on sugars & weightier liquorice; **b23.5** a full bodied classic bourbon which undulates over the palate. 57.15% (114.3 proof)

Old Fitzgerald Very Special 12 Years Old (93) n24 t23.5 f22.5 b23. There is always something that makes the heart sing when you come across a whiskey which appears so relaxed in its excellence. At the moment my heart is in the shower merrily lathering itself... 45%

Old Forester Birthday Bourbon dist Spring 93, bott 2005 (94) n24 t23 f23 b24 One of the most rye-studded stars in the bourbon firmament and wholly in keeping with the fabulous quality for which this brand has now become a byword. 40%

Old Grand-Dad (90.5) n22 t23 f23 b23.5. This one's all about the small grains. A busy, lively bourbon, this offers little to remind me of the original Old Grand-Dad whiskey made out at Frankfort. That said, this is a whisk(e)y-lover's whiskey: in other words the excellence of the structure and complexity outweighs any historical misgivings. Enormously improved and now very much at home with its own busy style. 43%

Old Grand-Dad Bonded 100 Proof (94.5) n22.5 light rye spices and citrus fruit pop around the glass. One of those weighty yet delicate bourbons, but here the small grain appear at full throttle; t24 impossible not to be blown away. Exactly like the nose, you are expecting from first impact thundering, almost bullying oak. Instead your taste buds are mesmerised by a fabulous infusion of busy rye: a thousand tiny, crisp explosions in every quarter of the mouth followed by a layering of coconut strands dipped in lightly charred, molten sugars...; f23.5 very toasty with the oak now unflinchingly taking the rye on; b24.5 obviously Old Grand-dad knows a thing or two about classy whiskey: this is a magnificent version, even by its own high standards. It was always a winner and one you could bet your shirt on for showing how the small grains can impact upon complexity. But this appears to go a stage further. The base line is a touch deeper, so there is more ground to cover on the palate. It has been a whiskey-lover's whiskey for a little while and after a few barren years, has been inching itself back to its great Frankfort days. The fact that Beam's quality has risen over the last decade has played no insignificant part in that. 50% (100 proof)

Old Rip Van Winkle 10 Years Old (93) n24 t23 f23 b23. A much sharper cookie than it once was. And possibly a Maryland Cookie, too, what with the nuts and chocolate evident. As graceful as it is entertaining. 45% (90 Proof). Buffalo Trace.

Old Weller Antique 107 (96) n24.5 only pour this one if you have a good half hour to spare: the nose absolutely mesmerises as it changes shape and depth continuously. The honeys are soft and graceful, never dominating but rounding edges. The spices are well mannered yet condiment. The fruit takes the direction of apple and mango. Together they create a near faultless harmony; t24 the wheat is vibrant, pressing bold spices into a honeyed core. The layering accentuated by the liquorice and hickory which balance the sweeter elements with rare panache; f23.5 long with varying textures of oak. Never dries too much while refusing to allow the bountiful sugars the upper hand. All the time the spices throb... b24 this almost blew me off my chair. Always thought this was pleasant, if a little underwhelming, in the past. However, this bottling has had a few thousands volts past through it as it now comes alive on the palate with a glorious blending of freshness and debonair aging. One of the surprise packages of 2012. 53.5% (107 proof)

⋯ **Orphan Barrel 'Barterhouse' 20 Years Old** (91) n22.5 elegant, almost playful, lavender and mint notes combine to give the softest outline to the big tannins; t22.5 mouth-watering delivery despite age with only a gentle degree of spice. The oak bites but ample molasses absorb the shockwaves; f23 the over-eagerness of the oak is stifled only by that impressive, dry molasses. The spice doesn't lose confidence...; b23 to think: this was still white dog when I first visited Old Stitz! 45.1%.

⋯ **Orphan Barrel 'Old Blowhard' 26 Years Old** (95) n23.5 fabulous, classic old bourbon: like the stuff I used to get from the inside of ancient barrels many years ago, seemingly still having something of the char on the nose as well as the profound burnt honeycomb and liquorice; t24 brilliant delivery: thick almost rummy Demerara, liberally laced with spice, vanilla and toasted coconut; f23.5 a sharp, almost acrid intensity to the toastiness now. But near sludgy molasses and manuka honey finds just enough sweetness to guarantee balance; b24 I do get my hands on a few samples of very old bourbon, but this seems to have a style more recognisable in the 1980s and early to mid '90s than now. Time warp whisky in every sense. Wonderful! 45.35%. Bottled in Tullahoma, aged 26 years, "found in Stitzel Weller".

Pappy Van Winkle's Family Reserve 15 Years Old (96) n24.5 the usual blood oranges by the cartload...the lilting mix of plum juice and white bread kneaded until it has become a sweet, sugary ball. All that plus a shy spiciness and some broad oak. But what makes it all work is the lightness of the mix...so big...yet so delicate...; t23.5 lush but with those threatening oaks on the nose exploding on impact. For a moment just a little OTT, but then several huge waves of cocoa-lined vanilla and marmalade puts the world to rights again...; f24 long and back to unbridled elegance. Cocoas flit around, as do those wheated softly, softly spices and layers of thinned manuka honey... stunning...; b24 at a book signing in Canada earlier this year a Bible enthusiast asked me which well-aged, wheated bourbon he should look for. I told him Pappy 15. He looked at me quizzically and said: "Well, that's what I thought, but in the Bible you have it down as rye-recipe." I told him he was wrong... until I checked there and then. And discovered he was right. Of course, Pappy has always been wheated and the lushness on the palate and spices radiating from it has always confirmed this. I'll put it down to not spitting enough. Or perhaps the speed at which I type whilst tasting. Sometimes you mean one thing – then another word comes out. Like when a member of my staff asks for a pay rise. I mean no. But somehow say yes. So apologies to any other I fooled out there. For not only is this a wheated bourbon. With its improbable degree of deftness for something so big, it has edged up a notch or two into a truly world great whiskey...whatever the recipe. 53.5% (107 proof)

⫶⫶ **Parker's Heritage Collection "Promise of Hope" Single Barrel 10 Years** db (95) n24 hard to imagine how so much complexity can evolve from a single barrel...a deep aroma lightened by sublime layering of sugars, mainly muscovado, aided and abetted by watered maple syrup. Gentle hints of orange and marzipan add depth and direction t24 this has "Parker Beam" stamped all over the taste buds: a man who prefers his whisky lush, sweet and profound; a whiskey which the average north American bear would make a lethal swipe for, so full it is of yummy honey. But it needs the injection of almost perfectly infused spices to launch this to the next level and act as the perfect counter to the blend of ulmo and manuka honeys which, combining with the liquorice, make for a sublime experience of riches engulfing the palate; f23 thins as the corn oils accelerate, but the spices persist; b24 in an age when masters Distillers assume that noble title after about ten minutes in the job and for marketing reasons alone, it is touching to find a whiskey bottled in honour of a genuine Master Distiller, a man who has probably forgotten more about whiskey than the majority of the recent intake have so far learned. It is no less touching that part of the money raised from the sale of this whiskey will go to ALS charities, a condition under which Parker Beam now labours. 48%.

Parker's Heritage Collection Sixth Edition Master Distillery's Blend Of Mashbills Aged Since 2001 db (94.5) n24 my word! The small grains have a field day: the rye really ups the crisp fruit levels while the wheat shovels on the spice; elsewhere its big, sweetened liquorice to confirm the dozen years in barrel; t23.5 the sugars arrive as though blasted from a cannon: hard as rock and crystalline they positively burrow into the taste buds and if explosives are required the wheat provides it with some wicked spices; that all said, the mid-ground is a depositary for the more elegant, teasing by-products; f23 settles contentedly along a vanilla route. Some burnt toasty notes, as expected; the sugars more even now, almost quiet with a lovely fried yam fade...and spice, of course! b24 shows plenty of muscle, but subtlety and sophistication in equal measures, too. 63.5% (127 proof). ncf.

Parker's Heritage Collection Wheated Mash Bill Bourbon Aged 10 Years (97) n24 t24 f24.5 b24.5. Hard to find the words that can do justice. I know Parker will be immensely proud of this. And with every good reason: I am working exceptionally hard to find a fault with this either from a technical distillation viewpoint or a maturation one. Or just for its sheer whiskeyness...A potential World Whisky of the Year. 62.1% (124.2 Proof). ncf.

Ridgemont Reserve 1792 Aged 8 Years (94.5) n23.5 throbbing, pulsing oak is kept comfortably in check with a soft honey and mint restraint. Fabulous depth and even a hint of salt to season the effect; t24 Barton's unique rye and Demerara combo is in full swing here and contrasts fascinatingly with the deeper, vaguely bitterish oak notes; f23.5 back to a vanilla and rye thread here, oscillating with the house brown sugars; the pulsing of the spice is sublime; b23.5 now here is a whiskey which appears to have come to terms with its own strengths and, as with all bourbons and malts, limitations. Rarely did whiskey from Barton reach this level of maturity, so harnessing its charms always involves a bit of a learning curve. Each time I taste this it appears a little better than the last...and this sample is no exception to the rule. Excellent. 46.85% (93.7 Proof)

Rowan's Creek Batch 13-88 (82) n20 t21.5 f20.5 b20. A modest bourbon short on complexity and weight but big on spice and delicate sugars. 50.05% (100.1 proof)

Russell's Reserve Single Barrel (94) n23.5 t24 f23 b23.5. Old-fashioned, thick as treacle bourbon. Delicious. 55%. ncf. Wild Turkey.

Russell's Reserve Small Batch 10 Year Old (92.5) n24.5 t23 f22 b23. Had the quality and complexity on the palate followed on from the nose I may well have had the world's No 1 whisky for 2012 in my glass. Just slum it with something quite wonderful, instead. Still waiting for an official explanation as to why this is a miserly 90 proof, when Jimmy Russell's preferred strength is 101, by the way... 45%. Wild Turkey.

⫶⫶ **Smooth Ambler Old Scout Straight Bourbon Aged 7 Years** bott 13 (94.5) n23.5 brilliant nose: the rye compartment is next door to the clean, crisp Demerara. Fruity, sharp and pulsing; t23.5 fresh, again showing its rye recipe credentials to the full. Fabulous clarity with a Jim Beam style intensity to the sugared liquorice; f23.5 long, with a beautifully controlled sweetness and late, elegant hickory flourish; b24 there is an argument that if you wanted to present someone with a bottle of bourbon to show them all its main and unique characteristics, this should be the one: very useful, indeed. 'Andy Ambler – a lion among the scouts. 49.5% WB15/372

⁛ **Smooth Ambler Old Scout Straight Bourbon 10 Years Old** batch 2, bott 4 May 13 **(95.5) n24** fruity: citrus and pear juice-calmed; light vanilla and even lighter spice; **t24** one of the softest bourbon deliveries at this strength I have encountered for a good while: the sugars are of the melt-on-impact variety, thickened only by the lightest touch of ulmo honey and broadened by a slow evolving of cream fudge and molasses. The liquorice is playful and the oak is from the butterscotch school; **f23.5** quietens further. A spicy buzz rumbles and forms the backdrop to the slowest possible fade of the delivery; **b24** one of the most delicate and sophisticated bourbons of the year. Absolutely every aspect of this glorious whisky is disarmingly understated...how un-American! 50% WB15/374

Spring 44 Straight Bourbon batch 2 **(84.5) n21 t22.5 f20.5 b20.5.** A straight Kentucky bourbon blended from two distinctly different rye recipe styles. The result is something very different, indeed – and sadly doesn't always work. In short, chocolate orange meets Yorkshire Tea. Odd. 45% (90 proof)

Spring 44 Single Barrel Bourbon batch 2, barrel no 8 **(93) n22 t23.5 f23.5 b24.** Pure entertainment. Ticks many of the boxes the Spring 44 bourbon misses. And, to be brutally honest, barrels properly blended should always outperform a single one. 50% (100 proof)

Stagg Jn (91.5) n22.5 t24 f22.5 b22.5. A whiskey of staggering brinkmanship. Who will blink first? The massive oak or the taste buds. To be honest, this is the kind of bourbon that sorts out the men from the boys, the women from the girls. Doesn't have quite enough covering sweetness of varying type and intensity to match the complexity found in the original Stagg. One that needs a very long time to get to the bottom of. 67.2% (134.4 proof)

Very Old Barton 90 Proof (94) n23 t24 f23.5 b23.5. One of the most dangerously drinkable whiskeys in the world... 45% (90 proof)

Very Old Barton 6 Years Old (92) n23 t23 f23 b23. One of those seemingly gifted bourbons that, swan-like, appears to glide at the surface but on closer inspection has loads going on underneath. 43%

Virgin Bourbon 7 Years Old (96.5) n24 so Wild Turkey-esque in style it is almost untrue: just loads of honey spilling out of the glass, backed up by big rye and leathery oak; **t24.5** hold on to the arm of your seats...the mouth feel is massive with chocolate honeycomb surrounded by juicy dates and figs; liquorice has been piled high with really thick molasses...quite incredible; **f24** the corn oils carry the sugars to the very end. But like distant thunder beyond the limestone hills, comes the spices and that liquorice, now with a touch of hickory, rumbling to the last...; **b24** this takes me back nearly 40 years to when I first began my love affair with bourbon and was still a bit of a whisky virgin. This was the very style that blew me away: big, uncompromising, rugged...yet with a heart of honeyed gold. It is the type of huge, box-ticking, honest bourbon that makes you get on your hands and knees and kiss Kentucky soil. 50.5% (101 proof)

Virgin Bourbon 15 Years Old (92.5) n23.5 t23 f23.5 b23. The kind of bourbon you want to be left in a room with. 50.5% (101 proof)

Virginia Gentleman (90.5) n22 t23 f23 b23.5. A Gentleman in every sense: and a pretty sophisticated one at that. 40% (80 Proof)

Weller 12 Years Old (93) n24 t23.5 f22.5 b23. Sheer quality. And an enormous leap in complexity and grace from the 7-y-o. 45%

⁛ **Western Gold 6 Year Old Bourbon Whiskey (91.5) n22** heavy liquorice and faintly burnt toast; dry and debonair; **t23** early spice pricks through the light layering of manuka honey and hickory. Overall, deep, though with the Demerara acting as peacekeeper as the spices continue to thrust; **f22.5** soft oils and light buzzing spice; **b23** taken from barrels sitting high in the warehouse, that's for sure. You get a lot for your six years... 40%.

Wild Turkey 101 (91) n22 t23.5 f22.5 b23. By far the best 101 I have tasted in a decade: you simply can't do anything but go weak at the knees with that spice attack. 55.5% (101 proof)

Wild Turkey American Spirit Aged 15 Years (92) n24 t22.5 f22.5 b23. A delightful Wild Turkey that appears under par for a 100 proofer but offers much when you search those nooks and crannies of your palate. 50% (100 proof)

Wild Turkey Rare Breed bott code L0049FH **(94) n22.5 t24.5 f23 b24.** It is hard to credit that this is the same brand I have been tasting at regular intervals for quite a long while. Certainly nothing like this style has been around for a decade and it is massively far removed from two years ago. The nose threatens a whiskey limited in direction. But the delivery is as profound as it is entertaining. Even on this bottling's singular though fabulous style, not perhaps quite overall the gargantuan whiskey of recent years. But, seeing as it's only the nose which pegs it back a point or two, still one that would leave a big hole in your whiskey experience if you don't get around to trying. 54.1%

Willett Family Estate Bottled Single Barrel Bourbon 14 Years Old white oak barrel, cask no. 1067 **(96) n24** drier, more liquorice; **t23.5** intense delivery with a superb balance between the drier hickory-liquorice combo and the much more open, wider-reaching sugar. Some serious maple syrup in with the molasses here..; **f24.5** that is brilliant: exactly what bourbon should be about! No off notes, no bitterness. Just a complex but fading massaging of the taste buds, with neither those drier tones nor the sweeter ones – and all with the same characteristics as earlier) dominating...classic stuff...; **b24** if I didn't have a book to write I could taste this all day... *57.6%. sc. Special bottling for "Mr Bourbon" (Heinz Taubenheim). 72 bottles.*

Willett Pot Still Reserve barrel no. 2421 **(95.5) n24.5 t23 f24 b24.** Another fabulous whiskey from Willett. You can so often trust them to deliver and here they have given us a bourbon showing serious oak injection, yet a sweetness which counters perfectly. *47%. 273 bottles.*

William Larue Weller dist Fall 1998, bott Fall 2011 **(97.5) n24 t24 f25 b24.5.** Wow! This is becoming a must experience whiskey for hardcore bourbon lovers. Well, whisk(e)y lovers period, really! A bourbon which absolutely takes you to the wire with a "will it or won't it" type brinkmanship taking the flavours as far as they will go in an oaky direction without veering off the road and crashing down the cliff side. Majestic. Or, as it's American, perhaps I should say: Presidential.. *66.75% (133.5 Proof)*

William Larue Weller (97) n24 t24 f25 b24. Among the best wheated mash bill bourbon I have ever encountered. Why some whiskeys work better than others is the stuff of long debate. The reason for this particular bottling is relatively simple: you have an almost breathless intensity, yet somehow the constituent parts of the complexity can be individually identified and savoured. That is quite rare in any whiskey with this degree of weight. *67.4% (134.8 proof). ncf.*

William Larue Weller (97.5) n24 weightier than last time out, though only fractionally, and here much more dependent on a coffee framework backed by wonderfully crystallised dark sugars. Plenty of hickory and little cough sweet thicken the soup; **t24.5** it is probably impossible to get more types of dark sugars into the delivery of whiskey. This is so mesmerizing, you find yourself chuckling as the taste buds are asked to identify the myriad sugar and honey styles which pass through. I have counted eight with some form of certainty...though I'm sure I've missed a few, too; **f24** to make this whiskey work, you now need the finale to be moderately dry...to the point of sophistication. And that is exactly what you get. You can almost taste the char, though it is, like on the nose, the hickory which shapes the finish, comfortably cradling the spices which are dying to burst out; **b25** for any whiskey with a proof of 123.4, the only way is up...! Last year's Whisky Bible World Whisky of the Year Runner-up is going for the full title big time, no holds barred. Again, this is absolutely supreme class. *61.7% (123.4 proof). ncf.*

⠶ **William Larue Weller** dist Spring 2001 db **(97.5) n24.5** almost too profound for words: you nose this as you might peel an onion, simply by stripping away layer upon layer. The sugars are of the heaviest duty imaginable: a mix of treacle and molasses. But this is met by a toasty almost meaty thrust of oak and spice. So dense, outwardly, but give it time and you will be royally entertained; **t24.5** no less massive on delivery. As ever, the sugars are in mesmerising form; thick, dark, brooding, restrained and holding onto the chunky oak to somehow up the intensity. Like on the nose, it is the dark sugars which perform, now with some manuka honey entering the fray; the spices, now buzzing and nipping, are truly glorious; **f24** just a fraction more restrained and simplistic than before. The oak has made more of a fist of this and is determined to end the complexity of the sugars; **b24.5** I always save this as one of the last whiskeys I taste for each Bible. In life you always need something to look forward to... *68.1%. Buffalo Trace Antique Collection.*

⠶ **Woodford Reserve Batch 98 (85.5) n23 t21.5 f20 b21.** The promise of the nose, full of the kind of liquorice and mollasess lovers of Old Forester rightly drool over will be as disappointed as I at the bitterness which digs in hard from the mid-point onwards. *43.2%.*

⠶ **Woodford Reserve Batch 115 (90) n22** soft, delicate. Perhaps missing some complexity; mainly lemon-soaked vanilla; **t22** soft delivery; some citrus and coconut water amid the deeper tannin; **f23** late praline with no shortage of oily depth and demerera; really lovely spices come into their own as the story unfolds; **b23** for those who prefer their bourbons a little nutty and creamy. And spicy... *43.2%*

⠶ **Woodford Reserve Batch 124 (87) n22.5 t22 f21 b21.5.** Pleasant enough bourbon. Perhaps the tannins could do with a little muzzling, as they have too much to say when there are so few counter notes. The thickness of the oils hardly helps, either. Enjoyable squeezes of citrus and do enjoy the cocoa and lime theme. *43.2%*

⠶ **Woodford Reserve Batch 126 (87.5) n21.5 t23 f21.5 b22.** A very tame bourbon poodling along the Bourbon Highway at a steady 40mph. A slight over dependence on sugars make for a limitation in complexity, badly requiring some of the oak prevalent in batch 124 to make things happen. This lack of body allows a degree of over bitterness at the end. But plenty of citrus and at the late middle a welcome, if short-lived, burst of mocha. With plenty of Demerera, of course... *43.2% . WB15/172*

Woodford Reserve Distiller's Select batch 95 (**91**) **n23 t23 f22 b23**. Few bourbons so beautifully pits sweet against dry to such excellent effect. 43.2%

Woodford Reserve Master's Collection Four Grain (**95**) **n24 t24 f23 b24**. Sod's law would have it that the moment we removed this from the 2006 Bible, having appeared in the previous two editions without it ever making the shelves, it should at last be belatedly released. But a whiskey worth waiting for, or what? The tasting notes are not a million miles from the original. But this is better bourbon, one that appears to have received a significant polish in the intervening years. Nothing short of magnificent. 46.2%

Tennessee Whiskey
BENJAMIN PRICHARD
Benjamin Prichard's Tennessee Whiskey (**83**) **n21.5 t21 f20 b20.5**. Majestic fruity rye notes trill from the glass. Curiously yeasty as well; bounding with all kinds of freshly crushed brown sugar crystals. Pleasant enough, but doesn't gel like Prichard's bourbon. 40%

GEORGE DICKEL
George Dickel Superior No 12 Brand Whisky (**90.5**) **n22.5 t23 f22.5 b22.5**. A different story told by George from the last one I heard. But certainly no less fascinating. 45%

JACK DANIEL
Jack Daniel's 120th Anniversary of the White Rabbit Saloon (**91**) **n22.5** lighter ulmo honey to this, which just lowers the temperature and intensity of the liquorice. Complex stuff...; **t23.5** magnificent delivery: early corn oil carries the deft molasses; both black and red liquorice slowly builds but the middle is pure vanilla; **f22** a mix of dry molassed notes and a little muscovado. Excellent late balance; **b23** on its best-behaved form. After the delivery, the oils are down a little, so not the usual bombastic offering from JD. Nonetheless, this is pure class and the clever use of sugars simply make you drool... 43%. Brown-Forman.

⁙ **Jack Daniel's Holiday Select 2013 Limited Edition** db (**91.5**) **n23** probably the most well-seasoned nose I have ever experienced from JD. Less oil apparent allowing the herbs, spices and black cherry free reign. Almost as though perfumed...surely not...! **t23** remarkably dry delivery with the tannins biting deep and with very little sugar for support. Those which do come through are of the molassed variety; **f22.5** back to the spicy, seasoned style apparent on the nose; **b23** just never seen a JD like this...some pretty well cooked barrels in play here. Doubtless all this is by judicious barrel choice. Now the Americans are tampering with their casks, for the first time ever I began to wonder if the flavouring wasn't all natural. I am sure it is, but see what happens once you begin trying to change the rules...? 49% WB15/381

Jack Daniel's Old No.7 Brand (Black Label) (**92**) **n23 t23 f22.5 b23.5**. Actually taken aback by this guy. The heavier oils have been stripped and the points here are for complexity...that should shock a few old Hell's Angels I know. 40%

⁙ **Jack Daniel's Master Distiller Series No 1** db (**90.5**) **n24** wonderful dose of extra tangy kumquat over the normal JD signature; something of the fruity cough sweet about this one; **t22** a massive, pleasantly oiled mix of molassed fudge and liquorice; **f22** drier, toastier hickory; **b22.5** no mistaking the JD pedigree. Just a few telling extra degrees of fruit. 43% WB15/387

Jack Daniel's Single Barrel 12-5660 bott 15 Oct 12 db (**92.5**) **n23.5** such clarity to the crystallised Demerara sugar, even though some molasses seems to have got into the act; slight cloves and hickory fumble the mocha's blouse buttons; **t23.5** silk delivery, very much putting the onus on the crisp sugars to forge a bright path, along which the very light oils (certainly lighter than of old) travel, as well as a gentle fruit rye kick which acts as the rudder; **f22.5** much gentler than of yore with some spices amid the vanillas; **b23** I'll tell you something about JD. A number of "whisky specialist" I know rubbish this whiskey. With a passion. In fact, they can barely bring themselves to call it whiskey at all. But their single barrel range really does show what magnificent stock they have maturing in their warehouses. As this random bottling testifies... Magnificent stuff. And sod the so-called experts, I say...just enjoy it! 45%

Jack Daniel's Single Barrel Select cask no. 12-0451, bott 31 Jan 12 (**93.5**) **n23.5 t23.5 f23 b23.5**. Absolutely bang on the money. Gets the liquorice bite and sugars in superb combination to create a signature like no other distillery in the world. 45% (90 proof)

Corn Whiskey
Dixie Dew (**95**) **n22.5** corn whiskey...???? Really...??? The corn oils form a bit of a sweet blob, but elsewhere it is all about graduated degrees of cocoa and hickory...and all rather lovely. **t24** good grief!! Have not tasted a profile such as this: healthy corn oils but then a welter of Columbian Santander Cacao and rye-rich spices interject. Absolutely unique and astonishing...; **f24** the corn plays out its long farewell but the spices don't listen and take

up the main ground; a few juicy sultanas fly in...from goodness knows where; **b24.5** I have kept in my previous tasting notes for this whiskey as they serve a valuable purpose. The three matured corn whiskeys I have before me are made by the same distillers. But, this time round, they could not be more different. From Mellow Corn to Dixie we have three whiskeys with very differing hues. This, quite frankly, is the darkest corn whiskey I have ever seen and one of world class stature with characteristics I have never found before in any whiskey. Any true connoisseur of whisk(e)y will make deals with Lucifer to experience this freak whiskey. There is no age statement...but this one has gray hairs attached to the cob... 50%

Georgia Moon Corn Whiskey "Less Than 30 Days Old" (83.5) **n21.5 t22 f20 b20.** If anyone has seen corn whiskey made – either in Georgia or Kentucky – then the unique aroma will be instantly recognisable from the fermenters and still house. Enjoyable stuff which does exactly what it says on the jar. *50%*

J. W. Corn (92.5) **n23 t23.5 f23 b23.** In another life this could be bourbon. The corn holds the power, for sure. But the complexity and levels are so far advanced that this – again! – qualifies as very high grade whiskey. Wonderful that the normal high standard is being maintained for what is considered by many, quite wrongly, as an inferior spirit. *50%*

Mellow Corn (83) **n19 t21 f22 b21.** Dull and oily on the nose, though the palate compensates with a scintillating array of sweet and spicy notes. *50%*

Single Malt Rye
ANCHOR DISTILLERY
Old Potrero Single Malt Straight Rye Whiskey Essay 10-SRW-ARM-E (94) **n24 t23 f24 b23** The whiskey from this distillery never fails to amaze. With the distillery now under new management it will be fascinating to see what lands in my tasting lab. Even at 75% quality we will still be blessed with astonishing whiskeys. *45% (90 proof)*

Straight Rye
Benjamin Prichard's Tennessee Rye Whiskey (86) **n20 t21.5 f23 b21.5.** Bit of a scruffy nose, but polishes up pleasantly. The rye itself is not of the sharp variety and at times is hard to identify. But the ulmo honey and lush butterscotch offer the gloss at the finish. *43%*

Bulleit 95 Rye (96) **n25** only the rye from the Lawrenceburg Indiana distillery can conjure a perfect rye aroma such as this...and that is exactly where it is from. Cinnamon and crunchy muscovado sugar crystal on green apple...so soft...so rigid...so unique...; **t24.5** exactly as the nose is fashioned, so is the delivery. At once liltingly soft yet absolutely granite hard...the rye offers both fruity and spicy branches...both lead to a salivating trunk; **f22.5** echoes of firm grain and fruit but pretty quick by comparison to what has gone on before...**23.5** this is a style of rye, indeed whiskey, which is unique. Buffalo Trace makes an ultra high-quality rye which lasts the course longer. But nothing compares in nose and delivery to this...in fact few whiskies in the world get even close... 45%. Straight *95% rye mash whiskey.*

Colonel E.H. Taylor Straight Rye (97) **n24** how can a breezy whiskey, seemingly so light and full of sparkle, also have such an intensely dark side? The rye grains appear to have a spotlight on them following their every elegant movement; the spices, at first docile, build and build. Yet all the time, the grain appears to revel in its cut-glass sugary clarity. A little mystifying, too, as the vague clove and eucalyptus lurking in the background reveals an oak presence found nowhere else in the tasting experience; **t24.5** almost all you want from a rye: so clean, so intent in purpose, that the grain seems to transform into Demerara granules with the most polite oils and (for the oak) ulmo honey notes spreading all far and wide and with sensational eight; **f24** all is left to the muscovado sugar and quietly persistent ulmo honey to ensure no bitterness or any other wayward notes can infringe upon the charmingly sweet and still lively finish; **b24.5** reminds me of the younger ryes when Sazerac Handy first hit the shelves, with the emphasis on the clarity of the grain and the fallout of oak and spice. Really, a bottle which should never be left on a liquor store shelf. *50%*

Cougar Rye (95) **n25 t24 f23 b23.** The Lawrenceburg, Indiana Distillery makes the finest rye I have ever tasted - and that is saying something. Here is a magnificent example of their astonishing capabilities. Good luck hunting the Cougar. 37%. *Foster's Group, Australia.*

⠿ **Crater Lake Rye Whiskey Batch no. JA 08** db (83.5) **n20 t22 f20.5 b21.** A distinctly warming, peppery whiskey with an obvious high rye content. Would do itself better justice as a 100 proof whiskey as here the oils are broken down a little too enthusiastically, allowing unhelpful freedom to a tobacco note. Good early use of dark sugars, though. One to keep an eye on. *40%.*

Devil's Bit Seven-Year-Old Single Barrel (93.5) **n22.5 t24 f23 b24.** A must-find rye from one of the most impressive small distilleries in the world. 47.7%. *Edgefield Distillery.*

High West 12 Years Old Rye (92.5) **n22 t24 f23 b23.5.** A very clever rye which will hit a chord of appreciation for those who savour this whiskey style. *46%*

⁙ **High West Whiskey Rendezvous Rye Batch 12431** db (94.5) n23.5 sharp, classic rye. Hard as nails and brittle on the nose, the fresh fruity rye leaps from the glass; t24 and that sharpness translates perfectly onto the palate. A younger style than before, with far more salivating grain. The molasses is something else; f23 still profound and sharop b24 after a few disappointing batches, this one appears to have found that vital spark. It could be a whole new set of whiskeys, a change of one barrel, or even the same whiskey re-stirred before bottling. It doesn't matter: something has clicked. 46%. ncf. WB15/176

High West Rocky Mountain 21 Year Old Rye (95) n23 how sexy is that dance between the milky cocoa and the piercing rye...? t25 just about everything you could wish for: the rye (as is the case in the very best ones) offers a dual role: it both firms up and fruit enriches, and here refuses to overly play either hand. The sugars are pure melt in the mouth; honeydew melon and liquorice dry out towards a toasty butterscotch-hickory middle; f23 relaxes to let the vanillas (aided by a little cocoa) take charge; b24 bizarrely, tastes a whole lot younger than the 16-years-old. Lighter in both colour and character, here you get to see the full personality of an absolutely outstanding rye whiskey. 46%

Pappy Van Winkle's Family Reserve Rye 13 Years Old (94) n24 outwardly, the aroma basks in a crisp rye flourish; scratch below the surface and there are darker, more sinister oaky forces at work; t23.5 crisp, almost crackling rye offers both the fruity-clean and burned fruitcake options; f23 dulls out a bit as the liquorice/toffee oak takes hold but remains alluringly spicy and sensual; b23.5 uncompromising rye that successfully tells two stories simultaneously. A great improvement on the Winkle rye of old. 478%

Rittenhouse Very Rare Single Barrel 21 Years Old (91) n25 t23 f21 b22. I may be wrong, but I would wager quite a large amount that no-one living has tasted more rye from around the world than I. So trust me when I tell you this is different, a genuine one-off in style. By rights such telling oak involvement should have killed the whisky stone dead: this is like someone being struck by lightning and then walking off slightly singed and with a limp, but otherwise OK. The closest style of whisky to rye is Irish pot still, a unique type where unmalted barley is used. And the closest whiskey I have tasted to this has been 35 to 50-year-old pot still Irish. What they have in common is a massive fruit base, so big that it can absorb and adapt to the oak input over many years. This has not escaped unscathed. But it has to be said that the nose alone makes this worthy of discovery, as does the glory of the rye as it first melts into the tastebuds. The term flawed genius could have been coined for this whisky alone. Yet, for all its excellence, I can so easily imagine someone, somewhere, claiming to be an expert on whiskey, bleating about the price tag of $150 a bottle. If they do, ignore them. Because, frankly, rye has been sold far too cheaply for far too long and that very cheapness has sculpted a false perception in people's minds about the quality and standing of the spirit. Well, 21 years in Kentucky equates to about 40 years in Scotland. And you try and find a 40-year-old Scotch for £75. If anything, they are giving this stuff away. The quality of the whiskey does vary from barrel to barrel and therefore bottle to bottle. So below I have given a summary of each individual bottling (averaging (91.1). The two with the highest scores show the least oak interference...yet are quite different in style. That's great whiskey for you. 50% (100 proof). ncf.

Barrel no. 1 (91) n25 t23 f21 b22. As above. 50%
Barrel no. 2 (89) n24 t23 f20 b22. Dryer, oakier. 50%
Barrel no. 3 (91) n24 t23 f22 b22. Fruity, soft. 50%
Barrel no. 4 (90) n25 t22 f21 b22. Enormous. 50%
Barrel no. 5 (93) n25 t23 f22 b23. Early rye surge. 50%
Barrel no. 6 (87) n23 t22 f20 b22. Juicy, vanilla. 50%
Barrel no. 7 (90) n23 t23 f22 b22. Even, soft, honeyed. 50%
Barrel no. 8 (95) n25 t24 f23 b23. The works: massive rye. 50%
Barrel no. 9 (91) n24 t23 f22 b22. Sharp rye, salivating. 50%
Barrel no. 10 (93) n25 t24 f22 b22. Complex, sweet. 50%
Barrel no. 11 (93) n24 t24 f22 b23. Rich, juicy, spicy. 50%
Barrel no. 12 (91) n25 t23 f21 b22. Near identical to no.1. 50%
Barrel no. 13 (91) n24 t24 f21 b22. Citrus and toasty. 50%
Barrel no. 14 (94) n25 t24 f22 b23. Big rye and marzipan. 50%
Barrel no. 15 (88) n23 t22 f21 b22. Major oak influence. 50%
Barrel no. 16 (90) n24 t23 f21 b22. Spicy and toffeed. 50%
Barrel no. 17 (90) n23 t23 f22 b22. Flinty, firm, late rye kick. 50%
Barrel no. 18 (91) n24 t24 f21 b22. Big rye delivery. 50%
Barrel no. 19 (87) n23 t22 f21 b21. Major coffee input. 50%
Barrel no. 20 (91) n23 t24 f22 b22. Spicy sugar candy. 50%
Barrel no. 21 (94) n24 t23 f24 b23. Subtle, fruity. 50%
Barrel no. 22 (89) n23 t22 f22 b22. Mollased rye. 50%
Barrel no. 23 (94) n24 t23 f24 b23. Soft fruit, massive rye. 50%

Barrel no. 24 (88) n23 t22 f21 b22. Intense oak and caramel. *50%*
Barrel no. 25 (93) n25 t22 f23 b23. Heavy rye and spice. *50%*
Barrel no. 26 (92) n23 t23 f23 b23. Subtle, delicate rye. *50%*
Barrel no. 27 (94) n25 t23 f23 b23. Delicate rye throughout. *50%*
Barrel no. 28 (96) n25 t24 f23 b24. Salivating, roasty, major. *50%*
Barrel no. 29 (88) n23 t22 f21 b22. Hot, fruity. *50%*
Barrel no. 30 (91) n24 t23 f22 b22. Warming cough sweets. *50%*
Barrel no. 31 (90) n25 t22 f21 b22. Aggressive rye. *50%*

Rittenhouse Rye Single Barrel Aged 25 Years (93.5) n24.5 t24 f22 b23. This is principally about the nose: a thing of rare beauty even in the highest peaks of the whiskey world. The story on the palate is much more about damage limitation with the oak going a bit nuts. But remember this: in Scottish years due to the heat in Kentucky, this would be a malt well in excess of 50 years. But even with the signs of fatigue, so crisp is that rye, so beautifully defined are its intrinsic qualities that the quality is still there to be clearly seen. Just don't judge on the first, second or even third mouthful. Your taste buds need time to relax & adjust. Only then will they accommodate and allow you to fully appreciate and enjoy the creaky old ride. At this age, though, always worth remembering that the best nose doesn't always equal the best tasting experience... 50% (100proof).

Barrel no. 1 (93.5) n24.5 t24 f22 b23. As above. *50%*
Barrel no. 2 (88) n22 t24 f20 b22. Intense. Crisp, juicy; a tad soapy, bitter. *50%*
Barrel no. 3 (89.5) n23 t23.5 f21.5 b21.5. Fabulously crisp. Fruity. Mollassed. *50%*
Barrel no. 4 (85) n21.5 t21.5 f21 b21. Subdued fruit. Massive oak. *50%*
Barrel no. 5 (90.5) n25 t22.5 f21.5 b21.5. Complex. Mega oaked but spiced, fruity. *50%*
Barrel no. 6 (91.5) n24.5 t22 f23 b22. Tangy. Honeyed and hot. Spiced marmalade. *50%*
Barrel no. 7 (83.5) n20 t22 f20.5 b21. Treacle toffee amid the burnt apple. *50%*
Barrel no. 8 (90) n23.5 t23.5 f21 b22. Flinty, teeth-cracking rye. Crème brulee. *50%*
Barrel no. 9 (91) n23.5 t23.5 f22 b22. Massive ryefest. Mocha coated. *50%*
Barrel no. 10 (86.5) n22 t23 f20 b21.5. Early zip and juice. Tires towards caramel. *50%*
Barrel no. 11 (89) n24 t22 f23 b22. Honeycomb. Hickory. Caramel. Oil. *50%*
Barrel no. 12 (84.5) n22.5 t21 f20 b21. Delicate. Vanilla and caramel. Light. *50%*
Barrel no. 13 (89.5) n22.5 t23 f22 b22. Succulent. Yet rye remains firm. *50%*
Barrel no. 14 (88) n22 t23 f21 b22. Very similar to 13 but with extra caramel. *50%*
Barrel no. 15 (86) n21 t23 f20.5 b21.5. Lazy grain. Warming but flat. Caramel. *50%*
Barrel no. 16 (92) n23 t23 f23 b23. Sculpted rye: sugared fruit; a twist of juniper. *50%*
Barrel no. 17 (86.5) n22.5 t21.5 f21 b21.5. Fizzy, fruity spice calmed by caramel. *50%*
Barrel no. 18 (91) n23.5 t23.5 f21.5 b22.5. Pristine rye. Spice. Juicy molasses. Crisp. *50%*
Barrel no. 19 (96) n24 t23.5 f24.5 b23.5. Concentrated honeycomb and chocolate. *50%*
Barrel no. 20 (89.5) n23 t22 f22.5 b22. Cream toffee. Fruit and spice. *50%*
Barrel no. 21 (85) n21 t20 f23 b21. Severe oak delivery. Recovers with mocha toffee. *50%*
Barrel no. 22 (81) n20 t20 f21 b20. Mild sap. Fruity. Oily. *50%*
Barrel no. 23 (94) n23.5 t24 f23.5 b23. Rich. Fruity. Juicy. Clean. Corn oil. Cocoa. *50%*
Barrel no. 24 (88.5) n22.5 t22 f21 b22. Huge vanilla. Slow spice. *50%*
Barrel no. 25 (88) n22.5 t21.5 f22 b22. Custard and sugared fruit. Sharpens. *50%*
Barrel no. 26 (90.5) n22 t23 f23 b22.5. Classic crisp rye. Big, manageable oak. *50%*
Barrel no. 27 (88) n23 t22 f21.5 b21.5. Huge, honeyed oak. Oily. Dries at end. *50%*
Barrel no. 28 (91) n22.5 t23.5 f22.5 b22.5. Exemplary honeycomb-rye delivery. Spices. *50%*
Barrel no. 29 (94) n23.5 t24 f23 b23.5. Juicy rye; crisp sugar-vanilla-hickory fade. *50%*
Barrel no. 30 (94.5) n23 t24 f24 b23.5. Thick rye. Cocoa. Spices. *50%*
Barrel no. 31 (79) n21 t20 f19 b19. Lethargic. Bitter. *50%*
Barrel no. 32 (88) n21.5 t22.5 f22 b22. Relaxed honeycomb. Hint of mint. *50%*
Barrel no. 33 (88.5) n22.5 t22 f22 b22. Powering oak-rye battle. *50%*
Barrel no. 34 (84) n23 t21 f20 b20. Thick oak throughout. Corn oil. *50%*
Barrel no. 35 (93.5) n22.5 t23.5 f24 b23.5. Big rye. Demerara-hickory. Complex. *50%*
Barrel no. 36 (77) n21 t19 f18 b19. Bitter oak. *50%*

Russell's Reserve Rye 6 Year Old Small Batch bott. code L0194FH) (93.5) n24 t23.5 f22.5 b23.5. Has lost none of its wit and sharpness: in fact has improved a notch or two in recent times. Wonderful! 45% (90 proof)

Sazerac Kentucky Straight Rye Whiskey 18 Years Old bott Fall 2010 (95) n23.5 t24 f23.5 b24. Some ego-driven, know-nothing commentators who for some mysterious reason claim an expertise with whiskey wonder how people can give different scores each year for a rye which has been living in a stainless steel vat. Of course, it would not occur to them that each time the vat is stirred before bottling the mix reveals subtle differences, depending on where the molecules fall. Line up Sazerac 18, one after the other from the last few years, and tell me which one is identical to the other. They are all quite different, and this one appears to have more than its fair share of sawdust and tannin. 45% (90 Proof)

Sazerac Kentucky Straight Rye Whiskey 18 Years Old dist Spring 1985, bott Fall 2011 (96.5) n24.5 t24 f24 b24. If you are looking to climb the Everest of rye whiskeys, then good luck in scaling the lofty, jagged peaks. 45% (90 Proof)

Sazerac Kentucky Straight Rye Whiskey 18 Years Old bott 2012 (95.5) n24 yet again a fascinating, subtle difference to previous years. This time a vague nougat toffee underpins the much brighter fruity and crispy rye; a little more earthy, also; t23 probably a first: wild cherries are plucked ripe and bulbous from the delivery, the intense fruity sharpness – with a just so touch of sweetness - masking the semi-aggressive roasty oak which accompanies it, though about half a beat behind. The mid-ground, despite a launching of tingling spices, remains juicy and mouth-watering, even though the grumbling oak tries to negate the freshness; f24 the vanillas which show first midway through now make a much more confident grip. Like a kind of cherry trifle, the finale sweetens and delights; b24.5 unquestionably showing a different side to its personality this time out, allowing the rye to show its fruity personality to the full. 45%

⋅∷⋅ **Sazerac Rye 18 Year Old** bott Fall 2013 db (97) n24.5 if you are studying whiskey and need to know exactly how a straight rye should nose, stick your beak above a glass of this: sparkling grain, crisp, refined, unsullied by caramel and crystalline; t24.5 heavier now than the nose: the oak has made inroads and forges a delightful partnership with the light oils. Again, the sweetness is spot on, just enough muscovado to make the rye almost three dimensional in its sharpness; f24 settles for a softer touch now, though the spices compensate. Hard to imagine a better rye-oak balance, though; b24 another stir of the pot and up comes Sazerac 18 polished and wallowing in its own enormity. Rye whiskey exactly how it should be. 45%. Buffalo Trace Antique Collection.

⋅∷⋅ **Smooth Ambler Old Scout Straight Rye Aged 7 Years** batch 17, bott 9 Nov 13 (82) n21 t22 f19 b20. Now this is odd. What do you get when you combine the characteristics of rye and gin? Something, probably, like this. Never been to these guys in West Virginia, though I'll try and make a point of paying a visit when next in that stunning state. No idea if they are involved with gin. But something about the botanical feel to the nose and finish in particular suggests they might. Intrigued. 49.5% WB15/373

⋅∷⋅ **Sonoma County Rye** pot distilled from grain db (83.5) n21 t21.5 f20 b21. Sweet nougat, heavy duty, wide-cut oily. Quite German in style. 48%. 1512 Spirits. WB15/384

Thomas H. Handy Sazerac Straight Rye Whiskey (97) n24 t25 f24 b24. It has taken me over three hours to taste this. Were all whiskies and whiskeys like this, the Bible, quite simply, would never see the light of day. Beyond enormous. A whiskey which located taste buds I had no idea I actually possess... Just like his near namesake, Thomas Hardy, Thomas Handy has come up with a rambling, immortal classic. 64.5% (129 proof). ncf.

Thomas H Handy Sazerac Straight Rye Whiskey dist Spring 2005, bott Fall 2011 (97.5) n24 t24.5 f24.5 b24.5. A real slow burner. Takes a bit of time on the nose to leave the launch pad. But once off the ground it just doesn't stop travelling. Superb! 64.5% (128.6 Proof)

Thomas H. Handy Sazerac Straight Rye Whiskey (97.5) n24 heavy on the spice and honey and quite light on the flinty rye which can often be found here. Entangled, enticing, beguiling....; t24.5 hold on to your hats, the chair...nail yourself to the ground...this is going to be some ride. The rye appears to have been to the gym and grown a few extra muscles: this is big and the spice will demolish the lily-livered beyond comprehension. The rye grains are always at the centre, even when a little liquorice forms towards the midpoint; f24.5 long and now back to the grain once more with the varying sugar strains head in all directions; a slightly dry finish as, at last, the oak gets a word in but the countering sweetness is ulmo honey at its deftest; b24.5 this was World Whisky of the Year last year and anyone buying this on the strength of that will not be disappointed. Huge whiskey with not even the glimmer of a hint of an off note. Magnificent: an honour to taste and rye smiles all round. 66.2%. ncf.

⋅∷⋅ **Thomas H. Handy** dist Spring 2007 db (93) n22.5 a charming nose, but dull by Thomas Handy standards with the usual bright rye being outmuscled by some intimidating caramel; t24.5 much more like it on delivery with the rye, gleaming but still not quite at its brightest, now thudding heavily on the palate; less juicy than normal: mocha sweetened by fudge and treacle; f23 a quiet, restrained finale with toffee again to the fore; b23 can't remember the last time I found so much natural caramel at every turn of a Thomas Handy. 64.2%.

Van Winkle Reserve Rye Aged 13 Years Old (94.5) n23.5 beautiful amalgamation of floral and fruit; t24.5 juicy, crisp brown sugar laced with hickory and then a storming middle of spice, tannin and toffee-liquorice; so like an ultra first class Jamaican pot still rum...; f23 with so little corn evident the twilight is shortish, but the sunset is nothing but pure dazzling rye; b23.5 magnificent. 45% (90 proof)

Whistlepig Aged 10 Years db (88) n21 a little untidy and, though clean, a little short of rye character; t22 much better with the grain making the firm impact demanded and the right kind of firm brown sugars hit the target; f23 very pleasant blend of vanilla and intensifying grain; b22 having tasted this after the Sazerac beasts, this could have disappeared without trace. But had enough sharpness and rye freshness to make for a very pleasant and worthwhile experience. *50% (100 proof)*

Willet Family Estate Bottled Rye Barrel Proof Single Barrel 3 Years Old (91.5) n23.5 t24 f21.5 b22.5. What it loses in complexity, it makes up for in bay-faced freshness and charm. Ryes rarely come more juicy or puckering than this...a must locate rye! *577% (115.4 proof)*

Willett Family Estate Bottled Single Barrel Rye 4 Years Old Barrel no 45 (94) n23.5 pretty much how you'd like a 4-y-o rye to show: crisp, uncluttered, the rye pounding out crystalline dark sugars and hints of spice; t24 spot on. Again, almost too clean with all the desired sharp cutting edges yet with truly magnificent mouth-watering qualities. Just as you begin salivating, the spices kick in. Some real boiled sweet quality here while the oak softens the grain only a fraction; f23 relatively short, though the oils are fuller and spices consistent; even some cocoa filters through; b23.5 truly satisfying rye which has in style more than a passing resemblance to the old Jim Beam yellow label rye of about 15 years ago. *55%*

Straight Wheat Whiskey
Bernheim Original (91.5) n22 t23 f23 b23.5. By far the driest of the Bernheims I have encountered showing greater age and perhaps substance. Unique and spellbinding. *45%*

American Microdistilleries
ALASKA DISTILLERY Wasilla, Alaska
Alaska Outlaw Whiskey (78.5) n20 t20 f19 b19.5. A surprisingly clean whiskey with a thin body and even thinner finale. So clean, in fact, that if you put it in a dirty glass, it'll probably end up sparkling. *40%*

ALLTECH Lexington, Kentucky.
Pearse Lyons Reserve (85) n22 t21 f21 b21. A fruity, grainy, pleasant whisky with the higher notes citrus dominant. Never quite finds a place to land or quite tells its story. Attractive but incomplete. *40% (80 proof)*

Town Branch Kentucky Straight Bourbon (88.5) n22.5 red liquorice, under-ripe greengages, nutmeg and polished oak floors...mmmm! t21.5 a soft landing with lashing of vanilla and muscovado; f23 thickens out as the treacle and liquorice re-emerge; some kumquats, too; b22 a delicious Kentucky bourbon of considerable depth and charm. I think they have found their niche: bourbon. In Kentucky. Go for it, guys! *40% (80 proof)*

AMERICAN CRAFT WHISKEY DISTILLERY Redwood Valley, California.
Low Gap Clear Malted Bavarian Wheat Whiskey batch 2010/3B, dist 30/07/10, aged 357 minutes in oak (90.5) n23 t23 f22 b22.5. In 20 years of doing this professionally, I'm pretty sure I have never come across something that has spent so little time in the oak. Very impressed and pray they have set some of this distillate aside for proper maturation. *42.7%*

Low Gap Whiskey Distilled from Malted Rye Aged 204 Minutes dist 20 Sep 2012 (87.5) n22 t22 f21.5 b22. Very attractive and working on a surprising number of levels despite the lack of body. Excellent sugars throughout while the rye generates shape and backbone. *42.6%*

Low Gap Bavarian Hard Wheat Aged 2 Years dist 31 Dec 10, bott 23 Jan 13 (76.5) n18 t21 f18.5 b19. There appears to be butyric on the nose and the finish bitters uncompromisingly. Despite the odd juicy, spicy high spot, not this distillery's finest moment. *43.1%*

ARIZONA DISTILLING Tempe, Arizona
Desert Derum Wheat Whiskey 10 gallon cask barrelled 2013 (89) n22 toasted...toast! A few old barrels comes to mind, too; t22.5 the delivery lulls you somewhat , as the sugars and oils are playful. Then....whuuumph!!! Along comes the spice, rammed home with the full weight of the oak; f22 still a little oaky bitter, the spices sizzle, the sugars sooth...; b22.5 a desert storm of a whiskey. The small barrel punches some pretty towering tannins into the mix, but credit to the distiller for producing a spirit with enough balls to take it. *46%. ncf.*

Desert Durum Wheat Whiskey Batch no. 2 db (87.5) n21.5 t23 f21.5 b21.5. Another hairy-chested gung-ho whiskey which pins you back in your chair. And my notes for the first edition fits this one equally as well. Except here it loses out slightly by having a slightly too wide cut, meaning the feints bite on the nose and finish. But still about as macho as a whiskey gets. And as chocolatey, too. *46%.*

BAINBRIDGE ORGANIC DISTILLERS Bainbridge Island, Washington
Battle Point Organic Washington Wheat Whiskey (88.5) n21 surprisingly placid with a light spice nibble; t23 brilliant delivery, full of quick-tempered spicy attitude. The oils are sublime and the sugars mostly of a muscovado bent; f22 some vanilla and butterscotch show light oaky intent while the sugars remove the spices completely; b23 soft and satisfying. The

spices demanded from wheat whiskey, though short-lived, hit all the right spots. Very well made and impressive. *43%*

BALCONES DISTILLERY Waco, Texas.

Balcones Baby Blue Corn Whisky batch no. BB 12.9, bott 10 Oct 12 db *(79.5)* **n**20 **t**21 **f**19 **b**19.5. A small move in the right direction. The oils are still too cumbersome but the sugars at least outbox the nougat. *46%*

Balcones Brimstone Texas Scrub Oak Smoked Corn Whisky batch no. BRM11-2, bott. 1/11/11 *(94)* **n**23 **t**23.5 **f**24 **b**23.5. Smoked bacon lovers, or devotees of Rupp smoked Alpine cheese, will be in their element. *53%*

Balcones Brimstone Texas Scrub Oak Smoked Corn Whisky batch BRM 1200, bott 10 July 12 *(95.5)* **n**24 **t**24 **f**23.5 **b**24. When a distillery goes out of its way to offer something different, and then does so on a silver platter, one can only stand back and applaud. Take a bow distiller Chip Tate and the team: you are doing the whisky world a great service. *61.5%*

Balcones Brimstone Texas Scrub Oak Smoked Corn Whisky batch no. BRM 12.9, bott 12 db *(95.5)* **n**23.5 once had a smoky bacon aroma. Now the stakes have risen and we have a real Arbroath Smokie feel to this that anyone from the north east of Scotland will recognise and swoon at, though there is some serious sugars at play, too; **t**24 just adore that delivery: no prisoners taken, no compromise. It is all about the toasty oak with, it seems every last piece of burnt sugar extracted. The corn oil remains the perfect conduit through which the sweetness travels; **f**23.5 the usual hints of chocolate and fruit. But the smoke lasts the course now with a degree of elegance; **b**24.5 probably one of the most satisfying of all the world's whiskies. *53%*

⫶⫶⫶ **Balcones Crooked Texas Bourbon Barrel** American Oak, cask no. 3017, bott 21/01/14 db *(96)* **n**24 black cherry and toasted honeycomb; **t**24.5 more black cherry – entire tree-fulls of it. That toasted honeycomb is also evident but is dwarfed by the impact of the liquorice and molasses combination; **f**23.5 much drier with spiced mocha on slightly burnt toast... with a glazed cherry on top... rare to find so many sugars completing the journey; **b**24 like a concentrated form of bourbon, though with far more sugars evident than is normal. Profound. And ridiculously yummy. *62.8%. ncf. no age statement.*

⫶⫶⫶ **Balcones Fifth Anniversary Single Barrel Texas Straight Malt** American oak, rumble cask reserve finish, barrel no. 2653, bott 12/20/13 db *(84.5)* **n**22 **t**22.5 **f**19 **b**20.5. Does pretty well until it gets to the finish, when the bitterness and fizzy, fuzzy finale gives the game away. Profound start both on nose and delivery with lots of rich, vaguely gristy juiciness. But not sure the cask finish helped here at all. *57.5%. ncf. no age statement. 181 bottles.*

⫶⫶⫶ **Balcones Fifth Anniversary Single Barrel Texas Straight Malt** American oak, Brimstone Resurrection finish, cask no. 2696, bott 20/12/13 db *(93)* **n**23.5 the lively and forthright barley must manfully step up to the plate to make any impact on the dizzying depth of the oak: it does; **t**24 near perfect weight on delivery: rarely do the sugars of the oak and concentrated, juicy riches of barley gather together so gorgeously; **f**22.5 spiced, molassed and feeling the effects of the usual wide cut; **b**23 you could stand a knife and fork as well as a spoon up in this. The depth of sugar is startling. *58.3%. ncf. no age statement. 204 bottles.*

⫶⫶⫶ **Balcones Fifth Anniversary Single Barrel Texas Straight Bourbon** American oak cask no. 1613, bott 05/07/13 db *(91.5)* **n**23.5 fascinating nose: it is as if someone and blended together all the heavier, impenetrable sugars and honey, those deep brown chappies, and tied it together with a spicy, molassed bow...; **t**23.5 the delivery needs a cutlass to hack your way through: massive oils from a dangerously generous cut ensure there is a persistent fizz to the toasty fudge; **f**21.5 and it fizzes feintily onwards... **b**23 just so profound. Had the cut been just a little more niggardly, might well have had an award-winner here. But early days for this great but young distillery: they will learn. *64.2%. ncf. no age statement. 176 bottles.*

⫶⫶⫶ **Balcones Fifth Anniversary Single Barrel Texas Straight Bourbon** v.ii American oak, cask no. 1142, bott 11/18/13 db *(93.5)* **n**23.5 red liquorice enjoys top billing as the sugars veritably crunch across the nose; you can count the layers of oak as you might tree rings...; **t**24.5 ye gods...!!! All my Christmasses and birthdays have come at once. The kind of delivery which sends you back in your chair through shock, then into a slump as you melt into its profound beauty. It is the harmony between the depth and softness of touch which ethralls. The usual generous cut ensure the oils are there to support the weight of the fudgy, molassed sugars; maple syrup tries to thin out the hickory; **f**22 vague feints cling to the throat as the drier vanilla-oak elements mop up the remaining sugars; **b**23.5 a bourbon version of a Texas steak: pleasing fat, full of succulent red juice and absolutely bloody enormous... *65.7%. ncf. 167 bottles.*

⫶⫶⫶ **Balcones Fifth Anniversary Single Barrel Brimstone Resurrection Straight Corn Whisky** American oak, cask no. 1200, bott 10/80/13 db *(94)* **n**23 huge, strangely uncluttered, big char effect held together superbly with elegant honeyed layerings amid the corn oil; **t**24 immense delivery as thick as a sea fog with the sugars showing enormous strength despite their polite interplay with the manuka-ulmo honey blend; the liquorice begins to form just as quietly; f23.5 a bourbon-style spice kick begins to build, though the corn oil refuses to recede; b23.5 when you start your tasting day 5.30am, as I do, there are fewer whiskies more capable of waking you up - or sending you straight back to bed – than this. Absolutely shakes the body and mind into submission... Beautiful. 60.5%. ncf. no age statement. 167 bottles.

Balcones Texas Single Malt Whisky Special Release finished in yard aged American/ French oak, batch SM12-3, bott 24 Apr 12 **(91)** n22 t23.5 f22.5 b23. A delicious malt that needs a lot of time and chewing. 52.9%. ncf

Balcones True Blue 100 Corn Whisky batch no. TB100 12.4, bott 25 Oct 12 db **(86)** n21.5 t22 f21 b21.5. Strangely, a more conservative bottling than others. Maybe the strength, maybe just the batch. Certainly a little conservative instead of honeycomb and I feel, also, the fermentation had a bit to play in this. 50%

Balcones True Blue Cask Strength Corn Whisky batch no. TB10-5, bott. 11/05/10 **(93.5)** n22 t23.5 f24.5 b23.5. Made from 100% Blue Corn, you could call this cornagraphic. It is certainly naked and gives you a rough, full-bodied ride...but also seduces you and caresses more tenderly than you could ever believe. A fabulous experience that will have you gasping for more...Believe me: a Texas star is born... 63%

Balcones True Blue Cask Strength Corn Whisky batch TB/6/3 1 date: 10 July 12 **(95.5)** n24 t24.5 f23 b24. When they get it right, Balcones are unquestionably the masters of big whisky in the USA outside Kentucky and Tennessee. And certainly ahead of the game in the use of feints to positively steer the experience. What a character whisky...! 68.6%

BALLAST POINT San Diego, California
Devil's Share Single Malt Aged Four Years (batch 001) **(84)** n20 t22.5 f20.5 b21. Enough feints on the nose and finish to take the gloss off an attractive first bottling from Ballast Point. Beyond the nougat, plenty of honey around to enjoy. But every distiller should remember that to move from a decent to a very good whiskey, the devil is in the detail... 46%

BENJAMIN PRICHARD'S DISTILLERY Kelso, Tennessee.
Benjamin Prichard's Lincoln County Lightning Tennessee Corn Whiskey (89) n24 t22.5 f21 b22. Another white whiskey. This one is very well made and though surprisingly lacking oils and weight has more than enough charm and riches. 45%

BERKSHIRE MOUNTAIN DISTILLERS Great Barrington, Massachusetts.
Berkshire Bourbon Whiskey (91.5) n23 t23.5 f23 b23. A bourbon bursting with character: I am hooked! Another micro-gem. 43%

BRECKENRIDGE DISTILLERY Breckenridge, Colorado.
Breckenridge Colorado Bourbon Whiskey Aged 2 Years (86) n22.5 t22 f20.5 b21. Full of character, big-hearted, chewy, slightly rugged bourbon where honey and cocoa thrives and spices make a telling impact. How apposite that probably the one and only town in Colorado named after a Kentuckian should end up making bourbon. Being close on 10,000 feet above sea level you'd think ice would come naturally with this one. But it does pretty well without it, believe me... 43%

CATOCTIN CREEK DISTILLERY Loudoun County, Virginia.
Catoctin Creek Cask Proof Roundstone Rye Organic Single Barrel Whisky batch B12E1 **(88.5)** n21 t23 f22 b22.5. A truly huge rye that, from a technical standpoint, fails its exams. But through a combination sheer delicious belligerence and chutzpah has your taste buds swooning. Great fun! 58%. Distilled from 100% rye. 134 bottles.

CEDAR RIDGE DISTILLERY Swisher, Iowa.
Cedar Ridge Iowa Bourbon Whiskey barrel no. 124 **(87.5)** n21.5 t23 f21 b22. Intriguing and entertaining, a complex bourbon which really maximizes the input of the small grains. 40%

CHARBAY DISTILLERY Napa Valley, California.
Charbay Hop Flavoured Whiskey release II, barrels 3-7 **(91)** n22 t22 f23 b24. Being distilled from beer which includes hops, it can – and will - be argued that this is not beer at all. However, what cannot be disputed is that this is a rich, full-on spirit that has set out to make a statement and has delivered it. Loudspeaker and all. 55%

CLEAR CREEK DISTILLERY Portland, Oregon.
McCarthy's Oregon Single Malt batch W11-01, bott 11 **(95)** n23 t23.5 f24.5 b24 Simply adorable whiskey. Not only consistent - has stayed exactly on course though I hadn't tasted it for a couple of years - but refuses to stint on its complexity. Remains an American institution. 42.5%

McCarthy's Oregon Single Malt Single Barrel Cask Strength cask no. 158, bott 1 Nov 10 (94.5) n23.5 t24 f23 b24. Probably the most Islay-style of all the McCarthy offerings. Rather than the trademark smoky bacon, here we get an unmistakable sea-salty edge to this both on nose and delivery. But, above all, it is the evenness of the smoke, its patient building of phenols which impresses most. Attach that to the sublime softness of the mouth feel and you have a single malt cask of almost outrageous elegance. *49%. sc.*

McCarthy's Oregon Single Malt Aged 3 Years batch W10-01, bott 8 Nov 10 (95) n23.5 t24 f23.5 b24. I am not sure any micro whisky distillery in the US can do charm and elegance quite like Clear Creek does with its McCarthy's. Here is another bottling which puffs out far bigger smoke than you at first realize, rather in the way Ardbeg does. And in this non-smoky bacon style, Ardbeg is its closest relation in style. A masterful single malt which keeps you smokily spellbound. *42.5%*

McCarthy's Oregon Single Malt Aged 3 Years batch W12-01, bott 7 May 2012 (95) n24 t23 f24 b24. I doubt if you could find, outside of the tropics, such a relatively young whisky with so vibrant and complex a personality. *42.5%*

McCarthy's Oregon Single Malt Aged 3 Years batch W13-01 bott Feb 13 (93.5) n23.5 no one does smoky bacon quite like Clear Creek...; t23 the smoke arrives upfront and vanishes for a second before regrouping. The intervening moments are filled with thick fudge and vanilla; f23.5 the spice and sugars which had been around since the first moments now get a chance to shine in the smoke...if you see what I mean...; b23.5 McCarthy's in its usual irresistible form. 42.5%

McCarthy's Oregon Single Malt Aged 3 Years batch W13-02 (90.5) n22 a very modest degree of smoke this time round, with the sugars also curiously absent; t22.5 silky delivery with the accent firmly on the fudge; toasty dry middle; f23 the smoke and spice take time to gather, but when they arrive, they do so with some zip and intent; b23 one of the lighter bottlings I have come across over the years. The spices, though, don't take a day off. Failed to grab hold of any 2014 bottlings. But will chase them down for the 2016 edition. *42.5%*

COLORADO GOLD DISTILLERY Cedaredge, Colorado.
Colorado Gold Straight Bourbon Over Two Years Old Single Barrel bott 8 Oct 11 (86.5) n21 t23 f21 b21.5. A bit of a whippersnapper of a bourbon. The nose and finish may lack depth. But it is a whisky bursting with personality and the delivery is an understated treat. A light mocha thread weaves in and out of the muscovado. Fun. *40%*

COPPER FOX DISTILLERY Sperryville, Virginia.
Copper Fox "Rye Whisky" Aged 14 Months bott 11 Jul 13 (91) n22.5 crisp, meaningful rye with bells on. Minty spice and earthy, too; t23 those rye notes really do gang together. Sublime firmness; all you could wish for. The mint is back for the middle, pleasantly cradled in chocolate; f22.5 soft oils, and a few muscovado notes trill with the rye; b23 when is rye whisky not a rye whisky? When it is matured in ex-bourbon barrels, rather than virgin oak for a start. Like this whisky is. So the quote marks are mine, not the label's. That said, purely from a tasting perspective: beautiful! Probably as good a rye type yet to come out of Sperryville. Just need to work on the balance... *45%*

Wasmund's Distiller's Art Series Single Malt Spirit dist 03/03/11, less than 30 days old (92) n23.5 t23 f22.5 b23. The light smoke of 60% applewood and 40% cherrywood really makes itself count, especially on the quite sexy nose. A beautifully characterful and superbly weighted spirit. *62%*

Wasmund's Single Malt Whisky 13 Months Old batch 94 (94.5) n23 the cherry wood both offers tannin and sweetness in equal measure, while the apple grapples with the spice; t23.5 sublime oils and sugars on delivery making the weight spot on and enough sweetness around to absorb the big tannin session which crashes like a tree in a forest; the middle now really concentrates on the ulmo honey, complete with light waxy train; f24 almost perfect. The smoke has gathered softly, the honey glows, the wood elements join the heavier phenols to create the base...gorgeous! b24 distiller Rick Wasmund gets flavours into and out of his whisky like a magician conjures a dove from a hat. Here he has exceeded himself by removing the taughtness which comes with over aging or overdoing the apple and cherry wood smoke. Here he has called it right. Superb. *48% (96 Proof) ncf*

Wasmund's Single Malt Whisky 14 Months Old Batch No. 52 (91.5) n22 t23 f23 b23. Makes a huge lightly honeyed statement: superb! *48%. ncf.*

CORNELIUS PASS ROADHOUSE DISTILLERY Hillsboro, Oregon.
McMenamins C.P.R. White Owl Distillery (93) n23.5 t23 f23 b23.5. Top dollar White Dog. Huge amount of copper helps expose all the honey available, especially on the nose. Superbly distilled and surging with barley and spice. *49.3%*

CORSAIR ARTISAN DISTILLERY Nashville, Tennessee.

Corsair Rye Moon (85) n20 t22.5 f21 b21.5. A sweet, well-weighted white dog with surprisingly little bite. The odd intense, crystalline rye moment is a joy. *46% (92 proof)*

Corsair Aged Rye (73.5) n18 t18 f19 b18.5. Hot and anarchic, not as well made as the Rye Moon. But has enough playful character to keep you guessing what's coming next. *46%*

Corsair Triple Smoke (92.5) n24 t23 f22 b23.5. The odd technical flaw, to pick nits. But, overall, a lovely whiskey with a curiously polite smoke style which refuses to dominate. Teasingly delicate and subtle...and different. *40%*

DARK CORNER DISTILLERY Greenville, South Carolina

Dark Corner Moonshine Corn Whiskey (77.5) n18.5 t22 f18 b19. Full blooded sweet corn on delivery. But could do with some extra copper elsewhere. *50%*

DARK HORSE DISTILLERY Lenexa, Kansas

Dark Horse Reserve Bourbon Less Than Four Years Old Batch 2 **(93)** n23 huge vanilla and toffee apple; ticks every bourbony box with a lovely toasted honey buzz; t23.5 exceptional. The tannins arrive in tandem with the molasses. The liquorice is clean and deep, the manuka honey keeps a watchful eye. A slow spice arrival; f23 back to colossal vanilla with a spiced cream toffee finale; b23.5 Even though they appear to have used oak chips to bolster the overall richness of this bourbon, there is no taking away that this is the closest any whiskey produced by a microdistiller comes to the true Kentucky style. But even there, there are few which display so much vanilla. *44.5% (89 proof)*

Dark Horse Reunion Rye Less Than Four Years Old Batch 2 **(89)** n22 rye on heat and a hint of clove; t23 the rye grain is so sharp you can cut your tongue on it: it is first to hit the taste buds and the last to leave. There is a little more extra oil than desired, bringing toasted honeycomb; f22 big oils again, though remains juicy and spicy; b22 another enormous, and truly memorable, offering from Dark Horse which is unambiguous in its style. Here, though, the cut was perhaps a little over generous (costing a point or two) with the very sharpest notes sacrificed. That said: just so big and delicious! *44.5% (89 proof)*

Long Shot White Whiskey bourbon mash **(88.5)** n22 t22.5 f22 b22. Seriously good, honest white dog: well made and gives the corn a free hand to shine. Love it. *40% (80 proof)*

DISTILLERY 291 Colorado Springs, Colorado.

❖ **291 Colorado Bourbon Whiskey Aspen Stave Finished** distilled from a bourbon mash, aged less than 2 years, barrel no. 1 db **(91)** n23 decent rye kick to the recipe; confident, thick and complex; a vague hoppy note; t23.5 thicker and meatier than your average bourbon due to the fat oils. But the honeycomb and molasses play their part, as does the rye amid the soft grains which at times pulses on the palate and is occasionally pleasingly crisp; f22 lots of spice buzz from the softening oil; b22 the usual house style of taking the cut as far as it can go and maybe a fraction more: serious brinkmanship but, again, some very serious whiskey, too. Excellent! *50%*

291 Fresh Colorado Whiskey Batch 13 **(87.5)** n21.5 t22 f22 b22. As near as damn it identical to the notes above! Talk about consistency! *45% (90 proof)*

❖ **291 Colorado Whiskey Aspen Stave Finished** rye malt mash, barrel no. 21 db **(86)** n23.5 t21.5 f20 b21. A pretty wide cut on the still means every element from the rye has been magnified. But so has much else. Which means a dry whiskey at its happiest when nosing. A huge rye curiously still dry despite the massive honeycomb. Astonishingly herbal, too. *50%*

❖ **291 Colorado Whiskey Aspen Stave Finished** distilled from a rye malt mash, aged less than 2 years, barrel no. 22 db **(92)** n24 dazzling, crisp rye: far cleaner than barrel 21. Classically sharp and strengthened by sublime muscavado notes; t23 full bodied delivery, this time revealing a little extra from the cut. The rye screams from every direction, bolstered by the extra oils, though the sharpness has now been blunted; f22 dries a little as the spices and cocoa take position; b23 wow! A rye whiskey for those who prefer theirs warts and all. 50.5% and 50.8% (two bottlings). *50.8%*

❖ **291 Colorado Whiskey Aspen Stave Finished** distilled from a rye malt mash, aged less than 2 years, barrel no. 23 db **(91.5)** n22 a big whoosh of tannin actually outguns the rye – which take some doing; t23 the cut is generous, but not wide enough to do damage. Instead the rye, alternately hard as diamond or soft as silk, swoops around the palate with rare abandon. Heavy, pleasantly oiled and spiced enough to show the oak back at work again; f23 enters into wonderful chocolate mousse territory; b23.5 a rye whiskey of broad sweeps rather than the usual pinpoint, rapier thrusts. Technically not as good as barrel 22, but.... *50.8%*

291 Colorado Rye Whiskey White Dog Aged Less than a week, batch 10 **(86.5)** n21 t21 f23 b21.5. A much tamer version of the last one I got my hands on. The rye gets bullied by other factors more easily, too. The finish, though, is superb. *50.8% (101.7 proof)*

291 Colorado Whiskey Aspen Stave Finished rye malt mash, barrel no. 2 **(94) n23 t24 f23.5 b23.5**. A superb, enigmatic rye which ticks every box: they are obviously fast learners! 50.8%

American Whiskey Aged 3 months **(73) n18 t19 f18 b18**. Busy. Spices aplenty. But nothing sits right. 43% (86 proof)

Bad Guy Bourbon aged 379 days barrel # 1 **(95.5) n23.5** huge cloves (from oak, usually!) abound; massive wall of rye and muscovado sugar... just so bloody enticing; **t24.5** what the f***!!! Flip, that's the word I was looking for... How can you get such an avalanche of advanced flavours from something so juvenile? Again, cloves and cinnamon to the fore followed by a gallery of crisp sugars. The ulmo honey moving in just takes the Mickey. Pure, clean, intense, fruity, sugary and...stunning! **f24** the spices are in overdrive, the sugars act only as a counterpoint. Still the cinnamon and cloves rumble. How the heck have they done that? **b24** arguably the most astonishing whisky of its age worldwide of the year. That a whiskey just a year old can be this good is obscene. But just imagine: the bad guys always win... 56.1%

Black Mountain Colorado Bourbon aged 9 months barrel #1 **(87) n22** big rye and cloves; **t21.5** so young, it should be illegal! Mouth-watering, fresh and youthful with firm corn and firmer rye; **f22** now oils up dramatically with cinnamon and cloves at finale; **b21.5** oily and in your face, despite the big colour, it has been unable to entirely shrug of the white dog bark. That said, the sheer abandon of the cough sweet sugars combined with surging spice – with cinnamon and cloves prevalent - makes for gripping sipping. 46% (92 proof)

Colorado Bourbon (Aspen stave finished) **(85) n20.5 t21.5 f22 b21**. A very young, sweet dude but thin bodied and, though attractive, somewhat over reliant on the manuka honey. 52.5% (105 proof)

Colorado Whiskey from rye malt mash **(86.5) n19 t22 f23 b22.5**. The nose may be worryingly thin and young. But the magnificence and intensity of the stark rye on delivery and follow-through makes for astonishing drinking. For all of its obvious limitations, its mixture of intensity and youth somehow catapult you back to a time when Colorado was first being colonised. This is probably the closest thing to true, unadulterated, frontier whiskey I've ever tasted. Now, where've I put those dirty glasses....? 56.8% (113.6 proof)

Colorado Whiskey from rye malt mash **(84) n20 t22 f21 b21**. This soaring eagle of a whiskey is just too bald, too often. 57.5% (115 proof)

DELAWARE PHOENIX DISTILLERY Walton, New York.
Rye Dog Batch 11-1 (78.5) n19 t21.5 f18 b19. Sweet, distinctive rye tang but a little short on copper sheen. 50% (100 proof)

DOWNSLOPE DISTILLING Centennial, Colorado.
Double Diamond aged 3 Years American/French oak batch RV-003 dist 1 June 2010 **(91.5) n22.5** all kinds of fruit and fruitcake covers the nose, but burnt raisin mostly; the oak is profound...; **t22** and on the delivery, also, though it settles quickly into a more creamy mocha-style; the fruit forms a healthy sub stratum; **f23** the spices grab hold and give the fudge and raisin attitude; finishes with chocolate milkshake; **b24** the degree of oak is a challenge. But in the end you finish shaking your head in wonderment as to how so many vastly different and unlikely aspects of a whiskey somehow fit together. Good going, guys! 50.5% (101 proof)

Double Diamond aged 3 Years French oak batch SR-005A dist 10 May 2010 **(87) n21.5** any more oak and I'll be having splinters extracted from my nose for the next six months...a little fruit soothes; **t21.5** puckering oak – no surprise. Didn't see that juicy malt and grape coming, though; **f22.5** at last settles into a rhythm as the spices dig into the figs and sultanas; **b21.5** in your face oak. Yet somehow salivating. You don't find that very often! A drunkard of dram, staggering without a script...but what fun! 52% (104 proof)

DRY FLY DISTILLING Spokane, Washington
Dry Fly Bourbon 101 (88) n21.5 busy tannin: very heavy oak bias with the corn an afterthought; **t23** superb delivery using its power to good effect. Here the small grains twinkle and the oak goes through some sugary gears before going into a cocoa-based autopilot; **f21.5** like the nose, thins to surprisingly basic elements; **b22** a well made bourbon which, with a bit of extra complexity, would stand above some of its Kentucky colleagues. 50.5%

Dry Fly Cask Strength Straight Wheat Whiskey (94.5) n23 busy aroma, similar to the Washington wheat bottling with toasted Hovis, except here a couple of slices have been forgotten for a minute or so in the toaster; **t24** beautifully intense sugar and spice on delivery. The same rich sugar cane, except with a little molten muscovado in the mix as well; a cake mix with gentle oils and a squeeze of citrus forms the middle; **f23.5** back to lightly salted butter on brown toast...with a drizzle of sugars; **b24** quite beautiful whiskey. One every whisky lover should experience to further their understanding of this multi-faceted spirit. 60%

Dry Fly Port Finish Wheat Whiskey (89) n22 plum and strawberry jam on toast; t23 silky delivery allowing soft sugars to form before the spices punch their way through; f22 chocolate liqueur finale; b22 if you mixed whiskey and jam you might end up with this little charmer. *50% (100 proof)*

Dry Fly Straight Triticale Rye Wheat Hybrid (86) n22 t22 f21 b21. Pleasant and easy going. But very surprising degree of natural caramels fill in the gaps and shaves off the higher notes expected from the rye. *44% (88 proof)*

Dry Fly Washington Wheat Whiskey (89) n22 beautifully toasty: warm Hovis with a caramel and maple spread; t22 succulent with a slow release of the expected spices. Juicy sugar cane begins to gather weight as the drier oaky elements begin to form; f22.5 superb bittersweet fade just as the first light oils gather. Some rich Dundee fruit cake makes a late stand; b22.5 hugely impressive, well weighted and balanced and a much better use of wheat than bread, for instance... *40%*

EASTSIDE DISTILLING Portland, Oregon

Burnside Bourbon 4 Year Barrel-Aged bott 2012 **(92)** n24 t23.5 f22 b22.5. "Put some sideburns on your face!" screams the back label. Well, a whiskey far too gracious to put hairs on your chest though it would be a close shave to choose this or a Kentucky 4-y-o as one of the best young bourbon noses of the year...Just bristles with charm. *48%*

EDGEFIELD DISTILLERY Troutdale, Oregon.

Edgefield Hogshead Whisky 100% malted barley, batch 12-B **(94)** n23.5 chocolate and Lubec marzipan; honeycomb nougat; a little kumquat accumulates with air; t24 superb texture with an almost perfect degree of oil. The barley has as much scope as it needs to shine; there is a juicy element as well as a weightier oakiness, inevitably heading towards a heather-honey sweetness; f23 an elegant fade with more nougat honey and mocha; still heavy on the oils; b23.5 been a little while since I lasted Edgefield. At that time they were seriously getting their act together. Now they deserve star billing in any bar. This is sheer quality and even though the cut is very fractionally wide, the two years in new oak has ensured something bordering magnificence. *46%*

FEW SPIRITS DISTILLERY Evanston, Illinois.

⁙ **FEW Bourbon Whiskey** batch 13-808, aged in charred new oak barrels for less than four years db **(86)** 13-808 n21 t22 f21.5 b21.5. A thick, chewy bourbon with a vague hint of botanicals on the nose and a delivery leaving little to the imagination. The small grains are busy while little has been spared on the liquorice and molasses content. Reduce the oils a little and this would be a belter. *46.5% WB15/377*

⁙ **FEW Rye Whiskey** batch 13-910, aged in charred new oak barrels for less than four years db **(87)** n22 t22 f21.5 b21.5. Few! What a scorcher! Big fresh rye fills every crevice of the palate, the house style oils ensuring it hangs around, too. The buzzing spice at the finale is indicative of the wide-ish cut which ensures a busy tang to the salivating, ultra juicy rye. Still not quite one for the purist, but the entertainment level is high. *46.5% WB15/375*

⁙ **FEW Single Malt Whisky** batch 10-13, aged in reused cooperage for one year db **(84.5)** n21.5 t20 f22 b21. This writing year, 2014, marks the 40th anniversary of when I first tasted an American single malt: it was in Maryland and had been made locally by a rye distillery. That was, I remember, a very simple, malty affair. This, by stark contrast, isn't. First you have to get through a nutty phase before the barley makes itself heard, but when it does, it is eloquent in its sheer maltiness. As usual, the oils have a big say. *46.5% WB15/376*

FINGER LAKES DISTILLING Burdett, New York.

Glen Thunder Corn Whiskey (92.5) n23.5 t23 f23 b23. Beautifully distilled, copper rich, Formula 1 quality, absolutely classic corn white dog. *45% (90 proof)*

White Pike Whiskey Aged 18 Minutes (91) n22.5 t23.5 f22 b23. Top notch white dog more full of flavour than any pike you are ever likely to catch. Maybe 19 minutes in cask might have just taken the edge of the complexity. So well done, boys. Beautifully made distillate, even if slightly copper challenged, where the grains really do stand and be counted and the sugars are slick and sing to you. Created from organic spelt, corn and malted wheat ostensibly as a mixing spirit: that would be a waste. *40%*

FLORIDA FARM DISTILLERS Umatilla, Florida

Palm Ridge Reserve Handmade Micro Batch Florida Whiskey orange and oak wood Less the 1 Year Old batch 29 **(94.5)** n23 big rye signature to the nose: fruity, light and easy on the corn oils. Some hints of marzipan, trimmed apple and very old marmalade; aggressive tannin; t24 I doubt if I will experience a more gentle landing on the palate for any US whiskey this year. Just enough oil to absorb the impact of the small grains and, again, the ryes run riot ensuring a juicy, spicy theme throughout. A little Parma Violet candy represents an earthiness which balances the complex, non-specific fruit doing the rounds; **f23.5** no great age to this guy (and I wrote that before I spotted the admitted maturation!), but the way the ulmo, manuka and orange-blossom honeys combine, depth is maintained; **b24** I can see why everyone heads to Florida in the winter: obviously to try and grab one of the meager 6,000 bottles of this on offer each year. This is beautifully crafted, truly adorable whiskey where fruit appears to constantly have its hand on the tiller. And rather than blast in like a Hurricane from the sea, it breezes gently around the glass and palate with an easy elegance. I have relatives in Florida: about time I gave them another visit... *45% (90 proof)*

GARRISON BROTHERS Hye, Texas.

Garrison Brothers Texas Straight Bourbon 2010 Aged Two Years Spring 2013 **(91) n23** what an improvement over two years! Virtually feint free and bursting with bourbon-ness in every direction. Particularly big on the manuka honey and cough sweet departments, some spice also makes an introductory ahem; **t23** similar to how I remember it a couple of years back with a big, oily statement and massive Demerara sugars. A little marmalade and marzipan also take a bow; **f22** the "virtually" bit of the feint free turns up, but so intense is the hickory and cocoa, it remains seriously enjoyable; **b23** a fascinating bourbon, made from local organic corn, which for a two-year-old is simply brimming with personality. The intensity and balance of the sugars and more bitter toastiness is a constant delight. Still room for improvement, but just love this magnificent stuff. Mind you, still waiting for the Hye Rye... *47%*

⁙ **Garrison Brothers Texas Straight Bourbon 2010 Aged Two Years** dist 2010, bott Spring 2014 db **(91.5) n22.5** a staggering degree of maple syrup sweetens the trademark high end bourbon development; waxy and nutty; **t23.5** hard to imagine a bourbon packing so many intense flavour traits hitting the palate so softly. The silky delivery seems to underscore the rich mocha and honeycomb; **f22.5** a tad bitter from light feints which reveal themselves late on. Some accompanying spices, too; **b23** has not come close to outgunning their Cowboy bourbon which re-wrote the manual as far as micro distilleries are concerned. But there is still so much to savour here. Delicious. *47%.*

Cowboy Bourbon Texas Straight Bourbon Whiskey Aged Three Years (96) n23.5 could be a blueprint for a solid bourbon aroma: beautifully waxy and nutty with a gathering of ever more intensifying tannins, the spice always well proportioned; **t24** massive. Not exactly Stagg like, as this has some very helpful sweetness to lessen the impact. And there is obviously less age involved. But, again, the weight and pace of the heavier notes, the citrus-studded hickory, even hints of burnt fruit cake (presumably from the rye) are all set to ensure maximum flavour fulfillment; treacle tinged with ulmo honey; **f24** now lightens to allow the liquorice and Sumatra coffee to mix and relax; the treacle lessens to Demerara and manuka honey; the waves just keep on lapping for a ridiculously long finish; **b24.5** I always know when I have a truly great whiskey on my hands: it takes every ounce of my professionalism to spit it out! This has, and make no mistake, raised the bar for bourbon made by the micro distillers: it is truly world class, three year old or not. In fact the name is a misnomer: there are no cowboys at work here. This is darned tootin' fine whiskey. Yesiree! *68%. 600 bottles.*

GOLDEN NORTHWEST DISTILLERY Bow, Washington.

Golden Artisan Spirits Single Barrel Cask Strength (88) n20.5 a little gruff, but redeemed by some coconut and maple syrup; **t22.5** and it's the maple syrup which is first out of the trenches backed by decimated coconut drenched in manuka honey; **f23** the highpoint by a distance as the honey is joined by deep liquorice...and welcome spice; **b22** much more like it! Not exactly textbook but excellent body and some lovely honey touches. *62.3%*

Golden Reserve Samish Bay Single Malt (85.5) n20 t23 f21 b21.5. From the nougat, molasses and chocolate school of distilling. Some honeycomb around, too. Actually, quite like its roughhouse antics on the palate. *40% (80 proof)*

Samish Bay Peated Single Malt (79) n19 t20 f20 b20. The lightest smoke imaginable is somewhat overshadowed by the nougat and honey feints. Pleasant if a bit rough and unready. *43% (86 proof)*

GRAND TRAVERSE DISTILLERY Traverse City, Michigan

Bourbon Whiskey (88.5) n21 a bit of youth makes for a slightly green, peppery aroma with limited harmony....; **t22** which cannot be said of the delivery. Young, for sure, but small-grain punchy and with chocolate honeycomb. The spices sprint off from the start while muscovado sugars form; **f23** we are now in deepest bourbon territory; thick liquorice, huge surges of vanilla, hints of molasses; **b22.5** an absolute charmer which just gets better as it goes along. *46% (92 proof)*

Ole George Straight Rye Whiskey (80) n19 t21 f20 b20. Hard to mark this one. As a rye, it marks relatively low. As a gin, it would be higher. Not sure why, but there seems to be all kinds of botanical aromas and flavours involved here. Pleasant as a spirit – and I love the mouth feel. But the flavour make up is skewed. *46.5% (93 proof)*

GREAT LAKES DISTILLERY Milwaukee, Wisconsin.
KinnicKinnic A Blend of American Whiskies (87) n21.5 t22.5 f21 b22. The bitterness is replaced by an extra dollop of nougat and honey. *43% (86 proof)*

HIGH WEST DISTILLERY Park City, Utah.
High West Silver Oat (86) n20 t22 f22 b22. A white whiskey which at times struggles to find all the copper it needs. But so delicious is that sweet oat – a style that has enjoyed similar success in Austria – that some of the technical aberrations are forgiven. Soft and friendly. *40%*

HOUSE SPIRITS DISTILLERY Portland, Oregon
Westward Oregon Straight Malt Whiskey 2 Years Old batch 1 **(92.5) n23** a coating of vanilla to the intense barley and maple syrup; **t23.5** superb degree of oils ensure the barley clings thickly to the plate. Ulmo honey and light hickory intermingle as the spices begin a gentle journey; **f23** the spices now fizz a little and a delicate, non-specific fruit tang attaches to the big barley; the vanillas are confident and creamy; just a tad too much lasting bitterness; **b23.5** two years old, perhaps. But absolute star quality with the barley pulsing at every turn: just so satisfyingly mouth-filling and palate teasing. Another great whiskey from Portland. *45%*

KINGS COUNTY DISTILLERY Brooklyn, New York.
Kings County Moonshine Corn Whisky (92) n23 t23 f23 b23. Absolutely spot on corn whiskey: sweet, clean, berry-fruity, very well made; does exactly what it says on the tin. *40%*

KOVAL DISTILLERY Chicago, Illinois.
⬦ **Koval Single Barrel Four Grain Whiskey** cask no. 613, organic. Mashbill: Oat, Malted Barley, Rye, Wheat db **(88.5) n21.5** grassy and busy a slight tobacco note is offset by dancing small grain alongside marmalade and castor sugar; **t23** almost slung back in my chair by the depth of delivery: instantly salivating with the grains fussing sharply about the palate; a wave of toffee strikes and calms things; **f21.5** lots of caramel on show still, but enough grain escapes to continue the mouth-watering until an oily bitterness creeps in; **b22.5** at times a seriously complex whiskey: a delightful experience. *47%. sc.*

⬦ **Koval Single Barrel Rye Whiskey** cask no. 531, organic. db **(77) n19 t20 f19 b19.** Organic maybe. But, sadly, not orgasmic. Unbelievably sweet and flat with little or no rye sharpness whatsoever. *40%. sc.*

⬦ **Koval Single Barrel Bourbon Whiskey** cask no. 506, organic. db **(86.5) n21.5 t22 f21.5 b21.5.** Koval's whiskeys are nothing if not idiosyncratic. Hard to pick out a traditional, recognised bourbon character here. The nose abounds with citrus, the delivery eye-watering sugars until some drying feints appear at the death. Attractive but don't expect something Kentuckian in style. *47%. sc.*

LOST SPIRITS DISTILLERY Monterey County, California.
⬦ **Leviathan III Under 4 Years** db **(86) n21 t22 f22 b21.** Not sure I am a great fan of three things wishing to dominate at once: peat, fruit and oak. In the end there is too much cancelling of each other out. Pleasant enough, though, and very sweet. *53%. sc.*

⬦ **Umami Under 4 Years** Peat smoked barley fermented in salt water. db **(94) n23** that sharp smoky bacon type smoke those who drink McCarthy's from Oregon will immediately recognise: something of a west coast thing...; **t24** some peat whiskies sooth and caress the palate: this arrives like an exocet blasting any phenols any taste buds which dare show its head above he parapet; quite possibly the spiciest arrival of any malt whisky made in the USA to date; **f23** calms as the fruits begin to find room to show; a tad off key towards the finish, though rights itself as the molasses arives. But then mixing sherry and peat is a very brave thing to do...; **b24** a chair with arm rests essential: you will be gripping them for dear life! If you are seeking a gentle, delicate little flower of a malt you have found the wrong bottle. This is a heat exuding missile...and your palate will be well and truly a-salted... *59%. Cask Strength.*

MISSISSIPPI RIVER DISTILLERY Le Claire, Indiana
Cody Road Bourbon 2013 Batch 1 **(91.5) n23.5** toasted brown wheat bread with a perfectly understated sublime manuka- and ulmo honey sweetness. Wow! **t23** the delivery offers both spice and molten muscovado sugars in equal measure; the midground thickens and becomes almost doughy; **f22** a little bitterness counters the continuing sugars; **b23** you

really don't need to be told this is a wheat recipe bourbon! A fabulously made whiskey of rare character. *45% (90 proof)*

Cody Road Rye 2013 Batch 4 **(86.5) n23 t22.5 f20 b21.** The clean, fruity unambiguous rye on the nose is stunning. There is nothing too shoddy about the crisp, juicy grain on delivery, either. Just bitters out a little too enthusiastically from the midpoint onwards. *40%*

MOYLAN'S DISTILLING COMPANY Petaluma, California.
Moylan's 2004 Cherry Wood Smoked Single Malt Cask Strength (94) n24 easily one of the most subtle of all America's micro distillery whiskeys and is unusual in not trying to make an early statements of intent. The smoke does no more than furnish a thin, earthy gloss to the delicate array of lightly fruited vanillas: absolutely beguiling; **t23.5** more of the same: a distinctive sharp kumquat note injects life into the vanilla; **f23** long yet without a hint of oil with light spices and cocoa playing happily together; again there is a faint, fruity glass to the finale; **b23.5** a top drawer, quite beautifully distilled and matured, malt which goes much easier on the smoke than you'd expect but is bubbling with personality...and quality. Bravo! *49.5%*

NEW HOLLAND BREWING COMPANY Holland, Michigan.
Beer Barrel Bourbon (86.5) n21.5 t22 f21.5 b21.5. A distinctly different bourbon, not least because it has been finished for three months in beer barrels. This really only becomes evident on the latest moments of the finish, when a slightly hoppy roast barley character emerges. The base Indiana-originating bourbon is decent enough, though you get the feeling the higher notes and rough edges have been blunted by the beer. *40% (80 proof)*

Bill's Michigan Wheat (85.5) n22 t21 f21.5 b21. A wheat whisky named in honour of an old friend of mine, Bill Owens, a shining beacon in the world of micro distilling. Kind of a fitting tribute, too, as the somewhat oily and bitter marmalade characteristics are always more likely to be found on a small still than from the big Kentucky boys. *45% (90 proof)*

Brewer's Whiskey Malt Whiskey Aged Six Months batch 3 **(87) n21.5** a curious mix of mocha and distant hop; **t22.5** beautiful delivery; the body is exceptional, as is the early, teasing spice. The sugars start out alone but are eventually caught up by pleasing praline and more spice; **f21** a hint towards kumquats towards the end...as well as hard, semi-bitter hop!! **b22** in the previous Bible, we had batch 1 of their Double Down Barley: this is, effectively batch 3. A better working this time, though the late finish is still challenging. *45% (90 proof)*

PEACH STREET DISTILLERS Pallisade, Colorado.
Colorado Straight Bourbon Aged More Than Two Years batch 40 **(92.5) n22.5** sharp hickory and caramel, flinty fruit and almost Indian-style spiced nuts; **t23.5** has that soothing mouth-feel on delivery of the oozy inside of a throat lozenge, except the flavours differ dramatically. For the odd moment you feel that malt is present, but soon we go into familiar manuka honey territory, as well as liquorice; the spices pick up pace with aplomb; **f23** a quality finale, with the spices gently raging, the rye notes riling and other familiar bourbon tones tantalising...; **b23.5** the last bottle I tasted was around the batch 20 mark and was an impressive intro to this distillery. Remarkably, this batch enjoys an almost identical thumb print. But now there is much more sharpness and definition. Superb! *46% (92 proof)*

RANGER CREEK DISTILLING, San Antonio, Texas
Ranger Creek .36 Texas Bourbon (93) n23 mega honey & liquorice: superbly weighted; **t23.5** again huge liquorice, perhaps pepped by the odd aniseed ball, before manuka honey and treacle weigh in; there are chewy vanillas to break up the intensity as well as chocolate toffee; **f23** scorched honeycomb & marzipan with just the right amount of sugars to make for a comfortable finale; **b23.5** I would so love to get back to Texas and have this wash down a plate-filling, half cooked ribeye. It's pretty obvious they have used small barrels to create a gentle giant like this – even before you find confirmation on the bottle. This comes under their Small Caliber series of whiskeys. Don't you believe it: this is a howitzer of a bourbon. *48% (96 proof)*

Ranger Creek Rimfire Mesquite Smoked Texas Single Malt batch 1 **(85) n21.5 t22 f20.5 b21.** As I have never tasted anything smoked with mesquite before – especially whiskey – I will have to guess that it is the tree of the semi-desert which is imparting a strange, mildly bitter tang on the finish. Whether it is also responsible for the enormous degree of creamed toffee, I am also not sure. Enjoyable, fascinating even...but something the ol' taste buds need a bit of acclimatising to. *43% (86 proof)*

RANSON SPIRITS Sheridan, Oregon.
Whipper Snapper Oregon Spirit Whisky (86.5) n21.5 t22 f21.5 b21.5. A curiously thin offering for all the obvious corn apparent. Some walnut oil and light Demerara do offer some meat on the vanilla. *42%*

ROCK TOWN DISTILLERY Little Rock, Arkansas.

Arkansas Hickory Smoked Whiskey batch 8 **(87.5)** n21.5 a very different kind of sweet smoke, spreading sugar on the bacon; **t21** thin delivery and sharp. Takes about the fourth flavour wave for the oils to gather and the smoke to fall back into place; **f23** delicious smoked chocolate; **b22** a bit of a screwball whiskey on delivery but the finale is to die for. 45%

Arkansas Young Bourbon Whiskey batch 12 **(89)** n22.5 now that has a very serious bourbon thumbprint; **t22** fizzing, nipping tannin and then a line of soft brown sugars and maple syrup to kiss the taste buds better; **f22** corn oily and late liquorice; **b22.5** gentle, sweet and all-round adorable. 46% (92 proof)

⸬ **Arkansas Bourbon Whiskey Batch 23** db **(89)** n22 t22 f22.5 b22.5. These guys have a tendency to do bourbon rather well. Again, a generous cut slightly oils up proceedings. But the magnitude of the liquorice/hickory/molasses combination is real stand-your-spoon-up-in fun. No insipid half-hearted stuff here. 46%.

⸬ **Arkansas Rye Whiskey Batch 5** db **(80)** n21.5 t21 f19 b19.5. A powerful whiskey with a determined rye bent. But like so many microdistiller's ryes, falls into the trap of over-widening the cut. This can be either from the fact they don't have much to distil from, so try maximise their resources. Or so powerful is flavour of the spirit, they have not yet worked out exactly where the middle is. Sometimes it is a bit of both. 46%.

⸬ **Arkansas Single Barrel Reserve Bourbon Whiskey** cask #163 db **(90)** n22.5 the tannins queue up, but happy to let the dark sugars ahead first...; **t22** liquorice concentrate, lightened by hickory; the molasses rolls in like sea mist; **f23** thins sufficiently for major complexity, especially when the spiced vanilla enters the fray; **b22.5** major bourbon with the passive aggressive oak pulling the strings. 57.81%.

⸬ **Arkansas Single Barrel Reserve Bourbon Whiskey** cask #167 db **(89.5)** n22 t23 f22 **b22.5**. As 163. Except here the sugars take far more of the load, resulting in a lighter and slower finish, but only after a bigger tannin crescendo. 57.14%.

⸬ **Arkansas Single Barrel Reserve Bourbon Whiskey** cask #173 db **(87.5)** n22 t22 f21.1 **b22**. This guy has hairs on it. The tannins are a little too up front for the overall good of the bourbon, meaning some displaced sugars. The black cherry is irresistible, however. If you like a whiskey with its own built in tooth picks, this is for you. 56.93%.

⸬ **Arkansas Single Barrel Reserve Bourbon Whiskey** barrel #181, cask strength db **(92.5)** n22 t23 f23.5 b24. Odd isn't it: I castigate cask 173 for over exuberant use of oak...and here is a bourbon in which you can count the tree rings...and I am praising it to the hilt. The secret is the balance: for every log of tannin to chew on there is magnificent blend of sugars, vanillas and fruits to counter it. The liquorice and molasses have to be experienced to be believed. And though this is OTT on the tannin, somehow it works rather beautifully. 56.2%.

⸬ **Arkansas Single Barrel Reserve Bourbon Whiskey** barrel #190, cask strength db **(96.5)** n23.5 t24 f24.5 b24.5. The only bourbon I have ever tasted which comes close to this in profile is 23 years of age and from Heaven Hill distillery. This breaks every rule in the book... or, rather, appears content to have re-written the rules. This is absolutely enormous whiskey. It is beautifully made with not a hint of an off note, so the cut must be nigh on perfection. The oak it has matured in is top dollar, and they have extracted every cent's worth of its favourable aspects: the liquorice is borderline creosote yet so thick are the molasses, so clever is the use of manuka honey, so compelling the toasted honeycomb and so busy the spices, the balance and bitter-sweet interplay could hardly be bettered if created on computer rather than in cask. Unquestionably one of the great microdistillery bourbons of all time: a bottling which will put Arkansas and Rock Town in particular on the world whisky map. 56.08%.

⸬ **Hickory Smoked Whiskey** db **(82.5)** n21 t20 f21 b20.5. Nowhere near as good as the last smoked offering I had from them. A tobacco note has replaced the bacon. Some pleasant Ovaltine and muscovado notes towards the finale. 45%.

ROGUE SPIRITS Newport, Oregon

Dead Guy Whiskey Aged One Month (73) n21 t22 f14 b16. Salt and honey, especially on delivery, make for a lovely opening gambit. The finish, alas, takes you via the graveyard. 50%

Shatoe Rogue Oregon Single Malt Aged 3 Months (76.5) n18.5 t19 f20 b19. Needs a bit more copper to brighten the experience. The growing sugars help. 40% (80 proof)

ROUGHSTOCK DISTILLERY Bozeman, Montana.

Roughstock Black Label (92.5) n22.5 t23.5 f23 b23.5. A very beautiful malt whiskey very well made which underlines the happy marriage between barley and virgin oak. A stunner! 64%

ST GEORGE SPIRITS Alameda, California.

St George Single Malt Lot 10 (90) n22 t23 f22.5 b22.5. Welcome back, my old friend! One of the grand-daddies of the micro distilling world and sticking to its guns for one of the fruitiest of all the malts out there. Even if not technically perfect, this is a three course meal of a malt. And so fruity, this one will appeal to rye lovers, too. In fact, it'll slay you... 40%

⁘ **Breaking & Entering Bourbon** New American charred oak, bott 08/08/2013 db (82) n21.5 t21.5 f19 b20. An arresting first attempt by St George. Vaguely butyric , but through the oils can be located some very decent bourbon strains. Needs a bit of tinkering, though. 43%. *Batch no.130824/ 19,900 bottles.*

⁘ **St Georges Single Malt Lot 11** bott 26/08/2011. db (90) n22.5 from the apple-achians...no California! Some decent oak present; t23 juicy barley on first contact, then a slow injection of oily, buttery toffee; f22 a little buzz and the oils thicken from a wide-ish cut; b22.5 not so heavily fruit-laden as some of their previous offerings. But bursting through the barrel with flavour and personality. 43%. *Approximately 3,100 bottles.*

⁘ **St Georges Single Malt Lot 12** bott 20/04/2012. db (88.5) n22 the barrel of green apples in evidence; sharp and clean; t22.5 massive juicy wave of castor sugar leading on to barley sugar candy; f22 remains malty, but a generous cut is again evident; b22 unquestionably their maltiest every offering, having now for the most part eschewed their traditional fruit style. Maybe the odd crack on the distillate is apparent, but the intensity of the barley more than compensates. 43%. *Approximately 3,500 bottles.*

⁘ **St Georges Single Malt Lot 13** bott 14/08/2013. db (91) n22.5 slightly overcooked butterscotch tart; light acacia honey and caramel; t23.5 huge delivery: a thick cascade of toffeed malt thumps against the taste buds and takes time to unravel. As it does, the barley in is full salivating mode while toasted fudge adds weight; f22 long with a late spice buzz and vanilla finale; b23 technically by far and away their best bottling for a very long time – both in production and maturation, even though not quite perfect. Genuinely high quality single malt. And delicious with it, too... 43%. *Approximately 3,000 bottles.*

SAINT JAMES SPIRITS Irwindale, California.
Peregrine Rock (83.5) n21 t20.5 f21.5 b20.5. Fruity and friendly, the wine and smoke combo work well-ish enough but the thumping oak injection highlights that maybe there isn't quite enough body to take in the aging. Perhaps less time in the barrel will reduce the bitter orange finale. 40%

SANTA FE SPIRITS Santa Fe, New Mexico.
⁘ **Colkegan Single Malt Whisky** once used American white oak batch no.2. db (73) n18 t20 f17 b18. I have been looking forward to seeing the latest from Santa Fe after encountering their strange Coyote whisky. This is another encounter which has me scratching my head wondering how some of the flavours were achieved – I really must get down to New Mexico to check this out: they are achieving results using just malt and oak I have never before seen. Can't say I go a bundle on the nose, or the finish come to that, with so much caramel and unidentified spice. Reminds me of some local whiskies I run across in India. 46%.

STEIN DISTILLERY Joseph, Oregon.
Straight Rye Whiskey Aged 2 Years cask no. 7 (88) n23 t22 f21 b22. A whiskey which offers up the grains to the full spotlight. A little more care with the cut and we have something special on our hands. 40%

STONE BARN BRANDYWORKS DISTILLERY Portland, Oregon.
Hard Eight Unoaked Rye Whiskey (86.5) n22.5 t21.5 f21 b21.5. The excellent fruity-rye nose does not quite show the width of the cut which creates a buzzing oiliness. Good brown sugar balance. 40%

STRANAHAN DISTILLERY Denver, Colorado.
Stranahan's Colorado Whiskey Small Batch dist Dec 05, cask no. 225 (94.5) n24 t23.5 f23 b24. Absolutely magnificent; a malt which never stays still in the glass. By the way, boys: the message on the label to me brought a lump to my throat. Thank you. 47% (94 Proof). sc.

Stranahan's Colorado Whiskey Batch No. 59 dist Jul 08 (92) n21.5 t24 f23 b23.5. Very complex. Very classy. The interplay of the sugars and spice is utterly world class and the bourbon notes which sing at regular intervals do so with a very clear voice. 47%

Stranahan's Colorado Whiskey Batch No. 60 dist Jul 08 (94.5) n23 t24.5 f23 b24. Two whiskeys obviously distilled on the same day (see Batch 59)...and a fascinating variance... This is Stranahan at its most communicative. And brilliant! 47% (94 Proof)

Stranahan's Colorado Whiskey Batch No. 61 dist Aug 08 (90.5) n22 t22.5 f23 b23. Back to its mega fudge state. Lovely whisky. 47% (94 Proof)

Stranahan's Colorado Whiskey Batch No. 62 dist Sep 08 (92) n23 t23.5 f22.5 b23. They appear to have hit a rich seem of consistency. My word: I love this distillery...! 47% (94 Proof)

Stranahan's Colorado Whiskey Batch #67 dist 30 Dec 08 **(96) n24 t24.5 f23.5 b24.** You can tell Colorado is in the mountains: this rocks! *47%*

Stranahan's Colorado Whiskey Batch #68 dist 15 Feb 09 **(91) n22 t23 f23 b23.** Mines every last caramel atom from the oak. Soft, sexy, understated and complex. *47%*

Stranahan's Colorado Whiskey Batch #72 dist 20 Mar 09 **(92) n22.5 t23.5 f23 b23.** Honey-nut bar nose and delivery; complex sugars; silky, spiced mocha finish. Superb! *47%*

Stranahan's Colorado Whiskey Batch #74 dist 2 Sept 09 **(90.5) n22.5 t23 f22 b23.** Full bodied, mouthwatering and chewy. Celebrates the sugar and spice element to the max. *47%*

Stranahan's Colorado Whiskey Batch #75 dist 11 Oct 09 **(94.5) n23 t24 f23.5 b24.** A striking whiskey which stops you in your tracks. Glorious! *47%*

Stranahan's Colorado Whiskey Batch #78 dist 17 Dec 09 **(91.5) n22 t24 f22.5 b23.** Relaxed, softly spoken, classy and brimming with sugary intent. Muscovado sugars meet liquorice and manuka honey head on. *47%*

Stranahan's Colorado Whiskey Batch #83 dist 20 Mar 10 **(95) n23.5 t23.5 f24 b24.** A rare example of where the malt element of the whisky overcomes the bourbon aspect. Magnificent complexity: just shows what a marginally thinner cut can do... *47%*

Stranahan's Colorado Whiskey Batch #86 dist 10 May 10 **(92.5) n22.5 t24 f23 b23.** Clean, malty with brown sugars which decorate the big vanilla spine. Elegant, intense, complex. *47%*

Stranahan's Colorado Whiskey Batch #89 dis 13 June 10 **(88) n22 t22 f22 b22.** Another slightly earthy offering; this time ulmo honey and molasses spring to the rescue. *47%*

Stranahan's Colorado Whiskey Batch #90 dist 19 Apr 09 **(96) n23.5 t24 f24 b24.5.** One of those liquid golden nuggets they find now and then in them thar Rocky Mountain hills. *47%*

Stranahan's Colorado Whiskey Batch #91 **(85.5) n21 t21 f22 b21.5** Curious with a much lighter body. Picks up in flavour intensity as the sugars merge with the spicy mocha. *47%*

Stranahan's Colorado Whiskey Batch #92 **(88.5) n22 t22 f22.5 b22** All about the sugars and the acacia honey and liquorice middle. Good oils from a brave cut. Chewy. *47%*

Stranahan's Colorado Whiskey Batch #93 **(83) n20 t21 f21.5 b20.5** Similar to #91 except the thicker build carries a vague feint. Some nougat and chocolate towards the end. *47%*

Stranahan's Colorado Whiskey Batch #94 **(94) n23.5** spot degrees of muscovado sugars amid the thick malt; the oak offers a little kumquat to lighten things; **t23** soft oil, glide over the plate while spices sparkle. the sugars stand guard; **f23.5** fabulous complexity as the malt goes into Malteser overdrive, the milk chocolate silky; **b24** 94 points for #94. If Stranahan's could hit this style complex, clean as a benchmark and stick to it, they'd be world beaters! *47% (94 Proof)*

Stranahan's Colorado Whiskey Batch #96 **(87.5) n22.5 t22 f21.5 b21.5** Back to something a little more austere, despite the efforts of the sugary oils. Enjoyable, though. *47%*

Stranahan's Colorado Whiskey Batch #97 **(88.5) n21 t22.5 f22 b23** Recovers wonderfully from a feinty nose to offer a glittering assortment of heavy brown sugars to chew on and teasing spice. *47% (94 Proof)*

Stranahan's Colorado Whiskey Batch #99 **(84) n20 t22 f21 b21** They appear to have got the slight OTT feints on nose and finish and irresistable big sugared middle off pat. *47%*

Stranahan's Colorado Whiskey Batch #100 **(93) n23.5** nutty: walnut oil and top quality north European marzipan; **t23** textbook oils show both malt and vanilla in a rich light. Biscuity...; **f23** the finish takes a surprise turn towards tangy marmalade **b23.5** a three course meal of a malt. And leaves you wanting seconds... *47% (94 Proof)*

Stranahan's Colorado Whiskey Batch #101 **(87.5) n22 t22 f21.5 b22** More playing dare with the cut. Here it pays off as the oils go into molasses overdrive. A dessert whiskey. *47%*

Stranahan's Colorado Whiskey Batch #102 **(92) n22.5** butterscotch, toffee, ulmo honey and spice; **t23** juicy barley which spices up beautifully; **f23** long, back to the ulmo honey again; the vanillas are creamy and complex; **b23.5** superb whisky of almost perfect weight and pace. *47% (94 Proof)*

Stranahan's Colorado Whiskey Batch #103 **(88) n21 t22.5 f22 b22.5** Another vanilla, butterscotch and honey-ladened gem once the light feints are overcome. *47% (94 Proof)*

Stranahan's Colorado Whiskey Batch #104 **(84.5) n21 t21.5 f21 b21** Just a little tight with the crisp sugars outflanked by the slightly bitter, blood-orange feints. *47% (94 Proof)*

Stranahan's Colorado Whiskey Batch #105 **(90) n22 t22 f23 b23** Interesting to see them continue along this orangey-citrus route. Malts show integrity. Spiced. Complex. *47%*

Stranahan's Colorado Whiskey Batch #106 **(86) n21.5 t22 f21 b21.5** Back to the big oils and cumbersome sugars and nougat. Marmalade on the finale, though. *47% (94 Proof)*

Stranahan's Colorado Whiskey Batch #109 **(92) n22 t23.5 f23 b23.5** Beautifully flighted malt with a rich seam of molassed sugars and raisins. Vanilla topping and spice. *47%*

Stranahan's Colorado Whiskey Batch #110 **(91.5) n22 t23 f23 b23.5** Lovely interplay between crispy grain and even crispier sugars. Two-toned . Juicy and gorgeously spiced. *47%*

Stranahan's Snowflake Cab Franc **(95.5) n24 t24.5 f23 b24.** A celebration of great whiskey, and a profound statement of what the small distilleries of the USA are capable of. *47%. sc.*

Stranahan's Snowflake Desire dist 3 Jan 07 **(94.5) n24 t24 f23 b23.5.** These guys do know how to pick a good barrel... And, frankly, make an exceptional whiskey... 47%. sc.

Stranahan's Snowflake Mount Shavano (85.5) n22 t21 f21.5 b21 The malt vanishes under a cartload of plums. Flat. 47% (94 Proof)

Stranahan's Snowflake Mount Silverheels (89) n22.5 t22 f22.5 b22 Another fruity job showing a pithy dryness in tandem with liquorice and treacle. A real mouthful of a malt. 47%

Stranahan's Snowflake Paladise/Grand Mesa dist Apr 05 **(94) n23 t24 f23 b24.** Seriously impressive. I know this distillery makes something a little special, but this is such a sure footed move away from the norm I am stunned. This is my first-ever Stranahan Snowflake... so named because it simply dissolves on touch...? 47%. (94 Proof). sc.

Stranahan's Snowflake Solitude dist Mar 08 **(93) n23 t23 f23.5 b23.5** I chose this as my 1,111th new whisky of the 2012 Bible, because there is a lot of ones in that. And when you spend three months on your own, virtually cut off from all others, one is number you get used to. So sampling a whisky called "Solitude" strikes home...whatever it tastes like. 47%. sc.

Stranahan's Snowflake Tempranillo (91) n21.5 t22 f24 b23.5 A bold malt with a liquorice and greengage delivery backed by a big treacle middle. Molasses wherever you look! 47%. (94 Proof)

SQUARE ONE BREWERY & DISTILLERY St. Louis, Missouri
J J Neukomm Missouri Malt Whisky Single Barrel (88.5) n21 sharp, smoky, intriguing – but a bit of a mess; **t23** juicy sugars with seemingly cherry at the heart make for soft footfall on delivery, but the intensity of the malt really surprises; **f22** rabidly spicy and threatens to bitter out. But cherry drops to the rescue; **b22.5** it was like being transferred back to Sperryville, Virginia, where Copper Fox whiskey is made. The cherry wood smoked malt has a highly distinctive voice, and here it is again. Except this really does appear to have dark cherry notes at work on the palate. Annoyingly, although single barrel, there is no distinguishing reference number. 45% (90 proof)

TUTHILLTOWN SPIRITS Gardiner, New York.
❖ **Hudson Baby Bourbon Year 13 Batch E1 (86) n21 t21.5 f22 b21.5.** A big, heavy duty bourbon. Feinty, though nothing like as oily as some previous bottlings I've encountered from these guys over the years. Enough toasted honeycomb and liquorice for this to make a few lovely noises. 46%. WB15/174

❖ **Hudson Four Grain Bourbon Year 13 Batch E1 (90.5) n22.5** busy with a small grain attack but the weightier cocoa and manuka honey hits the spot; **t22** a tad oily from the generous cut but this is overcome by a series of outlandish waves of muscovado sugar, maple syrup and treacle combining with the classic bourbon liquorice and hickory notes **f23** settles into a more delicate phase where complexity returns and the small grains are back on track; **b23** a really excellent whiskey, despite the odd technical weakness, which concentrates on complexity...and succeeds. An accomplished, big-hearted bourbon. 46%. WB15/175

❖ **Hudson Manhattan Rye** pot-distilled from rye grain, year 13, batch E2 **(89) n23** the rye flies at you: does what it says on the tin. A little feinty, but the firmness of the rye outmuscles it; **t22.5** a macho arm wrestle between thick rye and treacle; **f21.5** bitters as the feints show their hand slightly; **b22** rich, dense and pretty impressive. 46% WB15/383

TRIPLE EIGHT DISTILLERY Nantucket, Massachusetts.
The Notch Aged 8 Years dist 2000, bott Aug 08 db **(93) n24 t23.5 f22.5 b23.** Very few distilleries make their international bow with a single malt this sublime and superbly constructed. $888 dollars a bottle it may be, but for a taste of America's very first island malt... well, is there really a price? A head turner of a whisky, and every time it's towards the glass. Do we have a world classic distillery in the making...? 44.4% (88.8 proof)

The Notch Aged 8 Years db **(95.5) n24.5 t24.5 f23 b23.5.** Only six bottles of this were produced for a special dinner at the distillery. It is possible one escaped. I admit I had a hand in putting this one together, selecting samples from about half a dozen casks on the warehouse and blending them to certain percentages. Perhaps the closest it might be compared to is a Cardhu, though with a touch extra fruit. For the doubters, proof that this distillery is quite capable of whisky of the very highest calibre. 40% (80 proof)

WESTLAND DISTILLERY Seattle, Washington.
❖ **Westland American Single Malt Whiskey** dist Jun 11, bott Sept 14 db **(95) n23.5** even with the complex, buzzing oaky notes the marriage between profound citrus-tinted vanilla and intense barley is a happy one; the overt bourbon tones does give the malt an extra flourish; **t24.5** you rather lovely little smoothie, you....! Hard to imagine I'll find many deliveries as silky soft as this, especially taking into account the overall weight. Just so salivating, you

don't know whether to swallow or kiss it...; the sugars offer prefect weight to the malt, mainly of a maple syrup theme, but something more heavy and toasty besides; **f23** back to vanilla – custard cream biscuits, to be precise. **b24** the label makes the dangerously bold claim that this is a whisky which "can stand with the best whiskies in the world". As it happens, their pride may not be entirely misplaced... *46%. nc ncf.*

⬩⬩⬩ **Westland Deacon Seat American Single Malt Whiskey** dist Jun 11, bott Aug 13 db **(82)** **n21 t22.5 f18.5 b20.** Sweet – perhaps a little overly so early on. Soft in the house style. But way too flat and furry especially at the death. Sorry. No great fan of the effect the fruitiness has on this guy. *46%. 5000 bottles.*

⬩⬩⬩ **Westland First Peated American Single Malt Whiskey** dist Dec 11, bott Jan 14 db **(89)** **n22.5** a wonderfully different style of peated malt: the phenols positively ping off the thrusting tannin. The smoke does envelope gently, but there is a rigidity to the main theme, and a little kumquat, too; **t23.5** charming delivery which, like the nose, makes a point of entering new whiskey territory. The sugars are crisp and of a molassed disposition; the oak is forthright, firm and hickory fuddled. Before and after the briefest burst of spice the smoke doesn't appear sure whether to thrust or sit back and massage: in the end it does both...deliciously...; **f21** some cocoa-dusted liquorice rounds off a quite idiosyncratic malt; **b22** a very acceptable first forage into the smokier depths of the world's whiskies. If, in future bottlings, they can do something about the rock hard, unyielding finale they really will have something special here. *46%. nc ncf.*

WILLIE HOWELL SPIRITS
WH32137 (73.5) n15 t21 f18.5 b19. As big and intense as you'd expect from any spirit with a cut as wide as this. Very sweet corn oil ensures an uplifting body. *42.5%*

WOODINVILLE WHISKEY CO. Woodinville, Washington
Mash Bill No 9 Bourbon Batch 2 **(90) n22** no shrinking violet here. And on the subject of violets: pretty floral, though the spice rack has much to say too. Genuinely oak-laden and busy; **t23.5** if the nose has a lot to say, this positively grinds out the speeches and proclamations. Massive whiskey choc-a-bloc with varied citrus notes of different weights and density. The spices are outwardly delicate but cluster into something serious and meaningful, though the corn has a slightly miserly quality; **f22** thins a shade too fast, though the natural caramels and residual sugars do their best to keep the party going; **b22.5** a bourbon quite impossible not to love. Excellent fare from a new distillery to watch! *46%*

WOODSTONE CREEK DISTILLERY Cincinnati, Ohio.
Woodstone Creek 10 Year Old Peated Malt (92) 24 23 22 23. Just read the previous tasting notes. There is nothing I can either add nor subtract. Quite, quite wonderful... *46.25%*

Woodstone Microspirit 5 Grain Straight Bourbon Single Barrel No. 3 (95) n24 mega complex nose with just the right degree of liquorice and manuka honey to get you in a bourbon mood. The small grains are in dizzying perpetual motion; **t24** small still copper sharpness meets a rye-recipe style small grain juiciness with a wheat-recipe style spice. The oak also digs deep and does nothing to lessen the complexity, chipping in with a molten chocolate filling; **f23** softens as the oils filter through but we are back now to a liquorice/hickory feel, sweetened with orange blossom honey; **b24** you can tell Cincinnati borders Kentucky: of all the micro distillery bourbons I have ever tasted, this comes closest to the original big distiller style. Had I tasted blind, for the odd moment or two I might have called this as well aged stock from the Tom Moore distillery in Bardstown. Astonishing. And delightful! *47%*

YAHARA BAY DISTILLERY Madison, Wisconsin.
Sample No 1 (87) n22.5 t22 f20.5 b22. A disarmingly elegant whiskey. *40%*

American/Kentucky Whisky Blends
Ancient Age Preferred (73) n16.5 t19 f19.5 b18. A marginal improvement thanks mainly to a re-worked ripe corn-sweet delivery and the cocoa-rich finish. But still preferred, one assumes, by those who probably don't care how good this distillery's whisky can be... *40%*

Beam's Eight Star (69.5) n17 t18 f17 b17.5. If you don't expect too much it won't let you down. *40%*

Bellows (67) n17 t17.5 f16 b16.5 Just too thin. *40%*

Calvert's Extra (79) n19 t20 f20 b20. Sweet and mega-toffeed. Just creaking with caramel but extra marks for the late spice. *40%*

Carstair's White Seal (72) n16.5 t18.5 f19.5 b17.5 Possibly the cleanest blend about even offering a cocoa tang on the finale. Pleasant. *40%*

Kentucky Dale (64) n16 t17 f15 b16. Thin and spineless, though soft and decently sweet on delivery. The grain spirit completely dominates. *40%*

Kessler (84.5) n20 t21 f22 b21.5. "Smooth As Silk" claims the label. And the boast is supported by what is in the bottle: a real toffee-mocha charmer with a chewy, spicy depth. *40%*

PM Deluxe (75) n18 t18 f19 b18. Pleasant moments as the toffee melts in the mouth. *40%*

Sunny Brook (79.5) n20 t21 f19 b19.5. An entirely agreeable blend with toffee and lightly oiled nuts. Plus a sunny disposition... *40%*

Whiskey Distilled From Bourbon Mash

Angels Envy Bourbon Finished in Port Barrels (84) n20 t22 f21 b21. Almost like a chocolate raisin candy and fruitcake. Silky textured and juicy. *43.3% (86.6 proof)*

Angels Envy Cask Strength Bourbon Finished in Port Barrels Cask Strength (86.5) n21.5 t24 f20 b21. The problem with cask finishing most things, and bourbon in particular it seems, is that something is lost in the complexity - especially the small grain interaction, as well as balance between the spirit and oak - which is not quite compensated for with the lushness of extra fruit. Much better than the standard bottling, though, and the juiciness and cushioned enormity on delivery and spice at the midpoint is certainly worth discovering. *60.5%*

Big Bottom Straight Bourbon Finished in Port Casks 91 (86.5) n21.5 t24 f20 b21. Subtract over enthusiastic toastiness and withering dryness and for a while we have a genuinely stunning mouth feel backed by spectacular spiced apricot and ulmo honey. The odd few moments of genius there. *45.5% (91 proof) ncf*

Big Bottom Straight bourbon Finished in Zinfandel Casks 91 (85) n21 t22 f21 b21. A flat nose and delivery comes alive about eight or nine flavour waves in when the fruit comes to a compromise with the grains. The burnt raisin finish is just a little too bitter. *45.5%. ncf.*

⁙ **Woodford Reserve Master's Collection Four Wood** db (78.5) n20 t22.5 f18 b18. As much as they seem to want to kid us that this is bourbon – and let us be in no doubt: it isn't – it would help their misguided cause if whatever this was being offered proved an attractive experience. Apart from the immediate honey-rich delivery which is very pleasant indeed, the nose and finish have all the charisma of a 59-year-old train spotter going home to his empty house to make his sandwiches for the next day. Flat, characterless and spectacularly devoid of complexity. Basically, all the things bourbon cannot normally be accused of... *47.2% WB15/379*

Whiskey Distilled From Malt Mash

⁙ **Woodford Reserve Master's Collection Classic Malt** distilled from a malt mash db (79.5) n20 t21 f19 b19.5. Ok. So let me get my head around this. If their label and neck blurb is to believed, a spirit distilled from malt in the US and placed into used casks is a "whiskey distilled from a malt mash" while, as written on another product, a bourbon transferred into used casks is a bourbon. That appears to be Woodford's stance. Sorry, guys. Don't buy that argument for a second. If anyone argued that there appears to be more politicising, tactical manoeuvring and precedential games being played here as there is careful fermentation, distilling and blending, it would be hard to disagree. Says it is malt. But doesn't help by saying malt what. Presumably barley, as the nose offers nothing other than freshly cut hay. Which in a Scotch or Irish might be regarded as a problem, often pointing an accusing finger at fermentation. Sadly, the drinking experience, as sweet as it is, doesn't get much better. *45.2% WB15/382*

Whiskey Distilled From Rye Mash

Angels Envy Rye Finished in Caribbean Rum Casks (78) n18.5 truly a unique nose in my 24 years of professional tasting and 38 years of sampling the world's whisk(e)ys. Kind of perfumed burnt orange and toasted vanilla mallow filling in the rye peaks...; t20.5 what the hell...?? Yes, the rye bites through the clutter, and does it well. But there is still a bizarre background noise that just about defies description. Oily, sugary...odd; f20 a soft, lightly pulsing oil; b19 frankly, I was hardly expecting to have any teeth left after this sample. The hardest, most crisp of all whiskeys is rye. And if you want to give any whisk(e)y an extra degree of exoskeleton, then just finish it in a rum cask. And here we have the two together : yikes! Some twenty years ago I gave then Jack Daniel's blender Lincoln Henderson his first-ever taste of peated whisky: a Laphroaig. He hated it! I think he's waited a long time to return the compliment by showing me a style I did not know could exist. Beyond fascinating. Weird, even - hence the full tasting notes. One for the ladies with this liqueur-style smoothie. *50%.*

Other American Whiskey

⁙ **Abraham Bowman Double Barrel Bourbon** dist 12/06 bott 03/14. db (85) n23 t23 f19 b20. What does double barrel mean here? Well, in this instance thankfully it does not involve sherry or other wine casks. This is bourbon x2: the spirit is matured in virgin oak for a few years before being dumped into a fresh one. So this really is bourbon. If the great Truman Cox, the former distiller at Bowman, was still with us I'd have fun telling him why I think this is not something that has been done too often in the past. Not least because of the double dose of oak-induced sugars which means, sadly, a cloying, over-the-top sweetness and overall lack of charm and complexity. The saving grace on the palate is the delivery which packs enough spicily explosive punch to cut through the concentrated sugar candy to create something meaningful, if only temporarily so. The uncompromisingly dry finish is way off beam, so to speak, and even off-handedly bitter. One hundred proof, I'm afraid, that you can have too much of a good thing. If you do end up with a bottle, do make the most of the nose and test it only after it has aired and oxidised for about 20 minutes: it is like dipping your head into the spice cupboard in which the ginger has been knocked over and spilled. Ginger beer barrel...who needs it? 50%.

⋰ **Abraham Bowman Pioneer Spirit 'Gingerbread Beer Finished Bourbon'** charred white oak, dist 21/04/2006 bott 14/08/2013 db (**89**) n22 most ginger cake lurks at ever corner of this dry, gently spiced nose...; t22 again, a dry delivery with a build up of yapping if dull spice; big tannin signature though the hickory finds it hard to make its mark f23 even drier – almost like toasted brown bread. The ginger, now more pronounced, shimmers... b22 as gingerbread beer finished whiskey goes, rates highly... 45%.

⋰ **Abraham Bowman Virginia Limited Edition Whiskey "Port Finished Borboun"** dist 30/03/01 bott 17/08/13. db (**84.5**) n20 t23 f20.5 b21. I imagine this at one time was an entertaining bourbon. However, it reaches us as something of a dullard. The nose is instantly forgettable with the fruit and grains cancelling the other out; likewise the finish does little to stretch the imagination or taste buds other than some persistent spices. Only on delivery does this work as we are treated to a virtuoso display of dark sugars and jam vying for top spot. But the question needing answering for me is simple: why are the Americans trying to ape the Scots at a time when, quality-wise, Kentucky boots are firmly trod on kilted windpipes? 50%.

Buffalo Trace Experimental Collection 19 Year Old Giant French Oak Barrel 135 gallon French oak barrel, dist 27 Jan 93, bott 28 Jun 12 db (**84.5**) n21.5 t22 f20 b21. Conservative and tight on the nose and finish in particular. But for the sugary rush on delivery, not something you would have hoped to have uncovered after 19 years... 45% (90 Proof). sc.

Buffalo Trace Experimental Collection 23 Year Old Giant French Oak Barrel 135 gallon French oak, dist 89, bott 12 db (**91**) n23 big, winey number with a touch of the noble rot about it; t23 ballsy delivery with the oak and fruit right up there, tight and compact, rounded and determined to hang about together. A touch of salt...; f22.5 more salty fruit: figs, dates and, finally, rye crispness; b22.5 different. And, unlike the 19-y-o, this works... 45% (90 Proof). sc.

Buffalo Trace Experimental Collection 1989 Barrels Rediscovered white oak with seasoned staves, dist Nov 89, bott Dec 10 (**91.5**) n24 t23 f22.5 b22.5. A whispering bourbon of exceptional subtlety which makes minimum fuss of its antiquity. 45% (90 Proof)

Buffalo Trace Experimental Collection 1991 Barrels Rediscovered white oak with seasoned staves, dist Oct 91, bott Dec 10 (**93.5**) n24 t23.5 f23 b23. Pretty classic stuff. 45%

Buffalo Trace White Dog Mash #1 (**93**) n23 t23 f24 b23. Exceptionally high quality spirit, fabulously weighted, neither too sweet nor dry and with the distinctive cocoa character of the very best grain distillate. Beats the crap out of vodka. "White Dog" is the name for spirit which has run off the still but not yet been bottled: "New Make" in Scotland. It is not, therefore, whiskey as it has not been in any form of contact with oak. But what the hell... It must be at least 15 years ago that I told the old plant manager, Joe Darmond, that he should bottle this stuff as it would sell fast. BT brought it out initially for their distillery shop...and now it is in demand worldwide?! If you are reading this, what did I tell you? and about rye come to that! 62.5%

High West Son of Bourye blend of bourbon & rye (**95**) n23 the rye notes are as crunchy as a muscovado sugar driveway; t24.5 the kind of salivation factor that brings you to your knees in a state of grainy euphoria. The radiating brown sugars are as clean as they are exemplary; f23.5 only now does the bourbon get a word in edgeways, though can offer only a half-hearted honey, caramel and liquorice mix; b24 this son, presumably called Ryebon, is a stunningly stylish chap which comprehensively eclipses its lackluster parent... 46%

High West Campfire rye, bourbon & Scotch malt, batch no. 3 (**93**) n23.5 t22.5 f23.5 b23.5. An enchanting, hugely complex dram...the sort of thing I conjure up in my tasting room every day, in fact, by mixing differing whisky styles from around the world. Here the rye dominates by some margin, creating the backbone on which the sweeter bourbon tones hang. The peated malt ensures a wonderful background rumble. Well blended...and great fun! 46%

⋰ **High West Whiskey American Prairie Reserve Blend of Straight Bourbon** batch 13DQ3 db (**91**) n22.5 warm and rich, there is an unusually heavy copper content; red currents sits well with the spiced honeycomb; the hefty tannins in a brand called Prairie Reserve add a degree of irony; t23 exceptionally dry, tingling delivery with the sugars apparent but usually keeping their distance; f23 cream fudge and a return to a heftier type of tannin; b23 not often you find a predominantly dry bourbon...must have something to do with the Prairie...which ten percent of post tax profit will help to preserve. 46%. ncf. WB15/177

Canadian Whisky

It is becoming hard to believe that Canadian was once a giant among the world whisky nations. Dotted all over its enormous land large distilleries pumped out thousands upon thousands of gallons of spirit that after years in barrel became a clean, gentle whisky.

It was cool to be seen drinking Canadian in cocktail bars on both sides of the pond. Now, sadly, Canadian whisky barely raises a beat on the pulse of the average whisky lover. It would not be beyond argument to now call Canadian the forgotten whisky empire with column inches devoted to their column stills measured now in millimetres. It is an entirely sad, almost heartbreaking, state of affairs though hopefully not an irreversible one. The finest Canadian, for me, is still whisky to be cherished and admired. But outside North America it can be painfully hard to find.

Especially seeing how whiskies containing the permitted 9.09% of non-Canadian whisky (or whisky at all) had been barred from the European market. So just to ensure Jim Murray's Whisky Bible remained on the ball I spend as much time in Canada as possible keeping abreast of any changes I can find in the limited range of new bottlings to emerge each year. There appears now to be a distinct divergence of styles between traditionalist whisky like Alberta Premium, which realy is made from rye, and a more creamy textured, fruit-enhanced corn or wheat distilled product once confined to the USA but now found in Canada itself. The trouble is, apart from the Bible, there is little way of knowing which is which.

BRITISH COLUMBIA

ALBERTA

MANITOBA

Alberta

Vancouver

Calgary

Okanagan

Palliser

Gimli

Key
- ● Major Town or City
- ⛰ Distillery
- † Dead Distillery

However, there is no doubt that we are seeing a change in the perception of Canadian by drinkers who had previously confined themselves to top quality Scotch malt. Following the award of Jim Murray's Whisky Bible Canadian Whisky of the Year 2006 to Alberta Premium, I had the chance to spend time in television and radio studios around the country talking about the exceptionally high quality of top Canadian whiskies. It led to a string of emails from readers telling me they had since tasted Alberta and been somewhat shocked to find a world classic whisky lurking so unobtrusively - and cheaply - on their shelves. For many, this had led to further exploring of Canadian, and uncovering of further gems. For the Jim Murray's Whisky Bible 2013, 2014 and 2015 the winning Canadian asked many questions of just what is happening at Alberta. In July 2012 a knock out blind tasting of 16 award-winning whiskies from around the world I conducted had the people of Sun Peaks in British Columbia's Rocky Mountains speechless when they discovered they had voted Alberta Premium the finest whisky of the evening. No surprise, then, that it is rye from Alberta that not only won top Canadian billing in the Bible, but got through to the last six taste off for World Whisky of the Year. Yet, Masterson's 10-year-old is a label owned by an independent bottler: Alberta's official own new offering, Dark Horse, was anything but a thoroughbred by comparison.

Perhaps one of the things that makes Canadian whisky compelling is its ever-changing face. Many brands do have a tendency to move around in style slightly more than you might expect. However, there is an interesting development from Kentucky which contradicts that in an unorthodox manner. Buffalo Trace has decided to bottle some casks of Canadian in their inventory as a single barrel product. They sent me and others some samples back in their developmental stage and asked us for our input. Now, contrary to what anyone tells you, or claim they know, a Canadian single cask whisky called Bush Pilot was around some 15 years ago, the product of Canadian Club's Okanagan distillery. And each bottling was natural and fascinatingly different. The same can't quite be said for the new Caribou Crossing, a pleasant enough whisky which sports a thumping degree of unionizing caramel while the Canadian whisky lover, or potential convert, is little helped by every bottle looking identical with no cask details. Buffalo Trace have done little wrong in the last decade; indeed, in that time have become the most consistently excellent and exciting distillers in the world taking both bourbon and rye to new heights in my lifetime, and in Drew Mayville (a Canadian, incidentally) they have a blender at the top of his game. But the usual BT sure-footedness appears to have found a hole in the ice - for you can't help thinking that this perfect chance to win over hearts and minds to Canadian has not been fully grasped. Both Drew and I learned our Canadian from the very same school of past Canadian blending masters – and I use the term carefully – so we tend to have very similar views on matters Canadian/Canadien. When last in Frankfort I was unable to discuss this with him as we had the small matter of the Single Oak Project to dissect. Next time though I will be locking friendly Caribou horns with him.

QUEBEC

Glenora

ONTARIO

NOVA SCOTIA

Valleyfield

Quebec

Montreal

Canada Mist

Toronto

Kittling Ridge

Walkerville

Canadian Single Malts
GLENORA

Glen Breton db (81) n19 t21 f20 b21. Ultra sweet malt, in almost concentrated form with a tantalising whiff of smoke hanging around; mildly spiced and slightly oily, soapy finale. *43%*

Glen Breton Ice Aged 10 Years db (85.5) n21.5 t21 f22 b21. Tasting both a full strength bottled Canadian, and one that had been matured in Icewine barrels, I was nearly blown through the back of my seat and into the wall. One of the biggest shocks to hit you on the Canadian whisky scene today, there is no denying that this whisky offers sufficient panache and lucidity to genuinely impress. Hardly an exercise in perfect balance, it certainly celebrates the art of surprise and, late on, charm. The cocoa-dusted butterscotch really is a rare treat and, thanks to the fruity world it finds itself in, a truly unique and enjoyable experience. *57.2%*

Glen Breton Rare db (80) n18 t21 f20 b21. Caramel nose a bit soapy but the buttery, sweet malt, with its vanilla fizz, makes for a pleasant experience. *43%*

Glen Breton Rare Aged 10 Years bott 10 db (89.5) n22 t23 f22 b22.5. An impressive whisky: one of the best bottlings of this age for some while and showing the malt at full throttle. *43%*

Glen Breton Rare Aged 14 Years db (92) n23.5 t22.5 f23 b23. What is there not to enjoy? Some exceptionally good casks involved here. *43%*

Glen Breton Battle Of The Glen Aged 15 Years Special Edition db (94) n23.5 t23.5 f23 b24. I really did know they were capable of bottling something this good: there isn't a single barrel of this vintage I have not tasted in their warehouse at one time or another during its maturation cycle. This watermark bottling from then is an essentially sweet whisky, tasting all the sweeter as it marks the little distillery's victory over the Goliath that is the Scotch Whisky Association in their rightful battle to retain the right to use the name of their brand. Just sometimes there is evidence there just may be a god... *43% 4200 bottles.*

Glen Breton Ice Aged 17 Years aged in Icewine barrels bott 2010 db (90.5) n22.5 t24 f21.5 b22.5. A different animal to the 10-y-o Icewine version, though having much more to do with the spirit than the casks. Yet never before has this distillery sent me such a box of wonderful delights such as these barley... It is as though their victory over the Scotch industry has lifted a cloud of self-doubt. Glenora appears to have come of age. *54.6%*

Glen Breton Rare Cabot Links Reserve Aged 19 Years db (86.5) n21 t22.5 f21 b22. You know when astronomers build a super-powerful new telescope that gives them a clearer view of when the universe began. This bottling is a bit like that... taking us back to the days of the Glen Breton Big Bang. Lots of dramatic barley to view. But, naturally, all the more basic and primitive elements are there on show, also... *46%*

OKANAGAN SPIRITS CRAFT DISTILLERY

⋄ **Laird of Fintry Single Malt Whisky** French & American oak. db (84) n21 t22 f20 b21. A tangy, aromatic whisky where the oak appears to have a disproportionate say. Interesting marmalade depth. *40%. First Batch. 264 bottles.*

POTTER DISTILLING CO.

⋄ **Cadenhead's World Whiskies Canada Potter Distilling Co. Aged 24 Years** Bourbon barrel, bott Feb 14 (94.5) n23 though from a bourbon cask and distilled from corn, you cannot escape a delicate fruit note, as though from boiled candy. This suggests the cask might have spent some time in the distant past maturing in a warehouse in Canada with fruit distillate alongside; t24 gorgeous delivery with the corn ramping up both the flavour profile and the oils; the sugars are a mix of maple syrup and ulmo honey. Again, that vague unspecified fruitiness catches the palate offering a silky hue; f23.5 now the spices are in play yet the salivation levels do not drop despite the polite oak intervention via the drying vanilla; b24 a true classic of the Canadian rye style...though of course without any rye at all. As a whisky, a little bit of a mystery. When at Potter distillers in British Columbia about 17 years ago, I remember they then had no maturing stock of their own as they did not distil large enough quantities. But they did have casks of maturing Canadian whisky they had bought in from the nearby Okanagan Distillery which, for a while, had made Canadian Club for the west coast and Far East market. No guarantees, but chances are it could be that – and they did make very good whisky there, evidenced by the outstanding old Bush Pilot single cask brand. *56.5%. 126 bottles. WB15/178*

STILLWATERS DISTILLERY

⋄ **Stalk & Barrel Single Malt Whisky** cask 11 db (87.5) n21.5 t22 f22 b22. Attractively intense barley has all the space it requires to flourish thanks to a well distilled spirit impressively cut. Only a lack of complexity fails to crank the score a little higher. But if it's a malt whisky you want, with the accent on the malt, here's your man. *62.3%. sc.*

⋰∴⋱ **Stalk & Barrel Single Malt Whisky** cask 13 db **(77)** n20 t21 f17 b19. Not quite the delight that is cask 11. Not sure if that is because the weaker strength means the water has broken up the oils a little bit too much for their own good, exposing a few feints. Or if the cut wasn't quite as carefully made this time round. Still plenty of malt to get on with, though. *46%. sc.*

Canadian Blended Whisky

Alberta Premium (95.5) n24 throbbing, pulsing rye on a variety of levels: full and juicy, dull and dusty, firm and flinty. Unique and unmistakable; **t25** my first whisky of the day – and it needs to be. The tastebuds are given such a working over that they need to be fully tuned and fit to take this on. Again it is all about the rye: the first three flavours to pound the mouth are all rye-related. The very first are juicy with a minute sweetness. The second, hanging onto the coattails of the first are Rockies hard and brittle, clattering into the tastebuds with zero yield. Next comes a quick follow through of explosive peppers, but again leaving in their wake a semi-sweet juicy, fruitiness, almost certainly from the malted rye. No other whisky unleashes this combination of grainy punches around the palate. The words beautiful and complex don't even begin to do this whisky justice; **f22.5** dulls down, probably because of the needless caramel added, but there is slightly more depth than before thanks most probably to the malted rye. The spices continue to fizz as the Demerara-tipped vanillas make their mark; **b24** it has just gone 8am and the Vancouver Island sky is one of clear blue. My windows are open to allow in some chilly, early Spring air and, though only the first week of March, an American robin sits in the arbutus tree, resplendent in its now two-toned leaves, calling for a mate, as it has done since 5.15 this morning, his song blending with the lively trill of the house finches and the doleful, maritime anthem of the gull. It seems the natural environment of Alberta Premium, back here to its rye-studded best after a couple I tasted socially in Canada last year appeared comparatively dull and restrained. I am tasting this from Bottle Lott No L93300197 and it is classic, generating all I expect and now demand. A national treasure. *40%*

Alberta Premium bott lott L1317 **(96)** n24 t25 f23 b24. Tasting this three years on from the sample above, there is absolutely nothing to add or subtract (except the finish is fractionally more engrossing): the consistency and brilliance defies belief. *40%*

Alberta Premium bott lott L2150 **(94)** n23.5 t24 f23 b23.5. Fractionally duller than the 2011 bottling sampled above with less emphasis on the crystalline rye and more on cane sugar. Still a treat! *40%*

Alberta Premium 25 Years Old (95) n24 t23 f23 b25. Faultless. Absolutely nothing dominates. Yet every aspect has its moment of conquest and glory. It is neither bitter nor sweet, yet both. It is neither soft nor hard on the palate yet both elements are there. Because of the 100% rye used, this is an entirely new style of whisky to hit the market. No Canadian I know has ever had this uncompromising brilliance, this trueness to style and form. And, frightening to think, it could be improved further by bottling at least 46% and un-chillfiltered. For any whisky lover who ever thought Canadian was incapable of hitting the heights among the world's greats. *40%. Alberta Distillers.*

Alberta Premium 30 Years (88.5) n23 t23.5 f20 b22. It doesn't take much to tip the balance of a whisky this delicate on the nose and delivery. Five extra years in the cask has nudged the oak just a little too far. However, savour the nose and delivery which are to die for. *40%*

Alberta Premium Dark Horse (84) n18 t22 f22 b22. The blurb on the back says it is crafted for the "next generation of whisky connoisseur". Fine. But personally, I'd always shape a whisky for the true connoisseurs of today... I have not spoken to the blending team at Alberta to discuss this and, as the book has to be finished within a week or two, I won't get a chance. But this is the most extraordinary development in Canadian I have seen for a while. The nose is not great: it really does seem as though fruit cordial has been given the lead role. But the taste really does challenge, and I have to say there are many aspects I enjoy. It is as though some peated malt has been added to the mix as the finish does have distinctive smokiness. And the balance has been expertly worked to ensure the sugars don't dominate while the spices are persistent. But if it falls down anywhere, the over reliance on the fruit apart, it is the fact that Alberta makes the best spirit in Canada by a very great distance....yet someone has forgotten to ensure that fact is made clear in the taste and the nose especially. *45%*

Alberta Springs Aged 10 Years (83) n21 t21 f20 b20. Really appears to have had a bit of a flavourectomy. Sweet but all traces of complexity have vanished. 40%.

Barton's Canadian 36 Months Old (78) n19 t20 f19 b20. Sweet, toffeed, easy-going. *40%*

Bowman's Canadian Whisky (90.5) n22 t22 f23.5 b23. A delicious, honest Canadian for chocoholics. *40%*

Black Velvet (78) n18 t20 f20 b20. A distinctly off-key nose is compensated for by a rich corn and vanilla kick on the palate. But that famous spice flourish is a distant memory. Another big caramel number. *40%*

Campbell & Cooper Aged a Minimum of 36 Months (84.5) n21.5 t22 f20 b21. Huge flavour profile. An orchard of oranges on the nose and profound vanilla on delivery. 40%

Canadian Club 100 Proof (89) n21 t23 f22 b23. If you are expecting this to be a high-octane version of the standard CC Premium, you'll be in for a shock. This is a much fruitier dram with an oilier body to absorb the extra strength. An entertaining blend. 50%.

Canadian Club Premium (92) n23 t22.5 f23 b23.5. A greatly improved whisky which now finds the fruit fitting into the mix with far more panache than of old. Once a niggardly whisky, often seemingly hell-bent on refusing to enter into any form of complexity: but not now! Great spices in particular. I'm impressed. 40%

Canadian Club Aged 6 Years (88.5) n21.5 t22 f22.5 b22.5. Not at all bad for a Canadian some purists turn their nose up at as it's designed for the American market. Just brimming with mouth-watering enormity and style. Dangerously moreish. 40%

Canadian Club Reserve Aged 10 Years (86) n20 t22 f21.5 b22. Odd cove, this. The nose is less than welcoming and offers a hotchpotch of somewhat discordant notes giving a jumbled message and less than well defined statement of intent. Decent delivery, though, shifting through the gears with some impressive and sultry fruit tying in well with a rare grain onslaught found in Canadian these days. The finish, though, just can't steer away from the rocks of bitterness, alas. Again, as so often appears to be the case with CC, the spices star. 40%

Canadian Club Classic Aged 12 Years (91.5) n22 t24 f21.5 b23.5. A confident whisky which makes the most of a honeycomb theme. 40%

Canadian Club Small Batch Classic 12 Aged 12 Years batch C12-020 (75.5) n21 t22.5 f15 b17. A syrupy whisky which talks a great game on the back label, but fails to deliver in reality. Big fruit, perhaps a little too heavily accented as other avenues of complexity are limited. The bitter, tangy finish is not great at all. 40%

Canadian Club Aged 20 Years (92.5) n24 t21 f23.5 b23. In previous years, CC20 has ranked among the worst whiskies I have tasted, not just in Canada, but the world. Their current bottling, though, is not even a distant relation. Sure, it has a big sherry investment. But the sheer elan and clever use of spice make this truly magnificent. Possibly the most pleasant surprise in my latest trawl through all Canada's whiskies. 40%

Canadian Club Sherry Cask batch no. SC-018 (76) n18 t20 f20 b18. Twice as strong as you can normally buy Sherry yet somehow has only half the body. As I say, I really don't know what to make of this. Nor do I get the point. 41.3%

Canadian Five Star Rye Whisky (83) n21 t22 f20 b20. An entirely tame, well behaved Canadian which celebrates the inherent sweetness of the species. That said, the immediate impact on the palate is pretty delicious with a quick, flash explosion of something spicy. But it is the deft, satin-soft mouthfeel which may impress most. 40%

Canadian Hunter (85.5) n20.5 t21 f22 b22. Remains truly Canadian in style. The toffee has diminished, allowing far more coffee and cocoa to ensure a delightful middle and finish. 40%

Canadian Mist (78) n19 t20.5 f18.5 b20. Much livelier than previous incarnations despite the inherent, lightly fruited softness. 40%

Canadian Pure Gold (82) n21.5 t20.5 f20 b20. Full-bodied and still a notably lush whisky. The pure gold may have more to do with the caramel than the years in cask but the meat of this whisky still gives you plenty to chew over. I especially enjoy the gradual building of spices. 40%

Canadian Spirit (78) n20 t20 f19 b19. A real toffee-fest with a touch of hard grain around the edges. 40%. Carrington Distillers (Alberta Distillers).

Caribou Crossing Single Barrel (84) n20 t22.5 f20 b21.5. While the nose offers an unholy battle between some apple-fruity rye notes and dry, dusty caramel, there is a real pulsating delivery with the sharper spices helped along the way by the silkiness of the body. Though the caramel offers a toffee-fudge backdrop, a countering dry date sweetness does more than enough to keep it at bay. However, the finish dulls out as the caramel gains the upper hand, though the twitching spices do ensure a light, throbbing beat. An enjoyable Canadian, undoubtedly, I am somewhat perplexed by it. There is no reference to the barrel number so you won't know if you are buying from different casks. Also, if it is single barrel what is the point of the caramel? If it is to make all the casks taste the same, or similar, then why not just blend them together. A badly missed opportunity. 40%. Sazerac.

Centennial 10 Year Limited Edition (88.5) n21.5 t23 f22 b22. Retains its usual honey-flavoured breakfast cereal style, but the complexity has increased. Busy and charming. 40%

Century Reserve 8 Years Old Premium (82) n20 t21 f20 b21. Clean vanilla caramel. 40%

Century Reserve Custom Blend 15 Years Plus (88.5) n21.5 t22 f23 b22. After two days of being ambushed in every direction, or completely steamrollered by Canadian caramel, my tastebuds are in total shock. Caramel kept to an absolute minimum so that it hardly registers at all. Charming and refined drinking. 40%

Century Reserve 21 Years Old (91.5) n23.5 t23 f23 b22. Quite beautiful, but a spirit that is as likely to appeal to rum lovers as whisky ones. 40%

Century Reserve Custom Blend lot no. 1525 **(87) n21.5 t22 f21.5 b22.** An enjoyable whisky which doesn't quite reach its full potential. *40%*

Corby's Canadian 36 Months Old (85) n20 t21 f22 b22. Attractive with fine bitter-sweet balance and I love the late spice kick-back. *40%. Barton. Interesting label: as a keen ornithologist, I had no idea there were parrots in Canada. Must be related to the Norwegian Blue.*

Crown Royal (86) n22 t23.5 f19.5 b21. The Crown has spoken and it has been decreed that this once ultra grainy old whisky is taking its massive move to a silky fruitiness as far as it can go. It was certainly looking that way last time out; on this re-taste (and a few I have unofficially tasted) there is now no room for doubt. If you like grape, especially the sweeter variety, you'll love this. The highpoint is the sublime delivery and starburst of spice. The low point? The buzzy, unhappy finale. The Grain Is Dead. Long Live The Grape! *40%*

Crown Royal Black (85) n22 t23 f18.5 b21.5. Not for the squeamish: a Canadian which goes for it with bold strokes from the off which makes it a whisky worth discovering. The finish needs a rethink, though. *45%*

Crown Royal Cask No 16 Finished in Cognac Casks (85.5) n21.5 t21 f22 b21. Clean cut and very grapey. The nose is unique in the whisky world: it is one of Cognac. Otherwise struggles to really find its shape and rhythm. A perfect Canadian for those who prefer theirs with an air of grace and refinement but very limited depth. In fact, those who prefer a Cognac. *40%*

Crown Royal Limited Edition (87) n22 t22.5 f20.5 b22. A much happier and productive blend than before with an attractive degree of complexity but the more bitter elements of the finish have been accentuated. *40%*

Crown Royal Special Reserve (96) n24 a clean and attractively spiced affair with cinnamon and the faintest pinch of allspice leading the way: rye at work, one presumes; the fruit is clean and precise with weightier grape overshadowing a green apple freshness; **t24** a spicier element to the usual rye and fruit delivery, much more in keeping with the nose, but that fabulous, contrary mouth-feel of harder grain and softer fruit continues to do the business. The spices build slowly but with an impressive evenness and determination: one of the most outstanding Canadians on the palate of them all; **f24** the finish has been tidied up and with stunning effect: no more sawdust and eye-watering dryness. Both grain and soft fruit ensure a magnificently mouth-watering end to an amazing journey; **b24** complex, well weighted and simply radiant: it is like looking at a perfectly shaped, gossamer clad Deb at a ball. The ryes work astonishingly well here (they appear to be of the malted, ultra-fruity variety) and perhaps to best effect after Alberta Premium, though now it is a hard call between the two. *40%*

Crown Royal XR Extra Rare lot no. L7064 N4 **(93.5) n24 t23 f23 b23.5.** Just about identical to the previous bottle above. The only difference is on the finish where the rye, fortified with spice, decides to hang back and battle it out to the death; the toffee and vanilla make a controlled retreat. Either the same bottling with a slightly different stance after a few years in the bottle, or a different one of extraordinary high consistency. *40%*

⁂ **Crown Royal XO (87.5) n22 t21 f22.5 b22.** With an XO, one might have hoped for something eXtraOrdinary or at least eXOtic. Instead, we have a Canadian which carried on a little further where their Cask No 16 left off. Always a polite, if rather sweet whisky, it falls into the trap of allowing the Cognac casks a little too much say. Only on the finish, as the spices begin to find channels to flow into, does the character which, for generations, set Crown Royal apart from all other Canadians begin to make itself heard: complexity. *40% WB15/398*

Danfield's Limited Edition Aged 21 Years (95) n24 t24 f23.5 b23.5. A quite brilliant first-time whisky. The back label claims this to be small batch, but there is no batch number on the bottle, alas. Or even a visible bottling code. But this is a five star performer and one of this year's whiskies of the world. *40%*

Danfield's Private Reserve (84.5) n20 t21.5 f22 b21. A curious, non-committal whisky which improves on the palate as it goes along. An overdose of caramel (yawn!!) has done it no favours, but there is character enough for it to pulse out some pretty tasty spice. Seamless and silky, for all the toffee there underlying corn-rich clarity is a bit of a turn on. *40%*

8 Seconds Small Batch (86) n20 t22 f22.5 b21.5. Fruity, juicy, luxurious. And perhaps one of the few whiskies on the market anywhere in the world today which could slake a thirst. *40%*

Forty Creek Barrel Select (86.5) n21.5 t22 f21 b21.5. Thank goodness that the sulphur taint I had found on this in recent years has now vanished. A lush, enjoyable easy-goer, this juices up attractively at the start and ends with an almost sophisticated dry pithiness. *40%*

Forty Creek Confederation Oak Reserve lot 1867-B **(94.5) n23.5 t24 f23.5 b23.5.** Those who tasted the first batch of this will be intrigued by this follow up. The shape and intensity profile has been re-carved and all now fits together like a jigsaw. *40%*

Forty Creek Copper Pot Reserve (91.5) n23 t23.5 f22 b23. One of the beauties of John hall's whiskies at Forty Creek is that they follow no set pattern in the whisky would: they offer flavour profiles really quite different from anything else. That is why they are worth that bit of extra time for your palate to acclimatise. Here you are exceptionally well rewarded... *43%*

Forty Creek Double Barrel Reserve lot 247 **(86)** n21.5 t22.5 f20.5 b21.5. The usual juicy ride and plenty to savour early on. But there is something slightly off balance about the finish here. 40%

Forty Creek Port Wood Reserve lot 61 **(95.5)** n24.5 oh my word! Very highest quality Turkish Delight with some pretty top score chocolate; the fruit hangs off the frame full of juice and muscovado sugars. It demands spices...and gets them – with the right pizzazz! t24 the delivery is pure silk in texture and the most stunning fruit and spice on delivery. Hard to know whether to suck as it melts in the mouth, or chew as the background depth is outrageously nutty, with more cocoa to thicken. It is the astonishing spice that really mesmerises, as it is of almost perfect intensity; f23 dries into an attractive crushed grape pip dryness, again with the spices lingering; b24 John P Hall has got his ducks in a row. Magnificent! 45%

Forty Creek Three Grain (76) n19 t20 f18 b19. Not quite as well assembled as some Three grains I have come across over the last few years. There is a lopsidedness to this one: we know the fruit dominates (and I still haven't a clue why, when surely this of all whiskies, just has to be about the grains!) but the bitterness interferes throughout. If there have been sherry casks used here, I would really have a close look at them. 40%

Fremont Mischief Whiskey batch MPJ-0803, bott 11 **(77)** n19 t20 f19 b19. Though this whisky was from the Mischief distillery in Seattle, USA, the whiskey was produced in Canada. Overly sweet, overly toffeed and bereft of complexity. Like Alberta Springs on a very bad day. 40%

Gibson's Finest Aged 12 Years (77) n18 t20 f19 b20. Unlike the Sterling, going backwards rather than forwards. This is way too syrupy, fruity and toffee impacted. Despite the very good spice, almost closer to a liqueur than a true whisky style. 40%

Gibson's Finest Rare Aged 18 Years (95.5) n24 close your eyes and sniff and you would swear you have a bourbon-rye mix: simultaneously crisp and soft, the sharpness of the rye and apple-style fruitiness is sublime and as enticing as it gets; t24.5 and a perfect transfer onto the palate: spectacularly juicy with all kinds of clean rye and corn notes bobbling around in a gorgeous gentle Demerara sugar backdrop; f23.5 impressive vanilla and long strands of grain and bitter liquorice; b23.5 so far ahead of both Sterling and the 12, it is hard to believe they are from the same stable. But make no mistake; this is pure thoroughbred: truly world class. 40%

Gibson's Finest 100th Grey Cup Special Edition (87) n21 t23 f21 b22. When the label tells you there is a hint of maple, they aren't joking... 40%

Gibson's Finest Canadian Whisky Bourbon Cask Rare Reserve (89) n23 t21 f23 b22. A much better version than the first bottling, the depth this time being massively greater. 40%

Gibson's Finest Sterling (86.5) n22 t22.5 f20.5 b21.5. A massively improved Canadian that had me doing the equivalent of a tasting double take: had to look twice at this to check I had the right stuff! Much firmer now in all the right places with the corn making sweeping statements, the golden syrup melting into all the required crevices and spices exploding at the appropriate moments. Just need to sort the heavy toffee and bitter finish out and this would be up in the Canadian Premier League. 40%

Gibson's New Oak (88) n22 t21 f23 b22. Distinctly different from any other Canadian doing the rounds: the oak influence makes a wonderful and clever impact. 40%

Highwood Pure Canadian (84) n20 t21 f22 b21. A decent, ultra-clean Canadian with markedly more character than before. Certainly the caramel has been seriously reduced in effect and the wheat ensures a rather attractive spice buzz while the cane juice sweetness harmonises well. Perhaps most delightful is the wonderful and distinct lack of fruit. 40%

Hiram Walker Special Old (93) n22.5 t24 f23 b23.5. Even with the extra degree of all-round harmony, this remains the most solid, uncompromising Canadian of them all. And I love it! Not least because this is the way Special old has been for a very long time with obviously no intentions of joining the fruity bandwagon. Honest, first class Canadian. 40%

James Foxe (77.5) n20 t19.5 f19 b19. James could do with putting some weight on... 40%

Lord Calvert (72.5) n19 t18.5 f17 b18. Truly eccentric aristocracy, this. Comes from the most noble of homes, Alberta Distillery, and the pedigree of the rye is evident in patches on both nose and delivery. Then marries something very fruity well beneath its class. 40%

Lot No 40 Malted Rye Whisky (93) n24 the intensity of the malted rye element powers through, offering several variations of sharp honey concentrate, from manuka down to acacia. The tannins are pretty staggering for a Canadian and much more of the Kentucky/Indiana style. Simplistic yet so devastatingly beautiful... t23.5 there we go....like a rocket of rye, firing off in three stages with the softer intensity of the oilier malted rye being propelled by the far more rigid unmalted into orbit; about half way through they meld and then the cocoa-vanilla oak stage bursts through, as well as a playful spiciness which dries towards a serious dark chocolate middle; f22.5 being a miserable git, I'd say the oak tries too hard for world dominance here, allowing the bitterness to slightly overpower and over dry the crisper, toastier brown sugars. But on the other hand, those cocoa notes are pretty gorgeous and just enough oil allows it to level out across the palate; b23 an old friend – almost a long lost son – has returned and has brightened up my glass with colossal Canadianness. This is of a style unique to this country, though here the high levels of oak have perhaps dimmed the flame of the rye slightly. Welcome home, my son...!!! 40%

Masterson's 10 Year Old Straight Rye batch 003 **(96.5) n24** fizzing with fruity finesse, there is little doubting the grain involved here; almost a bubble gum sweetness to the fruit and through the melting softness lurks a note as firm and sharp as a sabre; **t24** just about as mouth-watering as it is spellbinding, the taste buds are immediately immersed in a stellar degree of crisp, sparkling rye notes; vanilla pods pop as it soaks in the juicy, clean rye; **f24** if you want to see an almost perfect degree of spice at work in a whisky, you really can't do better than savour the finish of this gorgeous bottling. Helped along by deft oil, the crystalline sugars and light vanillas just carry on their hypnotic dance; **b24.5** a magnificent whisky without any shadow of doubt. Rye is my favourite whisky type and this displays the style to a degree of excellence which is truly memorable in terms of a commercial bottling. Someone has done an outstanding job in selecting these casks. Interesting, however, that they don't actually state on the bottle that this is Canadian and confuse things a little further by spelling it "whiskey". My understanding is that this is unmalted rye from the outstanding Alberta Distillery in Calgary. What is certain is that this is a true classic of its style. And not so much Masterson's but Masterful. 45%

McGuinness Silk Tassel (79.5) n20 t21 f19.5 b19. Silk or satin? The corn oils offer a delightful sheen but still the caramel is over enthusiastic. 40%

McLoughlin and Steele Blended in the Okanagan Valley (87.5) n22 t22 f21.5 b22. As straight as a die: a Canadian Rye... without any discernible rye. 40%. McLoughlin and Steele.

Wm Morrison Imported Canadian Rye (87.5) n22 t22 f21.5 b22. Still a lovely Canadian, though the toffee needs toning down. Not sure what "Full Strength" is doing on the label when bottled at 40%, though... 40%.

Mountain Rock (87) n22 t20.5 f22.5 b22. Still a soft Canadian cocking a melt-in-the-mouth snook at its name. But this time the fruit is just over anxious to be heard and a degree of its old stability has been eroded. 40%. Kittling Ridge.

Okanagan Spirits Canadian Rye (88.5) n23 t22.5 f21 b22. A crisp, quite beautiful whisky with a youthful vision. Sort the thin finish out and we'd have something to really remember! Not, by the way, a whisky distilled at their new distillery. 40%

Pendleton Let'er Buck (91.5) n22.5 t23 f22.5 b23.5. A significantly improved whisky from the ultra-sweet, nigh on syrupy concoction of before. Here the surprisingly complex and sensual grains take star billing, despite the caramel: it almost makes a parody of being Canadian, so unmistakable is the style. For those who affectionately remember Canadian Club from 20-30 years ago, this might bring a moistening of the eye. 40% (80 proof). Hood River Distillers.

Pike Creek 10 Years Old finished in port barrels **(80) n21.5 t22.5 f17 b19.** The delivery is the highlight of the show by far as the fruit takes off backed by delicate spices and spongy softness. The nose needs some persuading to get going but when fully warmed, gives a preview of the delivery. The furry finish is a big disappointment, though. 40%

Potter's Crown (83) n19 t21.5 f21.5 b21. Silky and about the friendliest and most inoffensive whisky on this planet. The dusty aroma and thick, chewy toffee backbone says it all but still impossible not to enjoy! 40%

Potter's Special Old a blend of 5 to 11 year old rye whisky **(91) n23.5 t23 f22 b22.5.** More Canadian than a hockey punch-up – and, for all the spice, somewhat more gentle, too. 40%

Potter's Special Old Rye (85.5) n21 t23.5 f20 b21. Not quite the force majeure of a year or two back, the grains are now thinner and starker despite the beautifully striking delivery on the palate. The soft honey tones are an attractive compensation but the austerity on nose and finish takes a little getting used to when remembering previous incarnations. 40%

Proof Whisky charred oak barrels **(87.5) n22 t22 f21.5 b22.** The Proof is in the tasting, and this is a Canadian which should attract those who enjoy Bombay-style gin, too. 42%. .

Rich and Rare (79) n20 t20 f20 b19. Simplistic and soft. One for toffee lovers. 40%

Rich and Rare Reserve (86.5) n19.5 t21 f23.5 b22.5. Actually does what it says on the tin, certainly as to regard the "Rich" bit. But takes off when the finish spices up and even offers some ginger cake on the finale. Lovely stuff. 40%

Royal Canadian (87.5) n22 t22.5 f21 b22. Now there's a whisky which is on the up. 40%

Royal Canadian Small Batch (88) n22 t22.5 f21.5 b22. A big Canadian with a pleasing silk and steel pulse. 40%. Sazerac.

Royal Reserve (84.5) n19 t22.5 f21.5 b21.5. No question that the delivery is much richer, fresher and entertaining than before with the spices, dovetailing with subtle fruit, ensuring a complexity previously lacking - especially at the death. Frustratingly, the caramel seems to be biting deeper on the nose, which has taken a backward step. A much more enjoyable and satisfying experience, though. 40%

Royal Reserve Gold (94.5) n24 t23.5 f23 b24. Retains its position as a classy, classy Canadian that is an essay on balance. Don't confuse this with the much duller standard bottling: this has been moulded in recent years into one of the finest – and among its country's consumers - generally most underrated Canadians on the market. *40%*

Sam Barton Aged 5 Years (83.5) n19 t21.5 f22 b21. Exceptionally sweet session whisky with a lovely maple syrup glow and some complexity on the finish. Friendly, hospitable and impossible not to like. *40%. La Martiniquaise, France.*

Schenley Golden Wedding (92) n22 t24 f22 b23. Like a rare, solid marriage, this has improved over time. Always consistent and pleasant, there now appears to be a touch of extra age and maturity which has sent the complexity levels up dramatically. Quite sublime. *40%*

Schenley OFC (90) n22 t22.5 f23 b22.5. Notice anything missing from this whisky? Well the 8-year-old age statement has fallen off the label. But this is still a truly superb whisky which would benefit perhaps from toning down the degree of sweetness, but gets away with it in spectacular fashion thanks to those seductive oils. Not as complex as the magnificent old days, but a whisky that would have you demanding a refill nine time out of ten. *40%*

Seagram's Canadian 83 (86.5) n21 t22 f21.5 b22. A vastly improved blend which has drastically cut the caramel to reveal a melt-in-the-mouth, slightly crisp grain. There are some citrusy edges but the buttery vanilla and pleasing bite all go to make for a chic little number. *40%*

Seagram's VO (91) n22 t23.5 f22.5 b23. With a heavy heart I have to announce the king of rye-enriched Canadian, VO, is dead. Long live the corn-dominant VO. Over the years I have seen the old traditional character ebb away: now I have let go and have no option other than to embrace this whisky for what it has become: infinitely better than a couple of years back; not in the same league as a decade ago. But just taking it on face value, credit where credit is due. This is an enjoyably playful affair, full of vanilla-led good intention, corn and complexity. There is even assertive spice when needed and the most delicately fruity edge...though not rye-style. Thoughtfully blended and with no little skill, I am impressed. And look forward to seeing how this develops in future years. A treat which needs time to discover. *40%*

Snake River Stampede 8 Years Old dist 12 Dec 99, bott. 18 Jul 08 **(87.5) n22.5 t22.5 f21 b21.5.** A bit concerned when I read in the blurb that they finish this Canadian whisky in sherry butts. But no need; as clean as a perfectly lassoed colt. As silky as a cowboy's kerchief. *40%*

Still Waters Special 1+11 Blend batch 1204, bott 2012 **(92) n23.5 t23 f22.5 b23.** If the boys at Still Waters distillery end up with a whisky as enjoyable as this when theirs has matured, Canadian whisky will have flourished. *40%. 1200 bottles.*

Tangle Ridge Aged 10 Years (69) n18.5 t19.5 f15 b16. Decidedly less in your face than of old, unless you are thinking custard pies. For all the cleaned up aroma and early injection of spiced sultana, the uncompromisingly grim finish remains its usual messy self. An unpleasant reminder as to why I only taste this when it's Bible time... *40%*

Tesco Canadian Whisky (75) n18 t18 f20 b19. Sweet, clean, uninspiring. *40%*

Western Gold Canadian Whisky (91) n23 t23 f22.5 b22.5. Clean and absolutely classic Canadian: you can't ask for much more, really. *40%*

White Owl (77.5) n19 t19.5 f20 b19. White whisky: in others words, a whisky the same colour as water. To both nose and taste somewhat reminds me of the long gone Manx whisky which was casks of fully matured scotch re-distilled and bottled. Sweet and pleasant. But I doubt if connoisseurs will give two hoots... *40%*

Windsor (85.5) n21 t22 f21 b21.5. A whisky you could usually bet your week's wages on for consistency and depth. Here, though, the usual rye fruity, crispness has been dumbed down and though there are enough spices to make this a pleasant affair, the impact of the caramel is a tad too significant. The usual custard sweetness has also changed shape and dry vanilla at the death is the compromise. *40%*

Windsor (86) n20 t21 f23 b22. Pleasant but the majority of edges found on the Canadian edition blunted. Some outstanding, almost attritional, spice towards the middle and finale, though. Soft and desirable throughout: a kind of feminine version of the native bottling. *40%.*

Winn Dixie Canadian Whisky (80) n19 t20 f21 b20. Soft, sweet, toffeed and boasting a little spice...but with minimum fuss. *40%*

⋅∷⋅ **Wiser's 18 Year Old** db **(94) n22.5** dusty, fruity, busy. Soft, fruity sawdust to the sugars; **t24** excellent early bite, though the oils make their mark early. Salivating and silky despite the spice build and a little cocoa to accompany the fruit; **f23.5** comfortable, with a pleasing acceleration of spice; **b24** exceptionally creamy but maintains the required sharpness. Very decent blending. *40%. Case no. 2959 of 3500.*

Wiser's Very Old 18 Years Old (90.5) n24 t23 f21.5 b22. Much better than the last bottling I encountered, which in itself was no slouch. Here, though, the blender has written bolder what he is trying to achieve. *40%*

Wiser's De Luxe (86) n20 t22.5 f21.5 b22. Still nothing like the classic, ultra-charming and almost fragile-delicate Wiser's of old. But this present bottling has got its head partly out of the sand by injecting a decently oaked spiciness to the proceedings and one might even fancy detecting shards of fruity- rye brightness beaming through the toffeed clutter. Definitely an impressive turn for the better and the kind of Canadian with a dangerous propensity to grow on you. If they had the nerve to cut the caramel, this could be a cracker... 40%

Wiser's Legacy (95) n24 even by Canadian standards, a little different: coriander and juniper give a slight gin-style edge to this, though waiting in the wings is a subtle, spicy wine quality. The teasing sweetness, not entirely without a bourbon style new-oakiness and hint of rye-fruitiness, has all the intensity of Mona Lisa's smile...; **t24.5** there is a crystalline quality to the nose, and it transfers immediately to the palate. One is reminded of absolutely unblemished First Growth Bordeaux in the way the grape–fruitiness announces itself before progressing into greatness. After that, it takes, thankfully, a very different course except perhaps in the way the spices unfold: first no more than a shadow, then blossoming out into something profound, deep and always in sync with all else that is going on. Cocoa notes arrive early and stay while the grains offer a salivating edge...nothing short of glorious...; **f22.5** serious but high quality and contained oak: dry and toasty but always a light dusting of slightly sweetened vanilla; **b22.5** when my researcher got this bottle for me to taste, she was told by the Wiser's guy that I would love it, as it had been specially designed along the lines of what I considered essential attributes to Canadian whisky. Whether Mr Wiser was serious or not, such a statement both honoured and rankled slightly and made me entirely determined to find every fault with it I could and knock such impertinence down a peg or two. Instead, I was seduced like a 16-year-old virgin schoolboy in the hands of a 30-year-old vixen. An entirely disarming Canadian which is almost a whisky equivalent to the finest of the great French wines in its rich, unfolding style. Complex beyond belief, spiced almost to supernatural perfection, this is one of the great newcomers to world whisky in the last year. It will take a glass of true magnificence to outdo this for Canadian Whisky of the Year. 45%

Wiser's Red Letter (95) n24 t24 f23.5 b23.5. The recent trend with Canadian whisky has been to do away with finesse and cram each bottle with fruit. This returns us to a very old fashioned and traditional Canadian style. And had the rye been upped slightly and the caramel eschewed entirely it might have been a potential world whisky of the year...Even in this form, however, it is certainly good enough to be Canadian Whisky of the Year 2010. 45%

⁘ **Wiser's Red Letter 2013 Release** Virgin oak finish, cask 6075 db **(90.5) n22** fruit and toffee; **t24** vibrant delivery: a low spice hum which becomes louder and warmer as the experience progresses; salivating grains but always a backdrop of light, medium sweet fruit; **f22** long, good sweet-dry-spice ratio, though a little tangy; **b22.5** the axis of this blend has moved away from a classical style recognisable three decades ago to a more contemporary fruity number. Alas. Superb delivery, though. 45%. ncf.

Wiser's Reserve (75) n19 t20 f18 b18. The nose offers curious tobacco while the palate is uneven, with the bitterness out of tandem with the runaway early sweetness. In the confusion the fruit never quite knows which way to turn. A once mighty whisky has fallen. And I now understand it might be the end of the line with the excellent Wiser's Small Batch coming in to replace it. So if you are a reserve fan, buy them up now. 43%

Wiser's Small Batch (90.5) n21.5 t24 f22 b23. A real oddity with the nose & taste on different planets. The fruity onslaught promised by the drab nose never materialises and instead we are treated to a rich, grainy explosion. It's the spices, though, that take the plaudits. 43.4%

Wiser's Special Blend (78) n19 t20 f19 b19. A plodding, pleasant whisky with no great desire to offer much beyond caramel. 40%

⁘ **Wiser's Spiced Whisky Vanilla** db **(51) n16 t12 f11 b12.** The policy of the Whisky Bible is to not accept any spiced distillate as, by definition, being whisky. Only Canadian can escape that ban, as they are allowed to put up to 9.09% of whatever into their spirit and still call it whisky. That does not mean to say I am going to like it, though. And, believe me when I tell you I really can't stand this cloyingly sweet liqueur-like offering. Indeed, it may have "whisky" on the label, but this is about as much that great spirit as I am the next Hollywood pin up. 43%

Canadian Wheat Whisky

⁘ **Masterson's 12 Year Old Straight Wheat Whiskey** batch 001 **(92) n23** some spices, but not quite what I was expecting. Much lighter and more vanilla based. Gentle, but with a bit of attitude...; **t23** soft and silky, the maple syrup makes the running while the spices lag behind. A little heather honey springs from nowhere as the oaky vanillas begin to gather momentum; **f22.5** drier, yet remains delicate and quietly complex; **b23.5** I have chosen this as my 1,000th new whisk(e)y for Jim Murray WB 2015 because a couple of years back I uncorked their Rye...and tasted everything a great Canadian should be: indeed, it was a contender for my World Whisky of that year. Here I have their new wheat bottling. No it is not the blockbuster the rye bottling was: rye when distilled and matured to its fullest possibilities probably cannot be touched by any other grain. But this is a soft, melodious whisky, perfect for ending any day on a quiet high... 50% WB15/380

Japanese Whisky

How fitting that in the age when the sun never sets on where whisky is produced it is from the land of the Rising Sun that the finest can now be found.

Japan has, for the first time ever, won Jim Murray's World Whisky of the Year with its insanely deep and satisfying Yamazaki Sherry Cask(s) 2013, a result which will cause consternation among more than a few. And, doubtless, a degree of surprise in Japan itself.

It reminded me of when, about 15 years ago, I took my old mate Michael Jackson and a smattering of non-friends on a tour of the Yoichi distillery on Hokkaido, pointing out to them that here was a place where a malt could be made to mount a serious challenge to the best being made anywhere in the world. While there, a local journalist asked me what Japanese distillers could learn from Scotland. I caused a bit of a sharp intake of breath – and a pathetically gutless but entirely characteristic denial of association by some whisky periodical executive or other who had a clear idea which way his bread was buttered – when I said it was the other way round: it was more what the Scots could learn from the Japanese.

The reason for that comment was simple: the extraordinary attention to detail and tradition that was paid by Japanese distillers, those at Yoichi in particular, and the touching refusal to cut costs and corners. It meant that it was the most expensive whisky in the world per unit of alcohol to produce. But the quality was astonishingly high – and that would, surely, eventually reap its rewards as the world learned to embrace malt whisky made away from the Highlands and islands of Scotland, which was still to happen.

Ironically, it was the Japanese distillers' habit to ape most things Scottish – the reason why there is a near century-old whisky distilling heritage there in the first place - that has meant that Yoichi, or the magnificent Hakushu, has yet to pick up the Bible's World Whisky of the Year award I expected for them. Because, sadly, there have been too many bottlings over the last decade tainted by sherry butts brought from Spain after having been sulphur treated. So I was also pleasantly surprised when I first nosed – then nosed again in near disbelief – then tasted the Yamazaki 2013 sherry offering. There was not even the vaguest hint that a single one of the casks used in the bottling had been anywhere near a sulphur candle. The result: something as close to single malt perfection as you will have found in a good many years. A single malt which no Scotch can at the moment get anywhere near and, oddly, takes me back to the Macallans of 30 years ago.

The problem remains that it is still far too hard to find Japanese whisky on easily accessible whisky shelves outside its home country. You might find one brand, but that may be a token gesture by a supermarket chain: you will struggle to find a rival Japanese by its side.

A Japanese custom of refusing to trade with their rivals has not helped. Therefore a Japanese whisky, if not made completely from home-distilled spirit, will instead contain a percentage of Scotch rather than whisky from fellow Japanese distillers. This, ultimately, is doing the industry no favours at all. The practice is partly down to the traditional work ethics of company loyalty and an inherent, and these days false, belief that Scotch whisky is automatically better than Japanese. Back in the late 1990s I planted the first seeds in trying to get rival distillers to discuss with each other the

Yamazaki

Osaka

Fukuoka

Yoichi ●Sapporo

Sendai

Shirakawa

Karuizawa

Hakushu   Hanyu

Mars Shinshu

Gotemba

●Tokyo

Key
● **Major Town or City**
▲ Distillery

possibility of exchanging whiskies to ensure that their distilleries worked more economically.

So it can only be hoped that the deserved lifting of the Jim Murray's Whisky Bible World Whisky of the Year crown, and the associated international press that will receive, will help put the spotlight back on the great whiskies coming from the east. Because unless you live in Japan, you are likely to see only a fraction of the fabulous whisky produced there. The Scotch Malt Whisky Society should have a special medal struck as they have helped in recent years with some memorable bottlings from Japan, single cask snapshots of the greatness that is still to be be fully explored and mapped. A two-pronged attack would be useful: one by whisky outlets to actively track down and stock the widest Japanese stock they can afford. And the distillers themselves, always on the conservative side of marketing probably through a mis-placed lack of belief, show us what they have.

And I don't mean just with malts. Because even better still would be if the outside world could have at last access to the higher class blends produced there. But the Japanese whisky industry are themselves slow coming forward. Just perhaps, with Yamazaki atop the world's whisky very own Mount Fuji, there will be enough confidence to at last unleash upon us those hidden, majestic whiskies of Japan.

Single Malts
CHICHIBU

⁙ **Chichibu 'The Peated' 2013** dist 2010 bott 2013 db **(96.5) n24.5** a dry intensity to this, perhaps suggesting a high phenol content. Earthy and a little floral – not unlike bluebell woods – or freshly watered African violets. Deep, intense and very intact; **t24.5** anyone old enough to remember the original, now demolished, Caol IIa will recognise a returning ghost: the similarity is startling. Sublimely weighted, gently spices and the peat offering both the background and the lead, though operating on different levels; the sugars levels, and their ability to dissolve then reappear is a thing of beauty; **f23** long thanks to the most subtle of oils with smoke drifting off the cocoa; some late oaky bitter tang; **b24.5** clean, elegant, does exactly what it says on the tin...and a lot, lot more besides... *53.5%.*

⁙ **Chichibu 'On The Way'** dist 2010 bott 2013 db **(93) n23.5** an elegant display of red liquorice and crisp grist; a little citrus on the wing; **t24** intense delivery with the malts in concentrated form. The oaky tones reverberate around the palate to a surprising degree but the sugars soften; **f22.5** a little gristy, a touch of milk chocolate...; **b23** a malt which has already travelled far... *58.50%. Number One Drinks Company.*

⁙ **Chichibu Port Pipe** dist 2009 bott 2013 db **(66) n17 t18 f15 b16.** A port pipe in an awful, off-key storm. *54.5%. Number One Drinks Company.*

Golden Horse Chichibu Aged 12 Years bott 08 db **(95.5) n24 t24.5 f23 b24.** Immaculate, faultless (OK, nearly faultless), whisky. And, rarely for Japanese, bottled at exactly the right age. Had this not been bottled in 2008, a contender for World Whisky of the Year. Guys! You have to get this to me sooner!!! For the record, it kind of took me back to the mid 1970s when I was first studying whisky, for here I felt I was learning about this distillery for the very first time... Oh, and for the best effects: don't bother warming in the glass – just pour...and score... *56%*

Ichiro's Malt Chichibu Floor Malted 2009 (85.5) n23 t22.5 f20 b21. Big, pre-pubescent malt and barley statement, though barely in unison. The bitterness on the finish is unchecked. *50.5%.*

Ichiro's Chichibu Peated 2009 (91.5) n23 t23.5 f22 b23. You can stand your chopsticks up in this one...works so beautifully in so many department. *50.5%*

Number One Asama 1999/2000 (71) n17 t19 f16 b19. Sulphured. *46%*

⁙ **Scotch Malt Whisky Society Cask 130.1 Aged 4 Years** 1st fill barrel. dist 16 Jun 09. **(94.5) n23** malted milk biscuits meets muscly tannin head on....; **t24** before you even get to the flavours, you are blown away by the adorable mouth feel, a kind of sumptuous, massaging light oiliness. Next are the sugars and spices standing shoulder to shoulder, each refusing to take the lead....; a little ulmo honey goes a long way in the midground while a wave of maple syrup ripples gently; all the while the barley salivates; **f23.5** lightly salted butter fade. If anything, the spices warm and prickle with greater belief now. The remnants of the honey stretches to the end while the malted milk biscuit reappears late on as the tannin re-emerges; **b24** not sure anyone on this planet does milky malt like Chichibu. Another remarkable whisky from them. *62%. nc ncf sc. 227 Bottles.*

FUJI GOTEMBA 1973. Kirin Distillers.
The Fuji Gotemba 15 Years Old db **(92) n21 t23 f24 b24.** Quality malt of great poise. *43%. Kirin.*

HAKUSHU 1973. Suntory.
Hakushu Heavily Peated Aged 9 Years bott 2009 db **(92.5) n22.5 t23.5 f23 b23.5.** Nothing like as heavily peated as some Hakushus it has been my pleasure to sample over the years. But certainly superbly orchestrated and balanced. *48%*

Hakushu Single Malt Whisky Aged 12 Years db **(91.5) n22.5 t23.5 f22.5 b23.** Just about identical to the 43.3% bottling in every respect. Please see those tasting notes for this little beauty. *43.5%*

Hakushu Single Malt Aged 12 Years db **(91) n22 t23 f23 b23.** An even more lightly-peated version of the 40%, with the distillery's fabulous depth on full show. *43.3%*

Hakushu Single Malt Whisky Aged 12 Years bott 2011 db **(95.5) n24 t24.5 f23.5 b24.5.** A prime example of what makes this such a magnificent distillery. One of the most complex and clever 12 year old malts to be found anywhere in the world this year: a great whisky that could be easily overlooked. *43%*

The Hakushu Single Malt Whisky Aged 15 Years Cask Strength db **(95) n24 t23 f24 b24.** Last time round I lamented the disappointing nose. This time perhaps only a degree of over eagerness from the oak has robbed this as a serious Whisky of the Year contender. No matter how you look at it, though, brilliant!! *56%*

The Hakushu Single Malt Whisky Aged 25 Years db **(93) n23 t24 f23 b23.** A malt which is impossible not to be blown away by. *43%*

Hakushu Single Malt Whisky Aged 25 Years bott 2011 db (**91**) n23.5 t23.5 f21 b23. Just one slightly off butt away from total magnificence. *43%*

Hakushu 1984 db (**95**) n22 t25 f24 b24. A masterpiece of quite sublime complexity and balance. The sort of experience that gives a meaning to life, the universe and everything... *61%*

Hakushu 1988 db (**92**) n21 t24 f23 b24. Like all great whiskies this is one that gangs up on you in a way you are not expecting: the limited complexity on the nose is more than compensated for elsewhere. Superb. If this were an Islay malt the world would be drooling over it. *61%*

Scotch Malt Whisky Society Cask 120.05 Aged 17 Years 1st fill barrel, dist Dec 91 (**94**) n23 t24 f23.5 b23.5. Amazingly, this is a less than perfect cask deployed. But so absurdly good was the spirit filled into it, you barely notice...or care. *59%. 104 bottles.*

Suntory Pure Malt Hakushu Aged 20 Years db (**94**) n23 t24 f23 b24. A hard-to-find malt, but find it you must. Yet another huge nail in the coffin of those who purport Japanese whisky to be automatically inferior to Scotch. *56%*

HANYU

Hanyu Final Vintage 2000 cask no. 6309, bott 2010 (**94.5**) n23.5 t24 f23.5 b23.5. A fabulous exhibition in just how a sherry whisky should be: blemish free and exploding from the glass with personality. A fabulous malt made for this kind of strength. *59.7%. sc. Venture Whisky Co.*

Hanyu Single Malt 2000 hogshead refilled into Japanese oak, bott 2011 db (**91.5**) n21.5 t24; f23.5 b23.5. About as sweet a whisky can go and still be in total control. An after dinner malt if ever there was one... *60.9%. For 'Whisky Live Tokyo 2011'.*

Ichiro's Card "Four of Spades" Japanese oak "Mizunara" puncheon finish, dist 2000, bott 2010 (**95**) n24 t24.5 f23.5 b23.5. I have often heard the Japanese accused of trying to mimic scotch whisky. On this evidence, it's the Kentuckians who should be looking over their shoulder... *58.6%. Venture Whisky Ltd.*

Ichiro's Card "King of Hearts" PX finish, dist 1986, bott 2009 (**95.5**) n23.5 t24 f24 b24. This King of Hearts had some smoky tarts...delicious and complex almost beyond measure! *55.4%*

Ichiro's Card "Ten of Hearts" Hanyu 2000 Madeira hogshead finish, bott 2011 (**91**) n22.5 t23 f22.5 b23. Thank you, Madeira... *61%*

Ichiro's Card "Three of Hearts" Hanyu 2000 Port pipe finish, bott 2010 (**90**) n23 t23.5 f21 b22.5. Delicious, but an astonishing degree of toffee is created in the process. *61.2%. Venture Whisky Ltd.*

Ichiro's Malt Aged 20 Years (**95.5**) n24 t24 f23.5 b24. No this finish; no that finish. Just the distillery allowed to speak in its very own voice. And nothing more eloquent has been heard from it this year. Please, all those owning casks of Hanyu: for heaven's sake take note... *57.5%. Venture Whisky Ltd.*

Ichiro's Malt Aged 23 Years (**92.5**) n23 t23.5 f23 b23. A fabulous malt you take your time over. *58%*

One Single Cask Hanyu 1990 cask no. 9305, bott 2009 (**90.5**) n23 t23 f22.5 b22. Huge whisky but borderline OTT oak. The infused sugars do the trick. *53.4%. Number One Drinks Co.*

One Single Cask Hanyu 1991 Japanese oak, cask no. 370, bott 2009 (**91.5**) n22 t23.5 f23 b23. Unmistakable style: I found myself muttering " ah, local oak!" to myself (tasting close on 800 malts in a couple of months does that to you...) before I spotted the label. Quite beautiful. *57.3%. Number One Drinks Co.*

∴ **Scotch Malt Whisky Society Cask 131.2 Aged 13 Years** 1st fill barrel. dist 30 Jun 00. (**87**) n22 sweeping ultra rich fruitcake statements, heavy on the toasted raisin. The odd flicker of a sulphur fault; t22.5 swashbuckling grape, with a spices rampaging all over the deck. Loses points in the mid-ground as the fault on the nose begins to appear; f20.5 a faulty sulphur gene; b22. A malt which almost gets away with it. Despite the obvious and regrettable flaw, this really does have some outstanding attributes. *55%. nc ncf sc. 646 bottles.*

KARUIZAWA 1955. Mercian.

Karuizawa 1964 sherry cask, cask no. 3603, dist 1 Sep 64, bott 24 Dec 12 (**95.5**) n24.5 t24 f23 b24. A number one example of premier class, unsullied sherry butt from the Number One company. And Japanese Whisky of the Year without doubt. *57.7%. nc ncf sc. Number One Drinks Company. 143 bottles. Poland.*

Karuizawa 1967 Vintage sherry cask, bott 2009 db (**96**) n24 t24.5 f23.5 b24. Another engaging, engrossing and, frankly, brilliant malt from this distillery, equalling the oldest I have ever encountered from Karuizawa. If you find it, sell your body, sell your partner's body... anything...just experience it! *58.4%*

Karuizawa 1982 sherry, bott 2009 db (**90**) n23 t24 f22 b22. Forget the sherry. Forget the distant, nagging "S" word. Just home in on that astonishing middle: like a million Maltesers dissolving in your mouth all at once...there is nothing else like it in the whisky world. And no other distillery is capable. Alas. *56.1%. Speciality Drinks Ltd bottled for TWE's 10th Anniversary.*

Karuizawa 1983 Noh Bottling cask no. 7576, bott 2012 **(90.5) n23 t23 f22 b22.5.** Truly astonishing: an absolute one off. Unquestionably the most sea-salty whisky – malt or otherwise – I have ever tasted in my life. By several thousand fathoms... *57.2%. sc.*

Karuizawa Pure Malt Aged 17 Years db **(90) n20 t24 f23 b23.** Brilliant whisky beautifully made and majestically matured. Neither sweetness nor dryness dominates, always the mark of a quality dram. *40%*

Noh Whisky Karuizawa 1976 cask no. 6719, bott 09 **(91) n22 t24 f22.5 b22.5.** Sticks religiously to the malty house style despite the grape trying to enter from every angle. A beautiful whisky, reminding me what a special year 1976 was for Japan. Happy 35th in April. *63%.*

The Spirit Of Asama sherry cask **(71.5) n17 t19 f17 b18.5.** Sulphur hit. *48%.*

The Spirit Of Asama sherry cask **(75) n18 t20 f18 b19.** Lots of sultanas. Sweet. Pleasant in part. But it isn't just Scotland suffering from poor sherry butts. *55%.*

⁘ **Scoth Malt Whisky Society Cask 132.1 Aged 28 Years** refill butt. dist 30 Aug 84 **(96.5) n23.5** some dizzy bourbon notes with its leaning towards hickory and liquorice but the malts also make a stand; the vaguest hint of something smoky adds weight...or is that the hickory in another form...? **t24.5** near perfect mouth feel and delivery with a blend of heather and ulmo honey combining for a deepening of the depth; the barley pings around and even offers a salivating corner to this hugely complex experience; **f24** very long with the ulmo honey and gristy barley continuing to conjure something rich and salivating. Again a hint of something smoky lurks and the bourbon notes add a friendly subtleness to the oak **b24.5** long overdue on the SMWS portfolio, this is another Japanese malt which, with the care and attention of its make and maturation, put many of its Scottish counterparts to shame. What a way to make your SMWS debut!! *59.8% nc ncf sc. 229 bottles.*

⁘ **Scotch Malt Whisky Society Cask 132.2 Aged 22 Years** refill butt. diss 04 Sep 91. **(92.5) n23.5** gristy peat spread over lime marmalade on toast; **t24** the delivery, with its near perfect layering of smoke and its intense ulmo honey and concentrated grist is the stuff of Japanese fable; **f22** bitters slowly at the death; **b23** a rare case of peat and light fruit working for the benefit of the other. Superb. *62.4% nc ncf sc. 335 Bottles.*

⁘ **Scotch Malt Whisky Society Cask 132.3 Aged 20 Years** refill butt. diss 21 Jul 93 **(94.5) n23.5** intriguing. Nothing takes the lead, there is a puff of smoke here and there, though nothing you can grasp and all this punctuated by bursts of fresh fruit; **t24** eye-wateringly sharp and tart delivery. And on the subject of tarts, a touch of undercooked Bramley apple at work here; a little maple syrup stirred in with the ulmo honey; **f23** long, but principally vanilla and deft smoke, thick dark chocolate with a late fruit flourish; **b24** pure fun as a malt, no little complexity and keeps the taste buds on their toes from beginning to end. *61.1% nc ncf sc. 344 Bottles.*

⁘ **Scotch Malt Whisky Society Cask 132.4 Aged 17 Years** refill butt. diss 08 Jul 96 **(92) n23** boiled fruit sweets; a little sawdust and vanilla; **t24** the intense grape makes an immediate impact but it is the spice which explodes with a delayed entry, and then makes up for lost time by dominating entirely; the palate salivates through a mix of barley and succulent black grape but the tong throbs as the black peppers incinerate; the sugars are clever and complex, but mainy of the Demerara style; **f22** limited with a little tang to the tiring oak; **b22.5** not just a sherry influence, but something of a big Demerara rum about this one. If you like your whisky naturally spiced, then you'll forever regret missing out on this. *61.7% nc ncf sc. 346 Bottles.*

⁘ **Scotch Malt Whisky Society Cask 132.5 Aged 14 Years** refill butt. diss 25 Jun 1999 **(69) n17 t19 f16 b16.** Not just sulphured, but cloying, too. *58.6% nc ncf sc. 495 Bottles.*

⁘ **Scotch Malt Whisky Society Cask 132.6 Aged 12 Years** refill butt. diss 32 Dec 2000. **(84.5) n21 t23 f19 b21.5.** Fabulous delivery. Surprisingly youthful in some ways, with echoes of a new make maltiness, but there is a vividity to the barley which really deserves better than the nose appears a little perfunctory and dull and a finish which is disappointingly tangy. *63% nc ncf sc. 553 Bottles.*

KIRIN

Kirin 18 Years Old db **(86.5) n22 t22 f21.5 b21.** Unquestionably over-aged. Even so, still puts up a decent show with juicy citrus trying to add a lighter touch to the uncompromising, ultra dense oak. As entertaining as it is challenging. *43%. Suntory.*

KOMAGATAKE

Komagatake 1992 Single Cask American white oak cask, cask no. 1144, dist 1992, bott 2009 db **(93.5) n24.5 t23 f22.5 b23.5.** You know when you've had a glass of this: beautiful and no shrinking violet. *46%. Mars.*

MIYAGIKYO *(see Sendai)*

NIKKA

⠿ **Nikka Coffey Grain Whisky** db **(94.5) n24** molten muscovado sugar; **t24.5** soft oils carry the thinned golden syrup aloft. Almost a semi-liqueur, but with that indefinable whiskyness which sets it apart..; **f22.5** the slight bitterness of the cask jolts the serenity of the oily sugars; **b23.5** whisky, from any part of the globe, does not come more soft or silky than this... *45% WB15/401*

SENDAI 1969. Nikka.

Miyagikyo 15 Years Old batch 02I10D db **(91.5) n23 t23.5 f22 b23**. A much lighter, more refined and elegant creature than before. Despite a minor sherry butt blemish, fabulous. *45%*

Scotch Malt Whisky Society Cask 124.03 Aged 13 Years refill butt, dist 20 Jul 99 **(88) n22.5 t22 f21 b21.5**. Seriously feisty. I'm off to chew a jalapeno to cool down... *61.9%. nc ncf sc. 509 bottles.*

SHIRAKAWA

Shirakawa 32 Years Old Single Malt (94) n23 t24 f23 b24. Just how big can an unpeated malt whisky get? The kind of malt that leaves you in awe, even when you thought you had seen and tasted them all. *55%. Takara.*

WHITE OAK DISTILLERY

White Oak Akashi Single Malt Whisky Aged 8 Years bott 2007 db **(74.5) n18.5 t19.5 f17.5 b19**. Always fascinating to find a malt from one of the smaller distilleries in a country. And I look forward to tracking this one down and visiting, something I have yet to do. There is certainly something distinctly small still about his one, with butyric and feintiness causing damage to nose and finish. For all the early malty presence on delivery, some of the off notes are a little on the uncomfortable side. *40%*

YAMAZAKI 1923. Suntory.

Yamazaki 1984 bott 2009 db **(94) n24 t24 f22.5 b23.5**. If you like your whisky boringly neutral, lifeless and with nothing to say other than that it has been ruined by sulphur, then this will horrify you. Though there is a little blemish at the very death, there is still no taking away from this being a sublime 25-year-old. When this distillery is on form it makes for compelling whisky and here we have a bottling showing Yamazaki at its brightest. *48%*

The Yamazaki Single Malt Whisky Aged 12 Years bott 2011 db **(90) n23 t22 f22.5 b22.5**. A complex and satisfying malt. *43%*

The Yamazaki Single Malt Whisky Aged 15 Years Cask Strength db **(94) n23 t24 f23 b24**. An extraordinary bottling that far exceeds any previous version I have encountered. Stunning. *56%*

Suntory Pure Malt Yamazaki 25 Years Old db **(91) n23 t23 f22 b23**. Being matured in Japan, the 25 years doesn't have quite the same value as Scotland. So perhaps in some ways this can lay claim to be one of the most enormously aged, oak-laden whiskies that has somehow kept its grace and star quality. *43%*

⠿ **The Yamazaki Single Malt Whisky Puncheon** bott 2013 db **(87) n22 t22 f21 b22**. Not to be confused with former Millwall footballer Jason Puncheon who scored a hat-trick against Crystal Palace a couple of years back. Does not possess his guile, balance or explosive finish. Even so, a pleasant dram even if you'd like to see it do more than just offer a sugary glow offset by some half decent spices. *48%. ncf WB15/179*

⠿ **The Yamazaki Single Malt Whisky Sherry Cask** bott 2013 db **(97.5) n24.5** when they say sherry, they are not joking: huge oloroso signature, nutty, thick, dry as rounded as a snooker ball. A nose that was not uncommon in the warehouses of Scotland three decades ago, but now as rare as...well, an unsulphured sherry butt...; **t24.5** every bit as silky as the nose promises. The sugars, spices, plum walnut cake and moist Melton Hunt Cake combine for something rather special; **f24** long, juicy dates, more walnuts, sultanas as big as a small planet...a light, teasing spice; **b24.5** one of the first sherry casks I have seen from Japan not in any way, shape or form touched by sulphur for a very long time. It is as if the oloroso cask was still half filled with the stuff when they filled with Yamakazi spirit. If anyone wants to find out roughly what the first Macallan 10-year-old I had in 1975 tasted like, then grab a bottle of this... *48%. ncf. WB15/180*

YOICHI 1934. Nikka.

Yoichi Key Malt Aged 12 Years "Peaty & Salty" db **(95) n23 t25 f23 b24**. Of all the peated whiskies of the world, only Ardbeg can stand shoulder to shoulder with Yoichi when it comes to sheer complexity. Here is an astonishing example of why I rate Yoichi in the best five whiskies in the world. Forget the odd sulphur-tarnished bottling. Get Yoichi in its natural state with perfect balance between oak and malt and it delivers something approaching perfection. And this is just such a bottling. 55%. Nikka.

Yoichi Single Malt 12 Years Old batch 14F36A db (**91**) n22 t23 f23 b23. Best when left in the glass for 10-15 minutes: only then does the true story emerge. 45%

Yoichi 15 Years Old batch 06I08B db (**91.5**) n22 t23.5 f23 b23. For an early moment or two possibly one of the most salivating whiskies you'll get your kisser around this year. Wonderfully entertaining yet you still suspect that this is another Yoichi reduced in effect somewhat by either caramel and/or sherry. When it hits its stride, though, becomes a really busy whisky that gets tastebuds in a right lather. But I'm being picky as I know that this is one of the world's top five distilleries and am aware as anyone on this planet of its extraordinary capabilities. Great fun; great whisky – could be better still, but so much better than its siblings... 45%

Yoichi 20 Years Old db (**95**) n23 t23 f25 b24. I don't know how much they charge for this stuff but either alone or with mates get some for one hell of an experience. What makes it all the more remarkable is that there is a slight sulphury note on the nose: once you taste the stuff that becomes of little consequence. 52%. Nikka.

Nikka Whisky Yoichi 1986 20 Years Old (**94**) n23 t24 f23 b24. Now this is unambiguous Yoichi :exactly how I have come to know and adore this distillery. 55.0%

Scotch Malt Whisky Society Cask 116.17 Aged 25 Years First fill sherry butt, dist 20 Mar 1987, bott Sep 2012 (**96**) n24.5 I have very rarely encountered a nose like it: every last atom is oak enriched. Unlikely you'll find so many orange notes in one glass, all of them intensifying to the point of creating their own black holes; elsewhere green tea from a Sahara campfire permeates proceedings; t24.5 wonderful maple-syrup infused oils cushion the palate for the oaky onslaught. Spices threaten but vanish as quickly as they arrive while an unusual Turkish Delight with sugar almonds middle pulse complex layers of depth; f23 the drying over-exuberance of the oak begins to take its toll. But still plenty of vanilla to make for a picturesque final journey; b24 not as mouth-puckering as I expected from the nose. The sugars ensure this incredible celebration of all things oak works memorably well. 59.2%. nc ncf sc. 485 bottles. Nikka.

Scotch Malt Whisky Society 116.18 Aged 18 Years refill butt, dist 2 Feb 94 (**89**) n23 t23 f21 b22. Not one of the truly great Yoichis in its traditional style but a salty, oaky beast of a malt. 64.4%. nc ncf sc. 410 bottles.

Unspecified Malts

"Hokuto" Suntory Pure Malt Aged 12 Years (**93**) n24 t24 f23 b24. Another example of Suntory at its most feminine: just so seductive and beautiful. Although a malt, think Lawson's 12-y-o of a decade ago and you have the picture. 40%

Nikka Whisky From the Barrel batch 12F32C db (**91**) n22 t24 f22 b23. Truly great whisky that mostly overcomes the present Japanese curse of big caramel finishes. 51.4%

Nikka Whisky Single Coffey Malt 12 Years (**97**) n23.5 forget all about the malt: it's the big bourbon, hickory and honey sweet oak which wins hands down; t25 hold on to your hats: it's flavour explosion time...on first tasting it's simply too much to comprehend. Only on third or fourth mouthful do you really get an idea. First, the delivery is pretty close to perfection: the soft oils seem to draw every last nuance from the barley; then when it has done that, it manages to mix it with myriad delicate sweet notes radiating from the oak. This includes some of those allied to bourbon, especially chocolate honeycomb and very deep molassed notes usually associated with Demerara Coffey still rum; a unique combination absolutely perfectly displayed; f24 long...just so long. One mouthful, especially at 55%, last for about six or seven minutes. So impressive here is the delicacy of the fade: after a delivery so large, the finesse is extraordinary. The flavours in effect mirror the earlier delivery. Except now some vanilla does come in to dry things a little; b24.5 the Scotch Whisky Association would say that this is not single malt whisky because it is made in a Coffey still. When they can get their members to make whisky this stunning on a regular basis via their own pots and casks, then perhaps they should pipe up as their argument might then have a single atom of weight. 55%

Vatted Malts

All Malt (**86**) n22 t21 f21 b22. The best example by a mile of an almost unique style of vatted whisky: both malt and "grain" are distilled from entirely malted barley, identical to Kasauli malt whisky in India. Stupendous grace and balance. 40%. Nikka.

All Malt "Pure & Rich" (**89**) n22 t24 f21 b22. Not unlike some bottlings of Highland Park with its emphasis on honey. If they could tone down the caramel it'd really be up there. 40%. Nikka.

All Malt Pure & Rich batch 14F24A **(77) n19 t20 f19 b19**. My former long term Japanese girlfriend, Makie (hope you enjoyed your 30th birthday in April, by the way), used to have a favourite saying, namely: "I am shocked!" Well, I am shocked by this whisky because it is much blander than the previous bottling (04E16D), with all that ultra-delicate and complex honeycomb lost and lovely gristiness removed. For me, one of the biggest surprises – and disappointments - of the 2007 Bible. But proof that, when using something so potentially dangerous as caramel, it is too easy to accidentally cross that fine line between brilliance and blandness. Because, had they gone the other way, we might have had a challenger for World Whisky of the Year. 40%. Nikka.

Hokuto Pure Malt 12 Years (86) n20 t22 f22 b22. An oaky threat never materialises: excellent mixing. 40%. Suntory.

Ichiro's Malt Double Distilleries bott 2010 **(86.5) n22.5 t22 f21 b21.** Some imperious barley-rich honey reigns supreme until a bitter wood note bites hard. 46%. Venture Whisky Ltd.

Ichiro's Malt Mizunara Wood Reserve (76) **n19 t21 f18 b19**. I have my Reservations about the Wood, too... 46%. Venture Whisky Ltd.

Malt Club "Pure & Clear" (83) **n21 t22 f20 b20.** Another improved vatting, much heavier and older than before with bigger spice. 40%. Nikka.

Mars Maltage Pure Malt 8 Years Old (84) **n20 t21 f21 b22.** A very level, intense, clean malt with no peaks or troughs, just a steady variance in the degree of sweetness and oak input. Impossible not to have a second glass of. 43%. Mars.

Nikka Malt 100 The Anniversary Aged 12 Years (73) **n18 t19 f18 b18.** The depressing and deadly fingerprint of sulphur is all over this. Shame, as the spices excel. 40%

Nikka Pure Malt Aged 21 Years batch 08I18D db **(89) n23 t22.5 f21.5 b22.** By far the best of the set. 43%

Nikka Pure Malt Aged 17 Years batch 08I30B db **(83) n21 t21 f20 b21.** A very similar shape to the 12-years-old, but older - obviously. Certainly the sherry butts have a big say and don't always do great favours to the high quality spirit. 43%

Nikka Pure Malt Aged 12 Years batch 10I24C db **(84) n21.5 t21 f20 b21.5**. The nose may be molassed, sticky treacle pudding, but it spices up on the palate. The dull buzz on the finish also tells a tale. 40%

Pure Malt Black batch 02C58A **(95)** **n24 t23 f23 b25**. Well, if anyone can show me a better-balanced whisky than this you know where to get hold of me. You open a bottle of this at your peril: best to do so in the company of friends. Either way, it will be empty before the night is over. 43%. Nikka.

Pure Malt Black batch 06F54B **(92) n24 t24 f21 b23**. Not the finish of old, but everything else is present and correct for a cracker! 43%. Nikka.

Pure Malt Red batch 02C30B **(86) n21 t21 f22 b22**. A light malt that appears heavier than it actually is with an almost imperceptible oiliness. 43%. Nikka.

Pure Malt Red batch 06F54C **(84) n21 t22 f20 b21.** Oak is the pathfinder here, but the oily vanilla-clad barley is light and mouth-watering. 43%. Nikka.

Pure Malt White batch 02C30C **(92) n23 t24 f22 b23.** A big peaty number displaying the most subtle of hands. 43%. Nikka.

Pure Malt White batch 06J26 **(91) n22 t23 f22 b24.** A sweet malt, but one with such deft use of peat and oak that one never really notices. Real class. 43%

Pure Malt White batch 10F46C **(90) n23 t23 f22 b22.** There is a peculiarly Japanese feel to this delicately peated delight. 43%

Southern Alps Pure Malt (93) n24 t23 f22 b24. This is a bottle I have only to look at to start salivating. Sadly, though, I drink sparingly from it as it is a hard whisky to find, even in Japan. Fresh, clean and totally stunning, the term "pure malt" could not be more apposite. Fabulous whisky: a very personal favourite. 40%. Suntory.

Super Nikka Vatted Pure Malt (76) **n20 t19 f19 b18**. Decent and chewy but something doesn't quite click with this one. 55.5%. Nikka.

Taketsuru Pure Malt 12 Years Old (80) **n19 t22 f19 b20.** For its age, heavier than a sumo wrestler. But perhaps a little more agile over the tastebuds. Lovely silkiness impresses, but lots of toffee. 43%. Nikka.

Taketsuru Pure Malt 17 Years Old (89) n21 t22 f23 b23 Not a whisky for the squeamish. This is big stuff – about as big as it gets without peat or rye. No bar shelf or whisky club should be without one. 43%. Nikka.

Taketsuru Pure Malt 21 Years Old (88) **n22 t21 f22 b23.** A much more civilised and gracious offering than the 17 year old: there is certainly nothing linear about the character development from Taketsuru 12 to 21 inclusive. Serious whisky for the serious whisky drinker. 43%. Nikka.

Zen (84) **n19 t22 f22 b21.** Sweet, gristy malt; light and clean. 40%. Suntory.

Japanese Single Grain

Kawasaki Single Grain sherry butt, dist 1982, bott 2011 db **(95.5) n23.5** clean thick grape offering several layers of depth and intensity. Salty and sharp, too. My god, this is very much alive and kicking...; **t24** classic! Faultless grape arm in arm with rich, fruity fudge. Some spices arrive on impact and slowly spread out with the marauding sugars; **f24** chocolate fudge and garibaldi biscuit...carried far on usual oils for a grain...amazing! **b24** my usual reaction to seeing the words "sherry" and "whisky" when in the context of Japanese whisky, is to feel the heart sinking like the sun. Sulphur is a problem that is no stranger to their whiskies. This, however, is a near perfect sherry butt, clean and invigorating. Grain or malt, it makes no difference: excellent spirit plus excellent cask equals (as often as not) magnificence. 65.5%.

Blends

Ajiwai Kakubin (see Kakubin Ajiwai)

Black Nikka Aged 8 Years **(82) n20 t21 f21 b20.** Beautifully bourbony, especially on the nose. Lush, silky and great fun. Love it! 40%. Nikka.

The Blend of Nikka (90) n21 t23 f22 b24. An adorable blend that makes you sit up and take notice of every enormous mouthful. Classy, complex, charismatic and brilliantly balanced. 45%

Evermore (90) n22 t23 f22 b23. Top-grade, well-aged blended whisky with fabulous depth and complexity that never loses its sweet edge despite the oak. 40%. Kirin.

Ginko (78.5) n20.5 t20 f19 b19. Soft – probably too soft as it could do with some shape and attitude to shrug off the caramel. 46%. Number One Drinks Company.

Golden Horse Busyuu Deluxe (93) n22 t24 f23 b24. Whoever blended this has a genuine feel for whisky: a classic in its own right and one of astonishing complexity and textbook balance. 43%. Toa Shuzo. To celebrate the year 2000.

Hibiki (82) n20 t19 f23 b20. The grains here are fresh, forceful and merciless, the malts bouncing off them meekly. Lovely cocoa finale. A blend that brings a tear to the eye. Hard stuff – perfect after a hard day! Love it! 43%. Suntory.

Hibiki Aged 12 Years bott 2011 **(89) n22.5 t22 f22 b22.5.** A sensual whisky full of lightly sugared riches. 43%. Suntory.

Hibiki Aged 17 Years bott 2011 **(84.5) n22 t21 f20.5 b21.** Big oaks and a clever degree of sweetness. But takes the lazy big toffee option. 43%. Suntory.

Hibiki 50.5 Non Chillfiltered 17 Years Old (84) n22 t22 f20 b20. Pleasant enough in its own right. But against what this particular expression so recently was, hugely disappointing. Last year I lamented the extra use of caramel. This year it has gone through the roof, taking with it all the fineness of complexity that made this blend exceptional. Time for the blending lab to start talking to the bottling hall and sort this out. I want one of the great whiskies back...!! 50.5%. Suntory.

Hibiki Aged 21 Years bott 2011 **(96) n24** cherry fruitcake...with more black cherries than cake. Spiced sherry notes embrace the oak with a voluptuous richness; **t24.5** virtually perfect texture: seemingly silk-like but then a massive outbreak of busy oaky vanilla and juicy barley; the creamy mouth feel supports a mix of maple syrup and muscovado sugars; the middle moves towards a walnut oiliness; **f23.5** long, spicy with a gentle date and walnut fade; **b24** a celebration of blended whisky, irrespective of which country it is from. Of its style, it's hard to raise the bar much higher than this. Stunning. 43%. Suntory.

Hibiki Aged 30 Years (88) n21 t22 f22 b23. Still remains a very different animal from most other whiskies you might find: the smoke may have vanished somewhat but the sweet oakiness continues to draw its own unique map. 43%

Hokuto (86) n22 t24 f19 b21. A bemusing blend. At its peak, this is quite superb, cleverly blended whisky. The finish, though, suggests a big caramel input. If the caramel is natural, it should be tempered. If it is added for colouring purposes, then I don't see the point of having the whisky non-chillfiltered in the first place. 50.5%. ncf. Suntory.

Ichiro's Blend Aged 33 Years (84) n20 t22 f21 b21. Silky and sweet. But the creamy fudge effect appears to wipe out anything important the oak may have to say. Pleasing spices towards the end. 48%. Venture Whisky Ltd.

Ichiro's Malt & Grain bott 2011 **(85) n21 t22 f21 b21.** A clean though curious blend with the grain dominating and forming a jammy-sweet but thin structure. Pleasant throughout. 46%. Venture Whisky Co.

Imperial (81) n20 t22 f19 b20. Flinty, hard grain softened by malt and vanilla but toffee dulled. 43%. Suntory.

Kakubin (92) n23 t23 f22 b24. Absolutely brilliant blend of stunningly refreshing and complex character. One of the most improved brands in the world. 40%. Suntory.

Kakubin Ajiwai (82) n20 t21 f20 b21. Usual Kakubin hard grain and mouthwatering malt, with this time a hint of warming stem ginger. 40%. Suntory.

Kakubin Kuro 43º (89) n22 t23 f22 b22. Big, chewy whisky with ample evidence of old age but such is the intrusion of caramel it's hard to be entirely sure. *43%. Suntory.*

Kakubin New (90) n21 t24 f21 b24 seriously divine blending: a refreshing dram of the top order. *40%. Suntory.*

Kirin Whisky Tarujuku 50° (93) n22.5 t24 f23 b23.5. A blend not afraid to make a statement and does so boldly. A sheer joy. *50%. Kirin Distillery Co Ltd.*

Master's Blend Aged 10 Years (87) n21 t23 f22 b21. Chewy, big and satisfying. *40%.*

New Kakubin Suntory *(see Kakubin New)*

Nikka Master Blend Blended Whisky 12 Years Old 70th Anniversary (94) n24 t23 f24 b23. An awesome blend swimming in top quality sherry. Perhaps a fraction too much sweetness on the arrival, but I am nit-picking. A blend for those who like their whiskies to have something to say. And this one just won't shut up. *58%. Nikka.*

The Nikka Whisky Aged 34 Years bott 1999 (93) n23 t23 f24 b23. A Japanese whisky of antiquity that has not only survived many passing years, but has actually achieved something of stature and sophistication. Over time I have come to appreciate this whisky immensely. It is among the world's greatest blends, no question. *43%. Nikka.*

Nikka Whisky Tsuru Aged 17 Years (94) n23 t24 f23 b24. Unmistakingly Tsuru in character, very much in line, profile-wise, with the original bottling and if the caramel was cut this could challenge as a world whisky of the year. *43%*

Robert Brown (91) n22.5 t23 f22.5 b23. Just love these clean but full-flavoured blends: a real touch of quality here. *43%. Kirin Brewery Company Ltd.*

Royal 12 Years Old (91) n23 t23 f22 b23. A splendidly blended whisky with complexity being the main theme. Beautiful stuff that appears recently to have, with the exception of the nose, traded smoke for grape. *43%*

Royal Aged 15 Years (95) n25 t24 f22; b24. Unquestionably one of the great blends of the world that can be improved only by a reduction of toffee input. Sensual blending that every true whisky lover must experience: a kind of Japanese Old Parr 18. *43%*

Shirokaku (79) n19 t21 f20 b19. Some over-zealous toffee puts a cap on complexity. Good spices, though. *40%. Suntory.*

Special Reserve 10 Years Old (94) n23 t24 f23 b24. A beguiling whisky of near faultless complexity. Blending at its peak. *43%. Suntory.*

Special Reserve Aged 12 Years (89) n21 t24 f21 b23. A tactile, voluptuous malt that wraps itself like a sated lover around the tastebuds, though the complexity is compromised very slightly by bigger caramel than the 10-y-o. *40%. Suntory.*

Suntory Old (87) n21 t24 f20 b22. A delicate and comfortable blend that just appears to have over-simplified itself on the finale. Delicious, but can be much better than this. *40%*

Suntory Old Mild and Smooth (84) n19 t22 f21 b22. Chirpy and lively around the palate, the grains soften the crisp malts wonderfully. *40%*

Suntory Old Rich and Mellow (91) n22 t23 f23 b23. A pretty malt-rich blend with the grains offering a fat base. Impressive blending. *43%*

Super Nikka (93) n23 t23 f23 b24. A very, very fine blend which makes no apology whatsoever for the peaty complexity of Yoichi malt. Now, with less caramel, it's pretty classy stuff. However, Nikka being Nikka you might find the occasional bottling that is entirely devoid of peat, more honeyed and lighter in style (21-22-23-23 Total 89 – no less a quality turn, obviously). Either way, an absolutely brilliant day-to-day, anytime, any place dram. One of the true 24-carat, super nova commonplace blends not just in Japan, but in the world. *43%. Nikka.*

Super Nikka Rare Old batch 02I18D (90.5) n22 t23 f22.5 b23. Beautiful whisky which just sings a lilting malty refrain. Strange, though, to find it peatless. *43%. Nikka.*

Torys (76) n18 t19 f20 b19. Lots of toffee in the middle and at the end of this one. The grain used is top class and chewy. *37%. Suntory.*

Torys Whisky Square (80) n19 t20 f21 b20. At first glance very similar to Torys, but very close scrutiny reveals slightly more "new loaf" nose and a better, spicier and less toffeed finale. *37%. Suntory.*

Tsuru (93) n23 t24 f22 b24. Gentle and beautifully structured, genuinely mouthwatering, more-ish and effortlessly noble. If they had the confidence to cut the caramel, this would be even higher up the charts as one of the great blends of the world. And with Japanese whisky becoming far more globally accepted and sought after, now would be a very good time to start. As it is, in my house we pass the ceramic Tsuru bottle as one does the ship's decanter. And it empties very quickly. *43%. Nikka.*

The Whisky (88) n22 t22 f21 b23. A rich, confident and well-balanced dram. *43%. Suntory.*

White (80) n19 t21 f20 b20. Boring nose but explodes on the palate for a fresh, mouth-watering classic blend bite. *40%. Suntory.*

Za (79) n19 t21 f19 b20. Some lively boisterous grain offers a suet-pudding chewiness. A little bitter on the finish. *40%. Suntory.*

European Whisky

The debate about what it means to be European is one that seemingly never ends. By contrast, the discussion on how to define the character of a European whisky is only just beginning.

And as more and more distilleries open throughout mainland Europe, Scandinavia and the British Isles the styles are becoming wider and wider.

Small distillers in mainland Europe, especially those in the Alpine area, share common ground with their US counterparts in often coming into whisky late. Their first love, interest and spirit had been with fruit brandies. It seemed that if something grew in a tree or had a stone when you bit into it, you could be pretty confident that someone in Austria or California was making a clear, eye-watering spirit from it somewhere.

Indeed, when I was writing Jim Murray's Complete Book of Whisky during 1996 and 1997 I travelled to the few mainland Europe distilleries I could find. Even though this was before the days of the internet when research had to be carried out by phone and word of mouth, I visited most – which was few – and missed one or two... which was fewer still.

Today, due mainly to the four solid months it now takes to write the Bible, I can scarcely find the time to go and visit these outposts which stretch from southern Germany to Finland and as far abreast as France to the Czech Republic. It is now not that there is just one or two. But dozens. And I need my good friends Arthur Naegele, Julia Nourney and Birgit Bornemeier to whizz around capturing samples for me just to try and keep up to date.

It is a fact that there is no one style that we can call European, in the way we might be able to identify a Kentucky bourbon or a Scotch single malt. That is simply because of the diversity of stills – and skills – being deployed to make the spirit. And a no less wide range of grains, or blends of grains, and smoking agents, from peat to wood types, to create the mash.

The distillers who have made major financial investments in equipment and staff appear to be the ones who are enjoying the most consistent results. In the Premier League we have the now firmly established Mackmyra in Sweden and Penderyn in Wales, both of whom use female blenders or distillers, curiously. Newly promoted to the highest tier comes St George's in England and just joining them quality-wise, though not quantity, alas, is their British counterpart Hicks and Healey. In fact, St. George's has established themselves quality-wise in the world's whisky elite. All but the odd one or two of their bottlings have been staggeringly good and their Chapter 6 suite of bottlings had been the best ever not to pick up a major gong in the Whisky Bible's history. Never before have I been confronted with one bottling after another meriting a score of 90 plus: so unusual was the phenomenon that I had to taste them all over again a week later to ensure my radar was working correctly. It was. Remarkable, of course, is the youth of the whisky itself. But also the way in which a man fresh to making whisky has so seemlessly copied from an old master. The first distiller to set the distillery on the right path was Iain Henderson of Laphroaig fame. He was also, incidentally, the distillery manager who made the malt at Old Pulteney which over 21 years later was to be awarded World Whisky of the Year in the 2012 Whisky Bible. His successor, David Fitt, a former brewer at Greene King, has now proved himself to be unquestionably one of the best distillers in the world and confirmed that with Chapter 14 picking up the Bible's European Whisky of the Year 2015. The fact his spirit has matured into something so technically excellent in so short a time is truly remarkable: Iain Henderson obviously did a very good teaching job. St George's is not just a distillery to watch. It is also in many respects an inspiration to would-be major distillers.

Another distillery which maintains exceptionally high standards is the Belgian Owl. This is smaller concern than some, but now bigger than most, and the output of their single malt is consistent, beautifully made, and brimming with personality. It may be true that you can count internationally famous Belgians on one hand, but the whisky-loving world would immediately recognise two fingers of its owl... Some of the most remarkable whisky came from Liechtenstein, the country which was once unable to furnish me – anywhere within its borders – with a decent hotel room but now offers a three-year-old malt which, but for the wideness of its cut, nearly walked off with an award. The Telser distillery has a long history and its move into whisky has been an impressive one. Perhaps that big, malty, slightly oily and lush style is something of an Alpine trait: another distillery to watch is Interlaken with their Classic, Swiss Highland Single Malt. Which, with a brand name like that, is as likely to stir up the good folk at the Scotch Whisky Association as anything else.

AUSTRIA
ACHENSEE'R EDELBRENNEREI FRANZ KOSTENZER Maurach. Working.
Whisky Alpin Grain Whisky Hafer db (86.5) n20.5 t23 f21 b22. A glutinous dram, full of thick wheat oils but a surprising lack of spice, though the little which forms works well within the hot cross bun sweetness. 40%

Whisky Alpin Rye & Malt db (88) n22 t22 f22 b22. Needs to settle in the glass a little while for the malt to be at its best. But worth the wait. 40%

Whisky Alpin Single Rye Malt db (81) n19 t21 f20 b21. Creamy and spicy. Good Demerara sugar thread, but the rye itself struggles to convince. 45%

BRENNEREI ROSSETTI Schwaz. Working.
⠿ **Rosetti Young & Fine Pure Single Malt** bott code L482 db (85) n21 t22 f20.5 b21.5. It's young. And fine by me... Clean, thin almost, delicate in its sweetness and salivating, though a slight tang to the finish. Don't expect too much back story. 43.5%

BROGER PRIVATBRENNEREI Klaus. Working.
⠿ **Broger Burn Out Heavily Peated Malt Getreidebrand** bott code: L BO-12 db (89) n22.5 a unique peat nose: tight, acidic and acrid, it is as though a clod of turf was recently aflame in your glass. I assume the peat level was off the scale here. The trouble is...where's the whisky...? Damn it! I'll just enjoy the ride, anyway; t22 well, it makes an appearance on delivery mainly through a stream of crisp sugars. There is a light gristiness, too, which lightens the heavy load; f22.5 vanilla and...peat... b22 now, that really was something very different... Beautifully distilled, though elsewhere technically not brilliant; but a guaranteed quadruple orgasm to the hard core peatophiles out there... 42%.

⠿ **Broger Distiller's Edition Whisky** Madeira Cask bott code: L DE-09 db (81) n21 t22 f18 b20 Under-sugared gooseberry tart. Or should that be: under-sugared tart gooseberry? Either way, shame about the slightly furry finish. 58.7%.

⠿ **Broger Triple Cask Gerstenmalz-Whisky** bott code: L TC-09 db (63) n14 t17 f16 b16. Just awful on so many levels. But mainly through very poor distillate. 42%.

DACHSTEIN DESTILLERIE Radstadt. Working
⠿ **Mandlberggut Rock Whisky 5 Years** (82) n20 t21.5 f20 b20.5. Rock by name and nature. A massively crisp whisky, as though you are crunching on crystals of sugar and grains of barley. The slight tobacco note means it never quite gets into full song but if owners Bernhard and Doris perhaps slow the stills a tad and cut a little finer, they might have on their hands a rock of ages to come... db 40%.

DESTILLERIE GEORG HIEBL Haag. Working.
George Hiebl Mais Whisky 2004 db (93) n23 t23.5 f23 b23.5. More bourbon in character than some American bourbons I know...!! Beautifully matured, brilliantly matured and European whisky of the very highest order, Ye..haahhhh!! 43%

DESTILLERIE KAUSL Mühldorf, Wachau. Working.
Wachauer Whisky "G" Single Barrel Gerste (Barley) bott code L6WG db (90.5) n22 t23 f22.5 b23. Absolutely charming and well made malt. 40%

DESTILLERIE ROGNER Rappottenstein. Working.
Rogner Waldviertel Whisky 3/3 db (86.5) n20 t22 f22.5 b22. Plane sailing once you get past the tight nose. A beautiful display of crisp sugars and come-back-for more grainy juiciness. Lovable stuff, for all its gliches. 41.7%. ncf.

DESTILLERIE WEIDENAUER Kottes. Working
⠿ **Waldviertler Classic Haferwhisky** bottle code L05 db (88) n21 fruity, a hint of butyric, but the oats are powering; t23.5 several layers of sugars, all of them light and watery...then into the serious oatiness; f21 a slight tang from the production; dries as the oats take hold to the cost of the sugars; b22.5 a busy oat whisky of no little distinction, despite the lightest degree of butyric. Still, they have been making from this grain for a long time... 42%

⠿ **Waldviertler Dinkelmalz** Dinkelwhisky mit 2/3, bottle code L08 db (83.5) n20 t22.5 f20 b21. Big, boisterous and, at times, bruising. The spice is out in force, as you might expect. But despite the enormity of the character, the thicker-than-desired cut works against it – on the nose and finish especially. 42%

⠿ **Waldviertler Dinkelwhisky** bottle code L09 db (94) n23 lovely wheaty spice, a little earthy but balanced with a stunning, understated, acacia honey and molasses mix t23.5 textbook weight on delivery: the oils slip over the palate and do nothing to obscure the crispness of those sugars, or the brittleness of the spelt grain; **f23.5** so long, thanks to those oils. The sugars crumble, while the vanilla adds surprising weight and the correct degree of dryness. But the spices pick up and play gently, underlining the wheaty influence; **b24** a beautifully made and matured whisky. So, so subtle... *42%*

⫶⫶⫶ **Waldviertler Hafermalz** Haferwhisky mit 2/3 bottle code L09 db **(91)** **n22** a hinty whisky: hints citrus, hints of coconut, hints of black pepper...but no hinting at all at the oat, which comes through pretty loud and clear; **t23.5** marvellously intense; the light golden syrup meets a tangerine-tinged, deliciously oiled grain; **f22.5** tangy oak but the concentrated, sugared porridge prevails; **b23** every last drop of flavour successfully extracted. Lovely! *42%*

⫶⫶⫶ **Waldviertler Limited Edition Hafermalz** bottle code L08 db **(94)** **n22** slightly off key, but the voluptuousness of the oils and sugars win through; **t24.5** good grief...!! The nose may have had the odd blemish, but those oils certainly ensure a delivery and follow through to remember. Not sugar if it is the esters or the intrinsic sugars which give this such a continuous still Demerara feel...but there is something distinctly rummy about this. The honey is two-toned in intensity, though it is the light manuka which has the biggest say; **f23.5** long, still estery and enjoys a wonderful lime freshness to the oily oatiness; the late tang is a reminder of the earlier blemish. But it is piffling stuff... **b24** one of a type. Every whisky collector should hunt this down. Superb. *42%*

⫶⫶⫶ **Waldviertler Maiswhisky** 100% Maisbrand, bottle code L09 db **(88.5)** **n21.5** dry: a touch of tobacco in there somewhere; black liquorice supports a vague bourbon feel; **t23** big delivery with that distant bourbon quality still on track. Some acacia honey and golden syrup combine with a distinctly coppery-metallic richness; **f22** decent length, a little spicy buzz, but that could be the copper also. The sugars are of the treacle tart variety; **b22** a busy whisky with reasonable pretentions towards a bourbon style. *42%*

⫶⫶⫶ **Waldviertler Single Malt** dunkel Hafer-Whisky bottle code L09 db **(81.5)** **n20 t22 f19 b20.5**. Massive flavours. But the over generous cut offers a metallic edge. *42%*

DESTILLERIE WEUTZ St. Nikolai im Sausal. Working.
Franziska bott code. L070206/02 db The 5% elderflower means this is 100% not whisky. But a fascinating and eye-opening way to create a spirit very much in the young Kentucky rye style, especially in the nose. They certainly can do delicious... For the record, the scoring for enjoyment alone: **(93)** **n23.5 t23 f23.5 b23**. *48%. Malt refined with 5% elderflower.*

LEBE & GENIESSE Lagenrohr. Working
⫶⫶⫶ **Bodding Lokn** cask no. 8, dist 2010, bott 2014 db **(88)** **n22** a light, and delicately malty spirit allows the oak a big say; nutty and pretty zesty, too; **t22.5** gristy and young, in line with the nose. A few mocha moments begin to accumulate; **f21.5** thin, though some remnants of toasted, buttered farmhouse bread does up the depth a little; **b22** tight and toasty. But very young. *42%.*

⫶⫶⫶ **Bodding Lokn Double Cask** cask no. 6/11, dist 2010, bott 2014 db **(82)** **n20 t22 f20 b20**. Pleasant-ish, decently made whisky but way too young for its own good. The nose and finale underscore the serious lack of balance to this. Youthful whisky is acceptable if there is a rhythm to enjoy. Here we have a problem with two different types of oak being flung together yet hardly on speaking terms while at the same time the malt and oak have yet to find any meaningful sync and totter about like Bambi. The single redeeming highlight is the gristy sugars on delivery. But it is always worth remembering that to make the very most of a whisky it invariably needs patience and understanding.

MICHELEHOF Vorarlberg. Working.
⫶⫶⫶ **Micheles Single Malt 6 Years Old** 100% barley, dist 2008, bott code L8121 db **(78.5)** **n19 t21 f19 b19.5**. An oily, nutty affair which struggles hard to get over the effect of the wide cut. A few attractive salivating fudgy moments at about the halfway point. *43%*

PETER AFFENZELLER Albendorf. Working.
⫶⫶⫶ **Peter Affenzeller Blend** dist 2009, bott code L-1031132 db **(86)** **n20 t22 f22 b22**. A thinner, though more complex yet clean, version of the tannin-rich single malt bottling. Here, though, the spices strafe the taste buds from the first moment. Curiously satisfying, though. *42%*

⫶⫶⫶ **Peter Affenzeller Grain** dist 2009, bott code L-0821021 db **(82.5)** **n19 t21 f21.5 b21**. Silky soft delivery and mouth feel. Again, the tannins have full control and it is not unpleasant toasty nuttiness which prevails. *42%*

⫶⫶⫶ **Peter Affenzeller Single Malt** dist 2009, bott code L-1031102 db **(81.5)** **n18 t21 f21.5 b21**. Sweet, nutty and all kinds of tannins at play of a singular European style though, intriguingly, sometimes not always easily recognisable as oak. On the downside the malt is lost under the wood while the nose needs a bit of work. *42%*

⣿ **Peter Affenzeller White** bott code L-0821011 db **(84.5) n21 t21.5 f22 b20.** A pleasant, dry, well-made white spirit with a few decent sugar notes running into cocoa. Not sure how new make like this can be called whisky, though... *42%*

PFANNER Vorarlberg. Working.

⣿ **Pfanner Single Malt** dist 2009, bott code L 212 db **(74) n19 t20 f16.5 b18.5.** Nutty and some hefty feints late on puts a Pfanner in the works... *43%*

REISETBAUER Axberg, Thening. Working.

Reisetbauer Single Malt 7 Years Old Chardonnay and sweet wine cask, bott code LWH 099 db **(85.5) n19 t21 f23.5 b22.** A less than impressive nose is followed by a rocky delivery. But the panning out is truly spectacular as harmony is achieved with a rich honey and nougat mix, helped along the way with pecan nuts and figs. The finish is like a top rank trifle and fruitcake mix. A whisky of two halves. *43%*

WHISKY-DESTILLERIE J. HAIDER Roggenreith. Working.

Single Malt J.H. bott code L SM/06 **(91.5) n22 t23 f23.5 b23.** It must be over a dozen years now since I first went to their distillery. But this is their best batch of whiskies yet... *41%*

Single Malt Selection J.H. bott code L7/02 db **(94) n23 t23 f24 b24.** One of their cleanest, most understated bottlings to date. A gem. *46%*

⣿ **Single Malt J.H. Rare Selection** bott code L SM 09 SG db **(91) n22.5** a good deal of the house nougat-bourbon on show; **t23** thick and multi-layered as usual, the big oils make the most of the manuka honey and liquorice; **f22.5** the still liquorice dominates, even with a vague hint of Fisherman's friend. But now the spices hold the moment...; **b23** as usual, no shrinking violet! *46%*

⣿ **Single Malt J.H. Rare Selection** bott code L SM 06 TR db **(94) n23** at once subtle and delicate, yet chunky. Much more emphasis on the honey than normal, a little dry diced coconut and a slight hint of treacle; **t24** a sublime delivery with that honey-treacle combination arriving early. But it is the way the malt slowly takes the upper hand – seemingly by tiny degrees at a time – really makes for an exceptional Austrian experience. Near perfect weight with the intensity of the malt; the layering and pace can hardly be bettered; **f23.5** long and boasting spice prickle yet still those honeys and malt radiate, allowing in at last the chalky oaks sign off a very pretty picture; **b23.5** one of the best malts of all time from JH. *46%*

Special Single Malt Selection J.H. bott code L15/02 db **(93) n22.5 t23 f23.5 b24.** It is obvious that the JH whiskies are coming of age: they are consistently now of a very high standard – and just full of honeyed riches. *46%*

Original Rye Whisky J.H. L19/05 db **(91.5) n23.5 t23 f22 b23.** Their Original Rye was last year close to bringing home to Austria the Bible's European Whisky of the Year. This is another outstanding bottling. Perhaps not as sharp and mouth-watering as last time, but the marriage between the rye and toffee-honeycomb is a blissful one. Superb yet again! *41%*

Original Rye Whisky J.H. bott code L R/06 **(92.5) n23 t23.5 f23 b23.** This distillery can produce a Kentuckian style rye better than any other distillery outside the US. here is another gorgeous example. *41%*

⣿ **Original Rye Whisky Selection** bottle code L R 05. db **(91.5) n22** a little of the old tobacco style about this, but moves on fast...to rye-soaked nougat; **t23.5** glorious delivery of crick rye dipped in honey; **f23** long as the oils spread; cocoa arrives and deepens; **b23** pure entertainment! *46%*

Pure Rye Malt J.H. bott code LPR 07 db **(95.5) n24 t24 f23.5 b24.** Clean, unerring and screams "rye" at you. Magnificent. *41%*

Special Rye Malt Selection Nougat J.H. bott code L SPR 07 SL db **(84.5) n20 t22 f21 b21.5.** Big and cumbersome, the nougat effect dulls the rye to a telling degree. No shortage of spices, though. *46%*

DESTILLERIE WEIDENAUER Kottes. Working.

Waldviertler Hafer-Malz (2007 Gold Medaille label on neck) db **(91) n22 t22.5 f23 b23.5.** One of those whiskies that just gets better the longer it stays on the palate. Also, a master class in achieving near perfection in the degree of sweetness generated. *42%*

BELGIUM
THE BELGIAN OWL

⣿ **The Belgian Owl Single Malt 'New Make'** dist 06/13. db **(93) n23 t24 f23 b23.** Intensely sweet and rather beautifully made with enormous emphasis on concentrated clean, gristy barley. Looks as though they produce better New Make from the Caperdonich stills in Belgium than they could ever manage in Speyside. Strange... *70%*.

⸖ **The Belgian Owl Single Malt '8 Months'** db **(85)** n20 t21.5 f23 b20.5. Typically imbalanced for its age with the first sugary tannins lurching about the malt both blindly and seemingly without a map. Good finish though to this sometimes lush piece. 70%.

The Belgian Owl Single Malt Age 4 Years 1st fill bourbon cask, bott code. 270910 db **(94.5) n24 t23.5 f23 b24.** A Belgian treat. 46%. nc ncf.

The Belgian Owl Single Malt 48 Months 1st fill bourbon cask, bott code. L 260312 db **(86)** n21.5 t22 f21.5 b21. A much thinner bottling than of recent years with the sugars in the ascendancy and the barley devoid of muscle. Attractive and easy, though. 46%. nc ncf.

The Belgian Owl Single Malt 48 Months 1st fill bourbon cask no. 4275933 db **(90.5) n22.5 t23 f22 b23.** This is quite probably the most powerful bottled whisky I have encountered anywhere in the world in my entire career. Perhaps what is most remarkable is the beautifully delicate nature of the nose and flavour profile, despite the scary alcohol levels. A unique and, if you have the nerve, wonderful experience. 76.5%. nc ncf sc.

The Belgian Owl Single Malt Age 55 Months 1st fill bourbon cask no. 4275890 db **(92.5) n22 t23.5 f23.5 b23.5.** Fantastic whisky with more twists and turns than a corkscrew. At times like the Hubble telescope looking back to the Belgian Big Bang – the beginning of the dedicated whisky universe in the country. The picking up of extra copper shows it is getting closer to those very first moments at Belgian Owl... 74.3%. nc ncf sc.

The Belgian Owl Single Malt Age 53 Months 1st fill bourbon cask no. 4275986 db **(90.5) n23 t23 f22 b22.5.** Enormous whisky, unsurprisingly, as deeply satisfying. 74.1%. nc ncf sc.

The Belgian Owl Single Malt 60 Months cask no. 4276140 db **(94) n23.5 t23 f24 b23.5.** Carries out the dual purpose of giving you the big barley fix of the day...and dissolves any plaque that may have formed around your gums. Breathtaking...in every sense. 76.1%. nc ncf sc.

⸖ **The Belgian Owl Single Malt '60 Months'** db **(91.5)** n22.5 teasing vanilla pulls at the beard of the barley. The spice prickle is playful and polite; the sugars supportive rather than manipulative; **t23** anyone who fondly remembers butterscotch tart at school will have a soft spot for this. The body is as yielding as a sex-starved nurse and no less therapeutic to sugar-starved taste buds; **f23** now just a stream of light vanillas and thinned-out tannins. Quite chalky towards the delicate but still malty finish; **b23** after being introduced to this distillery's 60 month old at 76.1%abv last year, this is positively a Guardian-reading sop and pacifist by comparison. Gentle and genteel with none of the passion displayed by the previous, unadulterated, version. Something of the Belgian Owl and Pussycat.... 46%. nc ncf.

The Belgian Owl Single Malt 64 Months 1st fill bourbon cask no. 4275982 db **(90.5) n23 t23.5 f22 b22.5.** Demure and elegant. 50%. nc ncf sc.

⸖ **The Belgian Owl Single Malt '64 Months'** db **(96)** n23.5 ignore the dizzying degree of alcohol: concentrate on the nutty, malty notes and it all makes sense. Quite balmy flaked almonds mixed in with diced green apple and grist...; **t24** and it is the grist first up on delivery, followed by the juice of Williams' Pear. The sugars condense slightly at this point, but most are of an apple origin before the malt really ramps up the intensity; **f24.5** the star turn. Deft oils lengthen the effect f the malt; the sugars are bright yet polite and major on cane juice but still that barley makes its unerring mark...; **b24** what a delicious way to clean your teeth in the morning! Has more class and flair than the Belgian World Cup squad. And that is saying something...73.7%. nc ncf sc.

DESTILLERIE RADERMACHER

Lambertus Single Grain Aged 10 Years db **(44)** n12 t12 f10 b10. This is whisky...? Really???!!!!????? Well, that's what it says on the label, and this is a distillery I haven't got round to seeing in action (nor am I now very likely to be invited...). Let's check the label again... Ten years old...blah, blah. Single grain... blah, blah. But, frankly, this tastes like a liqueur rather than a whisky: the fruit flavours do not seem even remotely naturally evolved: synthetic is being kind. But apparently, this is whisky: I have re-checked the label. No mention of additives, so it must be. I am stunned. 40%

FILLIERS DISTILLERY

Goldly's Belgian Double Still Whisky Aged 10 Years db **(88)** n21.5 t23 f21.5 b22. Having actually discovered this whisky before the distillers – I'll explain one day...!! – I know this could be a lot better. The caramel does great damage to the finish in particular, which should dazzle with its complexity. Even so, a lovely, high-class whisky which should be comfortably in the 90s but falls short. 40%

IF GOULDYS

⸖ **Gouldys 12 Years Old Amontillado Finish First Release** bott 2012 db **(89.5)** n23.5 flawless nutty grape with no shortage of must; **t22** hugely rich sherry on a background of chocolate mousse; **f22** more chocolate – now spiced; **b22** a pleasant, gentle experience celebrating a non-sulphur involvement. But the grape influence is just a little too great even for the considerable character of Fillers' grain to show through to advantage. Easy does it, chaps. *43%. ncf nc. WB15/388*

⋰ **Gouldys 12 Years Old Distillers Range** cask no. 2600 db **(96) n24** is it the clarity of the sherry or the punchiness of the grain which grips first? Hard to say. But the refreshing grape does nothing to distract from the crispness of the rye element. The result is stunning...; **t24.5** the best sherry-influenced delivery I have tasted so far this year. A gorgeous viscosity to the grape works brilliantly against the firmness of the rye whilst the other grains chime in with confidence. Hard to find a whisky where the sugars, most of them of a Demerara style, work so well with the frothing spice...; **f23.5** now much more sedate, though the length defies belief as the grape and rye interweave seemingly into infinity; **b24** an essay in complexity. A faultless sherry butt influencing some of the best distillate in Europe: a triumph! *43.7%. ncf nc. WB15/390*

⋰ **Gouldys 12 Years Old Manzilla Finish First Release** bott 2012 db **(90) n23** flawless but heavy duty Manzanilla; **t23** superb spices warm the thick, chewy grape. The grains are indistinct but can be detected for a second or two; **f23** sweetens and softens, though the spices chatter on; **b21** another delightful whisky despite falling into the trap of overwhelming the grain with the grape. Pretty impossible not to love, though. *43%. ncf nc. WB15/389*

CZECH REPUBLIC
Single Malt
RUDOLF JELÍNEK DISTILLERY
Gold Cock Single Malt Aged 12 Years "Green Feathers" bott 27/05/09 db **(89.5) n22 t23.5 f22 b22**. From my first ever malt-related trip to the Czech Republic nearly 20 years ago, it was always a pleasure to get hold of my Gold Cock. I was always told it went down a treat. And this is no exception. Not a particularly big whisky. But since when has size counted? *43%*

STOCK PLZEN - BOZKOV S.R.O.
Hammer Head 1989 db **(88.5) n22 t22.5 f22 b22**. Don't bother looking for complexity: this is one of Europe's maltiest drams...if not the maltiest... *40.7%*

Blends
Gold Cock Aged 3 Years "Red Feathers" bott 22/06/09 db **(86) n22 t21 f21.5 b21.5**. Sensual and soft, this is melt-in-the-mouth whisky with a big nod towards the sweet caramels. *40%.*

Granette Premium (82) n21 t22 f19 b20. Lighter than the spark of any girl that you will meet in the Czech Republic. Big toffee thrust. *40%*

Printer's Aged 6 Years (86.5) n21.5 t22.5 f21 b21.5. Blended whisky is something often done rather well in the Czech Republic and this brand has managed to maintain its clean, malty integrity and style. Dangerously quaffable. *40%*

DENMARK
STAUNING DISTILLERY Skjern. Working.
Brigantia 3 Years Old bott code L-12/12 db **(79) n19 t21 f19 b20**. Huge malt statement, as is the distillery style. But it appears someone decided to try and extract as much spirit as possible, because the cut seems to be a little too wide for comfort here: the oils are unforgiving. *43%*

Stauning 1st Edition Peated dist 2009, bott 2012 **(94) n22.5 t24 f24 b23.5**. I didn't know whether to taste this, the first whisky from Stauning on the first birthday of my first grand-daughter, Islay-Mae, or make this the 999th new whisky I have tasted for 2013 Whisky Bible in recognition that I played a (very!) small part in its foundation....though only by offering encouragement. As fate dictates, both fell on the same day. Ah, this dram before me really is the stuff of history...and though not technically spot on, is the equivalent to half an hour in the gym for the taste buds. A malt of genuine character. Absolutely adore it! *62.8%*

Stauning 2nd Edition Traditional bott 2013 db **(85) n20 t21 f22.5 b21.5**. Always interesting to see how a malt develops with time. Compared to a year ago, this has lost a little balance, with the barley just a little too ferocious on the nose and the sugars, though ultimately enjoyable, almost to a liquor-ish degree, are too far removed from the hay-like malt. *55%*

Stauning 2nd Edition Peated dist 2009, bott 2013 db **(94.5) n23 t23.5 f24.5 b24**. If there are awards given for sheer cleverness within peaty malt, then this would win hands down. No matter how many times you taste it, you can never quite decide whether the smoke is simply a charming accompaniment, or actually has its hands on the tiller of the direction of the whisky. Now that is what I call complexity...and a very classy act! *55%*

⋰ **Stauning 3rd Edition Peated Single Malt** dist 2009, bott 2014 db **(94) n23** some serious complexity here: a huge cliff of tannin (surprising for the age) being battered by waves of peat of ever-varying intensity; the hay-malt noticeable on the standard bottling also has room to flourish; **t24** the sugars rise on the palate like the famous mountains of Denmark: just attractive little hills here and there undulating with the even smoke and quite early mocha, which I think last year took longer to evolve; those sugars range from lightly smoked muscovado to, briefly, lightly smoked treacle; **f23.5** a light heather honey strain can be heard as the smoke slowly disperses; **b23.5** such a delightful experience: a peated malt which appears to wish to be inclusive of many other traits. *50%.*

⠸⠇ **Stauning 3rd Edition Traditional Single Malt** dist 2009/2010, bott 2014 db **(87) n22 t22 f21 b22.** A malt on the march. Definitely a notch up from their previous bottling with the grassy malt signature on both nose and delivery standing out starkly against the spices. Still plenty of room for improvement as they progress. *49%.*

Stauning Peated Single Malt oloroso cask finish, dist 10, bott 13 **(93) n22.5 t23 f23.5 b24.** Can't say I'm the world's greatest fan of peat and sherry. But the finish on this one really is the stuff of smoky dreams. So impressive. *49.4%*

Stauning Peated Single Malt Pedro Ximenez cask finish, dist 2010, bott 13 **(85) n21 t22 f21 b21.** Can't say I'm a fan of PX and big peat being thrown together and this does little to alter my view. Simply too much: the tightness of the sugars appears to strangle the life out of any further development. Decent delivery and early shockwaves. But your taste buds feel like they are in a sugary straightjacket. *47.1%*

Stauning Rye Third Solution dist 2009/2010, bott 2012 **(92) n23 t23.5 f23 b22.5.** No doubting the grain used here: the rye bursts from the glass with massive, sharp fruity intent. Unlike some I have seen made elsewhere, this is very much in the Kentuckian mould and if the cut had been a little more precise, may well even have passed off as such. Not yet whisky, some of the spirit being a little less than the required three years, this bottling sends a very clear message: clean the distillate very slightly and bottle at full age and they will have one of Europe's great whiskies on their hands. This is beautiful stuff which even in this form delights from a multitude of angles. Also, this could well be their trademark whisky as it has the potential to out polish the peated and unpeated barley styles. Are we seeing the formative process of a potential world classic? It wouldn't surprise me. *50.5%*

Stauning Young Rye dist 10 & 11, bott Oct 12 db **(92.5) n23 t23 f23.5 b23.** An interesting change in gear from the last bottling, with this being far more in brown sugar-beech honey mode *49.3%*

Stauning Young Rye dist 2010, bott Aug 12 db **(94.5) n23.5 t24 f23.5 b23.5.** As this is too young be a whisky, no room for tasting notes. But there deserves to be. This is absolutely brimming with all the in-your-face chocolate-fruitiness you expect from a top rye. Not difficult to see an award-winner of the near future here. The intensity of the kumquat/liquorice/spice as the rye gets into full stride has been one of my treats of the year. Magnificent. *50.8%*

Stauning Young Rye dist 10/11, bott Jun 13 **(77) n19 t20 f19 b19.** Time to be a little careful, guys. The nougat on the nose means that perhaps a few corners have been cut...and the oils clinging to the finish confirms this. Maybe, after making some earlier excellent malte, an eye went off the ball: it is too easy to think that the making of great whisky has been mastered and it is easy. It never is! For rye to achieve its greatest clarity and crispness, the cut has to be precise and never too early. The intensity of the rye goes some way to saving the day. *51.2%*

⠸⠇ **Stauning Young Rye** dist 2010/2012, bott Jun 14 db **(91) n22** oily and full bodied, the fruity charm of the intense rye is almost three dimensional; **t22.5** maybe a bit of a wide cut. But only just: the toasted honeycomb and treacle just add to the ripping rye which offers both soft oils and crisp fruit...gosh! **f24** much cleaner towards the end where the oak and grain really do make the most of each other; **b22.5** if no-one has ever told this distillery they do rye rather well, about time they did. And, better still, they can make it cleaner than this, too... *53.3%*

ENGLAND
ADNAMS

⠸⠇ **Adnams Southwold Triple Grain Whisky No 2** American oak, bott 2013 **(87) n22 t22 f21 b22.** For my 999th new whisky for Bible 2015 I wanted, as this book's custom dictates, to choose something a little unusual. And here we have the first-ever Suffolk whisky, made at one of my favourite breweries in the world, Adnams. Not sure what happened to the first bottling but I have the second. And beside me is Percy, my Meyers parrot born in Norfolk not far from the Suffolk border while this cask was maturing. The most remarkable thing to report is the nose. It is, and I really have to find out how, the closest whisky I have ever encountered on nose that matches a decent biryani in its subtle Asian spicy complexity. To taste it is a lot more straightforward: a tad feinty, but those oils conjure up the spices which sit well with the intense sugars. The finish, naturally enough, is a little bitter and foggy from the feints...but with no uncomfortable edges. For now I shall stick to their almost incomparable bitter beer. But I shall be keeping a close eye... *43%. ncf. WB15/407*

HEALEY'S CORNISH CYDER FARM Penhallow. Working.

Hicks & Healey Cornish Single Malt 2004 Cask #29 (94.5) n24.5 t24 f22.5 b23.5. Fascinatingly, picking up much more apple here than I did at the distillery, mainly because of the ambient aromas around me there: a great example why all tasting notes I carry out are in controlled environments. Back in January I headed down to the distillery and after going through their casks suggested this one was, like their very finest apples, exactly ripe for picking. The most noticeable thing was that there, in the still house, I picked up only a fraction of the apple I get here in the controlled environment of my tasting room. The distillery makes, above all else, cider brandy, so the aroma is all pervasive. However, my instincts were probably correct, for the apple (doubtless absorbed from the environment of maturing with apple brandy casks, something like the fruit apparent on the whisky of St George's distillery, California) to be found here only contributes positively rather than detracts, especially on the nose...which I have upgraded from excellent then to near faultless now. As new distilleries go, this rates among the best debut bottlings of the last decade. That is not least because most distillers try and launch on three years to get money back as soon as possible. Here they have more than doubled that time and are reaping the benefit...with interest. A dram, then, to keep your nocturnal cinema going on classic mode: "Last night I dreamt I went to Penhallow again." Hang on: twelve syllables... I feel a book coming on... and a film... *61.3%.* sc.

Hicks & Healey Cornish Whiskey 2004 Cask #32 dist 13 Feb 04, bott Feb 12 db **(96)** n24 t24.5 f23.5 b24. I picked this one up absent-mindedly, nosed...and was carried to Cornwall. I knew what it was without even opening my eyes. Unmistakable. And just so stunningly beautiful... *60.2%.* ncf.

ST. GEORGE'S Rowdham. Working.

The English Whisky Co. Chapter 6 English Single Malt (unpeated) cask no. 163, 165, 171 & 173, dist May 07, bott Jun 10 db **(91)** n22 t23 f23.5 b22.5. Further confirmation that this distillery is on course for true excellence. Here, by comparison to earlier bottlings, the distillate shows some evidence that the stills have been run just a little faster and the cut thinned a little, meaning a laser-sharp crispness to the barley. So reminds me of Glen Grant at this age. *46%*

The English Whisky Co. Chapter 6 English Single Malt ASB casks, cask no. 573, 574, 613 & 614, dist May 08, bott Sep 11 db **(92)** n23 t23.5 f22 b23.5. Hugely enjoyable, very well made, excellently matured single malt. As simple as that! *46%.* nc ncf.

The English Whisky Co. Chapter 6 English Single Malt ASB casks, cask no. 478, 479, 480 & 481, dist Aug 08, bott Oct 11 db **(92.5)** n24 t23 f22.5 b23. But for one cask betraying the rest with that loose bitterness on the finish and this would have been Liquid Gold.... *46%.* nc ncf.

The English Whisky Co. Chapter 6 English Single Malt Not Peated ASB casks, cask no. 001, 002, 003, 004, dist May 09, bott Jan 13 db **(95)** n23.5 t24 f23.5 b24. Shows what maturing in truly great casks can do. Any more stylishly English and you'd think it was distilled in Jermyn Street... *46%.* nc ncf.

The English Whisky Co. Chapter 6 English Single Malt Not Peated ASB casks, cask no. 005, 006, 007, 008, dist May 09, bott Feb 13 db **(96)** n24 t24 f24 b24. You taste the Chapter 6 casks 1-4 and think it doesn't get any better...and then...this!!! Truly flawless distillate matured in high quality casks. Not just free of a single off note...free of a hint of a rumour of an off note. Truly sublime whisky showing that youth, when well brought up, can only delight. One of the finest examples of unpeated single malt whisky to have hit the market worldwide in the last three or four years... *46%.* nc ncf.

The English Whisky Co. Chapter 6 English Single Malt Not Peated ASB casks, cask no. 0193, 0194, dist Apr 10, bott Apr 13 db **(95)** n23.5 t25 f23 b23.5. I'm not sure if anything since Supertramp brought out Crime of the Century and Crisis What Crisis? back in the mid 1970s has two, or in this case three, back to back releases been so seamless or faultless. Let me say it and, as an Englishman, say it proudly: this whisky borders genius. *46%.* nc ncf.

⋰ The **English Whisky Co. Chapter 6 Unpeated** cask no. 248, 249, 250, 251, dist Oct 10, bott Nov 13 db **(89.5)** n22.5 a light honey thread distracts from the slightly new-makey breeze; t22 outrageously juicy on delivery, but the malt is febrile and takes time to happily link with the oak; f23 the slow pulsing of the dry cocoa is sublime though, unusually, this is from the spirit rather than the oak. Just how good the original spirit was becomes clear as the maltiness makes its mark; b22 a very solid score, though anything under 90 seems like a failure for this particular distillery. A rare occurrence where the youth of the spirit and the influence of the oak have been detached. Still a thing of youthful beauty when all is said and done. *60.2%.* WB15/183

⋰ The **English Whisky Co. Chapter 7 Rum Cask** cask no. 765, 766, dist Oct 09, bott May 14 db **(92)** n22.5 confidently crisp rum influence from the kickoff: a light, sugary shell encrusts the beautifully defined barley; t23 mmmm...!! Such a glorious fanfare of intense barley on delivery, which intensifies even further with a chunky gristiness during the slow progression; f23.5 quite wonderful finish: the rum remerges somewhat with a light sugary sheen to the charming chalky oak and citrus gristy mix; **b23** an essay in understated deliciousness. A near perfect use of delicate sugar. *46%. nc ncf. 550 bottles. WB15/188*

⠿ **The English Whisky Co. Chapter 7 Rum Cask** cask no. 0765, 0766, dist Oct 09, bott May 14 db **(94) n23 t23.5 f24 b23.5.** Of all the English Whisky bottlings to its sister version (above), this is the closest in style despite the alcohol leap. Everything here, though, is more polished, concentrated and vivid....as you might expect. Quite superb. *59.9%. 96 bottles. WB15/187*

The English Whisky Co. Chapter 7 Cask Strength rum casks, cask no. 0457, 0458, dist May 2009, bott Apr 2013 db **(94.5) n23 t24.5 f23.5 b24.** If you want proof that adding water to whisky does not necessary improve it, try this cask strength version against the friendly fellow at 46%, above. Here a fruitier element comes into play while some heavier oak notes, via cocoa, batters away with greater success at the inherent sugars offered by the rum. The spices also play their part with far more conviction while the barley has more freedom to shine. Another bottling which is showing that St George's has moved into the very highest echelons of world whisky. *59.9%*

The English Whisky Co. Chapter 7 Rum Finish ASB & rum cask nos. 024/025, dist Mar 07, bott Oct 10 db **(94) n23.5 t24 f23 b23.5.** Absolutely exceptional. A near faultless whisky where the youth of the malt and the sweet finesse of the rum casks were born for each other. The kind of light and juicy whisky I, frankly, adore. *46%. nc ncf.*

T**he English Whisky Co. Chapter 7 Rum Finish** ASB & rum casks, cask no. 0457, 0458, dist May 09, bott Apr 13 db **(91.5) n22 t23.5 f23 b23.** You have to be confident when maturing in rum: this has a propensity to tighten a malt until little but the sugars are heard. This though is 92% proof that St George can slay that particular dragon. *46%. nc ncf.*

The English Whisky Co. Chapter 7 Rum Cask Limited Edition bott 2011 db **(94) n23.5 t23.5 f23 b24.** Tight, disciplined, crisp...I have never had the experience, but this (I have been told) seems just what it is like when bound and whipped by a mistress. Britain's judiciary should be on their way to Norfolk en masse... Absolutely delicious!! *46%. nc ncf sc.*

The English Whisky Co. Chapter 9 English Single Malt (peated) cask no. 102, 115, 124 & 144, dist May 07, bott May 10 db **(93.5) n23 t23.5 f24 b23.** Frankly, it would be churlish to ask any more of a malt whisky of this age. Three years old only, yet going through the gears of complexity like an old 'un. The secret, though, is in the quality of the distillation and the very decent casks used. So exceptional is this, you would almost think that this was created by the guy who made Laphroaig for many a year... *46%*

The English Whisky Co. Chapter 9 Peated/Smokey ASB casks, cask no. 0501 & 0489, dist 08, bott 12 db **(95) n23.5 t24 f23.5 b24.** World class whisky with the weight and finesse making all the right noises. For its age, it writes itself in the annals of English whisky folklore. Beyond superb, this wins my Percy Award for things of stunning beauty coming from Norfolk! *46%. nc ncf.*

The English Whisky Co. Chapter 9 Peated/Smokey ASB casks, cask no. 62, 65, 449, 451, dist Apr 09, bott Jun 12 db **(88) n22 t23 f21 b22.** As sweet as a peaty nut! Just the odd sub-standard cask lets the side down a little. *46%. nc ncf.*

The English Whisky Co. Chapter 9 Peated ASB casks, cask no. 064, 065, 066, 103, dist Oct 09, bott Feb 13 db **(92.5) n23.5 t23 f23 b23.** A growling, grumbling, curmudgeonly dram which wants to keep to a separate path from the sugars. *46%. nc ncf.*

The English Whisky Co. Chapter 10 Sherry Finish Oloroso sherry hogshead, cask no. 488/489, dist Oct 07, bott Oct 10 db **(91) n23.5 t23 f22 b22.5.** A spotlessly clean oloroso cask ensures a beautiful malt, though not quite hitting the very highest forms of excellence as the host whisky has not yet formed sufficient muscle to carry the grape without the odd sideways stagger. That said, not a whisky you'd ever say "no" to the offer of a top-up... *46%. nc ncf.*

The English Whisky Co. Chapter 11 "Heavily Peated" ASB cask no. 645/647/648, dist 08, bott 11 db **(92) n23 t23.5 f22.5 b23.** As the 59.7% version below. Only for wimps. *46%. nc ncf.*

The English Whisky Co. Chapter 11 Heavily Peated ASB casks, cask no. 639, 640, 641 & 642, dist Mar 08, bott Nov 11 db **(91.5) n22.5 t23 f23 b23.** One of the sweetest English whiskies for the last century... *46%. nc ncf.*

The English Whisky Co. Chapter 11 Heavily Peated ASB casks, cask no. 0062, 0065, dist Apr 09, bott Jul 12 db **(81) n19 t22 f21 b19.** A rare blemish. This malt is very much less than the sum of its parts as not enough attention was made in balancing out the peats and the sugars. Brief harmony as the sugars and oils hit the palate, but on the nose and for long periods in the mouth this is a free for all: young malts are temperamental. And here the balance has not been found. *46%. nc ncf.*

The English Whisky Co. Chapter 11 Heavily Peated ASB casks, cask no. 0104, 0107, dist Nov 09, bott Feb 13 db **(93) n22 t24 f23.5 b23.5.** Superbly made and makes the most of some honey casks. If anything, perhaps too much honey...! *46%. nc ncf.*

The English Whisky Co. Chapter 11 "Heavily Peated" Cask Strength db **(94) n23.5 t24 f23 b23.5.** What can you say? A whisky only three years old yet carrying itself with the wisdom of an elder statesman. The pace of the peat is absolutely textbook; the marriage between the smoke and sugars the stuff of dreams. Proof that great – or even intermediate - age is not always the deciding factor. Sometimes, when a distiller has got all his sums right, a whisky can be plucked from the cask at a positively infantile age and still it can have the capacity to knock you off your chair. As this, indeed, does. And if you require proof that adding water to whisky doesn't do a whisky many favours, just try the 46% version... *59.7%. nc ncf.*

The English Whisky Co. Chapter 11 Heavily Peated Cask Strength ASB casks, cask no. 639, 640, 641 & 642, dist Mar 08, bott Nov 11 db **(93) n23 t23.5 f23 b23.5.** Feels very at home at this strength. impossible not to enjoy! *59.7%. nc ncf.*

⫶⫶ **The English Whisky Co. Chapter 13 Heavily Peated** cask no.527, 528, 827, 830, dist 2008, bott 2013 db **(92.5) n23.5** what a tease: the smoke caresses and whispers, though some of its speech is childish: the youth of this whisky is occasionally transparent; just look for that lime on the barley, though! At other times, the conversation is more mature with slightly overcooked raspberry pie out there; **t23.5** that fabulous, slightly buttery feel of cake mix nicked from the mixing bowl, but now with peaty grist sprinkled in; at all times, though, salivating barley refreshes; **f22** just a little bitterness creeps in from the oak. The delicate, citrusy sugars and fingerprints of peat try to counter; **b23.5** take your time with this: like all the best whiskies, this is a moving target never sitting still and with so many elements camouflaged before being spotted. *49%. ncf nc. WB15/397*

⫶⫶ **The English Whisky Co. Chapter 13 St. George's Day Edition** db **(91) n22** a telling light furriness tells me to be on the lookout for more fruit characteristics, which are to be found, intriguingly, with a slightly salty tang. More herb garden than fruit, though the delicate molasses heads in the direction of a dry, two-days-on-the-plate Melton Hunt cake....; **t24** the spices rise early on an oily bed which makes for a friendly, though far from docile opening. A mix of malt, red liquorice and hickory forms the van of the attack but deeper fruitier notes rumble, especially the magnificent walnut and dates; **f22** spicy still but the dryness has an unwelcome catch, though a few chocolate fruit and nut notes repairs some of the damage; **b23** the nose suggests sherry butts at work here, as does the slightly furry finale. But this is a superficial wound and the overall composition is rather lovely. *45%. nc ncf. WB15/181*

⫶⫶ **The English Whisky Co. Chapter 14 Not Peated** cask no. 450, 451, 452, 453, dist Feb 09, bott May 14 db **(96) n24** thick: you need a knife to cut your way through the honey-marmalade mix and wire-cutters to penetrate the barley; **t24.5** the citrus on the nose arrives ahead of the concentrated barley cavalry. Absolutely no need to tell you this is malt whisky: this is the densest malt you will taste this year from any distillery; some cocoa strands arrive relatively early but still cannot distract from the grain: for its age, as near as damn it faultless...; **f23.5** tangy oak gets a word in edgeways; thins at last but that barley still controls with varying intensity. A little salty, oddly enough, and a little Milky Way candy filling sits rather beautifully with the delicate cocoa; **b24** any distiller in the world would give his right hand to lay claim to malt of such exceptionally high quality. *58.8%. 299 bottles. WB15/185*

The English Whisky Co. Chapter 14 English Single Malt (unpeated) cask no. 582-585, dist 08, bott 13 db **(95) n23.5 t23.5 f24 b24.** This is great whisky in its simplest form – even the complexity, though evident, is untaxing. If you are not an age snob, this, for its gentle elegance, will blow you away. *58.8%. nc ncf.*

The English Whisky Co. Chapter 14 English Single Malt (unpeated) cask no. 582-585, dist May 08, bott Jul 13 db **(93) n23 t23 f23.5 b23.5.** Now there's a thing. Nosed and tasted then and thought: "that's weird! Just about identical to the last one. Gorgeous, but just doesn't quite hit the high notes when singing, or have quite so much bass." Then discovered it was the same whisky, but reduced to 46%. Says it all, really. *46%. nc ncf.*

The English Whisky Co. Chapter 15 English Single Malt (peated) db **(94.5) n23.5 t24 f23 b24.** If you could take that single flaw out of the equation, you'd have just about perfect whisky for a five-year-old. As it is, you'll just have to make do with bloody magnificent.... And make no mistake: this is no poor man's Islay. It stands up with the world's elite. *58.4%. nc ncf.*

The English Whisky Co. Chapter 15 English Single Malt (peated) cask no. 615-618, dist Apr 08, bott Jul 13 db **(92.5) n23.5 t23.5 f22.5 b23.** A drier, more inert version of the cask strength bottling. Here the peat is a little more dusty, though the gristy sugars do show up better. Simply enjoyable, high class peaty whisky however you look at it. *46%. nc ncf.*

The English Whisky Co. Classic (unpeated) db **(88.5) n22 t22 f22.5 b22.** Sweet, young and innocent. *43%. nc ncf.*

The English Whisky Co. Limited Edition "Ibisco Decanter" bourbon cask, dist Nov 06, bott Dec 09 db **(91.5) n22 t24 f23 b22.5.** Quite adorable. Beautifully made whisky from stills small enough to add almost invisible but vital weight. One of the true fun whiskies of the year which further raises the expectations of what this distillery is capable of. *46%*

The English Whisky Co. Peated db **(93) n23 t23.5 f23 b23.5.** A young whisky which proves, again, that it is the quality of the distillate – especially when peated – which can count over the years. *43%. nc ncf.*

Founders Private Cellar cask no. 0005 db **(94.5)** n23.5 t24 f23 b24. This is the first whisky from this distillery to be bottled at the grand old age of five! And this old timer bears the most eloquent testimony possible to the skills of veteran distiller Iain Henderson: it is a stunner! I drink this to your health, old friend. 60.8%. nc ncf sc.

Founders Private Cellar cask no. 0116, dist 12 Sep 07, bott 8 Apr 13 db **(94.5)** n24 t23.5 f23 b24. Yet another bottling from this remarkable distillery which almost defies belief. So clean and proffers the innocence of youth with unsullied beauty. 60.8%. nc ncf sc.

Founders Private Cellar Port Cask, cask no. 0859, dist 20 Jun 07, bott 10 Apr 13 db **(88.5)** n22 t23 f21.5 b22. Technically, this is not A1 spirit at work. However the influence of the Port pipe is so impressive, much, if not all, is forgiven... 59.3% nc ncf sc.

St George's to Commemorate the Royal Coronation db **(87)** n21 t23.5 f20.5 b22. It has just gone 8.30pm on Monday July 22nd 2013 and BBC Radio 4 has just announced that Kate the Duchess of Cambridge, has given birth to a baby boy, and both mother and child are doing well. Of course, that baby boy will be a future King of England; one, as a man in his mid-fifties, I hope never to see on the throne as his father should still be fully ensconced when it my time to grab my percentage of the angel's share. However, such joyous news meant that I made a rapid change to the whiskies I was due to taste. And I thought it only fitting that I should taste from the distillery closest to Cambridge and in which county the royal family have long had a family home, Sandringham. I not only taste this whisky but raise a glass of it to Prince Charles, with whom I have had the pleasure of meeting on several occasions, and welcome him to the joyous world of grandfatherhood. And of course the little, as yet un-named, baby in London, his eyes still unopened, and all around him a confused, cotton wool-minded, mystery. I wish you, Your little Highness, a long, happy and healthy life. Oh, and here's a little exclusive: just spoken to David Fitt who created this whisky. Originally it was meant to be bottled to celebrate the announcement of the expected royal baby. But they decided to switch it to the Coronation in order not to jinx the birth. So, how Fitting.... 46%. 1850 bottles.

Stephen Notman Whisky Live Taipei 2013 The English Whisky Co db **(95.5)** n24 t24 f23.5 b24. A ridiculously stunning cask which I selected from St George's to celebrate Stephen Notman's impressive five year stewardship of Whisky Live in Taipei... making this a very English Whisky affair. Bewildering and beguiling for a four-year-old, where the peat is confident yet elegent, the body crisp yet lush and the complexity and balance beyond comprehension for its age. It was a pleasure to help promote not just the best of Bristish, but truly world-class whisky to an appreciative Taiwanese audience. And just shows what magic happens when near perfect spirit meets a near perfect cask. 50.6%

Whisky Live Taipei 2013 Founders Release B1/416, dist 7/4/09 **(93)** n23.5 t23 f23.5 b23. Beautifully made; excellent sweetness and beautifully smoky. A quietly satisfying malt. 50.6%

FINLAND
PANIMORAVINTOLA BEER HUNTER'S Pori. Working.

Old Buck cask no. 4, dist Mar 04, bott Apr 10 db **(95)** n24 t23 f24 b24. Just read the tasting notes to the second release because, a dose of what almost seems like corn oil and ancient Demerara rum combined apart, oh - and an extra dose of oak, there is barely any difference. I will never, ever forget how I got this sample: I was giving a tasting in Helsinki a few months back to a horseshoe-shaped audience and a chap who had been sitting to my right and joining in with all the fun introduced himself afterwards as I signed a book for him as non other than Mika Heikkinen, the owner and distiller of this glorious whisky. I had not been told he was going to be there. His actual, touchingly humble words were: "You might be disappointed: you may think it rubbish and give it a low score. It just means I have to do better next time." No, I am not disappointed: I am astonished. No, it isn't rubbish: it is, frankly, one of the great whiskies of the year. And if you can do better next time, then you are almost certainly in line for the Bible's World Whisky of the Year award. 70.6%

TEERENPELI

Teerenpeli Single Malt Aged 8 Years oak cask db **(86)** n21.5 t22 f21 b21.5. Has moved on a notch or two from the five-year-old. A soft, simplistic experience, dependent on fudgy cream toffee and hazelnut. 43%

Teerenpeli Kaski Single Malt sherry cask db **(90.5)** n23 t23.5 f21.5 b22.5. A pristine sherry butt ensures massive fruit. Impressed. 43%

FRANCE
Single Malt
DISTILLERIE BERTRAND

Uberach db **(77)** n21 t19 f18 b19. Big, bitter, booming. Gives impression something's happening between smoke and grape... whatever it is, there are no prisoners taken. 42.2%

DISTILLERIE DES MENHIRS

Eddu Gold db (93) n22 t23 f24 b24. Rarely do whiskies turn up in the glass so rich in character to the point of idiosyncrasy. Some purists will recoil from the more assertive elements. I simply rejoice. This is so proud to be different. And exceptionally good, to boot!! 43%

⠶ **Eddu Silver** db (81) n20 t22 f19 b20. A curiosity of a whisky, though not up to the distillery's normal high standards. The base spirit hasn't been cut to advantage, so the feints tend to damage both nose and finish. Some astonishing sugars on deliver, though. 40%.

⠶ **Eddu Silver Broceliande** db (92.5) n23 both gentle and busy, the spices pepper but are charming about it; elsewhere there is a tandem between barley and greengage; t23 wow..! So juicy. A stunning mixture of salivating barley juice and something fruitier, thinned with lime; f23 heavier now with the spices much more attack-minded. Some caramel tart topped with stewed apple and raisin; b23.5 pure silk. A beautiful and engaging experience. 40%.

DISTILLERIE GLANN AR MOR

Glann Ar Mor Taol Esa 3ed Gwech 12 first fill bourbon barrel db (76) n18 t20 f18 b18. Sweet, oily, feinty. 46%. nc ncf. 674 bottles.

Glann Ar Mor Taol Esa 4ed Gwech 12 first fill bourbon barrel db (80.5) n19 t21 f20.5 b20. A very generous cut, but I can live with this. The malt is intense and is well backed by brooding, spiced tannins. 46%. Nc ncf. Celtic Whisky Ccompagnie. 949 bottles.

⠶ **Glann Ar Mor Taol Esa 4ed Gewch 13** first fill bourbon barrel db (78) n18 t21 f19 b20. Looks like the distiller wanted to get as many flavours as he could from the cut. 46%.

Glann Ar Mor Taol Esa 2l Gwech 13 first fill barrel db (73) n17 t19.5 f18 b18.5. I had hoped the feints might have taken a backward step: they haven't. 46%. nc ncf. 955 bottles.

⠶ **Glann Ar Mor Taol Esa 1an Gwech 14** first fill bourbon barrel db (79) n18 t20 f21 b20. Keeps up its feinty tradition. Ultra malty, though. 46%.

⠶ **Kornog 2013 For The Auld Alliance** first fill bourbon barrel db (94.5) n23 salty rock pools; t24 one of the most eye-wateringly intense deliveries produced by any European mainland distiller this year. The enormity of the barley is immeasurable, then ramped up even further by a big spoon-full of salt; entirely salivating and mind-blowing; f23.5 calms for the malt now to merely bathe in its own glow; some spices evolve but the usual mocha sweetness (and even a light hint of smoke) sees the malt out, perhaps helped along with gentle manuka honey; b24 an extraordinary whisky worthy of seeking and enjoying. In a style of its own. And when I say style...I mean style.... Specially tasted on 6th June 2014 to mark the 70th anniversary of the New Alliance... 58.7%.

⠶ **Kornog Saint Erwan 2014** first fill bourbon barrel db (88) n23 the usual rather wonderful salty-malty affair from this distillery; t23 a malt bomb exploding all over the palate; f20.5 long, spicy, though a tad bitter; b21.5 a slightly simplistic malt. But entirely charming. 50%.

Kornog Single Malt Whisky Breton Sant Ivy 2011 db (94) n23 t24 f23.5 b23.5. The nose, at least, says it was distilled on Islay. To a Frenchman, is that an honour or an insult...? For I have to say, this is the closest to a Scotch whisky I have ever tasted outside those cold, windswept lands..To be honest, this is better than your average Caol Ila, as the oak is of finer quality. Frankly, this is a never to be forgotten whisky. 578%. nc ncf sc. 249 bottles.

⠶ **Kornog Single Malt Saint Ivy 2014** first fill bourbon barrel db (94) n23.5 busy vanilla and ulmo honey. The smoke enters by the back door...and leaves again without anyone really noticing; the light sprinkling of salt on the marzipan is a masterstroke; t23 beautifully sumptuous malt, thickening almost into a Malteser candy, complete with milky chocolate; the smoke again keeps the very lowest profile imaginable. Despite this light enough for some salivating barley; f23.5 fabulously complex fade with the understated peat now helping the spices along; lilting mocha signs off; b24 what an elegant and quite delightful whisky. 58.9%.

Kornog Single Malt Tourbé Whisky Breton Sant Erwin 2013 first fill bourbon barrel db (87.5) n22.5 t22 f21.5 b21.5. Kind of lurches around the palate a bit. 50%. nc ncf sc.

Kornog Single Malt Tourbé (Peated) Whisky Breton Sant Ivy 2012 first fill bourbon barrel db (92) n22.5 t23 f23 b23.5. With the usual time constraints of writing this book and the number of awful, sulphured whiskies which blight my path, I had kept this back as something to look forward to: last year their 2011 bottling was a masterpiece: out-Islaying Islay. This, though, has its own French fingerprint upon it. Sweeter, more diffuse. But, Mon Dieu! A corker nonetheless! 599%. nc ncf sc. 260 bottles.

Kornog Single Malt Whisky Breton Sant Ivy 2013 first fill bourbon barrel db (94.5) n23.5 t24 f23 b24. An Ivy Leaguer in every respect. Remembered this from last time out....in some ways this is even better: as precise as a Michel Platini shot in off the post... 58.6%. nc ncf sc. Celtic Whisky Compagnie. 271 bottles.

Kornog Single Malt Tourbé Whisky Breton Taouarc'h An Hañv 2012 first fill ex bourbon cask db (93) n23 t23.5 f23 b23.5. Pulsing, phenolic and phenomenal. 58.7%.

Kornog Single Malt Tourbé (Peated) Whisky Breton Taourc'h Trived 12BC first fill bourbon barrel db **(95) n24 t23.5 f23.5 b24.** No off notes. No bitterness. Complexity on fill volume. I really do have to get to their distillery this year... now, where's that British Airways timetable...? *46%. nc ncf sc. 334 bottles.*

Kornog Taouarc'h Kentan db **(94.5) n24 t24 f23 b23.5.** Not sure there has been this number of perfectly rhapsodic notes coming out of France since Saint Sans was in his pomp... *57.1%*

Kornog Taourc'h Kentan 13 BC first fill barrel db **(90) n22 t22.5 f22 b23.5.** As soft as sun cream being spread over you while basking on a French beach. *46%. nc ncf. 907 bottles.*

⋰⋱ **Kornog Taouarc'h Kentan 14 BC** db **(92) n23** soft smoke drifting into a pool of brine; **t22** a sharp delivery, principally because of the slightly chunky distillation; the smoke enters the fray to sooth and settle; struggles a bit at first; **f24** much better now. There is a lovely milky mocha drift to this, aided by impressive Demerara; the smoke is now perfectly poised and elegant; **b23** only the other day I was telling someone about how this distillery's peated malt has a distinctly Islay feel to it. Well, that was before I tasted this: a malt which has very much its own signature and provenance. Incidentally, I tasted this, with all the other Kornog whiskies, on 6th June 2014 to mark the 70th anniversary of the D-Day landings. My late father, after battling Rommel in Africa, was fighting in Italy at the time. So I will use this whisky – combining British influence with the peat, American oak and French water and craftsmanship – to toast all those who showed bravery beyond anything we can possibly imagine. And, in particular, those – on whichever side - who never returned to tell the tale... *46%.*

Kornog Taourc'h Pevared 12 BC first fill barrel db **(92) n23.5 t23 f22.5 b23.** The language of peat is pretty universal. Laphroaig lovers in particular will rather like this one... *46%. nc ncf. 1007 bottles.*

DISTILLERIE GUILLON

Guillon No. 1 Single Malt de la montagne de Reims db **(87) n22 t21 f22 b22.** Right. I'm impressed. Not exactly faultless, but enough life here really to keep the tastebuds on full alert; By and large well made and truly enjoyable. Well done, Les Chaps! *46%*

DISTILLERIE MEYER

Meyer's Whisky Alsacien Blend Superieur db **(88.5) n22.5 t22.5 f21.5 b22.** Impressively clean, barley-thick and confident: a delight. *40%*

DISTILLERIE WARENGHEM

Armorik db **(91) n23 t22 f23 b23.** I admit it; I blanched, when I first nosed this, so vivid was the memory of the last bottling. This, though ,was the most pleasant of surprises. Fabulous stuff: one of the most improved malts in the world. *40%*

Armorik Double Maturation finished in oloroso casks db **(75) n18.5 t20 f18 b18.5.** Dull and decidedly out of sorts. *46%. ncf.*

Armorik Millésime Matured for 10 Years cask no. 3261 db **(92) n22.5 t23 f23 b23.** Never quite know what you are going to get from these messieurs. Didn't expect this bottle of delights, I must say. The sweetness is a bit OTT at one point, but just copes. *56.1%. sc.*

Armorik Sherry Finish db **(92) n22.5 t23.5 f23 b23.5.** The first sherry finish today which has not had a sulphur problem...and I'm in my eighth working hour...! Bravo guys! If their Classic was a note on sophistication, then this was an essay. *40%*

DOMAINE MAVELA

P&M Corsican Single Malt Aged 7 Years dist 05, bott 12 **(95) n23.5 t24 f23.5 b24.** Not been to this distillery yet and I don't speak much meaningful French. So not sure about the oak, though if I was a gambling guy (which I'm not) then it has the resonance of French oak, and it is this which appears to give the whisky its bold character. A distillery I must get to soon: it is rare to find a malt with this level of complexity and charm. Delightful: an absolute, near faultless joy of a malt. *42%*

KAERILIS

Kaerilis Le Grand Dérangement 15 Ans db **(78) n18 t22 f19 b19.** A breakdown of the oils doesn't help reveal the weaknesses from the distillate. A must for fans de nougat. *43%. nc ncf sc.*

Kaerilis l'Aube du Grand Dérangement 15 Ans db **(83.5) n20 t22.5 f20 b21.** Misfires when the revs are up, but purrs for moment on two on delivery as the sugar and barley kicks in to delicious effect. An enigmatic fruitiness enriches. *57%. nc ncf sc.*

WAMBRECHIES DISTILLERY

Wambrechies Single Malt Aged 8 Years db **(83) n20 t21 f21 b21.** There's that aroma again, just like the 3-y-o. Except how it kind of takes me back 30 years to when I hitchhiked across the Sahara. Some of the food I ate with the local families in Morocco and Algeria was among the best I have ever tasted. And here is an aroma I recognize from that time, though I can't say specifically what it is (tomatoes, maybe?). Attractive and unique to whisky, that's for sure. I rather like this malt. There is nothing quite comparable to it. One I need to investigate a whole lot more. 40%

Blends
P&M Blend Supérieur (82) n21 t21 f20 b20. Bitter and botanical, though no shortage of complexity. 40%. *Mavela Distillerie.*

P&M Whisky (89) n22 t23 f22 b22. No mistaking this is from a fruit distillery. Still quite North American, though. 40%

Vatted Malts
KAERILIS
Kaerilis Ster Vraz No 9 4 Year Old db **(80) n22 t21 f18 b19.** Plenty of salt and no little citrus. But undone by an oaky bitterness. 45%. nc ncf.

Kaerilis Ster Vraz No 9 4 Year Old db **(87) n21.5 t23.5 f20 b22.** What the hell was that...??? Something different, for sure. At its best, quite stunning. At its worst – at the death – hmmm, not great. Get your bucket and spade out for this one. 61.8%. nc ncf.

GERMANY
AV BRENNEREI ANDREAS VALLENDAR Wincheringen. Working.
Threeland Whisky dist 2007, bott code L-Wtr200701 db **(83) n19.5 t22.5 f20 b21.** Whilst pleasant enough in its own right, my eyes opened up at this one, as I remember last year's bottling as being one of the best from anywhere in Europe. That, I recall, was so wonderfully fresh and clean. This one, sadly, is bigger and oilier with evidence that the distiller has included some heads and tails which were excluded last time out. Still malty and mouth watering. But a useful lesson in learning the vital difference between good and great whisky. 46%

BAULAND BRENNEREI ALT ENDERLE Rosenburg. Working.
∷ **Alt Enderle Neccarus 8 Years Old Single Malt Whisky** db **(90.5) n22** surprisingly salty; **t23** one of Europe's most distinguished deliveries, being both gentle and rounded yet lively. Spicy but with a feel of boiled cherry sweets; **f23** more cough sweet depth, the salt lingers as the oaks arrive; **b22.5** a gently complex, delightful malt. Had it been scotch, I would have thought it was a coastal dram. Odd...! 43%

∷ **Alt Enderle Neccarus 12 Years Old Single Malt Whisky** db **(94) n23.5** a rich, fruity incarnation; **t23.5** superbly clean malt flushes the palate with myriad lively fruit notes of grape, cherry and plum. The spices are just about perfect in terms of intensity; **f23** long, good vanilla and butterscotch addition, though the fruit and spice carries the load; **b24** technically, among the best malt I have ever encountered from Germany. 43%

∷ **Alt Enderle Neccarus 15 Years Old Port Fass Single Malt Whisky** db **(92.5) n23** another salty Neccarus: dry grape skin comes over in waves; **t23.5** eye-watering fruit and saline mix; the sugars are subdues and of a fudgy style before mocha begins to soften the moment; **f23** a lovely chocolate and raisin fade; **b23** a chocolate mousse is on the loose. 51%

∷ **Alt Enderle Neccarus 15 Years Old Sherry Fass Single Malt Whisky** db **(86.5) n21 t22 f21.5 b22.** Clean sherry. But, after the mouth-watering delivery, relatively sweet and simple with just not enough gear changes. Pleasant, if not up to the standard of the other Neccarus. 49%

BIRKENHOF-BRENNEREI Nistertal. Working.
Fading Hill The Fourth bourbon casks, cask no. 22 & 23, dist Jul 08, bott 14 Mar 12 **(90.5) n22.5 t22 f23 b23.** Less Fading Hill: more F***ing Hell...!! Can't remember when I was taken down such a scary part of my past before: some of the aromas and flavours are like a time machine...! beautiful stuff. 45.7%. nc ncf.

BOSCH EDELBRAND Unterlenningen. Working.
Bosch Edelbrand Schwäbischer Whisky db **(83.5) n19 t22.5 f21 b21.** Could really do with making the cut a little more selective: has the promise to become a pretty high quality whisky. This shows some outstanding depth and honey for some time after the first, impressive delivery. 40%

BRANNTWEINBRENNEREI WEINBAU ADOLX KELLER Ramsthal.
A.K Whisky bott code L10209 db **(89.5) n22 t23 f22 b22.5.** Hardly faultless from a technical point of view. But if you can't enjoy something as raunchy and ribald as this, you might as well stop drinking whisky. 40%

BRENNEREI ANTON BISCHOX Wartmannsroth. Working.

Bischof's Rhöner Whisky bott code L-24 db **(75.5)** n17.5 t20 f18 b19. That unique blend of feints and intense, biscuity grains. Just checked: I see I gave it the same score as last year. Not only unmistakable, but consistently so! 40%

BRENNEREI DANNENMANN Owen. Working.

⁙ **Danne's Single Grain Schwäbischer Whisky Vom Bellerhof** dist 2006, bott L 0011 db **(85)** n21 t22 f21 b21. A rock hard whisky which crunches its way around the palate giving off flavours as flint might sparks. Eye-watering in places, though the rigid Demerara sugars are a treat. 43%

⁙ **Danne's Single Grain Schwäbischer Whisky Vom Bellerhof** dist 06, cask strength, bott 11 db **(88.5)** n22 big oak statement: almost bourbon in its liquorice and hickory firmness; t22.5 the house crash-bang-wallop delivery can be expected from the 43% abv bottling. Liquorice and hickory coated oils make the Demerara a softer prospect and helps it stick to the palate longer, though the spices have a bit of clout; f22 thick finale with the accent back on the bourbon: some cocoa teams up with the spiced hickory; b22 a good example of how reducing a whisky can damage it: compare this to the 43% version and here you see the oils unbroken and softening the flavour procession. 51.1%

⁙ **Danne's Single Malt Schwäbischer Whisky Vom Bellerhof** dist 09, bott code L 0017 db **(81)** n19 t21.5 f20 b20.5. A strange combination of nougat and thinness to the body: the over-widening of the cut usually results in nougat and heavy oils. Never finds a happy rhythm. 43%

⁙ **Danne's Single Malt Schwäbischer Whisky Vom Bellerhof** dist 09, cask strength, bott code L 0017 db **(87)** n20 t23 f22 b22. A huge whisky which kicks a lot harder than its 55% abv. Works a lot better than its sister 43% bottling, making the most of the golden syrup and grist mix, and the spiced cocoa fade. Pretty enjoyable. 54.9%

BRENNEREI ERICH SIGEL Dettingen. Working.

Original Dettinger Schwäbischer Whisky db **(88)** n21.5 t22.5 f22 b22. Softly sophisticated. 40%

BRENNEREI FABER Ferschweiler. Working.

Whisky aus der Eifel Aged 6 Years American oak, dist 2003 db **(91)** n23 t23 f22.5 b22.5. A riveting whisky of uncommonly high quality. 46%

BRENNEREI FRANK RODER Aalen - Wasseralfingen. Working.

Frank's Suebisch Cask Strength 2008 db **(91)** n22 t23 f23 b23. Frank has really got the hang of how to make the most of his still...a little stunner! And his cleanest yet. 57%

Frank's Suebisch Single Grain 2007 db **(86.5)** n21.5 t22 f21.5 b21.5. Consistent, gristy, mouth-watering fare. Does not try to be spectacular. More dissolving sugars this time. 40%

BRENNEREI HACK Pinzberg. Working.

Walburgis Franken db **(78)** n17 t20 f21 b20. While the nose puts the 'aahhhh!' in nougat, the sweet walnut-cake nuttiness on delivery and beyond makes some amends. 40%

BRENNEREI HENRICH Kriftel, Hessia. Working.

Gilors Fino Sherry Cask sherry cask, bott code L13032, dist Apr 10, bott May 13 db **(89.5)** n21 t22.5 f23 b23. Bravo! A sherry butt with not a hint of sulphur! 44%. sc. 866 bottles.

Gilors Port Cask sherry, bott code L13033, dist 2010, bott 2013 db **(86)** n20 t22 f22.5 b21.5. Thoroughly enjoyable and full of depth and no little fruit and spice. But the wide cut, apparent in the sherry version, is not tamed in quite the same effortless way. 44%. sc. 893 bottles.

BRENNEREI HÖHLER Aarbergen, Kettenbach. Working.

Whesskey Hessischer aus Stammwürze 4 Years Old db **(90)** n21 t22.5 f24 b22.5. There are so many things right with this whisky, but you also get the feeling – even when it as amazing as this - that something is wrong. Either way, bottling like this enliven any evening and give tired taste buds a new lease of life and a will to live... 57%

BRENNEREI HÖNING Winnweiler, Donnersbergkreis. Working.

Taranis Single Cask Limited Edition Aged 3 Years Limousin-Eiche barrel, cask no. 1, dist Sep 08 **(84)** n21 t21.5 f20 b21.5. Anyone for sweetened lemon tea? Pretty refreshing dram – though unusual! 46%. sc. 679 bottles.

BRENNEREI HÜBNER Stadelhofen, Steinfeld. Working.
Hubner Los Nr 3 db **(80.5) n20 t22.5 f18 b20**. Overwhelmed by fruit as far as complexity is concerned, but there is a distinctive smoky, salivating theme to this nonetheless. The balance has been trashed and if it were a novel, you'd have to read it three times...and still make no sense of it. A David Lynch film of a whisky...and I love it, though I have no idea why. 40%

BRENNEREI LOBMÜLLER Talheim. Working.
Schwäbischer Whisky Single Grain cask no. 7 db **(86.5) n20 t22.5 f22 b22**. A friendly, big-hearted, soul full of toffee-chocolate chewiness. Highly enjoyable. 41%

BRENNEREI MARTIN MEIER Neuravensburg. Working.
Mein 9. Fass db **(84) n19 t21.5 f22 b21.5**. The light spices and dissolving sugars melt beautifully into the malt. Nose apart, this is a ja, nicht ein 9... 42%

BRENNEREI MARTIN ZIEGLER Baltmannsweiler. Working.
Esslinger Single Malt Aged 8 Years db **(85) n20.5 t22 f21 b21.5**. Malty, nutty, a decent degree of sweetness and toffee marzipan. A well-made malt which you appreciate more as you acclimatise to its compact style. 42%

BRENNEREI RABEL Owen. Working.
Schwäbischer Whisky db **(76.5) n17 t21.5 f18 b20**. Here's something different. While the nose, or at least the getting it right, is a work in progress, the delivery and body are much more on the ball thanks mainly to a rich treacle and prune element which sees off the thicker distillate. The finish, though, confirms the fault lines. 40%

BRENNEREI VOLKER THEURER Tübingen-Unterjesingen. Working.
Sankt Johann Single Barrel Aged 8 Years bott code BL-2010 db **(85) n19.5 t22 f21.5 b22**. Fabulous fun. Once it gets over the drying tobacco nose the inevitable nougat is delivered. But it comes with a milk-creamy mocha which develops in intensity and with just the right doses of treacle to keep the sweetness at desired levels. Good background spices too. A very likeable character, this Saint Johann. 46.5%

BRENNEREI ZAISER Köngen. Working.
Zaiser Schwäbischer Whisky db **(83) n23 t21.5 f19 b19.5**. Surprisingly dry and constricted in development considering the beautiful soft sugars on the nose which also boast excellent clarity. 40%

BRENNEREI ZIEGLER Freudenberg, North Württemberg. Working.
Aureum 1865 Single Malt 5 Years Old db **(86) n20.5 t22.5 f21.5 b21.5**. Mocha with plenty of grist and muscovado stirred in. 43%
Aureum 1865 Vontage Single Malt 2008 db **(90.5) n20 t24 f23**. Still one enormous barley orgy, though a little bit of chalky butterscotch and cocoa tries to offer a towel of modesty; **b23.5** after a less than great start on the nose it truly blows you away with a massive impact. 53.9%. ncf.

DESTILLERIE DREXLER Working.
Drexler Arrach No. 1 Bayerwald Single Cask cask no. 262, dist May 07, bott May 10 db **(88.5) n21 t23 f22 b22.5**. Very good bitter-sweet marriage, but better still is the luxuriant mouth-feel. A well constructed malt. 46%. 210 bottles.

DESTILLERIE HERMANN MÜHLHÄUSER Working.
Mühlhäuser Oberwalder Single Grain bott code L0612 db **(86.5) n22 t22 f21 b21.5**. An enjoyable whisky, showing sturdy and at times sophisticated oak and good early sugar structure. The grain is a bit on the shy side, though: may have had a better chance to shine at 46%. 40%
Mühlhäuser Schwäbischer Whisky aus Korn bott code L1012 db **(85) n21 t21 f21.5 b21.5**. Clean, crisp, sweet, honeyed: am I the only one who thinks this tastes like distilled Golden Grahams...? 40%
Mühlhäuser Schwäbischer Whisky aus Korn db **(90.5) n23 t23 f22 b22.5**. Another stunning bottling from this excellent distiller. You have to admire the subtlety of the complexity of this whisky. 41%
Mühlhäuser Schwäbischer Whisky aus Korn db **(90) n22.5 t23 f22 b22.5**. So different! If you are into this, it'll be pastoral perfection. 40%

EDELBRAENDE-SENFT Salem-Rickenbach. Working.

SENFT bott code L-SW36, dist Jun 09, bott Aug 12 db (76.5) n18 t20.5 f19 b19. From the chewy nougat school of malt. Lots of toffee, too. But limited in scope. *42%. nc ncf.*

⁙ **Senft Bodensee Whisky** dist Dec 2010, bott Dec 2013, bott code L-SW37 db (83.5) n21 t22 f20 b21. Usual feints but really good distribution of sugared almonds. *42%. nc.*

⁙ **Senft Bodensee Whisky** dist Dec 10, bott Jul 14, bott code L-SW38 db (84) n21 t22 f20 b21. Intriguing and attractive mixture of citrus and celery. Some feinty cocoa around. *42%. nc.*

⁙ **Senft Bodensee Whisky Fabstáke** db (87.5) n21 t22.5 f22 b22. Despite the obvious feintiness, strikes out with an impressive boldness. A mysterious smokiness adds lustre to the muscovado sugars and extra weight. *55%. nc.*

EDELBRENNEREI PETER HOHMANN Nordheim, Rhön. Working.

Rhöner Grain Whisky Aged 6 Years db (89) n21 t22.5 f23 b22.5. Impressively made and matured with a quite lovely marriage between the sugars and spices. *40%*

EDELOBST-BRENNEREI ZIEGLER Freudenberg. Working.

AVREVM db (83) n21.5 t21 f20 b20.5. A most peculiar, though not unattractive, marriage of marmalade and hops. *43%. 1000 bottles.*

FEINBRENNEREI SEVERIN SIMON Alzenau-Michelbach. Working.

Simon's 10 Years Old Bavarian Pure Pot Still db (86.5) n21.5 t21.5 f22.5 b21. Not a whiskey to rush. Takes several hours to get to know this chap. When they say Pure Pott Still, I am sure they mean a mixture of malted and unmalted barley. Because that is the only style that offers a whiskey as rock hard as this with virtually no give on the palate. If there is any yield, it comes in a vaguely fruity form but this is a whiskey which sets up an impenetrable barrier and defies you to pass. Fascinating and very different. *40%*

FINCH HIGHLAND WHISKY DISTILLERY Nellingen, Alb-Donau. Working.

Finch Destillers Edition barrique matured/bourbon finish, bott Apr 12 db (94.5) n24 t23.5 f23 b24 These guys know exactly what they are doing... *40%*

Finch Schwäbischer Highland Whisky dist 06, bott 13 db (88) n23 t21.5 f21 b22.5. Not quite a perfect sherry butt, but one that adds an interesting spice side show. *41%. 449 bottles.*

Finch Schwäbischer Highland Whisky Destillers Edition dist 07, bott Feb 13 db (87.5) n22.5 t22.5 f21 b21.5. Chirpy, but not entirely on song... *41%.*

⁙ **Finch Schwäbischer Whisky Single Malt Barrel Proof 3/14** db (89) n22.5 big oak spice kick, backed up with some commanding dark sugars; a hint of French toast; t22.5 serious delivery full on and toasty (non-French!) at first. Again the dark sugars about, including manuka honey. Some serious treacle tart amid the oils of a slightly generous cut on the stills; f22 the spices – and feints - linger with intent; b22 this distillery has upped its game. Hugely impressive whisky, even if liberties have been taken with the spirit run: you got away with it! Well done, chaps! *54%.*

⁙ **Finch Schwäbischer Whisky Single Malt Destillers Edition 03/14** db (93) n22.5 a soft mosaic of malt and toffee, enriched by the odd strand of something a little grassy; t23 silky soft delivery, the odd hint of raisin in the creamy fudge; f24 long with the cream bun fade, perhaps with a hint of juicy sherry trifle: delicate and elegant to a fault...and topped with a sublime late spice; b23.5 from inside my tasting room I am looking out onto my quintessential English garden, ancient-walled and rose clad; and the thousand year old church which stands a few tombstones back strikes four bells. The birds continue their frenzy of feeding their young. I am regarding a goldfinch now, its golden wing and red face reflecting the afternoon sun and below it, on the feeders, are greenfinches gorging on the sunflower colonels. Below them, hopping around on the ground are chaffinches, mopping up the fallen seeds. Finches, finches everywhere. Even in my tasting room. And all of them gladdening my heart... *40%*

Finch White Label barrique barrels db (91) n23 t22.5 f22 b23 When I read my first books on archaeology and Iron Age man some 45 years ago, I wondered why they grew spelt and tried to imagine what it tasted like. Now I understand. I look forward to someone unearthing the first Iron Age pot still... A Finch which sings most beautifully *40%. Spelt and wheat.*

GUTSBRENNEREI AGLISHARDT Nellingen. Working.

HFG Dinkelwhisky Single Cask No 2 db (87.5) n21.5 t22 f22 b22. good, honest whisky with plenty of charm from the grain. *41.5%*

HAMMERSCHMIEDE Zorge. Working.

The Alrik Smoked Hercynian Single Malt 4 Years Old db (95) n24 t23.5 f23.5 b24 Beautiful weight, just-so sweetness, different...and simply adorable. *52.3%. nc ncf.*

∴ **The Alrik Edition 1912 The Early Bird** matured in 1st-fill PX hogsheads, finished in fresh 1st-fill PX Butts db **(84) n21 t22 f20 b21.** I have long struggled with PX and peat together. Just find it too much: a bit like having sex while someone is tickling your feet. Certainly this K2 of a malt has its merits, as it is rather wonderfully distilled and the early sugars are a delight. But I have to say the other "s" word is in there also, though under this smoky onslaught, it nearly gets away with it. *52.3%. nc ncf. 1111 bottles.*

∴ **The Alrik Edition 1913 Mittsommer** matured in three 1st-fill Marsala hogsheads, finished in one 1st-fill PX butt db **(92) n23** a genuine punch to the peat: Fisherman's Friends and boiled fruit candy combine impressively; as it dries towards ashy phenols a little Rota Rua hoves into view...; **t23.5** the delivery is no less in your face than the nose, though far more sugars at play. Demerera leads – even with a nod towards its rum counterpart – and there is a distinct treacle tart mid-ground. Smoked, of course; **f22** that little off note on the nose is just about detectable through the peaty swamp but no the spices really sizzle; **b23.5** an enormous, salivating whisky which makes light of the odd defect. Concentrate on the sugar and smoke mix and you will be blown away. *49.7%. nc ncf. 666 bottles.*

∴ **The Alrik Edition 1912 Mittwinter** matured in 1st-fill PX hogsheads, finished in fresh 1st-fill Château d'Yquem db **(89) n23** rich almost beyond words: the grape is on a sugary plateau...and smoke is everywhere. Huge...; **t23.5** and no shrinking violet on the plate. The molasses is colossal, yet somehow the peat does find a way to offer some form of alternative distraction of enormity. And at times, the two giants appear on the same wavelength; oh, and did I mention the liquorice...? Well, it's big...; **f20** undone a little with sulphur; **b22.5** nothing too bleak about this Mittwinter... *49.7%. nc ncf. 275 bottles.*

∴ **The Glen Els Banyul Aged 5 Years Cask Strength** cask no. 6/11, dist 26 May 2008, bott 24 Jun 2013, bott code. L1551 db **(92) n23** delicately smoked pear in syrup; **t23** dense enough to stand a spoon in, there is enough fruit to take away from the sugary edge to make this a comfortable delivery. When the spices rock up they are pretty full on; **f22.5** spiced vanilla as it dries; **b23.5** love the way the sugars are controlled throughout. And a clean wine cask goes a long way... *46.6%. sc.*

∴ **The Glen Els Cream Sherry Aged 5 Years Cask Strength** cask no. 135, dist 03 Jun 08, bott 04 Mar 14, bott code. L1590 db **(87) n21 t23 f22 b21.** An interesting one, this. As you know, I bang on big time angered by the use of sherry-treated casks in whisky. Here we have a cream sherry cask which appears innocent of any such possible charges against it. It is, to all intents and purposes, clean. Yet on this occasion it disappoints. Like the Malaga bottling it is rounder than a billiard ball and softer than blancmange. But, unlike the Malaga, it doesn't have quite enough personality to entertain. A little bit of a one trick pony, with its toffee-raisin nose, delivery and finish. Enjoyable, but travels over some flat and featureless land. *48.2%. 294 bottles.*

The Glen Els Dark Sherry Aged 5 Years woodsmoked, cask no. 77, dist 17 jan 08, bott 15 Feb 13 db **(82) n22 t22 f18 b20.** At its best when the smog (or should that be frog?) of the syrup of dates and prunes and smoke begins to thin slightly. But a faulty cask doesn't help. *47.1%. nc ncf sc. 244 bottles.*

∴ **The Glen Els Moscatel Aged 5 Years Cask Strength** cask no. 146, dist 03 Jun 08, bott 24 Jul 13, bott code. L1552 db **(86) n22.5 t21.5 f21 b21.** A busy little so-and-so. Perfectly enjoyable and clean. But one of those occasions where the fruit and woodsmoke fail to find a common land, a bit like David Cameron and Angela Merkel at any given moment, meaning there is little room for compromise and plenty for discord. *46%. -sc. 251 bottles.*

The Glen Els Dulce Negro Malaga Aged 5 Years Cask Strength cask no. 42, dist 26 Sep 07, bott 26 Oct 12 db **(87.5) n22 t23 f22 b20.5.** The single malt whiskies of Glen Els are not exactly shrinking violets: indeed, it is hard to think of any malt distillery in the world bottling such hairy-chested, challenging drams. As is the nature of the beast, some work, others don't. This, once the taste buds have time to overcome the shock and adjust, works. Just... *45.8%. nc ncf sc. 258 bottles.*

∴ **The Glen Els Rivesaltes Aged 5 Years Cask Strength** cask no. 126, dist 26 May 08, bott 22 Apr 13, bott code. L1597 db **(93) n23.5** there is almost a coastal feel to this: salt on the wind mingling with the smoke of log fires. Fruity, too with some pretty ripe greengage and prune juice. Rather satisfying...; **t23** luscious and soft: there is a sharpness to both fruit and grain which satisfies deeply; **f23** the smoke returns to rumble and now we have a more fruitcakey fade; **b23.5** it is just coming u to two in the afternoon and I have been tasting since 7:30am. And this is the first genuinely enjoyable whisky of the day: thank you Glen Els! *46.6%. sc. 246 bottles.*

The Glen Els Elements Air db **(90.5) n22.5 t22 f23 b23.** A beautifully refined malt. But I just hope that Glen Els is the name of the actual living, breathing distiller, not the brand... otherwise I see the good ol' Scotch Whisky Association finding another reason not to tackle their own problems and instead try to drown at birth a foreign distiller straying into the dangerous field of Scottish nomenclature... 45.9%. 600 bottles.

The Glen Els Ember woodsmoked, bott code. L1541 db **(93) n23 t23.5 f23 b23..5.** Bold, rich and proudly idiosyncratic. Really can't fault it! 45.9%. nc ncf.

The Glen Els Four Seasons 2013 claret, bott code. L1546 db **(89.5) n22 t23 f22.5 b22.5.** Vintage toffee... 45.9%. nc ncf sc. 250 bottles.

The Glen Els Four Seasons 2013 Dark Sherry bott code. L1530 db **(77) n19 t20 f19 b19.** I know, I know...some will ram raid any store carrying this. But for me: simply doesn't work as the profound sugars, the smoke and grape just never gel and find a happy balance. 45.9%. nc ncf sc. 250 bottles.

⁘ **The Glen Els Four Seasons 2014 Rich Madiera** bott code. L1591 db **(75) n19 t20 f18 b18.** Fruity, for sure. But spoiled by the all too familiar invasion of sulphur. Many Germans, though, will interpret this as "smoke". In this case, no smoke without ire... 45.9%. 264 bottles.

⁘ **The Glen Els Four Seasons 2014 Ruby Port** bott code. L1589 db **(90) n22** vanilla with spiced fruit dripping from every corner; **t23** rich delivery with more than a hint of garibaldi biscuit...and spice; **f22** maybe a sliver of ginger on the oily vanilla; **b23** a miniscule hint of feints on nose and finish but otherwise a malt which really makes the most of the high quality Port influence. 45.9%. 400 bottles.

The Glen Els The Journey European oak casks, bott code L1532 db **(94) n24 t24 f22.5 b23.5.** So date rich, probably the first whisky that'd appeal to a Tuareg... Ironically, as I taste this my parrot, Percy, is in the next room listening to Rachmaninoff's Piano Concerto #2 – which was used, I think, in Brief Encounter. I assume The Journey, then, is by train...to the Tuaregs... 43%. nc ncf sc.

The Glen Els Moscatel Aged 5 Years cask no. 79, dist 17 Jan 08, bott 18 Jan 13 db **(86.5) n21.5 t22.5 f21 b21.5.** Oddly enough, this comes from a cask which is in supreme nick and displaying not the vaguest hint of sulphur: a rarity. However, the smoke and the Moscatel are not the happiest of bed fellows: very tight, especially with the eye-watering sugars, with niggardly development. The more harmonious passages, aided by sultana and praline, are a treat, though. 46.1%. nc ncf sc. 257 bottles.

The Glen Els Pedro Ximenez Woodsmoked Aged 5 Years Cask Strength cask no. 65, dist 6 Nov 07, bott 17 Apr 13 db **(77) n19 t21 f18 b19.** Not technically the greatest butt of all time. But the enormity of the PX, the chocolate and the smoke...just too much. Of everything. 46.6%. nc ncf sc. 252 bottles.

⁘ **The Glen Els Rare & Special Malaga Single Cask Release Aged 6 Years** cask no. 83, dist 17 Jan 2008, bott 22 Apr 14, bott code L1596 db **(94) n24** succulent juice but attractively dry. Elements of liqueurice and coffee, too. The spices make a polite cough in the background; **t23** and succulent juice on delivery, also. Like the nose, the sugars are controlled tidily and the fruit is more linear to chewing grape and plum skins; **f23.5** subtle, lightly spiced with a delicate mocha fade; **b23.5** if there was a "Soft As A Baby's Bum" award in this book, this'd probably walk away with it... 46.6% 348 bottles.

⁘ **The Glen Els Rarities 2013** bott code. L1578 db **(88.5) n22** salted sandalwood; a plethora of herbs; **t22** a busy, spicy delivery with a rich moist fruitcake follow through; spices out towards the middle; **f22.5** spiced vanilla and toasted fudge; **b22** should be called Varieties: after all, it is the spice of life... 45.9%. nc ncf. 222 bottles.

The Glen Els Rich Claret Aged 5 Years woodsmoked, cask no. 78, dist 17 jan 08, bott 18 Jan 13 db **(92) n23.5 t24 f21.5 b23.** As though distilled by Dali, there are wonderful eccentricities to the overall piece. The secret, though, is the superb barrel choice: breathtakingly high quality despite having been treated, gently, somewhere en route. A Grand Cru of European whisky... 45.9%. nc ncf sc. 261 bottles.

The Glen Els Unique Distillery Edition First Fill Sherry Casks, bott code. L1547 db **(89) n22 t23 f21.5 b22.5.** Truly awash with sherry. But the pounding spices and rich cherry fruitcake makes up for the slight furriness towards the end. 45.9%. nc ncf sc.

The Glen Els Unique Single Dulce Negra Malaga cask no. 93, dist 08, bott 12 db **(92) n22.5 t23.5 f22.5 b23.5.** Glen Els may have got a few of their other wine casks slightly around their necks. But this has worked astonishingly well. In over 15,000 whiskies tasted in the last decade, I cannot find another whisky as a reference point. Truly unique. 44.4%. nc ncf sc. 384 bottles.

⁘ **The Glen Els Wayfare The Cask Strength** bott code. L1587 db **(93) n22.5** a slight touch of feint, but the intensity of the sugars and spice is like looking into the distance and seeing some kind of pitch black storm cloud heading your way...; **t23** the delivery confirms some heavy oils which reveal how borderline the cut is, but packs with it an astonishing array of dark sugars and chewy liquorice, all enlivened by very warming spice; **f24** adorable finale of molasses stirred into a cup of minty chocolate; **b23.5** some kind of oily, hallucinogenic, sugar, cocoa and spice concoction which plays is played out at maximum volume. The word "big" hardly does it justice... 57.9%. nc ncf.

HELMUT SPERBER Rentweinsdorf. Working.

Sperbers Destillerie Malt Whisky dist 2002 db **(77.5) n17.5 t20 f21 b19**. Very similar to the 46% except the sugars are much more eccentric. *59%*

KINZIGBRENNEREI MARTIN BROSAMER Biberach. Working.

Kinzigbrennerei Martin Brosamer Single Malt oak cask, dist Apr 05, bott Sep 08 db **(84) n20.5 t21 f21.5 b21**. For all the obvious nougat, the barley is given a clear stage from which to make its sweet speech. *42%. 120 bottles.*

KLEINBRENNEREI FITZKE Herbolzheim-Broggingen. Working.

Derrina Dinkel Schwarzwälder Single Grain bott code. L11108 db **(85) n22 t22 f20 b21**. Many European distillers working with spelt have come unstuck over the years. This is a better bottling than most, as they have coped better with the grain during fermentation. There a genuinely complex layering to the understated sugars which allows the soft chewiness of the grain to come through with ease. However, unusually for this distillery, less than wonderful oak has a deleterious effect on the finale. *43%*

Derrina Einkorn Schwarzwälder Single Grain bott code. L11209 db **(96) n23.5 t24.5 f24 b24**. Not every day one gets to taste Einkorn whisky. On this evidence, and when so carefully distilled, a great pity. For this is one of the great whiskies of the world. *43%*

Derrina Gerste Schwarzwälder Single Grain bott code. L5508 db **(80.5) n19 t21 f20 b20.5**. No little irony that a distillery which specialises so brilliantly in obscure grains gets it slightly wrong when it comes to barley. The juniper on the nose gets this off to a gin-style start...and finish. The intervening cocoa is the high spot. *43%*

Derrina Grünkern Schwarzwälder Single Grain bott code. L11009 db **(94.5) n23 t24 f23.5 b24**. This may be Green Spelt from the Black Forest. But this tastes as though it has been matured by a Blue Lagoon by Golden Sands. The most coastal whisky I have ever encountered from a land-locked European mainland distillery. Ein stunner! *43%*

Derrina Hafer Schwarzwälder Single Grain bott code. L6205 db **(91) n22.5 t24 f22 b22.5**. No faulting a beautifully made, complex malt. Any fan of oak whisky, like myself, will not be disappointed. *43%*

Derrina Hirse Schwarzwälder Single Grain bott code. L6507 db **(87.5) n21 t22.5 f22 b22**. By strange coincidence, my Meyer's parrot, Perseus, is tucking into some millet while I sample its distilled form. This is enjoyable (and very different!) but I think Percy is enjoying his experience more than me... *43%*

Derrina Reis Schwarzwälder Single Grain bott code. L10309 db **(84) n21 t21.5 f20.5 b21**. Purists argue that distilled rice isn't whisky. Well it's a grain, so surely, in my book, that counts. Whether it makes good distillate is another matter and the lack of body, complexity and anywhere for it to go is clear for all to see. Some pleasant sugary, chocolate moments, though. *43%*

Derrina Triticale Schwarzwälder Single Grain bott code. L 10409 db **(95) n23 t23.5 f24 b24.5**. A very different, but wonderful experience, conjured by a very rare and unusual grain. On this evidence, would love to see it in greater use for this, make no mistake, is a world classic... *43%*

Derrina Dinkelmalz Schwarzwälder Single Malt bott code. L5509 db **(93.5) n22 t23.5 f24.5 b23.5**. A wonderful essay in flavour development. A genuine treat of a malt. *43%*

Derrina Emmermalz Schwarzwälder Single Malt bott code. L6809 db **(90) n22 t23 f22.5 b22.5**. Another form of spelt and this one is comfortable and relaxed on the palate, allowing a really pleasing complexity. *43%*

Derrina Gerstenmalz Schwarzwälder Single Malt bott code. L5409 db **(89) n20 t22 f24 b23**. Splutters around on the nose and delivery but when it finds the map it finds the most satisfyingly complex of all routes. *43%*

Derrina Hafermalz Schwarzwälder Single Malt bott code. L6709 db **(87.5) n21.5 t22 f22 b22**. Lush and far from shy. *43%*

Derrina Roggenmalz Schwarzwälder Single Malt bott code. L5609 db **(85.5) n21 t21 f22 b21.5**. The oils are heavy and ponderous, swamping many of the more intrinsically fruity tones to be expected from the grain. Enjoyable, but could have been so much better. *43%*

Derrina Torf-Rauchmalz Schwarzwälder Single Malt bott code. L11309 db **(85.5) n19 t22 f22.5 b22**. Not quite the greatest nose, with the peat offering a stale tobacco aroma. But pedals hard to make up for lost ground with a sweet, gristy smokiness which charms as it relaxes. Lots of maple syrup fills in the cracks. *43%*

Derrina Weizenmalz Schwarzwälder Single Malt bott code. L5709 db **(88) n22 t21.5 f22.5 b22**. You expect spice from wheat whisky – and here you get it, believe me! *43%*

Schwarzwälder Whisky Weizenmalz bott code. L5706 db **(94) n23 t23 f24 b24**. Superbly made whisky with thumping character despite its fresh and delicate nature. One of Europe's finest, for sure. *43%*

KORNBRENNEREI WAGNER Dauborn. Working.

Golden Ground Grain Whisky Original Dauborner dist 2005 db **(88) n21 t23 f22 b22.** A little extra feints has worked well for the rich and complex body. 46%

KOTTMANN´S EDELDESTILLAT-BRENNEREI Bad Ditzenbach. Working.

Schwäbischer Whisky lot no. 120705 **(78.5) n19 t20 f19 b19.5.** Heavy, oily and with much nougat to chew on. 40%

MÄRKISCHEN SPEZIALITÄTEN BRENNEREI Hagen. Working.

Bonum Bono New Make Fassgelagert db **(89) n22 t23 f22 b22.** Malteser candy in distilled form. Unbelievably malty, helped along by thin milk chocolate and some compelling beech honey. 55%

⋰ **Tronje Von Hagen Single Malt Höhlenwhisky** cask number 1 db **(94.5) n23.5** uncompromisingly fruity. Pears, apples, grape skins all add to an increasingly dense and increasingly impermeable aroma; **t24** an outpouring of early sugars cover the range from icing sugar light to molasses viscous; some manuka honey gets in there but as the spices begin to rise, a few liquorice and treacle elements arrive; **f23** plateaus out allowing in, at last, the malt against a simple background of vanilla; **b24** this is a monumental whisky: to a degree one of the sweetest of the year without losing shape or direction. A triumph for a brand new whisky distillery. And entirely fitting as the one I tasted on the eve of the 2014 World Cup Final weekend. Might have a glass of this in hand while watching to see if Germany can carry on where they left off against Brazil. And if their display is as good as this malt, then the cup is theirs... 55%

NORBERT WINKELMANN Hallerndorf. Working.

Fränkischer Rye Whisky db **(93.5) n24 t24 f22.5 b23.** For the record, the nose is so good to this that I kept it with me one evening after a badly sulphured cask from another distillery had ruined my tasting for the day. The fruity beauty of this was not just balm, but a reminder of just how wonderful whisky should touch you. 42%

NORDPFALZER EDELOBST & WHISKYDESTILLE Höning. Working.

⋰ **Taranis Pfalzer 4 Years Old Single Malt Whisky** Amarone Cask Finished dist Sept 09 db **(88.5) n22** big, a little feinty, but the spiced fruit stars; **t23.5** when the feints work in your favour: a huge, sumptuous honey-sweetened tide of chocolate and raisin; **f21** and when they don't: tangy from the wide cut, sadly. But at keast the fruit now offers a trifle and custard finale...with spices, of course; **b22** big and rather beautiful, in its own cumbersome way... especially in its delivery of fruit. 50.80%. 440 bottles.

OBSTBRENNEREI MÜCK Birkenau. Working.

Old Liebersbach Smoking Malt Whisky bott code. L1105 db **(83.5) n21 t21.5 f21 b20.** Good heavens! Don't find many whiskies like this one around the world. Almost a Sugar Fest in part, especially in the earlier stages, then bitters out with an almost shocking suddenness. Fascinating and dramatic, though perhaps not for the purist. 43%

PRIVATBRENNEREI SONNENSCHEIN Witten-Heven. Demolished.

Sonnenschein 15 db **(79.5) n19.5 t21 f19 b20.** So, it's back!! In its youth, this was a tough whisky to entertain. Many years on and some of the old faults remain, but it has picked up a touch of elegance along the way. 41%

BRENNEREI REINER MÖSSLEIN Zeilitzheim. Working.

Fränkischer Whisky db **(91) n23 t23 f22.5 b22.5.** Rich, earthy, pungent, full of character and quite adorable. Perhaps an acquired taste for single malt stick-in-the-muds, though... 40%

SEVERIN SIMON Alzenau-Michelbach, Aschaffenburg. Working.

Simon's Bavarian Pure Pot Still Whiskey bott code L0011 db **(84) n20 t22.5 f20 b21.5.** Have been looking forward to locking horns with this one again; the last time we met my teeth almost shattered against its rigidity. A different animal this time, with the pine and lemon nose reminding me I have washing up to do. The first minute after delivery is the high point, where for a short while everything comes together for a sweet and tart chewy treat. But the finish carries on with the pine... 40%

SLYRS Schliersee-Neuhaus. Working.

Slyrs Bavarian Single Malt Sherry Edition No. 1 finished in Oloroso, lot no. L00354, bott 2013 **(86) n20 t22 f22 b22.** Anyone out there who loves cream toffee and spice? This malt has your name on it. 46%

Slyrs Bavarian Single Malt Sherry Edition No. 1 finished in Pedro Ximénez, lot no. LO2491, bott 2013 (88.5) n21 t23 f22 b22.5. Can't say PX is usually my favourite cask for whisky maturation. But I doff my feathered hat to these clever Bavarians: it has done the trick here! 46%

SPREEWALD-BRENNEREI Schlepzig. Working.
Sloupisti 4 Years (Cask Strength) db (94) n23 t24 f23 b24. A mind-blowing fruitfest. Just love the clarity to the flavours. This is such great fun...!! 64.8%

STAATSBRAUEREI ROTHAUS AG Grafenhausen-Rothaus. Working.
Black Forest Single Malt Whisky bourbon cask, dist Dec 07, bott Mar 11 db (79.5) n19 t20.5 f20 b20. This is one of the distilleries in Germany I haven't yet visited. So puzzled by what was in my glass, I called my dear friend Julia Nourney who sent me the sample. "Julia. Do they distill from beer, including the hops?" "You asked me exactly the same question last year", she replied. I had forgotten, until she reminded me. Apparently they don't. But it kind of tells a story in itself. 43%

STEINHAUSER DESTILLERIE Kressbronn, Baden-Württemberg. Working.
Brigantia 3 Years Old bott L-12/12 db (79) n19 t21 f19 b20 Huge malt statement, as is the distillery style. But it appears someone decided to try and extract as much spirit as possible, because the cut seems to be a little too wide for comfort here: the oils are unforgiving. 43%

STEINWÄLDER BRENNEREI SCHRAML Erbendorf. Working.
Stonewood 1818 dist 1999 db (91) n22.5 t23 f22.5 b23. Consistant throughout with a superb and endearing degree of sweetness. High quality stuff. 45%

UNIVERSITÄT HOHENHEIM Working.
Hohenheim Universität Single Malt (82) n21 t20 f20 b21. The aroma is atractively nutty, marzipan even, and clean; the taste offers gentle oak, adding some weight to an otherwise light, refreshing maltiness. Pleasant if unspectacular. 40%. Made at the university as an experiment. Later sold!

WEINGUT MÖßLEIN Kolitzheim. Working.
Weingut Mößlein Fränkischer Whisky 5 Years Old bott code L01/11 db (91.5) n22.5 t22 f23 b23. A joyous whisky but something very odd about it.... 40%

WHISKY DESTILLERIE LIEBL Bad Kötzting. Working.
Coillmór Kastanie Single Cask chestnut cask, cask no. 19, dist 24 Feb 06, bott code. LB0311 db (91.5) n22 t23 f23.5 b23. This is a distillery capable of making whisky at both ends of the quality scale. This beautifully intense malt is the best yet produced by the distillery and most definitely Bundeslige...! Hang on! Just noticed it is from a chestnut cask (hence the chestnuts????) Bugger! It ain't whisky, folks! 50.2%. 60 bottles.

WHISKY-DESTILLERIE ROBERT FLEISCHMANN Eggolsheim. Working.
Austrasier Single Cask Grain cask no. 1, dist Jun 98, bott May 11 db (91) n22 t22.5 f23.5 b23. I really don't know whether the Germans are able to knight someone for their services to whisky. But if they can't they should change the law. Another wonderful piece of high quality whisky fun. 40%. sc.

Austrasier Single Cask Grain cask no. 1, dist Jun 98, bott Apr 12 db (95.5) n23.5 t24 f24 b24.5. Big, thick, pulsing... this is one macho whisky that is sweet enough for the ladies to like. This distillery's finest hour... or two... 40%. nc ncf sc.

Blaue Maus 20 Years Old cask no. 1, db (89) n23 t22 f22 b22. Doesn't enjoy the same bourbon-rich vibrancy of the 20-y-o Spinnaker, which is a sweeter herr altogether. 40%. sc.

Blaue Maus 20 Years Old db (87) n22 t22.5 f21 b21.5. The first whisky of the longest day of the year – and it might take me all the hours the sun is up to work my way through this one...Good grief...technically flawed, yet compelling and strangely enjoyable!!! 45.5%

Blaue Maus 25 Years Old cask no. 1, dist Apr 88 db (94) n23.5 t24.5 f22.5 b23.5. Try not to adore this: Mission impossible. 40%. sc.

Blaue Maus Single Cask Malt cask no. 2, dist Jun 02 db (88) n21 t23 f21.5 b22.5. The mouse is at its nibbly-est. 40%. sc.

Blaue Mause Single Cask Malt 2 Fassfüllung cask no. 1, dist May 98, bott May 11 db (92.5) n22.5 t24 f23 b23. Methinks Blau Mause has sailed recently to Jamaica. 40%. sc.

Blaue Maus Single Cask Malt 2 Fassfüllung cask no. 1, dist Mar 04 db (89.5) n21.5 t23.5 f22 b22.5. All round, just lovely whisky of its style. 40%. sc.

Blaue Maus Single Cask Malt Fassstärke cask no. 2, dist Jun 92, bott Apr 12 db **(91) n22 t23 f23 b23.** Suffers a bit of early identity crisis. Whatever it thinks it is, it ends up as a very big experience. *49.3%. nc ncf sc.*

Elbe 1 Single Cask Malt cask no. 1, dist Jun 97, bott Jun 12 db **(91) n22 t23.5 f23 b23.** One of the most restrained, simplistic yet effective malts I have seen from this distillery for a while. *40%. nc ncf sc.*

Elbe 1 Single Malt Cask cask no. 1, dist Jul 00 db **(88) n20 t23 f22.5 b22.5.** Deep, complex and satisfying. Distilled Ledkuchen biscuit, in fact. *40%. sc.*

Grüner Hund Single Cask Malt cask no. 2, dist Jun 01 db **(79) n20 t19 f20 b20.** All kinds of German style biscuit spices. But the oil runs too deep. *40%. sc.*

Krottentaler Single Cask Malt cask no. 2, dist May 02 db **(88.5) n22.5 t22 f22 b22.** Another big oily Germanic beast, but works the toffee to full advantage. *40%. sc.*

Old Fahr Single Cask Malt cask no. 2, dist Jun 00, bott May 11 db **(94.5) n23.5 t23.5 f24 b23.5.** An object lesson in excellent whisky making. Robert, you have excelled...! *40%. sc.*

Old Fahr Single Cask Malt cask no. 5, dist Jun 00, bott Jun 12 db **(89) n22.5 t22.5 f22 b22.** Beginning to become one of my favourites from this distillery. Very consistent. *40%. nc ncf sc.*

Old Fahr III dist Jul 02 db **(89) n22.5 t22 f22 b22.5.** A complex battle of a dram. *40%*

Schwarzer Pirat Single Cask Malt cask no. 2, dist Jun 99 db **(81.5) n20 t21 f20 b20.5.** Loads of molassed sugar at work and pretty nutty, too. *40%. sc.*

Seute Deern Single Cask Malt cask no. 1, dist May 00 db **(87) n22 t22 f21.5 b21.5.** Incredibly soft. And one of the most single-mindedly toffeed whiskies on the market. Especially after the early sugars burn off. *40%. sc.*

Seute Deem Single Cask Malt cask no. 2, dist 00, bott 12 db **(94) n23.5 t23 f23.5 b24.** Gets its act together with some of the distiller's softer themes effortlessly uniting. Leave this in the glass for about 15-20 minutes in a warm room for the most beautiful results. *40%. nc ncf sc.*

Spinnaker 20 Years Old cask no. 1, dist Jul 92 db **(95) n23 t24 f24 b24.** The softest and most elegant of German malts. One to remember. *40%*

Spinnaker 25 Years Old cask no. 1, dist May 88 db **(94.5) n23.5 t24 f23 b24.** Tasted on the day Sabine Lisicki made it through to the Wimbledon final (indeed, just been interrupted by a phone call from someone who has just left the centre court), and although this may not be as graceful, powerful or beautiful, it may make you smile like tennis' most charming competitor of all time. *40%. sc.*

Spinnaker Single Cask Malt cask no. 2, dist Jul 99, bott May 11 db **(93) n22 t23.5 f24 b23.5.** Aha! Spinnaker's back! Seams a couple of years since I last had a new bottling of this German whisky mainstay. A much cleaner version than I remember: none of the normal nougat and better distillation. Quite superb! *40%. sc.*

Spinnaker Single Cask Malt cask no. 2, dist Jul 96, bott Jun 12 db **(91) n22 t23.5 f22.5 b23.** Seriously yummy whisky. *40%. nc ncf sc.*

Spinnaker Single Cask Malt cask no. 2, dist Jun 01 db **(86) n22 t21.5 f21 b21.5.** A big honey and spice job, though sometimes the sweetness becomes a tad too enthusiastic and borders a little too close to the liqueur line. Delicious, though! *40%. sc.*

ITALY
PUNI

The Italian Single Malt White marsala casks db **(87.5) n22 t22 f21.5 b22.** Not whisky. Yet. But a very promising early marriage between spice and fruit with perhaps the rye making the only noticeable impact of the three grains used - though the spice may be a wheat by-product. Can't wait to see the distillery in action... their maturation process in particular. *40%*

The Italian Single Malt Red 3-36 months Italian Marsala Cask db **(86) n21.5 t21.5 f21.5 b21.5.** A decent new make from the vanguard of Italian whisky. The grains of local barley, wheat and rye could do with making more of an impact but good scope for the oak to make an early entry. Might be much more interesting at full strength. *40%*

⸰⸰⸰⸰ **Puni Alba** db **(82) n20 t21 f20.5 b20.5.** Much more feinty, nutty and basic than their first offerings. Very decent body, though. *43%*

Puni Alba Masala pinot noir & muscat d'alexandrie db **(84) n20 t22 f21 b21.** The nose has the new make somewhat accentuated but the delivery is far more harmonious with a soothing combination of soft oils, sugars and grape. *43%*

⸰⸰⸰⸰ **Puni Opus I** db **(89.5) n22.5** a gentle smokiness melts into a malty mass. The sugars are similar to those in lava form on porridge; **t23.5** the first notes are so young its voice hasn't yet broken. But then the incredible intensity of the barley shakes you while a smoky coffee strokes the taste buds; **f22** thins as the vanillas arrive. But keeps its shape...and the light smoke; **b22.5** a really exuberant whisky just choc-a-bloc with character. Bellissimo! *53.72%. nc ncf. 350 bottles.*

Puni Pure Italian Triple Malt pot stills db **(86.5) n20.5 t22.5 f22 b22.** Forget the neo-grappa nose, the spontaneity of the barley on delivery and the richness of the maltshake follow through is a joy! *43%*

LATVIA
LATVIJAS BALZAMS Riga. Working.

L B Lavijas Belzams db **(83) n20 t22 f20 b21.** Soft and yielding on the palate, this is said to be made from Latvian rye, though of all the world's rye whiskies this really does have to be the softest and least fruity. I'll be astonished if there isn't a fair degree of thinning grain in there, too. *40%*

LIECHTENSTEIN
TELSER Triesen. Working.

Telsington IV 3 Years Old dist 2008 db **(94) n23.5 t23 f23.5 b24.** It seemed only right that the 999th new whisky for the 2012 Whisky Bible, a very big number I think you agree, should come from the world's smallest whisky distilling nation. And also because they have the ability to make above average spirit and this, technically, is their best yet. For good measure they have matured it in a first rate cask. The result is a distinguished malt of rare sophistication worthy of the trust I placed in it. *42%. sc.*

Telsington V 4 Years Old Pinot Noir Cask db **(88.5) n22 t22.5 f22 b22.** An friendly satisfying malt. The pinot is a bit tight, but the fruit has just enough shine and clarity. *43.5%.*

⁘ **Telsington Moosalp Edition Single Malt Whisky** bott 2014 db **(92) n22.5** beautifully constructed: very slight nougat betrays the still while gentle toasted hazelnut and honeycomb balance things well; **t23** a soft silkiness is soon overtaken by a grander, far more robust blast of liquorice, muscovado sugar and treacle – though, cleverly, of limited sweetness. Throughout, the grain ensures a salivating edge while a darker, drier, date and vanilla thread runs confidently through; **f23.5** by far and away the classiest finish from Telser yet: the sugars remain of the right weight an intensity...and somehow last to the very end despite the nudging butterscotch; **b23** benefitting from the use of an excellent cask, a big whisky from a little country. Very distinguished. Just like the Moosalp restaurant. *42%. 50 bottles.*

⁘ **Telsington VI Single Cask Malt**, 5 Years Old Pinot Noir cask, Swiss oak db **(94.5) n24** a nose deserving a very long study: the use of Swiss oak imparts an unusual softness to the proceedings, with the tannins willing to caress and filter rather than confront. The spices, fruit, vanilla and even barley all appear to gently drift, though tethered together. This is major sophistication at work...; **t23.5** the barley downs its fruity cape to make the first solo speech on delivery. Soon both fruit and vanilla are back in harness. Just adore the balance between the drier, though never bitter, oak and the proud sugar-gristiness of the barley. The fruit adds the background choir; **f23** long, with a slight tang from the grape but the just-so oils spread the most gentle spices imaginable and late milky mocha; **b24** I wonder if the chap at the top of the hill in that big castle above Vaduz has ever tasted this. For there is something effortlessly regal to this whisky. *43.5%. sc.*

⁘ **Telsington VII 5 Years Old Pinot Noir Finish** db **(73.5) n18 t20 f17.5 b18.** A poor wine cask has strangled the life out of this one. A shame, as a few lovely mocha notes can be heard in the distance. Telser VI had to be better than this...where is it? *43.5%. sc.*

⁘ **Teslington Single Cask Malt Black Edition**, 5 Years Old Pinot noir cask, French Oak db **(86) n22.5 t22 f20 b21.5.** The trouble, often, with French oak is that its tendency to dominate, even bully, shortens the complexity and ability to experience the full personality of the characters taking part. Sharp, sometimes shrill on the palate, it is certainly big. *43.5%. sc.*

⁘ **Telser Single Cask 100% Rye Malt**, 2 Years Old db **(89.5) n22.5** the rye pulses from the glass, heavy, fruity and unmistakable; **t23.5** no other grain on the planet conjours up such intensity of flavour as malted rye – not even peated malt. That is because there is an added intensity from the sugars, usually of a Demerara bent, that amplifies the crisp, sharpness of the grain; a little spiced coffee towards the middle; **f21.5** just drops a degree or two as the heavier oils from the distillate begin to get a grip; **b22** a remarkably memorable first try at malted rye: had the cut been a tad narrower this would have been a very distinguished dram. *42%. sc.*

⁘ **Telsington Single Cask Rye Whisky Aged 3 Years Islay** cask finish db **(90) n23** wine must: skins and pips aplenty, softened by the most gentle smoke. The rye itself cannot yet be heard....; **t23**...ah! Now it can. Not so much with the rye itself, though it does penetrate the fruit now and then, but the crispness of the backbone; **f20.5** at last: tangible, juicy rye and light smoke: intriguing and lovely; slight furriness to the finale; **b23.5** rye meets Islay, surely a match made in heaven as my two favourite whisky styles marry. I presume it had been in some kind of wine cask first, though, as there is high fruit dominance. Ticks many a box for me: well distilled, good fruit, firm grain and the most delicate smoke. Just a niggle on the finish, I fear. *42%*

LUXEMBOURG
DISTILLERIE DIEDENACKER Niederdonven. Working.

Diedenacker Number One 2006 Aged 5 Years Luxembourg white wine French oak barrique, cask no. 2, dist Jan 06, bott Apr 11 db **(90.5) n22.5 t23.5 f22 b22.5.** Congratulations to this new distillery – and what a way for Luxembourg to become a whisky nation. A whisky bursting with character and complexity. 42%. nc ncf sc. 450 bottles.

Diedenacker Number One Rye Malt 2008 Aged 5 Years db **(86) n22 t22 f21 b21.** Not quite hitting the heights of their first bottling, but the nut and nougat is balanced well by crystallised treacle. 42%. 450 bottles.

THE NETHERLANDS
ZUIDAM Baarle Nassau. Working.

⋅⋅⋅ **Millstone Aged 12 Years** Sherry Cask dist 26 Feb 99, bott 22 Mar 13 db **(95) n24** superb age on this: almost like opening a bottle of 20-year-old sherry and breathing in the plump spices seeing the world for the first time in decades.... Near perfect on the sweet-dry balance: sublime; **t23.5** fresh, lively grape slowly infiltrated by much heavier and drier tannins. The vanillas really do have a big say and sway; **f23.5** stays dry, with a hint of grape must. Decidedly raisin shortcake biscuit on the finale; **b24** after last year's disappointing sherry bottling, thought I'd need some Dutch courage to tackle this one. But, instead, an excellent cask at work here which ensures an overflow of character. Just underlines the difference between putting a good quality spirit into a less than impressive cask or filling into top quality oak So, so elegant... 46% WB15/399

Millstone 1999 Aged 14 Years sherry cask, cask no. 1355, dist 26 Feb 99, bott 15 Mar 13 **(73) n18.5 t19 f17 b18.5.** Those with a penchant for German spiced biscuits will love this. Personally, I have a problem with those types of spices which can also be tasted in some Indian whiskies. 46%. sc. Distillery Region Netherlands. Milroy's Of Soho.

⋅⋅⋅ **Millstone 100 Rye Whisky** new American oak, cask no. 603, dist Jan 04, bott 12 Feb 14 db **(90) n22** a shade more wildly spiced than I remember last year's bottling, still with cinnamon biscuit, but the rye is a little oilier and lighter; **t23.5** much more like it: the rye fair cracks against the teeth with added Demerara sugar flintiness. Salivating, rye-fruity and simply pulses with that forceful grain; **f22** the small still oils accumulate to form a thickening backdrop. The spices buzz...; **b22.5** not quite as finely tuned as the 2013 bottling, but really makes a very big statement. 50% WB15/400

Zuidam Dutch Rye Aged 5 Years cask no. 446-683, bott no. 81, dist Jan 05, bott Aug 10 **(92.5) n23.5 t23 f22.5 b23.5.** This bottle stays in my dining room. There is a new classic European to be found. 40%

Zuidam 2007 Dutch Rye virgin American oak barrel, cask no. 449, dist 07, bott 13 **(91.5) n24 t23 f22 b22.5.** Another impressive bottling from a distillery which proves it certainly knows how to make rye. 46%. sc. Distillery Region Netherlands.

SPAIN

DYC Aged 8 Years (90) n22 t23 f22.5 b22.5. I really am a sucker for clean, cleverly constructed blends like this. Just so enjoyable! 40%

SWEDEN
MACKMYRA Gästrikland. Working.

Mackmyra Brukswhisky db **(95.5) n24 t24 f23.5 b24.** One of the most complex and most beautifully structured whiskies of the year. A Mackmyra masterpiece, cementing the distillery among the world's true greats. 41.4%

Mackmyra Den Första Utgåvan (The First Edition) Swedish oak db **(93.5) n23.5 t23.5 f23 b23.5.** Only Mackmyra combines voluptuousness and severity in such knee-weakening proportions. Like being whipped by a busty blond dominatrix with a thick Scandinavian accent. Or so a judge friend of mine tells me... 46.1%

Mackmyra Moment "Glöd" (Glow) bott code MM-011 db **(96.5) n24.5 t24.5 f23 b24.5.** Technically, from a fermentation, distillation and maturation perspective: outstanding. From a blending viewpoint: masterful. Truly idiosyncratic: uniquely Mackmyra! If you are lucky enough to locate one of the remaining 1,088 bottles of this, pay what it takes... 51.2%.

Mackmyra Moment "Jord" bott code MM-004 db **(93) n23 t24 f23 b23.** Anyone with a fondness for bourbon might just have to get a case of this... hard to believe better casks have been used in maturation anywhere in the world this year. 55.1%

Mackmyra Moment "Källa" bott code MM-010 db **(89) n22 t23 f22 b22.** A bit pie-in-the-face with the avalanche of syrupy sugar. The vaguest fruitiness, but really a whisky for those looking for deliciously unsubtle power. 53.4%. 1065 bottles.

⁂ **Mackmyra Moment "Malström"** db **(96) n24** crisp muscovado sugar but camouflaged by a complex array of malty, vanilla notes of varying hues and perhaps the most subtle spice of the year worldwide. Unusually oak dependent here, though the sweet-dry balance is exceptional; **t24.5** salivating barley in almost traditional malt whisky style, but then a more examining series of deft vanilla-honey tones all wrapped as a parcel in an outer skin of heather honey. It is, unusually for a Mackmyra, the intensity of the barley which remains a constant; **f23.5** long, still with crisp though controlled sugar abounding, the edge dulled by butterscotch tart. Meanwhile, that malt just keeps on giving... **b24** more like "Femalstrom": very gentle and sexy..yet that self-assured power is always there: of its type an unequalled, and dominant malt. World class. *46.4%*

Mackmyra Moment "Mareld" (Sea Fire) bott code MM-013 db **(95) n23.5 t24 f23.5 b24.** Mesmerising. They say not all the wonders have been yet discovered from the sea. Here is one that apparently just has....A malt for people with time on their hands. Anything less than an hour will do you and the whisky a disservice... *52.2%. 1600 bottles.*

⁂ **Mackmyra Midnattssol Single Malt Art No MC-002** db **(93.5) n23.5** a happy three-way marriage (how 1970s Swedish!) between malt in the form of breakfast cereal, complete with toasted hazel nuts, oak (displaying a bent towards caramel) and honey, in an ulmo-cum-heather format; **t24** pretty fruity and juicy on delivery with an over-ripe plum squash and raspberry jelly mixing it with a more robust saline-topped vanilla and barley mix; a few nutty, spicy notes arrive late; **f23** tangy, with the odd grumble of a tired cask, but repaired by Brazilian coconut biscuit and a vague echo of burnt raisin; the warm spices nibble contentedly; **b23.5** fitting that this should be my 750th new whisky for the 2015 Bible: I had scheduled to hit that landmark by midsummer's day, but find myself tasting this just over two weeks later (thanks for nothing, the world's sulphured casks...!). However, this didn't drop into my lab until a few days ago, so it has worked out rather neatly. A silky number, this, with every character met by a calming influence. *46.1%*

⁂ **Mackmyra Midvinter Single Malt Art No MC-001** db **(94.5) n23.5** fabulously delicate teasing of nutmeg, the lightest paprika and salted cashews...all with an undercurrent of malt, redcurrant and liquorice...wow! **t24** near perfect weight to the delivery with just-so oils filling the mouth and softening things all round: almost ridiculously soft. The spices on the nose buzz, test and tease. Again the malt comes through with clarity despite the hubbub surrounding it. Pretty salty, though the sugars take the strain, offering a slightly caramelled touch to absorb the growing oak; **f23** a little tangy as the oak gets to work; but a more buttery and traditional touch to this now; **b24** how fitting: probably the most Swedish of all the Mackmyra whiskies yet: reminds me of light-challenged days in that country when, at night, you would retreat to a restaurant and finish the evening with an aquavit, spiced to the owner's liking. The seasoning and smoking here takes us very close to that uniquely Swedish style. The sophistication takes the breath away... *46.1%*

Mackmyra Moment "Morgondagg" (Morning Dew) bott code MM-012 db **(93) n24 t23 f22.5 b23.5.** Another masterful Mackmyra experience. Above all, you get the feeling of a heavyweight pulling its punches... *51.1%. 1600 bottles.*

Mackmyra Moment "Rimfrost" db **(95.5) n24 t24 f23.5 b24.** I thought that they had got the name "Rimfrost" from sitting on a Stockholm park bench in the middle of a Swedish winter. Apparently not. *53.2%. 1,492 bottles.*

Mackmyra Moment "Skog" db **(95.5) n24 t24.5 f23 b24.** With a name like "Skog" I wasn't sure if I was supposed to taste this stuff or simply wield the hefty bottle above my head and brain somebody in good Viking tradition. Fortunately I settled for the former...and made the correct choice. Although the latter always remains an open option to anyone who tries to steel this bottle from me. It is by far one of the most beautiful whiskies I have tasted this year... *52.4%. 3,000 bottles.*

Mackmyra Moment "Solsken" db **(92.5) n22.5 t23.5 f23 b23.5.** A treat of a malt. Scandinavian sophistication at its height. *52.6%. 3,000 bottles.*

Mackmyra Moment "Urberg" bott code MM-002 db **(95) n24 t23.5 f23.5 b24.5.** Beautifully distilled, superbly matured, clever flavour profile, first-rate packaging: the complete deal. Certainly one of the most intense, complex, compelling and simply enjoyable whiskies I have tasted this year. Truly a magic Moment... *55.6%*

Mackmyra Reserve Cask ex-sherry cask, cask no. 08-0689, dist 22 Dec 08, bott 28 Aug 12 **(89) n23 t22 f22 b22.5.** The first ever Mackmyra which, on tasting blind, I mistook for an Islay. A very easy mistake to make. *51.7%. Carpets Crawlers Choice.*

Mackmyra Special 09: "Vildhallon" (Wild Raspberries) bott Autumn 12, bott code MS.009 db **(89.5) n22.5 t22 f22.5 b22.5.** How interesting. First words to enter my head on nosing this was "meaty, cocoa" and on since checking the Special 08, I see I noted identical attributes. Absolutely no coincidence, that: the hallmark of a blender knowing exactly what she is setting out to achieve. *46.1%*

359

Mackmyra Special 10: "Kaffegök" bott Spring 13, bott code MS.010 db **(81.5)** n19 t23.5 f19 b20. Mackmyra do this from time to time: throw in a bottling which, I think, misses the target. The problem is the use of a cask or two of spirit which is not distilled with quite the same accuracy as normal. The plus side is that you are unlikely to find any malt this year which kicks off offering such a gorgeous and uninterrupted stream of acacia honey. But those extra oils are ultimately a little too burdensome for greatness. 46.1%

Mackmyra Svensk Rök bott code MR-001 db **(93)** n23 t23.5 f23 b23.5. A very different Mackmyra in both style and sensory texture. Subtlety is the key and time is the lock. Definitely need a good half hour to unpick this one. 46.1%

SPIRIT OF HVEN

Hven Dubhe Seven Stars Single Malt No 1 db **(84)** n21 t21.5 f20.5 b21. Very light malt displaying rich fudgy caramels. As simple as it gets, with a slight bitterness at the death. 45%

⠵ **Hven Seven Stars Single Malt No. 2 Merak** db **(92.5)** n23 growling smoke which gathers and intensifies; elsewhere the oak joins the cherry pie to ensure there is no letting up in the weight; t23.5 a fresh delivery, with dark cherry and juicy barley giving way to both smoke and some tingling spice; f22.5 dries as the oak holds control; excellent light spice to outline the phenols; b23.5 a far better bottling than their first effort, this is one which really commands attention. High quality stuff. Well done! 45% WB15/391

SWITZERLAND
ANDREAS VON OW DISTILLERY Busingen. Working.

⠵ **Munot Malt** dist Aug 10, bott 19 Sep 13 db **(87.5)** n22 t22 f21.5 b22. Sturdy and steady. The nose appears to offer more as a bourbon than malt and there is plenty of oak to chew on the palate. But the youthfulness is hinted at by firm oils and the light cocoa finish. 46%. sc.

BRAUREREI LOCHER Appenzell. Working.

Säntis Malt Swiss Highlander cask no. 1144, bott 26 Apr 13 db **(96.5)** n23.5 t23.5 f25 b24.5. When this distillery gets it right, their malt really is something to behold. An absolute joy and one of the great whiskies of 2013/14. 57.5%. sc. 570 bottles.

Säntis Malt Swiss Highlander Edition Alpstein 5 Aged 6 Years Merlot finish, 15 Apr 13 db **(87)** n22.5 t22.5 f20 b22. A real softie. 48%. 700 bottles.

⠵ **Säntis Malt Edition Alpstein No. VIII Aged 7 Years** pinot noir finish, bott 09 May 14 db **(93)** n24 astonishing: we appear to have a mix of bourbon – and every trademark note that possesses – in perfect tandem with fresh, sparkling grape. Yep, there is not a hint of discord or battling for supremacy, despite the massive egos on show; then, to top it all, we have that spiciness peculiar to central Europe including, here, orange and celery...; t23 sharp flavours, especially the kumquat and orange blossom honey; f22.5 a little bitteress creeps in, as do a few cocoa notes; b23 profound whisky, almost three dimensional. Every aspect of it comes at you in the most vivid form imaginable. 48%. 2000 bottles.

Säntis Malt Swiss Highlander Edition Alpstein 9 Aged 6 Years Merlot finish db **(88.5)** n22 t22.5 f21.5 b22.5. Note; I tasted this at the pre-bottling 48.5%. I don't see it changing much from this toffee fest, though. 48%. 455 bottles.

Säntis Malt Swiss Highlander Edition Dreifaltigkeit db **(96.5)** n24 t24.5 f24 b24. Such is the controlled enormity, the sheer magnitude of what we have here, one cannot help taste the whisky with a blend of pleasure and total awe. 52%

Säntis Malt Swiss Highlander Edition Sigel oak beer casks db **(91.5)** n23.5 t23 f22 b23. High quality whisky which balances with aplomb. 40%

⠵ **Snow White Limited Edition No 2. Cherry Finish** db **(86)** n21 t22 f21.5 b21.5. Dwarfed by the central European spices. At times tastes like a German, Austrian or Swiss Christmas cake. Add that to the sweetness and we have something a little more like a liqueur. 45%

BRENNEREI HOLLEN Lauwil. Working.

Hollen Single Malt Aged Over 6 Years matured in white wine casks db **(90.5)** n23 t23.5 f21.5 b22.5. Many facets to its personality, the nose especially, shows more rum characteristics than malt. A won't-say-no glassful if ever there was one, though, and made and matured to the highest order. Indeed, as I taste and write this, my BlackBerry informs me that Roger Federer is on his way to another Wimbledon title: the similarities in the quiet dignity, elegance and class of both Swiss sportsman and whisky is not such a corny comparison. 42%

BRENNEREI SCHWAB Oberwil. Working.

Bucheggberger Single Malt cask no. 23, bott no. 10 db **(74)** n17 t21 f17 b19. Decent malty lead, but the intensely bitter finish makes hard work of it. 42%

BRENNEREI URS LÜTHY Muhen. Working.

Dinkel Whisky pinot noir cask db **(92.5) n23 t24 f22 b23.5.** A big, striking malt which is not afraid to at times make compellingly beautiful statements. *61.5%*

BURGDORFER GASTHAUSBRAUEREI Burgdorf. Working.

Reiner Burgdorfer 5 Years Old cask no. 4 db **(82.5) n18 t22 f21 b21.5.** Recovers from the mildly feinty nose to register some wonderfully lush cocoa notes throughout the coppery, small still development on the palate. *43%*

DESTILLERIE EGNACH Egnach. Silent.

Thursky db **(93) n24 t23.5 f22.5 b23.** Such a beautifully even whisky! I am such a sucker for that clean fruity-spice style. Brilliant! *40%*

DESTILLERIE HAGEN-RÜHLI Hüttwilen. Working.

Hagen's Best Whisky No. 2 lot no. 00403/04-03-08.08 db **(87) n19 t23.5 f22 b22.5.** Much more Swiss, small still style than previous bottling and although the nose isn't quite the most enticing, the delivery and follow through are a delight. Lovely whisky. *42%*

BRENNEREI-ZENTRUM BAUERNHO Zug. Working.

Swissky db **(91) n23 t23 f22 b23.** While retaining a distinct character, this is the cleanest, most refreshing malt yet to come from mainland Europe. Hats off to Edi Bieri for this work of art. Moving stuff. *42%*

Swissky Exklusiv Abfüllung L3365 db **(94) n23 t23 f24 b24.** A supremely distilled whisky with the most subtle oak involvement yet. Year after year this distillery bottles truly great single malt, a benchmark for Europe's growing band of small whisky distillers. *40%*

ETTER SOEHNE AG Zug. Working.

Johnett Swiss Single Malt 2008 dist May 08, bott Aug 12 db **(84.5) n21.5 t22.5 f20 b20.5** Peaks on delivery with a series of gorgeous rich sugar, semi-gristy notes. Just not enough body, though, to sustain the complexity. *42%*

HUMBEL SPEZIALITÄTENBRENNEREI Stetten. Working.

⋆ **OURBEER Single Malt Whisky** dist 10, bott 23 Jul 14 db **(82) n20 t21.5 f20 b20.5.** A pretty unique aroma and flavour profile, strongly scented with spiced citrus and with a late herbal tang to the standard toffee. *43%*

KOBELT Marbach, St. Gallen. Working.

Glen Rhine Whiskey db **(88) n21 t22.5 f21.5 b22.** Try and pick your way through this one... can't think of another whisky in the world with that kind of fingerprint. *40%. Corn & barley.*

LANGATUN DISTILLERY Langenthal, Kanton Bern. Working.

Langatun Old Bear Châteauneuf-du-Pape cask, dist Apr 08, bott Jan 12, bott code L1201 db **(96) n24 t24 f23.5 b24.5.** Whisky for the gods... *64%*

RUGENBRAU AG Matten bei Interlaken. Working.

Interlaken Swiss Highland Single Malt "Classic" oloroso sherry butt db **(95) n23.5 t24 f23 b24.** Hugely impressive. I have long said that the finest whiskies made on mainland Europe are to be found in Switzerland. Game, set and match... *46%*

Top Of Europe Swiss Highland Single Malt "Ice Label" bott 2011 **(93.5) n23 t24 f23 b23.5.** I get a lot of stick for heaping praise on European whisky. OK, there is the odd technical flaw in the distillation – though in some ways it works to its advantage. But how many casks do you find like this in Scotland? For sheer quality of its output, this distillery must rate as high as an Alpine peak... *58.9%. sc.*

SANTISBLICK DESTILLERIE

⋆ **Single Malt Madeira** cask, bott code 91 von 300 db **(34) n1 t16 f8 b9.** This, without question, offers the scariest nose I have ever encountered on a commercially bottled whisky. Appallingly aggressive, I'll make this the last whisky I'll taste today (at least) - for I know I will regret it and my senses will need time to recover. Nosed at a safe distance, if such a thing exists, it appears to have been matured in a petrol barrel, though closer, braver inspection suggests it is peat of some sort at work. The palate gives some lie to this terrifying aroma, as my teeth still seem to be intact. Some burnt fudge running alongside the "smoke" makes the delivery not only bearable but for a few moments quite acceptable. But the finish, by contrast, is dry and after a short while you feel your tongue aflame...and it takes a while to put out the blaze. The Swiss are known as a peaceful people with a history of neutrality. Hardly surprising: with stocks of this stuff at hand, it is unlikely anyone will ever dare invade. 48%

⊰⊱ **Whisky 3 Years Old** bourbon cask, bott code L-130001 db **(83.5) n21 t22 f21.5 b19.** An odd but attractive whisky where the maltiness has been ramped up to nuclear strength. Best of all, though, is the body and overall mouth feel which is highly satisfying. A peculiar experience, though. 43%

⊰⊱ **Whisky 3 Years Old** sherry cask, bott code 83 von 300 db **(59) n13 t18 f12 b15.** Probably the weirdest sherry matured whisky I have ever encountered. Words fail me for the nose and finish, the former being unreal and the latter being only too real in its grimness. 43%

SPEZIALITÄTENBRENNEREI ZÜRCHER Port. Working.
Zürcher Single Lakeland 3 Years Old dist Jul 06, bott Jul 09 db **(88.5) n21.5 t23 f21.5 b22.5.** This distillery never fails to entertain. Not as technically perfect as usual, but none of the blemishes are seriously damaging and even add a touch of extra character. 42%

WEINGUT CLERC BAMERT Ruteli im Buobental. Working.
⊰⊱ **Weingut Clerc Bamert Whisky Finest Pure Malt 8 Years Old** db **(87) n22 t22 f21 b22.** Splutters and misfires on the finish, though not as badly as the single engine plane that has just gone, worryingly, overhead. Elsewhere some lovely malt, black cherry and caramel makes for a soft landing. 40%. sc nc.

WHISKY CASTLE Elfingen. Working.
Whisky Castle Vintage cask no. 485, dist Sep 06 db **(90.5) n22 t23 f23 b22.5.** Imagine a whisky angel gently kissing your palate...this is all about very good spirit (with a slightly wide cut) spending time in what appears to be either a high quality virgin cask, or something very close to one. Brimming with character and charisma. 43%

Vatted Malts
LANGATUN DISTILLERY
Langatun Old Eagle Cask Proof Pure Rye Whisky French oak charred, bott code L0113, dist 08, bott 13 db **(92) n21.5 t24 f23 b23.5.** To be honest, not quite a perfect distillation here and doesn't hit the unbelievable heights of the bottling last year. But this is infused with so much character that when it gets it right, as on the palate it pretty often does, you are lavishly and sometimes outrageously entertained. 51.7%. nc sc. 200 bottles.

The Swiss Malt (95.5) n23 t24 f24 b24.5. Sumptuous and the stuff for late night naval gazing. When Orson Welles, as Harry Lime in the immortal Third Man, made a disparaging summary of all Switzerland's achievements over the centuries as the invention of the cuckoo clock, it was obvious he had never tasted this. A whisky the Swiss distilling nation can be rightly proud of. 50.2%. From 20 Swiss Distillers. 175 miniatures.

WALES
PENDERYN Penderyn. Working.
Penderyn bott code 092909 **(93.5) n23 t23.5 f24 b23.** Just couldn't have been more Welsh than any potential offSpring of Catherine Zeta Jones by Tom Jones, conceived while "How Green Is My Valley" was on the DVD player and a Shirley Bassey CD playing in the background. And that after downing three pints of Brains bitter after seeing Swansea City play Cardiff City at the Liberty Stadium, before going home to a plate of cawl while watching Wales beating England at rugby live on BBC Cymru. Yes, it is that unmistakably Penderyn; it is that perfectly, wonderfully and uniquely Welsh. 46%. ncf. Imported by Sazerac Company.

Penderyn bott code 1131008 (750ml) db **(93.5) n22.5 t23.5 f23.5 b24.** The light cocoa infusion just tops this off perfectly. A truly classic Penderyn; more charm than Tom Jones, hitting just as many pure notes...and just being a fraction of his age 46%. US Market.

Penderyn Bourbon Matured Single Cask cask no. 227B, dist 06 db **(89.5) n22 t23 f22 b22.5.** Definitely a much bigger Penderyn than you might be used to, and that is only partly because of the cask. 62%. ncf sc.

Penderyn Grand Slam Edition 2012 bott 3 Dec 12 db **(91) n22.5 t23 f22.5 b23.** Like the Welsh XV of 2012: tries...and succeeds. 46%

⊰⊱ **Penderyn Icons of Wales Dylan Thomas Sherrywood** db **(91) n21.5** chalky, perhaps a tad too astringent and dry; **t24** the delivery is a complete contrast to the aroma: immediately sweet and superbly weighted. Lush without being oily, sultanas abound to magnificent effect; **f23** now reverts to something between the nose and delivery: delicate and dry, with vanillas handily placed but the fruit always pushing, probing and allowing in a little ulmo honey at the end; **b23** from an unpromising start comes something of a tone poem. 41%. ncf. WB15/402

Penderyn Icon of Wales Red Flag Madeira finish bott Nov 12 db **(94) n22.5 t24 f23.5 b24.** I thought this was dedicated to Cardiff City, the "red birds" for their promotion to the Premiership. But apparently not... though this year I was in the boardroom there watching Millwall and celebrating Neil Kinnock's 70th birthday. So maybe the whisky should represent both these landmarks, after all... 41%. ncf.

Penderyn Madeira released 7 Jul 10 db **(92) n21.5 t23.5 f23.5 b24.** This bottling is a testament to how far this whisky has moved over the years. There appears to be much more Madeira influence than was once the case, indicating that the malt is being allowed a little longer to mature. This is lush, beguilingly complex whisky of the very top order. 46%. ncf.

Penderyn Madeira released 9 Sep 10 db **(91) n21.5 t23.5 f23 b23.** Practically a re-run of the July bottling, with the odd tweak here and there. My curiosity spiked, I contacted the Welsh Whisky Company who confirmed they were now, as I was very much suspecting, using a tank to store the vatted casks before bottling... and thus creating a minor solera system. This explains the continuity of style with the slight variation from month to month, rather than the sometimes violent lurches in style from one bottling to the next that had hitherto been the hallmark of Penderyn. Higher quality, for sure...if slightly less excitement and nosing into the unknown for me...! I shall miss its Russian roulette idiosyncrasy... 46%. ncf.

Penderyn Madeira released 4 Oct 10 db **(92.5) n22 t23.5 f23.5 b23.5.** Very much in the same mould as the September release, above, but here the fruit has a warmer, softer, say while the milk chocolate is ramped up a notch or two. A very classy act. 46%. ncf.

Penderyn Madeira released 1 Feb 11 db **(94.5) n23.5 t23.5 f23.5 b24.** One of the great standard Peneryn bottlings. 46%. ncf.

Penderyn Madeira bott code. Mar 11 db **(92) n22.5 t23 f23.5 b23.** Almost like a chocolate mousse poured over a fruit pudding. And a spicy one at that. Not quite hitting the overall heights of the previous monster bottling. But sensational nonetheless. 46%

Penderyn Madeira bott 11 db **(95) n23.5 t23.5 f24 b24.** Concentrates on the fruity side of matters; the nose is a wonderful marriage (did I just put the words" marriage" and "wonderful" in the same sentence?....(shudder)) of rather over-ripe mango and fit-to-burst greengage while the delivery makes maximum gain from the sublime grape and peach lucidity. The finish is aided by the softest oils imaginable which inject the barley this is crying out for. Then a cocoa and raisin fade. It is a whisky that makes you sigh...and for all the right reasons. 46%. ncf.

Penderyn Madeira bott Jul 11 db **(91.5) n23 t23 f22.5 b23.** Perhaps if I was asked to pour a Penderyn to display its expected personality in full swing, with little grapey twists here, lightly sugared oaky turns there, this would sum the distillery up almost too well... And not least because of some extra viscosity allowing those sugars to expand as far as they are ever likely to go. 46%. ncf.

Penderyn Madeira bott Sep 11 db **(91) n23 t23 f22 b23.** You really have to take your hats off to these guys: the consistency is now absolutely top draw and here they appear to have that delicate balance between drier crushed grape pithiness of the Madeira completely in harmony with the sweeter elements of both oak and barley. Here, though, the spices season, entertain and bring alive, something like pepper on a piece of Welsh Rarebit. 46%. ncf.

Penderyn Madeira bott Oct 11 db **(94) n23 t23.5 f24 b23.5.** Penderyn with its tie off and top button undone. Relaxed from the moment it hits the palate – or I should say caresses – with a wonderfully soft barley-led fruitiness and then a mercurial display of complex spices and then vanilla-topped mocha. In this form unquestionably one of the easiest-drinking whiskies in the world. the remainder of this bottle won't be going back into my warehouse: this will be sitting in my dining room amid some accomplished others! 46%. ncf.

Penderyn Madeira bott Nov 11 db **(93) n22.5 t24 f23 b23.5.** Never quite settles like the October bottling, but through choice and design rather than fault. Edgy, dry and at times pretty nutty, with gorgeous walnut oil and chocolate fudge ramping up the complexity on the vanilla and burnt raisin. A malt which fidgets from one part of the palate to the next. But the quality is stunning. We have entered, without doubt, a purple period for Welsh Whisky. It is a bit like the national rugby team of the early 70s and Swansea City of the present: just a joy to behold. 46%. ncf.

Penderyn Madeira bott Feb 12 db **(92) n21.5 t23 f24 b23.5.** It is as though the gratingly dry character of the previous bottling had been noted and something has been done to make amends. The texture is much softer yet the grape both sturdier and sultana intense. The spices here are as big as any I can remember from this distillery and though they take no prisoners they successfully riddle the malt with complexity. Quite brilliant! 46%. ncf.

Penderyn Madeira bott Mar 12 db **(91.5) n22.5 t22.5 f23.5 b23.** The even-ness here suggests more casks than normal as we have a white noise on the nose of many of the Penderyn fixtures, though some cancelling others out. There is enough left over, though, to mesmerise. The delivery is also astonishingly well composed with barley and madeira striking an unusual balance of practically going halves in dominance. With the clear, grassy barley actually making this one of the most juicy Penderyns of all time, it is a malt which takes a little time to learn to fly, but when it does, it swoops and rises with elegant abandon. 46%. ncf.

Penderyn Madeira bott 2 Jun 12 db **(76)** n18 t21 f18 b19. Juicy in part. And some cocoa notes. But way, way off the pace by Penderyn's normal spot on standards. 46%

Penderyn Madeira bott 3 July 12 db **(94.5)** n23.5 t24.5 f23 b23.5. Probably the best delivery of any standard Penderyn since the product was launched. Absolutely marvellous whisky just bursting with depth and character. 46%. ncf.

Penderyn Madeira bott 7 Aug 12 db **(87.5)** n22.5 t22 f21.5 b21.5. Big barley lift, attractive, but not quite up to the ever-improving standards. 46%. ncf.

Penderyn Madeira bott 10 Oct 12 db **(88)** n23 t23 f20 b22. What's Welsh for "a juicy beast..."? 46%. ncf.

Penderyn Madeira bott 2 Jan 13 db **(91)** n22.5 t23.5 f22 b23. A rumbustious version which peaks several times before the final fade. 46%. ncf.

Penderyn Madeira bott 4 Feb 13 db **(95)** n23 t24 f23.5 b24.5. Just gorgeous! And simply faultless. 46%. ncf.

⠿ **Penderyn Madeira** bott May 13 db **(87.5)** n23 an unusual sprinkling of spice on the fruit-dappled oak; t22 some astonishingly delicate oils help ramp up the scant sugars. The oak hits with a dry buzz midway through; f20.5 a real tang to the grape and citrus; b22 drier than recent previous bottlings. 46%.

⠿ **Penderyn Madeira** bott Jul 13 db **(95)** n23.5 lush, with muscular grape, always rounded and even a touch of muscatel evident; gentle spices warble in the background; t24 the highly usual delivery style of being both rich and thick on the palate and salivating – all at the same time. The spices are screened slightly by the vanillas-clad oak while gorgeous cocoa notes begin to form; f23.5 the spicies become more confident and are joined by the fruit which has found a second wind; b24 makes up for the relative limitations of the May 13 bottling. Penderyn at its most irresistible. A real mouth filler....! 46%.

⠿ **Penderyn Madeira** bott Aug 13 db **(91)** n22.5 pretty firm barley, encased by a mellow, lazy almost, grape. The prickle is of semi-bourbon variety...; t22.5 delicate with the fruit at first lethargic but then volumises. Salivating throughout with the spices backing off after a confrontational start; f23 chewy, though dries at a steady lick. The spices rides again as something akin to a butterscotch tart meets with Madeira trifle...; b23 about as crisp and sturdy as Penderyn ever gets. 46%.

⠿ **Penderyn Madeira** bott Sept 13 db **(91.5)** n22.5 identical to Aug 13 edition!! t23 ah! Now this is softer bodied but slightly more emboldened than the previous bottling; f23 later spice and slightly more emphasis on coacoa. But otherwise very similar to Aug 13... b23 an almost identical set to Aug 13 edition, only the furniture has been moved around a bit. 46%.

⠿ **Penderyn Madeira** bott Oct 13 db **(89)** n22 dense with a few extra tannins at play; there is a some black pepper bouncing around with the earthy floral notes; t23.5 rarely does the Madeira have such an early say: here it is clean and pinging with juicy goodness, with the sugars let of their leash in most un-Penderyn style: a bit like a Jose Mourinho side playing attractive, all out attacking football....; f21 the flip side is a dull finale with a tanginess hanging onto the remaining spices; b22.5 perhaps not one of the most complex Penderyn experiences, but certainly one of the fruitiest and, early on, sweetest. 46%.

⠿ **Penderyn Madeira** bott Nov 13 db **(91.5)** n22.5 quiet on the fruit front. Certainly a little more oak noise than usual; t22 dry delivery but a gorgeously rounded mouth feel. Some serious complexity formulates in the mid term...; f24 now goes into complexity overdrive as the Venzualan cocoa mingles with pithy nut colonels and fruit skins. Rarely has such a dry finsh been so lively and salivating...; b23 rarely has a Penderyn quite come so much into its own at the death. 46%.

⠿ **Penderyn Madeira** bott Dec 13 db **(88.5)** n21.5 some orange pith and tobacco: perhaps a touch too dry and tight; t22 sumptuous delivery: soft but thinner than the previous month, though spices go on the charge early on; f23 there is a firm rattle of something not unlike Irish Pot Still here – cuious. Plenty of fruit and nut chocolate – but sexed up with spice, too; b22 in recent years Penderyn has been working hard to ensure a close proximity from one bottling t the next. Here we have a situation where the Dec version is not just on a different page, but a completely new book. I get the feeling they have tried to correct the lack of fruit in the previous month's incarnation. 46%.

⠿ **Penderyn Madeira** bott Jan 14 db **(95)** n23.5 a few molassed sugars tumble around with the ripe plums; t24 salivating and sensuous, again the sugars and fruit appears locked in arms. Some vanilla, butterscotch and ulmo honey combine to made an important and, frankly, eye-rollingly delicious contribution; f23.5 dries, as it should, but not enough to undermine the mocha which always seems to appear in this distillery's better moments and the walnut and muscovado fade; b24 a charming little tease of a malt which has got the sugars just right and the change of complexity at a wonderful pace. Standard Penderyn at its very best. 46%.

⠿ **Penderyn Madeira** bott Feb 14 db **(87.5) n22 t23.5 f20 b21.5**. A strange bottling this, neither fish nor foul. Absent-mindedly you register some tiny degree of smoke on the nose, which then comes into sharper focus on the palate. But it is no more than a hint which works well on thetop-hole, fruit-laden delivery, but falls flat on the disappointingly out of sorts and disjoined finale. 46%.

⠿ **Penderyn Madeira** bott Mar 14 db **(92.5) n21.5** dried kumquat and fizzy oak; a little austere; **t24** that more like it. Some serious barley at play here – offering the most malt Penderyn for a while; stage right the fruit tries to nudge its way in, but finds its path barred by the drying oak; pretty salivating for a large part of the journey; **f23** remains barley-rich. And a little fizzy spice peps u the fruit; **b24** a most un-Penderyn-like maltfest. But just love the squabbling between the fruit and oak on the palate. 46%.

⠿ **Penderyn Madeira** bott Apr 14 db **(93) n22** usual dry, slightly nipping aroma involving crushed fruit stones and peel; **t23.5** usual, fruity, juicy velvet-soft delivery which slowly takes on board a soothing mocha countenance...; **f23.5** usual bowing in the presence of vanilla and other drying oaks and spices; **b24** the last half dozen or so batches of Penderyn have been, by and large, pretty wonderful. This is business as usual... 46%.

Penderyn 41 db **(91.5) n22 t23 f24 b22.5**. Don't think for one moment it's the reduction of strength that makes this work so well. Rather, it is the outstanding integration of the outlandishly good Madeira casks with the vanilla. At usual strength this would have scored perhaps another couple of points. Oh, the lucky French for whom this was designed... 41%

Penderyn 41 Madeira bott Jun 11 db **(90.5) n22 t23 f22.5 b23** Penderyn at its most demure but also in this case showing it has a few claws, too. Works better at this strength than the Port Wood, probably because there is far more going on between the counter weight of grape and oak . The delivery, though, is the star as early cocoa notes pop up, welded to crunchy muscovado sugars and even a hint of stem ginger. 41%. ncf.

Penderyn Bourbon Matured Single Cask dist 2000 **(96) n24 t24.5 f23.5 b24**. Penderyn as rarely seen, even by me. This is as old a Welsh whisky that has been bottled in living memory. And it is one that will live in the memory of this current generation. For I have encountered very few whiskies which revels in a controlled sweetness on so many levels. This is so good, it is frightening. 61.2%

Penderyn Peated bott Oct 11 db **(90.5) n22 t23 f22.5 b23**. So few whiskies are quite so well-mannered as this... 46%. ncf.

Penderyn Peated bott Nov 11 db **(93.5) n23.5 t23 f23 b24**. The nose has rarely been the ace in the deck for Penderyn, but here it strengthens the hand considerably. This is the first Penderyn with some genuine peaty grunt. 46%. ncf.

Penderyn Peated bott 2 Nov 12 db **(95) n23.5 t24 f23.5 b24**. One of the most delicate whiskies you will experience this year. The fact it is smoked makes it even more remarkable. 46%. ncf.

Penderyn Peated bott 3 Feb 13 db **(88) n22 t22.5 f21.5 b22**. Almost a Laphroaig-style malt, complete with oaky bitterness at the death, too. 46%. ncf.

Penderyn Portwood bott 1 Nov 12 db **(96) n23 t24.5 f23.5 b25**. Oh, the colour...the colour...!!! The most Port wood Rose I have ever seen...what would this have been like at 46 or cask strength? I wonder. Probably nearer Port...Curiously the blurb on the label describes the colour as "golden". Must have been looking at a ring. For "ruby", like the Port, might have been closer. As for the whisky itself, more importantly, what can one say? Another bottling which is truly world class for sure. Certainly one of the greatest variations of this distillery, the subtlest and best balanced without doubt, and one that now sits in my dining table amongst the world's elite drams. 41%. ncf.

⠿ **Penderyn Portwood** bott Mar 13 db **(95.5) n24** the kind of heady mix between chunky Demerera sugars, higher, intense bourbon notes and thick, well matured fruitcake which almost makes the head spin. The spices are as little more than standard bearers for the chunky oak which controls itself with aplomb; **t24** thick and rich delivery but always light enough for the more delicate elements to filter through. You could swear some malt pings about a bit, but so do does under-sugared redcurrant jam. Stewed under-ripe greengages adds to the mix; **f23.5** a little mocha and marzipan is added to the Cadbury Fruit and Nut...; **b24** a mesmerising whisky, changing in the glass every two or three minutes. Not quite to the same breathtaking level as last year's effort, But really does take your palate through its paces. 41%

⠿ **Penderyn Portwood** bott Oct 13 db **(81.5) n20.5 t22 f19 b20**. A Portwood that has hit a bit of a storm. Some very decent plummy moments. But far too many off key ones for a malt of Penderyn's high standards. 41%

Penderyn Portwood Swansea City Special db **(96.5) n23.5 t24.5 f24 b24.5**. On Saturday 30th April 1966 I was taken by my father to see my very first football game: Millwall versus Swansea Town, as they were then known. On 30th April 2011 I celebrated 45 years of agony and ecstasy (though mainly agony!) with my beloved Millwall with a dinner at The Den as we hosted.... would you believe it? Yep, Swansea! The Swans won that day on their march to deserved promotion to the Premier League and it was my honour to be at Wembley to see them overcome Reading in the Play Off Final to book their place among the elite. I have met their Chairman Huw Jenkins on occasion but not yet had the chance to wish him well in his new rarified environment. I toast you and your grand old club, Huw, with this quite stunning, absolutely world class malt, as Welsh now as laverbread, and look forward to the day when the Lions are back among the Swans...Oh, and in the newly acquired knowledge from a discovery I made while tracing back some of my family history over Christmas 2011 that, as fate would have it, my paternal grandmother's family hail in the 19th century from Neath, on the outskirts of Swansea...; that there is not a jot of Scots in me as we Murray's previously believed, but a whole load of Welsh! Perhaps goes to explain why I have so long been such a fan of Penderyn! Or, just maybe, this fabulous whisky does... 59.4%. ncf sc.

Penderyn Sherrywood released 1 Jan 11 db **(94) n23 t23.5 f23.5 b24.** Drier than the lips of a Welsh Male Voice Choir singing in the Sahara. But a whole lot more harmonious. 46%. ncf.

Penderyn Sherrywood bott Feb 12 db **(94) n22 t24 f24 b24.** Fascinating how this sherry works in an entirely different way to the one bottled in October, offering different structure and focus points. But certainly no less quality. I am delighted for Penderyn when I taste this. But I wish some key people from the scotch whisky industry, as well as one or two commentators, would grab hold of this to learn just how a clean, entirely non-sulphured, sherry butt should actually be...if they have the ability to tell the difference (which in some cases I doubt), they will be in for a major shock. Mind you: there are none so blind than those who wish not to see... 46%. ncf.

Penderyn Sherrywood bott 20 oct 12 db **(89.5) n21.5 t23 f22.5 b22.5.** A faultless sherry butt ensures some marvellous moments, but the scope is a little limited. So enjoyable, though. 46%. ncf.

Penderyn Sherrywood bott 1 feb 13 db **(93) n23.5 t24 f22 b23.5.** A malt which really must be tasted at body temperature for the very best results. 46%. ncf.

Penderyn Sherrywood Limited Edition cask no. 546 db **(95) n24 t24 f23 b24.** This is one of the world great whiskies. Penderyn's consultant, Jim Swan, is responsible for the use and selection of this cask. As was the case with the other single cask selections. It meant an entire four hour tasting afternoon was been spent simply analysing these astonishing casks. If all the world's whiskies were this good I'd never be able to get even close to completing the Bible. The three single casks included here confirm that Penderyn has entered the stratosphere of magnificent whisky. Ignore this distillery entirely at your peril. 50%. ncf sc.

Scotch Malt Whisky Society Cask 128.1 Aged 6 Years 1st fill port barrique, cask no. PT3, dist 2003 **(93.5) n21.5 t24.5 f23.5 b24.** For those single malt fundamentalists who think the SMWS have welshed on their ideals, here is confirming proof: Welsh whisky. But tell me. The drunken nose apart, which has probably robbed it of an award, just which part of this whisky is not fabulous...? 55.6%. sc. 233 bottles.

Scotch Malt Whisky Society Cask 128.3 Aged 5 Years first fill barrel, cask no. 600, dist 06 **(96) n24 t24 f24 b24.** If this doesn't get Penderyn to bring out a succession of full strength cask whiskies, I don't know what will. This is, without question, world class... 61.3%. sc.

Scotch Malt Whisky Society Cask 128.4 Aged 7 Years first fill port barrique, cask no. 32, dist 2004 **(92) n22 t22.5 f24 b23.5.** Hardly a malt for the faint-hearted, but one many in the Scotch whisky industry, along with 128.3, can take a long hard look at. I'll give you a clue, boys: it is the quality of the casks. That area where the Scotch whisky industry has let us down so badly... 59.4%. sc.

British Blends

⋰ **The One British Blended Whisky (84.5) n22 t21.5 f20 b21.** Although it doesn't say so on the bottle, I understand this is made from a blend of malts from England, Ireland, Scotland and Wales. It says "blend" which implies the use of grain, though this is probably not so...another example of the confusion caused by the brainless and arrogant change of terminology from "vatted" to denote a blend of malts insisted upon by the Scotch Whisky Association. Not yet checked, but would have thought that as not scotch, they still would have been entitled to call it a vatting. The mind boggles over what they will do with this whisky if Scotland votes for independence in a few weeks' times. Doubtless the SWA will make some kind of noise... Anyway, back to the action. The label does claim this is a whisky of "intriguing complexity". If true, the term will have to be redefined. The nose, sure enough, does offer just enough smoky and citrus twists and turns to wonder what will happen next. But the delivery on the palate is a disappointment, with any complexity desired submerged under a welter of dull caramels. Just too flat and soft for its own good: back to the drawing board....and possibly without scotch... 40% WB15/406

World Whiskies

I have long said that whisky can be made just about anywhere in the world; that it is not writ large in stone that it is the inalienable right for just Scotland, Ireland, Kentucky and Canada to have it all to themselves. And so, it seems, it is increasingly being proved. Perhaps only sandy deserts and fields of ironstone can prevent its make physically and Islam culturally, though even that has not been a barrier to malt whisky being distilled in both Pakistan and Turkey. While not even the world's highest mountains or jungle can prevent the spread of barley and copper pot.

Outside of North America and Europe, whisky's traditional nesting sites, you can head in any direction and find it being made. South America may be well known for its rum, but in the south of Brazil, an area populated by Italian and German settlers many generations back, malt whisky is thriving. In even more lush and tropical climes it can now also be found, with Taiwan and Thailand leading the way.

Japan has long represented Asia with distinction and whisky-making there is in such an advanced state and at a high standard Jim Murray's Whisky Bible has given it its own section - and World Whisky of the Year for 2015!. But while neighbouring South Korea has ended its malt distilling venture, further east, and at a very unlikely altitude, Nepal has forged a small industry to team up, geographically, with fellow malt distillers India and Pakistan. The main malt whisky from this region making inroads in world markets is India's Amrut single malt. Actually, inroads is hardly doing them justice. Full-bloodied trailblazing, more like. So good now is their whisky they were, with their fantastically complex brand, Fusion deservedly awarded Jim Murray's Whisky Bible 2010 Third Finest Whisky in the World. That represented a watershed not just for the distillery, but Indian whisky as a whole and in a broader sense the entire world whisky movement: it proved beyond doubt that excellent distilling and maturation wherever you are on this planet will be recognised and rewarded.

Africa is also represented on the whisky stage. There has long been a tradition of blending Scotch malt with South African grain but now there is single malt there, as well. Two malt distilleries, to be precise, with a second being opened at the Drayman's Brewery in Pretoria. I was supposed to have visited it a little while back, but the distiller, obviously not wanting to see me, went to the trouble of falling off his horse and breaking his thigh the actual day before. Wimp.

One relatively new whisky-making region is due immediate further study: Australia. From a distance of 12,000 miles, the waters around Australia's distilleries appear to be muddied. Quality appears to range from the very good to extremely poor. And during the back end of 2004 I managed to discover this first hand when I visited three Tasmanian distilleries and Bakery Hill in Melbourne which perhaps leads the way regarding quality malt whisky made south of the Equator, and had another squint ten years later when I popped over once more. Certainly green shoots are sprouting at the Tasmania Distillery which has now moved its operation away from its Hobart harbour site to an out of town one close to the airport. The first bottlings of that had been so bad that it will take some time and convincing for those who have already tasted it to go back to it again. However, having been to the warehouse – and having tasted samples from every single cask they have on site – I reported in previous Bibles that it was only a matter of time before those first offerings would be little more than distant – though horrific – memories. Well, as predicted, it is now safe to put your head above the parapet. The last cask strength bottling I tasted was a bloody beaut.

For Jim Murray's Whisky Bible 2015 I was again flooded with a disarming array of excellent malt whiskies with all the usual suspects chipping in with deliveries far better their cricketing countrymen. Limeburners, Sullivan's Cove, Lark Distillery and Timboon came out with staggeringly beautiful bottlings; while Nant has already thrown down the gauntlet with a series of the most massive yet gorgeous malts yet from the Southern Hemisphere. Together they represent some of the highlights of world whisky.

The remaining casks of Wilson's malt from New Zealand are disappearing fast, though they are not vanishing without without trace. The NZ Whisky Collection 1988 picked up 96.5 points and Southern hemisphere whisky of the Year in the 2015 Bible. Apparently the stills from there are not just making rum in Fiji but whisky as well. We are all aware of the delights of island whisky, but a Pacific Island malt? Which leaves Antarctica as the only continent not making whisky, though what some of those scientists get up to for months on end no one knows.

ARGENTINA
Blends
Breeders Choice (84) n21 t22 f21 b20. A sweet blend using Scottish malt and, at the helm, an unusually lush Argentinian grain. 40%

AUSTRALIA
BAKERY HILL DISTILLERY 1999. Operating.
Bakery Hill Classic Malt cask no. 5710 db (87.5) n22 t22.5 f21 b22. Not far off how I remember David's previous Classic malt, except now sporting a higher honey level. 46%

Bakery Hill Classic Malt cask no. 8212 db (94) n23 t22.5 f24.5 b24. Just so elegant and playful! Will win any heart. 46%

Bakery Hill Classic Malt Cask Strength cask no. 5710 db (96) n23.5 t23 f25 b24.5. As the 46% version, only here just about every aspect here is more vivid, the flavours brighter – polished by the most sublime oils which offer also a degree of spice absent at the lower strength. Just pour, and nose and taste at body temperature and...you'll never see Australian whisky quite the same way again...Magnificent! 60%

Bakery Hill Classic Malt Cask Strength cask no. 9112 db (90.5) n23 t22.5 f22 b23. Ooh, that mix of tannin and honey...makes you come over all unnecessary...! 60%

Bakery Hill Double Wood cask no. 5591 db (82.5) n20.5 t22.5 f19 b20.5. Not quite exact cut makes for an ungainly malt full of sultanas. 46%

Bakery Hill Double Wood bourbon & French oak cask no. 5855 db (86.5) n22.5 t22.5 f20.5 b21. Substantial whisky with a delightful chocolate fruit and nut core. 46%

Bakery Hill Double Wood cask no. 8256 db (88.5) n21.5 t23 f21.5 b22.5. Placid. 46%

Bakery Hill Double Wood cask no. 9078 db (94.5) n24 t24 f22.5 b24. This light fruit cake number is one of the better Double woods from Bakery Hill yet. And on the subject of Double Wood, Haddin has just been castled by my old nets partner Graham Swann for 1 (112 for 6), the double wood, presumably the two stumps hit by the ball...) actually, this whisky is so good, TWO wickets have fallen while tasting it...David: how about calling it "Bakery Hill Double Wicket"...? Actually, as I write this a third wicket has just gone.. 114 for 8...any Aussie will get through a bottle of this just to get over the shock!) 46%

Bakery Hill Peated Malt cask no. 6512 db (94.5) n24 t23.5 f23 b24. Like the cask strength version, only at medium pace. 46%

Bakery Hill Peated Malt cask no. 7011 db (86) n22 t22.5 f20.5 b21. After the usual honey-rich machinations, bitters out quite tellingly (just as Smith loses his wicket to Anderson to make it five down for just 109..how bitter can an Aussie get?). 46%

Bakery Hill Peated Malt cask no. 9212 db (85.5) n21.5 t22 f21 b21. The same as the cask strength version...only not quite so loud... 46%

Bakery Hill Peated Malt Cask Strength cask 6512 db (92.5) n24 t23.5 f23 b24. Began tasting this first Australian whisky of the year at exactly 11am on Wednesday 10th July. Henry Blofeld, Blowers, is at one end of a BBC microphone, I, Sniffers, exactly 46 miles away as one of his pigeons fly. It is the moment Pattinson bowled a wide for the first ball of the 2013 Ashes series. There is smoke in the air at Trent Bridge, with the Red Arrows having flown past displaying red white & blue. The first Ashes Test I ever saw was also at Trent Bridge, Nottingham, where these present day combatants have set up camp. Roughly about the same time I got the exclusive story about a guy who crashed his bi-plane into the River Trent having flown, illegally, under the bridge next to the historic ground with a girl walking the wing at the time...oh, the days of my comparative youth. A bit like this beaut of a malt. A touch of youth, but wily enough to entertain with aplomb. As I sign off from this first Australian of this edition, England, having decided to bat, have progressed to 16 for no wicket. Oh, that 1981 test at Trent Bridge? England lost, their only defeat in a 3-1 series victory. Bowling for Australia was Dennis Lilley; batting for England Ian Botham. You get the feeling they both would enjoyed a macho malt like this... 60%

Bakery Hill Peated Malt Cask Strength cask no. 9212 db (86.5) n22 t22.5 f21 b21. A real softie for its strength. Let down a little by the bittering oak. But the light honey lift to the smoke is delightful. 60%

BOOIE RANGE DISTILLERY
Booie Range Single Malt db (72) n14 t20 f19 b19. Mounts the hurdle of the wildly off-key nose impressively with a distinct, mouth watering barley richness to the palate that really does blossom even on the finish. 40%

HEARTWOOD DISTILLERS
Convict Unchained 11 Years Old port cask, cask no. HH0613, dist 01, bott 12 db (88.5) n23.5 t23 f20 b22. Had this cask been technically on the mark, this would have been a world beater. 58%. sc. Batch 1. 220 bottles.

⠿ **Heartwood 'Convict Redemption' Batch 2 Single Malt** port cask no. HH0611, bott Dec 13, db **(91.5) n23** didn't even have to see the back of the label before a sniff of this sang "Australian Port" to me. Fresh, plummy fruit – and I mean more plummy than a bowler-hatted city gent at Lord's...; **t23** glorious delivery with the fruit swooping early, accompanied by medium dark sugars; a little vanilla begins to register; **f22.5** light vanilla and spice; **b23** scientists have announced today that strong black, sugarless coffee (which I drink every day) is good for destroying plaque and surrounding bacteria. Well, if the coffee didn't do the full job this morning, this must have finished the little blighters off. A not so little beaut! 71.90%. sc.

⠿ **Hellyers Road Single Malt Whisky 12 Year Old Original** db **(84.5) n19 t22 f21.5 b22.** Forget the nose and get stuck into the massive malt. 46.2%.

⠿ **Hellyers Road Single Malt Whisky Henry's Legacy 'The Gorge'** db **(83) n21.5 t21 f20 b20.5.** Eye-wateringly sharp in places, its best bits hang on a vaguely smoky, molasses-sweetened coffee note. 46.2%.

⠿ **Hellyers Road Single Malt Whisky Original** db **(84) n20.5 t22 f20.5 b21.** Bolstered on last year's bottling thanks to a profound malt surge on delivery. Citrus fruity in part, but both nose the tingle at the finish demands more copper. 46.2%.

⠿ **Hellyers Road Single Malt Whisky Port Matured** db **(88) n22.5** spiced, juicy fruitcake; **t23** superb delivery with the grape ripping home onto the throat with spice, then soothing and kissing better with its salivating freshness; **f20.5** a tad off key but the spices are busy and biting; **b22** without question the direction this distillery should take. Some wonderful moments. 46.2%.

Release The Beast sherry cask, bott 7 Aug 12 db **(95.5) n24 t24.5 f23 b24.** As beasts go, for all its power, is a tame and gentle one. Just too gorgeous. 65.4%. sc.

Vat Out of Hell sherry/bourbon, cask no. LD446 & HH0040, dist Mar 03 & Nov 99, bott May 13 db **(89) n22 t24 f21 b22.** Rather than tasting this today, I had planned to be at The Oval to see the Tasmanian former Aussie skipper Ricky Pontin, representing my beloved Surrey, bring the curtain down to his first class career. But with the deadline looming I eschewed, with heavy heart, my natural instincts to catch the train to St Pancras and travel on to Kennington in order to carry on tasting and get this book out on time. So, as a compromise, I spent his batting hours tasting Tas whisky. Ponting finished the day and his career of gritty plundering with an extraordinary 169 not out, having batted the entire day. To mark the end of his magnificent career on the very same day that a young lad on debut called Ashton Agar created Test history by making 98 as a number eleven (oh, for the fearlessness of youth...!) the next bottling should be in their honour: Bat Out of Hell... 67.4%. nc ncf. ask strength. 320 bottles.

Velvet Hammer 13 Years Old bourbon cask no. HH0072, dist Nov 99, bott Mar 13 db **(95) n23.5 t24.5 f23.5 b24.** Absolutely superb! Bill Lark, my old mate...you have excelled yourself! 68.8%. sc. Cask strength, 172 bottles.

HELLYERS ROAD

Hellyers Road Original Aged 10 Years ex-American cask db **(80) n18.5 t22.5 f19 b20.** A degree of citrus and a light Demerara helps overcome some of the feintier, oilier aspects of the distillate. 46.2%. ncf. Hellyers Road Distillery.

Hellyers Road Peated ex-American white oak casks db **(87) n22 t22.5 f20.5 b22.** Clunky and dry...a very unusual whisky experience. 46.2%. ncf.

Hellyers Road Pinot Noir Finish ex-American cask db **(87.5) n22 t22.5 f21 b22.** Lovely fruit...Hell, yes! 46.2%. ncf. Hellyers Road Distillery.

Hellyers Road Original Roaring Forty ex-American cask db **(84.5) n21.5 t22 f20 b21.** Dry and a little creaky, as is the wont of the house style. But enough cream caramel and muscovado sugars around to soften the experience. 40%. ncf. Hellyers Road Distillery.

LARK DISTILLERY

The Lark Distillery Single Malt Whisky Cask Strength cask no. LD140, bott Feb 10 db **(80) n19.5 t18.5 f22 b20.** From tip to tail there is a note on this I can't quite put my finger on, or say I much approve of. But there is also a real coppery small still feel to this, bolstered by a late-developing honeycomb and Demerara sheen. 58%

⠿ **The Lark Distillery Single Malt Whisky Cask Strength** port cask, cask no. 473, bott 2014 db **(94) n24** a beautifully bright nose: the muscovado sugars are dripping with greengage and black cherry. Not sure the spices could be more effective or disarming; **t24** hold tight: the taste buds are under immediate bombardment from rabid spices which have not the slightest intention of taking prisoners; the rich, soft fruit looks on helplessly; thankfully a big dollop of ulmo honey early on helps cushion the blows; **f22.5** remains juicy to the end, though it takes a while for the spice to recede. A little blood orange bitterness creeps in; **b23.5** and I'd always thought Hobart was a friendly town... 58%.

The Lark Distillery Single Malt Whisky Distillers Selection cask no. LD109, bott Apr 10 db (86.5) n21.5 t21 f22.5 b21.5. A chunky affair with some attractive nougat and orange; the star turn is the Rolo candy finale. 46%

⋅⋅⋅⊳ The Lark Distillery Single Malt Whisky Distiller's Selection sherry barrel aged, cask no. 475, bott 2014 db (88.5) n23 mixed herbs and spices offer up a nose more likely to befound in a delicatessen than a whisky glass. Somewhat busy...; t22 and on delivery turns 180 degrees and offers little or no spice but, rather, a soft toffee-raisin massage. So soft...; f21.5 more toffee-raisin – tangy this time with spice growth; b22 don't go looking for complexity or a quickened pulse. A Steady Eddie dram 46%.

⋅⋅⋅⊳ The Lark Distillery Single Malt Whisky Limited Release sherry cask, bott 2014 db (86) n21.5 t23 f20 b21.5. A big fruit and nut ensemble. Not sure if this Lark's finest ever distillate, mind. 52.1%

⋅⋅⋅⊳ The Lark Distillery Single Malt Whisky Single Cask port barrel aged, cask no. 516, bott 2014 db (90) n23 beautifully rounded and balanced, the spices fit well with the cucmber and sultana; t23 spices arrive first, then several waves of gentle fruit. The vanilla really has a big say as the oak plays a guiding role; some coconut in syrup thickens and sweetens; f22 a little late bitterness but the fruit does hang on, though some late oils from the still also grab a foothold. Hence, probably, the bitterness... b22 an entertaining dram which doesn't always balance out the way it was probably planned but gets there in the end. 43%.

LIMEBURNERS

Limeburners Single Malt Whisky Barrel M23 bott no. 78 da (90.5) n22.5 t23.5 f22 b22.5. First time I've tasted anything from this Western Australian mob. G'day fellas! I have to admit, thought it might have been from France at first, as the aroma on nosing blind reminded me of brandy. And not without good reason, it transpires. This no age statement malt spent an unspecified amount of time in American brandy cask before being finished in bourbon casks. Does it work? Yes it does. But now that's torn it lads. You are supposed to start off with a bloody horrible whisky and get better. Now you have gone and made a rod for your own back. Good on you! 61%

Limeburners Single Malt Whisky Peated Barrel M58 ex-bourbon American oak cask db (89) n22.5 t23.5 f21 b22. Taken aback when I nosed this: saw the Limeburners tag, but hadn't spotted the style. The smoke gave me a jolt: not seen this from these guys before. Peatburners, more like...and an attractive smoky style the like of which I have never encountered before. 48%. ncf. 133 bottles.

⋅⋅⋅⊳ Limeburners Single Malt Whisky Barrel M61 Ex bourbon American oak/ Finished Australian Port Cask, dist 30 Sep 08, bott 12 Sep 13 db (94.5) n23.5 the oak positively growls from the glass; as heavy and impenetrable as a tropical jungle. A spiced fruitcake and manuka honey mix plots a safe course through the low-hanging branches; t24 second innings are usually played out on slightly worn tracks with ever less even bounce. And taking more spin. Well, there is still some nip and fizz to the delivery here, one that gets you on the back foot as you take extra time to cope with the steepling fruit; f23 an elegant final passage before stumps...oak stumps that is. Remains juicy and full bodied to the end, though; b24 I really must get out to Perth to see these guys. A very sound and harmonious whisky. I word of contradiction, though. Their back label urges you to add a little water. Don't. Just follow the Murray Method at the front of this Bible...and the whisky's splendour will be fully revealed in good time! 60%. 99 bottles. ncf.

Limeburners Single Malt Whisky M64 Muscat Finish db (92) n23.5 t23 f22.5 b23. Macho malt keeps in touch with its feminine side. Tasty and beautifully made. 61%. ncf.

Limeburners Single Malt Whisky Barrel M79 ex-bourbon American oak cask and finished in an old Australian sherry cask db (93.5) n23 t24 f23 b23.5. A rare exhibition of a happy marriage between bourbon cask and sherry. 61%. ncf. 113 bottles.

Limeburners Single Malt Whisky Barrel M91 ex-bourbon American oak barrique and finished in an old Australian sherry cask db (80) n19 t21 f20 b20. The stale tobacco on the nose and rumbling, off key finish says something about the feints involved. The delicious clarity of the fruit is a tick for the "sherry" cask. 43%. ncf. 355 bottles.

THE NANT DISTILLERY

The Nant Single Malt First Release bott 2010 db (91.5) n24 t23 f22 b22.5. Beyond excellent for a first go. The flavours and style could not be more clearly nailed to the mast. I'll be watching this distillery closely. 43%

The Nant 3 Year Old American oak/Port db (91.5) n22.5 t22 f23 b24. Beautifully well made whisky. Has the sophistication of a dry martini, but without the olive...yet maintaining the salt. Last year I set out to keep my eyes on these chaps. Not a bad move. 43%

The Nant 3 Years Old Cask Strength American oak bourbon db **(95.5) n23 t24 f24 b24.5** I have really got to get back to Oz to visit these guys. Something majestic is happening here. Whatever it is they are doing, I have to discover first hand...World class. *61.6%*

The Nant Distillery 5 Years Old French oak/Port **(92.5) n23.5 t23.5 f22 b23.5.** Not sure if this is talking French, Portuguese, Oz or a strange dialect incorporating all three. Lovely to listen to, whichever, and makes itself fully understood. *43%*

The Nant Distillery 5 Year Old Cask Strength American oak/sherry **(86.5) n21.5 t23 f20.5 b21.5.** A bit of a lollipop of a malt: suck at it and you get plenty of fruity sugar. However, unlike most Nants I have tasted previously, there is a bit of an imbalance between the intense sugar, spices and fuzzy oils from the cut. No faulting the juiciness of the fruit or liveliness of the spice, though. *63%*

The Nant Distillery 5 Year Old Cask Strength French oak/Port **(94) n23.5 t24 f23 b23.5.** If you are looking for a simple, straight up and down dram, you have opened the wrong bottle. This is one very complex offering... *63%*

OLD HOBART DISTILLERY

Overeem Port Cask Matured heavily charred quarter cask finish, cask no. OHD-010, dist 15 Aug 07, bott 15 May 12 db **(89) n23 t23 f21 b22.** A supreme toastiness works so well with the big fruit. *43%. sc.*

Overeem Port Cask Matured heavily charred ex-Port, French oak quarter cask, cask no. OHD-026, dist 08, bott 13 db **(90) n22 t23.5 f22 b22.5.** Heavily alcoholic sticky treacle pudding... *43%. sc.*

Overeem Port Cask Matured Cask Strength heavily charred quarter cask finish, cask no. OHD-018, dist 15 Aug 07, bott 15 May 12 db **(95) n24 t24.5 f23 b23.5** Just get it if you see it: a no brainer! *60%. sc.*

Overeem Port Cask Matured Cask Strength heavily charred ex-Port, French oak quarter cask, cask no. OHD-029, dist Apr 08, bott Jan 13 db **(91) n21.5 t24 f22.5 b23.** You don't get many whiskies like this turning up in a lifetime. A completely unique finger print for any malt, believe me. Hope I can find a full working day in the next year or so to give this the analysis it deserves. *60%. sc.*

Overeem Sherry Cask Matured medium charred quarter cask finish, cask no. ODG-005, dist 5 Jun 07, bott 1 Jun 12 db **(85.5) n21.5 t22 f21 b21.** No frills, either. *43%. sc.*

Overeem Sherry Cask Matured heavily charred ex-sherry, French oak quarter cask, cask no. OHD-030 db **(88.5) n21.5 t23 f22 b22.** Clean, massively enjoyable...but just needing a top up of complexity for greatness. *43%. sc.*

Overeem Sherry Cask Matured Cask Strength medium charred quarter cask finish, cask no. OHD-003, dist 6 Jun 07, bott 2 Mar 12 db **(91.5) n23 t23 f22 b23.5.** Must have stolen all the complexity and charisma from cask ODG-005. A treat! *60%. sc.*

Overeem Sherry Cask Matured Cask Strength heavily charred ex-sherry, French oak quarter cask, cask no. OHD-032 db **(95) n23 t24.5 f23.5 b24.** The key is the spice: from the first nose to the final pulse on the palate it intrigues and enriches. Brilliant! *60%. sc.*

SMALL CONCERN DISTILLERY

Cradle Mountain Pure Tasmanian Malt db **(87) n21 t22 f21 b23.** A knock-out malt from a sadly now lost distillery in Tasmania. Faultlessly clean stuff with lots of new oak character but sufficient body to guarantee complexity. *43%*

SOUTHERN COAST DISTILLERS

Southern Coast Single Malt Batch 001 db **(92.5) n23 t24 f22 b23.5.** "A hint of bushfire in the barley" claims the back label. Well, that one's got me stumped; I pride myself in nosing anything and everything, but that particular aroma has passed me by. Perhaps they mean the heather aroma...? Mind you, I did get pretty close to some scary forest fires near Marseilles nearly 30 years ago, but probably not the same thing... Anyway, back to this fabulous first effort. Wow! Could ask for more in a study of crisp brown sugars and sweet cocoa...; *46%*

Southern Coast Single Malt Batch 002 db **(96) n24 t23.5 f24.5 b24.** Is this the best Australian whisky ever to shamelessly masquerade as Demerara pot still rum? I should think so. Will it ever be beaten? I doubt it. In fact, just how many Demerara rums have I ever tasted of this refinement. One or two, at most. And I have probably tasted more than anyone in the whisky trade living. One of the most astonishing whiskies it has been my honour to taste. Frankly, I am on my knees... *46%*

Southern Coast Single Malt Batch 003 db **(79.5) n18 t19 f23 b19.5.** Third time unlucky. Lots of oils and berserk honey. But too feinty, though this went to some finishing school, believe me...! *46%. ncf.*

Southern Coast Single Malt Batch 004 db **(82.5)** n20 t22 f20.5 b20. An earthy, slightly musty dram with a pleasing essence of honey but struggles to find structure or balance. 46%

Southern Coast Single Malt Batch 005 db **(83.5)** n21.5 t22 f20 b20. Starts off like a Jack Hobbs or Brian Lara or Alec Stewart taking the Aussie quick bowling apart. There is even an unusual, but mightily attractive, sweetened Vegemite hint to this (not as strange as it sounds, actually). But the middle stump is removed by the hefty finish: the cricketing equivalent of an ungainly, head-over hoick to cow corner.... 46%

Southern Coast Single Malt Batch 006 db **(95)** n24 t24 f23.5 b24. When I saw these Southern Coast Whiskies before me, my eyes lit up. Here was my journey to Demerara. Much cheaper and less problem-riddled than any trip I normally make to Guyana..and with less chance of coming away with my normal stomach complaint. Batches 4 and 5 let me down. But Batch 6.... even the sun has come out for the first time in three days as I nose this... Georgetown, here I come... 46%

TASMAN DISTILLERY

Great Outback Rare Old Australian Single Malt db **(92)** n24 t24 f21 b23. What can you say? An Australian whisky distillery makes a malt to grace the world's stage. But you can't find it outside of Australia. This will have to be rectified. 40%

TASMANIA DISTILLERY

Old Hobart db **(69)** n16 t19 f17 b17. The nose still has some way to go before it can be accepted as a mainstream malt, though there is something more than a little coastal about it this time. However, the arrival on the palate is another matter and I must say I kind of enjoyed its big, oily and increasingly sweet maltiness & crushed sunflower seed nuttiness towards the end. Green (& yellow) shoots are growing. The whisky is unquestionably getting better. 60%

Sullivans Cove db **(61)** n13 t15 f17 b16. Some malt but typically grim, oily and dirty; awesomely weird. 40%. *Australia.*

Sullivans Cove American Oak Single Cask cask no. HH0152, dist 28 Jan 00, bott 25 Sep 12 db **(86)** n21.5 t23 f20.5 b21. A slightly wider cut than required makes for slightly more aggressive oils than required. But you can't help loving the trademark orange-blossom honey, especially when it ends up as tangy marmalade...! 47.5%. nc ncf sc.

Sullivans Cove American Oak Single Cask cask no. HH0211, dist 10 Mar 00, bott 10 Jan 13 db **(82)** n20 t23 f19 b20. Not quite up to their normal standards on the distilling side. But such is the intensity of the grist and fruity sugars, the delivery simply takes the breath away. Overly sweet to a degree, but that repairs some damage. 47.5%. nc ncf sc.

Sullivans Cove American Oak Single Cask cask no. HH0257, dist 14 Apr 00, bott 25 Sep 12 db **(91.5)** n23 t23.5 f22 b23. About as relaxed and natural (and slightly imperfect) as a 19-year-old making his test debut for Australia at number eleven after the last five wickets have fallen for nine runs... 47.5%

Sullivans Cove American Oak Single Cask cask no. HH0258, dist 14 Apr 2000, bott 17 Aug 2012 db **(90.5)** n23 t23 f22 b22.5. I know I shouldn't say it. But the most Scotch single malt in style of all the Aussie drams: try and distinguish blind between this and very decent Speysider. 47.5%. nc ncf sc.

⫶ **Sullivans Cove American Oak Single Cask** cask no. HH0014, dist 22 Oct 99, bott 24 Mar 14 db **(90.5)** n22 a lively – and lovely – green apple tinge to this while the barley has remained pure and focussed despite 14 passing years in a warm climate; t23 superb delivery with almost three dimensional clarity to the barley early on. A few juicy, honey-brushed malty notes really do add riches; f22.5 long, with a distinct lemon meringue tart flourish, especially as the vanilla builds; b23 clean, ultra malty, high quality whisky in anyone's currency. 47.5%

⫶ **Sullivan's Cove American Oak Single Cask** cask no. HH0015, dist 22 Oct 99, bott 13 May 14 db **(87.5)** n21.5 t21.5 f22.5 b22. Fractionally on the hot side. Barrel HH0014 was more forgiving and softened the burn by allowing the barley to flourish. Here the malt takes longer to get under control, though when it finally does, it makes for a mouth-watering and chewy finale. 47.5%

⫶ **Sullivan's Cove American Oak Single Cask** cask no. HH0016, dist 22 Oct 99, bott 21 May 14 db **(86.5)** n20.5 t21.5 f22.5 b22. From the same, even identical, mould as HH15 with the oak not quite able to extract the very best from the distillate. And again, despite the fiery background, the maltiness finally wins through impressively. Degree of copper intensity at work, too. 47.5%

⫶ **Sullivan's Cove American Oak Single Cask** cask no. HH0017, dist 22 Oct 99, bott 21 May 14 db **(86.5)** n21.5 t21.5 f22 b21.5. Another sound, juicy cask though the warmth is again a bit challenging. More comfortable on finish when a little mocha filters through to join the malt. 47.5%

⠿ **Sullivan's Cove American Oak Single Cask** cask no. HH0047, dist 9 Nov 99, bott 30 Apr 14 db **(95.5) n24** hard to imagine a malt whisky being more malt whiskier...the nose celebrates outstanding distilling and classic maturation in a fine cask. The barley is multi-faceted and just about perfectly balanced between barley intensity and the use of deft, still slightly gristy, sugars. The oak chimes in with delicious butterscotch and even a hint of ginger; **t24** few distilleries do weight on delivery better than this one. The intensity of the barley deserves a medal alone, its balance with the gentle vanilla-led oak a bar; **f23.5** long, with a light smattering of cocoa yet the barley still feigns to have a degree of youth...even now; **b24** exemplary malt whisky: absolutely beautiful. 47.5%

⠿ **Sullivan's Cove American Oak Single Cask** cask no. HH0442, dist 22 Aug 99, bott 30 Apr12 db **(85.5) n20 t22 f22.5 b21.** A dodgy cove, one might say. The nose suggests all is not quite right and, despite the big barley blast, balance remains at a premium for this warming dram. Plenty to enjoy, but probably would have been better served stirring up another, duller cask. 47.5%

⠿ **Sullivan's Cove American Oak Single Cask** cask no. HH00460,dist 5 Sep 00, bott 30 Apr 14 db **(92) n23** fabulous mix of ulmo and heather honey really allows the barley to show in a bright light; **t22.5** intense barley from the moment it hits the palate and doesn't cease as the early cocoa arrives; **f23** the spices have been busy from early on but come into their own here. German caramelized biscuit meets Weetabix and malt cereal as the Demerara sugars gain hold; **b23.5** out malts many a Scottish malt distillery. A lovely barrel, complimenting top quality distillate. An assured and wonderfully paced dram of great confidence. 47.5%

Sullivans Cove Bourbon Matured Cask Strength Single Cask barrel no: HH0602, barrel date 21 Feb 01, bott 10 Sep 09 **(81) n18 t24 f20 b19.** An outrageous maltfest, for all its obvious faults. "Distilled with Conviction" the label proudly states, a reference to Tasmania's penal past. But it looks as though the stillman has made his escape as the nose suggests the eye wasn't being kept on the ball as feints abound. Ironically, the resulting extra oils mean the youthful but hugely intense malt simply blows you away. Technically, a nightmare. But you know what? I just love it...!!! (To ramp it up about five or six points, pour into a glass and place in hot water to burn off the higher alcohols. What remains after about five minutes, depending on the temperature of the water, is a much cleaner, more honeyed version). 60%

⠿ **Sullivan's Cove Double Cask batch 71**, youngest barrel 14 Feb 01, bott 20 Mar 14 db **(89) n22.5** fruit candy; pears and pear drops; **t22** firm, almost aggressive barley aided with the inevitable spice and something not too dissimilar to sherbet; **f22** dries to offer a high cocoa content fruit and nut bar; **b22.5** a satisfying whisky offering penetration on the palate and some decent complexity. 40%

Sullivans Cove Rare Tasmanian Single Cask American oak bourbon cask, cask no. HH0128, dist 25 Jan 00, bott 21 Sep 11 db **(86) n21 t22.5 f21 b21.5.** A slightly wider cut that normally means a subtle degree of extra oil is floating around, enough to dull the sharper edges of the more complex notes from an obviously top quality cask. As usual from the distillery, though, the sugars make you groan with delight. 47.5%. sc. 246 bottles.

Sullivans Cove Rare Tasmanian Single Cask American oak bourbon cask, cask no. HH0326, dist 30 May 00, bott 12 Jan 12 db **(90.5) n23 t22 t23 f22.5 b23.** Easy going, sweet enough and with sufficient weight to be an anytime kind of a malt. Put it this way: I'd say yes to it anytime, for one...! 47.5%. sc. 256 bottles.

Sullivans Cove Rare Tasmanian Single Cask American oak bourbon cask, cask no. HH0329, dist 2 Jun 00, bott 17 Feb 12 db **(91.5) n23.5 t23 f22.5 b22.5.** Complex, in a limited kind of way. But beautifully made and the barley is a delight. 47.5%. 168 bottles.

Sullivans Cove Rare Tasmanian Single Cask American oak bourbon cask, cask no. HH0330, dist 2 Jun 00, bott 17 Feb 12 db **(92) n23 t23.5 f22.5 b23.** Makes muted attempts to head into Kentucky territory. Complex. 47.5%. 238 bottles.

Sullivans Cove Rare Tasmanian Single Cask French oak port cask, cask no. HH0425, dist 2000, bott 2012 **(86) n20.5 t23 f21 b21.5.** Huge wine involvement with the chocolatey grape running amuck with a gorgeously soft and rounded assault on the palate. Perhaps, though, could just do with another trick. Still, I'm happy to enjoy the unusual charms offered! 47.5%. sc. 487 bottles.

Sullivans Cove Rare Tasmanian Single Cask French oak port cask, cask no. HH0429, dist 11 Aug 00, bott 21 Sep 11 db **(84) n21 t21 f21 b21.** Pleasant. But straight lines just a little too much thanks to the natural caramels. 47.5%. sc. 453 bottles.

Sullivans Cove Rare Tasmanian Single Cask French oak port cask, cask no. HH0430, dist 15 Aug 00, bott 17 Feb 12 db **(77.5) n19 t20 f19 b19.5.** Just never quite gets its act together or feels right. 47.5%. sc. 546 bottles.

Sullivans Cove Rare Tasmanian Single Cask French oak port cask, cask no. HH0509, dist 6 Oct 00, bott 17 Feb 12 **(96.5) n24 t24 f24 b24.5.** Although this comes from a wine cask, the dominant forces at work here have much more in common with bourbon style whisky than malt. It is also, unquestionably, one of the world whiskies of the year... *47.5%. sc. 494 bottles.*

TIMBOON RAILWAY SHED DISTILLERY

Timboon New Make bott 16 Jun 13 db **(89) 22 t23 f21.5 b22.5.** Plenty of fruit on this clean make. Hard to find sweet barley in more concentrated form, either. *71.4%. sc.*

Timboon Single Malt Whisky Port cask, dist 12 Jul 2009, bott 16 Jan 2013 db **(96.5) n24.5 t24 f24 b24.** Way, way better bottling than their last Port cask offering. Huge doesn't even begin to tell the story....with plenty of character. And no fear of giving the taste buds a biff and a kiss almost at the same moment. Easily one of the whiskies of 2013. *68%. sc.*

Timboon Single Malt Whisky dist Aug 08, bott May 11 db **(93) n24.5 t23 f22 b23.5.** Imagine Tim Boon, the cricketer, going out to face the current England pace attack with one of those foot-long bats used exclusively for players to sign. That, basically, is what we have here with a malt underpowered for the type of job it is capable of doing. Yes, its technique is extraordinary. Certainly, it has moved to the pitch of the barley and is in line with what's coming with rare textbook elegance. But the strength is too feeble to translate into the highest score that it deserves. That said, quality is quality. And this is strictly First Class. *40%*

Timboon Single Malt Whisky bourbon barrel, dist 12 May 09, bott 17 Jun 13 db **(91) n23 t23.5 f22 b22.5.** A thinner offering than last time round. But the nuttiness, perhaps underlined by the slightest lack of copper, is a treat. Not sure if they mature the whisky in the same environment as fruit spirits, because the otherwise inexplicable fruitiness is quite telling... *70.4%. sc.*

∹ **Timboon Single Malt Whisky Bourbon Expression** oak barrel, dist 09 Jan 11, bott12 Jul 14 db **(87) n22 t21.5 f22 b21.5.** A thin chap by Timboon's usually robust standards, but at least the malt has muscles even if the body is lacking. Slightly youthful, too. *40.8%*

∹ **Timboon Single Malt Whisky Limited Edition Port Expression** oak barrel, dist 11 Sep 09, bott 11 Nov 13 db **(88.5) n21** an extraordinary mix of salted celery, prunes and ersatz coffee: **t22.5** a distinctive rum theme is aided by a seductively lush body and teasing spice; **f22.5** sweetens as the oak and spices get a firmer grip. Attractive mix of rum and raisin and coffee fudge mingles; **b22.5** the only time I have ever nosed anything like this was when I was crawling around the warehouses of a rum distillery in Guyana checking out some old Demerara. But pretty delicious, once you get used to its alarming idiosyncrasy... *46%*

∹ **Timboon Single Malt Whisky Port Expression** oak barrel, dist 7 Aug 10, bott 20 Jul 14 db **(95.5) n23** serious grape and must concentrate: the Port is easy to spot and spices buzz enticingly; **t24** serious Timboon-esque delivery of the highest order: massive grape swamping the palate, reinforced by hordes of spice running rampant and taking few prisoners; **f24** brilliant, highly intense mocha and Demerara finish which accentuates the treacle at the finale; **b24.5** another explosive Timboon experience of majestic quality. *69.9%*

YALUMBA WINERY

Smith's Angaston Whisky Vintage 1997 Aged 7 Years db **(88) n20 t22 f23 b23.** Easily one of the most delicate whiskies of the year and one that puts Samuel Smith on the map. Perfect for the hipflask for a night at the ballet. *40%*

Smith's Angaston Whisky Vintage 1998 Aged 8 Years db **(86) n20 t22 f22 b22.** Perhaps conscious that their first offering, a genuine touch of culture that it was, wasn't quite Australian enough, this one's showing bit of aggression. And I mean a bit, as this is no tackle from Lucas Neil. Because after the delivery it's back to the girlie stuff with some admittedly delicious Swiss Roll filling fruitiness. Lovely malt from a distillery I'm going to have to keep my eyes on. *40%*

Vatted Malts

Tasmanian Double Malt Whisky Unpeated (87.5) **n22 t22 f21.5 b22.** Not a chance of getting bored with this guy. A sweet tooth would be useful. *43%. The Nant Distillery.*

BRAZIL
HEUBLEIN DISTILLERY

Durfee Hall Malt Whisky db **(81) n18 t22 f20 b21.** Superbly made whisky; the intensity of the malt is beautifully layered without ever becoming too sweet. Very light bodied and immaculately clean. Good whisky by any standards. *43%*

UNION DISTILLERY

Barrilete db **(72) n18 t19 f18 b17.** Nothing particularly wrong with it technically; it just lacks vitality. Thin but extremely malt intense. *39.1%*

Blends

Cockland Gold Blended Whisky (73) n18 t18 f19 b18. Silky caramel. Traces of malt there, but never quite gets it up. *38%. Fante.*

Drury's Special Reserve (86.5) n21.5 t22 f21 b22. Deceptively attractive, melt-in-the-mouth whisky; at times clean, regulation stuff, but further investigation reveals a honeycomb edge which hits its peak in the middle ground when the spices mix in beautifully. One to seek out and savour when in Brazil. *40%. Campari, Brasil.*

Gold Cup Special Reserve (84.5) n21 t22.5 f20 b21. Ultra soft, easily drinkable and, at times, highly impressive blend which is hampered by a dustiness bestowed upon it by the nagging caramels on both nose and finish. Some lovely early honey does help lift it, though, and there is also attractive Swiss roll jam towards the finish. Yet never quite gets out of third gear despite the most delicate hint of smoke. *39%. Campari, Brasil.*

Gran Par (77) n19.5 t22 f17.5 b18. The nose boasts of vaguely malty glory. The remainder is thin and caramelled with no age to live up to the name. And with Par in the title and bagpipes and kilt in the motif, how long before the SWA buys a case of it...? *39%*

Green Valley Special Reserve batch 07/01 **(70)** n16 t19 f17 b18. A softly oiled, gently bittersweet blend with a half meaty, half boiled sweet nose. An unusual whisky experience. *38.1%.*

Malte Barrilete Blended Whisky batch 001/03 **(76)** n18 t20 f19 b19. This brand has picked up a distinctive apple-fruitiness in recent years and some extra oak, too. *39.1%.*

Natu Nobilis (81.5) n22.5 t20 f19 b20. The nose boasts a genuinely clean, Speyside-style malt involvement. But to taste is much more non-committal with the soft grain dominating and the grassy notes restricted the occasional foray over the tastebuds. Pleasant, but don't expect a flavor fest. *39%. Pernod Ricard, Brasil.*

Natu Nobilis Celebrity (86) n22.5 t22 f20.5 b21. A classy blend with a decent weight and body, yet never running to fat. Some spice prickle ensures the flavor profile never settles in a neautral zone and the charming, citrus-domiated malt on the nose is immediately found on the juicy delivery. A cut above the standard Natu Nobilis and if the finish could be filled out with extra length and complexity, we'd have an exceptionally impressive blend on our hands. Another blend to seek out whenever in Brazil. *39%. Pernod Ricard, Brasil.*

O Monge batch 02/02 **(69)** n17 t18 f17 b17. Poor nose but it recovers with a malty mouth arrival but the thinness of the grain does few favours. *38.5%. Union Distillery.*

Old Eight Special Reserve (85.5) n20 t21 f22.5 b22. Traditionally reviled by many in Brazil, I can assure you that the big bite followed by calming soft grains is exactly what you need after a day's birding in the jungle. *39%. Campari, Brasil.*

Pitt's (84) n21 t20 f22 b21. The pits it certainly aint!! A beautifully malted blend where the barley tries to dominate the exceptionally flinty grain whenever possible. Due to be launched later in 2004, this will be the best Brazil has to offer – though some fine tuning can probably improve the nose and middle even further and up the complexity significantly. I hope, when I visit the distillery early in 2005, I will be able to persuade them to offer a single malt: on this evidence it should, like Pitt's, be an enjoyable experience and perfect company for any World Cup finals. *40%. Busnello Distillery.*

Wall Street (84) n23 t22 f19 b20. Fabulous nose with a sexy citrus-light smoke double bill. And the arrival on the palate excels, too, with a rich texture and confident delivery of malt, again with the smoke dominating. But falls away rather too rapidly as the grains throw the balance out of kilter and ensures too much bitter oak late on. *38%. Pernod Ricard, Brasil.*

INDIA
AMRUT DISTILLERY

Amrut Bourbon cask no. 3436, dist 2 Jun 09, bott 2 Aug 13 **(84.5)** n21 t23 f19.5 b21. A classic case of a cask where the good has been extracted and we are now getting down to some milky undesirables. The astonishing sugar array on delivery is worth the experience alone, though. *41%*

Amrut Bourbon, cask no. 3441, dist 2 Jun 09, bott 1 Aug 13 **(94)** n23.5 t24 f23 b23.5. Simple impossible not to love: just so much that's good to keep you entertained. *46%*

Amrut Cask Strength oak barrels, bott no. 01, bott Jul 09 db **(89.5)** n23 t22.5 f22 b22. Another big malty tale from India. But there is a big surge of natural, oily caramels to this one which keeps the complexity levels marginally down. *61.8%*

Amrut Cask Strength batch 5, bott 10 db **(84)** n21 t22 f20 b21. Just a little extra aging here has brought a telling degree of caramel into play, swamping much else. Pleasant, but a reminder of just how fragile the line between greatness and just plain, old-fashioned good. *61.8%. nc ncf.*

Amrut Double Cask ex-bourbon cask no. 2874/2273, bott no. 44, bott Feb 10 db **(96)** n23 t24.5 f24 b24.5. Frankly, a malt I thought I'd never see: how can a whisky survive seven years under the unremitting Bangalore sun? I am proud of the very small part I played in seeing this wonderful whisky see the world: I tasted both casks, containing the oldest whisky Amrut had ever produced, in a cellar at the distillery earlier in the year and passed both not only fit but exceptional. But I made the observation that they would certainly be better still if mixed together as the personalities of both casks very much complimented the other. On the day the younger of the two casks turned seven years old, this they did and bottled it. And just to show how wonderful this whisky is, from now what must surely be from one of the top two or three malt whisky distilleries in the world, simply leave an empty glass of it by your bedside table and smell it first thing in the morning. *46%. 306 bottles.*

Amrut Fusion batch no. 01, bott Mar 09 db (**97**) **n24 t24 f24 b25.** One of the most complex and intriguing new whiskies of 2010 that needs about two days and half a bottle to get even close to fathoming. Not exactly a textbook whisky, with a few edges grinding together like tectonic plates. And there is even odd note, like the fruit and a kind of furry, oaky buzz, which I have never seen before. But that is the point of whiskies like this: to be different, to offer a unique slant. But, ultimately, to entertain and delight. And here it ticks all boxes accordingly. To the extent that this has to be one of the great whiskies found anywhere in the world this year. And the fact it is Indian? Irrelevant: from distillation to maturation this is genius whisky, from whichever continent... *50%*

Amrut Fusion batch 10, bott Mar 11 db (**94.5**) **n24 t24 f22.5 b23.5.** Superb whisky, though to be plotted on a different map to the now legendary Whisky Bible award-winning Batch 1. This is a much more delicate affair: more hints and shadows rather than statements and substance. Still, though, a fabulous malt whisky in Amrut's best style. *50%. nc.*

Amrut Greedy Angels dist 3 Oct 04, bott 15 Nov 12 db (**96**) **n25 t24 f23 b24.** So here we have it: an 8-year-old Indian whisky. Matured in a cellar, luckily, but still has the hallmarks often seen on certain Speysiders in their late 30s...a series of Caperdonichs from about five or six years ago spring to mind. Except their noses were never this good: in fact, few noses have ever been better – it is certainly unsurpassed this year...worldwide. A true whisky great of the last decade. *50%*

Amrut Herald cask no. 2857 db (**92**) **n23 t24 f22 b23.** Here is the news: Amrut have come up with another fabulous whisky. Actually, the news these days is when they don't... *60.8%. sc.*

Amrut Herald cask no. 3030 db (**93**) **n23 t24 f22.5 b23.5.** Here's the news: this has outscooped the last Herald I tasted! *58.4%. 219 bottles.*

Amrut Intermediate Sherry Matured bott no. 01, bott Jun 10 db (**96.5**) **n24.5 t24 f23.5 b24.5.** How do you get three freshly emptied oloroso butts from Jerez to Bangalore without the casks spoiling, and not use sulphur? Answer: empty two cases of Amrut cask strength whisky into each of the butts before shipping them. Not a single off note. No bitterness whatsoever. And the fruit is left to impart its extraordinary riches on a malt matured also in American oak. Amrut is spoiling us again... *57.1%*

Amrut Peated batch no. 1, bott Sep 08 db (**94**) **n23 t24 f23.5 b23.5.** Absolutely everything you could ask for a peated malt at this strength. The length and complexity are matched only by a train journey through this astonishing country. *46%*

Amrut Peated Cask Strength bott 08 db (**92**) **n22 t22.5 f24.5 b23.** A touch of youth to this guy but the finish, entirely uncluttered by unnatural caramel or deprived by filtration, confirms a degree of greatness. By the way: if you want to experience something really stunning, trying mixing the 07 and 08 peated. When you get the proportions right...well, watch out Islay! *62.78%*

Amrut Peated Port Pipe, cask no. 2713, dist 2 Jun 09, bott 2 Aug 13 (**88.5**) **n22 t22 f22.5 b22.** So big, it's exhausting... *41%*

Amrut Portonova db (**93**) **n22 t24 f24 b23.** This is a whisky so big, so blinding that when I first tasted it I was so dazzled I could barely see a thing. It was like coming out of the pitch black into a fierce light. My first instincts, while recoiling, was that there was too much oak at work. Only on acclimatisation did I work out what was going on here...and fall helplessly in love. There is still way too much oak, however you look at it and the nose, which neither improves nor worsens over time confirms that. Indeed, the entire thing is outrageous: I have never come across such a flavour profile before anywhere in the world. But my word: what a statement this makes... Unique. *62.1%*

Amrut PX Sherry, cask no. 2701, dist 2 Jun 09, bott 2 Aug 13 (**80**) **n20 t21 f18.5 b20.5.** Big, cloying, fruity but the sugar makes this a little tart. Not the finest finish, either. Just not really my cup of Darjeeling. *43%*

Amrut PX Sherry, cask no. 2702, dist 2 Jun 09, bott 2 Aug 13 (**71**) **n18 t19 f16 b18.** A poor, sulphury butt gives the fruit no chance to come alive. Dance with the devil...and you get burned... *42%*

Amrut Single Malt batch 27, bott Mar 11 db (**92.5**) **n23 t24 f22.5 b23.5.** An assured, elegant malt which now strides greatness with nonchalance. *46%. nc ncf.*

Amrut Single Malt batch 41 Apr 12 db (**94.5**) **n23.5 t24 f23 b24.** Just another Amrut bottling. Just another reminder of how good whisky should be. *46%*

⠐⠂ **Amrut Single Cask** peated barley, portpipe, cask no. 2713, dist Jun 09, bott Aug 13 db **(94.5) n23.5** just adore the gentle assuredness of the peat: firm and thick, yet never aggressive. The grape adds little more than a delicate stratum; **t24** works fabulously: the delivery is a near perfect marriage between hefty smoke, juicy barley and no less juicy grape. But such is the cleverness of the amalgamation, none bully the other; **f23** softens into a deftly smoked sherry trifle; **b24** Amrut showing its ability to a world class player. 59%. sc ncf nc. 346 bottles. Bottled exclusively for Europe. WB15/393

⠐⠂ **Amrut Single Cask** unpeated barley, bourbon, cask no. 3436, dist Jun 09, bott Aug 13 db **(89.5) n23** creamy marshmallow; a fresh cappuccino steams away in the background; gristy; **t23** fresh delivery: a conflicting battle of newish barley notes and much tangier age-enriched tannins; **f21** slight burnt toast; **b22.5** for the most part, a beautifully lush, stylish whisky, though the finish was an oversight I fear. 60%. sc ncf nc. 174 bottles.

⠐⠂ **Amrut Single Cask** unpeated barley, Px-Sherry, cask no. 2699, dist Jun 2009, bott Aug 2013 db **(81.5) n19 t23 f19 b20.5**. Not many distilleries can pull off bottling from PX, which is why I suggest they stay away from it. Either the sweetness of the sherry overwhelms and you end up with a stodgy sticky toffee pudding. Or the sulphur treatment does all kinds of damage. This appears to have elements of both. 62.8%. sc ncf nc. 311 bottles. Bottled exclusively for Europe. WB15/394

Amrut Two Continents Limited Edition bott Feb 09 db **(95) n23.5 t24 f23.5 b24.** Here we have a malt distilled in India and matured first on the sub-continent and then Scotland. Let's just say that it is a malt which has travelled exceptionally well...and arrived at greatness. This is exactly how I like my whisky to be. 46%. 786 bottles.

Amrut Two Continents 2nd Edition bott Jun 11 db **(95) n23.5 t24 f23.5 b24.** I didn't expect their 2nd edition of this to get anywhere near the first in quality: it has. Not because of any loss in faith in the distillery – quite the contrary, in fact – but because, if I have learned anything in 20 years reviewing whisky, distillers find it near enough impossible to recreate the sublime. This is a vaguely fruitier effort and all the more fascinating for that. 50%. nc ncf. 892 bottles.

Amrut 100 Peated Single Malt ex-bourbon/virgin oak barrels db **(92) n23 t23 f23.5 b22.5**. Ironically, though one of the older whiskies to come from this distillery, the nose shows a little bit of youth. A quite different style from Amrut's other peated offerings and it was obviously intended. Further proof that this distillery has grown not only in stature but confidence. And with very good reason. 57.1%. nc ncf.

The Ultimate Amrut 2005 Cask Strength bourbon barrel no. 1641, bott no. 174, dist Dec 05, bott Apr 10 db **(94.5) n23.5 t24 f23.5 b23.5**. It makes no difference whether made and matured in Islay or India, great malt whisky is just that. And this is near faultless. And, what's more, it appears to have a character and personality all its own. 62.8%

Blackadder Amrut Rum Cask Finish cask BA5/2009, bott Jul 09 **(91.5) n23 t24.5 f21.5 b22.5**. For every action there is an equal and opposite reaction; so sweet to start, so dry on the finish. 62.%. nc ncf. 245 bottles.

Milroy's of Soho Amrut 2003 cask no. 08/08/30-1, dist Jul 03, bott Jan 09 **(84) n21 t22 f20 b21**. Juicy in part and very malty. But this whisky struggles at this kind of age with the oak, especially through the flattening natural caramels, dumbing the beauty down. 46%. 210 bottles.

JOHN DISTILLERIES

Paul John Brilliance db **(94.5) n23.5 t24 f23.5 b23.5**. Yet another astonishing malt from India. 46%

Paul John Edited db **(96.5) n24.5 t24.5 f23.5 b24**. A new Indian classic: a sublime malt from the subcontinent. To be more precise: a world classic! Think of Ardmore at its most alluring: one of Scotland's finest and most complex single malts, yet somehow possessing a saltiness and depth more befitting Islay. Then stir in a small degree of ulmo honey and bourbon-style hickory and liquorice. Plus subtle chocolate mint. And there you have it...the smoke drifting around stirring up spicy tales of the east. A world class whisky to be talked about with reverence without doubt... 52.9%

Paul John Single Malt Cask No 161 Non Peated **(94) n22.5 t24.5 f23 b24**. A malt which has much to say but does so with a quiet intensity. This really is a class act... 57%

Paul John Single Malt Cask No 163 Non Peated **(94.5) n24 t24 f23 b23.5**. A sublime whisky which, just as it appears to be heading off into deepest Kentucky land, veers back on course with a malty explosiveness. Magnificent complexity...57%

Paul John Single Malt Single Cask No 164 Non Peated **(96) n24 t24 f24 b24**. It is hardly believable that this is a three year old single malt: the unstinting high humidity of Goa and even higher temperature, perhaps helped along by three months of monsoons, appears to have given this whisky a degree of complexity which, even in Kentucky, it might have taken a dozen years to compile. This is single malt, but one with a hint of paradise...57%

Paul John Peated Single Malt db (89) n23 t22 f21.5 b22.5. One of those delicately peaty guys which gangs up on you slowly. The smoke-infused layering of sugars is the star turn, though. 55.5%

⁘ **Paul John Single Malt Cask No 692 Peated** db (95.5) n24 rich smoky bacon, tightening as the intensity of the peat appears to thicken. There is also (and I have never before found this with a peated malt) a eucalypt present, giving this a very singular and reverential signature. Assorted spices nibble on the nose but the balance is achieved by the slow revealing of sultry Demerara undercurrent; t23.5 big, resounding delivery on the palate, sharpened by a degree of lingering copper: the sugars do not take long to make their mark and are helped by subtle oils; enough fresh barley is around to ensure some salivation; f24 now we enter complexity overdrive as the Demerara meets toasted fudge and the harder early notes soften. The oak is working hard on its vanilla-enriching objective while the smoke takes its foot off the pedal. The sugars, meanwhile, do their own thing...and do it well...; b24 hard to believe a whisky apparently so young in years can offer such complexity. But that's Goa for you... 58.5%

⁘ **Paul John Single Malt Cask No 777 Peated** db (95) n23.5 no doubting the smoke. But here it forms a medium weighted guard of honour for the delicate honey and custard notes which teasingly dominate. The sugars are gentle and help sweeten the lemon zest which further lightens the experience; t24 follows the nose's overture to the letter: the sugars, mainly muscovado, mix a little with light maple syrup and then intensifies as the smoky gristiness bites home to create a sublime middle; around this time, the first cocoa notes are detected and tingling spices are already well established; gentle manuka honey slowly takes the steering wheel; f23.5 smoked mocha ,big natural caramels and vanilla...sweetened with ulmo honey which has taken over from the manuka; b24 a Paul John which tries to offer as much delicate honey as the peat will allow. Something of rare, understated beauty. And though I often fly 777s, few take off as well as this and here there is no need for a seat belt... 59.7%

⁘ **Paul John Single Malt Cask No 780 Peated** db (96) n24 from the colour, you'd expect the oak to give a rough ride. But on the contrary: it is there in full force, yet delivers a beautiful blood orange and kumquat citrus blast, with some decent marmalade thrown in for good measure. All this, of course, is framed by soft but confident and compelling peak reek; t24 the delivery is one of profound contrast: on one hand it hits the palate running and in its maltiest form, resulting in instant salivation. And on the other there are drier, darker, threatening tones, the ones carrying the smoke, and you are a bit confused about what might happen next. The answer is that they spread out and form into a smoked cocoa mass....; f24 so long; so delicate after the sheer enormity of all that has gone on before. And just how many shades of smoked cocoa butter in the world are there...? b24 Warning. If you are a bit of a dithering, wishy-washy whisky drinker, don't go anywhere near this stuff: this bottling is for serious whisky drinkers only... 57.3%

⁘ **Paul John Single Malt Cask No 784 Peated** db (95.5) n23.5 a host of natural caramels and vanillas gang up to make the smoky impact just a little less daunting than it might. Subtle, soft and charmingly delicate; t23.5 despite a passing moment when the oaks really bite deep and hard, no less soft on delivery with the smoke taking its time to make its mark. Instead, the vanillas and delicate ulmo honey make the early running and ensure a malt of outstanding delicacy despite its strength; f24.5 another Paul John malt which is an essay in how a great finish should be: the oaks have stacked up higher now, allowing the tannins to drip through. But the dark sugars merge with the smoke to ensure not a hint of tiredness or bitterness gets through; b24 the understated smoke ensures an elegant yet chewy experience. 59.2%

⁘ **Paul John Single Malt Cask No 1444 Non Peated** db (95.5) n23.5 soft cereal notes dominate. The oak offers a butterscotch tart sweetness but takes a step back into the wings to allow the malt centre stage; t24 the kind of delivery which stops you in your tracks and makes you purr with delight. A succession of delicate sugar tones is stirred into the lively spice. But all the time, this is paying lip service to the malt, which starts robustly and almost in concentrated biscuit form but then, somehow, intensifies breathtakingly; f24 that intense barley keeps its foot on the throat of the oak, radiating riches far and wide. Spices do slowly gather momentum while the oak offers a hickory alternative; b24 among the most intensely malty Indian whiskies ever to have been bottled. Quite superb. 59.7%

⁘ **Paul John Single Malt Cask No 1844 Non Peated** db (94.5) n23 oak shapes the majority of the nose, at times reminding you of a 35-year-old Speysider, and, at others, something a lot younger from Kentucky. The sugars play a clever role, just doing enough to ensure a freshness to the malt is maintained; t24 sharp barley contrasts with the attractive bourbon-style oakiness. Lots of liquorice and Demerara-sweetened hickory at play here and enough oil to make for a pleasing chewiness; some delicate ulmo honey supports the fragile sugars; **f23.5** much drier now and even a shade spicy. A degree of bitterness has crept in but the deft toasty fudge and maple syrup (seemingly on scorched toast) keeps everything on an even keel; **b24** let someone taste this blind, tell them it is three years old...and see their reaction. A big malt showing elegance and good grace throughout. *60.5%*

⁘ **Paul John Single Malt Cask No 1846 Non Peated** db (96) **n23.5** a light citrusy breeze sweeps across the oaky plains. The malt, a little brittle and gristy, makes a teasing contribution; **t23** superb mouth feel with gentle oils helping the drier oak notes glide across the palate without leaving splinters. The sugars are profound, too, some from an intense malty gristiness. The others have a darker hue; **f25** a late scattering of increasingly warming spices works rather beautifully with the toasted oak and malt mix. The manuka honey and Demerara simply cannot be a better combination and now heads, sublimely, down an old Kentuckian path of controlled roastiness; **b24.5** a very deep, complex whisky with many hills and canyons to explore. The finish orbits and often touches perfection. A profound malt. 60.8%

Paul John Single Malt-Classic (Un Peated) db (95) **n23.5 t24 f23.5 b24**. Further evidence that Indian whisky is on the rise. Just so charming...and irresistible. *55.2%*

PONDA DISTILLERY
Stillman's Dram Single Malt Whisky Limited Edition bourbon cask no. 11186-90 (94) **n23 t23 f24 b24**. Well, I thought I had tasted it all with the Amrut cask strength. And then this arrived at my lab...!! I predicted many years back that India would dish out some top grade malt before too long. But I'd be stretching the truth if I said I thought it would ever be this good... *42.8%. McDowell & Co Ltd, India.*

Blends
Antiquity Blue Ultra Premium Whisky batch 175, bott 16 Sep 11 (77) **n19.5 t20 f18.5 b19**. Busy and nutty, a blend which sets its stall out by depending on a creamy, lush texture. Juicy malt-tinged delivery before spices develop. Bitters out towards the end. *42.8%.*

McDowell's Single Malt batch 33, bott June 11 (82) **n20.5 t21.5 f20 b20**. The malt is hugely intense and offers a degree of gristy juiciness and on the nose something approaching a faint puff of peat. The show is let down by what appears to be very old casks which refuse to offer the support and complexity the decent malt deserves. *42.8%*

McDowell's Single Malt batch 33, bott May 11 (78) **n19 t21 f19 b19**. A sharp, salivating malt which works hard to shrug off the tart intrusiveness of some baser cask notes. Silky in part, smoky in others, this malt struggles to find its balance. Curiously, this claims the same batch, 033, as the June bottling. Yet they are like chalk and cheese. This is much darker, too. *42.8%*

McDowell's No 1 Diet Mate batch 103, bott 24 Jun 11 (76.5) **n18 t19.5 f19 b20**. A genuinely odd whisky. The nose is scented like a tart's boudoir while the finish is simply tart. The delivery, though, does offer a nimble malt effect while the spices rumble with attractive intent. As a fan of McDowell, I can't say this is quite their finest moment. *42.8%. Blended*

Old Oak Aged 12 Years Premium Malt Whisky batch 76, bott Oct 11 (72) **n19.5 t18 f17.5 b17**. It claims "unique taste". Indeed, it has: a malt whisky totally devoid of any discernable malt flavour. Soft and big on caramel. As a whisky of sorts, OK. As an "Aged 12 Years Premium malt whisky" a bit pathetic. *42.8%. Adinco Distilleries.*

Peter Scot Malt Whisky (84) **n20 t21 f22 b21**. Enjoyable balance between sweetness and oak and entertainingly enlivened by what appears to be some young, juicy malt. *42.8%.*

Rendezvous (95.5) **n24 t24 f23.5 b24.5**. A new Indian classic. A sublime malt from the subcontinent. *46%*

Royal Challenge batch 276, bott 31 Jan 11 (82) **n21.5 t20 f20 b20.5**. The Challenge appears to have been to spread the malts as thinly as possible across the grains yet still make an impact: a kind of malty comb over. The malts used are pretty delicious, though, and makes for a satisfying and attractive blend. *42.8%. A blend of rare Scotch, select grain and mature Indian malts. Mandovi Distilleries for United Spirits Ltd.*

Royal Stag Barrel Select batch 212, bott 17 Feb 12 (75.5) **n20.5 t19 f17 b18**. Thin and sweet. But should be shot to put it out of its misery. *42.8% Mix of Scotch malt and India grain spirit.*

Seagram's Blender's Pride batch 672 bott 12/12/11 (85) **n21.5 t21 f21 b21.5**. A thoughtful composition of soft sugars and caramels. Excellent texture and, rare for an Indian admix, the finish actually ups in complexity and weight. Good spices and attractive playful smoke on the nose especially. *42.8%. Mix of Scotch malt and India grain spirit.*

Seagram's Blenders Pride Reserve Collection (77) **n19 t20 f19 b19**. Way too reliant on the grain and the malt submerged under the caramel. Soft, clean and painfully non-committal. *42.8%. Mix of Scotch malt and India grain spirit.*

Signature (81.5) **n22.5 t22 f17.5 b19.5**. Excellent, rich nose & delivery helped along with a healthy display of peat reek. But more attention has to be paid to the brutally thin finish. *42.8%*

NEW ZEALAND
THE NEW ZEALAND WHISKY COMPANY

The New Zealand Whisky Collection Milford Single Malt Aged 15 Years (86.5) n21 t23 f20.5 b22. Exceptionally malty, succulent and enjoys a decent malt-oak balance despite the lack of further complexity. *43%. Gordon and Macphail.*

The New Zealand Whisky Collection South Island Single Malt Aged 21 Years (95) n24 t23.5 f23.5 b24. If someone asked me how I would like my 21-year-old non-peated malt to come to me, it would probably be something like this: a top of the range 40-year-old!! Proof that the country in which a whisky is made is totally irrelevant... Great whisky is great whisky. End of.... *40%.*

The New Zealand Whisky Collection 1988 Single Malt (84) n21.5 t21 f21 b20. The hotness of the malt has nothing to do with the spice...much more the double quick speed at which this was distilled. Enough crusty barley and tannin to make for an attractive experience, though. *56.4%. sc. Gordon and Macphail.*

⁙ **The New Zealand Whisky Collection Willowbank 1988 25 Years Old** cask no. 64, bott 3/13 (96.5) n24 deft peat forms the most delicate shell imaginable over no less fragile citrus. Soft salt, still a little grist after all these years, background vanilla: almost something akin to a moist lemon drizzle cupcake...with a few atoms of smoke thrown in..; t24.5 the adroit citrus mingles with the most alluring malt imaginable. The shadow of smoke acts like a siren while the tannins just up their game slightly. Just so well integrated...; f23.5 long, with a feeble spice buzz. Evidence of the shortage of copper from the cask comes through only at the very death; b24.5 when I first encountered this whisky it would have been a six-year-old and the Dunedin distillery had a very uncertain future. Question marks hung over the quality of the stock, so they were a bit surprised when I assured them that the vast majority of what they were making was of very decent to high standard. Who then would have thought that some two decades on I would be tasting this as one of the most delicate and sophisticated and complex 25-year-olds imaginable? Only the untidy finish shows the distillery's Achilles: low copper content. On the other hand, it also ensured that it would never be short of character. One of the most poignant and enjoyable whiskies of the year. And memories of the only distillery I ever visited and then took a five minute drive to watch penguins surface from the sea... *55.1%. sc. WB15/396*

The New Zealand Whisky Collection 1989 Single Malt (86.5) n21.5 t22 f21.5 b21.5. Another competent and richly malted New Zealander which lacks some of the backbone of G&M's other bottlings. The central theme of juiciness is a delight, though. *52.8%.*

The New Zealand Whisky Collection 1990 Single Malt (91) n22 t24 f22.5 b22.5. A curious single malt which reminds me of some of the better rare Irish whiskies uncovered in the late 1980s. The oak treads that fine line between dominance and ruinous intrusiveness with a rare assuredness. *61.7%. Gordon and Macphail.*

The New Zealand Whisky Collection 1993 Single Malt (92.5) n24 t23 f22.5 b23. I probably saw and tasted this cask when just a few months old. Always great to meet an old friend after many years apart...and even better to find them in tip-top shape. *51.9%.*

The New Zealand Whisky Collection Doublewood 10 Years Old (78.5) n21 t20.5 f18 b19 Any thinner and it would vanish. *40%. Gordon and Macphail*

The New Zealand Whisky Collection South Island Single Malt Aged 18 Years (89) n22 t22.5 f22 b22.5. Minimal complexity. Maximum charm. *40%.*

THE SOUTHERN DISTILLING CO LTD

The Coaster Single Malt Whiskey batch no. 2356 (85) n20 t22 f21 b22. Distinctly small batch and sma' still with the accent very much on honey. Nosed blind I might have mistaken as Blue Mouse whisky from Germany: certainly European in style. Recovers well from the wobble on the nose and rewards further investigation. *40%*

The MacKenzie Blended Malt Whiskey (85) n20 t22 f21 b22. A vaguely spicier, chalkier, mildly less honeyed version of Coaster. Quite banana-laden nose. *40%*

THOMSON WILLOWBANK

Thomson Single Malt 10 Years Old ex-bourbon barrel (71) n18.5 t19 f16.5 b17. The sugars are working hard. But have nothing to work with. *40%. Thomson Whisky.*

Thomson Single Malt 18 Years Old (77) n19.5 t20 f18.5 b19. Pleasant, sweet but absolutely no body whatsoever. *46%. sc. Thomson Whisky.*

Thomson Single Malt 21 Years Old (84) n21 t22.5 f20.5 b20. Bit of a bimbo whisky: looks pretty and outwardly attractive but has picked up very little in its 21 years... *46%. sc.*

Thomson Whisky Two Tone European oak & American white oak (86) n22 t22 f21 b21. This one had promise. Started full of intent on both nose and delivery, boasting attractive citrus notes. But after a quick rush of clear honey, thins out like the most basic of blends. *40%.*

WILSON DISTILLERY

Cadenhead's World Whiskies Lammerlaw Aged 10 Years bourbon, bott 07 **(91.5) n22 t23.5 f23 b23**. Stunning bottlings like this can only leave one mourning the loss of this distillery. *48.9%*

Blends

Kiwi Whisky (37) n2 t12 f11 b12. Strewth! I mean, what can you say? Perhaps the first whisky containing single malt offering virtually no nose at all and the flavour appears to be grain neutral spirit plus lashings of caramel and (so I am told) some Lammerlaw single malt. The word bland has been redefined. As has whisky. *40%*.

Wilson's Superior Blend (89) n22 t23 f21 b23. Apparently has a mixed reception in its native New Zealand but I fail to see why: this is unambiguously outstanding blended whisky. On the nose you expect a mouthwatering mouthful and it delivers with aplomb. Despite this being a lower priced blend it is, intriguingly, a marriage of 60% original bottled 10-y-o Lammerlaw and 40% old Wilson's blend, explaining the high malt apparent. Dangerous and delicious and would be better still at a fuller strength...and with less caramel. *37.5%*.

SOUTH AFRICA
JAMES SEDGWICK DISTILLERY

Three Ships 10 Years Old db **(83) n21 t21 f20 b21**. Seems to have changed character, with more emphasis on sherry and natural toffee. The oak offers a thrusting undercurrent. *43%*

Three Ships Aged 10 Years Single Malt Limited Edition db **(91) n22.5 t22.5 f23 b23.5**. If you are looking for a soft, sophisticated malt whose delicate fingers can sooth your troubled brow, then don't bother with this one. On the other hand, if you are looking for a bit of rough, some entertaining slap and tickle: a slam-bam shag of a whisky - a useful port in a storm - then your boat may just have sailed in... Beware: an evening with this and you'll be secretly coming back for more... *43%*

Bain's Cape Mountain Single Grain Whisky db **(85.5) n21 t22 f21 b21.5**. A lively, attractively structured whisky with more attitude than you might expect. Some lovely nip and bite despite the toffee and surprising degree of soft oils. *43%*

Blends

Drayman's Solera (86) n19 t22 f23 b22. For a change, the label gets it spot on with its description of chocolate orange: it is there in abundance. If they can get this nose sorted they would be on for an all round impressive dram. As it is, luxuriate in the excellent mouthfeel and gentle interplay between malt and oak. Oh and those chocolate oranges... *43%*.

Harrier (78) n20 t20 f19 b19. Not sure what has happened to this one. Has bittered to a significant degree while the smoke has vanished. A strange, almost synthetic, feel to this now. *43%. South African/Scotch Whisky.*

Knights (83) n20.5 t21 f20 b20.5. While the Harrier has crashed, the Knights is now full of promise. Also shows the odd bitter touch but a better all-round richer body not only absorbs the impacts but radiates some malty charm. *43%. South African/Scotch Whisky.*

Knights Aged 3 Years (87) n22 t22 f22 b22. This now appears to be 100% South African whisky if I understand the label correctly: "Distilled Matured and Bottled in South Africa." A vast improvement on when it was Scotch malt and South African grain. Bursting with attitude and vitality. When next in South Africa, this will be my daily dram for sure. Love it. *43%*.

Three Ships Bourbon Cask Finish (90) n22 t23 f22.5 b22.5. A soft, even whisky which enjoys its finest moments on delivery. Clean with a pressing, toasty oakiness to the sweeter malt elements. Always a delight. *43%*

Three Ships Premium Select Aged 5 Years (93) n23 t23.5 f23 b23.5. What a fabulous whisky. The blender has shown a rare degree of craft to make so little smoke do so much. Bravo! *43%. James Sedgwick Distillery.*

Three Ships Select (81) n19 t21 f20 b21. Busy and sweet. But I get the feeling that whatever South African malt may be found in Knights does a better job than its Scotch counterpart here. *43%. James Sedgwick Distillery.*

TAIWAN
KAVALAN DISTILLERY

Kavalan db **(91) n23 t23 f22 b23**. A high quality, confident malt which underline's this distillery's enormous potential. *40%*

Kavalan Concertmaster Single Malt Port cask finish db **(87) n22 t23 f20.5 b21.5**. A malt which will split its audience. In Germany, for instance, the light sulphur note will win all kinds of standing ovations; to the purist there will be a preference that it was not there. Because this piece has many moments of beauty as the malt and grape mingle and interlink: together they are company, anything else is a crowd. Even so I envisage many an encore for this... 40%

Kavalan King Car Conductor db (89.5) n22.5 t23 f22 b22. Not quite sure where the salt comes from; this distillery is far enough inland not to be affected. But it is there and does no harm whatsoever. Not quite technically perfect, as at least some of the characteristics are so contra they occasionally jar. But still fabulous whisky and a journey entirely worth embarking on. 46%

Kavalan Podium Single Malt bott 27th Nov 12 db (96.5) n24 complex and gorgeously weighted, the nose is like an evening in which Richard Strauss and Ralph Vaughan Williams are on the same bill: subtle notes and ranges being practised and perfected...in an air bursting with expectation; t24 the cherry and malt concentrate mix opening bars are not quite what are expected, but there is never less than harmony. The degree of oiliness, which is able to ramp up the maple syrup and treacle sweetness is also a surprise package; f24 the start may have exploded like a Strauss in full melodramatic mode, but the finish is Williams at his most pastoral. The toasty and elegant sugars and baser tannins have here formed a cord, one that fades to the death, but not before a few false endings. The use of the molasses brings in the inevitable vanilla so that you barely notice until a light ulmo honey entry is the last note standing.... b24.5 bravo! Encore!!! 46%. nc ncf.

Kavalan Single Malt ex-Bourbon Oak bott 12th Dec 12 db (93) n23 t23 f23 b24. Big oak with a quite dynamic sweetness, always beautifully controlled with the accent invariably on complexity. 46%. nc ncf.

Kavalan Single Malt Whisky Sherry Oak bott 13th Dec 12 (95) n24 t24 f23 b24. The type of sherry-heavy malt not uncommonly found on Speyside over 20 years ago before the quality if the butts nosedived dramatically. I feel the judicious hand of Jim Swan at work here who has somehow managed to make this Taiwanese malt more top quality Scottish in character than anything of its age you can find in the Highlands. What a rare treat: not too rare in future one hopes! 46%. nc ncf.

⁙ **Kavalan Single Malt Whisky** cask no. 2922, dist 07 bott 09 Dec 13 db (96) n24 the smoke fingerprint is not so much unusual but unique: as though the tannins have blasted a toasted honeycomb and red liquorice sweetness into the phenols themselves, as opposed to accompanying them. The result is one of the most delicate, non-pungent peat reeks of all time; t23.5 massively busy delivery and when the onrush of tannin and golden syrup has died away, a much clearer view of the peat can be seen, at first a little dusty and lightly spiced, then carrying a cocoa edge; f24 a Taiwanese sunset of fragile smoke drifting over a semi-bourbon field, with the spices, light oak intensity and sugars all recognisable as a Kentucky trait. The result, however, is something uniquely Kavalanian, though... b24.5 a tightly compact malt which could easily fold under the weight of the oak but doesn't thanks to the myriad strands of complexity and, above all, the composure and balance. Such a beautiful thing... 55% King Car Food Industrial co. Ltd

Kavalan Solist Barique db cask no. W080218037 (90.5) n23 t24 f21 b22.5. This distillery is, in all the world, my favourite to visit. The drama of the geology in which it is set appears matched only by what one discovers from time to time in their warehouses. It has the potential for true world greatness, though this bottling, for all its magnificence, only nudges rather than grasps at the prospect. 59.2%. nc ncf sc. 237 bottles.

Kavalan Solist Fino Sherry Cask db cask no. S060814045, bott no. 079/500 (95) n24.5 t24.5 f22.5 b23.5. When Dr Jim Swan, the distillery's consultant, told me he thought he'd found a cask which could well be a world-beater, I had mixed feelings. On one hand he'd been right when he'd said the same thing when he found a port pipe for Penderyn which has now entered Welsh whisky folklore. But, on the other, there are many times during the year when those I have long known in the game, including some good friends, have called me after reading my review and asked why I had marked their Great Hope down. Jim, though, has got this one spot on. The natural colour is astonishingly un-fino-esque and the overall experience is one that you come across only too rarely in life – especially with sherry butts. The marriage between the sweeter malt and drier grape notes is a thing of not just beauty, but awe. This is a bottling which will place the King Car Yuan-Shan distillery on the world map of truly great distilleries. Because having an exceptional cask is one thing. You also have to have a spirit excellent enough to maximize the potential of that cask and not be overwhelmed by it. That is exactly what you have here. A great new whisky dynasty has been born... 58.5%. ncf nc.

Kavalan Solist Fino Sherry Cask db cask no. S060814021 (97) n24.5 t24 f24 b24.5. It might be argued that the one and only thing that makes this exceptional is the quality of the cask, rather than the actual malt it contains. Well, let me set the record straight in this one. Earlier this week I made a very rare escape from my tasting room and visited the Royal Albert Hall for the 34th Prom of the 2011 season. The highlight of the evening was Camille Saint-Saens Symphony No 3 – "Organ". Now some critics, when they can find time to extract themselves from their own rear ends, dismiss this as a commoners' piece; something to amuse the plebeian. What they appear to not have is neither the wit nor humanity to understand that Saint-Saens sewed into this work a degree of such subtle shade and emotion, especially in the less dramatic second movement, that it can, when treated correctly, affect those capable of normal warmth and feeling. With so many nerve endings tingling and nowhere to go Saint-Saens seemingly recognised that he required something profound – in this case the organ – to create a backbone. And someone able to use it to maximum effect. And there we had it the other day: the Royal Albert Hall's awe-inspiring organ, and Thomas Trotter to make it come alive: The Solist. And this is what we have here: a perfect fino sherry selected by the maestro Dr Jim Swan. But able to display its full magnificence only because the host spirit is so beautifully composed. Good whisky is, without question, a work of art; great whisky is a tone poem. And here, I beg to insist, is proof. *58.4%. nc ncf sc. 513 bottles.*

Ka Va Lan Solist Vinho Barrique cask W080218011 bott 08 Nov 11 (93) n23 t24 f22.5 b23.5 this distillery in a very short time has already planted its flag firmly at the peak of the world's best whiskies. *60%*

Other Brands Available In Taiwan

Eagle Leader Storage Whisky (81.5) n20 t21 f21 b20.5. Attractively smoky with a surprisingly long finish for a whisky which initially appears to lack body. By no means straightforward, but never less than pleasant. *40%*

Golden Hill Single Malt (75) n18 t20 f19 b18. An unwieldy heavyweight. *40%*

Good Deer (in Chinese Characters) *see McAdams Rye Whisky*

McAdams Rye Whisky bott Nov 09 (85.5) n21 t22 f21.5 b21.5. Thoroughly delicious stuff absolutely brimming with juicy, crisp grain notes. The body is lightly oiled and shapely while the finish is sweet and attractive. The odd green apple note, too. *40%. Note: Says it's made in Taiwan, but possesses a maple leaf on the label.*

Sea Pirates (77) n18 t21 f19 b19. More Johnny Depp than Errol Flynn. Attractive smoke, though. *40%*

URUGUAY

Dunbar Anejo 5 Anos (85.5) n20 t22.5 f21.5 b21.5. A clean, mouth-wateringly attractive mix where the grain nips playfully and the Speyside malts are on best salivating behaviour. Decently blended and boasting a fine spice prickle, too. *40%*

Seagram's Blenders Pride (83) n20.5 t22 f20b20.5. The busy, relatively rich delivery contrasts with the theme of the silky grains and caramel. Easy drinking. *40%*

MISCELLANEOUS

House of Westend Blended Whisky (67) n17 t18 f16 b16. No more than OK if you are being generous; some tobacco-dirty notes around. Doesn't mention country of origin anywhere on the label. *40%. Bernkasteler Burghof, Germany.*

Jaburn & Co Pure Grain & Malt Spirit (53) n14 t13 f13 b13. Tastes like neutral grain and caramel to me. Some shop keepers, I hear, are selling it as whisky though this is not claimed on the label. Trust me: it isn't. *37.5%. Jaburn & Co, Denmark.*

Prince of Wales Welsh Whisky (69) n17 t18 f17 b17. Syrupy aroma is compounded by an almost liqueurish body. Thin in true Scotch substance, probably because it claims to be Welsh but is really Scotch with herbs diffused in a process that took place in Wales. Interestingly, my "liqueur" tasting notes were written before I knew exactly what it was I was tasting, thus proving the point and confirming that, with these additives, this really isn't whisky at all. *40%*

Shepherd's Export Finest Blend (46) n5 t16 f12 b13. A dreadful, illdefined grain-spirit nose is softened on the palate by an early mega-sweet kick. The finish is thin and eventually bitter. Feeble stuff. *37.2%. "A superb blend of Imported Scotch Malt whiskies and Distilled N.Z. grain spirit", claims the label which originally gives the strength as 40%, but has been over-written. Also, the grain, I was told, was from the USA. Southern Grain Spirit, NZ.*

The Teeling Whisky Co. Hybrid Malt Whiskey No. 1 Edition (90) n23 t22.5 f22 b22.5. Adorable vibrancy and use of smoke. *44.1%. nc ncf.*

Slàinte

It seems as though you can't have a Bible without a whole lot of begetting. And without all those listed below – a Tour de Force of all the world's whisky people – this Jim Murray's Whisky Bible 2015 would never have been begot at all. A huge amount of blood, sweat and tears go into the production of each edition, more than anyone not directly involved could even begin to comprehend. So, as usual, I must thank my amazing team: Vincent Flint-Hill, Dean Ayotte, Billy Jeffrey and David Rankin. Also, a special thank you to Arthur Naegele for fearlessly contacting the distilleries of Europe on my behalf. Extra special thanks must be placed on record for the unfailing, glass half full support of Paul and Denise Egerton, Pete and Linda Mayne, Byron and Jo Rogers, and David Hartley and Julie who, collectively kept me going - and laughing - when the weight of whisky and expectation seemed so daunting. As always, a massive hug to Heiko Thieme. But, above all, a big kiss and thank you to my amazingly patient gal, Judy Davis, for putting up with five months very hard labour, even if it was mine.... And, finally, because the list of thank yous had exceeded two pages, we have started again with those who have helped in providing help and samples for the 2013 Bible onwards. For all those who have assisted in the previous decade, we remain indebted.

Mitch Abate; Ally Alpine; Kevin Atchinson; Duncan Baldwin; Clare Banner; Jan Beckers; Franz Benner; Kirsteen Beeston; Annie Bellis; Barry Bernstein; Stuart Bertra; Menno Bijmolt; Sonat Birknecker Hart; Rich Blair; Hans Bol; Etienne Bouillon; Birgit Bornemeier; Phil Brandon; Stephen Bremner; Stephanie Bridge; James Brown; Sara Browne; Michael Brzozowski; Alexander Buchholz; Ryan Burchett; Amy Burgess; Euan Campbell; Kimla Carsten; Bert Cason; Jim Caudill; Danilo Cembrero; Lisa Chandler; Yuseff Cherney; Julia Christian; Nick Clark; Fredi Clerc; Dr Martin Collis; Jason Craig; David Croll; Danni Cutten; Mike DaRe; Stephen Davies; Alasdair Day; Dick & Marti; Paul Dempsey; Marie-Luise Dietich; Rob Dietrich; Angela D'Orazio; Jean Donnay; Tim Duckett; Camille Duhr-Merges; Mariette Duhr-Merges; Gemma Duncan; Jonas Ebensperger; Ray Edwards; Carsten Ehrlich; Ben Ellefsen; James Espey; Jennifer Eveleigh; Thomas Ewers; Charlotte Falconer; Joanna Fearnside; Hans-Gerhard Fink; David Fitt; Kent Fleischman; Martyn Flynn; Danny Gandert; Patrick Garcia; Dan Garrison; Carole Gibson; John Glaser; John Glass; Emily Glynn; Rodney Goodchild; Jonathon Gordan; Lawrence Graham; Hannah Gregory; Andrew Grey; Rebecca Groom; Jason Grossmiller; Viele Grube; Jasmin Haider; Georgina Hall; Georges Hannimann; Scott E Harris; Alistair Hart; Andrew Hart; Donald Hart; Stuart Harvey; Steve Hawley; Ailsa Hayes; Ross Hendry; Jason Himstedt; Roland Hinterreiter; Bernhard Höning; Emma Hurley; Alex Huskingson; Kai Ivalo; Amelia James; Ulrich Jakob; Michael John; Celine Johns; Robert Joule; Serena Kaye; Colin Keegan; Sara Klingberg; Larry Krass; Armin Krister; Karen Kushner; Ryan Lang; Sebastian Lauinger; Darren Leitch; Christelle Le Lay; Lars Lindberger; Mark T Litter; Steven Ljubicic; Alistair Longwell; Claire Lormier; C. Mark McDavid; John Maclellan; Dennis Malcolm;Tim Marwood; Jennifer Masson; Leanne Matthews; Josh Mayr; Roxane Mazeaude; Stephen R McCarthy; Angela Mcilrath; Catherine McKay; Jonny McMillan; Douglas McIvor; Maggie Miller; Euan Mitchell; Paul Mitchell; Jeroen Moernaut; Henk Mol; Nick Morgan; Maggie Morri; Fabien Mueller; Michael Myers; Arthur Nägele; Andrew Nelstrop; Alex Nicol; Jane Nicol; Jennifer Nicol; Zack Nobinger; Rachel Showalter Inman; Soren Norgaard; Tom O'Connor; Richard Oldfield; Casey Overeem; Ted Pappas; Richard Parker; Sanjay Paul; Percy; Alexandra Piciu; Amy Preske; Rachel Quinn;Sarah Rawlingson; Guy Rehorst; Carrie Revell; Kay Riddoch; Massimo Righi; Nicol von Rijbroek; Patrick Roberts; James Robertson; Anton Rossetti; David Roussier; Ronnie Routledge; Jim Rutledge; Caroline Rylance; Paloma Salmeron Planells; Phil Prichard; Kirsty Saville; John Savage-Onstwedder; Mick & Tammy Secor; Ian Schmidt; Mike Sharples; Rubyna Shekh; Caley Shoemaker; Jamie Siefken; Sam Simmons; Alastair Sinclair; Sukhinder Singh; Barbara Smith; Gigha Smith; Phil Smith; Cat Spencer; Jeremy Stephens; Hawley Steve; Vicky Stevens; Karen Stewart; Katy Stollery; Henning Svoldgaard; Tom Swift; Shoko Takagi; Chip Tate; Marko Tayburn; Marcel Telser; Celine Tetu; Sarah Thacker; Hamish Torrie; Louise Towers; Richard Urquhart; Stuart Urquhart; CJ Van Dijk; Mariah Veis; Aurelien Villefranche; Anna Wilson; Nick White; Robert Whitehead; Stephanie Whitworth; Arthur Winning; Ellie Winters; Stephen Worrall; Kate Wright; Frank Wu; Tom Wyss; Junko Yaguchi; Ruslan Zamoskovny; Rama Zuniga. And, as ever, in warm memory of Mike Smith.